FROMMER'S

COMPREHENSIVE TRAVEL GUIDE

CARIBBEAN '93

by Darwin Porter
Assisted by Danforth Prince

PRENTICE HALL TRAVEL

NEW YORK • LONDON • TORONTO • SYDNEY • TOKYO • SINGAPORE

FROMMER BOOKS

Published by Prentice Hall General Reference
A Division of Simon & Schuster Inc.
15 Columbus Circle
New York, NY 10023

ISBN 0-13-333659-X
ISSN 1044-2375

Design by Robert Bull Design
Maps by Geografix Inc.

FROMMER'S CARIBBEAN '93
Editor-in-Chief: Marilyn Wood
Senior Editors: Judith de Rubini, Alice Fellows
Editors: Thomas F. Hirsch, Paige Hughes, Sara Hinsey Raveret, Lisa Renaud, Theodore
Stavrou
Assistant Editors: Margaret Bowen, Peter Katucki, Ian Wilker
Editorial Assistant: Retha Powers
Managing Editor: Leanne Coupe

Special Sales

Bulk purchases of Frommer's Travel Guides are available at special discounts. The publishers
are happy to custom-make publications for corporate clients who wish to use them as
premiums or sales promotions. We can excerpt the contents, provide covers with corporate
imprints, or create books to meet specific needs. For more information write to Special Sales,
Prentice Hall Travel, Paramount Communications Building, 15th floor, 15 Columbus Circle,
New York, NY 10023.

Manufactured in the United States of America

CONTENTS

LIST OF MAPS

INVITATION TO THE READERS

In researching this book, I have come across many wonderful establishments, the best of which I have included here. I am sure that many of you will also come across appealing hotels, inns, restaurants, guesthouses, shops, and attractions. Please don't keep them to yourself. Share your experiences, especially if you want to comment on places that have been included in this edition that have changed for the worse. You can address your letters to:

Darwin Porter
Frommer's Caribbean '93
c/o Prentice Hall Travel
15 Columbus Circle
New York, NY 10023

A DISCLAIMER

Readers are advised that prices fluctuate in the course of time and travel information changes under the impact of the varied and volatile factors that affect the travel industry. Neither the authors nor the publisher can be held responsible for the experiences of readers while traveling. Readers are invited to write to the publisher with ideas, comments, and suggestions for future editions.

SAFETY ADVISORY

Whenever you're traveling in an unfamiliar city or country, stay alert. Be aware of your immediate surroundings. Wear a moneybelt and keep a close eye on your possessions. Be particularly careful with cameras, purses, and wallets, all favorite targets of thieves and pickpockets.

CHAPTER 1

GETTING TO KNOW THE CARIBBEAN

The Caribbean dream of days spent lolling on palm-tree-shaded sandy beaches or snorkeling in crystalline waters and of nights spent dining and dancing to steel-band rhythms exists only a few hours by plane from North America on this string of islands often called the "Eighth Continent of the World."

The island nations are extremely diverse in their population, culture, history, and mood, so which island you choose will depend on who you are and what you like to do—sunbathe in the buff on the nudist beaches of Guadeloupe; snorkel and scuba dive off Bonaire; sail as Lord Nelson did from English Harbour on Antigua; explore the oldest city in the Americas, Santo Domingo; shop the winding alleys of the bazaars of St. Thomas and St. Croix in the U.S. Virgin Islands; or climb around a volcanic crater on Saba.

1. GEOGRAPHY, HISTORY & POLITICS

GEOGRAPHY

The Caribbean Sea is ringed by the Greater Antilles (Cuba, Jamaica, Hispaniola, and Puerto Rico) on the north, the Lesser Antilles on the east, the coasts of Venezuela, Colombia, and Panama on the south, and Central America and the Mexican Yucatán on the west. It spans one million square miles.

The amazing variety of form and structure of the islands—which stretch from 10° north of the Equator almost to the Tropic of Cancer—is reflected in their size, topography, and depths of the sea around them, but all are tropical islands.

The island groups are referred to by different names, such as the West Indies, the Greater or Lesser Antilles, the Windward Islands, the Leewards, and so on. The name West Indies has had a number of meanings since Columbus first named his discoveries "Las Indies Occidentales" (the West Indies), thinking he had reached Asia.

The Greater Antilles includes Cuba (once known as the "Pearl of the Antilles"), Jamaica, Hispaniola (Haiti and the Dominican Republic), Puerto Rico, and the Cayman Islands. The name Lesser Antilles was given to the remainder of the chain of islands: the Leeward Islands curving from Anguilla in the north to Dominica in the south, and the Windward Islands from Martinique to Grenada, but not including

Barbados. There is also a little island chain paralleling the South American coast embracing three of the six islands today called the Netherlands Antilles.

THE ISLANDS IN BRIEF   I have refined the names of the island groups even further by separating, for instance, the U.S. Virgin Islands from the British Virgin Islands, and differentiating between the British Leeward Islands, the Dutch Windwards in the Leewards, and the Dutch Leewards, and so on.

   Anguilla   (British Leewards): Five miles north of St. Martin, Anguilla is flat and arid with 12 miles of white sandy beaches. Named after the Spanish word for eel (*anguilla*), this Caribbean backwater became chic in the 1980s.

   Antigua   (British Leewards): The largest of the Leewards (108 square miles), Antigua, along with the tiny island of Barbuda (not to be confused with Barbados), comprise a nation. The island of Antigua (An-*tee*-gah) was formed by limestone and coral deposits and is famous for having a different beach for every day of the year. St. John's, on its northwestern coast, and historic English Harbour, on its southern coast, are its two main settlements. Most of its population of 80,000 is of African descent.

   Aruba   (Dutch Leewards): Only 18 miles off the coast of Venezuela, Aruba is the smallest and most westerly of the Dutch-connected "ABC" islands (Aruba, Bonaire, and Curaçao). The island, less than 32 miles long, has many posh resort hotels and casinos, most of them stretched along 7 miles of white sandy beaches on the northern shore. The island has scant vegetation and receives little rain (not even 20 inches a year). The population of 65,000 is culturally diverse and includes Spanish, Dutch, and Caribbean Indian. Oranjestad is the capital.

   Barbados: This coral island, with its white sandy beaches and rolling countryside, is the easternmost in the Caribbean. Formerly governed by Britain, it is independent now, but its 250,000 people retain many British traditions. Only 14 miles wide and 21 miles long, it is the most populated island in the West Indies, and its range of accommodations is the most plentiful south of Miami.

   Bonaire   (Dutch Leewards): Like Aruba, this "ABC" Dutch-affiliated island gets slightly more than 20 inches of rainfall a year. The second largest of the Netherlands Antilles, it is 24 miles long and 4 to 6½ miles wide and lies 50 miles north of Venezuela, outside the hurricane belt. Its rich underwater life has made it the scuba-diving capital of the West Indies. The capital is Kralendijk.

   British Virgin Islands: Still a British Crown Colony, this island chain— called the B.V.I.—contains some 50 islands (depending on how many rocks, cays, and islets you want to count). Tortola, with its capital at Road Town, is the chief island, followed by Virgin Gorda, which has some of the poshest hotels in the West Indies, including the Little Dix Bay Hotel developed by Laurance Rockefeller.

   Cayman Islands: Like the B.V.I., this, too, is a British Crown Colony, consisting of three main islands: Grand Cayman (the largest), Cayman Brac, and Little Cayman. Lying 150 miles south of Havana and 48 miles south of Miami, Grand Cayman, home of the islands' capital, George Town, is relatively flat, about 4 miles wide and 22 miles long. Its Seven-Mile Beach and great dive sites make it a tourist favorite for those seeking a relaxed holiday.

   Curaçao   (Dutch Leewards): Along with its other Dutch-affiliated islands, Curaçao forms the "C" in the ABC chain of Aruba, Bonaire, and Curaçao. The largest island in the Netherlands Antilles, it's 37 miles wide at its widest point. The landscape, which receives scant rain, is arid and relatively barren and features many cacti. The capital is Willemstad, and the island's population is 170,000.

   Dominica   (British Windwards): Between Guadeloupe and Martinique, Dominica (Doh-mi-*nee*-kah), the largest and most mountainous island of the Windwards, is not to be confused with the Dominican Republic (see below). A land of waterfalls and rain forests, it is not known for its beaches, which are few and mainly of volcanic black sand. But for many devotees it's the lushest and most fascinating island in the Caribbean. Some 82,000 people live here, including the 2,000 descendants of the once-fierce, cannibalistic Carib peoples. The capital is Roseau.

   Dominican Republic: Occupying the eastern two-thirds of Hispaniola, an island shared with Haiti, the mountainous country of the Dominican Republic is the second largest of the Caribbean. About two million of its seven million Spanish-speaking population live in the historic capital city of Santo Domingo. It's a Caribbean bargain.

Grenada (British Windwards): The southernmost nation of the Windward Islands, Grenada (Gre-*nay*-dah) is one of the lushest in the Caribbean. Called the "spice island" because of the large amounts of nutmeg, mace, and cloves grown here, it is also a tourist island with white sand beaches and fertile mountains and valleys. Once a British Crown Colony but now independent, the island nation also consists of two smaller islands—Carriacou, which has some tourist facilities, and Petit Martinique, famous as a smugglers' haven.

Guadeloupe (French West Indies): Shaped like a butterfly, the French island of Guadeloupe has its capital at Basse-Terre, although its main city is Pointe-à-Pitre. It's surrounded by the satellite islands of Marie-Galante, Le Désirade, and Les Saintes (the last has the most tourist facilities). With a population of some 340,000 people, it is a *département* of France. Guadeloupe is actually two islands separated by a small bridge spanning the strait of the Rivière Salée. Its highest point is the volcano of Grande Soufrière, which rises 4,580 feet.

Jamaica: Favorite of North American honeymooners, Jamaica is a mountainous island rising from the sea 90 miles south of Cuba and about 100 miles west of Haiti. Its 4,410 square miles make it the third-largest island in the Greater Antilles. With an estimated population of 2.3 million (90% of whom are of West African descent), it's an English-speaking island with a turbulent history and some British tradition remaining. The major resorts are Montego Bay, Negril, and Ocho Rios; the capital is Kingston.

Martinique (French West Indies): For some the most exotic French destination in the Caribbean, Martinique is 19 miles wide and 40 miles long. Part of the Lesser Antilles, it is volcanic in origin; in fact, one volcano here is still active. Its capital, Fort-de-France, presides over a population of 350,000. Famed for its cuisine, the island has a coastline dotted with coves and bays that open inland onto lush vegetation.

Montserrat (British Leewards): This tiny (only 11 miles long and 7 miles wide), pear-shaped "Emerald Isle," lying 27 miles southeast of Antigua, is a British Crown Colony. A mountainous volcanic island, it has beaches of both black and white sand. Plymouth is the capital, and the island population is 12,500 residents, most of African descent. The island has limited tourist facilities.

Puerto Rico: The smallest and most easterly of the Greater Antilles, 110 by 35 miles, the Commonwealth of Puerto Rico is under the jurisdiction of the United States. Lying 972 miles southeast of Miami, it's home to 3.3 million people whose major language is Spanish, although many, especially those in the tourist industry, also speak English. The island's interior is filled with ancient volcanic mountains—the highest peak is Cerro de Punta at 4,333 feet—but its coastline is ringed with beaches. The commonwealth also includes a trio of small offshore islands: Culebra, Mona, and Vieques (the last has the most tourist facilities). San Juan, the capital, has a population of one million, and with its Latin American culture and tradition, and its long and colorful history, is one of the major ports of call in the Caribbean.

Saba (Dutch Windwards in the Leewards): The Dutch island of Saba (*Say*-bah), part of the Netherlands Antilles, is only 5 miles square. It's most often visited on a day trip from St. Maarten, 28 miles north. Don't go for the beaches; go for the scenery and the mountains. The Bottom is the capital and is one of four little villages with characteristic white and green houses.

St. Barthélemy (also called St. Barts or St. Barths; French West Indies): Part of the French *département* of Guadeloupe, lying 15 miles from St. Maarten, St. Barts is in the Leewards. It has a small population of 3,500 people who live on 13 square miles. A small number of African descendants live harmoniously on this chic Caribbean island with descendants of Normans and Bretons and a colony of French expatriates. Considered an expensive stamping ground of the rich and famous, St.

N
0
200 mi.
320 km.
FLORIDA
Miami
Gulf of Mexico
Straits of Florida
THE BAHAMAS
Havana
Yucatan Channel
Cuba
Little Cayman
Cayman Brac
Grand Cayman
CAYMAN ISLANDS
Montego Bay
Jamaica
Kingston
Port-au-Prince
GREATER
HONDURAS
NICARAGUA
Lago de Managua
Lago de Nicaragua
COSTA RICA
Caribbean Sea
Panama Canal
PANAMA
COLOMBIA
North Pacific Ocean

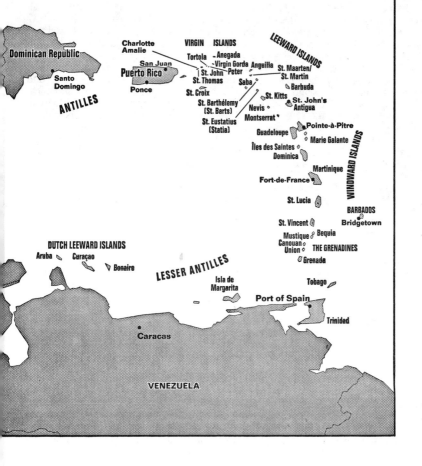

Atlantic

Ocean

Dominican Republic

Santo
Domingo

ANTILLES

Charlotte
Amalie

San Juan

Puerto Rico

Ponce

St. Croix

VIRGIN   ISLANDS

Tortola   – Anegada
~Virgin Gorda   Anguilla
St. John—Peter   Saba
St. Thomas

St. Barthélemy
(St. Barts)

St. Eustatius
(Statia)

LEEWARD ISLANDS

St. Maarten/
St. Martin

Barbuda

St. Kitts   St. John's
Nevis   Antigua
Montserrat

Guadeloupe   Pointe-à-Pitre

Îles des Saintes   Marie Galante
Dominica

Martinique

Fort-de-France

St. Lucia

WINDWARD ISLANDS

BARBADOS
St. Vincent   Bridgetown

Mustique   Bequia
Canouan
Union   THE GRENADINES
Grenada

DUTCH LEEWARD ISLANDS

Aruba   Curaçao
Bonaire

LESSER ANTILLES

Isla de
Margarita

Tobago

Port of Spain

Trinidad

Caracas

VENEZUELA

Barts has a "storybook" capital at Gustavia, named after a Swedish king (Sweden once ruled the island).

Sint Eustatius (known as Statia; Dutch Windwards in the Leewards): Another Dutch possession, like its neighbor Saba, Statia is only 5 miles long and 2 miles wide, and lies 35 miles south of Dutch-held St. Maarten. Among the poorest of the Windward Islands, with a population of 1,700, it has been slow to awaken to tourism. Its sleepy capital is Oranjestad.

St. Kitts and Nevis (British Leewards): Officially named St. Christopher, the island of St. Kitts is separated from its neighbor, Nevis, by a 2-mile strait, but together they form an island nation with traditional British affiliations. St. Kitts consists of 68 square miles and Nevis is 36 square miles. St. Kitts has more tourist facilities, but Nevis has more "inns of character," some formerly plantations. The capital of St. Kitts is Basseterre; the capital of Nevis is quiet little Charlestown. Both islands possess charm and unique personalities.

St. Lucia (British Windwards): St. Lucia (*Loo*-sha) is the second biggest of the Windward Islands, 24 miles south of Martinique. An island of great natural beauty, it has white and black sandy beaches, sulfur springs, and some of the most spectacular mountain scenery in the West Indies. Its twin mountain peaks, Gros Piton at 2,619 feet and Petit Piton at 2,461 feet, both ancient volcanos, are landmarks. The island, whose capital is Castries, spreads across 238 square miles and has a population of 140,000.

Sint Maarten/St. Martin (Dutch Windwards in the Leewards/French West Indies): Lying 144 miles east of Puerto Rico, this "twin nation" island of 37 square miles has been divided between the Dutch (Sint Maarten) and the French (St. Martin) since 1648. Regardless of how you spell it, it's the same island, although both sides of the unguarded border are quite different. Sint Maarten has many more shops and more intricately developed tourist facilities, whereas St. Martin, whose capital is Marigot, has some of the poshest hotels on the island as well as some of the best food in the Caribbean. The island is known for its beaches, casinos, and duty-free shopping. Shopping is best in the cruise port of Philipsburg, which is the capital of Sint Maarten.

St. Vincent and the Grenadines (British Windwards): Divers and the yachting crowd knew of the wonders of this mini-archipelago nation, but it was relatively slow to develop tourism. The largest and northernmost island of the British Windwards is St. Vincent, home to some 105,000 people, whose capital and major port is Kingstown. St. Vincent is 11 miles wide and 18 miles long. Stretching like a pearl necklace south of St. Vincent are some 32 neighbor islands called the Grenadines, including chic Mustique where Princess Margaret has a Caribbean home (which she often rents out). Others include Bequia, Canouan, Palm Island, and Petit St. Vincent.

Trinidad and Tobago: The southernmost of the West Indies, this two-island nation lies just 7 miles off the coast of Venezuela. Trinidad, known for its calypso music and exciting carnival, is one of the most culturally distinctive in the Caribbean. Covering 1,864 square miles, it's one of the most industrialized islands with a bustling capital at Port-of-Spain, but it is also known for its wildlife and flora. About 20 miles northeast of Trinidad, tiny Tobago (9 miles wide and 26 miles long) has its capital at Scarborough. Known for its beaches, it's much more of a "tourist island" than Trinidad.

U.S. Virgin Islands: Some 40 miles east of Puerto Rico and 1,100 miles southeast of Miami, these islands include St. Croix (the biggest), St. Thomas (considered the shopping mall of the Caribbean), and tiny St. John. Formerly Danish possessions, they became part of the United States in 1917.

HISTORY & POLITICS

EARLY HISTORY The indigenous peoples of the Greater Antilles, The Bahamas, and some of the Lesser Antilles were related to each other and all spoke forms of Arawak. They are thought to have come originally from South America's Amazon basin, driven out by the fiercer Carib peoples and risking their lives in oar-propelled dugout canoes to find better, safer places to live. The route the tribes followed over many centuries is thought to have led from South America via Puerto Rico to Hispaniola and Cuba. Among these Arawak-speaking tribes, the Taíno was one of the strongest and some traces of this tribe have been found in Cuba and Puerto Rico. Artifacts from other tribes have been found in Haiti, the Dominican Republic, and Jamaica. Some tribes even made their way as far north as the southern Bahamas. The Caribs themselves took control of some of the Lesser Antilles and Hispaniola.

THE EUROPEAN CONQUEST Columbus arrived in 1492 and many pictures have been painted of the unsuspecting natives showing no fear of the strange, overdressed (for the climate) men from across the sea. However, it didn't take the Spaniards long to wipe out the native population throughout the islands. Inflicting unspeakable cruelties on the natives, the conquistadores enslaved the survivors of small battles and used them as tools to dig precious metals from the ground, dive for pearls, and perform constant back-breaking labor. The Caribs, being warlike, lasted a little longer than did any of the Arawak tribes, but it was only about a century after Spanish claims were established before the native Caribbean islanders were almost entirely annihilated.

About the only places where traces of Arawak blood may still exist are Cuba and the Dominican Republic. The stronger Caribs have left their mark in Dominica and St. Vincent, where there are little groups of people called "black Caribs," of mixed African and West Indian blood. Also, on Aruba you'll meet many *mestizos,* whose blood is mixed Indian and white, but their ancestors probably came much later from South America than did the Arawaks and Caribs.

In the beginning, Spain, hungry for gold and with the support of the Catholic church, laid claim to everything in sight—and to a lot of lands only rumored to be in the area. On his four voyages, Columbus explored Cuba, Hispaniola (the whole island then being called Haiti, or "High Land," by the inhabitants), Dominica, Guadeloupe in the Lesser Antilles, Puerto Rico, the Cayman Islands, Jamaica, and Trinidad, as well as Central and South American territories. From the early 16th century, the Spaniards' quest for gold and silver led to some colonization of towns at the good natural harbors, but they were not really settlers in these new lands. The harbors served as ports on favorable sea lanes among the islands along which treasures were sent back to Spain. The newcomers spread their religion and their communicable diseases to the indigenous inhabitants, who died off rapidly as they were enslaved and brutalized by the Spaniards.

The treasures of the Antilles proved too tempting for other Europeans to pass up, and by the middle of the 16th century sea-going plunderers from various European nations were preying on the galleons bearing rich cargoes from the New World to fill the coffers of Spain. The Dutch, French, British—called variously corsairs, freebooters, pirates, privateers, filibusters, and buccaneers—prowled the seas and left a legacy of blood-spattered romance.

From the middle of the 17th century, assorted peoples from Western Europe began to settle in the new lands, which changed flags frequently. The British, French, Danes, and Dutch were chief among the claimants as Spain's power declined. The Dutch held Curaçao and the French kept Martinique, although the claims were long disputed. By 1670 Britain had seized Jamaica. The French government, following in the footsteps of freebooters, took over Hispaniola and renamed it Saint-Domingue.

As colonization took hold, the new landowners established sugar plantations, first in the Lesser Antilles and then on islands of the Greater Antilles. With the plantations came the slave trade—the importation of Africans as the labor force of the West Indies.

In 1763, after years of conflict (particularly between Britain and France), the treaty ending the Seven Years' War in Europe gave Britain the upper hand in many areas of the Caribbean, but it did not end the strife. Britain seized Guadeloupe. Major turmoil erupted in Hispaniola. As the 19th century dawned, the long discontent of Africans and mulattoes boiled up in revolt; the sons and daughters of Africa took eastern Hispaniola from Spain, which had regained control from France, but were soon forced to relinquish the prize. However, they threw off their chains of slavery and succeeded also in throwing off the yoke of French sovereignty in the western third of the island, establishing a republic and naming it Haiti.

Following the Napoleonic wars, treaties distributed the Caribbean islands as follows: France had only Martinique and Guadeloupe (and satellite islands) in the Lesser Antilles; the Netherlands finally got a clear claim to Curaçao; Britain held Jamaica, the Cayman Islands, and most of the Lesser Antilles (except for the French colonies and some small island possessions of the Danes and the Dutch); and Spain kept Puerto Rico, Cuba, and eastern Hispaniola, by now called Santo Domingo. The tribulations of Haiti were not over, although it was considered independent of European rule. The new republic kept trying to include eastern Hispaniola under its flag, but by the middle of the 19th century that part of the island had achieved independence from both Spain and Haiti, and the Dominican Republic had been set up. Hispaniola was henceforth an island of two separate republics.

By the time slavery was abolished by the various controlling nations, the African descendents were deeply rooted in the West Indies.

THE 20TH CENTURY   The United States became a presence in the Caribbean in 1898, not through colonization but by military and monetary power. Spain lost Cuba and Puerto Rico in the Spanish-American War. The U.S. occupied Haiti from 1915 to 1934 because of a bloody power struggle between blacks and mulattoes. It also occupied the Dominican Republic from 1916 to 1924 to protect U.S. interests. The people of Puerto Rico became U.S. citizens in 1917 and were granted limited self-government. In that same year the Danish Virgin Islands were bought by the United States as territories to be known as the U.S. Virgin Islands. The people there are U.S. citizens, but they cannot vote in federal elections. In 1952 the internally self-governing Commonwealth of Puerto Rico was established, and the island still may eventually become one of the United States of America.

With the end of colonialism in most of the Caribbean in the 20th century, many forms of self-government have emerged. The Netherlands Antilles now have internal self-government. Martinique and Guadeloupe were made overseas *départements* of France. Some of the former British colonies now have various forms of their own government. There are constitutional states, independent states, one presidential republic, one independent republic, and one British Associated State, all within the British Commonwealth. The British monarch is still head of state (represented by a governor) for the British Virgin Islands, the Caymans, and Montserrat, which are designated as Crown Colonies.

2. ART & LITERATURE

ART   Other Caribbean islands have followed Haiti's lead in producing—and selling—the primitive art of the people. You can see the work of the top artists, whose paintings command high prices, at galleries on a number of the islands, but you may be able to acquire a good and characteristic painting at a street show or even off the walls of some little café. Keep looking.

Wood carvings range from rough animal and human figures to fierce masks to smoothly finished statuary of mahogany and other native woods.

LITERATURE   Until this century, West Indies literature was limited to what missionary priests wrote about various aspects of the Caribbean islands. History, poetry, drama, and a few novels were written by people born on Guadeloupe, Martinique, Puerto Rico, the Dominican Republic, and Haiti during the 17th, 18th, and 19th centuries, but this early literary output, whether in English, French, or Spanish, had little originality of thought or form. In some cases the writers even sought to distance themselves from their island roots by seeking recognition in the capitals of the colonial empire rather than on the home scene. The lack of literary progress among the nonwhite islanders was largely due to the lack of education even after the abolition of slavery.

In this century a literature has developed in the Caribbean (and in Africa) in which individuality of expression and originality of subject matter have come to the fore. Called "the literature of negritude," it uses African forms and traditions and has played an important role in strengthening the racial pride and independence among the people of African ancestry.

A few of the leaders in the field of the literature of negritude are Jamaican Claude McKay, poet and the first professional Caribbean novelist; Jacques Roumain, essayist, poet, and novelist of Haiti; St. Lucia–born Trinidad-dweller Derek Walcott, playwright and poet; John Hearne, Canada-born Jamaican novelist; Roger Mais, Jamaican short-story writer, poet, and novelist; and George Lamming, novelist from Barbados.

Perhaps the spirit of the writers of the West Indies today was best voiced by Aimé Césaire, a poet born in 1913 on Martinique of poor peasants from Africa, one of the three founders of the negritude movement in Paris in 1937. He described his negritude by saying, "I want to rediscover the secret of great speech and of great burning. . . . The man who couldn't understand me couldn't understand the roaring of a tiger." At a conference on "Negritude, Ethnicity, and Afro Cultures in the Americas," held in 1988 at Florida International University at Miami, Césaire said, "Negritude, to my eyes, is not a philosophy, not metaphysics. It is the transfer of men from one continent to another, the debris of assassinated cultures." He continued that after centuries of "black diaspora," blacks must create a rehabilitation of their values themselves, rerooting themselves "within a history, within a geography, within a culture."

3. RELIGION & FOLKLORE

RELIGION   Although the slaves from Africa were forcibly "converted" to Christianity, they retained many beliefs and tribal customs of their native lands. This is seen in the mixture of pagan and Christian religious rites as observed by the voodoo followers on Haiti, santería on Cuba, and xango (shango) on Trinidad. The basic beliefs and rituals from Africa have been fitted in comfortably with Roman Catholic worship forms and figures. Protestant faiths, too, have also been strongly affected by the African heritage.

FOLKLORE   The folkloric tradition in the islands came from the memories and oral traditions from Africa that were passed down through the generations. The two most famous mythological figures of the Caribbean are the Obeah and the jumbie.

Basically, the Obeah is a "superstitious force" that natives believe can be responsible for both good and evil. It's considered prudent not to get on the bad side of this force, which might reward you or make trouble for you. If you encounter an old-time islander and ask, "How are you?" the answer is likely to be, "Not too bad." The person who may actually feel great says this so as not to tempt the force, which might be listening.

"Don't let the jumbies get ya!" is often heard in the islands, particularly when people are leaving their hosts and heading home in the dark. Like the Obeah, jumbies are also said to be capable of good or bad. These are supernatural beings that are believed by some to live around households. It is said that new settlers from the mainland of the United States never see these jumbies, and therefore need not fear them. But many islanders believe in their existence, and if queried, they may enthrall you with tales of sightings.

No one seems to agree on exactly what a jumbie is. "They're the souls of live people," one islander told me, "but they live in the body of the dead." It has also been suggested that a jumbie is the spirit of a dead person that didn't go where it belonged. The most prominent jumbies are "Mocko Jumbies." actually carnival stilt-walkers seen at all parades.

Weed women, who used old recipes handed down for generations, also have a firm place in the folklore of the islands. Apparently, some of their potions were amazingly effective, and some are still in use. They produced herbal teas and had "secret remedies" for any sickness or ailment, ranging from infertility to cancer.

4. CULTURAL & SOCIAL LIFE

Discoverers, fortune-hunters, pirates, planters, shipwrecked sailors, slaves, and free people have all splashed their colorful personalities across the canvas of the Caribbean. Long before the arrival of Columbus in 1493, the culture of the islands was already under way, as a result of the settlement by Arawak tribes and later the cannibalistic Caribs, who destroyed these kind people, either by working them to death as slaves or by eating them. With the advent of the European colonial powers, these cultures, along with these people, were completely wiped out.

Nothing was to shape the destiny and culture of the Caribbean more than the arrival of slaves from various parts of Africa, who brought their superstitions, fears, and gods with them. Although converted to Christianity, they kept their traditions alive in their fairs and festivals. The cultural and social life of the communities revolved almost completely around the church.

It was through storytellers that the past was kept alive for each new generation, since little of it was written down. However, since the coming of television, islanders rarely gather around to hear stories of the old days. Today some of the old stories are being collected and published in an attempt to preserve a cultural memory before it disappears completely.

Many British traditions are still maintained in the islands, especially on Barbados, as reflected in the judicial system and other matters. The legacy of Spain lives on in such islands as Puerto Rico and the Dominican Republic, which still have strong Latin traditions.

Of course, once the Americans took over the U.S. Virgin Islands and eventually made Puerto Rico a Commonwealth, American culture widely prevails. In fact, the big neighbor to the north has greatly affected all culture in the islands, as reflected by its big resort hotels, its cuisine, its films, and its television programs. In clothes, in cars, in food, in entertainment, and in currency, America dominates the islands.

But the annual festivals, the fungi bands, and even the belief in jumbies help to keep yesterday's culture alive.

THE PEOPLE After the indigenous population of the West Indies had been virtually annihilated, the population of the islands took on a variegated hue. Colonists brought European culture, customs, and languages of several nations, and many of these imports still exist, although inevitably they have been influenced by the tropical ambience. The colonists then imported the slaves from Africa by the hundreds of thousands, and today the majority of the islanders are descended from those African slaves.

After slavery was abolished, the British and French turned to a system of importing indentured servants from India, and some Chinese and Lebanese also came to the West Indies. These have added to the mixed bloodlines of the Caribbean populace, although some have maintained their ethnic purity, culture, religion, and customs through the years.

The ethnic heritage of the islands has enriched the cultural life of the Caribbean islands. Multinational influences are seen in architecture (places of worship, plantation great houses, villages, and huts), fine arts, and entertainment. Afro-Caribbean music, dancing, and painting (especially Haitian) are the most widely known art forms of the islands, but there is also Caribbean literature and other cultural expressions.

It's estimated that in the former British and French colonies over 90% of the population is made up of descendants of former slaves, with or without other ancestry. In the islands settled by Spain (Puerto Rico and Cuba), on the other hand, the white ancestry strongly predominates (less strongly in the Dominican Republic, which was affected by being twice made a part of black Haiti). There were fewer Africans in those islands in the colonial period because the plantation system did not develop there in the early days. By the time it did, slavery was no longer permitted, and the labor force for the Spanish-held islands came from the parent country and from the Canary Islands.

As to the East Indian population, it is mainly found in former British and French colonies. On Trinidad and Tobago you'll find that Asians make up some 40% of the count, and they are found in lesser numbers on Barbados, Curaçao, Grenada, Guadeloupe, Martinique, St. Lucia, St. Vincent, St. Kitts, Nevis, and a smattering in Haiti and Jamaica—and probably elsewhere.

Class distinctions throughout the islands were once based on race and color as well as wealth, but the system is changing. Instead of a small, mostly white, rich upper class and a large, poor, mainly black, mulatto, or otherwise mixed lower class, today a middle class is developing as a result of industrialization and other economic changes and improved education.

LANGUAGES   With such a melange of backgrounds, it's not surprising to find a linguistic mixture also. The language of the former colonial overlords is the official tongue of each island, even Haiti. There, the form is French, but the common speech is a French Créole. In fact the speech you'll hear when you travel in rural areas of many of the countries is heavily dependent on local dialects and patois, some with many phrases of African origin. Official languages of the islands are:

English—the Caymans, Jamaica, the U.S. and British Virgin Islands, Antigua, Barbuda, Montserrat, St. Kitts, Nevis, Anguilla, Dominica, St. Lucia, Barbados, Grenada, St. Vincent, the Grenadines, Trinidad, and Tobago.

Spanish—the Dominican Republic and Puerto Rico (where English is a second language), and Cuba.

French—Haiti, St. Martin, St. Barthélemy, Martinique, and Guadeloupe.

Dutch—Sint Maarten, Sint Eustatius, Saba, Aruba, Bonaire, and Curaçao.

5. PERFORMING ARTS

Calypso, reggae, and the beat of voodoo drums spring to mind when the music of the Caribbean is mentioned. The gutsy, aggressive beat and soul of African music was brought in with the cargoes of slave ships and long ago drowned out the tinkling harpsichord notes drifting through the great houses of plantations. The result was the music of the Caribbean.

Calypso music, which originated on Trinidad, is a mixture—basically African but with Afro-Spanish rhythms, English verses, and traces of French structure. The words to calypso tunes were originally (and sometimes still are) spontaneous improvisations, based on all sorts of subjects—love, sex, politics, whatever. Of more recent origin is **reggae,** which originated in Jamaica and is closely linked with the Rastafarian religious cult (whose messiah is the late emperor Haile Selassie, the Promised Land being Ethiopia). Reggae, developing out of an old form of folk music in Jamaica, embraces elements of music from Africa most strongly, but also uses ideas from Europe and India, calypso, the rumba, and the limbo. Reggae verses tend to accentuate views on politics, religion, social change, and antiwhite (where white equals imperialism) feelings.

The greatest single exponent of reggae music—and the person responsible for popularizing it around the world—is the late Bob Marley of Jamaica. The Marley family carries on his musical tradition today, along with countless imitators.

A basic source of Afro-Caribbean music is percussion, ranging from tom-toms to congas to the more modern steel drums. Other instruments of African inspiration are marimbas and banjos, while from Spain comes the infusion of guitar and wind instruments. Other sources of sound have been added as they came to hand: gourds, pots and pans, bamboo sticks, garbage cans and lids, cowbells, saws, even the jawbones of asses and horses and the trunks of trees. The making of music on old oil drums has become an art in itself when performed by the steel bands of the islands.

African dances, like the music, were mainly brought to the West Indies by slaves who had been born into the cultures of Dahomey and the Ashanti in what is now Ghana, along the Upper Guinea coast, and Nigerian Yoruba. Even today in Africa, especially in Ghana, the same kind of extempore verses are sung to the same rhythms as you'll hear in the calypso of the Caribbean. The **limbo** dance of the islands is a descendant of ancient tribal rites of Africa. Another dance form, seen mainly in Haiti, is the **merengue,** a dance ballad similar to calypso but usually more erotic in nature.

Spanish and Afro-Spanish influences are reflected in such dances as the **rumba, tango,** and **samba,** closely related to the Afro-French **calenda,** a dance whose movements were considered so suggestive by slave-owners in Martinique and Guadeloupe that they banned it. Outlawing the calenda didn't entirely kill it, however, and it even played a part in the development of the **béguine** in those islands.

The best way to enjoy the music and dancing of the Caribbean is at **carnival** time. In islands with strong Roman Catholic ties this is similar to Mardi Gras in New Orleans, with several days and nights of celebration and parades. For some islands, carnival lasts from Epiphany (January 6) to Ash Wednesday, with parades and dancing in the streets especially on each Sunday before Lent. On other islands, festivals, fiestas, and special days, many held in summer, take the place of carnival. For example, Barbados holds a Crop-Over Festival in June/July celebrating the end of the sugarcane harvest.

The carnivals and festivals are marked by flamboyant masqueraders parading and dancing to the pervasive island music, together with feasting on the foods common to the area. People of each island present folklore in song and dance at these events. If you can't be there for carnival, you may still have a chance to enjoy this bright facet of island life, as many hotels and nightclubs present abbreviated versions by folkloric groups as part of the entertainment program.

6. SPORTS & RECREATION

BEACHES   The Caribbean is known for having some of the finest beaches in the world. Nearly all the islands, except Saba and Dominica, have good ones, but on some islands, like Antigua, they are spectacular.

Among the most celebrated are Magens Bay Beach on St. Thomas, Lugillo Beach on Puerto Rico, and Trunk Bay on St. John. Cane Garden Bay on Tortola is acknowledged as the best stretch of beach in the British Virgin Islands. On Grand Cayman, many hotels are built to open onto Seven Mile Beach; and in the Dominican Republic, Playa Grande stretches along part of the north shore and is one of the least crowded beaches in the Caribbean.

For more details about beaches on the individual islands, see "Beaches" in the "Sports and Recreation" sections in the individual island chapters.

The Top 10 Beaches   Cane Garden Bay, Tortola, British Virgin Islands: One of the more spectacular stretches of beach, Cane Garden Bay extends for 1½ miles of white sand. A jogger's favorite, the beach is the rival of Magens Bay on St. Thomas.

Magens Bay Beach, St. Thomas, U.S. Virgin Islands: Known for its half-mile-long loop of brilliant white sand, and for its clear and calm waters, this public beach is the most popular in the U.S. archipelago. Two peninsulas protect the beach, and its flat, sandy bottom makes it safe for children.

Seven Mile Beach, Grand Cayman: It's really about 5½ miles, but the label of "seven mile" has stuck. Lined with condos and plush resorts, this beach is known for its array of water sports and its translucent aquamarine waters. Australian pines dot the background, and the average winter temperature of the water is 80°F.

Playa Grande, Dominican Republic: One of the Caribbean's least crowded beaches, but one of the best, Playa Grande, lies along the north shore. The long stretch of sand is powdery, and farther west is another beautiful beach at Sosúa, with calm waters and lots of tourist facilities.

Negril Beach, Jamaica: In the northwestern section of the island, this beach stretches for 7 miles along the sea and in the backdrop lie some of the most hedonistic resorts in the Caribbean, such as the appropriately named Hedonism II. Not for the conservative, the beach also contains some nudist "patches" along with bare-all Booby Island offshore. The nude beach areas are sectioned off, but some new resorts open onto these strands of sands for those wishing to take a look at the action from the ocean-view windows.

Luquillo Beach, Puerto Rico: This crescent-shaped public beach, 30 miles east of San Juan, is the local favorite. Much photographed because of its white sands and coconut palms, it also has tent sites and picnic facilities. These often fierce Atlantic waters are subdued by the coral reefs protecting the crystal-clear lagoon.

Trunk Bay, St. John, U.S. Virgin Islands: Protected by the rangers of the National Park Service, this is one of the Caribbean's most frequented beaches, a favorite with cruise-ship passengers. It's known for its underwater trail, where markers guide beachcombers along the reef lying just off the white sandy beach. Trunk Bay consistently makes "Top 10 Beaches" lists.

Shoal Bay, Anguilla: Often so empty it has been called "paradise" or "Eden," this silvery beach helped put Anguilla on tourist maps. Divers are drawn not only to the sands but also to the schools of iridescent fish underwater that dart among the coral gardens offshore.

St. Jean, St. Barts, French West Indies: A somewhat narrow but golden sandy beach, St. Jean is the nugget of this French-held island with a Swedish heritage. In spite of its French connection, however, nudity is strictly not permitted. Nevertheless, this is most often compared to a beach on France's Côte d'Azur. The beach strip is protected by reefs, making it ideal for swimming.

Le Diamant, Martinique, French West Indies: This bright white sandy beach stretches along for about 6½ miles, much of it undeveloped. It faces the landmark H.M.S. *Diamond Rock,* where people like to go swimming and enjoy picnics.

FISHING The Caribbean has some of the world's premier fishing grounds, containing an amazing variety of deep-sea game fish—wahoo, sailfish, tuna, marlin, and dolphin (the fish, not the mammal). Shallow-water fish pursued include tarpon, bonefish, pompano, and barracuda.

Spring through autumn is the best time to fish, although the sport is still practiced in winter.

Puerto Rico is virtually the fishing capital of the Caribbean—some 30 world records have been set here. Charters are plentiful in San Juan and Palmas del Mar.

Some of the other best fishing grounds are in the Cayman Islands, whose offshore waters are filled with tuna, yellowtail, marlin, and other catches; and the Dominican Republic, which attracts anglers in pursuit of sailfish, marlin, and bonito. Those in search of Marlin head for the north coast of Jamaica from September to April, whereas the south coast is favored in winter. Port Antonio is the major fishing center for Jamaica.

The U.S. Virgin Islands are also popular with vacationers pursuing allison tuna, bonita, marlin, and wahoo. Red Hook on St. Thomas is the major charter center, although St. John and St. Croix lure anglers as well.

GOLF Many people come to the West Indies just to play golf. Some of the world's major golf architects, including Robert Trent Jones (both Junior and Senior), Pete Dye, and others, have designed challenging courses in the Caribbean.

Perhaps the finest golf is offered at **Casa de Campo** in the Dominican Republic, where Peter Dye created his masterpiece. In Puerto Rico, the **Dorado Beach Golf Course** offers two state-of-the-art courses, although the Gary Player–designed

18-hole course at **Palmas del Mar,** near Humacao, is considered the island's most difficult challenge (6,690 yards, par 72). On St. Croix, in the U.S. Virgin Islands, the **Carambola Beach and Golf Resort,** designed by Robert Trent Jones, Sr., features several holes with water hazards. Another notable course is at **Tryall,** Jamaica, lying 12 miles from Montego Bay.

SAILING The Virgin Islands groups and the Grenadines are the best islands for sailing in the Caribbean. Both the U.S. island of St. Thomas, as well as Virgin Gorda and Tortola in the British Virgin Islands, are major yachting havens. The Grenadines is an archipelago of small islands (islets) stretching south from St. Vincent which governs them.

It is estimated that there are some 100 charter yachts in the B.V.I. as well as dozens upon dozens of bareboats. Bareboating, which is also popular on St. Thomas, usually costs about $75 a day in season (winter), or about $55 in summer. Cruising vacations on charter yachts can range to almost "anything" a day (the sky's the limit), but they start at about $150 for a no-frills outing.

SNORKELING & SCUBA DIVING Nearly all beach hotels rent snorkeling equipment, and dive shops, especially since the 1980s, have opened on virtually every island.

Bonaire is known for its spectacular dive sites, as are the Cayman Islands. Divers are also drawn to St. Croix, with its coral canyons and drop-offs at Davis Bay and Salt River, whereas snorkelers have only praise for Buck Island, a national park lying a short distance from Christiansted harbor. One of the best centers for snorkelers is Virgin Gorda's "The Baths." (See the individual island chapters for details.)

TENNIS Some resorts offer "tennis packages," with rooms and often meals at discounted rates. Ask travel agents about these. Securing "court time" in season can be difficult, but a tennis package will virtually guarantee time for you.

Several resorts are known for their tennis, including the luxurious **Buccaneer** on St. Croix, site of several annual tournaments. Tennis at the **Casa de Campo,** La Romana, in the Dominican Republic, is superb, with tennis packages available year round. Both Hyatt properties at Dorado, Puerto Rico—the **Cerromar Beach Hotel** and the **Dorado Beach Hotel**—are known as tennis resorts. Cerromar alone has 14 Laykold courts.

Also in Puerto Rico, **Palmas del Mar,** a complex of condos, offers 20 courts. In Antigua, the deluxe **Curtain Bluff** is the site of an annual spring tennis tournament.

The best tennis center on Jamaica is found at the **Half Moon Club** outside Montego Bay, with 13 courts.

Many courts are lit for night games.

7. FOOD & DRINK

ISLAND FOOD Hotel chefs prepare a presentable American and continental cuisine, but in recent years hotels have placed a greater emphasis on local dishes. Even so, it's still better to order a $15 meal at a local restaurant than it is to have a $50 dinner in a so-called gourmet restaurant at some deluxe resort.

Many recipes in the West Indies date back to the days of the Arawaks and Caribs, the original settlers who relied on what was available locally. Then came the conquerors from Europe and variations began to appear in the cuisine. African influences came with the slave trade, and even later influences included Hindu, Chinese, and Indonesian dishes.

Fruits and Vegetables The abundance of fruit in the islands is naturally reflected in the cuisine, which you'll see first at breakfast, usually freshly sliced on a platter. **Coconut,** for example, is used in everything from breads to soups. **Soursop** ice cream appears on some menus, and the guava might turn up in anything from juice to cheese. **Papaya** is called paw paw, and it will most often be your melon choice at breakfast. **Mango** is ubiquitous, used in chutney, but also in drinks and desserts. The **avocado,** most often called "pears," is used in fresh seafood salads and often stuffed with fresh crabmeat.

By now most visitors know that **plantain** (which is similar to a banana but red in color) is not eaten raw. These are served most often as a cooked side dish, the way we might present french fries. Puerto Ricans eat dried plantains, called *tostones,* from cellophane bags in lieu of potato chips. Plantains can also be served mashed or boiled, and they turn up in many desserts, especially when mixed with coconut and pineapple.

Two staples of the Caribbean islands have always been rice and pigeon peas. Balls of cornmeal, called **fungi,** also a staple of the West Indian diet, often accompany a salt-pork main dish known as **mauffay.** Sometimes these cornmeal concoctions will appear on the menus of local restaurants as *coo coo.* **Roast suckling pig** is nowhere better than on Puerto Rico and the Dominican Republic. Everything that appears unattractive and less desirable in the pig usually turns up in **souse,** most often including the head, tail, and feet, and it is usually served with black pudding.

One of the most common vegetables in the islands is **christophine** (sometimes called *foo foo*), a green, prickly gourd that tastes somewhat like zucchini. **Bread-fruit,** introduced to the islands by Captain Bligh (of *Bounty* fame) is green and ball shaped and is used much as we use potatoes. Potatoes and yams are also local favorites. The leaflike **callaloo** (regardless of how it's spelled) is one of the best-known vegetables in the West Indies. It's like spinach and is often served with crab, salt pork, and fresh fish with floating fungi as a garnish. You might call it the Caribbean version of bouillabaisse.

Seafood   Throughout the islands, warm-water lobster is the king of the sea and the most sought-after—and most expensive—main course to order. The "catch of the day" is most likely to be red snapper or grouper, but could also be shark or barracuda.

Caution is urged in eating barracuda. Barracuda north of Antigua tend to feed on copper deposits derived from eating a certain genus of seaweed. This genus is particularly concentrated along the Cayman Islands and Cuba. South of Antigua there tends not to exist these copper deposits, and locals consider barracuda fine eating. If the barracuda fights strongly during the net or line process, it is considered healthy. If it succumbs without a fight, it is viewed as sick and/or poisoned. Reputable fishermen throw sick fish back into the sea, and reputable restaurants tend to buy only from reputable fishermen. Sick fish can sometimes heal themselves in time, and later be judged "killer fighters" suitable for table consumption. The barracuda in south-lying Barbados are fine and usually very healthy.

Dolphin may also appear on the menu, but—never fear—this dolphin is a fish and not the playful mammal we usually associate with the term.

Créole Cookery   In a truly native restaurant in the Caribbean, you'll see hot peppers placed on the table. Be sparing. A selection of these hot pepper pastes is called **sambal.**

Créole cookery varies from island to island. For example, on Dominica and Montserrat, "mountain chicken"—sometimes known as **crapaud**—is a delicacy, but it's not chicken at all, it's large frogs' legs. The national dish of the Dominican Republic is **sancocho,** which is a soupy stew made with seven different kinds of meat.

On Puerto Rico the cuisine even today reflects the former inhabitants, ranging from the peaceful Taíno people to the Spanish conquerors. The most popular dish is **sopa de frijoles negros,** or black-bean soup. **Arroz con pollo,** or chicken with rice, long ago traveled north of the border. **Asopao** is a thick rice-based soup to which seafood has been added, and **mofongo** is a baseball-size patty made with plantains, pork rind, and lots of garlic.

Martinique and Guadeloupe are said to have the best food in the Caribbean. French dishes are served on both islands. Local cooks have created their own unique recipes, however, including crabes farcis (stuffed land crabs), colombo de poulet (a spicy chicken curry), and acrats de moure (salt codfish fritters).

In some areas you may be offered iguana or turtle. It would be better to choose another dish. Both the iguana and the turtle are endangered species, so please do not contribute to the extinction of these increasingly rare animals.

In Jamaica "jerk" cooking is the rage. **Jerk pork** is peculiar to country areas, where it is barbecued slowly over wood fires until crisp and brown. Traditionally, the meat is smoked for hours over pimiento (allspice) wood and leaves, which gives it a distinctive flavor—it's heavily spiced. **Jerk chicken** is also popular, and in recent years **jerk lobster** appears on many menus.

Your best bet when traveling through the islands is to sample what Barbadians call a **"cohoblopot,"** or a medley of "the best of it all."

ISLAND DRINKS Since the late 16th century, **rum** has been a legend, associated with slavery, Yankee traders, pirates, and bootlegging. A whole series of rum barons arose, with names that became famous around the world: Bacardí, González, Myers, and Barceló, to name only a few. "Kill-devil," as rum was once called, is of course the established drink of the islands.

Distilled in a not-very-complicated process from sugarcane, rum has played a major role in the history of the West Indies as the greatest naval powers of Europe struggled for supremacy. It can be argued that slavery even existed to service the flourishing intertwined industries of sugar, molasses, and rum. Today the rusted machinery and tumbledown ruins of distilleries are tourist stopovers on dozens of Caribbean islands.

The enormous crushing devices were powered, depending on the natural circumstances, by wind, water, or steam. The resulting mash was fermented in open vats and then distilled through long lengths of copper tubing. Conditions were far from sanitary, as everything from bat dung to spiders to crumbled leaves would routinely fall into the bubbling, foul-smelling mash.

Today's rum is made in modern distilleries using methods vastly more sanitary than those adopted by the colonials of a century ago. Each island seems to turn out its own type of rum, but when masked with the layers of fruit, syrup, and sugar that usually are included in a rum-based drink, it's difficult to tell the difference. While planter's punch is the most popular drink in the islands, the average bar in the Caribbean is likely to offer a bewildering array of rum-based drinks.

Don't think that the only **beer** you'll be able to find will be imported from Milwaukee or Holland. Of course, Heineken is ubiquitous, as is Amstel, especially in the Dutch islands, but Red Stripe from Jamaica is the most famous.

A *Word of Caution:* Be alert to your limits, especially if you're driving. The pastel-colored drinks can make neophytes lethally drunk on very short notice—partly because of their elevated sugar content and partly because of the heat of the Caribbean.

You can always drink **water.** Water is generally safe throughout the islands, but many tourists get sick from drinking it simply because it's different from the water they're accustomed to. If available, order bottled water.

8. RECOMMENDED BOOKS & RECORDINGS

BOOKS

GENERAL *Pirates of the Virgin Islands* and *Mavericks in Paradise,* by Fritz Seyfarth (Spanish Main Press), two books bound in one volume, capture all the daring exploits of the maritime gangsters who collected immense booty and made the West Indies a "private paradise."

Caribbean Pirates, by Warren Alleyne (Macmillan-Caribbean), tries to separate fact from fiction using some published letters and documents as sources.

Caribbean Style, the work of several authors (Crown Publishers), is a coffee-table book filled with Caribbean images, from decaying old plantation houses or balcony-fronted typical West Indian houses with peeling paint, to lush gardens and flowers.

FICTION Herman Wouk's *Don't Stop the Carnival* (in many editions) is "the Caribbean classic," and I recommend that anyone contemplating a visit to the Caribbean read this book before going there.

Caribbean, by James A. Michener (Fawcett paperback), is a grand epic from the master. His sweep of the Caribbean begins with the 1310 conquest of the peaceful Arawaks by the cannibalistic Caribs and ranges along seven centuries up to Castro.

Easy in the Islands, by Bob Shacochis (1985). Winner of the American Book Award in 1986, this collection of short stories giddily re-creates the flavor of the West Indies.

TRAVEL *Love and the Caribbean: Tales, Characters, and Scenes of the West Indies,* by Alec Waugh (Paragon House, 1991), is a vivid portrait of the Caribbean by a famous writer.

The Traveller's Tree: A Journey Through the Caribbean Islands, by Patrick Leigh Fermor (Quentin Crewe, 1950). Prize-winning author Fermor wrote this classic account of his now-famous journey through the West Indies in the 1940s.

HISTORY *From Columbus to Castro: The History of the Caribbean,* by Eric Williams (Vintage Books, 1970). The former prime minister of Trinidad and Tobago takes you on a grand tour of a region dominated by slavery, sugar, and often sheer greed.

Columbus and the Age of Discovery, by Zvi Dor-Ner with William G. Scheller (William Morrow, 1991), is the companion book to the PBS series broadcast on the explorer and is a good general survey of what is known about the voyages of Columbus.

The Caribbean People, by Reginald Honychurch (T. Nelson & Sons, 1981), in three volumes, is a well-balanced account written by one of the so-called new historians of the Caribbean.

RECORDINGS

Calypso and reggae, the sounds of the Caribbean, are famous. Less well known is *soca,* a rock-influenced calypso, and *zouk,* which is a fusion of all Caribbean music, with a touch of French melody thrown in for added measure.

Here's a representative list of recordings currently available in stores:

The Pan in Me, by the Amoco Renegades (Jit Somaroo) (Delos DE-4014).

Caribbean Medley: Sammy Did/Wings of a Dove/Mary Ann/Linstead Market/Amazing Grace, by the Cayman Allstars (Fiesta FCD 1018).

Brown Skin Girl, by Brutus Marcato and the Mardi Gras Orchestra (Fiesta FCD 1013).

Gaudeamus Igitur, by the Silver Stars (Delos DE-4012).

Welcome the Morning Sun, by the Five Star Cockspur Steel Orchestra (WIRL W-CD-002).

Soca Man, by the Success Stars (Delos DE-4012).

Hot Hot Hot, by the Five Star Cockspur Steel Orchestra (WIRL W-CD-002).

Bassa Roo, by Brutus Marcato and the Mardi Gras Orchestra (Fiesta FDC-1013).

Saturday Night, by the Cordettes–Sun Islanders Steel Orchestra (Fiesta FCD-1007).

Polanaise, by the Sunjet Serenaders Steelband (Columbia CS-9260).

Sunset, by the Steel Band of Trinidad & Tobago (Facet FICD 8201).

The Hammer, by the Steel Band of Trinidad & Tobago (Facet FICD 8201).

25th Anniversary, by "The Mighty Sparrow" (Francisco Flinger) (Charles Rawlston JAF001).

The Greatest, by "The Mighty Sparrow" (Francisco Flinger) (Charles Rawlston JAF1005).

Classics, Volume I, by "The Mighty Sparrow" (Francisco Flinger) (Charles Rawlston SCR7194).

Classics, Volume II, by "The Mighty Sparrow" (Francisco Flinger) (Charles Rawlston SCR3247).

Legend (Best Of), by Bob Marley, including such hits as the popular "Could You Be Loved" (Tuff Gong/Island Records 422846210-2).

Liberation, by Bunny Wailer, hailed by *Newsweek* as one of the three most important musicians in the Third World (Shanachie Records 43059).

Jahmakya, by Ziggy Marley & the Melody Makers, features such tunes as "Good Time" and "Drastic" (Virgin 2-91626).

Yellowman Strikes Again, by Yellowman, considered one of the pre-rap rappers or founders of rap music (VP Records VPCD 1078).

Earth Crisis, by Steel Pulse, including "Throne of Gold" (Elektra-Asylum 960315-2).

CHAPTER 2

PLANNING A TRIP TO THE CARIBBEAN

This chapter is devoted to the where, when, and how of your Caribbean trip—the advance-planning issues that need resolving before you leave home. It will explain how to get there, what it will cost, when to go, what health precautions to take, what insurance coverage is necessary, where to obtain more information, and more.

Before we begin, I'd like to make a recommendation. Since the islands are so diverse culturally and ethnically, I encourage you to island-hop rather than to stay in one place. It's easy to fly within the region, and will enrich your Caribbean vacation and help avoid sterile stopovers.

1. INFORMATION, ENTRY REQUIREMENTS, CUSTOMS & MONEY

INFORMATION

All the major islands have tourist representatives whom you can contact to obtain information before you go (see "Fast Facts" under the individual island listings). The **Caribbean Tourism Association,** 20 East 46th Streets, New York, NY 10017 (tel. 212/682-0435), can also provide general information.

You may also want to contact the State Department for background bulletins. Contact the Superintendent of Documents, **U.S. Government Printing Office,** Washington, DC 20402 (tel. 202/783-3238).

Other useful sources are **newspapers and magazines.** To find the latest articles published about the destination, go to your library and ask for the *Reader's Guide to Periodical Literature* and look under the island/country for listings.

A good **travel agent** can also provide information, but make sure the agent is a member of the American Society of Travel Agents (ASTA). If you have a complaint, write to the **ASTA Consumer Affairs Department,** P.O. Box 23922, Washington, DC 20006, for satisfaction.

ENTRY REQUIREMENTS

Even though the Caribbean islands are, for the most part, independent nations and thereby classified as international destinations, passports are not generally required. You do, however, have to have identity documents, and a passport is the best form of identification and will speed you through Customs and Immigration. Other acceptable documents include an ongoing or return ticket, plus a current voter registration card, or a birth certificate (the original or a copy that has been certified by the U.S. Department of Health). You will also need some photo ID, such as a driver's license or an expired passport; however, driver's licenses are not acceptable as a sole form of ID. Visas are usually not required, but some countries may require you to fill out a tourist card (see the individual island chapters for details).

Before leaving home, make two copies of your documents, including your passport and your driver's license; your airline ticket; and any hotel vouchers. If you're on medication, you should also make copies of prescriptions.

CUSTOMS

Each island has specific requirements. Generally, you are permitted to bring in items intended for your personal use, including tobacco, cameras, film, and a limited supply of liquor, usually 40 ounces.

U.S. CUSTOMS The U.S. government generously allows $1,200 worth of duty-free imports every 30 days from the U.S. Virgin Islands; those who go over their exemption are taxed at 5% rather than the usual 10%. The limit is $400 for such international destinations as the French islands of Guadeloupe and Martinique, and $600 for many other islands. If you visit only Puerto Rico, you don't have to go through Customs at all because of its status as an American Commonwealth.

Joint Customs declarations are possible for members of a family traveling together. For instance, if you are a husband and wife with two children, your exemptions in the U.S. Virgin Islands become duty free up to $4,800! Unsolicited gifts can be sent to friends and relatives at the rate of $100 per day in the U.S. Virgin Islands (or $50 a day on the other islands). As long as these gifts stay under the limit, they don't have to be declared on your Customs declaration. U.S. citizens 21 years of age and over are allowed to bring in duty free 200 cigarettes, 100 cigars (but not Cuban), and 1 liter of liquor (or wine).

Collect receipts for all purchases made abroad. Sometimes merchants suggest a false receipt to undervalue your purchase. *Warning:* You could be involved in a "sting" operation—the merchant might be an informer to U.S. Customs. You must also declare on your Customs form the nature and value of all gifts received during your stay abroad. It's prudent to carry proof that you purchased expensive cameras or jewelry on the United States mainland. If you purchased such an item during an earlier trip abroad, you should carry proof that you have previously paid Customs duty on the item.

If you use any medication containing controlled substances or requiring injection, carry an original prescription or note from your doctor.

For more specific guidance, write to the **U.S. Customs Service,** P.O. Box 7407, Washington, DC 20044, and request the free pamphlet "Know Before You Go."

CANADIAN CUSTOMS For total clarification, write for the booklet "I Declare," issued by Revenue Canada Customs Department, Communications Branch, Mackenzie Avenue, Ottawa, ON K1A 0L5. Canada allows its citizens a $300 exemption, and they can bring back duty free 200 cigarettes, 2 pounds of tobacco, 40 ounces of liquor, and 50 cigars. In addition, they are allowed to mail unsolicited gifts into Canada from abroad at the rate of $40 (Canadian) a day (but *not* alcohol or tobacco). On the package, mark "Unsolicited gift, under $40 value." All valuables you own and take with you should be declared before departure in Canada on the Y-38 form, including serial numbers. *Note:* The $300 exemption can be used only once a year, and then only after an absence of at least 7 days.

MONEY

CASH/CURRENCY   The U.S. dollar is widely accepted on many of the islands, and is the legal currency of the U.S. Virgin Islands, the British Virgin Islands, and Puerto Rico. Many islands use the Eastern Caribbean dollar, even though your hotel bill will most likely be presented in U.S. dollars. French islands use the French franc. Some countries have rather rigid currency requirements, especially Jamaica, which insists that all items purchased on that island be paid for with Jamaican dollars; currency in Jamaica should be changed at official bureaus or banks.
   For details, see "Fast Facts" in the individual island chapters.

TRAVELER'S CHECKS   Before leaving home, purchase traveler's checks and arrange to carry some ready cash (usually about $200).
   American Express (tel. toll free 800/221-7282 in the U.S. and Canada) is the most widely recognized traveler's check abroad; the agency imposes a 1% commission. Checks are free to members of the American Automobile Association.
   Bank of America (tel. toll free 800/227-3460 in the U.S., or 415/624-5400, collect, in Canada) also issues checks in U.S. dollars for 1% commission everywhere but California.
   Citicorp (tel. toll free 800/645-6556 in the U.S., or 813/623-1709, collect, in Canada) issues checks in U.S. dollars, British pounds, or German marks.
   MasterCard International (tel. toll free 800/223-9920 in the U.S., or 212/974-5696, collect, in Canada) issues checks in about a dozen currencies.
   Barclays Bank (tel. toll free 800/221-2426 in the U.S. and Canada) issues checks in both U.S. and Canadian dollars and British pounds.
   Thomas Cook (tel. toll free in the U.S. 800/223-7373, or 212/974-5696, collect, in Canada) issues checks in U.S. or Canadian dollars or British pounds. It's affiliated with MasterCard.

CREDIT CARDS   Credit cards are widely used in the Caribbean. VISA and MasterCard are the major cards used, although American Express and, to a lesser extent, Diners Club, are also popular.

2. WHEN TO GO — CLIMATE, HOLIDAYS & EVENTS

THE "SEASON"

More and more, the Caribbean is becoming a year-round destination. The "season" in the Caribbean runs roughly from mid-December to mid-April. Hotels charge their highest prices during the peak winter period, which is generally the driest season; however, it can be a wet time in mountainous areas, and you can expect showers especially in December and January on Martinique, Guadeloupe, Dominica, St. Lucia, on the north coast of the Dominican Republic, and in Jamaica's northeast section.
   For a winter vacation, make reservations 2 to 3 months in advance—or earlier for

trips at Christmas and in February. The mails are unreliable, so book through one of the many Stateside representatives all major and many minor hotels use or through a travel agent. You can also telephone or fax the hotel of your choice.

The temperature variations in the Caribbean are surprisingly slight, averaging between 75° and 85° Fahrenheit in both winter and summer, although it can get really chilly, especially in the early morning and at night. The Caribbean winter is usually like a perpetual May.

THE "OFF-SEASON"

The fabled Caribbean weather is balmy all year, with temperatures varying little more than 5° between winter and summer. The mid-80s prevail throughout most of the region, and trade winds make for comfortable days and nights, even without air conditioning.

Dollar for dollar, you'll spend less money by renting a summer house or self-sufficient unit in the Caribbean than you would on Cape Cod, Fire Island, Laguna Beach, or the coast of Maine. Sailing and water sports are better too, because the West Indies are protected from the Atlantic on their western shores, which border the calm Caribbean Sea.

20% TO 60% REDUCTIONS The off-season in the Caribbean—roughly from mid-April to mid-December (although this varies from hotel to hotel)—amounts to a summer sale. In most cases, hotel rates are slashed a startling 20% to 60%.

OTHER OFF-SEASON ADVANTAGES

- After the winter hordes have left, a less-hurried way of life prevails. You'll have a better chance to appreciate the food, the culture, and the local customs.
- Swimming pools and beaches are less crowded—perhaps not crowded at all.
- Year-round resort facilities are offered, often at reduced rates, and are likely to include snorkeling, boating, and scuba diving.
- To survive, resort boutiques often feature summer sales, hoping to clear the merchandise they didn't sell in February to accommodate stock they've ordered for the coming winter. Duty-free items in free-port shopping are draws all year too.
- You can often walk in unannounced at a top restaurant and get a seat for dinner, and since the waiters are less hurried, you'll get better service.
- No waiting for a rented car (only to be told none is available); no long tee-up for golf; more immediate access to the tennis courts and water sports.
- The atmosphere is more cosmopolitan because of the influx of Europeans; you'll no longer feel as if you're at a Canadian or American outpost.
- Some package-tour fares are as much as 20% lower, and individual excursion fares are also reduced between 5% and 10%.
- All accommodations, including airline seats and hotel rooms, are much easier to obtain.
- With school out, summer is the time for family travel.
- Finally, the very best of wintertime attractions remain undiminished—sea, sand, and surf, usually with lots of sunshine.

THE HURRICANE SEASON The curse of Caribbean weather, the "hurricane season" lasts—officially, at least—from June 1 to November 30. But there's no cause for panic. Satellite forecasts give adequate warnings so that precautions can be taken. Of course, there is always prayer: U.S. Virgin Islanders actually have a legal holiday in the third week of July, called Supplication Day, when prayers that the Virgin Islands will be spared another hurricane are said in churches islandwide. In late October, at the end of the season of danger, a supplemental Thanksgiving Day is celebrated.

To get a weather report before you go, call your nearest branch of the National Weather Service, listed in your phone directory under the "U.S. Department of Commerce." You can also call WeatherTrak; for the telephone number for your particular area, dial 900/370-8725 (a taped message gives you the three-digit access code for the place you're interested in).

HOLIDAYS

In addition to holidays normally observed by all islands, including Easter and Christmas, each island has special holidays. See "Fast Facts" in the individual island chapters.

CARIBBEAN CALENDAR OF EVENTS

JANUARY

☐ **Tennis Week,** Antigua. International tennis tournaments and clinics. First week of January.

☐ **Jamaica Classic Golf Tournament,** Tyrall Golf, Tennis & Beach Club, outside Montego Bay. This annual event draws golfers from around the world. Mid-January.

☐ **Curaçao Carnival.** The first of the West Indian carnivals, with costumed parades, music, and dancing. Late January to early February.

FEBRUARY

☐ **Holetown Festival,** Barbados. Commemorating the island's discovery in 1627, this week-long festival is filled with general revelry, street markets, and fairs. Mid-February.

☐ **Aruba Carnival.** This island-wide event features parades, street dancing, musical presentations, and the crowning of Carnival Queen. Mid- to late February.

☐ **Guadeloupe Carnival.** Carnival frenzy engulfs the island in a Mardi Gras aura, with parades, costumed "red devils," and general revelry, including a "King Carnival" burning on a funeral pyre. The rum flows, and there is feverish dancing. It begins as a pre-Lenten extravaganza and culminates on Ash Wednesday.

✪ ***MARTINIQUE CARNIVAL*** *For many, this is the biggest and best carnival in the West Indies—6 full weeks of zouks, or all-night revelries. Costumed dancers and ''she devils'' take to the streets, effigies burn, and the rum flows.*
   Where: *Throughout Martinique.* ***When:*** *Begins right after the New Year but doesn't reach fever pitch until just before Lent.* ***How:*** *Write to the Martinique Tourist Office (see Chapter 11) for more details.*

✪ ***TRINIDAD CARNIVAL*** *Filled with dazzling costumes and gaiety, hundreds of bands of masqueraders parade through the streets. It has been called a 48-hour orgy!*
   Where: *Throughout Trinidad and its neighbor island of Tobago.* ***When:*** *Monday and Tuesday preceding Ash Wednesday.* ***How:*** *Contact the National Carnival Committee, 41 Frederick Street, Port-of-Spain, Trinidad (tel. 809/623-7510), for more information.*

MARCH

☐ **Curaçao Regatta.** Racers from all over the world arrive in all types of boats. Dates vary.

☐ **St. Patrick's Day,** Montserrat. It's celebrated on the "Emerald Isle" of the Caribbean with much enthusiasm. Mid-March.

APRIL

☐ **Windsurfing Antigua Week.** Nine days of sailing and partying are followed by Sailing Week, when yachts from all over the globe converge at English Harbour for a regatta. Mid- to late April.

✪ *ST. THOMAS CARNIVAL* *The most spectacular carnival in the Virgin Islands, this annual celebration has roots in Africa. Over the years, the festivities have become Christianized, but the fun and gaiety remain. Mocko Jumbies, people dressed as spirits, parade through the streets on stilts, nearly 20 feet high. Steel and fungi bands, "jump-ups," and parades mark the event.*
   Where: Islandwide, but best on the streets of Charlotte Amalie. When: After Easter, sometime in April. How: Obtain a schedule of events from the tourist office on St. Thomas (see Chapter 5).

✪ *B.V.I. SPRING REGATTA* *The second leg of the Caribbean Ocean Racing Triangles events attracts everybody from the most dedicated racers to bareboat crews out for "rum and reggae." For the Caribbean boat crowd, the 3-day race is a major event.*
   Where: Tortola. When: Mid-April. How: For more information, contact the B.V.I. Spring Regatta Committee, P.O. Box 200, Road Town, Tortola, B.V.I. (tel. 809/494-3286).

MAY

☐ **Barbados Caribbean Jazz Festival,** in Bridgetown. A 3-day event with major performances. End of May.
☐ **Anguilla Day.** A day of boat racing, with many major competitions. May 30.

JUNE

☐ **Festival Pablo Casals,** San Juan, Puerto Rico. Although Spanish, Casals lived in Puerto Rico for many years, which inspired this gathering of cultural music artists from all over the world. Dates vary.
☐ **Aruba High-Winds-Pro-Am Windsurfing Tournament.** Many different races, including one to South America, characterize this event, followed by a major cultural event, the Aruba Jazz and Latin Music Festival in Oranjestad. Mid-June.

JULY

☐ **Carnival of St. John,** St. John, in the U.S. Virgins. Parades, bands, and colorful costumes lead up to the selection of Ms. St. John and King of Carnival. First week of July.
☐ **Antigua Carnival.** This carnival lasts for 10 days and includes steel bands and calypso, with parades and street dancing in costumes. Late July.
☐ **Crop Over Festival,** Barbados. This month-long event marks the end of the sugarcane harvest, with calypsonian competitions, flowing rum, and a "Cohobblopot," mixing dance, music, and theatrical presentations. Beginning in July but lasting into August (dates vary).

AUGUST

☐ **Virgin Islands Open Atlantic Blue Marlin Tournament.** Participants in this annual competition come from all over the world, some from as far away as Australia. Several marlin catches have set world records. Weekend closest to the full moon.
☐ **August Reggae Sunsplash International Music Festival,** Montego Bay,

Jamaica. Better attended every year, this brings all those stars who have followed in Bob Marley's footsteps together in an open-air concert. Dates vary.

☐ **B.V.I. Summer Festival.** Dancing to fungi and reggae bands, a Unity Day Parade, and general festivities sweep up the locals in their 3-day "big blast" for the year. First week in August.

SEPTEMBER

☐ **Fête-du-Vent,** St. Barthélemy. This annual event is an excuse for a good time marked with dances and fishing contests. Early September.

OCTOBER

☼ *CAYMAN ISLANDS PIRATES' WEEK*   *This national festival with cutlass-bearing pirates and sassy wenches storming George Town pays tribute to the island's past and cultural heritage.*
   Where: George Town. *When:* Late October. *How:* Contact the Pirates' Week Festival Administration, P.O. Box 51, Grand Cayman, B.W.I. (tel. 809/949-5078).

NOVEMBER

☐ **Statia/America Day,** St. Eustatius. The day Statians first saluted the American flag, the first foreign government to do so. Parades and historical pagaents mark the event. November 16.

DECEMBER

☐ **Run Barbados International Road Race Series.** A 26-mile, 385-yard marathon course draws competitors from around the world. First weekend of December.

☐ **Christmas on St. Croix.** This event launches the beginning of a 12-day celebration and festival that includes Christmas, the legal holiday December 26, New Year's Eve (called "Old Year's Day"), and New Year's Day. It ends January 6 at the observation of the Feast of the Three Kings, sometimes called Little Christmas, with a parade of flamboyantly attired carnival merrymakers marching through the streets of Christiansted. December 25 to January 6.

3. HEALTH, SAFETY & INSURANCE

HEALTH

Finding a good doctor in the Caribbean is not a problem, and most of them speak English. See "Fast Facts" for specific names and addresses on each individual island.

HEALTH PROBLEMS   If your medical condition is chronic, always talk to your doctor before leaving home. For conditions such as epilepsy, a heart condition, diabetes, or allergy, wear a **Medic Alert Identification Tag;** Medic Alert's 24-hour hotline enables a foreign doctor to obtain your medical records. A lifetime membership costs $35 and up. Contact the Medic Alert Foundation, P.O. Box 1009, Turlock CA 95381-1009 (tel. toll free 800/432-5378).

Although tap **water** is generally considered safe to drink, it's better to drink mineral water. Also, avoid iced drinks. Stick to beer, hot tea, or soft drinks.

If you experience **diarrhea,** moderate your eating habits and drink only mineral water until you recover. If symptoms persist, consult a doctor.

Sunburn   The sun can be brutal. Wear sunglasses to protect your eyes, a hat, and a coverup for your shoulders, and use a sunscreen. Experts also advise that you should limit your time on the beach the first day. If you do overexpose yourself, stay out of the sun until you recover. If your exposure is followed by fever or chills, a headache, or a feeling of nausea or dizziness, see a doctor.

Insects and Pests   One of the biggest menaces is the "no-see-ums," which appear mainly in the early evening. You can't see these gnats, but you sure can "feel-um." Screens can't keep these critters out, so carry your favorite bug repellent.

Mosquitoes are a nuisance. Malaria-carrying mosquitoes in the Caribbean are confined largely to Haiti and the Dominican Republic. If you're visiting either, consult your doctor for preventive medicine at least 8 weeks before you leave.

Other Possible Dangers   Dengue fever is prevalent in the islands, most prominently on Barbados, Cuba, the Dominican Republic, Haiti, and Puerto Rico. To date, no satisfactory treatment has been developed. You're told to avoid mosquito bites.

For prickly heat, athletes foot, and other **fungal infections,** use talcum powder and wear loose clothing.

Intestinal worms, such as hookworm, are relatively common and can be contracted by just walking barefoot on an infected beach. Schistosomiasis (also called Bilharzia), caused by a parasitic fluke, can be contracted by submerging your feet in rivers and lakes infested with a certain species of snail. This condition has been reported on St. Lucia, among other islands.

VACCINATIONS   Vaccinations are not required to enter the Caribbean if you're coming from the United States or Canada.

Infectious hepatitis has been reported on such islands as Dominica, Haiti, and Montserrat. Consult your doctor about the advisability of getting a gamma-globulin shot before you leave.

Ask your doctor about other shots, including typhoid, poliomyelitis, and tetanus. These are not common diseases, and most inoculations are recommended mainly to visitors planning to "rough it" in the wilds. If you're staying in a regular Caribbean hotel, such preventive measures are not generally needed.

MEDICINES   Take along an adequate supply of any prescription drugs that you need and a written prescription that uses the generic name of the drug—not the brand name. You may want to pack first-aid cream, insect repellent, aspirin, and Band-Aids.

SAFETY

Will I be safe in the Caribbean? This is one of the questions most often asked by the first-time visitor, and it's one of the most difficult to answer. Can a guidebook writer safely recommend traveling to New York or any major American city? Are you, in fact, free from harm in your own home?

In general, whenever you're traveling in an unfamiliar country, stay alert. Be aware of your immediate surroundings. Wear a moneybelt, carry traveler's checks, and keep your check numbers in a separate place. Store valuables in the hotel safe and keep your hotel-room doors locked. Also, lock car doors and never leave possessions in view in an automobile. Don't leave valuables, such as cameras and purses, lying unattended on the beach while you go for a swim. Caribbean tourist officials often warn visitors, "If you've got it, don't flaunt it." This will minimize the possibility of your becoming a victim of crime. Every society has its criminals. It's your responsibility to be aware and alert even in the most heavily touristed areas.

Tomorrow's headlines may carry the story of a Caribbean disaster. Let me point out, however, that trouble in, say, Kingston, Jamaica, doesn't mean trouble in Barbados, any more than a bombing in London means that you should cancel your trip to Munich.

CUSTOMS & MORES   The "attitude toward the visitor" takes on a wide range of meaning depending on whose attitude you're talking about. The Caribbean is composed of many nations, some of which have broken, at least on paper, from colonial powers that dominated their cultures for years; other nations have preferred to retain their safe links with the past, while still others prefer to seek help anywhere else but from their former colonial masters. But because their fragile economies depend on how many people their islands attract, many islands are taking steps to make their own people more aware of the importance of tourism and of treating their guests as they themselves would want to be treated if traveling in a foreign land.

Of course, many of the problems have come from the tourists themselves. Tourists should take care to treat the people of the Caribbean with respect and dignity. Many of the islanders are deeply religious and are offended by tourists who wear bikinis on shopping expeditions in town or appear nude on the beach.

Know that most of the people in the West Indies are proud, very proper, and most respectable, and if you treat them as such, they will likely treat you the same way. Others—certainly the minority, but a visible minority—can be downright antagonistic. Some islands are more hospitable to tourists than others; your greeting on Montserrat is likely to be friendlier than it is on the more jaded St. Thomas—but, then, Montserrat doesn't have five cruise ships a day docking at its harbor.

INSURANCE

Before purchasing insurance, check your current homeowner's, automobile, and medical insurance policies, and check the membership contracts of automobile and travel clubs, credit cards, and fraternal organizations. Sometimes these policies and contracts cover travel accidents, sickness, theft of luggage, and loss of such documents as your passport or your airline ticket. Coverage is usually limited to about $500 U.S. To submit a claim, remember that you'll need police reports or a statement from a local medical authority. Some policies provide advances in cash or arrange for immediate transferrals of funds.

If you feel you need additional insurance, check with the following companies:

Travel Guard International, 1145 Clarke Street, Stevens Point, WI 54481 (tel. toll free 800/826-1300, 800/634-0644 in Wisconsin), which offers a comprehensive 7-day policy that covers basically everything, including lost luggage. The cost of the package is $52, including emergency assistance, accidental death, trip cancellation and interruption, medical coverage abroad, and lost luggage. The rate for a family is $106. You should understand the restrictions, however, before you accept the coverage.

Travel Insurance Pak, Travelers Insurance Co., 1 Tower Square, 15 NB, Hartford, CT 06183-5040 (tel. 203/277-2381, or toll free 800/243-3174), offers $20,000 illness and accident coverage, beginning at $10 for 6 to 10 days. For lost or damaged luggage, $500 worth of coverage costs $20 for 6 to 10 days. You can also get trip-cancellation insurance for $5.50 per $100.

TRAVEL ASSISTANCE A number of companies now offer policies and help in case you're stranded abroad in an emergency. Each maintains a toll-free "800" number for out-of-state callers.

Wallach & Company, Inc., 107 West Federal Street, (P.O. Box 480), Middleburg, VA 22117-0480 (tel. 703/687-3166, or toll free 800/236-6615), offers "HealthCare Abroad," an insurance policy designed exclusively for individuals of any nationality traveling outside their own home country. This policy, good for 10 to 90 days, costs $3 a day and includes accident and sickness coverage to the tune of $100,000. Medical evacuation is also included, along with a $25,000 accidental death or dismemberment compensation. Trip-cancellation and lost or stolen luggage can also be written into this policy at a nominal cost.

Access America, Inc., 6600 W. Broad St., Richmond, VA 23230 (tel. 804/285-3300, or toll free 800/424-3391), has a 24-hour "hotline" in case of an emergency. This is a good company for those wanting family or individual policies. Medical coverage for 9 to 15 days costs $49 for $10,000 of coverage. If you want medical plus trip cancellation, the charge is $89 for 9 to 15 days. A comprehensive package for $111 grants blanket coverage for 9 to 15 days, including $50,000 worth of death benefits.

4. WHAT TO PACK

Comfortable clothing with the "casual but chic" look is the rule for the Caribbean. Cotton slacks or shorts are just fine for going around during the day. If you burn easily, bring a long-sleeved shirt and long pants.

Summer travelers don't need suits, but in winter men might want to wear a jacket with an open-neck shirt if they're dining in one of the more famous spots. Don't forget that evenings tend to be cooler, or you might go "up in the hills," so a light sweater or a jacket will come in handy. Sometimes restaurants and bars are overly air-conditioned. If you plan to visit nightclubs, casually chic dressy clothes are appropriate.

A wardrobe of lightweight cotton is preferable—avoid the synthetics or nylon which become hot and sticky in these climes. Khaki pants are acceptable for men in most places. Sometimes it's possible to get pressing done at hotels, but don't count on it. Take along at least two pairs of comfortable shoes.

If you want to bring along such items as an electric shaver or a hairdryer, check to see if you need an electrical transformer or adapter plugs.

Remember that airlines are increasingly strict about both carry-on items and checked suitcases. Checked luggage should not measure more than a total of 62 inches (width plus length plus height). Carry-on pieces must fit under your seat or in the overhead bin.

5. TIPS FOR THE DISABLED, SENIORS, SINGLES, STUDENTS & FAMILIES

FOR THE DISABLED   Hotels rarely give much publicity to what facilities, if any, they offer the disabled, so it's always better to contact the hotel directly, in advance. Tourist offices rarely have good data about such matters.

For more detailed information, try the **Travel Information Service,** Moss Rehabilitation Hospital, 1200 West Tabor Road, Philadelphia, PA 19141 (tel. 215/456-9600) (this service is not a travel agent). It charges $5 for a package of names and addresses of accessible hotels, restaurants, and attractions, often based on firsthand reports of travelers who have been there.

You can obtain a free copy of **"Air Transportation of Handicapped Persons,"** published by the U.S. Department of Transportation. Write for Free Advisory Circular No. AC12032, Distribution Unit, U.S. Department of Transportation, Publications Division, M-4332, Washington, DC 20590.

Specialized Tours   For names and addresses of operators of tours specifically for disabled visitors, contact the **Society for the Advancement of Travel for the Handicapped,** 347 Fifth Avenue, Suite 610, New York, NY (tel. 212/447-7284). Yearly membership costs $45 for senior citizens ($25 for students). Send a self-addressed, stamped envelope.

The **Federation of the Handicapped,** 211 West 14th Street, New York, NY 10011 (tel. 212/727-4268), offers summer tours for members, who pay a yearly fee of $4. Tours last 8 to 10 days.

For the blind, the best source is the **American Foundation for the Blind,** 15 West 16th Street, New York, NY 10011 (tel. 212/620-2000, or toll free 800/232-5463), which has information on travel. For those legally blind, it also issues identification cards for $6.

FOR SENIORS   Many discounts are available for seniors, some of which are detailed in a free booklet **"101 Tips for the Mature Traveler."** Write or phone Grand Circle Travel, 347 Congress St., Suite 3A, Boston, MA 02210 (tel. 617/350-7500, or toll free 800/221-2610).

SAGA International Holidays, 120 Boylston Street, Boston, MA 02116 (tel. toll free 800/343-0273), is known for its all-inclusive tours for seniors, preferably 60 years old or older. Insurance is included in the net price of any of their tours, except for cruises.

The **AARP Travel Experience from American Express,** 400 Pinnacle Way, Suite 450, Norcross, GA 30071 (tel. toll free 800/927-0111 for land arrangements, 800/745-4567 for cruises, or 800/659-5678 for TTD). This travel planner provides travel arrangements for members of the American Association of Retired Persons, 601 E Street NW, Washington, DC 20049 (tel. 202/434-AARP). Travel Experience provides members with a wide variety of escorted, hosted, go-any-day packages and cruises to most parts of the world. AARP members are offered individual discounts on car rentals and hotels, among other discounts, through the group's Purchase Privilege Program. This is a completely separate program from the product offered by Travel Experience.

Information is also available from the **National Council of Senior Citizens,** 925 15th Street NW, Washington, DC 20005 (tel. 202/347-8800). A nonprofit organization, the council charges $12 per person to join (couples pay $16) for which you receive a monthly newsletter, part of which is devoted to travel tips often featuring discounts on hotels and auto rentals.

FOR SINGLES Single travelers pay a penalty in an industry that's geared to "doubles." Jens Jurgen is founder of a company that has made heroic efforts to match single travelers with like-minded companions. He charges $36 to $66 for a 6-month listing. New applicants desiring a travel companion fill out a form stating their preferences and needs; they then receive a minilisting of potential partners. Companions of the same or opposite sex can be requested. His listings are extensive and it's very likely you'll find a suitable traveling companion. For an application and more information, contact Jens Jurgen, **Travel Companion,** P.O. Box P-833, Amityville, NY 11701 (tel. 516/454-0880).

Singleworld, 401 Theodore Fremd Avenue, Rye, NY 10580 (tel. 914/967-3334, or toll free 800/223-6490), operates tours for solo travelers. Two basic types of tours are available: youth-oriented tours for people under 35, and jaunts for any age. Annual dues are $25.

Grand Circle Travel, 347 Congress Street, Boston, MA 02210 (tel. 617/350-7500, or toll free 800/221-2610), offers escorted tours and cruises for retired people, including singles. Once you book one of their trips, membership is included, and in addition, you get vouchers providing discounts for future trips.

FOR STUDENTS Students can secure a number of travel discounts. The most wide-ranging travel service for students is **Council Travel,** a subsidiary of the **Council on International Educational Exchange (CIEE),** 205 East 42nd Street, New York, NY 10017 (tel. 212/661-1450), which provides details about budget travel, study abroad, work permits, and insurance. It also sells a number of helpful publications, including the *Student Travel Catalogue* ($1) and issues an International Student Identity Card (ISIC) for $12.95, plus $1.50 shipping, to bonafide students.

FOR FAMILIES The islands of the Caribbean contend for top position on the world list of family vacation places. There is something for everyone—shallow sea water and pools constructed for toddlers and endless sports activities and instruction for older children. Most resort hotels will advise you as to what there is in the way of fun for all ages, and many have play directors and supervised activities for the young of various age groups. However, there are some tips for making the trip a success which parents should attend to in advance:

Arrange ahead for cribs, bottle warmers, car seats, and cots. Find out if the hotel stocks baby food, and if not, bring it with you.

Draw up guidelines on bedtime, eating, keeping tidy, being in the sun, even shopping and spending, which can help make everybody's vacation more enjoyable.

Take along protection from the sun. For tiny tots, this should include a sun umbrella, while the whole family will need sunscreen (a "15" is a good idea) and sunglasses.

Take along anti-insect lotions and sprays. You'll probably need these both to repel the insects and to ease the itching and possible other after-effects of insect bites.

Baby-sitters can be found by most hotels, but you should insist that yours have a rudimentary knowledge of English.

For $35, you can order 10 issues of *Family Travel Times,* a newsletter about traveling with children. Subscribers to the newsletter can also call in with travel questions, but only from 10am to noon eastern standard time (later in the West) Monday through Wednesday only. Contact TWYCH (which stands for Travel With Your Children), 80 Eighth Avenue, New York, NY 10011 (tel. 212/206-0688).

6. ALTERNATIVE/ADVENTURE TRAVEL

EDUCATIONAL TRAVEL The best information is available from the **Council on International Educational Exchange (CIEE),** 205 East 42nd Street, New York, NY 10017 (tel. 212/661-1414). Request a copy of the 500-page *Work, Study, Travel Abroad: The Whole World Handbook,* which costs $12.95. If you'd like it mailed, add $1.50 for shipping. Some 1,000 study opportunities abroad are outlined.

Elderhostel, 75 Federal Street, Boston, MA 02110-1941 (tel. 617/426-7788), established in 1975, maintains an array of postretirement study programs, several of which are in the Caribbean. Most courses last for 2 or 3 weeks and include airfare, hotel accommodations in student dormitories or modest inns, all meals, and tuition. Courses involve no homework, are ungraded, and center mostly on the liberal arts. Participants must be age 60 or older, unless two members go as a couple, in which case only one member needs to be 60 or over. Write or call for their free newsletter and a list of upcoming courses and destinations.

A series of international programs combining travel and learning for persons over 50 years of age is offered by **Interhostel,** developed by the University of New Hampshire. Each program lasts 2 weeks and is escorted by a university faculty or staff member, and arranged in conjunction with a host college, university, or cultural institution. Participants can stay beyond 2 weeks if they wish. For information, contact the University of New Hampshire, Division of Continuing Education, 6 Garrison Avenue, Durham, NH 03824 (tel. 603/826-1147 between 1:30 and 4pm EST).

HOMESTAYS OR VISITS Meaning "to serve" in Esperanto, **Servas,** 11 John Street, Suite 706, New York, NY 10038 (tel. 212/267-0252), is a nonprofit, nongovernmental, international, interfaith network of travelers and hosts whose goal is to help build world peace, goodwill, and understanding by providing opportunities for personal contacts among people of diverse cultural and political backgrounds. Servas travelers are invited to stay without charge in private homes for visits lasting a minimum of 2 days. Visitors pay a $45 annual fee, fill out an application, and are interviewed for suitability; they then receive a Servas directory listing names and addresses of Servas hosts who will allow (and encourage) visitors in their homes. This program embraces 110 countries, including the Caribbean.

Friendship Force, 575 South Tower, 1 CNN Center, Atlanta, GA 30303 (tel. 404/522-9490), is a nonprofit organization that fosters and encourages friendship among people worldwide. Dozens of branch offices throughout North America arrange en masse visits, usually once a year. Because of group bookings, the airfare to the host country is usually less than the cost of individual APEX tickets. Each participant is required to spend 2 weeks in the host country. One full week is spent as a guest in the home of a family; most volunteers spend the second week traveling in the host country.

International Visitors Information Service, 733 15th Street NW, Suite 300, Washington, DC 20005 (tel. 202/783-6540), will send you a booklet for $5.95 listing opportunities for contact with local residents in foreign countries. It's called a *Meet the People* directory.

Experiment in International Living, Kipling Road (P.O. Box 676), Brattleboro, VT 05302 (tel. 802/257-7751), immerses high school (ages 15 to 20) and college students in other cultures for a summer or academic semester through a homestay. During that time they "become one of the family," and travel in the region or do academic study. Several of the 40 countries participating are in the Caribbean — namely, a service-focused program on St. Vincent for high school students and a Caribbean Area Studies and Development semester abroad in the Dominican Republic for college students.

TOURS FOR NATURALISTS Lectures on wildlife and the environment of Puerto Rico are offered by the **Commonwealth of Puerto Rico Department of Natural Resources,** especially for scientists and students. Also, private tours of nature reserves on the island are possible through prior arrangement. The name of the reserve you are interested in visiting should be specified in a request made to the Forest Service, Resident Biologist, at the Commonwealth of Puerto Rico Department of Natural Resources, P.O. Box 5887, Puerto de Tierra, San Juan, PR 00906 (tel. 809/724-8774).

ADVENTURE TOURS The number of cruise lines that regularly ply the waters of the Caribbean are about as numerous as casino chips at a roulette table. Many of them carry thousands of passengers and deliberately cater to nightlife and casino aficionadoes, who appreciate their massive size. Unfortunately, their enormous sizes and deep drafts usually require dockage at major and sometimes very congested ports, and the ensuing congestion evokes in many participants the urban stress they came to the Caribbean to avoid.

One noteworthy alternative to this system is offered by the **American Canadian Caribbean Line, Inc.,** P.O. Box 368, Warren, RI 02885 (tel. 401/247-0955, or toll free 800/556-7460 outside Rhode Island). The company was founded in 1965 by shipbuilder Luther H. Blount, who designed and built a trio of highly specialized (and highly idiosyncratic) cruise ships. Since then, both the National Geographic Society and the Library of Congress (which participated in one of its cruises in 1990 as part of a film documentary) have recognized A.C.C.L. for the quality and authenticity of its ecological and historical tours. Each ship is designed with shallow drafts of only 6 feet, and each contains space for no more than 65 to 80 passengers. Each can land on isolated shorelines without the pier and wharf facilities required for the disembarkation of larger cruise ships. Thanks to a specially designed 30-foot bow ramp, passengers can disembark directly onto the sands of some of the most obscure but pristine islands in the Caribbean — places that would otherwise require the chartering of a private yacht to reach.

Tours through the Caribbean are offered only between January and March, when the weather is supposedly perfect for this type of expedition. (In April and November, the ships move north to explore The Bahamas and the coastal sections of North America's eastern seaboard.) Caribbean tours focus on the British and U.S. Virgin Islands, and Puerto Rico and its offshore islands. Tours begin in either Mayagüez, Puerto Rico, or St. Thomas, and travel between the most beautiful and unspoiled cays and reefs of the archipelago, usually docking off coastlines that would almost never be visited by the average cruise line participant.

Cruises usually last 12 days and cost between $1,190 and $2,098 per person, double occupancy (with single occupancy beginning around $2,000), with all meals and port taxes included. Each itinerary includes lots of birdwatching, snorkeling, and nature appreciation.

HOME EXCHANGES House swapping keeps costs low if you don't mind a stranger living in your mainland home or apartment, and sometimes the exchange includes use of the family car.

Many home-exchange directories are published, but there is no guarantee that you'll find a house or apartment in the area you're seeking.

International Home Exchange Service, P.O. Box 590504, San Francisco, CA 94119 (tel. 415/435-3497), has a network spread over three dozen countries, with about 8,000 listings. For $45, you can obtain a trio of annual directories and can list your house on the exchange market. A photograph of your house can be printed for $11 extra. Senior citizens (65 or older) are charged $40.

Vacation Exchange Club, P.O. Box 820, Haleiwa, HI 96712 (tel. 808/638-8747, or toll free 800/638-3841), offers the same service but has fewer listings. For $50, you get four directories a year and you're listed in one.

FOR WOMEN SAILORS A program for women of all ages and levels of nautical expertise is offered by **Womanship, Inc.,** 410 Severn Avenue, The Boathouse, Annapolis, MD 21403 (tel. 301/268-0784, or toll free 800/342-9295). Originally established in 1984 and the first organization of its kind, it offers expert sailing instruction for all-women groups, up to a maximum of six "students" with two instructors. Participants sleep aboard the sailing vessel in shared accommodations containing two or more bunks. St. Thomas and Tortola are the ports of departure for the Caribbean divisions of this company, and most sailing instruction is taught in the many cays and estuaries of the British Virgin Islands. Most courses last a full week, although a series of less-frequently scheduled minicourses last for only a weekend. At the end of the course, participants are presented Cruising Certificates that can be used as evidence of expertise for future bareboat charters.

7. GETTING THERE

BY PLANE

All the biggest islands have air links to North America with regularly scheduled service, and the smaller islands are tied into this vast network through their own carriers. For details of how to reach each island, see the "Getting There" sections in the individual island chapters.

REGULAR FARES Always shop around to secure the lowest airfare, and keep calling the airlines. Sometimes you can purchase a ticket that is lower in price at the very last minute, because if the flight is not fully booked an airline will discount tickets to try to fill it up.

Most airlines charge different fares according to seasons. **Peak season,** which is winter in the Caribbean, is most expensive; **basic season,** in the summer, offers the least expensive fares. **Shoulder season** refers to the spring and fall months in between.

The assortment of fares ranges from first class, the most expensive, through business class to economy. The latter is the lowest-priced regular airfare carrying no special restrictions or requirements. Most airlines also offer promotional fares, which carry stringent requirements like advance purchase, minimum stay, and cancellation penalties. The most common such fare is the APEX (Advance Purchase Excursion). Land arrangements (prebooking of hotel rooms) are often tied in with promotional fares offered by airlines.

OTHER GOOD-VALUE CHOICES Proceed with caution through the next grab bag of suggestions. What constitutes good value keeps changing in the airline industry, and it's hard to keep up, even if you're a travel agent.

FROMMER'S SMART TRAVELER: AIRFARES

1. Shop all the airlines that fly to your destination.
2. Always ask for the lowest fare, not just a discount fare.
3. Keep calling the airlines. They would rather sell a seat than have it fly empty, so as the departure date nears, additional low-cost seats may become available.
4. Try to fly in summer, spring, or fall, when fares are lower.
5. Ask about the cost-conscious APEX (Advance Purchase Excursion) fare.
6. Find out if it's cheaper to fly Monday to Thursday.
7. Read the section on "Other Good Value Choices," which covers bucket shops, charter flights, and promotional fares.
8. Consider air-and-land packages, which offer considerably reduced rates.

Bucket Shops (Consolidators) The name originated in the 1960s in Britain, where the airlines gave that (then-pejorative) name to resalers of blocks of unsold tickets consigned to them by major carriers. "Bucket shop" has stuck as a label, but it might be more polite to refer to them as "consolidators." They exist in many shapes and forms. In its purest sense, a bucket shop acts as a clearinghouse for blocks of tickets that airlines discount and consign during normally slow periods of air travel. In the case of the Caribbean, that usually means from mid-April to mid-December.

Charter operators (see below) and bucket shops used to perform separate functions, but their offerings in many cases have been blurred in recent times. Many outfits perform both functions.

Tickets are sometimes—but not always—discounted from 20% to 35%. Terms of payment can vary, from anywhere from 45 days prior to departure to the last minute. Discounted tickets can also be purchased through regular travel agents, who usually mark up the ticket 8% to 10%, maybe more, thereby greatly reducing your discount.

A survey conducted of flyers who use consolidator tickets voiced only one major complaint: You can't arrange for an advance seat assignment, so you are likely to be assigned a "poor seat." The survey revealed that most flyers estimated their savings at around $200 per ticket off the regular price. Nearly a third of the passengers reported savings of up to $300 off the regular price. But—and here's the hitch—many flyers reported no savings at all, as the airlines will sometimes match the consolidator ticket with a promotional fare. The situation is a bit tricky and calls for some careful investigation on your part to determine just how much you are saving.

Bucket shops abound from coast to coast. Look for their ads in your local newspaper's travel section; they're usually very small and a single column in width. Just to get you started, here are some recommendations:

Access International, 101 West 31st Street, Suite 1104, New York, NY 10001 (tel. 212/465-0707, or toll free 800/827-3633), just may be the country's biggest consolidator, annually selling many thousands of discounted tickets.

Out west, you can try **Sunline Express Holidays, Inc.,** 607 Market Street, San Francisco, CA 94105 (tel. 415/541-7800), or **Euro-Asia, Inc.,** 4203 East Indian School Road, Suite 210, Phoenix, AZ 85018 (tel. 602/955-2742, or toll free 800/525-3876).

Charter Flights Charter flights allow you to travel at rates cheaper than on regularly scheduled flights. Many of the major carriers offer charter flights at rates that are sometimes 30% (or more) off the regular airfare.

There are some drawbacks, however. Advance booking of up to 45 days or more may be required, and there are hefty cancellation penalties, although you can take out insurance against emergency cancellations. Also, you must depart and return on your scheduled dates or you will lose your money. It will do no good to call the airline and tell them you're on Trinidad with yellow fever! If you're not on the plane, you can kiss your money good-bye.

Since charter flights are so complicated, it's best to ask a good travel agent to explain the problems and advantages. Sometimes charters require ground arrangements, such as the prebooking of hotel rooms.

Rebators   To confuse the situation even more, rebators have also begun to compete in the low-cost airfare market. These outfits pass along to the passenger part of their commission, although many of them assess a fee for their services. They are not the same as travel agents, but they sometimes offer roughly similar services, such as discounted land arrangements, including hotels and car rentals. Most rebators offer discounts averaging anywhere from 10% to 25% (but this could vary from place to place), plus a $20 handling charge.

Rebators include **Travel Avenue,** 641 West Lake Street, Suite 201, Chicago, IL 60606-3691 (tel. 312/876-1116, or toll free 800/333-3335); and **The Smart Traveller,** 3111 SW 27th Avenue, Miami, FL 33133 (tel. 305/448-3338, or toll free 800/226-3338 in Florida and Georgia only).

Promotional Fares   Airlines do announce promotional fares to the Caribbean. You'll need a good travel agent, or you'll have to do a lot of investigating yourself to learn what's available at the time of your intended trip.

Travel Clubs   Travel clubs supply an unsold inventory of tickets offering discounts in the usual range of 20% to 60%. After you pay an annual fee, you are given a "hotline" number to call to find out what discounts are available. Some discounts become available a few days in advance of actual departure, some a week in advance, and some as much as a month. Of course, you're limited to what's available, so you have to be flexible. Some of the best of these clubs include:

Discount Travel International, Suite 205, Ives Building, 114 Forest Avenue, Narberth, PA 19072 (tel. 215/668-7184, or toll free 800/334-9294), has an annual membership of $45.

Last Minute Travel Club, 1249 Boylston Street, Boston, MA 02215 (tel. 617/267-9800, or toll free 800/LAST-MIN in New England and New York but outside Massachusetts), literally offers "last-minute" bookings at slashed prices, with no membership fee—open bookings only.

Moment's Notice, 425 Madison Avenue, New York, NY 10017 (tel. 212/486-0500), has a members' hotline (regular phone toll charges) and a yearly fee of $45 per member.

Worldwide Discount Travel Club, 1674 Meridian Avenue, Miami Beach, FL 33139 (tel. 305/534-2082), presents a travelogue listing with about 200 discount possibilities every 25 days. Single travelers pay $40 annually to join but family membership is only $50.

Sears Discount Travel Club, 3033 South Parker Road, Suite 1000, Aurora, CO 80014 (tel. toll free 800/433-9383). For $49, members get a catalog (issued four times a year), along with maps, discounts at select hotels, and a 5% cash bonus on purchases.

BY CRUISE SHIP

Most cruises today appeal to the middle-income voyager who probably has no more than 1 or 2 weeks to spend cruising the Caribbean. Some 300 passenger ships sail the Caribbean all year, and in January and February that figure may go up another hundred or so. Pick up a copy of *Frommer's Cruises* for more detailed information, or consult a good travel agent.

BY CHARTERED BOAT

Experienced sailors and navigators can charter "bareboat," a term meaning a rental with a fully equipped boat but with no captain or crew. You're on your own, and you'll have to prove your qualifications before you're allowed to rent such a craft. Even an experienced skipper may want to take along someone familiar with local waters—waters that may in some places be tricky.

You can also charter a boat with a skipper and crew. Charter yachts, varying from 50 to more than 100 feet, can accommodate four to a dozen people.

Most yachts are rented on a weekly basis, with a fully stocked bar, plus equipment for fishing and water sports. However, more and more bareboat charterers are learning that they can save money and select menus more suited to their tastes by doing their own provisioning. Depending on the type of boat and the facilities offered, you can count on spending $50 to $100 per person daily bareboat (no crew or food included) or up to $120 to $180 per person daily for a boat with a crew. The average charter carries four to six passengers, and usually is reserved for a week. In summer, when business tends to be slow, you might be able to charter a boat for 4 or 5 days.

The Moorings, P.O. Box 139, Road Town, Tortola, B.V.I. (tel. 809/494-2331), or in the U.S., 19345 U.S. 19N, Suite 402, Clearwater, FL 34624 (tel. 813/530-5651, or toll free 800/535-7289 outside Florida), along with other charter services, has made the British Virgins the cruising capital of the world. Charlie and Ginny Cary started the first charter service in the B.V.I. You can choose from their fleet of sailing yachts which can accommodate up to three couples in comfort and style. Arrangements can be made for bareboating, with a skipper, or fully crewed with both a skipper and cook. The boats come equipped with barbecue, snorkeling gear, dinghy, windsurfer, and linens. The Moorings has an experienced staff of mechanics, electricians, riggers, and cleaners. In addition, if you're going out on your own, you'll get a thorough briefing session about Virgin Island waters and anchorages.

Windjammer Barefoot Cruises Ltd., P.O. Box 120, Miami Beach, FL 33119 (tel. 305/534-7447, or toll free 800/327-2601), offers 6- and 13-day sailing adventures on classic "tall ships" through the Caribbean. Its *Flying Cloud* island-hops the British Virgin Islands, its *Fantôme* travels the Grenadines and Tobago cays, its *Polynesia* and *Yankee Clipper* sail through the West Indies, and its *Mandalay* takes a leisurely 13-day cruise through the West Indies and Grenadines. Its supply ship, the *Amazing Grace,* carries 100 passengers island-hopping from Nassau to Grenada. Rates start at $675. Air-sea package deals are offered. S/V *Fantôme,* S/V *Mandalay,* and S/V *Polynesia* are registered in the British Virgin Islands; S/V *Flying Cloud,* S/V *Yankee Clipper,* and M/V *Amazing Grace* are registered in Honduras. All ships comply with international safety standards.

Nicholson Yacht Charters, 432 Columbia Street, Suite 21A, Cambridge, MA 02141-1043 (tel. 617/227-0555, or toll free 800/662-6066), or P.O. Box 103, St. John's, Antigua, W.I., one of the best in the business, handles charter yachts for use throughout the Caribbean basin, particularly the route between Dutch-held St. Maarten and Grenada, as well as the routes around the U.S. and British Virgin Islands. Specializing in boats of all sizes, they can arrange rentals of motor or sailing yachts of up to 298 feet. Especially popular are arrangements where two or more yachts, each sleeping eight guests in four equal double cabins, race each other from island to island during the day, anchoring near each other in secluded coves or at berths in Caribbean capitals at night. The price per week for renting a yacht depends on the number in your party and the size of the vessel. Rates range from $1,600 to $2,650 per person per week, depending on the time of the year.

You can also cruise in the Caribbean on larger yachts that have set sailing dates. On this type of craft, depending on its size, of course, there might be anywhere from 6 to 100 passengers.

Sunsail, 2 Prospect Park, 3347 NW 55th Street, Fort Lauderdale, FL 33309 (tel. toll free 800/327-2276), specializes in yacht chartering from its bases in Tortola (the British Virgin Islands) and St. Lucia, Marsh Harbour, Abaco, The Bahamas, and Phillipsburg, St. Maarten. Bareboat and crewed yachts between 32 and 80 feet are available. The charter manager suggests that reservations be made 4 to 6 months in advance (they require a $500 deposit). Clients who have flexible schedules need only reserve a month in advance. Insurance and full equipment will be included in the rates quoted to you.

PACKAGE TOURS

If you want everything done for you, and want to save money as well, consider taking a package tour. Besides general tours, many have specific themes—tennis packages, golf packages, scuba and snorkeling packages, and honeymooners' specials.

Economy and convenience are the chief advantage of a package tour—cost of transportation (usually airfare), a hotel room, food (sometimes), and sightseeing (sometimes) are combined under one price. There are extras, of course, but you'll know in advance roughly what the cost of your vacation will be, and can budget accordingly. The disadvantage is that you may find yourself stuck in a hotel you dislike. Choosing the right package can be a bit of a problem; it's best to go to a travel agent.

Packages are available because tour operators can mass-book hotels and make volume purchases. You generally have to pay the cost of the total package in advance. Transfers between your hotel and the airport are often included (some airports are situated a $40-or-more taxi ride from a resort). Many packages carry several options, including the possibility of low-cost car rentals. Nearly all tour packages are based on double occupancy.

Some of the leading tour operators to the Caribbean include:

Caribbean Concepts, 575 Underhill Bend, Syosset, NY 11791 (tel. 516/469-9800, or toll free 800/423-4433), offers several air-and-land packages to the islands, some including apartment, villa, or condo rentals. Car rentals and local sightseeing can also be arranged.

All year, **Aquarium Travel Consultants,** 816 King Street, Rye Brook, NY 10573 (tel. 914/939-2297, or toll free 800/955-6560 in New York City, 800/248-4141 outside New York City), offers packages to the Caribbean.

Carolina Express Tours, P.O. Box 12025, 407 East Boulevard, Charlotte, NC 28220 (tel. 704/347-1707, or toll free 800/643-2111), features tours year round.

Out of Florida, **Nationwide Leisure, Inc.,** 6970 Taft Street, Hollywood, FL 33024 (tel. 305/964-1000, or toll free 800/226-1700), also runs tours to the Caribbean.

You might also want to consider one of the many tours offered by **American Airlines** (tel. toll free 800/433-7300) or **American Express** (tel. 212/687-3700 in New York City).

8. WHERE TO STAY

Few travel destinations in the world offer such a wide range of accommodations: a tropical villa in St. Thomas, a millionaire's estate in Jamaica, a 17th-century great house in St. Kitts, a 200-year-old sugar warehouse in St. Vincent, or a beachfront apartel (an efficiency apartment for short-term rental) in Puerto Rico.

The number of guest rooms with private bathrooms has been given for establishments in the "Budget" category. All other guest units have private bathrooms unless otherwise noted.

HOTELS & RESORTS

There is no rigid classification of Caribbean hotels. The word "deluxe" is often used—or misused—when "first class" might have been a more appropriate term. "First class," itself, often isn't. I've presented fairly detailed descriptions of the properties so that you'll get an idea of what to expect once you're there. However,

---

WHAT THE ABBREVIATIONS MEAN

Travelers to the Caribbean may at first be confused by classifications on rate sheets. I've used these same classifications in this guide:

MAP (Modified American Plan) usually means room, breakfast, and dinner, unless the room rate has been quoted separately, and then it means only breakfast and dinner.

CP (Continental Plan) includes room and a light breakfast.

EP (European Plan) means room only.

AP (American Plan) is the most expensive rate of all because it includes your room plus three meals a day.

---

even in the deluxe and first-class properties, don't expect top-rate service and efficiency. Life in the tropics has its disadvantages. When you go to turn on the shower, sometimes you get water and sometimes you don't. You may even experience island power failures.

THE WEST INDIAN GUESTHOUSE

An entirely different type of accommodation is the guesthouse, where most of the Antilleans themselves stay when they travel. In the Caribbean, the term "guesthouse" can mean anything. Sometimes so-called guesthouses are really like simple motels built around swimming pools. Others are small individual cottages, with their own kitchenettes, constructed around a main building in which you'll often find a bar and a restaurant serving local food. Some are surprisingly comfortable, often with private baths and swimming pools. You may or may not have air conditioning.

For value, the guesthouse can't be topped. You can always journey over to a big beach resort and use its seaside facilities for only a small charge, perhaps no more than $3. Although bereft of frills, the guesthouses I've recommended are clean and safe for families or single women. The cheapest ones are not places where you'd want to spend time, because of their simple, modest furnishings.

SELF-CATERING HOLIDAYS

Particularly if you're a family or a group of friends, a housekeeping holiday can be one of the least expensive ways of vacationing in the Caribbean. Self-catering accommodations are now available on nearly all the islands. Some are individual cottages you can rent, others are housed in one building, and some are private homes rented when the owners are away. All have small kitchens or kitchenettes, so you can do your own cooking. Most self-catering places have maid service included in the rental, and you're given fresh linen as well.

RENTAL VILLAS & VACATION HOMES

CONDOS & VILLAS Even Princess Margaret rents out her private villa on Mustique in the Grenadines, providing you "have the proper references." Of course, she asks more than $8,000 per week, but throughout the Caribbean you can often secure good deals by renting privately owned villas and vacation homes.

Many villas have a staff, or at least a maid who comes in a few days a week, and they also provide the essentials for home life, including bed linen and cooking paraphernalia. Condos usually come with a reception desk and are often comparable to life in a suite in a big resort hotel. Nearly all condo complexes have swimming pools (some more than one).

Agencies specializing in these rentals include the following:

Villas of Distinction, P.O. Box 55, Armonk, NY 10504 (tel. 914/273-3331, or toll free 800/289-0900), is one of the best offering "complete vacations," including airfare, rental car, and domestic help. Some private villas have two to five bedrooms, and almost every villa has a swimming pool. Islands on which you can rent villas include St. Martin, Barbados, U.S. Virgins, Cayman Islands, and Anguilla, among others.

At Home Abroad, Suite 6-H, 405 East 56th Street, New York, NY 10022 (tel. 212/421-9165), has a roster of private homes for rent in the Caribbean, often with maid service included.

Caribbean Connections Plus, P.O. Box 261, Trumbull, CT 06611 (tel. 203/261-8603), offers many apartments and villas in the Caribbean.

Hideaways International, 1500 Goldsmith Street, Littleton, MA 01460 (tel. 508/486-8955, or toll free 800/843-4433), provides a 128-page guide with illustrations of its accommodations in the Caribbean so you'll get some idea of what you're renting. Most of its villas, which can hold up to three couples or a large family of about 10, come with maid service. You can also ask this travel club about discounts on plane fares and car rentals.

Sometimes local tourist offices will also advise you on vacation-home rentals if you write or call them directly.

PRIVATE APARTMENTS & COTTAGES   Private apartments are rented, either with or without maid service. This is more of a no-frills option than the villas and condos. The apartments may not be in buildings with swimming pools, and they may not have a front desk to help you. Cottages are the most free-wheeling way to live in these four major categories of vacation homes. Most of them are fairly simple; many open onto a beach, while others may be clustered around a communal swimming pool. Many contain no more than a simple bedroom with a small kitchen and bath. For the peak winter season, reservations should be made at least 5 or 6 months in advance.

Dozens of agents throughout the United States and Canada offer these types of rentals. You can also write to local tourist offices.

Travel experts agree that savings, especially for a family of three to six people, or two or three couples, can range from 50% to 60% of what a hotel would cost. If there are only two in your party, these savings don't apply. However, groceries are sometimes priced 35% to 60% higher than the average on the U.S. mainland because nearly all foodstuffs have to be imported. Even so, preparing your own food will be a lot cheaper than dining at restaurants.

9. WHERE TO DINE

The bad news is that dining in the Caribbean is generally more expensive than in either the United States or Canada; restaurant prices are more in tune with Europe than with America. Virtually everything has to be imported, except the fish or Caribbean lobsters that are caught locally. Service is automatically added to most restaurant tabs, usually 10% to 15%. Even so, if service has been good, it's customary to tip extra.

If you're booked into a hotel on the MAP (Modified American Plan, or half board), which is required by some establishments in peak winter season, you can sample some of the local restaurants at lunch.

In summer, only the more sophisticated and posh havens require jackets. Always ask about the dress code before you head to the restaurant, and check also to see if reservations are required. In winter you may find all the tables gone at some of the more famous places. At all places, wear a cover-up; don't enter a restaurant in a bikini.

Whenever possible, stick to regional food. Red meats are probably flown in and may have arrived in the islands long before you did.

When you do go out to dine, take a taxi. Roads in the Caribbean are not marked very well; they are also badly lit and very narrow, and on some islands you must drive on the left. The restaurant or hotel where you're dining will call a cab for you, which should arrive in within 30 minutes.

CHAPTER 3

THE CAYMAN ISLANDS

- **WHAT'S SPECIAL ABOUT THE CAYMAN ISLANDS**
- **FAST FACTS: THE CAYMAN ISLANDS**
1. **GRAND CAYMAN**
2. **CAYMAN BRAC**
3. **LITTLE CAYMAN**

Columbus first sighted the Cayman Islands in 1503. He called them Las Tortugas, or "the turtles." The name Cayman comes from a Spanish-Carib word, *caymanas,* or "crocodiles." The crocodiles, island historians believe, were not those animals at all, but were iguanas that used to live in the Caymans. The first colonists were a motley crew—bands of shipwrecked sailors and buccaneers, including the rollicking 17th-century Welshman, Sir Henry Morgan. Later, Scottish fishermen arrived and forged a quiet, peaceful settlement that today is a tranquil oasis at the western edge of the Caribbean.

Don't go to the Cayman Islands expecting fast-paced excitement. Island life focuses on the sea. Snorkelers will find a paradise; beach lovers will relish the powdery sands of Seven Mile Beach.

The Caymans, 480 miles due south of Miami, consist of three islands—Grand Cayman, Cayman Brac, and Little Cayman. Despite its name, Grand Cayman is only 22 miles long and 8 miles across at its widest point. The other islands are considerably smaller, of course, and contain very limited tourist facilities, in contrast to Grand Cayman which is well developed.

These islands were once a dependency of Jamaica, but when Jamaica gained independence in 1962, the Cayman Islands preferred to remain a British Crown Colony and a land without an income tax.

Appointed by Queen Elizabeth II, a governor heads the local government, and English is the official language of the islands, although it's often spoken with an English slur mixed with an American southern drawl and a lilting Welsh accent.

George Town on Grand Cayman is the capital, and is therefore the hub of government, banking (more than 500 banks operate in this tax haven), and shopping.

GETTING THERE

The Cayman Islands are easily accessible by air. Flying time from Miami is 1 hour 10 minutes; from Houston, 2¾ hours; and from New York, 3¾ hours. Only a handful of nonstop flights are available from the heartland of North America to Grand Cayman, so many visitors use Miami as their gateway.

Cayman Airways (tel. toll free 800/422-9626) offers the most frequent service to Grand Cayman with three or four flights daily from Miami, three nonstop flights a week from Tampa (two of which originate in Atlanta), two nonstop flights per week from Houston, and between three and five weekly flights from New York's JFK, depending on the season. It's also the only airline that offers service to Little Cayman and Cayman Brac. Round-trip fares to Cayman Brac are $77. If booked simultaneously, the airline can organize overnight and/or sightseeing packages that save money for visitors who want to see the country's isolated smaller islands.

WHAT'S SPECIAL ABOUT THE CAYMAN ISLANDS

Beaches

☐ Seven Mile Beach (in truth, 5½ miles) on Grand Cayman's west coast, one of the Caribbean's most famous and the site of posh hotels.

Great Islands/Towns

☐ Grand Cayman, the major tourist mecca of the three tiny coral islands.

☐ Cayman Brac, an old shipbuilding center, once the haunt of such pirates as Blackbeard.

☐ Little Cayman, the smallest island, where Philippe Cousteau found "one of the three finest diving spots in the world."

☐ George Town, capital of Grand Cayman and the offshore financial industry.

Sports and Recreation

☐ Grand Cayman, with 20 full-service dive operations, the largest single island in the Caribbean for dive tourism.

☐ Game fish—yellowfin tuna, wahoo, dolphin, and marlin—abound.

Ace Attractions

☐ Cayman Turtle Farm, the only commercial green sea turtle farm in the world.

☐ *Atlantis,* a 28-seat submarine that takes passengers to depths of 150 feet to see the marine life of a tropical reef.

Special Events

☐ Pirates' Week, a 7-day swashbuckling celebration in October with costumes and parades.

Many visitors opt for flights to Grand Cayman on **American Airlines** (tel. toll free 800/433-7300), which operates nonstop flights from Miami to Grand Cayman once a day.

Northwest Airlines (tel. toll free 800/225-2525) flies to Grand Cayman from Detroit, Minneapolis, and Memphis via Miami.

FAST FACTS: THE CAYMAN ISLANDS

Area Code To call the Cayman Islands from the mainland, dial 809, then the seven-digit number. This area code is not needed once you're in the Caymans. (See "Telephone," below, for information on making local calls.)

Business Hours Normally, **banks** are open Monday through Thursday from 9am to 2:30pm and on Friday from 9am to 1pm and 2:30 to 4:30pm. **Shops** are usually open Monday through Saturday from 9am to 5pm. Most **other businesses,** including government offices, operate Monday through Friday from 9am to 5pm.

Currency The legal tender is the **Cayman Islands dollar,** currently valued at $1.25 U.S. ($1 U.S. equals 80¢ C.I.). Canadian, U.S., and British currencies are accepted throughout the Cayman Islands. Most hotels quote rates in U.S. dollars. However, many restaurants quote prices in Cayman Islands dollars, which leads you to think that food is much cheaper. Unless otherwise noted, quotations in this chapter are in U.S. dollars, rounded off. The cost of living in the Cayman Islands is about 20% higher than in the U.S.

Documents No passports are required for U.S. or Canadian citizens, but proof of citizenship (voter registration card or birth certificate) and a return ticket are.

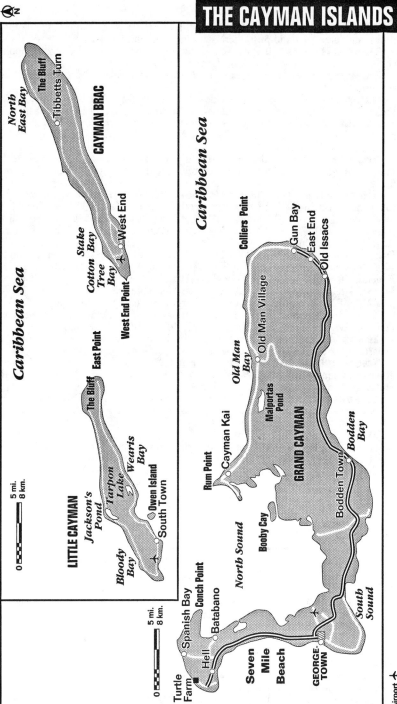

THE CAYMAN ISLANDS

N

Caribbean Sea

CAYMAN BRAC

The Bluff
Tibbetts Turn
North East Bay
Stake Bay
Cotton Tree Bay
West End
West End Point
East Point
The Bluff

Caribbean Sea

LITTLE CAYMAN

Jackson's Pond
Tarpon Lake
Wearis Bay
Bloody Bay
Owen Island
South Town

5 mi.
8 km.
0

GRAND CAYMAN

Caribbean Sea

Colliers Point
Gun Bay
East End
Old Issacs
Old Man Village
Old Man Bay
Malportas Pond
Bodden Bay
Bodden Town
Rum Point
Cayman Kai
Booby Cay
North Sound
South Sound
Conch Point
Spanish Bay
Batabano
Hell
Turtle Farm
Seven Mile Beach
GEORGE-TOWN

5 mi.
8 km.
0

Airport ✈

Drugs The Cayman Islands have strict laws on the use of marijuana and other drugs, and large fines and prison terms are imposed on offenders.

Electricity It's 110 volts AC, 60 cycles, so American and Canadian appliances will not need adapters or transformers.

Emergencies For **medical** emergencies, dial 555. Call 999 to summon the police.

Holidays Official holidays include New Year's Day, Ash Wednesday, Good Friday, Easter Monday, the third Monday in May, the Monday following the Saturday appointed as the official birthday of the reigning sovereign of the United Kingdom, the first Monday in July (Constitution Day), the Monday after Remembrance Sunday (in November), and Christmas Day.

Hospitals On Grand Cayman, the only hospital is **George Town Hospital,** Hospital Road (tel. 9-8600). On Cayman Brac, the only hospital is **Faith Hospital** (tel. 8-2243).

Information The **Cayman Islands Department of Tourism** has the following offices in the U.S.: P.O. Box 900024, Atlanta, GA 30329 (tel. 404/934-3959); P.O. Box 2602, Baltimore, MD 21215 (tel. 301/644-0855); P.O. Box 114, Boston, MA 02117 (tel. 617/431-7771); One Magnificent Mile, 980 N. Michigan Ave., Suite 1260, Chicago, IL 60611 (tel. 312/944-5602); 9794 Forest Lane, Suite 569, Dallas, TX 75243 (tel. 817/430-4221); Two Memorial City Plaza, 820 Gessner, Suite 170, Houston, TX 77024 (tel. 713/461-1317); 3440 Wilshire Blvd., Suite 1202, Los Angeles, CA 90010 (tel. 213/738-1968); 250 Catalonia Ave., Suite 401, Coral Gables, FL 33134 (tel. 305/444-6551); 420 Lexington Ave., Suite 2733, New York, NY 10170 (tel. 212/682-5582); and P.O. Box 824, Tarpon Springs, FL 34286 (tel. 813/934-9078). In Canada, contact Earl B. Smith, L. D. Day Travel Marketing Consultants, 234 Eglinton Ave. East, Suite 306, Toronto, ON M4P 1K5 (tel. 416/322-7824).

Taxes A government tourist tax of 6% is added to your hotel bill. Also, a departure tax of $7.50 (U.S.) is collected when you leave the Caymans.

Telegraph and Telex The Cable and Wireless, Anderson Square, George Town, on Grand Cayman (tel. 9-7800), is open from 8am to 5pm Monday through Friday, to 1pm on Saturday, and to 11am on Sunday.

Telephone A modern automatic telephone system enables Cayman operators to dial numbers worldwide 24 hours; international direct dialing is also possible. *In the islands, dial only the last five digits of the numbers given in this chapter.*

Time Eastern standard time is in effect all year—daylight saving time is not observed. Therefore, when Miami is on daylight saving time and it's noon there, it's still 11am in the nearby Cayman Islands.

Tipping Many restaurants add a 10% to 15% charge in lieu of tipping.

1. GRAND CAYMAN

Shipwrecked sailors, marooned mariners, and buccaneers founded Grand Cayman, once called "the island that time forgot." Today the largest of the three islands, a diving mecca, is one of the hottest tourist destinations in the Caribbean. With more than 500 banks, its capital, George Town, is the offshore banking center of the Caribbean. Retired people are drawn to the peace and tranquility of this British Crown Colony, site of a major condominium development. Almost all the Cayman Islands' population of 18,000 live on Grand Cayman. The civil manners of the locals reflect their British heritage.

Queen Elizabeth II, the official head of the island chain, is represented by a governor, who appoints three official members of the Legislature Assembly.

ORIENTATION

GETTING AROUND   By Taxi   All arriving flights are met by taxis. The rates are fixed by the director of civil aviation (tel. 809/949-7811) and typical one-way fares from the airport are $8 to George Town, $12 to the Holiday Inn on Seven Mile Beach, and $48 to Rum Point on the North Shore. Taxis (which can hold five people) will also take visitors on around-the-island tours.

By Bus   Service is erratic, but buses run every 30 minutes or so beside Seven Mile Beach. Vaguely defined official stops exist between West Bay and George Town, but most passengers simply wave down whichever bus happens to be heading their way. Fares are $1 C.I. ($1.25), and you can ride as far as you want. There are no buses on the eastern sections of the island. Information and schedules tend to be vague, but you can try phoning the Reliable Bus company (tel. 949-7865).

By Rental Car   Several car-rental companies operate on the island: **Avis** (tel. 9-2468 on Grand Cayman, or toll free 800/331-1084 in the U.S.), **Budget** (tel. 9-5605 on Grand Cayman, or toll free 800/654-3001), and **Hertz** (tel. 9-2280 on Grand Cayman, or toll free 800/654-3001). Each will issue the mandatory Cayman Islands driving permit, for $5 (U.S.). All three require that reservations be made between 6 and 36 hours before pickup. Avis and Hertz require that drivers be 18 and 25 years old, respectively, and Budget requires that drivers be between 25 and 65 years old. All three require the presentation of a valid driver's license and either a valid credit card or a large cash deposit.

Of the big three, Hertz offers the lowest rates, charging $162 a week (U.S.) for a Daihatsu Charade with automatic transmission and air conditioning. Although larger and more expensive cars are available, many readers opt for the smaller models because driving distances are short.

Each company charges between $7.25 and $10 per day for an optional collision-damage waiver, which will eliminate any financial responsibility you might have if you damage your car. (Check the coverage provided with your credit card, you *may* already have adequate coverage.) Extra medical insurance costs around $3 per day at each of the companies. All three maintain kiosks within walking distance of the airport, although most visitors find it easier to take a taxi to their hotels and then arrange for the cars to be brought to their hotels.

Remember to drive on the left and to reserve your car as far in advance as possible, especially in midwinter.

By Motorcycle or Bicycle   Honda motorcycles for two are popular and can be rented from **Caribbean Motors,** on North Church Street opposite Burger King (tel. 9-8878) for $18 C.I. to $27 C.I. ($22.50 to $33.75) per day. Bicycles are also rented here for $11 C.I. ($13.75) per day.

ESSENTIALS   The **Department of Tourism** is at Harbour Centre (P.O. Box 67), George Town, Grand Cayman, B.W.I. (tel. 809/949-7999). The best located pharmacy is **Cayman Drug,** Panton Street (tel. 9-2597) in George Town. Also in George Town, you'll find the **post office** and **Philatelic Bureau,** on Edward Street (tel. 9-2474), open Monday through Friday from 8:30am to 3:30pm and on Saturday 8:30 to 11:30am. The Philatelic Bureau (closed on Saturday) sells the postage stamps for which the Cayman Islands are famous.

WHERE TO STAY

True budget travelers will rent an apartment or condominium (shared with friends or families), so they can cut costs by cooking their own meals. Divers will want to find hotels or small resorts that include a half day's dive in their tariffs.

EXPENSIVE

CARIBBEAN CLUB, West Bay Rd. (P.O. Box 504), Grand Cayman,

B.W.I. Tel. 809/947-4099. Fax 809/947-4443. 18 villas. A/C MINIBAR TV TEL

$ Rates: Winter, $300–$325 single; $325–$375 double. Summer, $165–$250 single or double. Breakfast $10 extra. AE, MC, V. **Parking:** Free.

⭐ The Caribbean Club is actually an exclusive compound of luxuriously furnished one- and two-bedroom villas, each with a full-size living room, dining area, patio, and kitchen, but when the owners are away the units are rented to guests. The pink villas are 4 miles north of George Town, either on or just off the beach; oceanfront units are always more expensive, of course. At the core of the colony, the club center rises two stories with tall, graceful arches and picture windows that look out onto the lush grounds planted with palm trees and flowering shrubs.

Dining/Entertainment: Lantanas, the dining room, is open for dinner only (see "Where to Dine," below). There's also Ventana's Lounge.

Services: Room service (available only during open hours of Lantanas).

Facilities: Tennis court, water-sports center.

GRAND PAVILION HOTEL, West Bay Rd. (P.O. Box 1815), Grand Cayman, B.W.I. Tel. 809/947-4666. Fax 809/947-4919. 88 rms. A/C MINIBAR TV TEL

$ Rates: Winter, $290–$370 single or double. Summer, $180–$250 single or double. Breakfast $12 extra. AE, MC, V. **Parking:** Free.

An elegant five-star hotel, the Grand Pavilion offers luxuriously appointed bedrooms with Louis XV–style furniture, thick carpeting, French fabrics, and many other amenities. Within the glass-covered courtyard of the hotel is a splashing Tahiti-style fountain cluster, a small swimming pool, palm and date trees, and a thatch-covered bar. The hotel, 3 miles north of George Town, is not on the beach, but guests can reach West Bay Beach by crossing the highway near the hotel.

Dining/Entertainment: The hotel's major restaurant is the Living Reef Seafood Restaurant, complete with "living reef" saltwater aquariums and decor. There's also another restaurant, the Terrace Waterfall Café, and two additional bars.

Services: Room service, laundry.

Facilities: Exercise room, Jacuzzi, tennis courts, fitness center, swimming pool, sauna.

HOLIDAY INN GRAND CAYMAN, West Bay Rd. (P.O. Box 904), Grand Cayman, B.W.I. Tel. 809/947-4444, or toll free 800/421-9999. Fax 809/947-4213 215 rms. A/C MINIBAR TV TEL

$ Rates: Winter, $178–$278 single or double. Summer, $148–$208 single or double. Breakfast $10 extra. AE, MC, V. **Parking:** Free.

Three miles north of George Town and 5 miles from the airport, this modern, beachfront hotel boasts bedrooms with bright, tropical flair, done in floral prints. Most have sitting areas, and all have baths with dressing rooms. Each unit has a southern-style balcony whose white balustrades overlook a garden courtyard planted with palms and shrubs. Ocean-view and oceanfront rooms are more expensive, of course.

Dining/Entertainment: Chez Jacques is one of the island's best restaurants. At the Corsair's Wharf, the bar is set into the shell of a wooden boat and sheltered from the sun with a high roof from which swing hangman's nooses from a re-created ship's yardarm. Another bar, the Wreck of the Ten Sails, provides evening entertainment with a live band.

Services: Room service, baby-sitting, laundry.

Facilities: Lagoonlike swimming pool with arched bridges and poolside cocktails available; fully equipped dive shop; sailing, waterskiing, and deep-sea fishing available; four tennis courts (lit at night).

HYATT REGENCY GRAND CAYMAN, West Bay Rd. (P.O. Box 1698), Grand Cayman, B.W.I. Tel. 809/949-1234, or toll free 800/228-9000. Fax 809/949-8528. 236 rms, 40 villas. A/C MINIBAR TV TEL

$ Rates: Winter, $260–$375 single or double; $450 Regency Club double; $465

one-bedroom villa for two; $585–$690 two-bedroom villa for four. Summer, $165–$235 single or double; $305 Regency Club double; $275 one-bedroom villa for two; $380–$490 two-bedroom villa for four. Breakfast $12 extra. AE, DC, MC, V. **Parking:** Free.

By anyone's standards, this is the best-managed and most stylish hotel in the Cayman Islands. Opened in 1987, 2 miles north of George Town, the hotel is a major component in the 90-acre Britannia Resort community, which includes the Britannia Golf Course. Two acres front Seven Mile Beach. The hotel's design combines neoclassicism with modern art and a sort of British colonial airiness. Dozens of Doric arcades are festooned with flowering vines whose tendrils cascade beneath reflecting pools and comfortable teakwood settees. Low-rise buildings surround a large landscaped courtyard that contains gardens, waterfalls, and the swimming pool.

The Hyatt offers world-class luxury rooms with private verandas. Two buildings and 43 rooms are devoted to the posh Regency Club, which has 24-hour concierge service. The hotel also offers one- and two-bedroom luxury villas along the Britannia Golf Course or waterway, which have fully equipped kitchens and easy access to the resort's many facilities. Guests in the villas have their own private pool, whirlpool, cabaña, and patio area.

Dining/Entertainment: The resort offers several dining choices, including the Garden Loggia Café, which serves breakfast, lunch, and dinner (a buffet champagne brunch on Sunday is a special feature). There's a seafood restaurant, Hemingway's (see "Where to Dine," below), and you can also have lunch daily at the Britannia Golf Club and Grille, a few steps away from the first tea.

Services: Room service, baby-sitting, laundry.

Facilities: The most complete array of water sports in the Caymans (see "Sports and Recreation," below, for more information on the Hyatt's Red Sail Sports facility and its offerings); a one-third-acre swimming pool (with a whirlpool and swim-up bar); the Britannia golf course; tennis courts; croquet.

RADISSON RESORT, West Bay Rd. (P.O. Box 709), Grand Cayman, B.W.I. Tel. 809/949-0088, or toll free 800/333-3333. Fax 809/949-0288. 315 rms. A/C MINIBAR TV TEL

$ Rates: Winter, $225–$299 single or double. Summer, $155–$230 single or double. Breakfast $10 extra. AE, DC, MC, V.

One of the newest hotels on the island, opened in 1990, rises from an enviable position beside Seven Mile Beach, a 5-minute drive (2 miles) north of George Town. Its red-roofed, vaguely colonial design resembles a cluster of balconied town houses. Each of the bedrooms is decorated in blue and white and has views over the ocean or a garden courtyard.

Dining/Entertainment: There's a popular disco, the B.W.I. Club (see "Evening Entertainment," below), and two restaurants.

Services: Room service, laundry, baby-sitting.

Facilities: A swimming pool ringed with a beach bar/cabaña and sun parasols, located a few steps from the famous beach; a fully equipped dive shop.

RAMADA TREASURE ISLAND RESORT, West Bay Rd. (P.O. Box 1817), Grand Cayman, B.W.I. Tel. 809/949-7777, or toll free 800/228-9898. Fax 809/949-8489. 290 rms. A/C MINIBAR TV TEL

$ Rates: Winter, $220–$260 single or double. Summer, $155–$190 single or double. Breakfast $10 extra. AE, DC, MC, V. **Parking:** Free.

One of the largest hotels in the Cayman Islands, ideally located 1 mile north of George Town on Seven Mile Beach, opened in 1987. It offers extra-large bedrooms with two double beds or one king-size bed and a private balcony or patio. Water sports and diving are a specialty of the hotel.

Dining/Entertainment: The hotel has a trio of restaurants, including Chef John's beach barbecue and L'Escargot for more formal dining with fine china, silverware, and crystal. L'Escargot offers a French and continental menu. Silver's Night Club, with live music and entertainment, is the pride of the establishment (see "Evening Entertainment," below).

Services: Room service, baby-sitting, laundry.

Facilities: Scuba diving, windsurfing, parasailing, and waterskiing; two large swimming pools (one with a swim-up bar); two whirlpools; a wading pool for children; two tennis courts.

WEST INDIAN CLUB, West Bay Rd. (P.O. Box 703), Grand Cayman, B.W.I. Tel. 809/947-5255. Fax 809/947-5204. 6 units. A/C TV TEL Directions: Lies 2 miles north of George Town.

$ Rates: Winter, $170 efficiency for two; $280 one-bedroom unit for two; $360 two-bedroom unit for four. Summer, $125 efficiency for two; $180 one-bedroom unit for two; $230 two-bedroom unit for four. Minimum stay 1 week in winter, 5 days in summer. Children must be 10 years or older. AE, MC, V. **Closed:** Sept. **Parking:** Free.

Reached by an elegant drive lined with royal palms, this small private club is right on the beach and looks like an imitation Tara. It offers some of the poshest comfort on the island, with individually decorated housekeeping apartments. Each unit, furnished in a tropical decor, has a large living room with patio or balcony overlooking the beach. Best of all, each accommodation is assigned a personal maid, who will not only clean and do the laundry, but will also prepare local and standard American dishes (this service not available in the one efficiency).

MODERATE

THE BEACH CLUB, West Bay Rd. (P.O. Box 903G), Grand Cayman, B.W.I. Tel. 809/949-8100. Fax 809/947-5167. 41 rms. A/C MINIBAR TV TEL

$ Rates: Winter, $168–$235 single or double. Summer, $130–$190 single or double. MAP $35 extra per person daily. Scuba packages available. AE, DC, MC, V. **Parking:** Free.

Set 3 miles north of George Town across the road from its more glamorous (and more expensive) neighbor, the Hyatt Britannia Beach Hotel, the Beach Club is one of the oldest and best-located hotels on the island. Built in the early 1960s along Seven Mile Beach, it established a scuba-diving center and has since attracted a loyal clientele.

Designed like a large colonial plantation villa, it has a formal Doric portico, lots of lattices, and a popular bar that separates the hotel from the beach. There, calypso music and rum flow freely for a clientele who seem to be dressed in bathing suits throughout the day. The divers who opt for week-long scuba packages usually take one of the tile-floored villas clustered amid trees at the edge of the beach. Otherwise, most accommodations are simple but comfortable bedrooms in the main hotel. Each unit comes with furniture ranging from Caribbean rattan to reproductions of English Sheraton and a veranda.

CAYMAN DIVING LODGE, East End (P.O. Box 11), Grand Cayman, B.W.I. Tel. 809/947-7555, or toll free 800/852-3483. 17 rms. TEL

$ Rates: $90 single; $110 double. MAP $36 extra per person daily. AE, MC, V. **Parking:** Free.

In the southeast corner of the island, 20 miles east of George Town (take the A2) and 19 miles east of the airport, there is a haven for diving enthusiasts. The lodge is a two-story half-timbered building set amid tropical trees on a private coral-sand beach with a live coral barrier reef just offshore. Diving and snorkeling equipment are available for unlimited shore diving. Scuba and snorkeling trips can be arranged.

Ocean-view rooms are simple, yet modern and pleasant. Meals are prepared by Caymanian chefs who serve abundant portions and specialize in fish dishes. Laundry facilities are available.

VILLA CARIBE SEASIDE, Beachfront Resort, North Side (P.O. Box 16), Grand Cayman, B.W.I. Tel. 809/947-9636, or toll free 800/367-0041. Fax 809/947-9627. 14 rms. TV TEL **Directions:** From the airport, take the A2 west to the junction with the A1, and then the A1 north for 30 minutes.

$ Rates (including airport transfers and continental breakfast): Winter, $95–$115 single; $105–$125 double. Summer, $60–$75 single; $70–$85 double. MAP $35 extra per person daily. AE, MC, V. **Parking:** Free.

S On the uncrowded north side of the island lies "your country home by the sea," as host and owner James Terry calls it. All the rooms have private balconies overlooking the sea, maid service, and modern furnishings. Guests may snorkel near the shore with the inn's equipment or enjoy diving, fishing, boating, and island tours. The inn's dining room serves both local and American-style food and drink.

CONDOS

COLONIAL CLUB, West Bay Rd. (P.O. Box 320W), Grand Cayman, B.W.I. Tel. 809/947-4660. 24 units. A/C TEL
$ Rates: Winter, $350 unit for one or two; $400 unit for three or four. Summer, $280 unit for one or two; $280 unit for three or four. Minimum stay 5 nights Dec 16–Apr, 3 nights May–Dec 15. AE, MC, V. **Parking:** Free.

Although smaller than the hostelries flanking it on three sides, the Colonial Club occupies a highly desirable stretch of the famous beach. Built in 1985, it's a three-story condominium about 4 miles (5 minutes) north of George Town and some 10 minutes from the airport. First-class maintenance, service, and accommodations are provided in the apartments, all with kitchen fans, maid service, and laundry facilities.

Usually only 10 of the 24 apartments are available for rent—the rest are privately owned and occupied. You have a choice of units with two bedrooms and three baths or units with three bedrooms and three baths. Facilities include tennis courts (lit at night) and a freshwater pool.

HARBOUR HEIGHTS, West Bay Rd. (P.O. Box 688), Grand Cayman, B.W.I. Tel. 809/947-4295. Fax 809/947-5119. 18 units. A/C TV TEL
$ Rates: Mid-Dec to mid-Apr, $250 two-bedroom unit. Mid-Apr to mid-Dec, $165 two-bedroom unit. Extra person $15. Minimum stay 5 days (10 days at Christmas). AE. **Parking:** Free.

You can stay in style and comfort by the day, week, or month in this beachfront complex 6 miles north of George Town. You're on your own for meals, but there's a good-sized recreation area and a large free-form swimming pool with a surrounding tile terrace filled with white lounge furniture. Apartments are of generous size and can accommodate one to four guests. Each has a living room and dinette, an attractive and complete kitchen, two bedrooms, two baths, ample closet space, and its own balcony or patio. Furnishings are all in white tropical designs with decorative fabrics and accent rugs. Daily maid service is included.

PAN-CAYMAN HOUSE, West Bay Rd. (P.O. Box 440), Grand Cayman, B.W.I. Tel. 809/947-4002. Fax 809/947-4002. 10 units. A/C TEL
$ Rates: Winter, $250 two-bedroom unit for two to four; $315 three-bedroom unit for six. Summer, $155 two-bedroom unit for two to four; $220 three-bedroom unit for six. No credit cards.

The Georgian-style facade of this popular beachfront choice 4 miles north of George Town was attractively altered to suit its Caribbean setting. Each apartment has its own fully equipped kitchen, a private balcony or patio with an unrestricted view of the sea, and comfortable summer furniture. Hotel-type maid service is provided. This place is popular in winter, so reserve well in advance.

SILVER SANDS, West Bay Rd. (P.O. Box 205GT), Grand Cayman, B.W.I. Tel. 809/949-3343, or toll free 800/223-9815. Fax 809/949-1223. 42 units. A/C TEL
$ Rates: Winter, $280 two-bedroom unit for one to four; $360 three-bedroom unit for up to six. Summer, $165 two-bedroom unit for one to four; $250 three-bedroom unit for up to six. Extra person $20. AE, MC, V. **Parking:** Free.

This modern, eight-building complex is arranged horseshoe fashion directly on the beach 7 miles north of George Town. The apartments are grouped around a rectangular freshwater pool. The eight apartment blocks contain either two-bedroom/two-bath or three-bedroom/three-bath units. Each apartment comes with private sea-view balcony, fully equipped kitchen, and hotel-type maid service. The resident manager will point out the twin tennis courts and two utility rooms with washer-dryers.

TAMARIND BAY, West Bay Rd. (P.O. Box 30123), Grand Cayman, B.W.I. Tel. 809/949-8098, or toll free 800/232-1034. Fax 809/949-7054. 28 villas. A/C TV TEL

$ Rates: Winter, $355–$480 two-bedroom villa. Summer, $250–$295 two-bedroom villa. AE, MC, V. **Parking:** Free.

One of the most luxurious condominium complexes on the island occupies a stretch of Seven Mile Beach about 2 miles north of George Town. It resembles a series of modernized Tuscan villas, with zigzagging paths linking the curved walls of the swimming pool with privacy barriers of shrubs and trees. A pair of feathery casuarinas shade the beachside gazebos and surfside hammocks from the sun. The privately owned villas are beautifully furnished, flooded with sunlight, and impeccably maintained. Each contains two bedrooms, two baths, ceiling fans, and a private screened-in patio overlooking the sea, along with a fully equipped kitchen and maid service.

WHERE TO DINE

American and continental cooking predominate, although there is also a cuisine known as Caymanian, which features specialties made from turtle. (*Note:* Environmental groups consider this species to be endangered, although in the Cayman Islands it is bred for food, as opposed to being caught in the wild at sea.) Fresh fish is the star, and conch is used in many ways. Local lobster is in season from late summer through January. Since most dining places have to rely on imported ingredients, prices tend to be high.

EXPENSIVE

CHEF TELL'S GRAND OLD HOUSE, Petra Plantation, South Church St. Tel. 9-9333.
   Cuisine: AMERICAN/CARIBBEAN/GERMAN. **Reservations:** Required.
$ Prices: Appetizers $3.75–$6.95; main courses $13.95–$28. AE, MC, V.
   Open: Lunch Tues–Sun 11:45am–2:30pm; dinner daily 6–10pm. **Closed:** Sept.

This beautiful white mansion is a former plantation house constructed at the turn of the century by a Bostonian coconut merchant. It lies amid venerable trees 1 mile south of George Town past Jackson Point. Built on bedrock near the edge of the sea, it stands on 129 ironwood posts that support the main house and a bevy of gazebo satellites. Converted into a restaurant in 1969, it was purchased in 1986 by German-born chef Tell Erhardt as a showcase for culinary specialties that have been widely publicized throughout Europe and the United States. The Grand Old House is the island's premier caterer and hosts everything from lavish weddings and political functions to informal family celebrations.

Chef Tell specializes in conch fritters, Swedish gravlax, and spicy fried coconut shrimp. One of the favorite appetizers is grouper beignets (deep-fried grouper served with a minted-yogurt-and-curry sauce). Many dishes reflect Mr. Erhardt's origins, including roast duck with red cabbage and spätzle or schweinepfeffer (thin strips of pork sautéed, then finished with a cream and demi-glace sauce spiced with cracked peppercorns).

THE CRACKED CONCH, Selkirk Plaza, West Bay Rd. Tel. 7-5217.
   Cuisine: CARIBBEAN. **Reservations:** Not required.
$ Prices: Appetizers $1–$5 C.I. ($1.25–$6.25) at lunch, $1–$6 C.I. ($1.25–$7.50)

at dinner; main courses $4–$14 C.I. ($5–$17.50) at lunch, $11–$23 C.I. ($13.75–$28.75) at dinner. MC, V.
Open: Mon–Sat 11:30am–10pm.

Given the name, it's no surprise that this restaurant specializes in conch, prepared in every known way, ranging from conch burgers to conch fritters, from creamy conch chowder to Manhattan conch chowder, not to mention marinated conch and cracked conch, as well as conch stewed in coconut milk. If you *don't* like conch, you might begin with vichyssoise, followed by snapper meunière or the fish of the day. In addition, "heart health" menu selections emphasize cholesterol- and fat-free foods and preparation. You'll find the Cracked Conch about 3 miles northwest of George Town on the road that parallels Seven Mile Beach.

HEMINGWAY'S, in the Hyatt Regency Grand Cayman, West Bay Rd. at Seven Mile Beach. Tel. 9-1234.
Cuisine: SEAFOOD. **Reservations:** Recommended.
$ Prices: Appetizers $4–$8.50; main courses $12–$28. AE, MC, V.
Open: Lunch daily 11:30am–2:30pm; dinner daily 7–10pm.

Perhaps the finest seafood on the island can be found 2 miles north of George Town at Hemingway's, which is not only named after the novelist, but is also inspired by Key West, former residence of "Papa," in both decor and cuisine. For example, you might begin with a Key West salad, then follow with snapper tandoori. Hemingway's specialty is fresh fish based on the catch of the day, which might include snapper, swordfish, or tuna, char-broiled or "blackened." Caribbean spiny lobster is regularly featured, and the chef also prepares a superb Spanish paella.

LANTANAS, in the Caribbean Club, West Bay Rd. Tel. 7-5595.
Cuisine: AMERICAN SOUTHWEST. **Reservations:** Required.
$ Prices: Appetizers $2.75–$6.95; main courses $12.25–$28.50. AE, MC, V.
Open: Lunch Sun–Fri noon–2:30pm; dinner daily 6–10pm.

In the middle of Seven Mile Beach, 4 miles north of George Town, is one of the best dining choices on Grand Cayman, located in the Caribbean Club, already recommended for its accommodations. You might begin with Cayman conch fritters and chili mayonnaise or housemade lamb sausage served with Santa Fe red cabbage. Others prefer black-bean soup with green onions and sour cream. Main courses include grilled medallions of Texas venison, Santa Fe linguine with cilantro pesto, grilled swordfish with avocado and pineapple salsa, and pork tenderloin with "jerk" spices. Fresh fish is also available, and the restaurant has a good wine cellar. The restaurant is on two floors—the upstairs has a view of Seven Mile Beach and the downstairs has a southwestern decor.

LOBSTER POT, N. Church St. Tel. 9-2736.
Cuisine: SEAFOOD. **Reservations:** Required in winter.
$ Prices: Appetizers $4–$8.50; main courses $15–$30. AE, MC, V.
Open: Lunch Mon–Fri noon–2:30pm; dinner daily 5:30–10pm. **Closed:** Sun Apr–Dec.

One of the island's best-known restaurants overlooks the water from its second-floor perch at the western perimeter of George Town near the Fort George ruins. True to its name, it offers lobster prepared in many different ways: Cayman style, bisque, and salad; a lobster potpourri with conch, tuna, and shrimp is also included. Conch schnitzel and seafood curry are on the menu, together with turtle steak grown for food at Cayman Island kraals. The place is also known for its prime beef steaks. For lunch, you might like the English fish and chips or perhaps a seafood basket of fried oysters and shrimp. The Lobster Pot's pub is a pleasant place for a drink—you may find someone to challenge to a game of darts while you enjoy an English ale.

RISTORANTE PAPPAGALLO, West Bay Rd. Tel. 9-1119.
Cuisine: NORTHERN ITALIAN/SEAFOOD. **Reservations:** Recommended.
$ Prices: Appetizers $6.50–$8 C.I. ($8.15–$10); main courses $14–$25 C.I. ($17.50–$31.25). AE, MC, V.
Open: Dinner only, daily 6–10:30pm.

One of the island's most whimsically amusing and memorable restaurants is on the western edge of the island near the northern terminus of West Bay Road 8 miles north of George Town. Its designers incorporated Caymanian and Aztec weaving techniques in its thatched roof, whose soaring heights top glass doors, black marble, and polished brass, mixing a kind of Edwardian opulence into an otherwise Tahitian decor. A fountain shoots water skyward from the saltwater pond outside as you dine on black tagiolini with lobster sauce, fresh crab ravioli with asparagus sauce, lobster in brandy sauce, or perhaps Italian-style veal and chicken dishes. Good, too, for a nightcap.

MODERATE

CAPTAIN BRYAN'S, N. Church St. Tel. 9-6163.

Cuisine: INTERNATIONAL. **Reservations:** Not required.

$ **Prices:** Appetizers $3–$5 C.I. ($3.75–$6.25); main courses $10–$15 C.I. ($12.50–$18.75); sandwiches and lunch platters $3.75–$8 C.I. ($4.70–$10). AE, MC, V.

Open: Lunch daily 11:30am–3pm; dinner daily 6:30–9:30pm. Bar Mon–Fri 11am–1am, Sat–Sun 9am–midnight.

On a stony plot of land at the edge of the sea, within a 2-minute walk north of George Town, near the beginning of West Bay Road, Captain Bryan's isn't the island's most glamorous restaurant, yet many visitors quickly adopt it as their preferred hideaway for a drink, a simple meal, and a televised view of whatever rugby game happens to be broadcast from England at the time. Amid a setting of pine-sheathed walls draped with fish nets, you can order lunchtime platters of B.L.T. sandwiches, cracked conch, ham-and-cheese melts, or fried chicken in a basket. Dinners might include nacho platters or buffalo wings, seafood chowder, coconut-flavored grouper, curried chicken, or grilled steak. Dessert might be a heady brew of West Indian liqueur with Blue Mountain coffee.

CROW'S NEST RESTAURANT, South Sound. Tel. 9-9366.

Cuisine: CARIBBEAN. **Reservations:** Not required.

$ **Prices:** Appetizers $3.75–$4.50 C.I. ($4.70–$5.65); main courses $9–$14 C.I. ($11.25–$17.50). AE, DC, MC, V.

Open: Lunch Mon–Sat noon–2:30pm; dinner daily 5:30–10pm.

Recently enlarged with a boardwalk and terrace jutting outward onto the sands, with a view of both Sand Cay and a nearby lighthouse, this informal restaurant on the southwesternmost tip of the island, a 4-minute drive from George Town, is one of those places that evoke the Caribbean "the way it used to be." There's no pretense here. What you get is good, honest Caribbean cookery featuring grilled seafood. Try one of the daily specials or perhaps sweet, tender Caribbean lobster, the most expensive item on the menu. Other dishes might include grilled tuna steak with ackee or Jamaican chicken curry with roast coconut. For dessert, try the Key lime mousse pie, if it's available.

PERIWINKLE RESTAURANT AND LOUNGE, West Bay Rd. Tel. 7-5181.

Cuisine: INTERNATIONAL. **Reservations:** Required for dinner.

$ **Prices:** Appetizers $3.50–$8; main courses $12–$25. AE, MC, V.

Open: Lunch daily noon–2pm; dinner daily 5:30–10pm.

This pleasantly unpretentious bungalow, about 2 miles north of the center of George Town, on the road paralleling Seven Mile Beach, offers some of the finest Italian, seafood, vegetarian, and Caribbean cuisine in town. The establishment has an al fresco terrace, a cedar-lined bar with some of the best piña colada and tropical drinks on the island, and a pleasantly sunny but fully air-conditioned dining room. Main dishes might include grilled fresh swordfish, broiled fresh Caribbean lobster, and scampi provençal, and there's also a selection of vegetarian dishes. Some dishes are flambéed at your table.

THE WHARF, West Bay Rd. Tel. 9-2231.

Cuisine: CARIBBEAN/CONTINENTAL. **Reservations:** Recommended.

$ **Prices:** Appetizers $4–$7.50; main courses $12.50–$18. MC, V.

Open: Lunch Mon–Fri 11:30am–2:30pm; dinner daily 6:30–10pm.

Originally built in the 1950s, the Wharf, 2 miles north of George Town, has been everything from a dinner theater to a nightclub. In 1989 it became a leading restaurant on the island. Today it's decorated in soft Caribbean pastels and offers dining inside, out on an elevated veranda, or on a beachside terrace. The sound of the surf mingles with music from visiting calypso bands and the convivial chatter from the Ports of Call Bar located on the premises. Specialties include filet of fresh fish in a lime-butter sauce, seafood paella, softshell or stone crabs, commercially raised turtle steak, and an array of tropical drinks.

INEXPENSIVE

THE COOKRUM, N. Church St. Tel. 9-8670.

Cuisine: CAYMANIAN/CARIBBEAN. **Reservations:** Not required.

$ **Prices:** Appetizers $3–$6; main courses $8–$12. MC, V.

Open: Lunch Mon–Sat 11:30am–2:30pm; dinner daily 5:30–10pm.

One of the best of the local restaurants, the Cookrum is housed in an old Cayman home across from the Lobster Pot on the northern outskirts of George Town near the Fort George ruins. The owners guarantee that if you taste it, you'll like it. They almost always have commercially grown turtle steak along with such daily specials as red snapper and Cayman-style lobster. Other fresh fish is available, depending on the day's catch. Curried chicken and ackee and codfish are Jamaican-inspired dishes. You could begin with a soup of the day, perhaps red bean.

MORGAN'S HARBOUR, Batabano, West Bay. Tel. 9-3948.

Cuisine: CAYMANIAN. **Reservations:** Not required.

$ **Prices:** Appetizers $2.50–$3 C.I. ($3.15–$3.75); main courses $6–$10 C.I. ($7.50–$12.50). No credit cards.

Open: Lunch only, daily 11am–3pm. Bar Mon–Sat 9am–1am, Sun 1pm–1am.

Simple and unpretentious, with views of the sea, this family-run cabaña on the beach, within a 20-minute drive north of George Town in the hamlet of Batabano, serves island specialties every day at lunchtime; the rest of the time it's strictly a bar. Menu items include conch chowder, shrimp Créole, several different preparations of lobster, sandwiches, hamburgers, and salads. You can rub elbows with the islanders and the yachting folk from the marina at the veranda bar located on a pier that stretches out above the water. Service is good.

WELLY'S COOL SPOT, North Sound Rd. Tel. 9-2541.

Cuisine: CAYMANIAN. **Reservations:** Not accepted.

$ **Prices:** Appetizers $1.50–$4 C.I. ($1.90–$5); main courses $4–$9 C.I. ($5–$11.25). No credit cards.

Open: Breakfast/lunch Mon–Sat 7am–3pm; dinner Mon–Sat 6–10pm, Sun 6–10pm.

Near the airport, a short drive north of George Town, this is the place to go for local dishes, such as conch and commercially grown turtle. The cook also prepares lobster superbly, and offers different specials every night. If you give him advance notice, he'll do something particularly special—maybe curried goat.

WHAT TO SEE & DO

The capital, **George Town,** can easily be explored in an afternoon; it's visited for its restaurants and shops (and banks!)—not sights. The town does offer a clock monument to King George V and the oldest government building in use today, the post office on Edward Street. Stamps sold here are avidly sought by collectors.

The **Treasury Discovery Centre & Museum,** West Bay Road (tel. 7-5033), in front of the Hyatt Regency in the George Town Building, offers a wide assortment of displays, some relating to the discovery of the New World by Columbus. Other items concern sunken treasure and the "lore 'n legends" of pirates. Admission is $5 for adults and $3 for children. It's open Monday through Saturday from 9am to 5pm. There is also a gift shop.

Elsewhere on the island, you might **go to Hell!** That's at the north end of West Bay Beach, a jagged piece of rock named Hell by a former commissioner. There the postmistress will stamp "Hell, Grand Cayman" on your postcard to send back to the States.

The **Cayman Turtle Farm,** Northwest Point (tel. 9-3894), is the only green sea turtle farm of its kind in the world, and is also, with some 100,000 visitors annually, the most popular land-based tourist attraction in the Caymans. Once the islands had a multitude of turtles in the surrounding waters (which is why Columbus called the islands "Las Tortugas"), but today these creatures are sadly few in number (practically extinct elsewhere in the Caribbean) and the green sea turtle has been designated an endangered species. You cannot bring turtle products into the U.S. The turtle farm has a twofold purpose: to provide the local market with edible turtle meat and to replenish the waters with hatchling and yearling turtles. Visitors today can look at 100 circular concrete tanks in which these sea creatures can be observed in every stage of development; the hope is that one day their population in the sea will regain its former status. Turtles here range in size from 6 ounces to 600 pounds. At a snack bar and restaurant, you can sample turtle dishes. The turtle farm is open daily from 9am to 5pm. Admission is $5 for adults, $2.50 for children 6 to 12.

At **Botabano,** on the North Sound, fishermen tie up with their catch, much to the delight of photographers. If you've got your own kitchenette, you can buy lobster (in season), fresh fish, even conch. A large barrier reef protects the sound, which is surrounded on three sides by the island and is a mecca for diving and sports fishing.

If you're driving, you might want to go along **South Sound Road,** which is lined with pines and, in places, old wooden Caymanian houses. After leaving the houses behind, you'll find good spots for a picnic.

On the road again, you reach **Bodden Town,** once the largest settlement on the island. At Gun Square, two cannons commanded the channel through the reef. They are now stuck muzzle-first into the ground.

On the way to the **East End,** just before Old Isaac Village, you'll see the onshore sprays of water shooting up like geysers. These are called "blowholes," and they sound like the roar of a lion.

Later, you'll spot the fluke of an anchor sticking up from the ocean floor. As the story goes, this is a relic of the famous "Wreck of the Ten Sails" in 1788. A modern wreck can also be seen—the *Ridgefield,* a 7,500-ton Liberty ship from New England, which struck the reef in 1943.

Old Man Bay is reached by a road that opened in 1983. Head back to town along the cross-island road through savannah country, where royal palms sway in the breeze and the appearance is veldtlike. You might even spot the green Cayman parrot. At Old Man Bay, you can travel along the north shore of the island to **Rum Point,** which has a good beach and is as fine a place as any to end the tour.

An annual event, **Cayman Islands Pirates' Week,** is held in late October. It's a national festival with cutlass-bearing pirates and sassy wenches storming George Town, capturing the governor, thronging the streets, and staging a costume parade. The celebration, which is held throughout the islands, pays tribute to the nation's past and its cultural heritage. For information as to the dates of the festival each year, contact Pirates Week Festival Administration, P.O. Box 51, Grand Cayman, B.W.I. (tel. 809/949-5078).

SPORTS & RECREATION

What they lack in nightlife, the Caymans make up in water sports—fishing, swimming, waterskiing, and diving are among the finest in the Caribbean. *Skin Diver* magazine has written that "Grand Cayman has become the largest single island in the Caribbean for dive tourism." Coral reefs and coral formations encircle the islands and are filled with lots of marine life. However, the government bans scuba divers from taking any form of marine life.

It's easy to dive close to shore, so boats aren't necessary—but there are plenty of boats and scuba facilities available. On certain excursions I recommend a trip with a qualified divemaster. For rentals, the island maintains many "dive shops," but they will not rent scuba gear or supply air to a diver unless he or she has a card from one of the national diving schools, such as NAUI or PADI. Hotels also rent diving equipment to their guests, as well as arrange snorkeling and scuba-diving trips.

Universally regarded as the most up-to-date and best-equipped water-sports facility in the Cayman Islands, **Red Sail Sports,** in the Hyatt Regency Grand Cayman, West Bay Road (P.O. Box 1588) (tel. 809/947-5965), maintains headquarters in a gaily painted wooden house beside the beach.

Their deep-sea fishing excursions in search of tuna, marlin, and wahoo are arranged on a variety of air-conditioned vessels with an experienced crew. Tours depart at 7:30am and 12:30pm, last half a day, and cost $550 (a full day costs $750). The fee can be split among eight people.

Red Sail also rents 16-foot Hobie cats for $30 per hour, depending on the time of day. One of the best-designed sailing catamarans in the Caribbean is berthed in a canal a short walk from the water-sports center. Some 65 feet in length, with an aluminum mast 75 feet tall, it's fast, stable, and exhilarating. A sail to "Stingray City," with snorkeling equipment and lunch included in the price of $50 per person, leaves once daily. A sunset sail from 5 to 7pm, with hors d'oeuvres, costs $25 per person. A romantic 3½-hour dinner sail costs $66.

Red Sail offers beginners' scuba diving as well as excursions for longtime aficionados of the deep. A two-tank morning dive includes exploration of two different dive sites at depths ranging from 50 to 100 feet, lasts a full morning, and costs $55. Beginners can take advantage of a resort course offered daily and costing $100 per person. A full certification course, requiring a maximum of 5 days, costs $400.

Waterskiing can be arranged for $50 per half hour, and the cost can be divided among several people. Red Sail also offers parasailing at $35 per ride.

BEACHES   One of the finest in the Caribbean, Grand Cayman's ✪ **Seven Mile Beach,** which begins north of George Town, has sparkling white sands with Australian pines in the background. Beaches on the **east and north coasts** are also fine, as they are protected by an offshore barrier reef. In winter the average water temperature is 80°; it rises to 85° in summer.

FISHING   Grouper and snapper are most plentiful for those who bottom-fish along the reef. Deeper waters turn up barracuda and bonito. The flats on Little Cayman are said to offer the best bonefishing in the world. Sports people from all over the world come to the Caymans for the big ones—tuna, wahoo, and marlin. Most hotels can make arrangements for charter boats and experienced guides are also available.

A FITNESS CENTER   Set amid the island's densest concentration of hotels, near the island's only cinema and the Radisson Hotel, the **Nautilus Fitness Centre,** West Bay Road (tel. 9-5132), is open to visitors who want to release the kinks in their muscles. Activities include aerobics, dance classes, Nautilus machines, free weights, sauna, whirlpool, and shower facilities. Visitors register at the front desk, and pay $8 C.I. ($10) per day, $25 C.I. ($31.25) per week. The center is open Monday through Thursday from 6am to 9pm, on Friday from 6am to 8pm, on Saturday from 10am to 4pm, and on Sunday from 10am to 2pm.

GOLF   The only golf course on Grand Cayman is the **Britannia Golf Club,** next to the Hyatt Regency on West Bay Road (tel. 9-8020). The course, the first of its kind in the world, was designed by Jack Nicklaus and is unique in that it incorporates three different courses in one: a 9-hole championship layout, an 18-hole executive setup, and a Cayman course. The last was designed for play with the Cayman ball, which goes about half the distance of a regulation ball. Greens fees range from $40 to $55. Guests at the Hyatt and Britannia community can book a maximum of 72 hours in advance. Other players are allowed with 24-hour advance booking.

SCUBA DIVING   Established in 1957, the best-known dive operation in the

Cayman Islands is **Bob Soto's Diving Ltd.**, P.O. Box 1801, Grand Cayman (tel. 809/949-2022, or toll free 800/262-7686 to make reservations). Owned by Ron Kipp, the operation has grown to include full-service dive shops at the Holiday Inn and the Cayman Islander Hotel on Seven Mile Beach, the SCUBA Centre on North Church Street, and Soto's Coconut in the Coconut Place Shopping Centre. A resort course, designed to teach the fundamentals of scuba to beginners who know how to swim, costs $90. This requires a full day: The morning is spent in the pool and the afternoon is a one-tank dive from a boat. All necessary equipment is included. Certified divers can choose from a wide range of one-tank ($40 to $45) and two-tank ($55 to $60) boat dives daily, plus shore diving from the SCUBA Centre. Nondivers can take advantage of daily snorkel trips ($20). The staff are helpful and highly professional.

SUBMERSIBLES For a once-in-a-lifetime experience, you can take a deep dive in a submarine during your visit to the Cayman Islands—you can even choose between a submersible vessel that can go to a depth of 150 feet and others that can plunge downward to as deep as 800 feet.

One of the island's most popular attractions is the world's first commercial-service submarine, ✪ *Atlantis I,* a craft 50 feet long, weighing 49 tons, built at a cost of $1.8 million, with a capacity of 28 passengers. You drop 150 feet below the surface on 1-hour voyages. The cost is $69 per person for day or night dives (children 4 to 12 are charged $34.50). You can view the briny deep through large viewports 2 feet in diameter, eight on each side of the vessel, as it cruises along at a speed of 1½ knots. Attractions in this living world of a tropical reef, including a wrecked ship, are explained by a guide. At night, nocturnal marine life can be seen and colors not normally visible during the day come to vivid life under probing lights. The vessel makes 12 dives a day and leaves the dock on the hour from 9am to 8pm. Call 809/949-8383 for reservations or write P.O. Box 1043, Goring Ave., George Town, Grand Cayman, B.W.I. Closed the second or third week in September.

Deep Line, P.O. Box 1043G, Grand Cayman, B.W.I. (tel. 809/949-8296), operates *Deep Explorer 2* and *Deep Explorer 3,* two research submarines that each carry a pilot and two passengers on four dives a day. The subs go as deep as 800 feet, and their limit is 1,000 feet. Grand Cayman is the top of an underwater mountain, whose side, known as the Cayman Wall, plummets straight down for 500 feet before becoming a steep slope falling away for 6,000 feet to the bottom of the ocean. The *Deep Explorers,* in their 1½-hour trips, allow passengers to see the variety of sea life at different levels of the dive. Weather permitting, each trip goes down to the wreck of the *Kirk Pride,* a cargo ship that sank off George Town Harbour in 1976 and was lodged on a rock ledge of the wall at 780 feet. The submarines are dry and at one atmosphere pressure, so no previous experience is necessary. Each passenger receives a certificate of the dive and a sub crew T-shirt. It's possible to take pictures with 400 ASA film in your camera. The *Deep Explorer* trips cost $265 per passenger, and they're open to everyone over the age of 8. Reservations should be made at least a week in advance. The office is next door to the waterfront Burger King in George Town, and it's open Monday through Saturday from 8am to 5:30pm.

SAVVY SHOPPING

Shopping is not the most compelling reason to vacation in Grand Cayman, but it should be noted that there is free-port shopping, with merchandise from all over the world available in George Town stores. Often you'll find bargains in silver, china, crystal, Irish linen, French perfumes, British woolen goods, and such local crafts as black-coral jewelry and thatch-woven baskets. However, I have found the prices on many items to be similar to U.S. prices.

Don't purchase turtle products—they cannot be brought into the U.S.

BLACK CORAL AND . . . , Fort St., George Town. Tel. 9-0123.
Connoisseurs of unusual fine jewelry and unique objets d'art are drawn to the stunning black-coral creations of an internationally acclaimed sculptor, Bernard K. Passman, displayed here. In the past two decades the Iowa-born artist has created

pieces of exquisite black-coral and gold jewelry and sculptures. He produced the royal wedding gift for Prince Charles and Lady Diana—a 97-piece cutlery set of sterling silver with black-coral handles given to them by Queen Elizabeth II and Prince Philip. Pressman is credited with elevating the use of black coral from simple souvenirs to a prized art form in the Caribbean. The main gallery on Fort Street is a sightseeing attraction, and branches are at the Radisson Grand Cayman. Signed, limited-edition pieces are considered excellent investments.

BRIDGET'S FASHIONS AND FRAGRANCES, Harbour Dr., Freeport Plaza. Tel. 9-2699.

Opposite the cruise-ship passenger landing, Bridget's offers a selection of fashions from around the world, including Gottex swimwear from Israel, handcrafted batik from Bangkok, Irish linen, Cayman map wall hangings, and specially designed turtle ties, along with sportswear for men.

CARIBE ISLAND JEWELRY, North West Point, West Bay. Tel. 9-1077.

The locally made jewelry sold here is made from black coral, caymanite, whelk, and conch. The jewelry is produced in many forms, including necklaces, bracelets, and earrings. The store is on the way to the turtle farm. Closed in September.

CAYMANDICRAFT, S. Church St. Tel. 9-2405.

A 5-minute walk south of the center of George Town, this shop is probably the best established on the island for the fabrication and distribution of locally made gifts. Elizabeth Hurlston directs a staff who makes sewing kits, pincushions, handkerchief sets, stuffed animals, and decorative bookcovers. Also for sale are stylish fabrics, sold by the yard, from Liberty of London, as well as linens from Ireland and men's silk neckties.

CORAL ARTS COLLECTIONS, N. Church St. Tel. 9-3951.

This store offers rare and ancient coins, conch pearls, and a wide selection of jewelry. Designers use many types of coral—black, pink, angelskin, and oxblood—all crafted in 14- and 18-karat gold.

ENGLISH SHOPPE, Harbour Dr. Tel. 9-2457.

Duty-free perfumes, a fine collection of watches and other fine jewelry, Irish crystal, and collectors' items are the offerings here, all with prices quoted in U.S. dollars. T-shirts and souvenirs are also sold. The shop is in front of the cruise-ship landing.

KIRK FREEPORT PLAZA, Cardinal Ave. and Panton St. Tel. 9-7477.

The largest store of its kind in the Caymans, Kirk Freeport Plaza contains a treasure trove of gold jewelry, watches, china, crystal, perfumes, and cosmetics. The store holds a Gucci franchise for the island and has handbags, valises, and perfumes priced 15% to 35% less than suggested retail prices Stateside. Also stocked are crystal and porcelain priced 30% to 50% less than recommended retail prices Stateside, from such manufacturers as Wedgwood, Waterford, Lladró, Baccarat, Herend, and Daum.

VIKING GALLERY, S. Church St. Tel. 9-4090.

The largest establishment of its type in the Cayman Islands, this unusual boutique is owned by Finnish-born Rita Stroup and her mother, May. Established 20 years ago in a two-story building beside the waterfront, it sells hand-painted skirts; blouses; T-shirts and shorts for men and women; jewelry fashioned from black, pink, and white coral; an assortment of gift items; and Caribbean paintings. You'll find it directly on the waterfront in the center of George Town.

EVENING ENTERTAINMENT
THEATER

A varied program of productions by the **Cayman National Theatre Company** (tel. 9-5477) ranges from Cayman drama to *Macbeth*, as well as West Indian musicals and Broadway revues. Some presentations are at the Harquail Cultural Centre on

West Bay Road. The box office is on North Church Street, Grand Cayman. The theater season is from October to June, and ticket prices depend on the show.

PUBS & CLUBS

Because of its links with Britain, nightlife in the Caymans has a decidedly English tilt. Your options might include a sampling of rum-based drinks beneath swaying coconut palms or at a paneled bar whose accessories resemble those of a roadside pub.

B.W.I. CLUB, in the Radisson Hotel, West Bay Rd. Tel. 9-0088.

Although it sits, drydocked, in the Radisson Hotel, the B.W.I. Club has walls painted with Day-Glo fluorescent paint to simulate an underwater world. You'll drink and dance amid simulated strands of kelp and giant brain coral while the recorded dance music beats through the night. The club offers live music 5 nights a week, performed by local bands or groups from the States. You can dine in the much-awarded Regency Grille. Drinks cost $3.50 C.I. to $5 C.I. ($4.40 to $6.25). Open: Tues–Fri 8pm–1am, Sat 8pm–midnight.

Admission: Friday $3 C.I. ($3.75), Sat–Thurs free.

LONE STAR BAR & GRILL, West Bay Rd. Tel. 7-5175.

Everything about it represents a corner of the Texas Panhandle transported to some of the most richly gilt-edged real estate in the Caribbean. You can enjoy juicy hamburgers beneath the heavy trusses of the smoke-filled dining room, unless you prefer to head immediately for the bar in back. There, beneath murals of Lone Star beauties lassoing rattlesnake-entwined bottles of tequila, you can watch several sports events simultaneously on any of the establishment's 15 different TV screens. If nothing live is being broadcast at the time of your arrival, you might see a videotaped replay from last season. The house specialty drinks are lime and strawberry margueritas. Most guests order fajitas or Texas-style cheese steaks (hot chili peppers cost extra). Full meals begin at $12 C.I. ($15). Monday and Thursday are fajitas nights. Meals are served continuously during opening hours. Open: Mon 6pm–midnight, Tues–Sun 11:30am–midnight.

[LONG JOHN] SILVER'S, in the Ramada Treasure Island Resort, West Bay Rd. Tel. 9-7777.

The most innovative nightclub on the island is reached through the lobby of this previously recommended hotel. Designed with a recording studio on its upper balcony, Silver's uses the same acoustic principles as both the Grand Ole Opry in Nashville and La Scala, the opera house in Milan. At least 90% of its entertainment comes from live bands imported from abroad, whose music usually begins punctually at 9pm. Decorated in Caribbean-inspired colors, Silver's has two large bars and a dance floor. Beer costs $3 C.I. ($3.75) and up. Open: Mon–Fri 8pm–1am, Sat 8pm–midnight.

Admission: $5 C.I. ($6.25).

TEN SNAILS PUB AND COMEDY CLUB, in the Holiday Inn, West Bay Rd. Tel. 7-4444.

During the daytime, this place functions as an English-inspired pub, with platters of fish and chips (or chicken and chips) dispensed to a crowd of local office workers who head here during lunchtime. Several nights a week, however, the premises are transformed into the country's only comedy club, with comedic talent imported from the U.S. Swashbuckling murals of pirates and their treasure adorn the walls. A few steps from the pub's entrance, beside the hotel pool, a local musician ("The Barefoot Man") and his band play island music throughout the evening. Drinks begin at $4 C.I. ($5) each. Open: Pub, daily 11am–7pm; comedy club, Wed–Sun 8am–midnight, with performances 9–10:30pm.

Admission: Pub, free during the day; comedy club, $8 C.I. ($10) plus a two-drink minimum.

LORD NELSON RESTAURANT PUB, Trafalgar Place, West Bay Rd. Tel. 7-4595.

The Caribbean sunlight streams through windows, but the interior is fashioned after thousands of pubs found in the English countryside. Beneath blackened ceiling beams and polished saddle brasses, you can enjoy pub grub, foamy mugs of English ale, and the animated conversation of some of the island's British expatriates. A pint of ale costs $6.50 C.I. ($8.15) and might be accompanied by steak-and-kidney pie or fish and chips. Open: Daily noon–3pm and 5pm–1am; dinner daily 6–10pm.

ISLAND ROCK, in the Cayman Falls Shopping Centre, West Bay Rd. Tel. 7-5366.
The island's most frequented disco offers music nightly. It's a hot spot (usually), and attracts a lot of locals and any visitor who happens to find out about it. Open: Daily 9pm until "the wee hours," depending on business.
Admission: $6.

2. CAYMAN BRAC

The "middle" island of the Caymans is Cayman Brac, a piece of limestone and coral-based land 12 miles long and a mile wide, about 89 miles east-northeast of Grand Cayman. It was given the name Brac (Gaelic for bluff) by 17th-century Scottish fishermen who settled here. The bluff for which the island was named is a towering limestone plateau rising to 140 feet above the sea, covering the eastern half of Cayman Brac. Caymanians refer to the island simply as Brac, and its 1,200 inhabitants, a hospitable bunch of people, are called Brackers.

In earlier years, when Brac was a shipbuilding island (which ended with World War II), extremely hard wood used as the ribs for sailing ships came from the bluff, and there were little vegetable garden plots in pockets of fertile soil there. Today, since home-grown vegetables are not needed so much, the thick vegetation of the bluff—frangipani, century plants, and oleanders—is a winter home or stopover for migratory birds.

The big attraction of the bluff today isn't new. There are more than 170 caves honeycombing its limestone height. In the early 18th century the Caymans were occupied by pirates, and Edward Teach, the infamous Blackbeard, is supposed to have spent quite a bit of time around Cayman Brac. Some of the caves are at the bluff's foot while others can be reached only by climbing over jagged limestone rock. One of the biggest of them is Great Cave, with a number of chambers. Harmless fruit bats cling to the roofs of the caverns.

On the south side of the bluff you won't see many people, and the only sounds are the sea crashing against the lavalike shore. The island's herons and wild green parrots are seen here.

Most of the Brackers live on the north side, many in traditional wooden seaside cottages, some built by the island's pioneers.

The islanders must all have green thumbs, as attested to by the variety of flowers, shrubs, and fruit trees in many of the yards. On Cayman Brac you'll see poinciana trees, bougainvillea, Cayman orchids, croton, hibiscus, aloe, sea grapes, cactus, and coconut and cabbage palms. The gardeners grow cassava, pumpkins, breadfruit, yams, and sweet potatoes.

There are no actual towns on the island—only settlements such as Stake Bay (the "capital"), Spot Bay, the Creek, Tibbitt's Turn, the Bight, and West End, where the airport is located.

WHERE TO STAY & DINE

BRAC REEF BEACH RESORT, P.O. Box 56, Cayman Brac, B.W.I. Tel. 809/948-7323, or toll free 800/327-3835, 800/233-8880 in Florida. 40 rms. A/C TV TEL
$ Rates: Winter, $110 single; $120 double; $130 triple. Summer, $90 single; $100

double; $110 triple. All-inclusive packages available. Breakfast $10 extra. AE, MC, V.

On a sandy plot of land on the south shore 2 miles east of the airport, near some of the best snorkeling in the region, this resort contains motel-style units comfortably furnished with carpeting, ceiling fans, and modern baths. Once the location was little more than a maze of sea grapes, a few of whose venerable trunks still rise amid the picnic tables, hammocks, and boardwalks. On the premises are the rusted remains of a Russian lighthouse tower that was retrieved several years ago from a Cuban-made trawler.

Dining/Entertainment: A hideaway no guest should miss is the thatch-roofed two-story bar whose stout wooden columns rise from above the surf. Perfect for a moonlit tryst, it has a breezy interior where nightcaps are served to the occupants of boats moored alongside. Lunches are informal affairs accented with sunlight and water, while dinners are most often served buffet style under the stars.

Services: Laundry, maid service.

Facilities: Pool, Jacuzzi, water-sports facility.

DIVI TIARA BEACH RESORT, P.O. Box 238, Cayman Brac, B.W.I. Tel. 809/948-7553, or toll free 800/367-3484. Fax 607/277-3624. 71 rms, 13 apartments. A/C TV TEL

$ **Rates:** Winter, $140–$200 single or double; $255 apartment. Summer, $95–$130 single or double; $180 apartment. MAP $38 extra per person daily. AE, MC, V.

Part of the Divi Divi hotel chain, the Tiara, about 2 miles east of the airport, attracts divers and honeymooners. Many newcomers respond at once to the landscaping, which incorporates retaining walls of porous stone with fences of croton, bougainvillea, and palms. All accommodations are housed in motellike outbuildings; 13 of the units are luxury apartments, each with an ocean view, Jacuzzi, and king-size bed.

Dining/Entertainment: On piers on the beach is a Tahitian-style thatch-roofed bar where guests can gaze out to sea while sipping their drinks before heading to the Poseidon dining room to enjoy a Caribbean and American cuisine. There is entertainment at the hotel twice weekly.

Services: Laundry.

Facilities: An excellent Peter Hughes Dive Tiara operation; a swimming pool raised above a white sand beach where boardwalks run beneath groves of palms.

WHAT TO SEE & DO

The **Brack Museum,** in the former Government Administration Building (tel. 8-4222), has an interesting collection of Caymanian antiques, including pieces rescued after shipwrecks. The museum is open Monday through Friday from 9am to 4pm and on Saturday and Sunday from noon to 5pm. Admission is free.

Of course, the biggest lure to Cayman Brac is the variety of **water sports—** swimming, fishing, snorkeling, and some of the world's best diving and exploration of coral reefs. There are undersea walls on both the north and south sides of the island, with stunning specimens lining their sides. The best dive center is **Dive Tiara** at the Divi Tiara Beach Resort (see above).

3. LITTLE CAYMAN

The smallest of the Cayman Islands is Little Cayman, 10 miles long and about 1 mile across at its widest point, lying about 75 miles northeast of Grand Cayman and some 5 miles from Cayman Brac. This cigar-shaped island, which today has only about 30 permanent inhabitants, was first colonized in the 17th century by European adventurers. However, the settlers soon became the target of pirate raids and the little island was abandoned. With the stifling of pirate enterprise, settlers from Grand Cayman moved to Little Cayman in 1833, and it has been home to a few people ever since, although economic endeavors, including turtling and coconut growing, were not successful. It is believed that there may still be pirate treasure buried on the island, but it's in the dense interior of what is now the largest bird sanctuary in the Caribbean.

Little Cayman is home to a unique species of lizard that predates the iguana. It is the oldest species of New World reptile, and there are only 50 specimens in the world, two of which live under the generator shed and compressor/dive shop of Pirates Point Resort, recommended below. The entire island is coral and sand. Any rocks here were brought in from elsewhere, probably used as ballast in pirate ships.

The islands of the Caymans are mountaintops of the long-submerged Sierra Maestra Range, which runs north under the sea and into Cuba. The peaks were slowly built on by living corals after the drowning of the mountains, thus forming the islands of today and leaving subsea walls down the mountain precipices on which coral and other marine life grew for centuries, unseen and undisturbed. Little Cayman's Bloody Bay offers one of the walls nearest the surface—a stunning sight for snorkelers and scuba divers.

The island seems to have come into its own now that fishing and diving have been recognized as its main resources; this is a near-perfect place for such pursuits. The waters around the little island were hailed by the late Philippe Cousteau as one of the three finest diving spots in the world. Fine bonefishing is available just offshore, and a brackish inland pool can be fished for tarpon. Even if you don't dive or fish, you can row 200 yards off Little Cayman to isolated and uninhabited Owen Island, where you can swim from the sandy beach and picnic by a blue lagoon.

Blossom Village, the island's "capital," is on the southwest coast. There are no shops on Little Cayman and only two private phones and one pay phone.

GETTING THERE   Most visitors fly from Grand Cayman to Little Cayman. Cayman Airways (tel. 9-2311 on Grand Cayman, or toll free 800/422-9626 from the U.S.) is the reservations agent for **Island Air,** a charter company which charges between $77 and $122 (U.S.) round-trip, depending on circumstances. The lowest ($77) fare requires a 7-day advance reservation, and a stopover of between 7 and 21 days. Most flights are on six-seater propeller planes, which depart two or three times a day, with no service on Tuesday.

WHERE TO STAY & DINE

PIRATES POINT RESORT LTD., Little Cayman, Cayman Islands, B.W.I. Tel. 809/948-4210. Fax 809/948-4210. 6 rms.

$ Rates (including full board): Winter, $180–$220 single; $140–$180 per person double; $130 per person triple. Summer, $165 single; $125 per person double; $115 per person triple. Package rates (including full board and the activities described below), winter, $220 single; $180 per person double; $160 per person triple. Summer, $200 single; $160 per person double; $140 per person triple. 15% service and 6% tax extra. No credit cards.

For water activities or just relaxing, this resort directly west of the air strip, toward West End Point, offers a family environment with gourmet cuisine. The owner and manager, Gladys Howard, is a graduate of Cordon Bleu in Paris, has studied with such stars of the kitchen as Julia Child and James Beard, and has written several cookbooks. She uses fresh vegetables grown locally, as well as the bounty from the sea, in her menus.

The place has six remodeled and comfortably furnished rooms with private baths, usually rented by one to three guests (the third is often a child). The resort offers package holidays including room, three excellent meals per day with appropriate wines, and all alcoholic beverages, plus two-tank boat dives daily featuring the Bloody Bay Wall, the Cayman trench, and Jackson Reef. Nondiving activities include snorkeling, birdwatching, and exploring. Bonefishing, tarpon fishing, and an Owen Island picnic are available for an additional charge.

It was on Columbus's second voyage to the New World in 1493 that he sighted the island he called San Juan (St. John the Baptist), later renamed Puerto Rico. The island's government has undergone many changes since the days of its first governor, Ponce de León, to its present status as an American Commonwealth.

Lush, verdant Puerto Rico is only half the size of New Jersey and is located some 1,000 miles southeast of the tip of Florida. It's the hub of the Caribbean islands. With 272 miles of Atlantic and Caribbean coastline, and a culture dating back to the native Taíno peoples 2,000 years ago, Puerto Rico is a formidable attraction. Old San Juan is its greatest historic center, with 500 years of history, as reflected in its restored Spanish colonial architecture.

The oldest city in the Caribbean under the U.S. flag, San Juan is the world's second-largest home port for cruise-ship passengers. The old port of San Juan is being restored for $90 million, and the stately 19th-century Paseo de la Princesa will once again be a landscaped promenade of royal palms and fountains. However, the beauty and charm of the island have remained since the first navigators called it "the island of enchantment."

You'll find some of the best golf and tennis in the Caribbean at such posh resorts as the Hyatt Dorado Beach and Palmas del Mar. Accommodations have also greatly improved in smaller cities, such as Mayagüez with its Hilton. *Paradores*—government-sponsored inns—are sprinkled across the island for visitors who want a deeper look than that provided by the posh hotels and gambling casinos of San Juan.

Although San Juan is what comes to mind when one mentions Puerto Rico, the Puerto Rico Tourism Company (a government agency) has been quite successful in its efforts to promote Puerto Rico as "The Complete Island": There are 79 towns and cities, each with a unique charm and flavor. Puerto Rico has a rich countryside with many panoramas, centuries-old coffee plantations, sugar estates still in use, foreboding caves and enormous boulders with mysterious petroglyphs carved by the Taíno peoples (original settlers of the island), colorful but often narrow and steep roads, and meandering mountain trails leading out to tropical settings.

THE CUISINE

Although Puerto Rican cooking has similarities to both Spanish and Mexican cuisine, it has its own unique style, using such indigenous seasonings and ingredients as coriander, papaya, cacao, nispero, apio, plantains, and yampee.

Cocina Criola (Créole cooking) was initiated by the Arawaks and Taínos, the original inhabitants of the island. Long before Columbus arrived, these peaceful people thrived on diets of corn, tropical fruits, and seafood. When Ponce de León arrived with Columbus in 1493, the Spanish added beef, pork, rice, wheat, and olive

WHAT'S SPECIAL ABOUT PUERTO RICO

Beaches

- ☐ Luquillo Beach, 30 miles east of San Juan, the most famous—and arguably the best—beach on the island.
- ☐ Boquerón Beach, a mile-long west-coast beach of white sands, among the most beautiful in the Caribbean.

Great Towns/Villages

- ☐ San Juan, dating from 1521, with some of the New World's most authentic and carefully preserved examples of 16th- and 17th-century architecture.
- ☐ Ponce, the island's second-largest city, dating from 1692 and founded by the great-grandson of Ponce de León.
- ☐ San Germán, the second-oldest city on the island, with a colonial atmosphere and a church from 1606 that may be the oldest in the New World.

Ace Attractions

- ☐ El Yunque, sprawling across 28,000 acres, the only tropical rain forest in the U.S. National Forest System.
- ☐ Arecibo Observatory, a 20-acre site set into an ancient sinkhole containing the world's largest radiotelescope.
- ☐ Rio Camuy Caves, a 250-acre park with limestone caves of stalactites and stalagmites.

Offshore Islands

- ☐ Vieques, 6 miles to the east, with scores of palm-lined white sand beaches sharing space with U.S. military forces.
- ☐ Culebra, a mini-archipelago of 24 chunks of land, rocks, and cays, midway between Puerto Rico and St. Thomas.

---

oil to the island's foodstuffs. Soon after, the Spanish began planting sugarcane and importing slaves from Africa, who brought with them okra and taro, known in Puerto Rico as *yauita*. The mingling of flavors and ingredients passed from generation to generation among the different ethnic groups that settled on the island to create the exotic blend of today's Puerto Rican cuisine.

Lunch and dinner generally begin with sizzling hot appetizers such as *bacalaitos* (crunchy cod fritters), *surullitos* (sweet, plump cornmeal fingers), and *empanadillas* (crescent-shaped turnovers filled with lobster, crab, conch, or beef). Next, a bowl of steaming *asopao* (a hearty gumbo soup of rice with chicken or shellfish) may be followed by *lechón asado* (roast suckling pig), *pollo en vino dulce* (succulent chicken in wine), or *bacalao* (dried salted cod mixed with various roots and tubers and fried). No matter the selection, main dishes are served with *tostones* (deep-fried plantains, or green bananas) that are salted to taste, and plentiful portions of rice and beans.

The aroma that wafts from kitchens throughout Puerto Rico comes from *adobo* and *sofrito*—blends of herbs and spices that give many of the native foods their distinctive taste and color. Adobo, made by crushing together peppercorns, oregano, garlic, salt, olive oil, and lime juice or vinegar, is rubbed into meats before they are roasted. Sofrito, a potpourri of onions, garlic, and peppers browned in olive oil or lard and colored with *achiote* (annatto seeds), imparts the bright-yellow color to the island's rice, soups, and stews.

Dessert is usually a form of *flan* (custard) or perhaps *nisperos de batata* (sweet potato balls made with coconut, cloves, and cinnamon), or guava jelly and *queso blanco* (white cheese).

Finish your meal with Puerto Rican coffee, which is strong, black, and aromatic. Rum is the national drink, and you can buy it in almost any shade. In Puerto Rico it's quite proper to order a cold beer before even looking at the menu; one local choice is India, brewed in Mayagüez, famous for its pure water. However, most Puerto Ricans drink a golden brew known as Medalla.

GETTING THERE

Puerto Rico is by far the most accessible of the Caribbean islands, and it receives more incoming flights, with greater numbers of passengers, than many major cities on the U.S. mainland. **American Airlines** (tel. toll free 800/433-7300) has made San Juan its hub for both the Caribbean and most of Central and South America. American offers nonstop transport at least once a day from 14 U.S. gateways. Excellent connections are available from both Toronto and Montréal (through Chicago). Also available are direct flights from Los Angeles that touch down briefly in either Dallas or Miami.

Once you're on Puerto Rico, transport to neighboring islands is available on **American Eagle,** a wholly owned subsidiary of American Airlines. Using mostly smaller airplanes well suited to island-hopping, the airline offers frequent passage to 31 Caribbean and Bahamian destinations—more than any other airline.

Delta Airlines (tel. toll free 800/221-1212) operates between four and seven nonstop flights daily from Atlanta to Puerto Rico. Delta also operates a daily nonstop flight to San Juan from its hub in Orlando that departs late enough in the day so that connections can be made with other flights.

United Airlines (tel. toll free 800/468-8510) offers daily nonstop flights between Washington, D.C.'s Dulles International airport and San Juan.

Carnival Air Lines (tel. toll free 800/468-8510), a San Juan–based airline wholly owned by the Carnival Group (of cruise-line fame), flies to Ponce (Puerto Rico's second-biggest city) and to Aguadilla, on the island's northwestern coastline, from New Jersey's Newark and New York's JFK.

Trans World Airlines (tel. toll free 800/892-4141) has three nonstop flights a day from New York's JFK into San Juan, as well as one daily flight to San Juan from both Miami and St. Louis.

A handful of European carriers also fly into Puerto Rico, including **British Airways** (tel. toll free 800/247-9297) twice a week nonstop from London. **Lufthansa** (tel. toll free 800/359-5838) flies to San Juan two or three times a week, depending on the season, from Frankfurt. **Iberia** (tel. toll free 800/772-4642) flies to San Juan five times a week from Madrid, usually nonstop, and twice a week from San José, Costa Rica.

GETTING AROUND

BY PLANE   American Eagle (tel. 809/721-1747) flies from Isle Verde Airport to Mayagüez, which can be your gateway to the west of Puerto Rico. Most one-way fares are $40. For information about air connections to the offshore islands of Vieques and Culebra, see their individual sections, below.

BY PUBLIC TRANSPORTATION   *Públicos* are cars or minibuses that provide low-cost transportation and are designated with the letters "P" or "PD" following the numbers on their license plates. They run to all the main towns of Puerto Rico. Passengers are dropped off and picked up along the way. Rates are set by the Public Service Commission. Públicos usually operate during daylight hours, and depart from the main plaza (central square) of a town. Information about the públicos is available at **Lineas Sultana,** 898 Esteban Gonzalez, San Juan (tel. 809/767-5205).

**BY RENTAL CAR   **Some local rental-car agencies may tempt you with special slashed prices, but if you're planning to tour the island, you won't find any local branches should you run into car trouble. And some of the agencies advertising low-cost deals don't take credit cards and want cash in advance. You also have to watch out for "hidden" extras and the difficulties connected with regulating insurance claims which sometimes proliferate among the smaller and not-very-well-known firms.

If you're planning to do much touring on the island, it's best to stick to those old reliables: **Avis** (tel. 809/791-2500, or toll free 800/331-2112), **Budget** (tel.

PUERTO RICO

14 ml
22.5 km

Atlantic Ocean

Caribbean Sea

SAN JUAN

Ponce

Mayagüez

Arecibo

Isla Vieques

Pasaje de Vírgenes

Airport ✈

809/791-3685, or toll free 800/527-0700, and **Hertz** (tel. 809/791-0840, or toll free 800/654-3001). At press time, Hertz offered the lowest price on a subcompact car—around $180 per week (or $36 per day) with unlimited mileage. Budget made an attractive offer of $205 per week (or $36 a day). Avis was the most expensive, pricing its smallest car at $264 per week. The applicability of any special membership you might possess (such as AAA) sometimes grants discounts at the three companies, depending on their individual policies. Each of the "big three" car renters require a minimum age of 21, and Budget prefers not to rent to anyone over 75. Each company offers an optional loss/damage waiver priced at $10 or $11 per day. Even with its purchase, renters are required to pay the first $250 worth of damage to their rented car. (Paying for the rental with certain types of credit cards sometimes eliminates the need to buy this extra insurance; contact your credit card issuer directly to investigate.)

Each of the "big three" companies offers minivan transport to their airport offices and car depots. Added security comes from an antitheft double-locking mechanism that has been installed in most of the rental cars available on Puerto Rico. Car theft is high in Puerto Rico, so caution is always needed.

Distances are often posted in kilometers rather than miles (a kilometer is 0.62 miles), but speed limits are in miles per hour.

BY SIGHTSEEING TOUR **Borinquén Tours, Inc.,** 868 Ashford Avenue, Condado (tel. 809/725-4990), with offices at the Caribe Hilton Hotel and Condado Beach La Concha, operates bus tours that pick up people at their hotels.

One of the most popular half-day tours, leaving at 9am daily (and also at 1pm on Saturday), lasting 4 hours, and costing $18 per person, goes along the northeastern part of the island to El Yunque rain forest and later stops at Luquillo Beach.

A city tour of Old and New San Juan departs at 9am daily, and also at 1:30pm on Saturday, Sunday, and holidays. The 4-hour trip costs $20 per person. Another tour through Old San Juan takes you on a sightseeing jaunt and then to Bacardi's Rum Distillery, where you're treated to a complimentary rum drink. This tour, lasting 4 hours and costing $18 per person, leaves from hotels at 1:30pm Monday through Friday, except holidays.

For a sea excursion to the best beaches, reefs, and snorkeling in the area, contact **Capt. Jack Becker,** P.O. Box P, Villa Marina Yachting, Fajardo 00738 (tel. 809/860-0861). Captain Jack, a long-ago native of Washington, D.C., and a longtime resident of Puerto Rico, takes up to six passengers at a time on his twin-diesel-powered Bertram 31, the *Captain Jack B.* No deep-sea fishing is offered, but most participants appreciate the sun, the reefs, and the marine life. Before departure, guests are directed to a nearby delicatessen to buy drinks and a bagged lunch. The price for a five-hour swimfest is $40 per person. Call after 6pm any evening to make reservations.

FAST **PUERTO RICO**

American Express American Express Related Services is at 1035 Ashford Avenue, Condado (tel. 809/725-0565).

Area Code The telephone area code for Puerto Rico is 809. You don't use it for calls on the island.

Banks All major U.S. banks have branches in San Juan, and are open Monday through Friday from 8:30am to 2:30pm.

Currency The U.S. dollar is the coin of the realm. Canadian currency is accepted by some big hotels in San Juan, although reluctantly.

Documents Since Puerto Rico is part of the United States, American citizens do not need a passport or visa. Canadians, however, should carry some form of identification, such as a birth certificate.

Electricity The electricity is 110 volts A.C., as it is in continental U.S. and Canada.

Emergencies In an emergency, call the local **police** (tel. 343-2020), **fire**

department (tel. 343-2330), **ambulance** (tel. 343-2550), or **medical assistance** (tel. 754-3535).

Holidays Puerto Rico has many public holidays when stores, offices, and schools are closed. They include New Year's Day, January 6 (Three Kings' Day), Washington's Birthday, Good Friday, Memorial Day, July 4, Labor Day, Thanksgiving, Veterans' Day, and Christmas Day, plus such local holidays as July 25 (Constitution Day) and November 19 (Discovery Day).

Information Out in the island, it's best to go to the local city hall for tourist data. Ask for a copy of *Qué Pasa,* the official visitors' guide containing much useful information.

For information before you leave home, there are several tourist offices: 575 Fifth Ave., New York, NY 10017 (tel. 212/599-6262); 3575 W. Cahuenga Blvd., Los Angeles, CA 90068 (tel. 213/874-5991); 11 E. Adams St., Chicago, IL 60603 (tel. 312/922-9701); 200 SE First St., Miami, FL 33131 (tel. 305/381-8915); and 11 Yorkville Ave., Toronto, ON M4W 1L3 (tel. 416/925-5587).

Language English is understood at the big resorts and in most of San Juan. Out in the island, Spanish is still *numero uno.*

Newspaper The *San Juan Star,* an English-language newspaper, is published daily.

Safety Use common sense and take precautions. Muggings have been reported on the Condado and Isla Verde beaches in San Juan, so you might want to confine your moonlit beach nights to the fenced-in and guarded areas around some of the major hotels. The countryside of Puerto Rico is safer than San Juan, but caution is always the rule. Avoid small and narrow little country roads and isolated beaches, either night or day.

Taxes and Tips In addition to the government tax of 7% in regular hotels or 10% in hotels with casinos, some hotels add a 10% service charge to your bill. If they don't, you are expected to tip for services rendered. Tip as you would in the U.S. There is no airport departure tax.

Time Puerto Rico is on Atlantic standard time, which is 1 hour earlier than eastern standard time. However, when the eastern part of the U.S. goes on daylight saving time, Puerto Rico does not change its time.

Weather Puerto Rico's temperature is lower than that typical of the region as the island is cooled by trade winds blowing in from the northeast. Sea, land, and mountain breezes also help keep the temperatures at a comfortable level. The climate is fairly stable all year, with an average temperature of 76° Fahrenheit. The only variants are found in the mountain regions, where the temperature fluctuates between 66° and 76°, and on the north coast, where the temperature ranges from 70° to 80°.

1. SAN JUAN

San Juan, the capital of Puerto Rico, is today an urban sprawl, one municipality flowing into another to form a great metropolitan area. San Juan introduces you to Puerto Rico, and the look of this old city ranges from decaying ruins that recall the Spanish empire to modern, beachfront hotels that evoke Miami Beach.

San Juan roughly breaks down into several divisions, including the old walled city on San Juan Island; the city center on San Juan Island, which contains the Capitol building; Santurce, on a larger peninsula, which is reached by causeway bridges from San Juan Island (the lagoonfront section here is called Miramar); and Condado, the narrow peninsula that stretches from San Juan Island to Santurce.

The Condado strip of beachfront hotels, restaurants, casinos, and nightclubs is separated from Miramar by a lagoon. Isla Verde is near the airport, which is detached from the rest of San Juan by an isthmus.

ORIENTATION

GETTING AROUND   By Ferry   The *Agua Express* connects the old town of San Juan with Hato Rey and Catano across the bay. Ferries depart daily every 30 minutes from 6am to 9pm. The one-way fare to Hato Rey is 75¢ and the one-way fare to Catano is 50¢. Departures are from the San Juan Terminal at the pier in Old San Juan. Avoid traveling at rush hour, as hundreds of locals who work in town use this new ferry connection. Rides last about 10 minutes.

By Taxi   Taxis, operated by the Public Service Commission, are metered in San Juan, or else should be. The initial charge is $1, plus 10¢ for each one-tenth of a mile and 50¢ for every suitcase. A minimum fare is $3. Various taxi companies are listed in the *Yellow Pages* of the phone book under "Taxis," or you can call the PSC (tel. 791-3725) to request information or report any irregularities.

By Bus   The Metropolitan Bus Authority operates buses in the greater San Juan area. Bus stops are marked by upright metal signs or yellow posts, reading PARADA. Bus terminals in San Juan are in the dock area and at the Plaza de Colón. A typical fare is only 25¢. For more information about routes and schedules, call 767-7979.

By Limousine   These *limosinas* (their Spanish name) are operated by the Airport Limousine Service and offer cheaper transportation from the airport to various hotels than a privately rented taxi. However, you most often must share the vehicle. Basic fares are $3.50 into the old town, $3 to the Condado, and $2.50 to Isla Verde. Call 791-4745 for more information. One of the most popular services is operated by **Bracero Limousines** (tel. 740-0444).

ESSENTIALS   Tourist Information   Tourist information is available at the **Luis Muñoz Marín Airport** (tel. 809/791-1014). Another office is at **La Casita,** Pier 1, Old San Juan (tel. 809/722-1709). Out in the island, offices are at the **Casa Armstrong Poventud,** Plaza Las Delicias, Ponce (tel. 809/840-5695), and at **Rafael Hernández Airport,** Aguadilla (tel. 809/890-3315).

   Fast Facts   One of the most centrally located drugstores is the **Puerto Rico Drug Co.,** 157 San Francisco (tel. 725-2202), in Old San Juan. It's open Monday through Saturday from 8:30am to 9pm and on Sunday from 9am to 6pm. In a **medical emergency,** call 343-2550. Maintaining 24-hour emergency rooms are **Ashford Memorial Community Hospital,** 1451 Ashford Avenue (tel. 721-2160), and the **San Juan Health Center,** 200 De Diego Avenue (tel. 725-0202).

WHERE TO STAY

It's easy to spend $200 or more a day in San Juan, or get by for $35. There are package deals galore, and you may want to check with a travel agent to see if one fills your needs. For those interested in a hotel-sightseeing package that also includes cultural events, see the information on the Le Lo Lai Festival under "Evening Entertainment," below.

   Most of the hotels lie in Condado and Isla Verde, out by the airport. Both these sections border the beach.

   Note: All hotel rooms in Puerto Rico are subject to a 7% to 10% tax, which is *not* included in the rates listed in this chapter.

IN OLD SAN JUAN

GRAN HOTEL CONVENTO, calle del Cristo 100, San Juan, PR 00901.
   Tel. 809/723-9020, or toll free 800/468-2779. Fax 809/721-2877. 94 rms, 5 suites. A/C TV TEL **Bus:** A7, T1, or 2.
$ Rates: Winter, $125–$175 single; $150–$200 double; from $225 suite. Summer,

$85–$125 single; $95–$150 double; from $175 suite. Breakfast $7.95 extra. AE, DC, MC, V. **Parking:** $5.

⑤ Considered by many the "Grand Hotel of Puerto Rico," this 300-year-old Carmelite convent is authentically restored. It stands directly across the street from the building that was the original city hall in 1521 (during the Spanish colonial period) and a few steps from the cathedral where the remains of Juan Ponce de León are buried. Although not as lavishly accessorized as some of the resort giants of the Condado, it's the most historic hotel of Puerto Rico. Most of the historical landmarks of the colonial walled city are within walking distance.

Some of the guest rooms, furnished in a Spanish style of heavy wood, have a view of the old town square (Little Plaza of the Nuns) or of San Juan Bay, where one can spot modern ships and sailing schooners going past the ancient fortress of El Morro. There are no beach facilities, but transportation can be provided.

Dining/Entertainment: Cruise-ship passengers are fond of having lunch at El Patio Restaurant, which has a cool courtyard and a soup-and-sandwich menu. It's also a good choice for breakfast, when you can order a typically Puerto Rican breakfast called "macho." The more formal restaurant (operated independently) is Los Frailes, near the reception. In a setting of hand-painted tiles imported half a century ago from Spain, it's open daily from noon to 11pm and features a classic Hispanic menu. Los Frailes has a dark-wood bar, but at the front of the hotel is Romanticus, a modern cocktail lounge with a happy hour from 5:30 to 7:30pm.

Services: Room service, baby-sitting, laundry.
Facilities: Swimming pool, Jacuzzi.

IN PUERTO DE TIERRA

CARIBE HILTON, calle San Jerónimo, San Juan, PR 00901. Tel. 809/ 721-0303, or toll free 800/468-8585. Fax 809/725-8849. 616 rms, 52 suites. A/C MINIBAR TV TEL **Bus:** A7.
$ Rates: Winter, $250–$290 single; $275–$315 double; from $470 suite. Summer, $170–$210 single; $195–$235 double; from $500 suite. Children stay free in parents' room. Continental breakfast from $7.50. AE, DC, MC, V. **Parking:** $5.
The Hilton stands near the old Fort San Jeronimo, which has been incorporated into its complex. With Old San Juan at its doorstep and San Juan Bay at its backyard, the Hilton can be called the gateway to the walled city of San Juan. Built in 1949 in a 17-acre tropical park, it just underwent a major $40-million renovation. You can walk to the 16th-century fort or spend the day on a tour of Old San Juan, then come back and enjoy the beach and swimming cove. Some of the rooms are in the 20-story tower added in 1972, and the Garden Wing units have a tropical decor.

Dining/Entertainment: The Caribe Terrace restaurant complex features an international cuisine with a different menu each night. Other restaurants and entertainment facilities include El Batey del Pescador, a fish restaurant; Rôtisserie, devoted to continental cuisine; the Peacock Paradise Chinese Restaurant; and the Carib Bar, with deeply comfortable chairs and huge windows.

Services: Room service (6:30am–11pm), laundry/valet, baby-sitting.
Facilities: Two freshwater swimming pools, health club, lighted tennis courts.

RADISSON NORMANDIE, avenida Muñoz Rivera (at the corner of Rosales), San Juan, PR 00901. Tel. 809/729-2929, or toll free 800/333-3333. Fax 809/729-2930. 174 rms, 6 suites. A/C MINIBAR TV TEL **Bus:** A7.
$ Rates: Winter, $180–$210 single; $190–$220 double; from $440 suite. Summer, $130–$175 single; $150–$200 double; from $400 suite. Continental breakfast $6.50 extra. AE, DC, MC, V. **Parking:** $3.
Geared to the upscale business traveler, but also a haven for vacationers, the Normandie first opened in 1939 and reopened in 1989 after a $20-million renovation and reconstruction. Built in the shape of the famous French oceanliner, the *Normandie*, it is a monument to art deco. Adorned with columns, cornices, and countless decorations, it was originally built for a Parisian cancan dancer (who was married to a building tycoon). Next door to the Caribe Hilton, the hotel lies only 5

San Juan ★
PUERTO RICO

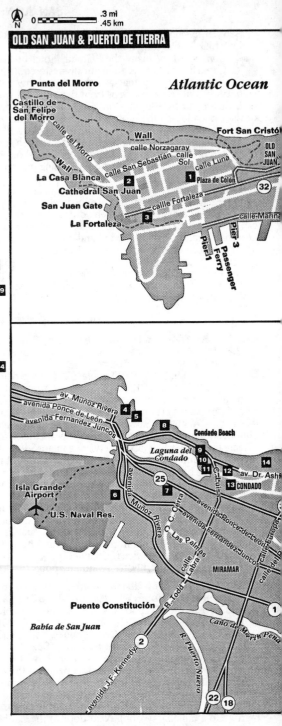

OLD SAN JUAN & PUERTO DE TIERRA

.3 mi
0 .45 km

Punta del Morro   *Atlantic Ocean*

Castillo de San Felipe del Morro

Wall   **Fort San Cristó**

calle del Morro

calle Norzagaray
calle San Sebastián   calle
Sol   calle Luna

OLD SAN JUAN

Wall   **1** Plaza de Colón

La Casa Blanca   **2**

Cathedral San Juan   **32**

San Juan Gate   calle Fortaleza   calle Marina

La Fortaleza   **3**

Pier 3
Pier 1
Passenger Ferry

av. Muñoz Rivera
avenida Ponce de León   **4**
avenida Fernandez Juncos   **5**

8   **Condado Beach**

Laguna del Condado   **9**

10
11   **12**   av. Dr. Ashf

Isla Grande Airport   **25**   **13 CONDADO**

6   **7**   avenida Ponce de León

U.S. Naval Res.

C. C. Cerra
avenida Muñoz Rivera
avenida Fernandez Juncos
C. Las Palmas
calle Labra
R. Todd

MIRAMAR

Puente Constitución   **1**

Bahía de San Juan   Caño de Merín Pena

2   R. Puerto Nuevo

avenida J. F. Kennedy   **22**   **18**

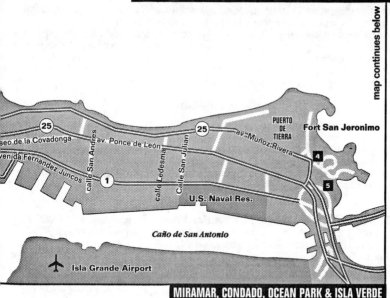

map continues below

PUERTO DE TIERRA

Fort San Jeronimo

seo de la Covadonga

av. Ponce de León

calle San Andrés

calle Ledesma

Calle San Julián

av. Muñoz Rivera

avenida Fernandez Juncos

25

25

1

4

5

U.S. Naval Res.

Caño de San Antonio

Isla Grande Airport

MIRAMAR, CONDADO, OCEAN PARK & ISLA VERDE

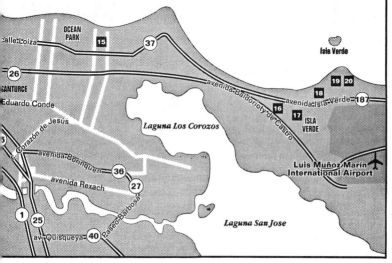

Atlantic Ocean

OCEAN PARK

calle Loiza

15

37

Isla Verde

26

SANTURCE

Eduardo Conde

avenida Baldorioty de Castro

avenida Isla Verde

187

19 20

18

16

17

ISLA VERDE

Corazón de Jesús

Laguna Los Corozos

avenida Borinquen

avenida Rexach

36

27

Luis Muñoz Marín
International Airport

1

25

av. Quisqueya

40

Paseo Barbosa

Laguna San Jose

Airport

minutes from Old San Juan, and its beachside setting adjoins the noted Sixto Escobar Stadium. The elegant and elaborate rooms are well furnished with private baths and all the amenities. The more expensive units are executive rooms.

Dining/Entertainment: There are two good restaurants, and the Atrium Lounge is set in a swirl of greenery. A French menu is served in the elegant Normandie Restaurant.

Services: Room service (to 11pm), laundry.

Facilities: Freshwater swimming pool and bar.

IN CONDADO

Once this area was devoted to residences for the very wealthy, but with the construction of the Puerto Rico Convention Center, all that changed. Private villas were torn down to make way for high-rise hotel blocks, restaurants, and nightclubs. The Condado shopping area, along Ashford Avenue and Magdalena Avenue, became the center of an extraordinary number of boutiques. There are good bus connections into Old San Juan, or you can take a taxi.

Expensive

CONDADO BEACH HOTEL, 1071 Ashford Ave., San Juan, PR 00907. Tel. 809/721-6090, or toll free 800/468-2775 for reservations. Fax 809/722-5062. 245 rms, 3 suites. A/C TV TEL **Bus:** T1.

$ **Rates:** Winter, $173–$420 single; $183–$250 double; from $230 suite. Summer, $121–$315 single; $142–$315 double; from $189 suite. Continental breakfast from $6 extra. AE, DC, MC, V. **Parking:** $5.

The jutting eaves, formal garden, and Spanish colonial design of this hotel evoke the feeling of an archbishop's palace. Built by the Vanderbilts as the first hotel (in 1919) along what is now the heavily congested Condado, the Condado Beach Hotel has been upgraded and modernized many times. Many of the bedrooms are in a rambling modern wing (invisible from the street) whose red-tile roof mimics the detailing of the original core. The oceanfront rooms in the west wing have private balconies. The higher tariffs are for the exclusive Vanderbilt Club "concierge floor," with rooms more expensive than a simple suite. During the day, many visitors ignore the nearby beach in favor of the sheltered pool area, where a double-tiered waterfall is ringed with miniature palms. This hotel is connected to El Centro with its casino.

Dining/Entertainment: On the premises is a handful of relaxing bars, including the Trade Winds. El Gobernador offers fresh seafood, among other dishes, and courteous service. El Café is for more informal dining. Flamenco shows are often presented.

Services: Room service (7am–11pm), baby-sitting, laundry.

Facilities: Outdoor swimming pool, tennis courts (next door), business center.

CONDADO PLAZA HOTEL & CASINO, 999 Ashford Ave., San Juan, PR 00907. Tel. 809/721-1000, or toll free 800/624-0420. Fax 809/253-0178. 544 rms, 15 suites. A/C MINIBAR TV TEL **Bus:** A7.

$ **Rates:** Winter, $225–$361 single; $245–$360 double; from $385 suite. Summer, $175–$305 single; $185–$315 double; from $350 suite. Continental breakfast $6.50 extra. AE, DC, MC, V. **Parking:** $5.

In this two-in-one hotel complex, the original oceanfront structure is linked by an elevated passageway across Ashford to its Laguna section. In the Laguna wing, which has its own lobby with direct access from the street, every room has a private terrace and king-size or double beds. The deluxe part of the hotel, the Plaza Club, has 75 units with five bilevel suites. This section has a VIP lounge reserved for the use of its guests and private check-in/check-out service. The least expensive rooms offered by the hotel are labeled Ashford, while the higher-priced units are called either Laguna View or Oceanfront.

The hotel has a link to the El San Juan Hotel (use of the facilities at one hotel can be charged to a room at the other), and a frequent shuttle service runs between the two hotels.

Dining/Entertainment: The Lotus Flower is one of the island's premier Chinese restaurants (see "Where to Dine," below). Sweeney is one of the better seafood houses and offers a choice of both Caribbean and Maine lobster along with Florida stone crab; one night a week it has a well-attended clambake. The Capriccio has northern Italian seafood as well as a collection of other classic Italian dishes. Las Palmas and Tony Roma's are other dining choices. La Posada, open 24 hours a day, is known for its prime beef and seafood. For nighttime entertainment, La Fiesta offers live Latin music, or you can dance to the disco beat at Isadora's.

Services: Room service, chaises longues and towels provided free at beach and pools, laundry.

Facilities: Five swimming pools, water sports, fitness center in the Laguna wing, two lit Laykold tennis courts.

CONDADO SAN JUAN HOTEL, 1045 Ashford Ave., San Juan, PR
00907. Tel. 809/724-5657, or toll free 800/468-2040. Fax 809/721-8230. 96 rms, 2 suites. A/C MINIBAR TV TEL **Bus:** A7 or 10.

$ Rates: Winter, $150–$190 single; $160–$200 double; from $300 suite. Summer, $95–$135 single; $105–$145 double; from $300 suite. Continental breakfast $4.95 extra. AE, MC, V. **Parking:** $5.

Catering to both vacationers and business travelers, this first-class hotel is right on the beach in the heart of the Condado section. Shopping, sights, and island nightlife are within walking distance or only a short ride away. Rooms are classified as standard, superior, or deluxe.

Dining/Entertainment: You can have lunch or drinks on the sun deck, and dance the night away in the Polo Lounge to live music alternating between Latin rhythms and soft romantic melodies. The intimate Polo Restaurant serves local specialties or continental fare from 6 to 11pm.

Services: Room service, baby-sitting, laundry.

Facilities: Swimming pool.

RADISSON AMBASSADOR PLAZA HOTEL & CASINO, 1369 Ashford
Ave., San Juan PR 00907. Tel. 809/721-7300, or toll free 800/468-8512. Fax 809/723-6151. 160 rms, 84 suites. A/C TV TEL **Bus:** A7.

$ Rates: Winter, $160–$300 single; $170–$310 double; from $385 suite. Summer, $145–$235 single; $155–$245 double; from $310 suite. Breakfast $7.50 extra. AE, DC, MC, V. **Parking:** $5.

Although it had always enjoyed an enviable spot in the heart of the Condado, the Ambassador emerged as a star-studded hotel after New York state entrepreneur Eugene Romano and his wife, Linda, poured more than $40 million into its restoration in 1990. The hotel offers rich doses of theatrical drama and big-time pizzazz, with Czech and Murano chandeliers; hand-blown wall sconces; acres of Turkish, Greek, and Italian marble; and yards of exotic hardwoods.

Accommodations are in a pair of high-rise towers, one of which is devoted to suites. Decors include inspirations from 18th-century Versailles, 19th-century London, Imperial China, and art deco California. Each unit has pay-for-view movies and a balcony with outdoor furniture.

Dining/Entertainment: The developers took care not to diminish from what might be the most famous Howard Johnson restaurant in the chain and the only one which caters to late-night gamblers. More intriguing is Giuseppe's northern Italian restaurant, the hotel's culinary highlight. The Jade Beach Chinese restaurant offers Szechuan and Cantonese cuisine. The casino has a higher percentage of slot machines than any other casino on the Condado, and a resident singer/pianist performs from a quiet corner bar.

Services: 24-hour concierge, VIP floors with extra amenities and enhanced services, a social programmer who offers a changing array of daily activities, room service (6:30am–midnight), baby-sitting, laundry.

Facilities: Penthouse-level fitness and health club; beauty salon; four different bar/lounges; rooftop swimming pool; business center staffed with typists, translators, guides, and stenographers.

Moderate

CONDADO LAGOON HOTEL, 6 Clemenceau St. (P.O. Box 13145), San Juan, PR 00908. Tel. 809/721-0170. Fax 809/724-4356. 46 rms, 2 suites. A/C MINIBAR TV TEL **Bus:** A7.

$ Rates: Winter, $85 single; $95 double; $150 suite. Summer, $70 single; $85 double; $120 suite. Breakfast from $3.50 extra. AE, MC, V. **Parking:** Free.

In Condado at the corner of Joffre Street, this hotel is small and personal. If you're booking from the States, allow plenty of lead time (2 or 3 weeks will do) since rooms go fast both in- and off-season. The suitably furnished rooms all have refrigerators, and guests are free to use the hotel's swimming pool. Meals can be enjoyed at the Ajilli Moijli restaurant, named after a garlic-and-onion sauce invented at the hotel. Although the hotel isn't on the beach, the sands are only a short walk away; it's a block from the main street of Condado. Baby-sitting is available, and room service is offered until 10pm.

Budget

EL CANARIO BY THE LAGOON HOTEL, 4 Clemenceau St., San Juan, PR 00907. Tel. 809/722-5058, or toll free 800/443-0266. Fax 809/723-8590. 40 rms (all with bath). A/C TV TEL **Bus:** 2 or A7.

$ Rates (including continental breakfast and morning newspaper): Winter, $80–$85 single; $90–$95 double. Summer, $60–$70 single; $70–$80 double. AE, DC, MC, V. **Parking:** Free.

A European-style hotel operated by the Olsons, this is in a quiet residential neighborhood just a short block from Condado Beach. The attractive rooms all have their own balconies, and the hotel has a guest laundry and an in-house tour desk. A relaxing informal atmosphere prevails.

EL CANARIO INN, 1317 Ashford Ave., San Juan, PR 00907. Tel. 809/722-3861, or toll free 800/443-0266. Fax 809/722-0391. 25 rms (all with bath). A/C TV TEL **Bus:** A7 or 10.

$ Rates (including continental breakfast and morning newspaper): Winter, $70 single; $80 double. Summer, $55 single; $65 double. Minimum stay 2 nights in winter. AE, DC, MC, V.

This inn offers one of the best bed-and-breakfast values in San Juan. You'll recognize the building by its arched veranda and the porte-cochère, which covers a side yard filled with plants, a fountain, and a gazebo. Keith and Jude Olson are the accommodating owners. The hotel, completely remodeled in 1988, consists of a main house and two nearby sets of servants' quarters, all linked by a terrace. On the premises are an outdoor breakfast bar and lots of quiet corners for conversation. Rooms contain two double beds, two twin beds, or one double bed. There is a communal kitchen, if you feel like cooking, although many restaurants are nearby. The beach is a short block away, and a tour desk is available in the lobby. Parking is not available.

CASABLANCA, calle Caribe 57, San Juan, PR 00907. Tel. 809/722-7139. Fax 809/722-7139. 7 rms (all with bath). **Bus:** T1, A7, or 2.

$ Rates: Winter (including continental breakfast), $50–$65 single; $60–$75 double. Summer, $35–$50 single; $45–$60 double. AE, MC, V.

This informal guesthouse occupies a valuable plot of land just a few paces from the Condado. Originally built as a guesthouse in the 1940s, it was expanded by a former resident of Massachusetts, Alex Leighton. You'll find it behind a wrap-around veranda, a wall, and a garden across Ashford Avenue. Inside, the small and simple guest rooms have ceiling fans (three are air-conditioned) and movie posters on the walls. An honor bar is open throughout the day, which turns the front porch into a social center for guests. You shouldn't expect the Ritz if you select this place, but you'll probably benefit from the cumulative advice that the management has assembled since they've been on the Condado. Only street parking is available.

MIRAMAR

Miramar, a residential sector, is very much a part of metropolitan San Juan, and a long brisk walk will take you where the action is. The beach, regrettably, is at least half a mile away.

HOTEL EXCELSIOR, 801 Ponce de León Ave., San Juan, PR 00907. Tel. 809/721-7400, or toll free 800/223-9815. Fax 809/723-0068. 130 rms (all with bath), 10 suites. A/C TV TEL **Bus:** T1 or 2.

$ Rates: Winter, $108–$134 single; $122–$148 double; from $161 suite. Summer, $80–$106 single; $93–$119 double; from $130 suite. Children under 10 stay free in parents' room; cribs free. Breakfast $4.95 extra. AE, MC, V. **Parking:** Free.

Handsome accommodations and good service are offered here. The bedrooms have been completely refurbished; many have fully equipped kitchenettes, and all have hairdryers, two phones (one in the bathroom), and marble vanities. Included in the rates are use of the swimming pool, daily coffee, a newspaper, shoeshines, and transportation to the nearby beach, as well as parking in the underground garage or the adjacent parking lot. The Excelsior is known for its excellent maintenance and meticulous housekeeping.

The award-winning Augusto's Restaurant serves lunch Tuesday through Friday and dinner Monday through Saturday, and breakfast is served at poolside daily at El Gazebo. A cocktail lounge, exercise room, and a beauty shop complete the hotel's facilities. Services include laundry and baby-sitting.

SAN JUAN CLARION HOTEL & CASINO, avenida Fernández Juncos 600, San Juan, PR 00907. Tel. 809/721-4100, or toll free 800/468-2491. Fax 809/721-6388. 124 rms (all with bath), 44 suites. A/C TV TEL

$ Rates: Winter, $140–$150 single; $150–$160 double; $180–$420 suite. Summer, $100–$140 single; $110–$150 double; $165–$310 suite. Breakfast $3.50 extra. AE, DC, MC, V. **Parking:** $5.

The tallest skyscraper in the Caribbean soars above a commercial and residential district 8 miles west of the airport (best reached by taxi). Its lobby and many of its public rooms are sheathed in marble. There's a swimming pool in back and a long tunnel leads to a pleasant restaurant, Adoquin. The uppermost story contains an elegant restaurant, Windows on the Caribbean. Each of the accommodations of this restored and redecorated hotel is done in stylish cream and pastels. Other facilities include a sauna and a health club, and services include laundry and room service. The hotel also has a casino.

OCEAN PARK

LA CONDESA INN, calle Cacique 2071, San Juan, PR 00911. Tel. 809/727-3698. 18 rms (all with bath), 3 suites. A/C TV **Directions:** Go by taxi.

$ Rates: Winter, $73 single; $85 double; from $95 suite. Summer, $48–$61 single; $73 double; from $85 suite. AE, MC, V.

The former private residence of the Spanish consul is now La Condesa Inn, located directly east of the airport in the residential Ocean Park–Condado area, just 60 yards from San Juan's most spacious beach and about a 5-minute taxi ride from most of the casinos, restaurants, and entertainment centers. Because this guesthouse is small, reserve and plan accordingly. All but the upstairs suites have their own private entrances. Some rooms contain complete kitchens and dining bars, though there is also a pool restaurant. Each has a clock radio. Room service is provided until 10pm. Only street parking is available.

ISLA VERDE

Beach-bordering Isla Verde is closer to the airport than the other sections of San Juan. Hotels here lie farther from the old town than do those in Miramar, Condado, and Ocean Park. However, a few of these establishments are among the deluxe showcases of the Caribbean. If you don't mind the isolation and want access to the fairly good beaches, then consider one of the following hotels.

CARIB-INN HOTEL, avenida Los Gobernadores, Isla Verde, San Juan, PR 00913. Tel. 809/791-3535, or toll free 800/548-8217. Fax 809/791-0104. 225 rms, 8 suites. TV TEL **Bus:** A7, T1, or 2.

$ Rates: Winter, $95–$135 single; $100–$140 double; from $250 suite. Summer, $60–$95 single; $65–$100 double; from $180 suite. Breakfast $3.95 extra. AE, DC, V. **Parking:** $2.

S The Carib-Inn Hotel is a complete tennis club and resort, just 8 minutes from the airport. This is the largest tennis facility in the San Juan area, and the sport is taken seriously here—you'll find a group of tennis pros at your command. Many of the high-ceilinged bedrooms and the cabañas have balconies, and most overlook a giant racquet-shaped swimming pool with a sunning and refreshment terrace, including the Bohío Bar. Rooms are traditionally furnished, most with two double beds. Accommodations are graded moderate, superior, or deluxe.

Dining/Entertainment: La Tinaja restaurant serves a local and international cuisine, and Cousin Ho's, a Chinese eatery, is one of the best Asian restaurants in the city. The Intimo Lounge provides live entertainment and dancing until the early hours.

Services: Room service (6:30am–11pm), laundry, baby-sitting.

Facilities: Swimming pool; eight tennis courts (4 professional Laykold-surfaced courts and four clay courts); health center with gym, steam room, and sauna.

DUFFY'S INN, 9 Isla Verde Rd., San Juan, PR 00913. Tel. 809/736-1415. 10 rms. A/C TV TEL **Bus:** T1.

$ Rates: Winter, $65 single; $75 double. Summer, $45 single; $50 double. Breakfast from $3.50 extra. AE, MC, V. **Parking:** Free.

Built as a private home in the 1930s but converted into a guesthouse in 1946, Duffy's resembles a secluded California bungalow compound hidden by flowering trees. You can leave your car in the parking area before heading in to meet the Rochester-born owner, Madeline Weiche. Everything is a bit time-worn, but that's what makes the place so low-key and mellow. The accommodations, which have ceiling fans and views of the vegetation, lie in a motellike conversion of an older house a few steps away.

Guests socialize in Duffy's Restaurant, where full dinners, costing up to $15 each, include grilled pork chops and chicken Cordon Bleu and are served from 5pm to midnight daily. The bar, open 24 hours a day, serves sandwiches and soup.

EL SAN JUAN HOTEL AND CASINO, Rte. 187 (P.O. Box 2872), San Juan, PR 00902. Tel. 809/793-1000, or toll free 800/468-2818. Fax 809/253-0178. 372 rms, 20 suites. A/C MINIBAR TV TEL **Bus:** T1.

$ Rates: Winter, $265–$365 single; $285–$385 double; from $435 suite. Summer, $195–$315 single; $215–$335 double; from $380 suite. Breakfast buffet $12.50 extra. AE, DC, MC, V. **Parking:** $5.

★ For dozens of reasons which involve more than its spectacular physical plant, this is considered the best hotel in Puerto Rico, and some say the best in the entire Caribbean basin. Built in the 1950s, it was restored with the infusion of $45 million. The hotel is surrounded by 350 palms, century-old banyans, and gardens. Its sandy beach with its almond trees is probably the finest in the San Juan area. At the hotel's river pool, currents and cascades evoke a freshwater jungle stream with lagoons.

The hotel's lobby is perhaps the most opulent and memorable in the Caribbean. Entirely sheathed in marble and hand-carved mahogany paneling, the public rooms stretch on almost endlessly.

The accommodations have intriguing touches of hi-tech and are decorated in Caribbean colors. Each includes dressing rooms, three phones, video-linked TVs, and ceiling fans. A few feature Jacuzzis. About 150 of the accommodations, designed as rustic but comfortable bungalows, are within the outer reaches of the garden. Known as casitas, they include Roman tubs, atrium showers, and access to the fern-lined paths of a tropical jungle a few steps away.

Dining/Entertainment: La Veranda Restaurant, near the sands, is open 24 hours. Dar Tiffany, a steak-and-seafood restaurant, is open nightly, or you might prefer Don Juan, an upmarket restaurant serving a nouvelle Caribbean cuisine. Good Italian food is served for lunch and dinner at La Piccola dining room. Or you can walk down a re-creation of a waterfront street in Hong Kong to a Chinese restaurant. The in-house casino is open daily from noon to 4am.

Services: 24-hour room service, dry cleaning, baby-sitting, massage service.

Facilities: Rooftop health club, water sports, steam room, sauna.

SANDS HOTEL & CASINO, 187 Isla Verde Rd., Isla Verde, PR 00913. Tel. 809/791-6100, or toll free 800/443-2009. Fax 809/791-8525. 420 rms, 17 suites. A/C TV TEL **Bus:** T1, A7, or 2.

$ Rates: Winter, $225–$305 single; $235–$315 double; from $400 suite. Summer, $145–$235 single; $160–$250 double; from $300 suite. AE, DC, MC, V. **Parking:** $5.

⭐ This spectacular resort evokes the high-rolling spirit of the Sands at Atlantic City and is the most lavish in the Caribbean. The public rooms are filled with museum-quality art, ranging from a 7-foot lion-headed bird from the royal palace of Singaraja in Indonesia to temple dogs from China. Everywhere you turn are pink-and-white marble floors, Lalique crystal, and tropical fabrics.

The deluxe rooms and luxurious suites have private balconies and either mountain or ocean views. Even more elegant is the Plaza Club, a wing of the hotel with private garden suites, sometimes called a hotel within a hotel. It has a private entrance, 24-hour concierge service, complimentary food and beverage buffets, and private spa and beach facilities.

Dining/Entertainment: The most elegant restaurant is Leonardo's, which serves a northern Italian cuisine. Tucano Restaurant, open 24 hours a day, is a light and breezy, informal place, where you can order Puerto Rican and international dishes. The hotel also offers Reina del Mar, an excellent seafood restaurant, plus the Dumpling House, with Chinese food. Its nightclub books some of the island's leading entertainment in winter, and it also operates one of the most frequented casinos in Puerto Rico.

Services: 24-hour room service, baby-sitting, laundry, limousine service, massage service.

Facilities: What is said to be the Caribbean's largest free-form swimming pool, with waterfalls and swim-up bar; business center; scuba-diving facilities.

WHERE TO DINE

In recent years San Juan restaurants have returned to a greater appreciation of Puerto Rican cooking. So now many of the leading restaurants feature local specialties as well as Stateside dishes.

OLD SAN JUAN

Expensive

LA CHAUMIERE, 367 Tetuan. Tel. 722-3330.

Cuisine: FRENCH. **Reservations:** Recommended. **Bus:** T1, A7, or 2.

$ Prices: Appetizers $5.50–$12.50; main courses $21.50–$29.50. AE, DC, MC, V.

Open: Dinner only, Mon–Sat 6pm–midnight. **Closed:** Aug–Sept.

⭐ Behind the Tapia Theater, La Chaumière is decorated like an inn in provincial France, with heavy ceiling beams, black-and-white checkerboard floors, and large rows of wine racks. Menu items include fresh goose liver in port wine sauce; rack of baby lamb provençal; chateaubriand for one; pâté maison made with pork, chicken, and duck liver; and daily specials, such as fish soup.

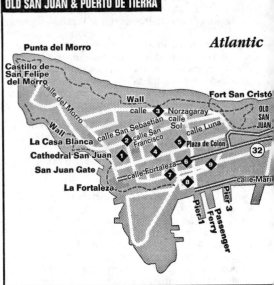

OLD SAN JUAN & PUERTO DE TIERRA

.3 mi
.45 km

0

Atlantic

Punta del Morro

Castillo de San Felipe del Morro

Wall

calle ❸ Norzagaray

Fort San Cristó

OLD SAN JUAN

calle del Morro

Wall

calle San Sebastián

calle Sol

calle Luna

La Casa Blanca

calle San Francisco

❷

❺ Plaza de Colón

Cathedral·San Juan ❶

❹

32

San Juan Gate

calle·Fortaleza

❻

❾

❼

❽

calle·Mari

La Fortaleza

Pier 3

Pier 1

Passenger Ferry

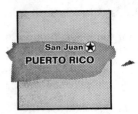

San Juan ⭐
PUERTO RICO

Al Dente ❽
Amadeus ❷
Augusto's ⑫
Back Street Hong Kong ㉔
Bombanera, La ❸
Butterfly People Café ❻
Caribe Hilton Hotel ⑩
Casona, La ⑲
Chart House ⑰
Chaumière, La ❾
Che's ㉓
Compostela ⑯
Criollissimo ⑳
Dar Tiffany ㉔
El Patio
 (Gran Hotel El Convento) ❶
El Patio de Sam ❷
Faisanes, Los ⑮
Giuseppe's ⑱
Howard Johnson's ⑱
L.K. Sweeney & Sons, Ltd. ⑬
Lotus Flower ⑬
Mallorquina, La ❹
Mona's Mexican Restaurant ㉑
NoNo's ❸
Ramiro's ⑮
Repostería Kassalta ㉒
Scotch & Sirloin ⑭
Sonny's Oceanfront Place
 for Ribs ㉕
Szechuan Restaurant ❼
Tasca del Callejon, La ❻
Tony's Room ⑬
Windows on the Caribbean ⑪

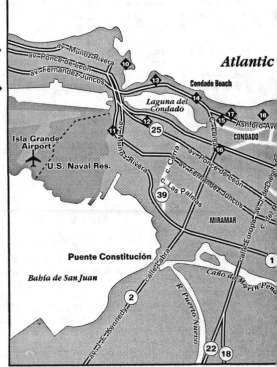

Atlantic

av-Muñoz-Rivera

av-Ponce-de-León

av-Fernández-Juncos

⑩

⑬

Condade Beach

Laguna del Condado

⑭

⑰

⑱

Ashford·Ave

⑪

⑮

CONDADO

25

Isla Grande Airport

av-Muñoz-Rivera

av-Ponce-de-León

⑯

U.S. Naval Res.

av-Fernández-Juncos

c. Cerra

c. c. Las Palmas

39

MIRAMAR

Puente Constitución

1

Bahía de San Juan

calle·Labra

Caño de Merín Peri

av-F.·Kennedy

2

R. Puerto Nuevo

22 18

map continues below

Ocean

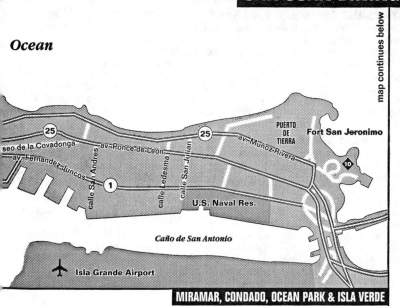

seo de la Covadonga
av. Ponce de León
av. Fernández Juncos
calle San Andrés
calle Ledesma
calle San Julián
25
25
av. Muñoz Rivera
PUERTO DE TIERRA
Fort San Jeronimo
10
1
U.S. Naval Res.
Caño de San Antonio
✈ Isla Grande Airport

MIRAMAR, CONDADO, OCEAN PARK & ISLA VERDE

Ocean

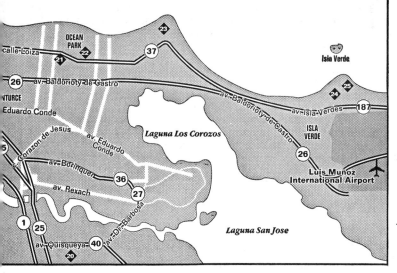

calle Loíza
OCEAN PARK
21
22
37
23
Isla Verde
26
av. Baldorioty de Castro
av. Baldorioty de Castro
24
25
av. Isla Verdes
187
NTURCE
Eduardo Conde
Laguna Los Corozos
ISLA VERDE
5
Jesus
Corazon de
av. Eduardo Conde
av. Botinquer
av. Rexach
36
27
26
Luis Muñoz International Airport ✈
1 **25**
av. Dr. Barbosa
av. Quisqueya **40**
20
Laguna San Jose

Airport ✈

Moderate

RESTAURANT AMADEUS, calle San Sebastián 106. Tel. 722-8635.
  Cuisine: CARIBBEAN. **Reservations:** Recommended. **Bus:** M2, M3, or T1.
$ Prices: Appetizers $2.75–$8.50; main courses $6.75–$17.50. AE, MC, V.
  Open: Daily noon–2am (kitchen closes at 12:30am).

Housed in a brick-and-stone building that was constructed in the 18th century by a wealthy merchant, Restaurant Amadeus offers Caribbean ingredients with a nouvelle twist. You might enjoy an appetizer of fried green plantains with caviar and fish mousse, fried dumplings in guava sauce, a cassoulet of shrimp with black beans and sausages, or rabbit with prunes and red wine sauce. The establishment lies in the heart of the old city, across from the Church of San José.

LA TASCA DEL CALLEJON, calle Fortaleza 317. Tel. 721-1689.
  Cuisine: SPANISH. **Reservations:** Recommended. **Bus:** T1, A7, or 2.
$ Prices: Tapas $3.50–$13; main courses $13.50–$20. AE, DC, MC, V.
  Open: Mon–Thurs noon–11pm, Fri–Sat noon–2am, Sun 5–11pm.

This is the only combination cabaret and taverna in Puerto Rico. In a large brick-sided room reminiscent of old Iberia, a battalion of attractive waiters and waitresses will interrupt their service to sing, dance, or play the guitar to a crowd enthusiastically applauding them.

The specialty here is tapas, an array of hot or cold appetizers which, when ordered in different combinations, make for a meal that is both satisfying and fun. Main dishes include cannelloni stuffed with pâté, octopus in vinaigrette, fabada asturiana (the bean dish of northern Spain), a hearty potato-and-kale soup called caldo gallego, grilled New York sirloin, and paella. No one will mind if you only order a single dish of tapas and drink the night away. Shows usually begin around 9:30pm and continue for several hours.

Inexpensive

LA BOMBONERA, calle San Francisco 259. Tel. 722-0658.
  Cuisine: PUERTO RICAN. **Reservations:** Recommended. **Bus:** M2, M3, or T1.
$ Prices: Main courses $4.35–$10.45. AE, MC, V.
  Open: Daily 7:30am–8:30pm.

⑤ This long-enduring favorite was established in 1902, and ever since it has been offering homemade pastries and endless cups of coffee (said to be the best served in the old town) in a traditional colonial decor. For decades it was a rendezvous for the island's literati and for old San Juan families, but now it has been discovered by foreign visitors. The food is authentic and inexpensive. They serve sandwiches, but most patrons prefer one of the main regional dishes, perhaps rice with squid, roast leg of pork, or a seafood asopao. For dessert, you might select an apple, pineapple, or prune pie, or one of many types of flan. Service is polite, if a bit rushed, and the place fills up quickly at lunchtime.

LA MALLORQUINA, calle San Justo 207. Tel. 722-3261.
  Cuisine: PUERTO RICAN. **Reservations:** Not required. **Bus:** 2, T1, or A7.
$ Prices: Appetizers $2.95–$6.95; main courses $9.95–$24.50. AE, DC, MC, V.
  Open: Lunch Mon–Sat noon–2pm; dinner Mon–Sat 8–10pm.

⑤ San Juan's oldest restaurant was founded in 1848. A bit of Old Spain transplanted to the New World, the restaurant is in a three-story, glassed-in courtyard with arches and antique wall clocks. Even if you've already eaten, you might want to have a drink at the old-fashioned wooden bar. The chef specializes in the most typical Puerto Rican rice dish—asopao. You can have it with either chicken, shrimp, or lobster and shrimp (if you're feeling extravagant). Arroz con pollo is almost as popular. Begin your dinner with garlic soup, or if that frightens you, gazpacho. Other recommended main dishes are grilled pork chop with fried plantain, beef tenderloin Puerto Rican style, and assorted seafood stewed in wine. Lunch is busy, and dinners are sometimes quiet.

EL PATIO DE SAM, calle San Sebastián 102. Tel. 723-1149.

Cuisine: AMERICAN/PUERTO RICAN. **Reservations:** Not required. **Bus:** T1, A7, or 2.

$ Prices: Appetizers $2.50–$6.75; main courses $8.50–$26.50. AE, DC, MC, V.

Open: Sun–Thurs 11am–2am (kitchen closes at 1:30am), Fri–Sat 11am–3am (kitchen closes at 2am).

Located across from the San José Church, the oldest building on the island faces the statue of Ponce de León, the island's first governor. This is a popular gathering spot for American expatriates, newspeople, and shopkeepers in the old town, and is known for having the best hamburgers in San Juan. Even though the dining room is not outdoors, it has been transformed into a patio. You'll swear you're dining al fresco: Every table is strategically placed near a cluster of potted, outdoor plants, and canvas panels and awnings cover the skylight. For a satisfying lunch, try the black-bean soup, followed by the burger platter, and topped with a Key lime tart. Other main dishes include various steaks, barbecued ribs, filet of sole stuffed with crab, and fish and chips.

SZECHUAN RESTAURANT, calle San Justo 257. Tel. 722-4929.

Cuisine: CHINESE. **Reservations:** Not required. **Bus:** T1, A7, or 2.

$ Prices: Appetizers $1.75–$6; main courses $9.75–$16.50. AE, DC, MC, V.

Open: Mon–Sat 11:30am–10pm, Sun 11:30am–9pm.

Here you'll find acceptable Asian food in the old town at half the price of the more highly touted Chinese restaurants in the Condado area. The cuisine is spicy and savory, and a section of the menu lists the chef's specials. You might begin with an excellent king crab and corn soup (properly flavored, not the usual bland variety), then follow with lobster fried rice, eggplant in a garlic sauce, or some of the choice meat, fish, and poultry selections. No one bothers much about decor—it's the food that counts here.

Budget

BUTTERFLY PEOPLE CAFE, calle Fortaleza 152. Tel. 723-2432.

Cuisine: CONTINENTAL/AMERICAN. **Reservations:** Not required. **Bus:** T1, A7, or 2.

$ Prices: Appetizers $3–$4; main courses $8–$9. AE, DC, MC, V.

Open: Lunch only, Mon–Sat 10am–6pm.

This butterfly venture with gossamer wings (see "Savvy Shopping," below) is on the second floor of a restored mansion in Old San Juan. Next to the world's largest gallery devoted to butterflies, you can dine in the café, which opens to a patio and has 15 tables. The cuisine is tropical and light European fare made with fresh ingredients. You might begin with gazpacho or vichyssoise, follow with quiche or one of the daily specials, and finish with chocolate mousse or the tantalizing raspberry chiffon pie with fresh raspberry sauce. A full bar offers tropical specialties featuring piña coladas, fresh-squeezed Puerto Rican orange juice, and Fantasias—a frappe of seven fresh fruits. Wherever you look, framed butterflies will delight you.

CONDADO

CHART HOUSE, 1214 Ashford Ave. Tel. 728-0110.

Cuisine: STEAK/SEAFOOD. **Reservations:** Required Sat–Sun, recommended Mon–Fri. **Bus:** 2, T1, or A7.

$ Prices: Appetizers $4–$9; main courses $15–$40. AE, DC, MC, V.

Open: Dinner only, Sun–Thurs 6–11pm, Fri–Sat 6pm–midnight.

The Chart House, one of the best restaurants on the island, attracts literally hundreds of locals on any night. It's housed in a lattice-trimmed villa built in 1910, which was once the home of the German consul. Today the heavy ceiling beams have been exposed, track lighting installed, and paintings added to create a warm ambience. The food is well prepared, and prime rib is a specialty. You can also order New England clam chowder, top sirloin, shrimp teriyaki, Australian lobster, Hawaiian chicken, and a copious salad. The special dessert is called "mud pie." The Chart House is part of a chain of restaurants based in California.

GIUSEPPE'S, in the Ambassador Plaza Hotel, 1369 Ashford Ave. Tel. 721-7300.
   Cuisine: NORTHERN ITALIAN. **Reservations:** Recommended. **Bus:** A7.
$ Prices: Appetizers $9–$12; main courses $15.50–$40. AE, DC, MC, V.
   Open: Lunch Mon–Fri noon–3pm; dinner Mon–Sat 6pm–midnight, Sun noon–10pm.

⭐ The most sophisticated Italian restaurant in San Juan caters to discerning diners who appreciate the nuances of fine cuisine and service. The decor of neutral colors, stucco arches, and gracefully unobtrusive *trompe l'oeil* murals. Menu items include just about the entire repertoire of northern Italian cuisine. You'll find a specialty version of Caesar salad; fresh mushrooms in garlic sauce; a succulent half-melted version of fresh mozzarella *in carozza;* many different preparations of seafood, veal, chicken, and beef dishes; and virtually any pasta dish known, which, if not on the menu, will be specially concocted with a flourish from the kitchen.

L. K. SWEENEY & SON, LTD., in the Condado Plaza Hotel, 999 Ashford Ave. Tel. 723-5551.
   Cuisine: SEAFOOD/INTERNATIONAL. **Reservations:** Recommended. **Bus:** A7.
$ Prices: Appetizers $10–$65; main courses $20–$29. AE, MC, V.
   Open: Dinner only, daily 6–11pm.

Stylish, and imbued with an architectural elegance probably derived from a Nantucket version of a London gentleman's club, this is one of the most desirable dining spots in a district loaded with unusual restaurants. Many diners opt for an apéritif (perhaps with a platter of clams, oysters, or shrimp) amid the burnished mahogany, stained glass, and polished marble of Sweeney's Oyster Bar, where a live pianist performs every night between 6pm and midnight. Specialties in the dining room include clams casino, chicken Michel (prepared with tarragon and cream), fresh fish imported daily from the markets of Boston and New York (sautéed, poached, or blackened), crab cakes, herb-laced Caribbean seafood stew, and thick and juicy steaks. Jackets for men are a good idea.

LOTUS FLOWER, in the Laguna wing of the Condado Plaza Hotel and Casino, 999 Ashford Ave. Tel. 722-0940.
   Cuisine: CHINESE. **Reservations:** Required. **Bus:** 2, T1, or A7.
$ Prices: Appetizers $2–$7; main courses $11–$25. AE, DC, MC, V.
   Open: Lunch Mon–Fri noon–3pm; dinner Mon–Sat 6–11:30pm, Sun 1–11:30pm.

⭐ One of the finest Chinese restaurants in the Caribbean overlooks the Condado Lagoon. The chef is equally at home in turning out Hunan, Szechuan, or Cantonese cookery. Specialties include lemon chicken, beef with scallops and shrimp in a hot sauce, and Szechuan Phoenix, made with prime beef and chicken in a hot sauce. Open your meal with the noodles in sesame sauce, a delectable dish.

RAMIRO'S, avenida Magdalena 1106. Tel. 721-9049.
   Cuisine: NEW CREOLE. **Reservations:** Recommended. **Bus:** 2, T1, or A7.
$ Prices: Appetizers $6.95–$12.95; main courses $20.95–$32.95; fixed-price five-course meal $42.95. AE, DC, MC, V.
   Open: Lunch Mon–Fri noon–3pm, Sun noon–3:30pm; dinner Mon–Thurs 6:30–10:30pm, Fri–Sat 6:30–11pm, Sun 6–10pm.

⭐ One of the most distinguished restaurants in Puerto Rico offers a refined cuisine and a touch of Old Spain. The elegant restaurant's owner and chef, Jesús Ramiro, prepares what he calls a *cocina imaginativa;* it has also been called "New Créole" cooking. You might begin with peppers stuffed with a blood-sausage mousse, ripe plantain croquettes, or green-pumpkin or cream of casava soup. For your main course, fish or meat can be charcoal-grilled upon request. Unusual main dishes include fresh fish prepared with a green sauce and served with clams, and jumbo shrimp with halibut mousse. Among the many homemade desserts are fresh strawberry sherbet and the chef's "fried" ice cream.

RESTAURANT COMPOSTELA, 106 avenida Condado. Tel. 724-6088.
   Cuisine: SPANISH/PUERTO RICAN. **Reservations:** Recommended. **Bus:** A7.
$ **Prices:** Appetizers $4–$11; main courses $17–$29. AE, DC, MC, V.
   Open: Lunch Tues–Sun noon–3pm; dinner Tues–Sun 6:30–10:30pm.

Set in a comfortably unpretentious pine-trimmed decor, this restaurant has a formality that evokes memories of Spain. Established by a family born in Galicia, who named it after their native region's most famous religious shrine (Santiago de Compostela, in northern Spain), the restaurant has gained an image as one of the most desirable in the capital. Specialties include roasted peppers stuffed with a salmon mousse, a mousse of land crab floating on a seafood sauce, brochettes of filet studded with truffles, grilled shellfish with brandy sauce, rack of lamb, duck with kiwi sauce, chicken breast stuffed with fresh lobster, roast pheasant, and paella. The wine list is appropriately international.

SANTURCE

LA CASONA, San Jorge 609, at the corner of Fernández Juncos. Tel. 727-2717.
   Cuisine: SPANISH/INTERNATIONAL. **Reservations:** Required. **Bus:** 1.
$ **Prices:** Appetizers $6–$12; main courses $17–$35. AE, DC, MC, V.
   Open: Mon–Fri noon–11pm, Sat 6 -11pm.

One of the finest dining rooms in Puerto Rico offers the kind of dining usually found in Madrid, complete with a strolling guitarist. Since 1972 the chefs here have dispensed their special blend of Spanish and international dishes in a turn-of-the-century mansion surrounded by gardens. The much renovated but still charming and sophisticated place draws some of the most fashionable diners in Puerto Rico. Paella marinara, prepared for two or more diners, is a specialty, as is a zarzuela de mariscos or seafood medley. Or you might select filet of grouper in Basque sauce, octopus vinaigrette, rabbit stew, or a rack of lamb.

MIRAMAR

AUGUSTO'S, in the Hotel Excelsior, 801 Ponce de León Ave. Tel. 725-7700.
   Cuisine: INTERNATIONAL. **Reservations:** Required. **Bus:** 2, A7, or T1.
$ **Prices:** Appetizers $4.50–$16; main courses $18–$24.50; fixed-price lunch $23–$35. AE, MC, V.
   Open: Lunch Tues–Fri noon–3pm; dinner Mon–Sat 7–9:30pm. **Closed:** July 7–Aug 1.

An interesting choice is a European enclave of aesthetics and cuisine in the middle of San Juan, although tropical ingredients are used as much as possible. It is operated by one of Puerto Rico's most successful chefs, Austrian-born August Schreiner, who first came to prominence on the island during his long stay at the Caribe Hilton, where he won many awards for outstanding international cuisine. The restaurant has a sophisticated decor with light-gray walls and masses of fresh flowers. The menu changes frequently, but you might begin with iced zucchini bisque or a Caesar salad with croutons, followed by fresh elk medallions in a juniperberry sauce or roast rack of lamb in a mustard-and-herb crust. For dessert, try, if featured, the chocolate soufflé. Other desserts are made from fresh fruits.

WINDOWS ON THE CARIBBEAN, in the Clarion Hotel & Casino, avenida Fernández Juncos 600. Tel. 721-4100.
   Cuisine: INTERNATIONAL. **Reservations:** Required. **Bus:** M3, M2, 9, or 10.
$ **Prices:** Appetizers $7–$9; main courses $18–$28. AE, DC, MC, V.
   Open: Dinner only, Tues–Sat 5–11pm.

You'll find this restaurant on the 27th floor of the tallest skyscraper in the Caribbean, the Clarion Hotel & Casino. In addition to being one of the city's finest restaurants, it also offers a sweeping view over the seacoast and San Juan (as does its popular piano bar). The chef specializes in such dishes as breast of chicken stuffed with crabmeat covered with a lobster sauce and medallions of filet of beef Cordon Rouge stuffed with pâté de foie gras in champagne sauce. The restaurant is also known for creating 13 variations of Valencian paella.

ISLA VERDE

BACK STREET HONG KONG, in the Hotel El San Juan, Rte. 187. Tel. 791-1224.
   Cuisine: MANDARIN/SZECHUAN/HUNAN. **Reservations:** Recommended. **Bus:** T1 or M4.
$ **Prices:** Appetizers $2–$10.50; main courses $14.50–$31.50. AE, MC, V.
   Open: Dinner only, Mon–Sat 6pm–midnight, Sun noon–midnight.
To reach this restaurant, you head down a disconcertingly realistic re-creation of a backwater street in Hong Kong. Disassembled from its original home at the 1964 New York World's Fair, it was rebuilt with the exposed electrical meters and lopsided facades of its original design intact. A few steps later you enter one of the best Chinese restaurants in the Caribbean. Beneath a soaring redwood ceiling, you can enjoy pineapple fried rice served in a real pineapple, a superb version of scallops with orange sauce, Szechuan beef with chicken, or a Dragon and Phoenix (lobster mixed with shrimp).

DAR TIFFANY, in the Hotel El San Juan, Rte. 187. Tel. 791-7272.
   Cuisine: SEAFOOD/AMERICAN. **Reservations:** Required. **Bus:** T1 or M4.
$ **Prices:** Appetizers $10.95–$12.95; main courses $16.95–$40. AE, DC, MC, V.
   Open: Dinner only, daily 6:30–11:30pm.
One of the best choices in San Juan for a taste of the good life, Dar Tiffany is usually jammed, especially on weekends, with the island's resident literati, glitterati, and beautiful people, including Joan Rivers, Eddie Murphy, and Raul Julia. On the ground floor of Puerto Rico's most glamorous hotel, it provides considerate service and an elegant etched-glass decor in a multilevel room, with lots of plants and tropical furniture. The wine list is actually more extensive than the food menu, which offers prime rib, filet mignon, veal chops, sea scallops, and filet of fresh Norwegian salmon. Prime dry-aged steaks are a specialty, as are live Maine lobsters and the fresh fish of the day. Salads are superb, especially the Caesar salad and spinach salad.

HATO REY

CRIOLLISSIMO, avenida F.D. Roosevelt 300. Tel. 767-3343.
   Cuisine: PUERTO RICAN. **Reservations:** Recommended.
$ **Prices:** Appetizers $3.50–$12; main courses $13–$23. AE, DC, MC, V.
   Open: Daily noon–11pm.
Established by a locally born lawyer, Adrian Marrero (who left a career in Washington to return to his native island), this is one of the most respected Puerto Rican restaurants in San Juan. The clientele includes the local *haute bourgeoisie,* former governors and ambassadors, and extended families dressed in their finery for a communal and traditional meal.
   On the main thoroughfare of the Hato Rey district, about a mile south of the beachfront of the Condado, at Criollissimo you'll dine in a garden decor while listening to a singer and a pianist. Specialties might include soups made from squash, pumpkin, or lentils; turnovers stuffed with ground meat or cowfish; piononos (slices of ripe plantain filled with meat and covered with egg batter); salads concocted from octopus, conch, or lobster; filet à la Criollissimo (stuffed with ham, onions, and tomatoes, and topped with a tomato-and-herb sauce); Mofongos (green plantains, deep-fried, mashed, and mixed with garlic, ground pork rinds, and olive oil, and then filled with chicken or shrimp); and pasteles (dough prepared by grating green plantains with a local vegetable called yautias, stuffed with beef, pork, or chicken, wrapped in plantain leaves, and boiled). Dessert might be lightly sugared beignets (buñuelos) flavored with anisette.

WHAT TO SEE & DO

The streets are narrow and teeming with traffic, but a walk through Old San Juan—in Spanish, El Viejo San Juan—is like a stroll through five centuries of history. You can do it in less than a day. In a seven-square-block historic landmark area in the westernmost part of the city you can see many of Puerto Rico's chief historical sightseeing attractions, and do some shopping along the way. Many of the museums in Old San Juan close for lunch between 11:45am and 2pm.

The Spanish moved to Old San Juan in 1521, and the city founded there was to play an important role as Spain's bastion of defense in the Caribbean. Once the city was called Puerto Rico (Rich Port), as the whole island was once called San Juan.

While I have outlined a walking tour of Old San Juan farther on in this section, here is an introduction to the sights you'll come across on it, as well as others you may wish to seek out yourself.

FORTS

FORT SAN CRISTOBAL, at the northeast corner of Old San Juan on calle Norzagaray. Tel. 729-6960.

This 1783 fort was built to defend San Juan against attacks by land, as well as to form backup support for El Morro if that fort were attacked from the sea. Composed of six independent units, the fort is connected to a central structure by means of tunnels and dry moats. You'll get the idea if you look at a scale model on display. On a site of 27 acres, the fort is overseen by the National Park Service. Be sure to see the Garita del Diablo, or the Devil's Sentry Box. The devil himself, it is said, would snatch away soldiers on guard duty at the box. Tours of the fort are given daily from 10am to 4pm.
Admission: Free.
Open: Daily 9am–6pm. **Bus:** T1.

CASTILLO SAN FELIPE DEL MORRO, calle Norzagaray. Tel. 729-6960.

Called El Morro, this fort stands on a rocky promontory dominating San Juan Bay. It was ordered built in 1540, and the original fort was a round tower which can still be seen inside the main bastion of the castle. More walls were added, a line of batteries installed, and by 1787 the structure reached its present stage. As one of the loftiest points in the old town, it is a labyrinth of dungeons, barracks, outposts, and ramps. A film in English and Spanish is presented, and guided tours are given daily from 10am to 4pm.
Admission: Free.
Open: Daily 9am–6pm. **Bus:** T1.

FORT SAN JERONIMO, east of the Caribe Hilton, at the entrance to Condado Bay.

Completed in 1788, this fort was badly damaged in the English assault of 1797. Reconstructed in the closing year of the 18th century, it has now been taken over by the Institute of Puerto Rican Culture. A museum here displays life-size mannequins wearing military uniforms. Ships' models and charts are also displayed.
Admission: Free.
Open: Wed–Sun 9am–noon and 1–4:30pm.

CHURCHES

CRISTO CHAPEL, calle del Cristo.

Cristo Chapel was built to commemorate what legend says was a miracle. Horse racing down calle del Cristo was the highlight of the fiestas on St. John's Day, the patron saint of the city. In 1753 a young rider lost control of his horse and plunged over the precipice. Moved by the accident, the secretary of the city, Don Mateo Pratts, invoked Christ to save the youth, and had the chapel built that same year. Today it's a landmark in the old city and one of its best-known historical monuments. The chapel's Campèche paintings and gold and silver altar can be seen through its glass doors.

Since the chapel is open only one day a week, most visitors have to settle for a view of its exterior. The chapel lies directly west of paseo de la Princesa.

Admission: Free.

Open: Tues 10am–4pm.

SAN JUAN CATHEDRAL, calle del Cristo 151 at caleta San Juan. Tel. 722-0861.

The San Juan Cathedral was begun in 1540 and has had a rough life. Restoration today has been extensive, so it hardly resembles the thatch-roofed structure that stood here until 1529, when it was wiped out by a hurricane. Hampered by lack of funds, the cathedral slowly added a circular staircase and two adjoining vaulted Gothic chambers. But along came the Earl of Cumberland in 1598 to loot it, and a hurricane in 1615 to blow off its roof. In 1908 the body of Ponce de León was brought here. After he'd died from an arrow wound in Florida, his body had originally been taken to the San José Church. The cathedral faces the Plaza de las Monjas (or the Nuns' Square), a tree-shaded spot where you can rest and cool off.

Admission: Free.

Open: Daily 8:30am–4pm.

DOMINICAN CONVENT, calle Norzagaray 98. Tel. 724-0700.

The Dominican Convent was started by Dominican friars in 1523, shortly after the city itself was founded. It was the first convent in Puerto Rico, and women and children often hid here during Carib attacks. The friars lived here until 1838, when the Crown closed down the monasteries and turned this building into an army barracks. The American army used it as its headquarters until 1966. Today it's the center of the Institute of Puerto Rican Culture, which promotes cultural events all over the island. On the ground floor is a permanent display of treasures, featuring a medieval altarpiece. Gregorian chants help re-create the long-ago atmosphere.

Admission: Free.

Open: Chapel Museum Wed–Sun 9am–noon and 1–4pm; Arts Museum, Mon–Sat 9:15am–4:15pm.

SAN JOSE CHURCH, in San José Plaza, calle del Cristo. Tel. 725-7501.

The San José Church is in San José Plaza, right next to the Dominican monastery. Initial plans were drawn in 1523 and work, supervised by Dominican friars, began in 1532. Before going into the church, look for the statue of Ponce de León on the adjoining plaza. It was made from British cannons captured during Sir Ralph Abercromby's unsuccessful attack on San Juan in 1797.

Both the church and its monastery were closed by decree in 1838, and the property was confiscated by the royal treasury. Later, the Crown turned the convent into a military barracks. The Jesuits restored the badly damaged church. The church was the place of worship for Ponce de León's descendants, who are buried here under the family's coat-of-arms The conquistador was interred here until his removal to the cathedral in 1908.

Although badly looted, the church still has some treasures, including *Christ of the Ponces,* a carved crucifix presented to Ponce de León. Packed in a crate, the image survived a terrible shipwreck outside San Juan Harbor. The church has four oils by José Campèche and two large works by Francisco Oller. Many miracles have been attributed to a painting in the Chapel of Belém, a 15th-century Flemish work called *The Virgin of Bethlehem.*

Admission: Free.

Open: Church, Mon–Sat 8:30am–3:30pm; Chapel of Belém, Mon–Fri 10am–4pm, Sun 11:30am–4pm.

MUSEUMS

PABLO CASALS MUSEUM, calle San Sebastian 101. Tel. 723-9185.

Adjacent to the San José Church, at the corner of Plaza San José, this museum is devoted to the memorabilia left by the artist to the people of Puerto Rico. The maestro's cello is here, along with a library of videotapes (played upon request) of some of his festival concerts. This small 18th-century house also contains manuscripts and photographs of Casals. Born in 1876, the maestro achieved fame as a cellist and also won glory as a conductor and composer. His annual Casals Festival draws worldwide interest and attracts some of the greatest performing artists; it's still held during the first 2 weeks of June.

Admission: Free.
Open: Tues–Sat 9:30am–5:30pm, Sun 1–5pm.

SAN JUAN MUSEUM OF ART AND HISTORY, calle Norzagaray. Tel. 724-1875.

Located at the corner of calle MacArthur, this is a contemporary cultural center today, but in the mid-19th century it was a marketplace. Local art is displayed in the east and west galleries, and audiovisual materials reveal the history of the often-beleaguered city. Sometimes major cultural events are staged in the museum's large courtyard. English-language audiovisual shows are presented Monday through Friday at 11am and 1:15pm.

Admission: Requested donation, $1 adults, 50¢ children.
Open: Mon–Fri 9am–noon and 1–5pm, Sat–Sun 10am–noon and 1–5pm.

MUSEUM OF THE UNIVERSITY OF PUERTO RICO, Ponce de León Ave., Recinto de Rio Piedras. Tel. 764-0000, ext. 2452.

Here you'll find good collections of paintings by Puerto Rican artists, including Francisco Oller and José Campèche, the first important artist of the country (18th century). There is also a large collection of pre-Columbian Puerto Rican native artifacts from the Ingeri, sub-Taíno, and Taíno civilizations. In the museum's temporary exhibition hall you can see the work of contemporary Puerto Rican artists, retrospectives of important aspects of Puerto Rican art, and exhibits of the work of other Puerto Rican and U.S artists.

Admission: Free.
Open: Mon–Fri 9am–9pm, Sat–Sun 9am–3pm.

HISTORIC SIGHTS

San Juan Gate, calle San Francisco and calle Recinto Oeste, built around 1635, just north of La Fortaleza, was the main gate and entry point into San Juan—that is, if you came by ship in the 18th century. The gate is the only one remaining of the several entries to the old walled city.

Plazuela de la Rogativa, caleta de las Monjas, basks in legend. In 1797 the British across San Juan Bay at Santurce held the old town under siege. However, that same year they mysteriously sailed away. Later, the commander claimed he feared that the enemy was well prepared behind those walls—he apparently saw many lights and believed them to be reinforcements. Some people believe that those lights were torches carried by women in a *rogativa,* or religious procession, as they followed their bishop. A handsome statue of a bishop, trailed by a trio of torch-bearing women, was donated to the city on its 450th anniversary.

The **City Walls,** calle Norzagaray, around San Juan were built in 1630 to protect the town against both European invaders and Caribbean pirates. The thickness of the walls averages 20 feet at the base and 12 feet at the top, with an average height of 40 feet. Between San Cristobal and El Morro, bastions were erected at frequent intervals. You can start seeing the walls from your approach from San Cristobal on your way to El Morro.

The **San Juan Cemetery,** calle Norzagaray, was officially opened in 1814 and has since been the final resting place for many prominent Puerto Rican families. The circular chapel, dedicated to Saint Magdalene of Pazzis, was built in the 1860s. Aficionados of old graveyards can wander among marble monuments, mausoleums, and statues—marvelous examples of Victorian funereal statuary. However, there are no trees or any form of shade in the cemetery, so don't go wandering in the noonday sun. In fact, the discreet tourist will not go wandering here at all, because it is often the venue for illegal drug deals and can be dangerous.

EL ARSENAL, La Puntilla. Tel. 724-5949.

The Spaniards used a shallow craft to patrol lagoons and mangroves in and around San Juan. Needing a base for these vessels, they constructed El Arsenal at the turn of the century, and it was at this same base that they, so to speak, staged their last stand, flying the Spanish colors until the final Spaniard was removed in 1898, at the end of the Spanish-American War. Exhibitions are held in the building's three galleries.

Admission: Free.
Open: Wed–Sun 9am–4:30pm.

LA CASA DE LIBRO, calle del Cristo 255. Tel. 723-0354.

This restored 19th-century house shelters a library devoted to the arts of printing and bookmaking, with examples of fine printing dating back eight centuries, as well as some medieval illuminated manuscripts. Special exhibits are usually shown on the first floor.

Admission: Free.
Open: Tues 11am–4:30pm and 7:30–10pm, Wed–Sat 11am–4:30pm.

LA FORTALEZA AND MANSION EJECUTIVA, calle Fortaleza, overlooking San Juan Harbor. Tel. 722-7945.

The office and residence of the governor of Puerto Rico is the oldest executive mansion in continuous use in the western hemisphere, and it has served as the island's seat of government for more than three centuries. Yet its history goes back farther, to 1553 when construction began for a fortress to protect San Juan's Spanish settlers during raids by Carib tribesmen and pirates. The original medieval towers remain, but as the edifice was subsequently enlarged into a palace, other modes of architecture and ornamentation were also incorporated, including baroque, Gothic, neoclassical, and Arabian. La Fortaleza has been designated a national historic site by the U.S. government. Informal but proper attire is required.

Admission: Free.
Open: Tours of the gardens (conducted in English and Spanish) Mon–Fri, every hour 9am–4pm.

CITY HALL, calle San Francisco. Tel. 724-1227.

City Hall was ordered built in 1604 and was rebuilt again in 1797 and 1841. The clock in the tower was installed in 1890.

Admission: Free.
Open: Tours by appointment Mon–Fri 8am–3pm. **Closed:** Hols.

CASA BLANCA, calle San Sebastián 1. Tel. 724-4102.

Ponce de León never lived here, although construction of the house (built in 1523) is sometimes attributed to him. The house was erected 2 years after the explorer's death, and work was ordered by his son-in-law, Juan Garcia Troche. The parcel of land was given to Ponce de León as a reward for services rendered to the Crown. Descendants of the explorer lived in the house for about 2½ centuries until the Spanish government took it over in 1779 for use as a residence for military commanders. The U.S. government as well used it as a home for army commanders. Today it's a museum that shows how Puerto Ricans lived in the 16th and 17th centuries.

Admission: Free.
Open: Tours given Tues–Sun 9am–noon and 1–4:30pm.

CASA DE LOS CONTRAFUERTES (House of the Buttresses), calle San Sebastián 101. Tel. 724-5949.

Adjacent to the Pablo Casals Museum, this building, which has thick buttresses, is believed to be the oldest residence remaining in El Viejo San Juan. The complex also contains a Pharmacy Museum, which existed in the 19th century in the town of Cayey. If you go upstairs, you'll find a Graphic Arts Museum, displaying an exhibition of prints and paintings by local artists.

Admission: Free.
Open: Wed–Sun 9am–noon and 1–4pm.

WALKING TOUR —— Old San Juan

Start: El Morro.
Finish: Fort San Cristobal.
Time: 2 hours (not counting stopovers).
Best Times: Any sunny day.
Worst Times: When several cruise ships are in port.

No other city in the Caribbean cries out for a pedestrian exploration as much as Old San Juan. Beneficiary of millions of dollars worth of restoration since the early 1970s, it flourishes as one of the world's best witnesses to the power and grandeur of an empire which at one time transformed the Caribbean into a Spanish lake.

Begin your walking tour at the:

1. **Castillo de San Felipe del Morro** ("El Morro"), the massive fortress whose treasury and strategic position was the envy of both Europe and the Caribbean. Here, Spain struggled to defend itself against the navies of Great Britain, France, and Holland, as well as the hundreds of pirate ships which wreaked havoc throughout the colonial Caribbean. The fortress walls were designed as part of a network of defenses which defined San Juan as La Ciudad Murada (the Walled City).
   The fortifications were financed by the Treasury of Mexico on orders from the King of Spain beginning in 1539. Built in a design inspired by French military strategist Vauban, it repulsed attackers who included English privateer Sir Francis Drake, who bombarded it in 1595, and a much larger English armada in 1797. The American navy finally subdued it during the Spanish-American War of 1898.
   After visiting the fort, descend the gentle slope of the long grassy field which leads from its gates to the heart of Old San Juan.
   Traveler's Advisory: Under no circumstances should you cross the stone wall that separates the fortress's lawns from the shantytown which clings to the steep and rocky slope descending to the sea. This warren of cement-sided buildings is considered one of the most dangerous and notorious drug zones of the Caribbean.
   From the windblown and open spaces that precede the fort, your pathway will slowly descend to intersect with an asphalt-topped road accessible to cars called:
2. **calle Norzagaray.** Turn left along this street, and proceed gently uphill on a high-altitude road which parallels the edge of the sea. Note that your access to certain of the imposing neoclassical buildings of Old San Juan might be complicated at this point by barricades that block your inland access because of urban restoration. In about 3 minutes you'll reach the severe stucco-sheathed walls that shelter the north entrance to the:
3. **Art and History Museum.** Its exhibits (and particularly the changing array of sculptures that ornament its central courtyard) might afford a diversion, unless you want to make a mental note to return later. (Note that if this northern entrance is closed at the time of your visit, the southern entrance, at the building's opposite end, might be open instead.) The building was originally built as a marketplace, but restored and transformed into its present function in 1985. After your visit, backtrack along calle Norzagaray and turn left (uphill) at any of the narrow alleyways. At least a few of these will be blocked because of urban renewal, but whichever is open will eventually lead, after a series of confusing twists and turns, to:
4. **calle San Sebastián.** (The best way to do this is by taking the unmarked alleyway leading between a massive pair of 19th-century neoclassical buildings

which emerge on the uphill edge of calle Norzagaray.) At the eastern end of calle San Sebastián, you'll find the dignified walls of the:

5. **Casa Blanca.** Built by his son-in-law as the island home of Ponce de León (who never lived here), this "White House" served as the home of the American governor of Puerto Rico for many years. Begun in 1521, it is reputed to be the oldest continuously inhabited house in the New World.

Climb the uphill slope of calle San Sebastián and continue in a westerly direction along it, admiring the solidly built antique houses that flank it on either side. The street will eventually deposit you before the statue of Ponce de León (cast from captured British cannon) which graces the center of the:

6. **Plaza San José.** The church which it prefaces is the Church of San José, where the coat-of-arms of the conquistador hangs above the altar. Established by the Dominicans in 1523, the church is one of the oldest places of Christian worship anywhere in the New World. Against one corner of the plaza is the:

7. **Pablo Casals Museum,** whose contents honor the life and work of the Spanish-born cellist who adopted Puerto Rico as his final home.

At this point, note the old and very worn steps that descend from calle San Sebastián from a point about a block to the west of the Plaza San José. The steps might (or might not) be marked as calle del Hospital. At their bottom, the steps will intersect with calle del Sol. Turn left for a short block, then descend yet another flight of steps which will be identified as:

8. **calle de las Monjas.** As you descend, notice the severe buff-colored walls of a five-story building which rises on your left. These walls shelter what was originally built as a Dominican convent during the 17th century and which today houses a:

REFUELING STOP   To appreciate the faded grandeur of the **Hotel El Convento,** turn left at the bottom of calle de las Monjas and note the graceful, plant-bordered steps that lead up to its reception area. Within the hotel's inner courtyard are a sun-flooded café/restaurant suitable for coffee, tea, or a drink, as well as a pair of Iberia-inspired bars where you can enjoy your refreshments.

After your refreshments, exit from the hotel and note the gracious proportions of the verdant and sun-dappled square in front of you. On the uphill edge of the square is the island's religious showplace, the:

9. **Cathedral of San Juan.** Recent restorations have brought the distinguished landmark back to its original Spanish beauty. In front of it, a gnarled tree was planted in dirt which was accumulated from dozens of North and South American nations, each of which contributed a handful of soil as a gesture of international friendship.

Now walk downhill along the well-worn bricks of the narrow street which descends from the lowest corner of Cathedral Square:

10. **caleta de San Juan.** Two centuries ago, the town houses that line its edges were among the most aristocratic in the Spanish-speaking Caribbean. At the street's bottom, pass beneath the thick stone-and-brick archway of the:

11. **Puerta de San Juan,** and notice the stone quays where ships were unloaded during the 18th and 19th centuries. You might stroll a short distance beside the harborfront, but once you return to the inner edge of the thick walls, turn left up a steep flight of narrow steps flanked on one side with grass. At the top of these steps, notice the heavily guarded iron gate which defends the entrance to the:

12. **Governor's Mansion (La Fortaleza),** the oldest executive mansion in the western hemisphere, home to some 170 governors of Puerto Rico. Originally built in 1533 as a fort, it was enlarged to its present size in 1846. Today it hosts some of the most glittering receptions anywhere in Puerto Rico.

From a stance near the mansion's entrance gate, you can admire a sweeping view of San Juan's colonial fortifications. A few steps away, notice the modern bronze statue of a bishop flanked with three female supplicants which sits in the center of a small park known as the:

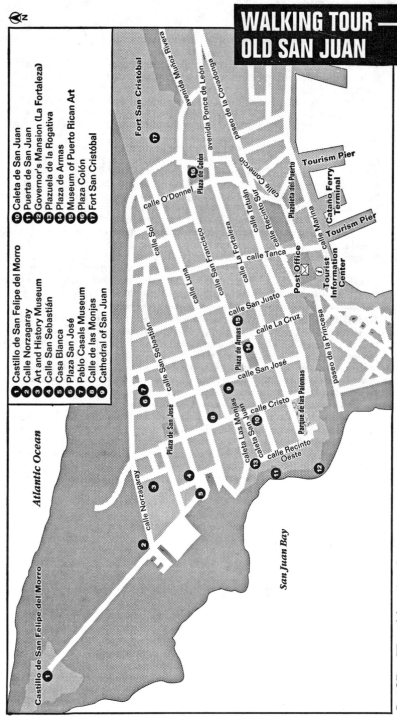

WALKING TOUR — OLD SAN JUAN

1 Castillo de San Felipe del Morro
2 Calle Norzagaray
3 Art and History Museum
4 Calle San Sebastián
5 Casa Blanca
6 Plaza San José
7 Pablo Casals Museum
8 Calle de las Monjas
9 Cathedral of San Juan
10 Caleta de San Juan
11 Puerta de San Juan
12 Governor's Mansion (La Fortaleza)
13 Plazuela de la Rogativa
14 Plaza de Armas
15 Museum of Puerto Rican Art
16 Plaza Colón
17 Fort San Cristóbal

Atlantic Ocean

San Juan Bay

Post Office ⊠   Information ⓘ

13. **Plazuela de la Rogativa.** The previously mentioned statue commemorates a time in 1797 when British soldiers fled when they mistook a religious procession for the arrival of Spanish reinforcements.

Descend once again to the Puerta de San Juan, then continue along the slope of a street which nearby signs will identify as the Recinto del Oeste. At the point where this street makes a sharp left-hand turn, a heavily guarded iron gate demarcates a second entrance to the Governor's Mansion (La Fortaleza). Turn left (the only direction allowable because of the barricade of the iron gate and the configuration of the street) and proceed eastward along calle San Francisco.

One of the streets which you'll intercept in your walk eastward is calle del Cristo, arguably the most famous street of the old town. Eventually you'll find yourself inside the expansive borders of San Juan's "outdoor living room," the:

14. **Plaza de Armas.** Designed along Iberian lines during the 19th century, it is a broad and open plaza. Two important buildings that flank this square include the neoclassic Intendencia (which houses certain offices of the U.S. State Department) and San Juan's City Hall (Alcaldia). Exit the square via the continuation of calle San Francisco. Within a few steps you'll pass the severe whitewashed walls and the small plaque that announces the entrance to the:

15. **Museum of Puerto Rican Art** (Museo de Arte y Historia de San Juan). (This is not to be confused with the earlier museum previously visited during this tour on calle Norzagaray.) A few steps later you'll pass the art nouveau, stained-glass signs marking the entrance to your next, much-awaited:

REFUELING STOP   Recognized as a landmark by hundreds of neighborhood residents, **La Bomoneria Puig & Abraham,** calle San Francisco 259 (tel. 809/722-0658), offers take-away baked goods as well as sandwiches, spicy platters of Puerto Rican food, and endless cups of richly scented coffee. No one will mind if you just order something to drink, but if you want lunch, the portions are copious and cheap. Don't expect an excessive formality; the place bustles, but no one goes away hungry.

Continue your promenade eastward along the length of calle San Francisco. It will eventually deposit you beside the very large:

16. **Plaza Colón.** At its center rises a stone column topped with a statue of Cristopher Columbus. Erected in 1893 to commemorate the 400th anniversary of the discovery of Puerto Rico, it is considered by some residents the most famous statue on the island. To the side of the square rises the Tapia Theater, restored to its original 19th-century elegance.

Continue to the end of calle San Francisco to the junction with calle Norzagaray and follow the signs to the:

17. **Fort San Cristobal.** When it was built along calle Norzagaray it was intended as an adjunct and defensive supplement to the previously visited El Morro. Today, like its twin, it is maintained by the National Park Service and can be visited throughout the day.

SAVVY SHOPPING

Puerto Rico has the same tariff barriers as the U.S. mainland. That's why you don't pay duty on items brought back to the United States. Nevertheless, you can still find great bargains in Puerto Rico, where the competition among shopkeepers is fierce. Even though the U.S. Virgin Islands are duty free, many readers report finding far lower prices on many items in San Juan than on St. Thomas.

The streets of the **old town,** such as calle San Francisco and calle del Cristo, are the major venues for shopping.

Native handcrafts can be good buys. Look for *santos* (hand-carved wooden religious figures), needlework (women no longer get 3¢ an hour for it!), straw work, ceramics, hammocks, guayabera shirts for men, papier-mâché fruit and vegetables, and paintings and sculptures by Puerto Rican artists.

The biggest and most up-to-date shopping plaza in the Caribbean Basin is **Plaza Las Americas,** which lies in the financial district of Hato Rey, right off the Las Americas Expressway. The complex, with its fountains and advanced architecture, has more than 200 shops, most of them upmarket. Open: Mon–Thurs and Sat 9:30am–6pm, Fri 9:30am–9:30pm.

ANTIQUES

JOSÉ E. ALEGRIA & ASSOCIATES, calle del Cristo 152-154. Tel. 721-8091.

Opposite El Convento Hotel, this shop is housed in an impressive old Spanish building dating from 1523 with rooms opening onto patios and courtyards. It displays antique furniture and paintings, and the collection is considered the finest in San Juan. The specialty here is 18th-century furniture and paintings, and there is also a collection of French furnishings and Spanish exhibits from the 16th to the 19th century. Intermingled are the paintings of contemporary artists who live in Puerto Rico or elsewhere. Prices are not low, but the quality is very high. There is a wine boutique in the old cellars.

ART

GALERIA BOTELLO, calle del Cristo 208. Tel. 723-2879.

A contemporary Latin American art gallery, Galería Botello is a living tribute to the success story of the late Angel Botello, considered one of the most outstanding artists in Puerto Rico, who died in 1986. Born in a small village in Galicia, Spain, he fled after the Spanish Civil War to the Caribbean and spent a 12-year period in the art-conscious country of Haiti. His paintings and bronze sculptures, evocative of his colorful background, are done in a style uniquely his own. This *galería* is his former home, and he restored the colonial mansion himself. It is today a setting to display his paintings and sculptures, and it also offers a large collection of Puerto Rican antique santos.

BOOKSTORES

THE BOOK STORE, calle San José 255. Tel. 724-1815.

This is the leading bookstore in the old town, with the largest selection of titles. It sells a number of books on Puerto Rican culture and also sells good touring maps of the island. You can ship purchases back to the States.

BUTTERFLIES (MOUNTED)

BUTTERFLY PEOPLE, calle Fortaleza 152. Tel. 723-2432.

Butterfly People is a gallery and café (see "Where to Dine," above) in a handsomely restored building in Old San Juan. Butterflies, sold here in artfully arranged boxes, range from $20 for a single butterfly to as much as $70,000 for a swarm. The butterfly wings are preserved by a secret formula, and the color lasts forever. The dimensional artwork is sold in limited editions, and the gallery ships boxes worldwide. This is the largest privately owned collection of mounted butterflies in the world, second only to the collection at the Smithsonian Institution. They don't use any endangered species, although butterflies come from virtually every tropical region of the world, the most beautiful coming from the densest jungles of Borneo and Malaysia.

CHINA & CRYSTAL

BARED AND SONS, calle Fortaleza 206 (corner of calle San Justo). Tel. 724-4815.

This outlet sells imported china and crystal at 30% to 40% less than what it would cost in the U.S. mainland, and they will pack, ship, and insure the goods. They carry Royal Doulton, Wedgwood, Limoges, Lalique, Baccarat, Waterford, Lladró, and Kaiser figurines.

CLOTHING

CASA CAVANAUGH, on the lobby level of the Condado Plaza Hotel, 999 Ashford Ave. Tel. 723-1125.

This outlet sells mostly women's clothing, including everything from beach attire and jogging suits to semiformal evening wear. For men, there are shorts, bathing suits, and jogging suits. Cavanaugh also maintains branches at the El San Juan Hotel (tel. 791-1000), the Sands Hotel (tel. 791-6100) and Palmas del Mar (tel. 852-6000).

HATHAWAY FACTORY OUTLET, calle del Cristo 203. Tel. 723-8946.

The selection of dress shirts, known for their "Red H," may vary widely in this factory outlet, but if you happen to be there shortly after stock is replenished, you can stock up at bargain prices on shirts that could easily cost twice as much back home. Most items are top-quality dress and knit shirts from the Hathaway factories in Waterville, Maine, but also included are articles by Chaps, Ralph Lauren, Christian Dior, and Jack Nicklaus, reduced by 35% to 50%.

GONZALES PADIN, Plaza de Armas. Tel. 721-5700.

This is the flagship for a 10-member chain of clothing stores scattered throughout the island. It contains three different floors of clothing for men, women, and children. Especially well stocked is the collection of guayabera shirts, which Puerto Rican men often substitute for jacket and tie.

JOLIE BOUTIQUE, 1015 Ashford Ave. Tel. 723-5575.

One of the best-known specialty shops on the island, Jolie Boutique offers a large selection of exclusively imported bathing suits, maillots, bikinis, and pareos, as well as high-fashion loungewear and beachwear. It's next door to the Condado Plaza Hotel and the Regency Hotel complex, with ample free parking.

LEVEL I, 1004 Ashford Ave. Tel. 725-0223.

Both formal and casual clothes for women by such designers as Johanna York and Teri Jon are sold here from a bustling commercial district near the Condado Beach Hotel and La Concha Hotel.

LONDON FOG, calle del Cristo 156. Tel. 722-4334.

London Fog often has discount sales on men's wear, including a wide selection of raincoats (which today are often made in Korea) and casual-wear winter jackets. Items for women are on the ground floor.

NONO MALDONADO, 1051 Ashford Ave. Tel. 721-0456.

Named after its owner, a Puerto Rican–born designer who worked for many years as the New York–based fashion director of *Esquire* magazine, this is one of the most fashionable and upscale haberdashers in the Caribbean. Selling both men's and women's clothing, it contains everything from socks to black tie, as well as ready-to-wear versions of Maldonado's twice-a-year collections. Both ready-to-wear and couture are available here. Although this is the main outlet for the designer (midway between the Condado Plaza and the Condado Beach Hotel), the establishment also maintains a somewhat smaller boutique in El San Juan Hotel.

POLO RALPH LAUREN FACTORY STORE, calle del Cristo 201. Tel. 722-2136.

This is one of the best shops in the old town if you're looking for sportswear for men, women, or children. At certain times of the year, discounts of 40% to 50% are offered.

HANDCRAFTS

DALINA, calle Fortaleza 65. Tel. 724-3215.

This store sells Lladró figurines and hand-embroidered tablecloths (made in China of cotton, linen, or polyester) at something like 25% to 30% less than similar items sold in the U.S.

PUERTO RICAN ARTS & CRAFTS, calle Fortaleza 204. Tel. 725-5596.

Owned and operated by the Amador-Gotay family, this is probably the premier outlet on the island for authentic artifacts from the Puerto Rican tradition. They sell costume jewelry, ceramics, sandals, and sculptures. Of particular interest are the papier-mâché carnival masks, usually made in Ponce, whose grotesque and colorful features were originally made to chase away evil spirits. Priced from $14 to $350, they are considered works of art.

OLÉ, calle Fortaleza 105. Tel. 724-2445.
Even if you don't buy anything, you can still learn a lot about the crafts displayed here. Practically everything that isn't made in Puerto Rico comes from South America, and all is artistically displayed in a high-ceilinged room decorated clear to the top. If you want a straw hat from Ecuador, hand-beaten Chilean silver, Christmas ornaments, or Puerto Rican santos, this is the place to buy them.

ROVERDALES, calle del Cristo 99. Tel. 722-5424.
Roverdales is big on brass, but also carries a wide selection of gift items, including a collection of inexpensive but authentic Puerto Rican santos, local handcrafts, and little easy-to-pack art objects from around the world.

JEWELRY

BARRACHINA'S, calle Fortaleza 104 (between calle del Cristo and calle San José). Tel. 725-7912.
Revered as the acknowledged birthplace, in 1963, of the piña colada, it offers a series of departments which sprawl over its single-floor emporium. A favorite of visiting cruise-ship passengers, it offers one of the largest selections of jewelry and gifts in San Juan. There's a patio for drinks, which serves as a calm oasis amid the commercial hubbub, where you can order a piña colada. There is a Bacardi rum outlet, a costume-jewelry department, a perfume outlet, a gift shop, and a section for authentic jewelry as well. Watches include Raymond Weil, Movado, Bulova, and Rado.

LETRAN, calle Fortaleza 201. Tel. 721-5825.
This store sells jewelry and watches, and is one of the best-established and most reputable jewelers in Old San Juan.

RIVIERA, calle Cruz 205. Tel. 725-4000.
This fine jewelry store specializes in first-class gemstones and excellent watches by Rolex and Patek Philippe. It does not sell costume jewelry.

200 FORTALEZA, calle Fortaleza 200, at the corner of calle Cruz. Tel. 723-1989.
Known as a leading place to buy fine jewelry in Old San Juan, this shop has famous-name watches, and you can purchase 14- and 18-karat gold chains, which are measured, fitted, and sold by weight and priced according to the gold market. You can buy your initial in diamonds set in 14-karat white and yellow gold, or even a 14-karat gold ring set with a diamond.

YAS MAR, calle Fortaleza 205. Tel. 724-1377.
This shop sells convincingly glittering fake diamonds for those who don't want to wear the real thing. They also sell real diamonds, emeralds, sapphires, and rubies.

LEATHER

LEATHER & PEARLS, calle del Cristo 202. Tel. 724-8185.
Majorca pearls and fine leather (including Gucci) are sold here from a location near the cathedral at discounted prices.

SHOES

DEXTER SHOE OUTLET, calle San José 252. Tel. 721-6079.

This is the factory outlet for a Maine-based shoe manufacturer. Shoes sometimes sell at 30% of what they'd cost retail in the U.S. The store stocks up to size 12 for women and up to size 15 for men.

LA FAVORITE, avenida Ponce de León 1501, Santurce. Tel. 723-0389.
This outlet sells a sophisticated collection of shoes for men and women from manufacturers in Spain, the U.S., Italy, and France.

EVENING ENTERTAINMENT

THE LE LO LAI FESTIVAL   This year-round vacation package grants savings to the visitor who plans to stay at least a few days in Puerto Rico. Le Lo Lai is a name created by the island people to express their love of song and dance and a cultural heritage that comes from Spanish, Native Caribbean, and African traditions. The government-sponsored Le Lo Lai Festival welcomes visitors to a complimentary week-long celebration, with the purchase of a 5-night stay from December 15 to April 14 or a 3-night stay from April 15 to December 14 at several participating San Juan hotels.

A 26-page discount booklet offers additional sightseeing suggestions and admission tickets to folkloric shows. The package also includes *paradores* (country inns) around the island, and free admission to museums and theme parks, all outside San Juan. The package of tickets is sold in San Juan at authorized travel agencies for those visitors who do not qualify for them on a free basis. The price is $8 for adults and $6 for children.

For further information, contact the Le Lo Lai Festival, P.O. Box 4435, San Juan, PR 00905 (tel. 809/723-3135).

THE PERFORMING ARTS

Qué Pasa, the official visitors' guide to Puerto Rico, lists cultural events, including music, dance, theater, film, and art exhibits. It's distributed free by the tourist office.

The **Condado Plaza Hotel & Casino,** 999 Ashford Avenue (tel. 721-1000), stages a San Juan de Fiesta every Sunday at 8pm, with Puerto Rican country music, dancing, and a show. The show starts at 8pm, and the $15 charged includes the price of entrance and two drinks. Children up to age 12 are charged only $8.

Every Monday at 7pm, the **Institute of Puerto Rican Culture** (Dominican Convent), calle Norzagaray 98 (tel. 724-0700), presents a folkloric show. Entrance for everybody is $8.50, and no drinks are served.

CENTRO DE BELLAS ARTES, avenida Ponce de León 22. Tel. 724-4747.
Built in 1981, in the heart of Santurce, the Performing Arts Center is a 6-minute taxi jaunt from most of the hotels on Condado Beach. Costing $18 million (relatively modest for such a complex), the center contains 1,883 seats in the Festival Hall, 760 in the Drama Hall, and 210 in the Experimental Theater. Some of the events here will be of interest only to those who speak Spanish, while others attract an international audience.

Admission: Tickets, $12–$30 (prices are determined by the producers of the various shows and can vary).

TEATRO TAPIA, avenida Ponce de León. Tel. 722-0407.
The Tapia Theater was paid for by taxes on bread and imported liquor. Standing across from Plaza de Colón, it is one of the oldest theaters in the western hemisphere, built about 1832. In 1976 a restoration returned the theater to its original look. Much of Puerto Rican theater history is connected with the Tapia, named after the island's first prominent playwright, Alejandro Tapia y Rivera (1826–82). Adelina Patti (1843–1919), the most popular and highly paid singer of her day, made her operatic debut here when she was barely 14.

Various productions—some musical—are staged here throughout the year and include drama, dances, and cultural events. You'll have to call the box office (open Monday through Friday from 9am to 5pm).

Admission: Tickets, $10 and up (prices are determined by the producers of the various shows).

THE CLUB & MUSIC SCENE

EL TROPICORO, in the Hotel El San Juan, Rte. 187, Isla Verde. Tel. 791-1000.

The format and nature of the shows presented here change frequently, although visitors can usually be assured of lots of glittering lights and plenty of theatricality. Currently, most of the shows include a bit of flamenco, as well as a bit of fashionably revealing décolletage from a bevy of feathered and beaded beauties. The hotel usually presents two shows a night, each of which lasts an hour, and which usually begin at 9pm and again at 11pm. An advance telephone call is strongly recommended, both for reservations and a description of the particular act slated for the night of your intended arrival.

Admission (including two drinks): $28.

EL CHICO BAR, in the Hotel El San Juan, Rte. 187, Isla Verde. Tel. 791-1000.

Located just off the expansive and richly paneled lobby of the most glamorous hotel in San Juan, this bar provides live music which percolates throughout most of the rest of the hotel's bustling lobby. Decorated in shades of scarlet, with risqué paintings evocative of a gilded age brothel in turn-of-the-century San Francisco, it is avidly appreciated by local residents of San Juan, who court, flirt, converse, celebrate, and dance on the sometimes-crowded dance floor. Drinks begin at $3.50. Open: Mon–Fri 9pm–1am, Sat–Sun 9pm–3am.

AMADEUS DISCO, in the El San Juan Hotel, Rte. 187, Isla Verde. Tel. 791-1000.

Its conservative art deco interior welcomes a widely divergent collection of the rich and beautiful, the merely rich, and the gaggle of onlookers pretending to be both. The Amadeus Disco is in the most exciting hotel in San Juan (see "Where to Stay," above), so a visit here could be combined with exploring the adjacent casino and the best-decorated lobby in Puerto Rico. The duplex area has one of the best sound systems in the Caribbean. Open: Tues–Sun 10pm–3:30am.

Admission (including two drinks): $10–$15.

CLUB MYKONOS, in the Hotel La Concha, Ashford Ave. Tel. 721-6868.

Club Mykonos dazzles with a decor that might be described as Pharaonaic. Don't expect to be admitted in sloppy clothes, since the owner has set a precedent for relative stylishness. Be sure to notice the frescoes near the entrance and above the bar and the hi-tech versions of Hellenistic columns whose summits flash strobes of multicolored lights. Open: Tues–Sat 9pm–2am.

Admission (including two drinks): $10–$15.

ISADORA'S, in the Condado Plaza Hotel & Casino, 999 Ashford Ave. Tel. 721-1000.

This is considered one of the most elegant and energetic discos and after-dark meeting points in Puerto Rico. Lit with strobe lights, accented in tones of red, and outfitted like a jungle garden, it contains lots of mirrors and enough padded corners to make anyone feel comfortable. Open: Bar (without any dance music) happy hour, Thurs–Fri and Sun 6:30–9:30pm, with half-price drinks; disco, daily 9:30pm–3am.

Admission (including two drinks): $10–$15, depending on whether there's live or recorded music.

PEGGY SUE, 1 Roberto H. Todd Ave. Tel. 722-4750.

This is one of the busiest nightclubs for the young, upwardly mobile, singles. There's a dance floor well worn by years of boogeying feet, although many visitors come only for drinks at the long and very accommodating bar. The decor is inspired by 1950s retro-chic, the music embraces most of the major musical movements since the 1960s, and people can usually meet and mingle without hindrances.

There's live music every Friday and Saturday night. No jeans are allowed. Its transformation from a bar into a crowded disco usually occurs around 9pm. Open: Daily 5pm–3am.

Admission (including one or two drinks): $5–$10, depending on the night of the week and the time you arrive.

BACHELOR'S CLUB, avenida Condado 112.

By anyone's estimate, this is the busiest, most glittering, and best-known gay disco in Puerto Rico, catering to a clientele of both gay men and lesbians who appreciate the chance to commingle. It sits in a neighborhood of bars and active nightlife, in the heart of some of the most gilt-edged real estate in the Caribbean. Drinks are served and the music begins every night around 9pm and stops late the next morning.

Admission (including first drink): $8.

THE BAR SCENE

FIESTA BAR, in the Condado Plaza Hotel & Casino, 999 Ashford Ave. Tel. 721-1000.

This bar succeeds at attracting a healthy mixture of local residents who mingle happily with hotel guests. The margueritas are appropriately salty, the rhythms are hot and appropriately Latin, and the admission usually helps you forget any losses you might have suffered in the nearby casinos. Drinks cost $5 to $7. Open: Sun–Thurs 5pm–1am, Fri–Sat 5pm–3am.

SHANNON'S IRISH PUB, 1503 Loiza St., Santurce. Tel. 728-6103.

The allure of Ireland and its ales gets tropicalized at this pub with a Latin accent. It's the regular watering hole of many of the island's university students, a constant supplier of high-energy rock-and-roll, and the after-hours hangout of the staff at many of the city's restaurants. Happy hours occur twice daily, from noon to 2pm and 4 to 9pm, when drinks are half price. There are pool tables, and a simple café serves inexpensive lunches daily from noon to 2pm. Beer costs $2.50, except during happy hour, when it's $1.25. Light lunches begin at $10 each. Open: Daily 11am–5am.

MARIA'S, calle del Cristo 204.

Perched on a stool here, you'll be served some of the coolest and most refreshingly original drinks in the capital—a banana, pineapple, or chocolate frost; an orange, papaya, or lime freeze; a mixed-fruit frappé. The students, TV personalities, writers, and models who gather here also enjoy Mexican dishes, such as chili with cheese, tacos, or enchiladas. If that sounds too heavy on a hot day, then I suggest the fruit salad. Tacos cost $3.25, enchiladas run $3.75, and most frothy drinks go for $3.50 and up. Open: Daily 11am–2am.

TIFFANY'S SALON, calle del Cristo 213. Tel. 722-3651.

Many young guests have wandered into this popular spot expecting a quick piña colada or daiquiri, only to stay all evening. Tropical drinks and frappes are also popular. The establishment is on one of the main streets of Old San Juan. Hard drinks start at $2.50. Open: Daily 11am–3am.

VIOLETA'S, calle Fortaleza 56. Tel. 723-6804.

Stylish, comfortable, and urbanized, Violeta's occupies the ground floor of a 200-year-old beamed house two blocks from the landmark Gran Hotel El Convento. A pianist at the oversize grand piano provides live music every Friday and Saturday night from 8pm to 1am, with a singer who performs in five different languages. An open courtyard in back provides additional seating. Margueritas, at $4, are probably the most popular drink. Open: Sun–Thurs 2pm–2am, Fri–Sat noon–4am.

CASINOS

These are one of the island's biggest draws. Many visitors come here on package deals and stay at one of the posh hotels at Condado or Isla Verde, with just one intent—to gamble.

One of the splashiest game rooms is at **El Centro,** the government-owned complex that connects the Condado Beach and La Concha hotels. All the other game rooms are in hotels, the plush ones certainly. Therefore you can try your luck at the **Caribe Hilton** (one of the better ones), **El San Juan,** at Isla Verde, and the **Condado Plaza Hotel & Casino.** The **Ambassador Plaza** is another deluxe hotel noted for its casino action. And there are no passports to flash, admissions to pay, or whatever, as there often are in European gambling casinos.

The largest casino on the island is the **Sands Casino** at the Sands Hotel & Casino at Isla Verde, on Isla Verde Road. Open from noon to 4am daily, this 10,000-square-foot gaming facility is an elegant rendezvous. One of its Murano crystal chandeliers is longer than a bowling alley. The casino offers 197 slot machines, 22 blackjack tables, five dice tables, six roulette wheels, two regular baccarat tables, and one mini-baccarat table. Puerto Rican law provides that a percentage of gaming revenues be set aside for education funding.

The best casinos "out in the island" are those at the **Hyatt Regency Cerromar Beach** and **Hyatt Dorado Beach.** In fact, you can drive to either of these hotels from San Juan to enjoy their nighttime diversions. There is also a casino at **Palmas del Mar** and yet another at the **Mayagüez Hilton** in western Puerto Rico.

Most casinos are open daily from 1 to 4pm and again from 8pm to 4am. Jackets for men are sometimes requested, as the Commonwealth is trying to keep a "dignified, refined atmosphere."

2. DORADO

The name itself evokes a kind of magic. Along the north shore of Puerto Rico, about a 40-minute drive (22 miles) west of the capital, a world of luxury resorts and villa complexes unfolds. The big properties of the Hyatt Dorado Beach Hotel and Hyatt Regency Cerromar Beach Hotel sit on the choice white sandy beaches here.

Many clients book into one of these hotels, and only pass through San Juan on arrival and departure. Others, particularly first-timers, may want to spend a day or so sightseeing and shopping in San Juan before heading for one of these complete resort properties, since, chances are, once at the resort, they'll never leave the grounds. The hotels are self-contained, with beach, swimming, golf, tennis, dining, and nightlife activities.

The site was originally purchased in 1905 by Dr. Alfred T. Livingston, a Jamestown, N.Y., physician, who had it developed as a grapefruit and coconut plantation of 1,000 acres. Dr. Livingston's daughter, Clara, widely known in aviation circles and a friend of Amelia Earhart, owned and operated the plantation after her father's death. It was she who built the airstrip here. The building housing Su Casa Restaurant (see "Where to Dine," below) was for many years the plantation home of the Livingstons.

If you don't have a car and need to use public transportation, call **Dorado Transport Coop** (tel. 796-1214) in San Juan. It offers limousine service to the area from the airport daily from 11:30am to 9:30pm. The charge is only $12 per passenger, but a minimum of four must take the trip.

WHERE TO STAY

HYATT DORADO BEACH HOTEL, Dorado, PR 00646. Tel. 809/796-1234, or toll free 800/233-1234. Fax 809/796-2022. 281 rms, 17 casitas. A/C MINIBAR TV TEL
$ Rates: Winter, $315–$420 single or double; from $555 casitas. Summer, $145–$195 single or double; from $235 casitas. MAP $56 extra per person daily. AE, DC, MC, V. **Parking:** Free.

✪ The Hyatt sprawls across the plantation filled with palms, pine trees, and purple bougainvillea, and a 2-mile stretch of sandy ocean beach. Located 22 miles west of San Juan, the Dorado Beach is a low-rise building and is the more tranquil of the two Hyatts here. Two side-by-side 18-hole championship golf courses, designed by Robert Trent Jones, are its big draw (see "Sports and Recreation Around the Island," below). The present hotel, originally a Rockefeller playground, opened in 1958, and many repeat guests, including celebrities, have been coming back ever since.

After several owners, Hyatt Hotels Corporation is in charge and has spent millions on improvements. The renovated bedrooms have marble baths and terra-cotta flooring throughout. Rooms are available on the beach or in villas tucked in and around the lushly planted grounds. Casitas are a series of private beach or poolside houses.

Dining/Entertainment: Breakfast can be taken on your private balcony and lunch on an outdoor ocean terrace. Dinner is served in a three-tiered main dining room where you can watch the surf. Hyatt Dorado chefs have won many awards, and the food at the hotel restaurants and Su Casa Restaurant (not included in the MAP) is considered among the finest in the Caribbean. And don't forget the casino.

Services: 24-hour room service, baby-sitting, laundry/dry cleaning.

Facilities: Two 18-hole golf courses; seven all-weather tennis courts; two swimming pools; a children's camp; a private airfield; one of the best windsurfing schools in Puerto Rico, the Lisa Penfield Windsurfing School (see "Sports and Recreation Around the Island," below).

HYATT REGENCY CERROMAR BEACH HOTEL, Dorado, PR 00646. Tel. 809/796-1234, or toll free 800/233-1234. Fax 809/796-4646. 461 rms, 43 suites. A/C MINIBAR TV TEL

$ Rates: Winter, $270–$380 single or double; from $580 suite. Summer, $140–$210 single or double; from $285 suite. MAP $56 extra per person daily. AE, DC, MC, V. **Parking:** Free.

✪ Near the elegant Hyatt Dorado Beach Hotel, this Hyatt stands on its own sandy crescent beach. The high-rise Cerromar is a combination of two words—*cerro* (mountain) and *mar* (sea)—and true to its name, you're surrounded by mountains and ocean. Approximately 22 miles west of San Juan, Cerromar shares the 1,000-acre former Livingston estate with the Dorado, so guests can enjoy the Robert Trent Jones golf courses as well as the other facilities at the next-door hotel; a shuttle bus runs back and forth between the two resorts every half hour.

All rooms have first-class appointments and are well maintained; the majority have private balconies. Floors throughout are tile and furnishings are casual tropical, in soft colors and pastels. All rooms have honor bars and in-room safes.

Dining/Entertainment: The outdoor Swan Café is triple level with a dramatic staircase. Some tables are at the edge of a lake, complete with swans and flamingos, paralleling the hotel's swimming pool. Other dining choices include the Ocean Terrace, the Surf Room, and the hotel's pride and joy, Medici's. The Flamingo bar offers a wide, open-air expanse overlooking the sea and the water playground.

Services: 24-hour room service, laundry/dry cleaning, baby-sitting.

Facilities: The water playground contains the world's longest freshwater swimming pool—a 1,776-foot-long fantasy pool inaugurated in 1986, with a current like a river because of differing heights in five connected free-form pools. It takes 15 minutes to float from one end of the pool to the other. There are also 14 waterfalls, tropical landscaping, a subterranean Jacuzzi, water slides, walks, bridges, and a children's pool. A full-service spa and health club provides services for both body and skin care, including Swedish massages and a "Powercise" machine that "talks" to you, coaching you during exercises and reporting your progress to other machines. In addition to 14 tennis courts, there is also a children's day camp for guests aged 3 through 13, open from mid-June to Labor Day, at Christmas, and at Easter.

WHERE TO DINE

EL MALECÓN, Rte. 693, Km 8.2. Tel. 796-1645.
Cuisine: PUERTO RICAN. **Reservations:** Not required.
$ Prices: Appetizers $3–$8.95; main courses $7.95–$29.95. AE, MC, **V.**
Open: Sun–Thurs 11am–10pm, Fri–Sat 11am–11pm.

If you'd like to find a local place serving a good Puerto Rican regional cuisine, then head for El Malecón, 2 miles east of the Hyatt Dorado Beach Hotel. It has a cozy family ambience, and is especially popular on weekends when live music is featured. The chef is best with fresh seafood.

MEDICI'S, in the Hyatt Regency Cerromar. Tel. 796-1234, ext. 3047.
Cuisine: NORTHERN ITALIAN. **Reservations:** Required.
$ Prices: Appetizers $4.50–$7.50; main courses $16.50–$24. AE, DC, MC, **V.**
Open: Dinner only, daily 7–9pm.

Medici's is an elegant 340-seat dining room. On the way to your table, you'll be torn between a view of the sprawling gardens and a look at the lavish antipasto table. Tables sit on tiers at several levels, each of which has been angled for views of one of the gardens. The staff sets the mood of relaxed formality, the music is "upbeat classical," and the wine cellar is diversified. Guests can take their pick—from steak to "spa cuisine," from osso buco to Caribbean flavors. The kitchen also turns out a light Italian cuisine, and most items, including pastas, are available as appetizers, or main or side dishes. Try grilled salmon on spinach with a dill sauce. Herb granita (Italian ice) is served between courses.

SU CASA, in the Hyatt Dorado Beach Hotel. Tel. 796-1234.
Cuisine: PUERTO RICAN/CONTINENTAL. **Reservations:** Required.
$ Prices: Appetizers $6.50–$19; main courses $24–$40. AE, DC, MC, **V.**
Open: Dinner only, daily 7–9pm. **Closed:** July–Oct.

Su Casa is the 19th-century Livingston family plantation home on the resort property. The Spanish colonial building with tile courtyards has been a favorite dining place for the rich and famous since the Rockefellers entertained guests at their posh Dorado Beach hideaway. Diners sit at candlelit tables and enjoy the serenade of strolling entertainers as they partake of Puerto Rican and classical European dishes. The chef produces an innovative cuisine, using Puerto Rican fruits and vegetables whenever possible, including plantain, spinach, and eggplant. Specialties include pastel de langosta (lobster fried in a corn tortilla with tomato-and-cilantro sauce), filete de res "Carlos V" (filet mignon with a Spanish brandy sauce on eggplant), and a house special dessert, Bien me sabe, made with Caribbean coconut and biscuit. Don't plan to rush through a meal at Su Casa—allow yourself enough time to enjoy the quality of your dinner in this relaxed tropical setting.

EVENING ENTERTAINMENT

When you tire of the casinos, try Puerto Rico's liveliest sports bar, **El Coquí,** in the Hyatt Regency Cerromar Beach Hotel (tel. 796-1234). An electronic temple to the sports-minded, it contains arrays of basketball simulators, board games, large-screen video TVs, and a high-amplification sound system left over from the establishment's original role as a disco. Drinks begin at $4, and the bar is open daily from 7pm to 2am.

3. PALMAS DEL MAR

Called the "Caribbean side of Puerto Rico," the residential resort community of Palmas del Mar lies on the island's southeastern shore, 45 miles from San Juan, outside the town of Humacao, about an hour's drive from the San Juan airport.

Once there, you'll find plenty to do: golf, tennis, scuba diving, sailing, deep-sea fishing, horseback riding, whatever. Hiking on the resort's grounds is another favorite activity. There is a forest preserve with giant ferns, orchids, and hanging vines. There's even a casino.

In fact, the resort has one of the most action-packed sports programs in the Caribbean (see "Sports and Recreation Around the Island," below, for more details).

The Humacao Regional Airport is 3 miles from the north boundary of Palmas del Mar. Its 2,300-foot strip will accommodate private planes. No regularly scheduled airline currently serves the Humacao Airport.

Palmas del Mar will arrange minivan or bus transport from Humacao to the San Juan airport for $16 each way for anyone who wants it. Call the resort if you want to be met at the airport.

WHERE TO STAY

Lying on 2,700 acres, **Palmas del Mar,** P.O. Box 2020, Humacao, PR 00661 (tel. 809/852-6000), is a former coconut plantation including a stretch of the Caribbean coastline. Guests are housed in villas built around a marina, the beach, a tennis complex, and a championship golf course. You have a choice of either rooms or villas, depending on your space needs. In the same complex are some privately owned condominium homes that the owners make available to guests when they're not living in them. In addition to the villas, guests can stay at the luxurious Palmas Inn or the Candelero Hotel. Most guests book in Palmas del Mar on a package plan, such as a golf package. Most packages are for 7 days/6 nights in winter and 4 days/3 nights in summer.

The New York sales and reservations office for the Puerto Rican resort of Palmas del Mar and its Candelero Hotel and Villas and the Palmas Inn is at 600 Third Avenue, 18th Floor, New York, NY 10016 (tel. 212/983-0393, or toll free 800/468-3331).

Once you arrive at Palmas del Mar, you can depend on free hotel shuttle service to get you to the properties recommended below.

CANDELERO HOTEL, Palmas del Mar (P.O. Box 2020), Humacao, PR 00661. Tel. 809/852-6000, or toll free 800/468-3331. Fax 809/850-4445. 102 rms. A/C TV TEL

$ Rates: Winter, $230–$270 single or double. Summer, $110–$160 single or double. MAP $50 extra per person daily. AE, DC, MC, V. **Parking:** Free.

Rooms here come in a variety of sizes, some with king-size beds. High cathedral ceilings accentuate the roominess, which is further extended by patios on the ground floor. Some of the superior and deluxe accommodations have private balconies. The main dining spot, Las Garzas, is detailed in "Where to Dine," below. The beach and golf course are near at hand. The hotel doesn't have the charm of the Palmas Inn, but many of its units are less expensive.

CANDELERO VILLAS, Palmas del Mar (P.O. Box 2020), Humacao, PR 00661. Tel. 809/852-6000, or toll free 800/468-3331. Fax 809/852-2230. Approximately 130 villas, depending on the policy of each individual owner regarding participation in the rental pool. A/C TV TEL

$ Rates: Winter, $310–$400 one-bedroom villa; $420–$525 two-bedroom villa; $550–$655 three-bedroom villas. Summer, $200–$250 one-bedroom villa; $270–$320 two-bedroom villa; $350–$400 three-bedroom villa. MAP $50 extra per person daily. Minimum stay 3 days. AE, DC, MC, V. **Parking:** Free.

Adjacent to the Candelero Hotel, this complex of red-roofed, white-walled Iberian-inspired villas might be suitable as the vacation headquarters for a family. Each villa is individually furnished and decorated according to the taste of its absentee owner and contains a full working kitchen and enough privacy to allow a feeling of relaxed well-being. Prices depend on the building's exposure to either the beachfront or the golf course; an additional handful of buildings are built against a steep hillside overlooking the tennis courts.

PALMAS INN, Palmas del Mar (P.O. Box 2020), Humacao, PR 00661.
 Tel. 809/852-6000, or toll free 800/468-3331. Fax 809/850-4445. 23 suites.
 A/C TV TEL
$ Rates: Winter, $390 double. Summer, $180 double. MAP $50 extra per person
 daily. AE, DC, MC, V. **Parking:** Free.
This gem contains only deluxe junior suites, each with a panoramic vista of sea and
mountains. The decor evokes that of a Mediterranean villa, with a spacious, airy
feeling; accommodations are decorated in a Spanish antique style. The inn also houses
the Azzurro Restaurant (see "Where to Dine," below) and La Galería lounge (see
"Evening Entertainment," below).

WHERE TO DINE

Moods for dining in Palmas del Mar come in a wide variety, depending on which
"village" you're staying in. The Azzurro Restaurant is arguably the best, serving
northern Italian food, but the choice is vast. Currently, MAP guests can select from a
choice of six specialty restaurants on the grounds, as well as five restaurants off the
property. They can also enjoy five theme nights, including a western night and a
Mexican night.
 The following is only a preview of the dining possibilities. You will discover several
more on your own. All the restaurants are open during the winter season; however, in
summer only three or four may be fully functioning.

**AZZURRO RESTAURANT, in the Palmas Inn, at the Palmas del Mar
 complex, at Humacao. Tel. 852-6000, ext. 13417.**
 Cuisine: NORTHERN ITALIAN. **Reservations:** Required.
$ Prices: Appetizers $4.50–$7.50; main courses $17.50–$23.50. AE, MC, V.
 Open: Dinner only, daily 6–11pm.
You might start your dinner here with homemade pasta, such as ravioli, tortellini, or
spaghetti carbonara, and then follow with red snapper, eggplant parmigiana, jumbo
shrimp, or veal cutlet valdostana. You dine on blue-and-white tiles, with the sea on
your side, in an enclosed courtyard. The setting is elegant, chic, and airy.

LE BISTROQUET, in Montesol. Tel. 852-6000, ext. 12510.
 Cuisine: FRENCH. **Reservations:** Required.
$ Prices: Appetizers $3.50–$7.50; main courses $13.50–$21.50. AE, MC, V.
 Open: Dinner only, Tues–Sun 7–10pm. **Closed:** May–Nov 15.
Near the tennis courts, Le Bistroquet is done in typical French-bistro style in the
atmosphere of the 1930s. Here Martine and Robert Gaffori serve French food in
air-conditioned comfort. You might choose as your main dish coq au vin, entrecôte
bordelaise, escargots, or lobster bisque.

CHEZ DANIEL/LE GRILL, Marina de Palmas del Mar. Tel. 852-3838.
 Cuisine: FRENCH. **Reservations:** Required.
$ Prices: Appetizers $4.50–$8; main courses $18.50–$24.50. AE, MC, V.
 Open: Lunch Wed–Mon noon–3pm; dinner Wed–Mon 6:30–10pm. **Closed:**
 June 15–July 10.
It's French, it's nautical, it's fun, and it's the preferred dining choice for occupants of
the yachts that moor at its adjacent pier. Daniel Vasse, the executive chef, presents a
menu that might begin with fish soup or stuffed mussels, followed by such main
courses as boneless red snapper sautéed with garlic and butter, or lobster and chicken
sautéed with butter in tarragon-and-lemon sauce. Filet mignon in a roquefort sauce is
another delectable dish.

LAS GARZAS, in the Candelero Hotel. Tel. 852-6000, ext. 50.
 Cuisine: PUERTO RICAN. **Reservations:** Not required.
$ Prices: Appetizers $4.95–$8.95; main courses $8.95–$30. AE, DC, MC, V.
 Open: Breakfast daily 7–11am; lunch daily noon–3pm; dinner daily 6–10:30pm.

Cooled by trade winds, this outstanding restaurant overlooks a courtyard and swimming pool and is an ideal choice for any meal. Lunch always includes sandwiches and burgers galore; if you want heartier fare, ask for the Puerto Rican specialty of the day, perhaps red snapper in garlic butter, preceded by black-bean soup. Dinner is more elaborate. Begin with a chilled papaya bisque served in half a coconut, and follow with a Caribbean lobster or shrimp in a sauce made with bananas, pineapple, and coconut. On Wednesday an island buffet features Puerto Rican specialties, and on Friday a lavish seafood buffet is presented. Saturday night a barbecue is held on the terrace.

EVENING ENTERTAINMENT

The most exciting nightspot in Palmas del Mar is **La Galería Disco Club,** near the casino. Here guests can drink and dance to the latest rhythms 5 nights a week, Wednesday through Sunday, from 8pm to 2am (perhaps later on Friday and Saturday). The $7 minimum includes your first drink.

The **casino** in the Palmas del Mar complex, near the Palmas Inn, is in the Culebra Room on the second floor of the building that houses La Galería bar. The casino has nine blackjack tables, two roulette wheels, a craps table, and dozens of slot machines. The place is open from 6pm to 2am daily (in summer, closed Monday and Tuesday). Guests are requested to dress with "casual elegance." Under Puerto Rican law, drinks cannot be served in a casino. You can have a drink in the lounge adjoining the gaming room or in La Galería downstairs.

4. RINCÓN

At the westernmost point of the island, Rincón, north of Mayagüez, has one of the most exotic beaches on the island that draws surfers from around the world. In and around this small fishing village are some unique accommodations.

If you choose to rent a car at the San Juan airport, it will take approximately 2½ hours to drive to the hotel via the busy northern Route 2, or 3 hours via the scenic mountain route (no. 52) to the south. I recommend the southern route through Ponce.

In addition, there are 15 daily flights from San Juan to Mayagüez on **American Eagle** (tel. toll free 800/433-7300). These flights take 30 minutes. From the Mayagüez airport, Rincón is a 30-minute drive to the north on Route 2 (go left or west at the intersection with Route 115).

WHERE TO STAY

HORNED DORSET PRIMAVERA HOTEL, P.O. Box 1132, Rincón, PR 00743. Tel. 809/823-4030. Fax 089/823-5580. 24 suites. A/C **Directions:** From the Mayagüez airport, take Route 2 north half a mile to the Anasco intersection; turn left onto Route 115 toward Rincón for 4 miles; after El Coche Restaurant, take a sharp left onto Route 429 and go about 1 mile; the hotel is on the left, at distance marker Km 3.

$ Rates: Winter, $225 single; $275–$300 double. Summer, $125 single; $170–$190 double. Third person $50. Breakfast $7.50 extra. AE, MC, V. **Parking:** Free.

Many Caribbean aficionados consider this the most sophisticated hotel in Puerto Rico, and (among the smaller properties) one of the most exclusive and elegant anywhere in the Caribbean. Established in 1987, its gracefully rambling headquarters evokes a much older building—an effect carefully contrived by the owners and architects who assembled it. It was built on the massive breakwaters and seawalls erected by a local railroad many years ago, and was named after a successful hotel (the Horned Dorset) which its owners still successfully maintain in upstate New York.

The hacienda evokes an aristocratic Spanish villa, with wicker armchairs, hand-painted tiles, ceiling fans, seaside terraces, and cascades of flowers spilling over the sides of earthenware pots. Management does not allow children under 12, most pets, radios, or televisions. Accommodations are in a series of suites which ramble uphill amid lush gardens. Decoration is tasteful, with four-poster beds and brass-footed tubs in marble-sheathed bathrooms.

Dining/Entertainment: The hotel's restaurant is one of the finest in the Caribbean (see "Where to Dine," below). There's a bar open throughout the day that serves some of the most delectable rum punches on the island. Guitarists and singers often perform during cocktail and dinner hours.

Services: Room service, concierge, laundry, massage, limousine and touring services.

Facilities: Probably the best hotel library in Puerto Rico (books on art, music, comparative literature, and poetry), swimming pool, secluded semiprivate beach, tennis courts, deep-sea fishing, golf, scuba diving.

PARADOR VILLA ANTONIO, Rte. 115, Km 12.3 (P.O. Box 68), Rincón, PR 00743. Tel. 809/823-2645, or toll free 800/443-0266. Fax 809/823-3380. 55 units. A/C TV **Directions:** Head north from Mayagüez along Route 2, then turn left (or west) at the junction with Route 115.

$ Rates: $60–$90 one-bedroom unit; $75–$95 two-bedroom unit. AE, DC, MC, V. **Parking:** Free.

Ilia and Hector Ruíz offer apartments by the sea with sand at your doorstep, privacy, and tropical beauty around you. The most sensible way to get here is by way of Mayagüez airport, just 15 minutes away by car. Facilities include a children's playground, two tennis courts, and a swimming pool. Surfing and fishing can be enjoyed just outside your front door. And you can bring your catch right into your cottage and prepare a fresh seafood dinner in your own kitchenette. There is no restaurant.

WHERE TO DINE

HORNED DORSET PRIMAVERA, Rincón. Tel. 823-4030.
    Cuisine: CLASSICAL FRENCH. **Reservations:** Recommended. **Directions:** Lies 6½ miles northwest of Mayagüez.
$ Prices: Lunch appetizers $5–$14; lunch main courses $9–$15; fixed-price seven-course dinner $40. AE, MC, V.
    Open: Lunch daily noon–2:30pm; dinner daily at 7, 8, and 9pm.

This place reigns without equal as the finest restaurant in western Puerto Rico, and is so alluring that diners sometimes journey out from San Juan for an intimate dinner. It is the Caribbean counterpart of an award-winning restaurant in Leonardsville, New York, the Horned Dorset. Amid the frangipani and oleander of an Iberian garden you can enjoy the kind of cuisine whose excellence can only be maintained through the constant hands-on supervision of a demanding team of owners. The restaurant is in the previously recommended hotel (see "Where to Stay," above). Meals are served beneath the soaring ceilings of what could be the dining room of an aristocratic Spanish home. A masonry staircase sweeps from the garden to reach the second-floor precincts.

Menu specialties change with the availability of the ingredients, but might include medallions of lobster in an orange flavored beurre-blanc sauce, grilled breast of duckling with bay leaves and raspberry sauce, piñon (a traditional Puerto Rican dish of sautéed plantains filled with seasoned ground meat and covered with a light mornay sauce), yellowfin tuna (hauled directly from the local piers within hours of being caught) grilled and served with a hot mustard/horseradish/cream sauce, and dorado (mahi-mahi) grilled and served with a ginger-cream sauce and served on a bed of braised Chinese cabbage. The famous desserts include Martinique cake, a light green confection concocted from sweet potatoes and coconuts, covered with chocolate and rum-flavored frosting, and served over a bed of strawberry sauce.

5. MAYAGÜEZ

Puerto Ricans have nicknamed their third-largest city the "Sultan of the West." This port city, not architecturally remarkable, was once considered the needlework capital of the island. There are still craftspeople who do fine embroidery and drawn-thread work, and the clever shopper can seek out some good buys in the older downtown shops that sell it.

Mayagüez dates from the mid-18th century. It was built to control the Mona Passage, a vital trade route for the Spanish empire. Queen Isabel II of Spain recognized its status as a town in 1836. Her son, Alfonso XII, granted it a city charter in 1877.

Mayagüez is the honeymoon capital of Puerto Rico. The tradition dates from the 16th century when, it is said, local fathers kidnapped young Spanish sailors who stopped here for provisions en route to South America—because of the scarcity of eligible young men, the farmers needed husbands for their daughters.

The major industry is tuna packing: 60% of the tuna consumed in the U.S. is packed here.

GETTING THERE   Motorcoaches are operated by the **Puerto Rico Motor Coach Co.** (tel. 809/725-2460), which provides the cheapest link between San Juan and the city of Mayagüez, with stops at both Aguadilla and Arecibo. Buses depart from Plaza Colón in San Juan every 2 hours from 6am to 6pm. A one-way fare is only $6, but you must call to reserve a seat.

There are 15 daily flights from San Juan to Mayagüez on **American Eagle** (tel. toll free 800/433-7300). These flights take 30 minutes.

If you rent a car at the San Juan airport, it will take approximately 2½ hours to drive to Mayagüez via the busy northern Route 2, or 3 hours via the scenic mountain Route 52 to the south. The southern route via Ponce is easier.

WHERE TO STAY & DINE

HILTON INTERNATIONAL MAYAGÜEZ, Rte. 104 (P.O. Box 3629), Mayagüez, PR 00709. Tel. 809/831-7575, or toll free 800/HILTONS. Fax 809/834-3475. 141 rms, 4 suites. A/C MINIBAR TV TEL **Directions:** Follow the signs at the northern approach to the city.

$ Rates: $143–$172 single; $166–$196 double; from $350 suite. Breakfast $8.50 extra. AE, DC, MC, V. **Parking:** $4.

This country club–style hotel is set on 20 acres of tropical gardens. Its grounds have been designated an adjunct to the nearby Mayagüez Institute of Tropical Agriculture by the U.S. Department of Agriculture. There are no fewer than five species of palm trees, including the royal palm (native to Puerto Rico), eight kinds of bougainvillea, and numerous species of rare flora. If you want to get deep into botany, the institute has the largest collection of tropical plants in the western hemisphere.

The hotel, at the edge of the city, was built in 1964 and has been completely refurbished. The well-appointed rooms open onto the swimming pool, and many units contain private balconies. Year-round rates depend on whether you take a standard, superior, or a deluxe accommodation.

Dining/Entertainment: The Rôtisserie Dining Room serves a blend of Puerto Rican and international specialties, and buffets are presented four times a week. In the corner of the restaurant is the Chef's Corner, a small gourmet restaurant. The Hilton is also the entertainment center of the city. There is a casino, established in 1987, which has free entrance and is open daily from noon to 4am. In addition, you can dance to the latest hits at the Baccus Music Club from 9:30pm to 3am or later Tuesday through Saturday; entrance is free for hotel guests, but nonresidents pay $8.

Services: Room service, laundry, baby-sitting.

Facilities: Olympic-size swimming pool; Jacuzzi; mini-gym; three tennis courts; physical-fitness trails; deep-sea fishing, skin-diving, surfing, and scuba diving can be arranged; 18-hole golf course at Borinquen Field, a former SAC airbase, about 30 minutes from the Hilton.

PARADOR EL SOL, calle Santiago Riera Palmer, 9 Este, Mayagüez, PR 00708. Tel. 809/834-0303. Fax 809/265-7567. 40 rms. A/C TV TEL
$ Rates: Winter, $55 single; $65 double. Summer, $45 single; $50 double. Breakfast $6 extra. AE, MC, V. **Parking:** Free.

This modern concrete building provides some of the most reasonable and hospitable accommodations in this part of Puerto Rico. Central to the shopping district and to all western-region transportation and highways, two blocks from the landmark Plaza del Mercado in the heart of the city, the seven-floor, restored hotel offers up-to-date facilities that include cable TV, a restaurant, and a swimming pool.

WHAT TO SEE & DO

The chief sight is the **Tropical Agriculture Research Station** (tel. 831-3435). At the administration office, ask for a free map of the tropical gardens, which contain one of the largest collections of tropical species useful to people, including cacao, fruit trees, spices, timbers, and ornamentals. The location is on Route 65, between Post Street and Route 108, adjacent to the University of Puerto Rico at Mayagüez campus and across the street from the **Parque de los Próceres** (Patriots' Park). The grounds are open free, Monday through Friday from 7am to 4pm.

The **Puerto Rico Zoological Garden,** Route 108 (tel. 834-8110), at Mayagüez, exhibits birds, reptiles, and mammals, plus a South American display, all contained in a tropical environment. Hours year round are 9am to 5pm Tuesday through Sunday, and admission is $1 for adults, 50¢ for children, plus $1 for parking.

Mayagüez might also be the jumping-off point for a visit to **Mona Island,** "the Galapagos of the Caribbean," which enjoys many legends of pirate treasure and is known for its white sand beaches and marine life. Accessible only by private boat or plane, the island is virtually uninhabited, except for two policemen and a director of the institute of natural resources. The island attracts hunters seeking pigs and wild goats, along with big-game fishers. But mostly it is intriguing to anyone who wants to escape civilization. Playa Sardinera on Mona Island was a nesting ground of pirates. On one side of the island, Playa de Pajaros, there are caves where the Taíno people left their mysterious hieroglyphs.

6. PONCE

Puerto Rico's second-largest city, Ponce—called "The Pearl of the South"—was named after Ponce de León. Founded in 1692, it is today Puerto Rico's principal shipping port on the Caribbean. The city is well kept and attractive, as reflected by its many plazas, parks, and public buildings. There is something in its lingering air that suggests a provincial Mediterranean town. Look for the *rejas,* or framed balconies, of the handsome colonial mansions.

GETTING THERE Ponce lies 70 miles southwest of San Juan and is reached by Route 52. There is no bus service between the two cities.

American Eagle (tel. toll free 800/433-7300) flies three times a day between San Juan and Ponce. Flights take about 30 minutes and cost $34 each way.

WHERE TO STAY

The Ponce Hilton may open in the lifetime of this edition. Check with a travel agent.

MELIÁ, 2 Cristina St., Ponce, PR 00731. Tel. 809/842-0260. Fax 809/841-3602. 74 rms. TV TEL
$ Rates (including continental breakfast): $55–$65 single; $60–$75 double. AE, DC, MC, V. **Parking:** $3.

A city hotel with southern hospitality, the Meliá—which has no connection with other hotels in the world bearing the same name—often attracts businesspeople. The location is a few steps away from Our Lady of Guadalupe Cathedral and from the Parque de Bombas (the red-and-black firehouse). The lobby floor and all stairs are covered with Spanish tiles of Moorish design. The desk clerks, oftentimes family members, are courteous and well versed in English. The rooms are comfortably furnished and pleasant enough, and most have a balcony facing either busy Cristina Street or the old plaza. Breakfast is served on a rooftop terrace with a good view of Ponce, and the hotel's dining room serves some of the best cuisine in town. You can park your car in the lot nearby.

WHERE TO DINE

RESTAURANT EL ANCLA, avenida Hostos Final, Playa Ponce. Tel. 840-2450.
Cuisine: PUERTO RICAN/SEAFOOD. **Reservations:** Not required.
$ Prices: Appetizers $1.50–$10; main courses $8–$21. AE, DC, MC, V.
Open: Daily 11am–10pm (when last orders are taken).

Established by members of the Lugo family in 1978, this is considered among the best restaurants of Ponce. Much of its allure derives from its position south of the city on soaring piers which extend from the rocky coastline out over the surf. As you dine, the sound of the sea rises literally from beneath your feet, which somehow seems to improve both the view of the maritime horizon and the flavor of the fish.

Specialties, made with the catch of the day, might include red snapper served with a pumpkin flan, dorado in a tomato-brandy sauce, seafood casserole and seafood paella (prepared only for two or more diners), and broiled lobster. Steak, veal, and chicken dishes are also available.

RESTAURANT LA MONTSERRATE, Sector Las Cucharas, Rte. 82. Tel. 841-2748.
Cuisine: PUERTO RICAN/SEAFOOD. **Reservations:** Not required.
$ Prices: Appetizers $1.50–$7; main courses $9–$20. AE, DC, MC, V.
Open: Daily 10:30am–10pm.

Beside the seafront, in a residential neighborhood about 4 miles west of the town center, this is probably the only restaurant in the area, and as such, draws a loyal clientele from the surrounding houses. Considered a culinary institution in Ponce, it occupies a large, airy, modern building divided into two different dining areas. The first of these is slightly more formal than the next. Most visitors, however, head immediately for the large room in back, where windows on three sides encompass a view of some offshore islands and where nobody minds if you spend a leisurely afternoon over food and wine.

Specialties, concocted from whatever fish is freshest on the day of your arrival, might include octopus salad, a platter containing seven different kinds of seafood swimming in butter sauce, four different kinds of asopao, a whole red snapper in Créole sauce, or (for diners who have already had their fill of seafood) a selection of different steaks and grills. The Velásquez family are the congenial owners.

WHAT TO SEE & DO

A $40-million restoration project is restoring more than 1,000 buildings to their original turn-of-the-century charm. Here architectural styles combine neoclassical with "Ponce Créole" and later art deco to give Ponce its distinctive ambience.

Any of the Ponceños will direct you to their ✪ **Museo de Arte de Ponce,** avenida Las Americas (tel. 848-0505). This excellent museum was donated to the people of Puerto Rico by Luís A. Ferré, a former governor. The building in which the museum is housed was designed by Edward Durell Stone (the designer of the New York Cultural Center), and it has been called the "Parthenon of the Caribbean." In spite of such a fanciful label, its collection represents principal schools of American and European art of the past five centuries. It's open Monday and Wednesday through Friday from 10am to noon and 1 to 4pm, on Saturday from 10am to 4pm, and on Sunday and holidays from 10am to 5pm (closed Tuesday). Adults pay $2.50; children under 12, $1.50.

Most visitors head for the **Parque de Bombas,** on the main plaza of Ponce. This old firehouse is fantastic—painted black, red, green, and yellow. It was built for a fair in 1883, and is today the headquarters for the government tourism agency's Ponce Information Office.

Around from the firehouse, the trail will lead to the **Cathedral of Our Lady of Guadalupe.** The church rises between two plazas.

The marketplace at Atocha and Castillo streets is colorful, the Perla Theater historic, and the Serralles rum distillery is worth a visit. The **tourist office** at Plaza Las Delicias (tel. 809/840-4141) will give you a map. Or perhaps you'll want to just sit on the plaza and watch the Ponceños at their favorite pastime—strolling in the plaza.

The **Serralles Castle Museum,** El Vigia 17 (tel. 259-1774), is the largest and most imposing building in Ponce, built high on a hilltop above town by the Serralles family (owners of a local rum distillery) during the 1930s. This is considered one of the architectural gems of Puerto Rico and probably the best evidence of the wealth produced by the turn-of-the-century sugar boom. Guides will escort you through the Spanish Revival house, where Moorish and Andalusian details include panoramic courtyards, a baronial dining room, a small café and souvenir shop, and a series of photographs showing the tons of earth that was brought in for the construction of the terraced gardens. It is open Tuesday through Sunday from 10am to 7pm. Admission is $3 for adults, $1.50 for children under 12, $2 for senior citizens over 65.

NEARBY ATTRACTIONS

The oldest cemetery in the Antilles, excavated in 1975, is on Route 503 at Km 2.7. The **Tibes Indian Ceremonial Center** (tel. 840-2255) contains some 186 skeletons, dating from A.D. 300, as well as pre-Taíno plazas from A.D. 700. Bordered by the Portugues River, the museum is open Tuesday through Sunday from 8am to 4pm. Admission is $2 for adults and $1 for children. Guided tours in English and Spanish are conducted through the grounds. Shaded by trees are seven rectangular ballcourts and two dance grounds. The arrangement of stone points on the dance grounds, in line with the solstices and equinoxes, suggests a pre-Columbian Stonehenge. A re-created Taíno village includes not only the museum but also an exhibition hall which shows a documentary about Tibes, a cafeteria where you can find refreshments, and a souvenir shop.

Built in 1833, **Hacienda Buena Vista** preserves an old way of life, with its whirring waterwheels and artifacts of 19th-century farm production. Once it was one of the most successful plantations in Puerto Rico, producing coffee, corn, and citrus. It was a working coffee plantation until the 1950s. Some 80 of the original 500 acres are still part of the estate. The rooms of the hacienda have been furnished with authentic pieces from the 1850s. Tours of Hacienda Buena Vista are conducted Friday through Sunday at 8:30 and 10:30am and at 1:30 and 3:30pm. Reservations are required; contact the Conservation Trust of Puerto Rico (tel. 809/722-5882). Tours cost $4 for adults, $1 for children. The hacienda lies in the small town of Barrio Magueyes, on Route 10 from Ponce to Adjuntas.

7. THE PARADORES (COUNTRY INNS)

Because of the efforts of Paradores Puertorriqueños, a chain of privately owned and operated country inns under the auspices and supervision of the Commonwealth Development Company, today everyone can enjoy the Puerto Rican countryside. These hostelries are easily identified by a Taíno grass hut in the signs and the logo of each inn. The paradores puertorriqueños are modeled after Spain's parador system.

The Puerto Rico Tourism Company established the program in 1973 to encourage tourism across the island. Each of the paradores is situated in a historic place or at a site of scenic beauty. Varying in size, the paradores are easily affordable, have hospitable staffs, and share a good standard of cleanliness.

While some paradores are in the mountains, others are by the sea, and most have swimming pools. They are known for their excellent Puerto Rican cuisine, with meals starting at only $12. Many of the paradores are within easy driving distance of San Juan.

For complete data on the paradores and to make reservations, contact **Paradores Puertorriqueños Reservation Office,** Old San Juan Station, San Juan, PR 00905 (tel. 809/721-2884, or toll free 800/443-0266).

AT CABO ROJO

PARADOR BOQUEMAR, Rte. 307, no. 103, Boquerón, Cabo Rojo, PR 00622. Tel. 809/851-2158. Fax 809/851-7600. 64 rms (all with bath). A/C TV **Directions:** Take Route 101 two blocks from Boquerón Beach.

$ Rates: $55 single; $75 double. Breakfast $5 extra. AE, DC, MC, V. **Parking:** Free.

Parador Boquemar lies near Boquerón Beach (considered one of the best bathing beaches on the island) in the southwestern corner of Puerto Rico, between Mayagüez and Ponce. The hotel is not right on the beach, but it's just a short walk away. There is also a swimming pool, popular with Puerto Rican families, in back of the hotel. The Boquemar offers comfortable bedrooms with modern furnishings. The parador has one of the best restaurants in the area, Las Cascadas, where it isn't necessary to make reservations. Meals begin at $15 and include such specialties as mofongo filled with lobster, and lobster asopao.

AT COAMO

PARADOR BAÑOS DE COAMO, P.O. Box 540, Coamo, PR 00640. Tel. 809/825-2186. Fax 809/825-4739. 48 rms (all with bath). A/C TV TEL **Directions:** From Route 52 out of San Juan, take Exit 76, then head north via Route 153; at the junction with Route 546, go west for about 1 mile.

$ Rates: $50 single; $60 double. Breakfast $5 extra. AE, DC, MC, V. **Parking:** Free.

Legend has it that the hot springs of Baños de Coamo were the fountain of youth sought by Ponce de León. It is believed that during pre-Columbian times the Taíno peoples held rituals and pilgrimages here as they sought health and well-being. For more than 100 years (1847 to 1958), the site was a center for rest and relaxation where many Puerto Ricans as well as others had enjoyable stays, some on their honeymoon, others in search of the curative powers of the thermal springs, which lie about a 5-minute walk from the hotel.

The spa is a parador offering hospitality in the Puerto Rican tradition. Buildings range from a lattice-adorned, two-story motel unit with wooden verandas to a pink stucco Spanish colonial building housing the restaurant. The cuisine is both Créole and international, and the coffee Baños style is a special treat. All units are roomy, and the decor has been restored to its original 19th-century style.

Coamo is inland on the south coast, about 2 hours from San Juan, and swimming is limited to an angular pool, but you can always drive to a nearby public beach. Horseback riding is unique at Baños de Coamo—here you can ride Paso Fino horses. This beautiful breed of Arabians is the pride of Puerto Rico's equestrian breeders. The Baños lists many notables among its past visitors, including F. D. Roosevelt, Frank Lloyd Wright, Alexander Graham Bell, and Thomas Edison.

AT JAYUYA

PARADOR HACIENDA GRIPINAS, Rte. 527, Km 2.5 (P.O. Box 387), Jayuya, PR 00664. Tel. 809/828-1717. 19 rms (all with bath). **Direc-**

tions: From Jayuya, head west via Route 144; at the junction with Route 527 go south for about a quarter of a mile.

$ Rates: $50 single; $60 double. Breakfast $5 extra. MC, V. **Parking:** Free.

A former coffee plantation about 2½ hours from San Juan in the heart of the Central Mountain Range, this parador is reached by a long, narrow, and curvy road. The home-turned-inn is a delightful blend of a hacienda of days gone by and the modern conveniences of today. The plantation's ambience is found everywhere—ceiling fans, splendid gardens, hammocks on a porch gallery, and more than 20 acres of coffee-bearing bushes. You'll taste the home-grown product when you order the inn's aromatic brew.

The restaurant features a Puerto Rican and international cuisine. Most of the modest rooms come with ceiling fans, and the prices are in effect year round. You can swim in the pool (away from the main building), soak up the sun, or go and enjoy the nearby sights, such as the Taíno Indian Ceremonial Ball Park at Utuado or the Pool of the Petroglyphs. Boating and plenty of fishing are just 30 minutes away at Lake Caonillas. The parador is also near the Río Camuy Cave Park.

AT LAJAS

PARADOR POSADA PORLAMAR, Rte. 304 (P.O. Box 405), La Parguera, Lajas, PR 00667. Tel. 809/899-4015. 18 rms (all with bath). A/C **Directions:** Drive west of Ponce along Route 2 until you reach the junction with Route 116; there, head south along Route 304.

$ Rates: $35 single; $50 double. AE, DC, MC, V. **Parking:** Free.

Life in a simple fishing village plus all the modern conveniences you want in a vacation are what you find at this "Guesthouse by the Sea" in the Parguera section of Lajas, in the southwestern part of the island. The area is famous for its Phosphorescent Bay and good fishing, especially snapper. The guesthouse is near several fishing villages and other points of interest. If you like to collect seashells, you can beachcomb. Other collectors' items found here are fossilized crustacea and marine plants. If you prefer fishing, you can rent boats at the nearby villages, and even bring your catch back to the guesthouse, where you can prepare it in your own kitchenette. Otherwise, no meals, not even breakfast, are served.

The drive to Lajas is 3 hours from San Juan, but if you prefer, you can fly from San Juan to Mayagüez and then take the much shorter drive to Lajas. Early reservations are necessary.

PARADOR VILLA PARGUERA, 304 Main St. (P.O. Box 273), La Parguera, Lajas, PR 00667. Tel. 809/899-7777. Fax 809/899-6040. 62 rms (all with bath). A/C TV TEL

$ Rates: Sun–Thurs $80.25 single or double; Fri–Sat $275 double-occupancy packages (including half board). Two children under 10 stay free in parents' room. AE, DC, MC, V.

Although the water in the nearby bay is too polluted for swimming, guests still benefit from a view of the water, and a swimming pool. Located on the southwestern shore of Puerto Rico, this parador is known for its seafood dinners, the comfort of its rooms, and its location beside the glistening phosphorescent waters of one of the coast's best-known bays. The dining room offers daily specials, including filet of fish stuffed with lobster and shrimp. Meals are served daily from noon to 5pm and 6 to 9:30pm. Rooms are simple and modern. Because the inn is popular with the residents of San Juan on the weekends, a special weekend package is offered for a 2-night minimum stay; it includes the price of the room, welcome drinks, breakfast, dinners, a bottle of champagne, flowers, and dancing with a free show.

AT LUQUILLO

PARADOR MARTORELL, 6A Ocean Dr., Luquillo, PR 00673. Tel. 809/

889-2710. 10 rms (4 with bath). TV **Directions:** After emerging from San Juan International Airport, turn left onto Route 26 until you reach the junction with Route 3; there, head west to Km 36.2 (a road marker), and then turn left and left again for four short blocks.

$ Rates (including continental breakfast): $49 single without bath; $59 double without bath, $64 double with bath. No credit cards. **Parking:** Free.

Back in 1800 the Martorell family came to Puerto Rico from Spain and fell in love with the island. Today their descendants own and manage the Parador Martorell in Luquillo, in the vicinity of the most impressive beach in all of Puerto Rico. When you arrive at the parador, you enter an open courtyard by a tropical garden. Meals served on the patio of the guesthouse come with fragrant flowers, the elusive hummingbirds, and the occasional music of the coquí, the tiny Puerto Rican tree frog that few people are privileged to see. The breakfast always features plenty of freshly picked fruit and baskets full of homemade breads and compotes. The main reason for staying at the Martorell is Luquillo Beach, which has shady palm groves, crescent beaches, coral reefs for snorkeling and scuba diving, and the surfing area.

AT QUEBRADILLAS

PARADOR EL GUAJATACA, Rte. 2, Km 103.8 (P.O. Box 1558), Quebradillas, PR 00742. Tel. 809/895-3070. Fax 809/895-3589. 38 rms (all with bath). A/C TV TEL

$ Rates: $72–$77 single; $75–$83 double. Breakfast from $2.50 extra. AE, DC, MC, V. **Parking:** Free.

You'll find this place along the north coast 70 miles west of San Juan along Route 2. Service, hospitality, and the natural beauty surrounding El Guajataca—plus modern conveniences and a family atmosphere—add up to a good visit. The parador is set on a rolling hillside which reaches down to the surf-beaten beach. Each room is like a private villa with its own entrance and private balcony opening onto the turbulent Atlantic.

Room service is available, but meals are more enjoyable in the glassed-in dining room where all the windows face the sea. Dinner is an experience, with a cuisine that's a mixture of Créole and international specialties. A local musical group plays for dining and dancing on weekend evenings. The bar is open daily from 11am to 10pm (until 1am on Friday and Saturday).

There are two swimming pools (one for adults, another for children), two tennis courts free to guests, plus a playground for children.

PARADOR VISTAMAR, P.O. Box T-38, Quebradillas, PR 00742. Tel. 809/895-2065. Fax 809/895-2294. 55 rms (all with bath). A/C TV TEL

Directions: From Quebradillas drive west on Route 2, then go left at the junction with Route 115 for half a mile.

$ Rates: $55 single; $85 double. Up to two children under 13 stay free in parents' room. Breakfast $6 extra. AE, DC, MC, V. **Parking:** Free.

High atop a mountain, overlooking greenery and a seascape in the Guajataca area, this parador, one of the largest in Puerto Rico, sits like a sentinel surveying the scene. There are gardens and intricate paths carved into the side of the mountain where you can stroll while you take in the fragrance of the tropical flowers. Or you may choose to search for the calcified fossils that abound on the carved mountainside. Visitors can also try their hand at freshwater fishing in the only river in Puerto Rico with green waters, just down the hill from the hotel. Flocks of rare tropical birds are frequently seen in the nearby mangroves.

A short drive from the hotel will bring you to the Punta Borinquen Golf Course. Tennis courts are just down the hill from the inn itself. Sightseeing trips to the nearby Ionospheric Observatory in Arecibo, with the largest radiotelescope in the world, and to Monte Calvario (a replica of Mount Calvary), are available. Another popular visit is to the plaza in the town of Quebradillas, where you can tour the town in a horse-driven coach. Back at the hotel, prepare yourself for a typical Puerto Rican dinner, or choose from the international menu, in the dining room with its view of the ocean. Rates are in effect all year.

AT UTUADO

PARADOR LA CASA GRANDE, P.O. Box 64, Caonillas, Utuado, PR 00761. Tel. 809/894-3939. Fax 809/724-4920. 20 rms (all with bath). **Directions:** From Utuado, drive south via Route 111 to Route 140, then head west to the junction with Route 612; there, go south for about half a mile.

$ Rates: $55 single or double. Breakfast $5 extra. AE, MC, V. **Parking:** Free.

Parador La Casa Grande lies in the district of Caonillas Barrios, in the mountainous heartland of the island, in the vicinity of the small town of Utuado. San Juan is about a 2½-hour drive east of Utuado. Set amid 107 acres of a former coffee plantation, the parador has a cocktail lounge, a restaurant with both Puerto Rican and international specialties, and a swimming pool. All the comfortably furnished bedrooms have ceiling fans.

8. TOURING THE ISLAND

Even though Puerto Rico is an island barely 100 miles long by 35 miles wide, it offers a variety of scenery, from the rain forests and lush mountains of El Yunque to the lime deposits of the north and the arid areas of the south shore, where irrigation is a necessity and the cactus grows wild. In Puerto Rico you will find some of the most complicated geological formations in the world.

While driving on the mountain roads of Puerto Rico, blow your horn before every turn, contrary to urban-zone regulations. Commercial road signs are forbidden, so make sure you take along a map and this guide to inform you of restaurants, hotels, and possible points of interest. There are white roadside markers noting distances in kilometers (.62 mile) in black lettering. Remember that speed limits are given in miles per hour.

Puerto Rico is a subtropical country, yet you can see seasonal changes. In November the sugarcane fields are in bloom, and in January and February the flowering trees along the roads are covered with red and orange blossoms. When spring comes, the Puerto Rican oak is covered with delicate pink flowers and the African tulip tree is ablaze with its deep-red blossoms. Summer is a flamboyant time when the roadsides seem as if on fire.

DINING AROUND THE ISLAND On your tour out in the island, you'll find few well-known restaurants, except those in the major hotels. However, there are plenty of roadside places and simple taverns.

Visitors to Puerto Rico longing for authentic island cuisine can rely on *mesones gastronómicos* (gastronomic inns). This established dining "network" sanctioned by the Puerto Rico Tourism Co. highlights restaurants recognized for excellence in preparing and serving Puerto Rican specialties at moderate prices.

Mesones gastronómicos are limited to restaurants outside the San Juan urban area that are close to major island attractions. Membership in the program requires that restaurants have attractive surroundings and comply with strict standards of good service. Members must specialize in native foods, but if you ask for any fresh fish dish, chances are you'll be pleased.

THE SAN JUAN ENVIRONS

I'll suggest a number of itineraries, beginning with a half-day trip around the metropolitan San Juan area to a rum distillery, Isla de Cabras, Loíza Aldea, and Boca de Cangrejos.

From San Juan, take Route 2 to Km 6.4. To the right you'll see a small park containing the ruins of the house erected in 1509 by Juan Ponce de León in Caparra, the first Spanish settlement in Puerto Rico.

Continue west on Route 2 until you reach **Bayamón.** Facing the town plaza is the old church, built in 1877, an excellent example of period architecture.

Afterward, continue north on Route 167 toward Catano and turn left at Km 5.2. Within a short distance you will find yourself at the **Barrilito Rum Distillery.** To the left you will see a 200-year-old mansion with grand outdoor staircases leading to the second-floor galleries. This is the original mansion of the Santa Ana plantation (which once covered 2,400 acres) and is still occupied by members of the family, owners of the distillery. There's an office on the right, near a tower that was originally a windmill from which the entire valley and bay could be seen. Along the bay is the **Bacardi Rum Plant,** where 100,000 gallons of rum are distilled each day. Guided tours are available.

Back on Route 167, drive until you reach Catano, then take Route 165 going west and turning left (hugging the shoreline) until you reach **Isla de Cabras.** From this point, you can see the entire bay of San Juan. At the end of the road in Isla de Cabras you will come upon **Fort Canuelo,** erected in 1610 and reconstructed in 1625 after the Dutch attack on Puerto Rico. Originally built on what was then a tiny islet, the fort seemed to be emerging from the water. Today, however, because of modern landfill techniques it's connected to Isla de Cabras. Picnic facilities are available. Here the breezes are cool and you have a good view of San Juan Bay and El Morro, built in 1539.

On the way back, drive toward Catano where you can take a short car-ferry ride to Old San Juan. Boats leave every half hour from 6:15am to 10:15pm, and the fare is 20¢ round-trip. A more extensive tour of the bay is offered by the Port Authority (tel. 788-1155); it leaves from the San Juan Terminal only on Sunday and holidays at 2:30 and 4:30pm. The tour takes you near the Coast Guard base, and you have a view of the governor's palace, the San Juan Door (Puerta de San Juan), and El Morro. The trip lasts 1½ hours and the price is $2.50 for adults and $1.50 for children.

From Catano, continue on Route 24 until the Caparra intersection with Route 20; then take Route 20 toward Guaynabo until you reach Route 21. After going past the psychiatric hospital, the medical center, and the state penitentiary, continue until the Río Piedras intersection and turn left toward Carolina by way of avenida 65 de Infantera (Route 3), from which you can see El Yunque. When you reach Km 18.3, turn onto the bridge and stay to the left to reach **Loiza Aldea.** If you're in Puerto Rico between July 19 and 29, the trip to Loiza Aldea will be quite an experience. This is when the whole town comes out to celebrate the feast day of its patron saint (Santiago Apostol). The festivities are unusual and bizarre—a mixture of pagan African Caribbean and Christian elements form part of the celebration and carnival.

The Church of San Patricio (St. Patrick), dating from 1645, in Loiza Aldea is in front of the road that leads you to the barge for crossing the Río Grande de Loiza. It's a bit of a thrill to cross this river (with your car) on a barge propelled by a man with ropes. Continue for half an hour on a sandy (but hard) road lined with coconut palms and shady trees until you reach the Nautical Club, then on to Santurce and San Juan.

THE RAIN FORESTS & BEACHES

From San Juan, if you have 2 days to explore, you can use the following itinerary. The first day you'll go to Trujillo Alto, Gurabo, El Yunque (rain forest), Luquillo Beach, and Fajardo. Perhaps you'll find the makings of a picnic lunch at one of the thatched "kiosks" along the road. On the second day you can explore Fajardo, Naguabo, Humacao, Yabucoa, Patillas, and Caguas, returning to San Juan in the late afternoon.

Water is considered one of Puerto Rico's most important resources; another is its fertile soil. During the period of a year, 400 billion cubic feet of rain falls on the island. The Spaniards nicknamed the island "The Land of Rivers." To harness this water for public consumption, many dams were built, creating lakes which can be visited.

DAY 1

From San Juan, go to Río Piedras and take Route 3 (avenida 65 de Infantera, named after the Puerto Rican regiment that battled in World War II and in Korea). Turn south on Route 181 toward Trujillo Alto, then take Route 851 up to Route 941. At the end of the valley you can spot the **Lake of Loíza.** Houses can be seen nestled on the surrounding hills. You can even see local farmers (*jíbaros*) riding their horses laden with produce on the way to and from the marketplace. The lake is surrounded by mountains.

Your next stop is the town of **Gurabo.** This is tobacco country, and you'll know you're nearing the town from the sweet aroma enveloping it (tobacco smells sweet before it's harvested). Part of the town of Gurabo is set on the side of a mountain, and the streets are made up of steps. One street has as many as 128 steps.

You leave the town by way of Route 30. Then get on Route 185 north, then Route 186 south. This road has views of the ocean beyond the valleys. At this stage you'll be driving on the lower section of the **Caribbean National Forest;** the vegetation is dense and you'll be surrounded by giant ferns. The brooks descending from El Yunque become small waterfalls on both sides of the road.

At about 25 miles east of San Juan, **۞ El Yunque** consists of about 28,000 acres and is the only tropical forest in the U.S. National Forest system. It is said to contain some 240 different tree species native to the area (only half a dozen of these are found on the mainland). In this world of cedars and satinwood draped in tangles of vines, you'll hear chirping birds, see wild orchids, and perhaps hear the song of the tree frog, the coquí. The entire forest is a bird sanctuary, and may be the last retreat of the rare Puerto Rican parrot.

El Yunque is 3,493 feet high, and the peak of El Toro rises 3,532 feet. You know you'll be showered upon, as more than 100 billion gallons of rain fall here annually. However, the showers are brief and there are many shelters.

You might go first to the **Sierra Palm Visitor Center** on Route 191, at Km 11.6. It's open daily from 9:30am to 5pm, and guides will give lectures and show slides. Groups, if they arrange in advance, can go on guided hikes. As the visitor center has no working telephone, call the administrative headquarters of the **El Yunque Ranger District** (tel. 887-2875) for information about the area.

To make your way back, head north along Route 191, connecting with Route 3. If you drive east for 5 miles, you'll reach **۞ Luquillo Beach,** lying about 30 miles east of San Juan. Edged by a vast coconut grove, this crescent-shaped beach is not only the best in Puerto Rico, it's also one of the finest in the Caribbean. You pay $1 to enter with your car, and you're allowed to rent a locker, take a shower, and have a place to change into your bathing suit. Luquillo gets very crowded on weekends, so if possible go on a weekday when you'll have more sand to yourself. Picnic tables are available as well. The beach is open Tuesday through Sunday from 9am to 5pm (closed Monday; if Monday is a holiday, then the beach will shut down on Tuesday that week instead). Before entering the beach, you may want to stop at one of the roadside thatched huts that sell Puerto Rican snacks and pick up the makings for a picnic.

From Luquillo, take Route 3 east toward Carolina and stay on Route 3 until the first exit to Fajardo, where you make a left onto Route 194. At the traffic light at the corner of the Monte Brisas Shopping Center, turn left; stay on this road until the next traffic light and turn right. Continue on this road until it intersects with Route 987. Turn left onto Route 987 and continue until you reach the entrance to **Las Cabezas de San Juan Nature Reserve,** better known as "El Faro," or the lighthouse. In the northeastern corner of Puerto Rico, north of Fajardo, it is one of the most beautiful and important areas of the island—unique because of the number of different ecological communities that flourish in proximity.

Surrounded on three sides by the Atlantic Ocean, the 316-acre site encompasses forest land, mangroves, lagoons, beaches, cliffs, offshore cays, and coral reefs. El Faro serves as a research center for the scientific community. Home to a vast array of flora and fauna (including sea turtles and other endangered species), it serves as a habitat for abundant underwater life and shore and migratory birds, and as an important spawning ground for fish and crustaceans. Guided tours of the reserve are available.

A winding walkway through dense mangroves, a lagoon illuminated by billions of light-emitting organisms, and a 19th-century lighthouse offering views of distant Caribbean islands are among the dramatic sights awaiting visitors.

The nature reserve is open Friday through Sunday, and reservations are required; call 809/722-5882. Admission is $4 for adults and $1 for children under 12 (parking included). Tours, lasting 2 to 2½ hours, are scheduled three times daily: at 9:30am, 10:30am, and 1:30pm.

After visiting the reserve, you can take the same road back until the highway directional signals (Route 3) point to **Fajardo,** a fishing port hotly contested in the Spanish-American War. Fishers and sailors are attracted to its shores and to nearby **Las Croabas,** which has a lot of fish restaurants. Puerto Ricans are found of giving nicknames to people and places, and for many years the residents of Fajardo have been called *cariduros* ("the hard-faced ones"). However, don't be misled by that—the people here are very friendly.

At Fajardo you can also rent boats or take the ferry ride to the islands of Vieques and Culebra (see below).

Where to Stay

PARADOR LA FAMILIA, Rte. 987, Km 4.2, Las Croabas, Fajardo, PR 00648. Tel. 809/863-1193. Fax 809/850-5345. 28 rms (all with bath). A/C
$ Rates: $52 single; $62 double. Breakfast $5 extra. AE, MC, V. **Parking:** Free.
This modern building lacks antique charm but offers comfortably furnished bedrooms with refrigerators. Seven of the rooms have balconies. Facilities include private parking, two swimming pools (one for adults and another for children), a cocktail lounge, and a good restaurant where lunch and dinner are served from 11am to 11pm. It's located near the beach in this northeastern fishing village, a major boating and sailing center. Close by are the coral-bordered offshore islands, the most popular being Icacos, a favorite among snorkelers and divers.

Where to Dine

ROSAS SEAFOOD, Playa Puerto Real, Fajardo. Tel. 863-0213.
   Cuisine: PUERTO RICAN/SEAFOOD. **Reservations:** Not required.
$ Prices: Appetizers 25¢–$6.95; main courses $8.95–$25. AE, MC, V.
   Open: Thurs–Tues 11am–11pm.

This is a simple *mesón gastrónomico* but it offers good food, especially the fresh-tasting fish dishes. A family favorite, it's located at the beach. Most items on the menu are inexpensively priced, except the expensive shellfish dishes. The restaurant is most popular on Sunday.

DAY 2

On the second day, continue south on Route 3, following the Caribbean coastline. At **Cayo Lobos,** not far from the Fajardo port, the Atlantic meets the Caribbean. Here the vivid colors of the Caribbean seem subdued compared to those of the ocean.

Go across the town of Ceiba, near the Roosevelt Navy Base, to reach **Naguabo Beach,** where you can have coffee and pastelillos de chapin, pastry turnovers used as tax payments in Spanish colonial days. At Km 70.9 briefly detour to Naguabo and enjoy the scented shady laurel trees from India in the town's plaza.

Continue on Route 3 and go through **Humacao** and its sugarcane fields. When the cane blooms around November and December, the tops of the fields change colors according to the time of day. Humacao is of little interest, but it has a balneario-equipped beach with changing facilities, lockers, and showers. From here you can detour to the 2,800-acre resort, Palmas del Mar (see Section 3, above).

After the stopover, continue until the town of Yabucoa, nestled among hills. The road suddenly opens up through **Cerro** (mountain) **La Pandura,** giving you some of the most spectacular sights in Puerto Rico. Take note of the giant boulders, beyond which you will see the Caribbean.

After passing the town of Maunabo along Route 181 (a tree-lined road that runs next to Lake Patillas), stay on the highway until you reach San Lorenzo, across the mountains. You take Route 183 to reach Caguas, then Route 1 for the scenic route back into San Juan, or, if you're tired, Route 52, which is faster.

THE KARST DISTRICT

The trip outlined below takes 2 days, as you cross an extraordinary limestone region, pass pineapple and coffee plantations, and explore caves. However, the itinerary can be cut down to 1 day if you eliminate a stay at the coffee plantation.

The trip takes you across the famous "Karst" district in Puerto Rico, one of the most developed regions of this type in the world. This area was formed by the wearing down of limestone by acids in the water, which left a maze of deep fissures and mounds. Some of the depressions in the area are 400 feet across and as deep as 160 feet. The radar/radiotelescope at the nearby **Arecibo Observatory** is built inside one of these craters, which is 160 feet deep and 1,300 feet wide (see below). Underground rivers are sometimes formed in this type of geological environment. An example of this is the Tanama River, which emerges and disappears at five different places.

DAY 1

From San Juan, take Route 2 heading west toward Manati, after which you'll pass the pineapple region. At Km 57.9, turn onto Route 140 south to Florida. At Km 25.5 you'll find a coffee cooperative where during harvest time the beans are processed, ground, and packed. At Km 30.7, turn right toward **Hacienda Rosas.** A coffee plantation is interesting at all times, but especially around harvest time (from September to December, sometimes as late as January) when the pickers, gathered in groups, walk under the bushes and pick the crimson beans while other workers process the already-picked yield.

Continuing, take Route 141 to Jayuya, where you can stay at the Parador Hacienda Gripinas (see "The Paradores," above).

After a restful day there, take Route 141 north until you're back on Route 140. Head west on Route 140 until you pass Lake Caonillas. There, turn onto Route 111 west, go through the town of Utuado, and continue to Km 12.3. Here you'll find the **Taíno Indian Ceremonial Ball Park.** Archeological clues date this site to approximately two centuries before the discovery of the New World. It is believed that Taíno Chief Guarionex gathered his subjects on this site to celebrate rituals and practice sports. Set on a 13-acre field surrounded by trees are some 14 vertical monoliths with colorful petroglyphs, all arranged around a central sacrificial stone monument. The ball complex also includes a museum, open daily from 9am to 5pm, charging no admission. There is also a gallery, Herencia Indígena, where visitors can purchase Taíno relics at very reasonable prices, including the sought-after Cemi (Taíno idols) and the famous little frog, the coquí.

Continue next on Route 111 up to Route 129 north and head toward Arecibo (going across the Karst region) until you reach Km 13.6. Take Route 489 south to **La Cueva de la Luz** (Cave of Light).

Next, follow Route 489 until the Barrio Aibonito, Pagan sector. If you have any doubts, ask anyone for **"La Cueva de Pagan Pagan" (Pagan Pagan's Cave).** A narrow road will lead you to its end at a general store, where anyone can help you find Pagan. Only the agile and those who like to explore should venture inside the cave. The cave is lit by daylight, but the floor is rough and irregular. (Wear slacks and sneakers or rubbersoles.) There are no bats in the cave. Inside, a stone vessel contains fresh water which some believe has rejuvenating qualities. Other caves in this area have not been explored fully, but native relics have been found. Return by way of Route 489 to Route 129 north, to Arecibo.

From Arecibo, take Route 10 south to Utuado, where you can find accommodations at Parador La Casa Grande nearby at Caonillas (see "The Paradores," above).

DAY 2

After a rest at the parador, drive north back to Arecibo and continue west on Route 2 to Hatillo, which takes you to the 300-acre ✪ **Rio Camuy Cave Park (Parque de las Cavernas del Río Camuy),** developed and operated by the Puerto Rico Land Administration to enable visitors to see Empalme Cave as well as the area of canyons, caverns, and sinkholes in a subterranean network. The third-largest underground river in the world, Río Camuy runs through the network of caves that were cut through the limestone base of the island over the course of millions of years. The caves were known to the Taíno peoples, the pre-Columbian inhabitants of the area, and to Puerto Rican farmers. The caves came to the attention of speleologists in the 1950s and were opened to the public in 1987. Gardens in the focal point of the park surround buildings where tickets can be purchased, after which a short film about the caves is shown in a theater. Visitors then descend to where open-air trolleys carry them on the downward journey to the actual caverns. The trip goes through a 200-foot-deep sinkhole, a chasm where tropical trees, ferns, and flowers flourish, to the delight of birds and butterflies. The trolley takes passengers to the entrance of Empalme Cave, one of the 16 in the Camuy Caves network, where they begin a 45-minute cave walk, viewing the majestic series of rooms rich in stalagmites, stalactites, and huge sculptures carved out and built up through the centuries. Other—some larger—caves in the network are being prepared for public viewing.

The caves are open Wednesday through Sunday from 8am to 5pm, with the last tour starting at 4pm. Tickets are $6 for adults, $4 for children 2 to 12. For information, phone the park at 756-5555.

If you want to drive to the park from San Juan, which takes 2½ hours, take Route 22 from San Juan, the Diego Expressway. At the end of the expressway, about 15 miles from San Juan, follow signs to Arecibo for about a quarter of a mile along Route 165, then go 27 miles on Route 2 to another section of the expressway. Watch for the exit from the bypass to Lares, the second exit to Route 129, and follow the signs for 11 miles to the park entrance on the left. Parking is $1. (Signs on the right are for the privately owned Cueva de Camuy, not for the park you are seeking.)

The ✪ **Arecibo Observatory,** the National Astronomy and Ionosphere Center of Cornell University (tel. 878-2612), the world's largest and most sensitive radar/radiotelescope, a 20-acre dish set in an ancient sinkhole, is a 2½-hour drive west of San Juan, not far from the Río Camuy Cave Park. The telescope, whose dish or "radio mirror" is 1,000 feet in diameter and 167 feet deep, allows scientists to examine the ionosphere, planets, and moon with powerful radar signals and to monitor natural radio emissions from distant galaxies, pulsars, and quasars. It has been used by scientists as part of the Search for Extraterrestrial Intelligence (SETI), whose basic proposition is that highly advanced technological civilizations throughout the universe might communicate via radio waves. Arecibo is called an "ear to the heavens."

Under the giant dish, vegetation flourishes, the rain and filtered sunlight encouraging a lush growth of ferns, grasses, and other plants, including wild orchids and begonias. Wildlife under the dish includes mongooses, lizards, frogs, dragonflies, and an occasional bird. Suspended above the dish is a 600-ton platform similar in design to a bridge. Hanging in midair on 12 cables, strung four each to reinforced concrete towers, it resembles a space station. The observatory is open to the public for self-guided tours Tuesday through Friday from 2 to 3pm and on Sunday from 1 to 4pm. It's a 35-minute drive south from the commercial city of Arecibo. Take Routes 129, 134, 635, and 625.

There is a souvenir shop on the grounds. The observatory is part of the National Astronomy and Ionosphere Center, a national research center operated by Cornell University under contract with the National Science Foundation.

From Arecibo, you can take Route 2 east back to San Juan.

THE WESTERN & SOUTHERN COASTS

More ambitious than the itineraries considered so far, this next trip follows the west and south coasts on the island and takes 5 days.

DAY 1

On the first day, follow Route 2 from San Juan west up to **Guajataca.** Just before reaching Km 103.4, you'll spot a sign for the Guajataca recreation area. Make a right turn and stay on the road to the parking area.

Go back to Route 2 and to the Guajataca Beach. It's so fine a beach you may want to stay here for at least 1 more day. (The Parador Guajataca is just above the hill from the beach.)

When you decide to continue, take Route 2 up to Km 91 and turn toward the south, across the Karst region (see the previous tour) until you reach the artificial Guajataca Lake. Follow the lake's shoreline for about 2½ miles and turn left at Km 19 to Route 455 until you reach a bridge spanning the Guajataca River, which runs through the lush mountainside.

Return by way of Route 119 and continue toward San Sebastián and to Route 109 across coffee plantations to Anasco. Turn onto Route 2 and head for Mayagüez for the night (see "Mayagüez," above).

DAY 2

Spend the morning exploring in and around Mayagüez (see "Mayagüez," above).

After touring Mayagüez, you can take Route 105 up to Route 120 as far as **Maricao.** The town is colorful and rather small. On the outskirts look for a sign that reads **"Los Viveros"** (The Hatcheries); then take Route 410. Here, the Commonwealth Department of Agriculture hatches as many as 25,000 fish for stocking the Puerto Rican freshwater lakes and streams.

Go back to Maricao to Route 120 south up to Km 13.8 until you reach the **Maricao State Forest** picnic area at a height of 2,900 feet above sea level. The observation tower provides a splendid view across the green mountain range up to the coastal plains. Continue on Route 120 across the forest to the town of Sabana Grande (Great Plain). Route 2 will then take you to ✪ **San German.** This town is a little museum piece. It was founded in 1512 and destroyed by the French in 1528. Rebuilt in 1570, it was named after Dona Germana de Foix, the second wife of King Ferdinand of Spain. Once it rivaled San Juan in importance, although it has now settled into slumber and is a living example of Spanish colonization. Gracious old-world buildings line the streets, and flowers brighten the patios as they do in Seville. Also as in a small Spanish town, the population turns out to stroll in the plaza in the early evening.

On a knoll at one end of the town stands the chapel of **Porta Coeli (Gate of Heaven)** (tel. 892-5845), dating from the 17th century, the oldest in the New World. Restored by the Institute of Puerto Rican Culture, it contains a museum of religious art which is open (admission free) Tuesday through Sunday from 9am to noon and 2 to 4:30pm. The museum has a collection of ancient santos, carved holy figures and saints. Guided tours are offered Wednesday through Sunday.

From San German, take Route 320 to Route 101. Then on to Lajas, where Route 116 will lead to Route 304, which will take you to La Parguera. There you can visit the **Phosphorescent Bay** (best on a moonless night). A boat leaves Villa Parguera pier nightly from 7:30pm to 12:30am, depending on demand. Tickets cost $6. The experience of seeing fish leave a luminous streak on the surface and watching the boat's wake glimmer in the dark is unique. The phenomenon, incidentally, is caused by a big colony of dinoflagellates, a microscopic form of marine life. They produce these sparks of chemical light when their nesting is disturbed.

For food and lodging, go to either Parador Villa Parguera or Parador Posada Porlamar, both at La Parguera, Laja (see "The Paradores," above).

DAY 3

On the third day, take Route 104 up to Route 116 to Ensenada. From there you can continue on Route 116 to **Guanica Bay.** Or you could turn off on Route 333 to **Cana Gorda Beach,** to have a swim or lunch. While there, look for the species of cacti typical of the region. Continue on Route 2 to Yauco, then take Route 132 and head for **Ponce,** where you can explore that city's attractions and spend the night (see "Ponce," above).

DAY 4

On the fourth and final day, leave Ponce by Route 1. As vast sugarcane fields fade from view, take Route 3 to **Guayama,** one of the handsomest towns in Puerto Rico.

The historical town of Guayama, on Puerto Rico's south side, is a beautiful small town with typical plants, steepled churches, and one of the finest museums around, **Museo Cautino.** The old mansion is a showplace of fine old turn-of-the-century furnishings, and pictures of prize horses for which the Guayama area is famous. The town is also just minutes from **Arroyo Beach,** a tranquil place to spend a day or afternoon.

Where to Stay

POSADA GUAYAMA, Rte. 3, Km 138.5, Vives Sector, Guayama, PR 00655. Tel. 809/866-1515. Fax 809/866-1515. 20 rms (all with bath). A/C TV TEL
$ Rates (including continental breakfast): Winter, $65 single; $85 double. Summer, $60 single; $65 double. AE, MC, V. **Parking:** Free.

Established in 1991 half a mile south of the center of Guayama, a 30-minute drive east of Ponce, this is among the newest government-supervised paradores in Puerto Rico. Built on 9 acres of land originally developed 200 years ago for the cultivation of sugarcane, it's a modern building filled with rattan furniture and dotted with jutting verandas. Within a 2-minute walk rises the stone tower of a windmill that many years ago helped crush the cane to extract the sweet juices. On the premises is a swimming pool, a tennis court, a basketball court, and a helpful staff. The nearest beach, at Arroyo, is within a 15-minute drive from the hotel.

DAY 5

The next day, drive north on Route 15. If you travel this road in either spring or summer, you'll be surrounded by the brilliant colors of flowering trees.

At Km 17.1, in Jajome, you can see the **governor's summer palace,** an ancient (now restored and enlarged) roadside inn. Continue on Route 15; then get on Route 1, which leads directly back to San Juan.

BEACHES ALONG THE ATLANTIC

An interesting scenic trip to the beaches between San Juan and Arecibo follows. Allow at least 5½ hours, not counting beach time.

The ever-changing colors of the Atlantic make this trip a memorable experience. Start on Route 2 to the Caparra intersection, where you turn onto Route 24 to Catano; then continue west on Route 165. El Morro and Old San Juan can be seen across the bay.

After passing a dense coconut grove, you'll reach Levittown City (a housing development). The sea turns a blue-green shade at this spot. Continue up to the river and the town of **Dorado** (see Section 2, above) by way of Route 690 north. Within a short distance, you will reach **Cerro Gordo Beach.** Watch your time, for you might be mesmerized by the natural beauty of this beach and stay longer than planned.

If you can break away from Cerro Gordo, take Route 688 back to Route 2 and head toward **Vega Baja** (founded in 1776). The residents of Vega Baja are nicknamed *melao-melao* ("molasses-molasses") because of the large amount of molasses produced in the town.

Route 676 north takes you to a spectacular beach in the west, where the water turns jade green with touches of purple and lots of white foam. Over to the east of this beach the water is less turbulent, held back by a giant rocky barrier where the waves crash thunderously. This beach is dotted with cabins and cabañas belonging to the local residents. Continue on Route 686 until you reach Route 648, which will take you to **Mar Chiquita,** where the high rocks enclose an oval lagoon perfect for swimming.

Return by way of Route 648 to Route 685, which will lead you to Route 2. Head north on Route 2 to Route 140 until you get to Barceloneta; then take Route 681 up to the **Plazuela sugar mill** and go through cane fields edged with almond trees.

Continue toward the beach and look for a sign pointing to **La Cueva del Indio (The Indian Cave).** Many Native American symbols can be seen on the cave walls.

Leave the area by way of Route 681 up to where it meets Route 2 in Arecibo. Route 2 east will take you back to San Juan through cane fields and perfumed pineapple plantations.

9. SPORTS & RECREATION AROUND THE ISLAND

Dorado Beach, Cerromar Beach, and Palmas del Mar are the chief centers for those seeking the golf, tennis, and beach life. San Juan's hotels on the Condado/Isla Verde coast also have, for the most part, complete water sports.

BEACHES With some 300 miles of coastline, both Atlantic and Caribbean, Puerto Rico obviously has plenty of beaches in addition to the ones mentioned above. Some, such as Luquillo, are overcrowded, especially on Saturday and Sunday. Others are practically deserted. If you find that secluded, hidden beach of your dreams, proceed with caution. On unguarded beaches you'll have no way to protect yourself or your valuables should you be approached by a robber or mugger, which has been known to happen. For more information about the island's many beaches, call the **Department of Sports and Recreation** (tel. 809/722-1551).

Beaches in Puerto Rico are open to the public, although you will be charged for parking and for use of *balneario* facilities, such as lockers and showers. The public beaches on the north shore of San Juan at **Ocean Park** and **Park Barbosa** are good, and can be reached by bus. **Luquillo,** on the north coast, some 30 miles east of San Juan, is discussed separately (see "Touring the Island," above; also see that section for more tips on beaches west from San Juan). Public beaches shut down on Monday. If Monday is a holiday, the beaches are open for the holiday but close the next day, Tuesday. Beach hours are 9am to 5pm in winter, to 6pm in summer.

Along the western coastal roads of Route 2, to the north of Mayagüez, lie what are reputed to be the best surfing beaches in the Caribbean. Surfers from as far away as New Zealand are attracted to these beaches. The most outstanding of all, comparable to the finest surfing spots in the world according to competitors in the 1988 World Surfing Championship held there, is at **Punta Higuero,** on Route 413 near the town of Rincón. In the winter months especially, uninterrupted Atlantic swells with perfectly formed waves averaging 5 to 6 feet in height roll shoreward, and rideable swells sometimes reach 15 to 25 feet.

DEEP-SEA FISHING It's top-notch! Allison tuna, white and blue marlin, sailfish, wahoo, dolphin, mackerel, and tarpon are some of the fish that can be caught in Puerto Rican waters, where 30 world records have been broken. Charter arrangements can be made through most major hotels and resorts.

It is said in Puerto Rico that **Capt. Mike Benitez** sets the standard by which to judge other captains. He is especially praised by marlin fishers. You can contact him directly at P.O. Box 5141, Puerta de Tierra, San Juan, PR 00906 (tel. 809/723-2292 daily until 9pm). The captain has chartered out of San Juan for almost 40 years. He takes his clients out on his 45-foot, air-conditioned, deluxe Hatteras, *Sea Born*. Fishing tours cost $395 for a half day, $695 for a full day, with a maximum of six passengers.

Some of the best year-round fishing in the Caribbean is found in the waters just off Palmas del Mar, the resort complex on the southeast coast of Puerto Rico. There, **Capt. Bill Burleson,** P.O. Box 8270, Humacao, PR 00792 (tel. 809/850-7442), operates charters on his fully customized 48-foot sport-fisherman, *Karolette,* which is electronically equipped for successful fishing. Burleson prefers to take fishing groups to Grappler Banks, 18 nautical miles away. The banks are two sea mounts, rising to about 240 feet below the surface and surrounded by deeps of 6,000 to 8,000 feet. They lie in the migratory paths of the wahoo, tuna, and marlin. The cost is $795 per day or $450 for a half day, for a maximum of six people. He also offers snorkeling expeditions to Vieques at a cost of $80 per person for a 6-hour trip.

GOLF   A golfer's dream, Puerto Rico has some splendid courses, too many for me to fully document here. Costs vary widely depending on the course and the season, ranging from $25 to $50 for 18 holes. The **Hyatt Resorts Puerto Rico** (tel. 796-1234), with 72 holes of golf, constitutes the greatest concentration of the sport in the Caribbean. The 18-hole Robert Trent Jones courses at the Hyatt Regency Cerromar and the Hyatt Dorado Beach are rated the finest anywhere.

The **Club de Golf,** at Palmas del Mar in Humacao (tel. 852-6000, ext. 2526), is one of the leading courses for golf in Puerto Rico. On Puerto Rico's southeastern coast, it has a par-72, 6,690-yard layout designed by Gary Player. Crack golfers consider Holes 11 through 15 "the toughest five successive holes in the Caribbean."

The **Mayagüez Hilton** (tel. 834-7575) makes arrangements for guests to play at a 9-hole course at a nearby country club. **Punta Borinquén,** at Aguadilla, the former Ramey Air Force Base, has an 18-hole public golf course which is open daily.

HORSEBACK RIDING   The equestrian center at **Palmas del Mar** (tel. 852-6000) has 42 horses, including English hunters for jumping, plus a variety of trail rides and instruction at all levels of ability (see "Palmas del Mar," above). The land set aside for equestrian pursuits abuts the resort's airstrip and is bounded on one side by a stream. Trail rides skirt this creek and follow paths through the coconut plantation and jungle, and along the beach. A trail ride lasts 1¼ hours and costs $20 per person.

HORSE RACING   Great thoroughbreds and outstanding jockeys compete all year at **El Comandante,** Route 3, Km 15.3 at Canovanas (tel. 724-6060), a modern track. Races are held on Wednesday, Friday, Sunday, and holidays at 2:30pm. Admission to the clubhouse is $4, and you pay only $1 for the grandstand. An air-conditioned terrace dining room opens at 12:30pm on each race day. Telephone for luncheon reservations. Most credit cards are accepted.

SCUBA & SNORKELING   The most comprehensive, accredited, and fully insured sports operation on the island is **San Juan Watersports,** at the Condado Plaza Hotel, 999 Ashford Avenue (tel. 809/724-5494). Under the direction of a PADI instructor, programs are available for everyone from novices to advanced divers. For a complete introduction to scuba, there is a half-day program, including classroom, pool, and underwater work. The PADI course requires 3 hours daily for a minimum of 5 days, and boat dives are available daily from the hotel. All equipment is included. In addition, the facility rents Yamaha Wave Runners and jet skis, and offers personalized harbor cruises on your own water vehicles, as well as banana-boat rides and catamaran rides, even aquacycles. Various half- and full-day snorkeling and diving excursions are offered, as is horseback riding on the beach and in the mountains. Evening harbor cruises are popular, and deep-sea fishing and video-camera rental can also be arranged.

A whole-day scuba trip to one of the eastern islands of Puerto Rico costs $119 per person with lunch and two dives included; snorkelers pay $69. To write for information, contact San Juan Watersports, Condominio Castillo del Mar, Suite 773, Isla Verde, PR 00913.

Coral Head Divers & Water Sports Center, P.O. Box C.U.H.F., Humacao, PR 00661 (tel. 809/850-7208, or toll free 800/255-8348), operates out of a building near the Candelera Hotel at Palmas del Mar. The dive center owns a trio of fully equipped boats, measuring 40 and 44 feet long. The center arranges snorkeling and scuba trips to offshore Vieques. A 6-hour snorkeling trip, including lunch and use of equipment, costs $70 per person. A scuba resort lesson costs $40.

TENNIS Again, the twin resorts of **Dorado** and **Cerromar** (tel. 796-1234) have the monopoly on this game, with a total of 21 courts between them. The charge is $12 an hour. Take your racquet and tennis outfit along (attire and equipment are often available in shops, but prices are high and the selection minimal). Lessons are available and cost $50 per hour.

In San Juan, the **Caribe Hilton,** the **Condado Plaza,** the **Carib Inn,** and the **Condado Beach and La Concha** have tennis courts. Also there's a public court at the old navy base, Isla Grande, Miramar. The entrance is from avenida Fernández Juncos at Stop 11.

The **Tennis Center** at Palmas del Mar in Humacao, the largest in Puerto Rico, features 20 courts. Court fees are $16 per hour for hotel guests during the day and $21 at night. Special tennis packages are available, including accommodations. Call 852-6000, ext. 51, for more information.

WINDSURFING The place to go if you're interested in windsurfing is **San Juan Watersports,** in the Condado Plaza Hotel & Casino, 999 Ashford Avenue, San Juan (tel. 724-5494). A 2-hour resort course goes for $50.

The best place along the island's north shore is on the manicured beachfront of the Hyatt Dorado Beach Hotel. Here the **Lisa Penfield Windsurfing School** (tel. 796-1234, ext. 3760) offers 90-minute private lessons for $55 each, and board rentals cost around $20 an hour. Well supplied with state-of-the-art windsurfers, plus many models designed specifically for children, it benefits from an almost uninterrupted exposure to the north shore's strong, steady winds, and an experienced crew of instructors.

10. VIEQUES

About 6 miles east of the big island of Puerto Rico lies Vieques (Bee-*ay*-kase), an island about twice the size of Manhattan with some 8,000 inhabitants and scores of palm-lined white sand beaches. Since World War II, some two-thirds of the 21-mile-long island has belonged to the United States military forces. Much of the government-owned land is now leased for cattle grazing, and when there are no military maneuvers the public can visit the beaches, which are sometimes restricted. Being allowed use of the land does not, however, totally cover local discontent and protest at the presence of the navy and marine corps personnel on the island.

ORIENTATION

GETTING THERE By Plane Four times a day **Vieques Air Link** (tel. 809/722-3735) flies between the Isle Grande Airport (not to be confused with San Juan's Luís Muñoz Marín International Airport) and the offshore island of Vieques for a round-trip fare of $55.

By Boat You can also go by ferryboat to Vieques with departures from the east-coast town of Fajardo. For information, consult the Fajardo Port Authority (tel. 809/862-0852), which runs the ferries on two daily trips each way (more on Saturday and Sunday when there is a demand). The voyage takes about an hour, at a round-trip cost of $4 for adults and $2 for children.

GETTING AROUND Public cabs or vans called **públicos** transport people around the island. **Car rentals** exist on the island, but most of them seem to be centered at someone's private home somewhere in Isabel Segunda. You'll see representatives at the airport. On one of my recent trips to Vieques, I had the feeling that I had rented a not very well maintained private car of a local family and deprived them of a long-awaited outing.

WHERE TO STAY

BANANAS, P.O. Box 1300, Barrio Esperanza, Vieques, PR 00765. Tel. 809/741-8700. 7 rms (all with bath), 1 suite.

$ Rates: Winter, $45 single; $45–$55 double; from $60 suite. Summer, $35 single; $35–$50 double; from $55 suite. Breakfast $5 extra. MC, V. **Parking:** Free.

During the 1986 making of the film *Heartbreak Ridge,* the actors and crew transformed this establishment's windswept porch into their second home. Located on the beach east of the U.S. Naval Reservation, and best known for its bar and restaurant, this guesthouse also has simple, clean, and comfortable rooms, some recently renovated. Each has a ceiling fan, and three are air-conditioned with their own screened-in porches.

The real heart of the place, however, is the pleasant veranda restaurant operated by the owners, Bill McCarthy and Don Campbell. Open daily from 11:30am to 1am in winter, the establishment serves meals and potent rum punches. You can choose from deli sandwiches, burgers, grilled Caribbean lobster, such local fish as snapper and grouper, and filet mignon, plus homemade desserts. Lunches cost $5 to $8, and dinners go for $12 to $20. Off-season the restaurant is likely to close at least 2 days a week—so call first.

LA CASA DEL FRANCES, P.O. Box 458, Barrio Esperanza, Vieques, PR 00765. Tel. 809/741-3751. Fax 809/741-0717. 18 rms (all with bath).

$ Rates: Winter, $80 single or double. Summer, $55 single or double. MAP available in winter only for $20 extra per person daily. AE, MC, V. **Parking:** Free.

S La Casa del Frances is about a 15-minute drive southeast of Isabel Segunda, just north of the center of Esperanza, east of the U.S. Naval Reservation. Set in a field near the southern coastline, its columns and imposing facade rise from the lush landscape surrounding it. It was completed in 1905 by a retired French general as the headquarters for his working sugar plantation. In the 1950s it was acquired by F. W. Woolworth, who installed a swimming pool and, with his partner, Franc Celeste, transformed 18 of its high-ceilinged bedrooms into old-fashioned hotel accommodations as an R&R oasis for his executives. Many rooms enjoy access to the sweeping two-story verandas ringing the white facade.

Scattered throughout the dozen acres attached to the main house are century-old tropical trees. The estate's architectural highlight is the two-story interior courtyard whose center is lush with bamboo, palms, philodendron, and Haitian art. The $15 fixed-price dinners are attended by many island residents who enjoy the Italian, barbecue, or Puerto Rican buffets which the staff presents with flair beneath a 200-year-old mahogany tree.

TRADE WINDS GUESTHOUSE, 107C Flamboyan (P.O. Box 1012), Barrio Esperanza, Vieques, PR 00765. Tel. 809/741-8666. 9 rms (all with bath), 1 studio.

$ Rates: $35 single; $40 double; $75 studio. Breakfast $7.50 extra. 3-night deposit by check or money order required. MC, V. **Parking:** Free.

Along the shore on the south side of the island east of the U.S. Naval Reservation, in the fishing village of Esperanza, this pleasant guesthouse offers nine units, four of them air-conditioned with terraces. The others have ceiling fans, and some also have terraces. The establishment is well known for its open-air restaurant overlooking the ocean and its hospitable atmosphere.

WHERE TO DINE

LA CAMPESINA ("The Country Place"), La Hueca. Tel. 741-1239.
Cuisine: INTERNATIONAL. **Reservations:** Recommended.

$ Prices: Appetizers $2.75–$6.75; main courses $9–$17. No credit cards.
Open: Dinner only, Tues–Sun 7–9:30pm. **Closed:** Early May to mid-Nov.

Designed to look like a native shack, this is an unusual and excellent restaurant built in the forest a few steps from one of the richest archeological deposits of Taíno artifacts in the Caribbean. The location is at the southwestern end of Route 201 (follow the signs to Esperanza) about 6 miles southwest of Isabel Segunda in the untrammeled fishing village of La Hueca. Occasionally a potent cocktail is available, perhaps a muleta made with rum and local fruits or a billi made with local quenapa, rum, and cognac. All the pasta is homemade, and the ravioli is delectable. Lobster is a specialty, as is a chayote relleño. For dessert, try the creamy "chocolate pot." The menu varies nightly.

RESTAURANT EL QUENEPO, Barrio Esperanza. Tel. 741-8541.

Cuisine: PUERTO RICAN. **Reservations:** Not required.
$ Prices: Appetizers $3.50; main courses $5.50–$14. No credit cards.
Open: Wed–Mon 9am–7pm.

Named after a large fruit tree growing between it and the nearby coastal road, this open-air pavilion is the year-round domain of Mario Abreu and his wife, Carmen. You dine beneath a raftered ceiling where revolving fans stir up a bit of the indolent air. Natives of Vieques, the Abreus prepare the specialties for which the island is best known: lobster and conch or an octopus salad, certainly a thick and spicy lobster soup (asopao), many varieties of locally caught fish, and several kinds of chicken. The restaurant is next to the Villa Esperanza Hotel on the south shore.

TRADE WINDS, Barrio Esperanza. Tel. 741-8666.

Cuisine: STEAK/SEAFOOD. **Reservations:** Recommended.
$ Prices: Appetizers $2.50–$4.50; main courses $8.50–$16.50. MC, V.
Open: Winter, lunch daily 11:30am–2pm; dinner daily 6:30–9pm. Off-season, dinner only, Wed–Sun 6:30–9pm. (Bar, year-round, daily 5pm–midnight.)

You'll find this restaurant at the ocean esplanade on the south side of the island in the fishing village of Esperanza (for my recommendation of its guesthouse, see "Where to Stay," above). It features the Topside Bar for relaxing drinks with a view of the water, and the Upper Deck for open-air dining. Menu items include surf and turf, several shrimp dishes, and fresh fish daily. Included in the price of a main dish are bread and butter, a salad, two fresh vegetables, and a choice of rice or potato.

WHAT TO SEE & DO

The Spanish conquistadores didn't think much of Vieques. They came here in the 16th century but didn't stay long, and they reported that the island and neighboring bits of land held no gold and were therefore "Las Islas Inutiles" (useless islands). The name Vieques comes from a native word for small island, *bieques.* Later Spanish occupation is attested to by the main town, **Isabel Segunda,** on the northern shore. The last Spanish fort in the New World was started around 1843 under the reign of the second Queen Isabella, for whom the town was named. The fort was never completed and is not of any special interest. The **Punta Mula Lighthouse** north of Isabel Segunda provides panoramic views of the land and sea. The island fishers and farmers conduct much of their business in Isabel Segunda.

On the south coast, **Esperanza,** once a center for the island's sugarcane industry, now a pretty little fishing village, lies near **Sun Bay (Sombe) public beach.** Sun Bay is a government-run, magnificent crescent of sand. The fenced area has picnic tables, a bathhouse, and a parking lot. Admission is $1 per car.

Few of the island's 40-some beaches have even been named, but most have their loyal supporters—loyal, that is, until too many people learn about them, in which case the devotees can always find another good spot. The U.S. Navy named some of the strands, such as **Green Beach,** a beautiful clean stretch at the island's west end. **Red and Blue Beaches,** also with navy nomenclature, are great jumping-off points for snorkelers. Other popular beaches are **Navia, Half Moon, Orchid,** and **Silver,** but if you continue along the water, you may find your own nameless secluded cove with a fine strip of sand. **Mosquito Bay,** sometimes called Phosphorescent Bay because it glows with phosphorescence on moonless nights, is a short way east of Esperanza. Less well known than the handful of other phosphorescent bays scattered throughout the Caribbean, the one at Vieques is in some ways the most vivid. The luminosity filling its waters is a function of millions of microorganisms—technically known as dinoflagellata—which thrive on the roots of red mangrove trees.

The best way to see this amazing light show is to negotiate locally with a boat operator to take you over at night (ask at your hotel). Those who decide to swim off the side of the boat are amazed at the way the whorls of churning water created by their moving bodies seem to come alive with an eerie glow.

11. CULEBRA

A tranquil little island, Culebra lies in a mini-archipelago of 24 chunks of land, rocks, and cays in the sea, halfway between Puerto Rico and St. Thomas, U.S. Virgin Islands. Just 7 miles long and 3 miles wide, with nearly 2,000 residents, the inviting little island is in U.S. territorial waters belonging to Puerto Rico, 18 miles away. This little-known, year-round vacation spot in what was once called the Spanish Virgin Islands was settled as a Spanish colony in 1886, but like Puerto Rico and Vieques, it became part of the U.S. after the Spanish-American War in 1898. In fact Culebra's only town, **Dewey,** was named for Adm. George Dewey, American hero of that war, although the locals call the fishing village **Puebla.**

For a long time, beginning in 1909, Culebra was used by the U.S. Navy as a gunnery range, and it even became a practice bomb site in World War II. In 1975, after years of protest over military abuse of the island's environment, the navy withdrew from Culebra, with the understanding that the island be kept as a nature preserve and habitat for the many rare species of birds, turtles, and fish that abound there. The four tracts of the Culebra Wildlife Refuge, plus 23 other offshore islands, are managed by the U.S. Fish and Wildlife Service. Culebra is one of the most important turtle-nesting sites in the Caribbean. Large seabird colonies, notably terns and boobies, are seen.

Today vacationers and boating people can explore the island's beauties, both on land and in the sea. (There's even a sailing school, described at the end of this chapter.) Culebra's white sand beaches (especially Flamenco Beach), the clear waters, and long coral reefs invite swimmers, snorkelers, and scuba divers. The landscape ranges from scrub and cactus to poincianas, frangipanis, and coconut palms.

Culebrita, a mile-long coral-isle satellite of Culebra, has a hilltop lighthouse and crescent beaches.

GETTING THERE By Plane Flamenco Airways (tel. 809/725-7707) flies from Isle Grande Airport to Culebra four or five times a day, depending on the season, for $40 to $50 round-trip (the lower rate is for cash payments). Most flights are on small aircraft holding no more than 10 passengers.

By Boat You can take an air-conditioned **passenger ferry** from Fajardo to Culebra that takes 1 hour and costs $5 for a round-trip. For information, phone 809/462-2005.

WHERE TO STAY

CLUB SEABOURNE, Fulladosa Rd. (P.O. Box 357), Culebra, PR 00645. Tel. 809/742-3169. Fax 809/742-3176. 14 units (all with bath). A/C **Directions:** From Puebla, follow Fulladosa Road along the south side of the bay for 1 ½ miles.

$ Rates (including continental breakfast): $65–$75 clubhouse double; $100 chalet and crow's nest double. AE, MC, V. **Parking:** Free.

Across the road from an inlet of the sea, about an 8-minute drive from the center of town, is a concrete-and-wooden structure set in a garden of crotons and palms, lying at the mouth of one of the island's best harbors, Ensenada Honda. It offers two chalets, a "crow's nest," and four rooms inside the clubhouse. Some rooms contain minibars and are air-conditioned. Dive packages and day sails can be set up at the office.

Overlooking Fulladosa Bay, the club's dining room features some of the best food on Culebra, with fresh lobster, shrimp, snapper, grouper, and conch, as well as steaks and other dishes (served nightly from 6 to 10pm). The inn also has a patio bar with a nightly happy hour, and the only freshwater swimming pool on the island.

FLAMENCO RESORT AND FISHING CLUB, 10 Pedro Marquez, Flamen-co Beach (P.O. Box 183), Culebra, PR 00645. Tel. 809/742-3144. 29 units (all with bath).
$ Rates: Winter, $75–$150 single or double. Summer, $65–$95 single or double. Breakfast from $3.50 extra. AE, MC, V. **Parking:** Free.
This is the only guesthouse or hotel near the white sands of one of the best beaches in the region, Flamenco Beach. It's located at the waterfront in Puebla. Each unit has access to a communal kitchen, and the place is ideal for a cluster of friends or an extended family, since the accommodations are arranged around spacious sitting rooms. The owner has studio apartments suitable for two, one-bedroom apartments suitable for two, and three-bedroom bungalows suitable for six. Nine units are air-conditioned. An array of supplemental diversions includes day trips on a sailboat to one of the nearby islands, snorkeling, and fishing expeditions.

WHERE TO DINE

Also consider the Club Seabourne (see "Where to Stay," above).

EL BATEY, 250 Carretera. Tel. 742-3828.
Cuisine: DELI. **Reservations:** Not required. **Directions:** Drive 5 minutes from the airport toward Puebla.
$ Prices: Appetizers $2.50–$3.50; main courses $8.50–$14; sandwiches $2–$3.50. No credit cards.
Open: Sandwiches daily 8am–2pm; dinner daily 6:30–9:30pm.
Across from the harbor is a large, clean place that maintains a full bar as well as an array of deli-style sandwiches, served until 2pm. Coffee and doughnuts are also served every morning. Beer is a popular drink, and the pool tables make the place lively, especially on weekends when many locals throng in. Breezes from the harbor cool the place. The owners, Digna Feliciano and Tomás Ayala, have many fans on the island. In the evening they offer full meals, including many fresh fish dishes.

WHAT TO SEE & DO

The **Culebra School of Sailing,** 7 Bahía Mosquito (tel. 809/742-3136), is owned and operated by Hugh and Diane Callum, who hail from Indiana and Québec, respectively. Daily sails cost $40 per person and include lunch. At their disposal is a speedboat and a fleet of four sailboats varying between 23 and 43 feet in length. Currently the only sailing school/rental on the island, it operates out of the Callums' home on Mosquito Bay, and they are happy to pick up their guests in town.

CHAPTER 5

THE U.S. VIRGIN ISLANDS

By a quirk of geographical demarcation, the U.S. Virgin Islands lie in two bodies of water: St. John is entirely in the Atlantic Ocean, St. Croix entirely in the Caribbean Sea, and St. Thomas separates the Atlantic and the Caribbean. These islands enjoy one of the most perfect year-round climates in the world. They lie directly in the belt of the subtropical, easterly trade winds. At the eastern end of the Greater Antilles and the northern tip of the Lesser Antilles, the U.S. Virgins are some 60 miles east of Puerto Rico, and 1,100 miles southeast of Miami. Some of their sugar-white beaches, experts say, are among the most beautiful on the globe.

Christopher Columbus (there's that name again) sighted the Virgin Islands on his second voyage to the New World, in 1493. He anchored at Salt River on St. Croix and named the islands for St. Ursula and her 11,000 virgins claimed to have been martyred by the Huns at Cologne in the Middle Ages.

In 1666 the Danes took formal possession of St. Thomas. According to Issac Dookan in *A History of the Virgin Islands of the United States,* the Danes departed the settlement after 19 months and then made a second attempt to colonize St. Thomas in 1672. That island, whose capital was renamed Charlotte Amalie in 1691, was divided into plantations, and an attempt was also made to colonize the island with convicts and prostitutes.

To help guard the Panama Canal, the United States purchased the islands in 1917 at a cost of $25 million, a price considered scandalously high at the time. Of course, the Americans feared German U-boat flotillas. These American outposts in the Caribbean today have territorial status, governed by an elected 15-member legislature and governor.

GETTING THERE

Nonstop flights to the U.S. Virgin Islands from either New York or Atlanta usually take 3¾ and 3½ hours, respectively. Flight time between St. Thomas and St. Croix is only 20 minutes. For information on how to proceed to St. John, see the "St. John" section in this chapter. Flying to San Juan from mainland cities and changing planes may save you money over the APEX nonstop fare.

American Airlines (tel. toll free 800/433-7300) offers one of the easiest and most comprehensive routes into St. Thomas and St. Croix from the U.S. mainland. A daily nonstop flight departs New York at 9:15am and arrives on St. Thomas in the early afternoon; passengers continuing to St. Croix remain on board for the final lap. American also offers eight (and sometimes nine) daily flights to St. Thomas from New

WHAT'S SPECIAL ABOUT THE U.S. VIRGIN ISLANDS

Beaches

- [ ] Magens Bay, St. Thomas, one of the most beautiful beaches in the world.
- [ ] Sapphire Beach, St. Thomas, with its luxury hotel complexes, one of the finest on the island and a favorite with windsurfers.
- [ ] Trunk Bay, St. John, wide and long, one of the most beautiful beaches in the West Indies.
- [ ] Caneel Bay, St. John, site of the famous Rockresort, with a string of seven beaches that stretch around Durloe Point to Hawksnest Caneel.
- [ ] Cormorant Beach, St. Croix, with some 1,200 feet of white sands and palm tree shade.
- [ ] Sandy Point, St. Croix, the biggest beach in the U.S. Virgin Islands, with shallow, calm waters.

Great Towns/Villages

- [ ] Christiansted, capital of St. Croix, a charming seaport filled with handsome 18th-century Danish colonial buildings.
- [ ] Frederiksted, "second city" of St. Croix, a gingerbread-studded monument to a long-ago mercantile prosperity.

- [ ] Charlotte Amalie, the capital of St. Thomas, one of the most beautiful port cities in the Caribbean.

Ace Attractions

- [ ] Coral World, a marine complex featuring a three-story underwater observation tower 100 feet offshore.
- [ ] Virgin Islands National Park, St. John, 9,500 acres filled with historical sites.

Historic Buildings

- [ ] Fort Christiansvaern, St. Croix, built on the foundations of a 1645 French fortress with fine harbor views from the battlements.
- [ ] The St. Thomas synagogue, second oldest in America, built by Sephardic Jews in 1833.
- [ ] Fort Christian, St. Thomas, constructed by the Danes in 1671 and named for King Christian V.

York, and almost as many on to St. Croix, that require a touchdown or a change of aircraft in San Juan or Raleigh/Durham. Seven daily flights depart from Miami, often with a brief change of equipment in San Juan. Connections from the West Coast to St. Thomas or St. Croix are made through Chicago or Miami.

American's tour desk can arrange discount air passage if a hotel reservation is made through American at the same time. American's lowest fare to St. Thomas requires a 14-day advance payment, and a delay of between 3 and 21 days before activating the return portion. A penalty will be imposed if you make any changes before departure from North America. APEX fares vary with the season, and travel in both directions on Monday through Thursday usually saves money. Requesting a change of aircraft at American's hub in Puerto Rico, or opting for an early-morning or late-night flight might also save you money. Flights from Puerto Rico to the U.S. Virgin Islands are usually on American's partner, **American Eagle** (tel. toll free 800/433-7300).

Delta (tel. toll free 800/221-1212) offers daily nonstop flights to St. Thomas from Atlanta. Hotel packages on St. Thomas are available to passengers who book air passage and hotel accommodations simultaneously either through Delta or a travel agent.

FAST THE U.S. VIRGIN ISLANDS

Since the Stars and Stripes fly over these islands with their old-world Danish towns, you don't have to worry about a language barrier or exchanging money.

Area Code It's 809 for the U.S. Virgin Islands, and you don't need it for calls within the islands.

Banks Several major banks are represented in the U.S. Virgins, although hours vary. They are usually open Monday through Thursday from 9am to 2:30pm and on Friday from 9am to 2pm and 3:30 to 5pm.

Customs Every U.S. resident can bring home $1,200 worth of duty-free purchases, including a gallon of alcoholic beverages per adult. If you go over the $1,200 limit, you pay a flat 5% duty, up to an additional $1,000. You can also mail home an unlimited amount in gifts valued at up to $100 per day, which you don't have to declare. (At other spots in the Caribbean, U.S. citizens are limited to $400 or $600 worth of merchandise and a single bottle of liquor.)

Driving Remember to *drive on the left*. This comes as a surprise to many visitors, who expect that U.S. driving practices will hold here. Of course, obey speed laws, which are 20 m.p.h. in towns, 35 m.p.h. outside.

Electricity It's the same as on the mainland: 120 volts AC, 60 cycles. No transformer, adapter, or converter is needed.

Holidays In addition to the standard legal holidays observed in the United States, the islanders also observe the following: January 6 (Three Kings' Day), March 31 (Transfer Day—transfer of the Danish Virgin Islands to the Americans), June 20 (Organic Act Day—in lieu of a constitution, they have an "Organic Act"), July 3 (Emancipation Day, commemorating the freeing of the slaves by the Danes in 1848), July 25 (hurricane supplication day), October 17 (hurricane thanksgiving day), November 1 (Liberty Day), and December 26 (Boxing Day to the British but called Christmas Second Day in the U.S. Virgins). The islands also celebrate two carnival days on the last Friday and Saturday in April: Children's Carnival Parade and Grand Carnival (adults') Parade.

Information Before you go, contact the **U.S. Virgin Islands Division of Tourism,** 1270 Ave. of the Americas, New York, NY 10020 (tel. 212/582-4520). Branch offices are at 235 Peachtree Center, Suite 1420, Atlanta, GA 30303 (tel. 404/688-0906); 122 S. Michigan Ave., Suite 1270, Chicago, IL 60603 (tel. 312/461-0180); 2655 Le Jeune Rd., Coral Gables, FL 33134 (tel. 305/442-7200); 3460 Wilshire Blvd., Suite 412, Los Angeles, CA 90010 (tel. 213/739-0138); and 1667 K St. NW, Suite 270, Washington, DC 20006 (tel. 202/293-3707).

Mail The Virgin Islands are part of the U.S. Postal System, so postage rates are the same as on the mainland.

Newspapers Daily newspapers from the mainland are flown in to St. Thomas and St. Croix every day, and local papers such as the *Virgin Island Daily News* also carry the latest news. St. Croix has its own daily newspaper, the *St. Croix Avis.*

Safety The U.S. Virgin Islands have more than their share of crime. St. John is safer than St. Thomas or St. Croix. But even on St. John there is crime, usually stolen possessions that were left unattended. One should exercise extreme caution both day and night when wandering the backstreets of Charlotte Amalie on St. Thomas and both Christiansted and Frederiksted on St. Croix—muggings are commonplace in those districts. Avoid night strolls or drives along quiet roads. Never go walking on the beaches at night.

Time When it's 6am in the Virgin Islands, it's still 5am in Florida. The U.S. Virgins are on Atlantic time, which places the islands an hour ahead of eastern standard time. When the East Coast goes on daylight saving time, Virgin Island clocks and those on the mainland record the same time.

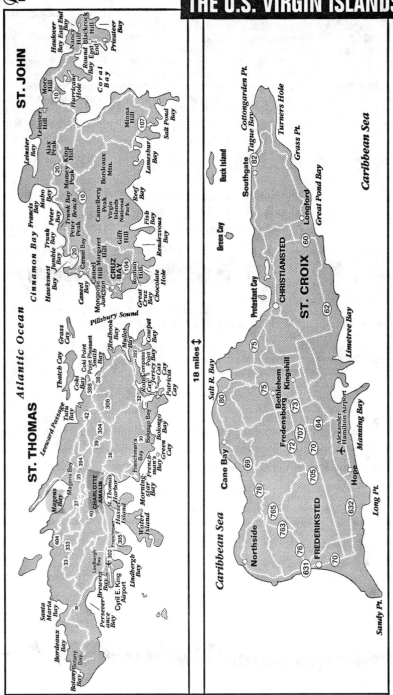

THE U.S. VIRGIN ISLANDS

ST. JOHN

Atlantic Ocean

ST. THOMAS

Leeward Passage

Pillsbury Sound

CHARLOTTE AMALIE

CRUZ BAY

Coral Bay

18 miles

Caribbean Sea

CHRISTIANSTED

ST. CROIX

FREDERIKSTED

Caribbean Sea

Tipping   As a general rule, it's customary to tip 15%. Some hotels add a 10% to 15% surcharge to cover service. When in doubt, ask.

Water   There is ample water for showers and bathing in the Virgin Islands, but you are asked to conserve. Hotels will supply you with all your drinking water. Many visitors drink the local tap water with no harmful after-affects. Others, more prudent or with more delicate stomachs, should stick to bottled water.

Weather   From November through February, temperatures average about 77° Fahrenheit. The average temperature divergence is 5° to 7°. Sometimes in August the temperature peaks in the high 80s, but the subtropical breezes keep it comfortably cool in the shade. The temperature in winter may drop into the low 60s, but this happens rarely.

1. ST. THOMAS

The busiest cruise-ship harbor in the West Indies, St. Thomas is the second largest of the U.S. Virgins, about 40 miles north of larger St. Croix. St. Thomas, with the U.S. Virgins' capital at Charlotte Amalie, is about 12 miles long and 3 miles wide. The capital is also the shopping center of the Caribbean (see "Savvy Shopping," below, on what to buy).

Hotels on the north side of St. Thomas face the Atlantic, and those on the south side front the calmer Caribbean. It's possible for the sun to shine in the south as the north experiences showers.

Holiday makers discovered St. Thomas right after World War II, and they've been flocking back in increasing numbers ever since. Shopping, sights, and sun prove a potent lure. Tourism has raised the standard of living here; it's now one of the highest in the Caribbean. Condominium apartments have grown up over the debris of bulldozed shacks.

St. Thomas is a boon for cruise-ship shoppers, who flood Main Street, the shopping center, basically three to four blocks long in the center of town. However, this center, which gets very crowded, is away from all beaches, major hotels, most restaurants, and entertainment facilities. At a hotel "out on the island," you can still find the seclusion you may be seeking.

If you're visiting in August, make sure you carry along mosquito repellent.

ORIENTATION

GETTING AROUND   By Plane   To hop over to St. Croix, St. John, or Tortola (the capital of the British Virgin Islands), call **Virgin Islands Seaplane Shuttle** (tel. 809/773-1776, or toll free 800/524-2050, 800/595-9504 in Puerto Rico).

By Bus   St. Thomas has the best public transportation of any island in the U.S. chain. A new system, **Vitran buses** now leave from the center of Charlotte Amalie and fan out east and west along all the most important highways on the island. Vitran stops are found beside the roads. You rarely have to wait more than 30 minutes during the day, and they run between 6am and 9pm daily, charging 75¢. This is an excellent and comfortable form of public transportation. Sometimes you are not necessarily delivered door to door, however, and may still have to walk a good way to your destination—perhaps to a hotel lying down along the beach.

St. Thomas also has an open-air **"safari bus,"** which leaves Red Hook dock every 60 minutes from 7:15am to 5:15pm daily for Charlotte Amalie. They also depart from the Market Place at the intersection of Main Street and Strand Gade in Charlotte Amalie for Red Hook once an hour from 8:15am to 5:15pm. A one-way ticket costs $3.

The **Manassah Country Bus** goes between Charlotte Amalie and Red Hook nearly every hour. Daily service starts at 6am from Charlotte Amalie and ends with the last run at 8pm from Red Hook, all for a one-way cost of 75¢. Throughout the day, other buses depart from Rothschild Francis Square in Charlotte Amalie and head across St. Thomas as far west as Bordeaux, with a one-way passage costing 75¢. For information about exact schedules, call 774-5678.

By Taxi The chief means of transport is the taxi, which is unmetered; agree with the driver before you get into the car. Actually, taxi fares are $30 for two passengers for 2 hours of sightseeing; each additional passenger pays another $12. For 24-hour radio-dispatch service, call 776-0496.

By Rental Car Partly because of its status as a U.S. territory, St. Thomas has many leading North American car-rental firms at the airport, and competition is stiff. The big companies, however, tend to be easier to deal with in cases of billing errors. Before you go, compare the rates of the "big three": **Avis** (tel. toll free 800/331-2112), **Budget** (tel. toll free 800/472-3325), and **Hertz** (tel. toll free 800/654-3001). Currently, the cheapest rate is offered by Avis: $188 for a week. There is no tax on car rentals in the Virgin Islands.

St. Thomas has a high accident rate: Many visitors are not used to driving on the left, the hilly terrain shelters blind curves and entrance ramps, and sometimes the roads are too narrow and the lighting is poor.

Additional collision-damage insurance (strongly recommended considering the high accident rate) costs $10 extra per day, and additional personal accident insurance runs $3 extra per day. The fine print on insurance policies varies, with Budget requiring payment of the first $500 in accident damages even by clients who purchased the optional collision-damage waiver. (Check the coverage provided with your credit cards; you *may* already have adequate coverage.) The minimum age requirement for drivers is 25 at Avis, and 21 at both Budget and Hertz. (Budget also requires that renters be younger than 70.)

By Boat If you're getting around by private boat, then you may want to get the *Yachtsman's Guide to the Virgin Islands,* available at major marine outlets, bookstores, book departments of major yachting publications, or direct from Tropic Isle Publishers, Inc., P.O. Box 610935, North Miami, FL 33161-0938 (tel. 305/893-4277). The guide, revised annually, is supplemented by sketch charts, photographs, and landfall sketches and chartlets showing harbors and harbor entrances, anchorages, channels, and landmarks, plus information on preparations necessary for cruising the islands.

ESSENTIALS American Express service is provided by the **Caribbean Travel Agency, Inc.**/Tropic Tours, Guardian Building, Havensight Mall (tel. 774-1855). **St. Thomas Hospital** is at Sugar Estate, Charlotte Amalie (tel. 776-8311). St. Thomas receives both cable and commercial TV stations. Radio weather reports can be heard at 7:30pm and 8:30am on 99.5 FM.

WHERE TO STAY

Nearly every beach has its own hostelry. You may want to stay in the capital, Charlotte Amalie, or at any of the far points of St. Thomas. St. Thomas may have more inns of character than anyplace else in the Caribbean. There is a 7½% government hotel tax.

If you are interested in a condo rental, contact **Property Management Caribbean, Inc.,** Route 6, Cowpet Bay, St. Thomas, USVI 00802 (tel. 809/775-6220, or toll free 800/524-2038), which currently represents six condo complexes. The company maintains an information desk at the airport to assist late-night arrivals, and rental units range from studio apartments to four-bedroom villas suitable for up to eight people. Each has an equipped kitchen, although no food is provided. A minimum stay of 3 days is required in any season (10 nights around Christmas).

VERY EXPENSIVE

BOLONGO BAY BEACH & TENNIS CLUB, Bolongo Estate 50 (P.O. Box 7337), Bolongo Bay, St. Thomas, USVI 00801. Tel. 809/775-1800, or toll free 800/524-4746. Fax 809/775-3208. 77 rms, 65 suites. A/C TV TEL **Transportation:** Vitran bus.

$ Rates (including continental breakfast): Winter, $200–$215 single; $210–$225 double; from $250 suite. Summer, $145–$160 single; $160–$175 double; from $180 suite. AE, DC, MC, V. **Parking:** Free.

Bolongo Bay is a unique property on St. Thomas—it's a resort complex with a beachside location where you can stay in the only all-inclusive resort on the island, in a comfortable accommodation with up-to-date amenities and an efficiency kitchen, or in an all-suites "pocket of posh." The three facilities are the Bolongo Limetree Beach Hotel, Bolongo Bay Beach & Tennis Club, and Bolongo Elysian Beach Resort. The resorts are connected by an hourly complimentary service.

This is the original and perhaps the most successful of the three resorts. After only 1 day here, you'll know why it's called "Club Everything." The 10-acre property has probably welcomed more honeymooners than any other hotel on the island. It was built in a series of interconnected bungalows in an arc that follows the shoreline of an 800-foot white sand beach studded with palm trees. Each unit has a private balcony, comfortably unpretentious furniture, a private kitchenette, and big sliding glass doors opening onto a view of a tropical fantasy. The social center is a cabaña-type bar, restaurant, and pool complex set near the edges of the beach.

The all-suites resort of Bolongo Bay Villas offers luxurious accommodations with ocean views, kitchens, balconies, king-size or double beds, and electronic safes. Accommodations here are the largest rental units offered by the resort complex. Set at the distant edge of the beach, they are a bit isolated (which some guests consider a virtue). Included in the rates are Sunfish sailboats, floats, tennis, an introductory scuba lesson, and snorkel gear. If you stay 7 or more nights, you can take a complimentary cruise aboard the club yacht to St. John or Magens Bay. Ask about such specials as the honeymoon package and dive packages, or "Couples with Kids."

Dining/Entertainment: On the grounds, areas are set aside for do-it-yourself cookouts, but most guests prefer the generously served, good-tasting food at the Sea Shell Restaurant, which opens onto the pool area. You can also order food at Coconut Henry's, the beach grill.

Facilities: Swimming pool, snorkeling gear, Sunfish sailboats; *Mohawk II,* the club's yacht, which makes day and overnight trips to the British Virgin Islands.

BOLONGO ELYSIAN BEACH RESORT, Cowpet Bay, Red Hook (P.O. Box 51), St. Thomas, USVI 00802. Tel. 809/779-2844, or toll free 800/524-4746. Fax 809/775-3208. 175 suites. A/C MINIBAR TV TEL **Transportation:** Hotel-owned open-air shuttle.

$ Rates (including continental breakfast): Winter, $285–$295 single or double. Summer, $175–$185 single or double. AE, DC, MC, V. **Parking:** Free.

This elegant all-suite resort opened in 1989 on Cowpet Bay between a pair of upscale condo complexes in the East End. This resort has a Europeanized kind of glamour, and it's within a 20-minute drive of Charlotte Amalie. The thoughtfully planned bedrooms have kitchens and large balconies, and some offer sleeping lofts reached by a spiral staircase. The decor is sophisticated and tropical, with white ceramic-tile floors, rattan and bamboo furnishings, and natural-wood ceilings. Rooms are in a bevy of four-story buildings connected to lushly landscaped gardens.

Dining/Entertainment: A member of the Bolongo Bay Beach Resorts, the hotel offers elegant international dining in its Palm Court Restaurant, and also has weekly barbecues on the terrace. Other restaurants include La Trattoria, with an Italian cuisine, and the Sea Breeze Grill.

Services: Open-air shuttle to town, room service, laundry and dry cleaning, a masseur, baby-sitting.

Facilities: Fitness center, water-sports center, tennis court.

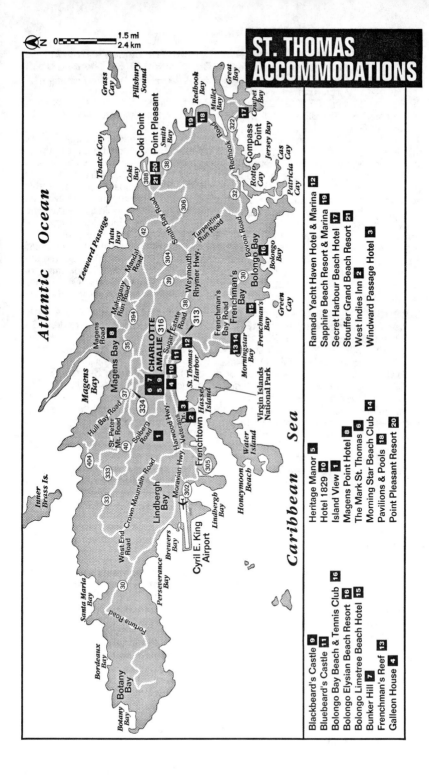

ST. THOMAS ACCOMMODATIONS

Blackbeard's Castle 9
Bluebeard's Castle 11
Bolongo Bay Beach & Tennis Club 16
Bolongo Elysian Beach Resort 16
Bolongo Limetree Beach Hotel 15
Bunker Hill 7
Frenchman's Reef 13
Galleon House 4

Heritage Manor 5
Hotel 1829 10
Island View 1
Magens Point Hotel 8
The Mark St. Thomas 6
Morning Star Beach Club 14
Pavilions & Pools 18
Point Pleasant Resort 20

Ramada Yacht Haven Hotel & Marina 12
Sapphire Beach Resort & Marina 19
Secret Harbour Beach Hotel 17
Stouffer Grand Beach Resort 21
West Indies Inn 2
Windward Passage Hotel 3

BOLONGO LIMETREE BEACH HOTEL, 100 Frenchman's Bay Estate (P.O. Box 7337), Frenchman's Bay Rd. (Route 30), St. Thomas, USVI 00801. Tel. **809/775-1800**, or toll free 800/524-4746. Fax 809/774-8485. 84 rms. A/C TV TEL **Transportation:** Taxi.

$ Rates: Winter, $2,800–$2,940 8-day/7-night all-inclusive package for two. Summer, $2,700–$2,905 8-day/7-night all-inclusive package for two. AE, DC, MC, V. **Parking:** Free.

This is the only all-inclusive resort on St. Thomas. Opening onto Frenchman's Cove just 10 minutes from Charlotte Amalie, its comfortable accommodations are in three-story villas set on two dozen beautifully landscaped acres. Walk across the "iguana bridge," and notice the pets of the property, a family of iguanas that will like you if you offer them their favorite food, hibiscus blossoms. The spacious and comfortable accommodations are decorated in an island motif, and some contain sleeping lofts.

The hotel quotes double rates only and requires a minimum booking of 4 days and 3 nights. Most clients reserve the 8-day/7-night package, which includes all meals, all drinks, wine with dinner, a PADI scuba course or two free dives, an all-day motor-yacht cruise to St. John, a half-day sail on a 52-foot catamaran with snorkeling, 1-day Budget car rental for an island tour, admission to Coral World, live entertainment and dancing every night, theme-night carnival buffets, and a wide range of sports activities, including tennis on two courts and Sunfish sailing. Other hotel facilities are a large swimming pool, Jacuzzis, and an exercise and weight room.

MARRIOTT'S FRENCHMAN'S REEF BEACH RESORT, 5 Estate Bakkeroe, Flamboyant Point (P.O. Box 7100), Charlotte Amalie, St. Thomas, USVI 00801. Tel. **809/776-8500**, or toll free 800/524-2000. Fax 809/776-3054. 424 rms, 19 suites. A/C MINIBAR TV TEL **Transportation:** Water or land taxi from Charlotte Amalie.

$ Rates: Winter, $260–$295 single or double; from $590 suite. Summer, $175–$210 single or double; from $420 suite. American breakfast $14 extra. AE, DC, MC, V. **Parking:** Free.

Frenchman's Reef has a winning southern position on a projection of land overlooking both the harbor at Charlotte Amalie and the Caribbean. Everywhere you look are facilities devoted to the good life. To reach the private beach, you take a glass-enclosed elevator. The bedrooms vary greatly, but are generally traditionally furnished in quite good taste.

Dining/Entertainment: Seafood with a continental flair is served in Windows on the Harbour, which resembles the inside of a cruise ship and has a view of the harbor. The Lighthouse Bar was once an actual lighthouse. Caesar's offers an Italian cuisine at surfside. In the evening, the Top of the Reef, a supper club, offers entertainment, or you can go to La Terraza lounge.

Services: Room service (7am–10:30pm), laundry, baby-sitting.

Facilities: Two swimming pools with poolside bar, tennis courts, water sports (snorkeling, scuba diving, sailing, deep-sea fishing).

MARRIOTT'S MORNING STAR BEACH CLUB, Frenchman's Reef Beach Resort, 5 Estate Bakkeroe, Flamboyant Point, Charlotte Amalie, St. Thomas, USVI 00802. Tel. **809/776-8500**, or toll free 800/BEACH CLUB. Fax 809/776-3054. 96 rms. A/C MINIBAR TV TEL **Transportation:** Water or land taxi from Charlotte Amalie.

$ Rates: Winter, $325–$425 single or double. Summer, $220–$270 single or double. MAP $48 per person extra. AE, DC, MC, V. **Parking:** Free.

Both its public areas and its plushly outfitted accommodations are among the most desirable on the island. They were built on the landscaped flatlands near the beach of the well-known Frenchman's Reef Beach Resort, as the elegant twin neighbor of the older hotel. The resort has five buildings, each containing between 16 and 24 units. Guests have the amenities and attractions of a large hotel nearby, yet maintain the privacy of an exclusive enclave. Each accommodation has rattan furniture; a color scheme of lilac, plum, and red mahogany; and views of the garden or beach. Swimming can be supplemented with a wide array of water sports.

Dining/Entertainment: The establishment's restaurant is the Tavern on the Beach.

Facilities: Guests have use of the Frenchman's Reef Beach Resort; water sports.

PAVILIONS & POOLS, Rte. 6, St. Thomas, USVI 00802. Tel. 809/775-6110, or toll free 800/524-2001. Fax 809/775-6110. 25 villas. A/C TV TEL **Transportation:** Taxi.

$ Rates (including continental breakfast): Winter, $230–$255 double. Summer, $175–$195 double. Honeymoon packages available. AE, DC, MC, V. **Parking:** Free.

⭐ Ideal for a honeymoon or an off-the-record weekend, this place seems the ultimate in small-scale luxury—your own villa, with floor-to-ceiling glass doors opening directly onto your own private swimming pool. The resort is a string of condominium units, built and furnished with good taste. After checking in and following a wooden pathway to your attached villa, you don't have to see another soul until you check out. The fence and gate are high, and your space opens into tropical greenery. Around your own swimming pool is an encircling deck. Inside, a high room divider screens a full, well-equipped kitchen. Each bedroom has its own style, with plenty of closets behind louvered doors. The bath has a garden shower where you can bathe surrounded by greenery, yet you are protected from Peeping Toms.

Dining/Entertainment: A small bar and barbecue area is the site for rum parties and cookouts. Occasionally a musician or singer will entertain.

Services: Helpful front desk books guided tours and day sails, and makes restaurant reservations.

Facilities: Free use of snorkeling gear, tennis courts, adjoining Sapphire Bay with its good beach.

POINT PLEASANT RESORT, Estate Smith Bay No. 4, St. Thomas, USVI 00802. Tel. 809/775-7200, or toll free 800/524-2300. Fax 809/776-5694. 134 rms. A/C TEL **Transportation:** Taxi.

$ Rates: $175–$240 single; $185–$270 double. Breakfast $10 extra. AE, MC, V. This very private, unique resort on Water Bay sits on the far northeastern tip of St. Thomas. From your living room you look out on a Virgin collection—Tortola, St. John, and Jost Van Dyke. The hotel complex is set on a bluff with flowering shrubbery, frangipani trees, secluded nature trails, and lookout points. Hummingbirds cheer your breakfast. The hotel offers villa-style accommodations, some with kitchens. The furnishings are light and airy, mostly rattan and floral fabrics. Currently, the rates are year round, but this is subject to change.

Dining/Entertainment: The Agave Terrace is one of the finest restaurants on the island and offers three meals a day. The menu is a blend of nouvelle American dishes with Caribbean specialties.

Services: Complimentary use of a car 4 hours a day; shopping and dinner shuttle available.

Facilities: Three freshwater swimming pools, night-lit tennis courts, snorkeling equipment, Sunfish sailboats.

SAPPHIRE BEACH RESORT & MARINA, Rte. 38, Smith Bay Rd. (P.O. Box 8088), St. Thomas, USVI 00801. Tel. 809/775-6100, or toll free 800/524-2090. Fax 809/775-4024. 171 suites and villas. A/C MINIBAR TV TEL **Transportation:** Taxi.

$ Rates: Winter, $295 suite for one or two, $320–$345 suite for three or four; $385 villa for two, $410–$435 villa for three or four, $460 villa for five. Summer, $190 suite for one or two, $215–$240 suite for three or four; $255 villa for two, $280–$305 villa for three or four, $330 villa for five. Children 12 and under stay free in parents' room. MAP $50 per person extra. AE, DC, MC, V. **Parking:** Free.

⭐ One of the finest modern luxury resorts in the Caribbean is this secluded retreat in the East End. Guests can arrive by yacht and occupy a berth in the 67-slip marina or else take a superb suite or villa. The accommodations open onto a horseshoe bay, with one of St. Thomas's most spectacular beaches, and exude casual elegance. The beaches are actually two crescents broken by the coral-reef peninsula of Prettyklip Point. The one-bedroom suites have fully equipped kitchens and microwaves, bedroom areas, living/dining rooms with queen-size sofa beds, and large, fully tiled outdoor galleries with lounge furniture. Villas are on two levels; the main one contains the same amenities as the suites while the upper level includes a second full bath, a bedroom and sitting area with a queen-size sofa bed, and a sun deck with outdoor furniture. Suites accommodate one to four guests, whereas villas are suitable for up to six guests.

Dining/Entertainment: Meals are served at the beach bar, and at night you can dine at the Seagrape, along the seashore, one of the island's finest eating places. Sometimes a 10-piece band is brought in for dancing under the stars.

Services: Beach towels, daily chamber service, guest services, desk, baby-sitting.

Facilities: Two swimming pools, snorkeling equipment, Sunfish sailboats, windsurfing boards, four all-weather tennis courts, waterfront pavilion with snack bar, complete diving center.

SECRET HARBOUR BEACH HOTEL, 2H25 Estate Nazareth (P.O. Box 7576), St. Thomas, USVI 00802. Tel. 809/775-6550, or toll free 800/524-2250. Fax 809/775-1501. 60 suites. A/C TV TEL **Transportation:** Vitran bus.

$ Rates: Winter, $255 studio suite; $325 one-bedroom suite; $460 two-bedroom suite. Summer, $162 studio suite; $192 one-bedroom suite; $289 two-bedroom suite. AE, MC, V. **Parking:** Free.

Secret Harbour is an all-suites resort on the beach at Nazareth Bay. The four contemporary buildings have a southwestern exposure and lie only a 15-minute ride east of Charlotte Amalie, 10 miles from the airport. At first you'll think you've arrived at a South Seas island beach resort in a setting of tall palms. Each unit has a private deck (or patio) and full kitchen. There are three kinds of accommodations and all are decorated by the individual owners: studio apartments with a bed/sitting-room area, patio, dressing-room area, and full bath; one-bedroom suites with a living/dining area, a separate bedroom and bath, plus a sun deck; and the most luxurious, a two-bedroom suite with two baths and a private living room.

Dining/Entertainment: The Eden Restaurant offers meals indoors or on an outdoor terrace in a setting on the beach, with peacock chairs and candlelight. For drinks you can go to the Beach Bar or Gazebo.

Services: Laundry, baby-sitting.

Facilities: Full water-sports/dive center on the beach, two all-weather tennis courts.

STOUFFER GRAND BEACH RESORT, Rte. 38, Smith Bay Rd. (P.O. Box 8267), St. Thomas, USVI 00801. Tel. 809/775-1510, or toll free 800/468-3571. Fax 809/775-3757. 261 rms, 36 suites. A/C MINIBAR TV TEL **Transportation:** Taxi.

$ Rates: Winter, $295–$415 single or double; from $595 suite. Summer, $195–$315 single or double; from $450 suite. MAP $65 per person extra. AE, DC, MC, V. **Parking:** Free.

Seven miles northeast of Charlotte Amalie, perched on a steep hillside above a 1,000-square-foot white sandy beach, this resort occupies 34 acres on the northeast shore of St. Thomas. Accommodations are in two separate areas, poolside and hillside. The two-story town-house suites and one-bedroom suites have Jacuzzis, and all units are stylishly outfitted. Each accommodation has cable color TV with HBO, a hairdryer, and an open balcony.

Dining/Entertainment: You can enjoy beachfront breakfast, lunch, and dinner at Bay Winds, featuring continental and Caribbean cuisine. Sumptuous breakfast buffets, mesquite-grilled dishes, and late-night desserts are served in Smugglers. Lighter fare is offered at the poolside snack bar. For cocktails, live entertainment, and nightly dancing, there's the Smugglers Lounge.

Services: Daily children's program, round-the-clock baby-sitting, laundry service, 24-hour room service, twice-daily chamber service, guest services desk/ concierge, newspaper and coffee with wake-up call, newsstand.

Facilities: Two swimming pools, boutiques, water-sports desk where you can rent sailboats or snorkeling equipment, scuba diving, windsurfing, deep-sea fishing, six lit tennis courts, exercise facility; 18-hole golf course 10 minutes away.

EXPENSIVE

BLUEBEARD'S CASTLE, Bluebeard's Hill (P.O. Box 7480), Charlotte Amalie, St. Thomas, USVI 00801. Tel. 809/744-1600, or toll free 800/524-6599. Fax 809/774-5134. 170 rms, 10 suites. A/C TV TEL

$ Rates: Winter, $129–$230 single or double; from $275 suite. Summer, $150– $185 single or double; from $235 suite. Extra person $30. MAP $50 per person extra. AE, DC, MC, V. **Parking:** Free.

Bluebeard's, almost a monument on St. Thomas, is a popular resort lying on one side of the bay overlooking Charlotte Amalie at the east end of the main street. The history of this spot dates from 1665. In the 1930s the U.S. government turned what had been a private home into a hotel which, on one occasion, attracted Franklin D. Roosevelt. Over the years Bluebeard's has had many additions and extensions to accommodate the ever-increasing throng of holiday makers. Bedchambers come in a wide variety of shapes and sizes—all pleasantly decorated.

Dining/Entertainment: The Terrace Restaurant commands a panoramic view and offers American and Caribbean specialties for open-air brunching, lunching, or late-night dining. Entre Nous, with views of the harbor, serves a continental cuisine.

Services: Free transportation to famous Magens Bay Beach.

Facilities: Freshwater swimming pool, two whirlpools, championship tennis courts.

MAGENS POINT HOTEL, Magens Bay Rd., St. Thomas, USVI 00802. Tel. 809/775-5500, or toll free 800/524-2031. Fax 809/776-5524. 31 rms, 23 suites. A/C TV TEL

$ Rates: Winter, $150–$160 single; $160–$176 double; $250 kitchenette suite for two; $300 kitchenette suite for three or four. Summer, $90–$103 single; $103– $115 double; $150 kitchenette suite for two; $235 kitchenette suite for three or four. Honeymoon packages available. Continental breakfast $6 extra. AE, DC, MC, V. **Parking:** Free.

Magens Point has a personality and charm of its own. On the northern shoreline, an 8-minute ride from downtown Charlotte Amalie and 6 miles north of the airport, it lies on a hillcrest overlooking Magens Bay with a beach that *National Geographic* called "one of the 10 best in the world." The hotel is small enough to retain its individuality, yet large enough to provide excellent holiday facilities. The main building is tastefully constructed with two rows of balconies and a shingled town-house style of roofing. The bedrooms and suites each come with two double beds, a large private balcony, framed watercolors, and Caribbean furnishings.

Dining/Entertainment: There's a wide, tree-shaded terrace with in- and outdoor dining. Buffets are often set out on long tables decorated with hibiscus bushes.

Overlooking the sea is the popular restaurant, the Green Parrot (unfortunately, a condominium blocks the view of the bay at sunset). Sometimes entertainment is provided. If you don't stay here and want to dine at the Green Parrot, call before striking out from Charlotte Amalie or wherever.

Services: Regularly scheduled transportation to and from the beach, the adjacent Mahogany Run Golf Course, and downtown free-port shopping.

Facilities: Swimming pool, lit tennis courts; golf, scuba diving, deep-sea diving, and sailing available.

MODERATE

BLACKBEARD'S CASTLE, 38-39 Dronningens Gade (P.O. Box 6041),

Charlotte Amalie, St. Thomas, USVI 00801. Tel. 809/776-1234, or toll free 800/344-5771. Fax 809/776-4321. 12 rms, 8 suites. A/C TV TEL
Directions: From the airport, turn right onto Route 30 which you take to Route 35, where you make a left turn; travel for half a mile until you see the sign pointing left to the hotel.

$ Rates (including continental breakfast): Winter, $110 single; $140 double; from $170 suite. Summer, $75 single; $95 double; from $120 suite. AE, MC, V. **Parking:** Free.

An Illinois businessman, Bob Harrington, transformed what had been a private residence into a genuinely charming inn that enjoys one of the finest views of Charlotte Amalie and the harbor, thanks to its perch high on a hillside above the town. In 1679 the Danish governor erected a soaring tower of chiseled stone here as a lookout for unfriendly ships. Legend says that Blackbeard himself lived in the tower half a century later. Each bedroom has a semisecluded veranda, a flat-weave Turkish kilim, terra-cotta floors, simple furniture, and a private bath. Guests enjoy use of a swimming pool, and the establishment's social center is the stylish bar and restaurant (see "Where to Dine," below).

HERITAGE MANOR, 1A Snegle Gade (P.O. Box 90), Charlotte Amalie, St. Thomas, USVI 00804. Tel. 809/774-3003, or toll free 800/828-0757. Fax 089/776-9585. 6 rms (4 with bath), 2 apartments. A/C

$ Rates (including continental breakfast): Winter, $70 single or double without bath; $95 double with bath; $110–$130 apartment. Summer, $50 single or double without bath; $80 double with bath; $85–$95 apartment. AE, V. **Parking:** Free.

This is a restored 150-year-old Danish merchant's town house in the historical district of Charlotte Amalie. The intimate hotel offers rooms—named Paris, Rome, London, New York, and San Francisco—with many extras, such as hairdryers and ceiling fans, and three of the accommodations have balconies with views of the harbor. The small inn has a freshwater pool installed in a former Danish bakery complete with a chimney.

HOTEL 1829, Kongens Gade (P.O. Box 1567), Charlotte Amalie, St. Thomas, USVI 00804. Tel. 809/776-1829, or toll free 800/524-2002. Fax 809/776-4313. 12 rms, 3 suites. A/C MINIBAR TV TEL

$ Rates (including continental breakfast): Winter, $70–$160 single; $80–$220 double; $280 suite. Summer, $50–$90 single; $60–$100 double; $180 suite. Children under 12 not accepted. AE, MC, V. **Parking:** Free.

Built by a French sea captain for his bride, this place was designed by an Italian architect in a Spanish motif. Danish and African labor completed the structure in 1829—hence the name. After a major renaissance, this once-decaying historical site has become one of the leading small hotels of character in the Caribbean. Right in the heart of town, it stands about 3 minutes from Government House and was built on a hillside with many levels and many steps (no elevator). It is reached by a climb. The 1829 has actually been a hotel since the 19th century and has entertained King Carol of Rumania (and his mistress, Madame Lupescu), Edna St. Vincent Millay, and Mikhail Baryshnikov.

Amid a cascade of flowering bougainvillea, you can reach the upper rooms which overlook a central courtyard with a miniature swimming pool. The units, some of which are small, are beautifully designed and comfortable. All have private baths, and most face the sea. In the restoration, the old was preserved whenever possible. A few have antiques, such as four-poster beds.

THE MARK ST. THOMAS, Blackbeard's Hill, Charlotte Amalie, St. Thomas, USVI 00801. Tel. 809/774-5511, or toll free 800/343-4085. Fax 809/774-8509. 8 rms, 1 suite. A/C TV TEL

$ Rates (including continental breakfast, airport transfer, and a welcome drink): Winter, $145 single or double; from $215 suite. Summer, $90–$150 single or double; from $160 suite. AE, DC, MC, V. **Parking:** Free.

Originally built in 1785 of bricks used as ballast in ships from Denmark, this was once the domain of a Danish-born merchant. The much-altered and expanded building stands today in the midst of pleasant gardens at the top of the island's famous 99 steps, at the east end of town. It is listed with the National Register of Historic Homes. In addition to a "great room" furnished with antiques, it rents comfortable bedrooms, each suitable for one or two occupants. An outlying cottage, the only accommodation without a sea view, has two bedrooms and can house up to four guests. Today the enclave is run by the New York partnership of Jack Hepworth and executive chief Ralph Cantito. The restaurant is recommended separately (see "Where to Dine," below).

RAMADA YACHT HAVEN HOTEL & MARINA, 4 Long Bay Rd. (P.O. Box 7970), St. Thomas, USVI 00801. Tel. 809/774-9700, or toll free 800/228-9898. Fax 809/776-3410. 151 rms, 3 suites. A/C TV TEL

$ Rates: Winter, $130–$180 single or double; from $250 suite. Summer, $90–$115 single or double; from $240 suite. Tax and service extra. Continental breakfast $5 extra. AE, DC, MC, V. **Parking:** Free.

This chain hotel is centrally located near the beaches and the shops at the east end of town. It is adjacent to one of the largest and best-equipped private marinas in the Caribbean and to the West Indies cruise-ship dock. Each of the spacious units contains extra-large twin or king-size beds, a bath, a radio, and a VCR. The hotel has a pool with a swim-up bar. The Bridge in the marina has a relaxed atmosphere for casual dining and offers a view of the yachts and cruise ships.

WEST INDIES INN, Villa Olga, Frenchtown, St. Thomas, USVI 00802. Tel. 809/774-1376, or toll free 800/448-6224. Fax 809/779-7040. 23 rms. A/C

$ Rates (including continental breakfast): Winter, $80–$150 single; $95–$170 double. Summer, $65–$105 single; $70–$115 double. AE, DC, MC, V. **Parking:** Free.

On a peninsula in Frenchtown, this unique waterfront hostelry provides modern lodging in a relaxed setting with good views and is convenient to many activities. The secluded yet central location directly west of town is just a short walk to town, major shops, inter-island ferries, and the seaplane shuttle. Each hillside room has a ceiling fan and a private bath. The freshwater pool with its large sun deck and flowering borders is terraced into the slope. Dinner can be ordered at the on-site Chart House (see "Where to Dine," below). The Joe Vogel Diving Company (see "Sports and Recreation," below) is located at the inn.

WINDWARD PASSAGE HOTEL, Veterans Dr. (P.O. Box 640), St. Thomas, USVI 00804. Tel. 809/774-5200, or toll free 800/524-7389. Fax 089/774-1231. 150 rms, 10 suites. A/C TV TEL

$ Rates (including buffet breakfast): Winter, $125–$150 single; $135–$160 double; from $180 suite. Summer, $90–$125 single; $100–$135 double; from $160 suite. AE, DC, MC, V. **Parking:** Free.

One of the best choices if you'd like to be in the center of Charlotte Amalie, only a 10-minute taxi ride east of the airport, this many-balconied hotel enjoys one of the highest rates of repeat reservations on the island. Built in 1968 and renovated in 1990, it has rooms arranged around a massive central atrium that contains a fountain, the Atrium Restaurant, a popular bar, and a rectangular swimming pool, with facilities for children. Some 54 harborfront rooms open onto beautiful views of some of the world's largest cruise ships. There is no beach nearby, but management runs frequent shuttle buses to the island beaches. Bedrooms are comfortably modern, with marble-trimmed bathrooms.

INEXPENSIVE

BUNKER HILL, Bunkers' Hill, 7 Commandant Gade, Charlotte Amalie,

St. Thomas, USVI 00802. Tel. 809/774-8056. 11 rms, 4 suites. A/C TV TEL

$ Rates (including continental breakfast): Winter, $70–$80 single; $80 double; from $90 suite. Summer, $60 single; $70 double; from $80 suite. MC, V. **Parking:** Free.

This clean and centrally situated guest lodge is suitable for students and others on a strict budget who don't want to sacrifice comfort and safety. Bunker Hill lies right in the heart of town, across from the post office, just a short walk from Main Street and all the major restaurants of Charlotte Amalie. A kitchenette is provided if you want to prepare your own meals.

GALLEON HOUSE, Government Hill (P.O. Box 6577), Charlotte Amalie, St. Thomas, USVI 00801. Tel. 809/774-6952, or toll free 800/524-2052. Fax 809/774-6952. 14 rms (12 with bath). A/C TV TEL

$ Rates (including continental breakfast): Winter, $59 single without bath, $105 single with bath; $69 double without bath, $115 double with bath. Summer, $49 single without bath, $69 single with bath; $59 double without bath, $79 double with bath. AE, MC, V. **Parking:** Free.

The main attraction of this place is its location, at the east end of Main Street, next to the Hotel 1829 on Government Hill, about one block from the main shopping section of St. Thomas. You'll walk up a long flight of stairs past a neighboring restaurant's veranda to reach the concrete terrace that doubles as this hotel's reception area. The rooms are scattered in several hillside buildings, and each contains a ceiling fan or air conditioning. There's a small pool on the grounds. The continental breakfast consists of fresh baked goods, juice, and coffee, and is served on the veranda overlooking the harbor.

ISLAND VIEW, 11-C Contant (P.O. Box 1903), St. Thomas, USVI 00803. Tel. 809/774-4270, or toll free 800/524-2023 for reservations only. Fax 809/774-6167. 14 rms (11 with bath), 1 suite. TEL **Directions:** From the airport, turn right to Route 33, then cut left and continue to Scott Free Road where you go left and look for the sign.

$ Rates (including continental breakfast): Winter, $58 single without bath, $90 single with bath; $63 double without bath, $95 double with bath. Summer, $40 single without bath, $63 single with bath; $45 double without bath, $68 double with bath. $4 surcharge for stays of only 1 night. AE, MC, V. **Parking:** Free.

You'll enter this guesthouse 545 feet up on Crown Mountain, overlooking St. Thomas Harbor and Charlotte Amalie, through a large gallery with a view. There are four main-floor rooms plus other poolside rooms. Six units are in a recent addition (three with kitchens and all with baths and balconies). The bedrooms are cooled by breezes and fans, and the newer addition has optional air conditioning. A self-service, open-air bar on the gallery operates on the honor system.

WHERE TO DINE

The cuisine on St. Thomas is among the top in the entire West Indies. Prices, unfortunately, are high, and many of the best spots can only be reached by taxi. With a few exceptions, the finest and most charming restaurants aren't in Charlotte Amalie but are out on the island.

IN CHARLOTTE AMALIE

BLACKBEARD'S CASTLE, 38–39 Dronningens Gade. Tel. 776-4321.
Cuisine: AMERICAN/SEAFOOD. **Reservations:** Recommended for dinner.
$ Prices: Appetizers $4.50–$9.50; main courses $16.50–$26. AE, MC, V.
Open: Lunch Mon–Sat 11:30am–2:30pm; dinner daily 6:30–10:30pm; brunch Sun 11am–3pm.

This previously recommended hotel at the east end of town offers an elegant dining room, with one of the best harbor views on the island, featuring seafood and nouvelle

ST. THOMAS DINING

Alexander's 3
Blackbeard's Castle 7
Café Normandie 3
Chart House Restaurant 4
East Coast 13
Eunice's 15
Fiddle Leaf 5

For the Birds 11
The Green Parrot 17
Hotel 1829 6
The Mark St. Thomas 8
Palm Court Restaurant 12
Piccola Marina Cafe 14
Raffles 10

Romano's Restaurant 16
Seagrape 18
Sugar Reef Cafe 2
Victor's Hide Out 1
Windjammer Restaurant 9

Airport ✈

American cuisine. Awarded three gold medals for ambience, Caribbean dishes, and overall food in local contests, owners Bob Harrington and Henrique Konzen offer one of the best Sunday brunches on the island. Dinners include frequently changing specials—sautéed duck with pink peppercorn demi-glace, and sautéed lobster with grapefruit beurre blanc and caviar. Pastas are available in half portions as appetizers. Lunches are slightly less elaborate and about one-third the price, and include salads, delicately seasoned platters, and frothy rum-based drinks. Don't miss the ornate cast-iron chandelier hanging in the anteroom of the bar.

FIDDLE LEAF, 31 Kongens Gade, Government Hill. Tel. 775-2810.

Cuisine: SEAFOOD/FRENCH/CARIBBEAN. **Reservations:** Recommended.
$ Prices: Appetizers $5–$9.50; main courses $16.75–$26. AE, MC, V.
Open: Lunch Mon–Fri 11:30am–2:30pm; dinner Tues–Sun 6:30–10pm.
Closed: Mid-Sept to mid-Oct.

Lushly filled with verdant plants, lots of lattices, and an open, contemporary Caribbean decor, this imaginative restaurant serves some of the most creative food on the island. Nestled next to the Hotel 1829, east of Main Street and up a hill, it offers a menu which rotates weekly according to whatever ingredients are flown in from the U.S. mainland. Especially flavorful is the array of fresh fish, the fresh-smoked breast of duckling, the roast rack of lamb with Caribbean herbs, fresh salads sometimes prepared at tableside, and a succulent version of filet mignon.

HOTEL 1829, Kongens Gade. Tel. 776-1829.

Cuisine: CONTINENTAL. **Reservations:** Required.
$ Prices: Appetizers $5.50–$12.50; main courses $22–$40. AE, MC, V.
Open: Dinner only, Mon–Sat 6–10pm.

At the east end of Main Street, the Hotel 1829 is graceful and historic (see "Where to Stay," above), and its restaurant serves some of the finest food on St. Thomas. Guests walk up the hill and climb the stairs of this old structure, and then head for the attractive bar for a before-dinner drink. Dining is on a terrace or in the main room, whose walls are made from ships' ballast. The floor is made of Moroccan tiles, two centuries old. For an appetizer, try escargots maître d'hôtel or one of the soups, such as cold cucumber or lobster bisque, made here fresh daily. Fish and meat dishes are usually excellent along with many grill dishes. The specialty of the house is the award-winning soufflé; try chocolate, amaretto, or raspberry.

THE MARK ST. THOMAS, Blackbeard's Hill. Tel. 774-5511.

Cuisine: CONTINENTAL. **Reservations:** Recommended.
$ Prices: Appetizers $4.50–$9.25; main courses $16.75–$21.50. AE, DC, MC, V.
Open: Dinner only, daily 5:30–10pm. **Closed:** Sun in summer.

Up a hill at the east end of Main Street in a previously recommended inn, the Mark St. Thomas has quickly become known as one of the finest in Charlotte Amalie. Guests dine on an open-air terrace of a room overlooking the harbor. Arrive early for a before-dinner drink. Built in 1785, the Mark was once a private residence for the many sea captains, traders, and merchants who have passed through here.

The chef is among the finest on the island, and he uses the freshest available ingredients for his classical dishes. Begin with a selection of tapas, Spanish hor d'oeuvres, or cold Chinese noodles with sesame, or pan-fried crab cakes. For a main dish, try New York strip steak, pan-fried scallops with chives, or roast duck with a Cassis sauce. The wine list has a good selection of Stateside and French vintages. Coconut tuile is the dessert specialty.

AT COMPASS POINT

FOR THE BIRDS, Scott Beach, near Compass Point. Tel. 775-6431.

Cuisine: TEX-MEX. **Reservations:** Not required.
$ Prices: Appetizers $2.50–$7; main courses $10–$30. AE, MC, V.
Open: Lunch daily 11am–3pm; dinner daily 6–10:30pm.

Set in a low-slung bungalow whose green roof matches the growth around it, this pleasant restaurant east of Charlotte Amalie offers reasonably priced, well-prepared food in gargantuan helpings. The surf and a sandy beach are a few steps away. Select heaps of nachos or an entire loaf of deep-fried onion rings, a plate of the best baby back ribs on the island, filet mignon, or southern fried catfish. There's also a selection of such Mexican specialties as beef or chicken enchiladas, chimichangas, and burritos. Margaritas are huge, 46 ounces, and beer comes in mason jars. Entertainment such as live rock 'n' roll is featured.

RAFFLES, 41 Frydenhoj, Compass Point. Tel. 775-6004.
   Cuisine: CONTINENTAL/SEAFOOD. **Reservations:** Required. **Transportation:** Taxi.
   $ Prices: Appetizers $5–$8; main courses $12–$22. AE, MC, V.
   Open: Dinner only, Tues–Sun 6:30–10:30pm.
Named after the legendary hotel in Singapore, this establishment is filled with tropical accents more evocative of the South Pacific than of the Caribbean. The furnishings include peacock chairs, lots of wicker, and ceiling fans. A pianist plays Gershwin and Porter during dinner, and showtime is at 10:30pm—a little risqué, with Noel Coward renditions, but it's lots of fun. You can choose from fresh seafood, beef, veal, lamb, chicken, and live Maine lobster. The fish of the day is freshly caught and well prepared, with various tasty sauces. The chef has also added Maryland softshell crabs and Florida alligator to the menu. Raffles nestles beside the lagoon at Compass Point, east of Charlotte Amalie.

WINDJAMMER RESTAURANT, 41 Frydenhoj, Compass Point Marina. Tel. 775-6194.
   Cuisine: GERMAN/AMERICAN. **Reservations:** Required. **Transportation:** Taxi.
   $ Prices: Appetizers $5.75–$6.50; main courses $7.50–$30. MC, V.
   Open: Dinner only, Mon–Sat 5–10pm. **Closed:** Sept–Oct.
Much of the paneling and the smoothly finished bar of this cozy place are crafted from thick slabs of island mahogany. The extensive menu features more than 30 main dishes of fish, shrimp, lobster, veal, chicken, and steaks; many reflect the restaurant's German heritage—snapper Adlon (a boneless snapper filet topped with shrimp and mushrooms), steak King Ludwig (a 14-ounce strip steak smothered in onions and mushrooms), rahmschnitzel (veal medallions in a heady cream sauce with fresh mushrooms), and chicken à la Bremen (a casserole of boneless chicken breast with bacon, mussels, peas, mushrooms, shrimp, and asparagus). Appetizers include what might be the best escargots on the island and a unique veal soup. The Key lime pie, wonderfully light and creamy cheesecake, chocolate layer cake, and apple strudel are all homemade.

AT FRENCHTOWN

ALEXANDER'S, rue de St. Barthélemy, Frenchtown. Tel. 774-4349.
   Cuisine: CONTINENTAL. **Reservations:** Recommended.
   $ Prices: Appetizers $5–$8; main courses $11–$18. AE, MC, V.
   Open: Lunch Mon–Sat 11:30am–5pm; dinner Mon–Sat 5:30–10pm.
Alexander's, west of town, will accommodate you in air-conditioned comfort with picture windows overlooking the harbor. It's named for its Austrian-born owner, Alexander Treml. The restaurant has only 12 tables, but it offers Austrian specialties served with flair. There's a heavy emphasis on seafood, including conch schnitzel. Other dishes include a mouth-watering wienerschnitzel, Nürnberger rostbraten, goulash, and homemade pâté. For dessert, try the homemade strudel, either apple or cheese, or the Schwartzwald torte. Lunch consists of a variety of crêpes, quiches, and a daily chef's special.

CAFE NORMANDIE, rue de St. Barthélemy, Frenchtown. Tel. 774-1622.
   Cuisine: FRENCH. **Reservations:** Required.
   $ Prices: Appetizers $4.50–$6; main courses $23.50–$40. AE, DC, MC, V.
   Open: Lunch Tues–Sun 11:30am–2:30pm; dinner Tues–Sun 6:30–9:30pm.
The fixed-price meals offered here are one of the best dining values on the islands.

Although there is a selection of à la carte hors d'oeuvres, the main courses (see above) are actually fixed-price dinners, and include soup, a fresh garden salad, and individually prepared main dishes. Your meal begins with hors d'oeuvres, perhaps made with seafood, plus soup, often French onion. Then you're served a salad and sorbet (to clear your palate) before your main course, which you select from specialties ranging from langouste to beef Wellington or chicken breast with champagne sauce. The dessert special (not featured on the fixed-price meal) is their original chocolate-fudge pie. Located west of town, the restaurant is air-conditioned, and the candlelight makes it quite elegant. It's beautifully run and the service is excellent. The dress code is informal, but don't show up in a bathing suit. A la carte meals are available too.

CHART HOUSE RESTAURANT, at the West Indies Inn, 8 Honduras, Frenchtown. Tel. 774-4262.
   Cuisine: STEAK. **Reservations:** Not accepted.
$ Prices: Appetizers $4.55–$8.35; main courses $11.25–$34.75. AE, DC, MC, V.
   Open: Dinner only, Sun–Thurs 5–10pm, Fri 5–11pm.

The restaurant is on the same property as this previously recommended hotel (the site of the Russian consulate in the 19th century), but is run separately. You may want to journey west of Frenchtown Village for dinner in this rebuilt Victorian villa. The dining gallery is a large open terrace fronting the sea. Cocktail service starts at 5pm 7 days a week, and the bartender will make you his special drink called a Bailey's banana colada. The restaurant features the best salad bar on the island, with a choice of 30 to 40 items, which comes with the dinner. Steaks are a specialty, but menu choices range from chicken to Australian lobster tail. Of course, this chain is known for serving the finest cut of prime rib anywhere. For dessert, order the famous Chart House "mud pie."

SUGAR REEF CAFE, 17 Crown Bay. Tel. 776-4466.
   Cuisine: CONTINENTAL. **Reservations:** Required.
$ Prices: Appetizers $6–$9; main courses $14–$32. AE, MC, V.
   Open: Lunch Mon–Fri 11:30am–2:30pm; dinner 6–10pm.

Just west of Frenchtown, on the waterfront off East Gregerie Channel, this restaurant is a good choice for a quiet afternoon of boat-watching. Guests anchor in at the mahogany bar beneath ceiling beams and swirling fans in a breezy open-sided pavilion. Drinks are served all day and often late into the night. Lunch is likely to include a choice of deli sandwiches, veal piccata, and omelets. The dinner menu features grilled yellowtail tuna, Caribbean lobster, sautéed veal medallions with dry vermouth and capers, and the Sugar Reef fresh catch of the day.

ON THE NORTH COAST

EUNICE'S, 67 Smith Bay, Rte. 38. Tel. 775-3975.
   Cuisine: WEST INDIAN. **Reservations:** Recommended for dinner.
$ Prices: Appetizers $6.50–$7.95; main courses $14.95–$24.95. AE, MC, V.
   Open: Lunch Mon–Sat 11am–4pm; dinner daily 6–10pm.

S A 30-minute taxi ride east of the airport, just east of the Coral World turnoff, is one of the best-known local restaurants, which went from a simple shack to a modern building. A hard-fisted collection of Stateside construction workers, West Indian locals, and dozens of tourists from nearby Stouffer's Grand Beach crowd into its confines for savory platters of island food served in generous proportions. A popular concoction called a Queen Mary (tropical fruits laced with dark rum) is a favorite. Dinner specialties include conch fritters, broiled or fried fish (especially dolphin), sweet-potato pie, and a number of chalkboard specials which are usually served with fungi, rice, or plantain. On the lunch menu are fishburgers, sandwiches, and such daily specials as Virgin Islands doved pork or mutton. (Doving, pronounced "*dough*-ving," involves baking sliced meat while basting with a combination of its own juices, tomato paste, Kitchen Bouquet, and island herbs.) Key lime pie is a favorite dessert.

THE GREEN PARROT, in the Magens Point Resort, Magens Bay Rd. Tel. 775-5500.
Cuisine: NOUVELLE AMERICAN/CARIBBEAN. **Reservations:** Recommended. **Transportation:** A 15-minute taxi ride west of Charlotte Amalie.
$ Prices: Appetizers $6–$7; main courses $14–$30. AE, MC, V.
Open: Breakfast/lunch Mon–Sat 8am–2:30pm; dinner daily 6–10pm; brunch Sun 10:30am–2:30pm (bar daily noon–midnight). **Closed:** June.
Arrive early for a before-dinner drink in the restaurant's bar overlooking Magens Bay. Breakfast and lunch are presented in the garden terrace daily, and Sunday's Louisiana brunch is often an island event with live jazz. Don't overlook the Green Parrot as an evening dining possibility either; take a taxi if you don't want to drive on the torturous Route 42 at night. Candlelit dinners are likely to include poached salmon, Caribbean duck, and local red snapper or other fresh fish. Try the delectable sweetbreads.

ROMANO'S RESTAURANT, 97 Smith Bay Rd. Tel. 775-0045.
Cuisine: ITALIAN. **Reservations:** Required.
$ Prices: Appetizers $6.95–$8.95; main courses $19.95–$24.95. AE, MC, V.
Open: Dinner only, Mon–Sat 6:30–10:30pm. **Closed:** Aug.
Located on the sandy-bottomed flatlands near Coral World, the sophisticated creation of New Jersey–born Tony Romano is skillfully decorated with exposed brick and well-stocked wine racks. Considered the best Italian restaurant on St. Thomas, it specializes in linguine con pesto, penne piancllo (with mushrooms, prosciutto, and pine nuts), osso bucco, scallopine marsala, and broiled salmon with white wine, lemon, tomatoes, and herb sauce. Many people say the best dish in the house is lingua de bue brasta (veal tongue gently sautéed with mushrooms, red wine, and fresh herbs).

SAPPHIRE BEACH

SEAGRAPE, in the Sapphire Beach Resort & Marina, Rte. 38, Smith Bay Rd. Tel. 775-9750.
Cuisine: CONTINENTAL/AMERICAN. **Reservations:** Recommended. **Transportation:** Taxi.
$ Prices: Appetizers $4.95–$10.95; main courses $16.95–$35. AE, DC, MC, V.
Open: Lunch Mon–Sat 11am–3pm; dinner daily 6–10pm; brunch Sun 10:30am–3pm.
One of the finest dining rooms along the eastern coast of St. Thomas is open to the sea breezes on one of the most famous beaches in the Virgin Islands. A well-trained staff and the quality of the food create an undeniable elegance. If you're enjoying the beach during the day, you can order from the luncheon menu which includes croissant sandwiches and crisp, freshly made salads; a children's menu is also offered. The dinner menu includes smoked Scottish salmon, lobster Fra Diavolo, tarragon chicken, red snapper filet, and filet mignon. A variety of local fish and seafood is prepared nightly and served with fresh vegetables cooked to perfection. For dessert, the chef is rightly proud of his Key lime pie. A steel band plays on Tuesday and Friday from 8 to 11pm. A Sunday brunch offers such delectable dishes as tortellini Alfredo and French toast Grand Marnier.

COWPET BAY

PALM COURT RESTAURANT, in the Bolongo Elysian Beach Resort, Cowpet Bay, Red Hook. Tel. 775-1000.
Cuisine: INTERNATIONAL. **Reservations:** Recommended. **Transportation:** Taxi.
$ Prices: Appetizers $4.25–$9.50; main courses $22–$28. AE, DC, MC, V.
Open: Lunch daily 11:30am–2:30pm; dinner daily 6:30–10pm.
The Palm Court is the premier restaurant of this previously recommended resort. The cuisine, decor, and service create a subtly Europeanized kind of glamour set in an open-sided pavilion near the sands of the beach. The lunch menu lists pastas, exotic salads, soups, sandwiches, and brochettes of chicken or

shrimp, with a good meal costing around $15. Dinner is more elaborate, and might include a spinach-and-oyster chowder; a vegetarian mousse of the day; spinach salad flambéed with Dijon mustard, Cointreau, and cognac; fricasée of monkfish garnished with scallops, crayfish, and Armagnac sauce; and medallions of veal with lobster, white asparagus, and Pernod.

RED HOOK

EAST COAST, Rte. 38 at Red Hook. Tel. 775-1919.
Cuisine: AMERICAN/SEAFOOD. **Reservations:** Not accepted. **Transportation:** Red Hook bus.
$ Prices: Appetizers $3.75–$5.75; main courses $6.75–$16.75. AE, MC, V.
Open: Dinner daily 5:30–11pm.

East Coast packs a Stateside crowd of beer-guzzling sports fans into its pine-sheathed interior nightly. They watch sports on TV and cheer their favorites. What is not readily apparent is that the adjacent restaurant serves very good meals. Leave your name with the hostess and then enjoy a beer at the bar. You can dine in a denlike haven or on an outdoor terrace in back. Start with a soup of the day, then follow with snapper native style or fresh Caribbean lobster. Habitués come here for the fresh grilled catch of the day, often a game fish such as wahoo.

PICCOLA MARINA CAFE, Rte. 38 at Red Hook. Tel. 775-6350.
Cuisine: ITALIAN/SEAFOOD. **Reservations:** Recommended in winter. **Transportation:** Red Hook bus.
$ Prices: Appetizers $4.95–$6.95; main courses $10.95–$18.95. AE, MC, V.
Open: Lunch Mon–Sat 11am–3pm; dinner daily 6–10pm; brunch Sun 11:30am–2:30pm.

A popular eatery, with an open veranda offering a view of the yachts moored at this marina, the Piccola offers lunch with various salads from Caesar to Greek, a fresh antipasto primavera, and an assortment of sandwiches, plus charcoal-broiled hamburgers. Sunday brunch offers everything from the traditional eggs Benedict to flaky croissants filled with Canadian bacon. All the food is homemade with only fresh ingredients. Fresh pasta dishes, such as Alfredo, carbonara, and pesto, and fresh fish, steak, chicken, and shrimp are on the dinner menu. Desserts include a homemade brownie specialty on Sunday and award-winning cheesecakes.

NEAR THE SUB BASE

VICTOR'S HIDE OUT, 32A Sub Base, off Rte. 30. Tel. 776-9379.
Cuisine: WEST INDIAN/AMERICAN. **Reservations:** Recommended. **Transportation:** Taxi.
$ Prices: Appetizers $3.50–$7.50; main courses $8.95–$29.95. AE, MC, V.
Open: Lunch Mon–Sat 11:30am–3:30pm; dinner daily 5:30–10pm.

Victor's is operated by Victor Sydney, who comes from Montserrat. You never know who's going to show up here—maybe Bill Cosby, perhaps José Feliciano. Victor's has some of the best local dishes on the island, but first you must find it, as it's truly a place to hide out. If you're driving, call for directions; otherwise, take a taxi. On a hilltop perch, the large, airy restaurant serves fresh lobster prepared Montserrat style (that is, in a creamy sauce) or grilled in the shell. You might also ask for a plate of juicy barbecued ribs. For dessert, try the coconut, custard, or apple pie.

WHAT TO SEE & DO

IN CHARLOTTE AMALIE

The color and charm of a real Caribbean waterfront town come vividly to life in the capital of St. Thomas, **Charlotte Amalie**, where most visitors begin their sightseeing on the small island. In days of yore, seafarers from all over the globe flocked to this old-world Danish town, as did pirates and members of the Confederacy, who used the port during the American Civil War. St. Thomas was also the biggest slave market in the world.

The old warehouses once used for storing pirate goods still stand, and, for the most part, house today's shops. In fact, the main streets (called "Gade" here in honor of their Danish heritage) are now a virtual shopping mall and are usually packed. Sandwiched among these shops are a few historic buildings, most of which can be covered on foot in about 2 hours (see the walking tour, below). Before starting your tour, stop off in the so-called Grand Hotel, near Emancipation Park. No longer a hotel, it contains, along with shops, a **visitor center** (tel. 774-8784).

WALKING TOUR — Charlotte Amalie

Start: King's Wharf.
Finish: Waterfront.
Time: 2½ hours.
Best Times: Any day between 10am and 5pm.
Worst Times: When major cruise ships are in port.

Begin your tour along the eastern harborfront at:

1. **King's Wharf,** site of the Virgin Islands Legislature, housed in the apple-green military barracks, which date from 1874. From here, walk away from the harbor up Fort Pladsen to:
2. **Fort Christian,** dating from 1672. Named after the Danish king, Christian V, the structure has been everything from a governor's residence to a jail. Many pirates were hanged in the courtyard of the fort. Some of the cells have been turned into the Virgin Islands Museum, which displays minor Native American artifacts. It's open Monday through Friday from 8am to 5pm and on Saturday from 1 to 5pm. Admission is free. Continue walking up Fort Pladsen to:
3. **Emancipation Park,** where a proclamation freeing African slaves and identured European servants was read on July 3, 1848. Facing the north side of the park is the:
4. **Grand Hotel,** where a visitor center dispenses information. When this hotel was launched in 1837, it was considered a rather grand address, but it later fell into decay and finally closed in 1975. Its former guest rooms upstairs have been turned into offices and a restaurant. Northwest of the park, at Main Street and Tolbod Gade, stands the:
5. **Central Post Office,** which displays murals by Stephen Dohanos, who became famous as a *Saturday Evening Post* cover artist. From the post office, walk east along Norre Gade to Fort Pladsen, to the:
6. **Frederik Lutheran Church,** built between 1780 and 1793. The original Georgian-style building, financed by a free black parishioner, Jean Reeneaus, was rebuilt in 1825 after a fire, and was rebuilt again in 1870 after it was damaged in a hurricane. After exiting the church, walk east along Norre Gade to Lille Taarne Gade. Turn left (north), climb to Kongens Gade (King Street), and pass through a neighborhood of law firms to:
7. **Government House,** the administrative headquarters for all the Virgin Islands. It's been the center of official life in the islands since it was built—around the time of the American Civil War. Visitors are allowed on the first two floors, Monday through Saturday from 8am to noon and 1 to 5pm. Some paintings by former resident Camille Pissarro are on display, as are works by other St. Thomian artists. Turn left on Kongens Gade. Directly to the left of Government House, on the same side of the street, stands the:
8. **Frederik Church Parsonage,** dating from 1725, one of the oldest houses on

the island. It's the only structure in the Government Hill district to retain its simple 18th-century lines. Continue to walk west along Kongens Gade until you reach:

9. Hotel 1829. The former Lavalette House, it was designed by one of the leading merchants of Charlotte Amalie. This is a landmark building, and a hotel of great charm and character that has attracted many of the island's most famous guests over the years.

REFUELING STOP **Hotel 1829,** Kongens Gade, provides a veranda with a view, ideal for a drink at midday but perfect for a sundowner. You may fall in love with the place, abandon the walking tour, and stick around for dinner—it's that special. Its bar is open daily from 10am to midnight, and drinks cost $2.75 and up.

Next door (still on the same side of the street) observe the:

10. Yellow-Brick Building, from 1854. It was built in what local architects called "the style of Copenhagen." You can go inside the building, as part of it is filled with shops.

At this point, you can double back slightly on Kongens Gade if you'd like to climb the famous:

11. 99 Steps. The steps, which were erected in the early 1700s, take you to the summit of Government Hill, from which you'll see the 18th-century:

12. Crown House, immediately to your right on the south side of the street. This was a stately home that was the residence of two of the past governors of the Virgin Islands. Here the rich and privileged lived in the 1700s, surrounded by Chinese wall hangings, a crystal chandelier from Versailles, and carved West Indian furniture. It was also the home of von Scholten, the Danish ruler who issued a proclamation of emancipation in 1848.

Walk back down the steps and continue right along Kongens Gade, then down a pair of old brick steps until you reach Garden Street. Across the way you'll pass the Straw Factory (see "Savvy Shopping," below). Go right on Garden Street and take a left onto Crystal Gade. On your left, at the corner of Nye Gade and Crystal Gade, you'll see:

13. St. Thomas Reformed Church, formerly Dutch and dating from 1844. Designed like a Greek temple, much of its original structure has been preserved intact. Continue up Crystal Gade. On your right (north side), you'll come to the:

14. St. Thomas Synagogue, the oldest synagogue in continuous use under the American flag. It still maintains the tradition of sand on the floor, commemorating the exodus from Egypt. Erected in 1833 by Sephardic Jews, it was built of local stone along with ballast brick from Denmark and mortar made of molasses and sand. It's open to visitors Monday through Friday from 9am to 4pm.

Retrace your steps to Raadets Gade, turn south toward the water, and cross the famous Vimmelskaft Gade or "Back Street" of Charlotte Amalie. Continue along Raadets Gade until you reach:

15. Main Street (Dronningens Gade), the most famous shopping street of St. Thomas and its major artery. Turn right and walk along Main Street until you come to the mid-19th-century:

16. Camille Pissarro Building, on your right side, at the Amsterdam Sauer Jewelry Store. Pissarro, a Spanish Jew who became one of the founders of French impressionism, was born in this building as Jacob Pizaro in 1830. Before moving to Paris and becoming involved with some of the greatest artists of his day, he worked for his father in a store along Main Street.

Continue along Main Street and on your right you'll pass the:

17. Enid M. Baa Public Library, the former von Bretton House, dating from 1818. Keep heading west until you reach:

18. Market Square, officially known as Rothschild Francis Square, at the point where Main Street intersects Strand Gade. This was the center of a large

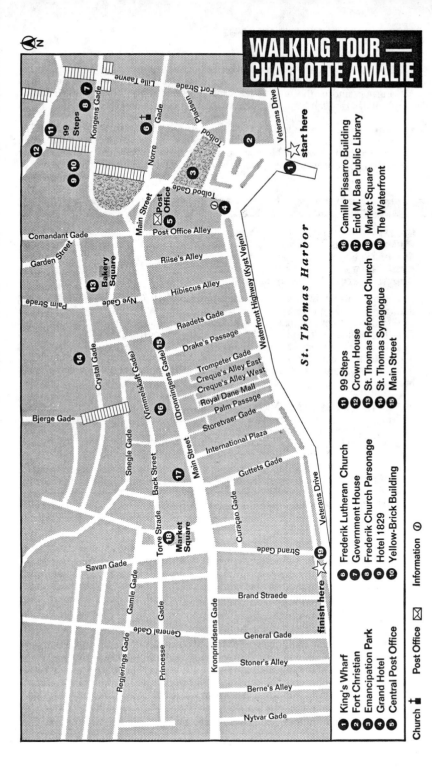

WALKING TOUR — CHARLOTTE AMALIE

St. Thomas Harbor

⊕ N

Church ✝   Post Office ⊠   Information ⊕

1. King's Wharf
2. Fort Christian
3. Emancipation Park
4. Grand Hotel
5. Central Post Office
6. Frederik Lutheran Church
7. Government House
8. Frederik Church Parsonage
9. Hotel 1829
10. Yellow-Brick Building
11. 99 Steps
12. Crown House
13. St. Thomas Reformed Church
14. St. Thomas Synagogue
15. Main Street
16. Camille Pissarro Building
17. Enid M. Baa Public Library
18. Market Square
19. The Waterfront

start here

finish here

slave-trading market before the emancipation was proclaimed. Today it's an open-air fruit and vegetable market selling, among other items, genips (break open the skin and suck the pulp off a pit). The wrought-iron roof came from Europe, and at the turn of the century covered a railway station. It's open Monday through Saturday, with Saturday its busiest day.

If the genip doesn't satisfy you, take Strand Gade down to:

19. The Waterfront (Kyst Vejen), where you can purchase a fresh coconut. The vendor will whack off the top with a machete, so you can drink the sweet milk from its hull. Here you'll have an up-close preview of one of the most spectacular harbors in the West Indies, which is usually filled with cruise ships.

DRIVING TOUR — St. Thomas

Start: Fort Christian.
Finish: Magens Bay Beach.
Time: 2½ hours.
Best Times: Sunday, when traffic is lightest.
Worst Times: Wednesday and Saturday, when traffic is heaviest.

Begin at Fort Christian in the eastern part of Charlotte Amalie and head west along the waterfront. To your left you'll see cruise ships anchored offshore and on your right will be all the stores that make Charlotte Amalie the shopping mall of the Caribbean. Continue on Route 30 and pass the Cyril E. King Airport on your left. As the road forks toward the airport, keep right along Route 30, which runs parallel to the airport, where you'll have a very close view of jumbo jets from the United States landing.

At about 2.4 miles from Fort Christian, the modern complexes on your right will be:

1. The University of the Virgin Islands, which is the major university in all the Virgin Islands. It is a modern complex with beautifully landscaped campus grounds. Continue along until you reach:

2. Brewers Bay, on your left, with its good sand beach. You may want to park near here and go for a swim, as this is considered one of the more desirable beaches on the island.

Continue 3.8 miles west, climbing uphill through scrub country along a hilly drive past the junction with Route 301. This far west Route 30 is called:

3. Fortuna Road, considered one of the most scenic areas of St. Thomas, with panoramic views of the water and offshore islands on your left. Along the way will be parking areas where you can pull off and enjoy the view. The one on Bethesda Hill is particularly spectacular. The names of the districts you pass through— Bonne Esperance and Perservance—come from the old plantations that used to stand here. The area is now primarily residential. At Bordeaux Hill, you descend sharply and the road narrows until you come to a dead end.

At this point, turn around and head back east along Route 30. The road is badly marked, and you'll probably need the *Official Road Map of the United States Virgin Islands*. Turn left and head northeast at the junction with Route 301. You'll come to the junction with:

4. Crown Mountain Road, the most scenic road in the Virgin Islands. Turn left at this junction onto Route 33. The road will sweep northward before it makes an abrupt switch to the east. You'll be traversing the most mountainous heartland of St. Thomas. Expect hairpin turns during your descent. You'll often have to reduce your speed to 10 m.p.h., especially in the Mafolie district. The road will eventually lead to the junction with Route 37, where you should go left, but only for a short distance, until you reach the junction with Route 40. At one point Routes 37 and 40 become the same highway, but when they separate, turn right and stay on Route 40 to Drakes Seat.

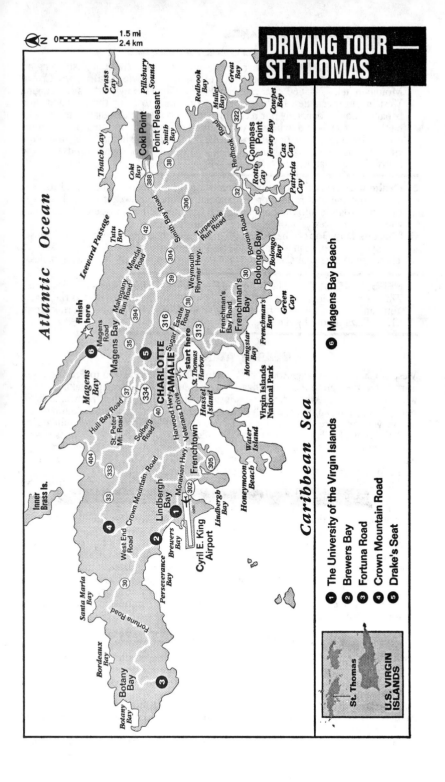

DRIVING TOUR —
ST. THOMAS

Atlantic Ocean

Caribbean Sea

St. Thomas Harbor

Charlotte Amalie

Magens Bay

Magens Bay Beach

1. The University of the Virgin Islands
2. Brewers Bay
3. Fortuna Road
4. Crown Mountain Road
5. Drake's Seat
6. Magens Bay Beach

St. Thomas

U.S. VIRGIN ISLANDS

start here

finish here

0   1.5 mi
     2.4 km

REFUELING STOP A former hotel which is now a traditional stopping-off point for mountain driving tours of St. Thomas, the **Mountain Top,** Crown Mountain (tel. 774-5660), is a cafeterialike place (lunch only) with daily changing West Indian specialties. But most people come here to enjoy the view and sip a banana daiquiri (definitely not recommended if you're the designated driver). The bar here, in fact, is said to be where the banana daiquiri was invented. The stopover is considered to be one of the most scenic perches in St. Thomas; it opens onto a view of Sir Francis Drake Channel, which separates the U.S. Virgin Islands from the British Virgin Islands.

5. **Drake's Seat** is the legendary perch where Sir Francis Drake is said to have figured out the best routes for the colonial European powers to take their ships from the Atlantic into the Caribbean Sea. Continue left onto Route 35. The road will veer northwest. Follow it all the way to:
6. **Magens Bay Beach,** hailed as one of the most beautiful beaches in the world. Here you can rent Sunfish sailboats, glass-bottom paddleboats, and windsurfers. There are lounge chairs, changing facilities, showers, lockers, and picnic tables.

REFUELING STOP The **Magens Bay Bar & Grill,** Magens Bay Beach (tel. 775-4669), is an ideal place for light meals, and the snack bar overlooks the beach. You can order sandwiches from $3.50, salads from $4.25, and soft drinks from $1.75. Pizza is sold by the slice.

NEARBY ATTRACTIONS

West of Charlotte Amalie, Route 30 (Veteran's Drive) will take you to **Frenchtown** (turn left at the sign to the Villa Olga). This was settled by a French-speaking people who were uprooted when the Swedes invaded and took over their homeland in St. Barts. They were known for the wearing of *cha-chas* or straw hats. Many of the people who live here today are the direct descendants of those long-ago immigrants.

This colorful village, many of whose residents engage in fishing, contains several interesting restaurants and taverns. Now that Charlotte Amalie has been deemed a dangerous place to be at night, Frenchtown has picked up the business, and it's the best choice for nighttime dancing, entertainment, and drinking.

The number-one tourist attraction of St. Thomas is a 20-minute drive north of St. Thomas. ✪ **Coral World Marine Park & Underwater Observatory,** Route 6, Coki Point (tel. 775-1555), is a marine complex that features a three-story underwater observation tower 100 feet offshore. Through windows you'll see sponges, deep-sea flowers, fish, and coral—underwater life in its natural state. In the Marine Gardens Aquarium, saltwater tanks display everything from sea horses to urchins: One 80,000-gallon reef tank features exotic marine life of the Caribbean; another tank is devoted to sea predators, with circling sharks and giant moray eels, among other creatures. Entrance is through a waterfall of cascading water. Also included in the marine park are a restaurant, Vista View Bar, duty-free shops, and a tropical nature trail. The complex is open daily from 9am to 6pm. Admission is $12 for adults, $7 for children.

SPORTS & RECREATION

BEACHES Chances are, your hotel will be right on the beach, or very close to one, and this is where you'll anchor for most of your stay. All the beaches in the Virgin Islands are public, and most lie anywhere from 2 to 5 miles from Charlotte Amalie.

The North Side I've already extolled the glory of ✪ **Magens Bay,** 3 miles north of the capital. Named one of the world's 10 most beautiful beaches, it charges 50¢ for adults and 25¢ for children. Changing facilities are available, and snorkeling gear and lounge chairs can be rented. Administered by the government, this beach is less than a mile long and lies between two mountains. There is no public transportation to reach it. From Charlotte Amalie, take Route 35 north all the way. The gates to the beach are open daily from 6am to 6pm (after 4 o'clock you'll need insect repellent).

In the northeast near Coral World, **Coki Beach** is good, but should be avoided when cruise ships are in port as it becomes overcrowded. Snorkelers are attracted here, as are pickpockets—so protect your valuables. Lockers can be rented at Coral World, next door. An East End bus runs to Smith Bay and lets you off at the gate to Coral World and Coki.

Also on the north side is **Stouffer Grand Beach,** one of the island's most beautiful, with the previously recommended hotel in the background. Many water sports are available at this beach, which opens onto Smith Bay and is in the vicinity of Coral World. The beach lies right off Route 38.

The South Side   On the south side near the Frenchman's Reef Hotel, **Morningstar** lies about 2 miles east of Charlotte Amalie. This is where you can wear your most daring swimwear. Or you can rent sailboards, sailboats, snorkeling equipment, and lounge chairs. The beach is reached by a cliff-front elevator at the Frenchman's Reef Hotel.

At the Limetree Beach Hotel, part of the Bolongo Bay Resorts, **Limetree Beach** has been called a classic, and lures those who like a serene spread of sand. You can feed hibiscus blossoms to iguanas, and rent snorkeling gear and lounge chairs. There is no public transportation, but the beach can easily be reached by taxi from Charlotte Amalie.

One of the most popular beaches, **Brewer's** lies in the southwest near the University of the Virgin Islands and can be reached by the public bus marked "Fortuna" heading west from Charlotte Amalie Road.

Near the airport, **Lindberg Beach** has a lifeguard, toilet facilities, and a bathhouse. It, too, lies on the Fortuna bus route heading west from Charlotte Amalie.

The East End   Small and special, **Secret Harbour** lies near a collection of condos whose owners you'll meet on the beach. With its white sand and coconut palms, it's a cliché of Caribbean charm. No public transportation stops here, but it's an easy taxi ride east of Charlotte Amalie heading toward Red Hook.

One of the finest on St. Thomas,   ✪ **Sapphire Beach** is set against the backdrop of the desirable Sapphire Beach Hotel complex, where you can lunch or order drinks. Windsurfers like it a lot, and snorkeling gear and lounge chairs can be rented. A large reef is found close to the shore, and there are good views of offshore cays and St. John. The beach of fine white coral sand opens onto beautiful views of the bay. To reach it, you can take the East End bus from Charlotte Amalie, going via Red Hook. Ask to be let off at the entrance to Sapphire Bay; it's not too far to walk from there toward the water.

BOATING   The biggest charter business in the Caribbean is done by Virgin Islanders. On St. Thomas most of the business centers around the Red Hook and Yacht Haven marinas.

Perhaps the easiest way to go out to sea is to charter "your yacht for the day" from **Yacht *Nightwind,*** Red Hook (tel. 809/775-4110, 24 hours a day), for $75 per person. You're granted a full-day sail with a champagne tropical lunch and open bar aboard this 50-foot yawl. You're also given free snorkeling equipment and instruction. Natives of New Jersey, Stephen and June March offer musical entertainment as well. If you're interested, ask about an attractive villa they have to rent.

New Horizons, whose office is at Suite 237, Red Hook Plaza (P.O. Box 16), Red Hook, St. Thomas, USVI 00802 (tel. 809/775-1171), offers windborne excursions amid the cays and reefs, which many visitors consider one of the high points of their trip. Classified as a two-masted 60-foot ketch, the ship was built in 1969 in Vancouver; it has circumnavigated the globe and has acted as a design prototype for other boats.

Owned and operated by Canadians Tim and Sue Krygsveld, it contains a hot-water shower, serves a specialty drink called a New Horizons Nooner (with a melon-liqueur base), and carries a complete line of snorkeling equipment for adults and children. A full-day excursion, with a "hot buffet Italian al fresco" and an open bar, costs $85 per person. Children aged 2 to 12, when accompanied by an adult, are charged $42.50. Excursions depart daily, weather permitting, from either the National Park Service Marina in Red Hook or from the Sapphire Beach Club Marina. Call ahead for reservations and information.

My Way (tel. 776-7751) is a 35-foot Pearson sloop which sails to the uninhabited island of Hans Lollick for $60 per person. Snorkeling equipment and instruction are provided, there's an all-day bar, and you have lunch on a deserted beach. Everything is included. Sailings leave from the north side of St. Thomas. Only four to six guests are taken.

True Love (tel. 775-6547) is a sleek 54-foot Malabar schooner that was used during the filming of *High Society* starring Bing Crosby and Grace Kelly (it gave its name to the Cole Porter duet they sang). It sails daily from 9am to 4pm from Red Hook into Pillsbury Sound. Bill and Sue Beer have sailed it since 1965. You can join one of Bill's snorkeling classes and later enjoy one of Sue's gourmet lunches with champagne. The cost is $75 per person.

Of course, if you want something more elaborate, you can go bareboating—that is, you can rent a craft where you're the captain. However, you must prove you're able to handle the craft before you're allowed to go out in it alone. On the other hand, if you'd like everything done for you, a fully crewed yacht with a captain at your service is the way to go on a charter plan. Either type of charter rental is available through **Avery's Boathouse,** P.O. Box 5248, Veterans Drive Station, Charlotte Amalie, St. Thomas, USVI 00803 (tel. 809/776-0113).

Rafting Adventures, Maritime Services International, 82 Red Hook Center, St. Thomas, USVI 00802 (tel. 809/779-2032), has been called "the most exciting boat trip in the Caribbean." Both half- and full-day tours are featured, and they visit such islands as St. John and Jost Van Dyke (the latter in the B.V.I.).

DEEP-SEA FISHING It's very good in the U.S. Virgins, and 19 world records have been set in recent years (8 for blue marlin). Sports fishing is offered on the *Fish Hawk* (tel. 775-9058). Captain Petrosky of New Jersey sails from Fish Hawk Marina Lagoon at the East End on his 48-foot diesel-powered craft, which is fully equipped with rods and reels. All equipment (but no lunch) is included in the rate of $350 per half day for up to six passengers. A full-day excursion, depending on how far the boat goes out, ranges from $700 to $800.

GOLF On the north shore, ✪ **Mahogany Run,** at the Mahogany Run Golf & Tennis Resort, Mahogany Run Road (tel. 775-5000), is an 18-hole, par-70 course. Designed by Tom and George Fazio, this is considered one of the most beautiful courses in the West Indies; cliffs and crashing sea waves are the ultimate hazards at the 13th and 14th holes. *Golf* magazine said, "There are 18 excellent reasons for golfers to visit St. Thomas, all at Mahogany Run." Greens fees depend on the time of year: January 1 to April 1 is the most expensive, when greens fees are $60; from July 1 to September 30 rates drop to their lowest point, $33 per 18 holes; in spring and autumn, greens fees are $45 for 18 holes.

SCUBA & SNORKELING With 30 spectacular reefs just off St. Thomas, the U.S. Virgins are rated as one of the "most beautiful areas in the world" by *Skin Diver* magazine.

St. Thomas Diving Club, Bolongo Bay Beach and Tennis Club (P.O. Box 7337), St. Thomas, USVI 00801 (tel. 809/776-2381), is a full-service, PADI five-star center, considered the best on the island. If you're a resident at Bolongo Bay Resorts (see "Where to Stay," above), you get such extras as a sail on the club's 52-foot *Heavenly Daze* to St. John, if you stay 7 or more nights. An open-water certification course, including four scuba dives, costs $350. An advanced open-water certification course, including five dives that can be accomplished in 2 days, costs $300. Every Thursday participants are taken on an all-day scuba excursion that includes a dive to the wreck of R.M.S. *Rhone* in the British Virgin Islands. This two-tank dive costs $150. You can also enjoy snorkeling for $25.

Joe Vogel Diving Co., P.O. Box 7322, St. Thomas, USVI 00801 (tel. 809/775-7610, or toll free 800/448-6224 to receive hotel/dive package materials), has been in business for some 30 years. The waterfront location is at the West Indies Inn, next to the Chart House Restaurant in Frenchtown. Ex-U.S. Navy frogman and company founder Joe Vogel still provides personal service and limits each group to seven divers for better safety and enjoyment. His 5-hour beginner scuba class, costing $60, is a classic in thoroughness. Other dives range from $32 to $42. Annual closing is mid-September to early October.

Dive In, in the Sapphire Beach Resort & Marina, Smith Bay Road, Route 38 (tel. 775-6100), is a well-recommended and complete diving center offering some of the finest diving services in the U.S. Virgin Islands, including professional instruction (beginner to advanced), daily beach and boat dives, custom dive packages, underwater photography and videotapes, snorkeling trips, and a full-service PADI dive center. An introductory resort course costs $55, an open-water certification course with four dives goes for $350, and a six-dive pass is $185. The location is especially convenient for clients of hotels on the East End.

TENNIS Outstanding courts are at the **Bolongo Bay Beach and Tennis Club,** Bolongo Bay (tel. 775-2489), which has four courts, two of which are lit until 11pm. It caters to members and hotel guests only, except for lessons, which cost $16 per half hour.

At **Frenchman's Reef Tennis Courts,** Flamboyant Point (tel. 774-8500, ext. 444), four courts are available and nonresidents are charged $10 a half hour per court. Lights stay on until 10pm.

At the famous **Bluebeard's Castle,** Bluebeard's Hill (tel. 774-1600), nonguests are charged $4 per hour to play on its two courts.

SAVVY SHOPPING

Shoppers not only have the benefits of St. Thomas's liberal duty-free allowances (Customs regulations are outlined in "Fast Facts," at the beginning of this chapter), but they also will find well-known brand names at savings of up to 60% off Stateside prices. However, to find true value, you often have to plow through a lot of junk. Many items offered for sale—binoculars, stereos, watches, cameras—can be matched in price at your hometown discount store. Therefore, you need to know the prices back home to determine if you're in fact making a savings.

Most of the shops, some of which occupy former pirate warehouses, are open Monday to Saturday from 9am to 5pm, regular business hours, and some stay open later. Nearly all stores close on Sunday and major holidays—unless a cruise ship is in port. Friday is the biggest cruise-ship visiting day at Charlotte Amalie (one day I counted eight at one time)—so try to avoid shopping then.

If you want to combine a little history with shopping, go into the courtyard of the old **Pissarro Building,** entered through an archway off Main Street. The impressionist painter lived here as a child, and the old apartments have been turned into a warren of interesting shops.

BLUE CARIB GEMS AND ROCKS, Bakery Square Shopping Mall. Tel. 774-8525.

For a decade the owners prospected for gemstones in the Caribbean, and these stones have been brought direct from the mine to you in this store behind Little Switzerland. The raw stones are cut, polished, and then fashioned into jewelry by the lost-wax process. On one side of the premises you can see the craftspeople at work, and on the other side view their finished products. A lifetime guarantee is given on all handcrafted jewelry. Since the items are locally made, they are duty free and not included in the $1,200 exemption. Incidentally, this establishment also provides emergency eyeglass repair.

CARDOW JEWELERS, 39 Main St. Tel. 774-1140.

Often called the Tiffany's of the Caribbean, Cardow boasts the largest selection of fine jewelry shown in the world. This fabulous shop, where there are more than 6,000 rings displayed, offers savings because of its worldwide direct buying, large turnover, and duty-free prices. Unusual and traditional designs are offered in diamonds, emeralds, rubies, sapphires, and Brazilian stones, as well as pearls and coral. Cardow has a whole wall of Italian gold chains. Also featured are antique coin jewelry and Piaget watches. The Treasure Cove has case after case of fine gold jewelry.

THE CLOTH HORSE, Bakery Sq., Back St. Tel. 774-4761.
The Cloth Horse will appeal to the decorator in you, with the French Oulivado fabric from Provence, as well as pine furniture from Denmark and wicker and rattan from the Caribbean. Some readers have reported a 40% savings over Stateside prices. You can also purchase Caribbean pottery, placemats, pillows, baskets, and mahogany from Haiti.

AL COHEN'S, 18A Estate Thomas. Tel. 774-3690.
At Al Cohen's big warehouse across from the West Indian Company dock, where cruise-ship passengers come in, you can purchase discount liquor, fragrances, T-shirts, and souvenirs. Your purchases are delivered free to the airport or your ship.

COKI, Compass Point. Tel. 775-6560.
Just outside Charlotte Amalie in the "East End," Coki is set in the midst of a little "restaurant row." An American, George McBride, employs island women who sew and stitch together pieces of canvas of hand-woven Madras cotton into the kind of chic resortwear suitable for yachting, beaching, or "hanging out." In season the shop is open daily from 9am to 9pm; summer hours are shorter.

COLOMBIAN EMERALDS INTERNATIONAL, Havensight Mall. Tel. 774-2442.
With another branch on Main Street at the waterfront, this outfit is renowned throughout the Caribbean for offering the finest collection of Colombian emeralds, both set and unset. Each Colombian Emeralds store offers a complete selection of loose stones, which are duty free for those returning to the U.S. mainland. In addition to jewelry, the shop offers a collection of some of the world's finest watches, including Raymond Weil and Seiko.

DOWN ISLAND TRADERS, 48 A-B Norre Gade. Tel. 776-4641.
The aroma of spices will lead you to Down Island Traders, at the location above or at 1-3 Wimmelskaffts Gade (tel. 774-4265). These outlets have an attractive array of spices, teas, seasonings, jams, and condiments, most of which are packaged from natural Caribbean products. Look also for candies and jellies. This is an original native market. The owner also carries a line of local cookbooks, as well as silk-screened island designs on T-shirts and bags, Haitian metal sculpture, children's gifts, Caribbean art, and jewelry.

THE ENGLISH SHOP, Main St. at Market Sq. Tel. 776-5399.
The location above, along with a branch at Havensight Mall (tel. 776-3776), has a wide selection of china, crystal, and figurines from the world's top makers.

IRMELA'S JEWEL STUDIO, in the Old Grand Hotel, at the beginning of Main St. Tel. 809/774-5875, or toll free 800/524-2047.
Irmela's has made a name for itself in the highly competitive jewelry business in St. Thomas. Here the jewelry is unique, custom-designed by Irmela, and handmade by her studio or imported from around the world. Irmela has the largest selection of cultured pearls in the Caribbean, including freshwater Biwa and South Sea pearls. Choose from hundreds of clasps and pearl shorteners. Irmela has a large selection of unset stones, such as rubies, sapphires, emeralds, and unusual ones including tanzanite and alexandrite. Diamonds range from pear-shaped to emerald cut, marquis, even heart-shaped, in sizes from tiny 2-pointers to several carats.

JAVA WRAPS, 24 Palm Passage, on the waterfront. Tel. 774-3700.
All white tiles, this store is done up with traditional Javanese matting decorated with exotic Balinese wood carvings on the walls. Locals and tourists alike buy the hand-batiked resortwear line specializing in shorts, shirts, sundresses, and children's clothing. Java Wraps is known for its sarong pieces and demonstrates tying them in at least 15 different ways.

THE LEATHER SHOP, INC., 1 Main St. and Havensight Mall. Tel. 776-0290.

Many handbags here are from chic Italian designers: Fendi, Bottega Veneta, Michel Clo, Furla, Prada, and Il Bisonte. You'll find a wide assortment of belts, sized to order with your choice of buckle. There are many styles of wallets, briefcases, and attaché cases, as well as all-leather luggage from Land.

THE LINEN HOUSE, 7A Royal Dane Mall. Tel. 774-8117.

The Linen House is considered one of the best stores for linens in the West Indies. It has another location at Palm Passage (tel. 774-8405). You'll find a wide selection of placemats, decorative tablecloths, and many hand-embroidered goods.

LION IN THE SUN, Riise's Alley. Tel. 776-4203.

It's one of the most expensive clothing stores on the island, but patrons shop here for its collection of designer-chic casual apparel. Whether it's tanks, tees, shorts, pants, or skirts, this store is likely to have what you're looking for, including clothes by such designers as Sonia Rykiel. But because of the prices, it's better to start your shopping at the sales rack. The owner is firm about prices as marked—no bargaining here.

LITTLE SWITZERLAND, 5 Main St. Tel. 776-2010.

Little Switzerland, with three stores in downtown Charlotte Amalie and one on the dock at Havensight Mall, sells fine watches, a wide selection of jewelry from Europe and Asia, and the best in crystal and china. They also maintain the official outlets for Hummel, Lladró, and Swarovski figurines.

LOUIS VUITTON, 24 Main St. at Palm Passage. Tel. 774-3644.

For fine leather goods, you can't beat Louis Vuitton, where the complete line by the world-famous French designer is available. Suitcases, handbags, wallets, and other accessories are carried here.

A. H. RIISE GIFTS, 37 Main St. at Riise's Alley. Tel. 809/776-2303, or toll free 800/524-2037.

This restored 18th-century Danish warehouse extends from Main Street to the waterfront. Special attention is given to the collection of jewelry, watches, crystal, and china from Europe's leading craftspeople. The perfume and cosmetics are in one of the largest parfumeries in the Caribbean, all at duty-free prices. Specialties also include Crabtree & Evelyn, Liberty of London, Oriental rugs, Hilda Icelandic woolens, liquor, tobacco, and duty-free art featuring a wide selection of Caribbean prints and note cards. Toll-free shop-by-phone service is available from the U.S.

ROYAL CARIBBEAN, 33 Main St. Tel. 776-4110.

With additional branches at 23 Main Street (tel. 776-5449), and Havensight Mall (tel. 776-8890), this is the largest camera and electronics store in the Caribbean. Since 1977 it has offered good values in top-brand cameras and electronic equipment, including all accessories. Royal Caribbean is the authorized Sony dealer. They also have good buys in famous-name watches, Mikimoto pearls, Dupont and Dunhill lighters, jewelry for both men and women, and gift items.

H. STERN JEWELLERS, Havensight Mall and Main St. Tel. 776-1939.

You'll find colorful gem and jewel creations at six locations in St. Thomas—two on Main Street, one in Havensight Mall, and branches at Bluebeard's Castle, the Stouffer Grand Beach Resort, and the Frenchman's Reef Hotel—as well as in a store at Sint Maarten, Netherlands Antilles. Every shop has the same duty-free prices, a considerable savings for visiting shoppers. Stern gives worldwide guaranteed service, including a 1-year exchange privilege.

THE STRAW FACTORY, 2A Garden St. Tel. 774-4849.

Just a stroll up from Post Office Square is the island's largest selection of straw hats, from classic Panamas to beachcomber bargains. There is a wide variety of handcrafted items, especially straw baskets of every size and description and hand-carved, brightly painted parrots and fish. The factory also has a big selection of handbags in straw and fabric, from huge totes to tiny purses and a wide choice of imprinted sportswear. Check their large assortment of dollar souvenirs. Stop at the counter outside for an ice-cream cone and eat it seated in the shade of the Straw Factory patio.

JIM TILLETT GALLERY, Tillett Gardens, Tutu. Tel. 775-1405.

A visit to the art gallery and craft studios of Jim Tillett is a sightseeing expedition. The Tillett compound was converted from a Danish farm called Tutu. The Tillett name conjures up high-fashion silk-screen printing by the famous Tillett brothers, who for years had their exquisite fabrics used by top designers and featured in such magazines as *Vogue* and *Harper's Bazaar*. Jim Tillett settled in St. Thomas, after creating a big splash in Mexico, where his work was featured in *Life* magazine. At his compound you can casually visit the adjoining workshops, where you can see silk-screening in progress.

Upstairs is an art gallery with an abundance of maps, paintings, sculpture, and graphics by local artists. Mr. Tillett created a series of maps on fine cotton canvas that are best-selling items. Arts Alive Fairs are held there three times a year—in spring, summer, and fall. These fairs give local artists a showcase for their work and offer crafts demonstrations and such special features as puppet shows for children; folkloric dancers; other dancing such as tap, ballet, and modern; steel bands; calypso music; and other activities.

TROPICANA PERFUME SHOPPES, 2 and 14 Main St. Tel. 809/774-0010, or toll free 800/233-7948.

These two stores stand at the beginning of Main Street near the Emancipation Gardens post office. The first is billed as the largest parfumerie in the world, and it offers all the famous names in perfumes and cosmetics, including Nina Ricci and Chanel for women and men. Men will also find Europe's best colognes and aftershave lotions here. When you return home, you can mail-order all these same fragrances by taking advantage of Tropicana's toll-free number.

EVENING ENTERTAINMENT

St. Thomas has more nightlife than any other island in the Virgin Islands, either U.S. or British, but it's not as extensive as you might think. The big hotels seem to offer the most varied programs.

THE PERFORMING ARTS

REICHHOLD CENTER FOR THE ARTS, University of the Virgin Islands, Brewer's Beach. Tel. 774-8475.

West of Charlotte Amalie is the artistic center of St. Thomas. You'll have to call the theater or check with the tourist office to see if one of the frequent performances staged here is being presented at the time of your visit. The theater itself is a Japanese-inspired amphitheater set into a natural valley, with seating for 1,200 spectators. The stage is used for presentations by several different repertory theaters of music, dance, and drama. Performances begin at 8 or 8:30pm (call the theater).

Admission: Tickets, $10–$40.

THE CLUB & MUSIC SCENE

BLUEBEARD'S CASTLE HOTEL, Bluebeard's Hill. Tel. 774-1600.

Overlooking the pool and yacht harbor, the Dungeon Bar offers piano-bar entertainment nightly and is a popular gathering spot for both residents and visitors. You can dance to a combo from 8pm to midnight on Thursday and from 8pm to 1am on Saturday. On Monday there's a steel band; other nights a piano player entertains. Drinks cost $2.50 to $4.50. Open: Sun–Fri 11am–midnight, Sat 11am–1am.

Admission: Free.

EPERNAY, rue de St. Barthélemy, Frenchtown. Tel. 774-5348.

Adjacent to Alexander's Restaurant, this stylish watering hole adds a touch of

Europe to the neighborhood of Frenchtown. With a color scheme of gray, black, and peach, you can order glasses of at least six different brands of champagne, and vintage wines by the glass. No main courses are served, but a list of appetizers, costing $6 to $10, seems tailor-made to accompany the flavors of the wine. Examples include sushi, caviar, and tempting desserts. Wines and champagnes begin at $5 a glass. Open: Mon–Sat 4pm–2am.

FRENCHMAN'S REEF, Flamboyant Point. Tel. 776-8500.

Frenchman's Reef enjoys a well-deserved reputation as one of the entertainment centers of St. Thomas. Occasionally major acts are imported to perform at the hotel's Top of the Reef Supper Club, Monday through Saturday, with dancing offered before and after the show until the early hours of the morning. Dinner, served there from 6:30 to 10:30pm, starts at $35. In addition, the hotel offers La Terraza, where a steel band often plays and a limbo show is staged. Check at the desk for what's on; there's almost always dance music from 9pm. Drinks cost $2.50 to $6. Open: Tues–Sun 9pm–2am.

Admission: Free.

GREENHOUSE, Veterans Dr. Tel. 774-7998.

Set directly on the waterfront, this bar and restaurant is one of the few nightlife venues recommended in Charlotte Amalie. You can park nearby and walk to the entrance. Each night a different entertainment is featured, ranging from oldies night to rock 'n' roll. Saturday night is the "big blast." Beer costs $2.50, with meals from $10. Open: Daily 7am–3am.

Admission: $2 Tues–Wed and Fri–Sat, $5 Thurs, free Sun–Mon.

IGGIE'S, in the Limetree Beach Resort Hotel, 100 Frenchman's Bay Rd., Frenchman's Bay. Tel. 776-4770.

Iggie's is the most electronically sophisticated nightclub on St. Thomas, and is part of a glittering trio of clubs that makes Limetree the number-one nightlife complex on the island. The secret is a complicated electronic device, imported at huge expense from Japan, called a karaoke machine. The orchestrations for hundreds of highly singable pop songs can be played while members of the audience temporarily enjoy center stage as lead singer. Drinks start at $3.50. Open: Mon–Sat 9pm–1am.

Admission: Free.

PARADISE ONE/PARADISE TWO, in the Bolongo Limetree Beach Hotel, 100 Frenchman's Bay Rd., Frenchman's Bay. Tel. 776-4770.

Located on an elevated and covered terrace near the lobby of this previously recommended hotel, these twin nightclubs are separated from one another only by a quasi-soundproof glass wall. Guests move freely from one area to another, each of which has a distinctly different ambience. Paradise I is a disco, with recent music. Paradise II has sit-down tables for better vantage points for watching live bands. The music is frequently West Indian, calypso, or reggae. Drinks begin at $4. Open: Tues–Sat 10pm–2am.

Admission (including both clubs): $5 Tues–Thurs, $10 Fri–Sat.

WALTER'S II, 3 Trompeter Gade. Tel. 774-5025.

This is the most recommendable of the clubs in Charlotte Amalie. Located in a town house built around 1935, about 100 yards from the island's famous synagogue, it was established by Nevis-born Walter Springette. The street-level disco plays recorded and highly danceable music. Later in the evening, a piano bar in the cellar provides live music from the 1950s, the 1960s, and the 1990s sound of contemporary jazz. On both levels, the preferred drink is calypso punch. Drinks begin at $4. Open: Daily 5pm–4am.

Admission: Free.

EASY EXCURSIONS

WATER ISLE The fourth largest of the U.S. Virgins, Water Isle is only half a mile long and about a half to 1 mile wide. At its nearest point, it comes about three-eighths of a mile from St. Thomas. Visitors go there to spend the day on **Honeymoon Beach,** where they swim, snorkel, sail, waterski, or just sunbathe on the palm-shaded beach and order lunch or a drink from the beach bar. The highest elevation is only 300 feet above sea level, and the Arawak peoples were the first to inhabit it. Originally the island had freshwater ponds from which sailing vessels replenished their casks. The army used Fort Segarra as a base in World War I.

It's possible to go on your own. A ferry runs between Water Isle Dock and the Sub Base at St. Thomas; the 7-minute ride costs $3.50 each way. Service is daily from 7am to midnight. For information, phone 774-1207.

UNDER THE SEA A major attraction is the ✪ *Atlantis* **submarine,** which takes you on a 1-hour voyage to depths of 90 feet, with a world of exotic marine life unfolding. For those who have never gone scuba diving, this is a unique experience. You can gaze on coral reefs and sponge gardens through 2-foot windows on the air-conditioned 65-foot-long sub, which carries 48 passengers (but no children under 4). You board a surface boat at the West Indies Dock, right outside Charlotte Amalie, which heads for the submarine, located near Buck Island (the St. Thomas version, not the more famous island near St. Croix). Both day and night sub dives are offered, and the view of the nocturnal ocean world is especially enchanting. The fare is $68 per person; children 4 to 12 are charged half fare. The *Atlantis* operates Tuesday through Saturday, and reservations are absolutely necessary. For tickets, go to the Havensight Mall, Building 6 (tel. 809/776-5650, or toll free 800/253-0493).

2. ST. JOHN

About 3 to 5 miles east of St. Thomas, depending on where you measure, St. John lies just across Pillsbury Sound. The island is about 7 miles long and 3 miles wide, with a total land area of some 20 square miles.

The smallest and least populated of the three main U.S. Virgins, St. John has more than half its land mass, as well as its shoreline waters, set aside as the Virgin Islands National Park, dedicated in 1956. Once it was slated for big development when it was under Danish control, but a slave rebellion and a decline of the sugarcane plantations ended that idea.

Ringed by a rocky coastline formed into crescent-shaped bays and white sand beaches, St. John hosts an array of birdlife and wildlife that is the envy of ornithologists and zoologists around the world. Its miles of serpentine hiking trails are dotted with spectacular views and ruins of 18th-century Danish plantations. Mysterious geometric petroglyphs incised into boulders and cliffs will be pointed out by island guides; of unknown age and origin, the figures have never been deciphered.

The boating world seeks out its dozens of sheltered coves for anchorages, swimming, and extended holidays. The hundreds of coral gardens that surround St. John's perimeter are protected as rigorously as the land surface by the National Park Service. Any attempt to damage or remove coral from these waters is punishable with large and strictly enforced fines.

ORIENTATION

GETTING THERE By Boat The easiest and most frequented way to go is by **ferry,** which leaves from Red Hook landing on St. Thomas; the trip takes about 20 minutes. Beginning at 6:30am (except on weekends and holidays, when departures begin at 8am), boats depart every hour. The last ferry back heads out of Cruz Bay at St. John at 11:15pm. Because of such frequent departures, even cruise-ship passengers, anchored in Charlotte Amalie for only a short time, can visit St. John for a quick island tour, perhaps a picnic and a swim at one of its fine sandy beaches, and return in time for dinner. The one-way fare is $3 for adults, $1 for children. Schedules can change without notice, so call 778-6111, ext. 220, for more information.

Should you ever get stranded, **water-taxi service** is available 24 hours a day for about $40 for two people, but this should be negotiated in advance. Call 775-6501.

To reach the ferry, you can take an **open-air shuttle** which departs from the Market Square in Charlotte Amalie. Monday through Saturday (not on Sunday) it will take you to the ferry dock at Red Hook. The fare is $3 per person each way.

It's also possible to board a **boat** directly at the Charlotte Amalie waterfront for a cost of $7 one way; the ride takes 45 minutes. The first boat departs St. Thomas at 9am; the last one to leave Cruz Bay heading for Charlotte Amalie is at 5:15pm.

Also, a **launch service** leaves from the dock at Caneel Bay on St. John and heads for the National Park Dock at Red Hook on St. Thomas. The one-way fare, however, is $9 per person, $12 to Charlotte Amalie. Telephone 776-6111 for times of departure.

GETTING AROUND By Public Transportation The most popular way to get around is by **surrey-style taxi.** If you just want to go from the ferry-landing dock to Trunk Bay, for example, the cost is about $7.50 for two. Between midnight and 6am fares are increased by 40%.

It's also possible to use the **bus** service, which runs from Cruz Bay to Maho Bay and stops at Caneel and Cinnamon bays. The one-way bus fare is $3.50 for adults.

By Jeep and Rental Car The extensive stretches of St. John's National Park have kept the edges of the island's roads undeveloped and uncluttered, with some of the most breathtaking vistas anywhere. Therefore many visitors opt to rent a vehicle (sometimes with four-wheel drive) to tour the island; most renters need a car for only a day or two.

One excellent source is **Budget Rent-a-Car** (tel. 776-7575, or toll free 800/527-0700). It operates from a kiosk beside Route 104, a 3-minute drive from Cruz Bay's ferryboat piers. Arriving passengers head for the company's pierside kiosk, where an employee will complete some paperwork and arrange for the immediate delivery to the dock of any vehicle. At Budget, both conventional and four-wheel-drive vehicles begin at $55 a day during high season (slightly less in summer), with unlimited mileage included. Collision-damage insurance costs around $6 a day, although renters will still be responsible for the first $500 worth of repair costs. Renters must be 25 years old to buy insurance, although the company will rent to 21-year-olds who present a valid credit card and driver's license and who want to risk driving with only limited insurance.

Gasoline at Budget and at most of the island's other car-rental agencies is not provided in the cost of the rental. (You're likely to be delivered a car with an almost-empty tank, just enough to get you to one of the island's two gas stations.) Because of the distance between gas stations, it's never a good idea to drive around St. John with less than half a tank of gas.

Hertz (tel. 776-6412, or toll free 800/654-3001) also rents vehicles from its office in Cruz Bay. Priced between $55 and $70 per day, a rental requires the presentation of a major credit card. Drivers must be at least 25 years old. Hertz has a more comprehensive insurance policy than Budget, offering a collision-damage waiver at $10 per day which charges no deductible in the event of an accident.

Also charging roughly similar rates on St. John is **Avis Rent-a-Car** (tel. 776-6374, or toll free 800/331-2112), at Cruz Bay. Drivers must be 25 or older for any rental. For about $50 per day during winter, Avis offers a sampling of conventional cars, but many visitors prefer to rent one of the slightly more expensive open-side four-wheel-drive vehicles simply because they are more fun. As they do at the competition, these begin at around $55 a day, with unlimited mileage included.

By Sightseeing Tour The **St. John Taxi Association** (tel. 776-6060) conducts a 2-hour tour of St. John, including swimming at Trunk Bay and a visit to the Caneel Bay resort, at a cost of $30 for one or two people. Depending on demand, tours depart Cruz Bay daily.

ESSENTIALS For **medical care,** the Morris DeCastro Clinic is in Cruz Bay (tel. 776-6252), and there is another clinic at Susannaberg (tel. 776-6400).

WHERE TO STAY

The choice of accommodations on St. John is limited, and that's how most people would like to keep it.

RESORTS

CANEEL BAY, Virgin Islands National Park (P.O. Box 720, Cruz Bay), St. John, USVI 00830. Tel. 809/776-6111, or toll free 800/223-9637. Fax 809/776-2030. 171 rms. MINIBAR

$ Rates: Dec 20–Mar, $325–$535 single or double. Summer, $190–$345 single or double. MAP $60 per person extra. AE, DC, MC, V. **Parking:** Free.

⭐ Caneel Bay was created out of a dream of an idealistic man, Laurance S. Rockefeller, and it's a remarkable achievement. Operated by Rockresorts, this is a luxurious resort on a 170-acre portion of St. John, in the national park, built on the site of a mid-1700s sugar plantation on the bay, with a choice of seven beaches. The main buildings are strung along the bays, with a Caribbean lounge and dining room at the core.

Other, separate units—really bedroom villas—stand along the beaches, so all you have to do is step from your private veranda onto the sands. Not all rooms, however, are on the beaches; some are set back on low cliffs or headlands. The decor is understated, with rich woods, hand-woven fabrics, elegant furnishings, and plantation fans. Gardens surround all buildings.

Dining/Entertainment: The choice dining spot at Caneel Bay is the Turtle Bay Estate House, part of the 18th-century Dutch sugar plantation. The other restaurants are described in "Where to Dine," below.

Services: Scheduled garden tours, fishing expeditions, diving excursions to offshore wrecks, deep-sea fishing, free snorkeling lessons, tennis lessons, baby-sitting, valet and laundry, massage, room service (breakfast only).

Facilities: Use of Laurance Rockefeller's family yacht for a morning, a day, or a week; full-service dive shop and water-sports activities desk, 11 tennis courts, free use of sailboats for windsurfing, outdoor swimming pool, seven beaches, endless hideaways for solitary or romantic interludes.

HYATT REGENCY ST. JOHN, Great Cruz Bay (P.O. Box 8310, Cruz Bay), St. John, USVI 00830. Tel. 809/776-7171, or toll free 800/233-1234. Fax 809/775-3858. 278 rms, 7 suites. A/C MINIBAR TV TEL **Transportation:** Taxi.

$ Rates: Winter, $295–$475 single or double, with mandatory MAP $55 per person extra; from $575 suite. Summer, $165–$275 single or double; from $375 suite. Children 18 and under stay free in parents' room. Breakfast $15 extra. AE, DC, MC, V. **Parking:** Free.

⭐ The Hyatt, the splashiest hotel on St. John, sits on 34 acres of what used to be scrub forest on the southeast side of the island. The 13 cedar-roofed postmodern buildings have ziggurat-shaped angles, soaring ceilings, and large windows. Herringbone-patterned brick walkways connect the gardens (where 400 palms were imported from Puerto Rico) with the beach and the most unusual swimming pool in the Virgin Islands. Each of the stylish accommodations contains fan-shaped windows, curved ceilings, and a color scheme of rose and mauve.

Dining/Entertainment: There is a handful of stylish restaurants and bars, including Fronds, which has a fine wine list and an exemplary cuisine. For Chow Bella, see "Where to Dine," below.

Services: Round-trip transfers from St. Thomas airport, supervised activities program for children, baby-sitting, laundry, room service.

Facilities: 11,000-square-foot swimming pool, six lit tennis courts, 1,200-foot beach, water sports, spa and health club.

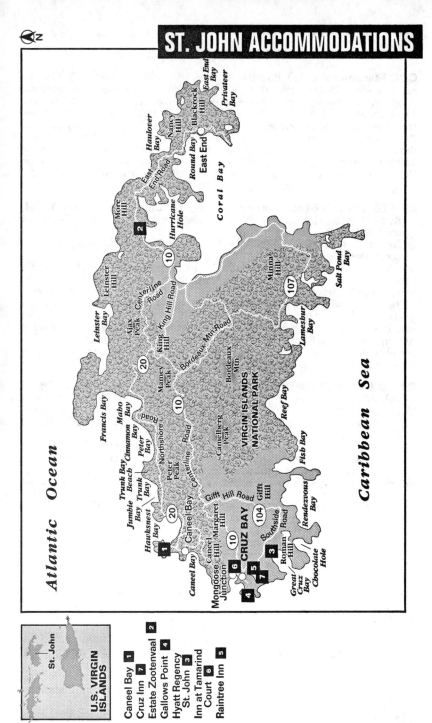

ST. JOHN ACCOMMODATIONS

Atlantic Ocean

Caribbean Sea

Coral Bay

U.S. VIRGIN ISLANDS

St. John

Caneel Bay 1
Cruz Inn 7
Estate Zootenvaal 2
Gallows Point 4
Hyatt Regency St. John 3
Inn at Tamarind Court 6
Raintree Inn 5

HOUSEKEEPING UNITS

CDC Management, P.O. Box 458, St. John, USVI 00831 (tel. 809/776-6152, or toll free 800/338-0987; fax 809/779-4044), is the island's biggest management company, with four small to medium-size resorts, all constructed in the last few years. These are affordable accommodations which cater to families with children (some resorts prohibit children). Properties include Cruz Views, Gifft Hill, Battery Hill, and Pastory Estates, the last a 16-unit resort condo on a private hill site about a 5-minute drive from Cruz Bay. With the exception of the private homes, the properties rent for less than $200 per night. For example, a two-bedroom unit suitable for four at Cruz Views costs $150 per night in season, and only $100 per night off-season. Kids under 6 stay free, and arrangements can be made for baby-sitters.

ESTATE ZOOTENVAAL, Hurricane Hole, St. John, USVI 00830. Tel. 809/776-6321, 216/861-5337 in the continental U.S. Fax 809/776-6321. 4 units. MINIBAR
$ Rates: $140–$175 double per day, $800–$1,000 double per week. No credit cards. **Parking:** Free.
Within the boundaries of the U.S. National Park, this complex sits at the edge of a horseshoe-shaped bay. Local mariners know that this bay is usually safe from even the most violent hurricane. Consisting of villas and a two-bedroom house, each painted driftwood gray with white trim, the complex sits within earshot of the waves on the grounds of what used to be a private estate called Zootenvaal. The accommodations have been renovated; each has its own color scheme, and all have Danish flatware, Arzberg china, and fully equipped kitchens. A few have housed novelists holing up to complete a manuscript. Maid service can be arranged for an extra cost, on an as-needed basis. There is a private beach for snorkeling.

GALLOWS POINT SUITE RESORT, P.O. Box 58, St. John, USVI 00830. Tel. 809/776-6434, or toll free 800/323-7229. Fax 809/776-6520. 60 units.
$ Rates: Winter, $250–$275 single or double. Summer, $140–$155 single or double. Extra person $25. Continental breakfast $5 extra. AE, DC, MC, V. **Parking:** Free.
The villa-style architecture of these appealing cottages ensures privacy. Nestled into a carefully cultivated garden, they were patterned after 18th-century Danish manor houses. The clapboards, latticework, fan-shaped windows, panoramic porches, and louvered French doors are stained a shade of putty. Each villa contains four separate units, the most desirable being on the top floor. These have massive exposed beams of Canadian cedar, sleeping lofts, and comfortable tropical furniture. The ground-floor (garden) units have sunken living rooms, wooden decks facing the water, and bathrooms full of greenery. Each has its own fully equipped kitchenette. You'll notice this complex of stylish buildings from the ferry as it enters the mouth of Cruz Bay.

GUESTHOUSES

Let's face it. Except for the campgrounds recommended next, the tabs at most of the establishments on St. John are far beyond the pocketbook of the average traveler. If you'll settle for just the minimum necessities, the following places will provide a low-cost holiday on St. John. These are places merely "to bunk."

THE CRUZ INN, P.O. Box 566, Cruz Bay, St. John, USVI 00830. Tel. 809/776-7449, or toll free 800/666-7688. 14 rms (5 with bath).
$ Rates (including continental breakfast): Winter, $50 double without bath; $65–$85 efficiency. Summer, $45 double without bath; $60–$75 efficiency. Minimum stay for efficiencies 3 days. Tax extra. MC, V. **Parking:** Free.
The Raintree Inn (see below) runs another low-priced accommodation, in the center of Cruz Bay, a bit of a walk from the ferry dock. Seven of the guest rooms are in the main building and share two baths; each has an overhead fan

and either a double or two twin beds. Other accommodations are efficiencies and apartments in the complex. Some of the units have cooking facilities (one, however, doesn't have hot water). Overlooking Enighed Pond, the inn also has a convivial bar and offers weekly entertainment.

INN AT TAMARIND COURT, P.O. Box 350, Cruz Bay, St. John, USVI 00830. Tel. 809/776-6378, or toll free 800/221-1637. 20 rms (13 with bath), 2 family suites.

$ Rates (including continental breakfast): Winter, $48 single without bath; $68–$78 single or double with bath; $98–$108 suite. Summer, $38 single without bath; $58–$63 single or double with bath; $88–$98 suite. Tax extra. AE, MC, V. **Parking:** Free.

Right outside Cruz Bay but still within walking distance of the ferry dock, Tamarind Court offers "back-to-basics" bedrooms. Activity centers around a courtyard bar, and accommodations are in both a small hotel and a little West Indian inn. If you need one, ask about renting a family room. Frankly, this isn't for everyone, but some adventurous young people like it.

RAINTREE INN, P.O. Box 566, Cruz Bay, St. John, USVI 00830. Tel. 809/776-7449, or toll free 800/666-7449. Fax 809/776-7449. 11 rms (all with bath).

$ Rates: Winter, $70 double; $95 efficiency. Summer, $60 double; $85 efficiency. Tax extra. Breakfast $3–$10 extra. Minimum stay for efficiencies 3 days. MC, V. **Parking:** Free.

Ⓢ In the center of Cruz Bay, next to the Catholic church, the Raintree also adjoins a reasonably priced restaurant next door, the inn's own Fish Trap, where Tuesday through Saturday you can order breakfast and lunch in season and dinner 11 months out of the year (it's closed in August). The simple rooms have private baths and overhead fans, and linen, towels, and soap are supplied. Maid service is extra. Three of the rooms have kitchenettes, and two twins are in a carpeted loft (you climb a ladder to reach them).

CAMPGROUNDS

CINNAMON BAY CAMPGROUND, P.O. Box 720, Cruz Bay, USVI 00830. Tel. 809/776-6330, or toll free 800/223-7637. Fax 809/776-6458.

$ Rates: Winter, $76 cottage for two; $59 tent; $12 bare site. Off-season, $50 cottage for two; $38 tent; $12 bare site. MC, V.

Established by the National Park Service in 1964, this campground is the most complete campground in the Caribbean. The site is directly on the beach, and thousands of acres of tropical vegetation surround you. Life is simple here, and you have a choice of three different ways of sleeping: tents, cottages, and bare sites. At the bare campsites, nothing is provided except general facilities. Canvas tents are 10 by 14 feet with floor, and a number of facilities are offered, including all cooking equipment. Even your linen is changed weekly. Cottages are 15 by 15 feet, a screened room with two concrete walls and two screen walls. They contain of four twin beds, and two cots can be added; cooking facilities are also supplied. Lavatories and showers are in separate buildings nearby. Camping is limited to a 2-week period in any given year. Near the road is a camp center office, with a grocery and a cafeteria (dinners for $10).

MAHO BAY, P.O. Box 310, Cruz Bay, St. John, USVI 00832. Tel. 809/776-6226, or toll free 800/392-9004. Fax 809/776-6504. 113 cottages. Directions: From Cruz Bay, take Rte. 20 to Maho Bay. There is also regularly scheduled bus service.

$ Rates: Mid-Dec to mid-Apr, $75 cottage for two; children staying in parents' cottage are charged from $10 each; 7-night minimum stay required. Mid-Apr to mid-Dec, $50 cottage for two; when staying in parents' cottage, children under 7 are charged $7, and children 7 and older, $10; no minimum stay required. Continental breakfast $3 extra. No credit cards.

S Maho Bay is an interesting concept in ecology vacationing, where you get close to nature, but with considerable comfort. The deluxe campground is set in the heart of the Virgin Islands National Park, an 8-mile drive from Cruz Bay. Utility lines and pipes are hidden underground.

The tentlike cottages, limited to two adults, are made of canvas. Each unit has a choice of a double bed or two movable beds, a couch, electric lamps and outlets, a dining table, chairs, a propane stove, and an ice chest (cooler). That's not all—you're furnished linen, towels, dinner service, and utensils. There's a store where you can buy (expensive) supplies. You do your own housekeeping and cooking, although you can eat at the camp's outdoor restaurant. Guests share a community bathhouse. Each unit is cantilevered over a thickly wooded area, providing a view of the sea, sky, and beach.

Maho Bay has a community center housing the Pavilion Restaurant, which always serves breakfast. Lunches are offered in winter, and the international dinner menu is changed nightly depending on what food is fresh. Both meat and vegetarian selections are offered. The Pavilion also functions as an amphitheater where various programs are featured. The camp has a good water sports program.

WHERE TO DINE
EXPENSIVE

CANEEL BAY BEACH TERRACE DINING ROOM, in the Caneel Bay Hotel. Tel. 776-6111.

Cuisine: INTERNATIONAL/SEAFOOD. **Reservations:** Required. **Transportation:** Taxi.

$ Prices: Appetizers $9.75–$12.75; main courses $25.50–$33.50; Mon night buffet $50; buffet lunch $25. AE, DC, MC, V.

Open: Lunch daily 11:30am–2:30pm; dinner daily 7–9pm.

Right below the Sugar Mill (see below) is an elegant choice with open-air tables overlooking the beach and the water. The self-service buffet luncheon is one of the best in the Virgin Islands. From November to May, men are required to wear jackets in the evening. Appetizers might include papaya with prosciutto, followed by excellently prepared soups. Salads are good, including the marinated green bean or the tossed garden greens mimosa. Main dishes are likely to include baked filet of red snapper or roast prime rib of blue-ribbon beef carved to order with natural juices. For dessert, try strawberry cheesecake or Boston cream pie. Menus change nightly. On Monday the chef offers a sumptuous buffet of West Indian, continental, and American dishes.

LE CHATEAU DE BORDEAUX, Centerline Rd., Bordeaux Mountain. Tel. 776-6611.

Cuisine: SEAFOOD/WEST INDIAN. **Reservations:** Required. **Transportation:** Taxi.

$ Prices: Appetizers $3.50–$5.95; main courses $5.95–$23. MC, V.

Open: Snacks daily 9am–5pm; dinner Mon–Sat 6:30–10pm. **Closed:** Sept–Oct 15.

Le Château de Bordeaux sits 1,424 feet above sea level near the center of the island. During the day an informal snack bar offers West Indian platters and burgers ranging from $5 to $8. An array of iron tables and chairs set beneath a sun shelter takes in a view down the valley to the distant sea. After dark, a more formal dining room opens, and the uncomplicated menu lists banana-conch fritters, filets of grouper or yellowtail snapper, conch in an onion-butter sauce, and an array of grilled steaks. The preferred drink is a passionfruit daiquiri.

CHOW BELLA, in the Hyatt Regency St. John, Great Cruz Bay. Tel. 776-7171.

Cuisine: ASIAN/ITALIAN. **Reservations:** Required. **Transportation:** Taxi.

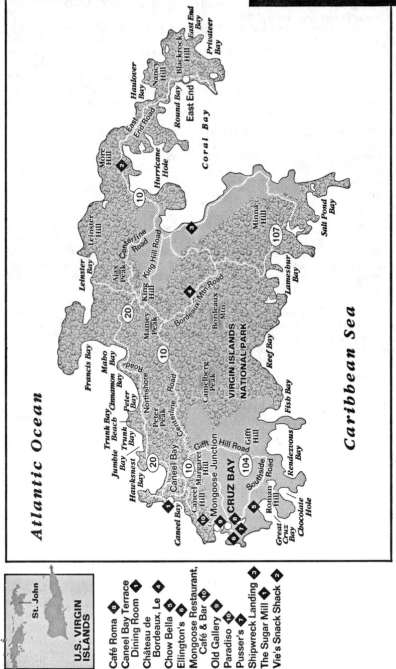

ST. JOHN DINING

Atlantic Ocean

Caribbean Sea

Café Roma **8**
Caneel Bay Terrace Dining Room **1**
Château de Bordeaux, Le **4**
Chow Bella **5**
Ellington's **6**
Mongoose Restaurant, Café & Bar **10**
Old Gallery **9**
Paradiso **10**
Pusser's **7**
Shipwreck Landing **3**
The Sugar Mill **1**
Vie's Snack Shack **2**

$ Prices: Appetizers $4.75–$8.25; main courses $14–$26.50. AE, DC, MC, V.
Open: Dinner only, daily 6–10pm.

Hypermodern marble tables are placed one floor above the most dramatic lobby in the Caribbean, with views down an atrium to an architectural column inspired by the ziggurats of ancient Egypt or Mesopotamia. Piano music filters from a spotlit dais from the restaurant to the lobby below as scents from the hotel's gardens filter upward. The cuisine mingles the traditions of Italy and the Far East and includes a farfalle agli aspargi (bow-tie pasta with asparagus and parmesan) with a platter of Thai pork and Japanese eggplant, fettuccine al prosciutto, stir-fried chicken with garlic, pollo Vesuvio, and shrimp with peanuts and bell peppers.

ELLINGTON'S, Gallows Point, Cruz Bay. Tel. 776-7166.
   Cuisine: CARIBBEAN/INTERNATIONAL. **Reservations:** Required.
$ Prices: Appetizers $7–$8.50; main courses $13–$23. AE, MC, V.
   Open: Breakfast daily 8–11am; lunch daily noon–3pm; dinner daily 6–10pm.

Ellington's is set near the neocolonial villas of Gallows Point, to the right after you disembark from the ferry. Its putty-colored exterior has the same kind of double staircase, fan windows, louvers, and low-slung hip roof found in an 18th-century Danish manor house. Drop in for a drink on the panoramic upper deck where a view of Cruz Bay unfolds. The establishment is named after a local radio announcer ("The Fat Man"), raconteur, and mystery writer whose real-estate developments helped transform St. John into a stylish enclave for the American literati of the 1950s and 1960s. Named Richard "Duke" Ellington (not to be confused with the great musician), he entertained his friends, martini in hand, around a frequently photographed table painted with a map of St. John. The tabletop today hangs in Ellington's dining room.

Lunch might include crab-salad sandwiches, hot Italian steak sandwiches, crisp salads, and New England conch chowder. Dinners are elegant, elaborate, and lighthearted affairs, which might begin with Caribbean conch chowder or black bean soup, then continue with swordfish scampi, beef Ellington (the house specialty, served only for two), or honey-mustard chicken.

PARADISO, Mongoose Junction. Tel. 776-8806.
   Cuisine: ITALIAN. **Reservations:** Recommended.
$ Prices: Appetizers $4.50–$7.50; main courses $15.95–$24.95. AE, MC, V.
   Open: Lunch Tues–Sun 11:30am–2:30pm; dinner Tues–Sun 6–10pm. **Closed:** Sept 1–21.

The most talked-about restaurant on St. John sits among the catwalks and lattices of the island's most interesting shopping center, Mongoose Junction, on the outskirts of Cruz Bay. It might remind you of a manor house, with a decor of brass, glowing hardwoods, nautical antiques, and what might be the most beautiful bar on the island. Menu items include pastas, Caesar salads, a platter of smoked seafood, baked stuffed sole with a lobster-cream sauce, lobster Fra Diavolo (with seafood and red chiles), and daily specials that depend on the delivery that day from the U.S. mainland.

THE SUGAR MILL, in the Caneel Bay Hotel. Tel. 776-6111.
   Cuisine: INTERNATIONAL. **Reservations:** Required. **Transportation.** Taxi.
$ Prices: Appetizers $5–$11.50; main courses $24–$38; lunch buffet $20; dinner buffet $50. AE, MC, V.
   Open: Lunch daily 11:30am–2:30pm; dinner daily 7–9pm.

This restaurant lies behind the bougainvillea-laden tower of an 18th-century sugar mill, where ornamental ponds with water lilies fill former crystallization pits for hot molasses. A flight of stairs leads to a monumental circular dining room, with a wraparound veranda and sweeping views of a park. In the center rises the stone column that horses and mules once circumambulated to crush sugarcane stalks.

From a brass-accented exposed kitchen come such specialties as peach daiquiris and one of the most lavish buffet tables on the island. Both the theme and the ingredients of the table change nightly, but might feature apricot-ginger soup, a seafood bar of shellfish, grilled kingfish with essence of tomato, grilled lobster tail, lamb chops, or steaks, and desserts.

MODERATE

CAFE ROMA, Cruz Bay. Tel. 776-6524.

Cuisine: ITALIAN. **Reservations:** Not required.
$ Prices: Appetizers $2.75–$6; main courses $8.50–$15.50. AE, MC, V.
Open: Dinner only, daily 5–10pm.

Diners climb a flight of concrete exterior steps to reach this restaurant in the center of Cruz Bay. You might arrive early and have a strawberry colada, then enjoy a pasta, veal, seafood, or chicken dish. Ask for their "white pizza," made without the red sauce. Different specialties are featured every night. Italian wines are sold by the glass or bottle, and you can end the evening with an espresso.

MONGOOSE RESTAURANT, CAFE, AND BAR, Mongoose Junction. Tel. 776-7586.

Cuisine: INTERNATIONAL. **Reservations:** Not required.
$ Prices: Appetizers $3–$8; main courses $9–$25. AE, DC, MC, V.
Open: Breakfast daily 8:30–11:30am; lunch daily 11:30am–5:30pm; dinner daily 5:30–10pm.

Some visitors compare this soaring interior design to a large Japanese birdcage because of the strong vertical lines, the 25-foot ceiling, and the setting among trees and above a stream. Many guests create a perch for themselves at the bar for a drink and sandwich; others sit on an adjacent deck where a canopy of trees filters the tropical sunlight. The bar offers more than 20 varieties of frothy island-inspired libations. Lunches include well-stuffed sandwiches, salad platters, and such main courses as seafood Créole, island fishcakes, and vegetable stir-fries. Dinners are more of the same but more expensive. The salad bar is served in an old-fashioned boat. The restaurant is on the outskirts of Cruz Bay, a 5-minute walk from the ferry dock.

OLD GALLERY, Cruz Bay. Tel. 776-7544.

Cuisine: WEST INDIAN/INTERNATIONAL. **Reservations:** Recommended.
$ Prices: Appetizers $6.50–$10; main courses $15–$23; fixed-price meal $9 at lunch, $16.95 at dinner. V.
Open: Lunch daily 11am–3pm; dinner daily 6:30–9:30pm.

The Old Gallery, a short walk from the ferry landing, is on the second floor of an old island building. Much of the nighttime scene passes under the balcony. You'll find no better bargain in Cruz Bay—cheaper, yes, but when it comes to the quality of the food and the generosity of the servings, Old Gallery is tops. There's always fish, a catch of the day, most often sautéed and served with lime butter. Other dishes might be conch in butter sauce, roast pork, and codfish. Johnnycakes (unleavened fried bread) accompany many dishes.

PUSSER'S, Wharfside Village, Cruz Bay. Tel. 774-5489.

Cuisine: INTERNATIONAL/CARIBBEAN. **Reservations:** Not required.
$ Prices: Appetizers $3.95–$7.95; main courses $5.95–$24.95. AE, MC, V.
Open: Lunch daily 11am–3pm; dinner daily 6–10pm.

A double-decker air-conditioned store and pub in Cruz Bay, Pusser's overlooks the harbor and is near the ferry dock. These stores are unique in the Caribbean, and they serve Pusser's Rum, a blend of five West Indian rums that the Royal Navy has served to its men for three centuries. Here you can enjoy traditional English fare, including steak and ale. Other dishes are Cajun barbecued chicken, crab ravioli, lobster medallions, and New York strip steak. Finish with Pusser's famous "mud pie."

INEXPENSIVE

SHIPWRECK LANDING, Rte. 107, Coral Bay. Tel. 776-8640.

Cuisine: SEAFOOD/CONTINENTAL. **Reservations:** Not required.
$ Prices: Appetizers $3.25–$6.25; main courses $10.25–$14.75. MC, V.

Open: Lunch daily 11am–4pm; dinner daily 6–10pm.

Ⓢ Eight miles east of Cruz Bay on the road to Salt Pond Beach, Shipwreck Landing is run by Michael and Julie Young. You dine amid palms and tropical plants on a veranda overlooking the sea. The intimate bar specializes in tropical frozen drinks. The menu includes conch fritter and scungilli salad, blackened red snapper, and surf and turf, along with daily seafood specials. Some Mexican and Asian dishes are also served. There's likely to be music featured on Tuesday night.

VIE'S SNACK SHACK, East End. Tel. 776-8033.
 Cuisine: WEST INDIAN. **Reservations:** Not required.
$ Prices: Appetizers $3.25; main courses $5–$6.50. No credit cards.
 Open: Daily 10am–5pm.
Vie's looks like little more than a plywood-sided hut on the island's East End, about 12½ miles east of Cruz Bay. Nonetheless, its charming and gregarious owner is known as one of the best local chefs on St. John. Her famous garlic chicken is considered the best on the island. She also serves conch fritters, johnnycakes, and coconut and pineapple tarts. Don't leave without a glass of homemade limeade made from home-grown limes. The place is open most days, but as Vie says, "Some days, we might not be here at all"—so you'd better call before heading out.

WHAT TO SEE & DO

Many visitors like to spend a lot of time at **Cruz Bay,** where the ferry docks. In this West Indian village there are interesting bars, restaurants, boutiques, and pastel-painted houses. It's pretty sleepy, but it's pleasant after the fast pace of St. Thomas. The **museum** (tel. 776-6359) at Cruz Bay isn't big, but it does contain some local artifacts and it will teach you some of the history of the island. It's at the public library, and can be visited Monday through Friday from 9am to 5pm; admission is free.

Most cruise-ship passengers dart through Cruz Bay and head for the island's biggest attraction, the **Virgin Islands National Park** (tel. 776-6201). But before going to the park, you may want to stop at the visitor center at Cruz Bay, which is open daily from 8am to 4:30pm. There you'll see some exhibits and learn more about what you can see in the park.

Today the Virgin Islands National Park is the only national park in the Caribbean. It totals 12,624 acres, including submerged lands and waters adjacent to St. John, and has a 20-mile trail system.

If time is limited, try to visit the **Annaberg Ruins,** Leinster Bay Road, where the Danes maintained a thriving plantation and sugar mill after 1718. It's located off North Shore Road east of Trunk Bay on the north shore. On certain days of the week (dates vary) from 10am to 1pm, St. John islanders show you their own style of native cookery and explain basketweaving.

Trunk Bay is considered one of the world's most beautiful beaches. It's also the site of one of the world's first marked underwater trails (bring your mask, snorkel, and fins). It lies to the east of Cruz Bay along North Shore Road. Beware of pickpockets.

Fort Berg (also called Fortsberg), at Coral Bay, dating from 1717, played a disastrous role during the 1733 slave revolt. The fort may be restored as a historic monument.

AN ORGANIZED TOUR Park rangers conduct several different **national park tours** of St. John. You must make a reservation for these tours by calling 776-6330. One tour explores a 2½-mile trail that goes by the mysterious petroglyphs carved on boulders, and the sugar mill ruins. Rangers also conduct a Reef Bay hike. A special 3-hour bus tour costing $15 per passenger leaves from the national park visitor center.

DRIVING TOUR — St. John

Start: Ferry docks in Cruz Bay.
Finish: Ferry docks in Cruz Bay.

Time: 3 to 7 hours, depending on beach time, bar stops, and pedestrian detours.
Best Times: Sunny days between 9am and 4pm, when you get the best light and driving conditions.
Worst Times: Rainy days, when bad roads become even worse.

Suggestion: Before you begin this tour, make sure you have at least three-quarters of a tank of gas, since there are only two gas stations on St. John, one of which is often closed. The more reliable of the two stations is in the upper region of Cruz Bay, beside Route 104. Ask directions when you pick up your rented vehicle. *Remember to drive on the left!*

Head out of Cruz Bay, going east on Route 20. Within about a minute you'll pass the catwalks and verandas of:

1. **Mongoose Junction.** Considered a sightseeing attraction as well as a shopping emporium, it contains some unusual art galleries and jewelry shops (see "Savvy Shopping," below).
    Two miles northeast of Cruz Bay, you'll see a pair of unmarked stone columns on your left, and an area of immaculate landscaping. This is the entrance to the island's most legendary resort:
2. **Caneel Bay.** Past the security guard, near the resort's parking lots, is an attractive gift shop, and a handful of bars and restaurants. In a mile you'll see the first of many spectacular panoramic vistas. Along the entire trajectory, note the complete absence of billboards and electrical cables (a rule rigidly enforced by the National Park Service). In less than 3 miles, you'll come to:
3. **Hawksnest Beach,** whose palms and salt-tolerant wild figs are maintained by the National Park Service. Stop to read the ecological signs and perhaps wet your feet in the water. There are some squat toilets (with lots of flies) at this point if you need them. Continuing your drive, you'll pass, in this order, Trunk Bay, Peter Bay (private), and Cinnamon Bay, all of which have sand, palm trees, and clear water. A few steps from the entrance to the Cinnamon Bay campground is a redwood sign marking the beginning of the:
4. **Cinnamon Bay Trail.** Laid out for hill climbers by the National Park Service, this is an optional 1.2-mile walk that takes about an hour. Its clearly marked paths lead through shaded forest trails along the rutted cobblestones of a former Danish road, past ruins of abandoned plantations.
    A short drive beyond Cinnamon Bay is the sandy sweep of Maho Bay, whose borders contain one of the most upscale campgrounds in the Caribbean.
    Shortly after Maho Bay, the road splits. Take the left fork, which merges in a few moments with an extension of Centerline Road. Off this road, on your left, will appear another National Park Service signpost marked DANISH ROAD, indicating a 5-minute trek along a potholed road to the ruins of an 18th-century school.
    At the next fork, bear right, toward Annaberg (make sure you don't go toward Francis Bay). You'll pass the beginning of a 0.8-mile walking trail to the Leinster Bay Estate, which leads to a beach said to be good for snorkeling. Within less than a minute, you'll reach the parking lot for the:
5. **Annaberg Historic Trail.** The historic highlight of this driving tour, the Annaberg Trail leads pedestrians within and around the ruined buildings of the best-preserved plantation on St. John. During the 18th and 19th centuries the smell of boiling molasses and the sight of hard-working slaves filled the area. About a dozen National Park Service plaques identify and describe each building in the compound. The walk around the grounds takes about 30 minutes. From a terrace near the ruined windmill, a map identifies the panorama to the north and names such landmasses of the British Virgin Islands as Little Thatch, Tortola, Watermelon Cay, and Jost Van Dyke.
    After your visit to Annaberg, retrace your route to its first major division and take the left fork. Soon a road sign will identify your road as Route 20 east. Stay on this road, forking left whenever possible, until you come, after many bends in the

road, to sandy bottomlands that contain an elementary school, a baseball field, and, on a hilltop, a simple barnlike building known as the:

6. **Emmaus Moravian Church,** with its yellow clapboards and red roof (it's often closed to visitors). Near its base yet another NPS walking trail begins (the 1½-mile Johnny Horn Trail), known for its panoramic views and steep hills. You will be now be about 12½ miles east of Cruz Bay.

The roads at this point are not very clearly marked. Don't drive beyond the elementary school below the church. That road, although beautiful, is long, and leads only to the barren and rather dull expanses of the island's East End. Instead, backtrack a very short distance to a cluster of signs that point to such restaurants as the Still and Shipwreck Landing. Follow these signs (i.e., head south) about a mile to:

7. **Coral Bay.** Claimed by the Danes in the 1600s, it still contains a crumbling stone pier that they used to unload their ships. It was also the site of the first plantation on St. John. Established in 1717 (and long ago abandoned), it predated the far-better-developed facilities of Cruz Bay. Coral Bay was the site of a state visit by a princess of the Danish royal family in the early 1700s.

Considered by yachting enthusiasts one of the most desirable harbors anywhere, Coral Bay shelters a closely knit community of boaters who moor here and live on their yachts between excursions to other parts of the Caribbean. Restaurants and bars ring its perimeter.

REFUELING STOP   An open-sided timbered pavilion close to the emerald waters of Coral Bay: **8. The Still,** 10-19 Estate Carolina (tel. 776-6866), provides shelter from the sun and open access to the trade winds blowing in from the sea. Its most famous drink? A Standstill Punch, a pink froth of three fruit juices, crème de cassis, and two different kinds of rum, priced at $3.50 each. Make sure the driver sticks to juices or soft drinks.

After your refueling stop, continue driving south beside Coral Bay, perhaps stopping in at another of the two or three shops and bars beside the road. (Shipwreck Landing, described in "Where to Dine," above, is a good choice.)

After you pass Shipwreck Landing, the road is passable for only another 5 or 6 miles. If you want, you can sightsee for a few miles along the eastern coastline (there are some churches and houses along the way), but eventually you'll have to retrace your route.

Conditions, of course, might have changed by the time you take this tour: Road signs on this end of the island are notoriously bad, so it's wise to ask directions at one of the Coral Bay bars, restaurants, or shops before making any firm conclusion about road conditions.)

Backtrack north along Coral Bay to a point near the Emmaus Moravian Church, which you'll see in the distance. At the cluster of restaurant signs, turn left onto Route 10 west (Centerline Road), which gives good high-altitude views in all directions as you follow it back toward Cruz Bay. (An alternative, although much steeper, way is Route 108, which merges later with Route 10 west.)

Within 7 or 8 miles, Route 10 merges with Route 104 (Gift Hill Road) just after the island's only hospital, the St. John Myrah Keating Smith Community Health Clinic. Take Route 104 and begin one of the steepest descents with the greatest number of blind curves of your driving tour. (Use low gear whenever possible, and honk around blind curves.) When the land levels off, on your left, you'll see the entrance to one of the most imaginative pieces of modern architecture on the island, the spectacularly postmodern:

9. **Hyatt Regency St. John.** If you're a gardening or architecture enthusiast, stop in for a look at a hotel whose inspiration included ancient Mesopotania, colonial Denmark, and the coast of California. What makes all of this even more impressive is the fact that it was built on land that was considered unusable swamp only a few

DRIVING TOUR — ST. JOHN

Atlantic Ocean

Caribbean Sea

VIRGIN ISLANDS NATIONAL PARK

Coral Bay

Hurricane Hole

Cruz Bay

East End Bay
Privateer Bay
East End
Blackrock Hill
Nancy Hill
Round Bay
Haulover Bay
East End Road
More Hill
Leinster Hill
Leinster Bay
Lebster Bay
Ajax Peak
Centerline Road
King Hill Road
King Hill
Mamey Peak
Bordeaux Mtn. Road
Bordeaux Mtn.
Minna Hill
Salt Pond Bay
107
Lameshur Bay
Reef Bay
Camelberg Peak
Fisb Bay
Northshore Road
Centerline Road
Peter Peak
Peter Bay
Cinnamon Bay
Mabo Bay
Trunk Bay
Trunk Beach
Jumbie Bay
Hawksnest Bay
Francis Bay
Caneel Bay
Caneel Hill
Margaret Hill
Gifft Hill Road
Gifft Hill
104
Southside Road
Rendezvous Bay
Great Cruz Bay
Chocolate Hole
Roman Hill

start here

finish here

U.S. VIRGIN ISLANDS
St. John

1 Mongoose Junction
2 Caneel Bay
3 Hawksnest Beach
4 Cinnamon Bay Trail
5 Annaberg Historic Trail
6 Emmaus Moravian Church
7 Coral Bay
8 The Still
9 Hyatt Regency St. John

✝ Church

years ago. A staff member will direct you to the hotel's scattering of bars (perhaps the Poolside Splash Bar) for a midafternoon quaff.

From here, a short drive along Route 104, through a slightly urbanized periphery of private homes, will return you to Cruz Bay.

SPORTS & RECREATION

Don't visit St. John expecting to play golf. Rather, anticipate some of the best snorkeling, scuba diving, swimming, fishing, hiking, sailing, and underwater photography in the Caribbean. The island is known for its coral-sand beaches, winding mountain roads, trails past old, bush-covered sugarcane plantations, and hidden coves.

BEACHES The lure is **✪ Trunk Bay,** already endorsed under "What to See and Do." It's the biggest attraction on St. John and a beach collector's find. To miss its great white sweep would be like touring Europe and skipping Paris. Trouble is, even though it's a beautiful stretch of sand, the word is out. It's likely to be overcrowded and there are pickpockets. The beach has lifeguards and offers rentals, such as snorkel gear. Beginning snorkelers in particular are attracted to its underwater trail near the shore. Both taxis and "safari buses" to Trunk Bay meet the ferry as it docks at Cruz Bay from Red Hook on St. Thomas.

As mentioned, **Caneel Bay,** the stamping ground of the rich and famous, fronts seven beautiful beaches on its 170 acres—but only one is open to the public. The previously recommended campgrounds of **Cinnamon Bay** and **Maho Bay** have their own beaches where forest rangers sometimes have to remind visitors to put their swimming suits back on. Snorkelers find good reefs here, and changing rooms and showers are available.

Hawks Nest Beach is a little gem of white sand, beloved by St. Johnians who let the tour groups fight it out for space on the sands at Trunk Bay. The beach is a bit narrow, but filmmakers long ago discovered its beauty. Close to the road are barbecue grills, and there are portable toilets. Safari buses and taxis from Cruz Bay will take you along the North Shore Road to reach this beach.

HIKING Hiking is the big thing here, and a network of trails covers the national park. However, I suggest a tour by Jeep first, just to get your bearings. At the visitor center at Cruz Bay, ask for a free trail map of the park. It's best to set out with someone experienced in the mysteries of the island. Both Maho Bay and Cinnamon Bay conduct nature walks (see "Campgrounds" in "Where to Stay," above).

TENNIS **Caneel Bay** (tel. 776-6111) has seven courts and a pro shop, but these courts aren't lit at night, and are used exclusively by guests. There are two public courts at Cruz Bay, however.

The **Hyatt Regency St. John,** Great Cruz Bay (tel. 776-7171), has six tennis courts, all lit at night.

WATER SPORTS The most complete line of water sports available on St. John is offered at the **Cinnamon Bay Watersports Center** on Cinnamon Bay Beach (tel. 776-6330). Specializing in sailing, the staff will charge $60 for a full day's outing ($30 for a half day) aboard the yacht *Gratia*. Snorkeling equipment and stopoffs at secluded reefs and uninhabited islands provide some of the most vivid underwater viewing in the region. Beer, soda, and snorkeling equipment are covered by the cost of the trip, but you must bring your own picnic lunch.

If you're interested in snorkeling, you can make trips on the M/V *Cinnamon Bay,* which circumnavigates St. John at least once a week, leaving at 9am every Wednesday. The cost is $30 to $35 per person.

Divers can ask about scuba packages at **Low Key Watersports,** Wharfside Village, P.O. Box 431, St. John USVI 00830 (tel. 809/776-7048). All wreck dives are two-tank, two-location dives. A one-tank dive costs $45 per person, with night dives going for $55. Snorkel tours are also available at $35 per person. The center uses its own custom-built dive boats. The center offers windsurfing lessons and specializes in water-sports gear, including masks, fins, snorkels, and "dive skins." It also arranges day-sailing charters and deep-sea sports fishing.

Cruz Bay Watersports, Cruz Bay (tel. 776-6234), is the only PADI five-star diving center on St. John, and offers daily dive trips year round. Certifications can be arranged through a divemaster. This outfit uses dive boats certified by the Coast Guard which explore gorgeous reefs ranging in depth from 30 to 80 feet. Reef dives cost $65 to $78, and a beginner's scuba course goes for $55. Night dives and "wreck dives" are also offered.

SAVVY SHOPPING

Compared to St. Thomas, it isn't much, but what's here is interesting. The boutiques and shops of Cruz Bay are individualized and quite special. Most of the shops are clustered at **Mongoose Junction,** in a woodsy area beside the roadway, about a 5-minute walk from the ferry dock. I've already recommended restaurants in this complex (see "Where to Dine," above), and it also contains shops of merit.

Before you set sail for St. Thomas, you'll want to visit **Wharfside Village,** just a few steps from the ferry-departure point on the waterfront, opening onto Cruz Bay. Here in this complex of courtyards, alleys, and shady patios is a mishmash of all sorts of boutiques, along with some restaurants, fast-food joints, and bars.

THE CANVAS FACTORY, Cruz Bay. Tel. 776-6196.

The Canvas Factory produces its own handmade, rugged, and colorful canvas bags in the "factory" at Mongoose Junction. Their products range from sailing hats to handsome luggage to an extensive line of island-made 100% cotton clothing. They are also the Caribbean agent for Lee sailmakers.

THE CLOTHING STUDIO, Mongoose Junction. Tel. 776-6585.

The Caribbean's oldest hand-painted–clothing studio has been in operation since 1978. You can watch talented artists create original designs on fine tropical clothing, including swimwear, daytime and evening clothing, for babies, children, men, and women.

FABRIC MILL, Mongoose Junction. Tel. 776-6194.

The Fabric Mill specializes in silk-screened and batik prints from around the world and it also carries locally silk-screened fabric displaying island motifs. Interesting accessories, soft sculptures, and unique gift items are also made in this studio shop.

D. KNIGHT & COMPANY, 258 Enighed Contant, Cruz Bay. Tel. 776-7958.

This establishment will interest only those readers who are intrigued by fine cabinetry and tropical hardwoods. In an industrial building on the east side of Cruz Bay on Route 104 you'll find one of the finest collections of exotic woods in the Caribbean. Mr. Knight's inventory includes beautifully striated Brazilian angelique, red locust from Dominica, honey-colored samaan, Burmese teak, ebony, black jacaranda, brown heart, green heart, purple heart, and rosewood. Unless you plan to buy massive quantities of the stuff, shipping it home will be a problem, but if you're just looking for a few boards for the top of something you're rebuilding in your workshop, Mr. Knight can arrange shipping through the mail. Closed: Sept.

R AND I PATTON GOLDSMITHING, Cruz Bay. Tel. 776-6548.

On the island since 1973, this is the oldest tourist business here. Next to the entrance to Mongoose Junction, it has a large selection of island-designed jewelry in sterling silver, gold, and precious stones.

PUSSER'S OF THE WEST INDIES, Wharfside Village, Cruz Bay. Tel. 774-5489.

This link in a famous chain was previously recommended for food and drink. The store offers a large collection of classically designed old-world travel and adventure clothing along with unusual accessories. It's a unique shopping trip for the island. Clothing for women, men, and children is displayed, along with T-shirts carrying

Pusser's colorful emblem. Nautical paintings and antiques from "all over" are also displayed.

DONALD SCHNELL STUDIO, Mongoose Junction. Tel. 776-6420.

In this working studio and gallery, Mr. Schnell and his assistants feature one of the finest collections of handmade pottery, sculpture, and blown glass in the Caribbean. The staff can be seen working daily and are especially noted for their rough-textured coral work. Water fountains are a specialty item, as are house signs. The coral pottery dinnerware is unique and popular. The studio will mail works all over the world. Go in and discuss any particular design you may have in mind—they enjoy designing to please customers.

3. ST. CROIX

The largest of the U.S. Virgin Islands, 84 square miles, St. Croix was a stop for Columbus on November 14, 1493, but the reception committee of Carib tribesmen was far from friendly. He anchored his ship off Salt River Point, on the north shore of St. Croix, before the Caribs drove him away. However, before leaving he named the island Santa Cruz (Spanish for Holy Cross). The cannibalistic Caribs made later colonizing parties less than eager to settle in St. Croix.

The Dutch, the English, the Spanish, and the French all claimed St. Croix at one time or another, but the Danes purchased the island in 1773, attracted to the site because of its slave labor and sugarcane fields. This marked the golden era for both planters and pirates. However, the sugar boom ended with eventual slave uprisings, the introduction of the sugar beet in Europe, and the emancipation of 1848. Even though seven different flags have flown over St. Croix, it is the nearly 2½ centuries of Danish influence that still permeates the island and its architecture.

At the east end of St. Croix, which, incidentally, is the easternmost point of the United States, the terrain is rocky and arid. The west end is lusher, with a rain forest of mango and mahogany, tree ferns, and dangling lianas. Rolling hills and upland pastures characterize the area lying between the two extremes. African tulips are just some of the flowers that add a splash of color to the landscape, which is dotted with stately towers that once supported grinding mills.

St. Croix has some of the best beaches in the Virgin Islands, and ideal weather. It doesn't have the sophisticated nightlife of St. Thomas, nor would its permanent residents want that.

ORIENTATION

GETTING AROUND By Bus At present there's no bus service on the island, but conditions could change—check locally. However, you can take a **public van** from the center of Christiansted to the shopping centers in the center of the island or to Frederiksted for $1.

By Taxi At Alexander Hamilton Airport you'll find official taxi rates posted. Per-person rates require a minimum of two passengers; a single person pays double the posted fares. Expect to pay about $10 for one or two riders from the airport to Christiansted and about $8 for one or two from the airport to Frederiksted. As the cabs are unmetered, agree on the rate before you get in.

The **St. Croix Taxicab Associations** (tel. 778-1088) offer door-to-door service.

By Rental Car This is a suitable means of exploring for some, but know that if you're going into "bush country," the roads are often disastrous. Sometimes the government smooths them out before the big season begins.

Car-rental rates on St. Croix are reasonable. However, because of the island's higher-than-usual accident rate (which is partly because many tourists aren't used to driving on the left), insurance costs might be higher than on the mainland.

Each of the "big three"—**Budget** (tel. toll free 800/472-3325), **Hertz** (tel. toll free 800/654-3001), and **Avis** (tel. toll free 800/331-2112)—maintains headquarters at the island's airport, with kiosks near the baggage-claim areas. All three require that renters be age 25 or older (and less than 70 at both Budget and Hertz) and that renters present a valid driver's license and a credit card at the time of rental. They each charge an additional $10 to $12 per day for collision-damage insurance, and around $3.50 a day for personal accident insurance. The issuer of your credit card *may* already provide this coverage; check with the issuer directly before your trip.

ESSENTIALS The **American Express** service representative is Southerland, Chandler's Wharf, Gallows Bay (tel. 773-9500). For medical care, try the **St. Croix Hospital,** Estate Ruby, Christiansted (tel. 778-6311).

WHERE TO STAY

All rooms are subject to a 7½% hotel room tax.

VERY EXPENSIVE

CORMORANT BEACH CLUB, 4126 La Grande Princesse, St. Croix, USVI 00820. Tel. 809/778-8920, or toll free 800/548-4460. Fax 809/778-9218. 34 rms, 4 suites. A/C TEL
$ Rates (including breakfast, lunch, and drinks before 5pm): Winter, $335 single; $360 double; $460 suite for two. Summer, $185 single; $235 double; $335 suite. AE, DC, MC, V. **Parking:** Free.

✪ The sumptuous setting, amid a colony of king palms on a 12-acre site about 3 miles northwest of Christiansted along Route 75 on Pelican Cove, strikes a perfect balance between seclusion and accessibility. Long Reef, one of the better-known zoological playgrounds of the Caribbean, is a few hundred feet from the hotel's sandy beachfront. In winter, children under 16 are politely discouraged, which many vacationers appreciate. Much of the success of the place is due to its manager, Larry Bathon, whose charm and welcome make you feel that you've made "the right choice" for your accommodations.

In well-maintained outbuildings, each room contains a spacious bath lined with coral blocks, cane and wicker furniture, and bouquets of seasonal flowers. Units are priced on a basis used nowhere else on St. Croix: Dubbed the CBC (Cormorant Beach Club) Plan, it includes breakfast, lunch, and all drinks until 5pm, tennis, snorkeling, and croquet.

Dining/Entertainment: In the tastefully airy dining room, large windows encompass a view of the beach. Dinners, served à la carte, feature a California and Caribbean cuisine costing about $30 per person and including fresh local fish, chicken, and steaks served with an interesting Caribbean accompaniment of mango, papaya, coconut, and Cruzan rum sauce.
Services: Laundry.
Facilities: Open-air clubhouse, well-stocked library, largest freshwater pool on St. Croix; golf, horseback riding, sailing, and scuba diving can be arranged.

VILLA MADELEINE, (P.O. Box 24190), Gallows Bay, St. Croix, USVI 00824. Tel. 809/773-8141, or toll free 800/548-4461. Fax 809/223-2518. 43 villas. A/C TV TEL

$ Rates: Winter, $320–$400 one-bedroom villa; $420–$500 two-bedroom villa. Summer, $225–$300 one-bedroom villa; $325–$400 two-bedroom villa. Breakfast $10 extra. AE, MC, V. **Parking:** Free.

Eight miles east of Christiansted, Villa Madeleine was built in 1990 on 6½ acres. Its focal point is a newly built great house whose Chippendale balconies and foursquare proportions emulate the designs of the Danish colonial era. Inside, a splendidly conceived decor incorporates the masses of English chintz and mahogany paneling you'd expect to find in the pages of *Architectural Digest*. The hotel is the creation of Gregory and Marcia Roncari.

The hotel rents one- and two-bedroom detached pale-yellow villas, each with its own privacy wall and plunge pool. Decorated in elegant 18th-century style, each unit has a four-poster bed, marble bathroom, and a richly accessorized kitchen. Thanks to the sloping terrain, none even hints at the proximity of its neighbors. Beachlovers willingly travel the third of a mile to the nearest beaches, Reef or Grapevine.

EXPENSIVE

BUCCANEER, Rte. 82, Estate Shoys (P.O. Box 25200) Gallows Bay, St. Croix, USVI 00824. Tel. 809/773-2100, or toll free 800/223-1108. Fax 809/778-8215. 150 rms, 11 suites. A/C MINIBAR TEL

$ Rates: Winter, $184–$325 single or double; from $600 suite. Summer, $140–$210 single or double; from $355 suite. AE, DC, MC, V. **Parking:** Free.

A large, family-owned resort in operation since 1948, the Buccaneer is 2 miles east of Christiansted, and its 240 acres contain three of the island's best beaches. The property was once a cattle ranch and a sugar plantation, and its first estate house, dating from the mid-17th century, stands near a freshwater swimming pool. Pink and patrician, the hotel offers a choice of accommodations in its main building or in one of the beachside properties. The baronially arched main building has a lobby opening toward drinking or viewing terraces, with a sea vista on two sides and Christiansted to the west. The accommodations effectively use modern construction materials and tropical furnishings to provide fresh, comfortable bedrooms which range from "standard" to "deluxe."

Dining/Entertainment: Breakfast and dinner are served at the Terrace Dining Room and at the Little Mermaid Restaurant. Lunch is also served at the Mermaid and at the Grotto, where hamburgers and hot dogs are available. There is entertainment nightly at the Terrace Lounge, with music ranging from Jimmy Hamilton's jazz to island steel drums. One of the most elegant places to dine is the resort's Brass Parrot Restaurant (see "Where to Dine," below).

Services: Room service (8am–9:30pm), laundry, baby-sitting.

Facilities: Best sports program on St. Croix—eight championship tennis courts with two lit at night, 18-hole golf course, horseback riding, sports fishing, scuba diving, snorkeling; excursions arranged to Buck Island's reef; outdoor swimming pool, 2-mile jogging trail.

MODERATE

ANCHOR INN, 58A King St., Christiansted, St. Croix, USVI 00820. Tel. 809/773-4000, or toll free 800/524-2030. Fax 809/773-4408. 32 rms, 4 suites. A/C MINIBAR TV TEL

$ Rates: Winter, $119–$134 single; $141–$156 double; $178 suite. Summer, $79–$90 single; $98 double; $109 suite. Continental breakfast $4.50 extra. AE, DC, MC, V. **Parking:** Public lot off King Street.

One of the few hotels in town directly on the waterfront is set in a quiet courtyard near Government House and the Old Danish Customs House, right in the heart of the shopping belt, between the Strand and Company Street. The space is so compact and intimate that you might not believe it holds 32 comfortably furnished units, each with refrigerator, radio, bath, and a small porch. A few units (without porches) have king- and queen-size beds.

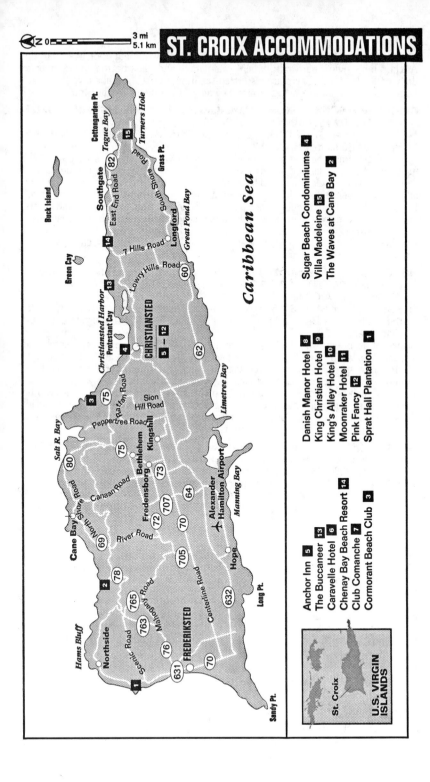

ST. CROIX ACCOMMODATIONS

3 mi
5.1 km

Caribbean Sea

Buck Island

Green Cay

Cottongarden Pl.
Turners Hole
Southgate
Tague Bay
East End Road
82
7 Hills Road
Longford
Great Pond Bay
Grass Pt.
South Shore Road
Lowry Hills Road
60
Christiansted Harbor
Protestant Cay
CHRISTIANSTED
62
Limetree Bay
Sion Hill Road
Peppertree Road
Kingshill
75
Bethlehem
Fredensborg
Alexander Hamilton Airport
Manning Bay
Canaan Road
73
64
72
707
70
Salt R. Bay
80
Cane Bay Road
North Store Road
River Road
705
Hope
632
69
78
Long Pt.
765
Centerline Road
Mahogany Road
Hams Bluff
Northside
763
Scenic Road
76
FREDERIKSTED
70
Sandy Pt.
631

Sugar Beach Condominiums **4**
Villa Madeleine **15**
The Waves at Cane Bay **2**

Danish Manor Hotel **8**
King Christian Hotel **9**
King's Alley Hotel **10**
Moonraker Hotel **11**
Pink Fancy **12**
Sprat Hall Plantation **1**

Anchor Inn **5**
The Buccaneer **13**
Caravelle Hotel **6**
Chenay Bay Beach Resort **14**
Club Comanche **7**
Cormorant Beach Club **3**

St. Croix

U.S. VIRGIN ISLANDS

Directly on the waterfront is a sun deck and small swimming pool, as well as the Anchor Inn's own boardwalk, where catamarans and glass-bottom boats operate daily to Buck Island. There are also deep-sea fishing boats, a scuba-dive shop, and honeymoon and family package tours. Dining is at Antoine's Anchor Inn.

CLUB COMANCHE, 1 Strand, Christiansted, St. Croix, USVI 00820. Tel. 809/773-0210, or toll free 800/524-2066. 43 rms. A/C TV TEL

$ Rates: Winter, $70–$115 single or double. Summer, $60–$98 single or double. Breakfast $6 extra. AE, DC, MC, V.

Club Comanche lives up to my idea of what a West Indian inn should be. Right on the Christiansted waterfront, a block off King Street, it's the domain of innkeeper Dick Boehm. The main house is old, but has been completely adapted to modern tastes in its remodeling and is a charming setting. Some of the bedrooms have slanted ceilings with handsomely carved four-poster beds, old chests, and mahogany mirrors. The newer addition, reached by a covered bridge spanning a shopping street, offers rooms in the poolside and harborfront buildings. There's a waterfront refreshment bar where you can order drinks and watch yachts come into dock.

HOTEL CARAVELLE, 44A Queen Cross St., Christiansted, St. Croix, USVI 00820. Tel. 809/773-0687, or toll free 800/524-0410. Fax 809/778-7004. 43 rms. A/C MINIBAR TV TEL

$ Rates: Winter, $105–$115 single; $115–$125 double. Summer, $78–$88 single; $88–$98 double. Breakfast from $5 extra. AE, DC, MC, V. **Parking:** Public lot off King Street.

Biggest of the downtown hotels, the Caravelle usually caters to a business clientele and is located between Church Street and King Cross Street. There's an Andalusian-style tile fountain splashing near the rectangular bar in the middle of the ground-floor reception area. The restaurant Banana Bay Club is a few steps away. Many resort activities, such as sailing, deep-sea fishing, snorkeling, scuba, golf, and tennis, can be arranged at the reception desk. A swimming pool and sun deck face the water, and all the shopping and activities of the town are close at hand. Each of the rooms has a private bath and is priced according to its view.

KING CHRISTIAN HOTEL, 59 King's Wharf (P.O. Box 3619), Christiansted, USVI 00822. Tel. 809/773-2285, or toll free 800/524-2012. Fax 809/773-9411. 24 superior rms, 15 no-frills rms. A/C TV TEL

$ Rates: Winter, $85 no-frills single, $115 superior single; $90 no-frills double, $125 superior double. Summer, $70 no-frills single, $88 superior single; $75 no-frills double, $94 superior double. AE, DC, MC, V. **Parking:** Public lot off King Street.

This is Betty Sperber's own special place, and she's one of the finest innkeepers on the island. The hotel is right in the heart of everything, directly on the waterfront. All its front rooms have two double beds, bathroom, cable color TV, refrigerator, room safe, and private balcony overlooking the harbor. No-frills economy-wing rooms have two single beds or one double and a bath, but no view or balcony.

On the premises is the Chart House, one of the best restaurants on St. Croix. You can relax on the sun deck, shaded patio, or in the freshwater pool. The staff will make arrangements for golf, tennis, horseback riding, and sightseeing tours, and there's a beach just a few hundred yards across the harbor, reached by ferry. Mile Mark Charters water-sports center, run by Betty's two sons, offers daily trips to Buck Island's famous snorkeling trail as well as a complete line of water sports.

KING'S ALLEY HOTEL, 57 King St., Christiansted, St. Croix, USVI 00820. Tel. 809/773-0103, or toll free 800/843-3574. Fax 809/773-4431. 23 rms. A/C TV TEL

$ Rates: Winter, $74–$128 single; $84–$140 double. Summer, $60–$105 single; $73–$116 double. DC, MC, V. **Parking:** Public lot off King Street.

Standing at water's edge, surveying Christiansted Harbor's yacht basin, the King's

Alley is furnished with a distinct Mediterranean flair. Many of its units overlook a swimming pool terrace surrounded by tropical plants. Each room has twin or king-size beds, and the galleries opening off them are almost spacious enough for entertaining. The hotel has a Marina Bar that serves drinks, and breakfast can be ordered if you walk to one of the nearby cafés.

PINK FANCY, 275 Prince St., Christiansted, St. Croix, USVI 00820. Tel. 809/773-8460, or toll free 800/524-2045. 13 rms.

$ Rates (including continental breakfast): Winter, $95–$125 single; $125–$150 double. Summer, $65–$75 single; $75–$90 double. MC, V. **Parking:** Off-street.

The Pink Fancy was restored and turned into this small, unique private hotel located one block from the Annapolis Sailing School. The oldest part of the four-building complex is a 1780 Danish town house, now one of the historic places of St. Croix. Years ago the building was a private club for wealthy planters. Fame came when Jane Gottlieb, the Ziegfeld Follies star, opened it as a hotel in 1948. In the 1950s the hotel became a mecca for writers and artists, including, among others, Noël Coward. Built on different levels, the efficiency rooms, with ceiling fans, are in four buildings clustered around the swimming pool. All but four units contain air conditioning.

INEXPENSIVE

DANISH MANOR HOTEL, 2 Company St., Christiansted, St. Croix, USVI 00820. Tel. 809/773-1377, or toll free 800/524-2029. Fax 809/773-1377. 36 rms (32 with bath), 2 suites. A/C TV TEL

$ Rates (including continental breakfast): Winter, $59 single without bath; $79–$89 single or double with bath; from $135 suite. Summer, $39 single without bath; $49–$59 single or double with bath; from $95 suite. AE, DC, MC, V. **Parking:** Public lot off King Street.

Built around an old Danish courtyard and a freshwater pool right in the heart of town, between King Street and Queen Street, this compound combines the very old and the very new. The hotel was erected on the site of a Danish West Indies Company's counting house. An L-shaped three-story addition stands in the rear, with spacious rooms with encircling balconies, ceiling fans, and cable TV and HBO. All units overlook an intimate courtyard dominated by an ancient mahogany tree. The entrance to the courtyard is through old arches.

MOONRAKER HOTEL, 43A Queen Cross St., Christiansted, St. Croix, USVI 00820. Tel. 809/773-1535. 12 rms (all with bath). A/C TV TEL

$ Rates: Winter, $65 single; $70 double. Summer, $50 single; $60 double. Extra person $10. Breakfast $5 extra. AE, DC, MC, V. **Parking:** Public lot off King Street.

A charming blend of old and new lies in the heart of Christiansted, between Church Street and King Cross Street. The hotel has been completely renovated and redecorated in a tropical motif. Bedrooms surround an old Danish courtyard shaded by a flourishing mango tree, and all have private baths and refrigerators. The hotel's Moonraker Lounge on the second floor is a favorite rendezvous for tourists and locals alike. Live entertainment is offered nightly in season. The Moonraker is close to the waterfront, free-port shopping, excellent dining, and nightlife.

A PLANTATION

SPRAT HALL PLANTATION, Rte. 63 (P.O. Box 695), Frederiksted, St. Croix, USVI 00841. Tel. 809/772-0305, or toll free 800/843-3584. 16 units (all with bath).

$ Rates: Winter $100 sea-view single; $110 sea-view double; $130 no-smoking room in great house; $140 cottage for one or two, $240 cottage for up to four. Summer, $70 sea-view single; $90 sea-view double; $120 no-smoking room in great house; $110 cottage for one or two; $160 cottage for up to four. MAP $30 per person extra. No credit cards. **Parking:** Free.

One mile north of Frederiksted is an accommodation that can never be duplicated. It is the oldest plantation "great house" in the Virgin Islands and the only French plantation house left intact. Dating back to the French occupation of 1650 to 1690, it's set on 20 acres of grounds, with private white sandy beaches. The plantation has room for about 40 people, depending on how many guests use the cottage units. Most rooms have air conditioning, radio, and TV, and some offer a minibar.

The three units in the great house have been designated for nonsmokers because of the value of the antiques. Sea-view rooms have been redecorated and carpeted. Room service is available to guests.

If you want more privacy, choose one of the Arawak units, with front porches for lounging or outdoor dining. There is full maid service daily, and guests have a choice of accommodations with king-size, double, or twin beds. Some of the Arawak group are two-bedroom cottages that can accommodate four to six people.

You can be sure of warm hospitality and good food, either at the Beach Restaurant at lunch or in the Sprat Hall great house restaurant, recommended below (see "Where to Dine"). On the grounds is the best equestrian stable in the Caribbean (see "Sports and Recreation," below). The Hurd Young family runs the operation and offers hiking and birdwatching, as well as snorkeling, swimming, and shore fishing. Scuba diving, deep-sea fishing, jet skiing, and waterskiing can be arranged.

CONDOS

In general, condominiums are rented at half or a third the going hotel rates, and if you wait until after April 15, prices are lowered even more.

CHENAY BAY BEACH RESORT, Rte. 82, East End Rd. (P.O. Box 24600), St. Croix, USVI 00824. Tel. 809/773-2918, or toll free 800/548-4457. Fax 809/773-2918. 50 cottages. A/C TV TEL

$ Rates: Winter, $175 cottage for two. Summer, $135 cottage for two. Continental breakfast $4.50 extra. AE, MC, V. **Parking:** Free.

With a quiet and "barefoot-casual" ambience, these West Indian–style cottages, new or newly renovated, are nestled on a 30-acre beach, with an open-air swimming pool. With one of the island's finest beaches for swimming, snorkeling, and windsurfing, Chenay Bay is just 3 miles east of Christiansted. Each cottage contains a fully equipped kitchenette, private bath, and ceiling fan. The Beach Bar and Grille is open for casual dining daily from 9am to 9pm. Children are welcome.

COLONY COVE, 221A Estate Golden Rock, St. Croix, USVI 00820. Tel. 809/773-1965, or toll free 800/828-0746. Fax 809/773-5397. 60 units. A/C TV TEL **Directions:** Travel east on Route 75, going toward Christiansted, to Five Corners, and then turn left and pass Mill Harbor; Colony Cove is the next driveway to the left.

$ Rates: Winter, $220–$280 single or double. Summer, $145–$205 single or double. AE, MC, V. **Parking:** Free.

Of all the condo complexes on St. Croix, Colony Cove is perhaps the most like a full-fledged hotel. About a mile west of Christiansted next to a palm-dotted beach, it's composed of four three-story buildings that ring a swimming pool. Each unit contains its own washer and dryer (rare for St. Croix), a kitchen, an enclosed veranda or gallery, two air-conditioned bedrooms, and a pair of bathrooms.

SUGAR BEACH CONDOMINIUMS, 3221 Estate Golden Rock, St. Croix, USVI 00820. Tel. 809/773-5345, or toll free 800/524-2049. Fax 809/773-1359. 46 units. A/C TV TEL

$ Rates: Winter, $150–$200 studio or one-bedroom unit for two; $250 two-bedroom unit for four; $295 three-bedroom unit for six. Summer, $90–$120 studio or one-bedroom unit for two; $150 two-bedroom unit for four; $190 three-bedroom unit for six. Maid service extra. AE, MC, V. **Parking:** Free.

This row of modernized one-, two-, or three-bedroom apartments is strung along 500 feet of sandy beach on the north coast off North Shore Road. When you tire of the sand, you can swim in the free-form freshwater pool nestled beside a sugar mill where rum was made three centuries ago. Under red-tile roofs, the apartments with enclosed balconies are staggered to provide privacy. All units open toward the sea, are tastefully decorated, and have completely equipped kitchens. The property has two Laykold tennis courts, and the Carambola golf course is minutes away.

THE WAVES AT CANE BAY, 112C Estate Cane Bay (P.O. Box 1749, Kingshill), St. Croix, USVI 00851. Tel. 809/778-1805, or toll free 800/545-0603. 12 units. A/C TV TEL **Directions:** From the airport, go left on Route 64 for 1 mile, right on Route 70 for 1 mile, left at the junction with Route 75 for 2 miles, and then a final left at the junction with Route 80 for 5 miles.

$ Rates: Winter, $115–$175 single or double. Summer, $70–$100 single or double. AE, MC, V. **Parking:** Free.

This intimate and tasteful property run by Suzanne and Kevin Ryan is about 9 miles from the airport, midway between the island's two biggest towns on a well-landscaped plot of oceanfront property on Cane Bay, the heart of the best scuba and snorkeling. Accommodations are in two-story units with screened-in verandas, all directly on the ocean. The Ryans host cocktail parties on the oceanside terrace and add many homelike touches. Units are high-ceilinged, with fresh flowers, well-stocked kitchens, private libraries, and thick towels. A two-room villa next to the main building has a large oceanside deck. The social center is a beachside bar ringed with stone and coral.

WHERE TO DINE

The island's independently owned restaurants are among the best in the Caribbean.

IN CHRISTIANSTED
Expensive

THE CHART HOUSE, 59 King's Wharf. Tel. 773-7718.
   Cuisine: STEAK/SEAFOOD. **Reservations:** Recommended.
$ Prices: Appetizers $7–$8.75; main courses $16–$25. AE, DC, MC, V.
   Open: Dinner only, daily 6–10pm.
In the center of town, off the wharf beneath the King Christian Hotel, this nautically decorated restaurant opens onto the waterfront in Christiansted and has a classy look of Oriental carpets and wicker chairs. Normally I don't like chain restaurants, but I always head for a Chart House. It has the best salad bar on the island, but I always order their celebrated prime rib. You might prefer their lobster, or barbecued beef ribs. Try their baked potato. The mud pie is justly renowned.

COMANCHE, 1 Strand. Tel. 773-2665.
   Cuisine: WEST INDIAN/CONTINENTAL. **Reservations:** Required.
$ Prices: Appetizers $3.50–$12; main courses $8.50–$25. AE, MC, V.
   Open: Lunch daily 11:30am–2:30pm; dinner daily 6–9:30pm.
Although relaxed, Comanche is quietly elegant and one of the best-liked restaurants on the island. A block from King Street, it's a very busy place. The menu is eclectic and is likely to include everything from fish and conch chowder to Cantonese shrimp balls. Each night a different special is featured, such as roast chicken with an oyster stuffing. Try bread pudding with rum sauce for dessert.

KENDRICKS, 52 King St. Tel. 773-9199.
   Cuisine: CONTINENTAL. **Reservations:** Recommended.
$ Prices: Appetizers $6.50–$8; main courses $16–$25. AE, V.
   Open: Dinner only Mon–Sat 6–10pm. **Closed:** June.
Kendricks is a fine restaurant in an old brick building in the heart of the town. Climb a flight of brick stairs to the second-floor dining room, which has a view of old Christiansted and the distant sea peeking out from above the rooftops. Meals might include grilled breast of duck with a molasses-and-black-peppercorn sauce, grilled rack of lamb with roasted garlic and thyme sauce, and grilled fresh fish

served with sun-dried tomatoes and a basil-flavor cream sauce. Desserts might include fresh apple crisp and a richly caloric mud pie.

TOP HAT, 52 Company St., opposite Market Sq. Tel. 773-2346.
  Cuisine: CONTINENTAL/SCANDINAVIAN. **Reservations:** Required.
  $ Prices: Appetizers $4–$10; main courses $13.50–$30. AE, DC, MC, V.
  Open: Dinner only, Mon–Sat 6–10pm. **Closed:** May–Nov.

Top Hat, on the second floor of a restored old merchant's house 2½ blocks from the wharf, has been operated by Bent and Hanne Rasmussen, two Scandinavians, since 1970. Look for daily specials, such as fresh seafood. A good selection of homemade desserts is offered, and there is an impressive selection of wines.

MODERATE

ANTOINE'S, 58A King St. Tel. 773-0263.
  Cuisine: GERMAN/AUSTRIAN/CARIBBEAN. **Reservations:** Required in winter.
  $ Prices: Appetizers $2.75–$8; main courses $8.75–$16.50. AE, MC, V.
  Open: Lunch daily 11:30am–2:30pm; dinner daily 6–10:30pm.

Antoine's was formerly known as the Anchor Inn Restaurant and Bar, and as such became famous in the Caribbean. In its latest incarnation, it's better than ever. The menu includes Austrian gulasch supper and knockwurst salad, but it still offers fresh local seafood and Caribbean lobster, as well as shrimp, scallops, and Maine lobster. It also includes a number of Cruzan food items, such as callaloo (a leaflike vegetable) and fish chowder. The bar is known for serving more than 35 frozen blender creations, ranging from piña colada to "raspberry poundcake" and the island's largest selection of beer. Live entertainment is provided in season. The location is right on King's Wharf, and the restaurant is on the second floor, with a covered terrace, so from your dining perch you can see the boats in the harbor.

BOMBAY CLUB, 5A King St. Tel. 773-1838.
  Cuisine: INTERNATIONAL. **Reservations:** Not required.
  $ Prices: Appetizers $4–$6.50; main courses $7–$15. AE, DC, MC, V.
  Open: Mon–Sat 11:30am–10pm.

The owners have managed to squeeze much miscellany into what has become one of the most enduring restaurants in Christiansted. Concealed from the street by the brick foundations of an 18th-century planter's town house, it includes a large photograph of John Lennon which greets visitors near the entrance, and such other ornaments as original paintings and tropical plants. You enter through a low stone tunnel and eventually find yourself near its bar and the courtyard which contains many of its tables. The food, while not overly fancy, is plentiful, flavorful, and reasonably priced. Menu items include the catch of the day, chicken Bombay, and a sauté of shrimp, beef, or chicken.

CAMILLE'S CAFE, Queen Cross St. Tel. 773-2985.
  Cuisine: DELI. **Reservations:** Not required.
  $ Prices: Appetizers $3.25–$4.25; main courses $3.95–$12.95; fixed-price dinner $12.95. No credit cards.
  Open: Mon–Sat 11am–10pm.

Near the intersection of Company Street, across from Government House, Camille's serves New York deli–type food. It's one of the best dining values in town, especially its fixed-price dinner. Crisp salads of shrimp and lobster are sold, or you might begin with a homemade soup. Sandwiches are also available for lunch. The place is a neighborhood enclave of convivial locals. Its brick walls and beamed ceilings were originally part of an 18th-century guesthouse.

DINO'S, 4C Hospital St. Tel. 778-8005.
  Cuisine: ITALIAN. **Reservations:** Required.
  $ Prices: Appetizers $5–$8; main courses $11–$18. No credit cards.
  Open: Dinner only, Mon–Wed and Fri–Sat 6–10pm. **Closed:** Sept.

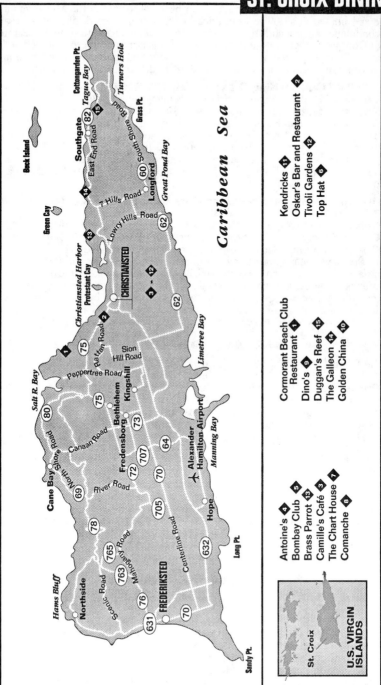

ST. CROIX DINING

N 0 3 mi
5.1 km

Caribbean Sea

Cottongarden Pt.
Tague Bay
Turners Hole
Grass Pt.
Southgate
East End Road
82
South Shore Road
Great Pond Bay
Longford
60
7 Hills Road
Lowry Hills Road
62
Christiansted Harbor
Protestant Cay
CHRISTIANSTED
12
3
62
Limetree Bay
Rattan Road
2
75
Sion Hill Road
1
Peppertree Road
Salt R. Bay
Kingshill
80
75
Bethlehem
Canaan Road
73
Cane Bay
North Shore Road
Fredensborg
707
64
Alexander Hamilton Airport
Manning Bay
69
72
70
River Road
705
Hope
78
Centerline Road
632
765
763
FREDERIKSTED
Melvin Road
76
Scenic Road
70
Hams Bluff
Northside
631
Long Pt.
Sandy Pt.
Back Island
Green Cay

Kendricks ◆11
Oskar's Bar and Restaurant ◆2
Tivoli Gardens ◆12
Top Hat ◆6

Cormorant Beach Club Restaurant ◆1
Dino's ◆9
Duggan's Reef ◆15
The Galleon ◆14
Golden China ◆10

Antoine's ◆4
Bombay Club ◆5
Brass Parrot ◆13
Camille's Café ◆3
The Chart House ◆7
Comanche ◆8

U.S. VIRGIN ISLANDS
St. Croix

One block east of Fort Christiansvaern is a bistro decorated in the Mediterranean style and housed in a 200-year-old brick building. It has two distinct sections: an air-conditioned interior and an open-air terrace in a commercial arcade in the heart of town. You might begin with a homemade pasta dish, then go on to veal piccata or breast of duck. A specialty is steak Dino, made with wild mushrooms and a flavoring of balsamic vinegar. Finish with a luscious Italian dessert or a cappuccino.

GOLDEN CHINA, 28 King Cross St. Tel. 773-8181.
    Cuisine: CHINESE. **Reservations:** Recommended Sat–Sun.
$ **Prices:** Appetizers $3–$7; main courses $9–$18. AE, MC, V.
    Open: Lunch Mon–Fri 11am–3pm; dinner daily 5–10pm.
On the water, Golden China serves food as fine as that enjoyed in the Chinatown of New York or San Francisco. The best experience is to get a group of six couples and arrange for the special Chinese banquet. Specialties include those from the Hunan and Szechuan kitchens. Each dish is prepared to order, and quality ingredients are used.

TIVOLI GARDENS, 39 Strand, upstairs over the Pan Am Pavilion. Tel. 773-6782.
    Cuisine: INTERNATIONAL. **Reservations:** Recommended for dinner.
$ **Prices:** Appetizers $3.50–$7; main courses $11.50–$19. AE, MC, V.
    Open: Lunch Mon–Sat 11:15am–2:30pm; dinner daily 6–9:30pm.
From this large second-floor porch festooned in lights you get the same view of Christiansted Harbor that a sea captain might. White beams hold up the porch of this favorite local rendezvous, and trellises and hanging plants add to the decor. The menu has everything from escargots provençals to a goulash inspired by a recipe concocted in the days of the Austro-Hungarian Empire. The Thai curry is also excellent. Save room for the wicked chocolate velvet cake. Often there is dancing from 7pm.

NEAR FREDERIKSTED

SPRAT HALL PLANTATION, Rte. 63. Tel. 772-0305.
    Cuisine: CARIBBEAN. **Reservations:** Required for dinner.
$ **Prices:** Main courses $16–$25; lunch $12. No credit cards.
    Open: Lunch daily noon–2:30pm; dinner Mon–Sat 7:30–8:15pm.
Some 1½ miles north of Frederiksted stands the oldest plantation great house in St. Croix. If you don't stay here (see "Where to Stay," above), you might want to call Mark and Judy Young to tell them you'd like to come by for dinner. Recommended by *Gourmet* magazine and considered one of the finest restaurants on the island, it has been feeding guests for years with the help of a bevy of West Indian cooks. Instead of appetizers, homemade muffins and a fresh salad made from the plantation's gardens are included in the price of the dinner. Main courses might be conch in sherry-butter sauce, loin of pork in a wild-orange sauce, grilled steaks, and local fish. Clients are requested to dress with decorum (no jeans or T-shirts, please).
    Lunches are less formal and are served almost directly on the white sands of a quarter-mile beach. Specialties include a basket of pumpkin fritters, conch salad, sandwiches, and curried chicken with coconut and raisins. Everything tastes better when preceded with a glass of Sprat Hall rum punch.

AROUND THE ISLAND

THE BRASS PARROT, in the Buccaneer Hotel, Rte. 82, Estate Shoys, Gallows Bay. Tel. 773-2100.
    Cuisine: INTERNATIONAL. **Reservations:** Required.
$ **Prices:** Appetizers $8–$12; main courses $20–$28. AE, DC, MC, V.
    Open: Dinner only, Thurs–Sun 7–9pm.
Two miles east of Christiansted along the coastal road and already previewed as one of the island's leading resorts (see "Where to Stay," above), this is the most formal and one of the best restaurants on the island; men must wear jackets. Named after the brass parrot that perches in the apéritif lounge, this air-conditioned, glassed-in cocoon

is set in the pink-sided great house of the hotel. Arched windows encompass views of both the hills and the sparkling faraway harbor of Christiansted. The kitchen is known for rack of lamb, chateaubriand for two, Caribbean lobster, and veal with crayfish.

CORMORANT BEACH CLUB RESTAURANT, 4126 La Grande Princesse. Tel. 778-8920.

Cuisine: CARIBBEAN/CALIFORNIAN. **Reservations:** Required.

$ Prices: Appetizers $5.50–$8.50; main courses $18–$28; Caribbean Grill Night $35; brunch Sun $22. AE, DC, MC, V.

Open: Lunch daily 11:30am–2pm; dinner daily 6:30–9:30pm; brunch Sun 11:30am–2pm.

Three miles northwest of Christiansted on Route 75, this restaurant could easily provide you with your most elegant—and best—dining experience on St. Croix. In a soaring wood pavilion open to a big-windowed view of the beach, it is especially romantic in the evening, when it flickers with candlelight. Entertainment begins every Thursday evening with an imported calypso singer who performs during the restaurant's Caribbean Grill Night, and it continues throughout the weekend until Sunday, when St. Croix's favorite brunch is enhanced with a steel-drum band.

The island's finest chef, Catherine Plav, blends the cooking of California with Cruzan ingredients and a touch of European flair. Whenever available, fresh ingredients from the seas and gardens of St. Croix are used in combination with the finest imports. Try the roast loin of pork stuffed with figs and cranberries and served with wild rice, or the ricotta cheese tortellini with grilled chicken, sun-dried tomatoes, zucchini, and walnuts in a sauce of fresh basil.

During the day, these dining facilities are open only to residents of the hotel.

DUGGAN'S REEF, Tague Bay. Tel. 773-9800.

Cuisine: AMERICAN/CARIBBEAN. **Reservations:** Recommended.

$ Prices: Appetizers $5–$10; main courses $16–$25. AE, MC, V.

Open: Lunch daily noon–3pm; dinner daily 6–10pm. **Closed:** Sept.

Duggan's Reef, owned by Frank Duggan, lies at Reef Beach 7 miles east of Christiansted at the eastern end of St. Croix (take Route 82). The bar, which is the most attractive feature of the place, begins inside the restaurant and ends on a wharf constructed over the water. For dinner, the most popular main dish is Duggan's Caribbean lobster pasta. You can also order a catch of the day, veal piccata, or a rack of lamb. Lunch is simpler and features soups, salads, and sandwiches.

THE GALLEON, East End Rd., Green Cay Marina, Estate Southgate. Tel. 773-9949.

Cuisine: CONTINENTAL/SEAFOOD. **Reservations:** Not required. Directions: Proceed east on Route 82 from Christiansted for 5 minutes; after going 1 mile past the Buccaneer Hotel, turn left into Green Cay Marina.

$ Prices: Appetizers $4–$8.50; main courses $13.50–$25. AE, MC.

Open: Dinner daily 6–10pm; brunch Sun 10am–2pm. **Closed:** July–Aug.

Overlooking the ocean, the Galleon is a local favorite—and deservedly so. The best cooking in Europe is found in northern Italy and France, and that's what's offered here, including carpaccio just as good as that served at Harry's Bar in Venice (but it's cheaper here). Freshly baked bread, two fresh vegetables, and rice or potatoes accompany main dishes. The menu always includes at least one local fish, or you can order a perfectly done rack of lamb carved at your table. Sunday brunch features a "groaning board" of delights, including chilled soup, fruit salads, and croissants. A baby grand is heard nightly until 11pm. The place has been called "casual but elegant."

OSKAR'S BAR AND RESTAURANT, La Grand Princesse, Rte. 75. Tel. 773-4060.

Cuisine: CONTINENTAL. **Reservations:** Not required. **Transportation:** Taxi.

$ Prices: Appetizers $2.50; main courses $8.50–$14.50. No credit cards.
Open: Lunch Mon–Sat 11am–2:30pm; dinner Mon–Sat 6–9pm.

Just outside Christiansted is a good, inexpensive restaurant. This Swiss-run place is often filled when other, better-known (and more expensive) establishments are empty. Meals, tasty and big ones, cost only $17. Try the special of the day, which might be roast pork with gravy, accompanied by mashed potatoes and corn. Or you may prefer bratwurst with sauerkraut, or even filet mignon. To finish your repast, why not Black Forest cake?

WHAT TO SEE & DO
IN CHRISTIANSTED

The picture-book harbor town of the Caribbean, Christiansted is an old Danish port, handsomely restored (or at least in the process of being restored). On the northeastern shore of the island, on a coral-bound bay, the town is filled with Danish buildings erected by prosperous merchants in the booming 18th century. These red-roofed structures are often washed in pink, ocher, or yellow. Arcades over the sidewalks make ideal shaded colonnades for shoppers. Government House—in fact, the whole area around the harborfront—has been designated a historic site and is looked after by the National Park Service.

WALKING TOUR — Christiansted

Start: Visitors' Bureau.
Finish: Christiansted harborfront.
Time: 1½ hours.
Best Times: Mondays to Saturdays, 10am to 4pm.
Worst Times: Sundays, when many places are closed.

Begin your tour at the:

1. **Visitors' Bureau,** a yellow building with a cedar-capped roof near the harborfront. It was originally built as the Old Scalehouse in 1856 to replace a similar, older structure which burned down. In its heyday, all taxable goods leaving and entering Christiansted's harbor were weighed here; the scales could accurately weigh barrels of sugar and molasses weighing up to 1,600 pounds each.
   In front of the Scalehouse is one of the most charming squares in the Caribbean, whose old-fashioned asymmetrical allure is still evident despite the masses of cars.
   With your back to the Scalehouse, turn left and walk through the parking lot to the foot of the white gazebo-inspired shell that sits in the center of a park named after Alexander Hamilton. The yellow-brick building with the ornately carved brick staircase is the:
2. **Old Customs House** (headquarters of the National Park Service). The gracefully proportioned 16-step staircase was added as an 1829 embellishment to an older building. (There are public toilets on the ground floor.)
   Continue climbing the hill to the base of the yellow:
3. **Fort Christiansvaern.** Considered the best-preserved colonial fortification in the Virgin Islands, it's maintained as a historic monument by the National Parks Service. Its original four-sided star-shaped design followed the most sophisticated military planning of its era.
   Exit from the fort and head straight down the tree-lined path toward the most visible steeple in Christiansted. It caps the appropriately named:
4. **Steeple Building** (Church of Lord God of Sabaoth), completed in 1753 as St.

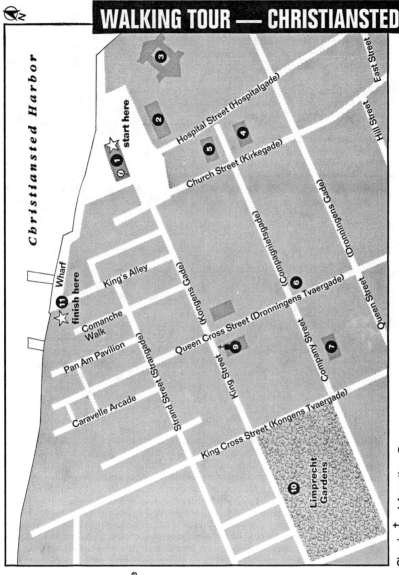

WALKING TOUR — CHRISTIANSTED

Christiansted Harbor

start here

Hospital Street (Hospitalgade)

Church Street (Kirkegade)

East Street

Hill Street

(Dronningens Gade)

(Compagnietsgade)

Wharf

finish here

King's Alley

Comanche Walk

Kongens Gade)

Queen Cross Street (Dronningens Tvaergade)

Queen Street

Pan Am Pavilion

Strand Street (Strangade)

King Street

Company Street

Queen Cross Street (Dronningens Tvaergade)

Caravelle Arcade

King Cross Street (Kongens Tvaergade)

Limprecht Gardens

Church ✝   Information ⊘

U.S. VIRGIN ISLANDS

Christiansted

St. Croix

1 The Visitors' Bureau
2 The Old Customs House
3 Fort Christiansvaern
4 Steeple Building
5 West Indies and Guinea warehouse
6 Bar Luncheria
7 Hendricks Square
8 Government House
9 Lord God of Sabaoth Lutheran Church
10 Limprecht Gardens and Memorial
11 Christiansted's harbor-front

Croix's first Lutheran church, and embellished with a steeple in 1794–96. The building was deconsecrated in 1831, and served at various times as a bakery, a hospital, and a school. A museum devoted to local history is inside.

Across Company Street from the Steeple Building is a U.S. Post Office. The building was built in 1749 as the:

5. West Indies and Guinea warehouse. It was once three times larger than today, and included storerooms and lodgings for staff. Go to the building's side entrance, on Church Street, and enter the rear courtyard if the iron gate is open.

For many years this was the site of the largest slave auctions in the Caribbean. From the post office, retrace your steps to Company Street and head west one block. On your left you'll pass the entrance to Apothecary Hall, 6 Company Street, which contains a charming collection of shops and restaurants.

REFUELING STOP The **6. Bar Luncheria,** Apothecary Hall, 6 Company Street (tel. 773-4247), is in a shedlike extension of an 18th-century building originally built of molasses-based mortar and local stone. Its tables sit in an enclosed courtyard in the shade of a handful of trees. The owners are considered the margarita specialists of the island and stock more types of tequila (15 plus) than any other bar in the neighborhood. Most margaritas begin at $2.50 each.

Exit Apothecary Hall and turn left onto Company Street. Cross Queen Cross Street (Dronningens Tuergade). Half a block later you'll arrive at the island's largest outdoor market:

7. Hendricks Square (Christian "Shan" Square), rebuilt in a timbered 19th-century style after the 1989 hurricane. Fruits and vegetables are sold here Monday through Saturday from 7am to 6pm.

Retrace your steps half a block along Company Street and turn left onto Queen Cross Street. Head downhill toward the harbor walking on the right-hand side of the street. In half a block you'll reach an unmarked arched iron gateway set beneath an arcade. If it's open, enter the charming gardens of:

8. Government House. Evocative of Europe, they contain very old trees, flowerbeds, and walkways. The antique building that surrounds the gardens was formed from the union of two much older town houses in the 1830s.

Exit the same way you entered, turn right, and continue your descent of Queen Cross Street. At the first street corner (King Street), turn left and admire the neoclassical facade of the:

9. Lord God of Sabaoth Lutheran Church, established in 1734. Continue walking southwest along King Street. In two blocks is the:

10. Limprecht Gardens and Memorial. For 20 years (1888–1908) Peter Carl Limprecht served as governor of the Danish West Indies. After the park, retrace your steps to King Cross Street and go left. One very short block later, turn right onto the Strand, which contains some interesting stones, including at least two different shopping arcades. The streets will narrow and the pedestrian traffic will be more congested. Pass beneath the overpass belonging to a popular bar and restaurant, the Club Comanche.

Continue down the meandering curves of King's Alley and within a block you'll be standing beside:

11. Christiansted's harborfront, on the boardwalk of its waterside piers.

IN FREDERIKSTED

This old Danish town at the western end of the island, about 17 miles from Christiansted, is a sleepy port town that comes to life only when a cruise ship docks at its shoreline.

Frederiksted was destroyed by a fire in 1879, and the citizens rebuilt it with wood frames and clapboards on top of the old Danish stone and yellow-brick foundations.

Most visitors begin their tour at russet-colored **Fort Frederick,** next to the pier. Some historians claim that this was the first fort to sound a foreign salute to the U.S. flag, in 1776. It was here on July 3, 1848, that Gov.-Gen. Peter von Schohen emancipated the slaves in the Danish West Indies. The fort, at the northern end of Frederiksted, has been restored to its 1840 look. You can explore the courtyard and stables, and an exhibit area has been installed in what was once the Garrison Room.

Just south of the fort, the **Customs House** is an 18th-century building with a 19th-century two-story gallery. Here you can go into the **visitors' bureau** and pick up a free map of the town.

Nearby, privately owned **Victoria House,** on Market Street, is a gingerbread-trimmed structure built after the fire of 1879. In the rebuilding, some of the original 1803 structure was preserved.

Along the waterfront Strand is the **Bellhouse,** once the Frederiksted Public Library. One of its owners, G. A. Bell, ornamented the steps with bells. The house today is an arts and crafts center and a nursery. Sometimes a local theater group presents dramas here.

The **Danish School,** on Prince Street, was adapted in the 1830s into a building designed by Hingelberg, a well-known Danish architect. Today it's the police station and Welfare Department.

Two churches are of interest: **St. Paul's Episcopal Church,** 28 Prince Street, was founded outside the port in the late 18th century, and the present building dates from 1812; **St. Patrick's Catholic Church,** on Prince Street, was built in the 1840s.

AROUND THE ISLAND

North of Frederiksted you can drop in at **Sprat Hall,** the island's oldest plantation, or else continue along to the rain forest, which covers about 15 acres, including the 150-foot-high **Creque Dam.** The terrain is private property, but the owner lets visitors go inside to explore. Most people want to see the jagged estuary of the northern coastline's **Salt River,** but other than bird life, there isn't much to see. This is where Columbus landed for a brief moment before being driven off by Caribs.

ST. GEORGE VILLAGE BOTANICAL GARDEN OF ST. CROIX, 127 Estate St., Kingshill. Tel. 772-3874.

Just north of Centerline Road, 4 miles east of Frederiksted at Estate St. George, is a veritable Eden of tropical trees, shrubs, vines, and flowers. Built around the ruins of a 19th-century sugarcane workers' village, the garden is a feast for the eye and the camera—from the entrance drive bordered by royal palms and bougainvillea to the towering kapok and tamarind trees. Restoration of the ruins is a continuing project. Two sets of workers' cottages provide space for a gift shop, rest rooms, a kitchen, and an office; these have been joined together with a Great Hall, which is used by the St. Croix community for various functions. Other completed projects include the superintendent's house, the blacksmith's shop, and various smaller buildings used for a library, a plant nursery, workshops, and storehouses.

Self-guided walking-tour maps are available at the entrance to the Great Hall.
Admission: $2 adults, $1 children 12 or under; donations welcome.
Open: Tues–Sat 10am–3pm. **Transportation:** Taxi.

CRUZAN RUM FACTORY, West Airport Rd. Tel. 772-0799.

This factory distills the famous Virgin Islands rum, which is considered by residents to be the finest in the world. Guided tours depart from the visitors' pavilion; call for reservations and information.
Admission: Free.
Open: Tours Mon–Fri 8:30–11:15am and 1–4:15pm.

ESTATE WHIM PLANTATION MUSEUM, Centerline Rd. Tel. 772-0598.

About 23 miles east of Frederiksted, this museum was restored by the St. Croix

Landmarks Society and is unique among the many sugar plantations whose ruins dot the island of St. Croix. This great house is different from most in that it's composed of only three rooms. With 3-foot-thick walls made of stone, coral, and molasses, the house is said by some to resemble a luxurious European château. Also on the premises is a typical woodworking shop, kitchen, gift shop, and a reproduction of a typical town apothecary. The ruins of the plantation's sugar-processing plant, complete with restored windmill, remain.

Admission: $5 adults, $1 children.
Open: Daily 10am–5pm.

DRIVING TOUR — East St. Croix

Start: Old Scalehouse, Christiansted.
Finish: Christiansted harborfront.
Time: 1½ hours.
Best Times: Early mornings or late afternoons.
Worst Times: Evenings.

Head east from Christiansted on Route 75 (some maps and some residents refer to this as East End Road). Within a few miles it will change its markings to Route 82. If you get confused at any time during this tour, remember to keep the ocean on your left.

Landmarks you'll pass on your way out of town will include Gallows Point and the:

1. **Buccaneer Hotel,** where you might want to return for one of the nightly musical performances which are among the best on the island.

   Suddenly the landscape will open into verdant countryside with grazing cows. An occasional mini-traffic jam might form as herds of goats cross the road. Continue driving and you'll pass:

2. **Green Cay Marina** (identified by a road sign), which you might want to visit to admire the yachts bobbing at anchor, or perhaps have a swim nearby at beautiful Chenay Bay. Nearby monuments include the Southgate Baptist Church, and a handful of stone towers that once housed the gear mechanisms of windmills that crushed the juice from sugarcane.

   About 7 miles along the route from Christiansted, you'll see the:

3. **Mountaintop aerie** of the island's most prominent socialite, the Contessa Nadia Farbo Navarro, the Romanian-born heiress to a great fortune. This opulent castle is the most outrageously unusual, most prominent, and most talked-about villa on St. Croix. Understandably, its privacy is rigidly maintained.

   A couple of miles farther you'll reach one of the most popular windsurfing beaches on St. Croix, Tague Bay. This is a good spot to take a break.

REFUELING STOP At Tague Bay, **4. Duggan's Reef** offers lunches, dinners, and a bar only 10 feet from the waves. Many guests claim that this is the best way to experience windsurfing without getting on a sailboard. See "Where to Dine" above, for details.

After your stop, continue driving east along Route 82 to the area that most residents consider the most peaceful and most dramatic on the island. It is especially beautiful at sunset.

At Knight Bay, near the eastern tip of the island, turn right onto Route 60 (Southside Road) and head west. One of the several lakes you'll pass is:

5. **Hartmann's Great Pond** (also known as Great Pond), a favorite of nesting seabirds. The sea vistas and the rolling grasslands are spectacular.

   Route 60 merges with Route 624 a short distance north of Great Pond. Fork left

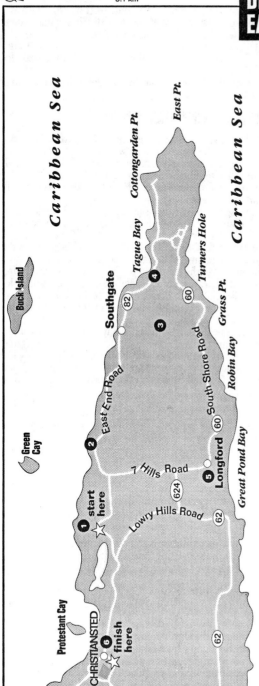

DRIVING TOUR — EAST ST. CROIX

0 | 3 mi
5.1 km

Caribbean Sea

Caribbean Sea

Buck Island

Green Cay

Protestant Cay

CHRISTIANSTED

East Pt.

Cottongarden Pt.

Tague Bay

Southgate

East End Road

7 Hills Road

Lowry Hills Road

South Shore Road

Turners Hole

Grass Pt.

Robin Bay

Great Pond Bay

Longford

82

60

60

624

62

62

1 start here

2

3

4

5 Longford

6 finish here

1 Buccaneer Hotel
2 Green Cay Marina
3 Mountaintop aerie
4 Duggan's Reef
5 Hartmann's Great Pond
6 Fort Christiansvaern

East St. Croix

U.S. VIRGIN ISLANDS

onto Route 624, and a short distance later, right onto Route 62 (Lowry Hill Road). You'll travel the mountainous spine of the island through districts named after former farms, such as Sally's Fancy, Marienhoj, and Boetzberg.

Within 2 miles, Lowry Hill Road merges with Route 82 again. Fork left and follow it as it turns into Hospital Gade and leads to the center of Christiansted. To your right will appear:

6. **Fort Christiansvaern,** as you pull into the parking lot in front of Christiansted's tourist office (Old Scalehouse).

SPORTS & RECREATION

BEACHES   Beaches are the big attraction. The drawback is that getting to them from Christiansted, center of most of the hotels, isn't always easy. It can also be expensive, especially if you want to go back and forth every day of your stay. Of course, you can always rent one of those housekeeping condos right on the water.

In Christiansted, if you want to beach it, head for the **Hotel on the Cay.** You'll have to take a ferry to this palm-shaded island.

Cramer Park, at the northeastern end of the island, is a special public park operated by the Department of Agriculture. Lined with sea-grape trees, the beach also has a picnic area, a restaurant, and a bar.

I highly recommend **Davis Bay** and **Cane Bay** as the type of beaches you'd expect to find on a Caribbean island—palms, white sand, and good swimming, and snorkeling. Cane Bay adjoins Route 80 on the north shore. Snorkelers and divers are attracted to this beach, with its rolling waves, coral gardens, and dropoff wall. No reefs guard the approach to Davis Beach, which draws bodysurfers but doesn't have changing facilities. It's off the South Shore Road (Route 60), in the vicinity of the Carambola Beach Resort.

Windsurfers like **Reef Beach,** which opens onto Tague Bay along Route 82, East End Road, a half-hour ride from Christiansted. Food can be ordered at Duggan's Reef. On Route 63, a short ride north of Frederiksted, **Rainbow Beach** invites with its white sand and ideal snorkeling conditions. In the vicinity, also on Route 63, about 5 minutes north of Frederiksted, **La Grange** is another good beach. Lounge chairs can be rented, and there's a bar nearby.

At the **✪ Cormorant Beach Club** (see "Where to Stay," above), about 5 miles west of Christiansted, some 1,200 feet of white sands are shaded by palm trees. Since a living reef lies just off the shore, snorkeling conditions are ideal. **Grapetree Beach** offers about the same footage of clean white sand on the eastern tip of the island (Route 60). Follow the South Shore Road to reach it. Water sports are popular here.

Two more beaches on St. Croix include **Buccaneer Beach,** 2 miles west of Christiansted, and **Sandy Point,** directly south of Frederiksted, the largest beach in all of the U.S. Virgin Islands. Its waters are shallow and calm, perfect for swimming. Jutting out from southwestern St. Croix like a small peninsula, Sandy Point is reached by taking the Melvin Evans Highway (Route 66) west from the Alexander Hamilton Airport.

FISHING   The fishing grounds at **Lang Bank** are about 10 miles from St. Croix. Here you'll find kingfish, dolphin, and wahoo. Using light-tackle boats along the reef, the catch is likely to turn up jack or bonefish. At Clover Crest, in Frederiksted, Cruzan anglers fish right from the rocks.

Serious sports fishers can board the *Ruffian,* St. Croix Marina, Gallows Bay (tel. 773-7165 during the day, 773-0917 at night), a 41-foot Hatteras convertible, available for half- or full-day charters with bait and tackle included.

GOLF   St. Croix has the best golfing in the U.S. Virgins. In fact, guests staying on St. John and St. Thomas often fly over for a day's round on the island's two 18-hole and one 9-hole golf courses.

The **✪ Carambola Golf Course** (tel. 778-5638), on the northeast side of St. Croix, was designed by Robert Trent Jones, who called it "the loveliest course I ever designed." The course, formerly the Fountain Valley and the site of "Shell's

Wonderful World of Golf," has been likened to a botanical garden. Its collection of par-3 holes is known to golfing authorities as the best in the tropics. Carambola's course record of 66 was set by Tom Kite in 1987. Greens fees in winter are $50 per person for a day, which allows you to play as many holes as you like. Rental of a golf cart is mandatory at $25 per 18 holes. In summer, greens fees are reduced to $30 per person for 18 holes, with carts costing $12.50 per person.

The other major course, at the **Buccaneer Hotel** (tel. 773-2100, ext. 738), 2 miles east of Christiansted (see "Where to Stay," above), is a challenging 6,200-yard, 18-hole course with spectacular vistas that allows the player to knock the ball over rolling hills right to the edge of the Caribbean. Nonguests who reserve pay $24 greens fees, and carts rent for $11. A golf pro is available for lessons, and there's a pro shop.

A final course is the **Reef,** at Tague Bay (tel. 773-8844), a 3,100-yard, 9-hole course charging greens fees of $12, with carts renting for $12. On the east end of the island, its longest hole is a 579-yard par 5.

HORSEBACK RIDING Offering more than 35 horses, **Paul & Jill's,** Sprat Hall Plantation, Route 63 (tel. 772-2880), is the largest equestrian headquarters in the Virgin Islands. Set on the sprawling grounds of the island's oldest plantation great house, it's operated by Paul Jojcie, and his wife, Jill Hurd, one of the daughters of this establishment's original founders. The stables are known for the quality of the horses and the beautiful trail rides through the forests, past ruins of abandoned plantation houses and sugar mills, to the tops of the scenic hills of St. Croix's western end. Most tours are accompanied by the operators, who give a running commentary on island fauna, history, and riding techniques. Beginners and experienced riders alike are welcome.

A 2½-hour trail ride costs $50 per person, with discounts granted to residents of the Sprat Hall Plantation. Tours usually depart daily at 10am and 4pm, with slight seasonal variations. Reservations at least a day in advance are important.

TENNIS Some authorities rate the tennis at the **Buccaneer Hotel** (tel. 773-2100, ext. 736) as the best in the West Indies. This hotel (recommended under "Where to Stay," above) offers a choice of eight courts, two lit for night games. They are open to the public. Nonguests pay $5 per person per hour; however, you must call to reserve a court. A tennis pro is available for lessons, and there is also a pro shop.

A notable selection of courts is also found at the **Carambola Golf Club** (tel. 778-5638), which has five clay courts, two of which are lit for night games. Open to the public, it charges $23 per hour for nonguests, around $30 at night. You must call to reserve. Both a pro shop and a tennis pro for lessons are available.

WATER SPORTS Spectacular sponge life, black-coral trees (considered the finest in the West Indies), and steep dropoffs into water near the shoreline have made St. Croix a diver's goal.

Buck Island, with an underwater visibility of more than 100 feet, is the site of the nature trail of the underwater national monument, and it's the major diving target (see "An Excursion to Buck Island" at the end of this chapter). All the minor and major agencies offer scuba and snorkeling tours to Buck Island. Divers also like to go to **Pillar Coral,** with its columns of coral spiraling up to 25 feet; **North Cut,** one of the tallest, largest coral pinnacles in the West Indies; and **Salt River Dropoff,** plunging to well over 1,000 feet deep, as well as **Davis Bay Dropoff,** with its unique coral and rock mound structures in grotesque shapes.

Dive St. Croix, 59 King's Wharf (tel. 773-3434, or toll free 800/523-DIVE), operates the 42-foot dive boat *Betty Ann*. The staff offers complete instructions from resort courses through full certification, as well as night dives. A resort course, including all equipment and a one-boat dive, is $65. A two-tank boat dive for the certified diver goes for $55.

V.I. Divers, in the Pan Am Pavilion, Christiansted (tel. 773-6045, or toll free 800/544-5911), is a PADI five-star dive center offering what *Skin Diver* magazine calls one of the "10 top dives in the Caribbean." For noncertified divers, an introductory dive costs $65; for certified divers, a two-tank boat dive goes for $60.

SAVVY SHOPPING
IN CHRISTIANSTED

In Christiansted, where the core of my shopping recommendations are found, the emphasis is on hole-in-the-wall boutiques selling one-of-a-kind merchandise; handmade items are strong. Of course the same duty-free stipulations, as outlined earlier, apply to your shopping selections on St. Croix.

Knowing that it can't compete with Charlotte Amalie, Christiansted has forged its own creative statement in its shops and has now become the "chic spot for merchandise" in the Caribbean. All the shops are easily compressed into half a mile or so. Most shops are open Monday through Saturday from 9am to 5pm.

CASA CARLOTA, Chandler's Wharf Mall, Gallows Bay. Tel. 778-8940.

Just east of Christiansted, Casa Carlota specializes in high-quality cotton garments for women. The distinctive collection of lightweight fashions features fine fabrics, meticulous craftsmanship, and outstanding styling. Included are Anokhi hand-blocked prints from Jaipur, India.

COLOMBIAN EMERALDS, 43 Queen Cross St. Tel. 773-1928.

Along with stunning emeralds, called "the rarest gemstone in the world," rubies and diamonds also dazzle here. Other gemstones are ametrine, blue topaz, opals, and amethyst. The staff will show you their large range of 14-karat gold jewelry, along with the best buys in watches, including Seiko quartz, Omega, and Porsche.

GROG AND SPIRITS LIQUOR STORE, in the King Christian Hotel building, 59 King's Wharf. Tel. 778-8400.

This is the place to go for beverages and snack foods. The owners can advise you on how much you can take back home with you in the liquor, liqueur, wine, and champagne line. Many times the prices here are so low that you'd be well off to buy here and pay duty if you go over the U.S. Customs limit. If you're making a trip to Buck Island from the dock next to the grog shop, you can purchase grocery items for a picnic, as well as beer and soda. Cigarettes are also sold here. You can have everything you buy packed in easy-to-carry boxes and delivered to your hotel.

The same operators also run **Portside Grog & Spirits,** Chandlers Wharf, Gallows Bay, Port Street (tel. 773-8485), across from the Gallows Bay Dock. This store features the largest wine and champagne selection in St. Croix.

ISLAND SPORT, in Club Comanche, Strand St. Tel. 773-5010.

Championship sportswear collections from Izod for men and women, casual resortwear from Renny, and lighthearted seaside prints from Boscali for women are available here. It also sells Ken Done's whimsical bright resortwear, plus bags, scarves, sunglasses, umbrellas, towels, posters, and housewares. Its T-shirt collection for both adults and kids is said to be the best on the island.

JAVA WRAPS, Strand and King St. Tel. 773-3770.

Selling perhaps the most avant-garde fashions in St. Croix is dedicated owner Twila Wilson, who spends 6 months of the year in Java and Bali overseeing the production of her resort designs made of hand-batiked prints. Twila, who naturally wears a sarong herself, says that her "designs and fabrics emphasize cool, easy-to-wear, clean good-looking things." You'll find kimonos, rompers, bikinis, shorts sets, sun dresses, and shirts for men and boys. But the bestseller is the one-size sarong. If you purchase it, you're given a sheet of instructions on how to wear it. Ask to see her antique Dorothy Lamour sarongs. She also has a collection of children's wear.

LAND OF OZ, 52A Company St. Tel. 773-4610.

This is the most enchanting store for children in the Caribbean. However, owner Joe Feehan says, "The store is for children of all ages." Variety is the keynote of this establishment, with emphasis on unusual items from around the world. An example is games, ranging from Wahree, one of the world's oldest games, to the latest advertised on TV. Some 3,000 different items are in stock. Shipping is available.

MANY HANDS, in the Pan Am Pavilion. Tel. 773-1990.
Devoted to Virgin Islands handcrafts, Many Hands also sells a collection of local paintings. You're invited to see their year-round "Christmas tree." Children get a lot of attention here, as there's an assortment of custom-made dresses and suits, along with stuffed toys. West Indian spices and teas are also sold, as are shellwork, stained glass, hand-painted china, ceramic switch plates, and handmade jewelry.

ONLY IN PARADISE, 5 Company St. Tel. 773-0331.
In this spacious air-conditioned store there's a choice assortment of gifts, such as art glass, linens, real and costume jewelry, and decorative items, as well as pearls however you want them—cultured, freshwater, or baroque. Its boutique, around back in a secluded courtyard, offers leather goods and cotton lingerie.

PEGASUS, 58 Company St. Tel. 773-6926.
Both a retail outlet and a jewelry workshop, Pegasus specializes in diamonds, gold, and gemstones, and can be trusted. In their undulating showcase they offer earrings, pendants, bracelets, and many one-of-a-kind pieces. Tariffs are based on the fluctuating price of gold. They also have a varied selection of handcrafted black coral, pink coral, and pearl jewelry.

VIOLETTE BOUTIQUE, in the Caravelle Arcade, 38 Strand. Tel. 773-2148, or toll free 800/544-5912.
A small department store with many boutique areas carrying lines known worldwide, Violette includes many exclusive fragrances and hard-to-find bath lines. It also has the latest in Cartier, Fendi, Seiko, Pequignet, Gucci, and Yves St. Laurent watches. A wide selection of famous cosmetic names are featured. Fendi has its own area for bags and accessories.

AROUND THE ISLAND

ST. CROIX LEAP, Mahogany Rd., Rte. 76. Tel. 772-0421.
On your tour of the island, especially if you're in western St. Croix near Frederiksted, you might want to stop off at St. Croix Leap for a fascinating adventure. In this open-air shop, you can see stacks of rare and beautiful wood being fashioned into tasteful objects. It's a St. Croix Life and Environmental Arts Project, dedicated to the natural environment through manual work, conservation, and self-development. The end result is a fine collection of Cruzan mahogany serving boards, tables, wall hangings, clocks, and sections of unusual pieces crafted into functional objects. They become a form of naturalistic art. St. Croix Leap is 5 miles from Christiansted, 2 miles up Mahogany Road from the beach north of Frederiksted. Large mahogany signs and sculptures flank the driveway. Visitors should bear to the right to reach the woodworking area and gift shop. It's open daily from 8am to 4pm. For inquiries, write to Leap, P.O. Box 245, Frederiksted, USVI 00841-0245.

WHIM GIFT SHOP, in the Estate Whim Plantation Museum, east of Frederiksted on Centerline Rd. Tel. 772-0598.
Offering a good selection of gifts and appealing to a wide age spectrum, the Whim Gift Shop has many imported items, but also many that are Cruzan made. Some were personally made for the Whim shop. And if you buy something, it all goes to a worthy cause: the upkeep of the museum and the grounds.

EVENING ENTERTAINMENT

St. Croix doesn't have the sophisticated nightlife of St. Thomas, so to find the action, you might have to hotel- or bar-hop or consult *St. Croix This Week.*

If he's playing, the one man to seek out is **Jimmy Hamilton,** Duke Ellington's "Mr. Sax." He and his quartet are a regular feature of St. Croix nightlife. Ask at your hotel if he's appearing locally at the time of your visit.

Also try to catch a performance of the **Quadrille Dancers,** the big treat of St. Croix. Their dances are little changed since plantation days; the women wear long dresses, white gloves, and turbans, and the men are attired in flamboyant shirts, sashes, and tight black trousers. When you've learned their steps, you're invited to join the dancers on the floor. Ask at your hotel if and where they are performing.

THE PERFORMING ARTS

ISLAND CENTER, half a mile north of Sunny Isle. Tel. 778-5272.
This 1,100-seat theater continues to attract big-name entertainers to St. Croix. Programs range from jazz, nostalgia, and musical revues to plays from Broadway, such as *Deathtrap.* The Caribbean Community Theatre and Courtyard Players perform here regularly. There aren't performances all the time, so you have to consult *St. Croix This Week* or call the center directly to see what's being presented and performance times.
Admission: Tickets, $15–$20, rising for really "big names."

THE CLUB & MUSIC SCENE

CORMORANT BEACH CLUB BAR, 4126 La Grand Princesse. Tel. 778-8920.
One of the most romantically positioned bars on the island is near the beach of La Grande Princesse at the entrance to this previously recommended hotel (see "Where to Stay," above), northwest of Christiansted. Guests sit at tables overlooking the ocean or around an open-centered mahogany bar in an enlarged gazebo. The decor is enhanced by wicker love seats, comfortable chairs, and soft lighting. After their drinks, some readers move into the adjacent restaurant (see "Where to Dine," above) for dinner. Excellent tropical drinks include margaritas and the house specialty, a Cormorant cooler, with champagne, pineapple juice, and Triple Sec. Drinks begin at $3.50. Open: Daily 5pm to "whenever."

HONDO'S BACKYARD/HONDO'S DISCO, 53 King St. Tel. 773-8187.
Most clients pass through the bar near the entrance to socialize in its fenced-in courtyard. On simple picnic tables outdoors, beer and rum punches flow freely, accompanied by such simple Tex-Mex or West Indian food as nachos, hamburgers, tacos, grilled chicken or ribs, mutton stew, and Cruzan meatloaf platters. Some clients eventually drift upstairs to Hondo's Disco (more frequently referred to simply as "Hondo's"). Platters of food cost $3.50 to $10; drinks go for $2.50 to $2.75. Open: Hondo's Backyard, Mon–Sat 11:30am–midnight, Sun 4pm–midnight; Hondo's Disco, Mon–Sat 8pm–2 or 4am (depending on business).
Admission: Disco, $3.

MOONRAKER LOUNGE, in the Moonraker Hotel, Queen Cross St. Tel. 773-1535.
On the upper balcony of one of Christiansted's most centrally located hotels, this place offers a view of the harbor, a happy hour from 7:30 to 8:30pm, and live entertainment (sometimes a guitarist in the style of Jimmy Buffett) beginning at 9pm. Drinks begin at $2.50, except during happy hour when they're reduced by about 40%. Open: Tues–Sat 7:30pm–1am.

THE SUNDOWNER, 40 LaGrange. Tel. 772-9906.
In an adaptation of one of the island's old houses, the Sundowner sits beside the water overlooking the piers, near the point where cars enter Frederiksted from Christiansted. This establishment really comes alive on Friday and Saturday at 5:30pm, when virtually every inhabitant of St. Croix shows up to drink, mingle, listen to live music—and watch the sun set. On Sunday between 5 and 9pm you can listen to rock 'n' roll, blues, and jazz. Drinks cost $2 to $3.50. Open: Mon–Sat 6am–9pm, Sun 9am–9pm.

THE TERRACE LOUNGE, in the Buccaneer Hotel, Rte. 82, Estate Shoys. Tel. 773-2100.
Every night this lounge off the main dining room of one of St. Croix's most upscale hotels welcomes some of the Caribbean's finest entertainers, including Jimmy Hamilton or a "down-island" steel band. Drinks cost $4 to $5. Open: Daily 8–11pm.

Admission: $4 for those who aren't staying in the hotel.

AN EXCURSION TO BUCK ISLAND

The crystal-clear water and the white coral sand of Buck Island, a satellite of St. Croix, are legendary. Slithering through its undergrowth in days of yore, you'd likely have run into Morgan, LaFitte, Blackbeard, or even Captain Kidd. Now the National Park Service has marked an underwater snorkeling trail. The park covers about 850 acres, including the land area, which has a sandy beach with picnic tables set out and pits for having your own barbecues, as well as rest rooms and a small changing room. There are two major underwater trails for snorkeling on the reef, plus many other labyrinths and grottoes for more serious divers. You can also take a hiking trail through the tropical vegetation that covers the island.

Only a third of a mile wide and a mile long, Buck Island lies only 1½ miles off the northeastern coast of St. Croix. A barrier reef shelters many reef fish, including queen angelfish and the smooth trunkfish. The attempt to return the presently uninhabited Buck Island to nature has been successful—even the endangered brown pelicans are producing young here.

Small boats run between St. Croix and Buck Island, charging $25 to $40, and snorkeling equipment is furnished. You head out in the morning, and nearly all charters allow 1½ hours of snorkeling and swimming.

One company that makes the trip is **Mile Mark Charters,** in the King Christian Hotel, 59 King's Wharf (P.O. Box 3045), Christiansted, St. Croix, USVI 00820 (tel. 809/773-2628). Owned and operated by two enterprising brothers, Miles and Mark Sperber, the company offers twice-daily tours to the aquatic wonders of Buck Island. Water-watchers can pick one of two ways to reach the reefs. One is aboard a glass-bottom boat departing twice daily (from 9:30am to 1pm and 1:30 to 5pm) from a point in front of the King Christian Hotel; the cost is $25 per person and all snorkeling equipment is included. A more romantic journey aboard one of the company's wind-powered trimarans offers the thrill of wind power to reach the reef for $35 per person. A full-day tour in the sailboat costs $45, and either Miles or Mark is happy to explain the fine point of underwater nature-watching.

Captain Heinz (tel. 773-3161 or 773-4041) is an Austrian-born skipper with some 20 years of sailing experience. His trimaran, *Teroro II*, leaves Green Cay Marina "H" Dock daily at 9am and 2:30pm, usually filled with small groups, never more than 24 passengers, who pay $35 per person. All gear and safety equipment are provided. The captain sailed the first *Teroro* across the Atlantic. He's a concerned host and will even take you around the outer reef, which the other guides do not, for an unforgettable underwater experience.

CHAPTER 6

THE BRITISH VIRGIN ISLANDS

With its small bays and hidden coves, once havens for pirates, the British Virgin Islands are considered among the world's loveliest cruising grounds by the yachting set. Strung over the northeastern corner of the Caribbean, about 60 miles east of Puerto Rico, are some 40 islands, although skeptics might consider many of these rocks, perhaps cays, and in some cases, "spits of land." Only a trio of the British Virgins are of any significant size: Virgin Gorda (the "Fat Virgin"), Tortola ("dove of peace"), and Jost Van Dyke. Other islands have such names as Fallen Jerusalem and Ginger. Norman Island is said to have been the prototype for Robert Louis Stevenson's *Treasure Island*. On Deadman Bay, a rocky cay, Blackbeard marooned 15 pirates and a bottle of rum, which gave rise to the ditty.

Columbus came this way in 1493, but the British Virgins apparently made little impression on him. Although the Spanish and Dutch contested it, Tortola was officially annexed by the English in 1672. Today, the British Virgin Islands are a British colony, with their own elected government and a population of about 11,000.

The vegetation is varied and depends on the rainfall. In some parts, palms and mangoes grow in profusion, while other places are arid and studded with cactus.

There are predictions that mass tourism is on the way, but so far the British Virgins are still a paradise for escapists. According to a report I once read, the British Home Office listed them as "the least important place in the British Empire."

GETTING THERE

BY PLANE There are no direct flights from New York to the British Virgin Islands, but you can make good connections from San Juan and St. Thomas to Beef Island/Tortola. (see Chapter 4 on Puerto Rico and Chapter 5 on the U.S. Virgin Islands for information on transportation to these islands.)

Your best bet to reach Beef Island/Tortola is to take **American Eagle** (tel. toll free 800/433-7300), which is probably viewed as the most reliable airline in the Caribbean and operates at least seven daily trips from San Juan to Beef Island/Tortola and its neighbor, Virgin Gorda. American Eagle also operates several daily nonstop flights between St. Thomas and both Tortola and Virgin Gorda.

Sun Air (tel. toll free 800/524-2094) operates small aircraft three times daily between St. Thomas and both Tortola and Virgin Gorda and between San Juan and both Tortola and Virgin Gorda.

You can sometimes make connections from a handful of other Caribbean islands on **Leeward Islands Air Transport (LIAT)** (tel. 809/462-0701). This Antigua-

WHAT'S SPECIAL ABOUT THE BRITISH VIRGIN ISLANDS

Beaches
☐ Cane Garden Bay, Tortola, which some beach aficionados rank as fine as St. Thomas's celebrated Magens Bay Beach.
☐ Apple Bay (also called Cappoon's Bay), Tortola, the surfer's favorite.

Great Towns/Villages
☐ Road Town, capital of Tortola and of the BVI, center for "stocking up" on everything for those heading for the remote islands.

Ace Attractions
☐ Guana Island, containing the richest fauna known for an island of its size in the West Indies—and maybe the world.

☐ Sage Mountain National Park, Tortola, with the highest mountain in the Virgin Islands (1,780 feet).
☐ The Baths, Virgin Gorda, clusters of massive prehistoric rocks forming cool, inviting grottoes, ideal for swimming and snorkeling.
☐ The wreck of the R.M.S. *Rhone*, off Salt Island, a royal mail steamer from 1807—the most celebrated dive site in the West Indies.

based carrier flies to Tortola from St. Kitts, St. Maarten, Antigua, and St. Thomas in small planes and is not acknowledged for frequency in service or adherence to any discernible schedule. Reservations are made through travel agents or through the large U.S.-based airlines which interconnect with LIAT hubs.

Flying time to Beef Island/Tortola from San Juan is 30 minutes; from St. Thomas, 15 minutes; and from the most distant of the LIAT hubs (Antigua), 60 minutes.

Beef Island, the site of the main airport for passengers arriving in the British Virgins, is connected to Tortola by the one-lane Queen Elizabeth Bridge.

BY BOAT You can travel from Charlotte Amalie (St. Thomas) by public ferry to West End and Road Town on Tortola, a 45-minute voyage along Drake's Channel through the islands. Services making this run include **Native Son** (tel. 809/495-4617), **Smith's Ferry Service** (tel. 809/494-4430), and **Inter-Island Boat Services** (tel. 809/776-6597).

FAST THE BRITISH VIRGIN ISLANDS

Area Code The area code for the British Virgin Islands is 809. (Also see "Telephone," below.)

Business Hours Generally, **banks** are open Monday through Thursday from 9am to 2:30pm and on Friday from 9am to 2:30pm and 4:30 to 6pm. Most **offices** are open Monday through Friday from 9am to 5pm; **government offices** are open from 8:30am to 4:30pm. **Shops** are generally open Monday through Friday from 9am to 5pm and on Saturday from 9am to 1pm.

Currency The **U.S. dollar** is the legal currency, much to the surprise of arriving Britishers who find no one willing to accept their pounds. *Note:* All prices in this chapter are given in U.S. dollars.

Documents U.S. and Canadian citizens need produce only an authenticated birth certificate or a voter registration card to enter the British Virgin Islands for a stay of up to 6 months, but they must possess return or ongoing tickets and show evidence of adequate means of support and prearranged accommodations during their stay.

Electricity   Your U.S.-made appliances can be used here, as the electricity is 110 volts AC, 60 cycles.

Holidays   January 1 (New Year's Day); Commonwealth Day (in March; dates vary); Easter Monday; Whit Monday; the Sovereign's Birthday (in June; the actual day of observance can vary); July 1 (Territory Day); Festival Monday, Festival Tuesday, and Festival Wednesday (in August); October 21 (St. Ursula's Day); November 14 (birthday of the heir to the throne); and December 25 and 26 (Christmas Day and Boxing Day).

Information   For more data on the British Virgin Islands, contact the **British Virgin Islands Tourist Board,** 370 Lexington Ave., Suite 511, New York, NY 10017 (tel. 212/696-0400, or toll free 800/835-8530). On the West Coast, contact the **B.V.I. Information Office,** 1686 Union St., San Francisco, CA 94123 (tel. 415/775-0344).

Language   English is spoken in this British colony.

Medical Care   Thirteen doctors practice on Tortola, and there is a hospital, **Peebles Hospital,** Porter Road, Road Town (tel. 809/494-3497), with x-ray and laboratory facilities. One doctor practices on Virgin Gorda. If you need them, your hotel will put you in touch with the islands' medical staff.

Prohibitions   Unlike some parts of the Caribbean, nudity is an offense punishable by law in the B.V.I. Drugs, their use or sale, are also strictly prohibited.

Reservations   One agency willing and able to streamline the reservations process at any of the B.V.I.'s hotels is the **B.V.I. Reservations Service** (tel. toll free 800/223-4483). Established by one of the country's most experienced tourist officials, Kenton Callwood, it maintains direct links to the reservations departments of all but a handful of the archipelago's hotels.

Safety   Crime is rare here: In fact, the B.V.I. is one of the safest places in the Caribbean. But crime does exist, and you should take all the usual precautions you would anywhere. Don't leave items unattended on the beach.

Taxes   A government tax of 7% is imposed on all hotel rooms. There is no sales tax. A $5 departure tax is collected from everyone leaving by air, $4 for those departing by sea.

Telephone   Each phone number in the islands begins with 49. *Note:* Once you are here, omit both the 809 and the 49 to make local calls; dial only the last five digits of the numbers given in this chapter.

Time   The islands operate on Atlantic standard time. In the peak winter season, when it's 6am in the British Virgins, it's only 5am in Florida. However, when Florida and the rest of the East Coast goes on daylight saving time, the clocks are the same in both places.

Weather   The islands, covering about 59 square miles, have a perfect year-round climate, with temperatures of 75° to 85° Fahrenheit, and the prevailing trade winds keep the islands from being too humid. Rainfall is infrequent, and even during the rainy season in early autumn, precipitation is generally heavy for only about 10 or 15 minutes and stops just as abruptly as it began.

1. ANEGADA

The most northerly and isolated of the British Virgins, 30 miles east of Tortola, Anegada has a population of about 250, none of whom have found the legendary treasure from the more than 500 wrecks lying off its notorious Horseshoe Reef. It's

BRITISH VIRGIN ISLANDS

Atlantic Ocean

Caribbean Sea

0 ___ 5 km
0 ___ 3 mi

N

Virgin Gorda

Necker Island

Eustatia

Prickly
Pear
Island

Mosquito Island

North
Sound

South Sound

Seal Dogs

George Dog

Great Dog

West Dog

Spanish
Town

Fallen
Jerusalem

Round
Rock

Ginger
Island

Scrub Island

Marina Cay

Cooper
Island

Salt Island

Great Camanoe

Little
Camanoe

Beef
Island

Salt
Island
Passage

Sir Francis Drake Channel

Guana
Island

Tortola East End

Peter Island

Norman Island

Road Town

Frenchman's
Cay

Flanagan
Passage

West End

Little
Thatch
Island

Great Thatch Island

Little Jost
Van Dyke

Jost Van
Dyke

**St. John
(U.S. Virgin Is.)**

Anegada

The Settlement

Anegada is 16 miles north of Virgin Gorda

different from the other British Virgins in that it's a coral-and-limestone atoll, flat, with a 2,500-foot airstrip. Its highest point reaches 28 feet, and it hardly appears on the horizon if you're sailing to it.

At the northern and western ends of the island are some good beaches, which might be your only reason for coming here. This is a remote little corner of the Caribbean: Don't expect one frill, and be prepared to put up with some hardships, such as mosquitoes.

GETTING THERE You can come by boat from Tortola; call **Speedy's** (tel. 809/495-5240) for schedules.

GETTING AROUND Limited **taxi** service is available on the island—not that you'll have many places to go. Round-trip fare from the Anegada Reef Hotel to West End Beach is $5 per person, or $6 per person to North Shore. From the Anegada Reef Hotel to the village costs $7 per person round-trip.

WHERE TO STAY

ANEGADA REEF HOTEL, Setting Point, Anegada, B.V.I. Tel. 809/495-8002. Fax 809/495-9362. 12 rms. A/C
$ Rates (including all meals): Winter, $160 single; $215 double. Summer, $150 single; $205 double. No credit cards. **Parking:** Free. **Closed:** Sept–Oct.

The only major accommodation on the island is 3 miles west of the airport and one of the most remote places in this guide. Guests who stay here are in effect "hiding out." It's a favorite of the yachting set, who enjoy hospitality provided by Lowell Wheatley. He offers large rooms with private porches opening onto the beach. Naturally, in such an isolated spot guests book in here on the AP (all meals included).

Inshore and deep-sea fishing (also bonefishing), along with diving and snorkeling, are possible. On party nights Mr. Wheatley brings in a fungi band (Afro-Caribbean musicians who improvise on locally available instruments) or he might have a barbecue on the beach. If you're going over for the day, you can order lunch at the beach bar. At night, the barbecued lobster is a favorite. If you plan to dine at the Reef, make a reservation early Dinner begins at $20 and is served at 7:30pm nightly.

WHERE TO DINE

NEPTUNE'S TREASURE, between Pomato and Saltheap Points.
Cuisine: SEAFOOD. **Reservations:** Recommended. **Transportation:** Taxi.
$ Prices: Fixed-price meal $7 at lunch, $12–$22 at dinner. No credit cards.
Open: Daily 8am–9pm.

You may want to visit this seaside restaurant run by the Soares family, who serve fresh fish and fresh lobster they catch themselves. One reader writes, "I had my first dogfish shark at this restaurant, and it was great!" The people are helpful in explaining to you how to explore their island. Their radio contact in the B.V.I. is on Tortola Radio, Channel 16 or 68.

The family also rents tents with single or double air mattresses if you'd like to camp on the island—and don't mind roughing it a bit. You can take a taxi to one of their sandy beaches and go snorkeling along their reefs.

2. JOST VAN DYKE

This rugged island, on the seaward (west) side of Tortola, was probably named for some Dutch pirate. In the 1700s a Quaker colony settled here to develop sugarcane plantations. One of the colonists, William Thornton, won a worldwide competition to design the U.S. Capitol in Washington, D.C. Smaller islands surround the place, including Little Jost Van Dyke, the birthplace of Dr. John Lettsome, founder of the London Medical Society.

About 130 people live on the 4 square miles of this mountainous island. On the south shore, White Bay and Great Harbor are good beaches. While there are only a handful of places to stay, there are several dining choices, as it's a popular stopping-over point for the yachting set.

GETTING THERE   Guests heading for the two hotels here fly first to Beef Island. From the airport, they take a taxi over the narrow bridge to West End or Road Town on Tortola; or they can take a ferry to West End from St. Thomas. At West End, a private launch picks up visitors (who must make arrangements to be met when making their hotel reservations) and transports them to the Sandcastle Hotel or Sandy Ground.

Those not staying on the island but who'd like to go over for a day trip can go on the M/V *Reel World* (tel. 809/495-9277 for reservations). It operates a regularly scheduled daily ferry service, departing West End, Tortola, at 9:30am and returning at 3pm. The fare is $14 round-trip.

WHERE TO STAY

Very casual types should also consider the simple accommodations offered by Rudy's Mariner's Rendezvous restaurant, listed under "Where to Dine," below.

SANDCASTLE HOTEL, White Bay, Jost Van Dyke, B.V.I. Tel. 809/494-0496. 4 villas. **Transportation:** 20-minute private motor-launch trip from Tortola.
$ Rates (including all meals): Dec 15–Apr 14, $235 single; $295 double. Apr 15–Dec 14, $175 single; $235 double. Tax and service extra. MC, V.

A perfect retreat for escapists, these cottages are surrounded by flowering shrubbery and bougainvillea and take advantage of the view. The small, personalized hotel caters to only a handful of guests. You're allowed to mix your own drinks at the beachside bar, the Soggy Dollar, but you'll also have to keep your own tab. Visiting yachting people often drop in to enjoy the beachside informality and order a drink called a "Painkiller." In the guest book you'll read: "I thought places like this only existed in the movies."

For reservations and information, call or write the Sandcastle, Suite 237, Red Hook Plaza, St. Thomas, USVI 00802 (tel. 809/775-5262).

SANDY GROUND, East End (mailing address: P.O. Box 594, West End, Tortola), B.V.I. Tel. 809/494-3391. Fax 809/495-9379. 8 villas. **Transportation:** Private water taxi from Tortola.
$ Rates: Winter, $1,150 double per week; extra person $150. Summer, $750 double per week; extra person $100. Tax extra. No credit cards.

On a 17-acre hill site on the eastern part of Jost Van Dyke are self-sufficient housekeeping units. The estates, as it is called, rents two- and three-bedroom villas. One of my favorites was constructed on a cliff that seems to hang about 60 or so feet over a good beach. If you've come all this way to reach this tiny outpost you might as well stay a week, which is the way the rates are quoted. The airy villas, each privately owned, are fully equipped with refrigerators, stoves, and their own electric generator. The managers help guests with boat rentals and water sports.

WHERE TO DINE

ABE'S BY THE SEA, Little Harbour. Tel. 5-9329.
Cuisine: WEST INDIAN. **Reservations:** Required. **Transportation:** *Reel World* (see above).
$ Prices: Sandwiches $3–$5; meals $12–$30. MC, V.
Open: Lunch daily noon–3pm; dinner daily 7–9:30pm.

In this local bar and restaurant the cook knows how to please the sailors with a menu of fish, lobster, conch, and chicken. Prices are low too, and it's money well spent, especially when a fungi band entertains you with its music and plays for dancing. For the price of the main course, you get peas and rice, along with coleslaw, plus dessert.

On Wednesday night in season, Abe's has a pig roast for $18, and these turn out to be festive nights. Friday is barbecue night. Approaching the harbor, you'll see Abe's restaurant on your right.

RUDY'S MARINER'S RENDEZVOUS, Great Harbour, Jost Van Dyke, B.V.I. Tel. 809/495-9282.
Cuisine: WEST INDIAN. **Reservations:** Required. **Directions:** At the western end of Great Harbour.
$ Prices: Dinner $12–$22. No credit cards.
Open: Dinner daily 7pm–1am.

Rudy's serves good West Indian food and plenty of it. A welcoming drink awaits sailors and landlubbers alike, and the food that follows is simply prepared and inexpensive. Conch always seems to be available, and a catch of the day is featured.

Beachcomber types will find three simple rooms to rent, with eight beds. Kitchenettes are provided, and there is hot and cold running water. In winter, on the AP (full board), a single costs $75 daily; a double, $125; a triple, $180; and a quad, $220. In summer, also with full board, the daily rate is $55 single, $75 double, $110 triple, and $180 quad.

SANDCASTLE, White Bay. Tel. 4-0496.
Cuisine: CONTINENTAL/AMERICAN. **Reservations:** Required—before 11am for lunch, before 4pm for dinner. **Transportation:** 20-minute trip by private motor launch from Tortola.
$ Prices: Dinner from $30, lunch from $15. MC, V.
Open: Lunch daily at 1:30pm; dinner daily at 7:30pm.
You don't have to bring a packed lunch to explore Jost Van Dyke—the previously recommended Sandcastle has excellent island food. Complete lunches are served in the open-air dining room, while lighter fare and snacks are available at the Soggy Dollar Bar. Dinner is by candlelight, featuring five courses, including duck à l'orange, chicken tarragon, and grouper piccata. Meals are served with seasonal vegetables and fresh pasta, along with a variety of salads and homemade desserts.

3. MARINA CAY

Near Beef Island, Marina Cay is a private 6-acre islet. Its only claim to fame was as the setting of the Robb White book *Our Virgin Isle,* which was filmed with Sidney Poitier and John Cassavetes. The island lies 5 minutes away by launch from Trellis Bay, adjacent to Beef Island International Airport. There are no cars on the island. I only mention the tiny cay at all because of the Marina Cay Hotel.

WHERE TO STAY

MARINA CAY HOTEL, Marina Cay (mailing address: P.O. Box 71, Road Town, Tortola), B.V.I. Tel. 809/494-2174. Fax 809/494-4775. 4 units.
Transportation: Private launch from Beef Island.
$ Rates (including MAP): Winter, $195–$395 double. Summer, $140–$340 double. AE, MC, V.
This small cottage hotel, opened in 1960 and extensively renovated, still has its original charm and conviviality. It houses guests in four double rooms with king-size beds, all overlooking a reef and Sir Francis Drake Channel, dotted with islands. Marina Cay is a tropical garden.

Dining is casual, with a good cuisine featuring continental and West Indian dishes. Activities include snorkeling on adjacent Mother Turtle Reef; sailing on Sunfish, windsurfers, and the J-24 sloop; scuba diving (with certification courses taught by a resident divemaster); castaway picnics on secluded beaches; and deep-sea fishing.

4. PETER ISLAND

Most of this 1,050-acre island, with its good marina and docking facilities, is devoted to the yacht club described below. The other part is deserted. Beach facilities are found at palm-fringed Deadman Bay, which faces the Atlantic but is protected by a reef. All goods and services are at the hotel. The island is so private that about the only creature a guest will encounter is an iguana or a wild cat, whose ancestors were abandoned generations ago by shippers (the cats are said to have virtually eliminated the rodent population).

GETTING THERE   A complimentary hotel-operated ferry picks up any overnight guest at the Beef Island airport. It departs from the pier at Trellis Bay, near the airport, and takes 45 minutes to cross. Other ferries depart eight or nine times a day from the CSY Dock in Road Town, Tortola, for a 20- to 30-minute crossing. Passengers must communicate their transportation needs to the hotel several hours in advance of their arrival or departure.

WHERE TO STAY & DINE

PETER ISLAND HOTEL AND YACHT HARBOUR, Peter Island (mailing address: P.O. Box 211, Road Town, Tortola), B.V.I. Tel. 809/494-2561, or toll free 800/346-4451. Fax 809/494-2313. 50 units, 1 bedroom villa. A/C MINIBAR TEL **Transportation:** See above.

$ Rates (including all meals): Winter, $350–$450 single; $450–$595 double; $2,750 villa for up to eight. Summer, $250–$350 single; $325–$425 double; $2,500 villa for up to eight. AE, MC, V.

On an 800-acre site, this self-contained village is completely devoted to hotel and marina facilities for the comfort of its guests and the yacht owners who moor their craft here. Its infrastructure was created by Peter Smidvig, the Norwegian shipowner, and is now owned by Amway of Michigan. After the 1989 hurricane, the owners spent a year on restoration and reopened in 1991. Luxurious and verdant, it has welcomed Nick Nolte, Robert Shaw, and Jacqueline Bisset, who stayed here during the filming of *The Deep*. Facilities (which include four different beaches) are interconnected by paths woven through tropical gardens.

The resort contains 30 units facing the bay and 20 larger units facing the beach. Amenities include ceiling fans, terraces or balconies, and comfortable furniture. A villa called the Crow's Nest overlooks Deadman Bay and crowns the peak overlooking the hotel. It offers four bedrooms, and has its own swimming pool.

Dining/Entertainment: Restaurant Tradewinds, the main dining room, serves breakfast and dinner throughout the year, and terrace lunches in winter only. Otherwise, most lunches are consumed at Deadman's Beach Bar and Grill, where grills, sandwiches, and salads are served beside the ocean. The main bar, Drake's Channel, is also open throughout the day and evening.

Services: Room service, laundry, baby-sitting.

Facilities: Fitness center, gift shop, freshwater pool, four tennis courts (two lit for night play), complete yacht marina; complimentary use of Sunfish, windsurfers, and 19-foot Squib day-sailers; scuba diving possible.

5. TORTOLA

On the southern shore of this 24-square-mile island, Road Town is the capital of the British Virgin Islands, the seat of Government House and other administrative buildings, but it seems more like a village. The landfill at Wickhams Cay, a 70-acre town center development and marina in the harbor, has brought in a massive yacht-chartering business and has transformed the sleepy capital into more of a bustling, sophisticated center.

The entire southern coast, including Road Town, is characterized by rugged mountain peaks. On the northern coast are white sandy beaches, banana trees, mangoes, and clusters of palms.

Close to Tortola's eastern end, **Beef Island** is the site of the main airport for passengers arriving in the British Virgins. The airstrip is 3,600 feet long and can accommodate the Avro 748 turbo-jet 48-seaters. The tiny island is connected to Tortola by the Queen Elizabeth Bridge, which the queen dedicated in 1966. The one-lane bridge spans the 300-foot channel that divides the little island from its bigger neighbor, Tortola. On the north shore of Beef Island is a good beach, Long Bay.

Because Tortola is the gateway to the British Virgin Islands, the information on how to get there is covered at the beginning of this chapter.

ORIENTATION

GETTING AROUND   By Taxi   Taxis meet every arriving flight. Your hotel can also call a taxi. The fare from the Beef Island airport to Road Town is $5 per person. A tour lasting 2½ hours costs $35 for one to three people. To call a taxi in Road Town, dial 4-2322; on Beef Island, 5-2378.

By Rental Car   Driving in the B.V.I. is only for those who enjoy hairpin turns. Canadian or American driver's licenses are accepted for car rentals, but in addition, you must pay $10 for a temporary British Virgins driving permit, which is valid for 3 months. At least in principle, this must be obtained at any of the island's police stations, although most car-rental companies usually maintain a stock of them in inventory, and will sell one to you. *Driving is on the left!*

To get the lowest price (and to guarantee getting a car at all during high season), reserve your rental car at least 14 days in advance. A handful of local operators will rent you a car, but because of the easier refund policies in case of billing error, damage disputes, or insurance claims, it's probably better to stick to one of the U.S.-based giants such as **Budget** (tel. toll free 800/527-0700), **Avis** (tel. toll free 800/331-2112), and **Hertz** (tel. toll free 800/654-3001). On Tortola, the well-recommended Budget is at 11 Wickham's Cay, Road Town (tel. 4-5150); Avis has offices opposite the police headquarters in Road Town (tel. 4-3322); and Hertz maintains offices on the island's West End, at the ferryboat docks (tel. 5-4405). All three companies require a minimum age of 25.

Among the "big three," the least expensive car is offered by Budget: $162 per week, with unlimited mileage. Hertz and Avis charge $180 and $222, respectively, plus tax. All three companies charge between $6 and $7 per day for a collision-damage waiver (CDW), although Hertz and Budget hold renters liable for between $500 and $600 worth of responsibility in the event of an accident, even if they purchased the waiver, whereas the policy at Avis brings the liability to zero.

By Bicycle and Scooter   If you can handle the rugged terrain, you'll find single and tandem bicycles for rent at **Hero's Bicycle Rental,** Pasea Estate, Tortola (tel. 4-3536). Bicycles cost $10 to $25 per day, and scooters go for $30.

ESSENTIALS   To cash traveler's checks, try the **Bank of Nova Scotia,** Wickhams Cay (tel. 4-2526), or **Barclays Bank,** Wickhams Cay (tel. 4-2171), both near Road Town. The local American Express representative is **Travel Plan Ltd.,** Waterfront Drive (tel. 4-2347).

Past & Presents, Main Street, over the J & C Department Store in Road Town (tel. 4-2747), has been called "one of the best bookstores in the Caribbean," and caters to boating vacationers. The best place for photographic needs is **Bolo's Brothers,** Wickhams Cay (tel. 4-2867). They have some of the best supplies on the island (stock up here on film if you're going to one of the other islands) and feature 1-hour developing service. If you need a drugstore, try **J. R. O'Neal Ltd.,** Main

Street, Road Town (tel. 4-2292). It is closed on Sunday. Stock up here on any prescribed medicines or other supplies you'll need if you're planning visits to the other islands.

WHERE TO STAY

None of the island's hotels is as big, as splashy, and as all-encompassing as the hotels in the U.S. Virgin Islands, although many of the island's repeat clients seem to like that just fine. All rates given in this unit are subject to a 10% service charge and a 7% government tax on the room.

EXPENSIVE

FRENCHMAN'S CAY HOTEL & YACHT CLUB, P.O. Box 1054, West End, Tortola, B.V.I. Tel. 809/495-4844, or toll free 800/235-4077. Fax 809/495-4056. 9 villas. TEL **Directions:** From Tortola, cross the bridge to Frenchman's Cay, turn left, and follow the road to the eastern tip of the cay.

$ Rates: Winter, $180 one-bedroom villa for two; $255 two-bedroom villa for three; $270 two-bedroom villa for four. Summer, $102 one-bedroom villa for two; $144 two-bedroom villa for three; $153 two-bedroom villa for four. Extra person using queen-size sofa bed $10 per day. Continental breakfast $4 extra. AE, MC, V. **Parking:** Free.

This luxury resort sits on the windward side of the little island of Frenchman's Cay that is connected to Tortola by a bridge. It enjoys year-round cooling breezes and views of the Sir Francis Drake Channel and the outer Virgins. The hotel, set in 12 acres of handsomely landscaped waterfront land, has one- and two-bedroom detached villas, elegantly furnished, each with a shady terrace, a full kitchen, a dining room, and a sitting room with a queen-size sofa bed suitable for two people. The two-bedroom units have two full baths.

For reservations or information, contact E & M Associates, 211 East 43rd Street, New York, NY 10017 (tel. 212/599-8280, or toll free 800/223-9832).

Dining/Entertainment: The Clubhouse restaurant and lounge bar is a true island structure, with a distinctive open-beam roof. Lunch is served from 11am to 2:30pm and dinner from 6:30 to 9pm daily. You can enjoy a drink while you watch the chef prepare one of the barbecue specialties.

Facilities: Freshwater swimming pool, tennis court; sailing, scuba diving, fishing tours, horseback riding, island tours, and car rentals can be arranged.

LONG BAY BEACH HOTEL, P.O. Box 433, Road Town, Tortola, B.V.I. Tel. 809/495-4252, or toll free 800/729-9599. Fax 809/495-4677. 72 units. A/C MINIBAR TEL **Transportation:** Taxi.

$ Rates (including MAP): Winter, $195–$290 double; $340 cottage for four. Summer, $145–$215 double; $230 cottage for four. AE, MC, V. **Parking:** Free.

On the north shore, about 10 minutes from the West End, is a low-rise hotel complex set in a 50-acre estate with nearly a mile of white sand beach. Available in a wide range of styles, shapes, and sizes, the accommodations, including regular and superior suites as well as cottages, are scattered up the side of a hill planted with shrubbery. Cottages come with two bedrooms (suitable for four guests), a bath and shower, a kitchen, and a living room overlooking the ocean. Beachfront deluxe rooms and cabañas are set at the edge of the white sands overlooking the ocean with a patio at beach level.

Dining/Entertainment: The beach restaurant offers breakfast and lunch, as well as informal à la carte suppers. The Garden Restaurant serves dinner by reservation only, and the food is of excellent quality.

Services: Room service (until midnight), laundry, baby-sitting.

Facilities: Oceanside saltwater swimming pool, beach house (which was once a distillery).

NANNY CAY RESORT & MARINA, P.O. Box 281, Road Town, Tortola, B.V.I. Tel. 809/494-4895, or toll free 800/786-4753. Fax 809/494-3288. 41 rms. A/C MINIBAR TV TEL **Transportation:** Taxi.

$ Rates: Winter, $150 single or double standard studio; $170 single or double deluxe studio. Summer, $90 single or double standard studio; $110 single or double deluxe studio. Extra person $15. Special packages available, including diving and honeymoon. AE, MC, V. **Parking:** Free.

On a 25-acre site adjoining a 200-slip marina, the Nanny Cay is located 3 miles from the center of Road Town and 10 miles from the airport. It offers regular rooms and studios with sitting areas and fully equipped kitchenettes. Units have ceiling fans, along with private balconies opening onto a view of the water, the marina, or the gardens. Accommodations, decorated in a West Indian motif, contain two big double or queen-size beds, along with many extras.

Dining/Entertainment: The hotel's Pegleg Landing Restaurant serves both lunch and dinner daily, featuring international dishes with a Caribbean flair. More casual food is offered at the poolside café and bar.

MODERATE

THE MOORINGS/MARINER INN, P.O. Box 139, Wickhams Cay, Road Town, Tortola, B.V.I. Tel. 809/494-2332, or toll free 800/535-7289 for reservations. 41 rms, 2 suites. A/C TV TEL **Transportation:** Taxi.

$ Rates: Winter, $140 single; $155 double; from $215 suite. Summer, $70–$80 single or double; from $100 suite. Breakfast from $7 extra. AE, MC, V. **Parking:** Free.

The Caribbean's only complete yachting resort is outfitted with 100 sailing yachts, some worth around $500,000. On an 8-acre resort, the inn was obviously designed with the yachting crowd in mind, offering not only support facilities and service but also shoreside accommodations (suites and lanai hotel rooms), a dockside restaurant, Mariner Bar, swimming pool, tennis court, beach club, gift shop, and dive shop that has underwater video cameras available for rent. Rooms are spacious and all have kitchenettes.

PROSPECT REEF RESORT, at the western end of Road Town (P.O. Box 104, Road Town), Tortola, B.V.I. Tel. 809/494-3311, or toll free 800/356-8937 for reservations. Fax 809/494-5595. 78 rms, 53 suites. TEL

$ Rates: Winter, $130–$160 single or double; from $175 suite. Summer, $66–$88 single or double; from $94 suite. Continental breakfast $4.50 extra. AE, MC, V. **Parking:** Free.

British-owned, this is the largest resort in the British Virgins. From this village built on a coral reef, 1 mile west of Road Town on Drake Highway, panoramic views of Sir Francis Drake Channel unfold. Attractively modern buildings have been set tastefully on 38 landscaped acres opening onto a bustling little private harbor. Built as condominiums, rental units consist of suites, town houses, villas, and apartments. Accommodations include private balconies or patios, private baths or showers, good-size living and dining areas, plus separate bedrooms or sleeping lofts. Some units are air-conditioned.

Food at the hotel restaurant, a combination of continental specialties and island favorites, was praised by *Gourmet* magazine. Diners usually begin their meals with an apéritif at the Drop Inn Bar by Prospect Harbour. Count on spending about $25 at dinner, if you don't order lobster. The water-sports desk can fill you in on what's available in day sailing, dinghy rental, snorkeling, scuba diving, or sport fishing. There are two swimming pools, plus sea pools for snorkeling or fish-watching, six tennis courts with lights, and a pitch-and-putt course.

THE SUGAR MILL, P.O. Box 425, Apple Bay, Tortola, B.V.I. Tel. 809/495-4355, or toll free 800/462-8834. Fax 809/495-4696. 16 rms, 4 family suites. TEL **Directions:** From Road Town, drive west for about 7 miles, then turn right over Zion Hill, heading north; at the T-junction opposite Sebastians, turn right; Sugar Mill is half a mile down the road.

$ Rates: Mid-Dec to mid-Apr, $125–$190 single; $135–$200 double; $215–$230

suite. Summer, $100–$140 single; $110–$150 double; $150–$180 suite. Breakfast $4–$10 extra. AE, MC, V. **Parking:** Free.

Set in lush foliage on the site of a 300-year-old sugar mill on the north side of Tortola, this cottage colony sweeps down the hillside to its own little beach, with flowers and fruits brightening the grounds. The estate is owned by Jeff and Jinx Morgan, formerly of San Francisco, who are travel, food, and wine writers.

Comfortable apartments climb up the hillside. At the center is a circular swimming pool for those who don't want to go down to the beach. The accommodations are contemporary and well planned, ranging from suites and cottages to studio apartments, all self-contained with kitchenettes, private terraces with views, and ceiling fans. The four suites are suitable for families of four.

Lunch or dinner is served down by the beach at the Islands, which serves dinner from 6:30 to 9pm daily from December to May, featuring Caribbean specialties along with burgers and salads. Dinner is also offered in the old Sugar Mill Restaurant (see "Where to Dine," below). Breakfast is served on the terrace. The bars are open all day, and snorkeling equipment can be used free.

TREASURE ISLE HOTEL, at the eastern end of Road Town (P.O. Box 68, Road Town), Tortola, B.V.I. Tel. 809/494-2501, or toll free 800/526-4789 for reservations. Fax 809/494-2507. 42 rms, 3 suites. A/C TEL **Directions:** Lies 1 mile east of Road Town.

$ Rates: Winter, $145 single; $155 double; from $215 suite. Summer, $80 single; $90 double; from $120 suite. MAP $39 per person extra. Daily package tours available to beaches and secluded islands nearby; dive and other hotel packages offered. Breakfast $7–$11 extra. AE, MC, V. **Parking:** Free.

The most complete and central resort on Tortola was built at the edge of the capital on 15 acres of hillside overlooking a marina. The core of the hotel is a rather splashy and colorful lounge and swimming pool area. The rooms, some with TVs, are on two levels along the hillside terraces; a third level is occupied by condominiums.

Adjoining the lounge and pool area is a covered open-air dining room overlooking the harbor. The cuisine is respected here, with barbecue, carvery, and full à la carte menus offered at dinner, 7 to 9pm Thursday through Tuesday. On Wednesday a West Indian buffet is served and entertainment and dancing are part of the fun. The hotel has a fully equipped dive facility that handles beginning instruction up to full certification courses.

WHERE TO DINE

EXPENSIVE

BRANDYWINE BAY RESTAURANT, Brandywine Estate. Tel. 5-2301.
   Cuisine: ITALIAN. **Reservations:** Required. **Directions:** Drive 3 miles east of Road Town (toward the airport) on South Shore Road.
$ Prices: Appetizers $5–$12; main courses $15–$25. AE, MC, V.
   Open: Dinner only, Mon–Sat 6:30–9:30pm. **Closed:** Sept–Oct.

On the south shore, 3 miles from the center of Road Town overlooking Sir Francis Drake Channel, this restaurant is set on a cobblestone garden terrace. Davide Pugliese, the chef de cuisine, and his wife, Cele McLachlan, the hostess, have earned a reputation on Tortola for their outstanding Florentine food. Once a fashion photographer, Davide changes his menu daily based on the availability of fresh produce. Typical dishes include beef carpaccio, homemade ravioli with pasta, his own special calves' liver dish (the recipe is a secret), pheasant, venison, and homemade mozzarella with fresh basil and tomatoes.

THE CLOUD ROOM, Ridge Rd. Tel. 4-2821.
   Cuisine: CONTINENTAL. **Reservations:** Required. **Transportation:** Private pickup from your hotel.

$ Prices: Appetizers $11–$19; main courses $22–$28. AE, MC, V.
Open: Dinner only, Mon–Sat 7:30–10:30pm. **Closed:** June–Oct.

A unique dining experience on Tortola, this restaurant and bar sits at the top of Butu Mountain, overlooking Road Town. When weather permits, which is practically every day of the year, the roof slides back and you dine under the stars. The road to the restaurant is bad and there's no place to park, so the owner, Paul Wattley, prefers to arrange to pick you up when you make your reservation. You'll get a selection of juicy sirloin steaks, fresh fish in season, shish kebab (the house specialty), and shrimp in Créole sauce.

SUGAR MILL RESTAURANT, Apple Bay. Tel. 5-4355.

Cuisine: CALIFORNIAN/CARIBBEAN. **Reservations:** Required. **Directions:** From Road Town, drive west for about 7 miles, take a right turn over Zion Hill going north, and then at the T-junction opposite Sebastians, turn right; Sugar Mill lies about half a mile down the road.

$ Prices: Fixed-price dinner $35; lunch from $20. AE, MC, V.
Open: Lunch daily noon–2pm; dinner daily 7–9pm.

You'll dine in an informal room that was transformed from a three-century-old sugar mill (see "Where to Stay," above). Works by Haitian painters hang on the old stone walls of the dining room, and big copper basins once used in distilling rum have been planted with tropical flowers. Before going to the dining room, once part of the old boiling house, I suggest a visit to the charming open-air bar.

Your hosts, the Morgans, know a lot about food and wine. Jinx Morgan supervises the dining room and is an imaginative cook herself. One of their most popular creations, published in *Bon Appétit,* is a curried-banana soup. They are likely to prepare delectable chicken breasts, seafood Créole, lobster crêpes, and a cold rum soufflé. Everything is homemade, and the Morgans have a herb and vegetable garden. Lunch can be ordered by the beach at the second restaurant, Islands, where dinner is also served from 6:30 to 9pm from December through May and features Caribbean specialties.

MODERATE

THE APPLE, Little Apple Bay. Tel. 5-4437.

Cuisine: WEST INDIAN. **Reservations:** Recommended.
$ Prices: Appetizers $3–$8; main courses $14–$30. AE, MC, V.
Open: Dinner only, Tues–Sun 6:30–9pm. **Closed:** Sept–Oct.

The Apple continues to please readers. Liston Molyneaux, a native Tortolian, will feed you well. You get West Indian fare with flair at this point about a 25-minute drive from Road Town on the northwest coast of Tortola where it opens onto charming Little Apple Bay. Diners can begin with a Virgin "souppy" made with soursop juice (from the famous Caribbean fruit) and rum, among other ingredients. Then they select from seafood dishes, including whelks (large marine snails) in garlic butter, conch B.V.I. style, or the catch of the day steamed and served with a Créole sauce.

MRS. SCATLIFFE'S RESTAURANT, Carrot Bay. Tel. 5-4556.

Cuisine: WEST INDIAN. **Reservations:** Required for dinner; call before 5:30pm. **Transportation:** Taxi.
$ Prices: Four-course fixed-price meal $20–$25. No credit cards.
Open: Lunch Mon–Fri noon–2:30pm; dinner daily 7–8:30pm.

For the best and most authentic West Indian cuisine (with a touch of the international kitchen), check out Mrs. Scatliffe's Restaurant. She offers meals on the deck of her island home, and some of the vegetables come right from her garden. You can begin with one of the best daiquiris on the island, made from fresh tropical fruit. Then you'll be served soup, perhaps spicy papaya, which will be followed by curried goat or "old wife" fish, perhaps chicken in a coconut shell. After dinner your hostess and her family will entertain you with a fungi-band performance.

IMPRESSIONS

Question: Where are the British Virgin Islands?
Answer: I have no idea, but I should think that they are as far as possible from
the Isle of Man.
—SIR WINSTON CHURCHILL

PUSSER'S LANDING, West End. Tel. 5-4554.

Cuisine: INTERNATIONAL. **Reservations:** Recommended. **Transportation:** Taxi.

$ Prices: Appetizers $3.50–$8.50; main courses $14.50–$26; lunch $6–$9. AE, MC, V.

Open: Daily 10am–1am.

Even more desirably located than Pussers Ltd. (see below), this place opens onto the water and offers a combination Caribbean/English-pub cuisine. In a charming nautically inspired setting you can select a soup made with seasonal ingredients, then follow with filet mignon, fresh grilled fish, West Indian roast chicken, or a live lobster from Pusser's tank. "Mud pie" is the classic dessert.

SKYWORLD, Ridge Rd. Tel. 4-3567.

Cuisine: INTERNATIONAL. **Reservations:** Recommended.

$ Prices: Appetizers $4–$7.50; main courses $6.75–$24; six-course fixed-price meal $34. AE, MC, V.

Open: Lunch daily 11:30am–5pm; dinner daily 6:30–9pm. **Closed:** Sept–Nov.

Skyworld is all the rage, and is certainly the worthiest excursion on the island. On one of the loftiest peaks on the island, at a breezy 1,337 feet, it offers views of both the U.S. and the British Virgins. The french fries and onion rings have been praised by *Gourmet* magazine. You might try the conch fritters, which are considered the best on the island. On the classic French-inspired menu, main dishes include lamb, quail, and fresh fish.

INEXPENSIVE

PUSSERS LTD., Main St., Road Town. Tel. 4-2467.

Cuisine: INTERNATIONAL. **Reservations:** Recommended.

$ Prices: Appetizers $2.50–$8; main courses $5.50–$10.50. AE, MC, V.

Open: Daily 10am–2:30am.

Standing on the waterfront across from the ferry dock, Pussers serves Caribbean fare, English pub grub, and good pizzas. The complete lunch and dinner menu includes English shepherd's pies and New York deli–style sandwiches. *Gourmet* magazine asked for the recipe for its chicken-and-asparagus pie. John Courage ale is on draft, but the drink to have here is the famous Pusser's Rum, the same blend of five West Indian rums that the Royal Navy has served to its men for more than 300 years.

WHAT TO SEE & DO

No visit to Tortola is complete without a trip to **Mount Sage,** a national park rising 1,780 feet. Here you'll find traces of a primeval rain forest and you can enjoy a picnic while overlooking neighboring islets and cays. The mountain is reached by heading west from Road Town.

Before you head out, go by the tourist office and pick up a brochure called "Sage Mountain National Park." It has a location map, directions to the forest (where there is a car park), and an outline of the main trails through the park.

Covering 92 acres, the park was established in 1964 to protect the remnants of Tortola's original forests not burned or cleared during the island's plantation era.

From the parking lot, a trail leads to the main entrance to the park. The two main trails are the Rain Forest Trail and Mahogany Forest Trail.

An organized tour may be your best way to see Tortola. **Travel Plan Tours,** Waterfront Plaza, Road Town (tel. 4-2347), will pick you up at your hotel (a minimum of four people is required) and take one to three persons on a 2½-hour tour of the island for about $45.

A **taxi tour** lasting 2½ hours costs $45 for one to three people. To call a taxi in Road Town, dial 4-2322; on Beef Island, 5-2378.

DRIVING TOUR — Tortola's West End

Start: Harbour Drive, in the center of Road Town.
Finish: Harbour Drive, in the center of Road Town.
Time: 2 hours, not counting stops.
Best Times: Mondays to Saturdays before 5:30pm.
Worst Times: Sundays, when many places are closed.

If you arrived on the island by plane, you landed at Beef Island's airport, off Tortola's northeastern tip, and you probably viewed much of the topography of the island's East End en route to your hotel. Therefore this tour concentrates on the West End, site of some of the lovelier beaches and vistas. Begin your tour at:

1. **Wickhams Cay,** site of the densest concentration of shops and restaurants of Road Town. Less carefully planned than many other Caribbean capitals, Road Town seems at first glance to be a scattered sprawl of modern buildings which form a crescent along the harborfront and up the hillsides. At Wickhams Cay, however, some of the town's charm might become more clear to you.

   From Road Town, head southwest along the coastal road past the capital's many bars and restaurants, including Pusser's, the Paradise Pub, and the local Struggling Man Restaurant. St. Paul's Episcopal Church (established 1937) and the Faith Tabernacle Church are other landmarks you'll pass.

   Less than 2 miles away, on your left, is the sandy peninsula containing the:
2. **Nanny Cay Hotel and Marina.** There's an attractive restaurant here (Pegleg Landing) and an opportunity to view some very fine yachts bobbing at anchor.

   Along the same road, 2½ miles southwest of Road Town, on your left spectacular views open of the combinations of sea and land that form the 5-mile-wide Sir Francis Drake Channel, beloved of yachters throughout the world. You'll now enjoy a frequently curving expanse of uncluttered road, one of the loveliest on the island, whose coastline is dotted with rocks, cays, inlets, and verdant uninhabited offshore islands.

   The crumbling antique masonry on the right side of the road (look through the creeping vegetation) is the ruins of a stone prison built by the English for pirates and unruly slaves. Lush St. John will appear in the distance on the opposite side of the channel.

   Keeping the water constantly on your left, you'll come to the unpretentious hamlet of:
3. **West End and the pier at Soper's Hole.** Yachters and boaters report to the Immigration and Customs officer stationed here. Turn left over the hamlet's only bridge to:
4. **Frenchman's Cay,** where there's a good view and, to the west, Little Thatch Island.

   Retrace your route toward Road Town, but at the first major intersection, turn left up Zion's Hill. This road's most prominent landmark, tucked into a hollow in the hillside, is the:
5. **Zion Hill Methodist Church.** Standing in rural isolation, with a devoted local following, it's one of many churches dotting the island.

   You'll soon be driving parallel to the island's northern coast, site of many of its least developed beaches, including Apple Bay, Little and Great Carrot Bays, and Ballast Bay. Stop at any of them and swim or snorkel wherever it looks safe. Churches you'll pass along the way include the Methodist Church of Carrot Bay and the Seventh Day Adventist Church of Tortola.

REFUELING STOP On the island's north coast: **6. Quito's Gazebo** is at Cane Garden Bay. Owned by Quito Rymer, one of the island's best musicians (who usually runs things), it serves piña coladas (either "virgin" or laced with liberal quantities of Callwood's local rum) from an enlarged gazebo built almost directly above the waves.

After Quito's, as the road cuts inland and climbs dramatically through forests and fields, a sweeping view will unfold behind you. Soon you'll be forced to make a turn. Fork left, and continue for a short distance along the rocky spine that runs down the length of the island. A sign will point to a platform that offers one of the finest views on Tortola:

7. Sky World. This eagle's-nest aerie has survived the most vicious hurricanes and offers unparalleled views of the entire island, as well as a succulent array of food and drink. Many visitors return to Sky World for a candlelit dinner. A small observatory near the parking lot has a memorial plaque you might want to read.

After Sky World, continue east for about 1 mile and fork right whenever possible. After the second right fork, the road will descend, passing houses, churches, suburbs, and schools, and eventually will join the main road running beside the waterfront at Road Town.

SPORTS & RECREATION

Tortola boasts the largest fleet of bareboat sailing charters in the world. It also offers some of the finest offshore diving areas anywhere.

BEACHES Beaches are rarely crowded on Tortola unless a cruise ship is docked. You can rent a car or a Jeep to reach these beaches, or else take a taxi (but arrange for it to return at an appointed time to pick you up). There is no public transportation.

The finest beach is **Cane Garden Bay** (see "An Excursion to Cane Garden Bay," below), which some aficionados have compared favorably to the famous Magens Bay Beach on the north shore of St. Thomas. It's directly west of Road Town, up and down some steep hills, but it's worth the effort.

Surfers like **Apple Bay**, west of Road Town. A hotel here, Sebastians, caters to a surfing crowd. January and February are the ideal time for visits.

Brewers Bay, site of a campground, is northwest of Road Town. Both snorkelers and surfers are attracted to this beach.

Smugglers Cove is at the extreme western end of Tortola, opposite the offshore island of Great Thatch and very close to the American island of St. John, directly to the south. Snorkelers also like this beach, sometimes known as Lowre Belmont Bay.

Long Bay Beach is on Beef Island, east of Tortola and the site of the major airport. Reached by taking the Queen Elizabeth Bridge, Long Bay is approached by going along a dirt road to the left before you come to the airport. From Long Bay you'll have a good view of Little Camanoe, one of the rocky offshore islands around Tortola.

BOATING The best for this is **The Moorings,** Wickhams Cay (P.O. Box 139), Road Town, B.V.I. (tel. 809/494-2332), whose 8-acre waterside resort is also recommended under "Where to Stay," above. Charlie and Ginny Cary, who started the first charter service in the B.V.I., rent a fleet of sailing yachts: Morgan 60, Moorings 500, and Moorings 51, which can accommodate up to three couples in comfort and style. Depending on your skills and inclinations, you can arrange a bareboat rental (with no crew or assistants of any kind); a rental fully crewed with a skipper, a staff, and a cook; or any variation in between. Boats usually come equipped with a portable barbecue, snorkeling gear, dinghy, windsurfer, linens, and galley equipment. The Moorings also has an experienced staff of mechanics, electricians, riggers, and cleaners.

To make reservations in the U.S., call toll free 800/535-7289; in Florida or outside the U.S., call 813/535-5651.

HORSEBACK RIDING **Shadow's Stables,** Todman's Estate (tel. 4-2262), offers horseback rides through Mount Sage National Park or down to the shores of Cane Gardens Bay. Call for details Monday through Saturday from 9am to 4pm. The cost is $25 per hour.

SCUBA & SNORKELING Divers are attracted to Anegada Reef, the site of many shipwrecks, including the *Paramatta* and the *Astrea*. However, the one dive site in the British Virgins that lures them over from St. Thomas is the wreckage of the ✪ **R.M.S. Rhone,** which sank in 1867 near the western point of Salt Island. *Skin Diver* magazine called this "the world's most fantastic shipwreck dive." It teems with beautiful marine life and coral formations and was featured in the motion picture *The Deep.*

For a good swimmer interested in taking his or her first dive under careful supervision, **Baskin in the Sun,** P.O. Box 108, Road Town, Tortola, B.V.I. (tel. toll free 800/233-7938), a well-equipped outfit, is the best choice in Tortola. It's a five-star dive center, established in 1969, and it has two locations: one at the Prospect Reef Resort near Road Town (tel. 4-2858) and another at Soper's Hole (tel. 4-5854) at the island's West End. The establishment offers a resort course for beginners which includes lessons in a pool and a one-tank reef dive lasting a full afternoon; the cost is $90. The operators provide expeditions to many dive sites, including the R.M.S. *Rhone,* and have a solid working knowledge of the best offshore dive sites.

Underwater Safaris (tel. 4-3235, or toll free 800/537-7032) takes you to all the best sites, including not only the R.M.S. *Rhone,* but also "Spyglass Wall" and "Alice in Wonderland." Its "Safari Base" office is located in Road Town and its "Safari Cay" office lies on Marina Cay. Get complete directions and information when you call. The center, connected with the Treasure Isle Hotel, offers a complete PADI training facility. An introductory resort course and one dive costs $80, and open-water certification, with 4 days of instruction and six open-water dives, goes for $300.

Marina Cay, off Tortola's East End, is known for its good snorkeling beach, and I also recommend the one at **Cooper Island,** across Drake's Channel. Underwater Safaris (see above) leads dives and snorkel expeditions to both sites, weather permitting.

SAVVY SHOPPING

Most of the shops are on Main Street, Road Town, on Tortola, but know that the British Virgins have no duty-free-port shopping. British goods are imported without duty, and the wise shopper will be able to find some good buys among these imported items, especially in English china. In general, store hours are 9am to 4pm Monday through Friday and 9am to 1pm on Saturday.

THE COCKLE SHOP, Main St., Road Town. Tel. 4-2555.

The Cockle Shop carries a wide range of souvenirs and gift items, maps, charts, T-shirts, books, games, Kodak film, and a large selection of the famous Wedgwood china from England.

LITTLE DENMARK, Main St., Road Town. Tel. 4-2455.

This is your best bet for famous names in gold and silver jewelry, and china, including Spode and Royal Copenhagen. Here you'll find many of the well-known designs from Scandinavian countries. There's also a collection of watches, but not at duty-free prices.

PUSSER'S COMPANY STORE, Main St. and Waterfront Rd., Road Town. Tel. 4-2467.

There's a long, mahogany-trimmed bar accented with many fine nautical artifacts and a souvenir store selling T-shirts, postcards, and upmarket gift items. Pusser's Rum is one of the best-selling items here, or perhaps you'd prefer polished brass mementoes of your visit.

SUNNY CARIBBEE HERB AND SPICE COMPANY, Main St., Road Town. Tel. 4-2178.
This lovely old West Indian building was the first hotel on Tortola, and its shop specializes in Caribbean spices, seasonings, teas, condiments, and handcrafts. Most of the products are blended and packaged on the island. You can buy two world-famous specialties here: West Indian hangover cure and Arawak love potion. A Caribbean cosmetics collection, Sunsations, is also available and includes herbal bath gels, island perfume, and sunshine lotions.

EVENING ENTERTAINMENT

Ask around to find out which hotel might have entertainment on any given evening. Steel bands and fungi or scratch bands (African-Caribbean musicians who improvise on locally available instruments) appear regularly, and nonresidents are usually welcome. Pick up a copy of **Limin' Times,** an entertainment magazine listing "what's happening" locally that's usually available at your hotel.

Bomba's Surfside Shack, Cappoon's Bay (tel. 5-4148), is the oldest, most memorable, and most uninhibited nightlife venue on the island and sits on a 20-foot-wide strip of unpromising coastline near the West End. By anyone's standards this is the "junk palace" of the island; it's covered with Day-Glo graffiti and laced into a semblance of coherence with wire and rejected odds and ends of plywood, driftwood, and abandoned rubber tires. Despite its makeshift appearance, the shack has the electronic amplification systems to create a really great party. The place is at its wildest on Wednesday and Sunday nights, when there's live music and an all-you-can-eat barbecue. A Bomba punch costs $3, and beer goes for $2. Barbecues are $7 per person. Open daily from 10am to midnight (or later, depending on business).

AN EXCURSION TO CANE GARDEN BAY

If you've decided to risk everything and navigate the roller-coaster hills of the B.V.I., then you need a destination. Cane Garden Bay is one of the choicest pieces of real estate on the island, long ago discovered by the sailing crowd. Its white sandy beach is a cliché of Caribbean charm, with sheltering palms. It's nearly always semideserted.

Rhymer's, Cane Garden Bay (tel. 5-4639), is the place to go for food and entertainment. Skippers of any kind of craft are likely to stock up on supplies here, but you can also order cold beer and refreshing rum drinks. If you're hungry, try the conch or whelk, or the barbecued spareribs. The beach bar and restaurant is open daily from 8am to 9pm and serves breakfast, lunch, and dinner, which costs $28 and up. On some nights a steel-drum band entertains the mariners. Ice and freshwater showers are available (and you can rent towels). Ask about renting Sunfish and windsurfers.

6. VIRGIN GORDA

The second-largest island in the cluster of British Virgins, Virgin Gorda is 10 miles long and 2 miles wide, with a population of some 1,400. It is 12 miles east of Road Town and 26 miles from St. Thomas.

In 1493, on his second voyage to the New World, Columbus named the island Virgin Gorda or "fat virgin" (the mountain that frames the island looks like a protruding stomach).

The island was a fairly desolate agricultural community until Laurance S. Rockefeller established the resort of Little Dix Bay Hotel in the early 1960s, following his success with St. John and Caneel Bay in the 1950s. He envisioned a "wilderness beach," where privacy and solitude reign, and he literally put Virgin Gorda on the map. Other major hotels followed in the wake of Little Dix, but privacy and solitude still reign supreme among visitors to the island.

In 1971 the Virgin Gorda Yacht Harbour opened. Operated by the Little Dix Bay Hotel, it accommodates 120 yachts.

ORIENTATION

GETTING THERE   **Virgin Air** (tel. toll free 800/522-3084) flies here from both St. Thomas and San Juan.

Speedy's Fantasy (tel. 5-5240) operates a ferry service between Road Town and Virgin Gorda; the ferry makes several trips daily and takes only half an hour.

ESSENTIALS   The local American Express representative is **Travel Plan Ltd.,** Virgin Gorda Yacht Harbour (tel. 5-5586).

WHERE TO STAY

BIRAS CREEK ESTATE, North Sound (P.O. Box 54), Virgin Gorda, B.V.I. Tel. 809/494-3555, or toll free 800/223-1108. Fax 809/494-8557. 16 cottages, 32 suites. **Transportation:** Hotel's private motor launch.

$ Rates (including continental breakfast): Winter, $375–$425 single; $475–$625 double. Summer, $275–$425 single; $375–$475 double. Honeymoon packages available off-season. AE, MC, V.

A magnificent resort stands at the northern end of Virgin Gorda like a hilltop fortress. On a 150-acre estate with its own marina, it occupies a narrow neck of land flanked by the sea on three sides. To create their Caribbean hideaway, Norwegian shipping interests carved out this resort in a wilderness, but wisely protected the natural terrain. The greenhouse on the grounds keeps the resort supplied with foliage and flowers. Cooled by ceiling fans, units have well-furnished bedrooms and divan beds with a sitting room and private patio, plus a refrigerator.

Dining/Entertainment: The food has won high praise, and the wine cellar is also good. The dining rooms and drinking lounge are quietly elegant, and there's always a table with a view. A barbecued lunch is often served on the beach.

Services: Laundry, baby-sitting; taxi service for guests arriving in Virgin Gorda to the hotel's motor launch; free trips to nearby islands.

Facilities: Swimming pool, snorkeling, Sunfish, paddleboards, tennis courts.

BITTER END YACHT CLUB, John O'Point, North Sound (P.O. Box 46), Virgin Gorda, B.V.I. Tel. 809/494-2746, or toll free 800/872-2392 for reservations. Fax 809/494-4756. 100 units.

$ Rates (including all meals): Winter, $320–$470 double; $700 suite. Summer, $250–$390 double; $610 suite. Packages available for longer stays. AE, DC, MC, V. **Parking:** Free.

This rendezvous point for the yachting set has hosted treasure hunter Mel Fisher and Jean-Michel Cousteau. The Bitter End offers an informal yet elegant life, as guests settle into one of the hillside chalets or well-appointed beachfront and hillside villas overlooking the sound and yachts at anchor. Forty units are air-conditioned. For something novel, you can stay aboard one of the 27-foot yachts, yours to sail, with dockage including daily maid service, meals in the Yacht Club dining room, and overnight provisions. Marina rooms are the same rates as live-aboard yachts—a good saving.

Dining/Entertainment: Dining is in the Clubhouse Steak and Seafood Grille or the English Carvery. The social hub of the place is the bar.

Services: Room service, baby-sitting, laundry; free trips to nearby islands; taxi service for guests arriving in Virgin Gorda to the hotel's motor launch.

Facilities: Unlimited use of Lasers, Sunfish, Rhodes 19s, J-24s, windsurfers, and outboard skiffs in sheltered waters; reef snorkeling; expeditions to neighboring cays; marine science participation.

FISCHERS COVE BEACH HOTEL, The Valley (P.O. Box 60), Virgin

Gorda, B.V.I. Tel. 809/495-5252. Fax 809/495-5820. 8 cottages. A/C **Transportation:** Taxi.
$ Rates: Winter, $120 single or double; $150 one-bedroom cottage; $250 two-bedroom cottage. Summer, $100 single or double; $195 cottage. MAP $40 per person extra. AE, MC, V. **Parking:** Free.

⑤ There's swimming at your doorstep in this group of cottages nestled near the beach of St. Thomas Bay. Erected of native stone, each house is self-contained, with one or two bedrooms and a combination living and dining room with a kitchenette. Six are air-conditioned. At a food store near the grounds you can stock up on your provisions if you're doing your own cooking. These are pleasant but simple rooms with views of Drake Channel. Each has its own private bath (hot and cold showers) and private balcony.

Lunch (from noon to 2pm) costs $12 and up, and dinner (from 7 to 10:30pm) begins at $22. A resident steel band provides entertainment most nights, and periodically a local scratch band plays.

GUAVABERRY SPRING BAY VACATION HOMES, Spring Bay (P.O. Box 20), Virgin Gorda, B.V.I. Tel. 809/495-5227. Fax 809/495-5283. 16 rms.
$ Rates: Winter, $120 one-bedroom house for two; $185 two-bedroom house for four. Summer, $80 one-bedroom house for two; $125 two-bedroom house for four. Extra person $20. Tax and service extra. No credit cards. **Parking:** Free.

Staying in one of these hexagonal white-roofed redwood houses built on stilts is like living in a treehouse, with screened and louvered walls to let in sea breezes. Each home, available for daily or weekly rental, has one or two bedrooms, and all have private baths, a small kitchenette, and dining area. The hosts will show you to one of their unique vacation homes, each with its own elevated sun deck overlooking Sir Francis Drake Passage. Within a few minutes of the cottage colony is the beach at Spring Bay, and the Yacht Harbour Shopping Centre is 1 mile away. It's also possible to explore "The Baths" nearby.

The owners provide a complete commissary for guests, and tropical fruits can be picked in season or bought at local shops. They will make arrangements for day charters for scuba diving or fishing, and will also arrange for island Jeep tours and saddle horses.

LITTLE DIX BAY HOTEL, on the northwest corner of the island (P.O. Box 70), Virgin Gorda, B.V.I. Tel. 809/495-5555, or toll free 800/223-7637. Fax 809/495-5661. 102 rms. A/C MINIBAR **Transportation:** Shuttle bus from the Virgin Gorda airport.
$ Rates: Winter, $450–$495 single or double. Summer, $280–$325 single or double. Continental breakfast $12 extra. AE, DC, MC, V. **Parking:** Free.

★ An embodiment of understated luxury, the Little Dix Bay Hotel is a resort discreetly scattered along a crescent-shaped private bay on a 500-acre preserve. It has the same quiet elegance as its fellow Rockresort, Caneel Bay Plantation on St. John in the U.S. Virgins. All rooms, built in woods, have private terraces with views of the sea or of gardens. Trade winds come through louvers and screens, and the units are further cooled by ceiling fans. Some units are two-story rondavels raised on stilts to form their own breezeways.

Dining/Entertainment: At the Pavilion, you can dine in the open or enjoy meals in the Sugar Mill Restaurant with its adjoining bar. If you're coming over for lunch at Sugar Mill, you can order Antilles fresh-fruit salad with coconut sherbet or sandwiches. On Thursday all the guests are transported by car or Boston whaler to Spring Bay for a barbecue luncheon with a steel band.

Services: Unequaled service with staff-to-guest ratio of one-to-one, laundry, room service.

Facilities: Sunfish, floats, snorkeling gear, Boston whalers that take you to beach of your choice with picnic lunch.

OLDE YARD INN, The Valley (P.O. Box 26), Virgin Gorda, B.V.I. Tel. 809/495-5544, or toll free 800/633-7411. Fax 809/495-5986. 14 rms.

$ Rates: Winter, $115 single; $160 double. Summer, $75 single; $95 double. MAP $35 per person extra. AE, MC, V. **Parking:** Free. **Closed:** Sept.

⑤ This little Caribbean inn 1 mile from the airport offers good value. Near the main house are two long bungalows with large renovated bedrooms, each with its own bath and patio. Scattered about are a few antiques and special accessories.

When you arrive you'll be asked about your interests. Perhaps you'll find a saddled horse waiting for a before-breakfast or a moonlight ride. Or you'll go for a sail on a yacht or a snorkeling adventure at one of 16 beaches, with a picnic lunch provided (perhaps lobster, pâté, champagne, or peanut-butter sandwiches).

Dining/Entertainment: Served under a banana-leaf thatched roof, the French-accented meals are one of the reasons for coming over. You can enjoy lunch from noon to 2pm, costing $12 and up. Dinners, from 7 to 9pm, begin at $18 but could run up to $30 if you want lobster. Movies are shown at 9pm daily in the library, and there is live entertainment twice a week in the dining room.

Facilities: Tennis courts, sailboat rentals.

WHERE TO DINE

BATH AND TURTLE PUB, Virgin Gorda Yacht Harbour, Spanish Town. Tel. 5-5239.
Cuisine: INTERNATIONAL. **Reservations:** Not accepted.
$ Prices: Appetizers $4.50; main courses $9–$15. AE, DC, MC, V.
Open: Daily 7:30am–midnight.
At the edge of the waterfront shopping plaza in Spanish Town, this is the most popular bar and pub on Virgin Gorda, with an active local trade whose interest is enhanced by its twice-daily happy hours (from 10:30 to 11:30am and again from 4:30 to 5:30pm). Even if you don't care about food, you might join the regulars over midmorning guava coladas or peach daiquiris. There's live music every Wednesday and Sunday (and also on Saturday in season) from 8pm to midnight (no cover charge). From its handful of indoor and courtyard tables, you can order fried fish fingers, nachos, very spicy chili, pizzas, reubens or tuna melts, and daily seafood specials.

CHEZ MICHELLE, the Valley. Tel. 5-5510.
Cuisine: CARIBBEAN. **Reservations:** Recommended.
$ Prices: Appetizers $6–$7.50; main courses $16–$27. MC, V.
Open: Dinner only, daily 6:30–9:30pm. **Closed:** Sept.
Chez Michelle lies beside the main road, a short walk north of the Yacht Harbour at Spanish Town. On the ground floor of a clean and modern breeze-filled house, it is considered the most competent and urbanized of the privately owned restaurants on the island. Menu specialties might include lobster Rémy (flambéed with a sauce of cognac, cream, and tomatoes), conch à la meunière (with a sauce of shallots, white wine, garlic, and lemon), pasta (such as fettuccine with chicken, burgundy wine, tomatoes, spinach, and mushrooms), and steaks. Desserts are considered one of the high points of a meal here, and there's a separate dessert menu.

TEACHER ILMA'S, the Valley. Tel. 5-5355.
Cuisine: WEST INDIAN. **Reservations:** Required for dinner; call before 3pm to order in advance.
$ Prices: Full meals $15–$22. No credit cards.
Open: Lunch daily at 1:30pm; dinner daily 7–8:30pm.
⑤ About half a mile south of Spanish Town, follow the road to the Baths and turn right at the sign to Teacher Ilma's. Mrs. Ilma O'Neal, who taught youngsters at the island's public school for 45 years, began her restaurant by cooking privately for visitors and island construction workers. Today she is the culinary grande dame of the island. Main courses, which include appetizers, might include stewed or roast chicken, lobster, johnnycakes, conch, pork, or grouper, followed by slices of guaveberry or coconut pie. Mrs. O'Neal emphasizes that her cuisine is not Créole, but

local in its origin and flavors. Meals are served on the screened-in veranda of Mrs. O'Neal's private home, near a pleasant bar and pool table.

WHAT TO SEE & DO

The northern side of Virgin Gorda is mountainous, with one peak reaching 1,370 feet. However, the southern half is flat, with large boulders appearing at every turn. The best **beaches** are at Spring Bay, Trunk Bay, and Devil's Bay.

Among the places of interest, **Coppermine Point** is the site of an abandoned copper mine and smelter. Because of loose rock formations, it can be dangerous, and you should exercise caution if you explore it. Legend has it that the Spanish worked these mines in the 1600s; however, the only authenticated document reveals that the English sank the shafts in 1838 to mine copper.

You'll find ✪ **The Baths** are on every visitor's list, and the area is known for its snorkeling. Equipment can be rented on the beach. These are a phenomenon of tranquil pools and caves formed by gigantic house-size boulders. As these boulders toppled over one another, they formed saltwater grottoes, suitable for exploring. The pools around the Baths are excellent for swimming.

Devil's Bay National Park can be reached by a trail from the Baths roundabout. The walk to the secluded coral-sand beach takes about 15 minutes through a natural setting of boulders and dry coastal vegetation.

The Baths and surrounding areas are part of a proposed system of parks and protected areas for the B.V.I. The protected area encompasses 682 acres of land, including sites at Little Fort, Spring Bay, the Baths, and Devil's Bay on the east coast.

The best way to see the island if you're over for a day trip is to call Andy Flax at Fischers Cove Beach Hotel (tel. 5-5252). He runs **Virgin Gorda Tours Associations,** which will give you a tour of the island for about $45 for one to three people. The tour leaves twice daily from the hotel's parking lot.

Kilbride's Underwater Tours (tel. 6-0111) is run by Bert and Gayla Kilbride. Bert has received prestigious NOGI awards for diving education. Today he offers the best diving in the B.V.I. at more than 40 dive sites, including Anegada Reef, the wreck of the *Chikuzen,* and the ill-fated R.M.S. *Rhone.* Prices start at $65 for a two-tank dive on one of the coral reefs. Tanks and weighted belts are supplied at no charge, and videos of your dives are available.

7. MOSQUITO ISLAND (NORTH SOUND)

The sandy, 125-acre Mosquito (also spelled Moskito) Island just north of Virgin Gorda wasn't named for those pesky insects we all know and few if any love. It took its name from the Mosquito (or Moskito) tribe, who were the only known inhabitants of the small land mass before the arrival of the Spanish conquistadors in the 15th century. Archeological relics of these peaceful people and their agricultural pursuits have been found here.

GETTING THERE Getting here requires taking a plane to the Virgin Gorda airport and Speedy's Taxi from there to Leverick Bay Dock. The taxi driver will radio ahead, and a boat will be sent from Drake's to take you on the 5-minute ride from the dock to the resort.

WHERE TO STAY

DRAKE'S ANCHORAGE RESORT INN, North Sound (P.O. Box 2510), Virgin Gorda, B.V.I. Tel. 809/494-2254, or toll free 800/494-2254 or 800/624-6651. Fax 809/494-2254. 10 rms, 2 suites.

$ Rates (including all meals): Winter, $330 single; $375 double; $475 suite. Summer, $225 single; $245 double; from $360 suite. AE, DC, MC, V.

Today the privately owned island is uninhabited except for Drake's Anchorage Resort Inn, which many patrons consider their favorite retreat in the British Virgins. The hotel offers comfortable rooms and suites with private baths and sea-view verandas. The resort's restaurant, attractively tropical in design, faces the water and offers a superb cuisine featuring local and continental dishes, including lobster and a fresh fish of the day.

Guests have free use of windsurfers, snorkeling equipment, and bicycles. For additional fees, you can go scuba diving, deep-sea fishing, and day sailing, or to the Baths at Virgin Gorda. The snorkeling and scuba here are considered so good that members of the Cousteau Society spend a month each year exploring local waters. There are four beaches on the island, each with different wave and water conditions.

8. GUANA ISLAND

This 850-acre island, a nature sanctuary, is one of the most private hideaways in the Caribbean. Don't come here seeking resort action; rather, consider vacationing here if you want to retreat from the world. Lying right off the coast of Tortola, this small island offers seven virgin beaches and nature trails ideal for hiking, and abounds in unusual species of plant and animal life. Its highest point is Sugarloaf Mountain at 806 feet, from which a panoramic view is possible. Arawak relics have been found on the island. It is said that the name of the island came from a jutting rock that resembled the head of an iguana.

GETTING THERE The Guana Island Club will send a boat to meet arriving guests at Beef Island airport (trip time: 10 minutes).

WHERE TO STAY

GUANA ISLAND CLUB (mailing address: P.O. Box 32, Road Town, Tortola), Guana Island, B.V.I. Tel. 809/494-2354, or toll free 800/544-8262. 15 rms.
$ Rates (including all meals): Nov–Dec 15, $355–$385 double. Dec 16–Mar, $480–$530 double. Apr–Aug, $345–$395 double. No credit cards. **Closed:** Sept–Oct.

The club dominates Guana Island, the sixth or seventh largest of the British Virgin Islands, which was bought in 1974 by Henry and Gloria Jarecki, dedicated conservationists who also run this resort. After your arrival on the island, a Landrover will transport you up one of the most scenic hills in the region, in the northeast of Guana. You arrive at a cluster of white cottages that were built as a private club in the 1930s on the foundations of a Quaker homestead. The stone-trimmed bungalows never hold more than 30 guests (and only two telephones), and since the dwellings are staggered along a flower-dotted hillside, the sense of privacy is almost absolute. Although water is scarce on the island, each airy accommodation has a shower; the decor is of rattan, wicker, and tile, and each unit has a ceiling fan. The panoramic sweep from the terraces is spectacular, particularly at sunset.

For reservations, contact the Guana Island Club, 10 Timber Trail, Rye, NY 10580 (tel. 914/967-6050).

Dining/Entertainment: Guests will find a convivial atmosphere at the rattan-furnished clubhouse. Casually elegant dinners by candlelight are served on the veranda, with menus that include home-grown vegetables and continental and Stateside specialties. Lunch is served buffet style every day. The self-service bars charge guests according to the honor system.

Services: Laundry.

Facilities: Seven beaches (some of which require a boat to reach), two tennis courts (one clay and one all-weather), fishing, snorkeling.

CHAPTER 7

THE DOMINICAN REPUBLIC

Five centuries of culture and tradition converge in the mountainous Dominican Republic, the fastest-growing tourist destination in the Caribbean. The 54-mile-wide Mona Passage separates the República Dominicana from Puerto Rico. In the Dominican interior, the fertile Valley of Cibao (rich sugarcane country) ends its upward sweep at Pico Duarte, formerly Pico Trujillo, the highest mountain peak in the West Indies, soaring to of 10,417 feet.

Nestled amid Cuba, Jamaica, and Puerto Rico, the island of Hispaniola (Little Spain) consists of Haiti, on the westernmost third of the island, and the Dominican Republic, which has a lush land mass equal to that of Vermont and New Hampshire combined.

Columbus sighted the coral-edged Caribbean coastline on his first voyage to the New World—"There is no more beautiful island in the world." The first permanent European settlement in the New World was founded here on November 7, 1493, and its ruins still remain near Montecristi in the northeast. Primitive native tribes called the island Quisqueya, "Mother Earth," before the Spaniards arrived to butcher them.

Much of what Columbus first saw still remains in a natural, unspoiled condition, but that may change. The country is building and expanding rapidly.

In the heart of the Caribbean archipelago, the country has an 870-mile coastline, about a third of which is given to magnificent beach. The average temperature is 77° Fahrenheit. August is the warmest month and January the coolest, although even then it's still warm enough to swim and enjoy the tropical sun. So why did it take so long for the Dominican Republic to be discovered by visitors? The answer is largely political. The country has been steeped in misery and bloodshed almost from the beginning, and it climaxed with the infamous reign of Rafael Trujillo and the civil wars that followed.

A BRIEF HISTORY The seeds of trouble were sown early. Hispaniola is divided today largely because a 1697 treaty with Spain granted the western part of the island to France. In 1795 another treaty between France and Spain granted the eastern part to France too.

But in the War for Reconquest the French colonials were defeated and the country was returned to Spanish domination. José Nuñez de Caceres in 1821 proclaimed the "Ephemeral Independence," but after that Charles Boyer, the Haitian president, declared the Dominican Republic a part of Haiti, an occupation that lasted for nearly a quarter of a century.

It wasn't until February 27, 1844, that "La Trinitaria" was founded. This freedom movement, begun by Juan Duarte, made him the father of the Dominican Republic. However, the country once more became a pawn in the colonial-possession game, and the Spanish claimed the country until they were ousted.

In 1916 the United States established a military occupation which lasted until

WHAT'S SPECIAL ABOUT THE DOMINICAN REPUBLIC

Beaches

☐ Boca Chica, a 30-minute ride east of Santo Domingo and crowded on weekends, where Dominicans go to flirt and frolic in the sun.

☐ The Amber Coast, north shore, a 70-mile stretch of white sandy beaches and splashy resorts.

☐ La Romana, south shore, with a trio of palm-fringed sandy beaches, including one on a desert island.

☐ Punta Cana, east shore, a 20-mile strand of pearl-white sand shaded by coconut palms, the longest beach strip in the West Indies.

☐ Sosúa, east of Puerto Plata, a favorite with Canadian beach buffs who are attracted to its gentle waters and long stretches of powdery white sand.

Great Towns/Villages

☐ Santo Domingo, one of the most historic cities in the Caribbean, famed for its Colonial Zone, where Spanish civilization in the New World began.

☐ Puerto Plata/Playa Dorada, center of the Amber Coast, playground of the country, with condos, villas, hotels, nightclubs, and casinos.

Ace Attractions

☐ Altos de Chavón, 3 miles east of Casa de Campo, a re-creation of a medieval Spanish village and site of an artists' colony.

☐ The Alcázar, Santo Domingo, a palace built for Diego, son of Columbus, governor of the colony in 1509, where Cortés, Ponce de León, and Balboa were feted.

Religious Shrines

☐ Cathedral of Santa María la Menor, in Old Santo Domingo, begun in 1514, the oldest cathedral in the Americas.

Sports and Recreation

☐ Casa de Campo, La Romana, 7,000 acres on the southeast coast, with a trio of Pete Dye–designed golf courses and 17 state-of-the-art tennis courts.

July 12, 1924. After the Americans' departure, Rafael Trujillo eventually overthrew the elected president in 1930 and gained power and dominated the country until his assassination in 1961. He wanted to be known as "El Benefactor," but more often his oppressed people called him "The Goat," because of his revolting excesses.

Today the Dominican Republic is rebuilt and restored, and it offers visitors a chance to enjoy the sun and sea as well as to learn about the history and politics of a developing society.

SEEING THE DOMINICAN REPUBLIC From Santo Domingo, there are two main tourist routes, east to La Romana or Punta Cana, or north to Puerto Plata and the string of emerging resorts that stretch east from there, including fast-growing Sosúa. Both La Romana and Punta Cana have airports, as does Puerto Plata, although you can drive to both sections of the island as well.

Heading East If you opt to go east, you'll first pass the beach of Santo Domingo, **Boca Chica,** some 16 miles from the capital. Set on a reef-protected shallow lagoon, it offers miles of white sand. On weekends the place is overcrowded, however. Continuing east, you pass **Juan Dolio,** another emerging resort development opening onto splendid beaches. Between Santo Domingo and the resort at La Romana lies **San Pedro de Macoris,** a sugar-export seaport on the Río Huguamo. Tourism is only beginning here. East of San Pedro is **La Romana,** with its luxurious

Casa de Campo, the premier tourist development on Hispaniola. It is also the site of **Altos de Chavón,** built in the Italian style and now an international artists' village.

Heading North If you opt to go north from Santo Domingo to Puerto Plata and its satellite resorts, take the highway, **Carretera Duarte,** going through Bonao, site of the country's best-known bus stop (many bus lines converge here). From there, the road continues north to La Vega, in the valley of Vega Real, then through Santiago de los Caballeros, the second-largest city in the Dominican Republic. It's also the commercial center of the Cibao Valley, which lies in the north-central part of the island. Because it's inland, it attracts few tourists.

At Santiago, the main highway splits, and the major artery heads northwest to Montecristi, a dreary little coastal town. Most visitors opt instead to take the secondary road northeast to **Puerto Plata,** the major resort of the Amber Coast which opens onto the Atlantic. Just east of Puerto Plata, 2½ miles from the airport, is the resort of **Playa Dorada,** which has experienced an incredible hotel boom. Eighteen miles east of Puerto Plata is another booming tourist development, **Sosúa,** with an excellent beach opening onto a small bay.

GETTING THERE

From New York's JFK Airport and New Jersey's Newark Airport, **American Airlines** (tel. toll free 800/433-7300) offers at least six daily flights to Santo Domingo or Puerto Plata; some are nonstop and others stop in Miami or San Juan, Puerto Rico. From Miami and San Juan, around 20 of American's flights wing into one of the Dominican Republic's two international airports each day.

Continental Airlines (tel. toll free 800/525-0280) flies nonstop several days a week from New Jersey's Newark Airport to both Puerto Plata and Santo Domingo.

The Dominican Republic is geared to mass tourism and offers all-inclusive packages for however many days you specify. These packages almost always save money over what you would have paid if you had booked your airfare and hotel accommodations separately. Call your travel agent or a major airline to hear what's currently available. American might be your best bet for this type of package.

If you want only airfare, deals depend on the market and the promotion. Currently, American's least expensive ticket is an Advance Purchase Excursion ticket, which requires a 14-day advance reservation and a stopover in the Dominican Republic of between 3 and 21 days before returning to your point of origin. During the midwinter high season, that round-trip ticket ranged from $412 to $452, plus tax; it decreased to between $372 and $412, plus tax, in low season.

A *Traveler's Advisory:* Arriving at Santo Domingo's Las Américas International Airport is confusing and chaotic. Customs officials tend to be rude and overworked, and give you a very thorough check! In addition, many readers have reported loss of luggage here to thieves. Beware of "porters" who offer to help. Hold on to your possessions carefully. Arrival at La Unión International Airport, 23 miles east of Puerto Plata on the north coast, is generally much easier, but it, too, requires caution.

For information on flights into Casa de Campo/La Romana, see the La Romana section of this chapter.

GETTING AROUND

This is not always easy if your hotel is remote. The most convenient means of transport is provided by taxis, rental cars, *públicos* (multipassenger taxis), and *guaguas* (public buses).

BY TAXI Taxis aren't metered, and determining the cost in advance (which you should do) may be difficult if you and your driver have a language problem (the official language is Spanish). Taxis can be hailed in the streets, and you'll definitely find them at the major hotels and outside the airport as you emerge from Customs.

BY RENTAL CAR The best way to see the Dominican Republic is by car: Island buses tend to be erratic, hot, and overcrowded; there's no rail transportation; and chartering a small plane is sometimes an expensive option. It's a very good idea to assure in advance that the car being proposed for your use has functioning safety belts.

Your Canadian or American driver's license is suitable documentation, along with a valid credit card or a substantial cash deposit. And unlike many places in the Caribbean, you *drive on the right.*

A Word of Warning: Although the major highways are relatively clear of obstacles, the country's secondary roads, especially those in the east, are disturbingly potholed and rutted. Plan a generous amount of transit time between destinations, drive carefully, and avoid alcohol.

At least three U.S.-based car-rental firms maintain branches in the Dominican Republic, usually at Puerto Plata, Santo Domingo, and La Romana.

The high accident and theft rate in recent years has helped to raise the price of car rentals substantially. Among the "big three" companies, the least expensive rentals tend to come from Budget: $372 a week with unlimited mileage, or $62 a day, plus tax; reservations must be made 1 week in advance to obtain that rate. The other car-rental firms offer slightly higher—even much higher—prices, but call around because prices are subject to change.

The big car-rental companies offer what might be the most expensive insurance policies in the Caribbean. Unless you buy a collision-damage waiver (CDW), priced between $6 and $16 per day, you're responsible for up to the full value of any damages in case of an accident. (In some cases, even if you buy the extra insurance, you're still responsible for the first $650 worth of damage. You should fully understand your insurance coverage (or lack thereof) and drive very, very carefully. Your credit card issuer *may* already provide you with this insurance; contact the issuer directly before your trip to find out.

For reservations and more information, call the rental companies at least a week before your departure: **Avis** (tel. toll free 800/331-2112), **Budget** (tel. toll free 800/527-0700), and **Hertz** (tel. toll free 800/654-3001).

BY PUBLIC TRANSPORTATION *Públicos* are a kind of unmetered multipassenger taxi that travels on main thoroughfares and stops to pick up people waving from the side of the street. You must tell the driver your destination when you're picked up to make sure the público is going to your destination. Watch for cars with a white seal on the car's front door.

Public buses, often in the form of minivans or panel trucks, are called *guaguas.* They provide the same service as públicos, but they are more crowded. Larger buses provide service outside the towns. Fares are dirt-cheap, but beware of pickpockets.

BY SIGHTSEEING TOUR One of the leading tour operators is **Prieto Tours,** avenida Francia 125 (tel. 685-0102), which will arrange a number of sightseeing excursions for you in and around Santo Domingo. A tour of the Colonial Zone costs $25, and a day at Casa de Campo and Altas de Chavón costs $60.

FAST FACTS THE DOMINICAN REPUBLIC

Area Code It's 809, and you don't need it for intra-island calls.

Currency The Dominican monetary unit is the **peso (RD$),** made up of 100 **centavos.** Coin denominations are 1, 5, 10, 25, and 50 centavos, and bill denominations are RD$1, RD$5, RD$10, RD$20, RD$50, RD$100, RD$500, and RD$1,000. Price quotations in this chapter appear sometimes in American and sometimes in Dominican currency, depending on the policy of the establishment— the use of any currency other than Dominican pesos is technically illegal, but few seem to bother with this mandate. As of this writing, you get about RD$12.50 to $1 U.S. (RD$1 equals about 8¢ U.S.), but this rate will surely fluctuate during the lifetime of this guide. Check with your bank or the tourist office before planning your budget

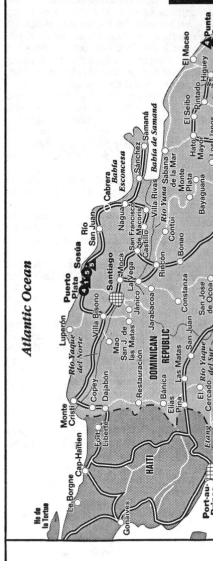

THE DOMINICAN REPUBLIC

0 —————— 65 mi
105 km

Atlantic Ocean

Caribbean Sea

Punta Cana

San Raphael de Yuma
Boca de Yuma
Isla Saona

El Macao

El Seibo
La Romana
San Pedro de Macorís
Isla Catalina
Rio Chavón
Higüey
Pintado

Juan Dolio

Boca Chica
Santo Domingo
Palenque
Las Calderas
Bahía de Ocoa

San Cristóbal
Bani

San José de Ocoa
Azua

Bayaguana
Monte Plata
Hato Mayor
Los Llanos
Sabana de la Mar

Villa Rivas
Contui
Bonao
Rincón
La Vega
Janico
Constanza
San Juan
Las Matas

Bahía de Samaná
Sánchez
Samaná
Cabrera
Bahía Esconcesa

Nagua
San Francisco de Macorís
Castillo
Moca
Santiago

Rio San Juan
Sosúa
San Juan

Puerto Plata
Luperón
Villa Bisono
Jarabacoa

Monte Cristi
Copey
Dajabón
Mao
San J. de las Matas
Restauración
Bánica
Elias Piña
El Cercado del Sur

Enriquillo
Oviedo
Barahona
Pedernales
Isla Beata

Neiba
Jimaní
Lago Enriquillo
Etang Saumâtre

DOMINICAN REPUBLIC

HAITI

Cap-Haïtien
Ête-Borgne
Île de la Tortue
Gonaïves
Fort Liberté
Pétionville
Port-au-Prince
Jacmel
Marigot

Rio Yaque del Norte
Rio Yuna
Rio Yaque del Sur

Airport

① Santo Domingo
② La Romana & Altos de Chavón
③ Punta Cana
④ Puerto Plata
⑤ Sosúa

BEACHES:
Amber Coast ▲1
Boca Chica ▲2
La Romana ▲3
Punta Cana ▲4
Sosua Beach ▲5

for the Dominican Republic. Bank booths at the international airports and major hotels will change your currency into Dominican pesos at the rate of exchange prevailing in the free market. You will be given a receipt for the amount of foreign currency you have exchanged. If you don't spend all your Dominican currency, you can present the receipt with the remaining pesos at the Banco de Reservas booth at the airport and receive the equivalent in American dollars to take out of the country. Payments by credit card are charged to you at the rate of exchange of the free market. Commercial banks can exchange dollars for pesos but not the reverse.

Documents To enter the Dominican Republic, citizens of the U.S. and Canada need only proof of citizenship, such as a passport or an original birth certificate. However, citizens may have trouble returning home without a passport; a reproduced birth certificate is not acceptable. Upon your arrival at the airport, you must purchase a tourist card for $10 U.S. To avoid waiting in line in the Dominican Republic, purchase this at the airport counter when you check in at your point of embarkation for your flight south.

Electricity The country generally uses 110 volts AC, 60 cycles, so adapters and transformers are usually not necessary for U.S. appliances. You might want to check with your hotel to be on the safe side.

Embassies All embassies are in Santo Domingo, the national capital. The **U.S. Embassy** is on calle Cesar Nicolas Penson (tel. 541-2171), the **British Embassy** is at Independencia 506 (tel. 682-3128), and the Canadian Embassy is at avenida Maximo Gomez 30 (tel. 685-1136).

Holidays The Dominican Republic celebrates the usual holidays, such as Christmas and New Year's, but also has some of its own: January 21 (Our Lady of La Altagracia), January 26 (Duarte's Birthday), February 27 (National Independence Day), Movable Feast (60 days after Good Friday, a Corpus Christi holiday), August 16 (Restoration Day), and September 24 (Our Lady of Las Mercedes).

Information Before your trip, contact any of the following **Dominican Republic Tourist Information Centers:** 1 Times Square Plaza, New York, NY 10036 (tel. 212/768-2481); 2535 Salcedo St., Coral Gables, FL 33134 (tel. 305/444-4592); 29 Bellair St., Toronto, ON N5R 2CB (tel. 416/928-9188); and 1464 Crescent St., Montréal, PQ H3A 2B6 (tel. 514/843-3418).

Language The official language is Spanish, but English is making inroads in the Dominican Republic.

Safety Once you've cleared the airports (see "Getting There," above), the Dominican Republic has more than its fair share of crime. Avoid unmarked street taxis, especially in Santo Domingo; you could be targeted for assault and robbery. While strolling around the city, you are likely to be accosted by hustlers selling various wares, and you can also be mugged. Pickpocketing is commonplace. Don't go walking in Santo Domingo after dark. Many will offer their services as a guide, and sometimes a loud refusal is not enough to shake their presence. Hiring an official guide from the tourist office can prevent this.

Taxes A departure tax of $10 U.S. is assessed and must be paid in U.S. currency. The government imposes an 11% tax on hotel rooms, and 7% on food and beverages.

Time It's Atlantic standard time throughout the country. When New York and Miami are on eastern standard time and it's 6am, it is 7am in Santo Domingo. However, during daylight saving time, when it's noon on the East Coast mainland, it is the same time in Santo Domingo.

Tips and Service In most restaurants and hotels, a 10% service charge is added to your check. Most people usually add 5% to 10% more, especially if the service has been good.

Weather The average temperature is 77° Fahrenheit. August is the warmest month and January the coolest month, although even then it's still warm enough to swim.

1. SANTO DOMINGO

Bartholomeo Columbus, brother of Christopher, founded the city of New Isabella (later renamed Santo Domingo) on the banks of the Ozama River on August 4, 1496, which makes it the oldest city in the New World. On the southeastern Caribbean coast, Santo Domingo—known as Ciudad Trujillo from 1936 to 1961—is the capital of the Dominican Republic. It has had a long, sometimes glorious, more often sad, history. At the peak of its power, Diego de Valásquez sailed from here to settle Cuba, Ponce de León went forth to discover and settle Puerto Rico and Florida, and Cortés was launched toward Mexico. The city today still reflects its long history—French, Haitian, and especially Spanish.

ESSENTIALS Tourist information is available from the **Centro Dominicano de Información Turística,** Arzobispo Merino 156 (tel. 809/687-8038), opposite the cathedral. In Santo Domingo, **24-hour drugstore service** is provided by San Judas Tadeo, avenida Independencia 57 (tel. 689-2851). An **emergency room** operates at Centro Médico Universidad, avenida Maximo Gomez 66 (tel. 682-1220). To summon the **police,** phone 682-3000.

WHERE TO STAY

Even the highest-priced hotels in Santo Domingo might be classified as medium priced in most of the Caribbean. *Remember:* Taxes and service will probably be added to your bill, which will make the rates substantially higher. When making reservations, ask if they are included in the rates quoted—usually they aren't.

EXPENSIVE

EL EMBAJADOR HOTEL CASINO, avenida Sarasota 65, Santo Domingo, Dominican Republic. Tel. 809/221-2131, or toll free 800/457-0067. Fax 809/532-5306. 272 rms, 44 suites. A/C MINIBAR TV TEL
$ Rates: $85–$115 single or double; from $125 suite. Breakfast $10 extra. AE, DC, MC, V. **Parking:** Free.

Trujillo had a luxury penthouse for his own use installed in this concrete-and-glass deluxe hotel. It was built 3 miles southwest of the city center on the grounds of a horse-racing track, but today modern high-rise buildings have encroached on the land where, in the Trujillo era, playboy Porfirio Rubirosa and El Jefe's son, Ramfis Trujillo, once played polo. The seven-story modern building has bedrooms done in French provincial style, with both king- and queen-size beds, walk-in closets, and private terraces.

Dining/Entertainment: Among the best restaurants in Santo Domingo are the Jade Garden, featuring Chinese cuisine, and the Embassy Club, a deluxe restaurant and disco with an international cuisine known for its flambé dishes. You can drink and dance in La Fontana lounge, and the casino is covered separately in "Evening Entertainment," below.

Services: Room service, laundry, baby-sitting.

Facilities: Tennis courts, undulating swimming pool with waterside terrace for refreshments, sauna and massage facilities.

HOTEL SANTO DOMINGO, avenida Independencia, Santo Domingo, Dominican Republic. Tel. 809/535-1511, or toll free 800/223-6620. Fax 809/535-4050. 220 rms, 12 suites. A/C MINIBAR TV TEL **Transportation:** Taxi.
$ Rates: Winter, $135 superior single or double; $155 Premier Club single or double. Summer, $118 superior single or double; $140 Premium Club single or double. Year round, $250 suite for one or two. Breakfast $10 extra. AE, DC, MC, V. **Parking:** Free.

✪ Run by Premier Resorts & Hotels, the Santo Domingo has a tasteful extravagance created by William Cox and the famed Dominican haute couturier, Oscar de la Renta. Their flair has made this ocher stucco structure, 15 minutes from the downtown area, a prestigious address that often attracts presidents of other Latin American countries. Opening onto the sea, this deluxe hotel stands on 14 acres of tropical landscaped grounds.

Rooms are in two structures, three stories tall and framing latticework loggias, one dedicated to orange trees. Most of the rooms open onto views of the water, but some face the garden, which isn't bad either. Premier Club rooms offer ocean-view balconies, personal service, complimentary breakfast, and other benefits.

Dining/Entertainment: Guests enjoy dinner at El Alcázar (see "Where to Dine," below). The hotel's gourmet restaurant is El Cafetal, and you can also enjoy a poolside lunch at Las Brisas. The piano bar, Las Palmas, draws a lively crowd at night.

Services: Room service, laundry, baby-sitting.

Facilities: Three professional tennis courts (lit at night), Olympic-size swimming pool, sauna.

RAMADA RENAISSANCE JARAGUA RESORT, CASINO & SPA, avenida George Washington 367, Santo Domingo, Dominican Republic. Tel. 809/221-2222, or toll free 800/228-9898. Fax 809/686-0503. 337 rms, 18 suites. A/C MINIBAR TV TEL

$ Rates: Winter, $170–$218 single or double; from $780 suite. Summer, $108–$135 single or double; from $505 suite. MAP $50 per person extra. AE, DC, MC, V. **Parking:** Free.

✪ "The pride of the Dominican Republic" was built on the 14-acre site of the old Jaragua ("Ha-*ra*-gua"), popular in Trujillo's day. Officially opened in 1988, the new hotel is a splashy waterfront palace. Located off the Malecón, convenient to the major attractions and shops of Santo Domingo, the hotel spreads its accommodations across two separate buildings: the 10-story Jaragua Tower (where there's butler service on the deluxe floors) and the two-level Jaragua Gardens Estate.

Seemingly no expense was spared in the luxuriously appointed rooms, as reflected by marble bathrooms with large makeup mirrors and hairdryers, three phones, refrigerators, and computerized door locks. And all this luxury is comparatively inexpensive, especially off-season.

Dining/Entertainment: The Jaragua boasts the largest casino in the Caribbean and a 1,000-seat Las Vegas–style showroom. For its restaurants—the Manhattan Grill, the Deli, Figaro, and Latino—see "Where to Dine," below.

Services: 24-hour room service and butler service on the deluxe floors of the Jaragua Tower.

Facilities: Swimming pool with 12 private cabañas, snack bar, and outdoor bar; one of the best tennis centers in Santo Domingo, with four clay courts (lit at night) and a pro shop; beauty parlor and barber; spa facility.

SHERATON SANTO DOMINGO & CASINO, avenida George Washington 365, Santo Domingo, Dominican Republic. Tel. 809/686-6666, or toll free 800/325-3535. Fax 809/687-8150. 260 rms, 8 suites. A/C TV TEL

$ Rates: Winter, $120–$130 single or double. Summer, $90–$110 single or double. Year round, from $150 suite. Breakfast from $7 extra. AE, DC, MC, V. **Parking:** Free.

The Sheraton is a high-rise set back from the Malecón. You travel along a tree-lined drive until you arrive at a vast lobby that's really a solarium. Bedrooms are equipped with hairdryers, and except for those on the third floor, all have ocean views.

Dining/Entertainment: The plant-filled Petit Café overlooks the lobby, and Yarey's Lounge is a piano bar with entertainment. Dining is at Antoine's (see "Where to Dine," below), an elegant continental place. Breakfast, lunch, and dinner are available at La Terraza coffeehouse, which has a terrace surrounding a large pool that opens onto views of the sea. Other additions to the hotel are La Canasta, featuring Dominican food, the Omni Disco, and a casino.

Services: 24-hour room service, baby-sitting, laundry, dry-cleaning.
Facilities: Complete business center.

MODERATE

HOTEL HISPANIOLA, avenida Independencia, Santo Domingo, Dominican Republic. Tel. 809/221-7111, or toll free 800/223-6620. Fax 809/535-4050. 215 rms, 5 suites. A/C MINIBAR TV TEL **Transportation:** 15-minute taxi ride from the center.

$ Rates: Winter, $135–$155 single or double; from $250 suite. Summer, $115–$135 single or double; from $225 suite. Breakfast from $5 extra. AE, DC, MC, V.
Parking: Free.

The Hispaniola has done an amazing Cinderella act and emerged from the shell of the Trujillo-era Hotel Pax (which once housed exiled Juan Peron) into its present reincarnation. Now operated by Premier Resorts & Hotels, it was practically rebuilt. Located on 10 beautifully landscaped acres across from the deluxe Sheraton Santo Domingo (already recommended), it's a six-story structure with well-furnished bedrooms. The top-floor rooms, which are preferable, offer seaside views.

Dining/Entertainment: The hotel's restaurant, La Piazzetta, serves Italian fare. The evening hot spots are the casino and the disco Neon 2002, which attracts many locals. In the thatched coffeehouse (a *bohío*) near the swimming pool, you can order breakfast, lunch, or drinks.

Services: Room service, laundry, baby-sitting.
Facilities: Swimming pool; use of the facilities at the Hotel Santo Domingo, including tennis courts.

HOTEL LINA, avenida Maximo Gomez and 27 de Febrero, Santo Domingo, Dominican Republic. Tel. 809/686-5000. Fax 809/686-5521. 217 rms, 8 suites. A/C MINIBAR TV TEL

$ Rates: Winter, RD$975 ($78) single; RD$1,040 ($83.20) double; from RD$1,800 ($144) suite. Summer, RD$780 ($62.40) single; RD$845 ($67.60) double; from RD$1,500 ($120) suite. Breakfast from RD$65 ($52) extra. AE, DC, MC, V.
Parking: Free.

Rising 15 floors in the heart of the capital, the Lina offers a wide range of services and facilities. All the rooms are junior or senior suites and contain full private baths, refrigerators, and full-size beds; at least 30% of the accommodations overlook the Caribbean. The hotel has attracted everybody from Julio Iglesias to David Rockefeller to Latin American presidents.

Dining/Entertainment: The hotel boasts one of the best-known restaurants in the Caribbean (see "Where to Dine," below), a cafeteria and snack bar, and a nightclub.

Services: 24-hour room service, laundry, baby-sitting.
Facilities: Two swimming pools, Jacuzzi, solarium, gym, sauna, tennis courts, shopping arcade.

PLAZA NACO HOTEL, Plaza Naco Mall, avenida Presidente Gonzalez (P.O. Box 30228), Santo Domingo, Dominican Republic. Tel. 809/541-6226. Fax 809/541-7251. 220 suites. A/C TV TEL **Transportation:** Taxi.

$ Rates: Winter, $100 single or double. Summer, $70 single or double. Breakfast from $5 extra. **Parking:** Free.

An ideal accommodation for commercial travelers or for visitors seeking a lot of space and facilities, the Plaza Naco offers handsomely decorated accommodations equipped with computer safe-lock doors, guest safes, kitchenettes with utensils, dining rooms, and hairdryers.

Dining/Entertainment: There is a good restaurant and a cafeteria. Those who want their own supplies for their suites can shop at the deli or the minimarket. Residents of the hotel are admitted free to the disco.

Services: 24-hour room service, laundry, dry-cleaning, bilingual secretarial and legal translation services, rental-car desk, tour desk.
Facilities: Sauna (with massages available), Jacuzzi, solarium, gym.

BUDGET

HOSTAL NICOLAS DE OVANDO, calle las Damas 53, Santo Domingo, Dominican Republic. Tel. 809/687-3101. Fax 809/688-5170. 52 rms (all with bath). A/C TV TEL

$ Rates: Winter, RD$600 ($48) single; RD$650 ($52) double. Summer, RD$600 ($48) single or double. Breakfast from $5 extra. AE, DC, MC, V. **Parking:** Free on street.

(S) In the shop-studded area of La Atarazana, in the old town, two 15th-century mansions have been converted into a hostal and named after the governor of Hispaniola, who lived here from 1502 to 1509. The structure is an example of a fortified house, with its own observation tower overlooking the Ozama River. The public rooms have heraldic tapestries, bronze mirrors, and colonial furnishings. Even if you can't stay in one of the comfortable rooms here, stop in for lunch at the Extramadura Restaurant during your visit to the old city.

HOTEL CERVANTES, avenida Cervantes 202, Santo Domingo, Dominican Republic. Tel. 809/688-2261. Fax 809/687-5764. 181 rms (all with bath). A/C TV TEL **Transportation:** Taxi.

$ Rates: RD$450 ($36) single; RD$580 ($46.40) double. Breakfast from $5 extra. AE, DC, MC, V. **Parking:** Free on street.

Long a favorite among budget travelers, the family-oriented Cervantes, staffed with a security guard, offers comfortably furnished bedrooms with refrigerators. It may not have the most tasteful decor in Santo Domingo, but is nevertheless clean and efficient and has a pleasant staff. The hotel has a swimming pool and is also known for its Bronco Steak House, which features both imported and local char-broiled beef.

HOTEL EL NAPOLITANO, avenida George Washington 51, Santo Domingo, Dominican Republic. Tel. 809/687-1131. Fax 809/689-2714. 72 rms (all with bath). A/C TV TEL

$ Rates: RD$607 ($48.55) single; RD$675 ($54) double. Breakfast from RD$55 ($4.40) extra. AE, DC, MC, V. **Parking:** Free.

El Napolitano is a safe haven and a good bargain along the Malecón, which is usually lively—and potentially dangerous—until the wee hours. Popular with Dominicans, the hotel rents comfortably furnished but simple units, many of which are large enough for families. All accommodations open onto the sea. There is a swimming pool on the second floor.

The café is open 24 hours a day, as is room service, and the hotel also has a good restaurant specializing in seafood (especially lobster). There is a disco and a piano bar, with both live and recorded music. If you like crowds, lots of action, and informality, El Napolitano may be for you.

WHERE TO DINE

In Santo Domingo, guests are not forced to dine every night in their hotels. The city has a host of restaurants serving good food, and most of the restaurants stretch along the seaside-bordering avenida George Washington, popularly known as the Malecón.

The national dish is *sancocho*, a thick stew made with meats (maybe seven different ones), vegetables, and herbs, especially marjoram. Another national favorite is *chicharrones de pollo*, pieces of fried chicken and fried green bananas flavored with pungent spices. One of the most typical dishes is *la bandera* (the flag), made with red beans, white rice, and stewed meat. Johnnycakes and mangú, the latter a dish inherited from people called *cocolos* who came to the Dominican Republic from the Windward and Leeward Islands, are frequently eaten. Johnnycakes can be bought on the street corner or at the beach, but you must ask for them as *vaniqueques*. Mangú, often included with hotel breakfasts, is a purée of green plantains.

A good local beer is called Presidente. Wines are imported, so prices tend to run high. Dominican coffee compares favorably with that of Colombia and Brazil.

EXPENSIVE

EL ALCAZAR, in the Hotel Santo Domingo, avenida Independencia. Tel. 535-1511.
Cuisine: INTERNATIONAL. **Reservations:** Recommended, especially for lunch buffet. **Transportation:** taxi (15-minute ride from the center).
$ Prices: Appetizers RD$28–RD$45 ($2.25–$3.60); main courses RD$140–RD$220 ($11.20–$17.60); fixed-price lunch buffet from RD$160 ($12.80). AE, DC, MC, V.
Open: Lunch daily noon–3pm; dinner daily 7–11pm.
Dominican designer Óscar de la Renta created El Alcázar in a Moroccan motif, with aged mother-of-pearl, small mirrors, and lots of fabric. Dishes are always good, and sometimes excellent; well-made sauces add zest to the meals. The presentation of the food and the service are two more reasons to dine here. Appetizers include onion soup and lobster bisque. The kitchen is known for its steaks and grills, such as filet mignon with béarnaise sauce. There is also a good selection of seafood, including grilled shellfish. The international lunch buffets provide one of the best food buys in the city.

ANTOINE'S, in the Sheraton Santo Domingo Hotel & Casino, avenida George Washington 361. Tel. 686-6666.
Cuisine: INTERNATIONAL. **Reservations:** Recommended.
$ Prices: Appetizers RD$30–RD$45 ($2.40–$3.60); main courses RD$140–RD$230 ($11.20–$18.40); lunch buffets RD$78–RD$96 ($6.25–$7.70). AE, DC, MC, V.
Open: Lunch daily noon–3pm; dinner daily 7pm–midnight.
This is where the well-dressed Dominican family goes to celebrate a special occasion. Of course, the well-run restaurant also draws the international crowd staying in this deluxe hotel, which is set back from the Malecón. Unusual appetizers include squid in garlic dressing. The waiters often suggest the lobster thermidor, but I've found the red snapper Basque style more interesting, and it costs less. If you don't want fish, try the tournedos Rossini. For dessert, I like Spanish coffee, but you might prefer baked Alaska.

DE ARMANDO, calle Santiago Esq. José Joaquín Perez 205, Gazcue. Tel. 689-3534.
Cuisine: INTERNATIONAL. **Reservations:** Required. **Transportation:** Taxi.
$ Prices: Appetizers RD$30–RD$45 ($2.40–$3.60); main courses RD$80–RD$105 ($6.40–$8.40). MC, V.
Open: Daily noon–midnight.
In a residential neighborhood, De Armando is operated by restaurateur Armando Rodríguez and offers dining indoors or outdoors. As an hors d'oeuvre, you might order seafood au gratin or the pumpkin soup. Filete Armando is meat served in a brandy-laced, herb-flavored mushroom sauce. Lamb, another good dish, is offered with a red wine sauce, and pollo merengon is chicken served in its own juices with steamed vegetables and olives. Desserts are made fresh every day, and the wine list ranges from French to Iberian. The restaurant is at its best in the evening, when there is live piano music.

FIGARO, in the Ramada Renaissance Jaragua Resort, Casino & Spa, avenida George Washington 367. Tel. 221-2222.
Cuisine: ITALIAN. **Reservations:** Recommended.
$ Prices: Appetizers RD$19–RD$50 ($1.50–$4); main courses RD$75–RD$295 ($6–$23.60). AE, DC, MC, V.
Open: Dinner only, daily 7:30–11pm.
Homemade pasta, including vegetable lasagne, may attract you to Figaro, which features northern and southern Italian fare, along with delectable pastries and cappuccino. Set on the lobby level of this previously recommended hotel set back from the Malecón, Figaro is now acclaimed as one of the best Italian restaurants in Santo Domingo. Cured ham with fresh mozzarella is one of the best

dishes. You might follow with either of the chef's specialties: lobster Fra Diavolo or sirloin steak. The atmosphere is that of an Italian trattoria, with an open kitchen, bright tiles, and hanging cheese.

LATINO, in the Ramada Renaissance Jaragua Resort, Casino & Spa, avenida George Washington 367. Tel. 221-2222.

Cuisine: DOMINICAN/SOUTH AMERICAN. **Reservations:** Recommended.

$ Prices: Appetizers RD$30–RD$85 ($2.40–$6.80); main courses RD$75–RD$225 ($6–$18). AE, DC, MC, V.

Open: Dinner only, daily 7:30pm–1am.

Latino features not only Dominican specialties but those of other Latin countries as well. You might begin with the increasingly popular Spanish tapas (hors d'oeuvres) or else black-bean soup, then follow with a Dominican favorite, "goat-in-rum." This small, cozy restaurant lies on the lobby level of this previously recommended hotel set back from the Malecón. Many gamblers come here for a late-night snack.

LINA RESTAURANT, in the Hotel Lina, avenida Maximo Gomez. Tel. 686-5000.

Cuisine: SPANISH/ITALIAN. **Reservations:** Required. **Transportation:** Taxi.

$ Prices: Appetizers RD$22–RD$125 ($1.75–$10); main courses RD$65–RD$250 ($5.20–$20). AE, DC, MC, V.

Open: Lunch daily noon–4:30pm; dinner daily 6:30pm–midnight.

The Lina is one of the most prestigious restaurants in the Caribbean. Spanish-born Lina Aguado originally came to Santo Domingo when it was Ciudad Trujillo; her culinary fame was so great in Madrid that she was hired as the personal chef de cuisine of the dictator Trujillo. She served El Jefe (as Trujillo was called) well until she left to open her own restaurant. It was a small place, but its fame grew, and she became the number-one restauratrice in the Dominican Republic.

Today this modern hotel and restaurant has nothing to do with the old place, except that Dona Lina taught the cooks her secret recipes. Four master chefs now rule in the kitchen. The cuisine is international and the service is first-rate. Try the paella valenciana or sea bass flambéed with brandy, or perhaps mixed seafood au Pernod cooked in a casserole—the repertoire is vast.

MANHATTAN GRILL, in the Ramada Renaissance Jaragua Resort, Casino & Spa, avenida George Washington 367. Tel. 221-2222.

Cuisine: STEAK. **Reservations:** Recommended.

$ Prices: Appetizers RD$50–RD$125 ($4–$10); main courses RD$130–RD$295 ($10.40–$23.60); lunch buffet RD$80 ($6.40). AE, DC, MC, V.

Open: Lunch daily noon–3pm; dinner daily 7:30–11pm.

The Manhattan Grill, the premier restaurant in this previously recommended hotel set back from the Malecón, isn't confined just to New York–type chow. Food ranges from New England (creamy clam chowder) to Louisiana (shrimp gumbo Cajun style). Meat cuts are imported from the U.S. Steak is a specialty, but both lobster and lamb are prepared in the open kitchen. The service is among the best in Santo Domingo. There's a daily lunch buffet of cold salads and hot dishes. The restaurant is a member of the Chaîne des Rôtisseurs.

REINA DE ESPAÑA, avenida Cervantes 103. Tel. 685-2588.

Cuisine: SPANISH/CREOLE/INTERNATIONAL. **Reservations:** Required.

$ Prices: Appetizers RD$45–RD$85 ($3.60–$6.80); main courses RD$85–RD$225 ($6.80–$18). AE, MC, V.

Open: Daily noon–midnight.

Chef Antonio Garcia made a sensation on San Juan's El Condado, and here he offers such culinary specialties as frogs' legs Romana, quail stew with herbs, and roast duck with mango sauce. Lobster is prepared almost any way you like it, and most fish dishes are excellent, including the seafood casserole. Local dishes aren't neglected; you might ask for a Dominican shrimp soup. For dessert, corn ice cream (that's right!) is a new taste sensation. Meals are among the most expensive in the capital, but patrons are usually satisfied, knowing they are getting quality ingredients handled by master chefs. The restaurant is near the Hotel Sheraton Santo Domingo.

VESUVIO I, avenida George Washington 521. Tel. 221-3333.
 Cuisine: ITALIAN. **Reservations:** Not accepted.
$ Prices: Appetizers RD$19–RD$50 ($1.50–$4); main courses RD$75–RD$195 ($6–$15.60). DC, MC, V.
 Open: Daily noon–2am.

Along the Malecón, the most famous Italian restaurant in the Dominican Republic draws crowds of visitors and local businesspeople. What to order? That's always a problem here, as the Neopolitan owners, the Bonarelli family, have worked since 1954 to perfect and enlarge their menu. Their homemade soups are excellent. The restaurant prepares fresh red snapper, sea bass, and oysters in interesting ways. Crayfish specialties include à la Vesuvio, which is topped with garlic and bacon. The broiled seafood platter is a sample of all their seafood, and the veal comes from the Bonarellis' own herd. A favorite dessert is tortelloni al vodka, but you may prefer a recent creation, choccolat fettuccine à la parra, a real chocolate pasta, only instead of sugar they've added salt.

The owner claims to be the pioneer of pizza in the Dominican Republic, and he makes a unique one next door in **Pizzeria Vesuvio**—a yard-long pizza pie! If you want to try their other Italian place, go to **Vesuvio II**, avenida Tiradentes 17 (tel. 562-6090).

MODERATE

LA BAHÍA, avenida George Washington 1. Tel. 682-4022.
 Cuisine: SEAFOOD. **Reservations:** Not required.
$ Prices: Appetizers RD$55–RD$125 ($4.40–$10); main courses RD$85–RD$195 ($6.80–$15.60). AE, MC, V.
 Open: Daily 9am until late.

You'd never know that this unprepossessing place right on the Malecón serves some of the best, and freshest, seafood in the Dominican Republic. One predawn morning as I passed by, fishermen were waiting outside to sell the chef their latest catch. Rarely in the Caribbean will you find a restaurant with such a diversity of seafood offerings. For your appetizer, you might prefer ceviche, sea bass marinated in lime juice, or lobster cocktail. Soups are likely to contain big chunks of lobster as well as shrimp. Specialties include kingfish in coconut sauce, sea bass Ukrainian style (a specialty—how did they get the recipe?), baked red snapper, and seafood in the pot. Conch is a special favorite with the chef. Desserts are superfluous, and the restaurant will stay open until the last customer departs for home in the early hours of the morning.

THE DELI, in the Ramada Renaissance Jaragua Resort, Casino & Spa, avenida George Washington 367. Tel. 221-2222.
 Cuisine: DELI. **Reservations:** Not required.
$ Prices: Appetizers $3.50–$6; main courses $7–$14. AE, DC, MC, V.
 Open: Daily 24 hours.

If you're playing at the Jaragua's casino, you can go to the Deli, which overlooks the hotel garden and falls and is set back from the Malecón. This busy place features corned beef and pastrami sandwiches, along with other fare associated with New York delis. It also offers some Dominican dishes, including peeled shrimp in a hot spicy sauce. Many visitors drop in just for the homemade ice cream and egg creams. Meals cost under $20.

FONDA LA ATARAZANA, calle Atarazana 5. Tel. 689-2900.
 Cuisine: CREOLE/INTERNATIONAL. **Reservations:** Not required.
$ Prices: Appetizers RD$12–RD$25 (95¢–$2); main courses RD$50–RD$85 ($4–$6.80). AE, MC, V.
 Open: Daily 10am–1am.

S For regional food in a colonial atmosphere, with night music for dancing as well, this patio restaurant often has folklore festivals. Just across from the Alcázar, it's a convenient stop as you're shopping and sightseeing in the old city. A cheap, good dish is chicharrones de pollo, which is tasty fried bits of Dominican chicken. Or you might try curried baby goat in a sherry sauce. Sometimes the chef cooks lobster thermidor and Galician-style octopus. If you don't mind waiting half an hour, you can order the sopa de ajo (garlic soup). Many fans come here especially for the fricasséed pork chops.

JADE GARDEN, in the Hotel Embajador, avenida Sarasota 65. Tel. 221-2131.
  Cuisine: CHINESE. **Reservations:** Recommended.
  $ Prices: Appetizers RD$55–RD$125 ($4.40–$10); main courses RD$85–RD$205 ($6.80–$16.40); fixed-price lunch RD$120 ($9.60). AE, DC, MC, V.
  Open: Lunch daily noon–3pm; dinner daily 7:30–11:30pm.
Jade Garden, 3 miles southwest of the center of town, is clearly in the front rank in Santo Domingo's Chinese cookery. The management even sent its cooks to Hong Kong to learn some of the secret methods of Peking and northern Chinese cuisine, and they returned to please customers with an array of delectables, such as minced pigeon, soya-bean chicken, sweet-corn soup (superb), lemon duck (even better!), sweet-and-sour pork, deep-fried fish, and fortune chicken, finished off with a toffee banana. The pièce de résistance is the Peking duck, which the chef roasts in an open-fire stove. The fixed-price luncheons are great buys.

BUDGET

CAFE ST. MICHEL, avenida Lope de Vega 24. Tel. 562-4141.
  Cuisine: FRENCH. **Reservations:** Recommended. **Transportation:** Taxi.
  $ Prices: Appetizers RD$34–RD$105 ($2.70–$8.40); main courses RD$98–RD$205 ($7.85–$16.40). AE, DC, MC, V.
  Open: Daily 11:30am–midnight.
S On a busy street in a north-central section of town called Naco is a popular restaurant which may have its finest hour daily at lunch, when the place is filled with local businesspeople. The interior is done in light-grained wood and stone trim, and there is an Italian-marble and wood bar. Menu items include beefsteak, red snapper, shrimp, lobster, green plantain vichyssoise, and chicken breast dishes stuffed in different ways. Dessert spectaculars are the chocolate soufflés and chocolate-nut tarts.

LA CANASTA, in the Sheraton Santo Domingo Hotel & Casino, avenida George Washington 365. Tel. 221-6666.
  Cuisine: DOMINICAN. **Reservations:** Not required.
  $ Prices: Appetizers RD$35–RD$95 ($2.80–$7.60); main courses RD$98–RD$185 ($7.85–$14.80). AE, DC, MC, V.
  Open: Daily 8pm–4am.
S The best late-night dining spot in the capital is set back from the Malecón, between the Omni Casino and the Omni Disco. It's not only economical but it also serves popular Dominican dishes culled from favorite recipes throughout the country, such as sancocho (a typical stew with a variety of meats and yucca) and mondongo (tripe cooked with tomatoes and peppers). Other unusual dishes are goatmeat braised in a rum sauce and pigs' feet vinaigrette Créole style.

RESTAURANT/BAR JAI-ALAI, avenida Independencia 411, at the corner of José Joaquín Pérez. Tel. 685-2409.
  Cuisine: INTERNATIONAL. **Reservations:** Not required.
  $ Prices: Appetizers RD$48–RD$180 ($3.85–$14.40); main courses RD$65–RD$180 ($5.20–$14.40). AE, MC, V.
  Open: Lunch daily 11:30am–4pm; dinner daily 6:30pm–midnight.
The original owner of this cosmopolitan restaurant behind the Sheraton left his home in Bilbao, Spain, when he was 18. After running a successful eatery in Lima, Peru, he

came to Santo Domingo and set up this restaurant named after the favorite sport of his Basque ancestors. Today the staff welcomes guests with a smile and a fluency in several languages. Shellfish is famous here, with such offerings as lobster Créole, shrimp Jai-Alai, seafood casserole, and oysters in red sauce. Other dishes include octopus Créole, garlic soup, Spanish-style pork chops, rabbit in garlic sauce, and sea bass, both Basque and Breton style. Before dinner you might enjoy a glass of the Peruvian pick-me-up called pisco.

WHAT TO SEE & DO

Santo Domingo, a treasure trove, is part of a major government-sponsored restoration. The old town is still partially enclosed by remnants of its original city wall. Its narrow streets, old stone buildings, and forts are like nothing else in the Caribbean, except Old San Juan. The only thing missing is the clank of the conquistadors' armor.

Old and modern Santo Domingo meet at the **Parque Independencia,** a big city square whose most prominent feature is its Altar de la Patria, a shrine dedicated to Duarte, Sanchez, and Mella, who are all buried here. These men led the country's fight for freedom from Haiti in 1844. As in provincial Spanish cities, the square is a popular family gathering point on Sunday afternoon. El Conde Gate stands at the entrance to the plaza and was named in 1955 for Count (El Conde) de Penalva, the governor who resisted the forces of Admiral Penn, the leader of a British invasion. It was also the site of the March for Independence in 1844, and holds a special place in the hearts of Dominicans.

In the shadow of the Alcázar, **La Atarazana** is a fully restored section which centered around one of the New World's finest arsenals, serving the conquistadors. It extends for a city block, catacombed with shops, art galleries (both Haitian and Dominican paintings), and boutiques, as well as some good regional and international restaurants.

Just behind river moorings, the oldest street in the New World is called **calle las Damas** (Street of the Ladies). Some visitors assume this was a bordello district, but actually it wasn't. Rather, the elegant ladies of the viceregal court used to promenade here in the evening. It's lined with colonial buildings.

Just north is the chapel of **Our Lady of Remedies,** where the first inhabitants of the city used to attend mass before the cathedral was erected.

Try also to see the **Puerta de la Misericorda.** Part of the original city wall, this "Gate of Mercy" was once a refuge for colonists fleeing hurricanes and earthquakes. To reach it, head four blocks west along calle Padre Billini and turn left onto calle Palo Hincado.

The **Monastery of San Francisco** is but a mere ruin, lit at night. That any part of it still is standing is a miracle; it was destroyed by earthquakes, pillaged by Drake, and bombarded by French artillery.

In total contrast to the colonial city, modern Santo Domingo dates from the Trujillo era. A city of broad, palm-shaded avenues, its seaside drive is called **avenida George Washington,** more popularly known as the Malecón. This boulevard is filled with restaurants, as well as hotels and nightclubs. *Warning:* Proceed with caution at night—there are pickpockets galore.

I also suggest a visit to the **Paseo de los Indios,** a sprawling 5-mile park with a restaurant, fountain displays, and a lake.

About a 20-minute drive from the heart of the city, off the Autopista de las Américas on the way to the airport and the beach at Boca Chica, is **Los Tres Ojos** or "three eyes," which stare at you across the Ozama River from Old Santo Domingo. There is a trio of lagoons set in scenic caverns, with lots of stalactites and stalagmites. One lagoon is 40 feet deep, another 20 feet, and yet a third—known as "Ladies Bath"—only 5 feet deep. A Dominican Tarzan will sometimes dive off the walls of the cavern into the deepest lagoon. The area is equipped with walkways.

The **Columbus Memorial Lighthouse,** avenida España, a monumental cruciform project on the water side of Los Tres Ojos, near the airport in the San Souci district, was opened in 1992 in honor of the 500th anniversary of the "Discovery of

America." A chapel holds "the bones" of Columbus, which have been moved here from the Cathedral of Santa María le Menor (see below). (It should be pointed out that other locations, including the Cathedral of Seville, also claim to possess the remains of the explorer.) A laser beam pierces the nighttime cityscape with a continuous saber of light. The site is the center of six minor museums.

You'll see a microcosm of Dominican life as you head east along calle El Conde from the Parque Independencia to Columbus Square, which has a large bronze statue honoring the discoverer. The statue was made in 1882 by a French sculptor. On the south side of the plaza, the ✪ **Cathedral of Santa María la Menor** (tel. 689-1920) begun in 1514 and completed in 1540, is the oldest cathedral in the Americas. Characterized by a gold coral limestone facade, it is a stunning example of the Spanish Renaissance style, with elements of Gothic and baroque. The cathedral, visited by Pope John Paul II in 1979 and again in 1984, was the axis for celebration of the 500th anniversary of the European Discovery of America marked in 1992. An excellent art collection of retables, ancient wood carvings, furnishings, funerary monuments, and silver and jewelry of the Treasure of the Cathedral can be seen.

THE TOP ATTRACTIONS

THE ALCÁZAR, calle Emiliano Tejera, at the foot of calle las Damas. Tel. 687-5361.

✪ The most outstanding structure in the old city is the Alcázar, a palace built for the son of Columbus, Diego, and his wife, the niece of Ferdinand, king of Spain. Diego became the colony's governor in 1509, and Santo Domingo rose as the hub of Spanish commerce and culture in America. Constructed of native coral limestone, it stands on the bluffs of the Ozama River. For more than 60 years it was the center of the Spanish court and entertained such distinguished visitors as Cortés, Ponce de León, and Balboa. After its heyday, it experienced two disastrous centuries as invaders pillaged it. By 1835 it lay in virtual ruins, and it was not until 1957, in Trujillo's day, that the Dominican government finally restored it to its former splendor. The nearly two dozen rooms and open-air loggias are decorated with paintings and period tapestries, as well as 16th-century antiques.

The same ticket entitles you to visit the **Museu Virreinal (Museum of the Viceroys),** adjacent to the Alcázar, which houses period furnishings and tapestries, as well as paintings dating from the colonial period.

Admission: RD$10 (80¢).
Open: Mon and Wed–Fri 9am–5pm, Sat 9am–4pm, Sun 9am–1pm.

CASA DEL CORDÓN (Cord House), at the corner of calles Emiliano Tejera and Isabel la Católica.

Near the Alcázar, the Cord House was named for the cord of the Franciscan order which is carved above the door. Francisco de Garay, who came to Hispaniola with Columbus, built the casa in 1503–04, which makes it the oldest stone house in the western hemisphere. It once lodged the first Royal Audience of the New World, which performed as the Supreme Court of Justice for the island and the rest of the West Indies. On another occasion, in January 1586, the noble ladies of Santo Domingo gathered here to donate their jewelry as ransom demanded by Sir Francis Drake in return for his promise to leave the city. The restoration of this historical manor was financed by the Banco Popular Dominicano, where its executive offices are found.

Admission: Free.
Open: Tues–Sun 8:30am–4:30pm.

NATIONAL PANTHEON, calle las Damas, near calle Mercedes.

The National Pantheon—a fine example of Spanish-American colonial architecture—was originally a Jesuit monastery in 1714, but it was later used as a tobacco warehouse, and even a theater. Trujillo restored the massive structure with austere lines in 1955, projecting it as his burial place, but instead one chapel preserves the ashes of the martyrs of June 14, 1959, who tried in vain to overthrow the dictator.

Admission: Free.
Open: Mon–Sat 9am–6pm.

MUSEO DE LAS CASAS REALES (Museum of the Royal Houses), calle las Damas, at corner of calle Mercedes. Tel. 682-4202.

Through artifacts, tapestries, maps, and re-created halls, including a courtroom, this museum traces Santo Domingo's history from 1492 to 1821. Gilded, elegant furniture, arms and armor, and other colonial artifacts, all inspected by King Juan Carlos of Spain in 1976, make it the most interesting of all museums of Old Santo Domingo. It contains replicas of the three ships commanded by Columbus, and one exhibit is said to hold part of the ashes of the famed explorer. You can see, in addition to pre-Columbian art, the main artifacts of two galleons sunk in 1724 on their way from Spain to Mexico, along with remnants of another Spanish ship, the *Concepción* (18th century).
Admission: RD$10 (80¢).
Open: Tues–Sat 9am–4:45pm, Sun 10am–1pm.

CASA DE TOSTADO (Tostado House), Padre Billini, at the corner of Arzobispo Merino. Tel. 689-5057.

The beautiful Gothic geminate (double) window in the Casa de Tostado is the only one existing today in the New World. The house was first owned by the scribe Francisco Tostado, and then was inherited by his son of the same name, a professor, writer, and poet who was the victim in 1586 of a shot fired during Drake's bombardment of Santo Domingo. The Casa de Tostado, which at one time was the archibishop's palace, now houses the **Museu de la Familia Dominicana** (tel. 689-5057), which focuses on life in the 19th century in a well-to-do household.
Admission: Museum, RD$10 (80¢).
Open: Thurs–Tues 9am–2pm.

MUSEO DEL HOMBRE DOMINICANO, Plaza de la Cultura, calle Pedro Henríquez Urena. Tel. 687-3622.

This museum houses the most important collection in the world of artifacts made by the Taíno peoples, who greeted Columbus in 1492. Thousands of magnificently sculptured ceramic, stone, bone, and shell works are on display.
Admission: RD$10 (80¢).
Open: Tues–Sun 10am–5pm.

MUSEO NACIONAL DE HISTORIA Y GEOGRAFIA (Museum of History and Geography), calle Pedro Henríquez Ureña. Tel. 686-6677.

Near the National Library, this museum contains personal belongings of Trujillo, such as clothing, handkerchiefs, French perfume, uniforms, combs, briefcases, and medals from Argentina, Spain, and Japan, as well as personal documents. A series of photographs traces the career of the former ruler. Also exhibited are artifacts of the conquistadors, the early colonists under Spanish rule, the Haitian invasion of the Dominican Republic, and other highlights of the nation's history. English-speaking guides are available.
Admission: RD$10 (80¢).
Open: Tues–Sun 9am–6pm.

GALLERY OF MODERN ART, Plaza de la Cultura. Tel. 682-8260.

The former site of the Trujillo mansion, the Plaza de la Cultura has been turned into a park and contains the Gallery of Modern Art, which displays national and international works (the emphasis is, of course, on native-born talent).

Also in the center are the **National Library** and the **National Theater** (tel. 687-3191), which sponsors, among other events, folkloric dances, opera, outdoor jazz concerts, traveling art exhibits, classical ballet, and music concerts.
Admission: RD$10 (80¢).
Open: Tues–Sat 9am–5pm.

JARDIN BOTANICO, avenida de los Proceres.

In the northern sector of Santo Domingo, the Botanical Gardens are the biggest in all of Latin America and contain flowers and lush vegetation of the Dominican

Republic. Seek out, in particular, the Japanese Park, the Great Ravine, and the floral clock. You can also tour the grounds by horse carriage or take a boat.

Admission: RD$5 (40¢).

Open: Daily 10am–6pm.

PARQUE ZOOLOGICO NACIONAL, avenida Maximo Gomez at avenida de los Proceres. Tel. 562-2080.

In 320 acres of parkland with the Isabella River at its northern boundary, you can see one of the largest zoos in Latin America, home to both native and exotic animals and birds. An aquatic bird lake, a crocodile pond, an aviary, a snake exhibit, and a huge "African Plain," where fauna from that continent roam, make the Santo Domingo zoo a fascinating place to visit. The zoo has a souvenir shop, snack bar, and rest areas.

Admission: RD$10 (80¢).

Open: Daily 10am–6pm. **Directions:** Take avenida Tiradentes, the busy thoroughfare that intersects avenida 27 de Febrero and runs past the Plaza Naco shopping center; go past avenida John F. Kennedy until you reach the zoo at the city's remote outskirts.

SPORTS & RECREATION

BASEBALL The national sport is baseball, and many of the country's native-born sons have gone on to the major leagues. From October through February, games are played at stadiums in Santo Domingo and elsewhere. Check the local newspaper for schedules and locations of the nearest game.

BEACHES The Dominican Republic may have some great beaches, but they aren't in Santo Domingo. The principal beach resort near the capital is at **Boca Chica,** less than 2 miles east of the international airport and about 19 miles from Santo Domingo. Clear, shallow blue water laves the fine white sand beach and a natural coral reef that protects the area from big fish. The east side of the beach, known as "St. Tropez," is popular with Europeans.

The great beaches are at **Puerto Plata,** but that's a rough, 3-hour drive or an easy flight from the capital, and at **La Romana,** a 2-hour drive to the east (see Sections 4 and 2, respectively, below).

Most of the major Santo Domingo hotels have swimming pools.

GOLF Serious golfers head for **Casa de Campo** with three 18-hole Pete Dye courses or the course that Robert Trent Jones designed at **Playa Dorada,** near Puerto Plata.

Golf is available in the capital at the **Santo Domingo Country Club,** an 18-hole course which grants privileges to guests of most of the major hotels. The rule here is members first, which means it's impossible for weekend games.

HORSE RACING Santo Domingo's race track, **Hipodromo Perla Antillana,** on avenida San Cristóbal (tel. 565-2353), schedules races on Tuesday, Thursday, and Saturday at 3pm. You can spend the day here and have lunch at the track's restaurant. Admission is free.

POLO Made so famous during Trujillo's day, polo is still a popular sport. Polo fields are in Santo Domingo at **Sierra Prieta,** where games are played on weekends, and in La Romana at **Casa de Campo,** where there are four fields.

SNORKELING & SCUBA Divers rate the Dominican Republic high for its virgin coral reefs, where you can explore ancient shipwrecks and undersea gardens with an endless variety of marine life.

Mundo Submarino, Gustavo Meja Ricart 99 (tel. 566-0344), is the best in Santo Domingo. It offers a snorkel tour daily from 9am to 1:30pm from the beach or a secluded cove. A minimum of four divers is required. Advanced scuba tours are featured at the same time—daily diving by boat, in both a shallow and a deep reef with steep walls. The possibilities for photography are excellent.

TENNIS   The major hotels have very good courts, especially the **Santo Domingo Sheraton, Embajador,** and **Lina.** Guests at the **Ramada Renaissance Hotel Jaragua** and **Hotel Santo Domingo** will find excellent courts set aside for residents. Some of these courts are lit for night games.

SAVVY SHOPPING

The best buys are in handcrafted native items, especially amber jewelry, the national gem, a petrified fossil resin millions of years old. The pine from which the resin came disappeared from the earth long ago. The origins of amber were a mystery until the beginning of the 19th century when scientists determined the source of the gem.

Look for pieces of amber with trapped objects, such as insects and spiders, inside the enveloping material. Colors range from a bright yellow to black, but most of the gems are golden in tone. Amber deposits in the Dominican Republic were only discovered in modern times. Fine-quality amber jewelry, along with lots of plastic fakes, is sold throughout the country.

A semiprecious stone of light blue (sometimes a dark-blue color), larimar is the Dominican turquoise. It often makes striking jewelry, and is sometimes mounted with wild boar's teeth, but you may prefer to make a less obvious statement with silver or gold.

Ever since the Dominicans presented John F. Kennedy with what became his favorite rocker, visitors have wanted to take home a rocking chair. To simplify transport, these rockers are often sold unassembled.

Other good buys include Dominican rum, hand-knit articles, macramé, ceramics, and crafts in native mahogany. Always haggle over the price, particularly in the open-air markets; no stallkeeper expects you to pay the first price asked. The best shopping streets are El Conde, the oldest and most traditional shop-flanked avenue, and avenida Mella.

In the colonial section, **La Atarazana** is filled with galleries and gift and jewelry stores, charging inflated prices. Duty-free shops are found at the airport, in the capital at the **Centro de los Héroes,** and at both the Hotel Santo Domingo and the Hotel Embajador. Shopping hours are generally 9am to 12:30pm and 2 to 5pm Monday through Saturday.

AMBAR MARIE, Caonabo 9, Gazcue. Tel. 682-7539.

In case you're worried that the piece of amber you like may be plastic, you can be assured of the real thing at Ambar Marie, where you can even design your own setting for your choice gem. Look especially for the tear-drop earrings and beautiful amber and gold necklaces. The shop is in a residential area, and is open during regular business hours Monday through Friday (closed weekends).

AMBAR TRES, La Atarazana 3. Tel. 688-0474.

In the colonial section of the old city, Ambar Tres sells jewelry made from amber, black coral, mahogany carvings, watercolors, oil paintings, and other Dominican products. The shop is open daily, but it closes at noon on Sunday.

GALERIA DE ARTE NADER, La Atarazana 9. Tel. 688-0969.

In the center of the most historical section of town is a well-known gallery that sells so many Dominican and Haitian paintings that they're sometimes stacked in rows against the walls. Don't miss the ancient courtyard in back if you want a glimpse of how things looked in the Spanish colonies hundreds of years ago.

EL MERCADO MODELO, avenida Mella.

Head first for the National Market, filled with stall after stall of crafts and spices, fruits, and vegetables. The merchants will be most eager to sell, and you can easily get lost in the crush. Remember to bargain. You'll see a lot of tortoise-shell work here, but exercise caution, since many species, especially the hawksbill, are on the endangered-species list and could be impounded by U.S. Customs if discovered in your luggage.

Rockers are for sale here, as are mahogany ware, sandals, baskets, hats, clay braziers for grilling fish, and so on.

NOVO ATARAZANA, La Atarazana 21. Tel. 689-0582.

Although the name would imply that it's new, this is actually one of the best-established shops in town. You can purchase pieces of amber, black coral, leather goods, wood carvings, and Haitian paintings. It's open 7 days a week.

PLAZA CRIOLLA, corner of 27 de Febrero and avenida Anacaona.

The Plaza Criolla is a modern shopping complex with a distinguished design theme. Shops are set in gardens with tropical shrubbery and flowers, facing the Olympic Center. The architecture makes generous use of natural woods, and a covered wooden walkway links the stalls together.

TU ESPACIO, avenida Cervantes 102. Tel. 686-6006.

One of the most charming shops in the capital is crammed with all sorts of goodies, including Taíno art (hand-carved reproductions, of course), Dominican and European antiques, monumental bamboo furniture, and odds and ends that Victorians used to clutter their homes with. If you're looking for that special trinket, you're likely to find it here. The merchandise is always changing.

EVENING ENTERTAINMENT
NIGHTCLUBS

LA FIESTA SHOWROOM, in the Ramada Renaissance Jaragua Resort, Casino & Spa, avenida George Washington 367. Tel. 221-2222.

La Fiesta features splashy Las Vegas–type multi-million-dollar revues with performances by top names. Show times in this 1,500-seat auditorium vary, but you'll be informed when you make your reservation. Seating is generally at 9pm with a 10pm showtime.

Admission (including first drink): RD$175–RD$500 ($14–$40), depending on the performer.

MESÓN DE LA CAVA, avenida Mirador del Sur. Tel. 533-2818.

This charming restaurant and nightclub built in a natural cave 50 feet under the ground provides live music for dancing. Shows with merengue music are offered. To reach it, you descend a perilous open-backed iron stairway.

At first I thought this was a mere gimmicky club until I sampled the food and found it among the best in the capital. For an appetizer you can choose from shrimp cocktail, onion soup, gazpacho, bisque of seafood, or red snapper chowder. Main courses include "gourmet" beefsteak, fresh sea bass in red sauce, tournedos, and coq au vin. You can finish with a sorbet. Meals average $30 per person, plus the cost of your drinks, which begin at RD$40 ($3.20). Hot food is served daily from noon to 3pm and 6pm to midnight. After midnight the waiters present a show of their own. The place is open every day.

Admission: Free.

DANCE CLUBS

Disco-hopping in the Dominican Republic is an after-dinner ritual.

LA BELLA BLU, avenida George Washington. Tel. 689-2911.

In keeping with the Malecón tradition, this place stays open until dawn. This is perhaps the best-known disco in Santo Domingo and draws both locals and an international crowd. The door policy is to deny entrance to "unsavory types." Though Bella Blu is relatively safe and can be a lot of fun, the boulevard on which it sits is not. Open: Mon–Sat 10pm–dawn.

Admission: RD$25 ($2).

NEON DISCOTHEQUE, in the Hotel Hispaniola, avenida Independencia. Tel. 535-7111.

One of the town's best-established dance clubs offers Latin jazz with different guest stars each week, although disco dancing under flashing lights is one of the main reasons for its popularity. The clientele tends to be very young, between 15 and 21, and includes many university students. The management reserves the right to accept only "well-behaved" clients. Drinks begin at RD$40 ($3.20). Open: Tues–Sun 9pm–4am.

Admission: RD$20–RD$25 ($1.60–$2).

OMNI DISCO, in the Sheraton Santo Domingo Hotel & Casino, avenida George Washington 361. Tel. 686-6666.

The Omni is popular with visitors and some of the sons and daughters of the country's most prestigious families who come here to drink and dance. Drinks begin at RD$20 ($1.60). Open: Wed–Mon 8pm–2am or later, depending on the crowd.

Admission: RD$30 ($2.40); free for hotel guests.

PUBS & BARS

MERENGUE BAR, in the Ramada Renaissance Jaragua Resort, Casino, & Spa, avenida George Washington 367. Tel. 221-2222.

In the glittering premises of this previously recommended hotel you'll find live music and colorful libations. A live band performs Monday through Wednesday from 5 to 9:30pm and Thursday through Sunday from 4 to 8pm, followed by a merengue band entertaining Monday through Wednesday from 9pm to 2am and Thursday through Sunday from 8pm to 2am. Drinks begin at RD$45 ($3.60). The bar is adjacent to the hotel casino.

RAFFLES PUB, calle Hostos 352. Tel. 686-3069.

When you're ready for a change, drop into Raffles Pub, an American bar across the street from the first western hemisphere hospital which will transplant you to Greenwich Village. The bar is decorated with murals by Dominican, Mexican, and Haitian artists, and you can wander a series of high-ceilinged Spanish-style rooms, with heavy beams and candlelight. You'll hear blues, rock 'n' roll, or video music; occasionally local musicians perform. Most local drinks cost RD$20 ($1.60). Open: Daily 8pm to early morning.

PIANO BARS

Most of the "chic stops" are in the big hotels.

FONTANA BAR, in the El Embajador Hotel, avenida Sarasota 65. Tel. 221-2131.

Here you can enjoy good music, whether it's by the piano player and vocalist early in the evening or by the trio later, with a variety of tunes for listening or dancing. The rhythms range from Dominican folk songs to samba to the merengue. The bar is inviting, and hard drinks begin at RD$40 ($3.20). Open: Daily 4pm–1am.

LAS PALMAS, in the Hotel Santo Domingo, avenida Independencia. Tel. 535-1511.

Las Palmas, the best piano bar in town, was decorated by the country's famous designer, Oscar de la Renta. Under a high-vaulted ceiling, mirrored walls are painted with palm fronds. A terrace, open to the sea, adjoins the bar. Romantic music is often played, and you can hear, on occasion, jazz, samba, and the bossa nova. Dance music is played on certain nights, and the staff wears Dominican colonial dress. Hard drinks cost RD$32 to RD$55 ($2.55 to $4.40). Happy hour is from 6 to 8pm, with free hors d'oeuvres. Open: Daily 5pm–1am.

CASINOS

Santo Domingo has several major casinos. The most spectacular is the **Jaragua Casino,** in the Ramada Renaissance Jaragua Resort, Casino & Spa, avenida George Washington 367 (tel. 221-2222), whose brightly flashing sign is the most dazzling light along the Malecón at night; you'll think you're on the Strip in Las Vegas. The most glamorous casino in the country is fittingly housed in the capital's poshest hotel. Action—blackjack, baccarat, roulette, slot machines—is from 4pm to either 2 or 3am daily, depending on business. You can gamble in either Dominican pesos or U.S. dollars.

Other casinos include **El Embajador Casino,** avenida Sarasota 65 (tel. 221-2131), where the popular games of blackjack, craps, and roulette are offered daily from 4pm to 5am. In between gaming sessions, you can have a drink at La Fontana, their casual bar where hors d'oeuvres are served.

Another casino is at the **Hotel Hispaniola,** avenida Independencia (tel. 221-7111), open daily from 4pm to 5am.

One of the most stylish casinos is the **Omni Casino,** in the Sheraton Santo Domingo Hotel & Casino, avenida George Washington 361 (tel. 686-6666). Its bilingual staff will help you play blackjack, craps, baccarat, and keno, among other games. It's open daily from 3pm to 7am.

2. LA ROMANA & ALTOS DE CHAVÓN

On the southeast coast of the Dominican Republic, La Romana was once a sleepy sugarcane town that also specialized in cattle raising, and unless one had business here with either industry, no tourist bothered with it. But when Gulf + Western opened (and later sold) a tropical paradise resort of refinement and luxury, the Casa de Campo, on its outskirts, La Romana soon became known among the jet-set travelers. Just east of Casa de Campo is Altos de Chavón, a village built specially for artists.

GETTING THERE   By Plane   If you're going just to Casa de Campo from North America, you'll find the easiest routing to La Romana via San Juan, Puerto Rico (see "Getting There" in Chapter 4, "Puerto Rico"). **American Eagle** (tel. toll free 800/433-7300) operates two daily nonstop flights to Casa de Campo/La Romana from San Juan. The cheapest ticket available costs $138 round-trip and requires no advance purchase, although clients are required to stay for 7 days. If you want to stay for between 7 and 21 days, the fare is $143. If you plan to visit for less than 7 days, an economy-class ticket with no restrictions costs $226 round-trip.

Oddly, the only flights operating between La Romana and other parts of the Dominican Republic are charters, which usually require elaborate special arrangements in advance.

By Car   If you're already in Santo Domingo, you can drive here in about an hour and 20 minutes from the international airport, along Las Américas Highway. (Allow another hour if you're in the center of the city.) Of course, everything depends on traffic conditions (watch for speed traps). Low-paid police officers openly solicit bribes whether you were speeding or not.

LA ROMANA
WHERE TO STAY

CASA DE CAMPO, La Romana, Dominican Republic. Tel. 809/523-3333,
or 305/856-7083 in Florida, or toll free 800/877-3643 in the U.S., Canada, Puerto Rico, and the Virgin Islands. Fax 809/523-8548. 278 casitas, 470 villas. A/C MINIBAR TV TEL

$ Rates: Winter, $200–$305 single or double casita; $495 one-bedroom villa. Summer, $100–$150 single or double casita; $210 one-bedroom villa. MAP $41 per person extra. AE, DC, MC, V. **Parking:** Free.

Translated as "House in the Country," Casa de Campo offers the greatest resort in the entire Caribbean area—and the competition is stiff. It brings a whole new dimension to a holiday. Gulf + Western took a vast hunk of coastal land, more than 7,000 acres in all, and carved out this chic resort, today operated by Premier Resorts & Hotels. The ubiquitous Miami architect, William Cox, helped create it, and Oscar de la Renta provided the style and flair. Tiles, Dominican paintings, louvered doors, and flamboyant fabrics decorate the interior.

The resort divides its accommodations into red-roofed, two-story casitas near the main building and more upscale villas that dot the edges of the golf courses, the gardens near the tennis courts, or the shores of the Atlantic. Some, within La Terrazza, are clustered in a semiprivate hilltop compound with views overlooking the meadows, the cane, and the fairways down to the distant sea.

Dining/Entertainment: At the core of everything is a wonderland swimming pool—four, in fact, each on a different level—with thatch huts on stilts to provide beverages and light meals. Perched over the pool is La Cana, the two-level bar and lounge, with a thatched roof but no walls. Dinner is on a rustic roofed terrace where you'll find some of the best food in the Dominican Republic. Perhaps they'll throw a roast suckling pig barbecue right on the beach. Most of the beef used is grown right on the plains of La Romana. See "Where to Dine," below, for recommendations of the resort's several other restaurants.

Services: 24-hour room service, laundry, baby-sitting.

Facilities: One of the most complete fitness centers on the island with weight and exercise machines, whirlpool and sauna (at $15 per hour), aerobics classes, and masseuses. See "Sports and Recreation," below, for the golf, tennis, water sports, fishing, and polo and horseback facilities.

WHERE TO DINE

EL PATIO, in Casa de Campo. Tel. 523-3333, ext. 2265.
Cuisine: CARIBBEAN/AMERICAN.
$ Prices: Full meals from $20. AE, DC, MC, V.
Open: Daily 7am–midnight.
Originally designed as a disco, El Patio now contains a shield of lattices, banks of plants, and checkerboard tablecloths. Technically, it's a glamorized coffee shop, but you can order some substantial daily specials. Meals might include ceviche, Cuban-style black-bean soup, sandwiches, salads, sirloin steaks, or pasta.

LAGO GRILL, in Casa de Campo. Tel. 523-3333, ext. 2266.
Cuisine: CARIBBEAN/AMERICAN.
$ Prices: Fixed-price breakfast $12; lunch $20. AE, DC, MC, V.
Open: Breakfast daily 7–11am; lunch daily noon–4pm.
The Lago Grill is ideal for breakfast; in fact, it has one of the best-stocked morning buffets in the country. Your view is of a lake, a sloping meadow, and the resort's private airport, with the sea in the distance. At the fresh-juice bar, a Dominican employee in colonial costume will extract juices in any combination you prefer from 25 different tropical fruits. Then you can select your ingredients for an omelet, and an employee will whip it up while you wait. Lunch includes sandwiches, burgers, sancocho (the famous Dominican stew), and fresh conch chowder. There is also a well-stocked salad bar.

TROPICANA, in Casa de Campo. Tel. 523-3333, ext. 3000.
Cuisine: CARIBBEAN. **Reservations:** Required.
$ Prices: Full meals $35. AE, DC, MC, V.
Open: Daily 7–11pm.
The most glamorous restaurant in the complex, Tropicana is a breezy pavilion known for its innovative "Caribbean Flair" and a wide range of seafood and exotic West Indian dishes.

SPORTS & RECREATION

At La Romana, on 7,000 acres of lush turf, you'll find three Pete Dye golf courses, a stable of horses with thrice-weekly polo, a private marina with deep-sea and river trips, snorkeling on live reefs, and a fitness center (at Casa de Campo, above), plus 13 tennis courts.

BEACHES A large, palm-fringed sandy crescent, **Bayahibe** is a 20-minute launch trip or a 30-minute drive from La Romana. In addition, **La Minitas** is a tiny, but nice, immaculate beach and lagoon. Transportation is provided on the bus, or you can rent a horse-drawn buckboard. Finally, **Catalina,** is a turquoise beach on a deserted island just 45 minutes away by motor boat.

GOLF The **Casa de Campo** courses are known to dedicated golfers everywhere—in fact, *Golf* magazine called it "the finest golf resort in the world." The course, Teeth of the Dog, has also been called "a thing of almighty beauty," and it is. The ruggedly natural terrain has eight holes skirting the ocean. Opened in 1977, the Links is the inland course, built on sandy soil away from the beach. A third Pete Dye course, La Romana Country Club, opened in 1989. A golf professional will answer your questions (dial extension 8115). For 18 holes, greens fees are $50 to $65. Hours are 7am to 7pm daily.

POLO & HORSEBACK RIDING Ever since the grand days when Dominican playboy Porfirio Rubirosa mounted some of the finest horses in the world, the Dominican Republic has been a polo-playing mecca. Today **Casa de Campo** is the best place in the Caribbean for playing, learning, and watching the fabled sport of kings and princes. On the premises are three full-size polo fields (one a practice field), a horse-breeding farm, and scores of polo ponies, as well as a small army of veterinarians, grooms, and polo-related employees. If during your visit you hear that a polo match will be played, by all means go.

Most serious polo players arrive with their own equipment, but beginners learn by watching more experienced players and participating in trail rides (which last 1 to 3 hours), as well as taking riding lessons at the resort's dude ranch. These cost $30 each.

TENNIS A total of 13 clay and four hard-surface courts at **Casa de Campo** are lit for night play. The courts are available daily from 7am to 10pm.

WATER SPORTS & FISHING **Casa de Campo** (tel. 523-3333) has one of the most complete water-sports facilities anywhere in the Dominican Republic. Reservations and information on any seaside activity can be arranged through the resort's concierge.

You can charter a boat for snorkeling or deep-sea fishing. The resort maintains eight charter vessels, with a minimum of eight people required per outing. Only four can fish at a time.

Patrons interested in river fishing on the Chavón can arrange trips there through the hotel as well. Some of the biggest snook ever recorded have been caught here.

ALTOS DE CHAVÓN

An international arts center known as Altos de Chavón was created 6 miles from La Romana and just east of Casa de Campo. At the edge of its acreage, on the high banks of the Chavón River, an entire town was built to house artisans who come here on a rotating basis and teach sculpture, pottery, silk-screen printing, weaving, dance, and music, among other artistic pursuits. Accomplished professional artists from many countries and disciplines compete for 20 3-month residencies here each year.

A 2-year college of the arts has its campus here, and artists can work in their craft shops and display their finished wares for sale. Construction of the center was under the energetic guidance of an Italian builder, who was seemingly inspired by a hill town in the Tuscan countryside, and he did a stunning job of creating an old-world village. To many, the village looks as if it has stood here for centuries.

In the center is the red-tile **Church of St. Stanislaus.** Surrounding it are "old" houses, along with restaurants on the main plaza, an inn, and other buildings, all overlooking the valley with its river. Arcaded shops sell merchandise, and stairways lead to studio apartments for the artisans and their private loggias.

Frank Sinatra inaugurated the 5,000-seat **auditorium,** an amphitheater modeled after the Greek antiquity at Epidaurus. Local and international artists appear here frequently. "Sunset performances" are usually on Friday and Sunday evening.

In addition, the **Museo Arqueologico Regional,** open daily from 9am to 9pm, is devoted to the legacy of the vanished Taíno peoples and displays artifacts found along the banks of the river.

A narrow walk leads down over a small arched bridge and wends its way to the river below. A large parking area is available before you arrive at the village, and a bus runs between Casa de Campo and Altos de Chavón every hour.

All telephones in Altos de Chavón operate through the Casa de Campo switchboard. To reach one of the extensions given below, dial 523-3333 and then the extension number. The hotel provides motorized transportation to reach the following recommendations:

WHERE TO DINE

CAFE DE SOL, Altos de Chavón. Tel. 523-3333, ext. 2346.
Cuisine: PIZZA/AMERICAN. **Reservations:** Not required.
$ Prices: Appetizers $5–$11; main courses $10–$30. AE, DC, MC, V.
Open: Daily 7am–9:30pm.

If you want a pizza after your exploration of the mosaic-dotted plaza near the church, you'll probably enjoy this stone-floored indoor/outdoor café. To reach it, you climb a flight of exterior stone steps to the rooftop of a building whose ground floor houses a jewelry shop.

CASA DEL RÍO, Altos de Chavón. Tel. 523-3333, ext. 2345.
Cuisine: FRENCH. **Reservations:** Required.
$ Prices: Appetizers RD$130–RD$195 ($10.40–$15.60); main courses RD$195–RD$325 ($15.60–$26). AE, DC, MC, V.
Open: Dinner only, daily 6:30–11pm.

The most glamorous restaurant at Altos de Chavón occupies the basement of an Iberian-style house whose towers, turrets, tiles, and massive stairs are entwined with strands of bougainvillea. Inside, brick arches support oversize chandeliers, suspended racing sculls, and filled wine racks. Piano music might accompany your meal. You could begin with an unusual presentation of escargots and gnocchi, or a soup, perhaps hearts of palm vichyssoise. Main courses are likely to include honey-flavored breast of duck or lobster lasagne.

EL SOMBRERO, Altos de Chavón. Tel. 523-3333, ext. 2353.
Cuisine: MEXICAN. **Reservations:** Recommended.
$ Prices: Appetizers $5–$11; main courses $12–$28. AE, DC, MC, V.
Open: Dinner only, daily 7–11pm.

In this thick-walled, colonial-style building, the jutting hand-hewn timbers and roughly textured plaster evoke a corner of Old Mexico. There's a scattering of dark, heavy furniture and an occasional genuine antique, but the main allure comes from the spicy cuisine. Most guests dine outside on the covered patio, within earshot of a group of wandering minstrels whose sombreros accentuate their lyrics. A margarita is an appropriate accompaniment to the tortillas, nachos, enchiladas, and burritos that are the house specialties. Grilled steaks and brochettes are also popular.

LA PIAZZETTA, Altos de Chavón. Tel. 523-3333, ext. 2339.
Cuisine: ITALIAN. **Reservations:** Required.
$ Prices: Appetizers RD$130–RD$185 ($10.40–$14.80); main courses RD$205–RD$305 ($16.40–$24.40). AE, DC, MC, V.
Open: Dinner only, Tues–Sun 7–11pm.

La Piazzetta snuggles happily in the 16th-century-style "village" set high above the Chavón River. Well-prepared Italian dinners might begin with an antipasto misto, followed with filet of sea bass with artichokes and black-olive sauce, chicken saltimbocca, or beef brochette with a walnut-and-arugula sauce. Your fellow diners are likely to be guests from the deluxe Casa de Campo nearby.

SHOPPING

BUGAMBILIA, Altos de Chavón. Tel. 523-3333, ext. 2355.

A staff of sales clerks will explain the origins of dozens of ceramic figures on display. Women have been sculpted in positions ranging from bearing water to carrying flowers to posing as brides; the female figures are crafted in the industrial city of Santiago as part of a long tradition of presenting peasant women without faces. Look, however, for an expression of dignity in the bodies of the figurines. The largest are packed but not shipped. The store also has a winning collection of grotesque papier-mâché carnival masks. Open: Daily 9am–9pm.

EVERETT DESIGNS, Altos de Chavon. Tel. 523-3333, ext. 8331.

The designs here are so original that many visitors mistake this place for a museum. Each piece of jewelry is handcrafted in a minifactory at the rear of the shop. Minnesota-born Bill Everett was the inspirational force for many of these pieces, which include Dominican larimar and amber, 17th-century Spanish pieces-of-eight from sunken galleons, and polished silver and gold. Open: Daily 10am–9pm.

OSCAR DE LA RENTA / FREYA BOUTIQUE, Altos de Chavón. Tel. 523-3333, ext. 2359.

With the exception of an outlet in Miami, this boutique is reputed to sell the creations of Señor de la Renta less expensively than anywhere else. Also for sale is a striking collection of purses and boxes cunningly fashioned from shell, bone, and cowhorn. Open: Mon–Sat 10am–6pm.

EVENING ENTERTAINMENT

GENESIS DISCO, Altos de Chavón. Tel. 523-3333, ext. 2340.

Genesis features just about every kind of music at least once each evening. Clients range from avant-garde artists to visitors from the corporate world. If you've always wanted to dance your way through the gamut from rock, blues, salsa, merengue, to a good dose of "music for lovers," this is the place for you. The illuminated and translucent dance floor is studded with multicolored pieces of coral. Open at 9pm each night, it's closed a few days a week off-season, so check before going there. Drinks begin at $10.

Admission: $20.

3. PUNTA CANA

Continuing east from La Romana, you reach Punta Cana, site of several major tourist developments, including Club Med, and more are projected at the easternmost tip of Hispaniola. This perhaps will one day become a formidable rival of Puerto Plata.

The area, known for its white sand beaches and clear waters, is an escapist's retreat, although resorts compete to have enough activities around the clock to keep guests on the premises.

When white sand bores you, head inland to the typical Dominican city of **Higüey,** 27 miles from Punta Cana, which hasn't been made pretty for tourists. There, you can see the **Basilica Nuestra Señora de la Altagracia,** with the largest carillon in the Americas. The founders of the church conceived the basilica to honor Our Lady of Altagracia, the patron saint of the Dominican Republic. The church is said to represent the best modern architecture on the island. It is reputedly the site of miracles.

Higüey was founded in 1494 by the conqueror of Jamaica, Juan de Esquivel, with immigrants brought in between 1502 and 1508 by Ponce de León to populate the land. It was from the castle he built here that the tireless seeker of the Fountain of Youth set out in 1509 to conquer Puerto Rico and in 1513 to check out Florida.

Toward the southern coast is **Saona Island,** where some 1,000 people live on 80 square miles of land, surviving primarily by fishing and hunting for pigeons and wild hogs—a healthy way to live, as attested to by the fact that Saona has the lowest mortality rate in the Dominican Republic.

GETTING THERE Scheduled flights to the Punta Cana airport were discontinued by its major traffickers, American Eagle, in 1991. Assuming that the airline's flights from San Juan have not been reinstated by the time you actually plan your trip (call American Eagle, toll free 800/433-7300, to be sure), you'll have to drive either from Santo Domingo (trip time: 2½ hours) or from the airport at La Romana (trip time: 1¼ hours). Most of the large hotels in Punta Cana will arrange for transportation upon request, usually in hotel-managed minivans.

WHERE TO STAY & DINE

BAVARO BEACH COMPLEX, Apartado Postal 1, Punta Cana, Higüey, Dominican Republic, Tel. 809/876-6612, or toll free 800/876-6612. Fax 809/686-5859. 1,168 rms, 126 one-bedroom units. A/C TV TEL
$ Prices (including MAP): Winter, $123–$208 single; $162–$226 double or one-bedroom unit. Summer, prices reduced by about 25%. Minimum stay 3 days. AE, DC, MC, V. **Parking:** Free.

This massive resort colony, the largest in the Dominican Republic, sits on one of the best beaches in the Caribbean, with 26 miles of white sands stretching in both directions. Built in a series of enlargements between 1985 and 1990, it contains four different low-rise sections, each of which lies parallel to the beachfront for maximum exposure to the sea. A series of one-bedroom apartments, each with a small kitchenette, lies within the establishment's gardens (not directly on the beach), and families with children often opt for these units. Each accommodation is equipped with a terrace, a safety-deposit box, and either two double beds or one double and one single bed. Clients appreciate the variety provided by their unrestricted access to the many bars, restaurants, swimming pools, and facilities of the resort's four different sections.

Dining/Entertainment: The resort contains four restaurants and at least six bars, one of which is transformed into a disco at night, where there always seems to be someone on hand to teach you the merengue. The resort has one of the largest casinos in the region, which opens every evening around 5pm and remains open till the last casino chip hits the roulette table.

Services: Laundry, baby-sitting, massage.

Facilities: Four swimming pools, daily aerobics sessions, scuba diving, snorkeling, sailing, windsurfing, waterskiing, children's camp.

CLUB MEDITERRANEE–PUNTA CANA, Apartado Postal 106, Province La Altagracia, Dominican Republic. Tel. 809/687-2767, or 212/750-1670 in New York, or toll free 800/CLUB-MED. Fax 809/687-2896. 334 rms. A/C
$ Rates (including all meals): Christmas and New Year's holidays, $1,380 per person double per week. Midsummer, $850 per person double per week. Rates at other times vary between these figures, depending on the particular week. 40%–50% discounts for children under 11. AE, MC, V. **Parking:** Free.

Some 145 miles east of Santo Domingo, Club Med opened in 1981 and put the far-eastern tip of the island of Hispaniola on the tourist map. The village lies along a reef-protected white sandy beach, which offers some of the best diving areas on the islands. It was here that the crews of *Niña, Pinta,* and *Santa Maria* are believed by some to have put ashore. Columbus wouldn't recognize the place today. Three-story clusters of bungalows are strung along the beach, contain twin beds, and open either on the sea or onto a coconut grove. Children under 11 are especially welcome.

Dining/Entertainment: The heart of the village is a combined dining room/bar/dance floor and theater complex facing the sea. A small restaurant and disco are located beside the sea. You get the usual Club Med activities here, including picnics, boat rides, nightly dancing, shows, and optional excursions.

Services: Laundry.

Facilities: Sailing, windsurfing, snorkeling, waterskiing, swimming, archery, 10 tennis courts (4 lit at night); Mini-Club for juniors 2 to 11, highlighting circus training and other activities.

4. PUERTO PLATA

Originally it was Columbus's intention to found America's first city at Puerto Plata and name it La Isabela. But a tempest detained him, and it wasn't until 1502 that Nicolas de Ovando founded Puerto Plata, or "port of silver," which lies 130 miles northwest of Santo Domingo. The port became the last stop for ships going back to Europe, their holds laden with treasures taken from the New World.

Puerto Plata appeals to a market that may shun more expensive resorts, and some hotels boast a nearly full occupancy rate almost all year. It's already casting a shadow on business at longer-established resorts throughout the Caribbean, especially in Puerto Rico.

Most of the hotels are not actually in Puerto Plata itself but are in a special tourist zone called **Playa Dorada.** The backers of this usually sun-drenched spot have poured vast amounts of money into a flat area between a pond and the curved and verdant shoreline. (It rains a lot in Puerto Plata during the winter, while the south and Punta Cana are drier.) There are major hotels, a scattering of secluded condominiums and villas, a Robert Trent Jones–designed golf course, and a riding stable with horses for each of the major properties.

ORIENTATION

GETTING THERE   By Plane   The international airport is actually not in Puerto Plata but is east of Playa Dorado on the road to Sosúa. For information about flights from North America, see "Getting There" at the beginning of this chapter.

By Car   From Santo Domingo, the 3½-hour drive directly north on Autopista Duarte passes through the lush Cibao Valley, home of tobacco industry and Bermudez rum, and through Santiago de los Caballeros, the second-largest city in the country, 90 miles north of Santo Domingo.

GETTING AROUND   For information on renting a car, see the discussion of car rentals in the Santo Domingo introduction. You might even find that a motor scooter will be suitable for transportation in Puerto Plata or Sosúa.

By Taxi   Make an agreement with the driver on the fare before your trip starts, as the vehicles are not metered. You'll find taxis on Central Park at Puerto Plata. At night it's wise to hire your cab for a round-trip. If you go in the daytime by taxi to any of the other beach resorts or villages, check on reserving a vehicle for your return trip.

By Motoconcho   The cheapest way of getting around is on a motoconcho, found at the major corners of Puerto Plata and Sosúa. This motorcycle "concho" or taxi offers a ride to practically anywhere in town for only RD$5 (40¢). For Puerto Plata to Playa Dorada (site of most of the hotels), it costs only RD$10 (80¢).

By Minivan   Minivans are another means of transport, especially if you're traveling outside town. They leave from Puerto Plata's Central Park and will take you all the way to Sosúa for just RD$5 (40¢). Vans operate Monday through Saturday from 6am to 5pm and on Sunday from 6am to midnight.

ESSENTIALS   Round-the-clock **drugstore** service is offered by Farmacía Deleyte, avenida John F. Kennedy 89 (tel. 571-2515). Emergency **medical service** is provided by Clínica Dr. Brugal, calle José del Carmen Ariza 15 (tel. 586-2583). Phone 586-2331 to summon the **police** in Puerto Plata.

WHERE TO STAY

EXPENSIVE

JACK TAR VILLAGE, Playa Dorada (Apartado Postal 368), Puerto Plata, Dominican Republic. Tel. 809/586-3557, or toll free 800/999-9182. Fax 809/586-4161. 284 rms. A/C TEL

$ Rates (including all meals and drinks): Winter, $160 single; $240 double. Summer, $150 single; $200 double. Children 3–12 $80 in winter and $90 in summer when sharing a room with two adults. AE, DC, MC, V. **Parking:** Free.

Owned by an investment group from Texas, this all-inclusive resort east of the airport is set at the edge of the sea and clustered around two swimming pools. The facility offers drinks, all meals, most water sports, and entertainment as part of its standard package, so you never have to leave the grounds. In the center of the resort, you'll find dozens of adults and children playing shuffleboard, cards, table tennis, and volleyball. If you prefer to linger beside one of the indoor/outdoor bars, where all your drinks are free, you'll have plenty of company. If you're more energetic, many water and land sports are offered, most of them included in the overall price of your accommodation.

Dining/Entertainment: In 1990 the resort opened a large, plush casino, one of the largest in the country, and a newly refurbished disco. Four nights a week, dinners are sit-down affairs in the high-ceilinged dining room with frequent musical entertainment. The rest of the time, and often at lunch, meals are buffet style. Drinks are free at the indoor and outdoor bars.

Services: Laundry.

Facilities: Two swimming pools.

MODERATE

DORADO NACO, Playa Dorada (Apartado Postal 162), Puerto Plata, Dominican Republic. Tel. 809/586-2019. Fax 809/586-3608. 141 units. A/C TV TEL

$ Rates: Winter, $110 one-bedroom suite; $150 two-bedroom suite, $180 one-bedroom penthouse. Summer, $60 one-bedroom suite; $100 two-bedroom suite; $130 one-bedroom penthouse. Children under 12 stay free in parents' room. Breakfast $7 extra. AE, DC, MC, V. **Parking:** Free.

When the Dorado Naco was built east of the airport in 1982, there was only one other hotel in the entire Playa Dorada area. After registering, you'll be ushered past the poolside bar and restaurant complex, down a series of flowered walkways into your room. Each unit contains comfortable furniture, a kitchen, and a creative arrangement of interior space. You can spend some of your evenings en famille, cooking at home. Many of the units are clustered along parapets or around well-planted atriums, and some of the larger ones include duplex floor plans and enough spacious luxury to satisfy any vacationer. One-bedroom suites accommodate one or two and two-bedroom suites and the penthouse can sleep up to four.

Dining/Entertainment: A wide range of entertainment is available, and a full range of activities is planned throughout the week in season. A beach bar and grill lie a short walk from every room. A nightly buffet is spread under a portico near the pool, and à la carte meals are available in the Flamingo Gourmet Restaurant and Valentino's Italian Restaurant. The hotel has live music every night and live shows twice weekly.

Services: Room service (7am–11pm), laundry, baby-sitting.

Facilities: Swimming pool, tennis court; water sports center for scuba diving, snorkeling, waterskiing, and sailing.

EUROTEL, Playa Dorada (Apartado Postal 337), Puerto Plata, Dominican Republic. Tel. 809/586-3663, or toll free 800/752-9236. Fax 809/586-4858. 316 rms, 186 junior suites. A/C MINIBAR TV TEL

$ Rates: Winter, $70–$165 single or double. Prices reduced about 20% in summer. Year round, $230 junior suite. Breakfast $7 extra. AE, DC, MC, V. **Parking:** Free.

Architects created a "Victorian Caribbean" design for the Eurotel, which sits east of the airport amid a garden of flowering plants, flagstone walkways, and a roughly textured rock wall from which a dozen artificial springs feed a pool. Each of the comfortable bedrooms has its own Spanish-style mirador (sheltered balcony) and the aura of a private apartment. Rooms and junior suites are rented as either singles or doubles.

Dining/Entertainment: A beachside entertainment center has its own bubbling whirlpool, an offering of water sports, a music platform for live entertainment, and a cluster of dining and drinking facilities. The resort has four restaurants, each with distinctive character. Of these, the Americas is the most formal and elegant.

Services: Room service, laundry, baby-sitting.
Facilities: Swimming pool.

PLAYA DORADA HOTEL & CASINO, Playa Dorada (Apartado Postal 272), Puerto Plata, Dominican Republic. Tel. 809/586-3988, or toll free 800/545-8089. Fax 809/586-1190. 249 rms. A/C TV TEL

$ Rates: Winter, $90 single or double; $20 extra person. Summer, $60 single or double; $10 extra person. Breakfast $8 extra. AE, DC, MC, V. **Parking:** Free.

This theatrically designed hotel east of the airport is one of the few in all the Caribbean that can boast nearly full occupancy during most of the year. The reception area is an air-conditioned oasis of Victorian latticework set beneath the soaring ceiling. The bedrooms are arranged along rambling corridors. More than two-thirds of the hotel's units are set into red-roofed wings that face the 1½-mile beach. The hotel also has specially designed rooms for disabled patrons. A sports package is included in the rates, so all the facilities are free.

Dining/Entertainment: In addition to La Palma restaurant, the many bars and entertainment facilities include a cocktail lounge, Las Olas, where live entertainment is presented every night, as well as one of the hottest discos in town on the premises. Around the swimming pool, the management hosts barbecues, buffet suppers, and weekly entertainment, which includes singers and dancers known throughout the Spanish-speaking world.

Services: Baby-sitting, laundry, valet.
Facilities: Boating, water sports, golf, three tennis courts (lit at night), swimming pool.

PLAYA DORADA PRINCESS GOLF, TENNIS & BEACH RESORT, Playa Dorada, Puerto Plata, Dominican Republic. Tel. 809/586-5350, or toll free 800/628-2216. Fax 809/586-5386. 251 rms, 7 suites. A/C MINIBAR TV TEL

$ Rates: Winter, $55–$85 single or double; $95 suite. Summer, $45–$75 single or double; $80 suite. AP $25 per person extra. AE, MC, V. **Parking:** Free.

This is one of the best of the modern complexes along this resort-studded coastline east of the airport. The hotel offers suites as well as standard rooms, all comfortably furnished and with private baths or showers.

Dining/Entertainment: Continental dining is offered at La Condesa until 11pm; barbecues are featured on a terrace, and a piano bar is host to dancing on an upper deck.

Services: Room service, laundry, baby-sitting, shuttle bus to beach.
Facilities: Water sports, seven all-weather tennis courts, gym, swimming pool with swim-up/walk-up bar; nearby 18-hole golf course.

VILLAS DORADAS BEACH RESORT, Playa Dorada (Apartado Postal 1370), Puerto Plata, Dominican Republic. Tel. 809/586-3000. Fax 809/586-4790. 170 rms, 32 suites. A/C TV TEL

$ Rates: Winter, $100 single or double; $120 junior suite. Summer, $70 single or double; $110 junior suite. Breakfast $7 extra. AE, MC, V. **Parking:** Free.

This collection of town houses east of the airport is arranged in landscaped clusters, usually around a courtyard. There's no beachfront here. Each unit is pleasantly furnished with louvered doors and windows.

Dining/Entertainment: A focal point of the resort is the restaurant Las Garzas, where a musical trio entertains guests every evening beneath the soaring pine ceiling. The management also features barbecues around the pool area, where a net is sometimes set up for volleyball games. Of course, it would be tempting never to leave the shade of the cone-shaped thatch-roofed pool bar, which is one of the most attractive and popular parts of the whole resort. El Pescador is a fish restaurant open for lunch beside the beach.

Services: Room service, laundry, baby-sitting.

Facilities: Swimming pool; sand beaches and golf facilities within walking distance.

BUDGET

MONTEMAR, avenida Circunvalación del Norte (Apartado Postal 382), Puerto Plata, Dominican Republic. Tel. 809/586-2800. Fax 809/586-2009. 95 rms (all with bath). A/C MINIBAR TV TEL

$ Rates: Winter, $90 single or double. Summer, $85 single or double. Breakfast $5 extra. AE, DC, MC, V. **Parking:** Free.

The Montemar complex east of the airport plays a double role: It's one of the pioneer resorts in the area and it houses the local hotel school. The lobby is one of the most distinctive in the area. Large bamboo chandeliers illuminate the upholstery, where images of birds flit across the comfortable couches and the naturalistic mural behind the reception desk. Most of the accommodations have views of palms and the sea. Your needs will be cared for by a battalion of students.

A lounge nearby engages a merengue band, which plays every night beside the illuminated palms. There are three tennis courts. Laundry, baby-sitting, and room service are provided, and there is free shuttle service to the airport.

WHERE TO DINE

EXPENSIVE

DE ARMANDO, calle Separación, at the corner of Antera Mota, Puerto Playa. Tel. 586-3418.

Cuisine: INTERNATIONAL. **Reservations:** Recommended.

$ Prices: Appetizers $2.90–$5.80; main courses $7–$20. AE, DC, MC, V.

Open: Daily noon–midnight.

Perhaps the most distinguished restaurant in Puerto Plata is De Armando, launched by Armando Rodríguez, who has a restaurant with the same name in Santo Domingo. In this elegant setting, you can select an appetizer such as escargots bourguignons or one of half a dozen soups, including lobster bisque. He serves excellent fish dishes. For that Dominican flavor, there is moro concho, rice and black beans served with pork fritters. Desserts are freshly made, and a trio entertains at night.

VALENTINO'S, in the Dorado Naco Resort Hotel, Playa Dorada. Tel. 586-2019.

Cuisine: ITALIAN. **Reservations:** Required.

$ Prices: Appetizers RD$35–RD$79 ($2.80–$6.30); main courses RD$49–RD$275 ($3.90–$22). AE, DC, MC, V.

Open: Daily noon–1am.

The specialties of this ristorante and pizzeria east of the airport are homemade pasta, such as lasagne verdi al forno, and brick-oven pizza. Against an elegant backdrop, with fountains and pink marble, it serves a savory cuisine. Have a drink on the terrace, perhaps the bartender's special called a Bloody Mary antipasto; then follow with one of the main dishes, such as risotto primavera with grilled chicken Venetian style.

INEXPENSIVE

JARDIN DE JADE, at the Villas Doradas Beach Resort, Playa Dorada. Tel. 586-3000.

Cuisine: CHINESE. **Reservations:** Recommended.
$ Prices: Appetizers RD$22–RD$100 ($1.75–$8); main courses RD$80–RD$230 ($6.40–$18.40); dinner buffet RD$125 ($10). AE, DC, MC, V.
Open: Dinner only, daily 6–11pm.

A high-ceilinged and airy, modern restaurant, the Jardin de Jade offers a Chinese buffet on Monday, Wednesday, and Friday. It is one of the best dining values at this resort east of the airport. Typical menu items include barbecued Peking duck, sautéed diced chicken in chili sauce, and fried crab claws. The chefs specialize in Cantonese and Szechuan cuisine.

JIMMY'S, calle Beller 72. Tel. 586-4325.

Cuisine: INTERNATIONAL. **Reservations:** Not required.
$ Prices: Appetizers RD$35–RD$85 ($2.80–$6.80); main courses RD$65–RD$275 ($5.20–$22). AE, DC, MC, V.
Open: Daily 11am–11pm.

One of the loveliest buildings in downtown Puerto Plata, Jimmy's is an alluring air-conditioned establishment that serves some of the best food in town. It lies behind lacy rows of cast-iron balustrades in a century-old building. The internationally inspired menu includes lobster "Jimmy's style," which is flambéed at your table with cream sauce, along with such steaks as tournedos and filet mignon. The kitchen turns out a delectable local cream of fish soup called sopita, several versions of chicken (including a "drunken" one with seven Dominican rums), and such spectacular desserts as bananas flambé and crêpes Suzette.

PORTO FINO, bulevar Las Hermanas Mirabal. Tel. 586-2858.

Cuisine: ITALIAN. **Reservations:** Not required.
$ Prices: Appetizers RD$8–RD$25 (65¢–$2); main courses RD$23–RD$150 ($1.85–$12). AE, MC, V.
Open: Daily 11am–11pm.

In this popular Italian restaurant just across from the entrance of the Hotel Montemar in Puerto Plata, parmesan breast of chicken, eggplant parmesan, ravioli, and pizzas are served in generous helpings. You'll get off cheap if you order only pizza. Locals and visitors mingle freely here.

ROMA II, calle Beller at Emilio Prud'homme. Tel. 586-3904.

Cuisine: INTERNATIONAL. **Reservations:** Not required.
$ Prices: Appetizers RD$24–RD$65 ($1.90–$5.20); main courses RD$43–RD$170 ($3.45–$13.60). AE, MC, V.
Open: Daily 11am–midnight.

This air-conditioned restaurant in the center of town is staffed by an engaging crew of well-mannered young employees, who work hard to converse in English. You can order from a selection of 13 varieties of pizza, topped with tempting combinations of cheese, shrimp, and garlic. Full meals include an array of seafood such as paella, seafood casserole, several preparations of lobster, sea bass, and octopus prepared Créole style or with vinaigrette. Beef dishes include Stroganoff or tenderloin.

VALTER'S, bulevar Las Hermanas Mirabal. Tel. 586-2329.

Cuisine: INTERNATIONAL. **Reservations:** Recommended.
$ Prices: Appetizers RD$24–RD$45 ($1.90–$3.60); main courses RD$70–RD$150 ($5.60–$12). MC, V.
Open: Lunch daily 11am–3pm; dinner daily 7–11pm.

Its low-slung Victorian porch, with its adjacent garden, seems like the ideal place for a romantic candlelit dinner in the center of town. Built about a century ago as a private home, it has ring-around gingerbread painted in vivid shades of lime green, an oversize veranda laden with dozens of tables, and a Neo-Victorian bar. Surf and turf is the house specialty, and you'll also find an array of classic pasta dishes. Many locals make dining here a special event.

WHAT TO SEE & DO

Fort San Felipe, considered the oldest fort in the New World, is a popular attraction. Philip II of Spain ordered its construction in 1564, a task that took 33 years to complete. Built with 8-foot-thick walls, the fort was virtually impenetrable, and the moat surrounding it was treacherous. The Spaniards sharpened swords and embedded them in coral below the surface of the water to discourage use of the moat for entrance or exit purposes. The doors of the fort are only 4 feet high, another deterrent to swift passage. During Trujillo's rule, Fort San Felipe was used as a prison. Standing at the end of the Malecón, the fort was restored in the early 1970s. Admission is RD$10 (80¢), and it's open Friday through Wednesday from 9am to noon and 3 to 5pm.

Isabel de Torres, a tower with a fort built when Trujillo was in power, affords a magnificent view of the Amber Coast from a point near the top, 2,595 feet above sea level. You reach the observation point by cable car (*teleférico*), a 7-minute ascent. Once there, you are also treated to 7 acres of botanical gardens. The round-trip costs RD$5 (40¢). The aerial ride is operated on Tuesday, Thursday, Friday, and Saturday from 8am to 5pm. *Be warned:* There is often a long wait in line for the cable car, and at certain times it's likely to be closed for repairs, so check at your hotel before going there.

You can see a collection of rare amber specimens at the **Museum of Dominican Amber,** calle Duarte 61 (tel. 586-2848). The museum, open Monday through Saturday from 9am to 5pm, is near Puerto Plata's Central Park. Guided tours in English are offered. Admission is RD$5 (40¢).

SPORTS & RECREATION

The north coast is a water-sports scene, although the sea here tends to be rough. Snorkeling is popular, and the windsurfing is among the best in the Caribbean. The resort of **Cabarete,** east of Puerto Plata, hosts an annual windsurfing tournament.

BEACHES You'll find superb beaches to the east and west of Puerto Plata. Among the better known are Playa Dorada, Sosúa, Long Beach, Cofresi, Jack Tar, and Cabarete.

GOLF Robert Trent Jones, Jr., designed the par-72, 18-hole **Playa Dorada championship golf course,** which surrounds the resorts and runs along the coast. Even nongolfers can stop at the clubhouse for a drink or a snack to enjoy the views. Instead of trying to call the course, it's best to make arrangements at the activities desk of your hotel.

TENNIS Some of the best facilities in the Playa Dorada area are available at the **Playa Dorada Princess Golf, Tennis, and Beach Resort** (tel. 586-5350), which has seven all-weather courts as well as a pro shop and club.

SAVVY SHOPPING

Unless otherwise cited, most shops are open Monday through Saturday from 9am to 6pm.

CENTRO ARTESANAL, calle J. F. Kennedy 3. Tel. 586-3724.

This is a nonprofit school for the training of future Dominican craftspeople, and it's also a promotion center for local crafts and jewelry. Selected student projects are for sale. Open: Mon–Sat 8am–noon and 2–5pm.

FACTORY GIFT SHOP, calle J. F. Kennedy 27. Tel. 586-2232.

A good place in town to purchase fairly priced samples of the two stones for which the Dominican Republic is noted is the Factory Gift Shop. Amber from the island's north shore and larimar turquoise from the south shore are sold in a wide and attractive variety, or you can buy black coral, bull's horn, or Dominican pictures. The

Ortiz family will show you their workshop, where they polish different grades of their raw material into cunningly shaped figures, such as frogs and rabbits. Some of the rare (and expensive) pieces contain well-preserved insects, and one even has in it a (petrified) lizard. Anything you buy can be mounted in silver or gold.

HARRISON'S, calle J. F. Kennedy 14. Tel. 586-3933.

The best-established place for fine gold jewelry is Harrison's, which also sells silver and black coral jewelry. The unusual designs have been worn by Madonna, Bruce Springsteen, and even Keith Richards of the Rolling Stones.

PLAZA ISABELA, Playa Dorada.

About 500 yards from the entrance to the Playa Dorada hotel complex, this collection of small specialty shops is constructed in the Victorian gingerbread style, but has a Spanish flair unique in the islands.

PLAZA TURISOL COMPLEX, Plaza Turisol.

The largest shopping center on the north coast has a multicolored roof and about 80 different outlets. Each week, or so it seems, a new store opens. You may want to head here to get a sampling of the merchandise available in Puerto Plata before going to any specific recommendation. The plaza lies about 5 minutes from the centers of Puerto Plata and Playa Dorada, on the main road heading east.

TOURIST BAZAAR BOUTIQUE, calle Duarte 61. Tel. 586-2848.

The neoclassical house sheltering the Amber Museum also contains the densest collection of boutiques in Puerto Plata. Merchandise is literally packed into seven competing establishments. A generous percentage of the paintings is from neighboring Haiti, but the amber, larimar, and mahogany wood carving are from the Dominican Republic. On the premises is a patio bar.

EVENING ENTERTAINMENT

DANCE CLUBS

PLAYA DISCO, in the Playa Dorada Hotel, Playa Dorada. Tel. 586-3988.

In one of the most animated nightspots in Puerto Plata, you're faced with a dance floor (which is usually packed by the end of the evening) and lots of banquette seating, tiny tables, and flashing lights. Open: Daily 8pm–3am.

Admission: RD$60 ($4.80) Fri–Sat, free Sun–Thurs.

VIVALDI'S, at the corner of bulevar las Hermanas Mirabel and the Malecón. Tel. 586-3752.

There's a restaurant on the upper floor, but most of the people who stream in head for the ground-floor disco, where everything from salsa to reggae to New York City's recent dance releases is played practically all night. The interior is ringed with what you might call wraparound neon. If you want a breath of cool air, there's a little-used terrace in front. A beer costs RD$30 ($2.40). It opens at 9pm.

Admission: RD$30 ($2.40).

CASINOS

JACK TAR VILLAGE, Playa Dorada. Tel. 586-3800.

Jack Tar joins the gaming flock with a casino and disco, along with a European-style restaurant. It's built in Spanish Mediterranean colonial style with a terra-cotta roof. Between bouts at the games tables, guests quench their thirst at one of five bars. No shorts or bathing suits are allowed in the casino. There is also an entertainment center that includes a 90-seat restaurant and a disco for 250 dancers. Open: Casino, daily 4pm–4am.

PLAYA DORADA CASINO, in the Playa Dorada Hotel, Playa Dorada. Tel. 586-3988.

The casino's entrance is flanked by columns and leads to an airy garden courtyard. Inside, mahogany gaming tables are reflected in the silver ceiling and ringed with mauve and pink walls. No shorts are permitted inside the premises after 7pm, and beach attire is never allowed. Open: Daily 4pm–4am.

PUERTO PLATA BEACH RESORT & CASINO, Malecón. Tel. 586-4243.
This was the first casino in Puerto Plata, and it's still one of the most charming, with high ceilings and tall French windows. Guests find craps tables, blackjack setups, roulette wheels, and two "big six" layouts. Gamblers can play in either pesos or U.S. dollars. Open: Daily 4pm–4am.

5. SOSÚA

About 15 miles east of Puerto Plata is one of the finest beaches in the Dominican Republic, Sosúa Beach, a strip of white sand more than half a mile wide in a cove sheltered by coral cliffs. The beach connects two communities, which together make up the town known as Sosúa. But, regrettably, you may not be allowed to enjoy a day on the beach in peace, as vendors and often beggars frequently annoy visitors.

At one end of the beach is **El Batey,** an area with residential streets, gardens, restaurants, shops, and hotels that can be visited by those who can tear themselves away from the beach. Real-estate transactions have been booming in El Batey and its environs, where many streets have been paved and villas constructed.

At the other end of Sosúa Beach lies **Los Charamicos,** a sharp contrast to El Batey. Here you'll find tin-roofed shacks, vegetable stands, chickens scrabbling in the rubbish, and warm, friendly people. This community is a typical Latin American village, recognizable through the smells, sights, and sounds in the narrow, rambling streets. All this may be changed even by the time you visit, however, as developers are eyeing the entire Sosúa area.

Sosúa was founded in 1940 by European Jews seeking refuge from Hitler, when Trujillo invited 100,000 of them to settle in his country on a banana plantation. Actually, only 600 or so Jews were allowed to immigrate, and of those, only about a dozen or so remained. However, there are some 20 Jewish families living in Sosúa today, and for the most part they are engaged in the dairy and smoked-meat industry the refugees began during the war. There is a local one-room synagogue, where biweekly services are held. Many of the Jews intermarried with Dominicans, and the town has taken on an increasingly Spanish flavor; women of the town are often seen wearing both the Star of David and the Virgin de Altagracia. Nowadays many German expatriates are also found in the town.

GETTING THERE Taxis, charter buses, and públicos from Puerto Plata and Playa Dorada let passengers off at the stairs leading down from the highway to Sosúa beach. Take the Autopista east for about 30 minutes from Puerto Playa.

WHERE TO STAY

PLAYA CHIQUITA BEACH RESORT, Sosúa, Dominican Republic. Tel. 809/571-2800. Fax 809/571-2470. 90 rms. A/C MINIBAR TV TEL
$ Rates: Winter, $35 single; $75 double. 25% reduction in summer. Breakfast $6 extra. AE, MC, V. **Parking:** Free.

In business since 1987, the "big hotel on the little beach" (Playa Chiquita means "little beach" in Spanish) has a harlequin facade of vivid Caribbean colors that greets guests who arrive in this relatively isolated spot on a private beach. Arranged around a lagoon-shaped pool, the private accommodations are bright, large, and cheery, and most open onto ocean views. Rooms have tiny kitchens, big baths, and little verandas. The hotel's formal air-conditioned restaurant, Iranja, is one of the finest in the resort and serves Dominican and continental specialties; its wines come from Chile and Italy. Tables are set with highly polished silver.

SAND CASTLE BEACH RESORT, Puerto Chiquito, Sosúa, Dominican

Republic. Tel. 809/571-2420, or toll free 800/446-5963. Fax 809/571-2000. 240 rms, 80 suites. A/C MINIBAR TV TEL

$ Rates: Winter, $70 single; $120 double; from $150 suite. 25% discounts in summer. Breakfast from $5 extra. MC, V. **Parking:** Free.

One of the most luxurious accommodations along the north shore opens onto views of the Atlantic and Puerto Chiquito Beach. The multilevel apartment-hotel was inaugurated in 1989. Created for an upmarket clientele as a "place to remember," it was constructed on a strip of land between the ocean and a saltwater pond. It offers two swimming pools and a Jacuzzi. The expensive decor includes stained glass, detailed mahogany work, and 10-foot-long full-length mirrors in every bath.

The hotel is known for the many facilities included as part of a stay here: horseback riding, windsurfing, snorkeling, tennis, bicycling, a daily program of entertainment, nightly shows, sailing, and entrance to the disco.

HOTEL SOSÚA, calle Dr. Alejo Martínez, El Batey, Sosúa, Dominican Republic. Tel. 809/571-2683. Fax 809/571-2442. 35 rms. A/C

$ Rates (including continental breakfast): Winter, $35–$40 single or double. Summer, $25–$27 single or double. No credit cards. **Parking:** Free.

The Sosúa lies in a suburban community about a 2-minute drive from the center of town. Its simple and attractive layout includes a reception area designed to conceal a flagstone-rimmed pool from the street outside. The bedrooms are strung along a wing extending beside the pool. The rooms contain ceiling fans and an occasional pine balcony.

SOSÚA BY THE SEA, Sosúa (Apartado Postal 361), Puerto Plata, Dominican Republic. Tel. 809/571-3222. Fax 809/571-3222. 81 rms, 7 suites. A/C MINIBAR TV TEL

$ Rates: Winter, $85 single or double; from $125 suite for two or three. Summer, $50 single or double; from $90 suite for two or three. Breakfast from $5 extra. AE, MC, V. **Parking:** Free.

The blue-and-white main building here is softened with inviting wooden lattices. The pool area opens onto Sosúa Bay, and the resort stands between two beaches. From the open-air rooftop lounge, you have a view of Mount Isabel de Torres. Accommodations lie along meandering paths through tropical gardens. Reached by elevator, the airy bedrooms are either well-furnished studios or one-bedroom suites, all with a compusafe. A formal restaurant serves both Dominican specialties and an international cuisine, and you can have lunch at the poolside bar and grill. The hotel has many amenities, including a sports clinic and a beauty salon.

VILLAS LOS CORALILLOS, Sosúa (mailing address: Apartado Postal 851, Santo Domingo), Dominican Republic. Tel. 809/571-2645. Fax 809/571-2129. 52 units. A/C TEL

$ Rates (including breakfast): Winter, $57 single or double; $75 suite; $125 villa. 25% discount in summer. AE, MC, V. **Parking:** Free.

The well-furnished accommodations here lie in a series of terra-cotta-tiled Iberian villas cantilevered over a bougainvillea-draped hillside. The action centers around the pool and main restaurant overlooking Sosúa Bay. Guests can request one- or two-bedroom villas, and the views from some of the villas are among the most spectacular in Sosúa. Each standard unit has twin beds and a small veranda. Dining is at the hotel's El Coral Restaurant (see "Where to Dine," below). Los Coralillos is the only hotel in town with direct access to the main Sosúa beach; if you tire of the pool, you can stroll to the sea through century-old mahogany and almond trees.

HOTEL YAROA, El Batey, Sosúa, Dominican Republic. Tel. 809/571-2651. Fax 809/571-2180. 24 rms. A/C

$ Rates: Winter, $40 single or double. Summer, $25 single or double. Breakfast from $5 extra. AE, MC, V. **Parking:** Free.

The Yaroa is named after a long-ago native village. Opened in 1986, it encompasses views of dozens of leafy trees that ring its foundations. Inside you'll find an atrium illuminated by a skylight, lots of exposed wood and stone, and a well-designed garden ringing a sheltered swimming pool. Each bedroom has a Spanish-style mirador (sheltered balcony) with a planter filled with local ferns, pine louvers for privacy, terra-cotta floors, lots of airy space, and a private bath. Two of the accommodations are designed like private cabañas at poolside. Breakfast, light lunches, and dinners featuring French cuisine are served in the dining room, Sonya (see "Where to Dine," below).

WHERE TO DINE

EL CORAL, El Batey. Tel. 571-2645.
  Cuisine: CARIBBEAN. **Reservations:** Recommended.
$ Prices: Appetizers RD$40–RD$55 ($3.20–$4.40); main courses RD$80–RD$110 ($6.40–$8.80). AE, MC, V.
  Open: Daily 7:30am–11pm.
The best and arguably the most pleasant restaurant in town is El Coral, in a Spanish-style building roofed with red tiles and set at the bottom of the garden near the end of Sosúa Beach. It offers a spacious area with terra-cotta tiles, wooden accents, and stark-white walls opening onto a panoramic view of the ocean. If you look out over the rear garden from one of the flowered terraces or through one of the big windows, you see a pool midway down the hill leading to the ocean. There's a bar in a room adjoining the dining room. The specialties include conch or octopus Créole style, pork chops with pineapple, and shrimp with garlic.

MARCO POLO BAR & RESTAURANT, calle Dr. Alejo Martínez 2, El Batey. Tel. 571-3680.
  Cuisine: DOMINICAN. **Reservations:** Not required.
$ Prices: Appetizers RD$27–RD$45 ($2.15–$3.60); main courses RD$80–RD$160 ($6.40–$12.80). AE, MC, V.
  Open: Dinner only, daily 5pm–midnight.
The Marco Polo opens onto one of the most spectacular views in the Caribbean. While sipping a rum punch or one of the mixed drinks, called "Shooters," you can enjoy Sosúa Bay from your cliffside perch. There is a happy hour at the bar daily from 5 to 7pm. Meals range from the succulent grilled honey chicken to fresh lobster and shrimp.

RESTAURANT MORUA MAI, Pedro Clisante 5, El Batey. Tel. 571-2503.
  Cuisine: CONTINENTAL/DOMINICAN. **Reservations:** Not required.
$ Prices: Appetizers RD$35–RD$75 ($2.80–$6); main courses RD$60–RD$275 ($4.80–$22). AE, MC, V.
  Open: Lunch daily 11:30am–5pm; dinner daily 7–11:30pm.
The patio here, which faces a popular intersection in the center of town, is the closest thing to a European sidewalk café in town. Inside, where occasional live entertainment is an important attraction, is a high-ceilinged, double-decked, and stylish space filled with touches of Neo-Victorian gingerbread, upholstered banquettes, and wicker furniture. Consider this place for a sun-washed drink or cup of afternoon tea in the side courtyard, where a cabaña bar serves drinks from beneath a palm-thatched roof. Pizzas, sandwiches, and light meals are the lunch fare, while dinner might include charcoal-grilled lobster, fish platters (with oysters, octopus, conch, and sea bass), Valencian paella, and grilled chicken with orange sauce.

RESTAURANT SONYA, in the Hotel Yarca, El Batey. Tel. 571-2651.
  Cuisine: DOMINICAN/INTERNATIONAL. **Reservations:** Recommended.
$ Prices: Appetizers RD$20–RD$50 ($1.60–$4); main courses RD$70–RD$185 ($5.60–$14.80). AE, MC, V.
  Open: Lunch Mon–Sat noon–4pm; dinner Mon–Sat at 6 and 8:30pm.
Sonya has a good-quality menu, not overly large but select, with well-chosen ingredients and fine service. The food is both Dominican and international, with an emphasis on French cuisine. You might try poached kingfish in a white-butter sauce, or filet steak with roquefort. For dessert, the crêpes Suzette are an experience.

CHAPTER 8

THE BRITISH LEEWARD ISLANDS

Once a British colony, the British Leeward Islands have moved into more independent seas, with the exceptions of Montserrat and Anguilla. The language of the Leewards, however, remains English.

Between French-controlled Guadeloupe and the U.S. Virgins, at a bend of an archipelago, the British Leewards consist of Antigua (in association with isolated Barbuda), Montserrat, the twin state of St. Kitts and Nevis, and little Anguilla. Of them all, Antigua, with its many beaches and resort hotels, is the best equipped for mass tourism and is a good base for going almost anywhere in the West Indies. However, the opening of more hotels and the addition of modern tourist facilities are drawing thousands to Montserrat, Nevis, and to more remote Anguilla, which is also becoming an increasingly chic address.

1. ANTIGUA & BARBUDA

Antigua boasts a different beach for every day of the year—365 of them. Most of these beaches are protected by coral reefs, and the sand is often sugar-white.

Antigua, Barbuda, and Redonda form the independent nation of Antigua and Barbuda, within the Commonwealth of Nations. (Redonda is an uninhabited rocky islet of less than a square mile located 20 miles southwest of Antigua; and sparsely populated Barbuda is covered at the end of this section.) Since its independence in 1981, this small state has had a British-style parliamentary government administered by a Cabinet of Ministers headed by a prime minister.

FAST FACTS ANTIGUA & BARBUDA

Area Code When calling from overseas, the telephone area code for Antigua and Barbuda is 809 (also, see "Telephone," below.)

Banking Hours Banks are usually open Monday through Thursday from 8am to 1pm and on Friday from 8am to 1pm and 3 to 5pm.

Currency The **Eastern Caribbean dollar (EC$)** is used on these islands. However, nearly all hotels bill you in U.S. dollars, and only certain tiny restaurants

WHAT'S SPECIAL ABOUT THE BRITISH LEEWARDS

Beaches

☐ Shoal Bay, Anguilla, called a "dream beach," miles of uncrowded silver sands lying off some of the Caribbean's best coral gardens.

☐ The beaches of Antigua, some 365 of them, all public, all white sand, with Pigeon Point and Dickenson Bay the best ones.

☐ The beaches of St. Kitts, miles of powdery white sand at the southern end of the island, the best being the twin beaches of Banana Bay and Cockleshell Bay, Frigate Bay, Conaree Beach, and Friar's Bay.

☐ Pinney's Beach, Nevis, 3 miles of uncrowded sand protected by a reef.

Ace Attractions

☐ Nelson's Dockyard, Antigua, one of the biggest attractions in the Caribbean, where Admirals Nelson, Rodney, and Hood found safe anchorage for their fleets.

Island Hideaways

☐ Barbuda, administered by Antigua, called "the last frontier of the Caribbean," today a pocket of posh.

☐ Montserrat, labeled "the way the Caribbean used to be," a volcanic island of lush forests and tropical vegetation.

☐ Sandy Island, off the coast of Anguilla, a palm-studded island retreat for escapists.

Special Events

☐ Summer carnival in Antigua in August, filled with fun and spectacle, including calypso and steel-band competitions.

---

present their prices in EC dollars. Make sure you know which dollars are referred to when you inquire about a price. The EC$ is worth about 37¢ in U.S. currency (EC$2.70 = $1 U.S.). Unless otherwise specified, rates quoted in this chapter are given in U.S. dollars.

Customs   Arriving visitors are allowed to bring in 200 cigarettes and 1 quart of liquor, plus 6 ounces of perfume.

Documents   U.S. and Canadian citizens do not have to have a passport, but they will be asked for some means of identification such as a birth certificate or voter registration card. An outbound transportation ticket is also required.

Electricity   Most of the island's electricity is 220 volts AC, 60 cycles. However, the Hodges Bay area and some hotels are supplied with 110 volts AC, 60 cycles.

Embassy   The **U.S. Embassy** is on Queen Elizabeth Hwy., St. John's, Antigua, W.I. (tel. 809/462-3511).

Emergencies   In an emergency, contact the **police** (tel. 2-0125), the **fire department** (tel. 2-0044), or an **ambulance** (tel. 2-0251).

Information   Contact the **Antigua and Barbuda Department of Tourism,** 610 Fifth Ave., Suite 311, New York, NY 10020 (tel. 212/541-4117); or 121 SE 1st St., Suite 508, Miami, FL 33131 (tel. 305/381-6762). In Canada, contact the **Antigua and Barbuda Department of Tourism & Trade,** 60 St. Clair Ave. East, Suite 205, Toronto, ON MT4 1N5 (tel. 416/961-3085).

Language   The official language is English.

Taxes and Service   A departure tax of $8 (U.S.) is imposed, and a 7% government tax is added to all hotel bills. Most hotels also add a 10% service charge.

Telephone   Each phone number on the islands begins with 46. Once you are here, omit both the 809 area code and the 46 prefix to make local calls and dial only the last five digits of the numbers given in this guide. A 24-hour-a-day telephone service links Antigua to all parts of the world.

Time Antigua is in the Atlantic time zone, so it's 1 hour ahead of eastern standard time, except when eastern daylight time takes over; then Antigua's time is the same as in the eastern United States.

Water Water generally is safe to drink here, but many visitors prefer the bottled variety.

Weather The average year-round temperature ranges from 75° to 85° Fahrenheit.

ANTIGUA

From a poverty-stricken sugar island, Antigua has risen to become a 20th-century vacation haven. Yankee millionaires seeking British serenity under a tropical sun turned Antigua into a citadel of elegance around the exclusive Mill Reef Club, where you will be accepted only if recommended by a member. The island has now developed a broader base of tourism and attracts not just the rich, but also the middle- and even lower-income voyager.

Rolling, rustic Antigua ("An-*tee*-gah") has as its highest point Boggy Peak, 1,360 feet above sea level. Stone towers, once sugar mills, dot the landscape; however, its inland scenery isn't as dramatic as on St. Kitts. But, oh, those beaches!

Discovered by Columbus on his second voyage in 1493, Antigua has a population of about 75,000 and an area of 108 square miles. The average year-round temperature ranges from 75° to 85° Fahrenheit.

Independence has come, but Antigua is still British in many of its traditions. English planters settled Antigua in 1623. In 1666 the French occupied the island, but Antigua was ceded to England the following year by the Treaty of Breda.

The **summer carnival** takes place on the first Monday and Tuesday in August and the preceding week. Included in this festival are a beauty competition; and calypso and steel-band competitions. Carnival envelops the streets in exotic costumes that recall the people's African heritage. The spring highlight is Antigua's annual **sailing week** in late April or May.

The capital is **St. John's,** a large, neatly laid-out town, 6 miles from the airport and less than a mile from the deep-water Harbour Terminal. The port is the focal point of commerce and industry, as well as the seat of government and tourist shopping. Trade winds keep the streets fairly cool, as they were built wide just for that purpose. Protected in the throat of a narrow bay, the port city consists of cobblestone sidewalks, weather-beaten wooden houses, corrugated iron roofs, and louvered West Indian verandas.

ORIENTATION

GETTING THERE The major airline flying to Antigua's V. C. Bird Airport, **American Airlines** (tel. toll free 800/433-7300) offers two daily nonstop flights to Antigua departing from San Juan, Puerto Rico, and one daily direct flight to Antigua from New York's JFK. (From New York, the aircraft touches down briefly in St. Maarten before continuing on to Antigua, although the flight from Antigua returns to New York without a stop.)

A vacation in Antigua can cost less if you book your air transport simultaneously with a hotel reservation; American's tour desk will provide these hotel bookings. If, however, you prefer to book your hotel independently, American's cheapest travel option to Antigua from New York costs between $451 and $370 round-trip (travel on Friday, Saturday, or Sunday usually costs a bit more than travel Monday through Thursday). This nonrefundable APEX fare requires a 7-day advance purchase and a

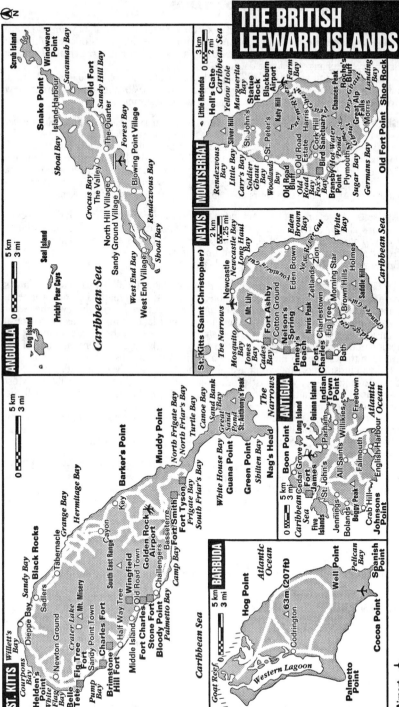

THE BRITISH LEEWARD ISLANDS

ST. KITTS

Willett's Bay, Courpons Bay, Helden's Point, White House Bay, Flag Bay, Belle, Tete, Dieppe Bay, Sandy Bay, Black Rocks, Sadlers, Newton Ground, Tabernacle, Grange Bay, Hermitage Bay, Fig Tree, Cayon, Key, Cranger Bay, Mt. Misery, South East Range, Sandy Point Town, Crater Lake, Barker's Point, Muddy Point, Pump Bay, Charles Fort, Half Way Tree, Middle Island, Wingfield, Old Road Town, Challengers, Golden Rock Airport, Fort Tyson, Frigate Bay, North Frigate Bay, North Friar's Bay, Turtle Bay, Brimstone Hill Fort, Fort Charles, Stone Fort, Bloody Point, Palmetto Bay, Camp Bay, Fort/Smith, Basseterre, Canoe Bay, Sand Bank, Great Bay, Sand Pond, St.Anthony's Peak, The Narrows, Nag's Head, South Friar's Bay, Shitten Bay, Green Point, Guana Point, White House Bay

ANGUILLA

Scrub Island, Windward Point, Savannab Bay, Snake Point, Old Fort, Sandy Hill Bay, Island Harbour, Shoal Bay, Forest Bay, The Quarter, Crocus Bay, The Valley, North Hill Village, Blowing Point Village, Sandy Ground Village, Rendezvous Bay, West End Bay, West End Village, Shoal Bay, Seal Island, Prickly Pear Cays, Dog Island

Caribbean Sea

ANTIGUA

Boon Point, Long Island, Indian Town Point, Parham, Willikies, Cedar Grove, Guiana Island, St. John's, Fort James, All Saints, Freetown, Falmouth, English Harbour, Five Islands, Jennings, Bolands, Boggy Peak, Crab Hill, Johnsons Point, Atlantic Ocean

Caribbean Sea

BARBUDA

Hog Point, Well Point, Codrington, △63m (207ft), Western Lagoon, Palmetto Point, Cocoa Point, Spanish Point, Pelican Bay, Goat Reef, Atlantic Ocean

St. Kitts (Saint Christopher)

The Narrows, Mosquito Bay, Jones Bay, Cades Bay, Fort Ashby, Mt. Lily, Nelson's Spring, Cotton Ground, Pinney's Beach, Fort Charles, Bath, Charlestown, Fig Tree, Nevis Peak, Zetlands, Morning Star, Saddle Hill, Brown Hills, Holmes, Zion, Eden Brown, Newcastle, Newcastle Bay, Long Haul Bay, Eden Brown Bay, White Bay, New River Gut, Gingerland

NEVIS

Caribbean Sea

MONTSERRAT

Little Redonda, Hell's Gate, Yellow Hole, Marguerita Bay, Silver Hill, Statue Rock, Blackburn Airport, Farm Bay, St. John's, Katy Hill, St. Peter's, Chances Peak, Dry Ghaut, Great Alp Falls, Rendezvous Bay, Little Bay, Carr's Bay, Soldier Ghaut, Woodlands, Old Road Bay, Cork Hill, Bird Sanctuary, Richie's Bluff, Morris, Old Road Estate, Harris, Hot Water Pond, Germans Bay, Sugar Bay, Plymouth, Bransby Point, Fox's, Old Fort Point, Shoe Rock, Old Road Bluff, Landing Bay

Caribbean Sea

Airport ✈

delay of between 3 and 21 days before activating the return portion of your ticket. No changes in itineraries or flight dates are permitted once this fare is booked, although several other cost-conscious tickets exist, for a few dollars more, which allow greater flexibility for changes in flight dates.

BWIA (tel. toll free 800/327-7401), the national airline of Trinidad and Tobago, offers daily nonstop service to Antigua from Miami. BWIA flies nonstop from New York every day in winter and three times a week in summer.

GETTING AROUND By Taxi Transportation isn't hard to find. Taxis meet every airplane, and drivers wait outside the major hotels. In fact, if you're going to be on Antigua for a few days, you may find that a particular driver has "adopted" you. Typical one-way fares from the airport to St. John's is $10, but to English Harbour it's $22 and up. The government of Antigua fixes the rates, and the taxis have no meters.

While it's costly, the best way to see Antigua is by private taxi as the drivers are also guides. Most full-day taxi tours cost $65 and up for one to four passengers.

By Bus Buses are not recommended for the average visitor, although they do exist and are cheap. Service seems erratic and undependable along impossibly bumpy roads. The official hours of operation between St. John's and the villages are daily from 5:30am to 6pm, but don't count on it. In St. John's, buses leave from the West Bus Station for Falmouth and English Harbour.

By Rental Car Newly arrived drivers quickly (and ruefully) learn that the island's roads are among the worst, most potholed, and most badly marked in the Caribbean. Many visitors will prefer to hire one of the island's battered taxis whenever they want to go somewhere. (Hotels and restaurants on the island summon taxis for patrons.) Considering the need to *drive on the left* (a holdover from the British tradition), the temptation to have one piña colada too many, and the high accident rate (one of the worst in the Caribbean Basin), renting a car in Antigua is usually not worth it.

If you insist on driving, you must obtain an Antiguan driver's license, which costs $12. To obtain one, you must produce a valid driver's license from home. Most car-rental firms are authorized to issue you an Antiguan license, which they usually do without a surcharge.

Several different car-rental agencies operate on Antigua, although they are sometimes precariously financed local operations with cars best described as "battered." The best of them are affiliated with major car-rental companies in the United States.

Avis (tel. toll free 800/331-2112) and **Budget** (tel. toll free 800/472-3325) are both represented on Antigua (but not Hertz). With a 2-day advance reservation, Avis charges about $124 a week for the cheapest car with unlimited mileage. Budget requires a 14-day advance reservation, and charges almost twice that rate, around $243 per week, for its cheapest car. Both companies charge between $10 and $11 per day for a collision-damage waiver (without it, you'll be liable for up to the full value of any accidental damage to the vehicle, and even if you buy it, depending on the company, you might still be liable for the first $1,000 worth of damage). Younger drivers usually head for Avis because of its minimum age of 21 (as opposed to a minimum age of 25 at Budget). All of this could change, so phone around before you go.

ESSENTIALS Antigua is generally safe, but that doesn't mean you should go wandering alone at night on the practically deserted streets of St. John's. Don't leave valuables unguarded on the beach.

The **Antigua and Barbuda Department of Tourism,** at Thames Street and Long Street in St. John's (tel. 2-0480), is open Monday through Thursday from 8am to 4:30pm and on Friday from 8am to 3pm.

The principal medical facility is **Holberton Hospital,** on Queen Elizabeth Highway (tel. 2-0251). **Telephone calls** can be made from hotels or from the office of Cable & Wireless, 42 St. Mary's Street in St. John's (tel. 2-9840). Faxes and telegrams can also be sent from here.

WHERE TO STAY

Antigua's hotels are among the best and most plentiful in the eastern Caribbean, and generally they are small—a 100-room hotel is rare on the island. Check summer closings, which often depend on the caprice of the owners, who may decide to shut down if business isn't good. Incidentally, air conditioning, except in first-class hotels, isn't as plentiful as some visitors think it should be. Chances are, your hotel will be on a beach. You can also rent an apartment or cottage if you want to cook for yourself.

Reminder: A 7% government tax and 10% service charge will probably be added to your hotel bill, which makes quite a difference in your final tab.

Very Expensive

BLUE WATERS, Soldier Bay (P.O. Box 256, St. John's), Antigua, W.I. Tel. 809/462-0292, or toll-free 800/372-1323. Fax 809/462-0293. 54 rms, 13 suites and villas. A/C MINIBAR TEL

$ Rates: Winter, $270–$310 single; $315 double; from $355 suite or villa. Summer, $110–$130 single; $135–$165 double; from $240 suite or villa. MAP $45 per person extra. AE, DC, MC, V. **Parking:** Free.

Blue Waters curves around a private sandy beach where you can lie in a hammock as a waiter serves you a rum punch. It's 4 miles (about a 15-minute drive) from St. John's, a 13-minute taxi ride south of the airport. All rooms are beachfront, surrounded by planting and coconut palms on the extensive grounds. Eight two- and three-bedroom villas were added in 1986.

Dining/Entertainment: The hotel's premier dining room is the Cacubi Room, cooled by ceiling fans, where you may want to dine even if you're not a guest at Blue Waters. The restaurant is known for its well-prepared continental dishes, which are topped by desserts flambéed at your table. Reservations are always necessary. The Sunday brunch at poolside is popular and includes entertainment by a steel band. There are also outdoor buffets and barbecues.

Services: $5 shuttle service to St. John's, laundry, baby-sitting, breakfast room service.

Facilities: Water sports, tennis, sailing, fishing.

CURTAIN BLUFF, Old Road (P.O. Box 288, St. John's), Antigua, W.I. Tel. 809/462-8400, or 212/289-8888 in New York. Fax 809/462-8409. 49 rms, 12 suites. TEL

$ Rates (including all meals): Mid-Dec to mid-Apr, $395–$625 single; $495–$725 double; from $795 suite. Oct 16 to mid-Dec and mid-Apr to May 15, $295–$450 single; $395–$625 double; from $695 suite. AE. **Parking:** Free. **Closed:** May 16–Oct 15.

Opened in 1961, this oasis of serenity and comfort is the home of Sailing Week and is the island's premier resort. It lies on the southwest shore 15 miles from the airport, in the village of Old Road, in the most tropical-looking section of the resort-studded island. Once a pilot for Texaco, founder Howard W. Hulford discovered his Shangri-La back in the 1950s while flying over it. It has remained the connoisseur's choice in Antigua.

In a setting like a subtropical forest, the resort offers beautifully furnished accommodations, including superior units with king-size beds, deluxe rooms with double beds, a terrace room with a king-size four-poster bed, plus suites. Ceiling fans and trade winds keep the rooms cool, and individual terraces open onto the water. Thoughtful amenities include wall safes, marble or tile floors, terry-cloth robes, bidets, tubs and showers, and fresh flowers daily (there's a plant nursery on the grounds). Rates include all meals (superb ones, at that), wine by the glass, soft drinks, tennis, water sports, laundry, and postage.

Dining/Entertainment: One reason guests check in here is for the food. Swiss-born Ruedi Portmann keeps his continental menu limited, so that all the food will be freshly prepared and artistically arranged. Curtain Bluff boasts the most extensive wine selection in the Caribbean, including every major red bordeaux. After dinner, guests can dance under the stars to a live band. Men are required to wear jackets and ties after 7pm. Once a week the resort hires a steel band to entertain guests down at the beach with a splendid buffet. Dinner on Sunday night is served at the Beach Club and features some Antiguan recipes. Local entertainers are featured on Sunday night.

Services: Room service (8am–10pm), laundry, baby-sitting.

Facilities: Sailing, waterskiing, skin diving, scuba diving (for certified divers only), tennis (four championship courts plus a pro shop and a full-time pro), squash, exercise room, aerobics classes—all at no extra charge.

GALLEY BAY, Five Islands (P.O. Box 305, St. John's), Antigua, W.I. Tel. 809/462-0302, or toll free 800/223-6510. Fax 809/462-1187. 30 rms. MINIBAR **Directions:** Leave St. John's on the harbor road south, pass through Five Islands Village, and turn right onto Galley Bay Road; it's a distance of 5 miles from the capital.

$ Rates (including all meals, drinks, service, and tax): Winter, Gauguin cottages, $285 single, $355 double; beachfront rooms, $335 single, $415 double. Summer, Gauguin cottages, $185 single, $255 double; beachfront rooms, $228 single, $298 double. AE, DC, MC, V. **Parking:** Free.

A retreat set on 40 acres of grounds, along half a mile of palm-fringed beach, Galley Bay offers a variety of accommodations. Gauguin Village, with 12 units, is 150 feet off the beach and built around a salt pond in a coconut grove. Each of its units consists of two grass-roofed villas—one the bedroom and the other the bath and dressing room. Directly on the beach are the other units, built in a more conventional style, and, as advertised, "only four seconds from bed to sea." Galley Bay operates on an all-inclusive rate covering three full meals, all bar drinks and house wines, and most sports.

Dining/Entertainment: There's a beachside bar, and the restaurant specializes in West Indian cuisine made with fresh local produce, including seafood.

Services: Laundry, baby-sitting.

Facilities: Water sports (such as windsurfing, snorkeling, and Sunfish sailing), tennis.

HALF MOON BAY, Half Moon Bay (P.O. Box 144, St. John's), Antigua, W.I. Tel. 809/460-4300, or toll free 800/223-6510. Fax 809/460-4306. 100 rms, 2 suites.

$ Rates (including AP): Winter, $235–$290 single; $310–$370 double; from $475 suite. Summer, $120–$165 single; $190–$240 double; from $305 suite. Special packages available AE, DC, MC, V. **Parking:** Free. **Closed:** Sept.

Although it's run like the country club of Antigua, Half Moon Bay is open to the public. Some 17 miles from St. John's (take Factory Road east out of St. John's and follow the signs), it's a neighbor to the exclusive Mill Reef Club, and for years has been recognized as one of the island's leading resorts. The hotel is on a three-quarter-mile-long, crescent-shaped beach of powdery sand. Over the years it has attracted many celebrities, including Paul McCartney. The oceanfront rooms have patios or balconies overlooking the ocean.

Dining/Entertainment: Nightly entertainment includes limbo and crab racing. An international cuisine is served on the all-inclusive plan, including Caribbean specialties. The menu is different every day. It's rather like "country club dining."

Services: Room service, laundry, baby-sitting.

Facilities: Nine-hole tropical golf course, five all-weather Laykold tennis courts, reef-protected beach, freshwater pool.

HAWKSBILL BEACH RESORT, Five Islands (P.O. Box 108, St. John's), Antigua, W.I. Tel. 809/462-1515. Fax 809/462-1515. 88 rms.

$ Rates (including breakfast): Winter, $235–$305 single; $285–$370 double. Summer, $135–$165 single; $160–$200 double. Dinner $32 per person extra. AE, DC, MC, V. **Parking:** Free.

Taking its name from an offshore rock that locals say resembles a hawksbill turtle, this resort has a former sugar mill, now turned into a boutique, on its 37-acre grounds. The resort is 10 miles west of the airport and 4 miles southwest of St. John's. Set on four beaches (one reserved for those who want to go home *sans* tan lines), it's a magnet for the sporting set, and also popular for weddings and honeymoons. The hotel revolves around an open-air, breezy central core and offers comfortably furnished bedrooms with ceiling fans and showers. The most expensive units are beachfront cottages, while the least costly accommodations open onto a garden.

Dining/Entertainment: There are two restaurants (one on the beach) and two bars. It's usually lively here if the crowd is right, with entertainment, such as limbo dancers and calypso singers, in season.

Services: Laundry, baby-sitting.

Facilities: Swimming pool, tennis court, Sunfish sailing, windsurfing, snorkeling, waterskiing (for a nominal charge).

THE INN AT ENGLISH HARBOUR, English Harbour (P.O. Box 187, St. John's), Antigua, W.I. Tel. 809/460-1014. Fax 809/460-1603. 28 rms. TEL **Directions:** From St. John's, head southeast along Fig Tree Drive and pass through Liberta until you reach the south coast.

$ Rates: Winter, $213–$288 single; $241–$316 double. Summer, $80–$125 single; $100–$155 double. MAP $42 per person extra. AE, MC, V. **Parking:** Free.

In a corner of Freeman's Bay, Peter and Ann Deeth offer guests a choice of pleasingly furnished rooms, or more expensive beachfront units. All accommodations are twins, but they can be rented as singles. The inn has one of the finest sites in Antigua, with views over Nelson's Dockyard and English Harbour from its terrace.

Dining/Entertainment: Have a before-dinner drink in the old-style English Bar, with its stone walls and low-overhead beams. Lunch is served both at the beach house and in the main dining room, and the inn is known for the quality of its cooking.

Services: Room service, laundry, baby-sitting.

Facilities: Water sports, including Sunfish sailing, waterskiing, snorkeling, rowing, deep-sea fishing, and scuba diving; tennis courts (lit at night), 5 minutes away.

JUMBY BAY, Long Island (P.O. Box 243, St. John's), Antigua, W.I. Tel. 809/462-6000, or toll free 800/421-9016. Fax 809/462-6020. 38 suites. MINIBAR **Transportation:** Taxi to "Beachcomber Dock" on the northeast coast of Antigua (northeast of the airport), then board the hotel's private launch to Long Island.

$ Rates (including all meals): Dec 23–Mar, $895 double. Oct 27–Dec 22 and Apr, $695 double. May–Aug, $525 double. **Closed:** Sept–Oct 26.

⭐ This exclusive little island resort, 300 acres in all, off the eastern coast of Antigua, is reached after a 12-minute launch ride. The site was selected for its white sandy beaches, along a coastline protected by coral reefs. The grounds have been handsomely landscaped in part with loblolly and white cedar trees. A Relais & Châteaux resort, it's on the site of the former private home of a sugarcane plantation owner.

Pampered guests are housed in junior suites, each with a large master bedroom and its own patio overlooking the water. Some even have a private "no curtains" shower courtyard.

As an ecological sideline, the Jumby Bay is engaged in an ongoing project to protect the endangered hawksbill sea turtle. Guests who are interested are encouraged to participate in the program by joining nightly patrols to tag, measure, and photograph the turtles.

Dining/Entertainment: In the 200-year-old vastly restored estate house, there is now a lounge, a library, and a games room. Dinner is served here and often attracts the yachting crowd who put into the 750-foot dock. The food is excellent, and picnic lunches can be arranged.

Services: Room service (7am–11pm), laundry.
Facilities: Snorkeling, scuba diving, tennis courts, fishing, sailing, waterskiing.

PINEAPPLE BEACH CLUB, Long Bay, near Willikie's Village (P.O. Box 54, St. John's), Antigua, W.I. Tel. 809/463-2006, or toll free 800/223-9815 in the U.S., 800/468-0023 in Québec and Ontario. Fax 809/463-2452. 125 rms, 8 suites. A/C **Directions:** Head east from the airport on Factory Road; Long Bay is at the east end of Willikie's Village.
$ Rates (including AP): Winter, $250–$320 single; $350–$420 double; from $440 suite. Summer, $170–$280 single; $250–$360 double; from $380 suite. AE, MC, V. **Parking:** Free.

On 45 acres of land, sloping down to a beach and a peninsula, this hostelry is furnished in part with woven cane pieces. Accommodations contain two double beds or one queen-size bed as well as a private bath. Rates are all-inclusive, covering room, meals, sports, and drinks.

Dining/Entertainment: On the premises are two restaurants, the Pelican Grill and a snack shop, the Outhouse, and three bars.

Facilities: Freshwater pool, tennis courts, health club, windsurfing school with both sailboat and sailboard instruction.

ST. JAMES'S CLUB, Mamora Bay (P.O. Box 63, St. John's), Antigua, W.I. Tel. 809/460-5000, 212/486-2575 in New York, or toll free 800/274-0008. Fax 809/460-3015. 128 rms, 20 suites. A/C MINIBAR TV TEL **Transportation:** Taxi.
$ Rates: Winter, $340–$490 single or double; from $740 suite. Summer, $190–$295 single or double; from $540 suite. Continental breakfast $10 extra. AE, DC, MC, V. **Parking:** Free.

The St. James, a luxurious resort on Mamora Bay, offers elegant ocean-view rooms and suites, all with complete baths and radios. Pricey villas and hillside homes are also rented. The resort's leisure facilities are among the best in the Caribbean.

Dining/Entertainment: The best of local and international dishes, freshly caught seafood, salads, barbecue grills, and tropical fruit are accompanied by cool white wine or dark rum cocktails. You can relax in elegant surroundings in the Rainbow Garden Restaurant or eat al fresco by candlelight at the Docksider Café overlooking Mamora Bay, enjoying lobster, barbecued chicken, or ribs. Take a little pasta in Piccolo Mondo, the hillside trattoria with views of the sunset over the bay. Lunch at the poolside Reef Deck is a social occasion and offers salads, burgers, and local delicacies. The Jacaranda nightclub will top off an evening for more active guests. Many enjoy gambling in the high-ceilinged European-style casino, whose walls are covered in a combination of Italian art deco columns and vertical stripes.

Services: Room service, laundry, baby-sitting.

Facilities: Water sports, including sailboats (Sunfish and Hobie cats), sailboards, aqua bikes, deep-sea fishing, waterskiing, snorkeling, scuba diving (with a scuba certification school offering American and European certification); seven hard tennis courts (lit for night play), with a center court for tournaments and the Martina Navratilova tennis program; stables with Texas quarterhorses and hillside trails; complete Universal-equipped gymnasium; Jacuzzi; massage facility; beauty salon; croquet court.

Expensive

THE COPPER AND LUMBER STORE, Nelson's Dockyard, English Harbour (P.O. Box 184, St. John's), Antigua, W.I. Tel. 809/460-1058. Fax 809/460-1529. 3 rms, 11 suites. Directions: Take Fig Tree Drive southeast to St. John's, going via Liberta.
$ Rates: Winter, $160–$180 single; $180–$240 double; $180–$280 suite. Summer, $80–$90 single; $80–$140 double; $120–$140 suite. Continental breakfast $5 extra. AE, MC, V. **Parking:** Free.

This 18th-century building was originally occupied by purveyors of wood and sheet copper for building and repairing the British sailing ships that plied the waters of the Caribbean. Today the guests recognize that in many ways this is the most understated, elegant hotel in Antigua. The store and its adjacent harbor structures were built of brick brought from England in the holds of ships as ballast. These bricks imbue the building with 18th-century English charm and sometimes serve to conceal its necessary modern amenities.

Each of the brick-lined period units has its own design and is named after one of the ships that fought at the Battle of Trafalgar. They're filled with fine Chippendale and Queen Anne reproductions, antiques, brass chandeliers, hardwood paneling, and hand-stenciled floors. Even the showers look like cabinetry in a sailing vessel, lined with thick paneled slabs of mahogany accented with polished brass fittings. All suites have kitchens, private baths (with showers only), and ceiling fans.

Dining/Entertainment: A traditional English pub adjoins the hotel and offers food daily from 10:30am to 9:30pm. The restaurant serves lunch and dinner.

Services: Room service, laundry, baby-sitting.

HALCYON COVE BEACH RESORT AND CASINO, Dickenson Bay (P.O. Box 251, St. John's), Antigua, W.I. Tel. 809/462-0256, or toll free 800/223-1588 in New York, 800/531-6767 in Canada. Fax 809/462-0271. 129 rms, 17 suites. A/C MINIBAR TEL

$ Rates: Winter, $200–$260 single; $220–$290 double; from $350 suite. Summer, $80–$140 single; $120–$180 double; from $200 suite. Continental breakfast $7 extra. AE, DC, MC, V. **Parking:** Free.

Halcyon Cove, a total resort with plenty of glamour, is 1½ miles west of the airport and 7 miles north of St. John's, about a 15-minute taxi ride. Most of the stylish bedrooms have a balcony or terrace; the majority of the units are set at beach level. Rooms range from garden rooms to superior rooms to poolside deluxe. The most expensive are called "oceanfront deluxe" and "oceanfront suites," the latter with color TV, mini-refrigerator, and a separate bedroom, living room, and dressing area.

Dining/Entertainment: The Arawak Terrace, the hotel's main dining room, is open for breakfast and dinner. You can also lunch or dine on the elongated Warri Pier, which stands on stilts 200 feet from the shore. Reached by a boardwalk over the sea, it serves three meals a day in season (no lunch off-season). Specialties are grilled lobster, steak, and fresh fish. There's also a beach barbecue for lunch (on Sunday night a steel band is brought in for a dinner barbecue). The Deli offers a coffee-shop menu. For a description of the gourmet restaurant, Clouds, see "Where to Dine," below. Live entertainment is offered nightly in season, and the resort also boasts a casino.

Services: Room service (at breakfast), laundry, baby-sitting.

Facilities: Half-mile beach, water-sports program (including a freshwater swimming pool, snorkeling, windsurfing, pedalboats, waterskiing, sailing, and scuba diving), four all-weather tennis courts (lit for night play).

JOLLY BEACH RESORT, Morris Bay (P.O. Box 744, St. John's), Antigua, W.I. Tel. 809/462-0061, or toll free 800/321-1055. Fax 809/462-1827. 464 rms, 16 suites.

$ Rates (including MAP): Winter, $110–$120 single; $190–$240 double; from $220 suite. Summer, $65–$70 single; $150–$180 double; from $180 suite. AE, MC, V. **Parking:** Free.

The liveliest and most action-oriented hotel in Antigua, especially for water sports, is 5 miles south of St. John's and 11 miles west of the airport. Set on 38 acres of grounds on a 1½-mile-long sandy beach, it's the most popular and the largest hotel on the island. You have a choice of rooms, beginning with the least expensive "minimum" room, which is quite small, up to standard and deluxe units. Surprisingly, in winter the most expensive double costs more than a suite.

Dining/Entertainment: In the older section, guests spend time around the beach bar, Coconut Wharf, and later enjoy dining in the Flamboyant Restaurant. In the newer section, the Palm Grill and the Palm Restaurant are popular dining spots and serve continental fare, Stateside specialties, and West Indian dishes. Buffets and barbecues are regular features. Night owls dance until the early hours at Jaybee's Disco or try their luck in the casino.

Services: Laundry, baby-sitting.

Facilities: Freshwater swimming pool, health club, scuba diving, water skiing.

LONG BAY HOTEL, Long Bay (P.O. Box 442, St. John's), Antigua, W.I. Tel. 809/463-2005, or toll free 800/223-1108. Fax 809/463-2439. 20 rms, 5 cottages.

$ Rates (including MAP): Winter, $268 single; $350 double. Summer, $150 single; $250 double. Cottages (without meals), from $290 winter, from $200 summer. Service extra. AE, MC, V. **Parking:** Free. **Closed:** Sept–Oct.

Dramatically situated on a spit of land between the open sea and a sheltered lagoon, Long Bay lies on the eastern shore 1 mile beyond the hamlet of Willikie's. It faces one of the best beaches on the island, as well as the sheltered waters of a reef-free lagoon that is considered exceptionally safe for water sports. Owned and operated by the Lafaurie family since 1966, it's more of an inn than a large-scale hotel. It features breeze-filled rooms as well as five furnished cottages for more reclusive guests.

Dining/Entertainment: The resort is centered around a hip-roofed clubhouse with a stone-walled dining room. The bar provides a relaxing environment. The hotel has a library and games room, a separate building for the dining room, and a beach house restaurant and bar.

Services: Room service, laundry, baby-sitting, special dinner sitting just for children.

Facilities: Championship tennis court, complete scuba facilities, rental sailboats; golf nearby.

RAMADA RENAISSANCE ROYAL ANTIGUAN RESORT, Deep Bay (P.O. Box 1322, St. John's), Antigua, W.I. Tel. 809/462-3733, or toll free 800/228-9898. Fax 809/462-3732. 282 rms, 2 suites, 12 poolside cottages. A/C MINIBAR TV TEL

$ Rates: Winter, $175–$275 single or double; from $600 suite; from $750 cottage. Summer, $135–$180 single or double; from $250 suite; from $350 cottage. Continental breakfast $7 extra. AE, DC, MC, V. **Parking:** Free.

On 150 acres on the crescent-shaped shores of Deep Bay on the northwestern coast of Antigua, the Ramada Renaissance is only a 25-minute ride west of the airport and 15 minutes south of St. John's. Set between Deep Bay and a lagoon, the resort creates the feeling of being on a private tropical island, and the main nine-story building is hidden from view by palm trees when you lie on the beach.

The guest rooms, one- and two-bedroom suites, and one-bedroom cottages with private patios or terraces have private baths, VCRs, and fire-security systems. The decor includes Italian furnishings, marble counters, and ceramic tile floors.

Dining/Entertainment: The most formal dining room, La Regènce, serves French and continental dishes. Andes on Deep Bay Beach restaurant specializes in fresh Caribbean catches and prime meats.

Services: Room service, dry cleaning, laundry, nightly turn-down.

Facilities: Beach, swimming pool with swim-up bar, drugstore/newsstand, beauty salon, health club; eight tennis courts (four lit at night); free snorkeling, windsurfing, and use of sailboats (waterskiing, deep-sea fishing, and powerboat cruises cost extra); use of nearby 18-hole Cedar Valley Golf Course can be arranged.

Moderate

ADMIRAL'S INN, English Harbour (P.O. Box 713, St. John's), Antigua, W.I. Tel. 809/460-1027, or toll free 800/223-5695. Fax 809/460-1534. 14 rms, 1 suite. **Directions:** Take the road southeast from St. John's, going via Fig Tree Drive and passing through Liberta to the south coast.

$ Rates: Winter, $78–$90 single; $96–$116 double; from $180 suite. Summer, $56–$64 single; $68–$82 double; from $100 suite. MAP $42 per person extra. AE, MC, V. **Parking:** Free. **Closed:** Sept.

Designed in 1785, the year Nelson sailed into the harbor as captain of the H.M.S. *Boreas,* and completed in 1788, the building here used to house dockyard services. Today it has been converted into one of the most atmospheric inns in Antigua. In the heart of Nelson's Dockyard, and loaded with West Indian charm, the hostelry is constructed of weathered brick brought from England as ships' ballast and has a terrace opening onto a centuries-old garden. The ground floor, with brick walls, giant ship beams, and island-made furniture, has a tavern atmosphere, with decorative copper, boat lanterns, old oil paintings, and wrought-iron chandeliers.

There are three types of character-filled accommodations. The highest tariffs are charged for some ground-floor rooms in a tiny brick building—on the site of a provisions warehouse for Nelson's troops—across the courtyard from the main structure. Each of these spacious rooms has a little patio and a garden entry as well as optional air conditioning. The same superior rate applies to front rooms on the first floor of the main building with views of the lawn and harbor. A medium rate applies to the back rooms on this floor, all of which have air conditioning. The lowest rate is for smaller chambers on the top floor, which may get warm during the day in summer but are quiet, with dormer-window views over the yacht-filled harbor. All rooms have twin beds, ceiling fans, and private baths and showers. The Joiner's Loft is an upstairs suite adjacent to the annex rooms of the inn, with a large living room looking out over the water; there are two bedrooms, two baths, and a full kitchen. Reservations are imperative.

Dining/Entertainment: For the inn's restaurant, see "Where to Dine," below. On Saturday night a steel band plays.

Services: Room service, laundry, baby-sitting, free transportation to two nearby beaches.

Facilities: Snorkeling equipment, Sunfish craft.

FALMOUTH HARBOUR BEACH APARTMENTS, English Harbour Village, Pigeon Point Rd. (P.O. Box 713, St. John's), Antigua, W.I. Tel. 809/460-1094. Fax 809/460-1534. 28 units. **Directions:** Take the road southeast from St. John's going via Fig Tree Drive and passing through Liberta to the south coast.
$ Rates: Winter, $86–$94 single; $110–$120 double. Summer, $60–$66 single; $78–$84 double. AE, MC, V. **Parking:** Free.

This might be what you're looking for if you'd like to be near historic English Harbour. On, or just above, a small sandy beach, it offers an informal Antiguan atmosphere and rents twin-bedded studio apartments. Each unit has a private bath with shower, ceiling fan, electric stove, refrigerator, oven, and terrace overlooking the water. A dozen units are directly on the beach, while the others lie on a hillside just behind. You can dine at the nearby Admiral's Inn (see "Where to Dine," below).

Inexpensive

BARRYMORE HOTEL, Fort Rd. (P.O. Box 244, St. John's), Antigua, W.I. Tel. 809/462-1055. Fax 809/462-4140. 34 rms.
$ Rates: Winter, $60–$68 single; $78–$86 double. Summer, $48–$56 single; $63–$70 double. Continental breakfast $6 extra. AE, MC, V. **Parking:** Free.

The Barrymore has its special niche in resort-crowded Antigua. It's a good bargain and offers an inexpensive holiday in an unpretentious setting. A bungalow colony with a freshwater swimming pool, it stands on 3 acres of private grounds 1 mile north of St. John's and about a mile from the nearest beach. Free transportation is provided to the beach, and waterskiing and windsurfing are available. Rooms and efficiencies are in modern white bungalows scattered about the grounds, bordered by flowering shrubbery. Bedrooms have motel-style modern appointments, along with private baths and patios. Some are air-conditioned and contain TV.

Condos & Villas

ANTIGUA VILLAGE, Dickenson Bay (P.O. Box 649, St. John's), Antigua, W.I. Tel. 809/462-4299, or toll free 800/223-1588. Fax 809/462-0375. 65 units. A/C

$ Rates: Winter, $170–$245 apartment for one or two; from $380 villa. Summer, $95 apartment for one; $115–$140 apartment for two; from $150 villa. AE, MC, V. **Parking:** Free.

On a peninsula stretching out into turquoise waters, 2 miles north of St. John's, Antigua Village is more of a self-contained condominium community than a holiday resort. A freshwater pool and a minimarket are on the premises, with a casino and restaurants within walking distance. You can use the neighboring tennis court, and there's an 18-hole golf course nearby. Water sports are free. The studio apartments and villas all have kitchenettes, patios or balconies, twin beds, and sofa beds in the living rooms.

DIAN BAY RESORT, Dian Bay (P.O. Box 230, St. John's), Antigua, W.I. Tel. 809/463-2003, or toll free 800/223-9815. Fax 809/463-2425. 30 units. MINIBAR

$ Rates (including continental breakfast): Winter, $200–$220 one-bedroom suite for two; $240–$260 two-bedroom suite for four. Summer, $130–$150 one-bedroom suite for two; $180 two-bedroom suite for four. Children under 12 stay free in parents' room. AE, MC, V. **Parking:** Free.

On the windswept eastern end of the island southeast of the airport is a remote hideaway on a sun-washed hilltop in an area filled with expensive private villas and flowering shrubs. All units have a veranda, a fully equipped kitchenette, and ceiling fans. Only two of the units are air-conditioned, but no one seems to mind because of the cooling trade winds.

A minimarket on the premises provides food staples for those interested in cooking in their units. The in-house restaurant enjoys a good reputation. A labyrinth of masonry walkways leads past a swimming pool to a sheltered lagoon, where windsurfing and snorkeling equipment are provided free to guests.

SIBONEY BEACH CLUB, Dickenson Bay (P.O. Box 222, St. John's), Antigua, W.I. Tel. 809/462-0806, or toll free 800/533-0234. Fax 809/462-3356. 13 suites.

$ Rates: Winter, $190 single; $220–$270 double. Summer, $90–$130 single; $130–$150 double. Tree house negotiable. MAP $42 per person extra. AE, MC. **Parking:** Free.

Owned by Australia-born Tony Johnson and his wife, Ann, the Siboney Beach Club is named after the Amerindian tribe predating the Arawaks. Set north of St. John's, on a thickly foliated acre of beachfront fronting the mile-long white sandy beach of Dickenson Bay, it's shielded on the inland side by what may be the tallest and most verdant hedge on the island. The club's social center is the Coconut Grove restaurant. The comfortable suites are in a three-story balconied building draped with bougainvillea and other vines. Some suites have optional air conditioning and all have fans and louvered windows for natural ventilation. There is no TV, but some suites have phones. All the units have separate bedrooms, living rooms, and balconies or patios, plus tiny kitchens behind moveable shutters. There is also a tree house—a single room with a king-size bed and jungle decor perched high in a ficus Benjamina tree.

WHERE TO DINE

Many independently operated restaurants serve West Indian food not readily available in the hotel dining rooms. Many dishes, especially the curries, show an East Indian influence, and Caribbean lobster is a specialty. In the 1980s "gourmet" restaurants started sprouting up on the island.

In St. John's

BIG BANANA HOLDING COMPANY, Redcliffe Quay. Tel. 2-2621.
Cuisine: PIZZA. **Reservations:** Not required.
$ Prices: Main courses $6–$12. AE, DC, MC, V.
Open: Mon–Sat 8:30am–10pm.
Some of the best pizza in the eastern Caribbean is served in what used to be slave quarters, now amid the most stylish shopping and dining emporiums in town, at the Heritage Quay Jetty. With its ceiling fans and laid-back island atmosphere, you almost expect Sydney Greenstreet to stop in for a drink (called "dwinks" on the menu). The frothy libations, coconut or banana crush, are practically desserts all by themselves. In addition to the zesty pizza, you can order overstuffed baked potatoes, fresh-fruit salad, or conch salad. On Monday and Thursday a reggae band entertains free.

Around the Island

ADMIRAL'S INN, in Nelson's Dockyard, English Harbour. Tel. 0-1027.
Cuisine: AMERICAN/CREOLE. **Reservations:** Recommended, especially for dinner in high season. **Directions:** Head southeast of St. John's along Fig Tree Drive via Liberta to the south coast.
$ Prices: Appetizers $1.50–$7; main courses $16–$25. AE, MC, V.
Open: Breakfast daily 7:30–10am; lunch daily noon–2:30pm; dinner daily 7:30–9:30pm. **Closed:** Sept to mid-Oct.
This historic building has already been previewed as a hotel (see "Where to Stay," above). In a 17th-century setting, lobster, seafood, and steaks are served. The favorite appetizer is pumpkin soup, which is followed by a choice of four or five main courses daily—perhaps local red snapper, grilled steak, or lobster. Before dinner, have a drink in the bar. There you can read the names of sailors carved in wood more than a century ago. The service is agreeable, and the setting is heavy on atmosphere.

LE BISTRO, Hodges Bay. Tel. 2-3881.
Cuisine: FRENCH. **Reservations:** Required especially in high season.
$ Prices: Appetizers EC$20–EC$30 ($7.40–$11); main courses EC$60–EC$70 ($22.20–$25.90). AE, MC, V.
Open: Dinner only, Tues–Sun 7–10:30pm. **Closed:** June–Aug 5.
This authentic bistro is the best on the island. Raffaele and Philippa Esposito run this little enclave of French cuisine on the north shore, 2 miles west of the airport on the road to Hodges Bay. Recognized for its superb fare by many international magazines, including *Gourmet*, it has a French chef, who named the maccheroni ziti Raffaele, made with cream, parmesan, and mushrooms, after one of the owners. Other dishes include red snapper baked in tin foil and a rack of lamb for two. Medallions of local lobster au basilic is another specialty.

CLOUDS, in the Halcyon Cove Beach Resort and Casino, Dickenson Bay. Tel. 2-0256.
Cuisine: NOUVELLE CARIBBEAN. **Reservations:** Required.
$ Prices: Appetizers $6.50–$8; main courses $22–$29. AE, DC, MC, V.
Open: Dinner only, Mon–Sat 7–9:30pm.
In this gourmet restaurant on a bluff overlooking the bay north of St. John's, you can begin with zucchini-and-carrot soup or the more classic lobster bisque. Then you can enjoy breast of chicken stuffed with duck and a pistachio mousse, filet of grouper steamed with leeks and shiitake mushrooms, or a medley of seafood blended with saffron cream and white wine. A pianist provides soft background music. Clouds is also a good place to visit for a sundowner or an after-dinner drink.

COCONUT GROVE, in the Siboney Hotel, Dickenson Bay. Tel. 2-0806.
Cuisine: CARIBBEAN/SEAFOOD. **Reservations:** Recommended, especially for dinner.
$ Prices: Appetizers $7–$10; main courses $17–$70. AE, MC, V.

Open: Lunch daily 11:30am–3pm; dinner daily 6:30–10:30pm.

Right on the beach are simple tables set on a flagstone floor beneath a thatch roof. North of St. John's, in a coconut grove (of course) and cooled by sea breezes, the restaurant is run by Bob and Julia England. They specialize in fresh lobster, fresh fish, and other seafood, but also offer good steaks and ribs in a spicy barbecue sauce. Continental dishes also appear on the menu, and shrimp fritters are a specialty. Live music is presented every night of the week.

COLOMBO'S RESTAURANT, in the Galleon Beach Club, English Harbour. Tel. 0-1452.
    Cuisine: ITALIAN. **Reservations:** Recommended. **Directions:** Head southeast from St. John's along Fig Tree Drive via Liberta to the south coast.
$ **Prices:** Appetizers $6–$14; main courses $20–$30. AE, DC, MC, V.
    Open: Lunch daily 12:30–2:30pm; dinner daily 7–10pm.
    Closed: Sept–Oct 5.

Colombo's serves up Italian food on a Polynesian-style open-air terrace sheltered by a ceiling crafted from woven palm fronds. It's only a few steps across the flat sands to the water. Lunches in this sprawling place might include spaghetti marinara, lobster salad, and sandwiches. Dinners are more elaborate, and include daily specials from a classic Italian inventory of veal scaloppine, veal pizzaiola, and lobster mornay. These can be accompanied by a wide assortment of French or Italian wines. Live music, including reggae, rock 'n' roll, jazz, and calypso, is often presented.

DUBARRY'S, in the Barrymore Hotel, Fort Rd. outside St. John's. Tel. 2-4063.
    Cuisine: AMERICAN/CARIBBEAN. **Reservations:** Required.
$ **Prices:** Appetizers $3.50–$9.50; main courses $10.50–$21.50. AE, MC, V.
    Open: Lunch Mon–Sat noon–3pm; dinner daily 7–11pm.

One of the best restaurants in town, 1 mile north of St. John's, is housed in a modern, low-slung building adjacent to the Barrymore Hotel. Dubarry's is divided into two distinctly different dining rooms and a paneled bar. On a chilly evening you'll be seated inside in a modern room capped with a ceiling of Douglas fir and pitch pine. In warm weather and during informal lunches, diners are seated behind an iron railing on an al fresco terrace overlooking an outdoor pool. Specialties include lobster bisque (from Antiguan lobster), several beef dishes, and the best catch of the fisherman's haul.

SHIRLEY HEIGHTS LOOKOUT, Shirley Heights. Tel. 3-1785.
    Cuisine: AMERICAN/SEAFOOD. **Reservations:** Not required.
$ **Prices:** Appetizers EC$10–EC$18 ($3.70–$6.65); main courses EC$35–EC$65 ($12.95–$24.05). AE, MC, V.
    Open: Daily 9am–10pm.

In the 1790s this was the lookout station for unfriendly ships heading toward English Harbour. To strengthen Britain's position in this strategic spot, Nelson ordered the construction of a powder magazine. Today the panoramic spot, directly east of English Harbour, is one of the most romantic in Antigua. Visitors sometimes prefer to be served on the stone battlements below the restaurant, though I'd rather dine under the angled rafters of the upstairs restaurant, where large, old-fashioned windows surround the room on all sides.

Specialties include pumpkin soup, grilled lobster in lime butter, garlic-flavored shrimp, and good desserts, such as banana flambé and carrot cake. Less expensive hamburgers and sandwiches are available in the pub downstairs. A tradition with residents and visitors alike is Sunday at the Heights. The "end of the week" barbecue that begins at 3pm features 6 hours of nonstop entertainment, with a steel-band concert from 3 to 6pm and a reggae band from 6 to 9pm. However, avoid it when cruise-ship passengers take over. It's best at lunch.

WHAT TO SEE & DO

ST. JOHN'S In the southern part of St. John's, the **market** is colorful and interesting, especially on Saturday morning. Vendors busy selling their fruits and vegetables bargain and gossip. The semi-open-air market lies at the lower end of Market Street.

Also in town, **St. John's Cathedral,** the Anglican cathedral, between Long Street and Newgate Street at Church Lane, has had a disastrous history. Originally built in 1683, it was replaced by a stone building in 1745. That, however, was destroyed by an earthquake in 1843. The present pitch-pine interior dates from 1847. The interior was being restored when, in 1973, the twin towers and structure were badly damaged by another earthquake. The towers and the southern section have been restored, but restoring the northern part is estimated to cost thousands of dollars, for which contributions are gratefully received. At the entrance, iron gates were erected by the vestry in 1789. The figures of St. John the Baptist and St. John the Divine, at the south gate, were said to have been taken from one of the Napoleonic ships and brought to Antigua by a British man-of-war.

The **Museum of Antigua and Barbuda,** Long Street and Market Street (tel. 2-1469), traces the history of the two-island nation—from geological birth to political independence. Housed in the old Court House building from 1750, exhibits include a wattle-and-daub house model, African-Caribbean pottery, and utilitarian objects of daily life. It's open Monday through Thursday from 8:30am to 4pm, on Friday from 8:30am to 3pm, and on Saturday from 10am to 2pm. Admission is free, but donations are welcome.

AROUND THE ISLAND   After leaving St. John's, the average visitor heads for one of the biggest attractions in the eastern Caribbean,   ✪ **Nelson's Dockyard.** It's open daily from 8am to 6pm and charges an admission of $1.60 for adults; children under 16 are admitted free. One of the safest landlocked harbors in the world, the restored dockyard was used by Admirals Nelson, Rodney, and Hood. It was the home of the British fleet at the time of the Napoleonic wars. From 1784 Nelson was the commander of the British navy in the Leeward Islands, and he made his headquarters at English Harbour. English ships used the harbor as early as 1671, for they found it a refuge from hurricanes. The era of privateers, pirates, and great sea battles in the 18th century revolved around the dockyard.

Restored by the Friends of English Harbour, the dockyard is sometimes known as a Caribbean Williamsburg. Its colonial naval buildings stand now as they did when Nelson was here (1784–87). However, Nelson never lived at **Admiral House** (tel. 3-1053)—it was built in 1855. It does contain what may have been his bed, a four-poster of gilded ivory-colored wood. The house has been turned into a museum of nautical memorabilia. (For accommodations at English Harbour, see "Where to Stay," above.) The museum is open daily from 8am to 6pm and charges $1.60 admission.

A footpath leads to **Fort Barclay,** the fort at the entrance to English Harbour. The path starts just outside the dockyard gate, and the fort is about half a mile away. The interesting fort is a fine specimen of old-time military engineering.

If you're at English Harbour at sunset, head for **Shirley Heights** directly to the east, named after General Shirley, governor of the Leeward Islands in 1781, who fortified the hills guarding the harbor. Still standing are Palladian arches, once part of the barracks. The Block House, one of the main buildings, was put up as a stronghold in case of siege. The nearby Victorian cemetery contains an obelisk monument to the officers and men of the 54th Regiment.

On a low hill overlooking Nelson's Dockyard, **Clarence House** was built by English stonemasons to accommodate Prince William Henry, later known as the Duke of Clarence, and even later known as King William IV. The future king stayed here when he was in command of the *Pegasus* in 1787. At present it's the country home of the governor of Antigua and is open to visitors when His Excellency is not in residence. A caretaker will show you through (it's customary to tip, of course), and you'll see many pieces of furniture on loan from the National Trust. Princess Margaret and Lord Snowdon stayed here on their honeymoon.

On the way back, take   ✪ **Fig Tree Drive,** a 20-some-mile circular drive across the main mountain range. It passes through lush tropical hills and fishing villages along the southern coast. You can pick up the road just outside Liberta, north of Falmouth. Winding through a rain forest, it passes thatched villages, and every hamlet has a church and lots of goats and children running about. However, don't expect fig trees—*fig* is an Antiguan name for bananas.

About half a mile before reaching St. John's you come to **Fort James,** which was begun in 1704 as a main lookout post for the port. It was named after James II in whose reign efforts were made to build the fort on the point known as St. John's.

Other places on the island worth seeking out include the following:

Parham Church, overlooking Parham Town, was erected in 1840 in the Italian style. Richly adorned with stucco work, it was damaged by an earthquake in 1843. Much of the ceiling was destroyed and very little of the stucco work remains, but the octagonal structure is still worth a visit.

Potworks Dam, holding back the largest artificial lake in Antigua, is surrounded by an area of natural beauty. The dam has a capacity of a billion gallons of water and provides protection for Antigua in case of a drought.

Indian Town, one of Antigua's national parks, is at a northeastern point on the island. Over the centuries Atlantic breakers have lashed the rocks and carved a natural bridge known as Devil's Bridge. It's surrounded by numerous blowholes spouting surf.

Megaliths, at Greencastle Hill, reached by a long climb, are said to have been set up by human hands for the worship of a sun god and a moon goddess. Some experts believe, however, that the arrangement is an unusual geological formation, a volcanic rockfall.

The **Antigua Rum Distillery,** at Rat Island, turns out fine Cavalier rum. Check at the tourist office about arranging a visit. Established in 1932, the plant is next to Deep Water Harbour. Its annual production rate is in excess of 250,000 imperial gallons.

SPORTS & RECREATION

BEACHES   Beaches, beaches, and more beaches—Antigua has some 365 of them. Some are superior, and all are public. There's a lovely beach at **Pigeon Point,** in Falmouth Harbour, about a 4-minute drive from Admiral's Inn. The beach at **Dickenson Bay,** near the Halcyon Cove Hotel, is also superior and a center for water sports; for a break, you can enjoy meals and drinks on the hotel's Warri Pier, built on stilts in the water. Chances are, however, you'll swim at your own hotel.

Other beaches are at the Curtain Bluff resort, with its long, sandy white **Carlisle Beach** set against a backdrop of coconut palms, and **Morris Bay,** which in addition to its sandy strip of white sands, has waters attracting snorkelers, among others. The beach at **Long Bay** is on the somewhat-remote eastern coast, but the beach here is beautiful, and most visitors consider it worth the effort to reach it. **Half Moon Bay,** site of the Half Moon Bay Hotel, is famous in the Caribbean and attracts what used to be called "blue bloods" to a stretch of sand that goes on for almost a mile. Site of such hotels as the Barrymore Beach, **Runaway Beach** is probably one of the most popular in Antigua, but because of its white sands it's worth fighting the crowds. **Five Islands** is actually a quartet of remote beaches with brown sands and coral reefs located near the Hawksbill Hotel.

Increasingly, readers complain of vendors hustling everything from jewelry to T-shirts, disrupting their time on the beach. The beaches are open to all, and hotels can't restrain beach use, so be duly warned.

GOLF   Antigua doesn't have the facilities of some of the other islands, but what it has is good. The 18-hole, par-72 **Cedar Valley Golf Club** (tel. 2-0161) is 3 miles out of St. John's, near the airport. The island's largest, with panoramic views of Antigua's northern coast, it was designed by the late Richard Aldridge to fit the contours of the area. Visitors can play on this semiprivate course by prior arrangement with the manager. Daily greens fees are $22 for 18 holes.

The other course of note is the nine-holer at **Half Moon Bay** (tel. 0-4300), on the southeastern corner of Antigua. In season, guests of the hotel are guaranteed a space—and nonguests may not be. Greens fees are $8 per day for the nine holes, and clubs rent for $6. In theory the caddy charge is $4, but it's advisable to pay yours more than that.

PARASAILING This sport is gaining in popularity in Antigua. Facilities are available during the day Monday through Saturday on the beach at **Dickenson Bay** (tel. 1-0945). There are also facilities at the **Jolly Beach Hotel** and **Ramada Renaissance Royal Antiguan Hotel.**

SAILING All major hotel desks can book you on a day cruise on the 108-foot "pirate ship," the *Jolly Roger,* Redcliffe Quay (tel. 2-2064). For $45 you are taken sightseeing on a fun-filled day, with drinks and a barbecue steak, chicken, or lobster. The *Jolly Roger* is the largest sailing ship in Antiguan waters. Lunch is combined with a snorkel trip. Dancing is on the poop deck, and members of the crew teach passengers how to dance calypso.

SCUBA DIVING & OTHER WATER SPORTS Scuba diving is best arranged through **Dive Antigua,** at the Halcyon Cove Beach Resort and Casino, Dickenson Bay (tel. 2-3483), Antigua's longest-established and most experienced dive operation. For $65 per person you can have instruction and a boat dive with all equipment provided.

You can also arrange scuba-diving trips at the **Jolly Beach Hotel** on Morris Bay (tel. 2-0061, ext. 111).

The **Long Bay Hotel** (tel. 3-2005), on the northeastern coast of the island at Long Bay, is a good location for various water sports—swimming, sailing, waterskiing, and windsurfing. The hotel also has complete scuba facilities. Both beginning snorkelers and experienced divers are welcomed, though Long Bay doesn't offer scuba courses for beginners. You're taken on snorkel trips by boat to Green Island and Great Bird Island (minimum of four). The shallow side of the double reef across Long Bay is ideal for the neophyte, and the whole area on the northeastern tip has many reefs of varying depths.

The **Blue Waters Beach Hotel,** Soldiers Bay (tel. 2-0290), has one of the best water-sports programs on the island. Waterskiing is available at about $20 per person per half hour. In addition, they offer snorkeling gear, fishing rods, windsurfers, pedaloes, Sunfish, Hobie Cats, and canoeing, all complimentary to Blue Waters guests.

TENNIS Tennis buffs will find courts at most of the major hotels, and some are lit for night games. I don't recommend playing tennis at noon—it's just too hot! If your hotel doesn't have a court, you'll find them available at the **Halcyon Cove, Half Moon Bay, Cedar Valley Golf Club, Jolly Beach,** and the **Ramada Renaissance Royal Antiguan** (the last two have eight courts each). If you're not a guest, you'll have to book a court and pay charges that vary from hotel to hotel. Residents of a hotel usually play free.

WINDSURFING The **Patrick Scales International Windsurfer Sailing Schools,** at the Halcyon Cove Beach Hotel, Dickenson Bay (tel. 2-0256), offers lessons for beginners, with a full range of boards and sails available, together with radio-assisted rescue facilities. He guarantees that you can learn to windsurf in just 2 hours. There's another branch of this outfit at the Lord Nelson Beach Hotel on Dutchmans Bay. The cost is $40 for a 2-hour lesson.

Another center for intermediate and advanced windsurfers is operated at the **Lord Nelson Beach Club,** Dutchmans Bay (tel. 2-3094). Onshore wind speeds vary from 12 to 25 knots, with a 2- to 3-foot chop off a quarter of a mile of white sandy beach. Instruction in jibing and other advanced windsurfer techniques is offered. Classes are offered daily from 10am to noon and 2 to 4pm.

SAVVY SHOPPING

Most of the shops are clustered on St. Mary's Street or High Street in St. John's. Some shops are open Monday through Saturday from 8:30am to noon and 1 to 4pm, but this rule varies greatly from store to store—Antiguan shopkeepers are an independent lot. Many of them close at noon on Thursday.

There are many duty-free items for sale, including English woolens and linens, and you can also purchase several specialized items made in Antigua, such as original pottery, local straw work, Antigua rum, and silk-screened, hand-printed local designs on fabrics, as well as mammy bags, floppy foldable hats, and shell curios.

If you want an island-made bead necklace, don't bother to go shopping; just lie on the beach—anywhere—and some "bead lady" will find you.

If you're in St. John's on a Saturday morning, you can attend the **fruit and vegetable market** at the West Bus Station. Handcrafts made locally are also offered for sale. One visitor said that "the incredibly sweet and juicy Antiguan black pineapple is worth the trip into town itself."

CO CO SHOP, St. Mary's St. Tel. 2-1128.

One of the best-equipped shops in town, this West Indian fashion center uses Sea Island cottons and even prints from Liberty of London. You can purchase these fabrics either made up or by the yard. Men's shirts have a tropical flair, and some of the carefree clothes are hand-embroidered. Men, women, and children will find a selection of shirts, dresses, blouses, and bikinis. The handcrafted ceramics are all made in Antigua. Ask for Antiguan Frangipani Perfume. A branch store is at the airport.

HARMONY HALL, Brown's Bay Mill, near Freetown. Tel. 0-4120.

This recent structure of cut stonework resembles a restored sugar mill and has views over Nonsuch Bay. Harmony Hall aims at promoting excellence in Caribbean art and craft by providing a special showcase in a distinctive setting. In addition to a circular bar and a large barbecue with seating in the shaded garden or the cut-stone dining room, Harmony Hall houses an art gallery, with regular exhibitions of Caribbean artists and sculptors. It also has a gift shop with many handcrafts. It is open daily from 10am to 6pm. The restaurant is closed on Monday but the bar, like the Gallery, is open daily. Dinner is offered Tuesday through Sunday by reservation only. To get there, follow signs along the road to Mill Reef and Half Moon Bay.

QUIN FARARA'S LIQUOR STORE, Long St. and Corn Alley. Tel. 2-0463.

Antigua has some of the lowest liquor prices in the Caribbean, and this shop has one of the largest collections of wines and liquors on the island. Often you'll save up to 50% on what you'd pay in the States. The staff will show you how to take home a "gallon," pay the duty, and still save. Don Diego (originally Cuban) cigars are also on sale.

SHIPWRECK SHOPS LTD., St. Mary's St., at Kensington Court. Tel. 2-1795.

The walls, ceilings, and counters are loaded with merchandise from either Antigua or some neighboring island. They carry everything—T-shirts, coverups, swimsuits, dresses, photo supplies, beach accessories, jewelery, wooden bowls, wood and ceramic figurines, glassware, hats, bags, postcards, and more. They also have daily newspapers, magazines, and many paperback books.

There are four other convenient locations: at Jardine Court, the Jolly Beach Hotel, the Halcyon Cove Hotel, and Heritage Quay.

SHOUL'S CHIEF STORE, St. Mary's St. Tel. 2-1139.

Opposite Barclays Bank is a cave of treasures. The store sells household items and appliances, a wide range of local and imported souvenirs, Antigua T-shirts, and fabrics of all colors, designs, and textures.

SUGAR MILL BOUTIQUE, Jardine's Court, St. Mary's St. Tel. 2-4523.

Here you'll find garments silk-screened or manufactured in Antigua. The designs include depictions of birds, fish, flowers, and shells indigenous to the region. The store also sells a wide variety of T-shirts for both children and adults.

WEST INDIAN SEA ISLAND COTTON SHOP, St. Mary's St. Tel. 2-2972.

Sea Island cotton products are good buys, and some of the best are found here. The shop is an outlet for the Romney Manor workshop on St. Kitts. The Caribelle label consists of batik and tie-dye beach wraps, swimwear, and head ties.

Shopping Centers

HERITAGE QUAY Antigua's first shopping-and-entertainment complex is a multi-million-dollar center featuring some 40 duty-free shops and a vendors' arcade in which local artists and craftspeople display their wares. Restaurants in Heritage Quay offer a range of cuisine and views of St. John's Harbour, while a "food court" serves visitors who prefer to feast on local specialties in an informal setting. You could start your shopping with any of these leading shops:

Colombian Emeralds (tel. 2-3462) is the largest retailer of Colombian emeralds in the world, with branches in the West Indies and The Bahamas. It offers an excellent variety of emeralds along with jewelry made from other precious stones, including sapphires and diamonds.

Little Switzerland (tel. 2-3108) is a name familiar to frequent travelers to the Caribbean. It sells the best selections of Swiss-made watches in Antigua, such as Rolex and Vacheron & Constantin. It also displays china and crystal made by Wedgwood and Baccarat.

The Land Shop, 53 Heritage Quay (tel. 2-0746), offers a wide selection of handbags, luggage, and leather clothing for both women and men.

"Sunseakers," 13 Heritage Quay (tel. 2-4523), is an elegant sportswear shop for women and men with an excellent collection of swimwear from such designers as Gottex, Jantzen, Catalina, and Triumph.

The **Windjammer Clothing Company,** 33 Heritage Quay (tel. 2-2607), offers casual dress for women, children, and men. The lightweight clothing is made in the West Indies and the designers use natural fibers and cotton.

Island Arts, Upstairs, Heritage Quay (tel. 2-2785), was founded by Nick Maley, a makeup artist who worked on *Star Wars* and *The Empire Strikes Back.* You can purchase one of his own fine-art reproductions, including the provocative *Windkissed & Sunswept.* Visitors are free to browse through everything from low-cost prints to works by artists exhibited in New York's Museum of Modern Art. Other outlets are found at the Ramada Renaissance Royal Antiguan Resort and the St. James's Club.

REDCLIFFE QUAY This historic complex is one of the best centers for shopping (or dining) in St. John's. Once, Redcliffe Quay was a slave-trading quarter, but after the abolition of slavery the quay was filled with grog shops and merchants peddling various wares. Now it has been redeveloped and contains a number of the most interesting shops in town, some in former warehouses.

Serendipity (tel. 2-2026) sells merchandise from England, Scotland, and Ireland, including handmade Scottish teddy bears, crofters' hand-woven lambswool blankets and shawls, scrimshaw, and a small selection of Irish pewter. They also sell items made of Montserrat Sea Island cotton.

A Thousand Flowers (tel. 2-4264) sells Indonesian batiks, crafted on the island into sundresses, knock-'em-dead shirts, sarongs, rompers, and swimwear. Many of the garments are designed into a one-size-fits-all motif of knots and flowing expanses of cloth appropriate for the tropics.

Jacaranda (tel. 2-1888) might tempt you with the art of John Woodland or placemats and prints by Jill Walker. The shop also stocks cosmetics from the islands along with herbs and spices.

The Goldsmitty (tel. 2-4601) presents the designs of Hans Smit in precious stones and gold. Each item is a treasure. Buyers can select from a wide array of merchandise, including necklaces, earrings, and rings in 14- or 18-karat gold. Closed in September.

EVENING ENTERTAINMENT

Most nightlife revolves around the hotels, unless you want to roam Antigua at night looking for that "hot native club." If you're going out for the night, make arrangements to have a taxi pick you up—otherwise you could be stranded in the wilds somewhere. Antigua has some of the best steel bands in the Caribbean.

MAIONE'S CASINO ROYAL ANTIGUAN, in the Ramada Renaissance Royal Antiguan, Deep Bay. Tel. 2-3733.
This 6,000-square-foot international casino has American games, including blackjack, baccarat, roulette, craps, and slot machines. Open: Daily from 8pm "until."
Admission: Free.

TROPIX, Redcliffe Quay. Tel. 2-2317.
In the leading disco on the island, dress is semiformal or sort of casually elegant. The place, once a warehouse used for storing tamarinds and sheepskins, now has a hi-tech format, plenty of flashing lights, and recently released music. Drinks begin at $4. Open: Wed–Sat from 9pm "until."
Admission (including one drink): $10.

BARBUDA

Known by the Spanish as Dulcina, sparsely populated Barbuda, part of the independent nation of Antigua and Barbuda, is considered the last frontier of the Caribbean. Charted by Columbus in 1493, the island lies 26 miles to the north of Antigua, and is about 15 miles long by 5 miles wide with a population of some 1,200 hardy souls, most of whom live around the unattractive village of **Codrington.**

Don't come here seeking lush, tropical scenery, as flat Barbuda consists of coral rock. There are no paved roads, few hotel rooms, only a handful of restaurants, and pastel-colored beaches, the most famous of which stretches for more than 17 miles.

The main town is named after Christopher Codrington, who was once the governor of the Leeward Islands. He is believed to have deliberately wrecked ships on the reefs circling Barbuda. What *is* known is that he used the island, which he'd received in 1691 from the Crown, for the purposes of breeding slaves. He was given the island in return for "one fat pig per year, if asked."

Barbuda has a temperature that seldom falls below an average of 75° Fahrenheit.

ORIENTATION

GETTING THERE The island is a 15-minute flight from Antigua's V. C. Bird Airport. Barbuda has two airfields: one at Codrington; the other a private facility, the Coco Point Airstrip, which lies some 8 miles from Codrington at Coco Point Lodge.

To reach Barbuda from Antigua, you can contact **Leeward Islands Air Transport (LIAT)** (tel. 809/462-0701), which operates two daily flights (usually around 8am and again around 4pm) from Antigua to Barbuda's Codrington Airport.

GETTING AROUND Many locals rent small Suzuki four-wheel-drive **Jeeps,** which are the best way to get around the island, meet incoming flights at Codrington Airport, and charge about $65 a day. An Antiguan driver's license (see above) is needed if you plan to drive.

WHERE TO STAY & DINE

K-CLUB, Barbuda, Antigua, W.I. Tel. 809/460-0300, or toll free 800/648-4097 for reservations in the U.S. Fax 809/460-0304. 40 bungalows. A/C MINIBAR TV TEL
$ Rates (including all meals and transportation from Codrington Airport): $1,000–$2,500 single or double. AE, DC, MC, V. **Parking:** Free. **Closed:** June–Nov.

☆ The most interesting—and *super*-expensive—hotel to open in the early 1990s in the Caribbean, this is a fusion of chic Italy into one of the most farflung backwaters of the Antilles. Located a 15-minute taxi ride from the airport and set on more than 200 acres, adjacent to the island's only other (strictly private) hotel, it's the creative statement of Italy's Krizia Mariuccia Mandelli whose sports and evening-wear empire have grossed one of the spectacular fashion fortunes of Europe.

The resort's architectural style, conceived by Italian architect Gianni Gamondi, consists of bungalows and a main clubhouse whose roof is supported by a forest of white columns. The resort's dominant color scheme is in the teal-blue and white that are the designer's trademark. Furnishings include lots of Hamptons-style wicker and a stylish insouciance. The resort was inaugurated in 1990 when a planeload of glitterati—spearheaded by Giorgio Armani—headed en masse for Barbuda.

Dining/Entertainment: The all-inclusive rates provide for all meals (but no drinks or wine). As for food, El Toulà restaurant group, one of the finest in Italy, helped Krizia develop the cuisine.

Services: Transportation from Codrington Airport.

Facilities: Two tennis courts, swimming pool, waterskiing, snorkeling, Sunfish sailing, windsurfing.

WHAT TO SEE & DO

Hunters, anglers, and just plain beachcombers are attracted to the island, as it has some fallow deer, guinea fowl, pigeons, and wild pigs. Those interested in fishing for bonefish and tarpon can negotiate with the owners of small boats who hire them out.

Trippers over just for the day usually head for **Wa'Omoni Beach Park,** where they can visit the frigate bird sanctuary, snorkel for lobster, and eat barbecue.

Indeed, the most impressive sight on Barbuda is the **frigate bird sanctuary,** one of the largest in the world, where visitors can see the birds, *Fregata magnificens,* sitting on their eggs in the mangrove bushes. The mangroves stretch for miles in a long lagoon accessible only by a small motorboat. Tours to the sanctuary can be arranged in Antigua at various hotels and resorts. Besides the frigate bird, the island attracts some 150 species of birds, including pelicans, herons, and tropical mockingbirds.

Other curiosities of the island include a **"Dividing Wall,"** which once separated the Codrington family from the black people, and the **Martello Tower,** which predates the known history of the island. Tours also cover interesting underground **caves** on the island. Stamp collectors might want to call at the **Philatelic Bureau** in Codrington.

2. MONTSERRAT

To see "the way the Caribbean used to be," visit Montserrat. Vacationers often fly to the volcanic island just for the day and then wish they could spend more time here. Called the "Emerald Isle of the Caribbean," Montserrat is some 27 miles southwest of Antigua, between Guadeloupe and Nevis. The pear-shaped island is mountainous with lush green forests, much tropical vegetation, and some licorice-colored beaches of volcanic sand that are powdery but black.

Montserrat was sighted by Columbus in 1493 and named after the famous sawtoothed mountain near Barcelona. However, it wasn't until 1632 that Irish settlers colonized the island, when Oliver Cromwell, it is believed, shipped out a band of reluctant colonists who had been captured after a rebellion. By 1648 Montserrat had also become home to 1,000 Irish families who fled their new homes on St. Kitts because of religious persecution. The Irish influence is shown in place names on the island and in the surnames of present-day residents.

The flag of Montserrat is the British Union Jack, but the official badge is the very Irish "Lady with the Harp." The shamrock is on the center gable of Government House, which can be visited, and it's also on the stamp with which Montserrat immigration people stamp your passport. The island even marks March 17 as a public holiday, but this is because the slaves in the early days staged a rebellion on St. Patrick's Day. Today Montserrat's more than 12,000 hard-working, friendly people, most of whom were descended from African slaves, often speak with an Irish brogue.

The island was captured by the French in 1644, restored to England in 1668, and retaken by the French in 1782, who ceded it to Britain in 1783. Today the officials have elected to remain a British Crown Colony, as they don't have the financial wherewithal to go it alone. The island is politically stable and is popular with retirees. The capital, **Plymouth,** is reputed to be one of the cleanest in the Caribbean; it's best viewed during market day on Saturday, when gossip is traded along with fruit.

George Martin, best known as the producer of the Beatles, has launched a contemporary electronic studio in a Belham Valley estate, and he uses Olveston House, the residence of an early lime-juice magnate, as a private residence for the Air Studios' recording company. So don't be surprised if, when exploring Montserrat, you encounter Paul McCartney, Elton John, Ringo Starr, Jimmy Buffett, Stevie Wonder, or Mick Jagger, who have all come here to record music and/or to "wind down."

ORIENTATION

GETTING THERE Antigua is by far the most popular gateway to Montserrat (for information on getting to Antigua, refer to "Getting There" in the "Antigua" section of this chapter). Once you're in Antigua, you can book any of the seven daily flights that are jointly maintained by a cooperative arrangement between **LIAT** (tel. 809/491-2200) and **Montserrat Aviation** (tel. 809/491-2362). The flying time between the two islands is about 15 minutes. LIAT also maintains an island-hopping service once a day which originates in Sint Maarten, touches down in St. Kitts, and eventually reaches Montserrat.

GETTING AROUND   By Taxi and Bus There are 150 miles of surfaced roads, and taxis and buses are the most popular means of transport. Taxi drivers meet every plane. Typical fares from the airport to Plymouth are $11 each way. Sightseeing tours cost about $11 per hour.

Buses run between Plymouth and most areas at fees ranging from $1 to $2.

By Rental Car To rent a car on Montserrat, you must go to the police station in Plymouth to get a temporary driver's license; you'll need to present a valid U.S. or Canadian license and pay $12. Visitors can also obtain these from the police officers at the Immigration department of the local airport. Incidentally, car rentals aren't allowed to operate out of the airport, so you must take a taxi to Plymouth.

Both **Avis** (tel. toll free 800/331-2112) and **Budget** (tel. toll free 800/527-0700) maintain branches in Montserrat. Currently, Avis has the lowest price, at $192 per week with unlimited mileage. A collision-damage waiver (CDW) costs $7 a day, although you'll still be liable for the first $200 of damage to your car. Avis requires that renters be between 25 and 75 years old, and present either a valid credit card or a cash deposit.

Budget charges $210 per week for its cheapest car, $10 per day for its CDW, and maintains more stringent insurance penalties (drivers are liable for the first $400 of damage). Drivers need to be 21 or older at Budget, with no maximum age requirement imposed. Rates at both companies are usually lower for clients who reserve in North America prior to their departure; for information once you reach the island, contact Avis (tel. 1-2345) or Budget (tel. 1-6065).

There are only two gas stations (they call it "petrol" here) on Montserrat. One is the Texaco station, north of Plymouth, and the other is opposite the public market, at the N & B Servicentre. Remember to *drive on the left.*

FAST FACTS MONTSERRAT

Area Code To call Montserrat from mainland North America, dial the Caribbean area code of 809, then 49 (the prefix for all phone numbers on the island), then the five-digit local number. For information on dialing numbers on the island, see "Telephone," below.

Currency All the British Leeward Islands use the **Eastern Caribbean dollar (EC$),** although most prices are given in U.S. dollars.

Drugstores Try **Lee's Pharmacy,** Marine Drive, in Plymouth (tel. 1-3274).

Electricity You'll need an electrical transformer and adapter for all U.S.-made appliances, as the island supplies 220–230 volts AC, 60 cycles. Check with your hotel, though, to see if they've converted their circuitry.

Hospitals The **Glendon Hospital,** Plymouth (tel. 1-2552), operates a 24-hour emergency room.

Information The **Department of Tourism** is on Church Street (P.O. Box 7), Plymouth, Montserrat, B.W.I. (tel. 809/491-2230).

Police Call 1-2552.

Safety As in the Caymans and the British Virgins, crime is rare here. It would be wise, however, to take the usual precautions about safeguarding your valuables.

Taxes The government charges a hotel tax of 7%. In addition, it imposes an $8 departure tax when you leave the island.

Telephone When dialing a number once you're on the island, omit the 809 area code and the 49 prefix, and dial only the last five digits.

Time Montserrat is on Atlantic standard time. When it's 6am in Plymouth, it's 5am in New York or Miami. However, island clocks match those of the eastern standard zone on the mainland when summer's daylight saving time is in effect in the U.S.

Tips and Service Most hotels and many restaurants add a 10% surcharge to your final tab to cover tips. If they don't, it's customary to tip 10% to 15%.

Weather The mean temperature of the island ranges from a high of 86.5° to a low of 73.5° Fahrenheit.

WHERE TO STAY

The trade winds, more than air conditioning, will keep you cool. Informality is the keynote.

HOTELS

Don't forget that the government imposes a 7% room tax on hotels, and usually a 10% service charge is also added. Ask about these charges when you make your reservation.

FLORA FOUNTAIN HOTEL, Lower Dagenham Rd. (P.O. Box 373), Plymouth, Montserrat, B.W.I. Tel. 809/491-6092. Fax 809/491-2568. 18 rms. A/C TEL

$ Rates: Winter, $60 single; $85 double. Summer, $50 single; $70 double. Breakfast $10 extra. AE, MC, V. **Parking:** Free.

Popular with business travelers who appreciate its central location in Plymouth, this hotel is built around a circular courtyard centered on a fountain whose illumination is computerized. There isn't much of a view, but each unit has its own balcony nonetheless, along with a private bath.

The hotel offers a fixed-price lunch from 11am to 2:30pm. Try to catch the Saturday-morning West Indian buffet breakfast, when you can feast on such local dishes as saltfish, bananas, breadfruit, souse, and blood pudding—or bacon and eggs.

VUE POINTE HOTEL, P.O. Box 65, Old Towne, Montserrat, B.W.I. Tel. 809/491-5210, or toll free 800/235-0709. Fax 809/491-4813. 40 units. MINIBAR TV TEL

$ Rates: Winter, $150 single; $165 double. Summer, $75 single; $95 double. Breakfast $6 extra. AE, MC, V. **Parking:** Free. **Closed:** Sept–Oct.

This family-run cottage colony 4 miles north of Plymouth consists of hexagonal, shingle-roofed villas, plus some interconnected rooms. They're set on 5 acres of sloping land near a black sand beach just 11 miles from the

Montserrat airport and about 2 minutes from the challenging seaside Montserrat Golf Club.

Most of the accommodations are constructed with natural lumber with open-beamed ceilings, and they're furnished with bamboo and modern pieces. Each has a private bath, a sitting-room area, and twin beds. A natural breeze sweeps through accommodations in lieu of air conditioning. The staff members are unobtrusive and well trained.

Dining/Entertainment: The cuisine is the best on the island, and everybody seems to show up for the West Indian barbecue on Wednesday night. Food is served family style, so you can ask for second helpings. There are two attractive bars: one at the rambling main house; the other, called the Nest, at water's edge. Dress is informal, except on Monday and Saturday nights in season when men should spruce up a bit. Sometimes there's music and dancing to a steel band, and sometimes movies are shown.

Services: Room service, laundry, baby-sitting.

Facilities: Freshwater swimming pool, two tennis courts; fishing, sailing, and snorkeling can be arranged.

CONDOS & VILLAS

BELHAM VALLEY HOTEL, P.O. Box 409, Old Towne, Montserrat, B.W.I. Tel. 809/491-5553. 3 units. TV TEL

$ Rates: Winter, $275 per week Jasmine studio; $450 per week Frangipani studio; $500 per week Mignonette unit. Summer, $225 per week Jasmine studio; $300 per week Frangipani studio; $350 per week Mignonette unit. AE, MC, V. **Parking:** Free.

These three apartments lie on a hillside 4 miles north of Plymouth, overlooking Belham Valley and its river, near the golf course. The beach is about a 7-minute walk, and you can also stroll over in the evening to the Vue Pointe Hotel. The Frangipani studio cottage, surrounded by tropical shrubs and coconut palm, can accommodate two guests and consists of a bedroom, living area, fully equipped kitchen, private bath, and a balcony facing the golf course and the sea. The Jasmine studio apartment also accommodates two and contains a large bed-sitting room, a small dinette, a private bath, a fully equipped kitchen, and a small private patio with views of the sea or mountains. A newer apartment, the Mignonette, accommodates four guests and has two bedrooms, a bath, and a living area with kitchen, plus a big patio facing the golf course and sea.

LIME COURT APARTMENTS, P.O. Box 250, Plymouth, Montserrat, B.W.I. Tel. 809/491-6985. Fax 809/491-6690. 12 units. TV TEL

$ Rates: Winter, $55 one-bedroom unit; $65 two-bedroom unit for four; $85 penthouse for two. Summer, $40 one-bedroom unit; $50 two-bedroom unit for four; $65 penthouse for two. Breakfast $5 per person extra. AE, MC, V. **Parking:** Free.

Right in the center of town, a 15-minute taxi ride north of the airport, this apartment colony is a short walk from the beach, shops, and restaurants. Fully furnished one- and two-bedroom apartments are available with well-equipped kitchens and electric cooking. Each unit has a hot-water shower, and all utilities and maid service are included. The most luxurious unit is no. 9, a well-furnished penthouse apartment offering a magnificent view of the harbor and a private patio. Neville Bradshaw, the manager, advises that in winter all bookings should be made at least 2 months in advance.

MONTSERRAT SPRINGS HOTEL, P.O. Box 259, Plymouth, Montserrat, B.W.I. Tel. 809/491-2481. Fax 809/491-4070. 40 units, 6 suites. TV TEL

$ Rates: Winter, $120–$140 single or double without kitchen; $160–$190 suite with kitchen. Summer, $85–$90 single or double without kitchen; $95–$105 suite with kitchen. MAP $40 per person extra. Children under 12 stay free in parents' room. AE, MC. **Parking:** Free.

Small and personalized, this hotel clusters accommodations into a series of interconnected, black-roofed town houses set a 25-minute taxi ride northwest of the airport
on steeply sloping land. Some are closer to the sea than others, but all are ringed with
carefully maintained landscaping. Each accommodation contains wicker furniture,
private bath, and balcony. The suites contain kitchenettes and washing machines and
are air-conditioned. Built on the site of natural springs, the premises contain a covered
duet of circular hot and cold baths, a 70-foot swimming pool, tennis courts, access to
the sands of Rendezvous Bay, a beach bar and a pool bar, and a dining room.

**SHAMROCK VILLAS, P.O. Box 58, Plymouth, Montserrat, B.W.I. Tel.
809/491-2431.** Fax 809/491-4660. 45 villas.

$ Rates: Dec–Apr, $450 per week one-bedroom unit for two; $550 per week
two-bedroom unit for four. May–Nov, $350 per week one-bedroom unit for two;
$400 per week two-bedroom unit for four. No credit cards. **Parking:** Free.

A condominium hillside colony at Plymouth, near the Montserrat Springs Hotel,
Shamrock Villas suggests an Iberian village of white, balcony-studded houses. Owners
have arranged for their villas to be rented in their absence. All villas have views of the
sea, the black sandy beaches, and Plymouth. Linen and cutlery are included, even for
short-term rentals. Maid service is available 2 days a week. Services are close by. Bread
comes fresh from the baker, and at the local market you can sample the produce
grown on the island, especially the tomatoes, carrots, and pineapples. A beach and
tennis court are adjacent.

**VILLAS OF MONTSERRAT, Isle Bay (P.O. Box 421), Plymouth, Montser-
rat, B.W.I. Tel. 809/491-5513.** 3 villas. TV TEL

$ Rates (including maid service, airfare from Antigua in summer, transfers to your
villas): Winter, from $2,000 per week. Summer, from $1,690 per week. No credit
cards. **Parking:** Free.

The island's most luxurious villa complex offers three deluxe villas, each with three
bedrooms, three baths (one with a Jacuzzi), a large living room with color TV and
stereo, a spacious dining area, and a kitchen with microwave oven and dishwasher.
They also have their own swimming pools, and there are washer/dryer facilities. The
villas can accommodate up to six guests, and prices provide inclusive services, with
rum punch drinks and a cold lobster and champagne dinner the first night. Your
breakfast, served on the patio, will be followed by a tour of the island. Maid service is
covered in the rates, and you can arrange for a private cook if you wish. The handsome
villas are on a hillside 4 miles north of Plymouth, with views of Isle Bay and the
Caribbean Sea as well as the Montserrat Golf Course.

WHERE TO DINE

Some of the best fruit and vegetables in the Caribbean are grown in the rich, volcanic
soil of Montserrat. The island is known for its tomatoes, carrots, and mangoes; and
"goat water" (a mutton stew) is the best-known local dish. Another island specialty is
"mountain chicken," as locally caught frogs' legs are called.

EXPENSIVE

BELHAM VALLEY RESTAURANT, Old Towne. Tel. 1-5553.
Cuisine: FRENCH/AMERICAN. **Reservations:** Recommended, especially for
dinner.

$ Prices: Appetizers $3–$6.75; main courses $15–$22.50. AE, MC, V.
Open: Lunch Tues–Sun noon–2pm; dinner Tues–Sun 6:30–11pm.

Near the Vue Pointe Hotel, 4 miles north of Plymouth, is the premier
restaurant of Montserrat. You can enjoy a local creamy pumpkin soup,
Montserrat conch fritters, escargots à la bourguignonne, or a combination of
seafood served in a rich vermouth sauce. The kitchen always prepares that ubiquitous
Montserrat "mountain chicken" (frogs' legs). Desserts are likely to include coconut-
cream cheesecake, a velvety-smooth mango mousse, and fresh coconut pie. The
setting is tropical, and the restaurant occupies a former private home on a hillside

overlooking the Belham River and its valley. It's convenient for guests at the Montserrat Golf Course.

THE OASIS, Wapping Rd., Plymouth. Tel. 1-2328.
  Cuisine: AMERICAN/SEAFOOD/VEGETARIAN. **Reservations:** Recommended.
$ Prices: Appetizers EC$7–EC$15 ($2.60–$5.55); main courses EC$9–EC$50 ($3.35–$18.50). No credit cards.
  Open: Lunch Thurs–Tues noon–2pm; dinner Thurs–Tues 6–10pm.
Nestled on the ground floor of an 18th-century stone house in the center of town, the Oasis is separated from the sea by a road, a copse of sea-grape coconut palms, and hibiscus. The cuisine is simple but full of flavor. You might be served sautéed jumbo shrimp, shrimp-stuffed filet of sole, a 12-ounce peppercorn T-bone steak, or boneless chicken breast flambéed with Cointreau.

MODERATE

THE IGUANA, Old Fort Rd., Wapping. Tel. 1-3637.
  Cuisine: AMERICAN/CREOLE/ITALIAN. **Reservations:** Recommended.
$ Prices: Appetizers EC$8–EC$15 ($2.95–$5.55); main courses EC$40–EC$65 ($14.80–$24.05). No credit cards.
  Open: Dinner only, Tues–Sun 6:30–10:30pm.
Set in a tropical garden near a cluster of other restaurants north of Plymouth, the Iguana serves some of the most creative cuisine in the neighborhood. Its core was originally built 200 years ago as a cotton mill, but today its dark stone-walled interior contains a nautical, somewhat spartan bar where you can have a before-dinner drink. Guests dine beneath a palm-thatched sun screen in the back garden. Specialties include "mountain chicken," Montserrat stingray with a local lobster Créole sauce, blackened redfish, and sautéed ribeye steak. Dessert is likely to be homemade ice cream.

VUE POINTE RESTAURANT, in the Vue Pointe Hotel, Old Towne. Tel. 1-5211.
  Cuisine: FRENCH/CARIBBEAN. **Reservations:** Recommended if you're not a hotel guest.
$ Prices: Appetizers $4–$9; main courses $12–$22; fixed-price dinner $26.50. AE, MC, V.
  Open: Lunch daily 12:30–2pm; dinner daily 7–9:30pm. **Closed:** Sept–Oct.
Graciously elegant and surrounded by the lawns and shrubbery of this previously recommended hotel, 4 miles north of Plymouth, this is one of the best-run restaurants on the island. Fixed-price dinners are available, or you can order à la carte. The Wednesday-night barbecue, an island event, is enlivened by a steel band. The kitchen turns out "mountain chicken," filet of kingfish, Créole-style red snapper, West Indian curried chicken with condiments, and filet of sole. Dessert might be a slice of lime cheesecake or a tropical fruit salad. A Sunday luncheon buffet contains barbecued spareribs, fresh fish, and chicken, among other selections.

BUDGET

BLUE DOLPHIN RESTAURANT, Parsons. Tel. 1-3263.
  Cuisine: AMERICAN/CARIBBEAN. **Reservations:** Required.
$ Prices: Main courses EC$25–EC$50 ($9.25–$18.50). AE, MC, V.
  Open: Lunch Mon–Sat noon–2pm; dinner Mon–Sat 6pm–midnight.
Serviced by a kind-hearted staff, the Blue Dolphin is on the side of a steep hillside near the medical school amid a lush landscape of plants. Main dishes, which are served with soup, such as pumpkin, include lobster, kingfish, "mountain chicken," pork chops, and breaded boneless breast of chicken, and are followed by coconut-cream pie with ice cream.

VILLAGE PLACE, Salem. Tel. 1-5202.

Cuisine: CARIBBEAN. **Reservations:** Not required.
$ **Prices:** Appetizers EC$18 ($6.65); main courses EC$25–EC$45 ($9.25–$16.65). No credit cards.
Open: Wed–Mon 7pm–midnight.

If you weren't looking for it, you might think these encircling hedges and thatch fences concealed a private house. Local lore says that Elton John proposed to his future wife at one of the outdoor tables. You can stand beneath the white cedar beams of the indoor bar and admire the musical memorabilia, or you can claim a table in the courtyard and listen to tree frogs. A meal might include chicken, an array of salads, or pumpkin or callaloo soup. If you just want a snack, order some of the most delectable barbecued chicken wings in the West Indies. The restaurant is north of Plymouth and directly east of Old Towne.

YACHT CLUB BAR & RESTAURANT, Wapping. Tel. 1-2237.
Cuisine: CARIBBEAN. **Reservations:** Not required.
$ **Prices:** Main courses EC$30–EC$35 ($11.10–$12.95); lunch from EC$17 ($6.30). No credit cards.
Open: Lunch Mon–Fri noon–2pm; dinner Mon–Sat 7:30–10pm.

These stucco-sided premises could hardly be less pretentious, but some of the most famous rock 'n' roll personalities—including Sting and Boy George—have swilled their beer on this oceanside veranda north of Plymouth. Eddie Edgecombe is the kind owner of this popular place near the sands, across from the Gallery Bar and Restaurant. Lunch includes lasagne, broiled kingfish, hamburgers, salads, and sandwiches. Dinner features lobster, roast beef with Yorkshire pudding, and several kinds of chicken. Live entertainment is offered on Thursday and Friday evenings.

WHAT TO SEE & DO

The island is small, only 11 miles long and 7 miles across at its widest point. Its gently rolling hills and mountains reach their zenith at **Chances Peak,** which rises to 3,000 feet. From its vantage point, a panoramic vista over the island unfolds. To climb the mountain, even serious hikers need a guide, which your hotel can arrange.

Galway's Soufrière, in the south-central region of the island, is a crater that bubbles and steams with sulfur smoke. A mountain road lined with tree ferns allows you to drive to within a 15-minute walk of the vents. Yellow sulfur spills over the side in stark contrast to the forest's green. Look also for the exotic incense tree. Again, you should have your hotel arrange a mountain guide.

On the way there, stop to explore **Galway's Plantation,** an archeological project directed by the Montserrat National Trust. In the 1660s David Galway, an Irishman from Cork, settled the land with Irish indentured servants who were later replaced by African slaves. He established a sugar plantation which reached its peak a century later; however, the plantation declined after the slaves were freed. The ruins remain today and include the old sugar-boiling house and the sugar mill.

Another natural wonder, the **Great Alps Waterfall,** is reached by first taking a 15-minute taxi ride south from Plymouth and then taking a leisurely hour's walk through a lush interior to a horseshoe-shaped formation with crystal water plunging some 70 feet into a mountain pool. The noonday sun turns the mist into rainbow colors and reflects the shadows of the rich surrounding foliage; the mystical effect is of great beauty and is worth the trek.

On the outskirts of Plymouth, **St. Anthony's Church**—the main Anglican church on the island—was built between 1632 and 1666, and then rebuilt in 1730. Freed slaves, upon their emancipation, donated the two beautiful silver chalices on display. Next to the church is a gnarled tamarind tree two centuries old.

About a 15-minute drive from town, the ruined **Fort St. George** dates from the 18th century. The fort is 1,184 feet above sea level and offers magnificent views.

At yet another fortification, **Bransby Point,** you can see restored cannons. The early earthworks date from 1640 to 1660. In 1693 a gun battery was built on this site, but it was destroyed by the French in 1712. In 1734 the British constructed a gun platform. By 1983 the restoration had been completed, after 200 years of destruction.

The **Montserrat Museum,** housed in an old sugar mill at Richmond Hill in Plymouth, displays a collection of Montserratian artifacts, including pictures of island life at the turn of the century. Some of the artifacts relate to the island's pre-Columbian history. The featured exhibit is a small replica of a wind-driven sugar mill. Admission is free, but donations maintain the museum. Hours are 2:30 to 5pm on Wednesday and Sunday.

Government House, on the south side of Plymouth above Sugar Bay, is one of the most interesting buildings on the island. The older parts date back to the 1700s, although it was substantially rebuilt in 1906 in the traditional gingerbread style. Unfortunately, its attractive terraced grounds are closed to the public.

SPORTS & RECREATION

BEACHES Perhaps you'll be drawn to the black sandy beaches (the soil is of volcanic origin) on the southern rim of the island. If you prefer your beaches in beige tones, head for the northwest coast where you'll find the three most frequented beaches: **Carr's Bay, Little Bay,** and **Rendezvous Bay.** The Vue Pointe Hotel can arrange day sails to these beaches.

GOLF The **Montserrat Golf Club,** Old Towne (tel. 1-5220), with 18 holes on some 100 acres in Belham Valley, is considered one of the finest in the eastern Caribbean. Greens fees are EC$50 ($18.50) per person per day. The second hole, the best known, is about 600 yards across two branches of the Belham River. Rental clubs and pullcarts are available, and you can visit the clubhouse and bar.

TENNIS Tennis buffs will find two asphalt courts at the previously recommended **Vue Pointe Hotel,** Old Towne. Residents play free, but nonresidents are charged EC$10 ($3.70). Two tennis courts are also available at the **Montserrat Golf Club** (see above) for those who pay a greens fee.

WATER SPORTS For windsurfing, **Danny Watersports,** at the Vue Pointe Hotel, Old Road Bay, Old Towne (tel. 1-5645), is your best bet. After Danny Sweeney taught the British rock star Sting to windsurf, Sting used Danny's name in the lyrics of one of his hit songs. Today Danny still teaches his techniques from a kiosk on the black sand crescent of the Vue Pointe Hotel's beach. Windsurfers rent for $10 per hour, and an introductory lesson costs $8. You can rent Sunfish at $10 per hour, or a day's snorkeling equipment for $5.

For **fishing,** ask at your hotel about the availability of small boats for rent.

SAVVY SHOPPING

There is no duty-free shopping, but some interesting locally made handcrafts are for sale. Straw goods and small ceramic souvenirs predominate, along with Sea Island cotton fabrics. Most shops are open Monday through Saturday from 8am to noon and 1 to 4pm, but they usually close at 12:30pm on Wednesday.

The **Montserrat Sea Island Cotton Company** sales outlet, at the corner of George Street and Strand Street (tel. 1-2557), offers exclusive locally hand-woven West Indian Sea Island cotton products, leather goods, and ceramics. The outlet is open from 8am, and closes at 4pm on Monday, Tuesday, Thursday, and Friday, and at noon on Wednesday and Saturday.

Outside town, the government-owned and -operated **Montserrat Leather Craft** (tel. 1-4934) is in an actual leathercraft shop at the Groves. On sale are artistic handcrafted locally tanned leather goods including belts, wallets, handbags, sandals, and purses. See in particular the batik belts. The factory is closed on Saturday and Sunday.

Tapestries of Montserrat (The John Bull Shop), Parliament Street, Plymouth (tel. 1-2520), sells handcrafted rugs, wall hangings, and tote bags with Caribbean designs. Products are handmade by skilled artisans, whom you can watch at work in the shop.

Carol's Corner, in a high-ceilinged public room of the Vue Pointe Hotel, Old Towne (tel. 1-5210), offers one of the most concentrated collections of Montserrat-related memorabilia on the island. They sell the famous stamps of Montserrat and copies of the difficult-to-obtain flag. There's a version of a Montserrat cookbook, *Goatwater,* which describes "how to skin and clean a fat female iguana." There's also a collection of roadmaps, summery dresses of Sea Island cotton, and a selection of local jams and honey. If you forgot your toothbrush, there are cosmetics and sundries as well.

EVENING ENTERTAINMENT

Montserrat may be sleepy during the day, but it gets even quieter at night. The most activity is at the **Vue Pointe Hotel,** Old Towne (tel. 1-5210), where a steel band plays every Wednesday night, and there is nightly entertainment by local musicians in season. At the Wednesday-night bash, a barbecue dinner costs EC$66 ($24.40) per person.

A West Indian disco that attracts the local crowd is **La Cave,** on Evergreen Drive in Plymouth (tel. 1-2685). This modest little place plays records for dancers and charges an entrance fee of EC$10 ($3.70). A beer costs EC$4 ($1.50). It's open daily from 11pm until the last customer leaves.

The Plantation, Wapping Road, Plymouth (tel. 1-7289), is less formal and a bit more raucous than the previously recommended Oasis Restaurant, downstairs. This establishment occupies the upper story of a 200-year-old stone-walled house. Popular with visiting musicians and local medical students, it's only a bar, with no food service. Open daily from 7:30pm until very late, it sometimes shows video movies as an accompaniment to the beer and rum drinks, which cost EC$5 ($1.85) and up.

3. ST. KITTS

The volcanic central island of the British Leewards is not really a resort mecca like Antigua. Its major crop is sugar, and has been since the mid-17th century.

At some point during your visit you'll want to eat sugar directly from the cane. Any St. Kitts farmer will sell you a huge stalk, and there are sugarcane plantations all over the island—just ask your taxi driver to take you to one. You strip off the hard exterior of the stalk, bite into it, chew on the tasty reeds, and swallow the juice. It's best with a side glass of rum.

The Caribs, the early settlers, called St. Kitts Liamuiga, or "fertile isle." Its mountain ranges reach up to nearly 4,000 feet, and in its interior are virgin rain forests, alive with hummingbirds and wild green vervet monkeys. The monkeys were brought in as pets by the early French settlers and were turned loose in the forests when the island became British in 1783. These native African animals have proliferated and can perhaps best be seen at the Estridge Estate Behavioral Research Institute. Another import, this one British, is the mongoose, brought in from India as an enemy of rats in the sugarcane fields. However, the mongooses and rats operate on different time cycles—the rats ravage while the mongooses sleep. Wild deer are found in the St. Kitts mountains.

Sugarcane climbs right up the slopes, and there are palm-lined beaches around the island. As you travel around St. Kitts, you'll notice ruins of old mills and plantation houses. You'll also see an island rich in trees and vegetation.

St. Kitts, 23 miles long and 6½ miles wide, rides the crest of that arc of islands known as the northerly Leeward group of the Lesser Antilles. It is separated from the associated state of Nevis by a 2-mile-wide strait, and its administrative capital is Basseterre.

On his second voyage in 1493, Columbus spotted St. Kitts and named it Saint Christopher, but the English later changed the name to St. Kitts. In 1623 Sir Thomas

Warner landed with his wife and son and a party of 14 farmers, and made St. Kitts the first British colony in the West Indies. When the island later sent out parties of settlers to neighboring islands, St. Kitts became known as the "mother colony of the West Indies."

Shortly after their arrival, the English were joined by the French. In 1627 they divided the island between them and, united, they withstood attacks from the Caribs and the Spanish. But in time the British and French fought among themselves, and the island changed hands several times until it was finally given to the British by the Treaty of Versailles.

In 1967 St. Kitts was given internal self-government and, along with Nevis, became a state in association with Britain. (Anguilla, included in this associated state at the time, broke away.)

The capital, **Basseterre,** an 18th-century-print port with its waterfront intact, lies on the Caribbean shore near the southern end of the island, about a mile from Golden Rock Airport, where you will land. With its white colonial houses with toothpick balconies, it looks like a Hollywood version of a West Indian port.

This British colonial town is built around a so-called Circus, the town's round square. A tall green Victorian clock tower stands in the center of the Circus. In the old days, wealthy plantation owners and their families used to promenade here.

At some point, try to visit the marketplace. There, country people bring baskets brimming with mangoes, guavas, soursop, mammy apples, and wild strawberries and cherries just picked in the fields. Tropical flowers abound.

Another major square is called Independence Square. Once a thriving slave market, it is surrounded by private homes of Georgian architecture.

ORIENTATION

GETTING THERE   Dozens of daily flights on **American Airlines** (tel. toll free 800/433-7300) land in San Juan, Puerto Rico. From there, **American Eagle** (same phone) makes two daily nonstop flights into St. Kitts, with departures at 1:45pm and 9:30pm.

BWIA (tel. toll free 800/327-7401), the national airline of Trinidad and Tobago, offers nonstop 4-hour flights from New York's JFK three times a week. On days when there are no nonstop flights to St. Kitts, BWIA offers a connection through Antigua. From Miami, BWIA provides a daily direct 3-hour flight to St. Kitts, with a touchdown (but no change of plane) in Antigua.

If you're already on St. Maarten and want to visit St. Kitts (with perhaps a side trip to Nevis), you can do so aboard one of the most remarkable little airlines in the Caribbean. Known by its nickname, **Winair (Windward Islands Airways International)** (tel. 809/465-0810) makes several flights a week from St. Maarten to St. Kitts and Nevis, as well as to nearly a dozen other destinations in the Antilles.

GETTING AROUND   By Plane   Most visitors to St. Kitts or Nevis like to spend at least 1 day on the neighbor island. **LIAT** (Leeward Islands Air Transport) provides daily morning and afternoon flights to and from Nevis at a cost of $15 per person one way. Make reservations at the LIAT office on Fort Street in Basseterre (tel. 809/465-2286) instead of at the airport.

By Ferry   The government passenger ferry M.V. *Caribe Queen* departs from each island between 7:30 and 8:30am on Monday, Tuesday, Wednesday, Friday, and Saturday, returning at 4 and 6pm (check the time at your hotel or the tourist office). The cost is $4 each way.

By Taxi   Since most taxi drivers are also guides, this is the best means of getting around. You don't even have to find a driver at the airport—one will find you. Drivers also wait outside the major hotels. Before heading out, however, you must agree on the price—taxis aren't metered. Also, ask if the rates quoted to you are in U.S. dollars or the Eastern Caribbean dollar. To go from Golden Rock Airport to Basseterre costs about EC$13 ($4.80); to Sandy Point, EC$36 ($13.30) and up.

You can negotiate with a taxi driver to take you on a tour of the island for about

$48 for a 3-hour trip, and most drivers are well versed in the lore of the island. Lunch can be arranged either at the Rawlins Plantation Inn or the Golden Lemon.

By Rental Car   None of the big three U.S.-based car-rental companies maintains facilities in St. Kitts. Filling in the gap are some well-organized local companies.

Delisle Walwyn & Co., Liverpool Row, Basseterre (tel. 809/485-8449), is a local company offering cars and mopeds. Daily charges range from $28 to $45.

Holiday Car Rentals, South Independence Square, Basseterre (tel. 809/465-6507), has a wide range of vehicles for rent. Prices range from $33 to $45 per day ($198 to $280 per week). Minibuses are available at $60 per day ($365 per week). Tax is $5 extra. Unlimited mileage is included. There is a free pickup and delivery service at the airport and at most of the island's hotels.

Reflecting British tradition, *driving is on the left!* However, you'll need a local driver's license, which can be obtained at the Traffic Department, Cayon Street in Basseterre, for $12; the car-rental agencies can also issue you one and will include the fee in their rates.

FAST FACTS   ST. KITTS

Area Code   To call St. Kitts from the North American mainland, dial the 809 area code, then the local number. You don't need the area code once you're on the island.

Banking Hours   If you want to exchange your dollars into Eastern Caribbean dollars, you'll find banks open Monday through Friday from 8am to noon and also on Friday from 3 to 5pm.

Currency   The local currency is the **Eastern Caribbean dollar (EC$),** exchanged at about $2.70 to the U.S. dollar. Many bills, however, including those of hotels, are quoted in U.S. dollars. Always determine which "dollar" locals are talking about.

Customs   You are allowed in duty free with your personal belongings. Sometimes luggage is subjected to a drug check.

Drugstores   The **Medics Pharmacy,** Fort Street, Basseterre (tel. 465-5404), is open Monday through Friday from 8am to 6pm (to 1pm on Thursday) and on Saturday from 8am to 8pm. When the pharmacy is closed, you can call 465-2810 for 24-hour prescription service.

Electricity   St. Kitts' electricity is 230 volts AC, 60 cycles, so you'll need an adapter and a transformer for U.S.-made appliances.

Emergencies   Telephone 99 from Basseterre main exchanges and 999 from all other exchanges.

Entry Requirements   U.S. and Canadian citizens can enter with proof of citizenship, such as a voter registration card or birth certificate.

Hospital   In Basseterre, there is a 24-hour emergency room at **Joseph N. France General Hospital,** Buckley Site (tel. 465-2551).

Information   Tourist information is available from the tourist board's Stateside office, 414 E. 75th St., New York, NY 10021 (tel. 212/535-1234). Other offices are at 3166 River Rd., Suite 33, Des Plaines, IL 60018; and at 11 Yorkville Ave., Suite 508, Toronto, ON M4W 1L3.

Language   English is the language of the island, and is spoken with a decided West Indian patois.

Police   Call 99 in Basseterre and 999 elsewhere.

Safety   This is still a fairly safe place to travel. Most crimes against tourists—and there aren't a lot—are robberies on Conaree Beach, so exercise the usual precautions. It would be wise to safeguard your valuables. Women should not go jogging along deserted roads.

Taxes   The government imposes a 7% tax on rooms and meals, plus another EC$20 ($8) airport departure tax (but not to go to Nevis).

Telecommunications Telegrams and Telexes can be sent from Skantel, Cayon Street, Basseterre (tel. 465-2219), Monday through Friday from 8am to 6pm, on Saturday from 8am to 2pm, and on Sunday and public holidays from 6 to 8pm. International telephone calls, including collect calls, can also be made from this office.

Time St. Kitts is on Atlantic standard time all year. That means that in winter when it's 6am in Basseterre, it's 5am in Miami or New York. When the U.S. goes on daylight saving time, St. Kitts and the East Coast mainland are on the same time.

Tipping Most hotels and restaurants add a service charge of 10% to cover tipping. If not, tip 10% to 15%.

Water The water supply of the island is generally safe, but the cautious traveler will drink mineral water instead.

Weather St. Kitts lies in the tropics, and its warm climate is tempered by the trade winds. The average air temperature is 79° Fahrenheit and the average water temperature is 80°. Average rainfall is 55 inches. Dry, mild weather is usually experienced from November to April; May through October it's hotter and rainier.

WHERE TO STAY

VERY EXPENSIVE

GOLDEN LEMON, Dieppe Bay, St. Kitts, W.I. Tel. 809/465-7260, or toll free 800/633-7411. Fax 809/465-4019. 14 rms, 8 suites. A/C

$ Rates (including MAP): Winter, $225–$300 single; $325–$375 double or twin; $380 one-bedroom suite. Summer, $175–$250 single; $260–$300 double or twin; $320 one-bedroom suite. 4-night minimum stay and 2-week maximum stay required in season. AE, MC, V. **Parking:** Free.

⭐ Arthur Leaman, one-time decorating editor of *House & Garden* magazine, has used his taste and background to create a tiny oasis that is a citadel of charm in this once-busy French shipping port. The 1610 French manor house with an 18th-century Georgian upper story is set back from a coconut grove and a black volcanic-sand beach beyond St. Paul's on the northwest coast of St. Kitts. Flanking the great house are the Lemon Court and Lemon Grove Condominiums, where you can rent luxuriously furnished suites, surrounded by manicured gardens. Some have private pools. The spacious rooms are furnished with antiques and cooled by ceiling fans, and always contain fresh flowers. Five units contain minibars. "Sophisticated" and "elegant" describe the Golden Lemon and its clientele.

Dining/Entertainment: The Golden Lemon Restaurant serves a continental and Caribbean cuisine (see "Where to Dine," below).

Services: Massage, laundry, baby-sitting.

Facilities: Swimming pool, scuba and waterskiing.

JACK TAR VILLAGE ST. KITTS BEACH RESORT & CASINO, Frigate Bay (P.O. Box 406), St. Kitts, W.I. Tel. 809/465-8651, or toll free 800/999-9182. Fax 809/465-1031. 241 rms, 3 suites. A/C TV TEL

$ Rates (including meals, drinks, golf, and most water sports): Winter, $160 single; $260 double; from $440 suite for three. Summer, $130 single; $180 double; from $270 suite for three. $50 child under 12 sharing parents' room. AE, MC, V. **Parking:** Free.

The largest hotel on St. Kitts, and certainly the showcase hotel of the much-touted Frigate Bay development, is 1½ miles east of the airport on a flat, sandy isthmus between the sea and a saltwater lagoon; it seems a lot like a private country club. The resort is almost completely self-contained. Each of the regular units has a patio or balcony and tropical furniture. Most visitors prefer the second-floor rooms because of the higher ceilings. When you check in, ID tags are usually issued in an effort to help you get acquainted with your fellow guests.

Dining/Entertainment: The resort has four restaurants, a number of bars, and the island's only casino. Throughout the day an enthusiastic staff keeps anyone who's interested hopping from one organized activity to another, including Scrabble and shuffleboard tournaments, scuba lessons, and toga contests.

Services: Laundry, baby-sitting.

Facilities: Two swimming pool areas (one for quiet reading, another for active sports), four tennis courts (lit at night); nearby golf course.

RAWLINS PLANTATION, P.O. Box 340, Mount Pleasant, St. Kitts, W.I. Tel. 809/465-6221, or toll free 800/621-1270. Fax 809/465-4954. 10 rms.

$ Rates (including MAP): Winter, $250 single; $375 double. Summer, $215 single; $225 double. No credit cards. **Parking:** Free.

Among the remains of a muscovado sugar factory, near Dieppe Bay just outside St. Paul's on the northeast coast, this former plantation is 350 feet above sea level and enjoys cooling breezes from both ocean and mountains. Behind the grounds the land rises to a rain forest and Mount Misery. A 17th-century windmill has been converted into a charming accommodation, complete with private bath and sitting room; and the boiling houses, formerly housing a caldron of molasses, have been turned into a cool courtyard where guests dine amid flowers and tropical birds. Accommodations are rented in the main house, as well as in pleasantly decorated cottages equipped with modern facilities. The owners welcome you to swim in their pool (fed from their own mountain spring). Laundry and baby-sitting are offered.

THE WHITE HOUSE, P.O. Box 436, St. Peter's, St. Kitts, W.I. Tel. 809/465-8162. Fax 809/465-8275. 8 rms.

$ Rates (including MAP and afternoon tea): Winter, $250 single; $350 double. Summer, $200 single or double. AE, MC, V. **Parking:** Free. **Closed:** July–Aug.

Small and special, the White House boasts a plantation great-house ambience at the foot of Monkey Hill overlooking Basseterre, directly west of Golden Rock Airport. Set in stone cottages, the guest rooms are bright and airy, with four-poster beds and Laura Ashley fabrics.

Dining/Entertainment: The dining room, dominated by a gigantic mahogany table, serves an excellent cuisine with many unusual dishes, such as chilled and zesty watermelon soup with citrus flavoring, and "drunken" beef made with rum.

Services: Room service, laundry, shuttle to the beach.

Facilities: Grass tennis court, swimming pool

EXPENSIVE

OCEAN TERRACE INN, P.O. Box 65, Fortlands, St. Kitts, W.I. Tel. 809/465-2754, or toll free 800/524-0512. Fax 809/465-1057. 54 rms, 8 suites. A/C TV TEL **Directions:** Go west along Basseterre Bay Rd. past Cenotaph.

$ Rates: Winter, $83–$149 single; $105–$204 double; $220 one-bedroom unit for two. Summer, $91–$145 single; $92–$149 double; $161 one-bedroom unit for two. Breakfast $4.60 extra. AE, DC, MC, V. **Parking:** Free.

The Ocean Terrace Inn is affectionately known as the "O.T.I." If you want to be near Basseterre, it's the best hotel around the port. The O.T.I. commands a view of the harbor and the capital, with oceanfront verandas. It's so compact that a stay here is like a house party on a great liner. Terraced into a well-landscaped hillside above the edge of Basseterre, the hotel has particularly beautiful gardens and grounds.

All the handsomely decorated bedrooms have a light, tropical feeling and overlook a well-planted terrace. In addition to its stylish rooms in the hillside buildings, the hotel offers the Fisherman's Wharf and Village, a few steps from the nearby harbor. These wooden apartments are filled with most of the comforts of home.

Dining/Entertainment: The flagstone-edged swimming pool has a row of underwater stools where you'll be served well-made drinks while still immersed. My favorite of the four bars is in the shadow of an elaborate aviary. For further details on the cuisine here, see "Where to Dine," below.

Services: Room service, laundry, baby-sitting.

Facilities: Two pools, Jacuzzi, scuba diving, waterskiing facilities.

OTTLEY'S ESTATE, Ottley's (P.O. Box 345, Basseterre), St. Kitts, W.I. Tel. 809/465-7234. Fax 809/465-4760. 15 units. A/C

$ Rates: Winter, $120–$180 single; $140–$260 double. Summer, $90–$120 single; $110–$170 double. MAP $40 per person extra. AE, MC, V. **Parking:** Free. **Closed:** Sept.

North of Basseterre on the east coast, beyond Hermitage Bay, 6 miles north of airport, Ottley's became one of the most desirable places to stay on the island shortly after it opened in 1989. For those seeking charm and tranquility, it occupies an unbeatable 35-acre site on a former West Indian plantation founded in the 18th century, near a rain forest. Nine rooms are in an 1832 great house and six are divided among three cottages, with air conditioning and overhead fans. One structure is called English cottage, in memory of a visit by Princess Margaret.

The innkeepers are Ruth and Art Keusch, who operated a chain of bookstores in the Northeast, and Nancy and Marty Lowell. The great house contains a dining room, sitting room, and library. Antiques and West Indian furnishings blend to form the English colonial decor, and chintz and wicker combine to create a light, airy, tropical motif.

Dining/Entertainment: The plantation operates one of the best restaurants on the island, the Royal Palm. The good chef prepares classic and contemporary dishes, many light in sauce and texture, along with local favorites. There is a Sunday champagne brunch, and high tea is served on the veranda. With a day's advance notice, the kitchen will prepare a box lunch with directions as to how to reach one of many secluded beaches on the southeastern peninsula.

Services: Room service, laundry, baby-sitting, massage; daily shuttles to beaches, tennis, shops, golf course, and casino.

Facilities: Spring-fed, granite-tiled, 65-foot swimming pool in an old sugar factory.

MODERATE

BIRD ROCK HOTEL, Bird Rock, Frigate Bay, St. Kitts, W.I. Tel. 809/465-8914, or toll free 800/621-1270. Fax 809/465-1675. 16 rms, 8 suites. A/C TV TEL **Directions:** Head due east of Bay Road from Basseterre.

$ Rates: Winter, $95–$110 single or double; $175 one-bedroom suite; $250 two-bedroom suite. Summer, $65–$80 single or double; $125 one-bedroom suite; $170 two-bedroom suite. MAP $38 per person extra. AE, DC, V. **Parking:** Free.

This small hideaway is tucked away on the cliffs of St. Kitts overlooking the surf of a secluded beach. Opened in 1990, it attracts those desiring a peaceful haven. The bedrooms are comfortably and attractively furnished, with private baths. Balconies open onto a view of the beach, and tennis and water sports are available.

In addition to a coffee shop, its Sunburst Restaurant offers carefully prepared fresh food in varying combinations of local fare and continental dishes. Facilities include a swimming pool and tennis court, and snorkeling and water sports can be arranged. Laundry, baby-sitting, and room service are available.

FORT THOMAS HOTEL, P.O. Box 407, Fortlands, Basseterre, St. Kitts, W.I. Tel. 809/465-2695, or toll free 800/223-9815. Fax 809/465-7518. 64 rms. A/C TEL

$ Rates: Winter, $85 single; $100 double. Summer, $75 single; $85 double. AE, DC, MC, V. **Parking:** Free.

The Fort Thomas has a sweeping view of the sea from its position 2 miles south of the airport above the northern edge of town. Its spacious rooms have two double beds and private balconies. The hotel's restaurant, carvery, and barbecue are known for their relaxed atmosphere, excellent cuisine, and seasonal evening entertainment.

Tennis and free transportation to the beach can be arranged at the front desk. From the Olympic-size freshwater pool and the terrace bar you have a clear view of the neighboring island of Nevis.

FRIGATE BAY BEACH HOTEL, P.O. Box 137, Frigate Bay, St. Kitts, W.I. Tel. 809/465-8935, or toll free 800/223-9815. Fax 809/465-7050. 40 rms, 16 suites. A/C TEL

$ Rates: Winter, $95–$120 single or double; $125–$310 suite. Summer, $55–$65 single or double; $75–$155 suite. Breakfast $6.50 extra. AE, MC, V. **Parking:** Free.

On a verdant hillside east of Basseterre, Frigate Bay has white condominium villas administered as hotel units for their absentee owners. The central core of the resort contains a pair of round swimming pools and a cabaña bar where you can enjoy a drink while partially immersed. An 18-hole golf course and tennis courts are within walking distance. Units are nicely furnished to the taste of the owner and painted in an array of pastel colors. They have cool tile floors, air conditioning and ceiling fans, sliding glass doors that lead onto verandas, and private baths.

LEEWARD COVE CONDOMINIUM HOTEL, P.O. Box 123, Frigate Bay, St. Kitts, W.I. Tel. 809/465-8030, or toll free 800/223-5695. Fax 809/465-3476. 10 rms, 6 units. A/C

$ Rates: Winter, $75 single; $110 double; $155 one-bedroom unit; $250 two-bedroom unit. Summer, $45 single; $55 double; $110 one-bedroom unit; $155 two-bedroom unit. Complimentary car included for each week's stay in one of the apartments. Continental breakfast $4.50 extra. AE, DC, MC, V. **Parking:** Free.

Leeward Cove has condos for rent or sale. Overlooking a championship golf course in the Frigate Bay area directly east of Basseterre, the units are self-catering apartments with one or two air-conditioned bedrooms, baths, dining areas, completely equipped kitchens, and living rooms with ceiling fans and convertible sofas, which makes them suitable for four to six people. Standard bedrooms with private bath are also available. Added conveniences are a laundry, daily maid service, a minimart next door, all water sports, and nearby restaurants and a casino.

WHERE TO DINE

Most guests eat at their hotels; however, St. Kitts has a scattering of good restaurants where you are likely to have spiny lobster, crab back, pepperpot, breadfruit, and curried conch. The drink of the island is CSR (Cane Spirit Rothschild), a pure sugarcane liqueur developed by Baron Edmond de Rothschild. Islanders mix it with Ting, a bubbly grapefruit soda.

EXPENSIVE

GEORGIAN HOUSE, Independence Sq., Basseterre. Tel. 465-4049.
Cuisine: MEDITERRANEAN. **Reservations:** Required.
$ Prices: Appetizers $3.50–$10.50; main courses $12–$22. MC, V.
Open: Tues–Sat 11am–9pm, Sun 6–9pm.

In the heart of Basseterre, this restored Georgian manor decorated with antique reproductions once housed the exclusive Planters' Club and is said to be the oldest habitable building in St. Kitts. New Yorker Roger Doche, the owner and chef, offers a well-prepared and sophisticated menu with specials that change nightly. Perhaps you'll begin with his French onion or chilled cucumber soups, continuing with chicken cacciatore or shrimp marseillaise. Desserts are luscious, especially Tía Maria chocolate cake.

THE GOLDEN LEMON, Dieppe Bay. Tel. 465-7260.
Cuisine: CREOLE/SEAFOOD. **Reservations:** Required.
$ Prices: Fixed-price dinner $25–$40; lunch appetizers $2.50–$4; lunch main courses $8.50–$25. AE, MC, V.
Open: Lunch daily noon–3pm; dinner daily 7–10pm.

⭐ If you're touring St. Kitts, the best luncheon stop is at the Golden Lemon, a 17th-century house converted into a hotel (see "Where to Stay," above), on the northern coast beyond St. Paul's. Enjoy your lunch either on the hotel's gallery or in the garden. The food is very good, and the service is polite. Dinner is served in an elegant, candlelit dining room. The cuisine features Créole, continental, and American dishes, with locally grown produce. The menu changes daily, but is likely to include baked Cornish hen with ginger, fresh fish of the day, and Créole sirloin steak with a spicy rum sauce. Dress is casual chic.

THE PATIO, Frigate Bay Beach. Tel. 465-8666.

Cuisine: CARIBBEAN/CONTINENTAL. **Reservations:** Required.
$ Prices: Appetizers $5–$12; main courses $23–$35. MC, V.
Open: Dinner Mon–Sat 7:15–11pm. **Closed:** June–July.

The Patio is at the private home of a likable Kittitian family, the Mallalieus, 6 minutes southwest of the airport. Cocktails are served in the lush flower garden just a few feet from the rear terrace of the house. The family's high-ceilinged modern living room is transformed with antique furniture, tablecloths, and kerosene lanterns into a dining room. Meals include home-grown vegetables and a fresh seafood menu that changes nightly. Flame-broiled mahimahi with shrimp is a specialty, as is pepperpot, a traditional local dish. If you have any special menu requests, Peter Mallalieu will probably follow them: each dish is prepared to order.

MODERATE

THE ANCHORAGE, Frigate Bay Beach. Tel. 465-8235.

Cuisine: SEAFOOD. **Reservations:** Not required.
$ Prices: Salads and sandwiches from $5; main courses $8.80–$19.80. No credit cards.
Open: Daily 8am–midnight.

This isolated beachfront restaurant on the rolling acres of Frigate Bay sits in the shadow of an enormous leafy tree. The Anchorage's many-peaked roof shelters its concrete-slab floor from sudden showers. The owners prepare rum-based drinks and seafood, with a menu that offers four different salads, broiled or thermidor lobster, steak, hamburgers, 13 kinds of sandwiches, fresh fish, and ice cream. If you're looking for an unspoiled beach with a casual restaurant nearby, this may be a good selection for you.

BALLAHOO RESTAURANT, The Circus. Tel. 465-4197.

Cuisine: CARIBBEAN. **Reservations:** Recommended.
$ Prices: Appetizers $2–$6; main courses $6–$20. AE, MC, V.
Open: Mon–Sat 6:30am–10pm.

Overlooking the town center Circus Clock and entered from Fort Street, the Ballahoo is about a block from the sea on the second story of a traditional stone building. Its open-air dining area is one of the coolest places in town on a hot afternoon, thanks to the sea breezes and the high ceiling. Meals might include fresh local lobster, chili, shrimp, "blue parrot" fish filets, seafood platters with a coconut salad and rice, chicken in red wine, or baby back ribs. For dessert, try the extraordinary rum-and-banana toasted sandwich with ice cream.

FISHERMAN'S WHARF SEAFOOD RESTAURANT AND BAR, Fortlands, Basseterre. Tel. 465-2754.

Cuisine: SEAFOOD/CARIBBEAN. **Reservations:** Not required.
$ Prices: Appetizers $3–$6; main courses $8–$18. AE, MC, V.
Open: Dinner only, daily 6pm–midnight.

⭐ At the west end of Basseterre Bay Road, the Fisherman's Wharf is between the sea and the white picket fence surrounding the Ocean Terrace Inn. Its heart and soul lie near the busy buffet grill, where hard-working chefs prepare fresh seafood. An employee will take your drink order, but you personally place your food orders at the buffet grill. Specialties are grilled lobster, shrimp in garlic sauce, shark steak with local herbs and spices, and grilled catch of the day. On Wednesday and

Friday there's a calypso seafood all-you-can-eat buffet with live entertainment, which costs $20 per person.

JONG'S, Conaree Beach. Tel. 465-2307.
   Cuisine: ASIAN. **Reservations:** Required.
$ Prices: Appetizers EC$2–EC$3.50 (75¢–$1.30); main courses EC$18–EC$30 ($6.65–$11.10). AE.
   Open: Lunch Tues–Sat noon–2:30pm; dinner Tues–Sat 7–11pm (bar Tues–Sat 11am–midnight).

Directly west of the airport, Jong's is combined with Cisco's Hideaway Bar and serves the best Asian food on St. Kitts. Dishes are well prepared, and the service is efficient. Main courses include chicken, beef, lobster, conch in garlic-butter sauce, and ginger chicken. Shrimp in oyster sauce is a specialty.

OCEAN TERRACE INN, Fortlands. Tel. 465-2754.
   Cuisine: CARIBBEAN/AMERICAN. **Reservations:** Required. **Directions:** Drive west on Basseterre Bay Road to Fortlands.
$ Prices: Appetizers $3–$10; main courses $8–$25; three-course fixed-price lunch $13; four-course fixed-price dinner $15. AE, DC, MC, V.
   Open: Lunch daily noon–2pm; dinner daily 7:30–10:30pm.

Some of the finest cuisine in Basseterre is found here, along with one of the best views, especially at night when the harbor is lit up. Your dinner might begin with curried chicken broth, followed by sliced hard-boiled eggs in a mushroom sauce served on the half shell. Then comes an order of tasty fish cakes, accompanied by breaded carrot slices, creamed spinach, a stuffed potato, johnnycake, a cornmeal dumpling, and a green banana in a lime-butter sauce, topped off by a tropical fruit pie and coffee! The kitchen also prepares French or English dishes along with some flambé specialties, including Arawak chicken, chateaubriand, steak Diane, and veal Fantasia, along with pepperpot. Each Friday a steel band plays, and each Wednesday a local fashion show is presented, and a band plays for dancing. Dining is on an open-air veranda.

OTI TURTLE BEACH BAR & GRILL, Southeastern Peninsula. Tel. 469-9086.
   Cuisine: SEAFOOD. **Reservations:** Recommended. **Directions:** Follow the Kennedy Simmonds Highway over Basseterre's Southeastern Peninsula, then follow signs to OTI Turtle Beach Bar.
$ Prices: Appetizers $4; main courses $8–$16; three-course fixed-price lunch or dinner $16. AE, MC, V.
   Open: Lunch daily noon–3:30pm; dinner daily 7–9:30pm.

Set directly on the sands above Turtle Beach, this airy and sun-flooded restaurant is part of the Ocean Terrace Inn (see "Where to Stay," above). Many clients spend the hour before their meal swimming or snorkeling beside the offshore reef; others simply relax beneath the verandas or shade trees (hammocks are available), perhaps with a drink in hand. Windsurfing and volleyball are possible, and a flotilla of rentable sailboats moor nearby. Menu specialties might include stuffed broiled lobster, conch fritters, barbecued swordfish steak, prawn salads, and an array of grilled steaks. The hotel sometimes runs a shuttle service between the restaurant and the hotel's reception area.

INEXPENSIVE

VICTOR'S, 9 Stainforth St., Basseterre. Tel. 465-2518.
   Cuisine: CREOLE. **Reservations:** Not required.
$ Prices: Main courses EC$18–EC$35 ($6.65–$12.95). No credit cards.
   Open: Lunch Mon–Sat 11:30am–2:30pm; dinner Mon–Sat 6:30–9:30pm.

Victor's is a totally Kittitian neighborhood restaurant set behind Basseterre's Church of the Immaculate Conception. Appetizers aren't featured, but main courses might include deep-fried or steamed fish, boneless beef, curried chicken, mutton, spareribs, and a local specialty known as goat water.

WHAT TO SEE & DO

The island's chief sight is ✪ **Brimstone Hill,** 9 miles west of Basseterre on Main Road, a 1690 English fortress built by thousands of slaves who toiled for more than a century. Once known as the "Gibraltar of the West Indies," the complex is one of the best preserved of its type in the Caribbean. Once you leave the parking area that's in the former parade grounds of the 38-acre fortress, be prepared for a long walk to the top.

One of the Caribbean's major battles between the French and the English took place here in 1782, when the English garrison, outnumbered eight to one, succumbed to a French force. The following year the fort was restored to the British under the Treaty of Versailles, and they restored it.

Today you can see the ruins of the officers' quarters, barracks, the ordnance store, a cemetery, and the redoubts. The history of St. Kitts from the Stone Age is traced in a small museum. Dominating the southwestern sector of St. Kitts, the fort offers a magnificent view with a radius of 70 miles, including Saba and St. Eustatius to the northwest, St. Barts and St. Maarten to the north, and Montserrat and Nevis to the southeast. There's a $5 admission fee (half price for children). Brimstone Hill is open daily from 9:30am to 5:30pm (on Thursday and Sunday from 2 to 5:30pm).

Rugged visitors also make the 8-hour excursion to **Mount Liamuiga,** for which you should hire a guide. A Land Rover will take you part of the way. After that, it's a long, steady climb to the lip of the crater at 2,600 feet (the peak is at 3,792 feet). Hikers can descend into the crater, clinging to vines and roots.

At the hamlet of **Half-Way Tree,** a large tamarind marked the boundary in the old days between the British-held sector and the French half.

It was near the hamlet of **Old Road Town** that Sir Thomas Warner landed with the first band of settlers and established the first permanent colony to the northwest at Sandy Point. Sir Thomas's grave is in the cemetery of St. Thomas Church.

A sign in the middle of Old Road Town points the way to **Carib Rock Drawings,** all the evidence that remains of the former inhabitants. The markings are on black boulders, and the pictographs date back to prehistoric days.

Two commercial tours might interest you. Get your driver to take you to the **Sugar Factory,** which is best visited February through July, when you can see raw cane processed into bulk sugar. As mentioned, a very light liqueur, CSR, is now being produced at the factory, and it's enjoyed with a local grapefruit drink, "Ting." You don't need a reservation.

Guests are also allowed to visit the **Carib Beer Plant,** an English lager beer-processing house. Carib Beer is considered the best in the West Indies, if sales are any indication. At the end of the tour through the plant, visitors are given a cold Carib in the lounge. Check before heading there to see if it's open.

SPORTS & RECREATION

BEACHES Beaches are the primary concern of most visitors, who find the swimming best at the twin beaches of **Banana Bay** and **Cockleshell Bay,** **Conaree Beach** (2 miles from Basseterre), **Frigate Bay** (north of Banana Bay), and **Friar's Bay** (a peninsula beach that opens onto both the Atlantic and the Caribbean). The narrow peninsula in the southeast that contains the island's salt ponds also boasts the best beaches. All beaches, even those that border hotels, are open to the public. However, if you use the beach facilities of a hotel, you must obtain permission first and will probably be assessed a fee.

GOLF At Frigate Bay, there is the **Royal St. Kitts Golf Club,** an 18-hole championship golf course (tel. 465-8339), designed by Robert Trent Jones and connected to Jack Tar Village. Greens fees are $30 per game.

TENNIS The **Olympic Club,** just around the corner from the Ocean Terrace

Hotel, has tennis courts on which visitors can play. Also downtown, at the **St. Kitts Lawn Tennis Club,** you can arrange for a temporary membership. Call 465-2754 for details.

WATER SPORTS A variety of activities is offered by **Pro-Divers** at the Ocean Terrace Inn, Wigley Avenue (tel. 465-3223). From Fisherman's Wharf, you can swim, sail, float, paddle, or go on scuba-diving and snorkeling expeditions.

Scuba trips, including all gear and guided dive trips by boat, cost $40 for one tank per person, $60 for two tanks per person per day, and $200 for eight tanks per person over 4 days. Total training in scuba diving is offered in a full certification course, including all gear and text for $260.

Snorkel trips take you in a safety-equipped boat to good spots to see the underwater life around St. Kitts. Mask, fins, and snorkel are included in the cost of $25 per person per 3 hours for a minimum of two people.

SAVVY SHOPPING

The good buys here are in local handcrafts, including leather items made from goatskin, baskets, and coconut shells. Some good values are also to be found in clothing and fabrics, especially Sea Island cottons. Store hours vary, but are likely to be 8am to noon and 1 to 4pm Monday through Saturday.

CARIBELLE BATIK, Romney Manor, Basseterre. Tel. 465-6253.
This place qualifies as a sightseeing attraction as well as a shopping expedition. Its workroom and sales showrooms are in the most romantic setting of any shopping recommendation in this guide—the entire Romney Manor, a plantation established in the 17th century. You'll need to take a taxi, as it's reached via a short, steep road off the coast; it's right off Old Road in the shade of a huge 350-year-old saman tree. On the way, ask your driver to show you the Carib petroglyphs carved on stones (right near Old Road Town).

In the showroom a chart explains the batik process, and you can watch as island workers apply different layers of molten wax and color, both required in the printing process. Also there are facilities for tie-dye fabrics. The shop offers wall hangings made of Sea Island cotton, beautiful caftans, T-shirts (preshrunk), and batik pictures. U.S. citizens may make duty-free purchases here. It's open Monday through Friday from 8:30am to 4pm.

CRAFTSHOUSE, Plaza Treasury Pier. Tel. 469-5505.
Craftshouse is an outlet for the handcrafts of St. Kitts and Nevis made by craftspeople working through the National Handicraft and Cottage Industries Development Board. They offer items in copper, wood, coir (a coarse fiber made from the outside of a coconut), and coconut, including furniture. The shops, found at the Golden Rock International Airport and the shoreline Plaza Treasury Pier (Bay Road), are open during regular business hours.

PALMCRAFTS, Princes St., Basseterre. Tel. 465-2599.
One of several shops at Palms Arcade, Palmcrafts sells selected Caribbean handcrafts, larimar, sea opal, coral, and amber jewelry, along with Dutch wax and Java prints, West Indian spices, teas, and perfumes. It also carries a collection of designer tropical clothes.

A SLICE OF THE LEMON, in the Palms Arcade at the Circus in Basse-terre. Tel. 465-2889.
Here you'll find luxurious shopping at affordable prices. The Slice offers duty-free perfumes, watches, jewelry, china, crystal, and pottery.

SPENCER CAMERON GALLERY, South Independence Sq. Tel. 465-1617.
In this gallery in the center of Basseterre, British Rosey Cameron-Smith produces watercolors and limited-edition prints of scenes from St. Kitts and Nevis. Captivated by the island's charms, she makes an effort to reproduce in art some of the essence of

true West Indian life. Rosey is well known on the island for her paintings of Kittitian Carnival clowns. She also produces greeting cards, postcards, and calendars, as well as first-day covers of the Christmas stamps of Carnival clowns and masqueraders she painted for the government. She also displays the works of some 20 other artists. Exclusive Spencer Cameron designs decorate T-shirts and dresses silk-screened by hand in the gallery's workshop. Hand-screened silks, cottons, and jerseys are sold by the length. The gallery staff will direct you to their fabric outlets in the Circus.

ST. KITTS PHILATELIC BUREAU, Social Security Bldg., Bay Rd., Basseterre. Tel. 465-2874.

Stamp collectors interested in what is essentially a new stamp-issuing country can find distinctive specimens bearing the name of St. Kitts at the St. Kitts Philatelic Bureau.

EVENING ENTERTAINMENT

Ocean Terrace Inn's (O.T.I.) Fisherman's Wharf, Fortlands (see above), has a live band every Friday night from 8 to 10pm and a disc jockey from 10pm. (O.T.I's) **Turtle Beach Bar and Grill,** on the southeast peninsula (see above), has a Saturday "theme night" every other Saturday night, and every Sunday is the popular seafood buffet with a live steel band from 1 to 3pm. There's no cover charge at (O.T.I.) Fisherman's Wharf or (O.T.I.) Turtle Beach Bar & Grill. Bar prices range from beer at $1.60 to mixed drinks at $2.20.

If you're in the mood to gamble, St. Kitts's only casino is at the **Jack Tar Village,** Frigate Bay (tel. 465-8651). It's open to all visitors, who can try their luck at roulette, blackjack, craps, and slot machines. The casino is open nightly from 6pm to 2am. Cover charge is $40, including unlimited drinks.

---

4. NEVIS

Two miles south of St. Kitts, Nevis ("*Nee*-vis") was sighted by Columbus in 1493. He called it Las Nieves, Spanish for "snows," because its cloud-capped mountains reminded him of the snow-capped range in the Pyrenees. When viewed from St. Kitts, the island appears like a perfect cone, rising gradually to a height of 3,232 feet. A saddle joins the mountain to two smaller peaks, Saddle Hill (1,250 feet) in the south and Hurricane Hill (only 250 feet) in the north. Coral reefs rim the shoreline, and there is mile after mile of palm-shaded white sandy beaches.

Settled by the British in 1628, the volcanic island is famous as the birthplace of Alexander Hamilton, the American statesman who wrote many of the articles contained in the *Federalist Papers* and was Washington's Secretary of the Treasury. He was killed by Aaron Burr in a duel.

In the 18th century, Nevis, the "Queen of the Caribees," was the leading spa of the West Indies, made so by its hot mineral springs.

Once Nevis was peppered with prosperous sugarcane estates, but they are gone now—many have been converted into some of the most intriguing character hotels in the Caribbean. Sea Island cotton is the chief crop today.

As you drive around the nostalgic island, through tiny villages such as Gingerland (named for the spice it used to export), you'll reach the heavily wooded slopes of Nevis Peak, which offers magnificent views of the neighboring islands. Nevis is an island of exceptional beauty and has remained unspoiled. Its people, in the main, are descendants of African slaves.

On the Caribbean side, Charlestown, the capital of Nevis, was very fashionable in the 18th century, when sugar planters were carried around in carriages and sedan chairs. Houses are of locally quarried volcanic stone, encircled by West Indian fretted verandas. A town of wide, quiet streets, this port only gets busy when its major link to the world, the ferry from St. Kitts, docks at the harbor.

ORIENTATION

GETTING THERE   By Plane   You can fly to Nevis on **LIAT** (tel. 809/462-0700), the only carrier that offers scheduled service to the island. Flights from St. Kitts, Antigua, and Montserrat are usually nonstop, while flights from St. Croix, St. Barts, and Anguilla usually require at least one intermediate stop before reaching Nevis. No leg of any flight takes more than 25 minutes. The cost of flying one of LIAT's three nonstop flights between St. Kitts and Nevis—a 5-minute flight in either direction—is $38 round-trip.

Some visitors opt for the personalized attention of a small Nevis-based charter airline, **Carib Aviation,** Newcastle Village, Nevis (tel. 809/469-9295), which makes itself available for quickly arranged and highly flexible charters to and from any of Nevis's neighbors. Most flights have two to nine passengers on board. With advance notice, Carib will wait for Nevis-bound passengers at the Antigua airport and then fly them directly to Nevis; thereby passengers can avoid the transfer in St. Kitts. Carib's charge for a chartered plane containing two passengers to Nevis from Antigua is $120 each way.

The airport lies half a mile from Newcastle in the northern part of the island.

By Ferry   You can also use the **inter-island ferry service** from St. Kitts to Charlestown on Nevis aboard the government passenger ferry M.V. *Caribe Queen.* For information on this service, see "Getting Around" in the "St. Kitts" section.

GETTING AROUND   By Taxi   Taxi drivers double as guides, and you'll find them waiting at the airport at the arrival of every plane. A taxi ride between Charlestown and Newcastle Airport costs EC$30 ($11.10); between Charlestown and Old Manor Estate is EC$26 ($9.60); and from Charlestown to Pinney's Beach, EC$10 ($3.70). Between 10pm and 6am, 10% is added to the prices for Charlestown trips. A 3½-hour sightseeing tour around the island will cost $40; the average taxi holds up to four people, so when the cost is sliced per passenger, it's a reasonable investment. No sightseeing bus companies operate on Nevis, but a number of individuals own buses that they use for taxi service.

By Rental Car   If you're prepared to face the winding, rocky, potholed roads of Nevis, you can arrange for a rental car from a local firm through your hotel. Or you can check with **Skeete's Car Rental,** Newcastle Village, near the airport (tel. 809/469-9458). Prices start at $35 per day.

To drive on Nevis you must obtain a permit from the Traffic Department, which costs EC$30 ($11.10) and is valid until December 31 no matter when it's purchased. Remember, *drive on the left side of the road.*

 NEVIS

Language, currency, and entry requirements have already been discussed in the "St. Kitts" section. Most visitors will clear Customs in St. Kitts, so arrival in Nevis should not be complicated.

Area Code   To call Nevis from the mainland, dial area code 809 and then the local number. Once on the island, you don't need the area code.

Banking Hours   Banks are open Monday through Saturday from 8am to noon and most are also open on Friday from 3:30 to 5:30pm.

Drugstores   Try **Evelyn's Drugstore,** Charlestown (tel. 469-5278), open Monday through Saturday from 8am to 5:30pm and on Sunday from 7am to 8pm.

Electricity   As in St. Kitts, an electrical transformer and adapter will be needed for most U.S. and Canadian appliances as the electricity is 230 volts AC, 60 cycles. However, check with your hotel to see if they have converted their voltage and outlets.

Emergencies   For the **police,** call 809/469-5391.

Hospitals A 24-hour emergency room operates at **Alexandra Hospital** in Charlestown (tel. 469-5473).

Information The best source is the **Tourist Bureau** on Main Street in Charlestown (tel. 809/469-5521). The **St. Kitts–Nevis Tourist Board** in the U.S. is at 414 E. 75th St., New York, NY 10021 (tel. 212/535-1234).

Language English is the language of the island and is often accented with a lilting West Indian patois.

Post Office The post office, on Main Street in Charlestown, is open Friday through Wednesday from 8am to 3pm and on Thursday from 8 to 11:30am.

Safety Although crime is rare here, protect your valuables and never leave them unguarded on the beach.

Taxes The government imposes a 7% tax on hotel bills, plus a departure tax of EC$20 ($8) per person. You don't have to pay the departure tax in Nevis if you're returning to St. Kitts.

Telecommunications Telegrams and Telexes can be sent from the **Cable & Wireless office,** Main Street, Charlestown (tel. 469-5000). International telephone calls, including collect calls, can also be made from the cable office. Hours are 8am to 6pm Monday through Friday, to noon on Saturday; closed Sunday and public holidays.

Time As on St. Kitts, Nevis is on Atlantic standard time, which means it's usually 1 hour ahead of the U.S. East Coast, except when the mainland goes on daylight saving time; then clocks are the same.

Tips and Service A 10% service charge is added to your hotel bill. In restaurants it's customary to tip 10% to 15% of the tab.

Water The water is generally safe to drink and in good supply.

Weather The information regarding climate given in "Fast Facts: St. Kitts" is also true for Nevis.

WHERE TO STAY

VERY EXPENSIVE

FOUR SEASONS RESORT, Pinney's Beach, Nevis, W.I. Tel. 809/469-1111, or toll free 800/332-3442 in the U.S., 800/268-6282 in Canada. Fax 809/469-1112. 179 rms, 17 suites. A/C MINIBAR TV TEL

$ Rates: Winter, $400–$450 single or double. Summer, $225–$275 single or double. Year round, from $500 suite. MAP $60 per person extra. Service and tax extra. Golf packages available. AE, DC, MC, V. **Parking:** Free.

On the west coast directly north of Charlestown is a member of the Toronto-based Four Seasons chain. On an island known for its small and intimate inns, this newly built resort stands out as the largest, most accessorized, and best financed in Nevis. Designed in harmony with the surrounding landscape, the accommodations are scattered in a dozen two-story beach cottages. Almost 90% of the accommodations have views of the beach, while the others overlook Nevis peak and one of the golf-course fairways. Each contains all the amenities you'd expect in an urban hotel (including hairdryers and bathrooms with double sinks) as well as such Caribbean accents as spacious verandas or terraces and ceiling fans.

Dining/Entertainment: The resort's centerpiece is the plantation-inspired great house, which contains the main restaurant and bar. Satellite restaurants and bars sit beside the beach and beside the resort's swimming pool.

Services: 24-hour room service, laundry, baby-sitting; employees will arrange for diving, deep-sea fishing, boating, hiking, or shopping excursions.

Facilities: 18-hole golf course designed by Robert Trent Jones, direct access to one of the finest beaches in the Caribbean, 10 tennis courts with three different surfaces, massage facilities, health club, sauna, whirlpool, beauty salon.

MONTPELIER PLANTATION INN, St. John Figtree (P.O. Box 474), **Montpelier, Nevis, W.I. Tel. 809/469-5462,** or toll free 800/243-9420. Fax 809/469-1932. 16 rms, 1 suite. TEL
$ Rates (including MAP): Winter, $255 single; $350 double; from $360 suite. Summer, $120 single; $175 double; from $185 suite. DC, MC, V. **Parking:** Free. **Closed:** Aug 10–Oct 7.

Seven hundred feet up the slopes of Mount Nevis, east of Charlestown, on the southwest corner of the island toward Gingerland, the Montpelier offers rooms with private terraces and baths in modern cottages kept cool and fresh by light breezes. Other portions are on the foundations of the ruins of the great Montpelier estate. Much use has been made of local stonework and traditional architectural styles. An 18th-century sugar mill is at the center of the magnificent and extensive gardens.

Dining/Entertainment: The hotel concentrates on the quality of its food and uses fresh local produce when available. In season, several nights a week there are dances at nearby establishments, and Montpelier itself occasionally has a grand intra-island party, featuring a local scratch band, where almost half of Nevis shows up.

Services: Laundry, baby-sitting, breakfast room service.

Facilities: Swimming pool and pool bar, hard tennis court, 17-foot Boston whaler with an 85-hp outboard engine for waterskiing and snorkeling; horseback riding, sailing, and deep-sea fishing can be arranged.

NISBET PLANTATION BEACH CLUB, Newcastle, St. James' Parish, **Nevis, W.I. Tel. 809/469-9325,** or toll free 800/344-2049. Fax 809/469-9864. 26 rms, 12 suites. TEL **Directions:** Turn left out of the airport and go 1 ½ miles.
$ Rates (including MAP): Winter, $198–$265 single; $298 double; from $398 suite. Summer, $126–$194 single; $200 double; from $290 suite. AE, MC, V. **Parking:** Free.

In this gracious estate house on a coconut plantation, gentility and a respect for fine living prevail. This is the former home of Frances Nisbet, who married Lord Nelson at the age of 22. Although enamored of Miss Nisbet when he married her, Lord Nelson later fell in love with Lady Hamilton, and Frances Nisbet died a bitter old woman in England.

The present main building on the 30-acre plantation was rebuilt on the foundations of the original 18th-century great house. The ruins of a circular sugar mill stand at the entrance, covered with cassia, frangipani, hibiscus, and poinciana. Set in the palm grove are guest cottages consisting of superior and deluxe rooms with showers and covered verandas, and a series of junior suites with private baths. All rooms are doubles.

Dining/Entertainment: Breakfast is served on a veranda with a view down the wide grassy lawn lined with sentinel palm trees leading to a half-mile-long sandy beach, one of the best in Nevis. A beach bar and restaurant, serving both lunch and dinner, overlooks the swimming pool and beach. Dinner is also served in the main-house dining room, which is furnished with English antiques. Local fish and lobster, as well as a continental and American cuisine, are featured. A steel band plays for Sunday barbecues on the beach.

Services: Laundry, baby-sitting, breakfast room service.

Facilities: Hard tennis court, 3 miles of beachcombing and shelling along two neighboring bays; swimming area with good snorkeling, protected by an offshore reef; horseback riding available.

EXPENSIVE

GOLDEN ROCK ESTATE, P.O. Box 493, Gingerland, Nevis, W.I. Tel. **809/469-3346,** or toll free 800/223-9815. Fax 809/469-2113. 15 rms, 1 suite.

$ Rates: Winter, $165 single; $175 double; from $200 suite. Summer, $85 single; $100 double; from $125 suite. Children under 2 stay free in parents' room. MAP $35 per person extra. AE, MC, V. **Parking:** Free. **Closed:** Sept.

⑤ A sugar estate built in 1815 high in the hills of Nevis, a 15-minute drive east of Charlestown, has been turned into one of the most charming and atmospheric inns in the Caribbean. You walk through a 25-acre garden in a tropical setting of about 150 acres. The original windmill, a stone tower, has been turned into a duplex honeymoon suite (or accommodations for a family of four or five), with an elaborate four-poster bed. Rooms are scattered about the garden, and each villa has four-poster king-size beds made of bamboo. Fabrics are island made, with tropical flower designs. In addition, rooms have large porches with views of the sea. The owner-manager is Pam Barry.

Dining/Entertainment: Wine is included at dinner, which is likely to be a West Indian meal (ever had stuffed pumpkin?) served at the 175-year-old "long house." Before dinner you can enjoy a drink in the hotel's bar. A separate facility at Pinney's Beach, the Carousel Bar, serves lobster, shrimp, grilled fish, and hamburgers with coconut-husk flavor; it's open daily during the winter season. Picnic lunches can be prepared in the hotel's kitchen.

Services: Laundry, baby-sitting; free round-trip shuttles to both beaches, with stops in Charlestown if requested.

Facilities: Freshwater swimming pool with a shady terrace (where tropical rum punches are served), tennis court, hiking through a rain forest; access to one beach on the leeward side, part of Pinney's Beach, and another beach on the windward side where there is surfing.

HERMITAGE PLANTATION, Hermitage Village, St. John's Parish, Nevis, W.I. Tel. 809/469-3477, or toll free 800/223-9815. Fax 809/469-2481. 10 rms, 4 suites. **Directions:** Proceed on the main island road 4 miles from Charlestown.

$ Rates: Winter, $180 single; $195 double; from $275 suite. Summer, $75 single; $100 double; from $180 suite. MAP $45 per person extra. AE, MC, V. **Parking:** Free.

★ This much-photographed, frequently copied historians' delight is said to be the oldest all-wood house in the Antilles and was built amid the high-altitude plantations of Gingerland in 1740. Here, former Philadelphian Richard Lupinacci and his wife, Maureen, have assembled one of the best collections of antiques on Nevis. Wide-plank floors, intricate latticework, and high ceilings add to the beauty of this hotel. Accommodations are in nine glamorous outbuildings designed like small plantation houses. Many contain huge four-poster beds, antique accessories, and colonial louvered windows. Gently sloping land inland from the sea, the property is protected by parallel rows of dry retaining walls.

Services: Laundry.

Facilities: Swimming pool, tennis court, thoroughbred stables.

MOUNT NEVIS HOTEL, Newcastle (P.O. Box 494), Charlestown, Nevis, W.I. Tel. 809/469-9373, or toll free 800/255-9684. Fax 809/469-9375. 32 rms. A/C TV TEL

$ Rates: Winter, $170 single or double; $210 deluxe studio for two. Summer, $120 single or double; $150 deluxe studio for two. Breakfast $5–$10 extra. AE, MC, V. **Parking:** Free.

On the slopes of Mount Nevis a 5-minute drive southwest of Newcastle Airport, this hotel offers rooms with private baths and VCRs. Private balconies open onto scenic views.

Dining/Entertainment: A beachfront restaurant, located 1 mile from the hotel, features excellent homemade pizzas, sandwiches, and salads. The Waves restaurant serves a Caribbean and continental cuisine. Local bands are often brought in to entertain.

Services: Beach shuttle, room service during mealtimes.

Facilities: Outdoor swimming pool; water-sports program with windsurfing, waterskiing, snorkeling, and deep-sea fishing.

OLD MANOR ESTATE, P.O. Box 70, Gingerland, Nevis, W.I. Tel. 809/ 469-5445, or toll free 800/223-9815. Fax 809/469-5388. 14 rms.

$ Rates (including MAP): Winter, $165 single; $245 double. Summer, $120 single; $185 double. AE, MC, V. **Parking:** Free.

East of Charlestown and north of Gingerland, at a cool and comfortable elevation of 800 feet, the Old Manor Estate has an old-world grace that makes it the most desirable hotel of its kind on Nevis. When Nevis was originally colonized, the forested plot of land on which the hotel sits was granted to the Croney family in 1690 by the King of England. The estate thrived as a working sugar plantation until 1936. Today the stately ruins of its great house, once dubbed by British historians as "the best example of Georgian domestic architecture in the Caribbean," complement the hotel's accurately and gracefully restored outbuildings. Scattered around the property are the rusted flywheels of cane-crushing machines whose bases are engraved "GLASGOW—1859–1861." The former smoke-house and jail were replaced by a rambling villa called the Overseer's Building.

Each of the accommodations contains wide-plank floors of tropical hardwoods, plushly comfortable colonial-reproduction furniture, and high ceilings. The resort is not recommended for children under 12, a fact much appreciated by many of the sophisticated guests. Owner Vicki Knorr is a considerate hostess.

Dining/Entertainment: A big part of the success of Croney's is the culinary inspiration of Mrs. Knorr. Her Cooperage dining room (see "Where to Dine," below) is the finest on the island. Breakfast is served daily in guests' bedrooms. Lunch is in the raftered dining room or beside an unusual swimming pool chiseled from fitted blocks of black volcanic rock. You serve yourself from a buffet table and a century-old grill in the plantation's colonial kitchens. Every Friday night there's a popular barbecue-and-buffet party.

Services: Beach and town shuttle.
Facilities: Swimming pool.

MODERATE

HURRICANE COVE BUNGALOWS, Oualie Beach, Nevis, W.I. Tel. 809/ 469-9462. Fax 809/469-9462. 9 bungalows, 1 villa.

$ Rates: Winter, $115 one-bedroom unit; $175 two-bedroom unit; $350 three-bedroom villa. Summer, $75 one-bedroom unit; $125 two-bedroom unit; $225 three-bedroom villa. No credit cards. **Parking:** Free. **Closed:** Sept.

These modern bungalows are nestled in a garden with a world-class view on the northernmost point of Nevis, a 20-minute drive east of the airport. Owners Mr. and Mrs. Bob Turner operate this little resort on a strictly EP arrangement, with a full-kitchen concept; most inns on the island operate on the MAP, so a stay at Hurricane Cove allows guests to dine at different inns every night or prepare their own meals in their kitchens or at a poolside barbecue grill. Bungalows are constructed of hardwood with tile roofs, each with a queen-size bed, covered porch, private bath, ceiling fan, and kitchen. Three contain TVs. On the grounds is a three-bedroom villa with a small private pool. A freshwater pool was built into the foundation of a 250-year-old fortification, and the beach is nearby.

WHERE TO DINE

The local food is good. Suckling pig is roasted with many spices, and eggplant is used in a number of tasty ways, as is the avocado. (*Note:* You may see turtle on some menus, but remember that this is an endangered species.)

THE COOPERAGE, in the Old Manor Estate, Gingerland. Tel. 469-5445.
Cuisine: AMERICAN/CARIBBEAN. **Reservations:** Recommended, especially for those not staying in the hotel.

$ Prices: Lunch from $15; dinner from $35. AE, MC, V.

Open: Lunch daily noon–3pm; dinner daily 7–9:30pm.

⭐ Directly east of Charlestown and north of Gingerland, the Cooperage is the previously recommended hotel's dining room, in a reconstructed 17th-century building where coopers once made barrels for the sugar mill. Under the sophisticated guidance of Ohio-born Vicki Knorr, the dining room has a high, raftered ceiling and stone walls. Lunch includes spinach salad, stuffed Caribbean lobster, and fruit desserts. At dinner, you might choose shrimp with coconut served on spinach, curried chicken breasts "Old Manor style" with homemade noodles, local fish bought fresh each morning, or a succulent variety of local shrimp.

HERMITAGE PLANTATION, Hermitage Village, St. John's Parish. Tel. 469-5477.

Cuisine: INTERNATIONAL. **Reservations:** Required. **Directions:** Proceed south on the main island road from Charlestown.

$ Prices: Lunch from $6–$15; dinner $35. AE, MC, V.

Open: Lunch daily noon–2:30pm; dinner daily at 8pm.

You can combine an excellent dinner with a visit to the oldest house on Nevis, now one of the island's most unusual hotels (see "Where to Stay," above). Meals are served on the latticed porch of the main house, amid candles and good cheer. Maureen Lupinacci, who runs the place with her husband, Richard, sees to combining continental recipes with local ingredients. Have a before-dinner drink in the colonial-style living room before you enjoy the likes of snapper steamed in banana leaves, carrot-and-tarragon soup, brown-bread ice cream, and a delectable version of rum soufflé. Nonresidents are accepted as dinner guests. Many turn up on Wednesday for the roast pig dinner.

MONTPELIER PLANTATION INN, Montpelier. Tel. 469-5462.

Cuisine: INTERNATIONAL. **Reservations:** Recommended for those not staying at the hotel.

$ Prices: Lunch buffet $20; fixed-price three-course dinner $40. DC, MC, V.

Open: Lunch daily noon–2:30pm; dinner daily at 8:15pm. **Closed:** Aug 10–Oct 7.

This previously recommended hotel (see "Where to Stay," above), on the southwest corner of the island toward Gingerland, offers some of the finest dining on the island. You dine on the veranda at this grand old West Indian mansion. Lobster and fish such as red snapper are served the day the catch comes in. The menu is eclectic, and sometimes you'll find roast beef and Yorkshire pudding. Suckling pig is also a specialty. The candlelit dinner has one seating, so try to show up on time. A buffet lunch is offered daily, and one of the local bands comes in to entertain about every 10 days.

OUALIE BEACH CLUB, Oualie Bay, Nevis, W.I. Tel. 469-9735.

Cuisine: SEAFOOD. **Reservations:** Not required.

$ Prices: Appetizers $2–$5; main courses $4–$15. AE, MC, V.

Open: Lunch daily noon–3pm; dinner daily 6–9pm.

⑤ The Oualie Beach Club, 5 miles north of Charlestown, offers dishes made from lobster, conch, fish, and shrimp, cooked using West Indian recipes with a hint of American or European influence. Daily specials are posted on the notice board and may include Créole conch stew or spinach-stuffed chicken breasts.

The club, owned by the Yearwood family, also offers 12 rooms built in the traditional West Indian style about 20 yards from the beach. Some units have kitchens. In winter, daily EP rates are $95 single and $115 double; summer EP rates are $65 single and $85 double. Tax and service are extra. Also on the premises is Scuba Safaris (see "Sports and Recreation," below).

UNELLA'S, Charlestown Harbour. Tel. 469-5574.

Cuisine: AMERICAN/CARIBBEAN. **Reservations:** Recommended.

$ Prices: Appetizers EC$12–EC$17 ($4.45–$6.30); main courses EC$20–EC$46 ($7.40–$17). MC, V.

Open: Lunch Mon–Sat 11:30am–3pm; dinner daily 6:30–11pm.

Homelike and hospitable, Unella's serves American-type food with a West Indian flavor. Owned by one of the island's younger matriarchs, Unella Archibald, it serves food continuously until "the customers are satisfied." Built long ago as a private house near the ferry pier, Unella's is made of brick and wood, with a prominent second-story balcony. Specialties are fish chowder, a succulent version of conch sautéed in garlic butter, curried lamb, and fresh fish and Caribbean lobster.

WHAT TO SEE & DO

When you arrive at the airport, negotiate with a taxi driver to take you around Nevis. The distance is only 20 miles, but you may find yourself taking a long time if you stop to see specific sights and talk to all the people who will want to engage you in conversation.

The major attraction is the **Birthplace of Alexander Hamilton,** on Main Street in Charlestown (tel. 469-5786), overlooking the bay. Mr. Hamilton was the illegitimate son of a Scotsman, James Hamilton, and Rachel Fawcett, a Nevisian of Huguenot ancestry. The family left the island in 1760 and never returned. The lava stone house by the shore has been restored, and a small museum, dedicated to Nevis history and Hamilton himself, has been established. The Archives of Nevis are housed there. The museum is open Monday through Friday from 8am to 4pm and on Saturday from 10am to noon. No admission is charged, but donations are accepted.

At Bath Village, about half a mile from Charlestown, stands the Bath Hotel, in serious disrepair, and its **Bath House,** which has been restored to use. The hotel was built in 1778 by John Huggins to accommodate some 50 guests, mostly wealthy planters in the West Indies who were afflicted with rheumatism and gout. The hotel had five hot baths built, in which temperatures ranged up to 108° Fahrenheit. It shut down in 1870. Both the hotel and the Bath House were acquired by the Nevis Island government in 1983, and the Bath House has been renovated and reopened for use under the management of the Ministry of Tourism; it has quickly become popular with both islanders and tourists.

Nearby, **St. John's Church** stands in the midst of a sprawling graveyard in Fig Tree Village. It is said to have been the parish church of Lady Nelson, wife of Horatio Lord Nelson. An 18th-century church of gray stone, it contains the record of Nelson's marriage to Frances Nisbet in the church register.

At Morning Star Plantation nearby, the **Nelson Museum** contains a large collection of Nelson memorabilia gathered by Robert D. Abrahams, a Philadelphia lawyer. Among items displayed is a faded letter written by Nelson with his left hand, after he lost his right one. Also exhibited are paintings depicting Nelson's romance with Lady Hamilton, plus dining chairs from the admiral's flagship, the *Victory.* See also a grandfather clock that was deliberately (and permanently) stopped the moment Queen Elizabeth II entered the museum on February 22, 1966. The museum can be visited free Monday through Saturday from 9:30am to 1pm.

Fort Ashby is now overgrown, but it was once used by Lord Nelson to guard his ships in Nevis while they took on fresh water and supplies. Nearby is **Nelson's Spring,** near Cotton Ground Village. In the 18th century, Nelson is said to have watered his ships here before they left to fight in the American Revolution. The fort, in sad disrepair, overlooks the site of Jamestown, an early settlement that was devastated by a 1680 tidal wave.

The **Eden Brown Estate,** about a mile and a half from New River, is said to be haunted. Once it was the home of a wealthy planter, whose daughter was to be married, but her husband-to-be was killed in a duel at the prenuptial feast. The mansion was then closed forever and left to the ravages of nature. A gray solid stone still stands. Only the most adventurous come here on a moonlit night.

Outside the center of Charlestown, the **Jewish Cemetery** was restored in part by an American, Robert D. Abrahams, the Philadelphia lawyer already mentioned. At the lower end of Government Road, it was the resting place of many of the early shopkeepers of Nevis. At one time, Sephardic Jews who came from Brazil made up a quarter of the island's population. It is believed that Jews introduced sugar production into the Leewards. Most of the tombstones date from between 1690 and 1710.

SPORTS & RECREATION

BEACHES The best beach on Nevis—in fact, one of the best beaches in the Caribbean—is the reef-protected **Pinney's Beach,** which has clear water and gradual slope, and is just north of Charlestown. You'll have 3 miles of sand (often virtually to yourself) that culminates in a sleepy lagoon. It's best to bring your own sports equipment; while hotels are stocked with limited gear, it may be in use by other guests when you want it.

GOLF The **Four Seasons,** Pinney's Beach (tel. 469-1111), has one of the most challenging and visually dramatic golf courses in the world. Designed by Robert Trent Jones, Jr. (who called it "the most scenic golf course I've ever designed"), this 18-hole championship golf course wraps around the resort and offers spectacular ocean and mountain views at every turn. From the first tee (which begins just steps from one of the most accessorized Sports Pavilions in the Caribbean) through the 660-yard, par-5, to the 18th green at the ocean's edge, the course is, in the words of one avid golfer, "reason enough to go to Nevis."

HORSEBACK RIDING Horseback riding is available at the **Nisbet Plantation Inn,** Newcastle (tel. 469-9325), discussed earlier. You can ride English saddle, and the cost is $25 per person for 1½ hours. With a guide, you're taken along mountain trails and you visit sites of long-forgotten plantations along the way.

MOUNTAIN CLIMBING This is strenuous, and is recommended only to the stout of heart. Ask your hotel to pack a picnic lunch and arrange a guide (who will probably charge about $25 for two hikers). Hikers can climb **Mount Nevis,** 3,500 feet up to the volcanic (extinct) crater and enjoy a trek to the rain forest to watch for wild monkeys.

TENNIS Most of the major hotels have tennis courts.

WATER SPORTS & FISHING For **snorkeling,** head for Pinney's Beach. You might also try the waters of Fort Ashby, where the settlement of Jamestown is said to have slid into the sea; legend has it that the church bells can still be heard and the undersea town can still be seen when conditions are just right. So far, no diver, to my knowledge, has ever found the conditions "just right."

Scuba Safaris Ltd., Oualie Beach (tel. 469-9518), offers scuba diving and snorkeling in an area rich in dive sites. They also offer resort and certification courses, dive packages, and equipment rental. A one-tank scuba dive costs $45. Glass-bottom-boat and snorkeling trips take you from Nevis across the narrows to St. Kitts. The 30-foot glass-bottom boat goes at a leisurely pace, and masks, fins, snorkels, snorkel vests, rum punch, and drinks are provided during the 2½-hour cruise. Boat charters to Basseterre, Banana Bay, Cockleshell Bay, and other beaches are offered, as well as deep-sea fishing trips on request. Scuba Safaris operates in conjunction with Oualie Beach Club, Oualie Bay (tel. 469-9735).

The **fishing** is excellent—especially for snapper, grouper, bonita, and kingfish. The best hotel for making boating arrangements is the **Golden Rock,** P.O. Box 493, Nevis, W.I. (tel. 809/469-5346), which takes diesel boats out in search of dolphin (the fish), wahoo, or Spanish mackerel. The cost is $150 for 4 hours of fishing. The Golden Rock has its own 16-foot Boston whaler for waterskiing, light offshore fishing, and snorkeling and scuba diving.

SAVVY SHOPPING

Normal store hours are 8am to noon and 1 to 4pm, but on Thursday some places close in the afternoon and on Saturday some stay open to 8pm. Most are closed Sunday.

NATIONAL HANDICRAFT AND COTTAGE INDUSTRIES DEVELOPMENT BOARD, Pinney's Industrial Site, Charlestown. Tel. 469-5505.

This branch of the Development Board's Craftshouse sales outlets offers a variety of handcrafted articles made of coconut shell. Open: Mon–Fri 8am–noon and 1–4pm.

NEVIS HANDICRAFT COOPERATIVE SOCIETY LTD., Cotton House, Charlestown. Tel. 469-1746.

In a stone building about 200 feet from the wharf, near the marketplace, this handcraft shop contains locally made gift items, including unusual objects of goatskin, local wines made from a variety of fruits grown on the island, hot-pepper sauce, guava cheese, jams, and jellies. Open: Mon–Fri 8:30am–12:30pm and 1:30–4pm, Sat 8:30am–12:30pm.

NEVIS PHILATELIC BUREAU, Head Post Office, Market St., Charlestown. Tel. 469-5535.

Those interested in stamp collecting can go to the Nevis Philatelic Bureau to see the wide range of colorful stamps. It lies next to the public market. Open: Mon–Fri 8:30am–4pm.

SOUTHERN CROSS DESIGNS, Walwyn Plaza. Tel. 469-5205.

Southern Cross Designs feature hand-embroidered styles and Nevis themes often form the motif in the patterns. Resort-type shirts and skirts are sold, and they're quite beautiful. The little industry provides work for many craftspeople on the island. Its label, Caribee Clothes, is sold in many fine West Indian boutiques and in the States.

THE SAND BOX TREE, Parkview Plaza, Charlestown. Tel. 469-5662.

Housed in a 100-year-old estate off Main Street overlooking Grove Park, this shop offers gifts, clothing, furniture, and works of art. It's also the home of the Cinnamon Hill Fabric Workshop where you can see cottons silk-screened by hand. The fabric is available by the yard and is suitable for garments, slipcovers, and curtains. Open: Mon–Fri 9am–4:30pm, Sat 9am–1pm.

TROPICAL TREASURES, Oualie Beach. Tel. 469-9638.

The place to shop on your way to the beach, Tropical Treasures offers a full line of bathing suits for men, women, and children, plus cover-ups and beach bags. Suntan lotions, sunglasses, snorkeling gear, and souvenirs make this the most complete beach store on Nevis. Open: Daily 10am–4:30pm.

SCHOOL FOR THE BLIND, Government Rd. Tel. 465-2584.

Heading up Government Road, you reach the School for the Blind, where the Nevisians make handcrafts for sale. Go only if you want to buy something. Open: Mon–Wed 9am–noon and 1–4pm, Sat 9am–noon.

5. ANGUILLA

It's small, serene, secluded, and special. The most northerly of the Leeward Islands in the eastern Caribbean, 5 miles north of St. Maarten, Anguilla (rhymes with "vanilla") is only 16 miles long, with 35 square miles in land area. Columbus may have spotted the island, and may have called it *anguilla* (Spanish for "eel") because of its elongated shape. Anguilla has very little rainfall so the soil is unproductive, with mainly low foliage and sparse scrub vegetation, but the beaches of white coral sand around the island are outstanding.

The little island has a population of some 7,000 people, predominantly of African descent but also some of European, particularly Irish. Most of the locals work in the tourist industry or in lobster fishing.

First colonized by the British in 1650, the island was subjected to sporadic raids by Irish and French freebooters. Attempted invasions by the French in 1745 and 1796 were repulsed, the latter by heroic Anguillans who fed their cannons with lead balls from their sprat nets. Once part of the federation with St. Kitts and Nevis, Anguilla gained its independence from that association in 1980 and has since been a self-governing British possession.

Anguilla used to be for the adventurous explorers attracted to its unspoiled nature. However, with the opening of some super-deluxe (and super-expensive) hotels in the 1980s, Anguilla was suddenly "discovered," and has become one of the most chic targets in the Caribbean. Recently some hotels have opened that are aimed at the "mid-market" price range. Not wanting to be "spoiled," Anguilla has controlled development so most operations are small and informal.

ORIENTATION

GETTING THERE By Plane Various airlines maintain more than 50 scheduled flights per week into Anguilla, not counting the many charter flights. Because there are no nonstop flights to Anguilla from mainland North America, visitors usually transfer through either San Juan, Puerto Rico, or nearby St. Maarten. Some visitors also come in from St. Kitts, Antigua, and St. Thomas.

One of the most reliable services into Anguilla is offered by **American Eagle** (tel. toll free 800/433-7300), the commuter partner of American Airlines, which offers twice-daily nonstop service to Anguilla from its hub in San Juan. Holding between 20 and 50 passengers, flights leave San Juan at 2:05 and 9:26pm. Return flights from Anguilla depart for San Juan at 8:30am and 3:50pm. Because schedules are subject to change, check with the airline or your travel agent.

From Dutch St. Maarten, **Winair** (Windward Islands Airways International) (tel. 775-0183 in Anguilla, or 5/54230 in St. Maarten) offers at least three scheduled flights daily, usually on Twin Otters. Winair also offers daily flights to Anguilla from St. Thomas.

Leeward Islands Air Transport (LIAT) (tel. 809/465-2286) offers three flights per week from Antigua and five flights per week from St. Kitts.

Air Anguilla (tel. 809/497-2643) and **Tyden Air** (tel. 809/497-2719) can arrange charters from Anguilla to and from all neighboring islands. Tyden Air is probably the more flexible and service-oriented of the two. It maintains a kiosk at the St. Maarten airport and is usually able to shuttle clusters of passengers—sometimes on short notice—between St. Maarten and Anguilla for around $30 per person.

Flying time from St. Maarten to Anguilla is 7 minutes; from San Juan and Antigua, 1 hour; from St. Thomas, 45 minutes; and from St. Kitts, 30 minutes.

By Ferry Ferries run between the ports of Marigot Bay, French St. Martin, and Blowing Point, Anguilla, at approximately 30-minute intervals daily. The first ferry leaves St. Martin at 8:10am and the last at 5:40pm; from Blowing Point, the first ferry leaves at 7:30am and the last at 5pm. Two night ferries from Marigot Bay (French St. Martin) depart at 7 and 10:45pm. The one-way fare for a day ferry is $8, and a night ferry, $12. There is a $5 departure tax. No reservations are necessary.

GETTING AROUND By Taxi The best way to get an overview of the island is on a taxi tour. In about 2 hours, a local driver (all of them are guides) will show you everything for $40 and up. If you're visiting just for the day (as most sightseers do), you can be let off at your favorite beach after a look around, and then be picked up and returned to the airport in time to catch your flight back to wherever.

By Rental Car To explore the island in any detail, it's best to rent a car. There are several rental agencies on the island that can issue the mandatory Anguillian driver's licenses, which are valid for 3 months. These are also issued at police headquarters in the Valley and at ports of entry. You'll need a valid driver's license from your home country, and pay a one-time fee of $6. Remember to *drive on the left!*

Most experienced visitors to Anguilla pay a taxi to carry them from the island's airport to their hotel, and then, the following day, arrange for a rental car to be delivered to wherever they're staying. Each of the island's car-rental companies delivers vehicles to anywhere on Anguilla for no extra charge, and each offers slight discounts for rentals of 7 days or more.

Two of North America's largest car-rental firms are represented on Anguilla, **Budget** (tel. toll free 800/527-0700) and **Avis** (tel. toll free 800/331-2112). Budget, located at Stoney Ground Road in Sandy Ground (tel. 497-2217), is the cheaper and more convenient of the two. With a 2-day advance reservation, Budget's cheapest car rents for $30 per day, with unlimited mileage, plus 6% tax. The optional but highly recommended extra insurance costs an extra $5 a day.

You can request a car through Avis's toll-free number, but no confirmation or guarantee will be issued unless you use a credit card or until you mail a deposit of $50 to $100 within 2 weeks to a month of the anticipated pickup of your car, depending on the season. Prices start at $35 per day plus 6% tax. The collision-damage insurance is mandatory and costs $7 extra per day. If you're interested, contact **Bennie & Sons,** Blowing Point, Anguilla, B.W.I. (tel. 809/497-6221).

A final possibility involves renting an automatic- or standard-shift car or Jeep from **Connor's Car Rental,** c/o Maurice Connor, P.O. Box 65, South Hill, Anguilla, B.W.I. (tel. 809/497-6433). Daily rates are $35 to $60. Mileage is unlimited, but gas is extra.

FAST FACTS ANGUILLA

Area Code Calls can be made directly from the U.S. by dialing the area code, 809, then 497 plus four digits. Don't use the area code when you're on the island.

Banking Hours Banks are open Monday through Thursday from 8am to 1pm and on Friday from 8am to 1pm and 3 to 5pm.

Currency The **Eastern Caribbean dollar (EC$)** is the official currency of Anguilla, although U.S. dollars are the actual "coin of the realm." The official exchange rate is EC$2.70 to each $1 U.S. (EC$1 = 37¢ U.S.).

Customs Even for tourists, duties are levied on goods imported into the island at varying rates: from 5% on foodstuffs to 30% on luxury goods, wines, and liquors.

Documents Visitors require a valid passport, or a birth certificate along with a photo ID such as a driver's license, or a voter registration card. All visitors must have an onward or return ticket.

Drugstores Go to the **Government Pharmacy,** in the Cottage Hospital, The Valley (tel. 497-2551). In addition, the **Paramount Pharmacy,** Waterswamp (tel. 497-2366), has a 24-hour emergency service, although standard hours are 8:30am to 8:30pm daily.

Electricity The electricity is 110 volts AC, so no converters or adapters are necessary for U.S. appliances. Except in the Valley area, electricity is usually provided by privately owned generators.

Holidays Special holidays include May 30 (Anguilla Day), August Monday (the first Monday in August), August Thursday (the Thursday after August Monday), Constitution Day (the Friday after August Monday), and December 19 (Separation Day).

Information Go to the **Anguilla Department of Tourism,** P.O. Box 60, The Valley, Anguilla, B.W.I. (tel. 809/497-2759). In the U.S., contact the **Anguilla Tourist Information & Reservations Office,** c/o Medhurst & Associates, Inc., 271 Main St., Northport, NY 11768 (tel. 516/261-1234, or toll free 800/553-4939). The **Anguilla Hotel and Tourism Association,** P.O. Box 104, The Valley, Anguilla, B.W.I. (tel. 809/497-2944), may also be useful.

Language English is spoken here, often with a West Indian accent.

Medical Care For medical services, there is a **Cottage Hospital,** The Valley (tel. 497-2551), plus several district clinics.

Police You can reach the police at their headquarters in the Valley (tel. 497-2333) or the substation at Sandy Ground (tel. 497-2354).

Post Office The main post office is in the Valley (tel. 497-2528). Collectors consider Anguilla's stamps valuable, and the post office also operates a philatelic bureau. Hours are 8am to noon and 1 to 3:30pm Monday through Friday, and 8am to noon on Saturday.

Radio   A daily broadcast service is provided by **Radio Anguilla,** which operates on a frequency of 1505 kHz (200m) with a power of 1,000 watts.

Safety   Although crime is rare here, secure your valuables; never leave them in a parked car or unguarded on the beach. Anguilla is one of the safest destinations in the Caribbean, but you should take the usual discreet precautions advised anywhere.

Taxes   The government collects an 8% tax on rooms and a departure tax of $6.25 U.S. or $16 E.C. if you leave the island by air.

Telecommunications   Telephone, cable, and Telex services are offered by **Cable and Wireless Ltd.,** Wallblake Road (tel. 497-2210), open Monday through Saturday from 7:30am to 10:30pm and on Sunday from 10am to 8pm.

Time   Anguilla is on Atlantic standard time, which means it's usually 1 hour ahead of the U.S. East Coast. When the mainland goes on daylight saving time, the clocks are the same.

Weather   The hottest months in Anguilla are July to October; the coolest, December to February. The mean monthly temperature is about 80° Fahrenheit.

WHERE TO STAY

Don't forget that an 8% government tax will be added to your hotel bill, plus 10% for service. In addition to the following, the Ferryboat Inn, listed under "Where to Dine" (see below), has reasonably priced accommodations.

VERY EXPENSIVE

CAP JULUCA, Maunday's Bay (P.O. Box 240), Anguilla, B.W.I. Tel. 809/497-6666, or toll free 800/323-0139. Fax 809/497-6617. 84 rms, 14 suites. A/C MINIBAR TEL.

$ **Rates** (including continental breakfast): Winter, $390–$600 single or double; $875–$1,500 one-bedroom suite for two; $1,350–$1,800 two-bedroom suite for four; extra person $150. Summer, $255–$390 single or double; $565–$975 one-bedroom suite for two; $880–$1,170 two-bedroom suite for four; extra person $100. AE. **Parking:** Free. **Closed:** Sept–Oct.

Cap Juluca is one of the most boldly conceived, most luxurious, and most pampering oases in the Caribbean. Named after the rain god (Juluca) of the island's long-ago inhabitants, the Arawaks, and occupying a rolling 179-acre site along the southwestern coast on one of the island's best beaches, Cap Juluca was the brainchild of half a dozen original investors who each achieved a measure of fame for their investment savvy on Wall Street. In their wake has followed a constant stream of Hollywood stars and financial barons.

The architects were given free rein to create a Moorish fantasy with white walls, palms, and bougainvillea. Accommodations are in villas evocative of Marrakesh, Morocco. Most have soaring domes, walled courtyards, labyrinthine staircases, and concealed swimming pools ringed with thick walls. Inside, a mixture of elegantly comfortable wicker furniture is offset with Moroccan accessories. Each unit faces one of the world's most perfect beaches, whose coral sands sprawl seaward toward a view of the blue-tinged mountains of French St. Martin. Most units can be expanded from deluxe doubles into one- or two-bedroom suites.

Expected amenities include air conditioning (or ceiling fans if you prefer), safety-deposit boxes, ice makers, king-size beds, marbled and mirrored bathrooms, and plenty of space.

Dining/Entertainment: A continental breakfast is served daily on your terrace.

On the premises are two interconnected restaurants: the less formal Italian terrace, Chatterton's, and the richly formal French/Caribbean restaurant, Pimms (see "Where to Dine," below). Live music is presented several times a week, and there's an informal lunch restaurant set beside the swimming pool.

Services: Laundry, massage, concierge, shuttle buses from the guest rooms to the hotel's restaurants and bars.

Facilities: Water sports (including waterskiing, fishing, windsurfing, Sunfish sailing, and snorkeling), championship tennis court, large pool.

MALLIOUHANA, Meads Bay (P.O. Box 173), Anguilla, B.W.I. Tel. 809/497-6111, or toll-free 800/422-1323. Fax 809/497-6011. 34 rms, 17 suites. MINIBAR TEL

$ **Rates:** Winter, $480–$600 single or double; from $600 suite for two. Summer, $240–$325 single or double; from $425 suite for two. 7-night minimum stay required Dec 18–Mar 31. Tax and service extra. Breakfast $12 extra. No credit cards. **Parking:** Free.

⭐ The Malliouhana is named for the Carib word for Anguilla, but this is all that's primitive about this deluxe and glamorous hotel, one of the most discreetly elegant in the Caribbean. Established in 1984 by the Anglo-French Roydon family, it occupies a rocky bluff jutting seaward between sandy beaches, in the southwest corner of the island beyond Long Bay, 8 miles northwest of the airport. Privacy plays a pivotal role at Malliouhana, where thick walls and shrubbery provide anonymity. The entire complex occupies 25 acres of sloping scrubland whose central core is landscaped into terraces and banks of flowers, pools, and fountains. At its edges sprawl almost 2 miles of white sand beaches.

Both public and private areas enjoy open-air themes ringed with plants and sea or garden views. A fine assemblage of Haitian art and the rest of the decorations were chosen by the famed "Boston Brahmin" decorator, Lawrence Carleton Peabody II. The spacious bedrooms and suites are distributed among the main buildings and outlying villas. Each room has tropical furnishings and wide private verandas. Each of the villas can be rented as a single unit or subdivided into three comfortable accommodations.

Dining/Entertainment: The resort's restaurant is considered one of the most prestigious in the Caribbean (see "Where to Dine," below). Scattered over the premises are a handful of bars for drinking and snacking throughout the day.

Services: Room service (7am–11pm), laundry, massage, tennis lessons from a qualified pro, concierge.

Facilities: Beauty salon, boutiques, TV room, library, water-sports center with instruction in practically everything, four tennis courts (two lit for night play), gym with resident instructor.

EXPENSIVE

CINNAMON REEF BEACH CLUB, Little Harbour, Anguilla, B.W.I. Tel. 809/497-2727, or toll free 800/223-1108. Fax 809/497-3727. 14 suites, 8 villas. A/C MINIBAR TEL

$ **Rates:** Winter, $250–$325 single or double; two-bedroom suite $400. Summer, $150–$225 single or double; two-bedroom suite $350. Extra person $60. MAP $50 per person extra. AE, MC, V. **Closed:** Sept–Oct.

⭐ One of the most sophisticated resorts in the British Leewards, this small and intimate hotel lies 2 miles west of the airport on the southern coast, astride a circular cove whose calm waters are said to be the best on the island for windsurfing. The resort's Mediterranean-inspired 7-acre core is set on 30 acres of rolling scrubland. Because of its limited size, and the personal attention of managers Norman and Marilyn Luxemburg, guests have the feeling of living in a pleasantly informal private estate. Accommodations are in white stucco villas and garden suites, where large archways lead onto private terraces. Each unit contains screened-in verandas, well-appointed bedrooms and dressing areas, ceiling fans, and spacious living rooms.

Dining/Entertainment: The Palm Court Restaurant and the rambling bar area are the focal points (see "Where to Dine," below). The views over the veranda are of the reef-sheltered harbor. Some entertainment and occasional dancing is offered at night.

Services: Room service (during meal hours), laundry.

Facilities: Freshwater pool, hot tub and Jacuzzi, two championship tennis courts, beach sheltered by a reef; free sailboats, paddleboats, windsurfers, and snorkeling and fishing equipment; scuba diving can be arranged.

COCCOLOBA, Barnes Bay (P.O. Box 332), Anguilla, B.W.I. Tel. 809/497-6871, or toll free 800/833-3559. Fax 809/497-6332. 9 rms, 2 suites, 40 cottages. A/C MINIBAR TEL

$ Rates (including American breakfast): Winter, $360 single or double; $460 ocean-view cottage for one or two; $760 one-bedroom suite for one or two. Summer, $195 single or double; $275 ocean-view cottage for one or two; $500 one-bedroom suite for one or two. Extra person $100. Taxes and service extra. Dinner $40 per person extra. Packages available. AE, MC, V. **Parking:** Free.

One of the island's most solidly comfortable resorts is built on a rocky headland which juts seaward between two of the island's excellent beaches, 7 miles west of the airport. Originally built on 30 acres of seaside scrubland by expatriate Iranian investors during the 1980s, it reminds many newcomers of a chic resort in the Mediterranean. Gaily striped parasols and awnings, an interconnected series of swimming pools, and an alluring swim-up bar contribute to the holiday flavor. The resort's reception lies under a soaring A-frame building. Accommodations ramble along a low-rise bluff above the sea, and most are in simple cottages with verandas and summer-inspired furniture.

Dining/Entertainment: The resort is justly proud of the Caribbean/Créole and French/American cuisine served in its only restaurant, the Pavilion. A pair of bars operate beside the pool and the beach.

Services: Room service (for continental breakfast only), laundry, massage, island tours.

Facilities: Freshwater pool with adjacent Jacuzzi and swim-up bar, two tennis courts (lit at night); deep-sea fishing, sunset-cruise trips, and waterskiing can be arranged.

THE MARINERS, Road Bay (P.O. Box 139), Sandy Ground, Anguilla, B.W.I. Tel. 809/497-2671, or toll free 800/223-0079. Fax 809/497-2901. 43 rms, 19 suites. TEL

$ Rates (including full board): Winter, $200–$285 single; $210–$490 double; from $710 suite for two. Summer, $135–$265 single; $145–$370 double; from $640 suite for two. AE, MC, V. **Parking:** Free.

Vacationers may be tempted to return again and again to this all-inclusive resort west of the airport. It occupies a flat sandy area beside an isolated beach whose access road winds between flowering shrubs and hillocks. Accommodations are in three two-story buildings and cottages delightfully embellished with gingerbread. All rooms have ceiling fans (some are air-conditioned), modern tile baths, and decor reminiscent of New England summer cottages in the 1930s.

Services: Room service, laundry.

Facilities: Swimming pool, tennis court, two Jacuzzis.

MODERATE

ANGUILLA GREAT HOUSE, Rendezvous Bay (P.O. Box 157), Anguilla, B.W.I. Tel. 809/497-6061. Fax 809/497-6019. 15 rms, 10 suites. TEL

Directions: From the main road at the airport, turn left and continue through two traffic circles; then follow the signs.

$ Rates: Winter, $185–$210 single; $200–$230 double; from $325 one-bedroom suite. Summer, $105–$110 single; $115–$120 double; from $215 one-bedroom suite. Breakfast $8.50 extra. AE, MC, V. **Parking:** Free.

You'll find a luxuriously modernized form of West Indian hospitality here. The buildings are typically Anguillan with gingerbread trim and painted shutters, and an informality pervades the place. Cooled by ceiling fans, the bedrooms have either twin or queen-size beds and are traditionally decorated with Victorian reproductions made in Jamaica. All accommodations open onto their own verandas, while some suites have their own living rooms and dining areas, plus fully equipped kitchenettes.

Guests enjoy food at the Great House Beach Bar & Restaurant, where both West Indian and continental cuisine are served. A variety of water sports can be arranged. Laundry, baby-sitting, and room service (9am to 9:30pm) are provided.

LA SIRENA, Meads Bay (P.O. Box 200), Anguilla, B.W.I. Tel. 809/497-6827. Fax 809/497-6829. 27 rms, 3 villas. TEL

$ Rates (including American breakfast): Winter, $120 single; $180–$215 double; from $240 villa. Summer, $70–$90 single; $95–$135 double; from $140 villa. AE, MC, V. **Parking:** Free.

Set only 300 feet from the beach, a 10-minute taxi ride from the airport, this resort is run by a Swiss couple. Each comfortable room has a ceiling fan and a balcony. Some of the more expensive units are villas with fully equipped kitchens. Villas contain TVs, and the hotel rooms have minibars. There is a swimming pool, tennis is available nearby, and laundry service and car rentals can be arranged. Opening onto Mead's Bay, the hotel operates two restaurants, the informal Coconuts and the more elegant Top of the Palms. The chef specializes in New American cuisine and seafood along with Swiss fondues and other international dishes. There's a Caribbean night each Thursday, with music and buffets, and a Sunday brunch with steel band music.

INEXPENSIVE

INTER-ISLAND GUEST HOUSE, Lower South Hill, Anguilla, B.W.I. Tel. 809/497-6259. Fax 809/497-5381. 10 rms, 4 suites. MINIBAR

$ Rates: Winter, $35 single; $50 double; from $85 suite. Summer, $25 single; $40 double; from $75 suite. Tax and service extra. Breakfast from $6 extra. AE, MC, V. **Parking:** Free.

Originally built in 1975 in a residential neighborhood near Sandy Ground, on the main road west of the airport, this two-story villa with upper and lower covered verandas overlooks the sea and neighboring French St. Martin. It's some 3 miles from the beach, so if you're a devoted sand buff you'll need a car. The guesthouse offers simple but comfortable bedrooms, each with a private bath and ceiling fans, and one- and two-bedroom apartments. Everything is kept sparkling clean. There's a restaurant and bar on the premises that serves a good West Indian cuisine.

CONDOS & VILLAS

Sunshine Villas in Anguilla, P.O. Box 142, Anguilla, B.W.I. (tel. 809/497-6149, or 215/565-3462 in the U.S.; fax 809/496-6021), is a widely scattered collection of elegant villas organized into one rental group by Canadian expatriates Jim and Judy Henderson. Currently they "market and manage" several houses, each of which has its own particular virtues. If you write to them, the Hendersons will send detailed information and sometimes photos, advertising special features of particular villas. Each comes with daily maid service. Year-round rentals for two usually range from $140 to $375.

CARIMAR BEACH CLUB, Meads Bay (P.O. Box 327), Anguilla, B.W.I. Tel. 809/497-6881, or toll free 800/235-8667. Fax 809/497-6071. 23 units.

$ Rates: Winter, $285 one-bedroom unit; $385 two-bedroom unit; $615 three-bedroom unit. Summer, $119 one-bedroom unit; $179 two-bedroom unit; $300 three-bedroom unit. AE, MC, V. **Parking:** Free.

Opening onto beautiful Meads Bay, this is considered the best of the small apartment hotels on the island, where you get the privacy of an apartment yet some of the comforts of a hotel. The well-appointed units are in two-story Mediterranean-style villas, each with a large living room, dining area, and patio or balcony overlooking mile-long Meads Bay Beach. For dinner, if you want to splurge, you can go over to the super-priced Malliouhana, nearby, for a meal. The hotel is west of the airport beyond Long Bay.

EASY CORNER VILLAS, South Hill (P.O. Box 65), Anguilla, B.W.I. Tel. 809/497-6433, or toll free 800/223-9815. Fax 809/497-6410. 22 units. TV

$ Rates: Winter, $160 one-bedroom unit; $195 two-bedroom unit; $240 three-bedroom unit. Summer, $125 one-bedroom unit; $155 two-bedroom unit; $195 three-bedroom unit. AE, MC, V. **Parking:** Free.

On the main road west of the airport, the Easy Corner Villas are owned by Maurice E. Connor, the same man who rents many of the cars on the island. The one-, two-, and three-bedroom units are in landscaped settings with sunset views of sailboats and beach frolickers from the private porches. All units have full kitchens, combination living/dining rooms, porches, large and airy rooms, ceiling fans (some are air-conditioned), private baths, and light rattan furniture. Children over the age of 2 are welcome, and daily maid service is available at an extra charge.

THE SEAHORSE, Rendezvous Bay (P.O. Box 17), Anguilla, B.W.I. Tel. 809/497-6751. Fax 809/497-6756. 5 units.

$ Rates: Winter, $680 per week for two. Summer, $420 per week for two. No credit cards. **Parking:** Free.

The Seahorse features five one-bedroom apartments, each spacious and well furnished, with a fully equipped kitchen, bath, and private gallery where you can view the sunset. Fans and the trade winds cool the rooms. At water's edge is a barbecue area for outdoor cooking or enjoying a drink. The location is west of the airport at the end of Rendezvous Bay, opening onto a 4-mile strip of almost-deserted white sandy beach with excellent swimming. Maid service is provided 6 days a week.

WHERE TO DINE

Order spiny lobster if you can get it—it's very good here and invariably fresh. Seafood lovers will also enjoy the crayfish, whelk, yellowtail, and red snapper. Home-grown vegetables accompany many local dinners, and the major resorts serve some of the most elegant continental fare in the West Indies.

VERY EXPENSIVE

MALLIOUHANA RESTAURANT, Meads Bay. Tel. 497-6111.

Cuisine: FRENCH/CARIBBEAN. **Reservations:** Required.

$ Prices: Appetizers $10–$27 at lunch, $12–$30 at dinner; main courses $12–$30 at lunch, $27–$32 at dinner. AE, MC, V.

Open: Lunch daily 12:30–3:30pm; dinner daily 7–10:30pm.

Eight miles northwest of the airport, the most Europeanized restaurant in Anguilla offers the most intensely structured service rituals, some of the finest food, and a clientele whose somewhat self-conscious glamour is perhaps the most theatrical on the island. Michel Rostang, the successful son of the legendary Jo Rostang, one of the most famous chefs of southern France, is in charge. You'll dine in an open-sided cedarwood pavilion built atop a rocky promontory jutting seaward. There's lots of space between tables, an ocean view, a superb wine list, and a splashing fountain that rambles against one edge of the dining area.

Menu items might include a fish soup with croûtons and a garlicky rouille sauce, a gratinée of pumpkin soup with sorrel, goat cheese wrapped in fresh salmon and served with a sweet-pepper sauce, grilled filet of snapper with fennel in a light anchovy sauce, a suprême of Bresse chicken with lemon spaghetti, or veal chop in its own curry-enriched juices. Dessert might be a caramelized pear with tea sauce and chocolate sorbet, or a confit of apples in crisp pastry served with apricot sauce.

PIMMS, in the Cap Juluca, Maunday's Bay. Tel. 497-6666.
Cuisine: FRENCH/CARIBBEAN. **Reservations:** Required.
$ Prices: Appetizers $9–$16; main courses $24–$32. AE.
Open: Dinner only, daily 6:30–9:30pm. **Closed:** Sept–Oct.

Pimms is the most elegant restaurant on Anguilla and one of the finest in the Caribbean. Set among the archways and domes of Anguilla's most spectacular resort, Cap Juluca, it blends the finest culinary standards of the Old and New Worlds with fresh and exotic ingredients flown in regularly. Tables overlook the island's most spectacular beach and are lit with flickering candlelight.

The menu might include a spicy and succulent version of beignets de crabe Pimms, a cannelloni of smoked salmon filled with a tartare of salmon and a coulis of fresh herbs, grilled tuna steak served with a coriander-and-ginger sauce, medallions of veal with a parsley-and-paprika sauce, or grilled sirloin of black Angus. Desserts feature pastries, mousses, and sherbets.

EXPENSIVE

BARREL STAY BEACH BAR & RESTAURANT, Sandy Ground. Tel. 497-2831.
Cuisine: FRENCH. **Reservations:** Recommended.
$ Prices: Appetizers $6–$20; main courses $16–$30. AE, MC, V.
Open: Lunch daily 11am–3pm; dinner daily 6:30–9:30pm.

This restaurant's walls, screens, tables, chairs, and bars are fashioned from barrels and disassembled barrel stays. The establishment sits beside the beach and has ample space for dining or drinking—there is an outdoor drink terrace and a smaller inner bar that sees most of its activity at night.

A favorite here is fish soup served in the French fashion, the conch maison, or the island fish with garlic sauce. You can also order barbecued lobster, steak au poivre, stuffed crab, or veal kidneys in the provençal style. A selection of French wines is offered at reasonable prices, along with rum drinks and beer.

MANGO'S, Barnes Bay. Tel. 497-6492.
Cuisine: NEW AMERICAN. **Reservations:** Recommended for lunch, required for dinner.
$ Prices: Appetizers $3.75–$7 at lunch, $3.75–$6 at dinner; main courses $10–$28 at lunch, $10–$29 at dinner, $8–$14.95 at Sun brunch. AE, MC, V.
Open: Lunch Wed–Mon noon–2:30pm; dinner Wed–Mon at 6:30–7pm and at 8:30–9pm; brunch Sun 10:30am–2:30pm. **Closed:** Aug–Oct.

In a white concrete and wood pavilion set a few steps from the edge of the sea on the northwest part of the island, this is probably the most alluring independent restaurant on Anguilla. The fun, unpretentious, charming restaurant is operated by the Blanchard family, who immigrated to Anguilla from Vermont after selling a company they founded that manufactured salad dressings. The pavilion was built in a West Indian style suited to the prevailing winds and sea views.

Lunch features open-face melted sandwiches, omelets, gazpacho, and salads. Dinner specialties might include blackened Anguillan lobster, grilled filets of whatever fish is freshest that day, Mango's calypso chicken, pepper-encrusted yellowfin tuna, and lots of richly caloric (and very tempting) desserts. You can order tropical drinks in the small cocktail area.

PALM COURT RESTAURANT, in the Cinnamon Reef Beach Club, Little Harbour. Tel. 497-2727.
Cuisine: NEW CARIBBEAN. **Reservations:** Recommended.
$ Prices: Appetizers $5–$12; main courses $6–$19 at lunch, $16–$30 at dinner. AE, MC, V.
Open: Lunch daily noon–2:30pm; dinner daily 7–9:30pm.

In one of the finest small hotels on Anguilla, this restaurant has earned an excellent reputation for the finesse of its cuisine. Tables are scattered before a sweeping view of an almost perfectly circular bay whose waters are sheltered by an offshore reef. Lunches are informal sun-flooded affairs and feature Anguillan lobster or chicken salads; succulent soups; seafood pasta made with grilled snapper, cream, and herbs; and sandwiches ranging from tuna burgers to lobster clubs.

The real allure of the cuisine, however, appears at dinner, with a coconut/chicken soup, a Caribbean-inspired pasta primavera made with only local pumpkin, cassavas, peppers, eggplants, and christophines; pan-seared filet of snapper with soy-laced beurre blanc sauce; a curried chicken pot pie; or perhaps a breast of duck with fresh pineapple-ginger sauce. Desserts might include mango puffs in caramel sauce or a mousse ringed with bananas flambéed at tableside.

PARADISE CAFE, Katouche Bay. Tel. 497-3210.
    Cuisine: INTERNATIONAL/ORIENTAL. **Reservations:** Recommended.
$ Prices: Appetizers $5–$8 at lunch, $6–$8 at dinner; main courses $6–$12.50 at lunch, $14–$25 at dinner. AE, MC, V.
    Open: Lunch daily noon–2pm; dinner daily 6:30–9pm.

Set amid what might be the most steeply inclined landscape on Anguilla, this independent restaurant has cantilevered terraces above a sweeping view of the sea. Attracting a clientele of movie stars, singers, politicians, the rich and famous, and a scattering of ordinary folks, it lies adjacent to the Masara Resort on the west coast near Crocus Bay and the Valley.

Lunches might include grilled burgers, Indonesian satays (heavily spiced beef, chicken, or seafood grilled on bamboo skewers), or fish soup with chili butter. Dinner specialties include a sizzling filet of rockfish with a sake-tamarind sauce, Szechuan beef with cherry-flavored oyster sauce, and such desserts as key lime pie or bread pudding with a whisky-rum sauce.

PAVILION RESTAURANT, in the Coccoloba Hotel, Barnes Bay. Tel. 447-6871.
    Cuisine: INTERNATIONAL. **Reservations:** Recommended.
$ Prices: Lunch appetizers $6–$8; lunch main courses $10–$17; fixed-price three-course dinner $36. AE, MC, V.
    Open: Lunch daily 12:30–2:30pm; dinner daily 7–9:30pm.

The Coccoloba Hotel's main dining room is open to visitors who telephone in advance. Seven miles west of the airport, it offers tables exposed to the sea breezes on two sides and whimsically elegant Caribbean style. Lunches are informal, with chilled lobster soup, avocado and grapefruit salads, and seafood sandwiches made from fresh salmon and tuna. Dinners are more elaborate and might include freshly marinated suprême of salmon, veal salad, grilled catch of the day, and chicken chiquita (boneless breast with ham and bananas, served on a julienne of carrots). Dessert might be Black Forest or coconut cake.

MODERATE

CHATTERTON'S, in the Cap Juluca, Maunday's Bay. Tel. 497-6666.
    Cuisine: NORTHERN ITALIAN. **Reservations:** Recommended.
$ Prices: Appetizers $3–$16; main courses $14–$25. AE, MC, V.
    Open: Lunch daily noon–2:30pm; dinner daily 6:30–9:30pm. **Closed:** Sept–Oct.

Set in a low-slung oceanside pavilion, west of Rendezvous Bay, this elegant but informal restaurant offers a lighthearted alternative to the intensely cultivated cuisine offered by Cap Juluca's main restaurant, Pimms. You'll dine within view of one of Anguilla's most spectacular beaches. The seafood-laden menu lists four different preparations of pasta; carpaccio of beef sprinkled with parmesan; a salad of smoked salmon with fresh tuna, capers, red onions, and salsa verde; stufadoti pesce, composed of fresh fish and shellfish in a herb-laden broth and served over pasta; tonno provenzale (grilled tuna on a bed of spinach, served with capers, black olives, vinaigrette sauce, and fettuccine); and pizzas.

FERRYBOAT INN, Cul de Sac Rd., Blowing Point (P.O. Box 189), Anguilla, B.W.I. Tel. 809/497-6613.
    Cuisine: CARIBBEAN/FRENCH. **Reservations:** Recommended. **Directions:**

Turn right just before the Blowing Point Ferry Terminal and travel 150 yards before making a left turn.

$ Prices: Appetizers $4.50–$16; main courses $6.50–$25. AE, MC, V.
Open: Lunch daily noon–2:30pm; dinner Mon–Sat 7:30–10pm. **Closed:** Sept (usually, but not always); Tues in summer.

Established by English-born John McClean with his Anguillan wife, Marjorie, and set directly on the beach a short walk from the Blowing Point ferry pier, this restaurant comes well recommended. Specialties are French onion soup, black-bean soup, some of the best lobster thermidor on the island (liberally laced with brandy, cream, and both parmesan and gouda cheese), and scallop of veal Savoyard (with white wine and fresh cream). Don't miss the house's special planter's punch.

The McCleans also rent nine simple but comfortable apartments, which (considering the high prices of Anguilla) represent good value. Single or double occupancy costs $150 to $180 per day, EP; in summer, prices are reduced to $85 to $125 single or double.

HIBERNIA, Island Harbour. Tel. 497-4290.

Cuisine: SEAFOOD/FRENCH. **Reservations:** Required.
$ Prices: Appetizers $5.50–$8.50; main courses $16–$28. AE, MC, V.
Open: Lunch Tues–Sun noon–2pm; dinner Tues–Sun 7–9pm. **Closed:** Sept–Oct.

Hibernia is a lovely little spot in a West Indian–style house with a veranda overlooking Scilly Cay, on the northeast corner of the island. Small and intimate, it contains only 10 tables. It's the personal statement of a French chef, Raoul Rodríguez, and Irish-born Mary Pat O'Hanlon. Local ingredients are used in the specialties, which include a plate of Caribbean fish smoked in exotic woods served as an appetizer, grilled crayfish with fresh lemongrass and a white wine sauce, queenfish wrapped in peppers and cabbage leaves and served with a sweet-pepper sauce, and both fish and Créole soup. Raoul even makes his own bread and ice cream.

LE FISH TRAP, Island Harbour Beach. Tel. 497-4488.

Cuisine: FRENCH. **Reservations:** Required.
$ Prices: Appetizers $4.50–$9.50; main courses $14.95–$24. AE, MC, V.
Open: Lunch daily noon–2pm; dinner daily 7–10pm.

In the extreme east end of Anguilla is one of the leading restaurants on the island. Chic and sophisticated, it's owned and operated by Veronica Leduc. From a table on the terrace, you'll have a view of the beach, the sea, the flat land mass of Scilly Cay, and the beached fishing boats. Full meals might include filet of yellowtail snapper, Créole-style conch, seafood platter, and such spicy appetizers as tomato pie or conch fritters. Entertainment is featured on certain nights.

KOAL KEEL, The Valley. Tel. 497-2930.

Cuisine: FRENCH/CARIBBEAN. **Reservations:** Recommended.
$ Prices: Appetizers $6.50–$13; main courses $18–$30. AE, MC, V.
Open: Lunch daily noon–3pm; dinner daily 7–10pm.

Originally built by an Englishwoman after the death of her husband in the 1780s, this place functioned for many years as the headquarters for a local plantation. Today it's considered one of the two oldest houses in Anguilla, and probably one of the most evocative of a bygone era. The Koal Keel restaurant lies on the ground floor of this historic building, nestled amid the most solidly constructed limestone foundations in Anguilla. (Incidentally, the restaurant is named after the stone oven, or keel, which long ago transformed coal into charcoal nearby.)

Decorated with a scattering of 19th-century island antiques, within view of a small garden, the restaurant serves lobster crêpes, seafood fettuccine, curried conch fritters, Créole-style conch, rack of lamb in a fresh thyme sauce with ratatouille, and grilled breast of duckling on a bed of mushrooms.

SMUGGLER'S RESTAURANT, Forest Bay. Tel. 497-3728.

Cuisine: INTERNATIONAL/CONTINENTAL. **Reservations:** Not required.
$ Prices: Appetizers $3.50–$8.75; main courses $11.50–$24. AE, MC, V.

Open: Dinner only, daily 6:30–9:45pm (last order).

Set atop pilings sunk deep into the waters of Forest Bay, east of the airport, this is probably the most deliberately nautical restaurant in all of Anguilla. In the establishment's center, a re-created sailing ship (complete with masts and spars) juts upward from the plank floor. Best of all, sweeping views of the ocean unfold on all sides.

You can stop here just for a drink (the rum punches and the views are memorable), but if you're hungry, you might opt for a fish-and-lobster soup (topped with bread and grilled cheese), a seafood quiche, shrimp Créole, lobster or shrimp brochettes, filet of snapper with tartar sauce, or grilled steak.

INEXPENSIVE

LUCY'S HARBOUR VIEW AND RESTAURANT, South Hill. Tel. 497-6253.

Cuisine: CARIBBEAN/INTERNATIONAL. **Reservations:** Recommended.

$ **Prices:** Appetizers $5–$9; main courses $18–$28. AE, MC, V.

Open: Lunch Mon–Sat 11:30am–3pm; dinner Mon–Sat 7–9:30pm. **Closed:** Late Aug to early Oct.

Not only does it boast the most attractive view on the island, but Lucy's also offers imaginatively prepared food. What makes it special is its owner, Lucy Halley, who lived in the French part of St. Martin and learned many secrets of the cuisine there. The 60-seat restaurant is in a converted home at the top of a steep hillside overlooking the salt ponds and houses of Sandy Ground. When you call (or after you arrive spontaneously), ask Lucy what she has in the larder, or tell her what kind of food you like. The menu usually contains homemade pumpkin soup, lobster salad, fresh Anguillan lobster (split and grilled), conch fritters, curried goat, kingfish, and T-bone steaks. Dishes are usually served with fresh vegetables and breadfruit pudding. This is a lively, fun, and very informal spot, painted in the signature green and white known throughout Anguilla as Lucy's trademark colors.

THE OLD HOUSE, George Hill Rd. Tel. 497-2228.

Cuisine: AMERICAN/CARIBBEAN. **Reservations:** Not required.

$ **Prices:** Appetizers $3.50–$4.95; main courses $4.50–$19.95. AE, MC, V.

Open: Lunch daily 11am–5pm; dinner daily 5–11pm. **Closed:** Wed in summer.

A pleasant restaurant with a reputation for good food and polite service, the Old House occupies a white plantation-style house overlooking the airport. Built in the 1950s as a private vacation home, the place offers such lunch choices as fish Créole, London broil, chef's salad, Anguillan pot fish, fish on a bun, and home-style barbecued beef. Dinner offers native lobster, West Indian breast of capon, fresh conch, barbecued steaks, and a limited selection of wine.

PALM PALM, Sandy Ground. Tel. 497-2253.

Cuisine: INTERNATIONAL. **Reservations:** Not required.

$ **Prices:** Appetizers $5; main courses $14–$28. AE, MC, V.

Open: Fri–Wed 11am–11pm.

Probably the least formal restaurant in Anguilla, Palm Palm is little more than an enlarged gazebo set directly on the sands of one of the island's most popular beaches. Perhaps because of that, many clients feel perfectly free to arrive here in bathing suits. Several evenings a week (usually Tuesday and Friday nights from 8:30pm till midnight) live music transforms the place into an indoor/outdoor entertainment bar. Anytime throughout the day or evening you can order club sandwiches, fish and chips, curried conch, T-bone steaks, goat Créole, red snapper, and kingfish, if it was brought in the night before. The place is painted in the signature green and white of the island restaurants owned and operated by Lucy (owner of the also-recommended Lucy's Harbour View).

ROY'S PLACE, Crocus Bay. Tel. 497-2470.

Cuisine: ENGLISH/CARIBBEAN. **Reservations:** Recommended, especially for dinner.

$ **Prices:** Appetizers $4.50–$7; main courses $4–$17.50 at lunch, $12.50–$26 at dinner. MC, V.

Open: Lunch Tues–Sun 11am–2pm; dinner Tues–Sun 6–9pm (bar Tues–Sun 11am–closing, usually between 10:30pm and midnight).

Considered the most authentic and uncompromisingly English pub in Anguilla, Roy's has absolutely no chic or elitist pretensions. It's the kind of pub you might find in Yorkshire or Devon, the two English home counties of owners Roy and Mandy Bossons. The indoor bar has a constantly busy trade (and a much-used dartboard), whether or not the restaurant is full. Dining is outside on a covered veranda overlooking the beach, with subdued lighting, occasional live music, and fresh fish. No one will mind if you just arrive for a pint or two of Double Diamond (English) lager, or perhaps a Foster's (Australian) lager, priced at $5 each, but if you want a meal, you might order fish and chips, or perhaps a steak sandwich with chips. Island-inspired dishes include barbecued breast of chicken, sirloin steak with vegetables, barbecued loin of pork with Créole sauce, local lobster, or lobster Créole. Chocolate rum cake is a favorite dessert.

The restaurant is on the northern edge of the island, between Road Bay and Shoal Bay.

WHAT TO SEE & DO

Boat trips can be arranged to **Sombrero Island,** 38 miles northwest of Anguilla. This mysterious island, with its lone lighthouse, is 400 yards wide at its broadest point, three-quarters of a mile in length. Phosphate miners abandoned it in 1890; and limestone rocks, now eroded, rise in cliffs around the island. The treeless, waterless terrain evokes a moonscape.

One of Anguilla's most festive, and certainly most colorful, annual festivals is **Carnival,** held jointly under the auspices of the Ministries of Culture and of Tourism. Boat races are Anguilla's national sport, and during Carnival they form 60% of the celebration. The island's people display the culture, drama, creativity, and love of their land. The festival begins on the Friday before the first Monday in August and lasts a week. Carnival harks back to Emancipation Day, or "August Monday" as it's called, when all enslaved Africans were freed.

SPORTS & RECREATION

BEACHES One of the most popular beaches is **Road Bay,** framed by the crescent-shaped village of Sandy Ground (the capital) and a large salt pond. There you can negotiate with one of the local fishermen to take you to **Sandy Island,** studded with palms, just 20 minutes from port. You can also go farther out to **Prickly Pear Cay,** which stretches like a sweeping arc all the way to a sand spit populated by sea birds and pelicans.

Other good beaches include ✪ **Shoal Bay,** which apart from its silver sands boasts some of Anguilla's best coral gardens, the habitat of hundreds of tiny fish with iridescent, brilliantly colored markings. **Crocus Bay** is a long, golden beach, where a fisherman might take you out in search of snapper or grouper, or ferry you to such wee islands as Little Scrub.

FISHING Fishing excursions can be made with the local fishermen. Your hotel can make the arrangements for you, but you should bring your own tackle. Agree on the cost before setting out, however, as some misunderstandings have been reported.

More organized deep-sea fishing trips are available at **Tamariain Watersports,** Sandy Ground (tel. 497-2020).

Malliouhana, Meads Bay (tel. 497-6111), has a 34-foot fishing cruiser, *Kyra,* that holds up to eight passengers at a time. It can be chartered for fishing parties. The cost is $340 for up to 4 hours, with a surcharge of another $90 for each additional hour. A box lunch can be packed for an additional charge, and all fishing gear is included as part of the package.

SCUBA DIVING Most of the coastline of Anguilla is fringed by coral reefs, and the island's waters are rich in marine life; off the shore are sunken coral gardens and brilliantly colored fish. Conditions for scuba diving and snorkeling on the island are ideal. Nature was given a helping hand by the government of Anguilla, which has systematically created artificial enlargements of the existing reef system, a first for the Caribbean. Never before have so many battered and outmoded ships been deliberately sunk in carefully designated places in efforts to enlarge the island's marine ecosystem. These artificial reefs act as nurseries for fish and lobster populations, and also provide new sites for divers.

Tamariain Watersports Ltd., Sandy Ground (tel. 497-2020), is Anguilla's only full-service scuba-diving center. It's a five-star PADI international training center and offers a complete line of PADI certification courses. They carry several lines of scuba equipment for sale or rental.

TENNIS Most of the resorts have their own tennis courts (see "Where to Stay," above). **Malliouhana,** Meads Bay (tel. 497-6111), has four championship Laykold tennis courts with a year-round tennis pro and shop.

There are also two courts at **Cinnamon Reef,** Little Harbour (tel. 497-2727). The cost to nonresidents is $20 per hour.

SAVVY SHOPPING

Anguillan handcrafts are simple. Handcrafted mats are quite beautiful, and table-cloths and bedspreads are woven into spidery lace designs—but many of these are grabbed up by shops on neighboring islands and sold there at high prices. Baskets and mats are made from stripped corn husks and sisal rope. Model schooners and small pond boats are also for sale, as are gifts made of shells and wooden dolls.

Stamp collectors should head to the already-mentioned Valley Post Office (tel. 497-2528), where they'll find unusual stamps from Anguilla.

SUNSHINE SHOP, in South Hill. Tel. 497-6164.

Opposite Connor's car-rental agency, this is easily identifiable by the "I-95 sign," as it is on I-95 West at the Blowing Point expressway exit. The shop stocks fine cotton wear, art, jewelry, and packable gift items. For men, there are unusual batik shirts and bathing briefs. The shop has an assortment of silk-screened items and lithographs of island houses, ready to frame. Look for a classic line of women's sportswear in the annex. The shop is closed in September.

THE BOUTIQUE, in the Malliouhana Hotel, Meads Bay. Tel. 497-6111.

Probably the most interesting and upscale boutique in Anguilla lies in one of the island's premier hotels. Here you'll find jewelry, sportswear and casual beachwear for men and women, evening dresses, gift items, and Gottex bathing suits.

CHEDDIE'S CARVING STUDIO, The Cove. Tel. 497-6027.

Completely devoted to the one-of-a-kind carvings of master woodcarver Cheddie Richardson, this shop relies on the artistic inspiration of its owner, who combs the island's shoreline for appropriately tortured tree roots bleached from the action of saltwater and sunlight, and then carves their ends into graceful interpretations of fish, hawk heads, and mermaids. These carvings are viewed by some critics as the most creative interpretations of driftwood in the West Indies. You'll find this shop and studio about 3 miles west of the airport. Carvings cost between $50 and $2,000.

EVENING ENTERTAINMENT

Of special interest is **Johnno's Beach Bar,** Sandy Ground (tel. 497-2728), which is a favorite of Michael J. Fox and other Hollywood types when they visit Anguilla. Open-air, with sunlight and sea winds wafting into its unpretentious premises, the club is open Tuesday through Sunday from 10am to 6pm for food service. You can order Beck's beer on the beach as well as spareribs nicely barbecued, grilled chicken, or fresh fish. Meals begin at $15. "Jump-up time," when live music entertainment is presented, is Wednesday and Saturday from 8pm to midnight and on Sunday from 2:30 to 7pm.

THE DUTCH WINDWARDS IN THE LEEWARDS

The Dutch Windwards have the same orientation to the northeast trades as the British Leewards (covered in Chapter 8). However, the islands of Sint Maarten, Sint Eustatius (called "Statia"), and Saba—no more than dots in the Antilles—are called "The Dutch Windwards." This is confusing to the visitor, but it makes sense in the Netherlands. The Dutch-associated islands of Aruba, Bonaire, and Curaçao, just off the coast of South America, go by the name of "The Dutch Leewards" (covered in Chapter 15). The three Windward Islands, along with Bonaire and Curaçao, form the Netherlands Antilles. Aruba is now a separate entity.

The Windwards in the Leewards were once inhabited by the fierce Carib peoples, who believed that one acquired and assimilated the strength of one's slain enemy by eating his flesh! Columbus, on his second voyage to America, is said to have sighted the group of small islands on the name day of San Martino (St. Martin of Tours), hence the present name of Sint ("Saint") Maarten.

Cooled by trade winds, the Windwards are comfortable to visit any time of the year.

1. ST. MAARTEN

It's small, only 37 square miles, about half the area of the District of Columbia. A split-personality island, St. Maarten is half Dutch, half French (who call their part St. Martin).

The divided island is considered the smallest territory in the world shared by two sovereign states (for more information on St. Martin, see Chapter 11 on the French West Indies). The only way you know you're crossing an international border is when you see the sign BIENVENUE, PARTIE FRANÇAISE—attesting to the peaceful coexistence between the two nations on the island.

The island was divided in 1648, and visitors still ascend Mount Concordia, near the border, where agreement was reached. Even so, St. Maarten changed hands 16 times before it became permanently Dutch.

Legend has it that a gin-drinking Dutchman and a wine-guzzling Frenchman

WHAT'S SPECIAL ABOUT THE DUTCH WINDWARDS

Beaches

☐ Mullet Bay Beach, St. Maarten, palm shaded and crowded on weekends, a white sandy beach with water-sports equipment rentals.

☐ Simpson Bay Beach, St. Maarten, crescent shaped with sugar-white sands, a center for water sports set against a fishing village.

☐ Oyster Pond, Dawn Beach, St. Maarten, a long white sand beach, a favorite of snorkelers for its underwater coral reefs and marine life.

☐ Maho Bay Beach, at Maho Beach Hotel and Casino, St. Maarten, a palm-shaded beach with chairs and facilities available.

Ancient Monuments

☐ Fort Orange, St. Eustatius, built in 1636, the first to salute the Stars and Stripes.

Ace Attractions

☐ Saba Marine Park, with coral reefs and a recreational zone for fishing, boating, swimming, and snorkeling.

☐ Shopping in St. Maarten, a duty-free port where prices are sometimes lower than anywhere else in the Caribbean.

Sports and Recreation

☐ Mullet Bay Resort Golf Course, St. Maarten, one of the most challenging in the Caribbean, providing both beauty and hazards.

☐ Diving on Saba, an island of underwater scenery, volcanic sands, and coral formations.

☐ Picnic sails from St. Maarten, including snorkeling and sightseeing, to nearby islands.

---

walked around the island to see how much territory each could earmark for his side in one day; the Frenchman outwalked the Dutchman, but the canny Dutchman got the more valuable piece of property.

Northernmost of the Netherlands Antilles, St. Maarten lies 144 miles southeast of Puerto Rico. A lush island, rimmed with bays and beaches, it has a year-round temperature of 80° Fahrenheit.

In addition to some 36 beaches, duty-free shopping and gambling casinos draw visitors to St. Maarten, where there has been a rush of hotel building in the past few years.

The Dutch capital, **Philipsburg,** curves like a toy village along Great Bay. The town lies on a narrow sand isthmus separating Great Bay and Great Salt Pond. The capital was founded in 1763 by Commander John Philips, a Scot in Dutch employ. To protect Great Bay, Fort Amsterdam was built in 1737.

The town still retains some of its unique shingled architecture. The main thoroughfare is the busy Front Street, which stretches for about a mile and is lined with stores selling international merchandise, such as French designer fashions and Swedish crystal. More shops are along the little lanes, known as *steegjes,* that connect Front Street with Back Street, another shoppers' mart.

ORIENTATION

GETTING THERE St. Maarten's **Juliana Airport** is the second busiest in the Caribbean, topped only by San Juan, Puerto Rico.

American Airlines (tel. toll free 800/433-7300) offers the most options and the most frequent service to St. Maarten. In addition to daily nonstop flights to St. Maarten from New York's JFK, American makes two daily connections (via San Juan) from New Jersey's Newark airport and two other daily connections via San Juan from JFK. Travelers from the West Coast can opt for American's direct daily service to San Juan from Los Angeles, or they can travel through Dallas. Other Caribbean islands are

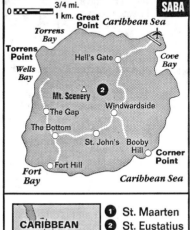

THE DUTCH WINDWARD ISLANDS

conveniently hooked into nearby San Juan via frequent shuttles on American's wholly owned subsidiary, **American Eagle** (same toll-free phone). Ask for one of the airline's tour operators, as you can save money by booking your airfare and hotel accommodation at the same time.

The least expensive tickets at American, as with most airlines, are sold to clients who reserve their seats at least 7 days in advance and who return after a predetermined number of days. Prices for round-trip transit from New York on a Thursday, Friday, or Saturday, for example, range from $458 to $498, plus tax. Fares for round-trip transit from New York to St. Maarten on any day between Monday and Thursday range from $388 to $428, plus tax. Of course, travel costs less in summer than in winter, and it's wise to compare prices with the competition.

Continental Airlines (tel. toll free 800/525-0280) flies daily to St. Maarten from Newark, New Jersey.

BWIA (tel. toll free 800/327-7401), the national carrier of Trinidad and Tobago, flies to St. Maarten via Antigua from Toronto. It also flies in from San Juan, Trinidad, and Miami.

ALM Antillean Airlines (tel. toll free 800/327-7230) offers nonstop daily service to St. Maarten from the airline's home base in Curaçao.

GETTING AROUND **By Taxi** Taxis are unmetered, but St. Maarten law requires drivers to have a list that details fares to major destinations on the island. Typical fares, say, from Juliana Airport to the Mullet Bay Resort and Casino are $4; from Philipsburg to Juliana Airport, $7. There are minimum fares for two passengers, and each additional passenger pays another $1. Passengers are entitled to two pieces of luggage free, and each additional piece is assessed 50¢ extra. Fares are 25% higher between 10pm and midnight, and 50% higher between midnight and 6am. Even if you're renting a car, taxi regulations require you to take a cab to your hotel, where your car will be delivered. For late-night cab service, call 22359.

By Minibus This is a reasonable means of transport in St. Maarten if you don't mind inconveniences, and at times overcrowding. Buses run daily from 7am to midnight and serve most of the major locations in St. Maarten. The most popular run is from Philipsburg to Marigot on the French side. Privately owned and operated, minibuses tend to follow specific routes, with fares ranging from $1 to $1.50, depending on where you're going.

By Rental Car Because of the island's size and diversity, car rentals in St. Maarten are practical, particularly if you want to experience both the Dutch and the French sides of the island. Be warned, however, that local taxicab unions, as well as the division of the island into Dutch and French zones, make renting a car complicated. For example, the taxi drivers' union strictly enforces a law that forbids anyone from picking up a car at the airport. As a result, every rental agency on the island is well equipped to deliver cars to a client's hotel, where an employee will complete all the necessary paperwork on the spot. You can also head for one of the rental kiosks which lie across the road from the airport.

Experienced visitors, however, reserve their car in the U.S. in advance (especially important in winter) and head immediately to their hotel by taxi, thereby bypassing the long lines at the car-rental kiosks near the airport, the numerous local car-rental hucksters, and the hassle of island navigation.

The twin nationality of the island also causes complication in some rentals. Both Hertz and Budget, for example, prefer not to rent a car on the Dutch side to a client staying on the French side—and each organization will ask for confirmation of a hotel booking on the Dutch side. If you're staying on the French side, both companies will refer you to the Budget office on the island's French side. The degree to which this rule is followed depends on the individual discretion of the various companies.

Prices tend to be competitive. Among the "big three" companies, currently **Hertz** (tel. 52314, or toll free 800/654-3131) offers the most economical price for its cheapest car: $192 per week, plus 5% tax. **Budget Rent-a-Car** (tel. 54224, or toll free 800/527-0700) charges $217 per week, plus tax, for its least expensive car. **Avis** (tel. 42322, or toll free 800/331-1212) charges the most of all, $240 per week, plus tax, for its least expensive vehicle. For the best rates at all three companies, clients should reserve at least 2 days in advance, especially in winter, and keep the car for a full week. A collision-damage waiver costs $10 to $11 at each of the three companies, but even if you purchase the waiver, you might still be responsible for up to $400 of repairs to your car. Your credit card issuer *may* provide this coverage; check with the company directly before your trip.

Warning: St. Martin has probably more car-rental charlatans than any other island in the Caribbean, and they may approach you at the airport or at your hotel. I have always found it safer, more convenient, and ultimately less costly to rent from one of the big three U.S.-based operators.

Drive on the right-hand side (on both the French and Dutch sides of the island), and don't drink and drive. Traffic jams are common near the island's major settlements, so be prepared to be patient. International road signs are observed, and there are no Customs formalities at the border between the island's political divisions.

By Sightseeing Tour   You can negotiate with a taxi driver who will also serve as your guide. One or two passengers are charged $30 for a 2½-hour tour, and an additional passenger pays around $7.50. It's cheaper to call **St. Maarten Sightseeing Tours** (tel. 22753), which offers a 2-hour tour for only $12 per person in a 20-passenger van.

FAST   ST. MAARTEN

Area Code   St. Maarten is *not* part of the Caribbean's 809 area code. For information on calling St. Maarten, see "Telephone," below.

Banking Hours   Most banks are open Monday through Thursday from 8:30am to 1pm and on Friday from 8:30am to 1pm and 4 to 5pm.

Currency   The legal tender is the **Netherlands Antilles guilder (NAf)**, and the official rate at which the banks accept U.S. dollars is 1.77 NAf for each $1 U.S. Regardless, U.S. dollars are easily, willingly, and often eagerly accepted in the Dutch Windwards, especially St. Maarten. *Note:* Prices in this chapter are given in U.S. currency unless otherwise designated.

Documents   To enter the Dutch-held side of St. Maarten, U.S. citizens should have proof of citizenship in the form of a passport (preferably valid but not more than 5 years expired), an original birth certificate with a raised seal or a photocopy with a notary seal, or a voter's registration card with photo ID. Naturalized citizens may show their naturalization certificate, and resident aliens must provide the alien registration "green" card or a temporary card which allows them to leave and reenter the U.S. All visitors must have a confirmed room reservation before their arrival and a return or ongoing ticket.

Electricity   Dutch Sint Maarten uses the same voltage (110 volts AC, 60 cycles), with the same electrical configurations as the U.S., so adapters and transformers are not necessary. However, on French St. Martin converters and adapters are definitely necessary. To simplify things, many hotels on both sides of the island have installed built-in sockets suitable for both the European and North American forms of electrical currents.

Emergencies   Call the **police** at 22222 or an **ambulance** at 22111.

Hospitals   The major hospital is **St. Rose Hospital,** Front Street, Philipsburg (tel. 5/22300).

Information   Before you go, contact the **St. Maarten Tourist Office,** 275 Seventh Ave., 19th Floor, New York, NY 10001 (tel. 212/989-0000). Once on the island, go to the **Tourist Information Bureau,** Cyrus Wathey Square (tel. 5/22337), open Monday through Friday from 8am to noon and 1 to 5pm.

Language   Even though the language is officially Dutch, most people speak English.

Safety Crime is on the rise on St. Maarten and, in fact, has become quite serious. If possible, avoid night driving—it's particularly unwise to drive on remote, usually unlit, back roads at night. Also, let that deserted, isolated beach remain so. It's safer in a crowd, although under no circumstances should you ever leave anything unguarded on the beach.

Taxes and Service A $5 departure tax is charged when you're leaving the island for St. Eustatius or Saba, and $10 is charged for international flights. A 5% government tax is added to hotel bills, and in general, hotels also add a 10% or 15% service charge. If service has not been added (unlikely), it's customary to tip around 15% in restaurants.

Telephone Neither Dutch St. Maarten nor French St. Martin is part of the 809 area code that applies to most of the Caribbean. To call Dutch St. Maarten from the U.S., if your long-distance telephone company is equipped to handle international direct dialing, dial 011 (the international access code), then 599 (the country code for the Netherlands Antilles), and finally 5 (the area code for all of St. Maarten) and the local number. If you cannot direct-dial internationally, dial 0 ("zero," for the operator) and tell the operator you wish to make an international call; once you are transferred to the international operator, state the 599 country code and then the area code and local number, and the operator will dial the call for you.

To make a call within St. Maarten you need only the five-digit local number. If you are calling "long distance" to the French side of the island, dial 06 and the six-digit French number; to call Dutch St. Maarten from the French side, dial 93 and then 5 (the area code) and the five-digit local number. *Note:* In this chapter, only the area code and the local number are given.

Time St. Maarten operates on Atlantic standard time year round. Thus in winter, when the U.S. is on standard time, if it's 6pm in Philipsburg it's 5pm in New York. During daylight saving time in the U.S., the island and the U.S. East Coast are on the same time.

Weather The island has a year-round temperature of about 80° Fahrenheit.

WHERE TO STAY

Remember, a government tax of 5% and a 10% to 15% service charge are added to your hotel bill. Ask about this when you book a room to save yourself a shock when you check out. See Chapter 11 on the French West Indies for my accommodations recommendations on French St. Martin.

VERY EXPENSIVE

BELAIR BEACH HOTEL, Little Bay (P.O. Box 140), Philipsburg, St. Maarten, N.A. Tel. 5/23362, or toll free 800/622-7836. Fax 5/25295. 72 suites. A/C MINIBAR TV TEL

$ Rates: Winter, $275–$375 single or double. Summer, $145–$175 single or double. Each extra person up to the maximum of six per suite, $55 per day in winter, $20 per day in summer. Off-season, children under 12 stay free in parents' room. AE, DC, MC, V. **Parking:** Free.

One of the most surprising things about this breezy, oceanfront hotel right on Little Bay Beach, a 10-minute taxi ride east of the airport, is the size of the accommodations—they're all suites. Each unit contains a spacious bedroom, one full bath with shower, a fully equipped kitchen including a microwave oven, a 21-foot patio or veranda with a sweeping view of the sea, and many extras, such as nightly turn-down of beds and fresh-daily towels.

Dining/Entertainment: The Sugar Bird Café serves breakfast, lunch, and dinner in a casual atmosphere. A grocery is on the premises. For vacationers who want more activities, the Divi Little Bay Resort and Casino is just a short walk down the beach.

Services: Laundry, baby-sitting, car-rental desk, water-sports desk.

Facilities: Beach, gift shop.

DIVI LITTLE BAY RESORT AND CASINO, Little Bay (P.O. Box 61), Philipsburg, St. Maarten, N.A. Tel. 5/22333, or toll free 800/367-3484. Fax 5-23911. 220 rms, 5 suites. A/C TV TEL

$ Rates: Winter, $255–$305 single or double; from $340 one-bedroom suite. Summer, $135–$165 single or double; from $190 one-bedroom suite. MAP $43 per person extra. AE, MC, V. **Parking:** Free.

The first of the island's resort hotels offers complete facilities, including its private 1,000-foot beach. It lies a 10-minute taxi ride east of the airport, within a short distance of the shops and restaurants of Philipsburg. The hotel opened in 1955 with only 20 rooms, and Queen Juliana and her husband, Prince Bernhard, were the first guests. Princess Margaret came here on her honeymoon, and Queen Beatrix has also stayed here.

Each unit is warm and inviting, with a private bath and terrace or balcony, and wall-to-wall carpeting. The best units are the beachfront accommodations.

Dining/Entertainment: There's a beach bar and a snack bar, appealing for a light lunch. Continental, American, and authentic Dutch and West Indian specialties are served in the Pappagallo Restaurant where diners enjoy a candlelit atmosphere with light music for listening or dancing.

Services: Laundry, baby-sitting.

Facilities: Water sports, beauty parlor, two freshwater pools, three tennis courts (lit for night play).

MULLET BAY RESORT AND CASINO, Mullet Bay (P.O. Box 309), Philipsburg, St. Maarten, N.A. Tel. 5/52801, or toll free 800/4-MULLET. Fax 5/54281. A/C TV TEL

$ Rates: Winter, $225–$265 single or double; $310–$360 one-bedroom suite; $495–$580 two-bedroom suite. Summer, $140–$165 single or double; $210–$225 one-bedroom suite; $330–$385 two-bedroom suite. MAP $55 per person extra. Golf, honeymoon, and other packages available. AE, DC, MC, V. **Parking:** Free.

Mullet Bay has been called "an island within an island"—it's so vast and complete that many guests never leave the 172-acre grounds. On the westernmost tip of St. Maarten, just a 5-minute ride west from Juliana Airport, it offers well-furnished and comfortable twins and doubles, but you may prefer a one- or two-bedroom apartment in one of the buildings or villas spread across the grounds. All accommodations have refrigerators. The apartments are especially luxurious, with complete living rooms, patios or balconies, and kitchens.

Dining/Entertainment: The Shipwreck and the Deli serve both breakfast and lunch, and there is also Little Italy. The Little Oceanreef features seafood and Créole cookery. The Frigate offers steaks and salads for dinner, and the Bamboo Garden, open only for dinner, serves cuisines from four regions of China. At night there's gambling at Grand Casino at Mullet Bay, plus dancing at Le Club.

Services: Baby-sitting.

Facilities: The island's only golf course, an 18-hole layout designed by Joseph Lee; 14 tennis courts (some lit for night games); water sports, including windsurfing, snorkeling, Sunfish sailing, and waterskiing; two swimming pools; food market.

ROYAL ISLANDER CLUB, Maho Bay (P.O. Box 2000), Philipsburg, St. Maarten, N.A. Tel. 5/52388, 212/969-9220 in New York City, or toll free 800/223-0757. Fax 5/53495. 110 units. A/C MINIBAR TV TEL

$ Rates: Winter, $215–$415 single or double. Summer, $155–$325 single or double. MAP $42 per person extra. AE, DC, MC, V. **Parking:** Free.

Half a mile west of the airport, the upscale twin of the also-recommended Maho Beach Hotel offers larger units, access to all the facilities of Maho Beach, and a combination of time-share and luxury hotel. All units face the bay and feature fully furnished one- and two-bedroom apartments with marble floors, balconies, baths, vanities, and fully equipped kitchens with microwave ovens and marble counter tops.

Dining/Entertainment: Dining facilities, a casino, disco, and nightclub are at nearby Maho.

Services: Car-rental desk, activities desk.

Facilities: Freshwater swimming pool; fitness center; water sports, tennis courts, and shopping arcade at nearby Maho.

EXPENSIVE

CARAVANSERAI, Maho Bay (P.O. Box 113), Philipsburg, St. Maarten, N.A. Tel. 5/52510, or toll free 800/223-6510. Fax 5/52378. 51 rms, 32 suites. A/C TV TEL

$ Rates: Winter, $165–$185 single or double; from $215 suite. Summer, $135–$170 single or double; from $195 suite. Continental breakfast $8 extra. AE, DC, MC, V. **Parking:** Free.

An elegant oasis on its own private coral promontory west of the airport, Caravanserai lies 6 miles west of Philipsburg. An occasional jet lands or takes off, but otherwise it's quiet around here. A long time ago it was the creation of an exiled New Yorker, Dave Crane, who turned it into one of the most urbane inns in the West Indies. Both Juliana and Beatrix, from the Dutch royal family, have stayed here. The decor uses natural woods and stone, with tropical furnishings. Accommodations come in a wide range—one-bedroom apartments and studios facing the Caribbean, 18 superior rooms also facing the sea, and 20 standard rooms opening onto the courtyard.

Dining/Entertainment: The larger pool opens onto a long, arched loggia, where you can have an American breakfast or an evening meal. The cuisine at La Fonda del Sol is international. The octagonal peak-roofed Ocean View bar is on the tip of the promontory.

Services: Room service, laundry.

Facilities: Two tennis courts, water sports, private beach, two swimming pools.

GREAT BAY BEACH HOTEL AND CASINO, Front St. (P.O. Box 310), Philipsburg, St. Maarten, N.A. Tel. 5/22447, or toll free 800/223-0757. Fax 5/23009. 285 rms. A/C MINIBAR TV TEL

$ Rates: Winter, $170–$215 single; $180–$225 double. Summer, $110–$135 single; $115–$145 double. MAP $42 per person extra. AE, DC, MC, V. **Parking:** Free.

This complete deluxe resort at the southwestern corner of Great Bay lies within walking distance of Philipsburg, ideal for shopping trips. The hotel was given a complete $10-million renovation; all guest rooms have been refurbished, and now contain designer furniture, a terrace or patio, and a king-size or two full-size beds. The corner ocean rooms are the most expensive. Bathrooms are decorated with Valentino-designed tiles.

Dining/Entertainment: The hotel has a casino and disco, and two restaurants, including a gourmet French dining room and a grill open nightly until 11pm.

Services: Laundry, baby-sitting.

Facilities: Two all-weather tennis courts, two freshwater pools.

MAHO BEACH HOTEL AND CASINO, Maho Bay, Philipsburg, St. Maarten, N.A. Tel. 5/52115, 212/969-9220 in New York City, or toll free 800/223-0757. Fax 5/53180. 700 rms. A/C TV TEL

$ Rates: Winter, $195–$230 single; $215–$250 double; from $340 suite for two. Summer, $140–$180 single; $155–$195 double; from $240 suite for two. MAP $42 per person extra. AE, DC, MC, V. **Parking:** Free.

Maho Beach added a 450-room wing in 1991, making it the largest hotel on the island. It's set about half a mile southwest of the airport in a greenbelt, which seems to showcase its pink-and-white facade. About a third of the rooms contain kitchenettes, and each has wicker furniture, Italian tiles, and plush upholstery. A few are in a separate cluster near the resort's tennis courts. Its only drawback is the thundering noise from the aircraft landing at the nearby airport several times a day.

Dining/Entertainment: On the premises are three stylish restaurants. One is the Lotus Flower, a branch of the well-known restaurant of that name in San Juan, and another, the Ristorante Roma, has, of course, an Italian cuisine. Its Casino Royale, across the main road, is the largest on the island.

Services: Laundry, baby-sitting.

Facilities: Tennis court, outdoor swimming pool with a view of Maho Bay, business center; sandy beach with water sports at the bottom of the hill.

OYSTER POND HOTEL, Oyster Pond (P.O. Box 239), Philipsburg, St. Maarten, N.A. Tel. 5/22206, 212/696-1323 in New York City, or toll free 800/372-1323. Fax 5/25695. 16 rms, 24 suites. TEL

$ Rates (including continental breakfast): Winter, $170–$290 double. Summer, $120–$230 double. AE, MC, V. **Parking:** Free. **Closed:** Sept.

Splendidly chic, this Caribbean Shangri-La, 8 miles east of Philipsburg, is reached by a twisting, scenic road. On the windward side of the island, on a circular harbor on the eastern shore near the French border, the fortresslike structure stands guard over a 35-acre protected marina and has a private half-moon sandy beach. There is a central courtyard and an al fresco lobby, with white wicker and fine paintings. More than half the units are suites or duplexes, and most have a West Indian decor. Bedrooms have balconies overlooking the pond or sea. The most elegant and expensive accommodation is a tower suite. Six rooms have air conditioning and 20 contain TV.

Dining/Entertainment: Off the courtyard, and opening onto the sea, is a bar/lounge, as warm and comfortable as a private home. The dining room is exceptional, and the chef turns out a well-prepared continental cuisine intermixed with some Créole dishes. All dining is à la carte.

Services: Laundry, baby-sitting.

Facilities: Tennis courts, salt-water swimming pool (22 by 44 ft.).

PELICAN RESORT AND CASINO, Simpson Bay (P.O. Box 431), Philipsburg, St. Maarten, N.A. Tel. 5/42503, or toll free 800/327-3286. Fax 5/42133. 655 units. A/C TV TEL

$ Rates: Winter, $205–$255 studio for two; $260–$320 one-bedroom unit for two; $420–$550 two-bedroom unit for four; $780 three-bedroom unit for six. Summer, $115–$150 studio for two; $160–$210 one-bedroom unit for two; $240–$330 two-bedroom unit for four; $330–$450 three-bedroom unit for six. 7-night minimum stay usually required in winter. AE, DC, MC, V. **Parking:** Free.

The Pelican is a seaside resort of varied architectural styles, west of Philipsburg. The village-style sections are well separated with walls of bougainvillea and hibiscus. Scattered among the 12 acres are a lily pond, many small waterways, and an orchid garden. All accommodations are privately owned and leased through the hotel management to vacationing guests. Each has one, two, or three bedrooms, a kitchen, and a VCR.

Dining/Entertainment: There's a convenience deli on the premises to make shopping easy, and a casino and restaurant, the Pelican Reef Seafood and Steak House. The Crocodile Café is another spot.

Services: Laundry, baby-sitting.

Facilities: Jacuzzi, six tennis courts, six swimming pools, 1,400 feet of ocean-front, marina; water sports can be arranged; L'Aqualigne, a unique health and beauty center (see "Revitalization Center" in "Sports and Recreation," below).

LA VISTA, Pelican Key Estates (P.O. Box 40), Philipsburg, St. Maarten, N.A. Tel. 5/43005, or toll free 800/223-9815. Fax 5/43010. 24 suites and cottages. A/C TV TEL

$ Rates: Winter, $190–$290 double. Summer, $100–$165 double. Continental breakfast $5 extra. AE, MC, V. **Parking:** Free.

La Vista is one of the golden nuggets of St. Maarten, although it's not well known.

The resort offers large and handsomely furnished junior suites, penthouse suites, and what it calls Antillean cottages. Each accommodation opens onto a sea view and contains a kitchenette with the necessary equipment, a generous living and dining area, and a good-sized balcony. The resort is about a 10-minute drive west of Philipsburg, longer if the traffic is heavy.

Dining/Entertainment: The complex features a lounge area, as well as an open-air restaurant, the Hideaway.

Services: Room service, laundry, baby-sitting.

Facilities: Freshwater swimming pool.

MODERATE

HOLLAND HOUSE, Front St. (P.O. Box 393), Philipsburg, St. Maarten, N.A. Tel. 5/22572, 212/545-8469 in New York City, or toll free 800/223-9815. Fax 5/24673. 54 units, 6 suites. A/C TV TEL
$ Rates: Winter, $140–$154 single; $153–$168 double; from $200 suite. Summer, $80–$89 single; $98–$127 double; from $152 suite. AE, DC, MC, V. **Parking:** Free.

With an urban-minded location 15 minutes east of the airport in the heart of town, this hotel rents cozy apartments decorated with furnishings from the Netherlands. Rates depend on the exposure to the street or to the beach, and each unit contains a tiny kitchenette, ideal for cooking an omelet but not a big dinner. You're right on the beach, where you can order drinks at the bar, and an open-air dining terrace fronts Great Bay. The hotel is near all the major restaurants and shops of Philipsburg. Even if you're not staying here, you might want to call and reserve a table for dinner; this is one of the few hotels that serves authentic Dutch specialties at its restaurant, Tulips.

MARY'S BOON, Simpson Bay (P.O. Box 2078), Philipsburg, St. Maarten, N.A. Tel. 5/54235. Fax 5/53316. 12 units. **Directions:** Take the first right turn from the airport toward Philipsburg.
$ Rates: Winter, $150 double. Summer, $75–$90 double. Continental breakfast $5 extra. No children under 16 accepted. No credit cards. **Parking:** Free.

This small, casual inn offers oversized stylish apartments with kitchenettes, designed as private villas. They lie directly on a 3-mile sandy beach, just south of the Juliana Airport and 15 minutes from Philipsburg. It's near the airport—but big planes are rare, and only land in the daytime. The rooms are decorated in rattan and wicker, and louvered windows open to sea breezes. Most rooms are in separate cottages, but there are two units in the main house. The efficiencies have ceiling fans.

There's a dining gallery fronting Simpson Bay in case you decide to take the half-board arrangement. The cuisine is Dutch-French/West Indian and is served in a restaurant with a panoramic view of the sea. In the bar you fix your own drinks on the honor system. Meals are not served from August 1 to October 15.

PASANGGRAHAN, 15 Front St. (P.O. Box 151), Philipsburg, St. Maarten, N.A. Tel. 5/23588, or toll free 800/365-8484. Fax 5/22885. 30 rms.
$ Rates: Winter, $114–$148 single or double. Summer, $68–$88 single or double. Breakfast $6.50 extra. AE, MC, V. **Parking:** Free. **Closed:** Sept.

Pasanggrahan is the Indonesian word for guesthouse, and this one is West Indian in style. A small, informal guesthouse, it's right on the busy, narrow main street of Philipsburg, toward the end of the mountain side of Front Street. It's set back under tall trees, with a building-wide white wooden veranda. The interior has peacock bamboo chairs, a pair of Indian spool tables, and a gilt-framed oil portrait of Queen Wilhelmina. So many guests asked to see the bedroom where the queen and her daughter, Juliana, stayed in World War II that the management turned it into the Sydney Greenstreet Bar. The newly renovated bedrooms have king-size beds and Saban bedspreads, each with a private bath, some in the main building, others in an adjoining annex. All accommodations have ceiling fans, and 26 rooms are air-conditioned.

Set among the wild jungle of palms and shrubbery is the dining area, the Ocean

View Restaurant. Service is from 11:30am to 3:30pm and 5:30 to 10pm daily. The private beach is only 50 feet away. Laundry is provided.

CONDOS & GUESTHOUSES

THE BEACH HOUSE, 160 Front St. (P.O. Box 211), Philipsburg, St. Maarten, N.A. Tel. 5/22456. Fax 5/30308. 8 rms. A/C MINIBAR TV
$ Rates: Winter, $85 single; $95 double. Summer, $58 single; $68 double. AE, MC, V. **Parking:** Free.

This little guesthouse sits on Windward Beach at Great Bay, 6 miles east of the airport. One-bedroom apartments, with fully equipped kitchenettes, daily maid service, and private balconies, are furnished in a simple Caribbean motif. Several of the best restaurants of St. Maarten are virtually at your doorstep.

HORNY TOAD GUEST HOUSE, Viaun St., Simpson Bay (P.O. Box 3029), Philipsburg, St. Maarten, N.A. Tel. 5/54323. Fax 5/53316. 8 units.
Directions: Follow the signs from the airport.
$ Rates: Winter, $190 single or double. Summer, $98 single or double. Extra person $40 in winter, $25 in summer. No credit cards. **Parking:** Free.

⑤   The Horny Toad was once an island governor's residence, and the present owners, Betty and Earle Vaughan, continue the tradition of hospitality. What you get here for your money makes it desirable, as it opens directly onto the beach at Simpson Bay. The second floor of the white frame building has an encircling covered West Indies balcony, and their efficiency units have kitchen areas and private baths. Six have separate bedrooms housing three guests per unit. Daily maid service is included. *Note:* The guesthouse is near the airfield and does have noisy moments.

Reservations: Contact Betty and Dave Harvey, 7 Warren Street, Winchester, MA 01890 (tel. 617/729-3171).

TOWN HOUSE VILLAS, 175 Front St. (P.O. Box 347), Philipsburg, St. Maarten, N.A. Tel. 5/22898, 212/545-8469 in New York City, or toll free 800/223-9815. Fax 5/22418. 11 units. A/C TV TEL
$ Rates: Winter, $250 unit for one to four. Summer, $125 unit for one to four. AE, MC, V. **Parking:** Free.

This group of two-story apartments lies at the edge of the restaurant and shopping district of Philipsburg. At your doorstep is Great Bay Beach, dotted with palms—it's all shut off from the main street by a rugged stone wall and a wrought-iron gate. The town houses are handsome, rather formal with slanted shingled mansard roofs. Each apartment has two large bedrooms and 1½ baths. There's a completely equipped kitchen, plus raised dining area in the long and well-furnished living room. Wide glass doors open onto a private terrace with lounge chairs. Whether dining or having conversation in the living room or drinks on your terrace, you can enjoy a view of the bay.

WHERE TO DINE

Half-Dutch, half-French St. Maarten/St. Martin has dozens of good international restaurants. See Chapter 11 on the French West Indies for restaurant suggestions on French St. Martin.

EXPENSIVE

ALBA, Lowlands, Cupecoy. Tel. 52100.
  Cuisine: ITALIAN. **Reservations:** Required.
$ Prices: Appetizers $6.75–$12.75; main courses $9–$19.75. AE, MC, V.
  Open: Lunch daily noon–3pm; dinner daily 6:30–11:30pm. **Closed:** Sept.

★   Adjacent to the Tap Five Superette, behind the Treasure Island Casino, Alba serves some of the best Italian food on the island, prepared by a master Italian chef. Pasta, fresh fish, and seafood are cooked with distinctive flair. Specialties include antipasto all italiano, an appetizer with four special meats, and filetto di pesce, a main course featuring grilled red snapper in a savory sauce. Alba is also a popular late-night gathering spot, featuring Brazilian entertainment and dancing.

ANTOINE'S, 49 Front St., Philipsburg. Tel. 22964.
Cuisine: FRENCH. **Reservations:** Recommended, especially in season.
$ Prices: Appetizers $4.75–$13.75; main courses $14.50–$23.95. AE, MC, V.
Open: Lunch Mon–Sat 11:30am–3pm; dinner Mon–Sat 6–10pm. **Closed:** Aug–Oct.

Antoine's offers *la belle cuisine* in an atmospheric building next to the Little Pier in the center of Philipsburg. Wear your casual-chic resortwear here at night. You can enjoy an apéritif in the cocktail bar. If the crowd is right (usually in winter), Antoine's takes on wordly sophistication, and the staff will prove that you don't have to cross the border for impressive wines, top-quality service, and a long list of Gallic specialties. Fresh local fish is always available, but well-sauced beef and chicken dishes are also served. The spiny Caribbean langouste is regularly featured, and prepared very well indeed.

LE BEC FIN, 119 Front St., Philipsburg. Tel. 22976.
Cuisine: INTERNATIONAL. **Reservations:** Required.
$ Prices: Appetizers $6–$16; main courses $16–$30. AE, MC, V.
Open: Dinner only, daily 6:30–10pm.

Le Bec Fin, in Museum Arcade, is one of the best restaurants in St. Maarten, on either the Dutch or the French side. You walk across a courtyard and ascend a flight of steps to reach this restaurant, which has a view over the harbor. You might start with seafood tagliatelli in a fresh ginger sauce, then follow with either peppersteak flambé or grilled red snapper. Grilled lobster is also regularly featured.

L'ESCARGOT, 84 Front St., Philipsburg. Tel. 22483.
Cuisine: FRENCH. **Reservations:** Recommended, especially in season.
$ Prices: Appetizers $8–$12; main courses $18–$22. AE, MC, V.
Open: Lunch daily noon–3pm; dinner daily 7–11:30pm.

L'Escargot is my favorite French bistro, and it's located right in the heart of Philipsburg where the competition is keen. It's perched in a gaily decorated 100-year-old Antillean house with a red tin roof. For good-tasting *bonne cuisine française,* and some of the nicest, friendliest people around, you'll do well here, and the prices, although not low, seem reasonable to most diners. If you arrive before your reservation, relax in the bar to your left before being shown to your candlelit table. The decor may appear too gimmicky to some, but the food is first rate: with snails served in pâté à choux, with mushrooms, in omelets, or in the more traditional escargots à la provençale; caviar blinis; duck in a pineapple-and-banana sauce; snapper in papillote; lobster thermidor; coq au vin; and a chocolate mousse for dessert.

FELIX RESTAURANT, Pelican Bay. Tel. 42797.
Cuisine: FRENCH. **Reservations:** Recommended.
$ Prices: Appetizers $6–$16; main courses $20–$28. AE, MC, V.
Open: Lunch daily 11:30am–2:30pm; dinner Thurs–Tues 6:30–10pm. **Closed:** Sept.

Opening onto the sea is one of the island's best choices for an al fresco meal. Margaret and Richard (Felix) Ducrot are the owners. This place is at its most romantic during candlelit dinners when seating choices range from intimate sheltered booths to outdoor tables set within sight and sound of the sea. Many of the seafood specialties come from the lobster tank. Choices might include chateaubriand for two, rack of lamb, fish caught locally and sometimes served with an exquisite sorrel-flavored hollandaise, and a Felix salad. The restaurant, on the road to the Pelican Resort and Casino, also has a lounge.

LE PERROQUET, 72 Airport Rd. Tel. 54339.
Cuisine: FRENCH. **Reservations:** Required.
$ Prices: Appetizers $5.50–$9.50; main courses $17.75–$24.75. AE, MC, V.
Open: Dinner only, daily 6–10pm. **Closed:** June and Sept.

⭐ Only a short walk from the airport sits the domain of M. Pierre Castagne, a French chef of exceptional ability. The name of this restaurant comes from the famed Chicago restaurant. The St. Maarten version is in a typical West Indian house with shutters open to the trade winds blowing around Simpson Bay Lagoon. Monsieur Castagne offers such dishes as ostrich breast (yes, that's right) and filet of boar, but you can also order more familiar fare, beginning with a savory fish soup or a fresh mâché salad, and moving on to mussels marinara, duck with a Grand Marnier orange sauce, or red snapper in a garlic sauce. Some of the specialties are wheeled in on a table, so you can make a visual selection, a nice touch.

THE RED SNAPPER, 93 Front St., Philipsburg. Tel. 23834.
   Cuisine: FRENCH. **Reservations:** Recommended.
$ **Prices:** Appetizers $6–$10; main courses $17–$24. AE, MC, V.
   Open: Tues–Sun 11:30am–10:30pm. **Closed:** Sept–Oct.
The Red Snapper, one of the premier restaurants of Philipsburg, located beside Antoine's, is a traditional French restaurant on the sea and is reached by passing through a narrow alleyway. Cool your thirst with an apéritif at a mahogany bar before going into the restaurant, open to a view of the harbor. The chef's specialties, prepared with flair, might be baked gratin of mussels, rack of lamb, or marinated sea scallops with hot goose liver. Fresh lobster is sautéed in a vermouth-flavored sauce.

SPARTACO, Almond Grove Plantation Estate. Tel. 45379.
   Cuisine: ITALIAN. **Reservations:** Recommended.
$ **Prices:** Appetizers $7–$12; main courses $20–$24. AE, MC, V.
   Open: Dinner only, daily 6:30–10pm. **Closed:** June–Oct.
You'll find Spartaco in a residential suburb midway between Philipsburg and the airport. Its limestone walls were originally built in 1803 as part of the West Indian manor house, but the decor today includes strong doses of 1930s art deco and some hi-tech design. Guests sit in the main dining room or on a breeze-filled wraparound veranda. The restaurant is the creation of an Italian entrepreneur from Siena, Spartaco Sargentoni, who is assisted by a handful of Italian chefs. They offer one of the most sophisticated menus on the island, including fresh black tagliolini (angel-hair pasta flavored with squid ink, served with shrimp, parsley, and garlic sauce), fresh green gnocchi with gorgonzola cheese, and swordfish Mediterranean (composed of parsley, garlic, capers, and an olive oil that Mr. Sargentoni imports from his relatives who produce it on a farm outside Florence). The antipasto makes a fine beginning.

MODERATE

CHESTERFIELDS, Great Bay Marina, Pointe Blanche. Tel. 23484.
   Cuisine: AMERICAN/CARIBBEAN. **Reservations:** Recommended.
$ **Prices:** Appetizers $5–$7; main courses $5.45–$19.95. No credit cards.
   Open: Breakfast daily 7:30–10:30am; lunch Mon–Sat 11:30am–2:30pm; dinner daily 6–10:30pm; brunch Sun 10:30am–2:30pm.
Chesterfield's has a special attraction other than its good food—which, incidentally, is among the best on the Dutch side. It offers pierside dining with a view of the harbor, on a trade wind–swept veranda near Great Bay Marina, east of Philipsburg. The yachting set gathers here, and everybody seems to know everybody else. The setting and the dress are both casual, and you dine on several international specialties, with fresh seafood and French-inspired cookery a highlight. Try the prime rib served with sautéed mushrooms, red snapper Créole or broiled, duck Chesterfield, or seafood pasta. In season, there's always some lively activity going on, such as champagne Sunday brunches with eggs Benedict or Florentine, or seafood omelets.

DON CARLOS RESTAURANT, Airport Rd., Simpson Bay. Tel. 53112.
   Cuisine: MEXICAN. **Reservations:** Not required.
$ **Prices:** Appetizers $4.55–$7.95; main courses $10.75–$24. AE, MC, V.
   Open: Daily 11am–11pm.
This restaurant is just a 5-minute walk east of the airport, and don't be deceived by its dusty parking lot and concrete facade. The place serves the only Mexican food on the

island. Owners Shenny and Carl Wagner invite you for a drink in their Pancho Villa Bar before your meal in their hacienda-style dining room. A trio plays live Mexican music.

THE GREENHOUSE, Bobby's Marina, Philipsburg. Tel. 22941.

Cuisine: AMERICAN. **Reservations:** Not required.

$ Prices: Appetizers $4.95–$6; main courses $10.95–$23; lunch from $12. AE, DC, MC, V.

Open: Lunch Tues–Sun 11am–4pm; dinner Tues–Sun 5:30–11pm.

Open to a view of the harbor, off Front Street, the Greenhouse is filled with plants, as befits its name. It's the best restaurant in the marina area, and probably one of the finest in its price category. As you dine, breezes filter through the open-air eatery. Lunches include the catch of the day, a wide selection of burgers, and conch chowder. Dinners might feature chunks of lobster in wine sauce, or a whole red snapper. Live entertainment is offered nightly from 10pm, when the copious rectangular bar fills up.

PARADISE CAFE, Maho Village. Tel. 52842.

Cuisine: INTERNATIONAL. **Reservations:** Not required.

$ Prices: Appetizers $3.25–$9.50; main courses $12.50–$24.90. AE, MC, V.

Open: Lunch Tues–Sun 11am–4pm; dinner daily 6pm–midnight in high season, 6:30–11pm off-season.

Set at the top of a hill near the airport, 200 yards from the Casino Royal and across from the Maho Beach Hotel, this has become a chic enclave. Near the bar, an elegant swimming pool is fed by a source splashing out of a terra-cotta urn. Visitors select a large peacock chair amid the caged birds and mahogany sheating. The menu features Mexican specialties, T-bone steaks, banana flambé, and frothy tropical drinks. A separate listing includes dishes grilled over mesquite wood, including kingfish steak, catch of the day, chicken, and beef dishes. Top off your meal with one of the specialty coffees.

THE WAJANG DOLL, 137 Front St., Philipsburg. Tel. 22687.

Cuisine: INDONESIAN. **Reservations:** Required.

$ Prices: 14-dish dinner $20; 20-dish dinner $35. AE, MC, V.

Open: Dinner only, Mon–Sat 6:45–10pm. **Closed:** Sept.

Housed in a wooden West Indian building on the main street of town, the Wajang Doll is one of the best Indonesian restaurants in the Caribbean. There's a low-slung front porch where you can watch the pedestrian traffic outside, and big windows in back overlook the sea. The restaurant is best known for its 20-dish dinner, known as a rijstaffel. The cuisine varies from West Java to East Java, and the chef crushes his spices every day for maximum pungency, according to an ancient craft. Other specialties include fried snapper in a chili sauce, marinated pork on a bamboo stick, and Javanese chicken dishes.

INEXPENSIVE

WEST INDIAN TAVERN, 8 Front St., Philipsburg. Tel. 22965.

Cuisine: AMERICAN/FRENCH. **Reservations:** Required.

$ Prices: Appetizers $3.95–$8; main courses $5–$32. AE, DC, MC, V.

Open: Dinner only, daily 5pm–12:01am.

Like a primitive island painting, the interior here is exploding with vibrant colors. A buccaneerish place, it was built from local cedar early in the 1800s on the site of a Jewish synagogue, making it St. Maarten's oldest restaurant. After 5pm, everybody in St. Maarten seems to gather here for a sundowner. You dine in a tree-shaded garden patio with bamboo and rattan chairs, tropical plants, overhead fans, old-world nautical prints, and a noisy parrot. The chef specializes in fresh local lobster; other dishes include fresh local grouper sautéed with bacon and hazelnuts and served in a cream sauce, yellowtail with medallions of lobster in a mornay sauce, and fisherman's pie (lobster, crab, shrimp, and snapper in champagne). The dessert specialty is real Key lime pie. Backgammon is played until 1am, and a West Indian trio provides entertainment.

SPORTS & RECREATION

See Chapter 11 on the French West Indies for information about sports and recreation on French St. Martin.

BEACHES   St. Maarten has 36 beautiful white sand beaches, and it's comparatively easy to find a part of the beach for yourself. *Warning:* If it's too secluded, be careful. Don't carry valuables to the beach; there have been reports of robberies on some remote beaches.

Regardless of where you stay, you're never far from the water. If you're a beach-sampler, you can often use the changing facilities at some of the bigger resorts for a small fee. (Nudists should head for the French side of the island, although the Dutch side is getting more liberal about such things.)

On the west side of the island, west of the airport, **Mullet Bay Beach** is shaded by palm trees and can get crowded on weekends. Water-sports equipment rentals can be arranged through the hotel.

Great Bay Beach is preferred if you're staying along Front Street in Philipsburg. This mile-long beach is sandy, but since it borders the busy capital it may not be as clean as some of the more remote beaches. Immediately to the west, at the foot of Fort Amsterdam, **Little Bay Beach** looks like a Caribbean postcard, but it, too, can be overrun with visitors from Divi Little Bay and Belair Resort.

Stretching the length of Simpson Bay Village, **Simpson Bay Beach** is shaped like a half moon with white sands. It lies west of Philipsburg before you reach the airport. Water-sports equipment rentals are available here.

North of the airport, **Maho Bay Beach,** at the Maho Beach Hotel and Casino, is shaded by palms and is ideal in many ways, if you don't mind the planes taking off and landing. Palms and sea grape provide shade, and food and drink can be purchased at the hotel.

The sands are pearly white at **Oyster Pond Beach,** near the Oyster Pond Yacht Club northeast of Philipsburg. Bodysurfers like the rolling waves here. In the same location, **Dawn Beach** is noted for its underwater tropical beauty (reefs lie offshore). The approach is through the Dawn Beach Hotel.

DEEP-SEA FISHING   Half-day deep-sea bottom-fishing excursions are offered aboard the **Black Fin** (tel. 22366), operating out of Bobby's Marina in Philipsburg. The vessel departs from the marina at the head of Front Street at 8am and returns at noon, Tuesday through Saturday. All bait and tackle are furnished, plus instructions for novices and an open bar. The cost is $375 per half day for four passengers.

GOLF   The **Mullet Bay Resort** (tel. 52801, ext. 370) has an 18-hole course, one of the most challenging in the Caribbean, designed by Joseph Lee. The fairways stretch along Mullet Pond and Simpson Bay Lagoon, providing both beauty and hazards. Greens fees for resort residents are $45 for 18 holes or $30 for 9 holes, including use of a cart. There are no caddies, but there are pros. In general, only residents of the resort are permitted to play on the course. However, cruise-ship passengers are allowed to play if they purchase an expensive golf package for $65.

HORSEBACK RIDING   At **Crazy Acres,** Wathey Estate, Cole Bay (tel. 42793), riding expeditions invariably end on an isolated beach where the horses, with or without their riders, enjoy the cool waters in an after-ride romp. Two experienced escorts accompany a maximum of eight people on the outings, which begin at 9:30am and 2:30pm Monday through Saturday and last 2½ hours. The price is $45 per person. Riders of all levels of experience are welcome, with the single provision that they wear bathing suits under their riding clothes for the grand finale on the beach. It's recommended that reservations be made at least 2 days in advance.

PARASAILING   **Lagoon Cruises & Watersports N.V.,** on the lagoon at Mullet Bay Resort (tel. 42801), offers a parasailing thrill—a 10-minute flight for $30 per person. Parasailing gives you a view of the island from above on closer terms than you get from an airplane. No experience is required, and Lagoon Cruises is open daily from 8:30am to 5pm.

PICNIC SAILS A popular pastime is to sign up for a day of picknicking, sailing, snorkeling, and sightseeing aboard one of several boats providing this service. The sleek sailboats usually pack large wicker hampers full of victuals and stretch tarpaulins over sections of the deck to protect sun-shy sailors.

The *Gabrielle* (tel. 23170) sails from Bobby's Marina in Philipsburg daily at 9am and returns at 5pm year round. The *Gabrielle* is a 46-foot ketch, with a spacious cockpit and large decks. Its $60-per-person price includes lunch, beer, French wine, and use of all equipment. A maximum of 12 people are taken to a secluded cove on a small island where you can sunbathe, swim, and snorkel. In most cases you can make reservations for any of these cruises at your hotel.

A REVITALIZATION CENTER **L'Aqualigne,** Pelican Resort and Casino, Simpson Bay (tel. 42426), is a health and beauty center with multiple services, specializing in the reduction of cellulite. Diets and aerobic exercises are just some of the services offered here, along with a program developed by cosmetologists. The center will send you full details. It's open daily from 9am to 6pm.

SAILING TO OTHER ISLAND COUNTRIES Experienced skippers make 1-day voyages to St. Barts in the French West Indies and to Saba, another of the Dutch Windwards in the Leewards; they stop long enough for passengers to familiarize themselves with the island ports, shop, and have lunch. To arrange a trip, ask at your hotel or at the **St. Maarten Tourist Bureau,** Cyrus W. Wathey Square in Philipsburg (tel. 22337).

The *Quicksilver* (tel. 22167), a 61-foot motor-sailing catamaran, leaves from Great Bay, Chesterfield's Marina, daily at 9am and returns around 5pm. It makes a 2-hour run to the French island of St. Barts, where you can visit the little capital of Gustavia, shop, and tour the island at your leisure. The $50 fare includes an open bar. A $5 departure tax is required. You can visit the *Quicksilver* at the dock before or after a cruise.

The *Eagle,* one of the most beautiful catamarans home-ported in Philipsburg at Great Bay Marina, measuring 67 feet long and 30 feet wide, sails for St. Barts daily at 9am and returns to St. Maarten at 5pm. The boat has double hulls painted black with gold trim and is propelled by a billowing spinnaker. The cruise includes snacks, open bar, use of snorkeling gear, and spectacular views. The cost is $50 per person, plus $5 departure tax.

The *Style,* Great Bay Marina (tel. 23248), sails Wednesday through Sunday at 9am for Saba and returns to St. Maarten at 5pm. The cost is $55 per person for a round-trip, with an open bar included. There is no departure tax, and the trip time is 90 minutes.

The *White Octopus* (tel. 23170 in the evening), a 75-foot motor-driven catamaran, offers spacious upper and lower decks for passengers going from St. Maarten to St. Barts, a trip lasting 1½ hours. The boat leaves Philipsburg Monday through Saturday at 9am and returns at 5pm. The cost is $50 per person, plus $5 departure tax. The boat docks at Bobby's Marina. This is said to be the island's fastest waterborne method of reaching St. Barts. There's an open bar, and snacks are served on the way back.

You can circumnavigate St. Maarten on the *Cheshire Cat* (tel. 22366), a luxurious catamaran that leaves from Bobby's Marina in Philipsburg at 10am and returns by 5pm Friday through Monday. The sail takes you on a trip "down island" in the lee of St. Maarten, then rounds Basse Terre, the most westerly part of the island, and sails into the Anguilla Channel, allowing views of bays and islands. The *Cheshire Cat* then takes passengers to the deserted island of Tintamarre (Flat Island), where for 30 years beginning in 1902 the locally dubbed "King of Tintamarre" and his 100 workers operated a cotton plantation. Here, you can relax on the long beach, swim, and snorkel—lessons are given to beginning snorkelers. A lunch of barbecued local fish, spareribs, or chicken is served with French wine. The homeward journey is along the windward side of the island. The trip includes lunch, open bar, sodas, snacks, and snorkeling gear, all for $75, plus $5 departure tax, for adults and $30 for children.

TENNIS You can try the courts at any of the large hotels, but the **Mullet Bay Resort** (tel. 52801, ext. 376) is the undisputed champion of both the French and Dutch sides of the island, with 14 tennis courts. Residents of the resort pay $9 per person hourly, and nonresidents are charged $25 per person per hour. Racquets are rented for $4 per hour. Two of the courts can be lit at night and cost $22 per hour.

WATER SPORTS **Windsurfing** and **jet-skiing** are especially popular on St. Maarten. The unruffled waters of Simpson Bay Lagoon, the largest in the West Indies, are ideal for these sports, as well as for **waterskiing.**

St. Maarten's crystal-clear bays and the countless coves make for great **snorkeling** and **scuba diving.** Underwater visibility reportedly runs from 75 to 125 feet. The biggest attraction for scuba divers is the 1801 British man-o-war, H.M.S. *Proselyte,* which came to a watery grave on a reef a mile off the coast. Most of the big resort hotels have facilities for scuba diving, and their staff can provide information about underwater tours, for photography as well as night diving.

One of the major water-sports centers, **Maho Watersports,** in the Mullet Bay Resort, Mullet Bay (tel. 54387), is the longest-established diving operation on the island. The center provides scuba lessons. A resort course—including beach instruction, all equipment, and a beach dive—costs $45. PADI or NAUI certification is available for $350, including 40 hours of instruction. A one-tank dive for certified divers is priced at $45. Dive packages are available on request. You can rent snorkel equipment and other dive items. Owned and operated by Tom Burnett, Maho Watersports is open daily from 8:30am to 5pm.

SAVVY SHOPPING

St. Maarten is not only a free port, but there are no local sales taxes. Prices are sometimes lower here than anywhere else in the Caribbean; however, you must be familiar with the prices of what you're looking for to know what actually is a bargain. Many well-known shops in Curaçao have branches here, in case you're not going on to the ABC islands (Aruba, Bonaire, and Curaçao).

Except for the boutiques at resort hotels, the main shopping center is in downtown Philipsburg. Most of the shops are on two leading streets, Front Street (called Voorstraat in Dutch), which is closer to the bay, and Back Street (Achterstraat), which runs parallel. Shopping hours in general are 8am to noon and 2 to 6pm Monday through Saturday. If a cruise ship is in port, many shops also open on Sunday.

SHOPPING CENTERS

MUSEUM ARCADE, 119 Front St.

This gallery of specialty shops is designed in an authentic old West Indian style and was built around St. Maarten's first museum. The museum is part of a foundation designed to promote excavations and other explorations on the island, as well as to carry out other projects related to the island's history and its cultural and artistic past. The museum is housed in a cottage on Front Street that dates from 1888 and was built in the West Indian gingerbread style. The museum is open Monday through Friday from 10am to 4pm and charges an admission of $1.

The Museum Arcade features six shops, a French café, and a French restaurant. The variety of items available ranges from Italian leather goods to French perfumes to novelty souvenirs. Crystal from the Scandinavian countries is also sold. If you're interested in unique gift items reflecting West Indian culture, then visit my favorite in the complex, Museum Classics, run by an American, Gail B. Knopfler, who has long been a promoter of St. Maarten. The arcade is next to the Sea Palace Hotel and has access from Front Street as well as Great Bay Beach. Visitors can enjoy the open-air terrace, breezy courtyard, and, perhaps more important, the public bathrooms.

OLD STREET SHOPPING CENTER, with entrances on Front St. and Back St. Tel. 24712.

The Old Street Shopping Center lies 170 yards east of the courthouse. Its lion's-head fountain is the most photographed spot on St. Maarten. Built in a West Indian–Dutch style, it features an array of shops and boutiques, including branches of several famous stores. Dining facilities include the Philipsburg Grill and Ribs Co., and Rick's Place Sports Bar, with satellite TV. The stores are open Monday through Saturday from 9:30am to 6pm, but the Philipsburg Grill and Ribs Co. and Rick's Place Sports Bar are open on Sunday as well, to 11pm.

SPECIALTY STORES

ANTILLEAN LIQUORS, Juliana Airport. Tel. 54267.

This duty-free shop attracts the last-minute shopper and is open daily 365 days a year, from 8am to 7pm. It has a complete assortment of all the leading brands of liquor and liqueurs, as well as cigarettes and cigars.

CARIBBEAN CAMERA CENTRE, 79 Front St. Tel. 25259.

The Caribbean Camera Centre has a wide range of merchandise, but it's always wise to know the prices charged back home.

COLOMBIAN EMERALDS INTERNATIONAL, Front St. Tel. 22438.

Here you can find stones from collector to investment quality. Unmounted duty-free emeralds from the rich mines of Colombia, as well as emerald, gold, diamond, ruby, and sapphire jewelry, will tempt your eye and pocketbook. There's another branch in the Old Street Arcade.

GUAVABERRY COMPANY, 10 Front St. Tel. 24497.

This place sells the rare island folk liqueur of St. Maarten that for centuries was made in private homes but is now available to everyone. Sold in square bottles, the product is made from rum that is given a unique flavor by use of rare, local berries usually grown in the hills in the center of the island. Don't confuse the guavaberries with guavas—they're very different. The liqueur is aged and has a fruity, woody, almost bittersweet flavor, and you can blend it with coconut for a unique guavaberry colada or pour a splash into a glass of icy champagne. Stop in at their shop and free-tasting house, which is open daily from 9am to 5pm.

H. STERN JEWELLERS, 56 Front St. Tel. 23328.

This is the Philipsburg branch of a worldwide firm that engages in mining, designing, manufacturing, exporting, and retailing jewelry for all occasions and in all price ranges. They use precious gems to create pieces in contemporary and traditional designs.

LITTLE SWITZERLAND, 42 and 69 Front St. Tel. 23530.

These fine-quality European imports are made even more attractive by the prices charged in Philipsburg. Elegant famous-name watches, china, crystal, and jewelry are for sale.

NEW AMSTERDAM STORE, 54 Front St. Tel. 22787.

In business since 1925, New Amsterdam offers extensive designer clothing, such as Polo by Ralph Lauren, Nautica, Jaime de Bettina, Gotcha, Gitano, and exotic swimwear from Gottex. It also features St. Maarten's largest linen department and carries Cuban cigars, although these can't be brought back to the U.S. Also available are Bally shoes from Switzerland.

LA ROMANA, Royal Palm Plaza, 61 Front St. Tel. 22181.

Arguably the most interesting international specialty boutique on the island, this shop offers an excellent selection of the famous line of La Perla swimwear/beachwear for men and women, the La Perla fine lingerie collection, and the latest Fendi fashion, bags, luggage, accessories, and perfume. The management states that prices are sometimes up to 40% less than U.S. prices.

SHIPWRECK SHOP, Front St. Tel. 23438.

Here you'll find West Indian hammocks, beach towels, steak plates, salad bowls, baskets, handmade jewelry, T-shirts, postcards, stamps, books, and much more. It's the home of wood carvings, native art, sea salt, cane sugar, and spices—in all, a treasure trove of Caribbean handcrafts.

YELLOW HOUSE [CASA AMARILLA], Wilhelminastraat. Tel. 23438.
Residents of the Dutch-speaking islands know this place as the branch of a century-old establishment in Curaçao. All kinds of perfumes and luxury items are sold here, including fine porcelain dishes and figurines. Everything is sold at duty-free prices.

EVENING ENTERTAINMENT

On the Dutch side of St. Maarten there are few real nightclubs. After-dark activities begin early here, as guests select their favorite nook for a sundowner—perhaps the veranda of the **West Indian Tavern** (see "Where to Dine," above) or the garden patio of **Pasanggrahan** (see "Where to Stay," above).
A favorite spot for sunset watching is at the luxury **Caravanserai** (see "Where to Stay," above). An airy octagonal gazebo caps a rocky outcropping at Burgeaux Bay. From here, guests watch for the legendary "green flash," an atmospheric phenomenon written about by Hemingway that sometimes occurs in these latitudes just as the sun drops below the horizon. Each evening guests wait expectantly, and have been known to break into a round of applause at a particularly spectacular sunset.
The big hotels, and some of the smaller ones too, sponsor **beachside barbecues** (particularly in season) with steel bands and native music and folk dancing. Outsiders are welcomed at most of these events, but call ahead to see if it's a private catered affair.

DISCOS & NIGHTCLUBS

LE CLUB, in the Mullet Bay Resort and Casino. Tel. 52801.
The most glamorous club of this sprawling resort stands next to the Shopping Plaza and Grand Casino. The joint rocks Tuesday through Sunday night, and every night happy hour is from 10 to 11pm, when drinks are half price. Otherwise, drinks begin at $4. Friends, St. Maarten's No. 1 recording band, might put in an appearance. Open: Daily 10:30pm "until. . . ."
    Admission (including one drink): $5 Sun–Thurs, $10 Fri–Sat.

THE COMEDY CLUB, in the Maho Beach Hotel and Casino, Maho Bay. Tel. 52115.
On the upper lobby of this previously recommended hotel, the Comedy Club presents shows Tuesday through Sunday at 9:30pm and again at 11:30pm. Management promises "the best young comedians from the Carson and Letterman shows and HBO and Showtime specials." There's also improvisation along with audience participation if you're game. (Check at the hotel desk for the times when the comedians from the U.S. go on.)
    Admission: $10.

CASINOS

Most of the combos and casinos are in the big hotels, such as the **Mullet Bay Resort and Casino,** the **Maho Beach Hotel and Casino** (with its glittering Casino Royale), and **Great Bay Beach Hotel and Casino** (see "Where to Stay," above, for descriptions and locations).
The **Casino Royale,** at the Maho Beach Hotel on Maho Bay, opened in 1975. It has 17 blackjack tables, 6 roulette wheels, 206 slot machines, and 3 craps tables. The Casino Royale also offers Caribbean stud poker. The casino is open from 1pm until 4am and accepts cash and checks.
Located at the Mullet Bay Resort, the **Grand Casino,** one of the Caribbean's

largest, offers both Atlantic City–and Las Vegas–style rules and features a wide range of games including baccarat, craps, double deck 21, and progressive slots. The Grand is open daily from 1pm until 3am.

A popular casino is at the **Pelican Resort and Casino** (tel. 42503), built to a Swiss design incorporating a panoramic view of Simpson Bay.

The Roman-themed **Coliseum Casino** on Front Street in Philipsburg (tel. 32102), which opened in 1990 as one of the newest casinos of St. Maarten, has taken several steps to attract gaming enthusiasts, especially "high rollers," and has the highest table limits on St. Maarten. In addition to offering all its patrons free limousine shuttle service from the Divi Little Bay Beach Hotel, the Coliseum arranges free limousine for "high rollers" from any hotel in St. Maarten. A private room with blackjack and roulette is reserved exclusively for those making high bets. Upon the management's approval, the Coliseum also offers credit lines for clients with a good credit rating at any U.S. casino. The Coliseum features 182 slot machines, 6 blackjack tables, and 2 roulette wheels. Several times a year the Coliseum holds special slot machine and blackjack tournaments. The Coliseum is open daily from 11am to 3am.

2. ST. EUSTATIUS

Called "Statia," this Dutch-held island is just an 8-square-mile pinpoint in the Netherlands Antilles, still basking in its 18th-century heritage as the "Golden Rock." One of the true backwaters of the West Indies, it is just awakening to tourism. The location is 150 miles east of Puerto Rico, 90 miles east of St. Croix, 38 miles due south of St. Maarten, and 17 miles southeast of Saba.

Two extinct volcanoes, the Quill and "Little Mountain," are linked by a sloping agricultural plain known as De Cultuurvlakte, where yams and sweet potatoes are grown.

Overlooking the Caribbean on the western edge of the plain, **Oranjestad** (Orange City) is the capital and the only village, consisting of both an Upper and Lower Town, connected by stone-paved, dogleg Fort Road.

Statia was sighted by Columbus in 1493, on his second voyage, and the island was claimed for Holland by Jan Snouck in 1640. The island's history was turbulent before it settled down to peaceful slumber under Dutch protection. From 1650 to 1816 Statia changed flags 22 times!

Once the trading hub of the Caribbean, Statia was a thriving market, both for goods and for slaves. Benjamin Franklin directed his mail to Europe through Statia.

Before the American Revolution the population of Statia did not exceed 1,200, most of whom were slaves engaged in raising sugarcane. When war came and Britain blockaded the North American coast, Europe's trade was diverted to the West Indies. Dutch neutrality lured many traders, which led to the construction of a mile and a half of warehouses in Lower Town. The Americans obtained gunpowder and ammunition shipped through Statia.

Statia's historical links with the United States are strong. Its Fort Oranje was the first fortress to salute the Stars and Stripes, flying from the 14-gun brigantine *Andrew Doria* on November 16, 1776. In reprisal, in 1781 Great Britain's Admiral Rodney seized and sacked Statia, and lured unsuspecting vessels into anchorage by continuing to fly the Dutch flag. It is estimated that when Rodney sailed away, he carried $15 million to $20 million of booty from Statia.

Contrary to legend, Statia was not destroyed by Rodney. After his forces left, the island bounced back to reach the pinnacle of its prosperity in 1790, with a population of 8,125. Its gradual decay came about when it was no longer needed as a transit port for the American colonies. Also it was bled by the exorbitant demands of interim French and English governments. Its unprotected warehouses eventually tumbled into the sea, and only their barest shells and raw foundations remain—skeletal stone walls that one historian dubbed "the Pompeii of the Caribbean."

ORIENTATION

GETTING THERE   St. Eustatius can be reached from Dutch St. Maarten's Juliana Airport via **Windward Islands Airways International (Winair)** (tel. 5/44230 in St. Maarten). The flying time to Statia's Franklin Delano Roosevelt Airport is only 20 minutes from St. Maarten, with flights five times a day. Once on Statia, connections can also be made for flights to either Saba or St. Kitts. There are often as many as four flights per day.

The little airline, launched in 1961, has an excellent safety record and has flown such passengers as David Rockefeller. The plane has 20 seats and is called a STOL (short takeoff and landing). At present the flight costs $50 per round-trip. You can visit just for the day, but I recommend that you spend more here. Always be certain that you reconfirm your return passage once you're on Statia.

LIAT (tel. 809/462-0700) has twice-weekly flights from St. Kitts, and from Antigua as well.

GETTING AROUND   By Taxi   Taxis are your best bet. They meet all incoming flights, and on the way to the hotel, I assure you that your driver will offer himself as a guide during your stay on the island. Taxi rates are low, probably no more than $3 to your hotel from the airport. If you book a 3½-hour tour (and in that time you should be able to cover all the sights on Statia), the cost is about $35 per vehicle.

By Rental Car   You'll find **Avis Rent-a-Car** represented through a local dealer, Rouse Enterprises, 8 Prinseweg (tel. 82421, or toll free 800/331-1212 in the U.S.), and is your best bet if you want to reserve a car in advance. With unlimited mileage included, Rouse's cheapest vehicle costs $50 per day. Drivers must be 21 years old and present a valid driver's license and credit card.

FAST FACTS   ST. EUSTATIUS

Area Code   St. Eustatius is *not* part of the Caribbean's 809 area code. For information on calling St. Eustatius, see "Telephone and Telegraph," below.

Banks   Barclay's Bank, Wilhelminastraat, Oranjestad (tel. 3/82392), the only bank on the entire island, is open from 8:30am to 1pm Monday through Friday and also from 4 to 5pm on Friday. On weekends, most hotels will exchange money for you.

Currency   The official unit of currency is the **Netherlands Antilles guilder (NAf),** at 1.77 NAf to each $1 U.S., but nearly all places will quote you prices in U.S. dollars.

Customs   There are no Customs duties as the island is a free port.

Documents   U.S. and Canadian citizens need proof of citizenship, such as a passport, voter registration card, or a birth certificate, along with an ongoing ticket. If you're using a birth certificate or voter registration card, you will also need some photo ID.

Electricity   It's the same as in the U.S., 110 volts AC, 60 cycles.

Information   Before you go, consult the **St. Eustatius Tourist Office,** c/o Medhurst & Associates, Inc., 271 Main St., Northport, NY 11768 (tel. 516/261-7474, or toll free 800/344-4606). On the island, the **Tourist Bureau** is at 3 Fort Oranjestraat (tel. 3/82433), open Monday through Friday from 8am to noon and 1 to 5pm.

Language   Dutch is the official language, but English is commonly spoken.

Medical Care   A licensed physician is on duty at the **Princess Beatrix Hospital,** 25 Princess Weg in Oranjestad (tel. 82211).

Safety   Although crime is rare here, it's wise to secure your valuables and take the kind of discreet precautions you would anywhere. Don't leave valuables unguarded on the beach.

Taxes   There is no departure tax if you're returning to the Dutch-held islands of St. Maarten or Saba; if you're going elsewhere, the tax is $5. Hotels on Statia collect a 5% government tax.

Telephone and Telegraph   Ask at your hotel if you need to send a cable. St. Eustatius maintains a 24-hour-a-day telephone service—and sometimes it takes about that much time to get a call through!

Statia is *not* part of the 809 area code that applies to most of the Caribbean. To call Statia from the U.S., if your long-distance telephone company is equipped to handle international direct dialing, dial 011 (the international access code), then 599 (the country code for the Netherlands Antilles), and finally 3 (the area code for all of Statia) and the five-digit local number. If you cannot dial direct internationally, dial 0 ("zero," for the operator) and tell the operator you wish to make an international call; once you are transferred to the international operator, state the 599 country code and then the area code and local number, and the operator will dial the call for you.

To make a call within Statia, only the five-digit local number is necessary. *Note:* In this chapter, only the area code and the local number are given.

Time   St. Eustatius operates on Atlantic standard time year round. Thus in winter, when the U.S. is on standard time, if it's 6pm in Oranjestad it's 5pm in New York. During daylight saving time in the U.S. the island keeps the same time as the U.S. East Coast.

Tipping and Service   Tipping is at the visitor's discretion, and most hotels, guesthouses, and restaurants include a 10% service charge.

Water   The water here is safe to drink.

Weather   The average daytime temperature ranges from 78° to 82° Fahrenheit. The annual rainfall is only 45 inches.

WHERE TO STAY

Don't expect deluxe hotels or high-rises—Statia is strictly for escapists. Sometimes guests are placed in private homes. A 15% service charge and 7% government tax are added to hotel bills.

AIRPORT APARTMENTS VIEW, Golden Rock, St. Eustatius, N.A. Tel. 3/82474. Fax 3/82517. 9 units. TV TEL
$ Rates: $55 single; $70 double. Breakfast $5 extra. AE, MC, V. **Parking:** Free.
Airport Apartments View has two locations: most units are in the Golden Rock area near the airport and four others are in Upper Town, Oranjestad, Princess Weg. The accommodations in the Golden Rock area all have fans, compact refrigerators, coffee makers, and private baths. They consist of five one-bed apartments for one or two people and four two-bed units for up to four guests. On the premises are a bar/restaurant and an outdoor patio with barbecue facilities.

In Upper Town, the accommodations consist of two three-bedroom units holding up to nine guests and two two-bedroom apartments for up to four people. They all have kitchens, living rooms, dining rooms, and baths.

GOLDEN ERA HOTEL, Lower Town, St. Eustatius, N.A. Tel. 3/82345. 20 rms.
$ Rates: Winter, $70 single; $88 double; $104 triple. Summer, $65 single; $80 double or triple. MAP $30 per person extra. MC, V. **Parking:** Free.
Set directly on the water, this modern hotel is clean, serviceable, and comfortable. The establishment, including its simply decorated bar and dining room, is operated by Hubert Lijfrock. Eight of the accommodations don't have a water view, but the remaining units offer a full or partial exposure to the sea; all are tasteful and spacious. There is also a swimming pool.
Lunch is from noon to 2pm and begins at $15 per person. Dinner, from 7 to 9pm

daily, goes for $20 and up per person and is likely to include stewed fish, curried lobster, and ice creams such as passion fruit and mango. The fruit punch, with or without rum, is delectable.

OLD GIN HOUSE AND MOOSHAY BAY PUBLICK HOUSE, Bay Rd. (P.O. Box 172), Lower Town, St. Eustatius, N.A. Tel. 3/82319. Fax 3/82555. 20 rms.
$ Rates: Winter, $110 single; $150 double. Summer, $85 single; $100 double. Continental breakfast $3.50 extra. AE, DC, MC, V. **Parking:** Free. **Closed:** Sept–Oct 15.

This is a two-in-one hotel, with half a dozen rooms facing the beach in Oranjestad, and the others built across the street, opening onto a pool. The Mooshay Bay Publick House—the hotel set back from the beach—is of more recent vintage than the Old Gin House. However, it was built on the ruins of 18th-century warehouses once used to store molasses. Run by John May, an expatriate American, the inn sports antiques mixed with practical pieces; a small pool was shaped from a decaying cistern and an old cannon discovered while digging the swimming hole has been retired to a peaceful nook.

The Publick House is brick and has a double row of balconies. An overseer's gallery has been turned into a library and backgammon room. Cooled by overhead fans and sea breezes, each accommodation has paintings and wrought-iron wall hangings from Haiti.

Across the street, the Old Gin House originally began as a hot-dog stand in 1972, but it grew and grew, and is now a six-room inn of character, small but special. A two-story unit faces the sea and the rooms are cooled by breezes. The ceilings are high and balconies open onto the waterfront.

WHERE TO DINE

L'ETOILE, 6 Van Rheeweg, northeast of Upper Town. Tel. 82299.
   Cuisine: CREOLE. **Reservations:** Required.
$ Prices: Appetizers $4–$5; main courses $6.50–$20. AE, MC, V.
   Open: Mon–Sat noon–10pm, Sun noon–6pm.

⑤ Caren Henriquez has had this second-floor restaurant with a few simple tables for some time. She is well known in Statia for her local cuisine, but you don't run into too many tourists here. Favored main dishes include the ubiquitous "goat water" (a stew), stewed whelks, mountain crab, and tasty spareribs. Caren is also known for her pastechis—deep-fried turnovers stuffed with meat. Expect a complete and very filling meal.

OLD GIN HOUSE AND MOOSHAY BAY PUBLICK HOUSE, Lower Town. Tel. 82319.
   Cuisine: CONTINENTAL. **Reservations:** Required for dinner.
$ Prices: Appetizers $3.50–$4.50; main courses $15–$30. AE, DC, MC, V.
   Open: Lunch daily noon–2pm; dinner daily 6:30–8pm. **Closed:** Sept–Oct 15.
Overlooking the beach, the Old Gin House and Mooshay Bay Publick House provide a nostalgic atmosphere where lunch guests can enjoy a shady treillage terrace. You might begin with a daiquiri before going on to order a luncheon special, perhaps lobster Antillean, or a hamburger. Lunches begin at $12.

At the Old Mooshay Bay dining room, continental cuisine is served poolside with candlelight and pewter. Sample the grapefruit mousse, snapper mousse, or rack of lamb. Try to arrive before the dinner hour so you can enjoy a drink in the pub, a structure of wooden beams and old ship ballast bricks.

STONE OVEN BAR & RESTAURANT, 15 Faeschweg, Upper Town. Tel. 82247.
   Cuisine: CREOLE. **Reservations:** Required.
$ Prices: Appetizers $3–$3.50; main courses $7–$13. No credit cards.
   Open: Lunch Tues–Sun 11am–2pm; dinner Tues–Sun 7–10pm (bar open Tues–Sun from 11am).

In this small house with a garden patio and a cozy Caribbean decor. Myrtle V. Suares, the manager, serves a variety of local and West Indian dishes. A specialty is red fish and rice. This is the liveliest place in town during "Jolly Time," every Friday from 9pm until they decide to close the doors.

TALK OF THE TOWN BAR & RESTAURANT, L. E. Saddlerweg, Golden Rock, St. Eustatius, N.A. Tel. 3/82236.
Cuisine: AMERICAN/CREOLE. **Reservations:** Not required.
$ Prices: Appetizers $3–$7; main courses $10–$18. AE, MC, V.
Open: Lunch daily 11:30am–2pm; dinner daily 7–10pm (bar stays open later).
In the Golden Rock area on the edge of town, about a 5-minute walk from the airport, this spot is owned by Nora and Koos Sneek, who serve red snapper, steaks, lobster stew, eggplant soufflé, spice crab backs, goat meat, and bullfoot soup. The bar is open from 11am "until."

Eight bedrooms above the restaurant are rented for $77 per couple in high season, $66 in low season. Prices include breakfast. All the rooms are air-conditioned and have private baths, phones, and TVs.

WHAT TO SEE & DO

The capital, **Oranjestad,** stands on a cliff looking out on a beach and the island's calm anchorage, where in the 18th century you might have seen 200 vessels offshore. **Fort Oranje** was built in 1636 and restored in honor of the U.S. Bicentennial celebration of 1976. Today, perched atop the cliffs, its terraced rampart is lined with old cannons. As mentioned, this fort was the first in the world to acknowledge the Stars and Stripes of the newly created republic of the United States of America. You'll see a bronze plaque honoring the fact that "Here the sovereignty of the United States of America was first formally acknowledged to a national vessel by a foreign official." The plaque was presented by Franklin D. Roosevelt. The fort is now used for government offices.

St. Eustatius Historical Foundation Museum, Upper Town (tel. 82288), is also called the de Graaff House in honor of its former tenant, Johannes de Graaff, who ordered the first-ever foreign salute to the Stars and Stripes at Fort Oranje (see above). After the British Admiral Rodney sacked Statia for its tribute to the United States, he installed his own headquarters in this 18th-century house. Today a museum, the former governor's house stands in a garden, with a 20th-century wing crafted from 17th-century bricks. Exhibits demonstrate the process of sugar refining, shipping and commerce, defense, archeological artifacts from the colonial period, and a pair of elegantly beautiful 18th-century antique furnished rooms. There is a section devoted to the pre-Columbian period. In the wing annex is a massive piece of needlework by an American, Catherine Mary Williams, showing the flowers of Statia. The museum is open Monday through Friday from 9am to 5pm and on Saturday and Sunday from 9am to noon; admission costs $1 for adults, 50¢ for children.

A few steps away, a cluster of 18th-century buildings surrounding a quiet courtyard is called **Three Widows' Corner.**

Nearby are the ruins of the first **Dutch Reformed church.** To reach it, turn west from Three Widows' Corner onto Kerkweg. Tilting headstones record the names of the characters in the island's past. The St. Eustatius Historical Foundation recently completed restoration of the church. Visitors may climb to the top level of the tower and see the bay as lookouts did many years before.

In the center, **Honen Dalim,** a Jewish synagogue, the second in the western hemisphere, can be explored, although it is in ruins. Once Statia had a large colony of Jewish traders. This house of prayer was begun about 1740 and was damaged by a hurricane in 1772; it fell into disuse at the dawn of the 19th century. The synagogue stands beside Synagogpad, a narrow lane whose entrance faces Madam Theatre on the square.

The walls of a *mikvah* (ritual bath) rise beside the **Jewish burial ground** on the edge of town. The oldest stone in the cemetery is that of Abraham Hisquiau de la

Motta, who died in 1742. The inscription is in both Portuguese and Hebrew. The most recent marker is that of Moses Waag, who died February 25, 1825. Most poignant is the memorial of David Haim Hezeciah de Lion, who died in 1760 at the age of 2 years, 8 months, 26 days; carved into the baroque surface is an angel releasing a tiny songbird from its cage.

In addition, a short ride from Oranjestad takes you to the road's end at White Wall. There on your left is **Sugarloaf,** a minireplica of Rio's famed cone. On the right is a panoramic view of St. Kitts.

At the base of the pink-gray cliff beneath Fort Oranje, **Lower Town** was the mercantile center of Statia in the 18th century. Bulging with sugar, rum, and tobacco, Lower Town was once filled with row upon row of brick warehouses. In some of these warehouses, slaves were held in bondage awaiting shipment to other islands in the Caribbean. You can wander at leisure through the ruins, and stop later at the Old Gin House for a drink (see "Where to Dine," above).

The Quill, an extinct volcano, called "the most perfect" in the Caribbean, shelters a lush tropical rain forest—a botanical wonderland—in its deep, wide crater. The Quill rises to 1,960 feet on the southern edge of the island. Hikers climb it, and birdwatchers come here for a glimpse of the blue pigeon, a rare bird known to frequent the breadfruit and cottonwood trees in the mountains.

SPORTS & RECREATION

BEACHES   Miles of golden sandy beaches are not the reason most visitors come to Statia. However, there are some, notably **Oranje Baai,** which has lots of black sand and fronts the Caribbean side of the island, off Lower Town. Other beaches include **Zeelandia** and **Lynch.** On the southwestern shore of Statia are the best volcanic beaches for swimming. Ask a taxi driver to take you to what he or she thinks is the best spot.

CRAB CATCHING   I'm perfectly serious. If you're interested, you can join Statians in a crab hunt. The Quill's crater is the breeding ground for these large crustaceans. At night they emerge from their holes to forage, and that's when they're caught. Either with flashlights or relying on moonlight, the "hunters" climb the Quill, catch a crab, and take the local delicacy home to prepare stuffed crab back.

HIKING   Perhaps this is the most popular sporting activity. Those with the stamina can climb the slopes of the Quill. The trip takes about half a day, and you can ask the tourist office to arrange for a guide for you, which will cost at least $20.

TENNIS   Tennis can be played at the **Community Center** on Rosemary Lane (tel. 82249). The court has a concrete surface and is lit for night games. Changing rooms are available. The court costs $5, and you must bring your own equipment.

WATER SPORTS   On the Atlantic side of the island, at Concordia Bay, the **surfing** is best. However, there is no lifeguard protection.

Snorkeling tours are available through the Caribbean Sea to explore the remnants of an 18th-century man-of-war and the walls of warehouses, taverns, and shops that sank below the surface of Oranje Bay more than 200 years ago.

Dive Statia is a fully equipped diving center on Fishermen's Beach in **Lower Town** (tel. 82435), near the Old Gin House, offering full certification, advanced certification, and specialty-course packages. Dive Statia's professional staff guides divers of all levels of experience to the reef formations and historic shipwrecks along with the ruins of 18th-century seaports now sitting on the ocean bottom. The establishment offers one- and two-tank boat dives. Snorkel trips are also available. A single dive costs $40.

SAVVY SHOPPING

Merchandise is very limited. Most shops, what few there are, are open Monday through Friday from 8am to noon and 1:30 to 5:30pm, and on Saturday from 10am to noon and 2:30 to 5:30pm. Of course, this could vary widely.

THE HOLE IN THE WALL, Upper Town. Tel. 82265.

This shop is literally built into a wall adjacent to the Catholic church grounds. It features local handcrafts, designed and hand-sketched by the owners. Available are hand-painted cotton resortwear (painted and designed on the premises by the owners), postcards, and jewelry made from natural local plants and some from "blue slave beads" from the 18th century. Also stocked are authentic 17th-century clay pipe-stem earrings. Open: Mon–Fri 10am–4pm.

MAZINGA GIFTSHOP, Upper Town. Tel. 82245.

Here you'll find an array of souvenirs—T-shirts, liquor, costume jewelry, handbags, Delft from Holland, and paperback romances. You may have seen more exciting stores in your life, but this is without parallel the best Statia offers.

PARK PLACE [ST. EUSTATIUS ARTS GALLERY], Upper Town. Tel. 82452.

Across from Kool Korner and near the tourist office is an art gallery. Managed by Barbara Lane, who is an artist in her own right and co-owner, Park Place carries the works of several local artists. Original watercolors, ceramics, textile art, and carved-wood and hand-painted items are all for sale. In addition, Park Place sells genuine locally made steel drums in regular and mini-sized tenor pans; embroidered items such as napkins, placemats, and bun warmers; straw items; Statia-made jewelry; and reproductions of antique Caribbean art.

3. SABA

An extinct volcano, exotic cone-shaped Saba is 5 square miles of rock carpeted in such lush foliage as orchids (which grow in profusion), giant elephant ear, and Eucharist lilies. At its zenith it reaches a height of 2,900 feet at Mount Scenery, which the locals call simply "The Mountain." The Dutch settled the island in the mid-17th century, and out of such an unusual piece of jagged geography they created an experiment in living that has continued to grow.

Saba is in the Netherlands' Windward Islands at the top of the Lesser Antilles arc. The location is 150 miles east of Puerto Rico and 90 miles east of St. Croix. Most visitors fly over from the Dutch-held section of St. Maarten, 28 miles to the north.

Columbus is credited with sighting Saba in 1493. Before it became permanently Dutch, it was passed back and forth among other European masters 12 times.

Sabans were known in days of yore to take advantage of their special topography— that is, they pelted invaders from above with rocks and boulders. Because of the influence of English missionaries and Scottish seamen from the remote Shetland Islands who settled on the island, Saba has always been English speaking. The official language, however, is Dutch. Also, because of those early settlers from Europe, 60% of the population is Caucasian, many with red hair and freckled fair skin.

ORIENTATION

GETTING THERE   By Plane   You can leave New York's JFK Airport in the morning and be at Captain's Quarters in Saba for dinner that night by taking a direct flight on either of the two airlines that currently fly from the U.S. to St. Maarten. From Juliana Airport there, you can fly to Saba on **Winair (Windward Islands Airways International)** (tel. 4/62255 on Saba or 5/54230 on St. Maarten). Flying time is between 15 and 20 minutes, and the round-trip fare is $50.

Arriving by air from St. Maarten, the traveler steps from Winair's 20-passenger STOL (short takeoff and landing) plane onto the tarmac runway of the **Juancho Yrausquin Airport.** The airstrip is famous as one of the shortest (if not *the* shortest) landing strips in the world, stretching only 1,312 feet along the aptly named Flat Point, one of the few level areas on the island.

Many guests at hotels on St. Maarten fly over to Saba on the morning flight, spend the day sightseeing, then return to St. Maarten on the afternoon flight. Winair connections can also be made in Saba to both St. Kitts and Statia.

By Boat   You can also travel between St. Maarten and Saba aboard the **M.V. Style,** a high-speed 52-foot luxury commuter yacht that makes the 90-minute journey on Wednesday and Sunday, departing at 9am from Great Bay Marina in St. Maarten (tel. 5/22167) and returning the same day at 3pm. Round-trip fare is $45. The *Style* has comfortable seating, an open bar, and taped music. Many visitors from St. Maarten visit Saba on a day trip, and enjoy the sea voyage almost as much as their time on land.

GETTING AROUND   By Taxi   Taxis meet every flight. The cost of a 2-hour tour is $7 per person if there are more than four passengers making the trip. One to four people pay $30.

By Rental Car   In the unlikely event that you should dare to drive a car on Saba, your hotel can make arrangements for you, for about $35 a day, or you can call the **Avis** representative, Windwardside (tel. 4/62289). You'll find a handful of tiny car-rental outfits on the island (some with no more than two cars), but most readers usually prefer to go through a branch of a U.S.-based agency. Because of the very narrow roads, the dozens of breathtaking cliffs, and the tight access roads, the danger of driving must be emphasized in advance. Don't drink and drive!

By Hitchhiking   Now frowned upon in much of the world, hitchhiking has long been an acceptable means of transport in Saba, where everybody seemingly knows everybody else. On recent rounds, my taxi rushed a sick child to the plane and picked up an old man to take him up the hill because he'd fallen and hurt himself—all on my sightseeing tour! I welcomed this cooperative spirit. By hitchhiking, you'll probably get to know everybody else, too.

On Foot   The traditional means of getting around on Saba is still much in evidence. But I suggest that only the sturdy in heart and limb walk from the Bottom up to Windwardside. Many do, but you'd better have some shoes that grip the ground, particularly after a recent rain.

FAST FACTS   SABA

Area Code   Saba is *not* part of the Caribbean's 809 area code. For information on calling Saba, see "Telephone and Telegraph," below.

Banks   The only bank on the island is **Barclays,** Windwardside (tel. 62216), open Monday through Friday from 8:30am to 12:30pm.

Currency   Saba, like the other islands of the Netherlands Antilles, uses the **Netherlands Antilles guilder (NAf),** valued at 1.77 NAf to $1 U.S. However, prices given here are in U.S. currency unless otherwise designated, since U.S. money is accepted by almost everybody here.

Customs   You do not have to go through Customs when you land at Juancho E. Yrausquin Airport, as this is a free port.

Documents   The government requires that all U.S. and Canadian citizens show proof of citizenship, such as a passport or voter registration card with photo ID. A return or ongoing ticket must also be provided.

Drugstore   Try **The Pharmacy,** The Bottom (tel. 63289).

Electricity   Saba uses 110 volts AC, 60 cycles, so most U.S.-made appliances do not need transformers or adapters.

Information   Glenn C. Holm is the chairman of the **Saba Tourist Board,** and he operates out of a small office, the **Tourist Bureau,** next door to the post office in Windwardside (tel. 4/62231), open Monday through Friday from 8am to noon and 1 to 5pm. For information before you go, consult the **Saba Tourist Office,** c/o Medhurst & Associates, Inc., 271 Main St., Northport, NY 11768 (tel. 516/261-7474, or toll free 800/344-4606).

Medical Care Saba's hospital complex is the **A. M. Edwards Medical Centre,** The Bottom (tel. 63239). To call a **doctor's office,** phone 63288.

Police Call 63237.

Safety Crime on this island, where everyone knows everyone else, is practically nonexistent. But who knows? A tourist might rob you. It would be wise to safeguard your valuables.

Taxes The government imposes a 5% tourist tax on hotel rooms. If you're returning to St. Maarten or flying over to Statia, you must pay a $1 departure tax. If you're going anywhere else, however, a $5 tax is imposed.

Telephone and Telegraph Cables and international telephone calls can be placed at the **Cable and Wireless** office in Windwardside (tel. 62225).

Saba is *not* part of the 809 area code that applies to most of the Caribbean. To call Saba from the U.S., if your long-distance telephone company is equipped to handle international direct dialing, dial 011 (the international access code), then 599 (the country code for the Netherlands Antilles), and finally 4 (the area code for all of Saba) and the five-digit local number. If you cannot direct-dial internationally, dial 0 ("zero," for the operator) and tell the operator you wish to make an international call; once you are transferred to the international operator, state the 599 country code and then the area code and local number, and the operator will dial the call for you.

To make a call within Saba, only the five-digit local number is necessary. *Note:* In this chapter, only the area code and the local number are given.

Time Saba is on Atlantic standard time, 1 hour earlier than eastern standard time. When the U.S. is on daylight saving time, clocks on Saba and the U.S. East Coast read the same.

Tips and Service Most restaurants and hotels add a 10% or 15% service charge to your bills to cover tipping.

Weather You'll encounter a temperature of 78° to 82° Fahrenheit. The annual rainfall is 42 inches.

WHERE TO STAY

CAPTAIN'S QUARTERS, Windwardside, Saba, N.A. Tel. 4/62201. Fax 4/62377. 10 rms.

$ Rates (including continental breakfast): Winter, $95 single; $125 double. Summer, $80 single; $95 double. MC, V. **Parking:** Free. **Closed:** Sept.

A restored 19th-century sea captain's house has been converted into a guesthouse where many visitors spend secluded holidays. Just off the village center of Windwardside, it's a complex of several guesthouses surrounding the main house with its traditional verandas and covered porches. You make your way here by going down a narrow, steep lane. Thrust out toward the water, almost as if ready to tumble down to the sea, is a freshwater swimming pool surrounded by a terrace where you can sunbathe or order refreshments from an open-air bar. The cool and refreshing dining room is nestled behind the main house amid a screen of plants. Service is polite and formal at the candlelit dinners.

The main house was built by a Saban sea captain and serves as office, library, sitting room, and kitchen on the first floor, with two private accommodations above (one is a honeymoon haven). The house is furnished with antiques gathered from many ports of the world. About half the bedrooms contain four-poster beds, and each is complete with a private bath and balcony overlooking the sea and Mount Scenery. Well-designed and cozy studio rooms stand in the garden. Everything seems a quaint reminder of New England.

CRANSTON'S ANTIQUE INN, The Bottom, Saba, N.A. Tel. 4/63218. 6 rms.

$ Rates (including breakfast): $44 single; $57.50–$69 double. No credit cards. **Parking:** Free.

Everyone congregates for rum drinks and gossip on the front terrace of this inn near the village roadway, on the west coast north of Fort Bay. It's an old-fashioned house, more than 100 years old at least, and every bedroom has antique four-poster beds. Mr. Cranston, the owner, will gladly rent you the same room where Queen Juliana once spent a holiday. Aside from the impressive wooden beds, the furnishings are mostly hit or miss.

Mr. Cranston has a good island cook, who makes use of locally grown spices. Local dishes are offered, such as roast pork from island pigs, red snapper, and broiled grouper. Meals begin at $10 and are served on a covered terrace in the garden. The house is within walking distance of Ladder Bay.

JULIANA'S APARTMENTS, Windwardside, Saba, N.A. Tel. 4/62269.

Fax 4/62389. 9 units. **Transportation:** Take a taxi from the center (a 10-minute ride).

$ Rates: Winter, $65 single; $85–$100 double. Summer, $55 single; $68 double. Continental breakfast $2–$6 extra. MC, V. **Parking:** Free.

Modern and immaculate, the accommodations here have private baths, balconies, and access to a sun deck for lounging. Each unit is simply but comfortably furnished. There's also a recreation room and a swimming pool.

SCOUT'S PLACE, Windwardside, Saba, N.A. Tel. 4/62205. Fax 4/62388. 15 rms.

$ Rates (including continental breakfast): $65 single; $85–$100 double. AE, DC, MC, V. **Parking:** Free.

Right in the center of the village, Scout's Place is hidden from the street. Set on the ledge of a hill, the place is owned by Diana Medora, who makes guests feel right at home. With only 15 rooms, it's still the largest inn on the island. The old house has a large covered but open-walled dining room, where every table has a view of the sea. It's an informal place, with a highly individual decor that might include everything from Surinam hand-carvings to peacock chairs in red-and-black wicker to silver samovars. Rooms open onto an interior courtyard filled with flowers, and each unit has a view of the sea.

WHERE TO DINE

CAPTAIN'S QUARTERS, Windwardside. Tel. 62201.

Cuisine: INTERNATIONAL. **Reservations:** Not required.

$ Prices: Appetizers $2.50–$10.50; main courses $12.50–$20. MC, V.

Open: Lunch daily noon–2pm; dinner Mon–Sat 6:30–9pm. **Closed:** Sept.

Dining is al fresco here; however, if it rains, don't worry—they have a roof. Large, hearty appetites are catered to at dinner. Perhaps you'll be there on the night they have fresh grouper or lobster. It's one of the best selections in the Caribbean. Soups are homemade and good. Fresh vegetables are regularly available, and the wine list has been extended.

SABA CHINESE RESTAURANT [MOO GOO GAI PAN], Windwardside. Tel. 62268.

Cuisine: CHINESE. **Reservations:** Not required.

$ Prices: Appetizers $2.50–$5.50; main courses $12.50–$18. No credit cards.

Open: Tues–Sun 11am–10pm.

Amid a cluster of residential buildings on a hillside above Windwardside, this place is operated by a family from Hong Kong headed by Yu Yuk Choi. It offers some 100 dishes, an unpretentious decor of plastic tablecloths and folding chairs, and a cookery so popular that many residents claim this to be their most frequented restaurant. Meals include an array of Cantonese and Indonesian specialties—lobster Cantonese,

Chinese chicken with mushrooms, sweet-and-sour fish, chicken with cashew nuts, conch chop suey, several curry dishes, roast duck, and nasi goreng.

SCOUT'S PLACE, Windwardside. Tel. 62205.
 Cuisine: INTERNATIONAL. **Reservations:** Required.
$ Prices: Main courses $16.50–$25; lunch from $12. AE, DC, MC, V.
 Open: Lunch daily at 12:30pm; dinner daily at 7:30pm.

For visitors over for the day, Scout's Place is a popular dining spot, but you should have your driver stop by early and make a reservation for lunch for you. Food at Scout's is simple and good, rewarding and filling, and the price is low too. Dinner is more elaborate, with tables placed on an open-side terrace, the ideal spot for a drink at sundown. Fresh seafood is a specialty, as is curried goat.

WHAT TO SEE & DO

On Saba, tidy white houses cling to the mountainside, and small family cemeteries adjoin each dwelling. Lace-curtained gingerbread-trimmed cottages give a Disneyland aura.

The first Jeep arrived on Saba in 1947. Before that, Sabans went about on foot, climbing from village to village. Hundreds of steps had been chiseled out of rock by the early Dutch settlers in 1640.

Engineers told them it was impossible, but Sabans built a single cross-island road by hand. Filled with hairpin turns, it zigzags from Fort Bay, where a deep-water pier accommodates large tenders from cruise ships, to a height of 1,600 feet. Along the way it has fortresslike supporting walls.

Past storybook villages, the road goes over the crest to **The Bottom.** Derived from the Dutch word *botte,* which means "bowl-shaped," this village is nestled on a plateau and surrounded by rocky volcanic domes. It occupies about the only bit of ground, 800 feet above the sea. It's also the official capital of Saba, a Dutch village of charm, with chimneys, gabled roofs, and gardens.

From the Bottom you can take a taxi up the hill to the mountain village of **Windwardside,** perched on the crest of two ravines at about 1,500 feet above sea level. This village of red-roofed houses, the second most important in Saba, is the site of the two biggest inns and most of the shops. From Windwardside you can climb steep steps cut in the rock to yet another village, **Hell's Gate,** teetering on the edge of a mountain. However, there is a serpentine road from the airport to Hell's Gate, where you'll find the island's largest church. Only the most athletic climb from here to the lip of the volcanic crater.

In Windwardside, the **Harry L. Johnson Memorial Museum** (tel. 62359) is in an old sea captain's home, with antique furnishings, evoking an 1890s aura. Filled with family memorabilia, the house can be visited for an admission of $1. The surprise visit of Jacqueline Kennedy Onassis is still vividly recalled. It's open Monday through Friday from 10am to noon and 1 to 3:30pm.

SPORTS & RECREATION

HIKING The island is as beautiful above the water as it is below. Mountain walking is the major sport, and the top of **Mount Scenery** is a wildlife reserve. Allow more than a day and take your time climbing the 1,064 concrete steps up to the cloud-reefed mountain. One of the inns will pack you a picnic lunch. The higher you climb, the cooler it grows, about a drop of $1°$ Fahrenheit every 328 feet; on a hot day this can be an incentive. The peak is 2,855 feet high.

If you don't want to set out on your own, **botanical tours** are offered, as well as other hikes with your special interests in mind, arranged by the Saba Tourist Bureau (tel. 62231) or Captain's Quarters (tel. 62201), costing $7.50 per person for up to four participants, $5 per person for larger groups. The botanical tour takes you to the top of Mount Scenery into the tropical rain forest where orchids bloom in winter and golden heliconia in spring. A shorter hike is possible to Maskehorne Hill, where huge rock formations covered with orchids and bromeliads lead to a view of

Windwardside. You can walk up the steps and cut through the terraced fields and forest of Big Rendezvous to an overlook of Crispeen. For a different view of the island, hike along Sandy Cruz, starting at Upper Hell's Gate and walking along the Deep Gut, with its blend of cultivated fields and windswept forest.

TENNIS   Tennis buffs will find a free **public court** (concrete, not grass) in the Bottom.

WATER SPORTS   Don't come here for beaches. Saba has only one sand beach, and it's about 20 feet long. Sports here are mostly do-it-yourself. Visitors such as John F. Kennedy, Jr., enjoy the underwater scenery and dark, volcanic sands and coral formations.

Stretching around the entire island to 200 feet below the highwater mark, the **Saba Marine Park,** Fort Bay (tel. 63295), has been established by the Saba government and the Netherlands Antilles National Parks Foundation to preserve the island's marine environment. The park is zoned for various purposes. There is an all-purpose recreational zone for boating, fishing, swimming, snorkeling, and diving, including Saba's only little beach which washes ashore only in summer—its sands disappear with the winter tides only to reappear in the late, late spring. Five recreational diving zones have been set up, with line- and spearfishing prohibited, and there is an anchorage and harbor, called the commercial zone. The park is intended to guarantee that coral reefs and the marine environment will be safeguarded for the future. The Saba Marine Park also maintains and operates a decompression chamber for diving accidents. The chamber was donated by the Dutch navy and is located in the Fort Bay.

Saba Deep Dive Center, Fort Bay (P.O. Box 22), Saba, N.A. (tel. 4/63347), a full-service dive operation, offers scuba diving, snorkeling, equipment rental and repair, and tank fills. It is staffed by both NAUI and PADI instructors and divemasters, and is open daily from 8am to 5pm. Whether 1 diver or 20, novice or experienced, Adrienne Gonia, Mike Myers, and their staff are concerned with individual attention Dive sites around Saba, all protected by the Saba Marine Park, have permanent moorings and range from very shallow to very deep: caves, ledges, overhangs, walls, and pinnacles, as well as coral and sponge formations and a wide variety of both reef fish and pelagic marine life. Dive packages are also available. A one-tank dive costs $45.

Sea Saba Dive Center, Windwardside (tel. 62246), is where Joan and Lou Bourque share with clients their knowledge of the underwater elkhorn forests and giant boulder gardens that make Saba "the unspoiled queen of the Caribbean" with regard to the sea world. The Bourques offer packages covering a variety of interests, including underwater photography, slide shows, marine biology seminars, and all PADI certification and resort courses. A one-tank dive costs $40.

SAVVY SHOPPING

After lunch you can go for a stroll in Windwardside and stop at the boutiques, which often look like someone's living room—and sometimes they are. Most stores are open Monday through Saturday from 9am to noon and 2 to around 5:30pm.

Stitched by Saban wives when their husbands are off to sea, the traditional **drawn threadwork** of the island is famous. You don't even have to go to a shop to find it. Chances are, your driver will stop along the road as women, mostly descendants of Europeans, crowd around.

Sometimes this work, introduced by a local woman named Gertrude Johnson in the 1870s, is called Spanish work, because it was believed to have been perfected by nuns in Caracas. Selected threads are drawn and tied in a piece of linen to produce an ornamental pattern. It can be expensive if a quality linen has been used.

Try to come home with some **"Saba Spice,"** an aromatic blend of 150-proof cask rum, with such spices as fennel seed, cinnamon, cloves, and nutmeg, straight from someone's home brew. It's not for everyone (too sweet), but will make an exotic bottle to show off at home.

AROUND THE BEND, at Scout's Place, Windwardside. Tel. 62259.

Housed in a charming little Saba cottage, this store is run by ex-Manhattanite Jean Macbeth, whose sophisticated taste is reflected in her hand-painted tops, hand-batiked casual wear, jewelry, scarves, tote bags, and a collection of amusing, locally made dolls and pillows.

SABA ARTISAN FOUNDATION, The Bottom. Tel. 63260.

In recent years the foundation has made a name for itself in the world of fashion with hand-screened resort fashions. The clothes are casual and colorful. Among the items sold are men's bush-jacket shirts, numerous styles of dresses and skirts, napkins, and placemats, as well as yard goods. Island motifs are used in many designs, and you might like a fern or casava-leaf print. Also popular are the famous Saba drawn-lace patterns. The fashions are designed, printed, sewn, and marketed by Sabans. Mail-order as well as wholesale distributorship inquiries are invited. Open: Mon–Fri 8am–noon and 1–5pm, Sat–Sun 10am–noon.

JAMAICA

Jamaica, 90 miles south of Cuba, is the third largest of the Caribbean islands, with some 4,400 square miles of predominantly green land, a mountain ridge peaking at 7,400 feet above sea level, and on the north coast, many beautiful white sand beaches with clear blue sea.

First populated in A.D. 700 by the Arawaks, gentle people from South America who named the island Xaymaca, Jamaica was sighted by Christopher Columbus, who called it "the fairest isle eyes have seen," in 1494. Spain settled the island in 1509. In due course, Africans were imported by the Spanish as slaves to supplement the native labor force, which was gradually depleted by European disease and overwork. By 1655, when the English captured the island, there were no Arawaks left.

Until 1962 Jamaica was a Crown Colony of Great Britain but long ago achieved full independence within the Commonwealth. The island's motto is, appropriately, OUT OF MANY, ONE PEOPLE. The islanders are mostly of African or African-European descent, with a minority of British, Chinese, Indians, Portuguese, Germans, and people from other West Indian islands, all intermarried to create one people. The government is similar to that of Great Britain: the queen is represented by a governor-general appointed on the advice of the prime minister of Jamaica, who is elected. English is the official language, but with delightful adaptations, and you'll probably hear "Jamaica talk" when you take your *bankra* (basket) and *dunny* (money) to the market or have a meal of fish tea, rundown, and skyjuice (see "Food and Drink," below).

Tourism has become the biggest industry in Jamaica, surpassing the traditional leaders, bauxite and aluminum.

The average Jamaican is friendly. Of course, there are rogues in every country, and common sense has to prevail when you travel. Don't call them natives, however. They feel it's insulting, and they are proud of just being called Jamaicans.

GETTING THERE

There are two **international airports** in Jamaica: Donald Sangster in Montego Bay and Norman Manley in Kingston. The most popular routings to Jamaica are from New York or Miami. Remember to reconfirm all flights, going and returning, no later than 72 hours before departure. Flying time from Miami is 1¼ hours; from Los Angeles, 5½ hours; from Atlanta, 2½ hours; from Dallas, 3 hours; from Chicago and New York, 3½ hours; and from Toronto, 4 hours.

THE MAJOR AIRLINES One of the most popular services to Jamaica is provided by **American Airlines** (tel. toll free 800/433-7300) through its hubs in New York and Miami. A daily nonstop flight departs from New York's Kennedy airport at 8:45am. Touching down in Montego Bay, it continues on without a change of aircraft to Kingston. Return flights to New York from Jamaica usually depart from Montego Bay, touch down in Kingston to exchange additional passengers, then continue

WHAT'S SPECIAL ABOUT JAMAICA

Beaches

- ☐ San San Beach, Port Antonio, voted by some members of the U.S. Navy as one of the best beaches in the world, with water sports galore and a favorite picnic area.
- ☐ Doctor's Cave Beach, Montego Bay, the beach that launched this resort in the 1940s and today the most crowded in town, with water sports and changing rooms.
- ☐ Walter Fletcher Beach, Montego Bay, one of Jamaica's premier beaches, a family favorite noted for its tranquil waters.
- ☐ Negril Beach, a 7-mile stretch of sand that is the pride of Jamaica, former carousing ground of the Caribbean's most infamous pirates.

Ace Attractions

- ☐ Dunn's River Falls, Ocho Rios, a 600-foot cascade which is sometimes referred to as the Niagara of the Caribbean, famous for its use by the film industry.
- ☐ Martha Brae's Rafters Village, Montego Bay, the departure point for freshwater rafting on a raised dais supported by interconnected bamboo logs.
- ☐ Rafting on the Río Grande, outside Port Antonio, a river sport launched by Errol Flynn during his residency nearby

Historic Homes

- ☐ Rose Hall, east of Montego Bay, former great house of that subject of Gothic horror, the notorious Annie Palmer.
- ☐ Firefly, St. Mary's Parish, former vacation home of Sir Noël Coward, British playwright, where he entertained the rich and famous of his day.

Great Towns/Villages

- ☐ Port Royal, at the mouth of Kingston Harbour, stamping ground of swashbuckling pirates and once known as "the wickedest city on earth."
- ☐ Spanish Town, oldest capital of Jamaica (1662–1872), originally established by colonists from Spain.
- ☐ Mandeville, called "English Town," lying on a plateau more than 2,000 feet above the sea in the island's tropical highlands.

Special Events

- ☐ Reggae Sunsplash Festival, an annual midsummer event in Montego Bay attracting disciples of the late Bob Marley from around the world.

nonstop back to Kennedy. From Miami, at least four daily flights depart at various times of the day and evening for both Kingston and Montego Bay.

Air Jamaica (tel. toll free 800/523-5585), the national carrier, operates nine flights a week from New York's JFK, which all stop at both Montego Bay and Kingston. More frequent are the flights that the airline operates to Jamaica from Miami (one flies nonstop to Kingston; the other three stop at both Montego Bay and Kingston) The airline also offers connecting service within Jamaica, to most of the country's smaller airports as well, from its two international airports.

Continental Airlines (tel. toll free 800/422-6232) offers nonstop service from its hub at Newark, New Jersey (a short ride from New York City) to Montego Bay, Jamaica.

Air Canada (tel. toll free 800/776-3000) departs for Jamaica from Toronto and from Montréal. Flights from Toronto depart four to seven times a week, depending on the season, and touch down at both Montego Bay and Kingston. Flights from

Montréal's Mirabel airport depart twice a week (usually on Saturday and Sunday) for Montego Bay. Montréal-based travelers bound for Kingston transfer aircraft in either Toronto or Montego Bay.

REGULAR AIRFARES American offers some of the most consistently reliable bargains. The least expensive fares are for Advance Purchase Excursion (APEX) tickets, whose definitions and restrictions come in a wide array of differing possibilities. Currently, American's least expensive ticket from New York to Montego Bay requires a 14-day advance purchase and a stopover in Jamaica of between 3 and 21 days. Fares for travel on weekdays (defined as Monday through Thursday) range from $305 to $350, while fares for travel on weekends (defined as any Friday, Saturday, or Sunday) range from $328 to $350, depending on the season, with tax included. It's important to watch for special promotional fares as well, and if you're flexible in your departure and return dates, you'll be able to profit from last-minute bargains.

Some airlines (including American) offer special rates at Jamaica's most interesting hotels, but only if the accommodations are reserved simultaneously with the airline tickets. Most of the hotels participating in American's program are recommended in this book, and the savings of simultaneous air and hotel bookings can be substantial.

GETTING AROUND

BY PLANE The majority of travelers to Jamaica, particularly tourists, enter the country via Montego Bay. The island's domestic air service is provided by **Trans-Jamaican Airlines Ltd.** (tel. 923-8680 in Kingston, 952-5401 in Montego Bay, 974-3254 in Ocho Rios, 993-2405 in Port Antonio, or 957-4251 in Negril), which offers 30 scheduled flights daily, covering all the major resort areas. Reservations can be made through overseas travel agents or through Air Jamaica. Incidentally, Tinson Pen Airport in the heart of downtown Kingston is for domestic flights only. Car-rental facilities are available only at the international airports at Kingston and Montego Bay.

BY TRAIN A leisurely sort of travel, but a marvelous way to see the country, is by rail from Kingston to Montego Bay. At each station, peddlers leap onto the train to sell their wares, and jump off at the last possible second as the train leaves the station. The trip between Kingston and Montego Bay takes 5 hours. There is no first class Monday through Friday. Tickets cost J$39.50 ($1.80). A first-class seat on Saturday and Sunday costs J$69 ($3.15). For information about departure times, phone the Jamaica Railway Corporation (tel. 922-6620 in Kingston or 952-4842 in Montego Bay).

BY TAXI & BUS Kingston has no city taxis with meters, so agree on a price before you get in. In Kingston and the rest of the island, special taxis and buses for visitors are operated by JUTA (Jamaica Union of Travellers Association) and have the union's emblem on the side of the vehicle. All prices are controlled, and any local JUTA office will supply a list of rates. JUTA drivers do nearly all the ground transfers, and some offer sightseeing tours. I've found them pleasant, in the main knowledgeable, and good drivers. There are many companies offering sightseeing tours of the island. Most of the cabs are of U.S. origin, but they're old.

BY RENTAL CAR Jamaica is big enough, and public transportation is unreliable enough, that a car is a necessity if you plan to do much independent sightseeing. (In lieu of this, you can always take an organized tour to the major sights and spend the rest of the time on the beaches near your hotel.) Subject to many variations depending on the road conditions, driving time for the 50 miles from Montego Bay to Negril is 1½ hours; from Montego Bay to Ocho Rios, 62 miles and 1½ hours; from Ocho Rios to Port Antonio, 60 miles and 2½ hours; from Ocho Rios to Kingston, 60 miles and 2 hours; from Kingston to Mandeville, 65 miles and 1½ hours; and from Kingston to Port Antonio, 68 miles and 2 hours.

For resolution of any accident claims that may result, and for the ease of any billing irregularities, it's best to stick to branches of U.S.-based rental outfits. Unfortunately,

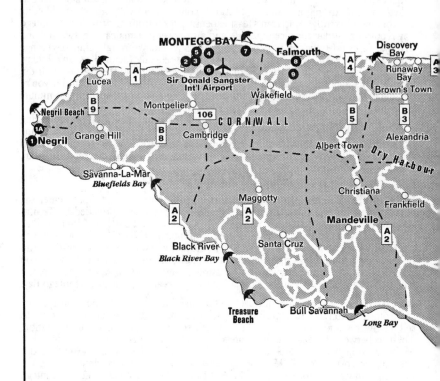

Caribbean Sea

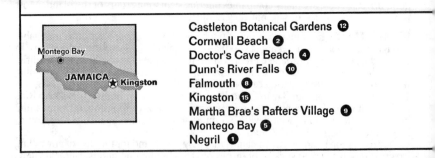

Castleton Botanical Gardens ⓬
Cornwall Beach ❷
Doctor's Cave Beach ❹
Dunn's River Falls ❿
Falmouth ❽
Kingston ⓯
Martha Brae's Rafters Village ❾
Montego Bay ❺
Negril ❶

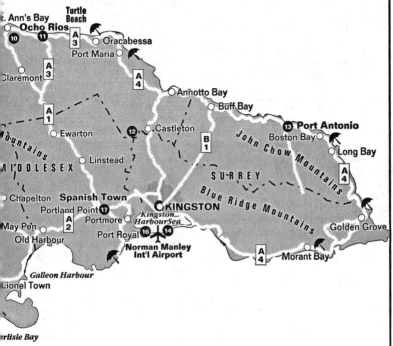

JAMAICA

Caribbean Sea

t. Ann's Bay · Turtle Beach
Ocho Rios
⑩ ⑪ A3 · Oracabessa
Port Maria
Claremont · A3
A4
A1 · Annotto Bay
Ewarton · Buff Bay
Mountains · ⑫ · Castleton
MIDDLESEX · Linstead · B1 · Port Antonio ⑬
Boston Bay
John Chow Mountains
S·U·R·R·E·Y · A4
Chapelton · Spanish Town
Portland Point ⑰ · Blue Ridge Mountains
May Pen · A2 · Portmore
Old Harbour · Kingston HarbourSea
Port Royal ⑯ ✈ ⑭ · Golden Grove
Norman Manley Int'l Airport
A4 · Morant Bay
Galleon Harbour
Lionel Town

rlisle Bay

Beach →

Airport ✈

Negril Beach ①Ⓐ
Norman Manley International Airport ⑭
Ocho Rios ⑪
Port Antonio ⑬
Port Royal ⑯
Rose Hall ❼
Sir Donald Sangster International Airport ❻
Spanish Town ⑰
Walter Fletcher Beach ❸

prices of car rentals in Jamaica have skyrocketed, making it one of the most expensive rental scenes in the Caribbean.

Avis (tel. toll free 800/331-1212) maintains offices at the international airports in both Montego Bay (tel. 952-4543) and Kingston (tel. 924-8013). The least expensive car requires a 2-day advance booking and costs $360 U.S. per week. The company's collision-damage waiver costs another $15 per day. If you choose not to accept it, you'll be responsible for up to the full cost of damage to your car, unless other insurance policies you already own become activated.

Budget Rent-a-Car operates branches in Ocho Rios (tel. 974-5617) and Montego Bay (tel. 952-1943). Only the branch in Montego Bay subscribes to Budget's toll-free reservations system (tel. toll free 800/527-0700); the branch in Ocho Rios must be phoned directly, and is often sold out because of heavy local demand. In Montego Bay, a small Subaru rents for $389 per week, with unlimited mileage, plus 10% tax. Three-day rentals are possible, at a net price of $189 plus tax, with unlimited mileage. Collision-damage waivers cost only $10 per day at Budget, but renters who buy them are still, as at Avis, responsible for the first $1,100 of damage to the rented car.

Hertz (tel. toll free 800/654-3131) operates Jamaican branches at the airports at both Montego Bay (tel. 979-0438) and Kingston (tel. 924-8028). Its least expensive subcompact car rents for $400 per week, plus 10% tax, with unlimited mileage included. A collision-damage waiver costs $15 extra per day, and will reduce the customer responsibility for any accident damage to the car from $2,000 to $500.

At all three companies, unless you give the imprint of your credit card you'll be required to pay a deposit of at least $1,000 in cash before you can drive away, and endure a sometimes-rigorous background check of your credit history and your employment record.

Be forewarned that in Jamaica *driving is on the left,* and you should exercise more than your usual caution here because of the unfamiliar terrain. Don't drink and drive, and be especially cautious at night. Speed limits in towns are 30 m.p.h., and 50 m.p.h. outside towns. Gas is measured by the Imperial gallon (a British unit of measurement that will give you 25% more than a U.S. gallon), and the charge is payable only in Jamaican dollars—most stations don't accept credit cards. Your own valid driver's license from back home is acceptable for short-term visits to Jamaica.

BY BIKE & SCOOTER　These can be rented in Montego Bay, and you'll need your valid driver's license. **Montego Honda/Bike Rentals,** 21 Gloucester Avenue (tel. 952-4984), rents Hondas for $35 a day, plus a $300 deposit. Scooters cost $30 per day. Deposits are refundable if the vehicles are returned in good shape. Hours are 7:30am to 5pm daily.

MEET THE PEOPLE

The Jamaica Tourist Board operates the Meet the People program in Kingston and the island's five major resort cities and towns. Through the program, visitors get the opportunity to meet Jamaican families who volunteer to host them free for a few hours or even a whole day. More than 650 families are registered in the project with the Tourist Board, which keeps a list of their interests and hobbies. All you have to do is give the board a rough idea of your own interests—birds, butterflies, music, ham radio, stamp collecting, or spelunking (there are many caves to explore)—and they will arrange for you to spend the day with a family with similar interests. Many lasting friendships have developed through this program.

Once with them, you go along with whatever they plan to do, sharing their life, eating at their table, joining them at a dinner party. You may end up at a beach barbecue, afternoon tea with the neighbors, or just sitting and talking far into the night. The program does not offer overnight accommodation.

It's important to know that this service is entirely free. You need not even take your host family a gift, but they will certainly appreciate a bunch of flowers after your visit.

In Jamaica, apply at any of the local Tourist Board offices (see "Information" in "Fast Facts," below).

FOOD & DRINK

There is great emphasis on seafood. **Rock lobster** appears on every menu—grilled, thermidor, cold, hot. **Saltfish and ackee,** the national dish, is a concoction of salt cod and a brightly colored vegetable that tastes something like scrambled eggs. **Escovitch** (marinated fish) is usually fried and then simmered in vinegar with onions and peppers. **Curried mutton and goat** are popular, as is **pepperpot stew,** all highly seasoned and guaranteed to affect your body temperature.

Jerk pork is peculiar to country areas, where it is barbecued slowly over wood fires until crisp and brown. Apart from rice and peas (which are really red beans), usually served as a sort of risotto with added onions, spices, and salt pork, vegetables are exotic: **breadfruit,** imported by Captain Bligh in 1723 when he arrived aboard H.M.S. *Bounty;* **callaloo,** rather like spinach, used in pepperpot soup (not to be confused with the stew of the same name); **cho-cho,** served boiled and buttered or stuffed; and green bananas and **plantains,** fried or boiled and served with almost everything. Then there is pumpkin, which goes into a soup or is served on the side, boiled and mashed with butter. Sweet potatoes appear with main courses, but there is also a sweet-potato pudding made with sugar and coconut milk, flavored with cinnamon, nutmeg, and vanilla.

You'll meet the intriguing **stamp and go,** saltfish cakes to eat as an appetizer; **dip and fall back,** salty stew with bananas and dumplings; and **rundown,** mackerel cooked in coconut milk, often eaten for breakfast. For the really adventurous, **manish water,** a soup made from goat offal and tripe, is said to increase virility. **Patties (meat pies)**—the best on the island are at Montego Bay—are another staple snack. Boiled corn, roast yams, roast saltfish, fried fish, soups, and fruits are sold at roadside stands.

"Tea" is a word used to describe any nonalcoholic drink in Jamaica, a tradition dating back to plantation days. **Fish tea** is actually a bowl of hot soup made from freshly caught fish. **Skyjuice,** a favorite treat with Jamaicans on a hot afternoon, is sold by street vendors from not-always-sanitary carts. It consists of shaved ice with sugar-laden fruit syrup and is sold in small plastic bags with a straw. **Coconut water** is a refreshing drink, especially when you stop by the roadside to have a local vendor chop the top from a fresh nut straight from the tree.

Rum punches are everywhere, and the local beer is **Red Stripe.** The island produces many liqueurs, the most famous being **Tía María,** made from coffee beans. **Rumona** is another good one to take home with you. **Bellywash,** the local name for limeade, will supply the extra liquid you may need to counteract the heat of the tropics. Blue Mountain coffee is the best, but tea, cocoa, and milk are usually available to round off a meal.

REGGAE SUNSPLASH FESTIVAL

The annual Reggae Sunsplash Festival, usually held in July or August in Montego Bay, features Jamaican artists. Arrangements to attend should be made by May of every year; many local hotels are fully booked for the festival, so advance reservations are necessary. The Jamaican Tourist Board's U.S. and Canadian offices (see "Information" in "Fast Facts," below) can give you information about packages and group rates for the festival. Other reggae concerts and festivals featuring top performers are held throughout the year in Jamaica. Ask the Tourist Board.

SPORTS & RECREATION AROUND THE ISLAND

If sports are important to your vacation, you may want to review the offerings of Jamaica before deciding on a particular resort. Sports are so spread out, and Jamaica so large, that it isn't feasible to go on a long day's excursion just to play golf, for example. The cost of most activities is generally the same throughout the island. Prices are in U.S. dollars, unless otherwise noted.

BEACHES Of course, many visitors will want to do nothing more "sporting" than lie on the beach. For specific recommendations of the best beaches in Jamaica, see the "What to See and Do" sections in the writeups of the individual resort areas.

DEEP-SEA FISHING Northern Jamaica waters are world renowned for their gamefish, including dolphin, wahoo, blue and white marlin, sailfish, tarpon, Allison tuna, barracuda, and bonito. The Jamaica International Fishing Tournament and Jamaica International Blue Marlin Team Tournaments run concurrently at Port Antonio every September or October. Most major hotels from Port Antonio to Montego Bay have deep-sea fishing facilities, and there are many charter boats.

At Port Antonio, **Juanita II** (tel. 993-3086) takes out up to four people for $150 per half day, $280 per day, with crew, bait, tackle, and soft drinks.

Seaworld Resorts Ltd., in Montego Bay (tel. 953-2180), operates flying-bridge cruisers, with deck lines and outriggers, for fishing expeditions. A half-day fishing trip costs $330.

At Ocho Rios, the **Sans Souci Hotel & Club** (tel. 974-2353) offers deep-sea fishing for $250 for six people.

GOLF Jamaica has the best courses in all the West Indies. Montego Bay alone has four championship courses. Here's a sampling:

The one at the **Wyndham Rose Hall Resort,** Rose Hall (tel. 953-2650), called "one of the top five courses in the world," is an unusual and challenging seaside and mountain course. Built on the shores of the Caribbean, its eighth hole skirts the ocean, then doglegs onto a promontory and a green thrusting 200 yards into the sea. The back nine is the most scenic and interesting, rising into steep slopes and deep ravines on Mount Zion. The 10th fairway abuts the family burial grounds of the Barretts of Wimpole Street, and the 14th passes the vacation home of singer Johnny Cash. The 300-foot-high 13th tee offers a rare panoramic view of the sea and the roof of the hotel, and the 15th green is next to a 40-foot waterfall, once featured in a James Bond movie. A fully stocked pro shop, a clubhouse, and a professional staff are among the amenities. In winter, rates are $45 for 18 holes; they drop to $30 in summer.

Other courses include the challenging **Tryall** (tel. 952-5110), in Hanover, 12 miles from town, where the Mazda Champions Tournament, with the biggest golf purse in the world, was played from 1985 through 1987 and the Jamaica Classic Annual was first played in January 1989. It is also the site of the Johnnie Walker Tournament. The course is said to be the best in Jamaica. In winter Tryall guests pay $55 for 18 holes and nonresidents are charged $125; in summer residents pay $40 for 18 holes, and nonresidents, $60.

The **Half Moon,** Rose Hall, Montego Bay (tel. 953-2560), has a championship course designed by Robert Trent Jones that opened in 1961, opposite the hotel. The course has manicured and diversely shaped greens. Off-season, 18 holes cost $35 for nonresidents of the Half Moon, although residents play free. Everyone pays $25 for the rental of a cart. A caddy costs $10. In winter, 18 holes costs $80 for nonresidents, while residents play free. The cost of a cart in winter is still $25, while the cost of a caddy rises to $12 for 18 holes. Golf lessons can be arranged for $50 for a full hour.

The **Ironshore Golf & Country Club,** St. James, Montego Bay (tel. 953-2800), less well known than the others, is another 18-hole course. It charges $25 for 18 holes in winter, $25 in summer.

Super Club's Runaway Golf Club, at Runaway Bay near Ocho Rios on the north coast (tel. 973-2561), charges greens fees of $20 per day year round.

Upton Golf Course & Plantation, Ocho Rios (tel. 974-2528), also welcomes visitors to play its 18 holes. It promises you're 700 feet up "and always cool." Golfers play amid beautiful scenery. Greens fees are $31 for 18 holes. There is a clubhouse and bar.

The **Manchester Country Club,** Caledonia Road, Mandeville (tel. 962-2403), has a nine-hole course where championship tournaments are played annually. Greens fees are J$100 ($4.55) for 18 holes.

HORSEBACK RIDING The best riding is in the Ocho Rios area. Jamaica's most complete equestrian center is **Chukka Cove Farm and Resort,** at Richmond Llandovery, St. Ann (tel. 972-2506), located less than 4 miles east of Runaway Bay. A 1-hour trail ride costs $23. The most popular ride is a 3-hour beach jaunt where, after riding over trails to the sea, you can unpack your horse and swim in the surf. Refreshments are served as part of the $45 cost of this trip. A 6-hour beach ride, complete with picnic lunch, goes for $70. Polo lessons are also available and cost $28 for 30 minutes.

Also good is the program at **Rocky Point Stables,** Half Moon Club, Rose Hall, Montego Bay (tel. 953-2286), which offers trail rides and riding lessons. Charges are $40 for 1½-hour rides, $50 for a 2½-hour combined trail ride and ocean swim for you and your horse.

TENNIS Most hotels have their own courts, many floodlit for night games. If your hotel does not have a court, expect to pay about $6 to $8 per hour at another hotel.

All-Jamaica Hardcourt Championships are played in August at the **Manchester Club,** 1 Caledonia Road (P.O. Box 17), Mandeville (tel. 809/962-2403). The courts are open for other play the rest of the year at J$20 (90¢) per person per game.

WATER SPORTS Water options for the sports lover proliferate throughout Jamaica, with many activities offered as part of all-inclusive packages by the island's major hotels. However, there are other well-maintained facilities for water sports not connected to the hotel offerings.

Jamaica has some of the finest diving waters in the world, with an average diving depth of 35 to 95 feet. Visibility is usually 60 to 120 feet. Most of the diving is done on coral reefs, which are protected by underwater parks where fish, shells, coral, and sponges are plentiful. Experienced divers can also see wrecks, hedges, caves, dropoffs, and tunnels.

In Falmouth, ✪ **Seaworld,** at the Trelawny Beach Hotel (tel. 954-2450), offers scuba-diving programs to the offshore coral reefs that are considered some of the most spectacular of the Caribbean. There are three NAUI-certified dive guides, one dive boat, and all the necessary equipment for either inexperienced or already-certified divers. Guests of the Trelawny benefit from free introductory lessons and the availability of a free daily dive; nonresidents are charged $30 per dive. Transportation is provided to all dive sites and night dives are also offered, costing $45. Trelawny Beach also offers free snorkeling, waterskiing, Sunfish sailing, windsurfing, and glass-bottom-boat rides to hotel guests; for others various fees are charged.

Negril Scuba Centre, in the Negril Beach Club Hotel, Norman Manley Boulevard (tel. 957-4425), is the most modern, best-equipped scuba facility in Negril. A professional staff of internationally certified scuba instructors and divemasters teach and guide divers to several of Negril's colorful and exciting coral reefs. Beginner's dive lessons are offered daily, as well as multiple-dive packages for certified divers. Full scuba certifications and specialty courses are also available.

A resort course, designed for first-time divers with basic swimming abilities, includes all instruction, equipment, a lecture on water and diving safety, and one open-water dive. It begins at 10am daily and ends at 2pm. Its price is $75. A one-tank dive costs $30 per dive plus $20 for the rental of equipment (not necessary if divers bring their own gear). More economical is a two-tank dive, which includes lunch. It costs $55, plus the (optional) $20 rental of all equipment. This organization is PADI-registered, although it accepts and recognizes divers certified from either NAUI or the YMCA dive course.

SunDivers is also at the Rock Cliff Hotel, West End Road, Negril (tel. 957-4331). There, a custom-built dive boat seats up to 20 divers. A choice of four shore dives is available. There is another Sundivers in Negril at the Poinciana Beach Hotel, Norman Manley Boulevard (tel. 957-4256), just after Sandals Negril. A resort course costs $60 and a one-tank dive is $40, plus $10 for equipment rental.

For water sports in Port Antonio, visit the **Navy Island Resort & Marina,** Navy Island, Port Antonio Tour Company Ltd. (PATCO), Port Antonio (tel. 993-2667). Snorkeling off Crusoe's Beach is offered, and visitors can rent masks, snorkels, and fins. Scuba diving with certified divers is available, and masks, fins, belts, and tanks are provided; they also give scuba lessons. Windsurfing, sailing, and deep-sea fishing are also part of the water-sports program.

Many hotels offer some of the water sports cited above free to their guests. In general, prices are as listed below.

Waterskiing   It costs $12 to $15 for a 15-minute ski run, and many hotels have training facilities.

Sunfish Sailing   Many hotels and some public beaches have Sunfish sailboats for rent at about $10 to $15 per hour. Hotels with their own fleets will charge less.

Snorkeling   Equipment is available in many places, for $12 per day.

Windsurfing   Some hotels have boards for windsurfing available. The best place for this sport is San San Beach in Port Antonio. It usually costs about $15 per hour.

FAST   JAMAICA

Area Code   To call Jamaica direct from North America, dial the area code, 809, then the local number. The area code is not needed for calls on the island.

Banks   Banks islandwide are open Monday through Friday from 9am to 5pm. There are **Bank of Jamaica** exchange bureaus at both international airports (Montego Bay and Kingston), at cruise-ship piers, and in most hotels.

Currency   The unit of currency in Jamaica is the **Jamaican dollar,** and it uses the same symbol as the U.S. dollar, "$." There is no fixed rate of exchange for the Jamaican dollar. Subject to market fluctuations, it is traded publicly. Visitors to Jamaica can pay for any goods in U.S. dollars. *Be careful!* Unless it is clearly stated, always insist on knowing whether a price is being quoted in Jamaican or U.S. dollars.

In this guide I've generally followed the price-quotation policy of the establishment, whether in Jamaican dollars or U.S. dollars. For clarity, I have used the symbol "J$" to denote prices in Jamaican dollars; the conversion to U.S. dollars follows in parentheses. When dollar figures stand alone, they are always U.S. currency.

Jamaican currency is issued in banknotes of J$1, J$2, J$5, J$10, J$20, J$50, and J$100. Coins are 1¢, 5¢, 10¢, 20¢, 25¢, and 50¢. At press time (but subject to change), the exchange rate of Jamaican currency is J$22 to $1 U.S. (J$1 equals about 5¢ U.S.).

You should use your immigration card (see "Documents," below) when making bank transactions and also when converting Jamaican dollars back into U.S. dollars. There is no limit to the amount of foreign currency you can bring in, but it is illegal to import or export Jamaican currency.

Customs   Do not bring in (or take out) illegal drugs from Jamaica. Your luggage is searched. Ganja-sniffing police dogs are found at the airport. Otherwise, you can bring in most items intended for personal use, including as much of your home currency as you desire, but *you cannot take Jamaican dollars out of the country.*

Documents   U.S. and Canadian residents do not need passports, but must have proof of citizenship (or permanent residency) and a return or ongoing ticket. Other visitors need passports, good for a maximum stay of 6 months.

Immigration cards, needed for bank transactions and currency exchange, are given to visitors at the airport arrivals desks.

Drugs   Although drugs are commonly sold in Jamaica, hard drugs and *ganja* (marijuana) are illegal and imprisonment is the penalty for possession. Some tourists have even attempted to bring *ganja* back into the United States, but U.S. Customs agents, well aware of the drug situation in Jamaica, have easily caught and arrested many chance-takers.

As to medications, prescriptions are accepted by local pharmacies only if issued by a Jamaican doctor. Hotels have doctors on call. If you need any particular medicine or treatment, bring evidence, such as a letter from your own doctor.

Drugstores   In Montego Bay, try **McKenzie's Drug Store,** 16 Strand Street (tel. 952-2467); in Ocho Rios, **Great House Pharmacy,** Brown's Plaza (tel. 974-2352); and in Kingston, the **Pegasus Hotel Pharmacy,** in the Jamaica Pegasus Hotel, 81 Knutsford Boulevard (tel. 926-8174).

Electricity   Most places have the standard electrical voltage of 110, as in the U.S. However, some establishments operate on 220 volts, 50 cycles. If your hotel is on a different current from your U.S.-made appliance, ask for a transformer and adapter.

Embassies   The **U.S. Embassy** is at Jamaica Mutual Life Centre, 2 Oxford Road, Kingston 5 (tel. 809/929-4850). The **Canada High Commission** is at Royal Bank Ltd. Building, 30 Knutsford Boulevard, Kingston 5 (tel. 809/926-1500), and the **United Kingdom High Commission** is at 26 Trafalgar Road, Kingston 10 (tel. 809/926-9050).

Emergencies   For the **police and air rescue,** dial 119; to report a **fire** or call an **ambulance,** dial 110.

Etiquette   For various reasons, some Jamaicans dislike having their pictures taken, so ask permission first. Don't call the locals "natives"; "Jamaicans" will do.

Hospitals   In Kingston, the **University Hospital** is at Mona (tel. 927-6621); in Montego Bay, the **Cornwall Regional Hospital** is at Mount Salem (tel. 952-5100); and in Port Antonio, the **Port Antonio General Hospital** is at Naylor's Hill (tel. 993-2646).

Information   Before you go, contact the **Jamaica Tourist Board** at the following addresses: 866 Second Ave., New York, NY 10017 (tel. 212/688-7650); 36 S. Wabash Ave., Suite 1210, Chicago, IL 60603 (tel. 312/346-1546); 3440 Wilshire Blvd., Suite 1207, Los Angeles, CA 90010 (tel. 213/384-1123); 1320 S. Dixie Hwy., Suite 1100, Coral Gables, FL 33146 (tel. 305/665-0557); 1315 Walnut St., Suite 918, Philadelphia, PA 19107 (tel. 215/545-1061); 26400 Lahser Rd., Lahser Center One, Suite 114A, Southfield, Detroit, MI 48034 (tel. 313/948-9557); 8214 Westchester, Suite 500, Dallas, TX 75225 (tel. 214/361-8778); and 300 W. Wienca Rd., Suite 100A, N.E. Atlanta, GA 30342 (tel. 404/250-9971). In Canada information offices are at 1 Eglinton Ave. E., Suite 616, Toronto, ON M4P 3A1 (tel. 416/482-7850); and 1110 Sherbrooke St. W., Montréal, PQ H3A 1G9 (tel. 514/849-6386).

Once in Jamaica, you will find **Tourist Board** offices at 21 Dominica Drive, Kingston (tel. 929-9200); Cornwall Beach, St. James, Montego Bay (tel. 952-4425); Ocean Village Shopping Centre, Ocho Rios, St. Ann (tel. 974-2582); City Centre Plaza, Port Antonio (tel. 993-3051), and Shop no. 20, Adrija Place, Negril, Westmoreland (tel. 957-4243).

Marrying   You can get a marriage license after 24 hours' residence on the island, and then marry as soon as it can be arranged. You will need your birth certificate, and, where applicable, divorce documents or death certificates. All documents must be properly certified—ordinary photostat copies will not be accepted. Most Jamaican hotels will make arrangements for your wedding and license. Otherwise, one of the headquarters of the Jamaica Tourist Board can assist you in meeting and making arrangements with a government marriage officer.

Nudity   Nude bathing is allowed at a number of hotels, clubs, and beaches (especially in Negril), but only where there are signs stating SWIMSUITS OPTIONAL. Elsewhere, the law will not even allow topless sunbathing.

Safety   You can get into a lot of trouble in Jamaica or you can have a carefree vacation—much depends on what you do and where you go. Major hotels have security guards who protect the grounds. Under no circumstances should you accept an invitation to see "the real Jamaica" from some stranger you meet on the beach. Exercise caution when traveling around Jamaica. Safeguard your valuables and never leave them unattended on a beach. Likewise, never leave luggage or other valuables in a car, or even the trunk of a car.

Shopping Hours   Hours vary widely, but as a general rule most business establishments are open Monday through Friday from 8:30am to 5pm (or in some places, earlier at 4:30pm). Some shops are open on Saturday until noon.

Taxes   The government imposes a 5% room tax, per room, per night. You will be charged a $16 departure tax at the airport, payable in Jamaican dollars.

Telephone   All overseas telephone calls incur a government tax of 15%.

Time   In winter, Jamaica is on eastern standard time. However, when the U.S. is on daylight saving time, at 6am in Miami it's 5am in Kingston.

Tips and Service   Tipping is customary. A general 10% or 15% is expected in hotels and restaurants on occasions when you would normally tip. Some places add a service charge to the bill. Tipping is not allowed in the all-inclusive hotels.

Water   It's usually safe to drink piped-in water, islandwide, as it is filtered and chlorinated; naturally, it's much more prudent to drink bottled water, if available.

Weather   Expect temperatures around 80° to 90° Fahrenheit on the coast. Winter is a little cooler. In the mountains it can get as low as 40°. There is generally a breeze, which in winter is noticeably cool. The rainy periods in general are October through November (although it can extend into December) and from May through June. Normally rain comes in short, sharp showers; then the sun shines.

1. KINGSTON

Kingston, the largest English-speaking city in the Caribbean, is the capital of Jamaica, with a population of some 650,000 people living on the plains between Blue Mountain and the sea.

The buildings are a mixture of very modern, graceful old, and plain ramshackle. It's a busy city, as you might expect, with a natural harbor that is the seventh largest in the world. The University of the West Indies has its campus on the edge of the city. The cultural center of Jamaica is here, along with industry, finance, and government. Now covering some 40 square miles, the city was founded by the survivors of the 1692 Port Royal earthquake, and in 1872 it became the capital, superseding Spanish Town.

WHERE TO STAY

Remember to ask if the 5% room tax is included in the rate quoted when you make your reservation. The rates listed below are year round, unless otherwise noted.

EXPENSIVE

Security-conscious Kingston now provides all leading hotels with guards, not unlike the deluxe apartment houses in New York.

JAMAICA PEGASUS, 81 Knutsford Blvd., Kingstown 5, Jamaica, W.I. Tel. 809/926-3690, or toll free 800/225-5843 in the U.S. and Canada. Fax 809/929-5855. 318 rms, 17 suites. A/C TV TEL
$ Rates: $179–$189 single or double; from $270 suite for two. MAP $40 per person extra. AE, DC, MC, V. **Parking:** Free.

A Forte hotel, the Jamaica Pegasus is a favorite with commercial travelers. It's located in the banking area—and a fine residential section—of Kingston, off Oxford Road. After its major renovation, the hotel is now better than ever, and is the site of many conventions and social events. With English style and Jamaican warmth, the hotel competes with any other hotel in town. The staff will arrange water sports and sightseeing.

Each of the well-furnished bedrooms contains coffee-making equipment and a radio. Several floors of luxuriously appointed suites form the Knutsford Club, which has special executive services.

Dining/Entertainment: The 4pm tea service at Le Pavillion Restaurant is considered a bit of a social event among some residents. See separate recommendation for dining. Country Kitchen is the "in" formal restaurant of the hotel, and it opens to the swimming pool where a splashing fountain cools the air. Less expensive than Le Pavillion and featuring Jamaican food and sandwiches, it adjoins a circular bar near the pool at which occasional barbecues are held.

Services: 24-hour room service, baby-sitting, laundry and dry-cleaning facilities, therapeutic massage.

Facilities: Jogging track, health club, tennis courts, outdoor pool.

OCEANA HOTEL AND CONFERENCE CENTRE, 3 King St., at Ocean Blvd. (P.O. Box 986), Kingston 10, Jamaica, W.I. Tel. 809/922-0920, or toll free 800/526-2422. Fax 809/922-3928. 238 rms, 12 suites. A/C TV TEL
$ Rates: $95 single or double; from $110 suite. Breakfast $6 extra. AE, DC, MC, V. **Parking:** Free.

Traditionally considered a well-managed commercial hotel, the Oceana has competed for the resort market since its refurbishment in 1986. It occupies an oceanfront neighborhood filled with prominent business and government buildings, a few steps from the cruise-ship piers in Kingston's harbor.

Rising 12 imposing stories, the hotel offers an array of vacation-oriented facilities in spite of its location in the center of town. The building is physically connected to Jamaica's largest and most modern conference center. The 10-sided freshwater swimming pool is ringed with modern verandas and shingle-capped pavilions, and the bedrooms are comfortable and well furnished.

Dining/Entertainment: The popular Fort Charles restaurant is recommended in "Where to Dine," below. A lobby-level bar, which converts to an evening disco, combines navy-blue murals of 18th-century Jamaican life with cool jazz and tall drinks.

Services: Laundry, massage, baby-sitting, fax service; newsstands, hairdresser and barbershop, and drugstore in an independently managed arcade a few steps from the hotel.

Facilities: Freshwater swimming pool; tour desk that organizes water sports, golfing, and tennis.

WYNDHAM KINGSTON HOTEL, 75 Knutsford Blvd. (P.O. Box 112), Kingston 10, Jamaica, W.I. Tel. 809/926-5430, or toll free 800/822-4200, 800/631-4200 in Canada. Fax 809/929-7439. 307 rms, 8 suites. A/C TV TEL
$ Rates: $130–$145 single or double; from $200 suite. Extra person $25. Children under 12 stay free in parents' room. Breakfast $9 extra. AE, DC, MC, V. **Parking:** Free.

In the center of New Kingston, the Wyndham rises in an imposing mass of pink stucco pierced with oversize sheets of tinted glass, and each unit has a white metal balcony. The engineers added an on-site generator, which is activated during the occasional city power failure. The hotel contains all the amenities to make what was a commercial hotel into an inner-city resort.

Dining/Entertainment: The hotel has two restaurants and two bars. The Rendezvous Piano Bar is a gathering place where live entertainment is presented in a setting of plants and soft lights. The Palm Court is an intimate restaurant created for business lunches and offers Italian specialties, steaks, kebabs, and a generous salad bar; the desserts are sinful, and the wine list—*c'est formidable!* Lunch and dinner, served Monday through Saturday, cost $12 to $25 and up. A less formal coffee shop, the Café Macaw, serves sandwiches, salads, and platters. A disco called the Jonkanoo (see "Evening Entertainment," below) provides evening conviviality.

Services: Laundry, valet, baby-sitting, massage, tour desk.

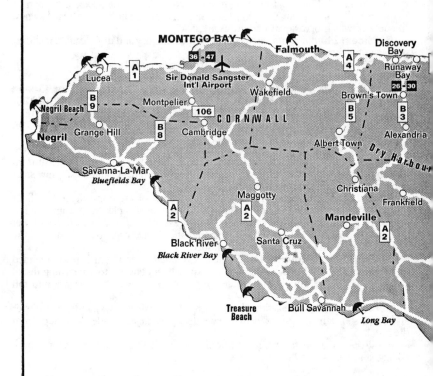

JAMAICA ACCOMMODATIONS

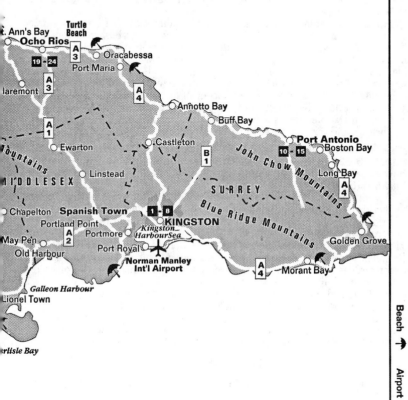

Caribbean Sea

t. Ann's Bay
Ocho Rios
Turtle Beach
A3
Oracabessa
Port Maria
19 - 24
A3
laremont

A4

Annotto Bay
Buff Bay

A1

Ewarton
Castleton
B1

Port Antonio
10 - 15
Boston Bay

ountains
Linstead
John Chow Mountains
Long Bay
A4

MIDDLESEX
SURREY

Chapelton
Spanish Town
Blue Ridge Mountains

Portland Point
A2
1 - 8
KINGSTON
Portmore
Kingston HarbourSea

May Pen
Old Harbour
Port Royal
Norman Manley Int'l Airport
Golden Grove

Galleon Harbour
Lionel Town
A4
Morant Bay

rlisle Bay

Beach →

Airport ✈

Facilities: Olympic-size swimming pool, floodlit tennis courts (free daily until 4pm, after which they rent for $2 per hour), fully equipped health club, business center (for typing, photocopying, and fax transmissions).

MODERATE

THE COURTLEIGH, 31 Trafalgar Rd., Kingston 10, Jamaica, W.I. Tel. 809/926-8174. Fax 809/926-7801. 78 rms, 2 suites. A/C TV TEL
$ Rates: $73 single; $76 double; from $89 suites. Breakfast from $6 extra. AE, MC, V. **Parking:** Free.

Housed in a symmetrical, white, two-story building set back from a busy street in the center of New Kingston, this Jamaican-owned establishment contains a covered reception area with no exterior walls, a plantation-inspired series of verandas and flowering gardens, and extended balconied wings holding the pleasant, simple, yet comfortable accommodations. The central core of all this is the flower-bordered pool area sheltered by shrubs and trees. Each of the rooms in the main building has a modern veranda or balcony of its own. An annex, which has its own swimming pool, is beautifully furnished, each unit a suite with one, two, or three bedrooms. On the premises is a popular disco, Mingles (see "Evening Entertainment," below), and the Plantation Terrace Restaurant (see "Where to Dine," below).

TERRA NOVA HOTEL, 17 Waterloo Rd., Kingston 10, Jamaica, W.I. Tel. 809/926-2211. Fax 809/929-4933. 33 rms. A/C TV TEL
$ Rates: $83–$94 single or double. Breakfast from $5 extra. AE, DC, MC, V. **Parking:** Free.

A gem among small, independently run hotels, this house on the western outskirts of New Kingston, built in 1924 as a wedding present for a young bride, has had a varied career. It was once the family seat of the Myers rum dynasty, and the birthplace and home of Christopher Blackwell, promoter of many Jamaican singers and musical groups, including Bob Marley and the Wailers and Millie Small. In 1959 the house was converted into a hotel, and, set in 2½ acres of well-kept gardens with a backdrop of greenery and mountains, it is now considered one of the best small Jamaican hotels.

Most of the bedrooms are in a new wing, and all have balconies or patios with views onto the gardens. Above the portico is a balcony roof bar. The Spanish-style dining room, with a stone floor, wide windows, and spotless linen, offers local and international food. Your à la carte breakfast is served on the balcony or in the dining room, and there is a swimming pool behind the hotel.

INEXPENSIVE

HOTEL FOUR SEASONS, 18 Ruthven Rd., Kingston 10, Jamaica, W.I. Tel. 809/929-7655. Fax 809/929-5964. 39 rms. A/C TV TEL
$ Rates: $62 single or double. Breakfast from $5 extra. AE, MC, V. **Parking:** Free.
Small and respectable, this hotel is in an old house with a colonial-style veranda along the front, with a view of mango trees and a garden through which you drive. It lies on the western outskirts of New Kingston. You'll enter into the reception and dining areas. Most guest rooms are simply decorated with contemporary furniture, and are in a modern wing added to the hotel in the 1960s.

Meals are served to both hotel guests and outsiders, either on the terrace or in the formal dining room. Monday through Friday, a buffet lunch offers hot dishes, vegetable salads, and desserts. The hotel has two bars (one inside, one out). Clients can arrange to swim in the pool belonging to the larger and more expensive Pegasus Hotel, about a 5-minute walk away.

INDIES HOTEL, 5 Holborn Rd., Kingston 10, Jamaica, W.I. Tel. 809/926-2952. 14 rms. A/C TEL
$ Rates: $42 single; $50 double. Breakfast from $5 extra. AE, MC, V. **Parking:** Free.
On one of the small side streets of New Kingston, near the intersection of Trafalgar

Road and opening onto a flower garden, this half-timbered building with double gables has a small reception area, a lounge, and a TV lounge. The bedrooms, restaurant, and bar are grouped around a cool patio, all spotless. The Indies has a reputation among the locals for friendly atmosphere and good-quality budget meals. Their fish and chips is renowned, and they specialize in pizza. They also serve steak with all the trimmings, and when they get fancy, lobster thermidor.

A NEARBY PLACE TO STAY AT PORT ROYAL

MORGAN'S HARBOUR HOTEL AND BEACH CLUB, Port Royal, Kingston 1, Jamaica, W.I. Tel. 809/924-8464. Fax 809/924-8562. 60 rms, 6 suites. A/C MINIBAR TV TEL **Transportation:** A public ferryboat, priced at J$2 (10¢) per person, departs every 2 hours from Victoria Pier on Ocean Boulevard. Many visitors arrive by car or taxi, or pay J$80 ($4) for the hotel's private boat to fetch them from any pier in downtown Kingston.

$ Rates: $107 single; $123 double; from $145 suites. Breakfast from $6 extra. AE, MC, V. **Parking:** Free.

This is the most visible building within the historic ruin of what was once believed to be the wickedest city on earth, Port Royal. Rebuilt after 1988's Hurricane Gilbert, Morgan's lies near the end of a long sandspit whose rocky and scrub-covered length shelters the harbor of Kingston. On the premises is a 200-year-old red-brick building originally built to melt pitch for the sailing ships of His Majesty's navy, a swimming area carefully defined by docks and buoys, and a rambling series of wings whose eaves are accented with hints of Neo-Victorian gingerbread. Set on 22 acres of flat and rock-studded seashore, the resort contains a breezy restaurant, a popular bar (where ghost stories about the old Port Royal seem especially lurid as the liquor flows on Friday night), and the largest marina facility in Kingston. Longtime residents quietly claim that the ghosts of those soldiers killed by a long-ago earthquake are especially visible on hot and very calm days, when British formations seem to march out of the sea accompanied by the jangling of keys.

The hotel rents well-furnished bedrooms, each furnished in an 18th-century Chippendale-Jamaican motif.

A NEARBY HOSTEL IN THE BLUE MOUNTAINS

WHITFIELD HALL, contact John Allgrove, 8 Armon Jones Crescent, Kingston 6, Jamaica, W.I. Tel. 809/927-0986 (preferably from 6 to 9pm). 7 rms (none with bath).

$ Rates: J$100 ($4.55) per person. No credit cards.

One of the most isolated and inconvenient hotels you're likely to find in Jamaica is Whitfield Hall, a high-altitude hostel and coffee estate about 6 miles from the hamlet of Mavis Bank. The main allure of this place is the opportunity to see the Blue Mountains from a hillclimber's point of view. Accommodations are about as basic as you can get, and there are no restaurant facilities once you get here. Be warned in advance that this is definitely an offbeat adventure.

To get here, you can drive to Mavis Bank, 20 miles from Kingston, leave your car at the police station, and walk; or order a Land Rover for J$200 ($9.10) for up to six passengers when you make your reservations. You can also get to Mavis Bank by bus from Kingston. Most readers request that they be picked up in Kingston by a Land Rover for J$400 ($20) each way for up to six passengers.

Located more than halfway up Blue Mountain, Whitfield Hall is an old coffee plantation dating from 1776, and is the last inhabited house before you get to the peak at some 4,000 feet above sea level. It provides accommodation for 30 guests in rooms containing two or more beds. Blankets and linen are provided, but personal items (like towels, soap, and food) are not. There is a deep freeze and a refrigerator as well as good cooking facilities, crockery, and cutlery. All water comes from a spring, and lighting is by kerosene pressure lamps called Tilleys. A wood fire warms the hostel and its guests, for it gets cold in the mountains at night. You bring your own food and share the kitchen.

Most visitors come to see the sunrise from the summit of Blue Mountain, which means getting up at around 2 or 3am to walk the additional 3,202 feet to the summit along a bridle path through the forest. The route is clearly marked, and you need a good flashlight and warm clothing, along with hiking boots or strong shoes. It's a 3-hour walk each way. It's also possible to hire a mule or a horse to make the jaunt, accompanied by a guide, for about J$180 ($8.20) round-trip for the 13-mile journey.

For reservations at the hostel, information, or a brochure, write or phone John Allgrove at the above address.

WHERE TO DINE
EXPENSIVE

BLUE MOUNTAIN INN, Gordon Town Rd. Tel. 927-1700.
    Cuisine: CARIBBEAN/SEAFOOD/STEAK. **Reservations:** Required.
$ Prices: Appetizers J$65–J$95 ($2.95–$4.30); main courses J$155–J$345 ($7.05–$15.70). AE, DC, MC, V.
    Open: Dinner only, daily 7–9pm.

About a 20-minute drive north from downtown Kingston is an 18th-century coffee plantation house set high on the slopes of Blue Mountain, surrounded by trees and flowers on the bank of the Mammee River. On cold nights, log fires blaze, and the dining room gleams with silver and sparkling glass under the discreet table lights. The inn is one of Jamaica's most famous restaurants, not only for food but also for atmosphere and service. Men are required to wear jackets (ties are optional), but the effort is worth it and the cool night air justifies it. Women are advised to take a wrap.

Menus change monthly and feature Caribbean dishes, fresh seafood, and U.S. steaks, all served with a selection of fresh vegetables; examples might include New Orleans bourbon-and-garlic shrimp, chicken Kiev, or an array of lobster dishes. Top off your meal with tropical fruit salad and ice cream, Tía Maria parfait, baked Alaska, or a more ambitious banana or pineapple flambé. The wine list includes European varieties together with local beverages.

LE PAVILLON RESTAURANT, in the Jamaica Pegasus Hotel, 81 Knutsford Blvd. Tel. 926-3691.
    Cuisine: CARIBBEAN/CONTINENTAL. **Reservations:** Recommended.
$ Prices: Appetizers J$20–J$105 (90¢–$4.75); main courses J$140–J$250 ($6.35–$11.35); three-course fixed-price lunch J$250–J$300 ($11.35–$13.65). AE, DC, MC, V.
    Open: Lunch Mon–Fri 12:30–3pm; dinner Mon–Sat 7–11pm.

Here you can enjoy first-rate dining from an à la carte menu on the lobby level of this previously recommended hotel in New Kingston. The decor is a modernized art nouveau. First courses such as smoked salmon or pepperpot could precede such main dishes as red snapper in lime butter or grilled lobster in garlic butter. It's open for dinner and entertainment, plus snacks, high tea, and pastries are available Monday through Friday from 4:30 to 7pm.

NORMA, 8 Belmont Rd. Tel. 929-4966.
    Cuisine: INTERNATIONAL. **Reservations:** Recommended.
$ Prices: Appetizers J$30–J$100 ($1.35–$4.55); main courses J$160–J$225 ($7.25–$10.25). MC, V.
    Open: Lunch Mon–Fri noon–4pm; dinner Thurs–Fri 7–11pm.

Norma has a sophisticated nouvelle cuisine, an open-air setting, and an enviable reputation as one of the most desirable and charming places for lunch anywhere in Kingston. The cuisine is a collection of creative recipes accumulated from around the world. Owner Norma Shirley holds forth in the rear garden of an unpretentious private house in New Kingston, about a 5-minute drive from the American Embassy. The parsley, thyme, and oregano used in many dishes are cultivated in a garden behind a screen of ficus. Typical dishes might include fettuccine with chicken and shrimp, grilled baby lamb chops, several creative combinations of smoked marlin, a fresh salad of the day, and several flavorful combinations of shrimp and/or lobster.

THE RESTAURANT AT TEMPLE HALL, Temple Hall Estate, Constant Spring. Tel. 942-2340.
   Cuisine: MODERN CARIBBEAN. **Reservations:** Required. **Transportation:** Complimentary pickup service from Kingston hotels (upon request), for a 25-minute ride north of Kingston.
$ Prices: Appetizers J$35–J$50 ($1.60–$2.25); main courses J$130–J$210 ($5.90–$9.55); five-course Sun brunch J$235 ($10.70). AE, DC, MC, V.
   Open: Dinner Mon–Sat 6:30–11:30pm; brunch Sun 11am–3pm.

Its cool whitewashed walls were originally built in 1728 as the headquarters for one of Kingston's most lavish plantations, on a high-altitude tract of rolling hills which experimented with the first coffee crops ever grown in Jamaica. Later it housed José Martí, hero of the Cuban Revolution, during that island's independence from the Spanish.

Today the lushly planted 114 acres that remain attached to the house contain the original stone aqueduct, gracefully covered with flowering vines, and stockyards and gardens that supply most of the herbs, produce, and meats that eventually wind up in creative combinations on your dining table.

The estate benefitted recently from its acquisition by a Swiss-owned consortium headed by three of the island's most talked-about restaurateurs, Swiss-born Valentino Salvi, André Niederhauser, and André's Jamaican-born wife (a former fashion model), Jacqueline Tyson. Together they produce an innovative combination of European culinary techniques coupled with Caribbean ingredients—the most intellectually stimulating cuisine in Jamaica. Examples include crayfish with yellow yams; fettuccine Boston (named after a famous North Shore beach known for the flavors of its jerk chicken), which combines homemade noodles with jerk chicken and ackee; shrimp à la mode (broiled over charcoal and served with sweet potatoes and oranges); and a succulent cheesecake covered in a tropical fruit sauce. These are served in an airy colonial-inspired dining room open to the activity in the kitchen

MODERATE

DEVONSHIRE RESTAURANT/THE GROGG SHOPPE, in Devon House, 26 Hope Rd. Tel. 929-7046.
   Cuisine: JAMAICAN. **Reservations:** Recommended for the Devonshire; not required for the Grogg Shoppe. **Directions:** Near Trafalgar Park.
$ Prices: Appetizers J$16–J$60 (75¢–$2.60) at lunch, J$20–J$175 (90¢–$7.95) at dinner; main courses J$65–J$175 ($2.95–$7.95) at lunch, J$95–J$300 ($4.30–$13.65) at dinner. AE, MC, V.
   Open: Daily 10am–midnight.

These two restaurants are in what were originally the brick-sided servants' quarters of Kingston's most-visited mansion, Devon House. The more formal of the two is the Devonshire, where you can eat on patios under the trees, in sight of the royal palms and the fountain in front of the historic great house.

Appetizers include a "tidbit" of jerk pork or a bowl of soup (perhaps Jamaican red pea—really bean—or pumpkin soup). Main dishes include Jamaican ackee and saltfish, barbecued chicken, or steamed snapper. Also tasty are their unusual homemade ice creams made of local fruits, such as soursop. Blue Mountain tea or coffee is served, and a 10% service charge is added to all bills. The bars for both restaurants serve 11 different rum punches and 10 fruit punches, such as a tamarind fizz or a papaya (paw-paw) punch. Especially popular is the "Devon Duppy," which combines into one pastel-colored glass virtually every variety of rum in the bartender's inventory. Rum drinks cost J$20 to J$25 (90¢ to $1.15) each. Many aficionadoes opt for these drinks on one of the Grogg Shoppe's two different terraces.

FORT CHARLES RESTAURANT, in the Oceana Hotel, 3 King St. Tel. 922-0920.

Cuisine: INTERNATIONAL. **Reservations:** Recommended.

$ **Prices:** Appetizers J$30–J$85 ($1.35–$3.85); main courses J$95–J$250 ($4.30–$11.35). AE, DC, MC, V.

Open: Daily 7am–11pm.

You can use it as a coffee shop for a quick snack or else as a more formal restaurant. Lunch includes a cold roast beef open-face sandwich, barbecued chicken, and the more exotic lobster thermidor, seafood Newburg, or rock lobster. From 7pm, the dinner menu includes a variety of appetizers, soups, steaks (called the juciest in town), and other meat dishes in addition to the daytime menu. Oceana seafood lasagne, smoked filets of marlin, and suprême of chicken stuffed with seafood are specialties. The restaurant is on the lobby level of the previously recommended hotel, at Kingston Harbour.

PLANTATION TERRACE, in the Courtleigh Hotel, 31 Trafalgar Rd. Tel. 926-8174.

Cuisine: INTERNATIONAL. **Reservations:** Not required.

$ **Prices:** Appetizers J$20–J$130 (90¢–$5.90); main courses J$95–J$230 ($4.30–$10.45); Sun night all-you-can-eat barbecue J$175 ($7.95). AE, MC, V.

Open: Breakfast daily 7–10am; lunch daily noon–3pm; dinner daily 7–11pm.

The Plantation Terrace is a pleasant place to dine and escape from the traffic of central New Kingston. Meals are served under a covered parapet lined with tropical plants near an outdoor cabaña-style poolside bar. Seated on iron armchairs you'll enjoy à la carte breakfasts, popular lunches, and candlelit dinners which include a Sunday-night barbecue. The other guests may include a scattering of businesspeople as well as the employees of the American consulate nearby. Specialties are pepperpot soup, chicken gumbo, pork piccata, chicken Cordon Bleu, baked crab backs, and many other dishes which vary according to the culinary culture being emphasized on a particular evening; there's even an occasional Chinese specialty, as well as a changing array of Jamaican dishes. Lunches are slightly less expensive than dinners. The restaurant sometimes has live music on Sunday evenings.

INEXPENSIVE

INDIES PUB AND GRILL, 8 Holborn Rd. Tel. 926-2952.

Cuisine: JAMAICAN. **Reservations:** Not required.

$ **Prices:** Appetizers J$15–J$20 (70¢–90¢); main courses J$20–J$120 (90¢–$5.45). AE, MC, V.

Open: Mon–Wed 10am–midnight, Thurs–Sat 10am–1:30am, Sun 4pm–midnight.

This informal neighborhood restaurant off Hope Road in New Kingston was designed around a garden terrace, which on hot nights provides the best (and coolest) place to sit. Of course, you can always go into the inner rooms, which are haphazardly but pleasantly decorated with caribou horns, tortoise shells, an aquarium sometimes stocked with baby sharks, and even a Canadian moosehead. The establishment offers a full sandwich menu at lunchtime. In the evening you can enjoy grilled lobster, fish and chips, barbecued quail, chicken Kiev, or roast beef. A bottle of Red Stripe, the Jamaican national brew, is the preferred beverage for practically everyone here, and is priced at J$18 (80¢).

TERRA NOVA HOTEL RESTAURANT, 17 Waterloo Rd. Tel. 926-9334.

Cuisine: INTERNATIONAL/JAMAICAN. **Reservations:** Recommended.

$ **Prices:** Appetizers J$21–J$89 (95¢–$4.05); main courses J$126–J$305 ($5.75–$13.85). AE, DC, MC, V.

Open: Lunch daily noon–2:30pm; dinner daily 7:30–11pm.

Set in one of the small and respectable hotels of New Kingston, off Hope Road, this restaurant welcomes a crowd of local businesspeople and other dignitaries at mealtimes into a formal dining room. Today the grandeur of the portico, the elaborate moldings of the hotel reception area, and the restaurant are souvenirs of the former affluent owners. There is an emphasis on fish and shellfish dishes, including mixed grill, pepper steak, seafood platters, and baked crab. The chef is also noted for his flambé dishes and his fondues.

BUDGET

CHELSEA JERK CENTRE, 9 Chelsea Ave. Tel. 926-6322.
   Cuisine: JAMAICAN. **Reservations:** Not accepted.
$ Prices: A jerk half-chicken J$42 ($1.90); a pound of jerk pork J$84 ($3.80). No credit cards.
   Open: Mon–Sat 11:30am–12:30am.
Located between the New Kingston Shopping Centre and the Wyndham New Kingston Hotel, this is the city's most popular provider of the Jamaican delicacies known as jerk pork and jerk chicken. You can order food to take away or eat in the comfortably battered dining room. Though no appetizers are served here, you might order a side portion of what the scrawled blackboard refers to as "Festival," which is fried cornmeal dumplings.

WHAT TO SEE & DO

Even if you're staying at one of the resorts, such as Montego Bay or Ocho Rios, you may want to visit Kingston for sightseeing, and for trips to nearby Port Royal and Spanish Town.

IN TOWN

One of the major attractions, ✪ **Devon House,** 26 Hope Road (tel. 929-6602), was built in 1881 by George Stiebel, a Jamaican who, after mining in South America, became one of the first black millionaires in the Caribbean. A striking classical building, the house has been restored to its original beauty by the Jamaican National Trust. The grounds contain craft shops (see "Shopping," below), boutiques, three restaurants (see "Where to Dine," above), and shops that sell the best ice cream in Jamaica in exotic fruit flavors, and a bakery and pastry shop with Jamaican puddings and desserts. The main house also displays furniture of various periods and styles. Admission to Devon House is J$22 ($1). The house is open Tuesday through Saturday from 10am to 5pm.
   Almost next door to Devon House are the sentried gates of **Jamaica House,** residence of the prime minister, a fine, white-columned building set well back from the road.
   Continuing along Hope Road, at the crossroads of Lady Musgrave Road and King's House Road, turn left and you'll see a gate on the left with its own personal traffic light. This leads to **King's House,** the official residence of the governor-general of Jamaica, the queen's representative on the island. The outside and front lawn of the gracious residence, set in 200 acres of well-tended parkland, is sometimes open to view Monday through Friday from 10am to 5pm. The secretarial offices are housed next door in an old wooden building set on brick arches. In front of the house is a gigantic banyan tree in whose roots, legend says, duppies (as ghosts are called in Jamaica) take refuge when they're not living in the cotton trees.
   Between Old Hope Road and Mona Road, a short distance from the Botanical Gardens, is the **University of the West Indies,** built in 1948 on the Mona Sugar Estate, the third of the large estates in this area. Ruins of old mills, storehouses, and aqueducts are juxtaposed with modern buildings on what must be the most beautifully situated campus in the world. The chapel, an old sugar factory building, was transported stone by stone from Trelawny and rebuilt on the campus close to the old sugar factory, the remains of which are well preserved and give a good idea of how sugar was made in slave days.
   The **National Stadium,** Briggs Park, of which Jamaica is justly proud, has an aluminum statue of Arthur Wint, national athlete, at the entrance. The stadium is used for such activities as soccer, field sports, and cycling. Beside the stadium is the

National Arena, used for indoor sports, exhibitions, and concerts, and there is an Olympic-size pool. Admission prices vary according to activities.

A mile above Kingston, if you go north on Duke Street, you come to **National Heroes Park,** formerly known as George VI Memorial Park. This was the old Kingston race course. An assortment of large office blocks, including the offices of the Ministries of Finance and Education, overlooks the park and the statues of Simón Bolívar and of national heroes, Nanny of the Maroons, George Gordon, and Paul Bogle, martyrs of the Morant Bay revolt. Norman Manley and Alexander Busta-Bustamente, national heroes of Jamaica, are buried here, as is Sir Donald Sangster, a former prime minister.

Just north of Heroes Park, on Marescaux Road, is **Mico College** (tel. 929-5260), a tertiary coeducational teacher-training institution. Lacy Mico, a rich London widow, left her fortune to a favorite nephew on the condition that he marry one of her six nieces. He did not, and the inheritance was invested. The interest was used to ransom victims of the Barbary pirates, but with the end of piracy in the early 19th century it was decided that the capital would be devoted to founding schools for newly emancipated slaves, and, among others, Mico College was established.

The central administrative offices of the **Institute of Jamaica,** founded in 1879, are between 12 and 16 East Street (tel. 922-0620), close to the harbor. Open from 8:30am to 5pm Monday through Thursday, to 4pm on Friday, the institute fosters and encourages the development of culture, science, and history in the national interest. The institute has responsibility for a Junior Centre, the Natural History Division (the repository of the national collection of flora and fauna), and the National Library. Those divisions and organizations located elsewhere are the Cultural Training Centre, 1 Arthur Wint Drive, with schools of music, dance, art, and drama; the African-Caribbean Institute, 12 Ocean Boulevard, which conducts research on cultural heritage; the Museums Division, with sites in Port Royal and Spanish Town, which have the responsibility for the display of artifacts of relevance to the history of Jamaica; the National Gallery, 12 Ocean Boulevard; and the Institute of Jamaica Publications Ltd., 2A Suthermere Road, which publishes a quarterly, the *Jamaica Journal,* as well as other works of educational and cultural merit.

The **National Library of Jamaica** (formerly the West India Reference Library), Institute of Jamaica, 12-16 East Street (tel. 922-0620), a storehouse of the history, culture, and traditions of Jamaica and the Caribbean, is the finest working library for West Indian studies in the world. It has the most comprehensive, up-to-date, and balanced collection of materials—including books, newspapers, photographs, maps, and prints—to be found anywhere in the Caribbean. Of special interest to visitors are the regular exhibitions that attractively and professionally highlight different aspects of Jamaica and West Indian life. September through June, it's open Monday through Thursday from 9am to 4:30pm, Friday from 9am to 4pm, and Saturday 9am to 1pm.

The **Bob Marley Museum** (formerly Tuff Gong Studio), 56 Hope Road (tel. 927-7056), is said to be the most-visited sight in Kingston, although unless you're a Bob Marley fan, it may not mean much to you. The clapboard house with its garden and high surrounding wall was the famous reggae singer's home and recording studio until his death. The museum is open on Monday, Tuesday, Thursday, and Friday from 9:30am to 4:30pm and on Wednesday and Saturday from 12:30 to 5:30pm. Admission is J$40 ($1.80) for adults and J$20 (90¢) for children 4 to 12. It's reached by bus no. 14.

PORT ROYAL

From West Beach Dock, Kingston, a ferry ride of 20 to 30 minutes will take you to Port Royal.

Port Royal conjures up pictures of swashbuckling pirates led by Henry Morgan, swilling grog in harbor taverns. This was once one of the largest trading centers of the New World, with a reputation for being the wickedest city on earth (Blackbeard stopped here regularly on his Caribbean trips). But the whole thing came to an end at 11:43am on June 7, 1692, when a third of the town disappeared under water as the result of a devastating earthquake. Nowadays, Port Royal, with its memories of the past, has been designated by the government for redevelopment as a tourist destination.

As you drive along the Palisades, you arrive first at **St. Peter's Church.** It's usually closed, but you may persuade the caretaker, who lives opposite, to open it if you want to see the silver plate, said to be spoils captured by Henry Morgan from the cathedral in Panama. In the ill-kept graveyard is the tomb of Lewis Galdy, a Frenchman swallowed up and subsequently regurgitated by the 1692 earthquake.

Fort Charles (tel. 925-0335), the only one remaining of Port Royal's six forts, has withstood attack, earthquake, fire, and hurricane. Built in 1656 and later strengthened by Morgan for his own purposes, the fort was expanded and further armed in the 1700s, until its firepower boasted more than 100 cannons, covering both the land and the sea approaches. After subsequent earthquakes and tremors, the fort ceased to be at the water's edge and is now well inland. In 1779 Britain's naval hero, Horatio Lord Nelson, was commander of the fort and trod the wooden walkway inside the western parapet as he kept watch for the French invasion fleet.

The **Fort Charles Maritime Museum** is in the former British naval headquarters where Nelson served. Scale models of the fort and ships of past eras are to be seen in the small museum. It's open from 10am to 4pm Monday through Friday, to 5pm on Saturday and Sunday. Admission is 50¢ for adults, free for children.

Part of the complex, **Giddy House,** once the Royal Artillery storehouse, is another example of what the earth's movements can do. Walking across the tilted floor is an eerie and strangely disorienting experience.

On the land side of the fort is the Old Naval Hospital, which now houses the **Archeological Museum and Research Centre** (tel. 924-8706). This building was completed in 1818 and is the oldest cast-iron prefabricated building in the western hemisphere. It contains many artifacts unearthed from digs and underwater searches around Port Royal, including a watch that had stopped at the moment of the 1692 earthquake, now in pieces; a Chinese porcelain madonna, of which only three exist in the world, recovered from the sea; Spanish armor; slave shackles; and much weaponry, together with models and descriptive tableaux of the Port Royal of the past. After gaining admission to the upstairs museum by ringing the 19th-century bell for the guide, you can see Prince Henry's Polygon Battery, the Old Coaling Wharf, the Jail House, and the Victoria and Albert Battery complex. It's open daily from 9am to 5pm. Admission is 50¢.

SPANISH TOWN

From 1662 to 1872 Spanish Town was the capital of the island. Originally founded by the Spaniards as Villa de la Vega, it was sacked by Cromwell's men in 1655 and all traces of papism were obliterated. The English cathedral, surprisingly retaining a Spanish name, **St. Jago de la Vega,** was built in 1666 and rebuilt after being destroyed by a hurricane in 1712. As you drive into the town from Kingston, the ancient cathedral, rebuilt in 1714, catches your eye, with its brick tower and two-tiered wooden steeple, which was not added until 1831. As the cathedral was built on the foundation and remains of the old Spanish church, it is half-English, half-Spanish, showing two definite styles, one Romanesque, the other Gothic.

Of cruciform design and built mostly of brick, the cathedral is historically one of the most interesting buildings on the island. The black and white marble stones of the aisles are interspersed with ancient tombstones, and the walls are heavy with marble memorials that are almost a chronicle of Jamaica's history, dating back as far as 1662. Episcopalian services are held regularly on Sunday at 7 and 10:30am and at 6:30pm, sometimes conducted by the bishop of Jamaica, whose see this is.

Beyond the cathedral, turn right and two blocks along you'll reach Constitution Street and the **Town Square.** This delightful little square is surrounded by towering royal palms.

On the west side is old **King's House,** gutted by fire in 1925, though the facade has been restored. This was the residence of Jamaica's British governors until 1972 when the capital was transferred to Kingston, and many celebrated guests—among them Lord Nelson, Admiral Rodney, Captain Bligh of H.M.S. *Bounty* fame, and King William IV—stayed here.

Behind the house is the **Jamaica People's Museum of Craft and Technology** (tel. 922-0620), open Monday through Thursday from 10am to 5pm and on Friday from 10am to 4pm. Admission is J$25 ($1.15). The garden contains examples of old farm machinery, an old water mill wheel, a hand-turned sugar mill, a coffee pulper, an old hearse, and a fire engine. An outbuilding contains a museum of crafts and technology, together with a number of smaller agricultural implements. In the small archeological museum are old prints, models (including one of King's House based on a written description), and maps of the town's grid layout from the 1700s.

On the north side of the square is the **Rodney Memorial,** perhaps the most dramatic of the buildings on the square, commissioned by a grateful assembly to commemorate the victory in 1782 of Baron George Rodney, English admiral, over the French fleet, which saved the island from invasion.

Opposite the Rodney Memorial was the **Court House,** the most recent of the four buildings. The court occupied the ground floor, and when in session, overflowed onto the pavement and road with an animated throng of court attendants, defendants, witnesses, and spectators. The courthouse was destroyed by fire in 1989, but it is to be rebuilt.

The final side of the square, the east, contains the most attractive building, the **House of Assembly,** with a shady brick colonnade running the length of the ground floor, and above it a wooden pillared balcony. This was the stormy center of the bitter debates for Jamaica's governing body. Now the ground floor is the parish library. Council officers occupy the upper floor, along with the Mayor's Parlour, all closed to the public.

The streets around the old Town Square contain many fine Georgian town houses intermixed with tin-roofed shacks. Nearby is the **market,** so busy in the morning you will find it difficult, almost dangerous, to drive through. It provides, however, a bustling scene of Jamaican life.

Driving to Spanish Town from Kingston on the A1 (Washington Boulevard), at Central Village you come to the **Arawak Museum,** on the right. The entrance appears to lead to a quarry, but don't be put off. Drive down to the museum, a hexagonal building on the site of one of the largest Arawak settlements on the island. It's open Monday through Thursday from 10am to 5pm and on Friday from 10am to 4pm. The small, well-planned museum contains drawings, pictures, and diagrams of Arawak life, plus old flints and other artifacts that help you to understand the early history or prehistoric period of Jamaica. Smoking of tobacco seems to have been a habit even in 1518, when Arawaks were recorded as lighting hollow tubes at one end and sucking the other. The visitor can also see signs of an original Arawak settlement at White Marl, around the museum's main building. Admission is J$2 (10¢).

SAVVY SHOPPING

Downtown Kingston, the old part of the town, is centered around Sir William Grant Park, formerly Victoria Park, a newly remodeled showpiece of lawns, lights, and fountains. North of the park is the Ward Theatre, the oldest in the New World, where the traditional Jamaican pantomime is staged from December 26 to early April. To the east is Coke Methodist Church and to the south, the equally historic Kingston Parish Church.

Cool arcades lead off from King Street, but everywhere there is a teeming mass of people going about their business. There are some beggars and the inevitable salespeople who sidle up and offer "hot stuff, mon," frequently highly polished brass lightly dipped in gold and offered at high prices as real gold. The hucksters do accept a polite but firm "no," but don't let them keep you talking or you'll end up buying. They're very persuasive!

On King Street are the imposing General Post Office and the Supreme Court buildings.

ART

For many years the richly evocative paintings of Haiti were viewed as the most valuable contribution to the arts in the Caribbean. There is within Jamaica, however, a rapidly growing perception of itself as one of the artistic leaders of the Third World. An articulate core of Caribbean critics are focusing the attention of the art world at large on the unusual, eclectic, and sometimes politically motivated paintings being produced in Jamaica.

MUTUAL LIFE GALLERY, Mutual Life Centre, 2 Oxford Rd. Tel. 926-9025.

One of the country's most prominent art galleries is in the corporate headquarters of a major insurance company. After you pass a security check, you can climb to the corporation's mezzanine level for an insight into the changing face of Jamaican art. The gallery's exhibitions are organized by Pat Ramsey, who encourages developing unknowns and showcases established artists. Exhibitions change once a month, but there is usually a stable of long-term exhibits. The Mutual Life Insurance Company donates the space for free as part of its own attempts to improve the status of the arts in the Caribbean. The gallery is a nonprofit institution. Open: Mon–Fri 10am–6pm, Sat 11am–3pm.

FRAME CENTRE GALLERY, 10 Tangerine Place. Tel. 926-4644.

This is one of the most important art galleries in Jamaica, and the founder and guiding force, Guy McIntosh, is widely respected today as a patron of the Jamaican arts. Committed to presenting quality Jamaican art, the gallery has three viewing areas and carries a varied collection of more than 300 works. It represents both pioneer and contemporary artists, some of which are internationally known—in addition, younger, newer talents are always on display here. Open: Mon–Fri 8:30am–5pm, Sat 11am–3pm.

CRAFTS

KINGSTON CRAFTS MARKET, at the west end of Harbour St., downtown.

A large, covered area of small stalls individually owned, the market is reached through such thoroughfares as Straw Avenue, Drummer's Lane, and Cheapside. All kinds of island crafts are on sale: wooden plates and bowls, trays, ashtrays, and pepperpots made from mahoe, the national wood of the island. Straw hats, mats, baskets are also on display. Batik shirts and cotton shirts with gaudy designs are sold. Banners for wall decoration are inscribed with the Jamaican coat-of-arms, and wood masks often have elaborately carved faces. Apart from being a good place to buy worthwhile souvenirs, the market is where you can learn the art of bargaining and ask for a *brawta*, a free bonus. However, be aware that, unlike in Haiti and the Hispanic islands, bargaining is *not* a Jamaican tradition. Vendors will take something off the price, but not very much.

THINGS JAMAICAN, Devon House, 26 Hope Rd. Tel. 929-7029.

Here you'll find a showcase of Jamaican handcrafts. Every item in the store is made in Jamaica—not only the paintings and sculpture, but also the sauces and liquor, including the best of Jamaican rum, and items in straw. Look also for their collection of pewter knives and forks, based on designs of original pewter items discovered in archeological exploration in the Port Royal area in 1965. In this collection you can buy items with the Tudor Rose seal and Lion Rampant spoons, among others. This reproduced Port Royal collection, however, is leadless, unlike the original. Even the imperfections have been reproduced. There is also an outlet in Montego Bay.

LIQUOR

SANGSTER'S OLD JAMAICA SPIRITS, 17 Holborn Rd. Tel. 926-8888.

A full array of unusual rum-based liqueurs is available in this well-scrubbed factory outlet on a side street off the modern uptown New Kingston business area. The entrance isn't well marked, but once you enter the showroom, you know from the hundreds of bottles on display that you're in a rum lovers' mecca. The prices vary, based on the quality and size of the container, not on the contents. You can purchase coconut rum, coffee-orange, coffee cream, coconut cream, and Blue Mountain coffee liqueurs. There's a large trolley filled with small cups of samples of the various rums and liqueurs, so you can taste before you buy. Open: Mon–Fri 8:30am–4:30pm.

A SHOPPING CENTER

NEW KINGSTON SHOPPING CENTRE, 30 Dominica Dr., New Kingston.
One of the most modern shopping centers in Jamaica, this is known for its assemblage of merchandise rather than for any particular merchant. It is sleek and contemporary, and stores are centered around a Mayan-style pyramid, down the sides of which cascades of water irrigate trailing bougainvillea. Fast-food outlets, fashion boutiques, and many shops are found here, and free concerts are often presented in the open-air theater. Open: Mon–Sat 10am–6pm.

EVENING ENTERTAINMENT

There are safer places to be. Use caution when going out.

THE PERFORMING ARTS

Kingston is called the cultural heart of the West Indies. There are several theaters presenting live performances, among them: the **Ward Theatre,** on North Parade (tel. 922-0453); and the **Little Theatre,** on Tom Redcam Drive near the National Stadium (tel. 926-6129). There is also the **Creative Arts Centre** at the University of the West Indies, Mona (tel. 927-1047). All the above stage local or imported plays and musicals, light opera, revues, and internationally acclaimed Jamaican dance and choral groups and pop concerts. The cost of tickets varies with the production. From downtown Kingston (Parade) and Cross Roads, bus nos. 90a and 90b run here.

Most entertainment of this sort is listed in the daily press, as is a host of other attractions, including colorful carnivals and festivals held islandwide throughout the year.

THE CLUB & BAR SCENE

Red Hills Strip, a suburban area of Kingston, has a number of nightclubs, all of which I make it a point to avoid.

JONKANOO, in the Wyndham Kingston Hotel, 75 Knutsford Blvd. Tel. 926-5430.
Although disco is the mainstay here, on some nights live entertainment is presented. Contemporary and elegant, and located in one of Kingston's most visible upmarket hotels, its offerings change according to the night of the week, including everything from sports events visible on a big-screen TV to live reggae bands. Beer costs J$20 ($1). Open: Mon–Sat 10pm–2am.
Admission: Fri–Sat J$50 ($2.25) men, J$20 (90¢) women; Mon–Thurs free.

MINGLES DISCO, in the Courtleigh Hotel, 31 Trafalgar Rd. Tel. 929-5320.
At the far end of the reception area of the hotel, this disco is furnished with a dark-grained decor of movable tables, parquet floors, and large expanses of both bar space and dancing areas. Live concerts are sometimes held here. A Red Stripe beer costs J$16 (75¢). Open: Mon–Thurs 5pm–2am or 3am, Fri–Sat 5pm to the wee hours.
Admission: J$40 ($1.80).

2. PORT ANTONIO

Port Antonio is a verdant and sleepy seaport on the northeast coast of Jamaica, 63 miles northeast of Kingston, where Tom Cruise filmed *Cocktail*. It has been called the Jamaica of 100 years ago. Port Antonio is the mecca of the titled and the wealthy, including European royalty and such stars as Linda Evans, Raquel Welch, Whoopi Goldberg (who came here to film *Clara's Heart*), Peter O'Toole, and Tommy Tune.

The small, bustling town of Port Antonio is like many on the island: clean and untidy, with sidewalks around a market filled with vendors; tin-roofed shacks competing with old Georgian and modern brick and concrete buildings; and lots of people shopping, talking, laughing, and some just loafing. The market is a place to browse among local craftwork, spices, and fruits.

In other days visitors arrived by banana boat and stayed at the Titchfield Hotel (which burned down) in a lush, tropical, unspoiled part of the island. Captain Bligh landed here in 1793 with the first breadfruit plants, and Port Antonio claims that the ones grown in this area are the best on the island. Visitors still arrive by water—but now it's in cruise ships that moor close to Navy Island, and the passengers come ashore just for the day.

Navy Island and the long-gone Titchfield Hotel were owned for a short time by film star Errol Flynn. The story is that after suffering damage to his yacht, he put into Kingston for repairs, visited Port Antonio by motorbike, fell in love with the area, and in due course acquired Navy Island, some say in a gambling game. Later, he either lost or sold it and bought a nearby plantation, Comfort Castle, still owned by his widow, Patrice Wymore Flynn, who spends most of her time there. He was much loved and admired by the Jamaicans and was totally integrated into the community. They still talk of him in Port Antonio—his reputation for womanizing and drinking lives on.

GETTING THERE To reach Port Antonio from the capital, you can take the A4 through Port Morant and up the east coast, or drive north on the A3 through Castleton and travel east along the north coast, where Jamaica's tourist industry started.

WHERE TO STAY

VERY EXPENSIVE

TRIDENT VILLAS & HOTEL, Rte. A4 (P.O. Box 119), Port Antonio, Jamaica, W.I. Tel. 809/993-2602, or toll free in the U.S. 800/237-3237, or 800/235-3505. Fax 809/993-2590. 11 rms, 15 suites. TEL

$ Rates: Winter, $210–$280 single; $250–$320 double; from $500 suite. Summer, $130–$170 single; $150–$190 double; from $300 suite. AE, MC, V. **Parking:** Free.

About 2½ miles east along Allan Avenue on the coast toward Frenchman's Cove stands an elegant rendezvous of the rich and famous. This deluxe hotel complex is one of the most tasteful and refined on the north shore. Sitting regally above jagged coral cliffs with a seaside panorama, the hotel is the personal and creative statement of Earl Levy, scion of a prominent Kingston family. Nearby he has erected a multi-million-dollar replica of a European château, known as Trident Castle, which can be rented as one unit. Here, guests are grandly housed in five large bedrooms beautifully furnished in plantation style.

The hotel's main building is furnished with many antiques, and flowers decorate the sea breeze–cooled lobby. Your accommodations will be a studio cottage or tower, reached by a pathway through the gardens. In a cottage, a large bedroom with ample sitting area opens onto a private patio with a view of the sea. All cottages and tower rooms have baths with tubs, showers, and toilets, plus ceiling fans and plenty of storage space. Jugs of ice and water are constantly replenished, and fresh flowers grace the dressing table. Singles are accommodated in either junior or deluxe villa suites, while two or three guests are lodged in junior, deluxe villa, prime minister's, or imperial suites.

There's a small private sand beach, and the immaculate gardens embrace a pool and a gingerbread gazebo. Lounges, tables, chairs, and bar service add to your pleasure.

Dining/Entertainment: The main building has two patios, one covered, where breakfast and lunch are served. You can also have breakfast on your private patio, served by your own butler. At dinner, when men are required to wear jackets and ties, silver service, crystal, and Port Royal pewter sparkle on the tables. Dinner is a many-course fixed-price meal, so if you are concerned with dietary restrictions, you should make your requirements known early so that alternative food can be served.

Services: Room service, laundry, baby-sitting.

Facilities: Swimming pool; tennis, horseback riding, and such water sports as sailing and snorkeling (included in the tariffs).

EXPENSIVE

FERN HILL CLUB, Mile Gully Rd., San San (P.O. Box 100), Port Antonio, Jamaica, W.I. Tel. 809/993-3222; for all reservations, 416/620-4666 in Toronto. Fax 809/993-2257. 38 units. A/C TV **Directions:** Head east along Allan Ave.

$ Rates: $98–$150 single or double. Breakfast buffet $10 extra. AE, MC, V. **Parking:** Free.

Attractive, airy, and panoramic, this resort occupies 45 forested acres high above the coastline. Technically classified as a private club, the establishment comprises a colonial-style clubhouse and five outlying villas, plus a comfortable annex at the bottom of the hill. The accommodations are highly private.

Dining/Entertainment: The Blue Mahoe Bar is named after the wood that sheathes it, and there's a patio for dining. The hotel restaurant offers an international menu.

Services: A shuttle bus makes infrequent trips down the steep hillside to the beach at Frenchman's Cove, and a less populated beach called San San.

Facilities: Four swimming pools, tennis court.

GOBLIN HILL VILLAS AT SAN SAN, San San (P.O. Box 26), Port Antonio, Jamaica, W.I. Tel. 809/993-3286, or toll free 800/423-4059. Fax 809/925-6248. 44 rms, 28 villas. A/C MINIBAR

$ Rates (including transfers and rental car): Winter, $1,780 one-bedroom villa per week; $2,080 two-bedroom villa for four per week. Summer, $1,480 one-bedroom villa per week; $1,880 two-bedroom villa for four per week. AE, MC, V. **Parking:** Free.

This green and sun-washed hillside once reputed to shelter goblins is now filled with vacation homes on San San Estate. The swimming pool is surrounded by a vine-laced arbor, which lies just a stone's throw from an almost-impenetrable forest. A long flight of steps leads down to the crescent-shaped sands of San San beach. The accommodations are town-house style against the landscape, and units have ceiling fans and king-size beds.

Dining/Entertainment: In the villas, housekeepers prepare and serve meals.

Services: Housekeepers attend to chores in villas.

Facilities: Two Laykold tennis courts, beach, swimming pool.

JAMAICA PALACE HOTEL, Williamsfield (P.O. Box 277), Port Antonio, Jamaica, W.I. Tel. 809/993-2021, 312/883-1020 in Chicago, or toll free 800/423-4095, Fax 809/993-3459. 21 rms, 44 suites. A/C TV TEL **Directions:** Head east on Allan Ave.

$ Rates: Winter, $110 single or double; $165 junior suite; $280 one-bedroom suite. Summer, $95 single or double; $145 junior suite; $240 one-bedroom suite. MAP $55 per person extra. AE, MC, V. **Parking:** Free.

Set on 5 tropically landscaped acres, this hotel opened in 1989. Rising like a stately mansion, the deluxe hotel commands a coastal view of Port Antonio. Its owner, German-born Siglinde von Stephani-Fahmi, set out to combine the elegance of a European hotel with the relaxed atmosphere of a Jamaican resort. The public rooms are filled with furnishings and art from Europe, including a 6-foot Baccarat crystal candelabra, and a pair of Italian ebony-and-ivory chairs from the 15th century. Outside, the Palace offers white marble columns (Tara style), sun-filled patios and balconies, and an unusual 114-foot swimming pool shaped like the island of Jamaica.

Accommodations include 21 deluxe rooms, 52 junior suites, 6 full suites, and an imperial suite. All rooms are large, with 12½-foot ceilings and oversize marble bathrooms. Suites are individually furnished with crystal chandeliers, Persian rugs, and original works of art.

Dining/Entertainment: Both continental and Jamaican food are served in the chic main dining room with its lighted "waterwall" sculpted from Jamaican cave stones, where men are requested to wear jackets and ties. There's also a poolside café with a barbecue area. Live dance music and calypso bands are featured.

Services: Room service, laundry, baby-sitting, massage facilities, fashion boutique (operated by Patrice Wymore Flynn, widow of Errol Flynn), complimentary shuttle service and admission to three nearby white sandy beaches.

Facilities: Swimming pool.

MODERATE

NAVY ISLAND RESORT & MARINA, Navy Island (P.O. Box 188), Port Antonio, Jamaica, W.I. Tel. 809/993-2667. Fax 809/993-2041. 7 studio cottages, 6 villas. **Transportation:** Private 24-hour ferry.

$ Rates: Winter, $90–$120 single; $115–$125 double; from $150 villa. Summer, $80 single; $100 double; from $140 villa. MAP $35 per person extra. AE, MC, V.

Jamaica's only private island getaway, this resort and marina on that "bit of paradise" once owned by actor Errol Flynn. Today this cottage colony and yacht club is one of the best-kept travel secrets in the Caribbean. To reach the resort, you'll have to take a ferry from the dockyards of Port Antonio on West Street for a short ride across one of the most beautiful and convoluted harbors of Jamaica. Guests of the hotel travel free, but temporary visitors pay J$40 ($1.80) for the round-trip. The ferry travels daily from 7am to 11pm.

Each accommodation is designed as a studio cottage or villa branching out from the main club. Ceiling fans and trade winds keep the cottages cool, and mosquito netting over the beds adds a plantation touch.

One of the resort's beaches is a secluded clothing-optional stretch of sand known as Trembly Knee Cove. You can leisurely explore the island, whose grounds are dotted with hybrid hibiscus, bougainvillea, and palms (many of which were originally ordered planted by Flynn himself).

Dining/Entertainment: At night, after enjoying drinks in the H.M.S. *Bounty* Bar, guests can dine in the Chuups Restaurant, which means "small kiss" in Jamaican patois. A five-course dinner is served nightly from 7 to 9pm and costs $26 to $32.

Services: Free ferry service.

Facilities: Swimming pool, two beaches, water sports (including scuba diving and windsurfing).

INEXPENSIVE

DE MONTEVIN LODGE HOTEL, 21 Fort George St., Port Antonio, Jamaica, W.I. Tel. 809/993-2604. 13 rms (3 with bath).

$ Rates: $35 single without bath, $45 single with bath; $63 double without bath, $68 double with bath. AE. **Parking:** Free.

This lodge, probably the most ornate and best-maintained version of a gingerbread house in town, stands on a narrow backstreet whose edges are lined with architectural reminders (some of them not well preserved) of the colonial days. Originally built as a sea captain's house in 1881, the hotel is really worth a photograph. Cast-iron accents and elongated red and white balconies set a tone for the charm you find inside: cedar doors, art deco cupboards, a ceiling embellished with lacy plaster designs, and the most elaborate cove moldings in town. Don't expect modern amenities here; your room might be a study of another, not-yet-renovated era.

WHERE TO DINE

All hotels welcome outside guests for dinner, but reservations are required.

DE MONTEVIN LODGE RESTAURANT, 21 Fort George St. Tel. 993-2604.
Cuisine: JAMAICAN. **Reservations:** Required.
$ **Prices:** Fixed-price meals J$80 ($3.65), J$100 ($4.55), and J$180 ($8.20). AE.
Open: Lunch daily 12:30–2pm; dinner daily 7–9pm.

Here you'll be able to order a true Jamaican dinner. Start with pepperpot or pumpkin soup, follow with curried lobster and chicken Jamaican style with local vegetables, and finish with coconut or banana-cream pie, washed down with coffee. I suggest an ice-cold Red Stripe beer with the meal, too. The menu changes according to the availability of fresh supplies, but the standard of cooking and the full Jamaican character of the meal are constant. Always call the day before to let them know you're coming.

FERN HILL CLUB, Mile Gully Rd. Tel. 993-3222.
Cuisine: INTERNATIONAL/JAMAICAN. **Reservations:** Required. **Directions:** Head east on Allan Ave.
$ **Prices:** Fixed-price meal $11 at lunch, $30 at dinner. AE, MC, V.
Open: Lunch daily 1–2pm; dinner daily 7:30–9:30pm.

One of the finest dining spots in Port Antonio has a sweeping view of the rugged coastline; sunset watching here is said to be the best at the resort. Well-prepared specialties are served: jerk chicken, jerk pork, grilled lobster, and Créole fish. Beach barbecues Monday and Friday cost $33 to $37, depending on the entertainment.

RAFTER'S RESTAURANT, St. Margaret's Bay. Tel. 993-2778.
Cuisine: JAMAICAN. **Reservations:** Not required.
$ **Prices:** Appetizers $2–$5; main courses $10–$20. AE, MC, V.
Open: Daily 7am–7pm.

Rafter's Restaurant lies at the edge of the river at the point where still waters provided a convenient resting point for the commercial raft operators who used to float goods downstream. Jean McGill and Beverley Dixon are the gracious managers of this establishment, where a flautist provides musical diversion throughout the day. The neoclassical pavilion housing the establishment was built in 1954 by a local architect for the Earl of Mansfield. The house drink is a Río Grande special, which combines four kinds of rum with fresh juice. Food includes sandwiches, burgers, an array of salads, steak or chicken, as well as grilled lobster. Fresh fish is served grilled, steamed, or pan-fried. The turnoff leading to this place is about 5 miles west of Port Antonio; follow the signs.

TRIDENT HOTEL RESTAURANT, Rte. A4. Tel. 993-2602.
Cuisine: INTERNATIONAL. **Reservations:** Required. **Directions:** Head east on Allan Ave.
$ **Prices:** Fixed-price dinner $50. AE, MC, V.
Open: Dinner only, daily 8–10pm.

The Trident Hotel Restaurant has for a long time been frequented by those seeking a high-level cuisine. Part of the main hotel building, the restaurant has an air of elegance. The high-pitched wooden roof set on white stone walls holds several ceiling fans that gently stir the air. The antique tables are set with old china, English silver, and Port Royal pewter. The formally dressed waiters will help you choose your wine and whisper the name of each course as they serve it: Jamaican salad; coconut soup; dolphin with mayonnaise and mustard sauce; steak with broccoli and sautéed potatoes; and peach Melba and Blue Mountain coffee with Tía Maria, a Jamaican liqueur. The six-course menu is changed every day. Tip at your discretion. Men are required to wear jackets and ties.

YACHTSMAN'S WHARF, 16 West St. Tel. 993-3053.
   Cuisine: INTERNATIONAL. **Reservations:** Not required.
$ **Prices:** Main courses J$90–J$140 ($4.10–$6.40). No credit cards.
   Open: Daily 7am–10pm, or later.
Beneath a thatch-covered roof at the end of an industrial pier near the departure point for the ferries to Navy Island, this rustic bar and restaurant is a favorite of the expatriate yachting set. Many of the ultra-expensive yachts whose crews have dined here have pinned their ensigns on the roughly textured planks and posts. It opens for breakfast, which begins at J$46 ($2.10), and stays open all day. Menu items include the usual array of tropical drinks, burgers, seafood ceviche, curried chicken, and ackee with saltfish. Main dishes include vegetables.

WHAT TO SEE & DO

SOMERSET FALLS, 8 miles west of Port Antonio, just past Hope Bay on the A4. Tel. 926-2950 (Albert Shaw).
The waters of the Daniels River pour down a deep gorge through the rain forest, with waterfalls and foaming cascades. You can take a short ride in an electric gondola to the hidden falls. A stop on the daily Grand Jamaica Tour from Ocho Rios, this is one of Jamaica's most historic sites; the falls were used by the Spanish before the English captured the island. Phone Albert Shaw at the above number or check with your Ocho Rios hotel or travel agent. At the falls, you can swim in the deep rock pools and buy sandwiches, light meals, soft drinks, beer, and liquor at the snack bar. The guided tour includes the gondola ride, a visit to a cave, and a visit to the freshwater fish farm.
   Admission: Tour, J$16 (70¢).
   Open: Daily 9am–5pm.

ATHENRY GARDENS AND CAVE OF NONSUCH, Portland. Tel. 993-3740.
These sights are south-southeast from Port Antonio: From Harbour Street in Port Antonio, turn south in front of the Anglican church onto Red Hassel Road and proceed approximately 1 mile to Breastworks community (fork in road). Take the left fork, cross a narrow bridge, go immediately left after the bridge, and proceed approximately 3½ miles to the village of Nonsuch. Twenty minutes from Port Antonio, it's an easy drive and an easy walk to see the stalagmites, stalactites, fossilized marine life, and evidence of Arawak civilization as well as signs of 1½ million years of volcanic activity. From the Athenry Gardens there are panoramic views over the island and the sea. The gardens are filled with coconut palms, flowers, and trees. Complete guided tours are given.
   Admission (including guide for gardens and cave): $5 adults, $2.50 children under 12.
   Open: Daily 9am–5:30pm (last tour at 4:30pm).

FOLLY GREAT HOUSE, on the outskirts of Port Antonio on the way to Trident Village, going east along the A4.
This house was built, it is said, in 1905 by Arthur Mitchell, an American millionaire, for his wife, Annie, daughter of Charles Tiffany, founder of the famous New York store. Sea water was used in the concrete mixtures of its foundations and mortar, and the house began to collapse only 11 years after they moved in. Because of the beautiful location, it's easy to see what a fine great house it must have been, but the years and vandals have not added to its attractiveness; decay and graffiti mar the remains of the two-story mansion.
   Admission: Free.

CRYSTAL SPRINGS, Buff Bay, Portland. Tel. 993-2609 (Stuart's Travel Service).
Privately owned Crystal Springs, lying on 156 acres of land, is part of a former plantation dating from the 17th century. Visitors can explore its grounds, and enjoy the landscaping, flowers, birds, and fish. Restaurant service is provided. For additional information, call Stuart's Travel Service in Port Antonio at the above telephone number.
Admission: J$20 (90¢).
Open: Daily 9am–5:30pm.

SPORTS & RECREATION

BEACHES Port Antonio has several white sand beaches open to the public, some free and some with a charge for use of facilities. **Boston Beach** is free, and often has light surfing, and there are picnic tables as well as a restaurant and snack bar. Before heading to this beach, stop nearby and get the makings for a picnic lunch at the most famous center for peppery jerk pork and chicken in Jamaica. These rustic shacks also sell the much rarer jerk sausage. A pound of any type, suitable for three or four people, begins at J$80 ($3.65). The dish was said to originate with the Maroons who lived in the hills beyond and occasionally ventured out to harass plantation owners. The location is east of Port Antonio and the Blue Lagoon.

Also free is **Fairy Hill Beach** (Winnifred), with no changing rooms or showers. **Frenchman's Cove Beach** attracts a chic crowd to its white sand beach combined with a freshwater stream. Nonhotel guests are charged a fee.

Navy Island, once Errol Flynn's personal hideaway, is a fine choice for swimming (one beach is clothing optional) and snorkeling (at **Crusoe's Beach**). Take the boat from the Navy Island dock on West Street across from the Exxon station. It's a 7-minute ride to the island, and a round-trip costs J$40 ($1.80). The ferry runs 24 hours a day. The island is the setting for the Navy Island Resort & Marina (see "Where to Stay," above).

San San Beach (tel. 993-3318) was voted by members of the U.S. Navy some years ago to be one of the best beaches in the world. Entrance is J$10 (45¢). There are changing rooms, showers, a picnic area with barbecue facilities, a full dive shop, and trained and licensed lifeguards. Water-sports facilities include windsurfers, Sunfish sailboats, paddleboats, canoes, and snorkeling equipment, all available for rent. If you're interested in scuba, and you're a PADI- or NAUI-certified diver, a one-tank dive costs $40.

RAFTING ✪ Rafting started on the Río Grande as a means of transporting bananas from the plantations to the waiting freighters. In 1871 a Yankee skipper, Lorenzo Dow Baker, decided that a seat on one of the rafts was better than walking, but it was not until Errol Flynn arrived that the rafts became popular as a tourist attraction. Flynn used to hire the craft for his friends, and he encouraged the drivers to race down the Río Grande, and bets were placed on the winner. Now that bananas are transported by road, the raft skipper makes one or maybe two trips a day down the waterway. If you want to take a raft trip, **Río Grande Attractions Limited** (tel. 993-2778) can arrange it for you.

The rafts, some 33 feet long and only 4 feet wide, are propelled by stout bamboo poles. There is a raised double seat about two-thirds of the way back for the two passengers. The skipper stands in the front, trousers rolled up to his knees, the water washing his feet, and guides the lively craft down the river, about 8 miles between steep hills covered with coconut palms, banana plantations, and flowers through limestone cliffs pitted with caves, through the Tunnel of Love, a narrow cleft in the rocks, then on to wider, gentler water.

The day starts at Rafter's Restaurant, west of Port Antonio at Burlington on St. Margaret's Bay. Trips last 2½ hours and are offered from 8:30am to 5pm daily at a cost of $40 per raft, which is suitable for two people. From the Rafter's Restaurant, a fully insured driver will take you in your rented car to the starting point at Grants Level or Berrydale, where you board your raft. The trip ends at Rafter's Restaurant, where you collect your car, which has been returned by the driver. If you feel like it, take a picnic lunch, but bring enough for the skipper, too, who will regale you with lively stories of life on the river.

3. OCHO RIOS

A 2-hour drive from Montego Bay or Port Antonio, Ocho Rios was once a small banana and fishing port, but in recent years tourism has become the leading industry. This north-coast resort is now Jamaica's cruise-ship capital. The bay is dominated on one side by a bauxite-loading terminal and on the other by a range of hotels with sandy beaches fringed by palm trees. Runaway Bay, once only a satellite of Ocho Rios but now a resort area in its own right, is presented in the next section.

Ocho Rios and neighboring Port Antonio have long been associated with celebrities. Its two most famous writers are Sir Noël Coward (who invited the world to his doorstep), and Ian Fleming, creator of James Bond (see "What to See and Do," below, for details about their homes here—Firefly and Goldeneye, respectively).

It is commonly assumed among Spanish-speakers that Ocho Rios was named for eight rivers, which is its Spanish translation. But it doesn't mean that in Jamaican. In 1657 British troops chased off a Spanish expeditionary force who had launched a raid from Cuba. The battle was near Dunn's River Falls, now the most important attraction of the resort. Seeing the rapids, the Spanish called the district *las chorreros*. That battle between the Spanish and the British forces was so named. The British and the Jamaicans weren't too good with Spanish names back then, so *las chorreros* was corrupted into "ocho rios."

Frankly, unless you are on a cruise ship, you may want to stay away from the major attractions on cruise-ship days. Even the duty-free shopping markets are overrun then, and the street hustlers become more strident in promoting their crafts, often junk souvenirs. Dunn's River Falls becomes almost impossible to visit at those times.

However, Ocho Rios has its own unique flavor and offers the usual range of sports, including a major fishing tournament every fall, in addition to a wide variety of accommodations.

WHERE TO STAY

VERY EXPENSIVE

JAMAICA INN, Main St. (P.O. Box 1), Ocho Rios, Jamaica, W.I. Tel. 809/974-2514, or toll free 800/243-9420. Fax 809/974-2449. 41 rms, 4 suites. A/C TEL

$ Rates (including all meals): Winter, $310 single; $350–$400 double; from $450 suite. Summer, $155 single; $200–$225 double; from $250 suite. No children under 14 accepted. AE, MC, V. **Parking:** Free.

Built in 1950, this is a long, low, U-shaped building set near the sea 1½ miles east of town and surrounded by grass and palm trees. Lovely patios open onto the lawns, and the bedrooms are reached along garden paths. The handsomely furnished rooms open onto balconies. The White Suite here was a favorite of Winston Churchill. Close to the shore, the sea is almost too clear to make snorkeling an adventure, but farther out it is rewarding.

Dining/Entertainment: The inn is proud of its cuisine. The European-trained chef prepares both international and Jamaican dishes. The management requires men to wear a jacket and tie at night.

Services: Room service, laundry.

Facilities: Swimming pool, wide white sand beach, tennis, comfortable lounge with books, games room with cards and jigsaw puzzles; golf close by at the Upton Golf Course.

PLANTATION INN, Main St. (P.O. Box 2), Ocho Rios, Jamaica, W.I. Tel. 809/974-5601, or toll free 800/237-3237. Fax 809/974-5912. 61 rms, 15 suites. A/C TEL

$ Rates: Winter, $210–$250 single; $250–$290 double; from $320 suite. Summer, $110–$135 single; $150–$175 double; from $193 suite. MAP $50 per person extra. No children under 12 in winter; no children under 7 in summer. AE, DC, MC, V. **Parking:** Free.

This magnificent hotel evoking a southern antebellum mansion is reached by a sweeping driveway and entered through a colonnaded portico, set above the beach in gardens 1½ miles east of town. All bedrooms open off balconies and have their own patios overlooking the sea. The double rooms are attractively decorated with chintz and comfortable furnishings, and there are also junior suites. Apart from the regular hotel, there are two units that provide lodgings: Plantana Villa above the eastern beach sleeps two to six people; Blue Shadow Villa on the west side accommodates up to eight guests.

Dining/Entertainment: There is an inside dining room, but most of the action takes place under the tropical sky. You can have breakfast on your balcony and lunch is served outdoors. English tea is served on the terrace every afternoon. On Thursday a Jamaica Night buffet is offered for $40, and you can feast, enjoy a local show, and dance to calypso music.

Services: Room service, facials, massages, waxing.

Facilities: Two private beaches (36 steps down from the garden; seats on the way provide resting spots), jungle gym with exercise equipment, sauna, two tennis courts; snorkeling, Sunfish sailing, windsurfing and a glass-bottom boat available; golf available at the Upton Golf Course.

SANS SOUCI HOTEL, CLUB & SPA, on the A3 (P.O. Box 103), Ocho Rios, Jamaica, W.I. Tel. 809/974-2353, or toll free 800/654-1337. Fax 809/974-2544. 38 rms, 73 suites. A/C MINIBAR TV TEL

$ Rates: Winter, $290 single; $230 double; from $380 suite. Summer, $145 single; $185 double; from $240 suite. MAP (full American breakfast and five-course dinner) $50 per person extra. AE, DC, MC, V. **Parking:** Free.

Sans Souci, French for "without a care," is one of the most luxurious and tasteful hotels in Ocho Rios. It's 3 miles east of town on a forested plot of land whose rocky border abuts the sea. Erected, demolished, and erected again, the resort witnessed the visits of some gilt-edged titles of Britain in the 1960s when the premises were leased as private apartments. In 1984, after a financial shuffle, it reopened as a deluxe resort terraced into a hillside. A cliffside elevator brings guests to an outdoor bar. There's a freshwater pool, plus a mineral bath big enough for an elephant, and a labyrinth of catwalks and bridges stretching over rocky chasms filled with surging water.

Each of the accommodations has its own veranda or patio, copies of Chippendale furniture, plush upholstery, and a subdued kind of colonial elegance. Some contain Jacuzzis.

Established in 1987, the resort's Spa (known in Jamaica as Charlie's Spa) grew out of the hotel's mineral springs, which had been frequented for their medicinal benefits since the 1700s. Considered effective for treatments of certain skin disorders, arthritis, and rheumatism, the spa features an 8-day/7-night spa program which allows only 10 clients to participate at a time. It's considered the finest place in Jamaica for a health-and-fitness vacation, and one of the finest in the entire Caribbean. The spa program also includes workouts (low-impact aerobics), weight training, "aquacize" classes in the mineral pools, massages, facials, and other invigorating body treatments. At night, spa clients can, if they wish, order low-calorie bar cocktails. The restaurant features a special spa menu, although since this is laidback Jamaica, no one will insist that you stick to it. In winter, the all-inclusive rate for 8 days and 7 nights is $3,358 for single occupancy and $4,616 for double occupancy; in summer, the price for the week-long spa program is $2,160 for single occupancy and $3,356 for double occupancy.

Services: Room service, laundry/valet, massages, baby-sitting.

Facilities: Three Laykold tennis courts (two lit at night); nearby croquet lawn; scuba diving, snorkeling, windsurfing, deep-sea fishing, and Sunfish and catamaran sailing available at the beach; guests can use 18-hole Upton Golf Course and watch polo matches while they take afternoon tea at the St. Ann Polo Club, Drax Hall.

MODERATE

SHAW PARK BEACH HOTEL, Cutlass Bay (P.O. Box 17), Ocho Rios, Jamaica, W.I. Tel. 809/974-2500. Fax 809/974-5042. 106 rms, 12 suites. A/C TEL

$ Rates: Winter, $138–$151 single; $150–$163 double; from $238 suite. Summer, $106–$118 single; $117–$172 double; from $200 suite. MAP $33 per person extra. AE, MC, V. **Parking:** Free.

All the comfortably furnished rooms in this elegant Jamaican Georgian property 1½ miles east of town are directly on the beach, facing the ocean. The reception area looks like a colonial version of a Georgian living room, and the terrace one floor below is built right up to the crashing waves. Most rooms have full bathrooms, but some in the east wing contain showers. There is a swimming pool, ocean water sports—sailing, fishing, windsurfing, waterskiing, snorkeling, and scuba diving—available from the beach at nominal charges, tennis courts, and reciprocity with the Upton Golf Course. It has three bars, two inside and the Beach Bar on the Caribbean Terrace under the sky. A resident band plays for dancing nightly, and floor shows are arranged most nights. The nightclub, Silks, vibrates to disco music and has an intimate Jockey Bar.

INEXPENSIVE

HIBISCUS LODGE HOTEL, 87 Main St. (P.O. Box 52), Ocho Rios, Jamaica, W.I. Tel. 809/974-2676. Fax 809/974-1874. 27 rms.

$ Rates: Winter, $62–$68 double; $92 triple. Summer, $52–$60 double; $75 triple. American breakfast $6 extra. AE, DC, MC, V. **Parking:** Free.

⑤ The Hibiscus Lodge Hotel offers more value for your money than any resort at Ocho Rios. It's an intimate little inn with character and charm, perched precariously on a cliffside three blocks from the Ocho Rios Mall, along the shore. All bedrooms, either doubles or triples, have private baths, ceiling fans, and verandas opening to the sea. Singles can be rented for the double rate.

After a day spent swimming in a pool suspended over the cliffs, with a large sun deck, guests can enjoy a drink in the unique swinging bar. On the 3-acre site are a Jacuzzi and tennis court, along with conference facilities. The owners, Richard Powell and Alfred Doswald, also provide two restaurants, Almond Tree and Red Poll (see "Where to Dine," below). The Grotto is a piano bar open daily from 5pm to 2am.

ALL-INCLUSIVE RESORTS

BOSCOBEL BEACH, P.O. Box 63, Ocho Rios, Jamaica, W.I. Tel. 809/974-3331, or toll free 800/858-8009. Fax 809/975-3270. 196 rms, 11 suites. A/C TV TEL

$ Rates (including all meals and drinks, airport transfers, and all activities): Winter, $540–$800 per person for 3 nights and 4 days (the minimum allowable stay). Summer, $450–$669 per person for 3 nights and 4 days. One child under 14 can stay free in parents' room. During certain high-volume weeks, 7-night minimum stay required. AE, MC, V. **Parking:** Free.

The name of this resort is old Spanish for "beautiful gardens by the sea"—it's that and more. Set on 14½ acres of prime seafront property, it stands 10 miles east of Ocho Rios. Children are encouraged and welcomed, with a big program set aside for them, including a children's center, a mini-zoo, and other activities. The resort also makes special rates for single parents traveling with children and is unique in promoting a special program for grandparents and their grandchildren. Naturally, baby-sitting can be arranged, too. But adults with no children are also given plenty of incentive to visit.

All the well-furnished and attractively decorated rooms are equipped with radios and refrigerators. Some of them feature large balconies and sunken bathtubs. A series of 44 lanai rooms (these are smaller) open right onto the beach.

Dining/Entertainment: Dinner is offered in an open-air dining room (a special children's meal is served earlier). There are also five bars on the property, including one at the beach that serves snacks throughout the day. A disco opens at 11pm. Live local entertainment is a nightly feature.

Services: Transfers to and from the airport, transfers to the golf course, baby-sitting, laundry.

Facilities: Children's facilities (see above), four tennis courts (lit for night play), fully equipped gym, exercise classes, aerobics, two Jacuzzis, reggae dance classes, windsurfing, sailing, waterskiing, scuba diving; golf nearby.

CIBONEY OCHO RIOS, Main St. (P.O. Box 728), Ocho Rios, St. Ann, Jamaica, W.I. Tel. 809/974-5600, or toll free 800/777-1800. Fax 809/974-5838. 36 rms, 162 one-bedroom suites, 18 junior villa suites, 26 two-bedroom villas, 4 three-bedroom villas, 14 honeymoon villas. A/C MINIBAR TV TEL

$ Rates (including all meals and drinks, most spa facilities, in-room video movies, land and water sports, and nightly entertainment): Winter, $285–$295 single; $370–$380 double; from $480 suite or villa. Summer, $260–$280 single; $340–$350 double; from $440 suite or villa. Minimum stay 3 nights. Children under 16 not allowed. AE, DC, MC, V. **Parking:** Free.

Newly opened in 1990, this all-inclusive resort is a Radisson-hotel franchise owned by Colony Hotels, one of the largest touristic conglomerates in Jamaica. It's a short drive (1½ miles) southeast of town on 45 acres of private estate dotted with red-tile villas and a great house in the hills overlooking the Caribbean sea. Across from the imposing gate near the entrance to the resort are the white sands of a private beach.

All but a handful of the accommodations are in one-, two-, or three-bedroom villas, each of which offers a private or semiprivate pool, fully equipped kitchen, and shaded terrace. Each villa is enhanced with the services of a personal attendant for service, cooking private meals, and cleaning. Honeymoon villas have their own Jacuzzis. Thirty-six of the accommodations are traditional single or double rooms on the third floor of the resort's social headquarters, the great house. Regardless of their location, accommodations are high-ceilinged, airy, and decorated in Caribbean colors. Throughout the property, a series of stone retaining walls hold the sloping grounds into carefully landscaped beds of flowering trees and vines. The rate structure is designed to encourage couples rather than singles. Multibedroom accommodations that can hold up to six occupants are also available.

Dining/Entertainment: There are four restaurants, including the resort's top-of-the-line Orchid's that specializes in a light-textured *cuisine naturelle*.

Services: Laundry, dry cleaning, massages, pedicures, manicures.

Facilities: European-inspired beauty spa with its own health-and-fitness center, several different conference rooms, six tennis courts (lit for night play), beach club offering an array of water sports, two swimming pools with swim-up bars (plus 90 other semiprivate swimming pools on the grounds), spa with 20 Jacuzzis; 18-hole Upton Golf Course nearby.

COUPLES, along the A3 (P.O. Box 330), Ocho Rios, Jamaica, W.I. Tel. 809/975-4271, or toll free 800/858-8009. Fax 809/975-4439. 172 rms, 6 suites. A/C TEL

$ Rates (including all meals, drinks, cigarettes, activities, and airport transfers):

Winter, $2,510–$2,860 a week per couple. Summer, $2,200–$2,400 a week per couple. No one 17 or under allowed. AE, MC, V. **Parking:** Free.

Don't come here alone—you won't get in! The management defines couples as "any man and woman in love." (While many coupled singles come here, I've been told that most couples are married, many on their honeymoons.) Everything is in pairs—even the chairs by the moon-drenched beach. Some couples slip away from the resort, which is an 18-minute drive (5 miles) east of town, to Couples' private island to bask in the buff.

Once you've paid the initial fee, you're free to use all the facilities—there will be no more bills. Even the cigarettes and whisky are free. You get three meals a day, including all the wine you want; breakfast is bountiful. And tips aren't permitted!

The bedrooms have either a king-size bed or two doubles and pleasantly traditional furnishings. Each has a patio, fronting either the sea or the mountains. The hotel accepts bookings for a minimum of 4 nights any day of the week, but most guests book in here on weekly terms.

Dining/Entertainment: Dinners are five courses, and afterward there is dancing on the terrace every evening, with entertainment. Guests have a choice of three restaurants.

Services: Breakfast-only room service, laundry.

Facilities: Five tennis courts (three lit at night), Nautilus gym, scuba diving, snorkeling, windsurfing, sailing, waterskiing.

SANDALS OCHO RIOS, Main St. (P.O. Box 771), Ocho Rios, Jamaica, W.I. Tel. 809/974-5691, or toll free 800/327-1991. Fax 809/974-5700. 237 rms. TV TEL

$ Rates (including all meals, "anytime" snacks, unlimited wine and drinks, airport transfers, and services and facilities listed below): Winter, $1,180–$1,390 double for 4 days and 3 nights (the minimum allowable stay). Summer, $1,145–$1,340 double for 4 days and 3 nights. AE, MC, V. **Parking:** Free.

Another Jamaican addition to the ever-expanding "couples only" empire of Gordon (Butch) Stewart, who pioneered similar properties in Montego Bay and Negril, Sandals Ocho Rios attracts a mix of coupled singles and married folk, including honeymooners. The resort uses the same formula: one price per male-female couple, including everything. On 13 well-landscaped acres, it offers comfortably furnished rooms with either ocean or garden views, and there are some cottage units, too. All rooms are reasonably large, with king-size beds, hairdryers, and radios. The resort is 1 mile west of the town center.

Dining/Entertainment: You can drink your free drinks at an oceanside swim-up bar, and nightly theme parties and live entertainment take place in a modern amphitheater. A unique feature of the resort is an open-air disco.

Services: Round-trip transfers from airport, tours to Dunn's River Ralls, massages, laundry.

Facilities: Three freshwater pools; private artificial beach; sporting equipment and instruction, including waterskiing, windsurfing, sailing, snorkeling, and scuba diving; paddleboats; kayaks; glass-bottom boat; Jacuzzi; saunas; fully equipped fitness center; two tennis courts.

WHERE TO DINE
EXPENSIVE

ALMOND TREE RESTAURANT, in the Hibiscus Lodge Hotel, 87 Main St. Tel. 974-2813.

Cuisine: CONTINENTAL. **Reservations:** Recommended.

$ Prices: Appetizers $3.50–$5.50; main courses $12–$28. AE, DC, MC, V.

Open: Lunch daily noon–2:30pm; dinner daily 6–9:30pm.

The Almond Tree is a two-tiered patio restaurant with a tree growing through the roof, overlooking the Caribbean at this previously recommended resort three blocks from the Ocho Rios Mall. Lobster thermidor is the most expensive item on the menu, but I prefer their bouillabaisse (made with conch and lobster). Also excellent are the roast suckling pig, medallions of beef Anne Palmer, and a fondue bourguignonne. Jamaican plantation rice is a local specialty. The wine list offers a variety of vintages, including Spanish and Jamaican. Have an apéritif in the unique "swinging bar" (swinging chairs, that is).

CARIB INN RESTAURANT, Main St. Tel. 974-2445.
   Cuisine: SEAFOOD/CONTINENTAL. **Reservations:** Recommended.
$ Prices: Appetizers $1–$9; main courses $10–$30; lunches from $10. AE, MC, V.
   Open: Daily 11am–10pm.
Located in the center of town, within walking distance of most hotels, the Carib Inn is nestled among crotons and coconut palms on 17 acres of streams and manicured lawns. For lunch, I suggest one of the daily specials such as curried goat and white rice, stewed beef, or ackee and codfish. For dessert, try a Tía Maria parfait (baked banana with coconut cream) or a baked Alaska. Lobster is a specialty, as is steak Diane. Bring your camera and swimwear and enjoy the private beach, the sea, and the Olympic-size freshwater swimming pool.

THE CASANOVA, at the Sans Souci Club, Spa, and Resort, along the A3, 3 miles east of Ocho Rios. Tel. 974-2353.
   Cuisine: INTERNATIONAL. **Reservations:** Recommended.
$ Prices: Appetizers $8.50–$11; main courses $13–$32; lunch from $18. AE, DC, MC, V.
   Open: Lunch daily 12:30–3pm; dinner daily 7–9:30pm.
In the main building of this previously recommended hotel, the Casanova is one of the most elegant dining enclaves along the north coast of Jamaica. In the late 1960s Harry Cipriani (of Harry's Bar fame in Venice) taught the staff some of his culinary techniques. The pasta is still made fresh daily, along with many of the other staples. Jazz from a lattice-roofed gazebo might accompany your meal. Typical dishes include smoked marlin, lobster bisque, grilled red snapper, and chicken suprême flambéed with whisky. Desserts are sumptuous, and might be followed by one of the house's four special coffees.

EVITA'S ITALIAN RESTAURANT, Eden Bower Rd. Tel. 974-2333.
   Cuisine: ITALIAN. **Reservations:** Recommended.
$ Prices: Appetizers $3–$5; main courses $7–$18.50. AE, MC, V.
   Open: Daily 11am–11pm.
Located a 5-minute drive south of the commercial heart of Ocho Rios, in a hillside residential neighborhood that enjoys a panoramic view over the city's harbor and beachfronts, this is the premier Italian restaurant of Ocho Rios and is one of the most fun restaurants along the north coast of Jamaica. Its soul and artistic flair come from Evita Myers, convivial former owner of some of the most legendary bars of Montego Bay, who established her culinary headquarters in this white, gingerbread Jamaican house in 1990. An outdoor terrace adds additional seating and enhanced views. More than half the menu is devoted to pastas, and the selection includes almost every variety known in northern and southern Italy. Other dishes include heartier fare, such as grilled steaks. Italian (or other) wines by the bottle might accompany your menu choice. The restaurant lies a few steps from one of the town's public parks, Carinosa Gardens.

RED POLL GRILL ROOM, in the Hibiscus Lodge Hotel, 87 Main St. Tel. 974-2676.
   Cuisine: STEAK/GRILLS. **Reservations:** Recommended in winter.
$ Prices: Appetizers $1.50–$7.50; main courses $9–$30. AE, DC, MC, V.
   Open: Dinner only, daily 6–10pm.
In Jamaican, *poll* means bull, and at this cliffside-hugging, open-air restaurant, you get some of the best beef in Ocho Rios. Sometimes it's grilled simply, as in the char-broiled T-bone steak, but at other times the chef prepares fancier concoctions, such as tournedos Rossini and kebab à la Hibiscus. Fish and lamb are also grilled, other dishes come from the "pork pit," and broiled lobster and seafood platters are

served. Interesting appetizers are terrine du pork and a classic onion soup. The restaurant is run by the same owners as the Almond Tree and is located in the center of town.

RUINS RESTAURANT, GIFT SHOP, AND BOUTIQUE, Turtle River, DaCosta Dr. Tel. 974-2442.

Cuisine: CHINESE/INTERNATIONAL. **Reservations:** Required.
$ Prices: Appetizers $1.80–$8.25; main courses $15–$30. AE, DC, MC, V.
Open: Lunch Mon–Sat noon–2:30pm; dinner daily 6–9:30pm.

Here you dine at the foot of a series of waterfalls in the center of town that can be considered a tourist attraction in their own right. In 1831 a British entrepreneur constructed a sugar mill on the site, using the powerful stream to drive his water wheels. Today, all that remains is a jumble of ruins, hence the restaurant's name. After you cross a covered bridge, perhaps stopping off for a drink at the bar in the outbuilding first, you find yourself in a fairyland where the only sounds come from the tree frogs, the falling water from about a dozen cascades, and the discreet clink of silver and china. Tables are set on a wooden deck leading all the way up to the pool at the foot of the falls, where moss and other vegetation line the stones at the base. As part of the evening's enjoyment you may want to climb a flight of stairs to the top of the falls, where bobbing lanterns and the illuminated waters below afford one of the most delightful experiences on the island. Menu items include a wide range of Chinese food, such as sweet-and-sour pork or chicken, several kinds of chow mein or chop suey, and a house specialty—lobster sautéed in a special sauce. International dishes include lamb or pork chops, chicken Kiev, steaks, and an array of fish.

MODERATE

HARMONY HALL RESTAURANT, Harmony Hall, Tower Isle, on the A3, 4 miles east of Ocho Rios. Tel. 975-4478.

Cuisine: CREOLE. **Reservations:** Not required.
$ Prices: Appetizers $1.50–$3.50; main courses $8.50–$15. AE, MC, V.
Open: Daily 10am–10pm.

This is both the leading art gallery in the area (see "What to See and Do," below) and a good moderately priced restaurant. Lunches are likely to begin with the soup of the day, followed by a Jamaican specialty. Dinner is more elaborate, including, on one occasion, lobster cocktail, chicken Oriental, and rum cake. Diners can order food either inside the 19th-century building, which is decorated in the tavern style, or on the patio, where they can enjoy the breezes.

LITTLE PUB RESTAURANT, 59 Main St. Tel. 974-2324.

Cuisine: JAMAICAN/INTERNATIONAL. **Reservations:** Recommended.
$ Prices: Appetizers $3.10–$4.50; main courses $13–$24. AE, MC, V.
Open: Breakfast daily 7–11am; lunch daily 11am–4:30pm; dinner daily 6pm–midnight.

Located in a red-brick courtyard with a fountain and a waterfall surrounded by souvenir shops in the center of town, this indoor-outdoor pub's centerpiece is a restaurant in the dinner-theater style. Top local and international artists are featured, as are Jamaican musical plays. No one will mind if you just enjoy a drink while seated on one of the pub's barrel chairs. But if you want dinner, proceed to one of the linen-covered tables capped with cut flowers and candlelight. Menu items include barbecued chicken, stewed snapper, and grilled kingfish. The chef is also known for his lobster specialties.

SIDNEY'S "ON THE BAY," Fisherman's Point. Tel. 974-5339.

Cuisine: JAMAICAN/INTERNATIONAL. **Reservations:** Recommended.
$ Prices: Appetizers $2–$5; main courses $5–$25. AE, MC, V.
Open: Daily 7am–11pm.

Part of a complex of rental units (Fisherman's Point), "On the Bay" lies in the heart of Ocho Rios, in the vicinity of Turtle Beach. The rather elegant dining spot was launched in 1987. For dinner, you can always count on "today's catch," perhaps

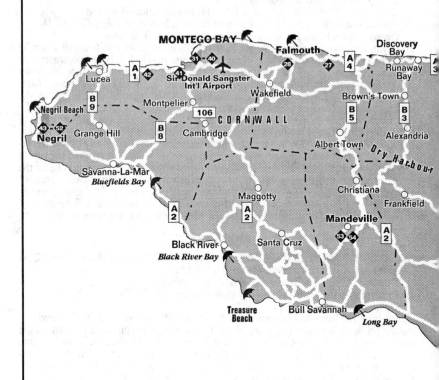

Caribbean Sea

Montego Bay

JAMAICA
★ Kingston

Almond Tree Restaurant ◆19
Ambrosia ◆29
Bill Laurie's Steak House ◆53
Blue Mountain Inn ◆1
Café au Lait (Mirage Cottages) ◆43
Calabash Restaurant ◆31
Carib Inn Restaurant ◆20
Casanova ◆18
Cascade Room ◆32
Chelsea Jerk Centre ◆2
Chicken Lavish ◆44
Cosmo's Seafood Restaurant
  & Bar ◆45
De Montevin Lodge Restaurant ◆12

Devonshire Restaurant/
  The Grogg Shoppe ◆3
Diplomat, The ◆33
Evita's Italian Restaurant ◆21
Fern Hill Club ◆13
Fort Charles ◆4
Georgian House ◆34
Glistening Waters Inn & Marina ◆2
Harmony Hall Restaurant ◆17
Indies Pub & Grill ◆5
Jade Garden ◆6
Julia's ◆35
Little Pub Restaurant ◆22
Lobster Bowl Restaurant ◆27

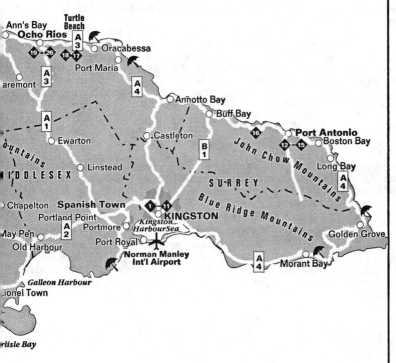

Caribbean Sea

Ann's Bay
Ocho Rios
Turtle Beach
A 3
Oracabessa
19 26 18 17
Port Maria
A 3
aremont
A 4
Annotto Bay
Buff Bay
A 1
Ewarton
Castleton
B 1
Port Antonio
16
John Chow Mountains
12 15
Boston Bay
ountains
Linstead
Long Bay
A 4
I'DDLESEX
S U R R E Y
Chapelton
Spanish Town
Blue Ridge Mountains
KINGSTON
1 11
Portland Point
Portmore
A 2
Kingston HarbourSea
Golden Grove
May Pen
Old Harbour
Port Royal
Norman Manley Int'l Airport
A 4
Morant Bay
Galleon Harbour
ionel Town
rlisle Bay

Beach → Airport ✈

Mandeville Hotel 54	Red Poll Grill Room 24
Marguerite's By the Sea 36	Richmond Hill Inn 39
Mariner's Inn & Restaurant 46	Rick's Café 50
Negril Jerk Centre 48	Round Hill Dining Room 42
Negril Tree House 47	Ruins Restaurant 25
Norma 7	Sidney's "On the Bay" 26
Paradise Yard 49	Sugar Mill Restaurant 30
Parkway Restaurant 23	Tan-Ya/Calico Jack's 51
Pavilion, Le 8	Temple Hall, The Restaurant at 10
Pier 1 37	Terra Nova Hotel Restaurant 11
Plantation Terrace 9	Town House 40
Pork Pit 38	Trident Hotel Restaurant 14
Rafter's Restaurant 16	Vendome, Le 52
Reading Reef Club Restaurant 41	Yachtsman's Wharf 15

Caribbean lobster, and certainly seafood chowder and marinated conch. Specialties are a flaming sword of seafood and paella. Or you can choose from the steak and chicken dishes, and perhaps finish with a chocolate soufflé. Breakfast begins at $4.50 and features such Jamaican specialties as saltfish and ackee.

INEXPENSIVE

PARKWAY RESTAURANT, 60 DaCosta Dr. Tel. 974-2667.

Cuisine: JAMAICAN. **Reservations:** Not required.

$ Prices: Appetizers $3.50–$4.25; main courses $6–$22.50. AE, MC, V.

Open: Daily 7:30am–11pm.

⑤ This popular establishment in the commercial center of town couldn't have a plainer facade. Inside, it continues to be unpretentious, but many local families and members of the business community know that they can get some of the best-tasting and least expensive local dishes here of any place in Ocho Rios. On clean napery, amid a serviceable decor, hungry diners are fed Jamaican-style chicken, curried goat, and filet of red snapper, and to top it off, banana-cream pie. Lobster and fresh fish are usually featured.

WHAT TO SEE & DO

BEACHES

Most visitors head for the beach. The most visited is the often-overcrowded **Mallards Beach** shared by hotel guests and cruise-ship passengers, but locals may steer you to **Turtle Beach** in the south.

ATTRACTIONS

A pleasant drive south of Ocho Rios along the A3 will take you inland through **Fern Gully.** This was originally a riverbed, but now the main road winds up some 700 feet among a profusion of wild ferns, a tall rain forest, hardwood trees, and lianas. For the botanist, there are hundreds of varieties of ferns, and for the less plant-minded, roadside stands offer fruit and vegetables, carved-wood souvenirs, and basketwork. The road runs for about 4 miles, and then at the top of the hill, you come to a right-hand turn, onto a narrow road leading to Golden Grove.

Head west when you see the signs pointing to Lydford. You'll pass the remains of **Edinburgh Castle,** built in 1763, the lair of one of Jamaica's most infamous murderers, a Scot named Lewis Hutchinson, who used to shoot passersby and toss their bodies into a deep pit built for the purpose. The authorities got wind of his activities, and although he tried to escape by canoe, he was captured by the navy under the command of Admiral Rodney and was hanged. Rather proud of his achievements (evidence of at least 43 murders was found), he left £100 and instructions for a memorial to be built. It never was, but the castle ruins remain.

Continue north on the A1 to **St. Ann's Bay,** the site of the first Spanish settlement on the island, where you can see the **Statue of Christopher Columbus,** cast in his hometown of Genoa, erected near St. Ann's Hospital on the west side of town, close to the coast road. There are a number of Georgian buildings in the town. The **Court House** near the parish church, built in 1866, is most interesting.

DUNN'S RIVER FALLS, on the A3. Tel. 974-2857.

✪ From St. Ann's Bay, follow the A3 east back to Ocho Rios and you'll pass Dunn's River Falls. There is plenty of parking space, and for a small charge, you can relax on the beach or climb with a guide to the top of the 600-foot falls. You can splash in the waters at the bottom of the falls or drop into the cool pools higher up between the cascades of water. The beach restaurant provides snacks and refreshing drinks, and dressing rooms are available. If you're planning to climb the falls, wear old tennis shoes, whatever, to protect your feet from the sharp rocks and to prevent slipping.

Admission: J$21 (95¢).

Open: Daily 8am–5pm.

PROSPECT PLANTATION, on the A3. Tel. 974-2058.

Three miles east of Ocho Rios along the A3, adjoining the 18-hole Prospect Mini Golf Course, is a working property. A visit to this plantation combines the opportunity to take an educational, relaxing, and enjoyable tour. On your leisurely ride by covered jitney through the scenic beauty of Prospect, you'll readily see why this section of Jamaica is called "the garden parish of the island." You can view the many trees planted by such visitors as Sir Winston Churchill, Dr. Henry Kissinger, Charlie Chaplin, Pierre Trudeau, Sir Noël Coward, and many others. You will learn about and see growing pimento (allspice), bananas, cassava, sugarcane, coffee, cocoa, coconut, pineapple, and the famous leucaena "Tree of Life." You'll see Jamaica's first hydroelectric plant and sample some of the exotic fruit and drinks.

Horseback riding is available on three scenic trails at Prospect. The rides vary from 1 to 2¼ hours. Advance booking of 1 hour is necessary to reserve horses.

Admission: Tours, $10 adults, free for children under 12; 1-hour horseback ride, $20.

Open: Tours, Mon–Sat at 10:30am, 2pm, and 3:30pm; Sun at 11am, 1:30pm, and 3pm.

BRIMMER HALL ESTATE, Port Maria, St. Mary's. Tel. 994-2309.

Twenty-one miles east from Ocho Rios, in the hills 2 miles from Port Maria, this is an ideal place to spend a day. You can relax beside the pool and sample a wide variety of brews and concoctions, including an interesting one called "Wow!" The Plantation Tour Eating House offers typical Jamaican dishes for lunch, and there is a souvenir shop with a good selection of ceramics, art, straw goods, wood carvings, rums, liqueurs, and cigars. All this is on a working plantation where you are driven around in a tractor-drawn jitney to see the tropical fruit trees and coffee plants, and learn from the knowledgeable guides about the various processes necessary to produce the fine fruits of the island.

Admission: Tours, $12.

Open: Tours, Daily at 11am, 1:30pm, and 3:30pm.

SHAW PARK GARDENS, in the hills west of town (there's no street name, but it's signposted).

On the site of an old plantation, these botanical gardens offer a fantastic view of Ocho Rios and Turtle Bay. You can stroll through the grounds where a 17th-century cannon will point you to the view. Other paths lead past rushing waterfalls and bushes that are a sanctuary for a rich variety of bird life.

Admission: J$22 ($1) adults, J$15 (70¢) children under 12.

Open: Daily 8am–5pm.

FIREFLY, in St. Mary, 20 miles east of Ocho Rios above Oracabessa.

Firefly was the home of Sir Noël Coward and his longtime companion, Graham Payn, who, as executor of Coward's estate, donated it to the Jamaica National Heritage Trust. The badly kept house is as it was on the day Sir Noël died in 1973, even to the clothes, including Hawaiian print shirts, hanging in the closet in his austere bedroom with its heavy mahogany four-poster. The library contains his large collection of books, and the living room is warm and comfortable with big armchairs and two grand pianos where he composed several famous tunes. When the English Queen Mother was entertained here, the lobster mousse Coward was serving melted, so he opened a can of pea soup. Guests—Coward's "bloody loved ones"—were housed in Blue Harbour, a villa nearer Port Maria where Sir Noël lived before building Firefly, and included Evelyn Waugh, Sir Winston Churchill, Errol Flynn and his wife, Patrice Wymore, Lord Laurence Olivier, Vivien Leigh, Claudette Colbert, Katharine Hepburn, and Mary Martin. Paintings by the noted playwright, actor, author, and composer adorn the walls. An open patio looks out over the pool and the sea, and across the lawn, on his plain, flat white marble grave is inscribed simply: "Sir Noël Coward, born December 16, 1899, died March 26, 1973."

Admission: J$20 (90¢).
Open: Daily 9am–5pm.

GOLDENEYE, Oracabessa, 13 miles east of Ocho Rios.

Coward was a frequent guest of Ian Fleming at Goldeneye, made fashionable in the 1950s. It was here that the most famous secret agent in the world, 007, was born in 1952. Fleming built the house in 1946, and wrote each of the 13 original Bond books in it. Through the large gates, with bronze pineapples on the top, came a host of international celebrities: Evelyn Waugh, Truman Capote, Graham Greene. The house was closed and dilapidated for some time after the writer's death, but its present owner, British music publisher Christopher Blackwell, has restored the property. It's furnished with "just the basics," the way Fleming wanted it. Unless you're a guest of the tenant, you aren't allowed to visit as it's private property. However, all 007 fans in this part of the world like to go by, hoping for a look. Look for the Esso (not Exxon) sign and take the narrow lane nearby going to the sea.

HARMONY HALL, Tower Isle, on the A3, 4 miles east of Ocho Rios. Tel. 975-4222.

Harmony Hall was built near the end of the 19th century as another one of the great houses of Jamaica, and was connected with a pimento estate. Today, after a restoration, it's a center for a gallery selling paintings and other works by Jamaican artists. High-quality arts and crafts are also sold—not the usual junky assortment you might find at the beach. A bar and restaurant are on the ground floor (see "Where to Dine," above). Watson's shopping shuttle stops at various hotels and makes a lunchtime trip Monday through Saturday.
Admission: Free.
Open: Gallery, daily 10am–6pm.

COLUMBUS PARK MUSEUM, Queens Hwy., Discovery Bay. Tel. 973-2135.

This is a large, open area between the main coast road and the sea at Discovery Bay. You just pull off the road and then walk among the fantastic collection of exhibits, which range from a canoe made of a solid piece of cottonwood in the same way the Arawaks did it more than five centuries ago, to a stone cross, a monument originally placed on the Barrett estate at Retreat by Edward Barrett, brother of poet Elizabeth Barrett Browning. You'll see a tally, used to count bananas carried on men's heads from plantation to ship, as well as a planter's strongbox with a weighted lead base to prevent its theft. Also among the exhibits are 18th-century cannons, a Spanish water cooler and calcifier, a fish pot made from bamboo, a corn husker, and a water wheel of the type used on the sugar estates in the mid-19th century for all motive power. You can follow the history of sugar since its introduction in 1495 by Columbus, who brought canes from Gomera in the Canary Islands, and see how Khus Khus, a Jamaican perfume, is made from the roots of a plant, and how black dye is extracted from logwood. Pimento trees, from which allspice is produced, dominate the park. There is a large mural by Eugene S. Hyde, depicting the first landing of Columbus at Puerto Bueno (Discovery Bay) on May 4, 1494. The museum is well worth a visit to learn of the varied cultures that have influenced the development of Jamaica.
Admission: Free.
Open: Daily 9am–5pm.

CIRCLE B FARM, Liberty District, near Priory, St. Ann, 8 miles west of Ocho Rios. Tel. 972-2988.

You can visit this model Jamaican small farm between Runaway Bay and Ocho Rios. Hilma and Bob Miller open their property to guided walking tours, including a welcome rum or fruit punch, fruits in season, and a buffet lunch. To look at the diversified farm operation and enjoy the Millers' hospitality takes about 2 hours.
Admission: $10 for tour, $20 for tour and lunch.
Open: Daily 10am–5pm.

BOONOONOONOOS

Boonoonoonoos is Jamaican for "very nice" or "super," and also stands for a "happening" in Jamaica.

A **Reggae Lobster Party** at Coconut Grove Great House, half a mile east of the center, is a Jamaican experience you can enjoy on Monday and Thursday from 7 to 11pm. Reggae music, a native floor show, an open Jamaican bar, and dinner are all part of the package, which costs $36 for adults and $18 for children. For information, contact Coconut Grove House Ltd. (tel. 974-2619).

Also presented by Coconut Grove Great House is an event promising "romance and adventure." All year on Sunday and Thursday at 7pm you can enjoy a **Jamaican Night on the White River,** 2 miles to the east of Ocho Rios. The boat trip takes you up the torchlit river for a picnic supper on the banks. There is an open bar, and a native folklore show precedes dancing under the stars. The cost is $36 for adults, $18 for children. Call 974-2619 for more details.

SAVVY SHOPPING

There are seven main shopping plazas. The originals are Ocean Village, Pineapple Place, and Coconut Grove. Newer ones include the New Ocho Rios Plaza, in the center of town, with some 60 shops. Island Plaza is another major shopping complex, as is the Mutual Security Plaza with some 30 shops. Opposite the New Ocho Rios Plaza is the Taj Mahal, with 26 duty-free stores.

Ocean Village Shopping Centre (tel. 974-2683): Here are numerous boutiques, food stores, a bank, sundries purveyors, travel agencies, service facilities— what have you. **Ruth Clarage Ltd.** (tel. 974-2874) specializes in beautifully colored hand-silk-screened prints. Many are embroidered by hand in her Montego Bay workshops. You can also buy ready-made dresses, evening wear, sports clothes, and matching ceramic jewelry. The **Ocho Rios Laundry Mart,** (tel. 974-2409) is where you can do your own laundry or leave it and your dry cleaning to be done for you. The **Ocho Rios Pharmacy** (tel. 974-2041) sells most proprietary brands, perfumes, plasters for sore heels, and suntan lotions, among its many wares.

Pineapple Place Shopping Centre, across from Planatation Inn, just east of Ocho Rios: This is a collection of shops in cedar-shingle-roofed cottages set amid tropical flowers.

Ocho Rios Craft Park: This is a complex of some 150 stalls through which to browse. At the stalls, an eager seller will weave you a hat or a basket while you wait, or you can buy from the mixture of ready-made hats, hampers, handbags, placemats, and lampshades. Other stands stock hand-embroidered goods and will make up small items while you wait. Alongside all this activity, wood carvers work on bowls, ashtrays, wooden head carvings, and statues chipped from lignum vitae, and make cups from local bamboo. Even if you don't want to buy, this lively and colorful park is worth a visit.

Coconut Grove Shopping Plaza: This collection of low-lying shops is linked by walkways and shrubs. The merchandise consists mainly of local craft items. Many of your fellow shoppers may be cruise-ship passengers.

Island Plaza: The **Frame Gallery,** 9 Island Plaza (tel. 974-2374), is the best art gallery at the resort and is a branch of the previously recommended one in Kingston. It presents quality Jamaican art Monday through Friday from 9am to 5pm and on Saturday from 10am to 5pm.

EVENING ENTERTAINMENT

Hotels often provide live entertainment to which nonresidents are invited. Ask at your hotel desk where "the action" is on any given night. Otherwise, you may want to look in on **Silks Nightclub,** in the Shaw Park Hotel, Cutlass Bay (tel. 974-2552), which has a smallish dance floor and a sometimes-animated crowd of drinkers and dancers. Nonresidents of this well-known hotel can enter for J$25 ($1.15) each. The club is open nightly from 10pm until 4am.

4. RUNAWAY BAY

Once this resort was a mere western satellite of Ocho Rios. However, with the opening of some large resort hotels, plus a colony of smaller hostelries, Runaway Bay is now a destination in its own right.

This part of Jamaica's north coast has several distinctions: It was the first part of the island seen by Columbus, the site of the first Spanish settlement on the island, and the point of departure of the last Spaniards leaving Jamaica following their defeat by the British. Columbus landed at Discovery Bay on his second voyage of exploration in 1494, and in 1509 Spaniards established a settlement called Sevilla Nueva (New Seville) near what is now St. Ann's Bay, about 10 miles east of the present Runaway Bay village. Sevilla Nueva was later abandoned when the inhabitants moved to the southern part of the island.

In 1655 an English fleet sailed into Kingston Harbour and defeated the Spanish garrison there. However, a guerrilla war broke out on the island between the Spanish and English in which the English prevailed. The remnants of the Spanish army embarked for Cuba in 1660 from a small fishing village on the north coast. Some believe that this "running away" from Jamaica gave the name Runaway Bay to the village. However, later historians believe that the name possibly came from the traffic in runaway slaves from the north-coast plantations to Cuba.

WHERE TO STAY & DINE
VERY EXPENSIVE

FDR (Franklyn D. Resort), the A1 (P.O. Box 201), Runaway Bay, St. Ann, Jamaica, W.I. Tel. 809/973-3067, or toll free 800/654-1FDR. Fax 809/973-3071. 67 suites. A/C MINIBAR TV TEL

$ Rates (including meals, bar drinks, beer, cigarettes, sports, and entertainment): Winter, $225–$235 per person in a one-bedroom suite; $213–$227 per person in a two- or three-bedroom suite. Summer, $180–$209 per person in a one-bedroom suite; $165–$200 per person in a two- or three-bedroom suite. AE, DC, MC, V. **Parking:** Free.

One of the newest all-inclusive resorts in Jamaica, FDR is geared to families with children and is dedicated to including all meals and activities in a net price. The resort, named after its Jamaican-born owner and developer (Franklyn David Rance), is on 6 acres of flat, sandy land dotted with flowering shrubs and trees, on the main seaside highway (the A1), 17 miles west of Ocho Rios. Each of the Mediterranean-inspired buildings has a terra-cotta roof, a loggia or outdoor terrace, Spanish marble in the bathroom, and a personal attendant whose cooking, cleaning, child-caring, and miscellaneous services come with each of the units. Although neither its narrow beach nor its modest swimming pools are the most desirable on the island, many visitors appreciate the spacious units and the wholehearted concern of the resort for the amusement of its resident children. Each unit contains a kitchenette where, if you want, meals can be prepared by the personal attendant.

Dining/Entertainment: A dining room serves free wine with lunch and dinner, a piano bar provides music every evening, and a handful of bars keep the drinks flowing. Live music is provided nightly.

Services: Baby-sitting (free 8am–5pm, $1 an hour at other times), children's supervisor in attendance at "Kiddies' Center" (where a computer center, kiddies' disco, and kiddies' dinners are regular features), scuba lessons, picnics, photography lessons, arts and crafts lessons, donkey rides.

Facilities: Water sports, illuminated tennis courts, satellite TV room, disco, Nintendo games, gym/health club with free use of bicycles for getting around the neighborhood.

JAMAICA, JAMAICA, P.O. Box 58, Runaway Bay, Jamaica, W.I. Tel.

809/973-2436, or toll free 800/858-8009. Fax 809/973-2352. 234 rms, 4 suites. A/C TEL

$ Rates (all-inclusive): Winter, $280 single; $460 double. Summer, $225 single; $240 double. Children under 16 not accepted. AE, DC, MC, V. **Parking:** Free.

Six miles west of Ocho Rios, this stylish incarnation of a resort that has known several identities since it was built operates on a price plan including three meals a day, all drinks, free cigarettes, and a galaxy of other benefits. Its long, low-lying clubhouse is approached by passing through a park filled with tropical trees and shrubbery. Inside the lobby is the best re-creation of the South Seas in Jamaica, with hanging wicker chairs and totemic columns. Each of the rooms has a view of a well-landscaped courtyard, with a private balcony overlooking the sea. Near the wide sandy beach is a mini-jungle with dangling hammocks, and the nearby swimming pool is traversed by a wooden footbridge. There's even a nearby nude beach.

Dining/Entertainment: Live music emanates from a stylish bar every evening at 6:30pm, and a nightclub offers live shows 5 nights a week at 10:30pm. You dine either in the beachside restaurant, or in the more formal re-creation of a colonial-era dining room.

Services: Reggae exercise classes held twice daily.

Facilities: Gym filled with Nautilus equipment, swimming pool, sports activities center (featuring scuba diving, windsurfing, and a golf school), 18-hole championship golf course.

EXPENSIVE

CHUKKA COVE RESORT, P.O. Box 160, Richmond Llandovery, Ocho Rios, Jamaica, W.I. Tel. 809/972-2506. Fax 809/974-5568. 6 villas. A/C MINIBAR TEL

$ Rates: Winter, $1,725 villa per week. Summer, $1,400 villa per week. No credit cards. **Parking:** Free.

Already mentioned (see "Sports and Recreation" at the beginning of this chapter) for its horse-riding tours, this is also an ideal equestrian center for horse lovers who'd like to live on the grounds. Located 4 miles east of Runaway Bay, it's often frequented by Capt. Mark Phillips, estranged husband of Britain's Princess Anne. On the estate's acreage lie six two-bedroom villas, each suitable for four guests, with a veranda, plank floors, and an architectural plan vaguely reminiscent of 18th-century models. Your pampering staff will prepare meals in your villa. Rates can be prorated for shorter stays. Snorkeling is also included. Taxis are necessary to get east to Ocho Rios or west to Montego Bay.

EATON HALL BEACH HOTEL, P.O. Box 112, Runaway Bay, St. Ann, Jamaica, W.I. Tel. 809/973-3503, or toll free 800/JAMAICA. Fax 809/973-2432. 52 rms. A/C

$ Rates (including three meals a day, airport transfers, taxes, tips, and use of facilities and services mentioned below): Winter, $140–$215 single; $97–$127 per person double. Summer, $130–$165 single; $90–$98 per person double. Children under 12 not accepted. AE, DC, MC, V. **Parking:** Free.

An original plantation great house has been restored and turned into this small hotel of charm and character, two blocks east of the town's main square. The brick foundation walls are probably those of an English fort dating from the 17th or 18th century. A subterranean passage, now bricked up, leads from the living room to the coral cliffs behind the house. The property is a successful coordination of old blended with new. Some of the bedrooms of the great house open onto an arched portico, and four units in the main house front the sea. On each side of the hall are bedroom wings with ocean views furnished with tropical designs and older mahogany pieces. Carved mahogany four-poster beds are found in some of the rooms. Directly over the sea are the villas, with four bedrooms and verandas extending out over a rocky ledge with the water 6 feet below. Some rooms have phones.

Dining/Entertainment: Entertainment, weekly floor shows, and a Jamaican buffet once a week are also part of the all-inclusive plan. There is one restaurant that offers American, Jamaican, and continental foods, and there are two bars.

Services: Airport transfers, laundry.

Facilities: Sunfish sailing, snorkeling equipment, scuba diving.

RUNAWAY H.E.A.R.T. COUNTRY CLUB, P.O. Box 98, Runaway Bay, St. Ann, Jamaica, W.I. Tel. 809/973-2671, or toll free 800/526-2422. Fax 809/973-2693. 20 rms. A/C TV TEL

$ Rates (including MAP): Winter, $408 single; $636 double for 4 days/3 nights. Summer, $390 single; $564 double for 4 days/3 nights (see text for details). AE, MC, V. **Parking:** Free.

Called "the best-kept secret in Jamaica," this place is located on the main road, opposite the public beach, and it practically wins hands down as the bargain of the north coast. One of Jamaica's few training and service institutions, the club and its adjacent academy are operated by the government to provide a high level of training for young Jamaicans interested in the hotel trade. The hotel is very well run with a professional staff, intermixed with trainees, who are helpful and eager to please, and offer perhaps the finest service of any hotel in the area.

The rooms are bright and airy and have either a king-size bed, a double bed, or twin beds. Accommodations open onto private balconies with views of well-manicured tropical gardens or vistas of the bay and golf course.

All package rates include round-trip airport transfers, unlimited golf greens fees, and use of a chaise longue at the pool or at a private beach, which is reached by a free beach shuttle.

Dining/Entertainment: Guests enjoy having a drink in the piano bar (ever had a cucumber daiquiri?) before heading for the dining room, the Cardiff Hall Restaurant, which has a combination of Jamaican and continental dishes. Nonresidents can also enjoy dinner, served nightly from 7 to 9pm; a well-prepared meal costs around $20. The academy has won awards for some of its dishes, including "go-go banana chicken" and curried codfish.

Services: Free beach shuttle, laundry.

Facilities: Swimming pool, golf course.

INEXPENSIVE

CARIBBEAN ISLE HOTEL, P.O. Box 119, Runaway Bay, Jamaica, W.I. Tel. 809/973-2364. Fax 809/974-1706. 23 rms. A/C

$ Rates (for standard rooms): Winter, $50 single; $70 double. Summer, $45 single; $55 double. Breakfast $3 extra. AE, MC, V. **Parking:** Free.

This small hotel, 1 mile west of Runaway Bay, has 8 superior and 15 standard rooms, with personalized service in an informal atmosphere. The rooms all have ocean views and private baths, and the superior units all have private balconies. The hotel has a TV in the bar-lounge and a dining room leading onto a sea-view patio. Meals are served from 8am to 9:30pm daily. Dinner includes lobster, fish, shrimp, pork chops, chicken, and local dishes prepared on request.

5. FALMOUTH

This port town, which lies on the north coast about 23 miles east of Montego Bay, is just beginning to be discovered by tourists. Of course, Trelawny (see "Where to Stay," below) has already put it on the tourist map. The town in itself is interesting but ramshackle. There is talk about fixing it up for visitors, but no one has done it yet. If you leave your car at Water Square, you can explore the town in about an hour or so. The present Courthouse was reconstructed from the early 19th-century building, and fisherfolk still congregate on Seaboard Street. You'll pass the Customs Office and a parish church dating from the closing years of the 18th century. Later, you can go on a shopping expedition outside town to Caribatik (see "Savvy Shopping," below).

WHERE TO STAY

TRELAWNY BEACH HOTEL, P.O. Box 54, Falmouth, Jamaica, W.I. Tel. 809/954-2450, or toll free 800/336-1436. Fax 809/954-2173. 350 rms. TEL

$ Rates (including MAP): Winter, $171–$199 single; $270–$300 double. Summer, $128–$156 single; $178–$206 double. Children 14 years or under stay free in parents' room. Honeymoon and wedding packages available. AE, DC, MC, V. **Parking:** Free.

This self-contained resort on 8 acres is about a 45-minute drive (30 miles) east of Sangster International Airport in Montego Bay, along the A1. Locally made materials, in keeping with the policy of the "New Jamaica," were used when possible, including wicker furniture along with floral fabrics. The 1,400-foot beach area was achieved with the leasing of 1,100 feet of adjacent frontage. Bohíos (open-sided huts) were built around the pool area, and many trees and flowers planted.

Accommodations are in rooms with private balconies and an ocean or mountain view. Bungalows by the pool area are also available at additional charges (these are more suited to families). Rates include the services and facilities listed below.

Dining/Entertainment: There is live entertainment nightly, and parties are often held for the guests. A Jamaican Night poolside barbecue is held on Tuesday and a Beach Party Spectacular on Thursday with food, bonfires, music, and dancing. A la carte dinners are served in the Jamaican Room and buffets on the Palm Terrace the rest of the week.

Services: Shuttle-bus service to and from Montego Bay; lessons in scuba diving, snorkeling, Sunfish sailing, windsurfing, waterskiing, and reggae dancing.

Facilities: Four lit Laykold tennis courts, swimming pool, children's activity center that offers supervised activities daily, water sports.

WHERE TO DINE

GLISTENING WATERS INN AND MARINA, between Falmouth and the Trelawny Beach Hotel. Tel. 954-3229.

Cuisine: SEAFOOD. **Reservations:** Not required.

$ Prices: Appetizers J$6–J$55 (25¢–$2.50); main courses J$40–J$130 ($1.80–$5.90). MC, V.

Open: Daily 10am–9pm.

Residents of Montego Bay often make the 22-mile drive out here, along the A1, just to sample an ambience of the almost-forgotten Jamaica of another era. The well-recommended restaurant with a veranda overlooking the lagoon is housed in what was originally a private clubhouse of the aristocrats of nearby Trelawny. The furniture here may remind you of a stage set for *Night of the Iguana*. Menu items may include local fish dishes such as snapper or kingfish, served with bammy (a form of cassava bread). Other specialties are three different lobster dishes, three different preparations of shrimp, three different conch viands, fried rice, and pork served as chops or in a stew. Many guests look forward to coming here because the waters of the lagoon contain a rare form of phosphorescent microbes which, when the waters are agitated, glow in the dark. Ask about night boat cruises, which cost J$50 ($2.25).

SAVVY SHOPPING

Two miles east of Falmouth on the north-coast road is **Caribatik Island Fabrics,** at Rock Wharf on the Luminous Lagoon (tel. 954-3314). You'll recognize the place easily, as it has a huge sign painted across the building's side. This is the private living and work domain of Keith Chandler, who established the place with his late wife, Muriel, in 1970. Today the batiks created by Muriel Chandler are viewed as stylish and sensual garments by the chic boutiques in the States.

In the shop there is a full range of fabrics, scarves, garments, and wall hangings, some patterned after such themes as Jamaica's "Doctor Bird" and various endangered animal species of the world. Muriel's Gallery continues to sell a selection of her original batik paintings. Either Keith or a member of the staff will be glad to describe the intricate process of batiking during their open hours: 10am to 3pm Tuesday through Saturday. They are closed from mid-May to mid-November, but during that time the place can be visited by telephone appointment.

AN EXCURSION TO RÍO BUENO

I suggest a visit to this little village near Falmouth, to stop at **Gallery Joe James,** Río Bueno, Trelawny, halfway between Ocho Rios and Montego Bay, 30 miles each way. Joe is one of those rare men in whose company you could happily spend a day or a year, listening to his talk about art, his life in England and Jamaica, his enthusiasm for painting and carving, and his hopes for the future development of art in Jamaica. At the woodcraft workshop, he personally supervises production of the sculptures and wood carvings which, with his own striking paintings, fill the gallery with color and life.

Note: Don't try to bargain for the items on sale here. Joe will voluntarily offer a discount if you buy a number of objects of reasonable value. Otherwise, the prices are as marked.

WHERE TO DINE

LOBSTER BOWL RESTAURANT, Río Bueno. Tel. 973-3563.
  Cuisine: JAMAICAN. **Reservations:** Not required.
$ Prices: Appetizers J$54–J$63 ($2.45–$2.85); main courses J$181–J$270 ($8.25–$12.25); fixed-price meal from J$280 ($12.75). AE, DC, MC, V.
  Open: Breakfast daily 7–10am; lunch daily 11am–2pm; dinner daily 5–10pm.
Lunch here is served inside or on the patio with the water almost lapping your feet. For dinner, the cost of a full meal includes soup, salad, dessert, coffee, and a Tía Maria, plus a main course of grilled fish, broiled lobster, or sirloin steak. The wine list includes a wide variety, or you can order Red Stripe beer. The menu is kept small so that the quality of each dish is high. The restaurant is along the A1.

6. MONTEGO BAY

Montego Bay first attracted tourists in the 1940s when Doctor's Cave Beach was popular with the wealthy who bathed in the warm water fed by mineral springs. The town, now Jamaica's second-largest city, is on the northwestern coast of the island. In spite of the large influx of visitors, it still retains its own identity with a thriving business and commercial center, and it functions as the market town for most of western Jamaica. It has cruise-ship piers and a growing industrial center at the free port. The history of Mo Bay, as the islanders call it, goes back to 1494 when it was discovered as an Arawak settlement.

As Montego Bay has its own airport, the Donald Sangster International Airport, those who vacation here have little need to visit Kingston, the island's capital, unless they are seeking its cultural pleasures. Otherwise, you have everything in Mo Bay, the most cosmopolitan of Jamaica's resorts.

WHERE TO STAY

VERY EXPENSIVE

HALF MOON CLUB, Rose Hall (P.O. Box 80), Montego Bay, Jamaica,
  W.I. Tel. 809/953-2211, or toll free 800/237-3237. Fax 809/626-0592. 92
  rooms, 117 suites and villas. A/C TEL
$ Rates: Winter, $210–$310 single; $250–$350 double; from $380 suite or villa.

Summer, $120–$140 single; $150–$170 double; from $190 suite or villa. Breakfast from $9 extra. MAP $50 per person extra. AE, DC, MC, V. **Parking:** Free.

⭐ Located about 8 miles east of Montego Bay's city center and some 6 miles from the international airport, the Half Moon Club is considered one of the 300 best hotels in the world. Attracting such distinguished guests as President George Bush over the years, the resort complex consists of spacious hotel rooms, suites, and private one- to three-bedroom villas scattered over 400 acres of fertile landscapes carefully arranged to provide maximum privacy. Each accommodation is comfortably furnished in an English colonial/Caribbean motif, including some mahogany four-poster beds, and many of the private villas here have private swimming pools.

Dining/Entertainment: The Sugar Mill restaurant is set beside a working water wheel from a bygone sugar estate (see "Where to Dine," below). The Seagrape Terrace (named after the 80-year-old seagrape trees which push up from the pavement that surrounds them) offers meals served outdoors. Nightly entertainment includes music from a resident band, and nightly folklore and musical shows. You can also easily taxi into Montego Bay to sample the nightlife there.

Services: Room service (7am–midnight), laundry, baby-sitting, lessons in various water sports.

Facilities: Shopping arcade (with a pharmacy and boutiques), beauty salon, sauna and massage facilities, a mile-long beach, sailing, windsurfing, snorkeling, scuba diving, deep-sea fishing, two freshwater swimming pools, 13 tennis courts (7 floodlit at night), four lit squash courts, 18-hole Robert Trent Jones–designed golf course.

ROUND HILL HOTEL AND VILLAS, on the A1 (P.O. Box 64), Montego Bay, Jamaica, W.I. Tel. 809/952-5150. Fax 809/952-2505. 36 rms, 27 villas. A/C TEL

$ **Rates:** Winter, $210–$290 single; $250–$330 double; from $440 villa. Summer, $110–$170 single; $150–$210 double; from $270 villa. MAP $50 per person extra. AE, DC, MC, V. **Parking:** Free.

⭐ Opened in 1954 and now a Caribbean legend, this is one of the most distinguished and legendary hotels in the West Indies. It stands on a lushly landscaped 98-acre peninsula 8 miles west of town, once part of Lord Monson's sugar plantation, which slopes gracefully down to a sheltered cove whose edges house the establishment's discreetly elegant reception area and social center. Distinguished guests have included the Kennedys, Sir Noël Coward, and Cole Porter, and more recently Paul McCartney, Jacqueline Onassis, Kim Basinger, Geraldo Rivera, and Ralph Lauren. Many evenings are defined as "informal," except Saturday, when a jacket and tie or black tie is required for men. Likewise, it's preferred that tennis players wear all white on the tennis courts.

Surrounded by beautifully landscaped tropical gardens, Round Hill accommodates some 200 guests, who enjoy its private beach, the views of Jamaica's north shore and the mountains, and the colonial elegance of the resort. Deluxe hotel accommodations lie in a richly appointed seaside building known as the Pineapple House. Each opens onto views of the water and beach.

There are also privately owned villas dotted over the hillside, most available for private rental when the owners are not in residence. Each contains two, three, or four individual suites with a private living area and/or patio; 17 of the villas have their own swimming pools. Each villa is individually decorated, sometimes lavishly so, and includes the services of a uniformed maid, a cook, and a gardener.

Dining/Entertainment: At a little sandy bay is an intimate straw hut and an open terrace where guests congregate for informal luncheons. Jamaican and continental dishes are served on a candlelit terrace or in the Georgian colonial room overlooking the sea. The entertainment is varied—a bonfire beach picnic on Monday, a calypso barbecue on Wednesday, a Jamaican night on Friday, and Round Hill's gala night every Saturday.

Services: Room service (7am–10pm), concierge, laundry, baby-sitting, valet service, in-villa preparations of meals.

Facilities: Swimming pool, top-quality tennis courts (lit for nighttime play), safety-deposit boxes, windsurfing, glass-bottomed boat rides, sailing, paddle boats, rubber-sided inflatable boats, waterskiing.

TRYALL GOLF, TENNIS AND BEACH CLUB, P.O. Box 1206, St. James, Montego Bay, Jamaica, W.I. Tel. 809/952-5110, or toll free 800/336-4571. Fax 809/952-0401. 52 rms, 45 villas. A/C TEL
$ Rates: Winter, $210–$370 single; $250–$410 double; from $3,750 per week two-bedroom villa for up to four. Summer, $110–$190 single; $150–$230 double; from $2,200 per week two-bedroom villa for up to four. MAP $60 per person extra. AE, DC, MC, V. **Parking:** Free.

Comprising more acreage than almost any hotel in Jamaica, this stylish and upscale resort sits on the site of a 2,200-acre former sugar plantation about 12 miles west of the heart of town. Known as one of the grand Jamaican resorts, the property lies along a 1½-mile seafront and is presided over by a 155-year-old Georgian-style great house. Accommodations lie either in modern wings or luxurious villas scattered throughout the surrounding acreage. Bedrooms are decorated in cool pastels with an English colonial decor. All contain ceiling fans, along with picture windows framing sea and mountain views. The resort's famous villas are set amid lush foliage and are designed for privacy. Each villa comes with a full-time staff, including a cook, a maid, laundress, and gardener. All have private swimming pools.

Dining/Entertainment: The more formal of the resort's eating areas is in the great house, where antiques evoke the grandeur and power of the plantation era. Less formal meals are served in a beachside café. A resident band plays everything from reggae to slow-dance music every night during dinner. Afternoon tea is served in the great house every afternoon from 4 to 6:30pm.

Services: 24-hour room service, baby-sitting, laundry, massage; lessons in golf, tennis, and water sports.

Facilities: Championship par-71 18-hole golf course (site of many world-class golf competitions and the pride of this elegant property), nine Laykold tennis courts, 2-mile jogging trail, swimming pool with a swim-up bar; available water sports include windsurfing, scubadiving, snorkeling, deep-sea fishing, paddle boats, and glass-bottom boats.

EXPENSIVE

WYNDHAM ROSE HALL RESORT, Rose Hall (P.O. Box 999), Montego Bay, Jamaica, W.I. Tel. 809/953-2650, or toll free 800/822-4200. Fax 809/953-2617. 469 rms, 19 suites. A/C TEL
$ Rates: Winter, $150–$180 single or double; from $400 suite. Summer, $100–$120 single or double; from $300 suite. MAP $47 per person extra. AE, DC, MC, V. **Parking:** Free.

Just 9 miles east of the Montego Bay airport, Wyndham Rose Hall is at the bottom of a rolling 30-acre site along the north-coast highway. On a former sugar plantation that once covered 7,000 acres, the hotel abuts the 200-year-old home of the legendary "White Witch of Rose Hall," now a historic site. Although it's popular as a convention site, the hotel also caters to a family market where children are considered an important part of the clientele. The seven-story H-shaped structure features numerous rooms with a sea view. Most units have two queen-size beds, and each accommodation has a private balcony.

Dining/Entertainment: There are three restaurants and a busy staff of social organizers. It's never more than a short walk to one of the many bars scattered around the hotel property.

Services: Room service (7am–1am), baby-sitting, laundry, massage.

Facilities: Three pools (one for wading, one for swimming, and a third for diving), sandy beach, complimentary sailboats, top-rated golf course meandering over part of the hotel grounds, tennis complex (with seven lit all-weather Laykold courts) headed by pros who offer a complete tennis program, open-air fitness center.

MODERATE

DOCTOR'S CAVE BEACH HOTEL, Gloucester Ave. (P.O. Box 94), Monte-go Bay, Jamaica, W.I. Tel. 809/952-4355. Fax 809/952-5204. 80 rms, 10 suites. A/C TEL

$ Rates: Winter, $121 single; $143 double; $176 suite for two. Summer, $84 single; $106 double; $140 suite for two. Breakfast from $8 extra. AE, DC, MC, V. **Parking:** Free.

Across the street from the well-known Doctor's Cave Beach in the bustle of the town's commercial zone, this hostelry has its own gardens, a swimming pool, a Jacuzzi, and a small gymnasium with a sauna. Rooms are simply but comfortably furnished, and suites have kitchenettes. The establishment's two restaurants include the Coconut Grove, whose outdoor terrace is floodlit at night, and the less formal Greenhouse. In the Cascade Bar, where a waterfall tumbles down a stone wall, you can listen to a piano duo during cocktail hours.

FANTASY RESORT, Gloucester Ave. (P.O. Box 161), Montego Bay, Jamaica, W.I. Tel. 809/952-4150. Fax 809/952-0020. 119 rms. A/C

$ Rates: Winter, $105 single; $115 double. Summer, $85 single; $95 double. MAP $57 per person extra. Children 12–15 staying in parents' room are charged $15 each; children 11 and under stay free in parents' room. AE, MC, V. **Parking:** Free.

In the heart of Montego Bay, in an angular blue-and-white building (which, with nine stories, is one of the tallest buildings in town), you'll find one of the most reasonably priced resorts at Montego Bay. If you turn your back to the busy boulevard outside and look only at the cliffs beyond, you'll think you're in the Jamaican countryside. Though some of the accommodations face the sea and the resort's busy main street, the majority look inward onto an inner courtyard built around a swimming pool. Each contains a private balcony and comfortable furniture. Facilities include a freshwater pool, two tennis courts, a disco, a piano bar, an exercise room, a Jacuzzi, a small-stakes casino, and nightly entertainment. The resort lies only a short walk from the town's most popular swimming area, Doctor's Cave Beach.

HOLIDAY INN, Rose Hall (P.O. Box 480), Montego Bay, Jamaica, W.I. Tel. 809/953-2485. Fax 809/953-2940. 516 rms, 5 suites. A/C TEL

$ Rates: Winter, $134–$177 single; $140–$185 double; from $250 suite. Summer, $83–$108 single; $88–$113 double, from $175 suite. Extra person $15–$20. Children under 12 stay free in parents' room. MAP $38 per person extra. AE, DC, MC, V. **Parking:** Free.

This oceanside stone hotel is separated from the busy street by a screen of palm trees. Located 7 miles northeast of Sangster International Airport (and 8 miles east of Montego Bay's center), the hotel ensures its guests' privacy by having a guard at the entrance to screen those coming in. Numerous amenities include a free-form pool whose narrowest section is spanned by an arched footbridge.

There are four bars, three restaurants, the Rhythm Disco, and live entertainment by the pool nightly. Laundry, room service (from 7am to 10pm), and baby-sitting are available. Facilities include a swimming pool, a sandy beach, water sports (glass-bottom boats, sailboats, and scuba and skin diving), tennis courts, a children's playground, a fitness center, and a gaming room with both slot machines and electronic games.

LIFESTYLES, Gloucester Ave. (P.O. Box 262), Montego Bay, Jamaica, W.I. Tel. 809/952-4703, or 305/925-8481 in Florida for reservations. Fax 305/966-3493. 80 rms, 20 cottages. A/C TEL

$ Rates: Winter, $85 single; $90 double; $115 cottage for one or two. Summer, $55 single; $85 double; $75 cottage for one or two. MAP $25 per person extra. AE, MC, V. **Parking:** Free.

Set on carefully landscaped grounds adjacent to the Montego Bay Craft Market, this hotel was created when an older hotel was enlarged with a series of modern wings and annexes containing upgraded accommodations. Although it stands on a hillside with no beach of its own (it does have a swimming pool), it lies within a 5-minute walk from the white sands of Walter Fletcher Beach. On the premises are a gym, two Jacuzzis, a steam and massage room, and both a tennis and basketball court. Rooms are simply but comfortably furnished and have a balcony or small terrace. The hotel's Victoria Terrace Restaurant serves an international cuisine. There are three bars, plus a disco, and live entertainment is provided on most nights.

READING REEF CLUB, the A1, at the bottom of Long Hill (P.O. Box 225), Reading, Montego Bay, Jamaica, W.I. Tel. 809/952-5909, or toll free 800/223-6510. Fax 809/952-7217. 20 rms, 8 suites. A/C TEL

$ Rates: Winter, $80–$150 single; $100–$185 double; $285 two-bedroom suite; $365 three-bedroom suite. Summer, $60–$110 single; $75–$125 double; $200 two-bedroom suite; $275 three-bedroom suite. MAP $35 per person extra. AE, MC, V. **Parking:** Free.

This pocket of posh was created by two Americans, Jo Anne and Bob Rowe. Jo Anne, a former fashion designer whose hobby is cooking, has a sense of style and a flair for cuisine that are reflected in the running of this hotel. Located on 2½ acres at the bottom of Long Hill Road, a 15-minute drive west of Montego Bay, the hotel opened in 1986 on a 350-foot sandy beach where people relax in comfort, unmolested by beach vendors. The complex of four buildings overlooks beautiful reefs praised for their aquatic life by Jacques Cousteau.

The accommodations, which include two- and three-bedroom suites, open onto a sea view. All have spacious private baths, ceiling fans, and a light Caribbean motif. See "Where to Dine," below, for the restaurant recommendation. There is also a bar lounge and a beachside luncheon barbecue specializing in Jamaican (jerk) sausages, English sausages, and Tex-Mex food. Services include laundry, valet, drivers for island tours, and massages. Guests also enjoy the freshwater swimming pool, a boutique selling gift items and T-shirts, a private beach, and free water sports including snorkeling on the Reading Reef, windsurfing, and sailing in a 12-foot sailboat.

WEXFORD COURT HOTEL, Gloucester Ave. (P.O. Box 108), Montego Bay, Jamaica, W.I. Tel. 809/952-2854, or toll free 800/237-3421. Fax 809/952-3637. 54 rms, 7 one-bedroom apartments. A/C TV TEL

$ Rates: Winter, $80–$90 single; $85–$100 double. Summer, $65–$75 single; $75–$85 double. MAP $30 per person extra. AE, DC, MC, V. **Parking:** Free.

On the main road about 10 minutes to downtown Mo Bay and close to Doctor's Cave Beach, this hotel has a pleasant pool and a patio where calypso is enjoyed in season. The apartments have living/dining areas and kitchenettes, so you can cook for yourself. All rooms have patios shaded by gables and Swiss chalet-style roofs. The Wexford Grill includes a good selection of Jamaican dishes, such as chicken deep-fried with honey. Guests can enjoy drinks in a bar nearby. The hotel is owned and operated by Godfrey G. Dyer, who has led an interesting life—he has been a policeman, a detective, and a taxi business entrepreneur.

WINGED VICTORY HOTEL, 5 Queen's Dr., Montego Bay, Jamaica, W.I. Tel. 809/952-3891. Fax 809/952-5986. 16 rms. A/C

$ Rates: Winter, $90–$110 single or double. Summer, $70–$90 single or double. MAP $34 per person extra. AE, MC, V. **Parking:** Free.

On the hillside road in Montego Bay, this tall and modern hotel delays revealing its true beauty until you pass through its comfortable public rooms into a Mediterranean-style courtyard in back. There, urn-shaped balustrades enclose a terraced garden, a pool, and a veranda looking over the faraway crescent of Montego Bay. The veranda's best feature is the Calabash Restaurant. The dignified owner, Roma Chin Sue, added hotel rooms to her already well-known restaurant in 1985. All but five have a private balcony or veranda, along with an attractively eclectic decor that is part Chinese, part colonial, and part Iberian.

INEXPENSIVE

HOTEL CORAL CLIFF, 165 Gloucester Ave. (P.O. Box 253), Montego

Bay, Jamaica, W.I. Tel. 809/952-4130. Fax 809/952-6532. 32 rms. A/C TEL
$ Rates: $52–$58 single; $54–$60 double. MAP $22 per person extra. MC, V.
Parking: Free.

For value received, the Hotel Coral Cliff may be your best bet in Montego Bay. The hotel grew from a colonial-style building that was once the private home of Harry M. Doubleday (of the famous publishing family). The location is about a mile west of the center of town but only 2 minutes from Doctor's Cave Beach. The Coral Cliff also offers its own luxurious swimming pool. Many of the light, airy, and spacious bedrooms open onto a balcony with a view of the sea. Rates are modest for what you get. The hotel's breeze-swept restaurant is appropriately called the Verandah Terrace, and it overlooks the bay. The food is good too, and includes lobster thermidor and pan-fried snapper.

OCEAN VIEW GUEST HOUSE, Sunset Blvd. (P.O. Box 210), Montego Bay, Jamaica, W.I. Tel. 809/952-2662. 12 rms. A/C
$ Rates: Winter, $24 single; $33–$35 double. Summer, $21 single; $29–$31 double. Breakfast from $4 extra. No credit cards. **Parking:** Free.
Originally established in the 1960s when the grandparents of the present owners began to rent extra rooms in their home, this super-bargain is half a mile west of the airport and the same distance from the public beach. Buses, marked Montego Bay, pass the door for the ride down into town, and the owner sometimes provides his own transportation to and from the airport. The simple and uncomplicated bedrooms are supplemented with a small library and TV room with satellite reception. All the rooms are air-conditioned and have fans, and most open onto a veranda or the spacious front porch. It's quietest at the back. The owner will arrange tennis, golf, and water sports for you. Dinners (priced from $6) are offered only to guests, and reservations must be made by 2pm. T-bone steak, pork chops, roast chicken, and fresh fish are often served.

ROYAL COURT HOTEL, Sewell Ave. (P.O. Box 195), Montego Bay, Jamaica, W.I. Tel. 809/952-4531. Fax 809/952-4532. 20 rms, 3 suites. A/C TEL
$ Rates: Winter, $50–$92 single; $60–$70 double; from $115 suite. Summer, $40–$58 single; $45–$68 double; from $90 suite. Breakfast from $6 extra. AE, MC, V. **Parking:** Free.
This budget accommodation is located on the hillside overlooking Montego Bay, above Gloucester Avenue and off Park Avenue. The rooms are furnished with bright, tasteful colors, and all have patios; the larger ones have fully equipped kitchenettes. Meals are served in the Pool Bar and Eatery. On Sunday evening, a Jamaican buffet is served around the swimming pool. Free transportation is provided to the town, the beach, and the tennis club. This hotel is clean and attractive, has a charming atmosphere, and is good value.

ALL-INCLUSIVE RESORTS

JACK TAR VILLAGE, Gloucester Ave. (P.O. Box 144), Montego Bay, Jamaica, W.I. Tel. 809/952-4341, or toll free 800/999-9182. Fax 809/952-6633. 128 rms. A/C TV TEL
$ Rates (including all meals, drinks, activities, taxes, service and—in winter only—airport transfers): Winter, $160–$190 single; $130–$160 per person double or triple; $80–$100 extra if child shares room with parents. Summer, $140 single; $100 per person double or triple; $70 extra if child shares room with parents. AE, MC, V. **Parking:** Free.
Called simply the "Village," this resort 2 miles north of the city center offers one of those "all-inclusive" package deals, including unlimited beer, wine, and liquor both day and night, and all the services and facilities mentioned below. This is one of the smallest resorts in the Jack Tar chain, a fact which probably adds a noticeable intimacy

to its bustling all-inclusive format. Each of the bedrooms sits a few steps from the beach, with a view of the water. Private balconies open directly onto Montego Bay, and guests practically live in their swimsuits.

Dining/Entertainment: Lunch is served at beachside or in the main dining room, and there is nightly entertainment.

Services: Reggae dance lessons, massages.

Facilities: Tennis clinic and tennis courts (for daytime), sauna, windsurfing, waterskiing, snorkeling, sailing, a freshwater pool.

SANDALS INN (formerly Carlyle on the Bay), Kent Ave. (P.O. Box 412), Montego Bay, Jamaica, W.I. Tel. 809/952-4140, or toll free 800/ SANDALS. Fax 809/952-6913. 52 rms. A/C TV TEL

$ Rates (including all meals, snacks, drinks, sports and entertainment activities, airport transfers, taxes, and services for 4 days/3 nights): Winter, $970–$1,045 double. Summer, $875–$940 double. AE, MC, V. **Parking:** Free.

The Sandals Inn is a couples-only (male and female) hotel built around a large pool and patio, with a beach a short walk across a busy highway. A transformation of an older hotel, this is the least expensive, least glamorous, least accessorized, least spacious, and least attractive of the five Sandals all-inclusive resorts scattered across Jamaica. The relative lack of plushness, however, is compensated by the nearby attractions of downtown Montego Bay, by the low cost, and by the ability of any guest to enter with free day passes (including free transportation) either of the other two Sandals resorts of Montego Bay.

Thirty-eight rooms open onto the swimming pool. All the accommodations contain king-size beds, private baths, hairdryers, and clock radios. Rates are all-inclusive, which means three meals a day, "anytime" snacks, unlimited drinks both day and night, even tips.

Dining/Entertainment: Food is served in bountiful portions in the resort's only dining room, and there is nightly entertainment.

Services: 24-hour room service, free round-trip airport transfers.

Facilities: Recreational and sports program, exercise room, saunas, Jacuzzi, tennis courts, swimming pool, room safes.

SANDALS MONTEGO BAY, Kent Ave. (P.O. Box 100), Montego Bay, Jamaica, W.I. Tel. 809/952-5510, or toll free 800/SANDALS. Fax 809/952-0816. 211 rms, 32 suites. TV A/C TV TEL

$ Rates (including all meals, drinks, activities, service, taxes, and airport transfers for 4 days/3 nights): Winter, $1,180–$1,390 double; from $1,435 suite for two. Off-season, $1,110–$1,210 double; from $1,335 suite for two. AE, MC, V. **Parking:** Free.

Located 5 minutes northeast of the airport, next to Whitehouse Village, this honeymoon haven may have the highest occupancy rate of all resorts in the Caribbean. The 19-acre site is a couples-only (male and female), all-inclusive resort, where everything—all meals, snacks, nightly entertainment (including those notorious toga parties), unlimited drinks night or day at one of four bars, tips, and round-trip airport transfers and baggage handling from the Montego Bay airport—is covered in the price.

In contrast to its somewhat more laid-back nearby counterpart (the Sandals Royal Caribbean; see below), this resort offers many different "fun in the sun" participatory activities for a clientele and staff which tends to be extroverted and gregarious; the Playmakers, as staff members are called, like to keep everybody amused and the joint jumping.

Accommodations are either in villas spread along 1,700 feet of white sandy beach or in the main house where all bedrooms face the sea and contain private balconies. All units are well furnished, with king-size beds, hairdryers, and radios.

Reserve as far ahead as possible.

Dining/Entertainment: Dinner is by candlelight on an al fresco terrace bordering the sea. Those who haven't tired themselves can head for the late-night disco, Skydome, which often has rum and reggae nights.

Services: Free shuttle bus to the resort's twin, Sandals Royal Caribbean, whose facilities are open without charge to residents here.

Facilities: Waterskiing, snorkeling, sailing, scuba diving, windsurfing, paddleboats and a glass-bottom boat, two freshwater pools, three Jacuzzis, tennis (available day or night), fully equipped fitness center.

SANDALS ROYAL CARIBBEAN, Mahoe Bay (P.O. Box 167), Montego Bay, Jamaica, W.I. Tel. 809/953-2231, or toll free 800/SANDALS. Fax 809/953-2788. 176 rms, 14 suites. A/C TV TEL

$ Rates (including all meals, snacks, drinks, taxes, service, activities, and airport transfers for 4 days/3 nights): Winter, $1,275–$1,440 double; from $1,510 suite for two. Summer, $1,150–$1,295 double; from $1,360 suite for two. AE, MC, V. **Parking:** Free.

Four miles east of town, this all-inclusive couples-only (male and female) resort is a reincarnation of what was once a prestigious Montego Bay hotel constructed in the Jamaican colonial style. The earlier hotel was once patronized by Queen Elizabeth and Prince Philip. The building lies on its own private beach (which, frankly, isn't as good as the one at Sandals Montego Bay). Some of the British colonial atmosphere overlay remains, as reflected by a formal tea in the afternoon, but there are modern touches as well, such as a private island reached by boat where clothing is optional.

The spacious rooms range from standard to superior to deluxe. Even higher in price are the deluxe beachfront accommodations or a junior suite. Amenities include hairdryers and radios. Packages and prices at this resort are exactly the same as for its counterpart at Sandals Montego Bay (see above).

Dining/Entertainment: A seven-course Jamaican dinner with white-glove service is offered nightly. There are four bars, plus food and drink available throughout the day. Live music by a local reggae band is presented.

Services: Laundry, massage; free shuttle bus to the resort's twin Sandals, whose facilities are available without charge to any resident; if you're not married to your companion when you arrive here, management can arrange (if you wish) for the wedding before you leave.

Facilities: Scuba diving, windsurfing, sailing, three tennis courts, swimming pool.

SEA GARDEN BEACH RESORT, Kent Ave., Montego Bay, Jamaica, W.I. Tel. 809/952-4780, or toll free 800/545-9001. Fax 809/952-7543. 97 rms. A/C

$ Rates (including all meals, snacks, drinks, activities, service, taxes, and airport transfers for 4 days/3 nights): Winter, $660 single; $463 per person double. Summer, $594 single; $417 per person double. AE, MC, V. **Parking:** Free.

About 1½ miles east of Montego Bay, this resort stands near some of the most popular public beaches. Designed in a British colonial style of Neo-Victorian gingerbread, tall columns, and white lattices, it is airy, comfortable, and stylish. A dining room is under a high arched ceiling sheathed in mahogany whose view opens onto a flagstone-covered courtyard. The accommodations lie in sprawling motellike units built around the pool in back. Each unit contains a private balcony or patio and simple mahogany furniture.

Dining/Entertainment: One main dining room is the venue for international meals. There are three bars, and a resident band plays nightly.

Services: Baby-sitting, laundry, free transportation to and from the airport.

Facilities: Two lit tennis courts; water sports, such as sailing, snorkeling, and windsurfing.

WHERE TO DINE

The resort area has some of the finest—and most expensive—dining on the island. But if you're watching your wallet, you'll find that food is often sold right on the street. For example, on Kent Avenue you might try jerk pork, a delicacy peculiar to Jamaica. Seasoned spareribs are also grilled over charcoal fires and sold with extra-hot sauce, and you'll want to order a Red Stripe beer to go with it. Cooked shrimp are also sold on the streets of Mo Bay; they don't look it, but they're very hotly spiced, so be warned. If you have an efficiency unit with a kitchenette, you can buy fresh lobster or the "catch of the day" from Mo Bay fishers.

EXPENSIVE

CALABASH RESTAURANT, in the Winged Victory Hotel, 5 Queen's Dr. Tel. 952-3891.
Cuisine: INTERNATIONAL/JAMAICAN. **Reservations:** Recommended.
$ Prices: Appetizers $4–$7; main courses $11–$22. AE, MC, V.
Open: Lunch daily noon–2pm; dinner daily 6pm "until."

Perched on the hillside road in Montego Bay 500 feet above the distant sea, this well-established restaurant has amused and entertained Peter O'Toole, Robert McNamara, Leonard Bernstein, Francis Ford Coppola, and Roger Moore. It was originally built as a private villa by a doctor in the 1920s. About 25 years ago owner Roma Chin Sue established its Mediterranean-style courtyard and its elegantly simple eagle's-nest patio as a well-managed restaurant. The seafood, Jamaican classics, and international favorites include curried goat, surf and turf, the house specialty of mixed seafood en coquille (served with a cheese-and-brandy sauce), and a year-round version of a Jamaican Christmas cake.

THE DIPLOMAT, 9 Queen's Dr. Tel. 952-3353.
Cuisine: CONTINENTAL/JAMAICAN. **Reservations:** Required. **Transportation:** Private restaurant van.
$ Prices: Appetizers $2.50–$6; main courses $21–$28; fixed-price seven-course Jamaican dinner $30. AE, DC, MC, V.
Open: Dinner only, Mon–Sat 6:30–10:30pm.

The Diplomat offers a delightful, informal, yet elegant evening. Hidden in a long white wall, gates lead to a sweeping driveway through clipped lawns, old trees, and colorful flower beds to a gracious house. Georg Kahl, your host, does not require ties and jackets for men, but shorts and T-shirts are frowned upon. Guests dine on the terrace overlooking a floodlit ornamental pool with fountains playing and trees silhouetted with lights leading down toward the sea. Typical dishes might include grilled rib lamb chops or grilled Jamaican lobster in a butter sauce. Liqueurs are served at your table or in the drawing room. This is a good place from which to watch Mo Bay's famous sunsets, and arrangements can be made for a van to pick you up when you make your reservation.

GEORGIAN HOUSE, 2 Orange St. Tel. 952-0632.
Cuisine: INTERNATIONAL. **Reservations:** Recommended. **Transportation:** Private restaurant van.
$ Prices: Appetizers $3–$6; main courses $21–$29. AE, DC, MC, V.
Open: Dinner only, daily 6–10:30pm.

The Georgian House brings a grand cuisine and an elegant setting to the heart of town. The 18th-century buildings were constructed by an English gentleman for his mistress, or so it is said. You can select either the upstairs room, which is more formal, or the garden terrace, with its fountains, statues, lanterns, and cut-stone exterior.

The international cuisine is backed by a fine wine list. You might begin with a typically Jamaican appetizer such as ackee and bacon, then follow with pan-barbecued shrimp (you peel the shrimp yourself, but are given a scented fingerbowl). Continental dishes such as tournedos Rossini are also prepared with flair. For dessert, try the English plum pudding with coconut sauce. When you make reservations, ask for the restaurant's round-trip transportation provided to and from most hotels.

JULIA'S, Julia's Estate, Bogue Hill. Tel. 952-1772.
Cuisine: ITALIAN. **Reservations:** Required. **Transportation:** Private restaurant van.

$ Prices: Fixed-price dinner $33. AE, DC, MC, V.
Open: Dinner only, daily 5:30–10:30pm.

The winding jungle road you take to reach this place is part of the before-dinner entertainment. After a jolting ride to a site high above the city and its bay, you pass through a walled-in park which long ago was the site of a private home built in 1940 for the Duke of Sutherland. Today the building that is the land's focal point is a long, low-slung modern house whose fresh decor encompasses sweeping views. When you make your reservation, you can ask for a van to come to your hotel and pick you up. Raimondo and Julia Meglio, drawing on the cuisine of their native Italy, prepare chicken cacciatore, breaded milanese cutlet with tomato sauce and mozzarella cheese, filet of fresh fish with lime juice and butter, and 18 different kinds of pasta.

READING REEF CLUB RESTAURANT, the A1, at the bottom of Long Hill Rd. Tel. 952-5909.

Cuisine: ITALIAN/CONTINENTAL/CARIBBEAN. **Reservations:** Required.
$ Prices: Appetizers $3–$10; main courses $12–$22. AE, DC, MC, V.
Open: Lunch daily noon–3pm; dinner daily 7–10pm.

There are those, and perhaps Lady Sarah Churchill was among them, who claim that the food served here in this second-floor terrace overlooking the bay is among the finest—perhaps the finest—in Montego Bay. The menu is the creative statement of Jo Anne Rowe (see "Where to Stay," above), who has a passion for cooking and menu planning, a skill she perfected while entertaining prominent people in Montego Bay at her private dinner parties. Today her cook specializes in seafood, Italian, continental, and Caribbean recipes, such as perfectly prepared scampi, along with imaginative pasta dishes, such as spaghetti with fresh ginger, garlic, and parmesan. Her food is excellent, including a catch of the day, perhaps snapper, yellowtail, kingfish, or dolphin. She also imports quality New York sirloin steaks, but whenever possible likes to use local produce. Dinner might begin with Jamaican soup, such as pepperpot or pumpkin, and the restaurant is known for its lime pie. Lunches are low profile with a more limited menu. The restaurant is 4 miles west of the town center along the main seafront road (the A1).

RICHMOND HILL INN, Union St. Tel. 952-3859.

Cuisine: INTERNATIONAL. **Reservations:** Recommended. **Directions:** Take a taxi (2-minute ride) uphill from the central square in town.
$ Prices: Appetizers $2.50–$8.50; main courses $22–$31. AE, MC, V.
Open: Lunch daily 11am–3pm; dinner daily 6–10pm.

The Richmond Hill Inn is an old plantation house built in the early 19th century above the bustle of the bay area. Music is muted and classical in the early evening, but calypso is introduced later on. You might begin with a shrimp-and-lobster cocktail, which for many years I have found to be their best appetizer. Dolphin (the fish, that is) is regularly featured among the catch of the day. If you're traditional, try the filet mignon or lamb chops.

ROUND HILL DINING ROOM, in the Round Hill Hotel and Villas, along the A1, 8 miles west of the center of Montego Bay. Tel. 952-5150.

Cuisine: INTERNATIONAL. **Reservations:** Required.
$ Prices: Appetizers $6.50–$10.50; main courses $22–$31.50. AE, DC, MC, V.
Open: Dinner only, daily 7:30–9:30pm.

Considered the most prestigious dining room in Montego Bay, this is the culinary retreat of some of the western hemisphere's most discreetly prestigious personalities. To reach the dining room, you'll have to pass through the resort's open-air reception area and proceed through a garden. Many visitors opt for a drink in the large and high-ceilinged bar area before moving on to their dinner, which is served either on a terrace perched above the surf or (during inclement weather) under an open-sided breezeway.

Specialties include fettuccine in a cream-coated prosciutto sauce; Maroon Town chicken (farm-raised local chicken basted with a peanut-and-pepper marinade and served with cucumber/yogurt sauce); lobster tail; rack of lamb roasted in a glaze of rosemary, sherry, and mustard; and coconut-fried shrimp. One of the most succulent of the restaurant's desserts is a coffee and rum-caramel custard flavored with a hint of nutmeg. Important note: Saturday nights, in winter only, the dress code at Round Hill is formal.

SUGAR MILL RESTAURANT, at the Half Moon Club, Half Moon Golf Course, Rose Hall, along the A1. Tel. 953-2314.
   Cuisine: INTERNATIONAL/CARIBBEAN. **Reservations:** Required.
$ **Prices:** Appetizers $4.50–$10.50; main courses $14–$26. AE, MC, V.
   Open: Lunch daily noon–2:30pm; dinner daily 7–9:30pm.

After a drive through rolling landscape, you arrive at a stone ruin of what used to be a water wheel for a sugar plantation 8 miles east of Montego Bay. Guests dine on an open terrace by candlelight, with a view of a pond, the water wheel, and plenty of greenery.

Although he came from Switzerland, it was with the produce of the Caribbean that chef Hans Schenk blossomed as a culinary artist. He has entertained everybody from the British royal family to Farouk, the former king of Egypt. Lunch, beginning at $15, can be a relatively simple affair, perhaps an ackee burger with bacon, preceded by Mama's pumpkin soup and followed with a homemade rum-and-raisin ice cream. Smoked north-coast marlin is a specialty. The chef is said to make the most elegant Jamaican bouillabaisse on the island, or elegant "jerk" versions of pork, fish, or chicken. Should you prefer something less exotic, he also prepares today's catch. You top your meal with a cup of Blue Mountain coffee. A minivan will be sent to most hotels to pick you up.

MODERATE

MARGUERITE'S BY THE SEA, Gloucester Ave. Tel. 952-4777.
   Cuisine: INTERNATIONAL. **Reservations:** Required for the dining room.
$ **Prices:** Appetizers $2.75–$5.25; main courses $17.50–$28. AE, DC, MC, V.
   Open: Dining room, dinner only, daily 6–10:30pm. Beer garden, daily 11am–10:30pm.

This two-in-one restaurant and beer garden across from Coral Cliff offers an international cuisine specializing in seafood. The beer garden is ideal for lunch, as it's on a breeze-swept terrace overlooking the sea. The menu includes sandwiches, salads, and hot food such as deep-fried lobster. Meals start at $10.

But at night the magic of the place comes alive next door in the dining room. The changing menu is often based on fresh produce, including a catch of the day—you can ask the chef to steam it in coconut milk if you prefer—with grilled New York sirloin steaks also available. You can finish with the house specialty, a coffee ice-box cake. This is one of the more popular Mo Bay restaurants.

RESTAURANT AMBROSIA, in the Wyndham Rose Hall Resort, Rose Hall. Tel. 953-2650.
   Cuisine: NORTHERN ITALIAN. **Reservations:** Recommended.
$ **Prices:** Appetizers $3–$9; main courses $11–$25. AE, MC, V.
   Open: Dinner only, daily 6:30–9:30pm.

The restaurant sits across from one of the largest hotels in Montego Bay 9 miles east of the airport. Its cedar-shingled design and its trio of steeply pointed roofs give the impression that the place is a clubhouse for some neocolonial country club. Once you enter the courtyard, complete with a set of cannons, you find yourself in one of the loveliest restaurants in the area. You'll enjoy a sweeping view over the rolling lawns leading past the hotel and down to the sea, interrupted only by Doric columns. The menu includes pasta, seafood, and continental favorites, including baked filet of fish, scampi, lobster, and boneless breast of chicken topped with mushrooms in a cognac-cream sauce.

TOWN HOUSE, 16 Church St. Tel. 952-2661.

Cuisine: JAMAICAN/INTERNATIONAL. **Reservations:** Recommended. **Transportation:** Free limousine service.

$ Prices: Appetizers $2.50–$6; main courses $11–$29. AE, DC, MC, V.

Open: Lunch Mon–Sat 11:30am–2:30pm; dinner daily 6–9:30pm.

This restaurant has recommendations from, among others, *Gourmet* magazine. The lovely old, red-brick house was built in 1765, and you find the bar and restaurant around at the back in what used to be the cellars, now air-conditioned with tables set around the walls. Old ship lanterns give a warm light, and pictures of bygone days and soldiers of the past adorn the walls. Additional dining is available in a formal upstairs room. The place is a tranquil, cool luncheon choice, if you want to dine lightly on sandwiches and salads—or on more elaborate fare if you're hungry. If you return for dinner, you'll find it more atmospheric, and you're faced with a wide and good selection of main courses. Everybody talks favorably of red snapper en papillotte (baked in a paper bag). You might also try Jamaican stuffed lobster. I'm fond of the chef's large rack of barbecued spareribs with the owner's special Tennessee sauce. Free limousine service is offered to and from many of the Montego Bay hotels.

INEXPENSIVE

CASCADE ROOM, at the Pelican, Gloucester Ave. Tel. 952-3171.

Cuisine: SEAFOOD/JAMAICAN. **Reservations:** Recommended.

$ Prices: Appetizers J$27.75–J$87.75 ($1.25–$4); main courses J$220–J$425 ($10–$19.30). AE, DC, MC, V.

Open: Dinner only, daily 6–10pm.

With an intimate setting and relaxing atmosphere, the Cascade Room is one of Montego Bay's best seafood restaurants. Rushing waterfalls and cool tropical foliage blend with the natural cedar of the interior to make dining an enjoyable experience. Excellent service combines with the finest of seafood, such as lobster in the shell, shrimp Créole, filet of red snapper, and ackee and codfish. There is bar service and an adequate choice of wines.

PIER 1, Howard Cooke Hwy. Tel. 952-2452.

Cuisine: JAMAICAN. **Reservations:** Not required. **Transportation:** Private minivan.

$ Prices: Appetizers $2.50–$4; main courses $8–$18. AE, MC, V.

Open: Mon–Sat 11am–midnight, Sun 4pm–midnight.

One of the major dining and entertainment hubs of Mo Bay was built on landfill in the bay. It's operated by Robert and Beverley Russell, whose Jamaican food is considered some of the best served in the area. Fisherfolk bring fresh lobster to them which the chef prepares in a number of ways, including Créole style or curried. You might begin with one of the typically Jamaican soups such as conch chowder or red pea (which is actually red bean). At lunch their hamburgers are said to be the juiciest in town, or you might find their quarter-decker steak sandwich with mushrooms equally tempting. The chef also prepares such famous island dishes as jerk pork or chicken, and Jamaican red snapper. Finish your meal with a slice of moist rum cake. You can drink or dine on the ground floor, open to the sea breezes, but most guests seem to prefer the more formal second floor. If you call, the Russells can arrange to have you picked up in a minivan at most hotels (you're also returned).

PORK PIT, Gloucester Ave. Tel. 952-1046.

Cuisine: JAMAICAN. **Reservations:** Not required.

$ Prices: Main courses 1 pound of jerk pork J$90 ($4.10). No credit cards.

Open: Daily 11am–11:30pm.

S The Pork Pit is the best place to go for the famous Jamaican jerk pork and jerk chicken, and the location is right in the heart of Montego Bay, near Cornwall Beach. In fact, many beach buffs come over here for a big lunch. Prices are reasonable; for example, you can order an entire jerk chicken for J$80 ($3.65). Picnic tables encircle a gazebolike building, and everything is open-air and informal. The menu also includes steamed roast fish.

WHAT TO SEE & DO
VISITING WITH THE ANIMALS

JAMAICA SAFARI VILLAGE, outside Falmouth. Tel. 954-3065 for reservations.

Continual, conducted tours are offered through a petting-zoo area and breeding centers, and alongside crocodile ponds. (Did you know that a 750-pound adult croc can move at 40 miles per hour?) You may get to hear the crocodile love call, which is original to say the least. Safari Village served as a film set for the James Bond thriller *Live and Let Die.*

Admission: Tours, J$85 ($3.05) adults, half price for children.
Open: Daily 8:30am–5:30pm.

ROCKLANDS FEEDING STATION, Anchovy. Tel. 952-2009.

Otherwise called Rocklands Bird Sanctuary, this was established by Lisa Salmon, known as the Bird Lady of Anchovy, and it attracts nature lovers and birdwatchers. It's a unique experience to have a Jamaican doctor bird perch on your finger to drink syrup, to feed small doves and finches millet from your hand, and to watch dozens of other birds flying in for their evening meal. Do not take children age 5 and under, as they tend to worry the birds. Smoking and playing transistor radios are forbidden. Rocklands is about a mile outside Anchovy on the road from Montego Bay.

Admission: $5.
Open: Feeding station, daily 3:15pm until half an hour before sundown.

THE GREAT HOUSES

Occupied by plantation owners, the great houses of Jamaica were always built on high ground so that they overlooked the plantation itself and could see the next house in the distance. It was the custom for the owners to offer hospitality to travelers crossing the island by road. Travelers were spotted by the lookout, who noted the rising dust, and bed and food were then made ready for the traveler's arrival.

ROSE HALL, Rose Hall Hwy. Tel. 953-2323.

The most famous great house in Jamaica is the legendary Rose Hall, a 9-mile jaunt east from Montego Bay along the coast road. The subject of at least a dozen Gothic novels, Rose Hall was immortalized in the H. G. deLisser book *White Witch of Rosehall.* The house was built about two centuries ago by John Palmer. However, it was Annie Palmer, wife of the builder's grandnephew, who became the focal point of fiction and fact. Called "Infamous Annie," she was said to have dabbled in witchcraft. She took slaves as lovers, and then killed them off when they bored her. Servants called her "the Obeah woman" (*Obeah* is Jamaican for "voodoo"). Annie was said to have murdered several of her coterie of husbands while they slept, and eventually suffered the same fate herself in a kind of poetic justice. Long in ruins, the house has now been restored and can be visited by the public.

Admission: $8.50 adults, $4 children.
Open: Daily 9am–6pm.

GREENWOOD, Hwy. A1. Tel. 997-5030.

Greenwood is even more interesting to some house tourers than Rose Hall. On its hillside perch, it lies 14 miles east of Montego Bay and 7 miles west of Falmouth. Erected in the early 19th century, the Georgian-style building was the residence of Richard Barrett between 1780 and 1800, who was of the same family as Elizabeth Barrett Browning. On display is the original library of the Barrett family, with rare books dating from 1697, along with oil paintings of the Barrett family, china made by Wedgwood for the family, and a rare exhibition of musical instruments in working order, plus a fine collection of antique furniture. The house today is privately owned but open to the public.

Admission: $8.80 adults, $4.40 children.
Open: Daily 9am–6pm.

ORGANIZED TOURS & EVENTS

A tour aboard the **Appleton Estate Express** is offered by Appleton Express, Howard Cooke Highway (tel. 952-6606). You ride in air-conditioned coaches into the interior of Jamaica through spectacular scenery, stop at Catadupa for shopping at the fabric market, then at Ipswich Caves, and then visit the Appleton distillery. Lunch and an open bar are included in the price of $60 per adult for the day's trip (half price for children). The company buses will pick you up at your hotel in the Montego Bay area.

The **Croydon Plantation,** Catadupa, St. James (tel. 952-4137), is a 45-minute ride from Montego Bay. It can be visited on a half-day tour from Montego Bay on Tuesday, Wednesday, and Friday. Included in the $40 price are round-trip transportation from your hotel, a tour of the plantation, a tasting of varieties of pineapple and tropical fruits in season, plus a barbecue chicken lunch. Most hotel tour desks can arrange this tour.

The **Miskito Cove Beach Picnic,** which takes place at the cove of that name, is offered on Wednesday and Saturday and might be the highlight of your visit. Hotel tour desks book the excursion, which leaves at 10am, returns at 3:30pm, and has pickups at Tryall and Round Hill. For $40 per person, you can enjoy an open Jamaican bar, buffet lunch, calypso band, a glass-bottom-boat ride, a raft ride with a calypso singer on board, and water sports including snorkeling with a guide and equipment provided, Sunfish sailing with trained captains, jet-skiing, and windsurfing.

For a plantation tour, go on a **Hilton High Day Tour,** with an office on Beach View Plaza (tel. 952-3343). Round-trip transportation on a scenic drive through historic plantation areas is included. Your day starts at the plantation with a continental breakfast served at the old plantation house on a patio overlooking the fields and hills. You can roam around the 100 acres of the plantation and visit the German village of Seaford Town or St. Leonards village nearby. A Jamaican lunch of roast suckling pig with rum punch is served at 1pm. The charge for the day is $50 per person for the plantation tour, breakfast, lunch, and transportation.

SPORTS & RECREATION

BEACHES   ✪ **Cornwall Beach** (tel. 952-3463) is Jamaica's finest underwater marine park and fun complex and is a long stretch of white sand beach with dressing cabañas. Water sports, scuba diving, and snorkeling are available. Admission to the beach is J$4.40 (20¢) per adult, half price for children, for the entire day. A bar and cafeteria offer refreshment. Hours are 9am to 5pm daily.

Across from the Montego Bay Club, ✪ **Doctor's Cave Beach** (tel. 952-2566) helped launch Mo Bay as a resort in the 1940s. Admission to the beach is J$5.50 (25¢) for adults, half price for children. You can participate in water sports here. Dressing rooms, chairs, umbrellas, and rafts are available from 9am to 5pm daily.

One of the premier beaches of Jamaica, ✪ **Walter Fletcher Beach** (tel. 952-5783), near the Pelican Grill in the heart of Mo Bay, is noted for its tranquil waters, which makes it a particular favorite for families with children. There are facilities for snorkeling and waterskiing as well. Changing rooms are available, as is lifeguard service. You can have lunch here in a restaurant. The beach is open daily from 10am to 6pm, with an admission of J$5 (25¢) for adults and J$1.50 (5¢) for children.

BOAT CRUISES   Fun cruises are offered aboard the *Mary-Ann* (tel. 952-5505). A morning cruise is at 10am: At the sound of the conch trumpet, played by a quartet blowing conch shells, you set out aboard the 57-foot Australian ketch on a scenic cruise across the bay, with a stop to see colorful coral and reef fish in marine gardens, swim, snorkel, and collect shells. The cruise costs $30 per person. The *Mary-Ann* also makes a sunset dinner cruise, which leaves at 3pm and also costs $30 per person. Both these jaunts sail from the Sandals Montego Bay Resort, with free pickup and return service provided.

Day and evening cruises are offered aboard the *Calico,* a 55-foot gaff-rigged wooden ketch that sails from Pier 1 on the Montego Bay waterfront. You can be transported to and from your hotel for either cruise. The day voyage, which departs at 10am and returns at 3pm, provides a day of sailing, sunning, and snorkeling (with equipment supplied), plus a Jamaican buffet lunch served on the beach, all to the sound of reggae and other music. The cruise costs $50 per person and is offered Tuesday through Sunday. On the *Calico*'s evening voyage, which costs $25 per person and is offered Wednesday through Saturday from 5 to 7pm, cocktails and wine are served as you sail through sunset. For information and reservations, call Capt. Bryan Langford, North Coast Cruises Ltd. (tel. 952-5860).

RAFTING   Rafting on the Martha Brae is an exciting adventure. To reach the starting point, drive east to Falmouth and turn approximately 3 miles inland to ✪ **Martha Brae's Rafters Village.** The rafts are similar to those on the Río Grande, and cost about $30 per raft, with two riders allowed on a raft, plus a small child if accompanied by an adult. The trips last about an hour and operate daily from 9am to 4pm. You sit on a raised dais on bamboo logs. The rafters supplement their incomes by selling carved gourds. Along the way you can stop and order cool drinks or beer along the banks of the river. There is a bar, a restaurant, and a souvenir shop in the village. Later you get a souvenir rafting certificate.

   Mountain Valley Rafting is offered at Lethe Property, about 10 miles from Montego Bay, daily from 8am to 4:30pm. For $36, two people can go rafting, and there are free donkey rides. The raft trip takes about an hour and is operated by Mountain Valley, 31 Gloucester Avenue (tel. 952-0527).

SAVVY SHOPPING

You can find good duty-free items here, including Swiss watches, Irish crystal, French perfumes, English china, Danish silverware, Portuguese linens, Italian handbags, Scottish cashmeres, Indian silks, and liquors and liqueurs. Appleton's overproof, special, and punch rums are excellent value. Tía Maria and Rumona (the one coffee-, the other rum-flavored) are the best liqueurs. Khus Khus is the local perfume. Jamaican arts and crafts are available throughout the resort and at the Crafts Market (see below).

   The main shopping areas are at **Montego Freeport,** within easy walking distance of the pier; **City Centre** (where most of the in-bond shops are, aside from at the large hotels); and **Holiday Village Shopping Centre.**

   The **Old Fort Craft Park,** a shopping complex with 180 vendors (all licensed by the Jamaica Tourist Board), fronts Howard Cooke Boulevard up from Gloucester Avenue in the heart of Montego Bay on the site of Fort Montego. A market with a varied assortment of handcrafts, it is ideal browsing country for both souvenirs and more serious purchases. You'll see a selection of wall hangings, hand-woven straw items, and hand-carved wood sculpture, and you can even get your hair braided. Fort Montego, now long gone, was constructed by the British in the mid-18th century as part of their defense of "fortress Jamaica." But it never saw much action, except for firing its cannons every year to salute the monarch's birthday.

   At the **Crafts Market,** near Harbour Street in downtown Montego Bay, you can find a wide selection of handmade souvenirs of Jamaica, including straw hats and bags, wooden platters, straw baskets, musical instruments, beads, carved objects, and toys. That "jipijapa" hat is important if you're going to be out in the island sun.

ARTS & CRAFTS

AMBIENTE ART GALLERY, 9 Fort St. Tel. 952-7919.

   A 100-year-old clapboard cottage set close to the road houses this gallery. The Austrian-born owner, Maria Hitchins, is considered one of the doyennes of the Montego Bay art scene. She has personally encouraged and developed scores of local artists toward prominence, yet many of her good paintings sell for under $300. Open: Mon–Sat 9am–5pm.

BAY GALLERY, St. James Place. Tel. 952-7668.

   The Bay Gallery lies on the upper floor of this airy shopping complex near the tourist office. Gilou Bauer always presents an interesting selection of local artists. Open: Mon–Sat 10:30am–6pm, Sun noon–5pm.

BLUE MOUNTAIN GEMS WORKSHOP, at the Holiday Village Shopping Centre. Tel. 953-2338.

Here you can take a tour of the workshops to see the process from raw stone to the finished product you can buy later.

NEVILLE BUDHAI PAINTINGS, Budhai's Art Gallery, Reading Main Rd., Reading.

This is the art center of a distinguished artist, Neville Budhai, the president and co-founder of the Western Jamaica Society of Fine Arts. A veteran artist, he has a distinct style, and is said to capture the special flavor of the island and its people in his artworks. The artist may sometimes be seen sketching or painting in Montego Bay or along the highways of rural Jamaica. His studio is 5 miles east of Montego Bay on the way to Negril. Open: Daily 8:30am until early evening. Bus: No. 11 from Mo Bay.

THINGS JAMAICAN, 44 Fort St. Tel. 952-5605.

Affiliated with the government and set up to encourage the development of Jamaican arts and crafts, Things Jamaican is a showcase for the talents of the artisans of this island nation. Here is displayed a wealth of the products of Jamaica, even food and drink, including rums and liqueurs along with jerk seasoning orange-pepper jelly. Look for Busha Browne's fine Jamaican sauces, especially spicy chutneys or planters spicy piquant sauce or spicy tomato (called *love apple*) sauce, which is not to be confused with catsup. These recipes are prepared and bottled by the Busha Browne Company in Jamaica just as they were 100 years ago. Many items for sale are carved from wood, including sculpture, salad bowls, and trays. You'll also find large hand-woven Jamaican baskets and women's handbags made of bark (in Jamaica, these are known unflatteringly as "old lady bags").

Also look for reproductions of the Port Royal collection. Port Royal, once described as "the wickedest city on earth," was buried by an earthquake and tidal wave in 1692. After resting in a sleepy underwater grave for 275 years, beautiful pewter items were recovered and are living again in reproductions (except that the new items are leadless). Some of the pewter came from the Netherlands, other items from Britain. Impressions were made, and molds were created to reproduce them. They include Rat-tail spoons, a spoon with the heads of the monarchs William and Mary, Splay-Footed Lion Rampant spoons, and spoons with Pied-de-Biche handles. Many items were reproduced faithfully, right down to the pit marks and scratches. To complement this pewter assortment, Things Jamaican created the Port Royal Bristol-Delft Ceramic Collection, based on original pieces of ceramics found in the underwater digs.

FASHION

JOLIE MADAME FASHIONS, 30 City Centre Building. Tel. 952-3126.

Its racks of clothing for women and girls might contain evening dresses, casual clothes, and beach attire. Many garments cost under $40. Norma McLeod, the establishment's overseer, designer, coordinator, and founder, is always on hand to arrange custom-made garments. Open: Mon–Sat 9am–6pm.

KLASS KRAFT LEATHER SANDALS, 44 Fort St. Tel. 952-5782.

Next door to Things Jamaican, this store offers sandals and leather accessories made on location by a team of Jamaican craftspeople. Many sandals cost under $30. Open: Mon–Fri 9am–5pm.

JEWELRY

GOLDEN NUGGET, 8 St. James Shopping Centre, Gloucester Ave. Tel. 952-7707.

The Golden Nugget is a duty-free shop with an impressive collection of watches for both women and men, and a fine assortment of jewelry, especially gold chains. Set in the manicured confines of one of Montego Bay's most modern shopping compounds, it is run by India-born Sheila Mulchandani. Open: Mon–Sat 9am–6pm, Sun 10am–2pm.

EVENING ENTERTAINMENT

There are a lot more activities to pursue in Montego Bay in the evenings than going to the discos, but the resort area certainly has those, too. Much of the entertainment is offered at the various hotels.

Pier 1, Howard Cooke Highway (tel. 952-2452), already previewed as a selection for Jamaican cookery (see "Where to Dine," above), might also be your entertainment choice for a night on the town. On Saturday night a live band, usually reggae, is brought in from 7:30pm to midnight, when a cover charge of $20 is imposed. Friday night sees disco action from 10pm "till daybreak." The club is open on other nights from 6pm to midnight. Usually a $5 cover charge is assessed on most disco nights. But entertainment schedules change, so call first.

The **Junkanoo Lounge and Disco,** at the Wyndham Rose Hall Resort (tel. 953-2650), is one of the liveliest spots in the Mo Bay area. The 180-seat club has an inviting atmosphere and the finest state-of-the-art audio and visual system featuring music videos and live entertainment. Drinks begin at $2.50, and it's open daily from 9pm to 2am. There is no cover charge.

Every Sunday, Tuesday, and Thursday, there's an **Evening on the Great River,** during which you ride in a fishing canoe up the river 10 miles west of Montego Bay. A torchlit path leads to a re-created Arawak village, where you eat, drink as much as you like at the open bar, and watch a floor show. The Country Store offers jackass rope (tobacco by the yard), nutmeg, cinnamon, brown sugar, and all sorts of country items for sale. The cost, with transportation, is $50 per person. The operator is Great River Productions, 29 Gloucester Avenue, Reading, St. James (tel. 952-5047).

An interesting Jamaican experience is **Lollypop on the Beach** at Sandy Bar, Hanover, half a mile west of Tryall, held every Wednesday from 7:30 to 11pm (also on Saturday if the demand is heavy). Your $45 includes round-trip transport to the beach from Mo Bay hotels, a glass-bottom-boat ride with a calypso band, dinner of seafood and jerk meats, and traditional dance groups performing cumina, reggae, the basket dance, the bamboo dance, the limbo, and dancing on the beach. The festivities are run by Sunmar Enterprise Ltd., Montego Bay (tel. 952-4121).

Boonoonoonoos Beach Party is held on Friday from 7 to 11pm on Walter Fletcher Beach, Montego Bay, costing $34 (not recommended for children). A live band, three-course Jamaican dinner, open Jamaican bar, and a floor show make for a festive evening. For information, call the Coconut Grove Great House, Ocho Rios (tel. 974-2619).

7. NEGRIL

Jamaica's newest resort, on the western tip of the island, is famed for its 7-mile beach, the pride of the area. A place of legend, Negril recalls Buccaneer Calico Jack (his name derived from his fondness for calico undershorts) and his carousings with the infamous women pirates, Mary Read and Ann Bonney.

Emerging Negril is 50 miles and about a 2-hour drive from Montego Bay's airport along a winding road, past ruins of sugar estates and great houses. From Kingston, it's about a 4-hour drive, a distance of 150 miles.

This once-sleepy village has turned into a tourist mecca, with visitors drawn to its beaches along three well-protected bays—Long Bay, Bloody Bay (now Negril Harbour), and Orange Bay. Negril became famous in the late 1960s when it attracted laid-back American and Canadian youth, who liked the idea of a place with no phones and no electricity; they rented modest digs in little houses on the West End where the local people extended their hospitality. But those days are long gone. Today a "new Negril," with its new, more sophisticated hotels and all-inclusive resorts such as Hedonism II and Sandals Negril, draws a better-heeled and less rowdy crowd, including hundreds of European visitors.

At some point you'll want to explore Booby Key (or Cay), a tiny islet off the Negril Coast. Once it was featured in the Walt Disney film *20,000 Leagues Under the Sea,* but now it's rampant with nudists from Hedonism II.

Chances are, however, you'll stake out your own favorite spot along Negril's 7-mile beach. You don't need to get up for anything, as somebody will be along to serve you. Perhaps it'll be the "banana lady," with a basket of fruit perched on her head. Maybe the "ice cream man" will set up a stand right under a coconut palm. Surely the "beer lady" will find you as she strolls along the beach with a carton of Jamaican beer on her head and a bucket of ice in her hand, and hordes of young men will seek you out peddling illegal *ganja* whether you smoke it or not.

There are really two Negrils: The West End is the site of many little eateries, such as Chicken Lavish, and cottages that still receive visitors. The other Negril is on the east end, the first you approach on the road coming in from Montego Bay. Here the best hotels, enjoying some of the most panoramic beachfronts, such as Negril Gardens, are giving Negril a touch of class.

WHERE TO STAY

In addition to the following, the Café au Lait/Mirage Cottages (listed under "Where to Dine," below) has accommodations for rent.

MODERATE

CHARELA INN, Norman Manley Blvd. (P.O. Box 33), Negril, Jamaica, W.I. Tel. 809/957-4277. Fax 809/957-4414. 39 rms. A/C

$ Rates: Winter, $110–$140 single; $130–$155 double. Summer, $72–$90 single; $98–$114 double. MAP $36 per person extra. 5-night minimum stay in winter. MC, V. **Parking:** Free.

A seafront inn reminiscent of a Spanish hacienda, this sits on the main beach strip on 3 acres of landscaped grounds. The building has an inner courtyard with a tropical garden and a round freshwater swimming pool opening onto one of the widest (250-ft.) sandy beaches in Negril. The inn attracts a loyal following of visitors seeking a "home away from home." Its dining room faces both the sea and the garden, and offers both an à la carte menu and a five-course fixed-price meal that is changed daily. Sunsets are toasted on open terraces facing the sea. Simplicity and a quiet kind of elegance are the keynote of the inn.

NEGRIL BEACH CLUB HOTEL, Norman Manley Blvd. (P.O. Box 7), Negril, Jamaica, W.I. Tel. 809/957-4220. Fax 809/957-4364. 50 rms, 38 suites. A/C

$ Rates: Winter, $72–$82 single; $80–$90 double; $100–$110 studio with kitchenette for one or two; from $130 suite. Summer, $50–$65 single; $60–$75 double; $80–$90 studio with kitchenette for one or two; from $110 suite. MAP $25 per person extra. AE, MC, V. **Parking:** Free.

This casual, informal resort is designed around a series of white stucco cottages with purple trim and exterior stairways and terraces. The entire complex is clustered like a horseshoe around a rectangular garden whose end abuts a sandy beach just north of Negril. There's ample parking on the premises and easy access to a full range of sporting facilities including snorkeling, a pool, volleyball, table tennis, and windsurfing. Other activities can be organized nearby, and beach barbecues and buffet breakfasts are ample and frequent. Accommodations range from simply furnished units to one-bedroom suites with kitchens. The well-appointed rooms each have private bath or shower; the less expensive units don't have balconies. The Seething Cauldron Restaurant on the beach serves barbecues, seafood, and such

Jamaican specialties as roast suckling pig and ackee and codfish. Because some of this establishment's units are devoted to time-share investors, some of the 88 accommodations are not always available for rentals.

NEGRIL CABINS, Rockland Point, Negril, Jamaica, W.I. Tel. 809/957-4350. 20 units.
$ Rates: Winter, $85 single or double. Summer, $60 single or double. MC, V. **Parking:** Free.

Except for the palms and the Caribbean vegetation, you might imagine yourself at a log-cabin complex in the Maine Woods. In many ways, this is the bargain hotel of Negril, suitable for the budget-conscious eager to get away from it all. The cabins are on the easternmost edge of Negril, beside the road leading in from Montego Bay, in a forest across the road from a beach called Bloody Bay, where the infamous 18th-century pirate, Calico Jack, was killed by the British. There are 10 small timber cottages, none more than two stories high, rising on stilts, and each containing two separate accommodations with balconies or patios. The complex is in a 4-acre garden planted with royal palms, bull thatch, and a rare variety of mango tree. The establishment's bar and restaurant serves tropical punch, a medley of fresh Jamaican fruits, and flavorful but unpretentious Jamaican meals.

NEGRIL GARDENS, Norman Manley Blvd., Negril, Jamaica, W.I. Tel. 809/957-4408, or toll free 800/223-9815. Fax 809/957-4374. 54 rms. A/C TV
$ Rates: Winter, $125–$135 single or double. Summer, $80–$90 single or double. MAP $38 per person extra. Two children stay free in parents' room. AE, MC, V. **Parking:** Free.

The Negril Gardens rests amid tropical verdure on the famous 7-mile stretch of beach. The two-story villas are well furnished, and rooms open onto a front veranda or a balcony with either a beach or a garden view. The units on the garden side are cheaper and face the beautiful swimming pool with a pool bar and a tennis court.

Directly on the beach is a Tahiti-style bar, and right behind it stands an al fresco restaurant serving some of the best food in Negril. Nonresidents are also invited to patronize this facility, where they can choose from Jamaican cookery and international dishes, such as various versions of conch, lobster, and other seafood, plus curried goat and stew peas, or chicken fricassee. Dinner is from 7 to 10:30pm nightly.

NEGRIL TREE HOUSE, Norman Manley Blvd. (P.O. Box 29), Negril, Jamaica, W.I. Tel. 809/957-4386, or toll free 800/423-4095. Fax 809/957-4386. 55 units, 12 suites.
$ Rates: Winter, $95–$125 single or double; $225–$255 family suite for up to four. Summer, $60–$90 single or double; $130–$150 family suite for up to four. Breakfast $7 extra. AE, DC, MC, V. **Parking:** Free.
Owned by Gail Y. Jackson, the Negril Tree House is a desirable little escapist retreat with an ideal beachfront location. Scattered across the property in 11 octagonal buildings are the comfortably furnished units, including 12 suites, each with tile baths and air conditioning or ceiling fans. Suites, as an added bonus, also have kitchenettes and TVs. The resort features a number of water sports, including parasailing, snorkeling, jet skiing, and scuba diving.

POINCIANA BEACH HOTEL, Norman Manley Blvd. (P.O. Box 44), Negril, Jamaica, W.I. Tel. 809/957-4256, or toll free 800/468-6728. Fax 809/957-4229. 122 units, 8 suites. A/C TV
$ Rates: Winter, $131 single; $150 double; $164 studio for one or two; from $260 suite. Summer, $104 single; $118 double; $126 studio for one or two; from $170 suite. Breakfast $7 extra. AE, MC, V. **Parking:** Free.
Located between the beach and the resort's main highway, 5 miles east of town, this hotel is set on 6½ acres of verdant landscaping in its own gardens, the centerpiece of which is a small L-shaped pool on a terrace above the ocean. Accommodations are scattered among about a dozen two-story buildings interspersed with flowering shrubs. Opened in 1983, the resort offers a beachfront bar, a pool, a restaurant, a

water-sports kiosk, and a tradition of live reggae and calypso music on some nights. Each of the studio apartments and suites contains a small kitchen, allowing visitors to save money by preparing some of their own meals.

SEASPLASH RESORT, Norman Manley Blvd., Negril, Jamaica, W.I. Tel. 809/957-4041, or toll free 800/526-2422. Fax 809/957-4049. 15 suites. A/C TV TEL

$ Rates: Winter, $180 single; $200 double; $220 triple; $235 quad. Summer, $115 single; $135 double; $155 triple; $175 quad. Breakfast $7 extra. AE, MC, V. **Parking:** Free.

Partly because of its small size, this resort often has a sense of intimacy and personal contact among the staff and the guests. In deliberate contrast to the mega-resorts nearby, it lies on a small but carefully landscaped sliver of beachfront land richly planted with tropical plants. The suites are spacious and stylishly decorated with wicker furniture and fresh pastel colors. Each unit is the same size and contains the same amenities—a kitchenette, a balcony or patio, large closets, and either a king-size bed or twin beds—although those on the upper floor have higher ceilings and an enhanced feeling of space.

The resort contains two different restaurants, Calico Jack's (a simple lunchtime *bohío*) and the more elaborate Tan-Ya (see "Where to Dine," below). Services include baby-sitting, laundry, and room service. Guests have use of a small gym, a Jacuzzi, and a swimming pool with a thatch-covered gazebo-style bar at one end, and there is immediate access to the beach.

ALL-INCLUSIVE RESORTS

GRAND HOTEL LIDO, Bloody Bay (P.O. Box 88), Negril, Jamaica, W.I. Tel. 809/957-4013, or toll free 800/858-8009. Fax 809/957-4317. 200 junior suites. A/C MINIBAR TV TEL

$ Rates (including all meals, snacks, drinks, entertainment, sports activities, taxes, service charges, and airport transfers for the minimum stay of 4 days/3 nights): Winter, $840–$970 single; $740–$870 per person double. Summer, $840–$928 single; $740–$828 per person double. AE, MC, V. **Parking:** Free.

Considered the grandest and most architecturally stylish hotel in its chain, the Grand Hotel Lido sits on a flat and lushly landscaped stretch of land adjacent to Hedonism II, at the easternmost end of the beach strip. Considered the most upscale and discreetly elegant of the string of resorts known as Jamaica's Super Clubs, it opened in 1989 to a richly deserved fanfare. Accommodations are probably as stylish, or more so, than those in any other hotel in Negril. Each contains a sophisticated stereo system, lots of space, and either a patio or balcony that (except for a few) overlook the beach. The smaller of the resort's two beaches is reserved for nudists, who, according to most accounts, seem to give the best cocktail parties, enjoy the most uninhibited humor, and make some of the greatest number of repeat visits to the resort. Only adults are welcome, but unlike many other all-inclusive resorts, especially Club Med, there is no resistance here to giving a room to a single occupant. Even after the resort's quartet of restaurants closes, there are three different dining enclaves that remain open throughout the night and are tucked into alluring corners of the resort, each with a bubbling Jacuzzi nearby.

Dining/Entertainment: In addition to the cavernous and airy main dining room is a trio of restaurants, including one devoted to nouvelle cuisine, another to continental food, and a third to Italian pasta. Guests also enjoy an all-night disco, the piano bar, and the dozens of pool tables and dart boards of no fewer than nine bars, so getting a drink here is never a problem.

Services: 24-hour room service, concierge, laundry, tour desk that arranges visits to other parts of Jamaica, instructors to teach tennis and sailing.

Facilities: Four tennis courts, two swimming pools, four Jacuzzis, gym/sauna/health club, two fine beaches lined with chaises longues; one of the most glamorous yachts in the West Indies, the M-Y *Zein*, offered long ago by Aristotle Onassis to Prince Rainier and Grace of Monaco as a wedding present.

HEDONISM II, Negril Beach Rd. (P.O. Box 25), Negril, Jamaica, W.I. Tel. 809/957-4200, or toll free 800/858-8009. Fax 809/957-4289. 280 rms. A/C

$ Rates (including all meals, drinks, activities, taxes, service charges, and airport transfers for 4 days/3 nights): Winter, $620–$695 single; $545–$620 per person double. Summer, $543–$641 single; $468–$566 per person double. AE, MC, V. **Parking:** Free.

Devoted to the pursuit of pleasure, Hedonism II packs "the works" into a one-package deal, including all the drinks and partying anyone might want. There is no tender of any sort, and tipping is not permitted. Of all the members of its chain, this is the most animated. The rooms are stacked in two-story clusters dotted around a sloping 22-acre site. Most of the guests, who must be above 16 years of age, are Americans. Closed to the general public, this is not a "couples-only resort," as singles are both accepted and encouraged. On one section of this establishment's beach, clothing is optional. The resort also has a secluded beach on nearby Booby Key (originally Cay) where guests are taken twice a week for picnics. The complex is beside Negril's main road stretching east toward Montego Bay, about 2 miles east of the center.

Dining/Entertainment: Nightly entertainment is presented, along with a live band, a high-powered and high-energy disco with a stage for the presentation of occasional live performers, and a piano bar. Buffets are lavish, and the cuisine is international.

Services: Massage.

Facilities: Sailing, snorkeling, waterskiing, scuba diving, windsurfing, glass-bottom boat, Jacuzzi, swimming pool, six tournament-class tennis courts (lit at night), two badminton courts, basketball court, two indoor squash courts, volleyball, table tennis, Nautilus and free-weight gyms, aerobics, indoor games room.

NEGRIL INN, Norman Manley Blvd., Negril, Jamaica, W.I. Tel. 809/957-4209. Fax 809/957-4365. 46 rms. A/C

$ Rates (including all meals, drinks, activities, taxes, service charges, and airport transfers): Winter, $180 single; $140 per person double; $130 per person triple. Summer, $140 single; $115 per person double; $105 per person triple. AE, MC, V. **Parking:** Free.

Located in the heart of the 7-mile beach stretch, about 3 miles east of the town center, beside the main road leading in from Negril, this is one of the smallest all-inclusive resorts in Negril. Because of its size, the atmosphere is more low-tech, calmer, and less energy-charged than the atmosphere in its larger competitors. The resort, *not* confined to couples only, offers guest rooms with private balconies, spread through a series of two-story structures in a garden setting. The helpful staff offers a host of activities, day and night. Children are not accepted in winter.

Dining/Entertainment: Included in the package are all meals, all alcoholic drinks (except champagne), and nightly entertainment (including a disco). Meals are consumed in the resort's only restaurant, although there are bars in the disco and beside the pool.

Services: Room service (for breakfast only), laundry, round-trip transfers to and from the airport at Montego Bay, filtered water from a 10,000-gallon plant on the premises.

Facilities: Windsurfing, waterskiing, scuba diving, snorkeling, hydrosliding, aqua bikes, glass-bottom boat, two floodlit tennis courts, piano room, Universal weight room, freshwater pool.

SANDALS NEGRIL, Rutland Point, Negril, Jamaica, W.I. Tel. 809/957-4216, or toll free 800/SANDALS. Fax 809/957-4338. 198 rms, 1 suite. A/C TV TEL

$ Rates (including all meals, snacks, drinks, activities, taxes, service charges, and airline transfers for a minimum stay of 4 days/3 nights): Winter, $1,355–$1,620 double; from $1,800 suite. Summer, $1,260–$1,510 double; $1,675 suite. AE, DC, MC, V. **Parking:** Free.

Sandals Negril is an all-inclusive, couples-only (male-female) resort, part of the expanding "empire" of the enterprising Gordon "Butch" Stewart, who pioneered similar operations in Montego Bay. The word "Sandals" in Jamaica has come to stand for a "no problem, mon" vacation, as they say locally. The resort occupies some 13 acres of prime beachfront land a short drive east of Negril's center, on the main highway leading in from Montego Bay. It's about a 1½-hour drive (maybe more) from the Montego Bay airport. Round-trip transfers to and from Montego Bay are part of the package deal.

The developers linked two older hotels into a unified whole with very little incentive to ever set foot off the property. The crowd is usually convivial, decidedly informal, and often young. There are five divisions of accommodations, rated standard, superior, deluxe, deluxe beachfront, and one-bedroom suite. The casually well-furnished rooms have a tropical motif, and hairdryers and radios.

Dining/Entertainment: Rates include all meals, even snacks, and unlimited drinks day and night at one of four bars (a swim-up pool bar is a special feature). Nightly entertainment, including theme parties, is also included.

Services: Laundry, massage.

Facilities: Two freshwater swimming pools, tennis courts for day or night, scuba diving, snorkeling, Sunfish sailing, windsurfing, canoeing, glass-bottom boat, fitness center with saunas and Universal exercise equipment.

SWEPT AWAY, Norman Manley Blvd. (P.O. Box 77), Negril, Jamaica, W.I. Tel. 809/957-4040, or toll free 800/545-SWEP. Fax 809/957-4060. 130 units. A/C TEL

$ Rates (including all meals, drinks, activities, taxes, airport transfers, and services): Winter, $371–$414 per couple. Summer, $365–$393 per couple. AE, MC, V.
Parking: Free.

Swept Away is the newest and perhaps the best-equipped hotel in Negril—it's certainly the one most conscious of sports, emotional relaxation, and physical and mental fitness. All-inclusive, with meals, drinks, and all activities covered in the price, it caters to couples (male-female) eager for an ambience with all possible diversions but absolutely no organized schedule of when or with whom to play them. The resort occupies 20 flat and sandy acres which straddle both sides of the highway leading in from Montego Bay 3½ miles to the west.

The accommodations (the hotel defines them as "veranda suites" because of their large balconies) are in 26 two-story villas clustered together and accented with flowering shrubs and vines, a few steps from the 7-mile beachfront. Each accommodation contains a ceiling fan, a king-size bed, and (unless the verdant vegetation obscures it) sea views.

Dining/Entertainment: The resort's social center is its international restaurant, Feathers, which lies inland, across the road from the sea. There's also an informal beachfront restaurant, and four bars scattered throughout the property.

Services: Room service (for continental breakfast only), laundry, tour desk for arranging visits to other parts of Jamaica.

Facilities: Racquetball, squash, and 10 lighted tennis courts; fully equipped gym; aerobics; yoga; massage; steam; sauna; whirlpool; billiards; bicycles; beachside swimming pool; scuba diving; windsurfing; reef snorkeling.

WHERE TO DINE
MODERATE

MARINERS INN AND RESTAURANT, West End Rd. Tel. 957-4348.
Cuisine: JAMAICAN/AMERICAN. **Reservations:** Not accepted.
$ Prices: Appetizers J$25–J$95 ($1.15–$4.30); main courses J$130–J$250 ($5.90–$11.35). AE, MC, V.
Open: Lunch daily 11am–3pm; dinner daily 5–11pm.

The main reason most guests come here is for the boat-shaped bar and the adjoining restaurant, entered through a tropical garden which eventually slopes down to the beach. As you drink or dine, the breezes will waft in adding to one of the most pleasant and relaxed experiences in Negril. Curried chop suey and chicken are available, as are cheese omelets, homemade pâté, and—if you really want to dine elegantly—lobster, cooked in white wine. Look also for the chef's specials of the day. The restaurant is along the West End strip.

NEGRIL TREE HOUSE, Norman Manley Blvd. Tel. 957-4287.

Cuisine: JAMAICAN. **Reservations:** Not required.
$ Prices: Appetizers $2.50–$4; main courses $7.50–$22. AE, MC, V.
Open: Daily 6:30am–10pm.

This informal beachfront place takes its name from a mamee tree that grows through the main building of this resort hotel. Dining is on the second floor, but guests can come early and have a drink in the beachfront bar. This is a lively center both day and night. At lunch you can ask for a homemade soup, perhaps pepperpot, or a sandwich, or else more elaborate fare such as a typically Jamaican dish of escovitched fish. Some of the produce comes from the owner's own farm in the country.

At night, Gail Y. Jackson, your hostess, offers her full repertoire of dishes, including a lobster spaghetti "worth a detour." You might begin with a callaloo quiche and later follow with roast chicken (a specialty) or conch steak. Try the Tía Maria parfait for dessert.

RESTAURANT TAN-YA/CALICO JACK'S, in the Seasplash Resort, Norman Manley Blvd. Tel. 957-4041.

Cuisine: JAMAICAN. **Reservations:** Recommended.
$ Prices: Appetizers $2.50–$8 at dinner, main courses $2.50–$6.50 at lunch, $10–$19 at dinner. AE, MC, V.
Open: Lunch daily 11am–6pm; dinner daily 6:30–10pm.

Set within the thick white walls of a previously recommended resort, these two restaurants provide well-prepared food and the charm of a small, family-run resort. Informal lunchtime food is served at Calico Jack's, whose tables are in an enlarged gazebo, near a bar and the resort's swimming pool. The resort's gastronomic showcase, however, is the Tan-Ya. There, specialties include lemon-flavored shrimp, Tan-ya's snapper with herb butter, three different preparations of lobster, smoked Jamaican lobster with a fruit salsa, and deviled crab backs sautéed in butter.

RICK'S CAFE, West End Rd. Tel. 957-4335.

Cuisine: SEAFOOD/STEAK. **Reservations:** Not required.
$ Prices: Appetizers $3–$7; main courses $14–$20. No credit cards.
Open: Daily noon–10pm.

At sundown, everybody in Negril seems to head down toward the lighthouse along the West End beach strip to Rick's Café—whether or not they want a meal. Of course, the name was inspired by the old watering hole of Bogie's *Casablanca;* the "Rick" in this case is owner Carl Newman. Here the sunset is said to be the most glorious at the resort, and after a few fresh-fruit daiquiris (pineapple, banana, or papaya), you'll give whoever's claiming that no argument. At this cliffside proximity to nature, "casual" is the word in dress.

There are several Stateside specialties, including imported steaks along with a complete menu of blackened dishes (Cajun style). The fish is always fresh, including red snapper, fresh lobster, or grouper, and you might begin with a Jamaican fish chowder. You can also buy plastic bar tokens at the door, which you can use instead of money à la Club Med.

LE VENDOME, in the Charela Inn, Negril Beach. Tel. 957-4277.

Cuisine: JAMAICAN/FRENCH. **Reservations:** Required for Sat dinner.
$ Prices: Appetizers $2.70–$6.50; main courses $8–$29; five-course fixed-price meal $21–$33. MC, V.
Open: Lunch daily 11am–3pm; dinner daily 6:30–10 or 11pm.

Some 3½ miles from the center, this establishment enjoys a good reputation for its food. Nonresidents are invited to sample the cuisine that's a combination of, in the words of owners Daniel and Sylvia Grizzle, a "dash of Jamaican spices" with a "pinch of French flair." Their wine and champagne are imported from France. You dine on a terra-cotta terrace, where you can enjoy a view of the palm-studded beach. You may want to order a homemade pâté, perhaps a vegetable salad to begin with, and then follow with baked snapper, duckling à l'orange, or a seafood platter.

INEXPENSIVE

CAFE AU LAIT/MIRAGE COTTAGES, Lighthouse Rd., West End, Negril, Jamaica, W.I. Tel. 809/957-4471.

Cuisine: FRENCH/JAMAICAN. **Reservations:** Not required.
$ Prices: Appetizers $2.30–$6; main courses $8.20–$28.50. MC, V.
Open: Lunch daily noon–3pm; dinner daily 5–10pm.

Daniel and Sylvia Grizzle, a Jamaican/French couple, prepare the cuisine as well as direct the smooth operation of this place, located 1½ miles from the town center along the West End beach strip. Menu items include quiches, escargots, lobster, and an unusual crêpe made with cheese and callaloo. There are four kinds of pizza, roast lamb, fish steak, and curried shrimp, and there is a wine list stressing French products. Dessert may be lime tart with fresh cream.

Set in 4½ acres of tropical garden, the property flanks both sides of the road. On the land side, there are two two-bedroom cottages, ideal for four to six people. On the sea side, where high cliffs dominate the coastline, they have one one-bedroom cottage, one duplex, and four large studio rooms with big balconies and views of the coast. All accommodations have private baths and ceiling fans. The studios are air-conditioned. Winter rates are $88 to $98 daily in a single and $95 to $110 in a double; summer tariffs range from $45 to $55 daily in a single, $55 to $66 in a double. There are sunning areas, three access ladders to the sea, and a gazebo for relaxing in the shade.

CHICKEN LAVISH, West End Rd. Tel. 957-4410.

Cuisine: JAMAICAN. **Reservations:** Not required.
$ Prices: Appetizers J$16 (75¢); main courses J$55–J$140 ($2.50–$6.35). MC, V.
Open: Daily 9am–10pm.

I've found that Chicken Lavish, whose name I love, is the best of the lot. Just show up on the doorstep and see what's cooking. It's located along the West End beach strip. Curried goat is a specialty, as is fresh fried fish. Fresh Caribbean lobster is prepared to perfection here, as is the red snapper caught in local waters. But the main reason I've recommended the place is because of the namesake. Ask the chef to make his special Jamaican chicken. He'll tell you, and you may agree, that it's the best on the island. What to wear here? Dress as you would to clean up your backyard on a hot August day.

COSMO'S SEAFOOD RESTAURANT & BAR, Norman Manley Blvd. Tel. 957-4330.

Cuisine: SEAFOOD. **Reservations:** Not required.
$ Prices: Appetizers J$5–J$20 (25¢–90¢); main courses J$60–J$190 ($2.75–$8.65). MC, V.
Open: Daily 11am–10pm.

One of the best places to go for local seafood is centered around a Polynesian thatched bohío open to the sea and bordering the main beachfront. This is the dining spot of Cosmo Brown, who entertains locals as well as visitors. You can order his famous conch soup, or conch in a number of other ways, including steamed or curried. He's also known for his savory kettle of curried goat, or you might order freshly caught seafood or fish, depending on what the catch turned up. It's a rustic establishment, and prices are among the most reasonable at the resort.

NEGRIL JERK CENTRE, West End Rd. Tel. 957-4847.

Cuisine: JAMAICAN JERKED MEATS. **Reservations:** Not accepted.
$ Prices: J$20–J$38 (90¢–$1.75) for a half-pound portion of jerked meat (a full meal for most diners). No credit cards.
Open: Daily 10am–11pm.

In a wood-sided hut beside the West End's only paved road, near the tourist office in the center of town, this is the town's premier outlet for the spicy, slow-cooked meats that are the culinary trademark of Jamaica. There is a handful of simple tables and chairs inside, although most diners opt for the take-out. Don't forget to look at the metal ovens in back, where large quantities of pork, beef, chicken, and fish slowly stew in their juices.

PARADISE YARD, Gas Station Rd. Tel. 957-4006.
  Cuisine: JAMAICAN. **Reservations:** Not required.
$ Prices: Appetizers J$15–J$45 (70¢–$2.05); main courses J$65–J$190 ($2.95–$8.65). No credit cards.
  Open: Daily 8am–11pm.

Set on the verdant flatlands of downtown Negril, near the police station and a 10-minute walk from the beach, this simple but welcoming restaurant is the undisputed domain of Jamaican-born chef and owner Lorraine Washington. Meals, served either on the outdoor terrace or in an airy and comfortable interior decorated with roughly textured boards and pink tiles, might include the house specialty, "Rasta Pasta" (defined as red and green "dreadlocks pasta" chosen in honor of the colors of the Jamaican flag, with tomatoes, pepper, and ackee), a succulent version of pasta with lobster, curried chicken (prepared either mild or in fiery degrees of hotness, depending on your taste), Mexican enchilladas, Jamaican "escovitched fish," and some of the best pumpkin soup in Jamaica.

---

8. MANDEVILLE

The "English Town," Mandeville lies on a plateau more than 2,000 feet above the sea in the tropical highlands. The commercial part of the town is small and is surrounded by a sprawling residential area popular with the large North American expatriate population mostly involved with the bauxite-mining industry. Much cooler than the coastal resorts, it's a possible center from which to explore the entire land.

Shopping in the town is a pleasure, whether in the old center or in one of the modern complexes, such as Grove Court. The market in the center of town teems with life, particularly on weekends when the country folk bus into town for their weekly visit. The town has several interesting old buildings. The square-towered church built in 1820 has fine stained glass, and the little churchyard tells an interesting story of past inhabitants of Mandeville. The Court House, built in 1816, is a fine old Georgian stone-and-wood building with a pillared portico reached by a steep, sweeping double staircase. See "What to See and Do," below, to read about Marshall's Pen, one of the great houses in Mandeville.

WHERE TO STAY

HOTEL ASTRA, 62 Ward Ave., Mandeville, Jamaica, W.I. Tel. 809/962-3265. 20 rms, 2 suites. TV TEL
$ Rates: $60–$85 single or double; from $90 suite. Breakfast $5 extra. AE, MC, V.
  Parking: Free.

My top choice for a stay in this area is this family-run hotel a mile west of the town center beside the access road leading in from Kingston. It's operated by the Pikes, who do all they can to ensure that visitors and local people alike are satisfied. Diana McIntyre-Pike, known to her family and friends as Thunderbird (she's always coming to the rescue of guests), happily picks up people in her own car and takes them around to see the sights, plus organizes introductions to people of the island. The accommodations are mainly in two buildings reached along open walkways.

The Zodiac Room, entered from the lounge area, offers excellent meals. Lunch or dinner is a choice of a homemade soup such as beef-and-vegetable or pumpkin, followed by shrimp rice, meatballs Italiano, or braised steak. The kitchen is under the personal control of Diana, who is always collecting awards in Jamaican culinary competitions, and someone is on hand to explain to you the niceties of any particular Jamaican dish. A complete meal costs $10 to $15. Dinner is served Monday through Friday from 6:30 to 9:30pm and on Saturday and Sunday from 7 to 10pm. Friday is barbecue night, when guests and townfolk gather around the pool to dine.

The Revival Room is the bar, where everything including the stools is made from rum-soaked barrels. Try the family's own homemade liqueur and "reviver," a pick-me-up concocted from Guinness, rum, egg, condensed milk, and nutmeg—guaranteed not to fail. Service is 11am to 11:30pm daily.

In addition to the pool, there is a sauna, or you can spend the afternoon at the Manchester Country Club, where tennis and golf are available. Horses can be provided for cross-country treks.

MANDEVILLE HOTEL, 4 Hotel St. (P.O. Box 78), Mandeville, Jamaica, W.I. Tel. 809/962-2138. Fax 809/962-0700. 53 rms, 9 suites. TV TEL
$ Rates: $50–$70 single or double; from $85 suite. Breakfast from $5 extra. AE, MC, V. **Parking:** Free.

The richly ornate hotel with the same name which preceded this modern establishment was established around the turn of the century, and for a while housed part of the British military garrison. In the 1970s the venerable hotel was replaced with this modern peach-colored substitute, which was completely refurbished in 1976. It lies in the heart of Mandeville, a short walk from the police station. Today, the modern hotel has a large outdoor bar and a spacious lounge, and good food and service. Activity centers mainly around the pool and the coffee shop, where substantial meals are served at moderate prices. There are attractive gardens, and golf and tennis can be played at the nearby Manchester Country Club. Horseback riding can also be arranged.

WHERE TO DINE

BILL LAURIE'S STEAK HOUSE, Bloomfield Gardens. Tel. 962-3116.
Cuisine: STEAK. **Reservations:** Not required.
$ Prices: Appetizers J$15–J$45 (70¢–$2.05); main courses J$65–J$190 ($2.95–$8.65). No credit cards.
Open: Lunch Mon–Sat 11am–2pm; dinner Mon–Sat 6–10pm.

Standing 100 feet above Mandeville is this long, two-story wooden house with a veranda stretching the length of the upper floor. Outside you are likely to find several cars, none less than 30 years old, including an old London taxi which used to take customers home after a heavy meal. The front end of an old Wolseley makes up the total count. Going upstairs to the bar and restaurant, you encounter more than 500 vehicle license plates, along with visiting cards by the thousand, beer mats, and model cars vying for space among pewter tankards left there permanently by regulars who are set in their ways.

The food consists of appetizers such as fruit punch or mango nectar, soups, and steaks varying in size and cut. Ground beef steak, mixed grill, and lamb chops are among the main-dish offerings. All meals are cooked to order and come with french fries, salad, and vegetables.

MANDEVILLE HOTEL, 4 Hotel St. Tel. 962-2460.
Cuisine: JAMAICAN. **Reservations:** Not required.
$ Prices: Appetizers $5–$7; main courses $10–$15. AE, MC, V.
Open: Breakfast daily 6:30–9:30am; lunch daily 12:30–2:30pm; dinner daily 7–9:30pm.

Close to the city center, near the police station, and popular with local businesspeople who use the coffee shop by the pool for a quick, appetizing luncheon stop, the Mandeville Hotel offers a wide selection of sandwiches, plus milkshakes, tea, and coffee. In the hotel restaurant the à la carte menu offers Jamaican pepperpot soup, lobster thermidor, fresh snapper, and kingfish. Potatoes and vegetables in season are included in the main-dish prices. A full Jamaican breakfast begins at $7. From the restaurant's dining room you'll have a view of the hotel's pool and the green hills of central Jamaica.

WHAT TO SEE & DO

Mandeville is the sort of place where you can become well acquainted with the people and feel like part of the community.

One of the largest and driest **caves** on the island is at Oxford, about 9 miles northwest of Mandeville. Signs direct you to it after you leave Mile Gully, a village dominated by St. George's Church, some 175 years old.

Among the interesting attractions, **Marshall's Pen** is one of the great houses, an old coffee plantation home some 200 years old and filled with antique furniture. The house is a history lesson in itself, as it was once owned by the Earl of Balcarres, the island's governor. It has been in the hands of the Sutton family since 1939; they farm the 300 acres and breed many Jamaican and red poll cattle. They also have a large collection of seashells, some fine Arawak relics, and a large general stamp collection. This is very much a private home and should be treated as such. Guided tours can be arranged. A contribution of J$50 ($2.25) is requested. For information or an appointment to see the house, contact Robert L. Sutton, P.O. Box 58, Mandeville, Jamaica, W.I. (tel. 809/962-2260).

At **Marshall's Pen cattle estate and nature reserve,** near Mandeville, 89 of Jamaica's 256 species of birds (including 23 endemic species and many North American winter migrants) can be seen. Groups can arrange guided birding tours of the scenic property *in advance,* for early morning or evening (to see nocturnal birds) or to go to other outstanding birding spots in Jamaica, at rates to be negotiated. For further information, contact Robert L. Sutton, P.O. Box 58, Mandeville, Jamaica, W.I. (tel. 809/962-2260).

Milk River Mineral Bath, Milk River, Clarendon (tel. 809/924-9544; fax 809/986-4962), lies 9 miles south of the Kingston–Mandeville highway. It boasts the world's most radioactive mineral waters, recommended for the treatment of arthritis, rheumatism, lumbago, neuralgia, sciatica, and liver disorders. These mineral-laden waters are available to guests of the Milk River Mineral Spa & Hotel, Milk River, Clarendon, Jamaica, W.I., as well as to casual visitors to the enclosed baths or the mineral swimming pool. The restaurant offers fine Jamaican cuisine, health drinks, and special diets in an old-world atmosphere of relaxation. The nearby Milk River affords boating and fishing. Accommodations are available at year-round MAP rates ranging from $62.50 to $68 daily in a single, $80 to $86 in a double. The cheaper rooms are without bath.

On Knockpatrick Road, 1½ miles from Mandeville, you can visit the octagonal, hilltop home of **Cecil Charlton** (tel. 962-2432), Sunday, Monday, Tuesday, Thursday, and Friday from 10am to 6pm. Mr. Charlton also has a collection of rare birds. There is no admission charge, but visitors may tip guides or give a donation to charity.

CHAPTER 11

THE FRENCH WEST INDIES

French charm and tropical beauty combine in the great curve of the Lesser Antilles. A long way from Europe, France's western border is composed mainly of Guadeloupe and Martinique, with a scattering of tiny offshore dependencies, such as the six little clustered Iles des Saintes.

Almond-shaped Martinique is the northernmost of the Windwards, while butterfly-shaped Guadeloupe is near the southern stretch of the Leewards. These are not colonies, as many visitors wrongly assume, but the westernmost *départements* of France, meaning that these *citoyens* are full-fledged citizens of *la belle France*.

Other satellites of the French West Indies include St. Martin (which shares an island with the Dutch-held St. Maarten; see Chapter 9), St. Barthélemy, Marie-Galante, and La Désirade, a former leper colony.

Unlike Barbados and Jamaica, the French West Indies are Johnny-come-latelies to tourism. Although cruise-ship passengers had arrived long before, mass tourism began in these islands only in the 1970s. Créole customs make these islands unique in the Caribbean. The inhabitants also serve some of the best food. Don't be afraid if I've sent you to a dilapidated wooden shack. You may find the *New York Times* food editor there too, sampling a sumptuous meal.

INFORMATION

For more information on these islands before you leave home, contact the **French West Indies Tourist Board,** 610 Fifth Ave., New York, NY 10020 (tel. 212/757-1125). You can also contact branch offices at 9454 Wilshire Blvd., Beverly Hills, CA 90212 (tel. 213/272-2661); 645 N. Michigan Ave., Chicago, IL 60611 (tel. 312/337-6301); 2305 Cedar Spring Rd., Suite 205, Dallas, TX 75201 (tel. 214/720-4010); and 1 Hallidie Plaza, Suite 250, San Francisco, CA 94102 (tel. 415/986-4161). Or you can telephone "France on Call" (tel. 900/420-2003, a toll call at 50¢ a minute). In Canada, visit 1981 avenue McGill College, Suite 490, Montréal, PQ H3A 2W9 (tel. 514/288-4264); or 1 Dundas St. W., Suite 2405, Toronto, ON M5G 1Z3 (tel. 416/593-4717).

1. MARTINIQUE

France's anchor in the Caribbean world, Martinique is the land of the Empress Joséphine. In her youth, Madame de Maintenon, mistress of Louis XIV, also lived here in the small fishing village of Le Prêcheur.

WHAT'S SPECIAL ABOUT THE FRENCH WEST INDIES

Beaches

- ☐ St. Jean, St. Barthélemy, two adjoining curves of golden sandy beach, great for French bikini watching (for both sexes).
- ☐ Pointe des Châteaux, Guadeloupe, on the eastern tip, an array of white sandy beaches, including the *au naturel* Pointe Tarare.
- ☐ Le Diamant, Martinique, 6½ miles of white sandy beach facing the landmark Diamond Rock, with snorkeling, swimming, and picnic areas.
- ☐ St. Martin, with 36 perfect white sandy beaches including Ilet Pinel, a tiny offshore island for beach recluses.

Great Towns/Villages

- ☐ Fort-de-France, Martinique, a combination New Orleans and French Riviera town, dominated by its handsome savannah.
- ☐ Marigot, capital of French St. Martin, famed for its gourmet restaurants and freeport shopping.
- ☐ Gustavia, capital of St. Barts, named for a Swedish king, today a picture-postcard town of elegance that attracts the yachting set.

Museums

- ☐ La Pagerié, Trois-Ilets, Martinique, mementoes of the most famous person in the island's history, the Empress Joséphine.
- ☐ Centre d'Art Musée Gauguin, Anse Turin, Martinique, commemorating the artist's stay in Martinique in 1887.

Ace Attractions

- ☐ Pointe-des-Châteaux, near where the Atlantic meets the Caribbean in Guadeloupe, a view evocative of France's Brittany coast.
- ☐ La Soufrière, the sulfur-puffing volcano of Guadeloupe that rises to a height of 4,800 feet.

Special Events

- ☐ Carnival in Martinique, right after the New Year, with costumes, parades, and "she-devils" of both sexes.

Columbus first charted Martinique, and the French settled the island when the king's gentleman, Belain d'Esnambuc, took possession in the name of Louis XIII in 1635. In spite of some intrusions by British forces, the French have remained in Martinique ever since. Emigration from France produced sugarcane plantations and rum distilleries.

In the beginning of their colonization, the French imported black slaves from Africa to work the plantations, but at the time of the French Revolution, slavery began to decline on Martinique. It wasn't until the mid-19th century, however, that its abolition was obtained by Victor Schoelcher, a Paris-born deputy from Alsace. Since 1946 Martinique has been a part of France.

Martinique is part of the Lesser Antilles and lies in the semitropical zone; its western shore faces the Caribbean and its eastern shore faces the livelier Atlantic. It's some 4,340 miles from France, 2,000 miles from New York, 2,300 miles from Montréal, and 1,450 miles from Miami.

The surface of the island is only 420 square miles—50 miles at its longest dimension, 21 miles at its widest point.

The ground is mountainous, especially in the rain-forested northern part where Mount Pelée, a volcano, rises to a height of 4,656 feet. In the center of the island the mountains are smaller, with Carbet Peak reaching a 3,960-foot summit. The high hills rising among the peaks or mountains are called *mornes*. The southern part of

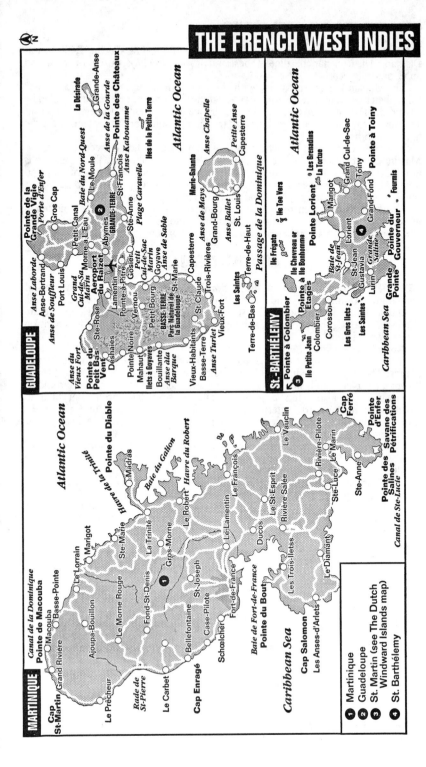

THE FRENCH WEST INDIES

MARTINIQUE

Atlantic Ocean

Canal de la Dominique
Pointe de Macouba
Cap
St-Martin Grand Rivière
Macouba
Basse-Pointe
Ajoupa-Bouillon
Le Lorrain
Le Morne Rouge
Marigot
Fond-St-Denis
Case-Pilote
Bellefontaine
Le Carbet
Schœlcher
Le Prêcheur
Rade de St-Pierre
Cap Enragé
Les Anses-d'Arlets
Le Diamant
Cap Salomon
Baie de Fort-de-France
Pointe du Bout
Fort-de-France
Le Lamentin
St-Joseph
Gros-Morne
Ste-Marie
La Trinité
Le Robert
Havre du Robert
Le François
Le Vauclin
Madras
Baie du Galion
Havre de la Trinité
Pointe du Diable
Pointe des Salines
Savane des Pétrifications
Canal de Ste-Lucie
Caribbean Sea
Les Trois-Îlets
Rivière-Salée
Ducos
Le St-Esprit
Rivière-Pilote
Le Marin
Ste-Luce
Ste-Anne
Le Vauclin
Cap Ferré
Pointe d'Enfer

GUADELOUPE

Atlantic Ocean

Grande-Anse
La Désirade
Anse de la Gourde
Pointe des Châteaux
Pointe de la Grande Vigie
Grande-Anse
Porte d'Enfer
Gros Cap
Baie du Nord-Ouest
Le Moule
Anse Kabouanne
Îles de la Petite Terre
St-François
Anse-Bertrand
Anse Laborde
Port Louis
Anse de Souffleur
Petit-Canal
Grand Cul-de-Sac Marin
Morne à l'Eau
Abymes
Aeroport du Raizet
Pointe-à-Pitre
Ste-Anne
St-Francois
Plage Caravelle
Pointe du Petit Bas-Vent
Anse du Vieux Fort
Ste-Rose
Deshaies
Pointe Noire
Mahaut
Îlets à Goyaves
Lamentin
Vernou
Petit-Bourg
Petit Cul-de-Sac Marin
Goyave
Anse de Sable
Capesterre
Ste-Marie
Bouillante
Anse à la Barque
BASSE-TERRE
Parc Naturel de la Guadeloupe
Vieux-Habitants
St-Claude
Basse-Terre
Anse Turlet
Trois-Rivières
Vieux-Fort
GRANDE-TERRE

Marie-Galante
Anse Chapelle
Petite Anse
Capesterre
Anse de Mays
Grand-Bourg
Anse Ballet
St. Louis
Les Saintes
Terre-de-Haut
Terre-de-Bas

Passage de la Dominique

St-BARTHÉLEMY

Atlantic Ocean

Pointe à Colombier
Île Petite Jean
Colombier
Corosso
Pointe à
Étangs
Les Gros Îlets :
Les Saintes
Lurin
Pointe du Gouverneur
Grande Pointe
Grande Saline
Gustavia
St-Jean
Baie de St-Jean
Marigot
Lorient
Pointe Lorient
Île Chevreau ou Île Bonhomme
Île Frégate
Île Toc Vers
Les Grenadins
La Tortue
Grand Cul-de-Sac
Toiny
Grand-Fond
Pointe du
Pointe à Toiny
Fourmis

Caribbean Sea

Caribbean Sea

① Martinique
② Guadeloupe
③ St. Martin (see The Dutch Windward Islands map)
④ St. Barthélemy

Martinique has only big hills, reaching peaks of 1,500 feet at Vauclin, 1,400 feet at Diamant. The irregular coastline of the island provides five bays, dozens of coves, and miles of sandy beaches.

The climate is relatively mild, with the average temperature in the 75° to 85° Fahrenheit range. At higher elevations it's considerably cooler. The island is cooled by a wind the French called *alizé*, and rain is frequent but doesn't last very long. From late August to November might be called the rainy season. April to September are the hottest months.

The early Carib peoples, who gave Columbus such a hostile reception, called Martinique "the island of flowers," and indeed it has remained so. The vegetation is lush, and includes hibiscus, poinsettias, bougainvillea, coconut palms, and mango trees. Almost any fruit that can grow in the ground sprouts out of Martinique's soil—pineapples, avocados, bananas, papayas, and custard apples.

Birdwatchers are often pleased at the number of hummingbirds. The mountain whistler, the blackbird, the mongoose, and multicolored butterflies are also spotted. After sunset, there's a permanent concert of grasshoppers, frogs, and crickets.

ORIENTATION

GETTING THERE Lamentin International Airport lies outside the village of Lamentin, a 15-minute taxi ride east of Fort-de-France and a 40-minute taxi ride northeast of Trois Ilets peninsula. Most flights to Martinique and Guadeloupe require a transfer on a neighboring island, although Air France operates a handful of nonstop flights from Miami.

American Airlines (tel. toll free 800/433-7300) flies into the hub in San Juan, where passengers transfer to an **American Eagle** flight heading to the French islands. The Eagle's schedule calls for a daily nonstop departure from San Juan at 8:40pm; the plane lands first on Guadeloupe and then continues on to Martinique. American Eagle also offers a separate daily nonstop flight from San Juan to Guadeloupe in the early afternoon. From there, Martinique-bound passengers transfer to one of the Air France commuter flights that shuttle frequently between the two islands.

Consult an American Airlines reservations clerk about booking your hotel simultaneously with your airfare, since substantial deductions sometimes apply if you handle both tasks at the same time.

Air France (tel. toll free 800/237-2747) flies from Miami to Martinique (with continuing service to Guadeloupe) twice every Sunday and twice every Monday. Passengers who need to return to the U.S. mainland any other day of the week usually request transfers at San Juan via American. Air France also flies separate daily nonstops from Paris's Charles de Gaulle airport to both Guadeloupe and Martinique.

Air Canada (tel. toll free 800/776-3000) has flights that depart from Canadian soil every Saturday. One of them originates in Toronto, touches down briefly in Montréal, then continues nonstop to Martinique. The other originates in Toronto late enough in the morning to permit transfers from Montréal, then flies nonstop to Guadeloupe.

Leeward Islands Air Transport (LIAT) (tel. 212/779-2731 in New York City, or toll free 800/253-5011), based in Antigua, flies from Antigua to both Martinique and Guadeloupe several times a day, sometimes with connections on to Barbados. Both Antigua and Barbados are important air-terminus links for incoming flights on either American (see above) or **BWIA** (tel. toll free 800/327-7401) from New York and Miami.

Minerve Airlines, a French charter company, operates direct weekly flights on Saturday from New York's JFK International Airport to Martinique and Guadeloupe. Most of the flights' seats, however, are offered in conjunction with 7-night packages available through several major Caribbean wholesalers. For more information, call **Council Charter,** 205 East 42nd Street, New York, NY 10017 (tel. 212/661-4546, or toll free 800/765-6065).

GETTING AROUND   By Bus and Taxi Collectif   There are two types of buses operating on Martinique. Regular buses, called *les grands busses,* hold about 40 passengers and cost 5F to 10F (95¢ to $1.95) to go anywhere within the city limits of Fort-de-France. But to travel beyond the city limits, *taxis collectifs* are used. These are privately owned minivans that traverse the island and bear the sign TC. Their routes are flexible and depend on passenger need. A simple one-way fare is 25.55F ($4.95) from Fort-de-France to Ste-Anne. Taxis collectifs depart from the heart of Fort-de-France from the parking lot of Pointe Simon. There is no phone number to call for information about this unpredictable means of transport, and there are no set schedules. Traveling in a taxi collectif is for the adventurous tourist—they are crowded and not very comfortable.

By Taxi   Travel by taxi is popular but expensive. Most of the cabs aren't metered, and you'll have to agree on the price of the ride before getting in. Most visitors arriving at Lamentin Airport head for one of the resorts along the peninsula of Pointe du Bout. To do so costs about 142F ($27.30) during the day, about 200F ($38.45) for two in the evening. Night fares are in effect from 8pm to 6am, when 40% surcharges are added.

   If you want to rent a taxi for the day, it's better to have a party of at least three or four people to keep costs low. Depending on the size of the car, expect to pay 510F ($98.05) and up for a 5-hour trip. Only a few of the drivers will be able to speak English, however.

By Rental Car   The scattered nature of Martinique's geography makes renting a car especially tempting. Martinique has several local car-rental agencies, but clients have complained of mechanical difficulties and billing irregularities. I recommend renting from one of America's "big three" (Hertz, Budget, and Avis). A valid driver's license, such as one from the United States or Canada, is needed to rent a car for up to 20 days. After that, an International Driver's License is required.

   Budget Rent-a-Car, Lamentin Airport Fort-de-France (tel. 51-22-88, or toll free 800/527-0700), usually offers slightly lower prices than its competitors. For example, Budget's least expensive car costs around $253 per week, plus tax. The lowest price for similar cars at **Hertz,** rue Ernest-Deproge, 24, Fort-de-France (tel. 51-28-22, or toll free 800/654-3001), and **Avis,** rue Ernest-Deproge, 4, Fort-de-France (tel. 70-11-60, or toll free 800/331-2112) is $304 and $266, respectively, plus tax.

   Remember that regardless of which company you choose, you'll be hit with a whopping 14% value-added tax (VAT) on top of the final bill. Collision-damage waivers (CDWs), an excellent idea in a country where the populace drives somewhat recklessly, cost an additional $9 to $11 per day, depending on the company.

   Each of the companies maintains a kiosk in the arrivals hall of the island's Lamentin Airport, with staffs willing to transport prospective renters to pickup depots a short drive away. Prices are usually lower if you reserve a car in North America at least 2 business days before your arrival. Renters must be 21 years old at Hertz and Avis, and 23 at Budget.

By Ferry   The least expensive way to go between Quai d'Esnambuc in Fort-de-France and Pointe du Bout is by ferry (*vedette*), costing 12F ($2.30) per passenger. Ferry schedules are printed in the free visitor's guide, *Choubouloute,* which is distributed by the tourist office. However, if the weather is bad, the service may be cancelled.

   Ferry service has been expanded between Fort-de-France and the little beach resorts of Anse Mitan and Anse-à-l'Ane, which are across the bay and are home to many small hotels and a multitude of Créole restaurants. A boat departs daily from Quai d'Esnambuc in Fort-de-France every 30 minutes from 6am to 7pm. The piers at Anse Mitan and Anse-à-l'Ane are departure points for those areas. The trip takes only about 15 minutes.

By Bicycle and Motorbike   In cooperation with local bike clubs, the **Parc**

Naturel Regional, boulevard Général-de-Gaulle, 9 (tel. 73-19-30), has designed some unusual itineraries. Bicycles and motorbikes are rentable from **Discount** in Pointe du Bout (tel. 66-33-05), as well as **Funny** in Fort-de-France (tel. 63-33-05). The new 18-speed VTT (*velo tout terrain,* or all-terrain bike) is revolutionizing cycling.

For tour information on the "mountain" bike, contact Jacques Vartel, **VT Tilt,** Anse Mitan (tel. 66-01-01). A tour in the rain forest, for example, costs 400F ($76.90).

THE CUISINE   Many travel-wise visitors wing in to Martinique just to sample its Créole cookery. The food served here, at least in my opinion, is the best in the Caribbean. The island's chefs have been called "seasoned sorcerers."

In honor of its African roots, Créole cooking is based on seafood, often bought by the chef "fresh from the Caribbean Sea." Out in the country, every cook has his or her own herb garden, as the Martinique cuisine is highly seasoned with herbs and spices. Except in the major hotels, most restaurants are family run, offering real homemade cooking. Best of all, you usually get to dine al fresco.

Stuffed, stewed, skewered, or broiled langoustes, clams, conchs, oysters, and octopuses are presented to you with French taste and subtlety but with martiniquais skill and invention. Every good chef knows how to make **colombo,** a spicy rich stew of poultry, pork, or beef, served with rice, herbs, sauces, and a variety of seeds. Another Créole favorite is **calalou** (callaloo in English), a soup flavored with savory herbs. Yet another traditional French West Indian dish is **blaff,** fresh seafood poached in clear stock and usually seasoned with hot peppers.

Incidentally, watch those Sunday closings.

CARNIVAL   If you like masquerades and dancing in the streets, you should attend carnival, or "Vaval" as it's known here. The event of the year, carnival begins right after the New Year, as each village prepares costumes and floats. Weekend after weekend, frenzied celebrations take place, reaching fever pitch just before Lent.

Fort-de-France is the focal point, and the spirit of the carnival envelops the island, as narrow streets are jammed with floats. On Ash Wednesday the streets of Fort-de-France are filled with *diablesses,* or she-devils (portrayed by members of both sexes). Costumed in black and white, they crowd the streets to form King Carnival's funeral procession. As devils cavort about and the rum flows, a funeral pyre is built at La Savane. When it's set on fire, the dancing of those "she-devils" becomes frantic (many are thoroughly drunk at this point).

Long past dusk, the cortège takes the coffin to its burial, ending carnival until another year.

FAST FACTS   MARTINIQUE

Area Code   Martinique is *not* part of the Caribbean's 809 area code. For information on telephone calls from North America, see "Telephone," below.

Banking Hours   Banks are open Monday through Friday from 7:30am to noon and 2:30 to 4pm.

Consulate   The **U.S. Consulate** is at rue Blénac, 14, in Fort-de-France (tel. 63-13-03).

Currency   The **French franc (F)** is the legal tender here. Exchange your money at banks because they give much better rates than hotels. Currency quotations in this chapter are both in U.S. dollars and French francs. At press time, 1 franc is exchanged for 19¢ U.S. (5.2F = $1 U.S.). Of course, exchange rates are subject to fluctuations and are quoted only for your general guidelines.

Currency Exchange   A money exchange service, **Change Caraïbes** (tel. 51-51-51, ext. 1141), operates daily at the Arrivals Building at Lamentin Airport.

Customs   Items for personal use, such as tobacco, cameras, and film, are admitted without formalities or tax if not in excessive quantity.

Documents   U.S. and Canadian citizens need proof of identity (a voter registration card or birth certificate, plus a photo ID, or a passport) for stays of less than 21 days. After that, a valid passport is required. A return or ongoing ticket is also necessary.

Drugstores   Try the **Pharmacie de la Paix,** at the corner of rue Perrinon and rue Victor-Schoelcher in Fort-de-France (tel. 71-94-83).

Electricity   Electricity here is 220 volts AC, 50 cycles, the same as that used on the French mainland. However, check with your hotel to see if they have converted the electrical voltage and outlets in the bathrooms (some have). If they haven't, bring your own transformer and adapter for U.S. appliances; don't count on the hotel's.

Emergencies   Call the **police** at 17, report a **fire** at 18, and summon an **ambulance** at 70-36-48.

Hospitals   There's a 24-hour emergency room at **Hôpital La Meynard,** Châteauboeuf, right outside Fort-de-France (tel. 50-15-15).

Information   The **Office Départmental du Tourisme** (tourist office) is at rue Ernest-Deproge (B.P. 520), 97206 Fort-de-France, Martinique F.W.I. (tel. 63-79-60).

Languages   French, the official language, is spoken by almost everyone. The local Créole patois uses words borrowed from France, England, Spain, and Africa. In the wake of increased tourism, English is occasionally spoken in the major hotels, restaurants, and tourist organizations. But don't count on driving around the countryside and asking for directions in English. The Martiniquais aren't that bilingual yet.

Medical Care   Health services and medical equipment are both modern and comprehensive. There are some 18 hospitals and clinics on the island. In an emergency, your hotel can put you in touch with the nearest one.

Safety   Crime is hardly rampant on Martinique, yet there are still those who prey on unsuspecting tourists. Follow the usual precautions here, especially in Fort-de-France (a large Caribbean city) or in the tourist-hotel belt of Pointe du Bout. It would also be wise to protect your valuables and never leave them unguarded on the beach.

Telephone   To call Martinique from the U.S., if your long-distance telephone company is equipped to handle international direct dialing, dial 011 (the international access code), then 596 (the country code for the French West Indies), and finally the six-digit local number. If you cannot direct-dial internationally, dial 0 ("zero," for the operator) and tell the operator you wish to make an international call; once you are transferred to the international operator, state the 596 country code and then the local number, and the operator will dial the call for you. To make a call within Martinique, only the six-digit local number is necessary. *Note:* In this chapter, only the local numbers are given.

Time   Martinique time is 1 hour later than eastern standard time, except when daylight saving time is in effect. Then Martinique time is the same as the East Coast of the United States.

Water   Potable water is found throughout the island.

Weather   The climate is relatively mild—the average temperature is in the 75° to 85° Fahrenheit range.

FORT-DE-FRANCE

A mélange of New Orleans and Menton (French Riviera), Fort-de-France is the main town of Martinique and lies at the end of a large bay surrounded by evergreen hills. Iron-grillwork balconies overflowing with flowers are commonplace here.

The people of Martinique are even more fascinating than the town. Today the

Créole women are likely to be seen in jeans instead of their traditional turbans and Empress Joséphine–style gowns, but they still have the same walk. Heads held high, shoulders up, they have a jaunty spring. They're a proud people, and I miss their massive earrings that used to jounce and sway as they sauntered along.

Narrow streets climb up the steep hills on which houses have been built to catch the overflow of the capital's more than 100,000 inhabitants.

WHERE TO STAY

Rates are sometimes advertised in U.S. dollars, sometimes in French francs, and sometimes in a combination of the two currencies. It depends on the individual hotel.

HOTEL LA BATELIERE, route 32, 97200 Schoelcher, Martinique, F.W.I. Tel. 61-49-49. Fax 61-62-29. 194 rms (all with bath), 6 duplexes and suite. A/C MINIBAR TV TEL
$ Rates (including breakfast): Winter, 1,050F–1,250F ($201.90–$240.40) single; 1,300F–1,400F ($250–$269.20) double; from 2,200F ($423.05) suite. Summer, 750F–980F ($144.25–$188.45) single; 920F–1,020F ($176.90–$196.15) double; from 1,650F ($317.30) suite. Buffet breakfast 65F ($12.50) extra. AE, DC, MC, V. **Parking:** Free.
This waterside French-modern hotel is a white stucco structure, set back in a garden from its wide private beach. The hotel lacks super-glamour but successfully offers many water sports, social activities, dining choices, and a nightlife scene complete with casino and disco. Each unit contains a tile bath, but best of all are the roomwide glass doors that open onto your own water-view terrace.

In the Blue Marine dining room, French, international, and Créole cuisine is served, and there's a pizzeria near the swimming pool. Scuba diving, snorkeling, windsurfing, sailing, and waterskiing are available at rates that depend on the season and duration. Tennis is free, except at night when there's a surcharge. On the premises are a beauty salon and barbershop and a sauna.

HOTEL L'IMPERATRICE, place de la Savane, rue de la Liberté, 97200 Fort-de-France, Martinique, F.W.I. Tel. 63-06-82. Fax 72-66-30. 24 rms (15 with bath). A/C TEL
$ Rates (including breakfast): 300F–355F ($57.70–$68.25) single without bath, 420F ($80.75) single with bath; 375F–420F ($72.10–$80.75) double without bath, 510F ($98.05) double with bath. MC, V. **Parking:** Free.
Favored by businesspeople, this stucco-sided hotel faces a landscaped mall in the heart of town, near the water's edge and close to the tourist office. Originally built in the 1950s and named in honor of one of Martinique's most famous exports (Joséphine), it has encircling balconies overlooking the traffic at the western edge of the sprawling promenade known as the Savane. The lounge has large, white wickerwork chairs and an adjoining bar. Or you may prefer the second-floor bar, whose trademark colors of green and white have been repainted (but never changed) since its original construction. The bedrooms are modern and functional, and many contain TV sets. The front rooms tend to be noisy; yet, to compensate, windows overlook the life along the Savane. The hotel's restaurant, Le Joséphine, does a brisk business with local shoppers in town for the day.

LE LAFAYETTE, rue de la Liberté, 5, 97200 Fort-de-France, Martinique, F.W.I. Tel. 73-80-50. Fax 60-97-75. 42 rms (all with bath). A/C MINIBAR TV TEL
$ Rates: Winter, 665F ($127.90) single; 820F ($157.70) double. Summer, 500F ($96.15) single; 600F ($115.40) double. Breakfast 30F ($5.75) extra. AE, DC, MC, V. **Parking:** Free.
You'll enter this modern hotel, located right on La Savane, through rue Victor-Hugo; the reception hall is up a few steps of terra-cotta. The dark-brown wooden doors are offset by the soft beige walls. Japanese wall tapestries decorate the bedrooms, and most rooms contain twin beds in a dark-brown wood. Bathrooms are in pure white, and the overall impression is of a neat, but simple hostelry.

WHERE TO DINE

EL RACO, rue Lazare-Carnot, 23. Tel. 73-29-16.
Cuisine: FRENCH/SPANISH. **Reservations:** Not required.
$ Prices: Appetizers 33F–120F ($6.35–$23.10); main courses 70F–160F ($13.45–$30.75). MC, V.
Open: Lunch Tues–Fri noon–3pm; dinner Mon–Sat 7–10pm. **Closed:** Aug.

Life seems little changed since 1945 in the commercial and residential neighborhood near La Savane where you'll find El Raco. For such a small place, the menu is elaborate. You can ask the chef to prepare a classic paella, perhaps preceded by gazpacho or Catalan eggs. Sophisticated vintages of wine can be selected by the glass.

LE COQ HARDI, rue Martin-Luther-King, 52. Tel. 71-59-64.
Cuisine: STEAK/GRILLS. **Reservations:** Recommended. **Transportation:** Take a taxi (2-minute ride) north from the main square (La Savane) of Fort-de-France.
$ Prices: Appetizers 50F–70F ($9.60–$13.45); main courses 80F–155F ($15.40–$29.80). AE, MC, V.
Open: Lunch Sun–Fri noon–2pm; dinner daily 7:30–11pm.

The premier steakhouse on Martinique is maintained by one of the island's most likable and realistic restaurateurs, Alphonse Sintive. Trained as a master butcher and *charcutier* before World War II on the French mainland, he can regale you, if he chooses, with stories of his experiences in the French Foreign Legion in Indochina and Algeria. The juicy steaks and chops are imported from France and grilled over a wood fire. You'll find this restaurant beside a steeply inclined traffic artery, which crisscrosses a residential hillside just outside the center of town. Hearty eaters will appreciate the large portions.

LE LAFAYETTE, in Le Lafayette Hôtel, rue de la Liberté, 5. Tel. 63-24-09.
Cuisine: CREOLE/FRENCH. **Reservations:** Recommended.
$ Prices: Appetizers 40F–70F ($7.70–$13.45); main courses 90F–140F ($17.30–$26.90); fixed-price three-course (plus coffee) meal 140F ($26.90). AE, DC, MC, V.
Open: Lunch Mon–Sat 12:30–2:30pm; dinner Mon–Sat 7:30–11pm.

Elegant and expensive, Le Lafayette offers a refined cuisine and many memories of mainland France. With its china, silver, and crystal, a profusion of beautiful flowers, and walls hung with original art, it's the most fashionable place to dine in Fort-de-France. The combination of the traditional Créole recipes with new and light renditions of classic French cuisine has won applause from many discerning critics. Try, if featured, the shrimp in puff pastry with spinach, salmon gros sel in olive oil, veal kidneys, or one of four or more sophisticated adaptations of Créole dishes.

WHAT TO SEE & DO

A museum credit card, sold for 35F ($6.75), at any of the island museums, allows entry to all others.

At the center of the town lies a broad garden planted with many palms and mangoes, **La Savane,** a handsome savannah with shops and cafés lining its sides. In the middle of this grand square stands a statue of Joséphine, "Napoleon's little Créole," made of white marble by Vital Debray. With the grace of a Greek goddess, the statue poses in a Regency gown and looks toward Trois-Ilets, where she was born.

After viewing her, you can head for the **St. Louis Roman Catholic Cathedral,** on rue Victor-Schoelcher, built in 1875. It's an extraordinary iron building, which someone once likened to "a sort of Catholic railway station."

A statue in front of the Palais de Justice is of the island's second main historical figure, Victor Schoelcher (you'll see his name a lot in Martinique). As mentioned, he worked to free the slaves more than a century ago.

The **Bibliothèque Schoelcher,** rue de la Liberté, also honors this popular hero. The elaborate structure was first displayed at the Paris Exposition of 1889.

However, the Romanesque portal in red and blue, the Egyptian lotus-petal columns, even the turquoise tiles were imported piece by piece from Paris and reassembled here.

Guarding the port is **Fort St-Louis,** built in the Vauban style on a rocky promontory. In addition, **Fort Tartenson** and **Fort Desaix** stand on hills overlooking the port.

The **Musée Départemental de la Martinique,** rue de la Liberté, 9 (tel. 71-57-05), the one bastion on Martinique that preserves its pre-Columbian past, has relics left from the early settlers, the peaceful Arawaks, and the cannibalistic Caribs. The museum is at the same location as the government-sponsored Caribbean Art Center, facing the Savane. The museum is open Monday through Friday from 9am to 1pm and 2 to 5pm, and on Saturday from 9am to noon, charging 8F ($1.55) for adults and 3F (60¢) for children.

Sacré-Coeur de Balata Cathedral, at Balata, overlooking Fort-de-France, is a copy of the one looking down upon Montmartre in Paris—and this one is just as incongruous, maybe more so. It's reached by going along route de la Trace (route N3). Balata is 6 miles north of Fort-de-France.

A few minutes away on route N3, **Le Jardin de Balata (Balata Garden)** (tel. 64-48-73) is a tropical botanical park. The park was created by Jean-Philippe Thoze on land the jungle was rapidly reclaiming around a Créole house that belonged to his grandmother. He has also restored the house, furnishing it with antiques and engravings depicting life in other days, and with bouquets and baskets of fruit renewed daily. The garden contains flowers, shrubs, and trees growing in profusion and offering a vision of tropical splendor. Balata is open daily from 9am to 5pm. Admission is 30F ($5.75) for adults, 10F ($1.95) for children.

The 15,000-square-foot Martinique Aquarium, boulevard de Marne (tel. 73-02-29) in Fort-de-France boasts 2,000 sea creatures of more than 250 species, offering visitors of all ages a chance to learn about the varied marine life that inhabits Martinique's surrounding waters, as well as the oceans of the world. Special features include a shark tank and a 59-foot aquaterrarium, home to a school of piranhas. Open daily from 9am to 7pm, it charges 38F ($7.30) for adults and 24F ($4.60) for children.

AN EXCURSION TO TROIS-ILETS

Marie-Josèphe-Rose Tascher de la Pagerié was born here in 1763. As Joséphine, she was to become the wife of Napoléon I and empress of France from 1804 to 1809. She'd been married before to Alexandre de Beauharnais, who'd actually wanted to wed either of her two more attractive sisters. Six years older than Napoleon, she pretended that she'd lost her birth certificate so he wouldn't find out her true age. Although many historians call her ruthless and selfish (certainly unfaithful), she is still revered by some in Martinique as an uncommonly gracious lady. Others have less kind words for her, because Napoleon is said by some historians to have "reinvented" slavery, and blame Joséphine's influence.

After 20 miles of driving south from Fort-de-France, you reach Trois-Ilets, a charming little village. One mile outside the hamlet, turn left to **La Pagerié,** where a small museum (tel. 68-34-55) of mementoes relating to Joséphine has been installed in the former estate kitchen. Along with her childhood bed in the kitchen, you'll see a passionate letter from Napoleon. The collection was compiled by Dr. Robert Rose-Rosette. Here Joséphine gossiped with her slaves and played the guitar.

Still remaining are the partially restored ruins of the Pagerié sugar mill and the church (in the village itself) where she was christened in 1763. The plantation was destroyed in a hurricane. The museum is open Tuesday through Sunday from 8:30am to 5pm, charging 15F ($2.90) for admission.

A botanical garden, **Parc des Floralies,** is adjacent to the golf course Golf de l'Impératrice Joséphine, as is the museum devoted to Joséphine described above.

Maison de la Canne, Pointe Vatable (tel. 68-32-04), stands on the road to Trois-Ilets. (From Fort-de-France, you can take a taxi or shuttle bus to La Marina, Pointe du Bout; from there, a bus heads for Pointe Vatable.) It was created in 1987 to

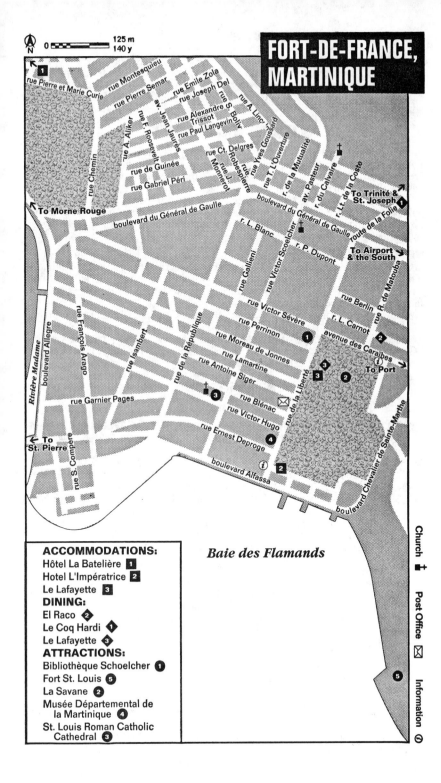

FORT-DE-FRANCE, MARTINIQUE

0   125 m / 140 y

N

rue Pierre et Marie Curie

rue Montesquieu

rue Pierre Semar

rue Emile Zola

rue Joseph Del

av. Jean Jaurès

rue F. Roosevelt

rue A. Aliker

rue Chemin

rue S. Boliv

rue Alexandre
Trissot

rue Paul Langevin

rue A. Linc

rue Ct. Delgres

rue de Guinée

rue Gabriel Péri

rue J. Monnerot

rue J. Robespierre

rue Yves Goussard

rue T. L'Ouverture

rue de la Mutualité

av. Pasteur

r. du Calvaire

r. Lt. de la Coste

**To Trinité &
St. Joseph**

route de la Folie

boulevard du Général de Gaulle

To Morne Rouge

boulevard du Général de Gaulle

r. L. Blanc

rue Victor Scœlcher

r. P. Dupont

**To Airport
& the South**

rue Galliéni

rue Berlin

R. de Matouba

rue Victor Sévère

rue Perrinon

r. L. Carnot

avenue des Caraïbes

rue Moreau de Jonnes

rue Lamartine

rue Antoine Siger

rue de la République

rue Isambert

rue François Arago

boulevard Allègre

Rivière Madame

rue Garnier Pages

rue S. Compère

rue Blénac

rue de la Liberté

To Port

rue Victor Hugo

rue Ernest Deproge

boulevard Alfassa

boulevard Chevalier de Sainte-Marthe

**To
St. Pierre**

Baie des Flamands

Church **✝**

Post Office **✉**

Information **ⓘ**

house a remarkable permanent exhibition that tells the story of sugarcane with panels, models, tools, a miniature slave ship, an ancient plow tethered to life-size models of two oxen, a restored carriage, and a copper still. Hostesses guide visitors through the exhibition. It's open Tuesday through Sunday from 9:30am to 5:30pm, with an admission of 15F ($2.90).

POINTE DU BOUT

Pointe du Bout is a narrow, irregularly shaped peninsula across the bay from Fort-de-France. Over the past few years it has become Martinique's primary resort area, primarily because of four major hotels—the PLM Azur Carayou, PLM Azur Pagerié, Bakoua, and Méridien.

In addition to these hotels and others, you'll find a Robert Trent Jones–designed golf course, a dozen tennis courts, several restaurants, a marina, a gambling casino, discos, swimming pools, and facilities for horseback riding, waterskiing, scuba diving, snorkeling, and volleyball.

GETTING THERE   To drive there from Fort-de-France, leave by route 1, which takes you for a few minutes along the autoroute. You cross the plain of Lamentin, the industrial area of Fort-de-France and the site of the international airport. Very frequently the air is filled with the fragrance of caramel because of the large sugarcane factories in the surrounding area.

After 20 miles of driving, you reach Trois-Ilets, Joséphine's hometown. Three miles farther on your right, take the D38 to Pointe du Bout.

For those who want to reach Pointe du Bout by sea, there's a ferry service (see "Getting Around," in "Orientation," above), running all day long (until midnight) from Fort-de-France for 12F ($2.30) fare.

WHERE TO STAY
Expensive

HOTEL BAKOUA-SOFITEL, Pointe du Bout, 97229 Trois-Ilets, Martinique, F.W.I. Tel. 66-02-02, or toll free 800/221-4542. Fax 66-00-41. 132 rms, 6 suites. A/C TV TEL

$ **Rates** (including breakfast): Winter, 1,500F–1,750F ($288.45–$336.55) single; 2,000F–2,500F ($384.60–$480.75) double; from 3,500F ($673.05) suite. Summer, 1,000F–1,250F ($192.30–$240.40) single; 1,500F–2,000F ($288.45–$384.60) double; from 2,500F ($480.75) suite. AE, DC, MC, V. **Parking:** Free.

Considered a famous and desirable hotel with a long history of glamour, this hostelry is known for the beauty of its landscaping and its position on a hillside somewhat removed from the bustle of the many hotels that surround it, 17 miles from the airport. Run by the Sofitel chain, this hotel consists of three hillside buildings in the center of a garden, plus another, bungalow-type building, right on the beach. Celebrities are often attracted to the hotel. The rooms are comfortable and conservatively modern.

Dining/Entertainment: A dramatically engineered bar, crafted into a perfect circle out of exotic Caribbean hardwood, is one of the ideal rendezvous points of Pointe du Bout. The hotel contains a beachside snack bar as well as an upscale and elegant French restaurant, Le Chateaubriand. Dinner is served nightly from 7 to 10pm.

Services: Concierge, laundry, baby-sitting, free twice-daily shuttle bus to the golf course.

Facilities: Swimming pool; active sports program, including a free golf lesson and a free driving lesson; diving center; waterskiing, jet skiing, golf, and horseback riding available nearby.

HOTEL MERIDIEN TROIS-ILETS, Point du Bout, Trois-Ilets (B.P. 894, 97245 Fort-de-France), Martinique, F.W.I. Tel. 66-00-00, or toll free 800/543-4300 in the U.S. and Canada. Fax 66-04-23. 286 rms, 8 suites. A/C TV TEL

$ Rates (including buffet breakfast): Winter, 1,360F–2,500F ($261.55–$480.75) single; 1,680F–2,500F ($323.05–$480.75) double; from 3,000F ($576.90) suite. Summer, 1,080F ($207.70) single; 1,400F ($269.20) double; from 3,000F ($576.90) suite. AE, DC, MC, V. **Parking:** Free.

The largest hotel in the resort community of Pointe de Bout, with some of the most extensive facilities, is a 16-mile drive from the airport. Owned and operated by Air France, it contains a dramatically spacious reception area which opens onto the palm-fringed swimming pool, the waters of the bay, and the twinkling faraway lights of Fort-de-France. The hotel is slightly angled to follow the contours of the shoreline, so each of its bedrooms overlooks either the Caribbean or the bay. The bedrooms were renovated late in 1990, and provide much comfort. Each contains a private balcony and conservatively modern furnishings with tropical accents. Farther out on the point is an old French colonial fort.

Dining/Entertainment: The Casa Créole offers gourmet meals served by Créole waitresses dressed in regional costume. The casino provides evening glitter every night between 9pm and 3am. Around the huge block of rooms are a waterside garden, a 100-foot marina, and a cabaña bar near the swimming pool. Every Thursday night the hotel hosts the vibrant Ballets Martiniquais in a sprawling pavilion near the pool. A Créole buffet supper follows this folklore show.

Services: 24-hour room service, laundry, concierge, massage.

Facilities: Swimming pool, two tennis courts, sauna, hairdressing salon; water sports (including scuba diving, sailing, snorkeling, waterskiing, and windsurfing).

PLM AZUR CARAYOU, Pointe du Bout, 97229 Trois-Ilets, Martinique, F.W.I. Tel. 66-04-04. Fax 66-00-57. 196 rms, 1 suite. A/C MINIBAR TV TEL
$ Rates (including breakfast): Winter, 770F–970F ($148.05–$186.55) single; 1,065F–1,480F ($204.80–$284.60) double; 2,600F ($500) suite. Summer, 520F ($100) single; 670F ($128.85) double; 2,000F ($384.60) suite. AE, DC, MC, V. **Parking:** Free.

When you enter this hotel, you'll think you've come for a walk in a tropical garden. The buildings are encircled by large lawns planted with coconut or palm trees and many flowering bushes. The rooms are in two-story bungalows, each with a balcony. The view from your abode will be of gardens, a marina, or the bay of Fort-de-France. It's near the Méridien Hôtel, 16 miles from the island's airport.

Dining/Entertainment: In the Café Créole, you can order a quick lunch without disrupting your suntanning schedule; it architecturally interconnects the beach to the pool. The café is also open for dinner, and serves excellent and attractively presented food. La Boucau, the hotel's principal restaurant, has an island atmosphere of white ceilings and wooden beams, with a sweeping view of the water and of a small stage where a local combo plays music during dinner. Créole cookery, particularly the preparations of fish, is done with flair here. Taking advantage of that bay view, La Paillote is a nicely decorated bar with nautical accessories.

Services: 24-hour concierge, laundry.

Facilities: Swimming pool, a small beach with safe swimming, water sports (including windsurfing, scuba diving, waterskiing, sailboat rentals, and snorkeling).

Moderate

PLM AZUR LA PAGERIE, Pointe du Bout, 97229 Trois-Ilets, Martinique, F.W.I. Tel. 66-05-30. Fax 66-00-99. 96 rms. A/C TV TEL
$ Rates: Winter, 551F ($105.95) single; 690F ($132.70) double. Summer, 325F ($62.50) single; 390F ($75) double. Breakfast 55F ($10.60) extra. AE, DC, MC, V. **Parking:** Free.

The facilities here are relatively modest compared to those in some of the larger and more expensive hotels of Pointe du Bout, but its guests are able to compensate by visiting the many restaurants, bars, and sports facilities that proliferate nearby. Set close to the gardens of the Hôtel Bakoua, within a 16-mile drive from the airport, this moderately priced hotel offers you your own personal apartment. Accommodations are neat and uncomplicated, with contemporary lines, tile floors, and splashes of color. Each has a small refrigerator and a balcony with a view opening onto the bay, and about half of the units contain tiny kitchenettes. (There is no price supplement for rooms with kitchenette. The hotel contains a small swimming pool and a small bar, open only in the evening, near the reception area, but there is no restaurant. Clients usually walk the short distance to the establishment's neighbor hotel, the PLM Azur Carayou.

Budget

AUBERGE DE L'ANSE MITAN, Anse Mitan, 97229 Trois-Ilets, Martinique, F.W.I. Tel. 66-01-12. Fax 66-01-05. 19 rms (all with bath), 6 studios. A/C TEL

$ Rates: Winter, 330F ($63.45) single; 420F ($80.75) double; from 450F ($86.55) studio. Summer, 260F ($50) single; 330F ($63.45) double; from 350F ($67.30) studio. AE, DC, MC, V. **Parking:** Free.

Many of its guests prefer its location at the isolated end of a road whose more commercial side is laden with restaurants and a bustling nighttime parade. The hotel was originally built in 1930, but it has been renovated several times since then by the hospitable Athanase family. What you see today is a three-story concrete-box-type structure. Six of the units are studios with kitchens; all have private shower. Outsiders are welcome to have a fixed-price meal if they phone ahead. Dinner is served every night from 7:30 to 9pm. The hotel also has a cozy bar.

LA MATADORE, Anse Mitan, 97229 Trois-Ilets, Martinique, F.W.I. Tel. 66-05-36. Fax 66-07-45. 8 rms (all with bath). A/C TEL

$ Rates (including breakfast): Winter, 325F ($62.50) single; 441F ($84.80) double. Summer, 235F ($45.20) single; 300F ($57.70) double. AE, DC, MC, V. **Parking:** Free.

The bedrooms offered by this small inn, beside the main highway about a mile southwest of the tourist complex at Pointe de Bout, are considered a kind of adjunct to the establishment's main focus, which is its Créole restaurant (for more information on the restaurant, see "Where to Dine," below). Bedrooms, however, are clean and uncomplicated, appropriate for clients who plan to spend lots of time at the local beach, which lies within a short drive. Nightlife, water sports, and the bustle associated with a large resort are at Pointe de Bout, less than a mile away.

WHERE TO DINE

DAVIDIANA, La Marina, Pointe du Bout. Tel. 66-60-54.
   Cuisine: FRENCH/CREOLE. **Reservations:** Usually not required.
$ Prices: Appetizers 45F–140F ($8.65–$26.90); main courses 85F–195F ($16.35–$37.50). MC, V.
   Open: Lunch Tues–Sun noon–2:30pm; dinner daily 7–10:30pm.

This is today's incarnation of the once-famous Chez Sidonie, whose namesake chef was the most acclaimed Créole cook in Martinique. Located beside the marina, across the road from the Hôtel Méridien, the restaurant offers an inexpensive and unpretentious café on its street level, and a more dignified dining room upstairs. You might begin with fish soup or accras of codfish, and then follow with a fricassée of crayfish or a colombo of lamb. Flavors are zesty and the service is usually polite.

LA MATADORE, Anse Mitan, Trois-Ilets. Tel. 66-05-36.
   Cuisine: FRENCH/CREOLE. **Reservations:** Recommended.
$ Prices: Appetizers 40F–60F ($7.70–$11.55); main courses 80F–120F ($15.40–$23.10). AE, DC, MC, V.
   Open: Dinner only, Thurs–Tues 7–10pm.

La Matadore has long enjoyed a position as one of the most solidly entrenched French and Créole restaurants in Martinique, and I want only to add to that well-deserved reputation. (The name is not Spanish, it's Créole for "arrogant woman in full dress.") The restaurant lies beside the main highway passing through the hamlet of Anse Mitan, about a mile southwest (and a 5-minute drive) of Pointe du Bout. It has a prominent covered terrace. François and Raymonde Crico, your sophisticated hosts, will serve you crabes farcis (a land crab that has been deviled and flavored with a hot seasoning and tossed in breadcrumbs, then baked in its own shell). Also popular is red snapper simmered in a well-flavored court bouillon, and a colombo (curried stew) of mutton or baby goat. In contrast to the Créole-inspired menu, the wine list is French.

LA MOUINA, route de Redoute, km 2.5. Tel. 79-34-57.
Cuisine: FRENCH/CREOLE. **Reservations:** Required. **Transportation:** Taxi.
$ Prices: Appetizers 45F–140F ($8.65–$26.90); main courses 85F–195F ($16.35–$37.50). MC, V.
Open: Lunch Mon–Fri noon–4pm; dinner Mon–Fri 7:30–9:30pm.

La Mouïna, whose name is a Créole word for a house of reunion, is a restaurant offering one of the finest luncheons on the island. Sitting next to the police station in the suburb of Redoute, this 50-year-old white colonial house shelters the culinary domain of one of the island's most experienced groups of chefs. You might begin with crabes farcis (stuffed crabs) or escargots de Bourgogne, then follow with tournedos Rossini, rognon de veau entier grillé (grilled kidneys), or duckling in orange sauce. The owners are particularly fond of their version of red snapper en papillotte. Ask at your hotel for good directions before setting out (or even better, hire a taxi) because it's a bit hard to find.

LE CANTONNAIS, La Marina, Pointe du Bout. Tel. 66-02-33.
Cuisine: CHINESE. **Reservations:** Not required.
$ Prices: Appetizers 35F–85F ($6.75–$16.35); main courses 80F–110F ($15.40–$21.15); fixed-price meal 85F ($16.35). AE, MC, V.
Open: Lunch Sun noon–1pm; dinner Wed–Mon 6:30–11pm.

Amid a classic Chinese decor of red and gold, this moderately priced restaurant across the road from the Méridien Hôtel offers Asian food whose flavors and colors are sometimes a welcome change from a constant diet of Créole and Caribbean food. Try broiled shark fin, chicken with salted-bean sauce, or steamed ribs with black-bean sauce. The restaurant's sliced duckling with plum sauce is excellent, too. Soups include braised bird's nest with minced chicken and a soothing version of egg drop.

THE SOUTH LOOP

We now leave Pointe du Bout and head south for more sun and beaches. Resort centers here include Le Diamant and Sainte-Anne.

On the way to them from Trois-Ilets, you can follow a small curved road that brings you to **Anse-à-l'Ane, Grande Anse,** and **Anse d'Arlet.** At any of these places are small beaches, quite safe and usually not crowded.

At Anse d'Arlet the scenery is beautiful. Fishing boats draw up on the beach, and the nets are spread out to dry in the sun.

From Anse d'Arlet, route D37 takes you to Diamant. The road offers pleasant scenery.

LE DIAMANT

This village offers quite a good beach open to the winds from the south. Diamond Rock juts from the sea rising to a height of 573 feet. In a daring maneuver in 1804, the British carried ammunition and 110 sailors to the top. There, in spite of French coastal artillery bombardment, they held out for 18 months and commanded the passage between the rock and Martinique. You can visit it, but the access by small boat is considered risky.

Diamond Beach is excellent, with surf and bathing possibilities. It's lined with the familiar groves of swaying palms.

Where to Stay & Dine

HOTEL DIAMANT-LES-BAINS, 97223 Le Diamant, Martinique, F.W.I.
Tel. 76-40-14. Fax 76-27-00. 25 rms. A/C TV TEL.
$ Rates (including breakfast): Winter, 380F–480F ($73.05–$92.30) single; 500F–

600F ($96.15–$115.40) double. Summer, 290F–400F ($55.75–$76.90) single; 400F–500F ($76.90–$96.15) double. MC, V. **Parking:** Free. **Closed:** Early Sept to early Oct.

This is a simple, unpretentious, family-style hotel based in a cluster of cottages grouped beneath palm trees at the edge of the water. The cultivated gardens surrounding the bungalows have lounge chairs and a swimming pool, where you can sit and enjoy the view of Diamond Rock. A handful of the units are motellike beachside bungalows. Most accommodations have red-tile floors, small refrigerators, built-in furniture made from polished fruitwoods, and lots of tilework.

The main building, with its upper-deck bedrooms, houses the restaurant where you can dine on the terrace with a view of the sea. You can sample classic Créole specialties, such as crab salad, spicy black pudding, and a fish blaff, and finish with a coconut flan. The cuisine is mostly Créole, with some French dishes. The chef features locally caught fish.

NOVOTEL LE DIAMANT, 97223 Le Diamant, Martinique, F.W.I. Tel. 76-42-42, or toll free 800/221-4542. Fax 76-22-87. 173 rms, 6 suites. A/C MINIBAR TV TEL

$ Rates (including buffet breakfast): Winter, 925F–1,235F ($177.90–$237.50) single; 1,070F–1,690F ($205.75–$325) double; from 2,200F ($423.05) suite. Summer, 655F ($125.95) single; 830F ($159.60) double; from 1,500F ($288.45) suite. AE, DC, MC, V. **Parking:** Free.

Two miles outside the village and 18 miles south of Fort-de-France on 6 acres of lushly forested land, the Novotel resort is in one of the most beautiful districts on Martinique—on a rock-bordered peninsula that was famous as an 18th-century stronghold of the (eventually defeated) English. Today it serves as one of the Novotel chain's most prominent and talked-about Caribbean properties.

From many of the bedrooms, the views are more evocative of the South Pacific than of the Caribbean. Units face either the pool or the coast, with its expansive view of Diamond Rock, and are tropical and elegant. The reception opens onto a large pool which you cross on a Chinese-style wooden bridge to connect with the dining facilities. Outside the hotel, the neighboring beaches aren't too crowded, and the view of the Caribbean is splendid in most directions. Lawns and gardens, as well as tennis courts, surround the hotel. Water sports are also offerd. The trip from the airport in a taxi should take about 35 minutes.

SAINTE-ANNE

As you follow the road south to Trois Rivières you'll come to **Sainte-Luce,** perhaps one of the island's most charming villages. Beautiful beaches surround the town, and it's the site of the Forêt Montravail. Continuing, you'll reach Rivière Pilote, quite a large town, and **Le Marin,** at the bottom of a bay of the same name.

From Le Marin, a 5-mile drive brings you to Sainte-Anne, at the extreme southern tip of Martinique. This is a sleepy little village, with white sand beaches. It opens onto views of the Sainte Lucia Canal, and nearby is the site of the Petrified Savannah Forest. The French call it **Savane des Pétrifications.** It's a field of petrified volcanic boulders in the shape of logs. The eerie, desertlike site, no-man's-land, is studded with cacti. The region is so barren you'll not want to linger long.

After passing Le Marin, you reach **Vauclin,** a fishing port and market town that is pre-Columbus. If you have time, stop in at the 18th-century **Chapel of the Holy Virgin.** Visitors like to make an excursion to **Mount Vauclin,** the highest point in southern Martinique. There they are rewarded with one of the most scenic panoramas in the West Indies.

Where to Stay

LA DUNETTE, 97227 Sainte-Anne, Martinique, F.W.I. Tel. 76-73-90. Fax 76-76-05. 18 rms. A/C TEL

$ Rates (including continental breakfast): Winter, $57–$73 single; $82–$109 double. Summer, $55–$65 single; $60–$73 double. MC, V. **Parking:** Free.

If you want to stay in Sainte-Anne, I recommend La Dunette, a motellike structure on the water a 50-minute drive south of the airport. It's near Club Med and the white sandy beaches of the Salines. The seaside inn is protected by a garden filled with flowers and tropical plants. The furnishings are in casual modern, and some of the units are quite small.

In the evening guests gather for drinks on the terrace above the sea. The restaurant is closed off-season. Water sports and excursions can be arranged for you, even a jaunt to watch a mongoose fight a snake.

LES BOUCANIERS [BUCCANEER'S CREEK] CLUB MEDITERRANEE, Point-Marin, 97227 Sainte-Anne, Martinique, F.W.I. Tel. 76-76-13, or toll free 800/258-2633. Fax 76-72-02. 313 rms. A/C

$ Rates (including all meals and sports): Winter, $820–$1580 per person per week, double occupancy, with increases at Christmas. Spring, summer, and fall, $770 per person per week, double occupancy. Single occupancy is granted in any season only if space is available, for a supplement of 30% over the going rate for the week of your visit. Children under 12 not accepted. AE, MC, V. **Parking:** Free.

Set on a peaceful cove at the southernmost tip of Martinique, about a 50-minute drive from the airport, this resort offers all-inclusive packages. Designed as a series of scattered outbuildings reminiscent of a Créole village, the club is set on the 48-acre site of a former pirate's hideaway at Buccaneer's Creek, amid a forest of coconut palms. Accommodations are in comfortable bungalows with twin beds and private shower baths. Although many Club Meds welcome children enthusiastically, this particular club is most fully geared to single guests or couples. The emphasis is often on group activities, with much ado over communal gatherings and conviviality, and meals are consumed at long tables whose seating plans are sometimes conducive to meeting other guests.

Dining/Entertainment: In a domed two-level building in the heart of the resort, you'll find an amusement center, a theater, dance floor, and bar. A walk along rue du Port (the main street of Club Med) leads to a conically roofed circular Tour du Port, a bar that overlooks the sailboat fleet anchored in the marina. Nonguests on a tour of Martinique are welcome to stop in and enjoy a large buffet with Créole specialties where you help yourself to all you want. The resort contains a communal dining room, as well as a pair of specialty dining rooms called the Yacht Club (specializing in beef and seafood), and the somewhat less formal Café du Port. A late-night disco stays open till the wee hours.

Services: Social director, massage.

Facilities: Sailing, waterskiing, snorkeling; part of beach reserved for nude sunbathing.

Where to Dine

AUX FILETS BLEUS, Point Marin, Sainte-Anne. Tel. 76-73-42.
Cuisine: CREOLE. **Reservations:** Required.

$ Prices: Appetizers 40F–60F ($7.70–$11.55); main courses 80F–120F ($15.40–$23.10). No credit cards.

Open: Lunch Tues–Sun 12:30–3pm; dinner Tues–Sun 7:30–10pm.

Set on a flat area close to the beach, a 50-minute drive south of the airport, is a family-run restaurant flanked by canopies and separated from the road by a hedge. Once you've entered, the seaside exposure of the al fresco dining room and its terrace makes you feel as if you're in an isolated tropical retreat, where the only sound is the splash of waves and the tinkling of ice in glasses. What appears to be a glass-covered reflecting pool set into the floor is actually a lobster tank. The menu features several preparations of lobster, stuffed crab, fried sea urchins, and many kinds of grilled fish.

THE NORTH LOOP

As we swing north from Fort-de-France, our main targets are Le Carbet, St-Pierre, Montagne Pelée, and Leyritz. However, I'll sandwich in many fascinating stopovers along the way.

From Fort-de-France there are three ways to head north to the Montagne Pelée. The first way is to follow route N4 up to St-Joseph. There you take the left fork for 3 miles after St-Joseph and turn onto the D15 toward Marigot.

Another way to Montagne Pelée is to take the N3 through the vegetation-rich *mornes* until you reach Le Morne Rouge. This road is known as "Route de la Trace," and is now the center of the Parc Naturel de la Martinique.

Yet a third route to reach Montagne Pelée is to follow the N2 along the coast Near Fort-de-France, the first town you reach is Schoelcher.

Farther along the N2 you reach Case Pilote, and then Bellefontaine. This portion, along the most frequented tourist route in Martinique—that is, Fort-de-France to St-Pierre—will remind many a traveler of the French Riviera. Bellefontaine is a small fishing village, with boats stretched along the beach. Note the many houses also built in the shape of boats.

EN ROUTE AT MORNE DES ESSES

Where to Dine

LE COLIBRI (The Hummingbird), allée du Colibri. Tel. 69-91-95.
Cuisine: CREOLE. **Reservations:** Not required.
$ Prices: Appetizers 35F–60F ($6.75–$11.55); main courses 70F–120F ($13.45–$23.10). AE, DC, MC, V.
Open: Lunch Tues–Sun noon–3pm; dinner Tues–Sun 7–11pm.

S In the hamlet of Morne des Esses, you might want to stop for lunch at Le Colibri, which is the home of Mme Clotilde Paladino and her daughters. If the terrace fills up with weekenders from Fort-de-France, you'll be seated on another smaller veranda where you can survey the cooking. The place is decidedly informal, and it exudes the warmth of madame. The typically Créole cookery is first class. You might begin with a calalou soup with crab or a sea urchin tart. I recommend a buisson d'ecrevisses (a stew of freshwater crayfish), stuffed pigeon, chicken with coconut, and roast suckling pig. For dessert, try a coconut flan. French wines accompany most meals. It lies on the northeastern coastline, near St. Aubin, about 20 miles from Fort-de-France.

LE CARBET

Leaving Bellefontaine, a 5-mile drive north will deliver you to Le Carbet. Columbus landed here in 1502, and the first French settlers arrived in 1635. In 1887 Gauguin lived here for 4 months before going on to Tahiti. You can stop for a swim at an Olympic-size pool set into the hills, or watch the locals scrubbing clothes in a stream. The town lies on the bus route from Fort-de-France to St-Pierre.

The **Centre d'Art Musée Paul-Gauguin,** Anse Turin, Le Carbet (tel. 77-22-66), is near the beach represented in the artist's two paintings, *Bord de Mer.* The landscape has not changed in 100 years. The museum, housed in a five-room building, commemorates the French artist's stay in Martinique in 1887, with books, prints, letters, and other memorabilia. There are also paintings by René Corail, sculpture by Hector Charpentier, and examples of the artwork of Zaffanella. Of special interest are faïence mosaics made of once-white pieces that turned pink, maroon, blue, and black in 1902 when the fires of Montagne Pelée devastated St-Pierre. There are also changing exhibits of works by local artists. The museum is open daily from 10am to 5pm, with an admission of 13F ($2.50).

ST-PIERRE

At the beginning of this century St-Pierre was known as the "Little Paris of the West Indies." Home to 30,000 inhabitants, it was the cultural and economic capital of Martinique. On May 7, 1902, the citizens read in their daily newspaper that "Montagne Pelée does not present any more risk to the population than Vesuvius does to the Neapolitans."

However, on May 8, at 8am, the southwest side of Montagne Pelée exploded into fire and lava. At 8:02am all 30,000 inhabitants were dead—that is, all except one. A convict in his underground cell was saved by the thickness of the wall. When islanders reached the site, the convict was paroled, and left Martinique to tour in Barnum and Bailey's circus.

St-Pierre never recovered its past splendor. Now it could be called the Pompeii of the West Indies. Ruins of the church, the theater, and some other buildings can be seen along the coast.

The **Musée Volcanologique,** rue Victor-Hugo, St-Pierre (tel. 78-15-16), was created by American volcanologist Franck Alvard Perret, who turned the museum over to the city in 1933. Here, in pictures and relics dug from the debris, you can trace the story of what happened to St-Pierre. Dug from the lava is a clock that stopped at the exact moment the volcano erupted. The museum is open daily from 9am to 5pm, with an admission of 10F ($1.95) for adults, 7F ($1.35) for children.

LE PRECHEUR

From St-Pierre, you can continue along the coast north to Le Prêcheur. Once the home of Madame de Maintenon, mistress of Louis XIV, it's the last village along the northern coast of Martinique. Here you can see hot springs of volcanic origin and the **Tombeau des Caraïbes (Tomb of the Caribs),** where, according to legend, the collective suicide of many West Indian natives took place after they returned from a fishing expedition and found their homes pillaged by the French.

MONTAGNE PELEE

A spectacular and winding road (route N2) takes you through a tropical rain forest. The curves are of the hairpin variety, and the road is twisty and not always kept in good shape. However, you're rewarded with tropical flowers, baby ferns, plumed bamboo, and valleys so deeply green you'll think you're wearing cheap sunglasses.

The village of Morne Rouge, right at the foot of Montagne Pelée, is a popular vacation spot for Martiniquais. From there on, a narrow and unreliable road brings you to a level of 2,500 feet above sea level, 1,600 feet under the round summit of the volcano that destroyed St-Pierre. Montagne Pelée itself rises 4,656 feet above sea level.

If you're a trained mountain climber, you can scale the peak to Grand Rivière—that is, if you don't mind 4 or 5 hours of hiking. Realize that this is a mountain, that rain is frequent, and that temperatures drop very low. Tropical growth often hides deep crevices in the earth, and there are other dangers. So if you're really serious about this climb, you should hire an experienced guide. As for the volcano, its death-dealing rain in 1902 apparently satisfied it—at least for the time being!

Upon your descent from Montagne Pelée, drive down to **Ajoupa-Bouillon,** which some describe, perhaps with justification, as the most beautiful town in Martinique. Abounding in flowers and shrubbery with bright yellow and red leaves, this little village is the site of the remarkable **Gorges de la Falaise.** These are mini-canyons on the Falaise River up which one can travel to reach a waterfall. Ajoupa-Bouillon also makes a good lunch stop.

Where to Dine

ABRI RESTAURANT, Ajoupa-Bouillon. Tel. 53-32-13.
   Cuisine: CREOLE. **Reservations:** Not required.
$ Prices: Appetizers 30F–40F ($5.75–$7.70); main courses 70F–115F ($13.45–$22.10). MC, V.
   Open: Lunch only, daily noon–3pm.
In the hills, about 7 miles northeast of the village of Lorrain, near Martinique's northern tip, is a large concrete building not unlike an aircraft hangar, whose rough edges are softened by potted plants. Originally a cockfight stadium, this restaurant serves meals that might begin with a glass of freshly squeezed sugarcane juice. The kitchen is known for its fricassée of crayfish, which is served to you and two or three others in a large bowl with herbs. You must shell the fish, then dip it into the sauce. It's a messy—and expensive—affair. You might prefer instead to order fish stuffed with

sea urchins and cooked in coconut fronds. To begin, you can order calalou soup with crab or many kinds of accras, ranging from sea urchins to pumpkin.

LEYRITZ

Continue east toward the coast, toward the town of Basse-Pointe in northeastern Martinique. A mile before Basse-Pointe, turn left and follow a road that goes deep into sugarcane country to Leyritz, where you'll find the best-restored plantation in Martinique, and perhaps stop by for lunch.

Where to Stay & Dine

HOTEL PLANTATION DE LEYRITZ, 97218 Basse-Pointe, Martinique, F.W.I. Tel. 78-53-92. Fax 78-92-44. 48 rms. A/C TEL

$ Rates (including continental breakfast): Winter, 540F ($103.85) single; 680F ($130.75) double. Summer, 370F ($71.15) single; 480F ($92.30) double. MC, V. **Parking:** Free. **Closed:** Sept.

⭐ This hotel, which offers spa facilities, was built around 1700 by a plantation owner, Bordeaux-born Michel de Leyritz. It was the site of the "swimming pool summit meeting" in 1974 between Presidents Gerald Ford and Valéry Giscard d'Estaing. It's still a working banana plantation, which was restored to its original character. There are 16 acres of tropical gardens, and at the core is an 18th-century stone great house. From the grounds, the view sweeps across the Atlantic and takes in fearsome Montagne Pelée. The owners have kept the best of the old, such as the rugged stone walls (20 inches thick), the beamed ceilings, and the tile and flagstone floors. They have created a cozy setting of mahogany tables, overstuffed sofas, and gilt mirrors. A few of the outbuildings, former slave quarters with bamboo roofs and stone walls, now house guests, and new ones have been added. I prefer the 10 units in the manor, because they are probably the most attractive, and are certainly the most authentic. You can also stay in the carriage house across the lawn. Don't expect luxury—that's not the style here.

Dining/Entertainment: The dining room is in a rum distillery, incorporating the fresh spring water running down from the hillside. Eating here is dramatic at night, and the cuisine is authentically Créole. Tour-bus crowds predominate at lunch, which costs 125F ($24.05) and up. On one visit I enjoyed a first-class Créole lunch that was really like a dinner. The main course was grilled chicken covered in coconut-milk sauce, along with oussous, a freshwater crayfish which came in an herb sauce. Vegetables consisted of sautéed breadfruit and sautéed bananas. Dinners go for 175F ($33.65) and up. Lunch is served from 12:30 to 2pm, and dinner is from 7:30 to 9pm, daily. Dinner is more elaborate, with both French and Créole dishes, including duck with pineapple, a colombo of lamb, and boudin (blood pudding) Créole.

Services: Laundry.

Facilities: Outdoor swimming pool.

BASSE-POINTE

At the northernmost point on the island, Basse-Pointe is a land of pineapple and banana plantation fields, covering the Atlantic-side slopes of Mount Pelée volcano.

Where to Dine

CHEZ MALLY EDJAM, Basse-Pointe. Tel. 78-51-18.

Cuisine: FRENCH/CREOLE. **Reservations:** Required.

$ Prices: Appetizers 30F–80F ($5.75–$15.40); main courses 80F–125F ($15.40–$24.05); fixed-price three-course lunch 70F ($13.45). AE, DC, MC, V.

Open: Lunch daily noon–3pm; dinner by special arrangement only. **Closed:** July.

⭐ This local legend operates from a modest house beside the main road in the center of town, 36 miles from Fort-de-France. Appreciating its exotic but genteel charm, many visitors prefer to drive all the way from Pointe du Bout to dine here instead of at the Leyritz Plantation. You sit at one of a handful of tables on the side porch, unless you prefer a seat in the somewhat more formal dining room.

Grandmotherly Mally Edjam (who is ably assisted by France-born Martine Hugé) is busy in the kitchen turning out her Créole delicacies. Both women know how to prepare all the dishes for which the island is known: stuffed land crab with a hot seasoning, small pieces of conch in a tart shell, and a classic colombo de porc (the Créole version of pork curry). Equally acclaimed are the establishment's lobster vinaigrette, the papaya soufflé (which must be ordered in advance), and the highly original confitures, which are tiny portions of fresh island fruits, such as pineapple and guava, that have been preserved in a vanilla syrup.

GRAND' RIVIÈRE

After Basse-Pointe, the town you reach on your northward trek is Grand' Rivière. From there you must turn back, but before doing so you may want to stop at a good restaurant right at the entrance to the town.

Where to Dine

CHEZ VAVA, blvd. de Gaulle. Tel. 75-52-81.
   Cuisine: FRENCH/CREOLE. **Reservations:** Recommended.
$ **Prices:** Appetizers 30F–80F ($5.75–$15.40); main courses 80F–130F ($15.40–$25). No credit cards.
   Open: Daily 7am–6pm.
Directly west of Basse-Pointe, with its bright-orange tiling, Chez Vava is easy to spot. You'll also find plenty of space to park your car. With a simple country-inn style, it's actually a *maison privé*. A la carte menu items include Créole soup, a blaff of sea urchins, lobster, and various colombos. An old rum punch, a specialty of the house, is also offered.

SAINTE-MARIE

Heading south along the coastal road, you'll bypass Marigot to reach a sightseeing stop in the little town of Sainte-Marie. The **Musée du Rhum Saint-James,** at the Saint James Distillery (tel. 54-62-07), displays engravings, antique tools and machines, and other exhibits tracing the history of sugarcane and rum from 1765 to the present. Guided tours of the museum also include a visit to the distillery and storage area, and a session of rum tasting. Admission free, the museum is open daily from 9am to 6pm.

TRINIT

If you head back south along the coastal route (N1) from Ste-Marie, you'll pass through the small village of Trinité on the Atlantic side of Martinique. It would hardly merit a stopover were it not for the Saint-Aubi Hôtel.

Where to Stay

SAINT-AUBIN HOTEL, 97220 Trinité, Martinique, F.W.I. Tel. 69-34-77.
   Fax 69-41-14. 15 rms. A/C TEL
$ **Rates** (including continental breakfast): Winter, 375F ($72.10) single; 540F ($103.85) double. Summer, 340F ($65.40) single; 480F ($92.30) double. AE, DC, MC, V. **Parking:** Free.
A former restaurant owner, Normandy-born Guy Forêt has sunk his fortune into restoring this three-story Victorian house and turning it into a three-star hostelry, one of the loveliest inns in the Caribbean. Painted a vivid pink with fancy gingerbread, it was once a plantation house. It sits on a hillside above sugarcane fields and Trinité's bay 14½ miles from the airport, 19 miles from Fort-de-France, and 2 miles from the seaside village of Trinité itself. There are 800 yards of private beach, plus there's a swimming pool on the grounds. All rooms sport wall-to-wall carpeting and modern (not antique) furniture. There are some family rooms as well. After dinner you can

relax on the veranda on the first and second floors. Rooms have a view of either the garden or the sea. The hotel restaurant and bar are reserved for use of hotel guests.

ACTIVITIES AROUND THE ISLAND
CAMPING

Camping is permitted in some places, including in the mountains and forests and on many beaches. Check with the local mayor's office or property owner before setting up camp. Campsites are usually basic, although comfortable camps with cold showers and toilets are on the southeast coast at Macabou; at Ste-Luce, Le Marin, and Ste-Anne on the south coast; and Anse-à-l'Ane near Trois-Ilets. Contact the **Office National des Forêts** (tel. 71-34-50) for more information.

SPORTS & RECREATION

The Martiniquais often don't work at their sports as hard as many North Americans do, but they do have an active sports program. Scuba diving, snorkeling, fishing, and waterskiing can be enjoyed all along the coastline. Golf clubs are at your disposal in all the first-class hotels (tariffs vary considerably, depending on the duration and season).

BEACHES The beaches south of Fort-de-France are white, while the northern strands are composed mostly of gray sand. Outstanding in the south is the 1½-mile **Plage des Salines,** near Ste-Anne, with palm trees and a long stretch of white sand, and the 2½-mile-long **Diamant,** with the landmark Diamond Rock offshore. Swimming on the Atlantic coast is for experts only, except at **Cap Chevalier** and **Presqu'île de la Caravelle Nature Preserve.**

The clean white sandy beaches of **Pointe du Bout,** site of the major hotels of Martinique, were created by the developers. However, to the south the white sand beaches at **Anse Mitan** have always been there welcoming visitors, including many snorkelers. Incidentally, nudist beaches are not officially sanctioned, although topless sunbathing is widely practiced at the big hotels, often around their swimming pools. Public beaches as a rule do not have changing cabins or showers. Some hotels charge nonguests for the use of changing and beach facilities, and request a deposit for rental of towels.

DEEP-SEA FISHING Increased facilities for deep-sea fishing have been developed in Martinique because of the demand created by fine catches of tuna, barracuda, dolphin, kingfish, and bonito. Most hotels will help make arrangements if given a day or two advance notice, and the Hôtel Méridien, for example, has daily trips.

Bathy's Club at the Méridien (tel. 66-00-00) sends out a 36-foot fishing boat, *Pink Diver,* every day at 6am for a 3½-hour trip. The excursions, primarily for recreational fishing, cost 1,400F ($269.20) for the boat, including gear and breakfast, but it's divided among four to eight participants. Barracuda is the most common catch on these trips, and by everyone's estimate, the period during which the fish will bite is already over before 10am. Breakfast is served after the return to the dock, around 9:30am.

GOLF The famous golf course designer, Robert Trent Jones, visited Martinique and left behind the 18-hole **Golf de l'Impératrice-Joséphine** at Trois-Ilets (tel. 68-32-81), a 5-minute, 1-mile drive from the leading resort area of Pointe du Bout and about 18 miles from Fort-de-France. This, the only golf course on Martinique, unfolds its greens from the birthplace of Empress Joséphine for whom it is named, across rolling hills with scenic vistas down to the sea. Amenities include a pro shop, a bar, a restaurant, and three tennis courts. Greens fees are 225F ($43.25) per person for 18 holes. Residents of certain hotels (including the Bakoua, the Méridien, and the Novotel Le Diamant) receive discounts on their greens fees, and pay between 150F and 175F ($28.85 and $33.65), depending on the policies in effect on the day they make their reservations.

HIKING Inexpensive guided excursions for tourists are organized by the personnel of the **Parc Naturel Régional de la Martinique** year round. Special excursions can be arranged for small groups by contacting the Parc Naturel Régional de la Martinique, Excollège Agricole de Tivoli, B.P. 437, 97200 Fort-de-France (tel. 64-42-59).

The **Presqu'île de la Caravelle Nature Preserve,** a well-protected peninsula jutting into the Atlantic Ocean, has safe beaches and well-marked trails to the ruins of historic Château Debuc and through tropical wetlands.

Serious hiking excursions to climb Montagne Pelée and explore the Gorges de la Falaise or the thick coastal rain forest between Grand' Rivière and Le Prêcheur are organized with local guides at certain times of the year by the park staff.

HORSEBACK RIDING   The premier riding facility on Martinique, **Ranch Jack,** Quartier Espérance, Trois-Ilets (tel. 68-37-69), offers morning horseback rides for both experienced and novice riders, at a cost of 290F ($55.75) per person for a 3½- to 4-hour ride. Jacques and Marlene Guinchard make daily promenades across the beaches and fields of Martinique, with a running explication of the history, fauna, and botany of the island. Cold drinks are included in the price, and transportation is usually free to and from the hotels of nearby Pointe du Bout. This is an ideal way to discover both botanical and geographical Martinique.

MONGOOSE VS. THE SNAKE   Some people say you've not really seen Martinique until you've attended a match between a mongoose and a snake. Said to have been imported by East Indian workers, this is a to-the-death struggle. If you attend such an event, you're to remain deadly still. Even lighting a cigarette is supposed to break the concentration of the combatants. Incidentally, the mongoose almost always wins. Even if the snake should win, the fight is still unfair, because another mongoose will be brought out to do combat with the snake. Some taxi drivers or small innkeepers on the island will tell you where to go to watch this "sport." Frankly, I prefer to skip it.

SAILING   While this is a big pastime in Martinique, it's also a big cost unless there are enough in your party. Only a select few can afford yacht charters, either crewed or bareboat. If you want to see the waters around Martinique, it's better to go on one of the sailboat excursions in the bay of Fort-de-France and on the southeast coast of the island. Ask at your hotel desk what ships are taking passengers on cruises in Martinique waters. These vessels tend to change from season to season.

On a smaller scale, many hotels (including the Méridien at Pointe du Bout) will rent Hobie Cats and Sunfish to their guests for around 140F ($26.90) per hour, but only if sailing competence can be demonstrated in advance.

SCUBA DIVING & SNORKELING   Scuba divers come here to explore the St-Pierre shipwrecks sunk in the 1902 volcano eruption and the Diamond Rock caves and walls. Small scuba centers operate at many of the hotels.

Snorkeling equipment is usually available free to hotel guests, who quickly learn that coral, fish, and ferns abound in the waters around the Pointe du Bout hotels.

Across the bay from Fort-de-France, in the Hôtel Méridien, **Bathy's Club** (tel. 66-00-00) is one of the major scuba centers for Pointe du Bout and welcomes anyone who shows up. Daily dive trips, depending on demand, leave from the Méridien Hôtel's pier. Prices include equipment rental, transportation, guide, and drinks on board. Dives are conducted twice daily, from 8am to noon and 2 to 6pm, and full-day charters can be arranged. The dive shop on the Méridien's beach stocks everything from weight belts and tanks to partial wetsuits and underwater cameras. Dives cost 250F ($48.10) per person. Initial instruction is offered for beginners.

Other Martinique hotels also have scuba centers.

Tropicalize is a dive center whose office is at the Hôtel La Batelière (tel. 61-49-49), just north of Fort-de-France. It offers guided dives of the St-Pierre shipwrecks, coral reefs, and ridges. Two trips depart daily, with single dives costing 250F ($48.10).

TENNIS   Each large hotel has courts. Residents play free during the day, and night games usually require a surcharge of around 40F ($7.70) for 30 minutes. Nonguests are faced with a playing-time charge that could range from 50F to 75F ($9.60 to $14.40) per half hour, although the tennis pros at Bathy's Club at the Hôtel Méridien in Pointe du Bout usually allow nonresidents to play for free if the courts are otherwise unoccupied—except at night when the charge is almost universally imposed.

Another good choice is to play at one of the three courts on the grounds of **Golf de l'Impératrice-Joséphine** at Trois-Ilets (tel. 68-32-81), a 5-minute drive from the major hotels at Pointe du Bout. The setting here is one of the most beautiful in Martinique.

WATERSKIING & WINDSURFING Waterskiing is available at every beach near the large hotels, and costs about 100F ($19.25) for 10- to 15-minute rides.

Windsurfing is the most popular sport in the French West Indies. Equipment and lessons are available at all hotel water-sports facilities, especially the **Hôtel Méridien,** Pointe du Bout (tel. 66-00-00), where 30-minute lessons cost 80F ($15.40). However, board rentals are only about 75F to 100F ($14.45 to 19.25) per hour.

SAVVY SHOPPING
In Fort-de-France

Your best buys in Martinique are French luxury imports, such as perfumes, fashions, Vuitton luggage, Lalique crystal, or Limoges dinnerware. Sometimes (but don't count on it) prices are as much as 30% to 40% below those in the U.S.

One cautious reader points out that if you pay in dollars store owners supposedly will give you a 20% discount; however, when you pay in dollars, the exchange rates vary considerably from store to store, and almost invariably they are far less favorable than that offered at one of the local banks. He writes: "The net result is that you received a 20% discount, but then they take away from 9% to 15% on the dollar exchange, giving you a net savings of only 5% to 11%—not 20%." He further notes, "Actually, you're probably better off shopping in the smaller stores where prices are 8% to 12% less on comparable items and paying in francs that you have exchanged at a local bank."

The main shopping street is **rue Victor-Hugo.** The other two leading shopping streets are **rue Schoelcher** and **rue St-Louis.**

Facing the tourist office and alongside **quai d'Esnambuc** is an open market where you can purchase local handcrafts and souvenirs. Many of these are tacky, however.

Far more interesting is the display of vegetables and fruit—quite a show—at the open-air stalls along **rue Isambert.** Don't miss it for its local ambience, and you can't help but smell the fish market alongside the **Levassor River.**

Gourmet chefs will find all sorts of spices in the open-air markets, or such goodies as tinned pâté or canned quail in the local *supermarchés.*

For the ubiquitous local fabric, madras, there are shops on every street with bolts and bolts of it, all colorful and inexpensive. So-called haute couture and resortwear are sold in many boutiques dotting downtown Fort-de-France.

Most shops are open Monday through Friday from 7:30am to 12:30pm and 2:30 to 5:30pm, and on Saturday from 8am to noon; closed Sunday. Try to postpone your shopping trip if a cruise ship is in town.

ROGER ALBERT, rue Victor-Hugo, 7. Tel. 71-71-71.

All the big names in perfumes from Paris are here, as well as crystal from Baccarat and Lalique, chinaware from Limoges, figurines by Lladró, and sportswear by Lacoste and Tacchini. The merchandise is of the highest quality and provides one of the finest selections in the Caribbean. Long established, just off the Savane, this is the best-known store in Martinique.

CADET-DANIEL, rue Antoine-Siger, 72. Tel. 71-41-48.

Cadet-Daniel, which opened in 1840, sells Christofle silver, Limoges china, and crystal from Daum, Baccarat, Lalique, and Sèvres. Like some nearby stores, it also offers island-made 18-karat gold baubles, including the beaded *collier chou,* or "darling's necklace," long a required ornament for a Créole costume.

LA CASE A RHUM, Galerie Marchande, rue de la Liberté, 5. Tel. 73-73-20.

Before leaving Martinique, you may want to purchase some rum, considered by aficionados to be one of the world's finest distilled drinks. Hemingway in *A Moveable Feast* lauded it as the perfect antidote to a rainy day. This shop is the best place for browsing, offering all the brands of rum manufactured in Martinique (at least 12), as well as several others famous for their age and taste. They offer samples in small cups to prospective buyers. I suggest that you try Vieux Acajou, a dark, mellow Old Mahogany, or a blood-red brown liqueurlike rum bottled by Bally.

MERLANDE, rue Victor-Schoelcher 10, near the cathedral. Tel. 71-38-66.

One of the finest department stores in the Caribbean, Merlande sells French fashions, along with china and crystal, and such famous names in perfume as Lanvin, Chanel, Jean Patou, and Guerlain.

The enterprise also has another store, **Au Sans Pareil,** rue Blénac 26 (tel. 71-52-32), which is known for its china, crystal, toys, beauty accessories, and luggage.

Elsewhere on the Island

If you're staying at one of the hotels on the peninsula of Pointe du Bout, you'll find that the Marina complex there has a number of interesting boutiques. Several sell handcrafts and curios from Martinique. They are of good quality, and are quite expensive, regrettably, particularly if you purchase some of their batiks of natural silk and their enameled jewel boxes.

There are the sturdy, attractive straw food baskets in the shops of **Morne-des-Esses,** the *vannerie* (basket-making) capital of Martinique.

POTERIE DE TROIS-ILETS, Quartier Poterie, Trois-Ilets. Tel. 68-17-12.

At Christmastime, many of the island's traditional foie gras and pastries are presented in crocks made by Martinique's largest earthenware factories, the Poterie de Trois-Ilets. At least 90% of its production is devoted to brickmaking. However, one small-scale offshoot of the company devotes itself to the production of earth-toned stoneware and pottery whose colors and shapes have contributed to the folklore of Martinique. In theory, the studios are open Monday through Saturday from 9am to 6pm, but it's a good idea to call before you set out to make sure they will accept visitors.

EVENING ENTERTAINMENT

Everybody who goes to Martinique wants to see the show performed by **Les Grands Ballets de la Martiniquais,** a bouncy group of about two dozen dancers, along with musicians, singers, and choreographers. This is probably the most interesting program of folk dances in the Caribbean. Launched in the early 1960s, this group performs the traditional dances of Martinique and has been acclaimed in both Europe and the States. With a swoosh of gaily striped skirts and clever acting, dancers capture all the exuberance of the island's soul.

The group has toured abroad with great success, but they perform best on home ground presenting tableaux that tell of jealous brides and faithless husbands, demanding overseers and toiling cane cutters. Dressed in traditional costumes, the island women and men dance the spirited mazurka, which was brought from the ballrooms of Europe, and the exotic beguine.

Cole Porter, incidentally, did not invent the beguine. It's a martiniquais dance—some would call it a way of life. Instead of having me try to explain it, it's best to see it. Or dance it, if you think you can.

Les Grands Ballets perform Monday at the Hôtel Diamant-Novotel, Wednesday at the PLM Azur Carayou, Thursday at the Méridien Trois-Ilets, Friday at the Bakoua

Beach, and Saturday at the Hôtel La Batalière, but this can vary so check locally. In addition, the troupe gives mini-performances aboard visiting cruise ships. The cost of dinner and the show is usually 250F ($48.10) per person. Most performances are at 9pm, with dinners at the hotels beginning at 7:30pm.

There's also a lot of nightlife revolving around the four major hotels at Pointe du Bout—**Bakoua Beach, PLM Azur Carayou, Méridien Trois-Ilets,** and **PLM Azur La Pagerié.** As mentioned, on certain nights you can watch Les Grands Ballets de la Martiniquais. In addition, musicians, some of them quite young, play nightly in the larger hotels.

Hotel guests are allowed in free at two of the nightclubs, **Vesou** in the PLM Azur Carayou and **Hutte** in the Bakoua. If you're not a resident of one of the hotels, you'll be charged an entrance fee of around 85F ($16.35), including your first drink. These clubs are open Monday through Saturday from 10:30pm. It's hard to say which club is the best, as a mainly young crowd wanders from one to the other on a warm night.

The **Casino Trois-Ilets,** on the premises of the Méridien Trois-Ilets, Pointe du Bout (tel. 66-00-30), is open every night from 9pm to 3am. Here you can try to win the cost of your vacation by playing roulette, blackjack, or chemin-de-fer. Some form of photo identification is required at the entrance. You present it along with 60F ($11.55).

You might also try your luck at the **Hôtel La Batelière Casino,** in Schoelcher, outside Fort-de-France (tel. 61-49-49). Not as glamorous as Las Vegas, it attracts a leisure crowd who play roulette, French chemin-de-fer, craps, or blackjack. An identity card such as a passport is required. The entrance fee is 60F ($11.55), and hours are 9pm to 3am daily.

I'd advise you to spend your nights in the big hotel clubs. There are other local clubs frequented by the Martiniquais. However, some "incidents" have been reported when tourists strayed in. If you insist on going to one of these clubs "to see the real beguine," I suggest that you go there with some local friends, if you've made any, who know the island.

2. GUADELOUPE

"The time is near, I believe, when thousands of American tourists will come to spend the winter among the beautiful countryside and friendly people of Guadeloupe." Or so Theodore Roosevelt accurately predicted on February 21, 1916. Guadeloupe isn't the same place it was when the Rough Rider himself rode through, but the natural beauty he witnessed, and certainly the people, are still there to be enjoyed.

Guadeloupe is part of the Lesser Antilles, about 200 miles north of Martinique, closer to the United States than its cousin. In addition to tourism, sugar production and rum beef up the local economy. The total surface of Guadeloupe and its satellite islands is close to 700 square miles. There is a lot of similarity in climate, animals, and vegetation between Martinique and Guadeloupe.

Guadeloupe is, in fact, formed by two different islands, separated by a narrow seawater channel known as the Rivière Salée. **Grande-Terre,** the eastern island, is typical of the charm of the Antilles, with its rolling hills and sugar plantations.

On the other hand, **Basse-Terre,** to the west, is a rugged mountainous island, dominated by the 4,800-foot volcano La Soufrière, which is still alive. Its mountains are covered with tropical forests, impenetrable in many places. Bananas grown on plantations are the main crop. The island is ringed by beautiful beaches, which have attracted much tourism.

Among the celebrities from the island, Saint-John Perse (alias Alexis Saint Leger) was born on St-Leger-des-Feuilles, a small islet in Pointe-à-Pitre bay, in 1887. The French diplomat was better known as a poet, and was the Nobel Prize winner in 1960. He wrote a constant song to the beauty of his island.

Guadeloupe was first called Karukera by the Arawaks, meaning "the island of the beautiful waters." On November 3, 1493, Columbus landed and named the island Santa María de Guadelupe de Estramaduros, which in time became Guadeloupe. The island's modern history is very much related to that of Martinique. Guadeloupe was settled by Sir Lienard de l'Olive and Sir Duplessis d'Ossonville, who were detached from Martinique by its commander, Belain d'Esnambuc. These men arrived with a group of some 500 settlers on June 18, 1635.

The British seized the island in 1759. They gave it back, but took it once more in 1794. A mulatto, Victor Hugues, attacked them with his revolutionary army of blacks and whites, but he faded after Napoleon came to power, who then allowed the British to move in again in 1810. The island returned to French hands in 1815.

For 100 years Guadeloupe was a dependency of Martinique. In 1946 Guadeloupe became a full-fledged French *département* (the French equivalent of an American state), and its people are citizens of France with all the privileges thereof.

ORIENTATION

GETTING THERE   Most of the flights to Guadeloupe require a transfer in a neighboring island, although Air France has a handful of nonstop flights from Miami.

American Airlines (tel. toll free 800/433-7300) has many flights into its hub in San Juan, and then **American Eagle** has flights on to the French islands. The Eagle's schedule calls for a daily nonstop departure from San Juan at 8:40pm. American Eagle schedules an arrival first in Guadeloupe and, after a short wait, a continuation to Martinique. American Eagle also offers a separate daily nonstop flight from San Juan to Guadeloupe in the early afternoon. Consult an American Airlines reservations clerk about booking your hotel simultaneously with your airfare, since substantial deductions sometimes apply if you handle both tasks at the same time.

Air France (tel. toll free 800/237-2747) flies from Miami to Martinique (with continuing service to Guadeloupe) twice every Sunday and twice every Monday. Passengers who need to return to the U.S. mainland any other day of the week usually fly American Eagle to San Juan and transfer there to American. Air France also flies separate daily nonstops from Paris's Charles de Gaulle airport to both Guadeloupe and Martinique.

Air Canada (tel. toll free 800/776-3000) has a flight that departs from Canadian soil every Saturday. It originates in Toronto late enough in the morning to permit transfers from Montréal, then flies nonstop to Guadeloupe.

Leeward Islands Air Transport (LIAT) (tel. 212/779-2731 in New York City, or toll free 800/253-5011), based in Antigua, flies from Antigua to both Martinique and Guadeloupe several times a day, sometimes with connections on to Barbados. Both Antigua and Barbados are considered important air-terminus links for incoming flights on either American (see above) or **BWIA** (tel. toll free 800/327-7401) from New York and Miami.

Minerve Airlines, a French charter company, operates direct weekly flights on Saturday from New York's JFK International Airport to Martinique and Guadeloupe. Most of the flights' seats, however, are offered in conjunction with 7-night packages available through several major Caribbean wholesalers. For more information, call **Council Charter,** 205 East 42nd Street, New York, NY 10017 (tel. 212/661-4546, or toll free 800/765-6065).

GETTING AROUND   By Bus   As in Martinique, there is no rail service. But buses link almost every hamlet to Pointe-à-Pitre. However, you may need to know some French to use the system. From Pointe-à-Pitre you can catch one of these jitney vans, either at the Gare Routière de Bergevin if you're going to Basse-Terre, or the Gare Routière de Mortenol if Grande-Terre is your destination. Service is daily from 5:30am to 7:30pm.

By Taxi   You'll find taxis when you arrive at the airport, but no limousines or buses waiting to serve you. From 9pm until 7am, cabbies are legally entitled to charge you

40% more. In practice, either day or night, the taxi drivers charge you whatever they think the market will bear, although technically fares are regulated by the government. Always agree on the price before getting in. Approximate fares are 60F ($11.55) from the airport to Gosier hotels, or 35F ($6.75) from the airport to Pointe-à-Pitre. Radio taxis can be called at 82-15-09, 83-64-27, or 84-37-65.

If you're traveling with people or imaginative in putting a party together, it's possible to sightsee by taxi. Usually the concierge at your hotel will help you make this arrangement. A 6-hour tour to Soufrière, for example, is likely to cost at least $95.

By Rental Car   Your access to a car enables you to circumnavigate Basse-Terre, which many aficionados claim is one of the loveliest drives in the Caribbean. Car-rental kiosks at the airport are usually open to meet international flights. Rental rates at local companies might appear lower, depending on the agency, but several readers have complained of mechanical problems and billing irregularities, and difficulties in resolving insurance disputes in the event of accidents. If you want to be sure to get a car when you arrive, it's often best to reserve one in advance through the nationwide toll-free numbers of North America's largest car-rental companies: **Hertz** (tel. toll free 800/654-3131), **Avis** (tel. toll free 800/331-2112), and **Budget** (tel. toll free 800/527-0700), each of which is represented on the island.

At all three, the best values are usually offered when you reserve at least 2 days in advance and keep the car for at least a week. If you decide to rent a car after your arrival on the island, each of the companies maintains its headquarters at the island's Raizet Airport. For information once you get there, contact Avis at 82-02-71, Budget at 82-95-58, and Hertz at 82-00-14.

Budget, followed in some categories by Avis, is usually the cheapest. Budget's least expensive vehicle costs $240 per week, plus a 14% government tax. Avis and Hertz charge $261 and $311, respectively, plus tax, for similar cars.

Hertz and Avis prefer that drivers be older than 21 before renting one of their cars, whereas renters must be 25 at Budget.

All three companies offer additional insurance in the form of a collision-damage waiver, priced at between $8 and $11 per day. Unless you have other forms of insurance, I highly recommend that you buy the extra coverage.

Driving is on the right side, and there are several gas stations along the main routes. Don't drink and drive.

 GUADELOUPE

Area Code   Guadeloupe is *not* part of the Caribbean's 809 area code. To phone Guadeloupe from the North American mainland, see "Telephone," below.

Currency   The official monetary unit is the **French franc (F),** although some shops will take U.S. dollars. At press time the exchange rate was 5.2F to $1 U.S. (1F = 19¢), and this was the rate used to calculate the dollar values given in this chapter. As this is sure to fluctuate a bit, use this rate for guidance only.

Customs   Items for personal use, "in limited quantities," can be brought in tax free.

Documents   For stays of less than 21 days, U.S. or Canadian residents need only proof of identity (a voter registration card or birth certificate with a photo ID, or a passport), plus a return or ongoing plane ticket. For a longer stay, a valid passport is required.

Drugstores   The pharmacies carry French medicines, and most over-the-counter American drugs have French equivalents. Prescribed medicines can be purchased if the traveler has a prescription. Drugstores operate on an around-the-clock basis, the schedule of which is always changing. The tourist office can tell you what pharmacies are open at what time.

Electricity   The local electricity is 220 volts AC, 50 cycles, which means that you'll need a transformer and an adapter. Some of the big resorts lend these to guests, but don't count on it. One hotel I know had only six in stock, and a long, long waiting list (and of the six, two were broken!). Take your own.

Emergencies   Call the **police** at 17, report a **fire** at 18, and summon an **ambulance** at 82-89-33.

Information   The major tourist office in Guadeloupe is the **Office Départemental du Tourisme,** 5 Square de la Banque, in Pointe-à-Pitre (tel. 82-09-30).

Language   The official language is French, and Créole is the unofficial second language. As in Martinique, English is spoken only in the major tourist centers, rarely in the countryside.

Medical Care   There are five modern hospitals in Guadeloupe, plus 23 clinics. Hotels and the Guadeloupe tourist office can assist in locating English-speaking doctors. A 24-hour emergency room operates at the **Pointe-à-Pitre Central Hospital,** Abymes (tel. 82-98-80).

Safety   Like Martinique, Guadeloupe is relatively free of serious crime. But don't go wandering alone at night on the streets of Pointe-à-Pitre; by nightfall they are relatively deserted and might be dangerous. Purse-snatching by fast-riding motorcyclists has been reported, so exercise caution.

Taxes   A departure tax, required on scheduled flights, is included in the airfares. Hotel taxes are included in all room rates.

Telephone   Guadeloupe, as a *département* of France, is *not* part of the 809 area code that applies to most of the Caribbean. To call Guadeloupe from the U.S., if your long-distance telephone company is equipped to handle international direct dialing, dial 011 (the international access code), then 590 (the country code for Guadeloupe), and finally the six-digit local number. If you cannot direct-dial internationally, dial 0 ("zero," for the operator) and tell the operator you wish to make an international call; once you are transferred to the international operator, state the 590 country code and then the local number, and the operator will dial the call for you. To make a call within Guadeloupe, only the six-digit local number is necessary. *Note:* In this chapter, only the local numbers are given.

Time   Guadeloupe time is 1 hour ahead of eastern standard time (when it's 6am in New York, it's 7am in Guadeloupe). When daylight saving time is in effect in the U.S., clocks in New York and Guadeloupe show the same time.

Tips and Service   Hotels and restaurants usually add a 10% to 15% service charge, and most taxi drivers who own their own cars do not expect a tip. Surprisingly, neither do hotel porters.

Tobacco   American tobacco and cigarettes are available at hotel shops, and Guadeloupe also has some *café-tabacs* selling foreign cigarettes.

POINTE-A-PITRE

The port and chief city of Guadeloupe, Pointe-à-Pitre lies on Grande-Terre. Unfortunately, it doesn't have the old-world charm of Fort-de-France in Martinique, and what beauty it does possess is often hidden behind closed doors.

Having been burned and rebuilt so many times, the port has emerged as a town lacking in character, with modern apartments and condominiums forming a high-rise backdrop over jerry-built shacks and industrial suburbs. The rather narrow streets are jammed during the day with a colorful crowd creating a permanent traffic tie-up. However, at sunset the town becomes quiet again and almost deserted.

The real point of interest in Pointe-à-Pitre is shopping. It's best to visit the town in the morning—you can easily cover it in half a day—taking in the waterfront and outdoor market (the latter is livelier in the early hours). Be careful about walking alone on the nearly deserted streets of Pointe-à-Pitre at night.

The town center is the **place de la Victoire,** a park shaded by palm trees and poincianas. Here you'll see some old sandbox trees said to have been planted by Victor Hugues, the mulatto who organized a revolutionary army of both whites and blacks to establish a dictatorship. In this square he kept a guillotine busy, and the death-dealing instrument still stood there (but not in use) until modern times.

With the recent completion of the **Centre St-Jean-Perse,** a $20-million project that has been on the drawing boards for many years, the waterfront of Pointe-à-Pitre, has been transformed from a bastion of old warehouses and cruise terminal buildings, into an architectural complex comprising a hotel, three restaurants, 80 shops and boutiques, a bank, and the expanded headquarters of Guadeloupe's Port Authority.

Named for Saint-John Perse, the 20th-century poet and Nobel Laureate who was born just a few blocks away, the centre is tastefully designed in contemporary French West Indies style which blends with the traditional architecture of Pointe-à-Pitre. It offers an array of French Caribbean attractions: duty-free shops selling Guadeloupean rum and French perfume; a renowned restaurant, La Canne à Sucre; small tropical gardens planted around the complex; and a location right near the colorful open-air markets and small shops of this bustling port of call. For brochures, maps, and data on sightseeing, the Guadeloupe tourist office is just minutes away.

WHERE TO STAY

HOTEL BOUGAINVILLEE, angle des rues Delgrès et Frébault, 97110 Pointe-à-Pitre, Guadeloupe, F.W.I. Tel. 90-14-14. Fax 91-36-82. 34 rms, 2 suites. A/C TEL

$ Rates: 490F ($94.25) single; 580F ($111.55) double; from 715F ($137.50) suite. Breakfast 45F ($8.65) extra. AE, DC, MC, V. **Parking:** Free.

It's concrete and without frills, but the Bougainvillée is clean and serviceable. Its location on a busy street corner guarantees a regular clientele of commercial travelers. Guests register in a wood-trimmed, renovated lobby before taking a cramped elevator to one of the bedrooms. They're all maintained, with white walls, heavy dark furniture, like something you'd find in Iberia, and each contains a private bath and shower. Ten rooms have a minibar, and several contain their own TV.

WHERE TO DINE

"Cuisine moderne" or modern French cooking has superseded "nouvelle" (which has been declared dead by French chefs of note) and refers to current culinary methods of preparing classic dishes with the best of the "nouvelle" techniques to bring out the natural flavors of the freshest ingredients without the more eccentric excesses.

LA CANNE A SUCRE, Quai no. 1, Port Autonome. Tel. 82-10-19.
Cuisine: MODERN FRENCH/CREOLE. **Reservations:** Recommended.
$ Prices: Street-level Brasserie, appetizers 40F–70F ($7.70–$13.45); main courses 50F–75F ($9.60–$14.40). Upstairs restaurant, appetizers 90F–135F ($17.30–$25.95); main courses 90F–155F ($17.30–$29.80). AE, MC, V.
Open: Brasserie, Mon–Sat 8am–midnight. Restaurant, lunch Mon–Fri noon–2pm; dinner Mon–Sat 7:30–10pm.

Three feet from the water's edge, beside the quays where the cruise ships deposit their passengers, this is one "sugarcane" that has created a local sensation. It's the most select rendezvous for superbly prepared local cuisine on the island. Gerard Virginius, along with his wife, Marie, moved in 1991 into a concrete-and-glass building with a view of the many cruise ships that dock a short distance from the shore. The style of both dining areas is a mixture of Créole with art nouveau. The street level contains an elegant brasserie, where sophisticated but informal food might include a brioche of red snapper covered with lobster sauce, duckmeat salad with raspberry vinegar, and red snapper in puff pastry with exotic mushrooms. Upstairs is a more formal, and more expensive, restaurant where menu items might include a filet of red snapper in a passionfruit sauce, filet of marlin with champagne sauce, breast of chicken stuffed with conch, and duckling basted with starfruit-enriched vinegar. Desserts are lavish and sinful: a soursop sherbet or a coupe Canne à Sucre (a rondelle with old rum, coconut sherbet, whipped cream, banana, caramel, and a touch of cinnamon). It's traditional to begin your meal with a small rum punch.

SAVVY SHOPPING

Frankly, I suggest that you skip a shopping tour of Pointe-à-Pitre if you're going on to Fort-de-France in Martinique, as you'll find far more merchandise there, and perhaps friendlier service. If you're not, however, I recommend the following shops, some of which line rue Frébault.

Of course, your best buys will be anything French—perfumes from Chanel, silk scarves from Hermès, cosmetics from Dior, crystal from Lalique and Baccarat. I've found (but not often) some of these items discounted as much as 30% below U.S. or Canadian prices. Shops, which most often will accept U.S. dollars, give these discounts only to purchases made by traveler's check. Purchases are duty free if brought directly from store to airplane. In addition to the places below, there are also duty-free shops at Raizet Airport selling liquor, rums, perfumes, crystal, and cigarettes.

Most shops open at 9am, close at 1pm, then reopen between 3 and 6pm. They are closed on Saturday afternoon, Sunday, and holidays. When the cruise ships are in port, many eager shopkeepers stay open longer and on weekends.

One of the best places to buy French perfumes, at prices often lower than those charged in Paris, is **Phoenicia,** rue Frébault, 8 (tel. 83-50-36).

Rosebleu, rue Frébault, 5 (tel. 82-93-44), has one of the biggest stocks in Pointe-à-Pitre of jewelry, perfumes, gifts, and fashion accessories. The best crystal made in France is sold here. If you pay with traveler's checks, you'll get discounts. Closed Monday.

Vendôme, rue Frébault, 8–10 (tel. 83-42-84), has imported fashions for both men and women, as well as a large selection of gifts and perfumes, including the big names. Usually you can find someone who speaks English to sell you a Cardin watch.

If you're adventurous, you may want to seek out some native goods in little shops along the backstreets of Pointe-à-Pitre. Considered collector's items are the straw hats or salacos made in Les Saintes islands. They look distinctly related to Chinese coolie hats and are usually well designed, often made of split bamboo. Native doudou dolls are also popular gift items.

Open-air stalls surround the **covered market** at the corner of rue Frébault and rue Thiers. Here you can discover the many fruits, spices, and vegetables that are enjoyable just to view if not to taste. A deep fragrance of a Créole market permeates the place. In madras turbans local Créole women make deals over their strings of fire-red pimientos. The bright fabrics they wear compete with the rich tones of oranges, papayas, bananas, mangoes, and pineapples. The sounds of an African-accented French fill the air.

MOVING ON

Saint-John Perse once wrote about the fine time sailors had when they arrived in Pointe-à-Pitre when it was used as a stopover anchorage on the famous route du Rhum. But since that day is long gone, you may not want to linger; you can take a different route instead, this one to the "South Riviera," from Pointe-à-Pitre to Pointe des Châteaux.

LE BAS DU FORT

The first tourist complex, just 2 miles east of Pointe-à-Pitre, is called Le Bas du Fort, near Gosier.

The **Aquarium de la Guadeloupe,** place Créole, Marina Bas-du-Fort (tel. 90-92-38), is rated as one of the three most important of France and is the largest and most modern in the Caribbean. Just off the main highway near Bas-du-Fort Marina, the aquarium is home to tropical fish, coral, underwater plants, and huge sharks and other sea creatures. The exhibits are all clearly labeled. Open daily from 9am to 7pm. Admission is 35F ($6.75) for adults, 25F ($4.80) for children 12 and under.

WHERE TO STAY

FLEUR D'EPEE NOVOTEL, Le Bas du Fort, 97190 Gosier, Guadeloupe, F.W.I. Tel. 90-81-49, or toll free 800/221-4542. Fax 90-99-07. 186 rms. A/C MINIBAR TV TEL

$ Rates (including continental breakfast): Winter, 960F–1,210F ($184.60–$232.70) single; 1,040F–1,640F ($200–$315.35) double. Summer, 605F ($116.35) single; 780F ($150) double. AE, DC, MC, V. **Parking:** Free.

This is the most visible branch in Guadeloupe of a France-based hotel chain whose financial success has inspired feature stories in newspapers around Europe. This branch stands beside a pair of crescent-shaped bays whose white sands are shaded by palms and sea-grape trees, near the center of the resort complex of Bas du Fort, about 3 miles south of Pointe-à-Pitre. Designed for the resort market, each bedroom is a well-scrubbed, modern, carefully tiled enclave of quiet, with private bath and a simple but functional floor plan which is duplicated in Novotels around the world. There's a breeze-filled restaurant on the premises, as well as about a dozen indoor/outdoor eateries within walking distance, many with views of the beach.

PLM AZUR MARISSOL, Le Bas du Fort, 97190 Gosier, Guadeloupe, F.W.I. Tel. 90-84-44. Fax 90-83-32. 200 rms. A/C MINIBAR TV TEL

$ Rates (including continental breakfast): Winter, 775F–930F ($149.05–$178.85) single; 1,090F–1,416F ($209.60–$272.30) double. Summer, 550F ($105.75) single; 700F ($134.60) double. AE, DC, MC, V. **Parking:** Free.

Near the entrance to the touristic complex of Bas du Fort, about 3½ miles south of Pointe-à-Pitre, is a secluded bungalow colony of two- and three-story structures that were originally built in 1975. The PLM Azur is set away from the main road and occupies the grounds that stretch between a secondary route and the shoreline. In a setting of banana trees and lawns, it offers first-class comfort, with rooms either in bungalows or in the two wings, which open onto a view of the parklike grounds or the water. The furnishings are sober and modern, the floors are tiled, the baths have a separate toilet, and all units have either twin or double beds.

Dining/Entertainment: Next to the pool is a circular bar, Le Wahoo. The hotel's deluxe restaurant, Le Grand Baie, opens onto a terrace where you can order local Créole specialties or traditional French cuisine. Sicali is an open grill lying halfway between the beach and the pool.

Services: Laundry, massage, baby-sitting, concierge.

Facilities: Small beach; large swimming pool; beauty and fitness center known as "Gym-Tropique," with a "hammam" steam room, exercise lessons called "gymnastique douce," relaxation exercises based on yoga, and hot-water baths with algae or oils; water-sports kiosk featuring windsurfing, sailing, and snorkeling; scuba diving can be arranged.

WHERE TO DINE

LA PLANTATION, Galerie Commerciale de la Marina, Le Bas du Fort. Tel. 90-84-83.

Cuisine: MODERN FRENCH. **Reservations:** Recommended.

$ Prices: Appetizers 70F–150F ($13.45–$28.85); main courses 105F–130F ($20.20–$25). AE, DC, MC, V.

Open: Lunch Mon–Fri noon–2:30pm; dinner Mon–Sat 7–10:30pm.

La Plantation is a stylish and sophisticated establishment whose main dining room overlooks the most impressive section of the resort's marina complex 3 miles south of Pointe-à-Pitre. In this intimate, air-conditioned setting, modern adaptations of French cuisine are presented by Gianni Ferraris, the Turin, Italy–born owner. He and his French-born chefs turn out delectable meals, which might include a lobster-and-sweetbreads salad with a seafood vinaigrette, a pot-au-feu of fish richly flavored with Glenfiddich scotch, breast of wild duckling stuffed with pistachio nuts, and a "biscuit" composed of crayfish soufflé interwoven with al dente vegetables. Traditionalists might appreciate this establishment's plantation-style conch or its medley of smoked fish.

GOSIER

Some of the biggest and most important hotels of Guadeloupe are found at this holiday center, with its nearly 5 miles of beach, stretching east from Pointe-à-Pitre.

For an excursion, you can climb to **Fort Fleur-d'Epée**, dating from the 18th century. Its dungeons and battlements are testaments to the ferocious fighting between the French and British armies in 1794 seeking to control the island. The well-preserved ruins command the crown of a hill. From there you'll have good views over the bay of Pointe-à-Pitre, and on a clear day you can see the neighboring offshore islands of Marie-Galante and Iles des Saintes.

WHERE TO STAY

ECOTEL GUADELOUPE, route de Gosier, 97190 Gosier, Guadeloupe, F.W.I. Tel. 90-60-00. Fax 90-60-60. 44 rms. A/C MINIBAR TV TEL
$ Rates (including continental breakfast): Winter, 580F ($111.55) single; 780F ($150) double. Summer, 380F ($73.05) single; 525F ($100.95) double. AE, DC, MC, V. **Parking:** Free.
A restful retreat surrounded by gardens, an 8-minute drive from the capital and 10 minutes (6 miles) east of the airport, the Ecotel Guadeloupe is maintained by students from the local hotel school. It's modern in styling, yet its restaurant (Jardin Gourmand), bar, and bedrooms are French West Indian in feeling. Each of the accommodations opens onto a view of the pool, the gardens, or the adjoining forest. The units contain many built-in pieces. The air conditioning is occasionally not strong enough for some guests, but it's silent.

Dining/Entertainment: At the restaurant, Jardin Gourmand, serving dinner only, you get not only student waiters but also student cooks, the latter under the tutelage of a trained chef from France. Among the specialties are a filet de machoiran, a fleshy fish shipped in from Guyana; the local red snapper done in a variety of ways; and a gâteau de langouste (spiny lobster) with whisky. If you choose, you can dine on lighter fare alongside the swimming pool at Pap-Pap. Breakfast is served on an al fresco extension of the comfortably furnished reception area.

Services: Room service (for breakfast), laundry, baby-sitting.
Facilities: Swimming pool, car-rental desk, shopping boutiques.

LA CREOLE BEACH HOTEL, Pointe de la Verdure, 97190 Gosier, Guadeloupe, F.W.I. Tel. 90-46-46. Fax 90-46-66. 319 rms. 6 duplexes. A/C MINIBAR TV TEL
$ Rates (including continental breakfast): Winter, $128 single; $156 double; from $348 duplex. Summer, $110 single; $150 double; from $242 duplex. AE, DC, MC, V. **Parking:** Free.
Sporting the nicest hotel design of any Gosier establishment, half New Orleans and half colonial, La Créole stands alongside two beaches in a setting of lawns and trees, as well as hibiscus and bougainvillea. The bedrooms are traditional in tone, with dark-wood pieces and carpeted floors. Your balcony will be large enough to be your breakfast spot or a perch for your sundowner.

Dining/Entertainment: The hotel restaurant, attractively decorated with plants, serves many local specials along with a more familiar international cuisine. During the day guests enjoy drinks at the poolside bar, St-Tropez, or a lunch at the beach snack bar.

Services: Room service (at mealtimes), laundry, baby-sitting.
Facilities: Swimming pool, tennis courts, scuba diving, waterskiing, sailboat rentals.

PULLMAN AZUR CALLINAGO BEACH HOTEL AND VILLAGE, P.O. Box 1, 97190 Gosier, Guadeloupe, F.W.I. Tel. 84-25-25. Fax 84-24-90. 40 rms, 115 apartments. A/C MINIBAR TV TEL

$ Rates (including breakfast in rooms but not in apartments): Winter, 625F–700F ($120.20–$134.60) single; 810F–940F ($155.75–$180.75) double; 740F–870F ($142.30–$167.30) apartment for two; 1,070F–1,300F ($205.75–$250) apartment for four. Summer, 370F ($71.15) single; 530F ($101.90) double; from 420F ($80.75) apartment for two; 740F ($142.30) apartment for four. MAP 150F ($28.85) per person extra. American buffet breakfast 65F ($12.50) extra for apartment occupants. AE, DC, MC, V. **Parking:** Free.

Named after a Carib military hero, and reminiscent of a small resort along the Mediterranean, this hotel stands along the Gosier beachfront between the Pullman Vieille Tour and the Arawak Hotel 2 miles east of Pointe-à-Pitre. Rooms are housed in pink-and-white stucco buildings, and contain private baths and balconies. Most of the accommodations, however, are in a separate compound designed somewhat like a small village. Contained within it are a series of spacious studios and duplex apartments with modern furnishings, a bathroom, and a complete kitchen. A sliding glass wall opens onto a small private balcony overlooking Gosier Bay. Each of the duplexes, suitable for three or four occupants, contains a spiral staircase which leads to an upstairs bedroom, with a private bath and another small terrace.

Dining/Entertainment: Although residents can prepare their meals within their own kitchens, there's a Créole/French restaurant on the premises, the Tomaly, whose name is translated from the Arawak as "Meal."

Services: Room service (for breakfast), laundry, baby-sitting.

Facilities: Beach, freshwater swimming pool, two tennis courts; waterskiing, sailing, snorkeling, pedalboating, and windsurfing available at an extra cost; market selling food supplies.

PULLMAN VIEILLE TOUR, Montauban, 97190 Gosier, Guadeloupe, F.W.I. Tel. 84-23-23. Fax 84-23-23. 158 rms, 2 suites. A/C MINIBAR TV TEL

$ Rates (including continental breakfast): Winter, 1,230F–1,170F ($236.55–$225) single; 1,825F–1,480F ($350.95–$284.60) double; from 2,500F ($480.75) suite. Summer, 660F ($126.90) single; 1,480F ($284.60) double; from 2,100F ($403.85) suite. AE, DC, MC, V. **Parking:** Free.

★ In this harmonious combination of the old and the practical new, you get vintage charm and an authentic Créole quality. Originally established by a local family, and recently acquired from them by the Pullman Hotel Chain, the complex was built directly east of Pointe-à-Pitre within the shadow of a sugar mill whose thick walls date from 1835. Today, the mill serves as the resort's reception area, and scattered throughout the grounds are the dented and rusted mechanical parts of the former mill. Modern annexes and wings have been added, which all seem to flow unobtrusively out into the surrounding gardens; each contains first-class rooms with balconies overlooking the gardens and a small private beach.

Dining/Entertainment: The resort contains two restaurants, the more formal of which is discussed in "Where to Dine," below. Breakfast and lunch are served in the poolside Ajoupa Restaurant. Sometimes limbo dancers are brought in, and buffets and barbecues are planned.

Services: Concierge, baby-sitting, laundry.

Facilities: Water sports from the hotel's small beach (including snorkeling, sailing, windsurfing, and swimming), tennis court (lit at night), swimming pool.

WHERE TO DINE

At some of these places you'll get Créole cookery with a relaxed atmosphere, and often relaxed service too.

AUBERGE DE LA VIEILLE TOUR, in the Pullman Vieille Tour Hôtel, Montauban, Gosier. Tel. 84-23-23.

Cuisine: FRENCH/CREOLE. **Reservations:** Recommended.

$ Prices: Appetizers 40F–80F ($7.70–$15.40); main courses 100F–190F ($19.25–$36.55); fixed-price meal 200F ($38.45). AE, DC, MC, V.
Open: Dinner only, daily 7–9:30pm.

⭐ One of the finest restaurants on the island is in a big-windowed pavilion near the swimming pool of the previously recommended hotel east of Pointe-à-Pitre. Decorated in the French style, it's staffed with a bevy of islanders dressed in traditional Créole garb. The menu changes but perhaps the fish soup with fennel will get you going, and might be followed by veal sweetbreads delicately braised with honey or roast lamb with a saffron sabayon. The locally caught red snapper is likely to be accompanied by cucumber balls and mango butter (yes, mango butter).

CHEZ ROSETTE, Lotissement des Gisors, route de Gosier. Tel. 84-11-32.
  Cuisine: FRENCH/CREOLE. **Reservations:** Recommended.
$ Prices: Appetizers 40F–80F ($7.70–$15.40); main courses 80F–120F ($15.40–$23.10); three-course fixed-price meal 120F ($23.10). MC, V.
  Open: Lunch daily noon–3pm; dinner daily 7–11:30pm.
Chez Rosette is in the center of the village of Gosier near many of the previously recommended hotels, whose guests, even though on the half-board plan, come here for dinner. They know they'll get zesty Créole cookery beautifully flavored with spices and herbs. Originally established on the front porch of an unpretentious island home, Chez Rosette is one of the largest Créole places on Guadeloupe. Rosette Limol is the owner today and is capably assisted by her many daughters. The restaurant is in a sprawling wood building with several wings, a handful of dining rooms, and a garden with outside tables.
  Known for its fish platters, which are often stewed or curried, the restaurant also serves seafood stew and colombos of goat, chicken, or conch. You'll be served by a bevy of Guadeloupiennes dressed in the traditional *madras et foulard*

CHEZ VIOLETTA, Perinette Gosier. Tel. 84-10-34.
  Cuisine: FRENCH/CREOLE. **Reservations:** Not required.
$ Prices: Appetizers 45F–80F ($8.65–$15.40); main courses 85F–135F ($16.35–$25.95). AE, DC, MC, V.
  Open: Lunch daily noon–3:30pm; dinner daily 7:30–11pm.

⭐ At the far-eastern end of Gosier village, en route to Ste-Anne, this is the most formally decorated of all the Créole restaurants on the island. It has Louis XIII-style velvet-covered chairs, striped wallpaper in rich but somber colors, and a decor that looks as if it had been transported from Burgundy. In spite of its neocolonial trappings, this is the domain of a high priestess of Créole cookery. Her name is Violetta, and her skill has become almost a legend on the island.
  On the à la carte menu, try her stuffed crabs, her blaff of seafood, and her fresh fish of the day (perhaps red snapper). For an appetizer, ask for cod fritters or beignets called accra. The classic blood sausage, boudin, is also served here. In addition, she does a fine conch ragoût, superb in texture and flavor; it's best when served with hot chiles grown on Guadeloupe. On occasion she'll even prepare a brochette of shark, if available. Fresh pineapple makes an ideal dessert, or you can try her banana cake. Waitresses dress in *madras et foulard*.

LA CHAUBETTE, route de la Riviera. Tel. 84-14-29.
  Cuisine: CREOLE. **Reservations:** Recommended.
$ Prices: Appetizers 12F–22F ($2.30–$4.25); main courses 55F–85F ($10.60–$16.35). MC, V.
  Open: Lunch Mon–Sat noon–4pm; dinner Mon–Sat 7–11pm.
Begin your meal here with a rum punch, made with white rum and served with a lime wedge and sugar. But don't order too much—it's lethal, and you won't be able to get through the rest of dinner. This is a "front porch" Créole restaurant with lots of local color. About a 12-minute run east of Pointe-à-Pitre, it's almost like the Guadeloupe version of a roadside inn, with its red-checked tablecloths and curtains made of bamboo. Mme Gitane Chavalin is in charge, and she's known in the area for her

Créole recipes. She uses the fish and produce of her island whenever possible. When it's available, her langouste is peerless, as is her hog's-head cheese with a minced-onion vinaigrette. Top off your fine meal with either coconut ice cream or a banana flaming with rum.

STE-ANNE

About 9 miles east of Gosier, little Ste-Anne is a sugar town and a small resort offering many fine beaches and lodging facilities. In many ways it's the most charming of the villages of Guadeloupe, with its town hall in pastel colors, its church, and its principal square, place de la Victoire, where a statue of Schoelcher commemorates the abolition of slavery in 1848.

WHERE TO STAY

CLUB MED–CARAVELLE, 97180 Ste-Anne, Guadeloupe, F.W.I. Tel. 88-21-00, or toll free 800/CLUB-MED. Fax 88-06-06. 329 rms. A/C TEL
Transportation: Free hotel shuttle meets passengers at the airport.
$ Rates (including all meals and activities): Winter, $970–$1,400 per person per week double. Summer, $900–$1,100 per person per week double. Higher rates over New Year's. Children under 12 in their parents' room, $1,030 in winter, $730 in summer. Single supplement 30% above the per-person rate for a double. AE, MC, V. **Parking:** Free.

St-Anne's best-known resort is Club Med–Caravelle, covering 45 acres along a cape covered with palm trees. Its beach is one of the finest in the French West Indies. Beads are legal tender here. Club Med vacations are open to members only, but membership is available. An all-inclusive vacation package is offered at one price, which depends on the time of year, and includes all-you-can-eat meals daily, with unlimited wine at lunch and dinner, plus use of all sports facilities, with expert instruction and equipment.

Note that during the summer (but a bit less so during the winter) this resort, more than any other Club Med in the Caribbean, markets itself almost exclusively to a French clientele through its sales outlets in Paris. Though North Americans are welcome, be warned that almost all midsummer activities here are conducted in French, which may or may not suit your particular vacation plans.

Dining/Entertainment: Throughout the year, food is a specialty at the resort. The breakfast and lunch buffet tables groan with French, continental, and Créole delicacies. Dinner is served in the main dining room, which has been enlarged and remodeled into a series of small, comfortable sections, or in La Beguine annex restaurant. There's a weekly folklore night when the dinner features specialties of the region, along with a performance by the Guadeloupe folklore ballet. Also in the evening, guests gather around the bar and dance floor, which becomes the theater for nightly entertainment. Afterward you can dance at the midnight disco.

Services: Laundry.

Facilities: Beach, windsurfing, sailing, snorkeling trips (leaving daily from the dock), sea excursions to explore the island's coastline, six tennis courts, archery, calisthenics, volleyball, basketball, table tennis.

HOTEL LA TOUBANA, Durivage (B.P. 63), 97180 Ste-Anne, Guadeloupe, F.W.I. Tel. 88-25-78. Fax 88-38-90. 32 bungalows. A/C MINIBAR TEL
$ Rates (including continental breakfast): Winter, 650F–1,090F ($125–$209.60) single; 850F–1,300F ($163.45–$250) double. Summer, 475–565F ($91.35–$108.65) single; 590F–700F ($113.45–$134.60) double. AE, DC, V. **Parking:** Free.

The Hôtel La Toubana is centered around a low-lying stone building on a cliff overlooking the bay. Many guests come here just for the view, which on a clear day encompasses Marie-Galante, Dominica, La Désirade, and the Iles des Saintes, but you'll quickly learn that there's far more to this charming place than just a panorama.

The red-roofed bungalows lie scattered among the tropical shrubs along the adjacent hillsides (*toubana* is the Arawak word for "small house").

Dining/Entertainment: The dining room offers both indoor and al fresco dining stretching right up to the edge of the pool.

Services: Room service (for breakfast), laundry, baby-sitting.

Facilities: Beach (a 5-minute walk from any lodging), tennis courts; deep-sea fishing and other water sports can be arranged.

LE RELAIS DU MOULIN, Châteaubrun, 97180 Ste-Anne, Guadeloupe, F.W.I. Tel. 88-13-78. Fax 88-03-92. 40 rms. A/C MINIBAR TEL

$ **Rates** (including continental breakfast): Winter, 535F ($102.90) single; 660F ($126.90) double; 615F ($118.25) single occupancy duplex, 765F ($147.10) double occupancy duplex. Summer, 400F ($76.90) single; 550F ($105.75) double; 615F ($118.25) single occupancy duplex, 765F ($147.10) double occupancy duplex. MAP 150F ($28.85) per person extra. AE, DC, MC, V. **Parking:** Free.

The 19th-century stone tower that serves as this establishment's centerpiece was originally built as the headquarters of a prosperous sugar plantation. Today it juts boldly above the hilly countryside on the outskirts of Ste-Anne, and serves as the registration desk and lobby for the resort. About half the units here are private bungalows with red roofs and white walls. The remainder are duplex apartments, grouped into interconnected clusters of four, whose white exterior walls are covered with trumpet vines and bougainvillea. Each unit has a private bath, terrace with a hammock, and refrigerator.

Dining/Entertainment: Guests congregate at the poolside breeze-filled bar. For a recommendation of the restaurant, Tap-Tap, see "Where to Dine," below.

Facilities: Swimming pool, free bicycles.

WHERE TO DINE

TAP-TAP, in Le Relais du Moulin, Châteaubrun, Ste-Anne. Tel. 88-23-96.
Cuisine: FRENCH. **Reservations:** Recommended.

$ **Prices:** Appetizers 30F–90F ($5.75–$17.30); main courses 90F–120F ($17.30–$23.10); fixed-price meal 140F–195F ($26.90–$37.50). AE, DC, MC, V.
Open: Lunch daily noon–2:30pm; dinner daily 7–10pm.

You dine in the shadow of a soaring mill, originally built in 1848, beneath a ceiling crisscrossed with heavy beams. Oversize windows flood the interior with sunlight at lunch. At night, the flickering candles give the room the aura of a Norman farm. The kitchen turns out a blend of Antillean-inspired French food. Specialties include accras de morue (codfish), freshwater crayfish flambéed in old rum, a court bouillon of red snapper, and an array of colombos (curries). The resort lies in the heart of some of the best-developed horse country in Guadeloupe, on the outskirts of Ste-Anne.

ST-FRANÇOIS

Continuing east from Ste-Anne, you'll notice many old round towers named for Father Labat, the Dominican founder of the sugarcane industry. These towers were once used as mills to grind the cane. St-François, 25 miles east of Pointe-à-Pitre, used to be a sleepy fishing village, known for its native Créole restaurants. Then Air France discovered it and opened a Méridien hotel with a casino. That was followed by the promotional activities of J. F. Rozan, a native, who invested heavily to make St-François a jet-set resort. Now the once-sleepy village has first-class accommodations, as well as an airport available to private jets, a golf course, and a marina.

WHERE TO STAY

HAMAK, 97118 St-François, Guadeloupe, F.W.I. Tel. 88-59-99. Fax 88-41-92. 56 suites. A/C MINIBAR TV TEL

$ **Rates:** Winter, $270–$310 single; $340–$400 double. Summer, $200–$250 single; $230–$280 double. Continental breakfast $15 extra. AE, MC, V. **Closed:** Aug 29–Oct 3. **Parking:** Free.

⭐ For people who care for independence, I suggest a bungalow at Guadeloupe's poshest property, 25 miles east of Pointe-à-Pitre and a quarter of a mile from the Méridien. Its sandy beach along the lagoon and its proximity to golf and a tiny airport make it popular with jet-setters from Europe and the U.S. "Les amis" like to be elegant, but informally so. It was the site of the 1979 international summit that brought President Carter and Giscard d'Estaing, among others, here. Spread on a 250-acre estate, the accommodations are in villas (each with two individual tropical suites with twin beds opening onto a walled garden patio where you can sunbathe *au naturel*). Each bungalow houses one to four guests.

Dining/Entertainment: Hamak has two dining rooms, one opening onto the beach, the other onto an enclosed garden. Outsiders can dine here if they reserve in advance.

Services: Room service, laundry, baby-sitting.

Facilities: 18-hole Robert Trent Jones golf course with a full-service clubhouse and snack bar, spa Jacuzzi pool, tennis courts, windsurfing, other water-sports facilities.

MERIDIEN ST-FRANÇOIS, 97118 St-François, Guadeloupe, F.W.I. Tel. 88-51-00. Fax 88-40-71. 258 rms, 9 suites. A/C TV TEL

$ Rates (including continental breakfast): Winter, 1,360F–2,500F ($259.60–$480.75) single; 1,680F–2,500F ($323.05–$480.75) double; from 2,000F–3,000F ($384.60–$576.90) suite. Summer, 1,100F ($211.55) single; 1,500F ($288.45) double; from 1,800F ($346.15) suite. AE, MC, V. **Parking:** Free.

The Méridien St-François was one of the first Méridien hotels built for Air France. It stands alongside one of the best beaches in Guadeloupe on 150 acres of land at the southernmost tip of the island, a 20-minute walk from the village of St-François. The climate, quite dry here, is refreshed by trade winds. The four-star hotel offers rooms overlooking the sea or the Robert Trent Jones–designed golf course with many amenities and furnishings in a modern style combined with Créole overtones.

Dining/Entertainment: Café Caribe, known for its sumptuous buffets, is a deluxe restaurant charging 220F ($48.40) and up for a good meal from the French or Créole repertoire. Or perhaps you'll prefer Balaou, a terraced restaurant in a more relaxed and exotic mood, where a fixed-price three-course meal costs around 195F ($37.50). In addition, the hotel has a grill and barbecue snack bar right on the beach, where the prices are quite high, especially if you order lobster.

Services: 24-hour room service, massage, baby-sitting, laundry.

Facilities: Swimming pool, tennis courts, windsurfers; golf available for an extra charge at the course next door (tel. 88-41-87 for information); near by marina; access to additional watersports; small airport for anyone wanting to charter flights to neighboring islands.

WHERE TO DINE

LA LOUISIANE, Quartier Ste-Marthe, outside St-François. Tel. 88-44-34.

Cuisine: FRENCH/CARIBBEAN. **Reservations:** Not required.

$ Prices: Appetizers 45F–85F ($8.65–$16.35); main courses 110F–130F ($21.15–$25). MC, V.

Open: Lunch Tues–Sun noon–2pm; dinner Tues–Sun 7–10pm.

The oldest building in this neighborhood about half a mile east of St-François, this century-old former plantation house is sheltered from the road by trees and shrubbery. When they emigrated, French owners Daniel and Muriel Hugon brought with them some of the best cuisine of their native regions, Provence and the Vosges. Full meals might include a filet of marlin with garlic sauce, sharkmeat with saffron sauce, filet of red snapper with a basil-flavored cream sauce, a gratin of lobster, veal escalope with shrimp, and scallops with ginger-and-lemon butter.

RESTAURANT LES OISEAUX, Anse des Rochers. Tel. 88-56-92.

Cuisine: FRENCH/ANTILLEAN. **Reservations:** Required.

$ Prices: Appetizers 45F–85F ($8.65–$16.35); main courses 115F–135F ($22.10–$25.95). V.
Open: Lunch Fri–Wed noon–3pm; dinner Fri–Sat and Mon–Wed 7–10:30pm.
Closed: Sept to early Oct.

Probably the best imitation of a Provençal farmhouse on the island stands on a seaside road about 3½ miles west of St-François on a scrub-covered landscape whose focal point is the sea and the island of Marie-Galante. Its walled-in front garden frames a stone-sided, low-slung building that produces an aroma of a southern French and Antillean cuisine worth the detour. This is the domain of Arthur Rollé and his wife, Claudette, who serve dishes like fish mousse, Créole-style beef, and a filet en croûte with red wine sauce. Try also the marmite Robinson, inspired by the tale of Robinson Crusoe, a delectable fondue of fish and vegetables which you cook for yourself in a combination of bubbling coconut and corn oil. Dessert might be a composite of four exotic sherbets or a crêpe.

POINTE DES CHATEAUX

Seven miles from St-François is Pointe des Châteaux, the easternmost tip of Grand-Terre, where the Atlantic meets the Caribbean. Here, where crashing waves sound around you, you'll see a cliff sculpted by the sea into castlelike formations, the erosion typical of France's Brittany coast. The view from here is splendid. At the top is a cross put there in the 19th century.

If you wish, you can walk to **Pointe des Colibris,** the extreme end of Guadeloupe. From there you'll have a view of the northeastern sector of the island, and to the east a look at La Désirade, another island which has the appearance of a huge vessel anchored far away. Among the coved beaches found around here, **Pointe Tarare** is the *au naturel* one.

LE MOULE

To go back to Pointe-à-Pitre from Pointe des Châteaux, you can use an alternative route, the N5 from St-François. After a 9-mile drive, you reach the village of Le Moule, which was founded at the end of the 17th century, and known long before Pointe-à-Pitre. It used to be a major shipping port for sugar. Now a tiny coastal fishing village, it never regained its importance after it was devastated in the hurricane of 1928, like so many other villages of Grand-Terre. Because of its more than 10-mile-long crescent-shaped beach, it's developing as a holiday center. Modern hotels built along the beaches have opened to accommodate visitors.

Specialties of this Guadeloupian village are palourdes, the clams that thrive in the semisalty mouths of freshwater rivers. Known for being more tender and less "rubbery" than saltwater clams, they often, even when fresh, have a distinct sulfur taste not unlike that of overpoached eggs. Local gastronomes prepare them with saffron and aged rum or cognac.

Nearby, the sea unearthed some skulls, grim reminders of the fierce battles fought among the Caribs and the French and English. It's called "the Beach of Skulls and Bones."

The **Edgar Clerc Archeological Museum** (tel. 23-57-57) shows a collection of both Carib and Arawak artifacts gathered from various islands of the Lesser Antilles. The admission-free museum is open on Monday, Tuesday, Thursday, and Friday from 9:30am to 12:30pm and 2:30 to 5:30pm.

To return to Pointe-à-Pitre, I suggest that you use the D3 toward Abymes. The road winds around as you plunge deeply into Grand-Terre. As a curiosity, about halfway along the way, a road will bring you to **Jabrun du Nord** and **Jabrun du Sud.** These two villages are inhabited by caucasians with blond hair, said to be survivors of aristocrats slaughtered during the Revolution. Those members of their families who escaped found safety by hiding out in Les Grands Fonds. The most important family here is named Matignon, and they gave their name to the colony known as "les Blancs Matignon." These citizens are said to be related to Prince Rainier of Monaco.

Pointe-à-Pitre lies only 10 miles from Les Grand Fonds.

A DRIVING TOUR NORTH FROM POINTE-A-PITRE

From Pointe-à-Pitre, head northeast toward Abymes, passing next through Moren à l'Eau; you'll reach **Petit Canal** after 13 miles. This is Guadeloupe's sugarcane country, and a sweet smell fills the air.

PORT LOUIS

Continuing northwest along the coast from Petit Canal, you come to Port Louis, well known for its beautiful beach, La Plage du Souffleur, which I find best in the spring, when the brilliant white sand is effectively shown off against a contrast of the flaming red poinciana. During the week the beach is an especially quiet spot. The little port town is asleep under a heavy sun, and it has some good restaurants.

Where to Dine

LE POISSON D'OR, rue Sadi-Carnot, 2, Port Louis. Tel. 22-88-63.
Cuisine: CREOLE. **Reservations:** Recommended. **Directions:** Drive northwest from Petit Canal along the coastal road.
$ Prices: Appetizers 45F–85F ($8.65–$16.35); main courses 110F–130F ($21.15–$25). No credit cards.
Open: Breakfast/lunch daily 9am–4:30pm; dinner daily 6–9pm.

You'll enter the little Antillean house by going down a narrow corridor and emerging into a rustic room. You can climb the steps to the second floor, where an open terrace overlooks the sea and the fishing boats. In spite of the simple setting, the food is excellent. Try the stuffed crabs, the court-bouillon, topped off by coconut ice cream, which is homemade and tastes it. The place is a fine choice for an experience with Créole cookery, complemented by a bottle of good wine.

ANSE BERTRAND

About 5 miles from Port Louis lies Anse Bertrand, the northernmost village of Guadeloupe. What is now a fishing village was the last refuge of the Carib tribes, and a reserve was once created here. Everything now, however, is sleepy.

Where to Dine

FOLIE PLAGE [CHEZ PRUDENCE], Anse Laborde. Tel. 22-11-17.
Cuisine: CREOLE. **Reservations:** Not required.
$ Prices: Appetizers 12F–25F ($2.30–$4.80); main courses 60F–75F ($11.55–$14.40). AE, DC, MC, V.
Open: Lunch daily noon–3pm; dinner daily 7–10pm.

About a mile north of Anse Bertrand at Anse Laborde, this place is owned by Prudence Marcelin, a *cuisinière patronne*, who enjoys much local acclaim for her Créole cookery. She draws people from all over the island, especially on Sunday when this place is its most crowded. Island children frolic in the pool, and in between courses diners can shop for handcrafts, clothes, and souvenirs sold by a handful of nearby vendors. Her court bouillon is excellent, as is either her goat or chicken (curried) colombo. The palourdes (clams) are superb, and she makes a zesty sauce to serve with fish. Her crabes farcis are done to perfection as well. The place is relaxed and casual. She also rents a handful of very basic bungalows for informal overnight stays.

LE CHATEAU DE FEUILLES, Campêche, Anse Bertrand. Tel. 22-30-30.
Cuisine: FRENCH/CARIBBEAN. **Reservations:** Required, especially in summer when meals are prepared only in anticipation of your arrival.

$ Prices: Appetizers 50F–100F ($9.60–$19.25); main courses 100F–200F ($19.25–$38.45). V.

Open: Lunch Tues–Sun in winter 11:30am–3pm. At night, at least 10 diners must reserve before they will open. **Closed:** Sept.

⭐ Set inland from the sea, amid 8 rolling acres of greenery and blossoming flowers, this gastronomic hideaway is owned and run by a Norman-born couple, Jean-Pierre and Martine Dubost. To reach their place, which is 9 miles from Le Moule on the Campeche road, motorists must pass the ruins of La Mahaudière, an 18th-century sugar mill. A gifted chef making maximum use of local ingredients, Monsieur Dubost prepares pâté of warm sea urchins, sautéed conch with Créole sauce, gigot of shark with fresh pasta and saffron sauce, and a sauerkraut of fresh fish with papaya.

CONTINUING THE TOUR

From Anse Bertrand, you can drive along a graveled road heading for **Pointe de la Grande Vigie,** the northernmost tip of the island, which you reach after 4 miles of what I hope will be cautious driving. Park your car and walk carefully along a narrow lane which will bring you to the northernmost rock of Guadeloupe. The view of the sweeping Atlantic from the top of rocky cliffs is remarkable—you stand at a distance of about 280 feet above the sea.

Afterward, a 4-mile drive south on quite a good road will bring you to the **Porte d'Enfer** or "gateway to hell." Once there, you'll find the sea rushing violently against two narrow cliffs.

After this kind of awesome experience in the remote part of the island, you can head back, going either to Morne à l'Eau or Le Moule before connecting to the road taking you back to Pointe-à-Pitre.

AROUND BASSE-TERRE

Leaving Pointe-à-Pitre by the N1, you can explore the lesser windward coast. After a mile and a half you cross the Rivière Salée at Pont de la Gabarre. This narrow strait separates the two islands that form Guadeloupe. For the next 4 miles the road runs straight through sugarcane fields.

At the sign, on a main crossing, turn right on the N2 toward **Baie Mahault.** Leaving that town on the right, head for **Lamentin.** This village was settled by corsairs at the beginning of the 18th century. Scattered about are some colonial mansions.

STE-ROSE

From Lamentin, you can drive for 6½ miles to Ste-Rose, where you'll find several good beaches. On your left, a small road leads to **Sofaia,** from which you'll have a splendid view over the coast and forest preserve. The locals claim that a sulfur spring here has curative powers.

Where to Dine

CHEZ CLARA, Ste-Rose. Tel. 28-72-99.
Cuisine: CREOLE. **Reservations:** Recommended.
$ Prices: Appetizers 30F–50F ($5.75–$9.60); main courses 60F–140F ($11.55–$26.90). MC, V.

Open: Lunch Thurs–Tues noon–2:30pm; dinner Thurs–Tues 8–10pm. **Closed:** Oct.

⭐ Chez Clara, on the waterfront near the center of town, is the culinary statement of Clara Lesueur and her talented and charming semiretired mother, Justine. Clara lived for 15 years in Paris as a member of an experimental jazz dance troupe, but she returned to Guadeloupe, her home, and set up her breeze-cooled restaurant. Try for a table on the open patio, where palm trees complement the color scheme.

Clara and Justine artfully meld the French style of fine dining with authentic, spicy Créole cookery. Specialties may include crayfish, curried skate, lobster, clams, boudin (blood pudding), ouassous (local crayfish), brochette of swordfish, palourdes (small clams), several different preparations of conch, and crabes farcis (red-orange crabs with a spicy filling). The "sauce chien" served with many of the dishes is a blend of hot peppers, garlic, lime juice, and "secret things" that go well with the house drink, made with six local fruits and ample quantities of rum. Your dessert sherbet might be guava, soursop, or passionfruit.

DESHAIES/GRAND ANSE

A few miles farther along, you reach Pointe Allegre, the northernmost point of Basse-Terre. At **Clugny Beach,** you'll be at the site where the first settler landed on Guadeloupe.

A couple of miles farther will bring you to **Grand Anse,** one of the best beaches in Guadeloupe. It's very large and still secluded, sheltered by many tropical trees.

At **Deshaies,** snorkeling and fishing are popular pastimes. The narrow road winds up and down and has a corniche look to it, with the blue sea underneath, the view of green mountains studded with colorful hamlets.

Nine miles from Deshaies, **Pointe Noire** comes into view. Its name comes from black volcanic rocks. Look for the odd polychrome cenotaph in town.

ROUTE DE LA TRAVERSEE

Four miles from Pointe Noire, you reach **Mahaut.** On your left begins the ✪ **route de la Traversée,** the Transcoastal Highway. This is the best way to explore the scenic wonders of **Parc Naturel de Guadeloupe** when traveling between the capital, Basse-Terre, and Pointe-à-Pitre. I recommend going this way, as you pass through a tropical forest.

To preserve the Parc Naturel, Guadeloupe has set aside 74,100 acres, or about one-fifth of its entire terrain. Reached by modern roads, this is a huge tract of mountains, tropical forests, and magnificent scenery.

The park is home to a variety of tame animals, including Titi (a raccoon adopted as its official mascot), and such birds as the wood pigeon, turtledove, and thrush. Small exhibition huts, devoted to the volcano, the forest, or to coffee, sugarcane, and rum, are scattered throughout the park.

The Parc Naturel has no gates, no opening or closing hours, and no admission fee.

From Mahaut you climb slowly in a setting of giant ferns and luxuriant vegetation. Four miles after the fork, you reach **Les Deux Mamelles (The Two Breasts),** where you can park your car and go for a hike. Some of the trails are for experts only; others, such as the Pigeon Trail, will bring you to a summit of about 2,600 feet where the view is impressive. Expect to spend at least 3 hours going each way. Halfway along the trail you can stop at Forest House. From that point, many lanes, all signposted, branch off on trails that will last anywhere from 20 minutes to 2 hours. Try to find the **Chute de l'Ecrevisse,** the "Crayfish Waterfall," a little pond of very cold water which you'll discover after a quarter of a mile.

After the hike, the main road descends toward Versailles, a hamlet about 5 miles from Pointe-à-Pitre.

However, before taking this route, while still traveling between Pointe Noire and Mahaut on the west coast, you might consider the following luncheon stop.

Where to Dine

CHEZ VANEAU, Mahaut/Pointe Noire. Tel. 98-01-71.
   Cuisine: CREOLE. **Reservations:** Not required.
$ **Prices:** Appetizers 15F–30F ($2.90–$5.75); main courses 60F–100F ($11.55–$19.25). AE, MC, V.
   Open: Daily noon–9pm, depending on business, with an early closing on Sun.

Set in an isolated pocket of forest about 18 miles north of Pointe Noire, far from any of its neighbors, Chez Vaneau offers a wide, breeze-filled veranda overlooking a gully, the sight of local neighbors playing cards, and steaming Créole specialties coming from the kitchen. This is the unquestioned domain of Vaneau Desbonnes, who is assisted by his wife, Marie-Gracieuse. Specialties include oysters with a piquant sauce, crayfish bisque, ragoût of goat, different preparations of octopus, and roast pork.

BOUILLANTE

If you don't take the route de la Traversée at this time but wish to continue exploring the west coast, you can head south from Mahaut until you reach the village of Bouillante, which is exciting for only one reason: You might encounter Brigitte Bardot, as she's a part-time resident.

Try not to miss seeing the small island called **Ilet à Goyave** or **Ilet du Pigeon.** Jacques Cousteau often explored the silent depths around it.

Facing the islet is the best choice for a luncheon on the whole island. After a meal at La Touna, you can explore around the village of Bouillante, the country known for its thermal springs. In some places if you scratch the ground for only a few inches you'll feel the heat.

Where to Dine Near Bouillante

CHEZ LOULOUSE, Malendure Plage. Tel. 98-70-34.
   Cuisine: CREOLE. **Reservations:** Not required.
$ Prices: Appetizers 15F–25F ($2.90–$4.80); main courses 40F–55F ($7.70–$10.60); fixed-price meals 80F–130F ($15.40–$25). MC, V.
   Open: Lunch daily noon–3:30pm; dinner daily 7–10pm.
Another good choice for lunch is Chez Loulouse, a staunchly matriarchal establishment with plenty of offhanded charm, beside the sands of the well-known beach, opposite Pigeon Island. Many guests prefer their rum punches on the panoramic veranda, overlooking a scene of loaded boats preparing to depart and merchants hawking their wares. A quieter oasis is the equally colorful dining room inside, just past the bar. There, beneath a ceiling of palm fronds, is a wraparound series of Créole murals that seem to go well with the reggae music emanating loudly from the bar.

This is the creation of one of the most visible and charming Créole matrons on this end of the island, Mme Loulouse Paisley-Carbon. Assisted by her children, she offers house-style Caribbean lobster, spicy versions of conch, octopus, accras, gratin of christophine (squash), and savory colombos (curries) of chicken or pork.

LA TOUNA, Malendure. Tel. 98-70-10.
   Cuisine: SEAFOOD/CREOLE. **Reservations:** Recommended on Sun. **Directions:** In the village of Mahaut, turn left on route 2 and drive south.
$ Prices: Appetizers 45F–60F ($8.65–$11.55); main courses 55F–145F ($10.60–$27.90). MC, V.
   Open: Lunch only, Tues–Sun noon–3pm. **Closed:** Sept.
Built on a narrow strip of sand between the road and the sea, its foundation almost touching the water, this charming restaurant has a marine panorama, which complements the seafood specialties that Francis and Françoise Ricart concoct so skillfully in the kitchen. Most of the dining tables are in a side veranda whose ceiling is covered with palm fronds. Many guests delay a meal until after a drink in the sunken bar whose encircling banquettes give the impression of a ship's cabin.

One of the most appealing rituals in Guadeloupe has become a habit here: You are brought a tray on which are seven or eight carafes, each filled with a rum-soaked tropical fruit, such as guava, maracoja, pineapple, and passionfruit. You select the ingredients you prefer and mix your own drink. Of course if you prefer the house specialty, you'll have a combination of fruit with or without rum, one of the most refreshing drinks on the island.

Menu items make use of the freshest ingredients, many of them brought in daily by the Ricarts' deep-sea-fishing business. Full meals might include a mousse of smoked swordfish, calamari provençal, stuffed crabs, stuffed sea urchins, kingfish au poivre, and stingray with black-butter sauce.

VIEUX HABITANTS

The winding coast road brings you to Vieux Habitants (Old Settlers), one of the oldest villages on the island, founded back in 1636. The name comes from the people who settled it. After serving in the employment of the West Indies Company, they retired here. But they preferred to call themselves inhabitants, so as not to be confused with slaves.

BASSE-TERRE

Another 10 miles of winding roads bring you to Basse-Terre, the seat of the government of Guadeloupe, lying between the water and La Soufrière, the volcano. Founded in 1634, it's the oldest town on the island and still has a lot of charm; its market squares are shaded by tamarind and palm trees.

The town suffered heavy destruction at the hands of British troops in 1691 and again in 1702. It was also the center of fierce fighting during the French Revolution, when the political changes that swept across Europe caused explosive tensions in Guadeloupe. (As it did in the mainland of France, the guillotine claimed many lives in Guadeloupe during the infamous Reign of Terror.)

In spite of the town's history, there isn't much to see in Basse-Terre except for a 17th-century cathedral and Fort St-Charles, which has guarded the city (not always well) since it was established.

Where to Stay En Route

RELAIS DE LA GRANDE SOUFRIERE, route de la Soufrière, 97120 St-Claude, Guadeloupe, F.W.I. Tel. 80-01-27. Fax 80-18-40. 22 rms. A/C TV TEL

$ Rates: 250F–300F ($48.10–$57.70) single; 400F–500F ($76.90–$96.15) double. Breakfast 30F ($5.75) extra. DC, MC, V. **Parking:** Free.

Originally built in the 1860s as the island residence of one of Guadeloupe's governors, Governor Favtier, this charming Créole mansion on the eastern outskirts of town was reopened in 1987 and makes an excellent place for a stopover. Graced with verandas, a flowering garden, high ceilings, and thick walls, the hotel offers comfortable bedrooms and an old-fashioned dining room. Each accommodation has a private bath and a view of the garden, an inner courtyard, or the faraway sea. The beach is a 10-minute drive away, although the mansion's location in the north-central residential section of St-Claude places it near most of the town's architectural points of interest.

Even if you're not a guest, you can visit for a meal served daily in the dining room from noon to 2pm and 7 to 9:30pm. Fixed-price meals range from 120F to 180F ($23.10 to $34.60), while à la carte dinners usually average around 230F ($44.25). Specialties include recipes from classic French cuisine as well as adaptations of Créole dishes.

Where to Dine

LE HOUELMONT, rue de la République, 34. Tel. 81-35-96.
Cuisine: INTERNATIONAL. **Reservations:** Required.
$ Prices: Appetizers 45F–60F ($8.65–$11.55); main courses 55F–150F ($10.60–$28.85); fixed-price meals from 110F ($21.15). MC, V.
Open: Lunch Mon–Sat noon–3pm; dinner Mon–Sat 7–10:30pm. **Closed:** Dinner in Oct.

Set in the monumental heart of town, across a boulevard from a massive government building called the Conseil General, is the oldest and best-established restaurant in the island capital, Le Houëlmont. After climbing a flight of stairs to the paneled second story, diners enjoy a sweeping view over the hillside, sloping down to the sea one block away. Mme Boulon, the owner, an old-time Guadeloupienne restaurateur, offers fixed-price and à la carte meals. Specialties include a medley of Créole food such as accras, court bouillon of fish, grilled fish, steaks, shellfish, and blood sausage, plus French and international dishes.

LA SOUFRIERE

The big attraction of Basse-Terre is the famous sulfur-puffing La Soufrière volcano, which is still alive, but dormant—for the moment at least. Rising to a height of some 4,800 feet, it's flanked by banana plantations and lush foliage.

After leaving the capital at Basse-Terre, you can drive to **St-Claude,** a suburb, 4 miles up the mountainside at a height of 1,900 feet. It has an elegant reputation for its perfect climate and tropical gardens.

Instead of going to St-Claude, you can head for **Matouba,** in a country of clear mountain spring water. The only sound you're likely to hear at this idyllic place is of birds and the running water of dozens of springs. The village was settled long ago by Hindus.

From St-Claude, you can begin the climb up the narrow, winding road the Guadeloupeans say leads to hell—that is, ✪ **La Soufrière.** The road ends at a parking area at La Savane à Mulets, at an altitude of 3,300 feet. That is the ultimate point to be reached by car. Hikers are able to climb right to the mouth of the volcano. However, in 1975 the appearance of ashes, mud, billowing smoke, and earthquakelike tremors proved that the old beast was still alive.

In the resettlement process, 75,000 inhabitants were relocated to Grande-Terre. However, no deaths were reported. But the inhabitants of Basse-Terre still keep a watchful eye on the smoking giant.

Even in the parking lot, you can feel the heat of the volcano merely by touching the ground. Steam emerges from fumaroles and sulfurous fumes from the volcano's "burps." Of course, fumes come from its pit and mud caldrons as well.

Where to Dine En Route

CHEZ PAUL DE MATOUBA, Rivière Rouge. Tel. 80-29-20.

Cuisine: CREOLE/INTERNATIONAL. **Reservations:** Not required. **Directions:** Follow the clearly marked signs—it's beside a gully close to the center of the village.

$ **Prices:** Appetizers 15F–30F ($2.90–$5.75); main courses 50F–90F ($9.60–$17.30). MC, V.

Open: Lunch only Tues–Sun noon–4pm.

You'll find good food in this family-run restaurant which sits beside the banks of the small Rivière Rouge (Red River). The dining room on the second floor is enclosed by windows, allowing one to drink in the surrounding dark-green foliage of the mountains. The cookery is Créole, and crayfish dishes are the specialty. However, because of the influence of the region's early settlers, East Indian meals are also available. By all means, drink the mineral or spring water of Matouba. What one diner called "an honest meal" might include stuffed crab, colombo (curried) chicken, as well as an array of French, Créole, and Hindu specialties. You're likely to find the place overcrowded in the winter season with the tour-bus crowd.

THE WINDWARD COAST

From Basse-Terre to Pointe-à-Pitre, the road follows the east coast, called the Windward Coast. The country here is richer and greener than elsewhere on the island.

To reach **Trois Rivières** you have a choice of two routes. One goes along the coastline, coming eventually to Vieux Fort, from which you can see Les Saintes archipelago. The other heads across the hills, Monts Caraïbes.

Near the pier in Trois Rivières you'll see the pre-Columbian petroglyphs carved by the original inhabitants, the Arawaks. They are called merely Roches Gravées, or "carved rocks." In this archeological park, the rock engravings are of animal and human figures, dating most likely from A.D. 300 or 400. You'll also see specimens of plants, including cocoa, pimento, and banana, that the Arawaks cultivated long before the Europeans set foot on Guadeloupe. From Trois Rivières, you can take boats to Les Saintes.

After leaving Trois Rivières, you continue on route 1. Passing through the village of Banaier, you turn on your left at Anse Saint-Sauveur to reach the famous ☼ **Chutes du Carbet,** a trio of waterfalls. The road to two of them is a narrow, winding one, along many steep hills, passing through banana plantations as you move deeper into a tropical forest.

After 3 miles, a lane, suitable only for hikers, brings you to Zombie Pool. Half a mile farther along, a fork to the left takes you to Grand Etang, or large pool. At a point 6 miles from the main road, a parking area is available and you'll have to walk the rest of the way on an uneasy trail toward the second fall, Le Carbet. Expect to spend around 20 to 30 minutes, depending on how slippery the lane is. Then you'll be at the foot of this second fall where the water drops from 230 feet. The waters here average 70° Fahrenheit, which is pretty warm for a mountain spring.

The first fall is the most impressive, but it takes 2 hours of rough hiking to get there. The third fall is reached from Capesterre on the main road by climbing to Routhiers. This fall is less impressive in height, only 70 feet. When the Carbet water runs out of La Soufrière, it's almost boiling.

After Capesterre, you can go along for 4½ miles to see the statue of the first tourist who landed in Guadeloupe, which stands in the town square of Ste-Marie. The tourist was Christopher Columbus, who anchored a quarter of a mile from Ste-Marie on November 4, 1493. In the journal of his second voyage he wrote, "We arrived, seeing ahead of us a large mountain which seemed to want to rise up to the sky, in the middle of which was a peak higher than all the rest of the mountains from which flowed a living stream."

However, when Caribs started shooting arrows at him, he left quickly.

After Ste-Marie, you pass through Goyave, then Petit Bourg, seeing on your left the route de la Traversée before reaching Pointe-à-Pitre. You will have just completed the most fascinating scenic tour Guadeloupe has to offer.

ACTIVITIES AROUND THE ISLAND
SPORTS & RECREATION

BEACHES Chances are, your hotel will be built right on a beach, or will lie no more than 20 minutes from a good one. There is a plenitude of natural beaches dotting the island from the surf-brushed dark strands of western Basse-Terre to the long stretches of white sand encircling Grande-Terre. Public beaches are generally free, but some charge for parking. Unlike hotel beaches, they have few facilities. Hotels welcome nonguests, but charge for changing facilities, beach chairs, and towels.

Sunday is family day at the beach. Topless sunbathing is common at hotels, less so on village beaches. Nudist beaches also exist, including at **Ilet du Gosier,** off the shore of Gosier, site of many leading hotels.

Outstanding beaches of Guadeloupe include **Caravelle Beach,** a long, reef-protected stretch of sand outside Ste-Anne, about 9 miles from Gosier.

Another nudist beach, **Plage de Tarare,** lies near the tip of Grand-Terre at Pointe des Châteaux, site of many local restaurants.

On Basse-Terre, one of the best beaches is **Grande Anse,** a palm-sheltered beach north of Deshaies on the northwest coast.

Other good beaches are found on the offshore islands, Iles des Saintes and Marie-Galante (see below).

DEEP-SEA FISHING The season for barracuda and kingfish is January to May. For tuna, dolphin, and bonito, it's December to March. Hotels will recommend such deep-sea fishing boats as the *Papyrus,* based in Bas du Fort at the Port de Plaissance Marina (tel. 82-74-94).

GOLF Guadeloupe's only golf course is the well-known **Golf de St-François** (tel. 88-41-87) at St-François, opposite the Hôtel Méridien, about 22 miles east of Raizet

Airport. The golf course runs alongside an 800-acre lagoon where windsurfing, waterskiing, and sailing prevail. The course, designed by Robert Trent Jones, is a 6,755-yard, par-71 course, which presents many challenges to the golfer, with water traps on 6 of the 18 holes, massive bunkers, prevailing trade winds, and a particularly fiendish 400-yard, par-4 ninth hole. The par-5 sixth is the toughest hole on the course; its 450 yards must be negotiated into the constant easterly winds. Greens fees are 250F ($48.10) per day per person, a cost which allows a full day of playing time. Clubs can be rented for 100F ($19.25), and an electrified golf cart costs 220F ($42.30) for each 18-hole cycle you use it for.

HIKING The **Parc Naturel de Guadeloupe** is the best hiking grounds in the Caribbean, in my opinion (see the touring notes on route de la Traversée in "Around Basse-Terre," above). Marked trails cut through the deep foliage of rain forests until you come upon a waterfall or perhaps a cool mountain pool. The big excursion country, of course, is around the volcano, La Soufrière. However, because of the dangers involved, I recommend that you go out only with a guide. Hiking brochures are available from the tourist office. Hotel tour desks can arrange this activity.

Warning: Hikers may experience heavy downpours. The annual precipitation on the higher slopes is 250 inches per year, so be prepared.

SAILING Sailboats of varying sizes, crewed or bareboat, are plentiful. Information can be secured at any hotel desk. Sunfish sailing can be arranged at almost every beachfront hotel.

SCUBA DIVING Scuba divers are drawn to Guadeloupe, and Jacques Cousteau described Guadeloupe's Pigeon Island as "one of the world's 10 best diving spots." During a typical dive, sergeant majors become visible at 30 feet, spiny sea urchins and dazzling green parrotfish at 60 feet, and magnificent finger, black, brain, and star coral come into view at 80 feet.

Other dive sites are Mouton Vert, Mouchoir Carré, and Cay Ismini. They are close to the major hotels, in the bay of Petit Cul-de-Sac Marin, south of Rivière Salée, the channel separating the two halves of Guadeloupe. North of the Salée is another bay, Grand Cul-de-Sac Marin, where the small islets of Fajou and Caret also boast fine diving.

Chez Guy, B.P. 4 Pigeon, 97132 Bouillante, Guadeloupe, F.W.I. (tel. 98-82-43), is Guadeloupe's only PADI dive center, lying directly on the Cousteau Underwater Reserve. This is world-class diving, with high-quality rental equipment. The center's boats make the 10-minute trip to the dive sites three times a day. Accommodations can be arranged, as can a 10-dive ticket at a considerable discount. The price of one dive is 150F ($28.85).

TENNIS All the large resort hotels have tennis courts, many of which they light at night for games. The noonday sun is often too hot for most players. If you're a guest, tennis is free at most of these hotels, but you will be charged for night play.

If your hotel doesn't have a court, you might consider an outing to **Le Relais du Moulin,** Châteaubrun, near Ste-Anne (tel. 88-23-96).

WINDSURFING & WATERSKIING Windsurfing is the hottest sport in Guadeloupe today, and it's available with lessons at all the major beach hotels, at a cost of 90F ($17.30) and up.

Most seaside hotels can arrange waterskiing at 110F ($21.15) for 30 minutes' boating time.

EVENING ENTERTAINMENT

Guadeloupeans claim that the beguine was invented here, not on Martinique. Regardless, the people dance the beguine as if they truly did own it. Of course, calypso and the merengue move rhythmically along—the islanders are known for their dancing.

Ask at your hotel where the folkloric **Ballets Guadeloupeans** will be appearing. This troupe makes frequent appearances at the big hotels, although they don't enjoy the fame of the Ballets Martiniquais, the troupe on the neighbor island already described.

Guests from surrounding hotels often head for the **Hôtel Salako,** Pointe de la Verdure (tel. 84-22-22). The after-dark attraction is the Disco Berdy, a disco nightclub. If the crowd is right, the place can be fun. For your first drink you pay 80F ($15.40), which includes the entrance fee. Open Tuesday through Sunday from 10:30pm to 4am.

Casino de la Marina (tel. 88-41-44) stands near the Hôtel Méridien St-François. It's open nightly from 9pm to 3am to persons 21 or over providing they have proof of identity—a driver's license with a photo or a valid passport. The entrance fee is 60F ($11.55), and once inside, you can play American roulette, chemin-de-fer, and blackjack. Dress is casual. The nightclub in the open garden offers dancing under the stars to a live band or disco. A free buffet is spread on Saturday night. Drinks begin at 40F ($7.70).

Another casino is **Gosier-les-Bains,** on the grounds of the Hôtel Arawak (tel. 84-18-36) in Gosier. Entrance fee is 60F ($11.55). Coat and tie are not required, but dress tends to be casually elegant. An identity card with photo is required for admission. It's open nightly from 9pm to 3am, and the most popular games are blackjack, roulette, and chemin-de-fer. There is not only a restaurant, but also a disco.

AN EXCURSION TO THE ILES DES SAINTES

A cluster of eight islands off the southern coast of Guadeloupe, the Iles des Saintes are certainly off the beaten track. The two main islands and six rocks are Terre-de-Haut, Terre-de-Bas, Ilet-à-Cabrit, La Coche, Les Augustins, Grand Ilet, Le Redonde, and Le Pâté; only Terre-de-Haut ("land of high"), and to a lesser extent Terre-de-Bas ("land below"), attract visitors.

If you're planning a visit, **Terre-de-Haut** is the most interesting Saint to call upon. It's the only one with facilities for overnight guests.

Some claim that Les Saintes has one of the nicest bays in the world, a lilliput Rio de Janeiro with a sugarloaf. The isles, just 6 miles from the main island, were discovered by Columbus (who else?) on November 4, 1493, who named them "Los Santos."

The history of Les Saintes is very much the history of Guadeloupe itself. In years past the islands have been heavily fortified, as they were considered Guadeloupe's Gibraltar. The climate is very dry, and until the desalination plant opened, water was often rationed.

The population of Terre-de-Haut is mainly Caucasian, all fisherfolk or sailors and their families who are descended from Breton corsairs. The very skilled sailors maneuver large boats called *saintois* and wear coolielike headgear called a *salaco,* which is shallow and white with sun shades covered in cloth built on radiating ribs of thick bamboo. Frankly, the hats look like small parasols. If you want to take a photograph of these sailors, please make a polite request (in French, no less; otherwise they won't know what you're talking about). Visitors often like to buy these hats (if they can find them) for use as beach wear.

Terre-de-Haut is a place for discovery and lovers of nature, many of whom stake out their exhibitionistic space on the nude beach at Anse Crawen.

ORIENTATION

GETTING THERE   By Plane   The fastest way to get there is by plane. The "airport" is a truncated landing strip that accommodates nothing larger than 20-seat Twin Otters. **Air Guadeloupe** (tel. 27-61-90) has two round-trips daily from Pointe-à-Pitre, which take 15 minutes.

By Ferry   Most islanders reach Terre-de-Haut via one of the several ferryboats that travel from Guadeloupe every day. Most visitors opt for one of the two boats that depart every day from Pointe-à-Pitre's Gare Maritime des Iles, on quai Gatine, across the street from the well-known open-air market. The trip requires 50 minutes each way, and costs 150F ($28.85) for round-trip passage. Three different ferryboats also depart from Trois Rivières, and two other ferryboats depart from the island's capital of Basse-Terre. Transit from either of these last two cities requires 25 minutes each way, and costs 75F ($14.40) for the round-trip passage.

The most popular departure time for Terre-de-Haut from Pointe-à-Pitre is at 8am Monday through Saturday, and at 7am on Sunday, with return at 4pm. (Be at the ferryboat terminal at least 15 minutes prior to the anticipated departure.) For more information and last-minute departure schedules, contact **Trans-Antilles Express,** Gare Maritime, quai Gatine, Pointe-à-Pitre (tel. 83-12-45).

GETTING AROUND On an island that doesn't have a single car-rental agency, you get about by walking or renting a **bike** or **motorscooter,** which can be rented at hotels and in town near the pier.

There are also minibuses called **Taxis de l'Ile** (eight in all), which take six to eight passengers.

WHERE TO STAY

BOIS JOLI, 97137 Terre-de-Haut, Les Saintes, Guadeloupe, F.W.I. Tel. 99-52-53. Fax 99-55-05. 25 rms, 5 bungalows.

$ Rates (including MAP): Winter, 475F–610F ($91.35–$117.30) double; 620F–1,100F ($119.25–$211.55) bungalow for two. Summer, 440F–525F ($84.60–$100.95) double; 580F–1,000F ($111.55–$192.30) bungalow for two. MC, V. **Parking:** Free.

On the western part of the island, 2 miles from the village overlooking a fine beach, Bois Joli sits in confectionery white, a stucco block on a palm-studded rise of a slope. Accommodations are in the main house and five bungalows on the hillside. Bold-patterned fabrics are used on the beds, and the rooms have modern furnishings. Twenty of the units are air-conditioned, with various combinations of shower and bath arrangements. Sixteen rooms have private phones. Families might be interested in renting one of the bungalows. The food is good Créole cooking. Mr. Blandin can arrange for waterskiing, sailing, boat trips to some of the islets or rocks that form Les Saintes, and snorkeling.

HOTEL LA SAINTOISE, 97137 Terre-de-Haut, Les Saintes, Guadeloupe, F.W.I. Tel. 99-52-50. 10 rms. A/C

$ Rates (including continental breakfast): 250F ($48.10) single; 350F ($67.30) double. AE, MC, V.

Originally built in the 1960s, La Saintoise is a modern, two-story building set near the almond trees and widespread poinciana of the town's main square, near the ferryboat dock, across from the town hall. As in a small French village, the inn places tables and chairs on the sidewalk, where you can sit out and observe what action there is. The owner will welcome you and show you through his uncluttered lobby to one of his bedrooms, each of which is outfitted with a tile bath. They are on the second floor, and the furnishings are admittedly modest. Everything is kept immaculately clean.

KANAOA, 97137 Terre-de-Haut, Les Saintes, Guadeloupe, F.W.I. Tel. 99-51-36. Fax 99-55-04. 14 rms. A/C

$ Rates (including continental breakfast): Winter, 440F ($84.60) single; 520F ($100) double. Summer, 380F ($73.05) single; 440F ($84.60) double. MC, V.

Named after the open-sided log canoes originally used by the Arawaks, this modern structure erected on a little beach at Pointe Coquelet is utterly plain and lies within a 10-minute walk north of town center. All accommodations have private showers and rather spartan furnishings; five have views of the sea and Anse Mire cove. A limited amount of English is spoken. The location is 1¼ miles from the airport. A garden with its own swimming pool lies near the hotel, and a pleasant restaurant serves breakfast, lunch, and dinner on the premises.

LE VILLAGE CREOLE, Point Coquelet, 97137 Terre-de-Haut, Les Saintes, Guadeloupe, F.W.I. Tel. 99-53-83. Fax 99-55-55. 22 rms. A/C MINIBAR TEL

$ Rates: Winter, 640F–780F ($123.05–$150) single or double. Summer, from 330F ($63.45) single or double. MC, V.

Owned and operated by a courteous family from the French mainland, this hotel was built on 3½ acres that border 130 yards of seashore, close to the foundations of Fort Napoléon, on the northern edge of town, at the mouth of the harbor. Each of the villas reflects the traditional architectural style of the island. Eleven villas are divided into two first-class duplexes, all with private bath, a washer-dryer, a flower-filled patio, and comfortable summery furniture. Daily maid service is also included. The owner prefers weekly rentals, but shorter or longer stays are possible. Bicycles can be rented and day trips planned.

WHERE TO DINE

Many French-speaking guests used to come to Terre-de-Haut to eat roast iguana, the large but harmless lizard found on many of these islands. But now that the species is endangered, it is no longer recommended that this dish be consumed. Instead, you'll find lots of conch (called lambi), Caribbean lobster, and fresh fish. Prices are reasonable—among the least expensive meals of any place in France. For dessert, you can sample the savory island specialty, tourment d'amour ("agony of love"), a coconut pastry available in the restaurants but best sampled from the barefoot children who sell the delicacy near the boat dock.

CHEZ JEANNINE [LE CASSE-CROUTE], Fond-de-Curé, Terre-de-Haut. Tel. 99-53-37.
   Cuisine: CREOLE. **Reservations:** Recommended for large groups only.
$ Prices: Fixed-price meal 60F ($11.55) for two courses, 75F ($14.40) for three courses. MC, V.
   Open: Breakfast/lunch daily 8am–3pm; dinner daily 6:30–10pm.

The creative statement of Mme Jeannine Bairtran, originally from Guadeloupe, this restaurant is in a simple Créole house decorated with modern Caribbean accessories, a 3-minute walk south of the town center. Only fixed-price meals are served, and they include an array of Créole-inspired dishes, such as avocado stuffed with crabmeat, a gâteau de poissons (literally "fish cake"), and several different varieties of curry-enhanced stews (including one made with goat). Crayfish and grilled fish (the ubiquitous catch of the day) appear daily on the menu. Local vegetables are used. The ambience is that of a Créole bistro—in other words, a hut with nautical trappings and bright tablecloths.

LA REDONDE/LE VERGER DES ILES, Terre-de-Haut. Tel. 99-54-96.
   Cuisine: CREOLE/SEAFOOD. **Reservations:** Recommended.
$ Prices: La Redonde, appetizers 25F–50F ($4.80–$9.60); main courses 45F–140F ($8.65–$26.90). Le Verger des Iles, fixed-price meals 70F–150F ($13.45–$28.85). MC, V.
   Open: Lunch Sat–Thurs noon–2pm; dinner Sat–Thurs 7–10pm.

This pair of restaurants lies across the street from one another in the heart of town beside the town's only church. Both offer excellent seafood, prepared in the Créole style and served in ample portions. Owned and operated by Georges Garçon (known to everyone in town as "Chicken Georges" because of a long-ago legal imbroglio), they comprise one of the most charming dining enclaves on the island. La Redonde is the more formal and expensive of the two. Contained in a tiny clapboard Créole house, it specializes in lobster, seafood paella, and a flavorful dish called La Redonde, which is prepared for a minimum of two diners. Simmered in a stewpot with the best of the day's local catch, it includes portions of conch, mussels, shrimp, octopus, two different kinds of fish, and lobster.

   Le Verger des Iles contains a scattering of tables and chairs set beneath parasols and the roof of an open-sided pavilion. There, an array of fixed-price meals includes a somewhat more limited selection of seafood and grills. Service in both places is easygoing, but one or two of the establishment's rum punches might help ease you into the slowed-down rhythms.

LES AMANDIERS, place de la Mairie. Tel. 99-50-06.
Cuisine: CREOLE. **Reservations:** Recommended.
$ Prices: Fixed-price meals 55F–100F ($10.60–$19.25). AE, MC, V.
Open: Lunch daily 11am–2:30pm; dinner daily 7–11pm.

Across from the town hall on the main square of Bourg is perhaps the most traditional Créole bistro on Terre-de-Haut. Conch (lambi) is prepared either in a fricassée or a colombo, a savory curry stew. Also available is a court bouillon of fish, a gâteau (terrine) of fish, and a seemingly endless supply of grilled crayfish, a staple of the island. The catch of the day is also grilled the way you like it. You'll find an intriguing collection of stews, concocted from fish, bananas, and christophene (chayote, to many readers.) A knowledge of French would be helpful around here.

WHAT TO SEE & DO

On Terre-de-Haut, the main settlement is at **Bourg,** a single street that follows the curve of the fishing harbor. A charming hamlet, it has little houses with red or blue doorways, balconies, and Victorian gingerbread gewgaws. Donkeys are the beasts of burden, and everywhere you look are fish nets drying in the sunshine. You can also explore the ruins of **Fort Napoléon,** which is left over from those 17th-century wars, including the naval encounter known in European history books as "The Battle of the Saints." You can see the barracks and prison cells, as well as the drawbridge and art museum. Occasionally you'll spot an iguana scurrying up the ramparts. Directly across the bay, atop Ilet-à-Cabrit, sits the fort named in honor of Empress Joséphine.

You might also get a sailor to take you on his boat to the other main island, **Terre-de-Bas,** which has no accommodations, incidentally. Or you can stay on Terre-de-Haut and hike to **Le Grand Souffleur** with its beautiful cliffs, and to **Le Chameau,** the highest point on the island, rising to a peak of 1,000 feet.

Scuba-diving centers are not limited to mainland Guadeloupe. The underwater world off Les Saintes has attracted deep-sea divers as renowned as Jacques Cousteau, but even the less experienced may explore its challenging depths and multicolored reefs. Intriguing underwater grottoes found near Fort Napoléon on Terre-de-Haut are also explored.

AN EXCURSION TO MARIE-GALANTE

This offshore dependency of Guadeloupe is an almost-perfect circle of about 60 square miles. Almost exclusively French-speaking, it lies 20 miles south of Guadeloupe's Grand-Terre and is full of rustic charm.

Columbus noticed it before he did Guadeloupe, on November 3, 1493. He named it for his own vessel, but didn't land there. In fact, it was 150 years later that the first European came ashore.

The first French governor of the island was Constant d'Aubigne, father of the Marquise de Maintenon. Several captains from the West Indies Company attempted settlement, but none of them succeeded. In 1674 Marie-Galante was given to the Crown, and from that point on its history was closely linked to that of Guadeloupe.

However, after 1816 the island settled down to a quiet slumber. You could hear the sugarcane growing on the plantations—and that was about it. Many windmills were built to crush the cane, and lots of tropical fruits were grown.

Now, some 30,000 inhabitants live here and make their living from sugar and rum, the latter said to be the best in the Caribbean. The island's climate is rather dry, and there are many good beaches. One of these stretches of sand covers at least 5 miles—brilliantly white. However, swimming can be dangerous in some places. The best beach is at **Petite Anse,** 6½ miles from **Grand-Bourg,** the main town, with an 1845 baroque church. The 18th-century Grand Anse rum distillery can be visited, as can the historic fishing hamlet of Vieux Fort.

GETTING THERE & GETTING AROUND **Air Guadeloupe** (tel. 27-61-90) will bring you to the island in just 20 minutes from Pointe-à-Pitre, landing at Les Basse Airport on Marie-Galante, about 2 miles from Grand-Bourg.

Trans-Antilles Express, Gare Maritime, quai Gatine, Pointe-à-Pitre (tel. 83-12-45), operates boat service to the island, with four daily round-trips between Pointe-à-Pitre and Grand-Bourg. The round-trip fare is 155F ($29.80). Departures from Pointe-à-Pitre are daily at 8am, with a return from Grand-Bourg at 4pm.

A limited number of taxis are available at the airport, but the price should be negotiated before you drive off.

WHERE TO STAY & DINE

There are only a few little accommodations on the island, which, even if they aren't very up-to-date in amenities, are clean and hearty. At least the greetings are friendly. They may also be bewildering if you speak no French.

AUBERGE DE SOLEDAD, 97112 Grand-Bourg, Marie-Galante, Guadeloupe, F.W.I. Tel. 97-75-45. 18 rms. TV
$ Rates (including continental breakfast): 225F–275F ($43.25–$52.90) single or double. No credit cards.
I prefer the Auberge de Soledad, which lies about 2 miles from the airport on the outskirts of Grand-Bourg. In a setting of sugarcane fields, it rents out simply furnished rooms, each with private shower. Rooms are also equipped with refrigerators and TV sets (the latter of little use to most English-speaking guests). The hotel also rents bicycles and small motorcycles to guests. On the grounds are tennis courts and a Créole restaurant.

L'AUBERGE DE L'ARBRE A PAIN, rue Jeanne-d'Arc, 32, 97112 Grand-Bourg, Marie-Galante, Guadeloupe, F.W.I. Tel. 97-73-69. 7 rms. A/C
Directions: At the harbor, take the first street going toward the church.
$ Rates: 240F–260F ($46.15–$50) single or double. MC, V.
Near the harbor in the middle of town, guests interested in a view of old colonial France will find respectable accommodations here. Each room has simple furnishings, a private bath, and easy access to nearby beaches. The hotel's restaurant is open continuously throughout the day for breakfast, lunch, and dinner, and offers such dishes as a court bouillon of fish, a soufflé of sea urchins, and a tempting array of fresh grilled fish. Full meals begin at 160F ($30.75), and you're welcome to have a meal here if you're visiting only for the day. Should you want a room, however, you should book well in advance.

AN EXCURSION TO LA DESIRADE

The ubiquitous Columbus spotted this *terre désirée* or "sought-after land" after his Atlantic crossing in 1493. Named La Désirade, the island, which is less than 7 miles long and about 1½ miles wide, lies just 5 miles off the eastern tip of Guadeloupe proper. This former leper colony is often visited on a day excursion (Club Med types like it a lot).

The island has fewer than 2,000 inhabitants, including the descendants of Europeans exiled here by royal command. Tourism has hardly touched the place, if you can forget about those "day trippers," and there are almost no facilities for overnighting, with a hardly recommendable exception or two.

The main hamlet is **Grande Anse,** which has a lovely small church with a presbytery and flower garden, and the homes of the local inhabitants. **Le Souffleur** is a village where boats are constructed, and at **Baie Mahault** are the ruins of an old leper colony from the early 18th century.

The best **beaches** are Souffleur, a tranquil oasis near the boat-building hamlet, and Baie Mahault, a small beach that is a Caribbean cliché with white sand and palm trees.

GETTING THERE From Pointe-à-Pitre, **Air Guadeloupe** (tel. 27-61-90) flies to La Désirade three times daily on a 20-minute flight. The airstrip on La Désirade accommodates up to 19-seat aircraft. Should you ever go by sea, the crossing is likely to be rough. A ferry leaves from La Darse in Pointe-à-Pitre; the crossing takes 1½ hours and costs 150F ($28.85) for a round-trip ticket. Telephone 83-32-67 for departure times. Usually it's possible to go from St-François at 8:15am and return from La Désirade at 3pm (trip time is 45 minutes).

GETTING AROUND   On La Désirade, three minibuses run between the airport and the towns. To get around, you might negotiate with a local driver. Bicycles are also available.

3. ST. MARTIN

Partitioned between the Netherlands and France, the divided island of St. Martin (Sint Maarten in Dutch) has a split personality. The 37-square-mile island is shaped like a lazy triangle. The northern part of the island, a land area of about 21 square miles, belongs to France, the southern part to the Netherlands.

The island has two jurisdictions, but there is complete freedom of movement between the two sectors. If you arrive on the Dutch side and clear Customs there, there'll be no red-tape formalities when crossing over to the French side—either for shopping, perhaps a hotel, or certainly for eating, as it has the best food (with some notable exceptions).

French St. Martin is governed from Guadeloupe and has direct representation in the government in Paris. Lying between Guadeloupe and Puerto Rico, the tiny island has been half French, half Dutch since 1648.

The principal town on the French side is **Marigot,** the seat of the subprefect and municipal council. Visitors come here not only for shopping, as the island is a free port, but also to enjoy the excellent cookery in the Créole bistros.

Marigot is not quite the same size as its counterpart, Philipsburg, in the Dutch sector. It has none of the frenzied pace of Philipsburg, which is often overrun with cruise-ship passengers. In fact, Marigot looks like a French village transplanted to the West Indies. The policeman on the beat is a gendarme. If you climb the hill over this tiny port, you'll be rewarded with a view from the old fort there.

About 20 minutes by car beyond Marigot is **Grand Case,** a small fishing village that is an outpost of French civilization with many good restaurants and a few places to stay.

St. Martin hardly has the attractions of St. Thomas, Puerto Rico, or Jamaica. You may ask "Why come here?" There are no dazzling sights, no spectacular nightlife. Even the sports program on St. Martin isn't as organized as it is on most Caribbean islands, although the Dutch side has golf and other diversions. Most people come to St. Martin just to relax on the island's many fine beaches.

For a description of the facilities and attractions of Dutch St. Maarten, refer to Chapter 9.

ORIENTATION

GETTING THERE   Most arrivals are at the Dutch-controlled **Queen Juliana International Airport,** St. Maarten. For a more detailed description of transportation on that side of the island, see "Getting There" in "Orientation" for on St. Maarten in Chapter 9.

If you're coming from St. Barts, however, **Air Guadeloupe** (tel. 27-61-90 on St. Barts or 90-37-37 on St. Martin) has 10-minute flights into French St. Martin's **Espérance Airport** in Grand Case (tel. 87-51-21), where you clear Customs.

GETTING AROUND   By Bus   It's much cheaper to get around on one of the island's buses, which run daily from 6am until midnight. One departs from Grande Case for Marigot every 20 minutes. There's a departure every hour from Marigot to the Dutch side. The one-way fare from Marigot to Philipsburg on the Dutch side is only $1, increasing to $1.50 from Grande Case.

By Taxi   For visitors, the most common means of transport is a taxi. A **Taxi Service & Information Center** operates at the port of Marigot (tel. 87-56-54). Always agree on the rate before getting into an unmetered cab. Here are some sample fares: from Espérance Airport to Grande Case Beach Club, $8; from Juliana airport to La Belle Créole, $16. These fares are in effect from 7am to 9pm; after that, they go up by 25% until midnight, rising by 50% after midnight.

You can also book 2½-hour sightseeing trips around the island, either through the organization listed above or at any hotel desk. The cost is $30 for one or two passengers, plus $7.50 for each additional.

By Rental Car   The division of the island into dual political zones makes car rentals a bit more problematic. Complicating the situation is a local law which forbids clients from picking up a rental car immediately upon arrival at Juliana airport. (This law was instigated, and is strictly enforced, by the island's union of taxi drivers.) Also, some companies, such as Budget, are reluctant to rent a car from its branch on the Dutch side to clients staying at hotels on the French side. Knowing this in advance, many visitors resign themselves to taking a taxi directly to their hotels as soon as they arrive at Juliana airport, and then the rental agency will either deliver a car directly to the renter's hotel, or a van will transport the renter to the depot where cars are stored.

Each of the largest North American car-rental companies maintains a branch on the island. **Avis** (tel. toll free 800/331-2112) usually sends a van from the Dutch side to pick up passengers. For more information on Avis, see "Getting Around" in "Orientation" for St. Martin in Chapter 9. **Budget Rent-a-Car** (tel. toll free 800/527-0700) insists that clients registered at hotels on the French side book their cars from Budget's office on the French side. Once you're on the island, call the office in French Cul-de-Sac in Marigot (tel. 87-38-22) and a car will be delivered to your hotel. Of the "big three," Budget's cars tend to be the least expensive, costing around $185 per week (plus 5% tax) for their cheapest car. A collision-damage waiver (CDW) costs around $10 a day, but even if you agree to buy it, you'll still be responsible for the first $600 of damage. It's best to book cars 14 days before your intended pickup to guarantee the lowest rate.

Hertz (tel. toll free 800/654-3001) maintains an office on French St. Martin, and usually arranges to deliver its cars directly to a client's hotel. To arrange this once you reach your hotel on the French side, call 87-73-01. Hertz charges around $192 per week, plus tax, with unlimited mileage included, for rentals of its least expensive cars. A collision-damage waiver is $11 per day, but even if you buy it, you'll still be liable for the first $1,500 of damage. Potential clients must be 25 or older to rent a car from Hertz.

The policies of each of these companies regarding dropoffs on the Dutch side differs, so it's best to check carefully before you rent. Avis, for example, is one of the island's most flexible car-rental companies and allows you to drop your car off near the Dutch section's Juliana airport (but not at the French side's Espérance airport) on the day of your departure. Most foreign driver's licenses are honored. One tank of gas should last a week.

FAST FACTS: ST. MARTIN

Area Code   St. Martin is *not* part of the Caribbean's 809 area code. For information on telephoning to and on the island, see "Telephone," below.

Banking Hours   Banks are generally open Monday through Thursday from 8:30am to 1pm and on Friday from 8:30am to 1pm and 4 to 5pm.

Currency   The currency, officially at least, is the **French franc (F),** yet U.S. dollars seem to be preferred wherever you go. Canadians should convert their money into U.S. dollars and not into francs. At press time, the exchange rate was 5.2F to $1 U.S.

Documents   U.S. and Canadian citizens should have either a passport, a voter registration card, or a birth certificate, plus an ongoing or a return ticket. With a birth certificate or voter registration card, you'll also need photo ID.

Electricity   The electricity is 220 volts AC, 50 cycles. Some hotels have altered the voltage and outlets in the bathrooms, so check. If not, don't count on the hotel; bring your own transformer and adapter if you plan to use your appliances such as a hairdryer.

Information   The tourist board, called **Syndicat d'Initiative,** is at Mairie de Saint-Martin at Marigot (tel. 87-57-21).

Language   English is widely spoken in St. Martin, although this is a French possession. A patois is spoken only by a small segment of the local populace.

Medical Care   There is a hospital in Marigot (tel. 87-50-07), and hotels will help visitors in contacting English-speaking doctors.

Safety   The crime wave hitting Dutch-held St. Maarten also plagues French St. Martin. Travel with extreme caution here, especially at night. Avoid driving at night along the Lowlands road. Armed patrols have helped the situation somewhat, but hotel safes should be used to guard your valuables.

Tax   A departure tax of 10F ($1.95) at Espérance airport is included in Air Guadeloupe's published fare.

Telephone   French St. Martin is linked to the Guadeloupe telephone system, which is *not* a part of the 809 area code that applies to most of the Caribbean. To call French St. Martin from the U.S., if your long-distance telephone company is equipped to handle international direct-dialing, dial 011 (the international access code), then 590 (the country code for Guadeloupe), and then the six-digit local number. If you cannot direct-dial internationally, dial 0 ("zero," for the operator) and tell the operator you wish to make an international call; once you are transferred to the international operator, state the 590 country code and then the local number, and the operator will dial the call for you.

To make a call within St. Martin only the six-digit local number is necessary; no codes are needed unless you are calling "long distance" to the Dutch side of the island, in which case dial 93 and the five-digit Dutch number. (To call French St. Martin from the Dutch side, dial 06 and the six-digit local number.) *Note:* In this chapter, only the local numbers are given.

Time   St. Martin operates on Atlantic standard time year round, 1 hour ahead of eastern standard time, which means that the only time the U.S. East Coast and St. Martin are in step is during the daylight saving time of summer.

Tips and Service   Your hotel is likely to add a 10% to 15% service charge to your bill to cover tipping. Likewise, most restaurants include the service charge on your bill.

Water   The water of St. Martin is safe to drink. In fact, most hotels serve desalinated water.

WHERE TO STAY

French St. Martin experienced a building boom in the 1980s and now has a wide range of accommodations, including three of the most luxurious hotels on the island (see below). Hotels here are more continental in flavor than some of the beachside hostelries outside Philipsburg in St. Maarten. On St. Martin, many little Antillean inns still exist where English is definitely the second language, if spoken at all.

Hotels on French St. Martin add a $4 government tax and a 10% service charge.

VERY EXPENSIVE

HOTEL LA SAMANNA, Baie Longue (B.P. 576, Marigot), 97150 St.

Martin, F.W.I. Tel. 87-51-22, or toll free 800/372-1323 in the U.S., 800/338-8782 in Canada. Fax 87-87-86. 15 rms, 70 apartments and villas. TEL

$ Rates: Winter, $350–$440 single; $480–$630 double; from $650 apartment or villa. Summer, $250–$350 single; $363–$440 double; from $495 apartment or villa. MAP $85 per person extra. AE, MC, V. **Parking:** Free. **Closed:** July–Oct.

⭐ The Hôtel La Samanna admits it's "not for everyone." However, if you're a person devoted to good, wholehearted, unabashed sybaritism—and have lots of money—you should fit in beautifully here. Set on a landscaped 55-acre piece of choice property northwest of Mullet Bay, La Samanna opens onto a mile and a half of white sandy beach. The resort, like so many places on St. Martin, is more evocative of the Côte d'Azur or Morocco than the Caribbean—it's what the French call *intime, tranquille, et informal.*

The hotel is a melange of styles. Arches and balconies in pure "Greek-fishing-village white" are set off effectively by the use of stunning royal-blue doors and umbrellas. Splashes of bold fabrics are used on the puffy cushions on the Haitian furniture, which is mostly in wicker and rattan. The colors are like a flamboyant flower garden. The choice of rooms is complicated. In the main building you'll find twin-bedded rooms with balconies that are screened from the terrace by a thatched ramada roof. Or you can ask for one of the two dozen one-bedroom apartments, one of the 16 two-bedroom units, or one of the six villas with three bedrooms—each with fully equipped kitchens, living rooms, dining areas, and large patios.

Dining/Entertainment: Dining is al fresco with a French cuisine prepared by some of the best chefs on the island. You eat out on a candlelit terrace overlooking Baie Longue. After dinner, the bar becomes a disco.

Services: Room service, laundry, baby-sitting, massages.

Facilities: Fitness and activity center, outdoor swimming pool, waterskiing, three tennis courts, sailboat rentals, shopping boutique.

LA BELLE CREOLE, Pointe des Pierres à Chaux (B.P. 578, Marigot), 97150 St. Martin, F.W.I. Tel. 87-58-66, or toll free 800/HILTONS. Fax 87-56-66. 138 rms, 18 suites. A/C MINIBAR TV TEL

$ Rates: Winter, $265 single; $395–$485 double; from $795 suite. Summer, $150 single; $225–$300 double; from $605 suite. MAP $48 per person extra. AE, DC, MC, V. **Parking:** Free.

⭐ Operated by Conrad Hotels, La Belle Créole is 2 miles from the French capital of Marigot and 5 miles from Juliana airport on the Dutch side. The deluxe Mediterranean-style resort, modeled after a fantasy Côte d'Azur fishing village, lies on a peninsula within view of the capital and is surrounded by three white beaches.

Stone walkways connect the central square of the resort to the accommodations housed in 21 separate three-story villas. Most units have private terraces. Five types of guest rooms are rented. All have either king-size or double beds, and five rooms are specially equipped for the disabled.

Dining/Entertainment: Seating 200 patrons, La Provence, the hotel's gourmet restaurant, offers continental and Créole cuisine, as well as three different "theme" nights.

Services: Laundry, baby-sitting.

Facilities: Gym, outdoor swimming pool, four tennis courts (lit at night) and a pro shop (operated by Peter Burwash Tennis International); water sports, including parasailing, windsurfing, waterskiing, jet skiing, and scuba diving.

MERIDIEN L'HABITATION DE LONVILLIERS, Marcel Cove (B.P. 581, Marigot), 97150 St. Martin, F.W.I. Tel. 87-33-33, 212/719-5750 in New York City, or toll free 800/543-4300. Fax 87-30-38. 248 rms, 52 suites. A/C MINIBAR TV TEL

$ Rates (including continental breakfast): Winter, $306–$346 single or double; from $584 suite. Summer, $177–$198 single or double; from $232 suite. AE, DC, MC, V. **Parking:** Free. **Closed:** Aug 31–Oct 1.

L'Habitation is a secluded sports- and spa-oriented retreat on a 150-acre flat of land between a 120-slip marina and 1,800 feet of white sand. Its isolated position was considered almost inaccessible until a crew of engineers cut a 2-mile road through some of the most rugged terrain on the island, 11 miles from Marigot and a 35-minute drive north of Juliana airport. Accommodations are in a string of Neo-Victorian buildings ringed with lattices, gingerbread, and verandas. Rental units consist of rooms, regular suites, marina suites, and two-bedroom suites. The rooms and suites are well equipped, each with its own kitchenette, soundproofing, balcony, two-sink bathroom, radio, internal video system, and a stylish decor of tropical furniture.

Dining/Entertainment: The pool bar resembles a tile-sheathed gazebo on stilts at the edge of the water. For casual dining, there's Le Balaou restaurant or Le BBQ on the beach. However, for a night of haute cuisine, head for the formal dining room, **La Belle France.**

Services: Room service, laundry, baby-sitting.

Facilities: Swimming pool; nearby health spa on a mountainside overlooking the hotel, with both a sports and fitness center and a dining and nightclub complex.

EXPENSIVE

ANSE MARGOT, Baie Nettle (B.P. 979, Marigot), 97150 St. Martin, F.W.I. Tel. 87-92-01. Fax 87-92-13. 58 rms, 38 suites. A/C MINIBAR TV TEL
$ Rates: Winter, $120–$235 single; $135–$235 double; from $195 suite. 20% reductions in summer. American breakfast $14 extra. AE, DC, MC, V. **Parking:** Free.

Luxurious and comforting, Anse Margot is set on a narrow sandy strip of seafront at Baie Nettle overlooking a saltwater lagoon, a 5-minute drive west of Marigot. The hotel consists of eight pastel-colored buildings, each adorned wedding-cake style with ornate balconies and gingerbread. Each of the beautifully furnished bedrooms has a French Antillean decor as well as a private bath and many other amenities.

Dining/Entertainment: The resort's social center rises like a miniature temple, with swimming pools flanking it on two sides. After dark, a pianist performs everything from Piaf to jazz. Sometimes local bands are brought in, especially on nights when the chef decides to offer a buffet. Otherwise, the hotel restaurant serves a French cuisine.

Services: Room service, laundry, baby-sitting.

Facilities: Scuba diving, outdoor swimming pool, waterskiing, sailboat rentals, shopping boutiques.

ESMERALDA RESORT, Lot 44, Baie Orientale, 97150 St. Martin, F.W.I. Tel. 87-36-36, 203/847-9445 in Connecticut, or toll free 800/622-7836. Fax 87-35-18. 47 rms, 7 suites. A/C TV TEL
$ Rates (including continental breakfast): Winter, $200–$300 single or double; $450–$550 suite for two, plus $50 each for third and fourth occupants. Summer, $150–$200 single or double; $250 suite for two, plus $25 each for third and fourth occupants. AE, MC, V. **Parking:** Free.

Originally conceived as a site for a single private villa, and then for a semiprivate club for like-minded guests of the owner, this hillside development a 25-minute taxi ride northeast of Juliana airport has blossomed into a full-scale resort with views over Orient Bay and a decidedly French focus. The landscaping includes palms, cactus, and an array of flowers. Up to a maximum of four separate vaguely Spanish mission-style accommodations is in one of 14 tile-roofed villas whose interior doors can be locked or unlocked as needed to create a variety of different-sized units. Each of the units contains a kitchenette, bathroom, private terrace, and a private entrance.

Dining/Entertainment: A bar and grill lie close to the nearby beach, and a more formal lunch and evening restaurant is on the property.

Services: Room service (for dinner), laundry, baby-sitting, massage.

Facilities: 14 swimming pools, tennis courts, scuba diving, waterskiing.

GRANDE CASE BEACH CLUB, Grand Case, 97150 St. Martin, F.W.I. Tel. 87-51-87. Fax 87-59-93. 56 rms, 18 suites. A/C TV TEL

$ Rates (including continental breakfast): Winter, $200–$250 room for one to four people; from $295 suite. Summer, $95–$125 room for one to four people; from $150 suite. AE, MC, V. **Parking:** Free. **Closed:** Sept–Oct 15.

Within walking distance of Grand Case, 12 miles from Juliana Airport, this is a beachfront condominium hotel, where most units open onto ocean-view terraces. You have a choice of ocean- or garden-view studios and one- and two-bedroom apartments. Each has a fully equipped kitchen, bath, and private patio. Units are airy, with tile floors, rattan furnishings, and daily maid service. The ambience at the hotel is informal. This is the type of place where you make friends with other guests and plan to see them "same time next year."

Dining/Entertainment: Café Panoramique, extending out on a bluff, overlooks Grand Case and the sunset, and serves three meals (French cuisine) a day. A guest lounge contains billiards and a giant TV for movies, news, and sports.

Services: Laundry, baby-sitting.

Facilities: Two beaches, beach boutique, grocery store, water sports (including waterskiing, snorkeling, and sailing), free use of the Caribbean's first artificial-grass tennis court.

HOTEL CAPTAIN OLIVER, Oyster Pond, 97150 St. Martin, F.W.I. Tel. 87-40-26. Fax 87-40-87. 39 bungalows. A/C MINIBAR TV TEL

$ Rates: Winter, $155–$175 single; $180–$200 double. Summer, $85–$105 single; $110–$130 double. AE, DC, MC, V. **Parking:** Free.

This hotel is named for Oliver Lange, who was a Paris restaurateur for nearly a quarter of a century before coming here. At the French-Dutch border 10 miles east of Juliana airport, near the prestigious Oyster Pond Hotel on the Dutch side, he constructed pink bungalows in a labyrinth of outlying cottages, each ringed with a suggestion of gingerbread and connected with boardwalks. High on a hill, the cottages command excellent views, and from the large terraces you can gaze over to St. Barts. Each unit is furnished in white rattan and decorated with local prints. The accommodations come with kitchenettes, marble baths, double sinks, large double closets, and many amenities. Each bungalow is provided with two beds, plus a sofa bed, which makes them possible family rentals.

Dining/Entertainment: See "Where to Dine," below.

Services: Room service, laundry, baby-sitting.

Facilities: Scuba-diving facilities, outdoor swimming pool, private taxi boat to beach, shopping boutiques.

MONT VERNON, Chevrise Baie Orientale (B.P. 1174, Marigot), 97150 St. Martin, F.W.I. Tel. 87-62-00, or toll free 800/233-0888. Fax 87-37-27. 394 suites. A/C TV TEL

$ Rates (including American breakfast): Winter, $190–$260 single or double. Summer, $115–$180 single or double. Children under 13 stay free in parents' room. AE, MC, V. **Parking:** Free.

Opened in 1990, this top-notch resort complex on the eastern coast of the island offers junior suites and two-room suites, with twin or king-size beds and private balconies opening onto the water. Each room has a private bath and a number of amenities, such as a refrigerator.

Dining/Entertainment: There's a 400-seat main restaurant, Le Créole; a 100-seat main bar and patio; a 50-seat beach bar; and a 100-seat pool snack bar with a barbecue, called Le Sloop. French, Italian, and a Créole cuisine are offered.

Services: Laundry, baby-sitting, massage.

Facilities: Duty-free shopping arcade, large swimming pool with a sun deck, tennis courts, archery, fitness club, water-sports center (where sailboats can be rented and deep-sea fishing arranged).

MODERATE

LAGUNA BEACH HOTEL, Baie Nettle, 97150 St. Martin, F.W.I. Tel. 87-91-75. Fax 87-81-65. 62 rms. A/C TV TEL

$ Rates: Winter, $116–$190 single; $155–$214 double. Summer, $75–$100 single; $92–$127 double. Continental breakfast $7 extra. AE, MC, V. **Parking:** Free.

On the road between Marigot and the Lowlands, the Laguna Beach Hotel, which opened in 1988, offers accommodations in a pair of two-level buildings. Rooms, for the most part, are spacious and include radios, VCRs, terraces, private safes, refrigerators, and hairdryers. Laguna has a central freshwater swimming pool and three tennis courts. Its dining room is open to the breezes. The public rooms are furnished in part with rattan and decorated with Haitian art. Room service, laundry, and baby-sitting are offered.

LA RESIDENCE, rue du Général-de-Gaulle (B.P. 679), Marigot, 97150 St. Martin, F.W.I. Tel. 87-70-37. Fax 87-90-44. 21 rms. A/C MINIBAR TV TEL

$ Rates (including continental breakfast): $96 single; $112 double. AE, MC, V. **Parking:** Free.

In the commercial center of town, La Résidence has a concrete facade enlivened with Neo-Victorian gingerbread fretwork. Rooms are arranged around a landscaped central courtyard, where a fish-shaped fountain splashes water into a bowl. A bar with a soaring tent serves drinks to clients relaxing on wicker and bentwood furniture. Each of the bedrooms contains minimalist decor, and all but a few have sleeping lofts and a duplex design of mahogany-trimmed stairs and balustrades. Room service is available.

LE PIRATE, B.P. 296, Marigot, 97150 St. Martin, F.W.I. Tel. 87-78-37. Fax 87-95-67. 57 rms. A/C TV TEL

$ Rates: Winter, $127–$155 single or double; $163–$182 triple or quad. Summer, $94–$114 single or double; $122–$137 triple or quad. Continental breakfast $5.50 extra. AE, DC, MC, V. **Parking:** Free.

Set on a narrow strip of sandy land between the open sea and a salt pond, Le Pirate lies on the main road from Marigot to the Lowlands, a 20-minute taxi ride north of Juliana airport. Its aim, as voiced by the management, is to combine "French savoir-vivre with Créole color." Each of its comfortably furnished bedrooms has a kitchenette, a private bath, and a balcony opening onto views over the harbor or marina. Studios and duplexes are rented, the latter suitable for three or four guests. The hotel has a small swimming pool a few paces from the beach. Laundry and baby-sitting are available.

LE ROYALE LOUISIANA, rue du Général-de-Gaulle, Marigot, 97150 St. Martin, F.W.I. Tel. 87-86-51. 54 rms, 14 duplexes. A/C TV TEL

$ Rates: 320F ($61.55) single; 440F ($84.60) double; 560F–700F ($107.70–$134.60) duplex. AE, DC, MC, V. **Parking:** Free.

Occupying a prominent position in the center of Marigot, 10 miles north of Juliana airport, this hotel is designed in a hip-roofed French-colonial Louisiana style; its rambling balconies are graced with ornate balustrades. Each accommodation contains a bathroom, big sunny windows, and modern furniture. Standard rooms have either king- or queen-size beds. Fourteen of the accommodations are duplexes. Ideal for families, these units have a bedroom and bath on the upper level and a sitting room with a fold-out sofa on the lower floor. Duplex rates are not based on the number of occupants. The hotel, a member of the French-owned Accor group, has a restaurant and bar, Le Hammock, where breakfast and lunch are served. For dinner, patrons can go to one of the nearby French restaurants in Marigot.

MARINE HOTEL SIMPSON BAY, Baie Nettle (B.P. 172, Marigot), 97150 St. Martin, F.W.I. Tel. 87-54-54, or toll free 800/221-4542 in the U.S. and Canada. Fax 87-92-11. 128 rms, 47 suites. A/C TV TEL

$ Rates (including American breakfast): Winter, $109–$129 single; $118–$138 double; from $186 suite. Summer, $89 single; $98 double; from $129 suite. AE, DC, MC, V. **Parking:** Free.

One of the most stylish hotels in its price bracket on the French side of the island is operated by the French hotel conglomerate Accor. The Marine occupies a flat, sandy stretch of land between a saltwater lagoon and the beach, 5 miles west of Juliana airport. Decorated in peach, turquoise, and maize, it was designed with five three-story buildings, each like a large, balconied Antillean house. In its center, two swimming pools serve as the focal point for a bar built out over the lagoon, an indoor/outdoor restaurant, and a flagstone terrace that hosts steel bands and cocktail parties in the evening.

The hotel offers accommodations with ceiling fans, private baths, wicker furniture, and kitchenettes set on outdoor patios. The most desirable accommodations, on the third (top) floor, contain sloping ceilings sheltering spacious sleeping lofts as well as two bathrooms. Room service, laundry, and baby-sitting are available.

RESIDENCE ALIZEA, Mont Vernon, 97150 St. Martin, F.W.I. Tel. 87-33-42. Fax 87-41-15. 26 units. A/C TV TEL **Directions:** After passing through Grand Case, turn left and follow the signs along the cul-de-sac.

$ Rates (including continental breakfast): Winter, $155 single; $169 double; $247 bungalow with garden. Summer, $109 single; $124 double; $182 bungalow with garden. AE, MC, V. **Parking:** Free.

On the northeastern end of the island, this is the smallest hotel in a district sparsely dotted with some of the biggest blockbusting resorts on the French side. The inn opens onto a panoramic vista of Orient Bay. A swimming pool is on the premises, but the beach is a 10-minute hike through fields and across a road. Each accommodation differs from its neighbors in size, but all contain a kitchenette set on an open-air veranda, a light and airy collection of wooden furniture, and a color scheme of Caribbean pastels.

The establishment is best known for its restaurant, where trade winds (known in French as *les alizés*), ceiling fans, rose-colored walls, and a two-sided view of the bay are the most important furnishings. Full meals begin at $45 each, and include French and Gallicized Caribbean dishes such as callalou-and-spinach soup with coconut, sea scallops in filo pastry on a bed of tomatoes and provençal herbs, and roast young rabbit served with pâté.

SOL HOTEL AMBIANCE, Oyster Pond, 97150 St. Martin, F.W.I. Tel. 87-38-10. Fax 87-32-23. 8 bungalows. A/C

$ Rates (including continental breakfast and one-way transport either to or from the airport): Winter, $110 single; $120 double; $150 triple. Summer, $70 single; $90 double; $115 triple. AE, MC, V. **Parking:** Free.

This pastel-ornamented building overlooks the yachts bobbing in the Oyster Pond right at the French-Dutch border 8 miles east of Juliana airport. Built in 1987, this remote outpost consists of bungalows done in traditional West Indian style. Although small, it aims to provide all the services of a large hotel, including a good-sized pool, daily maid service, and telefax. Each unit, offering either a king-size bed or twin beds, has a kitchenette and a private terrace.

BUDGET

BERTINE'S, La Savana, Grand Case, 97150 St. Martin, F.W.I. Tel. 87-58-39. Fax 87-58-39. 4 rms (all with bath), 1 apartment. **Directions:** Lies 3 miles outside Marigot on the road to Grand Case.

$ Rates (including continental breakfast): Winter, $50 single; $55 double; $80 apartment. Summer, $40 single; $45 double; $60 apartment. MC, V. **Parking:** Free. **Closed:** Sept–Oct.

Bertine's is best known for its restaurant (see "Where to Dine," below). In addition to its dining facilities, it offers several comfortable but simple accommodations, whose ambience is a lot like that of a lighthearted private home. Guests are given the use of a residents' lounge filled with wall-mounted fans and louvered windows. The location is isolated, the rooms aren't glamorous, and you'll need a car to get to the beach, but some guests return year after year.

WHERE TO DINE

The classic French haute cuisine, with a big touch of the West Indies, is waiting to greet your taste buds. St. Martin has some of the finest food in the Caribbean.

IN BAIE LONGUE

LA SAMANNA, Baie Longue. Tel. 87-51-22.
  Cuisine: FRENCH. **Reservations:** Required.
$ Prices: Appetizers 8F–195F ($1.55–$37.50); main courses 180F–240F ($34.60–$46.15). AE, MC, V. **Closed:** July–Oct.
  Open: Lunch daily 12:30–2:30pm; dinner daily 7–9:30pm.

⭐ Even though you may not be staying at La Samanna, northwest of Mullet Bay, you might want to make a reservation to enjoy a meal on the resort's dining terrace. Judges of this cuisine have declared it among the best in the Caribbean, matching the finest world-class restaurants in Paris. The high prices reflect its image. The dinner menu lists crevettes et épinards mimosa en salade, sauce gingembre et citron vert (shrimp and raw-spinach salad with ginger-and-lemon sauce), salade de langouste Baie Longue (lobster salad Baie Longue), and poisson grillé sauce Créole (grilled local red snapper with Créole sauce). The Dover sole and the oysters are flown in fresh from France, and the steaks are imported from New York. The al fresco dining terrace's zigzag parapet overlooks the sea, with dinner served by candlelight. Each table is set with Rosenthal china, lit by lamps from the *Orient Express,* and, at lunch, adorned with local flowers. (Lunches, where a theatrically prepared steak tartare is a favorite, are less expensive.)

The Indian Bar, which envelops guests under a billowing canopy of colorful Indian wedding tenting, is a cozy respite for cocktails. Located in the main building with a terrace overlooking the pool, the bar has no set hours. La Samanna's underground, air-controlled wine cellar houses more than 20,000 bottles from elite vineyards around the world.

IN & AROUND MARIGOT

Very Expensive

LA VIE EN ROSE, bd. France. Tel. 87-54-42.
  Cuisine: FRENCH. **Reservations:** Required.
$ Prices: Appetizers $8–$15; main courses $25–$50. AE, MC, V.
  Open: Lunch daily 11:30am–2:30pm; dinner daily 6:30–10pm. **Closed:** Sun off-season.
In this balconied second-floor restaurant, the cozy dining room, with ceiling fans and candlelight, evokes the nostalgia of the 1920s. If you don't like the parlor, you can gravitate to one of the tables on a little veranda overlooking the harbor, provided you requested one when you made a reservation. A French gourmet rendezvous, the restaurant offers dinner costing a steep $80 per person and up. The chefs prepare lobster fricassée, boneless chicken breast with capers, entrecôte in red wine sauce, and red snapper bedded in a spinach mousse. The soupe de poisson (fish soup) is served with a rouille sauce and garlicky croutons. The desserts are some of the best made on the island.

LE NADAILLAC, Galerie Périgourdine, rue de la Liberté. Tel. 87-53-77.
  Cuisine: FRENCH. **Reservations:** Required.
$ Prices: Appetizers $10–$15; main courses $20–$50. AE, MC, V.
  Open: Lunch Mon–Sat noon–2:30pm; dinner daily 6–11pm. **Closed:** Sept.
On the waterfront side of this gallery, a little terrace restaurant is like a transplanted pocket of France in the Caribbean. The chef-owner Fernand Malard, a native of the Périgord region of France (which is famous for its truffles and foie gras), operates a splendid but expensive restaurant. His skilled touch is seen in such dishes as giblet salad (it appears as salade de gésiers aux lardons) and in his preserved goose, or confit

d'oie. Portions of goose are cooked in goose fat and preserved in stoneware pots. He gets many of his products from France, but also has imaginative touches with what emerges from local waters, such as red snapper. You might also try filet mignon with green peppercorns.

Expensive

LA MAISON SUR LE PORT, rue de la République. Tel. 87-56-38.
Cuisine: FRENCH. **Reservations:** Recommended.
$ Prices: Appetizers $5–$10; main courses $17–$21. AE, MC, V.
Open: Lunch Mon–Sat noon–2:30pm; dinner Mon–Sat 6–10:30pm. **Closed:** Sun.

Christian Verdeau and his staff welcome people to enjoy their French cuisine in a refined atmosphere and elegant surroundings, with a view of a waterfall in the garden. The tables are dressed with snowy tablecloths and Limoges china. At lunch, when you are seated on the covered terrace, you can choose from a number of salads as well as fish and meat courses. Dinner choices include fresh fish such as snapper, salmon, or lobster; homemade pâté de foie gras; and filet of lamb, veal, or steak, each with a light sauce. Duck has always been a specialty of La Maison. You can order from a wine list with an extensive selection of imported French products at moderate prices, or you may want to try the house cocktail, made with blanc de blanc wine, fresh orange juice, Grand Marnier, and a splash of lemon juice. Many guests come here at sundown to watch the yachts bobbing in the harbor.

LE MINI CLUB, rue de la Liberté. Tel. 87-50-69.
Cuisine: FRENCH/CREOLE. **Reservations:** Required.
$ Prices: Appetizers $9–$40; main courses $18–$35; fixed-price dinner $30; Wed and Sat dinner buffet $40. AE, MC, V.
Open: Lunch Mon–Sat noon–3pm; dinner daily 7–10:30pm.

After you climb a sloped flight of wooden stairs, you'll find yourself in an environment once described as a treehouse built among coconut palms. Suspended on a wooden deck above the sands of the beach, this establishment is filled with Haitian murals and grass carpeting. The specialties include lobster soufflé (made for two or four people), an array of fish and vegetable terrines, red snapper with Créole sauce, sweetbreads in puff pastry, and many kinds of salad. Dessert might consist of bananas flambéed with cognac. Lavish buffets are held every Wednesday and Saturday night, with unlimited wine included. The restaurant is along the seafront at Marigot.

RESTAURANT JEAN DUPONT, Port La Royale. Tel. 87-71-13.
Cuisine: FRENCH/SEAFOOD. **Reservations:** Required.
$ Prices: Appetizers $6–$10; main courses $20–$35. AE, MC, V.
Open: Lunch Mon–Sat noon–3pm; dinner daily 6–11pm.

Monsieur Dupont, the proprietor who made his reputation at the very expensive Le Santal, operates this newer, less formal spot in a shopping and dining complex—not quite as pricy and romantically located as Le Santal. But the food is just as good here, and the service is excellent. Try, for example, sautéed scallops and shrimp in a light curry or a chicken suprême. For an appetizer, try the lobster soufflé on a bed of spinach with caviar.

Moderate

DAVID'S, rue de la Liberté. Tel. 87-51-58.
Cuisine: AMERICAN/FRENCH. **Reservations:** Required.
$ Prices: Appetizers $2.50–$7; main courses $8.50–$24. AE, MC, V.
Open: Lunch Mon–Sat 11:30am–3pm; dinner daily 6–10pm (bar, daily until midnight).

David's, one block from the post office in the center of town, attracts visiting yachting people to its casual expatriate ambience. A red, white, and blue spinnaker hangs from the rafters. Appetizers include everything from conch fritters to potato skins, and good soups are served too, especially fish chowder and baked onion. Fresh dorado is prepared in different ways, and local lobster is done by the chef any way you want it. The specialty of the house is beef Wellington, served with a red wine sauce. Chicken Kiev is a more recent addition, as is the wienerschnitzel. The steaks are prime quality and can be served with dijonnaise or black-pepper sauce.

LA BRASSERIE DE MARIGOT, rue du Général-de-Gaulle. Tel. 87-94-43.
  Cuisine: FRENCH/SEAFOOD. **Reservations:** Not required.
$ **Prices:** Appetizers $5–$10; main courses $10–$30. AE, MC, V.
  Open: Lunch Mon–Sat 11am–3pm; dinner daily 6–11pm.

This is where the real French eat. Opened in a former bank, it has a marble-and-brass decor, a sort of retro 1950s style with green leather banquettes. Meals include pot-au-feu, choucroûte (sauerkraut garni), blanquette de veau, cassoulet, even chicken on a spit and steak tartare. Lobster is the most expensive item on the menu. Naturally, you can order interesting terrines here, and wine is sold by the glass, carafe, or bottle. The brasserie, located in the center of town, is air-conditioned, with sidewalk tables overlooking the pedestrian traffic outside. It also features the most glamorous "take-out" service in St. Martin.

IN & AROUND GRAND CASE

This beach town, a scant mile-long brush stroke, has the greatest concentration of fine dining spots in the Caribbean. On the town's one and only street there are more than 18 restaurants serving the cuisines of at least half a dozen cultures.

Very Expensive

CHEZ MARTINE, bd. de Grand-Case. Tel. 87-51-59.
  Cuisine: FRENCH. **Reservations:** Required.
$ **Prices:** Appetizers $8.75–$20.25; main courses $22.75–$35. AE, MC, V.
  Open: Lunch daily noon–3pm; dinner daily 6:30–10pm. **Closed:** Sept.

Diners sit at a well-set table on a gingerbread terrace overlooking the sea at this very French Antillean place, and the staff gives capable service. You get a number of choices in cuisine. To begin your meal, try uncooked salmon (marinated in a sauce of fresh herbs), snails in garlic butter, or foie gras. The most tempting part of the menu is that listed under "Poissons." You can order grilled island lobster flambéed with cognac or sea scallops in a morel sauce. For dessert, try a French pastry.

HEVEA, bd. de Grand-Case. Tel. 87-56-85.
  Cuisine: FRENCH. **Reservations:** Required.
$ **Prices:** Appetizers $6–$15; main courses $30–$50; menu gourmand 299F ($57.50). MC, V.
  Open: Dinner only, daily 6:30–10pm. **Closed:** Mon Apr 15–Dec 14.

A small and intimate restaurant, with only 10 tables, Hévéa is owned by Jacqueline Dalbera. Here you can enjoy French cuisine in pleasant formal surroundings of French furniture. Dishes might include a marinated fresh raw salmon and sea scallops in lime juice and dill, sliced duck breast in a wine sauce with black currants, and a dessert specialty of chocolate marquise.

L'AUBERGE-GOURMANDE, bd. de Grand-Case. Tel. 87-55-45.
  Cuisine: FRENCH/SEAFOOD. **Reservations:** Required.
$ **Prices:** Appetizers $10–$15; main courses $20–$45. MC, V.
  Open: Dinner only, Thurs–Tues 6:30–10pm. **Closed:** Aug–Sept.

The chef-owner, Burgundy-born Daniel Passeri, runs this small romantic dining room that resembles a little French country inn. Classic French dishes, plus some with a touch of Burgundy, are served in this old Antillean home. Begin with a duck pâté with walnuts. The salads are well made here, with crisp fresh greens, often mixed with bits of ham, cheese, and walnuts. For a main course, the langouste is the most preferred and expensive selection, and the red snapper in port-wine sauce is equally as good. You might also try duck breast with three-berry sauce or scallops and shrimp with fresh sauce. For dessert, try apple crêpe drenched in Calvados. Trade winds cool the place in lieu of air conditioning.

Moderate

BERTINE'S, in La Savana, Grand Case. Tel. 87-58-39.
Cuisine: INTERNATIONAL. **Reservations:** Recommended.
$ **Prices:** Appetizers $6–$8; main courses $14–$28. MC, V.
Open: Dinner only, Mon–Sat 6–10pm. **Closed:** Sept–Oct.

S Previously recommended for its simple accommodations, Bertine's is better known as an unusual restaurant. It's angular concrete building sits atop a steep hill 3 miles from Marigot, 1½ miles from Grand Case, near the farming hamlet of La Savana. Its two separate sections are joined by a wide veranda whose hardwood sheathing is kept spotlessly polished by Bernard and Christine Poticha. Born in Chicago, they moved to a warmer climate, took up cooking, and today are known for their copious portions, good humor, and charm. Bernie does the cooking, while Christine serves and creates an ambience like a private dinner party. Between courses, guests watch the sunset glimmering over the sea between two hills. Dinner might include crab au gratin, hickory-smoked pork ribs Chicago style (with Bernie's special sauce), and a homemade chocolate-mousse pie. A novel house specialty is "steak on a hot rock."

IN COLOMBIER

LA RHUMERIE, Colombier. Tel. 87-56-98.
Cuisine: FRENCH/CREOLE. **Reservations:** Required.
$ **Prices:** Appetizers $6–$10; main courses $15–$50. AE, MC, V.
Open: Dinner only, daily 7–9:30pm. **Closed:** Sept–Oct.

✪ Minutes from Marigot, in the tiny hamlet of Colombier, is one of the best Créole restaurants on St. Martin. West Indies–born owner Francillette Le Moine continues a tradition established by her late husband, Yannick, from Brittany, in serving fine food with finesse—dishes that lead many residents on the island to declare this their favorite restaurant. For years I recommended the Le Moines' Chez Lolotte, which they ran in Marigot before taking a private home in this country setting. They transformed this home into a charming restaurant that also serves traditional French dishes, such as stuffed crab back, escargots, and onion soup gratiné. But the place is best known for Créole cuisine, including curried goat, a salad of coffre (a local fish), conch in fresh herbs, and poulet boucanne Créole (home-smoked chicken served with baked green papayas and christophine au gratin).

IN ANSE MARCEL

LA BELLE FRANCE, in the Méridien L'Habitation de Lonvilliers. Tel. 87-33-31.
Cuisine: FRENCH/SEAFOOD. **Reservations:** Required.
$ **Prices:** Appetizers $5–$6; main courses $22–$40. AE, MC, V.
Open: Dinner only, daily 7pm–midnight.

This beautifully appointed gourmet restaurant is tucked away in a remote corner of St. Martin (see "Where to Stay," above). You might begin with Caribbean lobster soufflé before going on to a delightful salad with quail and flap mushrooms. La Marmite Caraïbe is a selection of steamed local fresh fish and seafood, braised fresh duck liver is sautéed in raspberry vinegar, and you can also order steamed young guinea fowl with a sherry sauce.

IN OYSTER POND

CAPTAIN OLIVER RESTAURANT, in the Hôtel Captain Oliver. Tel. 87-30-00.
Cuisine: FRENCH/CREOLE. **Reservations:** Recommended.
$ **Prices:** Appetizers $6–$9; main courses $11.50–$46. AE, MC, V.
Open: Lunch daily noon–3pm; dinner daily 7–11pm.

Partially built on piers above the bay right at the Dutch border and overlooking a yacht-filled harbor, Captain Oliver is reached from either Marigot or Philipsburg along a twisting road. Once there, you'll find West Indian conch, "fish soup of the captain," a fisherman's platter, tuna steak grilled with caper sauce, and fresh grilled lobster. This place has been known to island gourmets since it opened in 1983. It adjoins a previously reviewed bungalow colony facing the island of St. Barts, and a marina adds to its appeal, particularly at night.

SPECIALTY DINING

Should the heat of the day get to you, stop in at **Etna Ice Cream Per Dolce Vita,** avenue Kennedy, 3, in Port La Royale (tel. 87-72-72). Here, Paolo and Betty Smiroldo operate a gelateria-pasticciere, with homemade ice creams created from fresh fruit. Their specialties cost 10F to 18F ($1.95 to $3.45). The tartufo is as good as the one served on the piazza Navona in Roma, and they also have spumoni, cassata, espresso, along with French croissants and mouth-watering pastries. A fresh-fruit drink, Frullato, is prepared in front of you, and you can also order homemade frozen yogurt. The "sweet life" holds forth here daily in winter from 8am to 10pm, to 6:30pm May to October.

SPORTS & RECREATION

BEACHES The island as a whole has 36 perfect white sandy beaches. The hotels, for the most part, have grabbed up the choicest sands, and usually for a small fee nonguests can use hotel beaches and changing facilities. Topless sunbathing is practiced commonly at the beaches on the French side. **Club Orient Hôtel** (tel. 87-53-85) has the only nudist beach on the island, but nude or mono-kini (as opposed to bikini) is relatively common, even though total nudity is not officially endorsed.

Ilet Pinel, a tiny island off St. Martin, is perfect for beach recluses. You can get there by negotiating with a passing fisherman to provide transport back and forth.

Beyond the sprawling Mullet Beach Resort on the Dutch side, **Cupecoy Bay Beach** lies just north of the Dutch-French border. On the western side of the island, it's a string of three white sandy beaches set against a backdrop of caves and sandstone cliffs that provide morning shade. The beach doesn't have facilities but is very popular. One section of the beach is "clothing optional."

Top rating on St. Martin goes to **Baie Longue,** a long beautiful beach that's rarely overcrowded. Chic La Samanna (see "Where to Stay," above) opens onto this stretch. The location is to the north of Cupecoy Beach, reached by taking the Lowlands road. If you're driving, don't leave any valuables in your car, as many break-ins have been reported. If you continue north along the highway, you reach the approach to another long and popular stretch of sand, **Baie Rouge.** Snorkelers are drawn to the rock formations at both ends of this beach. There are no changing facilities, but, for some, that doesn't matter as they prefer to get their suntan *au naturel.*

On the north side of the island, to the west of Espérance airport, **Grand Case Beach** is small but select. The sand is white and clean, but the previously recommended Grand Case Beach Club takes up a huge hunk of the beach.

For a description of beaches on the Dutch side, see "Sports and Recreation" in Section 1 on St. Maarten in Chapter 9.

SCUBA DIVING Scuba diving is excellent around St. Martin, with reef, wreck, night, cave, and drift diving; the depth of dives is 40 to 50 feet. Off the northeastern coast on the French side, dive sites include Ilet Pinel for shallow diving; Green Key, a barrier reef; Flat Island for sheltered coves and geologic faults; and Tintamarre, known for its shipwreck. To the north, Anse Marcel and neighboring Anguilla are good choices. Most hotels will arrange for scuba excursions on request. There is a PADI scuba-dive center, **Lou Scuba Club,** at the Marine Hôtel, Nettle Bay (tel. 87-22-58). Its dives costing from $45 and range from 25 to 50 feet.

You can also try the **Blue Ocean Dive Center,** Pirate Hôtel, in Marigot (tel. 87-89-73). A certified dive costs $45, including equipment. A PADI certification course is available for $350.

SNORKELING   The calm waters ringing the shallow reefs and tiny coves found throughout the island make it a snorkeler's heaven. The waters off the northeastern shores of St. Martin have been classified as a regional underwater nature reserve, **Reserve Sous-Marine Régionale.** The area, comprising Flat Island (also known as Tintamarre), Pinel Islet, Green Key, and Petite Clef, is thus protected by official government decree. The use of harpoons is strictly forbidden. Snorkeling can be enjoyed individually or on sailing trips. Equipment can be rented at almost any hotel.

At **Grande Case Beach Club** (tel. 87-51-87), a 1-hour snorkeling trip costs $10 to $15 per person, depending on the destination.

TENNIS   Tennis buffs heading for French St. Martin can play at most hotels. Once a rarity on the French side of the island, tennis is now a regular amenity.

L'Habitation has six courts, all lit for night play, and **La Belle Créole** has four, also lit. The Omnisport (artificial grass) court at **Grand Anse Beach Club** is also lit. There are three unlit courts at the exclusive **La Samanna.**

WATERSKIING & WINDSURFING   Most beachfront hotels have facilities for waterskiing or windsurfing as well as parasailing. Rides and lessons fall into the $20 to $30 range.

SAVVY SHOPPING

Many day-trippers come over to Marigot from the Dutch side just to look at the collection of boutiques and shopping arcades. Because it's a duty-free port, you'll find some of the best shopping in the Caribbean. There is a wide selection of French goods, including crystal, perfumes, jewelry, and fashions, sometimes at 25% to 50% less than in the U.S. and Canada. There are also fine liqueurs, cognacs, and cigars. Whether you're seeking jewelry, perfume, or St-Tropez bikinis, you'll find it in one of the boutiques, often in mellow old buildings, along rue de la République and rue de la Liberté in Marigot.

Most of the boutiques on the French side are open Monday through Saturday from 9am to noon or 12:30pm and from 2 to 6pm. When cruise ships are in port on Sunday and holidays, some of the larger shops open again.

Prices are often quoted in U.S. dollars, and salespeople frequently speak English Credit cards and traveler's checks are generally accepted. Look especially for French luxury items, such as Lalique crystal, Vuitton bags, and Chanel perfume.

IN MARIGOT

At harborside in Marigot there's a frisky **morning market** with vendors selling spices, fruit, shells, and local handcrafts.

At **Port La Royale,** the bustling center of everything, mornings are even more alive: Schooners unload produce from the neighboring islands, boats board guests for picnics on deserted beaches, a brigantine sets out on a sightseeing sail, and the owners of a dozen different little dining spots are getting ready for the lunch crowd. The largest shopping arcade in St. Martin, it has many boutiques, some of which come and go with great rapidity.

Another shopping complex, the **Galerie Périgourdine,** facing the post office, is again a cluster of boutiques. Here you might pick up some designer wear for both men and women, including items from the collection of Ted Lapidus.

GINGERBREAD GALLERY, Marigot Marina. Tel. 87-73-21.

Owner Simone Seitre scours Haiti four times a year to secure the best works of a cross section of Haitian artists, both the "old master" and the talented amateur. One of the most knowledgeable purveyors of Haitian art in the Caribbean, this sophisticated pan-European has promoted Haitian art at exhibits around the world. Even if you're not in the market for an expensive piece of art (the paintings come in all price ranges), you'll find dozens of charming and inexpensive handcrafts. The little gallery is a bit hard to find, on a narrow alleyway at the marina next to the Café de Paris, but it's worth the search.

HAVANE, Port La Royale. Tel. 87-70-39.

Havane offers exclusive collections of French clothing, both in sports and high-fashion designs for men and women.

LIPSTICK, Port La Royale, rue Kennedy. Tel. 87-73-34.

Try Lipstick for the largest assortment of duty-free fragrances and cosmetics, as well as beauty preparations by such name designers as Dior and Yves St. Laurent. You can also get facials and massages here. There's another branch of Lipstick along rue de la République in Marigot (tel. 87-53-92).

LITTLE SWITZERLAND, rue de la République. Tel. 87-50-03.

This is one of the best places on the island if you're seeking European imports at prices lower than in the U.S. You get not only name china and crystal, but also precision Swiss watches. The jewelry collection in both its Philipsburg branch and the one at Marigot is perhaps one of the largest in the West Indies. There are many gift items as well, and you can select your favorite fragrance.

MANEKS, rue de la République. Tel. 87-54-91.

Worth a stopover, Maneks has a little bit of everything: video cameras, tobacco products, liquors, gifts, souvenirs, radio cassettes, Kodak film, watches, T-shirts, sunglasses, and pearls from Majorca.

ORO DE SOL JEWELERS, rue de la République. Tel. 87-57-02.

In this well-stocked store is one of the most imaginative selections on St. Martin, including an array of gold watches by Cartier, Ebel, Patek Philippe, and the like, as well as high-fashion jewelry studded with precious stones.

The establishment also has a branch on the harborfront in Marigot (tel. 87-80-98), carrying all the perfumes and fragrances as well as china, Baccarat, Lalique, and Christofle. The owners buy their inventory from around the world.

LA ROMANA, rue de la République. Tel. 87-88-16.

In the heart of Marigot, this handsome landmark building has been transformed into a showcase for the line of La Perla swimwear/beachwear for men and women plus the beautiful La Perla lingerie collection, an extensive collection of the latest in Fendi bags, luggage accessories, and perfume.

SANDRINE BOUTIQUE, rue de la Liberté. Tel. 87-53-77.

Across from the post office in Galerie Périgourdine, this boutique features the latest fashions for men and women, as well as exclusive beachwear.

IN ORLEANS

ROLAND RICHARDSON, Orléans. Tel. 87-32-24.

Local artist Roland Richardson welcomes visitors into his house to view and purchase his original watercolors and prints of island vistas on Thursday from 10am to 6pm or by appointment. The premier local artist on the island, he is a promoter of the island's culture and tradition. In his work he captures and preserves the natural beauty of St. Martin.

EVENING ENTERTAINMENT

Some St. Martin hotels have dinner-dancing, cocktail-lounge music, and even discos. But the most popular after-dark pastime is leisurely dining.

Le Jardin de l'Atmosphere, Port Royale Marina (tel. 87-50-24), is appropriately named: It has an eagle's-nest position under a sloping roof overlooking the bobbing yachts of Marigot's marina. Inspired more by St-Tropez than by the Caribbean, it's often a late-night gathering place for the restaurant patrons searching for one final watering hole before calling it a night. Drinks start at 35F ($6.75) each. Entrance costs $15, and hours are daily from 10:30pm to 3am.

4. ST. BARTHELEMY

New friends call it "St. Barts," while old-time visitors prefer "St. Barths." Either way, it's short for St. Barthélemy—named by its discoverer Columbus in 1493 and pronounced "San Bar-te-le-*mee.*" The uppermost corner of the French West Indies, it's the only Caribbean island with a touch of Sweden in its personality.

French adventurers first occupied it, and then sold it to the Knights of Malta in 1651. When the Caribs pushed the knights out in 1656, France regained control, but eventually ceded its rights to Sweden, which ruled from 1784 to 1877. Once, in the 19th century, Britain also held control. However, in 1878 a plebiscite returned permanent control to France, and today St. Barts is a dependency of Guadeloupe, which in turn is an overseas *département* of France. As such, the citizens of St. Barts participate in French elections. It has its own mayor (elected every 7 years), a town constable, and a security force of six police officers and at most a dozen gendarmes.

For the most part, St. Bartians are descendants of Breton and Norman fisherfolk. Many are long-limbed and attractive, of French and Swedish ancestry, the latter showing in their fair skin, blond hair, and blue eyes. The mostly Caucasian population is small, about 3,500 living in some 8 square miles, 15 miles southeast of St. Martin and 140 miles north of Guadeloupe.

Occasionally you'll see St. Bartians dressed in the provincial costumes of Normandy, and when you hear them speak Norman French, you'll think you're back in the old country—except for the temperature. In little Corossol, more than anywhere else, you can see the following of traditions brought from 17th-century France. You might see elderly women wearing the starched white bonnets known as *quichenottes* or the *calèche.* This special headgear, brought from Brittany, was called *quichenotte,* a corruption of "kiss-me-not," and may well have served as protection from the close attentions of Englishmen or Swedes on the island. The bonneted women can also be seen at local celebrations, particularly on August 25, St. Louis's Day. Many of these women are camera-shy, but they offer their homemade baskets and hats for sale to tourists.

For a long time the island was a paradise for a few millionaires, such as David Rockefeller who has a magnificent hideaway on the northwest shore, and Edmond de Rothschild who occupies some fabulous acres at the "other end" of the island. The Biddles of Philadelphia are in the middle. Nowadays, however, St. Barts is developing a broader base of tourism as it opens more hotels. Nevertheless, the island continues as a celebrity favorite in the Caribbean, attracting the likes of Tom Cruise, Harrison Ford, and Steve Martin. In February the island guest list often reads like a roster from "Lifestyles of the Rich and Famous."

The island's capital is **Gustavia,** named after a Swedish king; in fact, Gustavia is St. Barts's only town and seaport. It's a landlocked, hurricane-proof harbor, looking like a little dollhouse-scale port.

ORIENTATION

GETTING THERE By Plane From the U.S., the principal gateways are St. Maarten (see Chapter 9), St. Thomas (see Chapter 5), and Guadeloupe (see Section 2 in this chapter). At any of these islands, connections to St. Barts can be made on inter-island carriers.

It's just a 10-minute flight from Juliana airport on Dutch-held St. Maarten. From

St. Maarten, the best way to go is on a flight of **Windward Islands Airways International (Winair)** (tel. 5/44230 on St. Maarten). This airline, which has carried such passengers as Queen Beatrix of Holland and Jacqueline Onassis, will fly you over to St. Barts in the morning and back around 5 in the afternoon. But I recommend that you spend more time, of course, to savor the special flavor of St. Barts.

If you're in Guadeloupe, you can fly in aboard **Air Guadeloupe** (tel. 27-61-90), a 1-hour trip. Air Guadeloupe also has regular service to St. Barts from the small Espérance airport on the French side of St. Martin.

It's also possible to fly with **Air St. Barts** (tel. 27-71-90) and **Virgin Air** (tel. 27-71-76, or toll free 800/522-3084), which have regular service to St. Barts from San Juan and St. Thomas. For information about these flights, phone Air St. Barts or Virgin Air at the St. Jean Airport on St. Barts.

Many jokes have been made about the makeshift landing strip on St. Barts. It's short, and accommodates small craft—the biggest plane it can land is a 19-seat STOL (short takeoff and landing craft). As a chilling sight, a cemetery adjoins the strip! Locals pray to the white cross that stands between two hills flanking the field. Your plane has to make a curving swoop through a hilltop pass. No matter, everybody seems to arrive in one piece.

Traveler's Advisory: Always reconfirm your return flight from St. Barts with one of the secondary carriers recommended above. If you don't, you'll find that your reservation has been canceled. Also, don't check your luggage all the way through to St. Barts or you may not see your belongings for a few days. Check your bags to your gateway destination, whatever island you are connecting through, most often Dutch St. Maarten. Then take your luggage to whatever carrier you're using and recheck your bags to St. Barts. You'll be glad you did.

By Boat   There is a variety of service between St. Barts and St. Maarten, but schedules vary with the season, so it's best to check on the spot. Contact the skippers of the *White Octopus* or *El Tigre,* who arrive in St. Barts around 11am after a 1-hour, often turbulent, crossing from St. Maarten. They depart the same afternoon, usually at 3pm. The price is $50 round-trip.

GETTING AROUND   By Taxi   Taxis meet all flights and are not very expensive, mostly because no one destination is all that far from any other. Dial 27-66-31 for taxi service.

By Rental Car   The hilly terrain, and perhaps the sense of adventure of the residents, combine to form a car-rental situation unique in the Caribbean. Never have I seen as many open-sided Mini-Mokes and Suzuki Samurais as I have on St. Barts. Painted in vivid colors, they're fast, fun, and very windy. You'll enjoy driving one too, as long as you're handy with a stick shift and don't care about your coiffure.

Budget Rent-a-Car (tel. 27-67-43, or toll free 800/527-0700) rents Daihatsu Charades for around $280 a week, with unlimited mileage included, and Mokes for a few dollars more. A collision-damage waiver, absolving renters of all but $150 of responsibility in the event of an accident, costs around $8 a day. For the lowest rate, you must reserve at least 2 business days before your arrival.

Budget's most aggressive competition, **Hertz** (tel. toll free 800/654-3001) operates in St. Barts through a local dealership, Henry's Car Rental. With branches at the airport and in St-Jean (tel. 27-60-21), it offers VW Beetles and the previously mentioned open-sided Samurais for around $300 a week.

At **Avis** (tel. 27-71-43, or toll free 800/331-2112), you'll need a reservation a full month in advance in high season, plus the advance payment of a $100 deposit. Its VW Golfs are priced at $350 per week. (Be warned that Avis is closed during most of September every year.)

Gas is extra. Tanks hold enough to get you to one of the two gas stations—the Shell station at the airport is the only one open on Sunday, and then only from 8 to 11am. All valid foreign driver's licenses are honored. No one will mind if you honk your horn furiously while going around the island's blind corners, a practice that avoids many sideswiped fenders. Drive slowly, carefully, and with consideration, and don't drink and drive.

By Motorbikes and Scooters Denis Dufau operates **Rent Some Fun** in Gustavia (tel. 27-70-59). A helmet is needed, and potential bikers must pay a $100 deposit as well as rental fee of 100F to 150F ($19.25 to $28.85) a day. A driver's license is also required.

By Sightseeing Tours Group tours are scaled to the island's size: eight passengers per minibus. A full-day, 8-hour tour, with a 2-hour break for lunch (at your own expense) or swimming, costs 500F ($96.15) per vehicle. Operators include **Constant Gumbs** (tel. 27-61-93) and **Claude Lédée** (tel. 27-75-32).

FAST FACTS: ST. BARTHELEMY

Area Code St. Barts is *not* part of the Caribbean's 809 area code. For details on calling to and on the island, see "Telephone," below.

Banks There are two banks on the island, both in Gustavia and both open Monday through Friday. The **Banque Française Commerciale**, rue du Général-de-Gaulle (tel. 27-62-62), is open from 8am to noon and 2 to 3:30pm. The **Banque Nationale de Paris**, rue du Bord-de-Mer (tel. 27-63-70), is open from 8:15am to noon and 2 to 4pm.

Currency The official monetary unit is the **French franc (F)**, but most stores and restaurants prefer payment in U.S. dollars. Most hotels also quote their rates in American currency at a discount from the rates as quoted in francs. For your reference, at press time the exchange rate was 5.2F to $1 U.S., and this is the rate used in this chapter. As this is sure to fluctuate a bit, use this rate for guidance only.

Customs You are allowed to bring in items for personal use, including tobacco, cameras, and film.

Documents If you're flying in, you'll need to present your return or ongoing ticket. U.S. and Canadian citizens need only photo identification or a passport.

Drugstores The **Pharmacie de Gustavia** is on rue de la République (tel. 27-61-82) in Gustavia.

Electricity Voltage is 200 AC, 50 cycles; therefore, American-made appliances require French plugs and transformers.

Information For information, go to the **Office du Tourisme,** Mairie de St-Barth, rue August-Nyman, in Gustavia (tel. 27-60-08).

Language French is the official language, and the type spoken by St. Bartians is a quaint Norman dialect. Some of the populace speak English, however, and there is seldom a language problem at major hotels, restaurants, and shops.

Medical Care Gustavia has five doctors and three dentists at the **Gustavia Clinic,** at the intersection of rue Sadi-Carnot and rue Jean-Bart (tel. 27-60-35).

Safety Although crime is rare here, it would be wise to protect your valuables. Don't leave them unguarded on the beach or in parked cars, even if locked in the trunk.

Taxes An airport departure tax of 15F ($2.90) is assessed. Hotels add a 7% room tax.

Telephone St. Barts is linked to the Guadeloupe telephone system, which is *not* part of the 809 area code that applies to most of the Caribbean. To call St. Barts from the U.S., if your long-distance telephone company is equipped to handle international direct dialing, dial 011 (the international access code), then 590 (the country code for the French West Indies), and finally the six-digit local number. If you cannot direct-dial internationally, dial 0 ("zero," for the operator) and tell the operator you wish to make an international call; once you are transferred to the international operator, state the 590 country code and then the local number, and the operator will dial the call for you. To make a call within St. Barts, only the six-digit local number is necessary. *Note:* In this chapter, only the local numbers are given.

Time When standard time is in effect in the U.S. and Canada, St. Barts is 1 hour ahead of the U.S. East Coast. Thus, when it's 7pm in St. Barts, it's only 6pm in New York or Toronto. When daylight saving time is in effect in the U.S., clocks in New York and St. Barts show the same time.

Weather The climate of St. Barts is ideal: It's dry with an average temperature of 72° to 86° Fahrenheit.

WHERE TO STAY

With the exception of a few super-priced hotels, most places here are homey, comfortable, and casual. Everything is small, as tiny St. Barts is hardly in the mainstream of tourism. In March it's often hard to get in here unless you've made reservations far in advance. Accommodations throughout the island, with some exceptions, tend to be exceptionally expensive, and a service charge and 7% tax are likely to be added to your bill. Ask about this beforehand to save yourself a parting surprise. Some hotels quote their rates in U.S. dollars, others in French francs.

St. Barts has a sizable number of villas, beach houses, and apartments for rent by the week or month. Villas are dotted around the island's hills—very few are on the beach. Instead of an oceanfront bedroom, you get a spectacular view. One of the best agencies to contact for villa, apartment, or condo rentals is **St. Barth Properties,** 22 Park Road, Franklin, MA 02038 (tel. 508/528-7789, or toll free 800/421-3396). There, Peg Walsh, who believes in "living your dream," will inform you of what's available and at what price, depending on the season. She can also make arrangements for car rental and air travel to St. Barts, and is very helpful in providing information about the island. Apartments begin at $420 weekly in summer, $910 weekly in winter.

VERY EXPENSIVE

FILAO BEACH, St-Jean (B.P. 167), 97133 St. Barthélemy, F.W.I. Tel. 27-64-84. Fax 27-62-24. 30 rms. A/C MINIBAR TV TEL

$ Rates (including continental breakfast and transfers to and from the airport): Winter, 1,600F–2,400F ($307.70–$461.50) single or double. Summer, 800F–1,500F ($153.85–$288.45) single or double. AE, DC, MC, V. **Parking:** Free. **Closed:** Aug 31–Oct 10.

In this crescent-shaped, white stucco beachside bungalow hotel on the main beach a 4-minute drive from the airport, each room is named after a château in France. This is the only Relais & Châteaux in the French West Indies. Try to reserve Bungalow 10 or 40, near the beach. All rooms are modern and elegantly simple, plushly carpeted, and well upholstered with large closets, private safes, ceiling fans, and sun-flooded terraces big enough to enjoy a leisurely breakfast.

Dining/Entertainment: A bar and restaurant overlooks St. Jean's Beach and serves both a French and international cuisine.

Services: Laundry and baby-sitting can be arranged.

Facilities: Swimming pool; scuba diving and waterskiing can be arranged.

HOTEL GUANAHANI, Anse de Grand Cul-de-Sac, 97133 St. Barthélemy, F.W.I. Tel. 27-66-60, 212/838-3110 in New York City, or toll free 800/223-6800. Fax 27-70-70. 49 rms, 15 suites. A/C MINIBAR TV TEL

$ Rates (including continental breakfast): Winter, $380–$470 single or double; from $650 suite. Summer, $240–$280 double; from $400 suite. AE, DC, MC, V. **Parking:** Free.

A member of the prestigious "Leading Hotels of the World," an organization representing the finest hotels around the globe, the Hôtel Guanahani, in the northeast part of the island, opened with Gallic fanfare in 1986 and became the largest and most deluxe hotel on the island. Well signposted, this beachfront resort is spread over 7 landscaped acres with pastel cottages trimmed in gingerbread. Its units include doubles, deluxe rooms, spa suites, and one-bedroom suites, all with private patios, small refrigerators, ceiling fans, and radios. The spa suites offer small outside spas (cold Jacuzzi), and the one-bedroom suites have their own private splash pools and are equipped with kitchens.

Dining/Entertainment: The Guanahani has two restaurants. The more formal is Bartolomeo (see "Where to Dine," below). Indigo is the poolside café, available for breakfast and lunch.

Services: Room service, laundry, baby-sitting, massages.

Facilities: Freshwater swimming pool and Jacuzzi with a good view of Grand Cul-de-Sac, two hard-surface tennis courts (lit at night); water sports available (some at an additional charge).

HOTEL MANAPANY COTTAGES, Anse des Cayes (B.P. 114), 97133 St. Barthélemy, F.W.I. Tel. 27-66-55. Fax 27-75-28. 32 rms, 20 suites. A/C TV TEL

$ Rates (including continental breakfast): Winter, $355–$390 single or double; from $505 suite. Summer, $200–$215 single or double; from $270 suite. AE, DC, MC, V. **Parking:** Free.

★ With a wide range of spa facilities, the Hôtel Manapany climbs a steep, well-landscaped hillside on the northwestern side of the island, a 10-minute taxi ride north of the airport. This is one of the most luxurious and stylish hotels in the Caribbean (the name, translated from Malagese, means "small paradise"). It offers a cluster of units on the hillside and another group along the water, all with red roofs and rambling verandas open to the sea. Wicker furniture combines tropical comfort with Gallic style. Behind sliding glass doors, you'll find either one or two bedrooms, a large-screen TV with in-house video movies, ceiling fans, a tile bath, and a kitchenette. You register in a villa at the base of a hill.

Dining/Entertainment: The restaurant, Ouanalao, is a crescent-shaped terrace overlooking the sea, featuring casual dining with light lunches and candlelit romantic dinners. Italian dishes and fresh pastas are the specialties. More formal meals are served in an elegant raftered dining room, the Ballahou (see "Where to Dine," below).

Services: Concierge, room service, laundry, baby-sitting.

Facilities: Swimming pool, tennis court; spa facilities, including massage, acupuncture, nerveotherapy, vertebrotherapy, lymphatic drainage, curative magnetism, and reflexology (foot massage), for $70 per hour.

SAPORE DI MARE, Morne Lurin (B.P. 60), 97133 St. Barthélemy, F.W.I. Tel. 27-61-73. Fax 27-85-27. 10 rms.

$ Rates (including continental breakfast): Dec 20–Apr 20, $165–$325 single or double; $540 villa. Summer, $120–$190 single or double; from $325 villa. No credit cards. **Closed:** Sept to mid-Oct.

★ A luxurious private retreat perched on a hillside, Sapore di Mare commands spectacular views of Gustavia harbor and the offshore islands. Built in the Provençal style, it is exclusive, exceptional, and the most durably chic resort on the island. It lies a steep 1.7 miles from the airport, about three-quarters of a mile from Gustavia.

This retreat of relaxed luxury houses its guests in a number of different accommodations, including two small bedrooms in the main building. Villas have two bedrooms, a gracious two-story living room with a marble floor, complete kitchens, tapedecks, baths with bidets, and a wide private terrace for that view. The price of this style comes high, however.

Dining/Entertainment: Even if you don't stay here, you might visit for dinner, as it serves some of the finest food on St. Barts. The cuisine is Italian. There is a bar for an apéritif.

Services: Room service, laundry, baby-sitting, massage.

Facilities: Swimming pool with a view, tennis courts; beach nearby at St-Jean (a 5-minute drive down the steep hill); sailboat rentals can be arranged.

EXPENSIVE

EL SERENO BEACH HOTEL, Grand Cul-de-Sac (B.P. 19), 97133 St. Barthélemy, F.W.I. Tel. 27-64-80. Fax 27-75-47. 20 rms, 9 villas. A/C MINIBAR TV TEL

$ Rates: Winter, $210–$265 single; $245–$315 double; $185–$275 villa. Summer, $115–$135 single; $135–$170 double; $100–$150 villa. Continental breakfast 60F ($11.55) extra. AE, DC, MC, V. **Parking:** Free. **Closed:** Sept–Oct 15.

El Sereno's low-slung pastel facade and its isolated location 4 miles east of Guastavia create the aura of St-Tropez in the Antilles. A lot of the Riviera crowd is attracted to it, partly because of its Lyon-born owner, Marc Llepez, and his wife, Christine. On the premises are accommodations with garden views, plus a trio of units overlooking the sea. Each unit contains two beds, an individual safe, a refrigerator, and video movies. In 1991 the hotel opened nine extra villas, each with a large bedroom, a living room, a kitchen, a wide terrace, and a private bath, along with air conditioning and phone.

Dining/Entertainment: The feeling is a bit like a private compound, whose social center is an open-air bar and poolside restaurant, La Toque Lyonnaise.

Facilities: Freshwater pool, in the center of which is a verdant island.

FRANÇOIS PLANTATION, Colombier, 87133 St. Barthélemy, F.W.I. Tel. 27-78-82. Fax 27-61-26. 12 bungalows. A/C MINIBAR TV TEL

$ Rates (including full American breakfast): Winter, $250–$380 single or double. Summer, $170–$200 single or double. AE, MC, V. **Parking:** Free. **Closed:** Sept–Oct.

This complex 2 miles northwest of Gustavia, a 10-minute ride from the airport, re-creates the plantation era. Set inland in a tropical garden (not on the beach) are 12 bungalows, each decorated in an elegant West Indian style, with reproduction antique four-poster beds. Each has a ceiling fan and safe. Eight of the units open onto sea views, while others front a garden vista. The owners are Françoise and François (you heard right) Beret, longtime residents of St. Barts.

Dining/Entertainment: The hotel also has an exceptional restaurant (see "Where to Dine," below).

Facilities: Swimming pool with view.

LA BANANE, l'Orient, 97133 St. Barthelemy, F.W.I. Tel. 27-68-25. Fax 27-68-44. 9 rms. MINIBAR TV TEL

$ Rates (including continental breakfast): Winter, 2,000F ($384.60) single; 2,400F ($461.50) double. Summer, 1,700F ($326.90) single; 2,000F ($384.60) double. AE, V. **Parking:** Free. **Closed:** Sept to mid-Oct.

About a mile from the airport on the outskirts of the village of l'Orient, off the shore road near Autour de Rocher, is this small, intimate, and well-furnished hotel, filled with some of the most stylish antiques on the island. The complex is ringed by a fence whose boundaries are a 3-minute walk from the beach. My favorite accommodation contains a large mahogany four-poster bed, whose trim was made from a little-known Central and South American wood called angelique. The other units are less spacious, but each has a VCR, some Haitian art, a mixture of antique and modern designs, a refrigerator, a private terrace, and louvered windows overlooking the garden.

Dining/Entertainment: The small inn operates a good French restaurant on the premises.

Services: Room service.

Facilities: Beach nearby.

L'HIBISCUS, rue Thiers, Gustavia, 97133 St. Barthélemy, F.W.I. Tel. 27-64-82. Fax 27-73-04. 10 bungalows. A/C MINIBAR TV TEL

$ Rates: Winter, 1,800F ($346.15) bungalow for two. Summer, from 800F ($153.85) bungalow for two. Continental breakfast 40F ($7.70) extra. AE, MC, V. **Parking:** Free.

Since L'Hibiscus is dramatically terraced into one of Gustavia's steep hillsides, visitors have the pleasure of surveying the entire town from a private panoramic terrace. This lovely place and its cottages stand immediately beneath a 200-year-old clock tower in the uppermost region of town (follow the signs from the main street in Gustavia). Set amid a labyrinth of terra-cotta walkways on steeply sloping ground, each cottage has its own veranda, kitchenette, living room, VCR, and tasteful accessories.

Dining/Entertainment: The hotel offers a fine French cuisine, served on an attractive dining terrace, Vieux Clocher. Many guests come early to enjoy the cocktail hour, as L'Hibiscus is considered one of the best spots in Gustavia for a sundowner. The open-air bar adjacent to the pool encompasses lattices, greenery, and that view of the port.

Services: Room service, laundry, baby-sitting.

Facilities: Swimming pool; although not on the water, the hotel can arrange scuba diving, waterskiing, and sailboat rentals.

MODERATE

EDEN ROCK, St-Jean, 97133 St. Barthélemy, F.W.I. Tel. 27-72-94. Fax 27-88-37. 6 rms. A/C **Transportation:** Taxi (a 3-minute ride from the airport).
$ Rates: Winter, $110–$165 double. Summer, $85–$100 double. No credit cards.
When the rock it sits on was purchased many years ago by the island's former mayor, Remy de Haenen, the seller was an old woman who laughed at him for paying too many francs for it. Today it's part of the island lore. The building capping its pinnacle looks like an idealized version of a Provence farmhouse, and offers some of the best panoramas. It's surrounded on three sides by the waters of St. Jean Bay. I prefer the terra-cotta terrace, especially in the glare of noon, when the frigatebirds are wheeling and diving for fish in the turquoise waters. Inside the stone walls is a collection of French antiques and paintings, including a few drawings by Monsieur de Haenen's father, a well-known turn-of-the-century illustrator. The de Haenen family offers six bedrooms, each with a sea view, air conditioning or ceiling fan, and plenty of old-fashioned charm. It's best to reserve in summer 1 month before arrival, and in winter, 2 months.

HOSTELLERIE DES 3 FORCES, Vitet, 97133 St. Barthélemy, F.W.I. Tel. 27-61-25. Fax 27-81-38. 8 bungalows. MINIBAR
$ Rates: Winter, $150–$170 single or double. Summer, $65–$75 single; $80–$90 double. Continental breakfast $8 extra. AE, MC, V. **Parking:** Free. **Closed:** Aug 15–Sept 7.
In this "new age inn," guests benefit from the gracious attention of the owner and resident astrologer, Hubert de la Mortte. The cedar-sided accommodations are scattered over a dry and sandy slope whose panorama encompasses rolling hills near the village of Vitet, 3 miles east of Gustavia. Each bungalow is ringed with Neo-Victorian gingerbread and contains a simple decor of exposed wood and roughly textured fabrics, big windows, and private bathrooms. Most units have terraces and air conditioning. On the premises is a swimming pool, and the restaurant is recommended separately (see "Where to Dine," below).

LE VILLAGE SAINT-JEAN, Baie de Saint-Jean (B.P. 23), St. Barthélemy, F.W.I. Tel. 27-61-39, or toll free 800/633-7411. Fax 27-77-96. 4 rms, 20 cottages, 1 Jacuzzi suite. A/C TEL
$ Rates (including continental breakfast in rooms but not in cottages): Winter, $115 single or double; $300 cottage or suite. Summer, $68 single or double; $180 cottage or suite. AE, MC, V. **Parking:** Free.

S Over the years this cottage colony hideaway, 1 mile from the airport in the direction of St-Jean, has attracted a distinguished clientele, including food critic Craig Claiborne. Lying in the most central part of St. Barts, it offers, in my opinion, the best value on this high-priced resort island. Its cottages, built of stone and wood, contain kitchens, sun decks or gardens, as well as terrace living rooms, plus balconies, private baths, and ceiling fans. The highest price cited is for the Jacuzzi suite, but the other accommodations are very satisfactory. Although the rate structure is modest compared to other places on the island, don't be surprised to see a movie star or a media headliner here; after all, some of them like to save money too.

The complex has an excellent restaurant and bar, Le Patio, with a terrace. The hotel's swimming pool has two decks overlooking the bay, cascading water, and a Jacuzzi. It's also a 2-minute walk down to the beach. Founded in the early 1960s, this was the first inn of its kind in St. Barts, and it is still administered by the Charneau family. You will probably be welcomed by the gracious and charming (also English-speaking) Catherine.

TROPICAL HOTEL, St-Jean (B.P. 147), 97133 St. Barthélemy, F.W.I. Tel. 27-64-87. Fax 27-81-74. 20 rms. A/C TV TEL

$ Rates: Winter, $150 single; $170–$195 double. Summer, $80 single; $100–$130 double. Minimum stay 4 days in high season, 1 week over the Christmas holidays. Continental breakfast $7 extra. AE, MC, V. **Parking:** Free. **Closed:** June–July.

This little picture-postcard inn, trimmed in gingerbread, offers an intimate and restful atmosphere. It's perched on a hillside about 50 yards above St. Jean Beach (a mile from the airport and a mile and a half from Gustavia). The hotel (almost a bungalow inn) rents twin-bedded units, each with private shower, tile floor, and a refrigerator to cool your tropical drinks. Nine of the units come with a sea view and balcony, and 11 contain a porch opening onto a garden that is so lush it looks like a miniature jungle.

There's a hospitality center, where guests read, listen to music, or order drinks at a paneled, inviting bar ringed with antiques. The freshwater swimming pool is small, but water sports are available on the beach. Breakfast is served at the poolside terrace, and from December to May guests can dine at Le Stromboli, which offers salads, skewers, broiled meats, and lobster.

BUDGET

HOTEL NORMANDIE, L'Orient, 97133 St. Barthélemy, F.W.I. Tel. 27-61-66. 8 rms (all with bath).

$ Rates: $50–$70 single or double. Continental breakfast $6 extra. No credit cards. **Parking:** Free.

This is what the French call an *auberge antillaise*. Set inland a good haul from the beach, 3 miles east of the airport, it offers bedrooms of casual comfort (some are air-conditioned and others contain ceiling fans). A modest, family-owned hotel, it presents a row of louvered shutters to the street outside. A swimming pool with a terrace is found in the rear. It's one of the least expensive places to stay in St. Barts.

WHERE TO DINE

For the most part, you're served an essentially French cuisine with local adaptations; I've found few truly local dishes. However, at a private home I was once served "Madame Jackass," a redfish dish with hot peppers. Be aware that many of these restaurants shut down on a whim if there's no business—especially in autumn.

IN GUSTAVIA

Expensive

AU PORT, rue Sadi-Carnot. Tel. 27-62-36.

Cuisine: FRENCH/SEAFOOD. **Reservations:** Recommended, especially for veranda tables.

$ Prices: Appetizers $6–$8; main courses $20–$50. AE.

Open: Dinner only, daily 7–11pm. **Closed:** Sept–Oct.

From the outside this looks like a consciously raffish harborfront building, with a narrow veranda jutting above the bumpy road outside. You climb a steep and tiled flight of stairs to reach its second-floor dining room, in the center of town at the waterfront, where a simple decor of blue-and-white walls and neocolonial charm act as the appropriate foil for the satisfying classic cuisine. You might begin with a fish soup with flavorings of Provence or a homemade pasta with duck-liver pâté. Among the main courses, try medallions of angler fish roasted in a garlic sauce, or beef tenderloin with foie gras sauce.

CARAIBES CAFE, rue Jeanne-d'Arc, 2. Tel. 27-80-34.
Cuisine: FRENCH. **Reservations:** Required.
$ Prices: Appetizers $10–$15; main courses $15–$60. AE, MC, V.
Open: Dinner only, daily 7–11pm.

One of the premier restaurants of Gustavia, the Caraïbes Café occupies a second-floor premises with a view of the yacht-filled harbor. The menu is a delightful combination of French dishes. Dishes are prepared to order, and most diners agree that it's worth the wait. Try the seafood platter, lobster served on a bed of lentils, jumbo shrimp with a Créole sauce, and a homemade dessert made fresh daily.

LE CREMAILLERE, rue du Général-de-Gaulle. Tel. 27-82-95.
Cuisine: FRENCH/SEAFOOD. **Reservations:** Required.
$ Prices: Appetizers $16–$20; main courses $10–$48. MC, V.
Open: Lunch Mon–Sat noon–3pm; dinner Mon–Sat 6:30–11pm. **Closed:** Lunch off-season.

In the center of town near Gustavia's harbor, Le Crémaillère is easily one of the island's finest restaurants in all respects—the service, the menu, the carefully selected ingredients, and the fine wine list. It's in a 200-year-old Swedish house, which the French-born owner transformed into a chic country hideaway with an undeniable tropical flair. You can dine on an eyrie-style balcony, but my favorite corner is inside the air-conditioned inner room. Specialties include crayfish bisque, lobster thermidor, steak au poivre, and house-style lobster, with chocolate cake for dessert.

LE SAPOTILLIER, rue Sadi-Carnot. Tel. 27-60-28.
Cuisine: FRENCH/SEAFOOD. **Reservations:** Required.
$ Prices: Appetizers 45F–80F ($8.65–$15.40); main courses 100F–180F ($19.25–$34.60). Fixed-price meal 185F ($35.60). MC, V.
Open: Dinner only, daily 6:30–11pm. **Closed:** Sun off-season; May to mid-Oct.

This West Indian house is the domain of Austrian-born Adam Rayner, who runs one of the finest restaurants in Gustavia. Set on the innermost embankment of the capital's harbor, Le Sapotillier is at the top of the list for every visiting gourmet. Named after a gnarled and wind-blown sapodilla tree in the courtyard, the restaurant offers diners a choice of seating locations. They can enjoy the candlelit patio or select a table in the old wood-sided Antillean bungalow that was transported to the site from the outlying village of Corossol on the shoulders of local laborers.

Mr. Rayner, in the best tradition of European innkeeping, pays strict attention to the quality and presentation of his food. His menu might begin with sautéed frogs' legs, then follow with filet of duck with raspberries or apples, or better yet, one of the fish selections such as assorted boiled fish in a ginger stock. A dessert specialty is a delicate warm apple pie served with vanilla sauce and vanilla ice cream.

L'ESCALE, La Pointe. Tel. 27-81-06.
Cuisine: FRENCH/ITALIAN. **Reservations:** Required in high season.
$ Prices: Appetizers 45F–75F ($8.65–$14.40); main courses 58F–140F ($11.15–$26.90). MC, V.
Open: Lunch daily noon–3pm; dinner daily 7pm–midnight. **Closed:** Sept 15–Oct 15.

Some villa owners cite L'Escale as their favorite restaurant on the island. On the wharf, where yachts tie up, it stands alongside another popular spot, Le Marine Café. Frankly, you can dine lightly and inexpensively here or spend a lot of money, depending on your menu selections and appetite. Typical fare might include one of their excellent salads, pizzas, or pasta dishes. Or at night, sitting on the restaurant's al fresco terrace, you can order one of their grilled-meat specialties or fresh fish "according to arrival."

RESTAURANT AUX TROIS GOURMANDS, La Pointe. Tel. 27-71-83.
Cuisine: FRENCH/SEAFOOD. **Reservations:** Required.
$ Prices: Appetizers $8–$10; main courses $20–$50. AE, MC, V.
Open: Lunch Mon–Sat noon–2pm; dinner daily 6:30–11pm. **Closed:** Mid-Aug to late Sept.

On the less congested side of the harbor, this place sits behind a gingerbread-laden facade whose awnings flutter at boats moored nearby. Diners enjoy drinks on the wicker sofas near the bar. Christophe Gasnier, a much-experienced chef de cuisine, serves fish soup, filet of red snapper, lobster salad, and faux filet with mustard sauce for lunch. Dinners might include mussel soup with saffron, fish pâté in a tarragon sauce, homemade pasta with fresh foie gras, breast of duck with a cassis sauce, boneless chicken breast in a truffles sauce, and lobster medallions sautéed with sweetbreads.

Moderate

EDDY'S GHETTO, rue du Général-de-Gaulle. Tel. 27-87-00.
Cuisine: FRENCH/CREOLE. **Reservations:** Not required.
$ Prices: Appetizers $5.50–$7.40; main courses $13–$15.75. No credit cards.
Open: Dinner only, Mon–Sat 7–10pm.

Priding itself on its role as the island's most unpretentious restaurant, whose only glamour comes from its simple white walls and open access to the Caribbean breezes, Eddy's Ghetto is in a small Antillean house near the harborfront. Meals, served at simple wooden tables, might include crab salad, ragoût of beef, and grilled filets of fish and chicken. Available wines include an array of passably good French vintages, which seem to go well with an atmosphere best described as laid-back and French. The owner is Eddy Stakelborough, who sells T-shirts from behind the establishment's bar.

LA LANGOUSTE, rue Bord-de-la-Mer. Tel. 27-69-47.
Cuisine: CREOLE/SEAFOOD. **Reservations:** Required.
$ Prices: Appetizers $8–$12; main courses $20–$40. MC, V.
Open: Lunch daily noon–2pm; dinner daily 7–10pm.

La Langouste used to be known as "Annie's." Annie, of the island family of Ange, is still around, but she prefers to name her place in honor of the clawless Caribbean lobster instead of herself. In a century-old building erected during the Swedish domain over the island, her zesty little restaurant is near the Gendarmerie. You get down-to-earth Créole cookery here, and that means stuffed land crabs, conch ragoût, cod fritters (called accra de morue), the namesake langouste, always-fresh fish, and curried chicken. Lunches are light, but dinner is a Créole delight.

TASTE UNLIMITED, rue du Général-de-Gaulle. Tel. 27-70-42.
Cuisine: DELI. **Reservations:** Not required.
$ Prices: Appetizers $2–$3; main courses $5–$10. No credit cards.
Open: Mon–Sat 7:30am–7pm. **Closed:** Sept.

The best deli on the island, set in a passageway in the center of Gustavia, this is a leading caterer to occupants of those expensive villas and also serves take-out meals. But it's no ordinary deli—the quality of its food is top-notch. It's an ideal place to pick up items if you're planning a boat excursion to a neighboring island.

ANSE DES CAYES

RESTAURANT BALLAHOU, in the Hôtel Manapany Cottages, Anse des Cayes. Tel. 27-66-55.
Cuisine: FRENCH/SEAFOOD. **Reservations:** Required for non-hotel guests.
$ Prices: Appetizers 119F–250F ($22.90–$48.10); main courses 80F–370F ($15.40–$71.15). AE, DC, MC, V.
Open: Lunch daily 12:30–3pm; dinner daily 7:30–9:30pm. **Closed:** May–Nov.

⭐ Named after a small variety of swordfish, this is one of the best and most elegant restaurants on the island, with a sun-flooded pink-and-white interior, a 5-minute drive north of the airport. To enter, you pass beneath a portal dripping in fanciful Caribbean gingerbread. Dining is under a high ceiling whose rafters curve around the perimeter of an oval swimming pool. Lunch, served more informally beside the pool, includes salads, stuffed land crabs prepared Créole style, air-dried alpine beef with lentils, and many variations of crayfish. Elaborate dinners are served by candlelight inside and are accompanied by live music. The specialties might include bisque of lobster, braised sweetbreads, duck with a sweet orange sauce, and kidneys cooked with Armagnac.

IN THE ST-JEAN BEACH AREA

CHEZ FRANCINE, Plage de St-Jean. Tel. 27-60-49.
Cuisine: FRENCH/CREOLE. **Reservations:** Recommended.
$ Prices: Appetizers 40F–50F ($7.70–$9.60); main courses 70F–160F ($13.45–$30.75); fixed-price lunch 110F ($21.15). MC, V.
Open: Lunch only, daily 11:30am–3:30pm. **Closed:** 2 weeks in midsummer.
Chez Francine, 1 mile east of the airport, maintains a delightfully informal atmosphere. People from all over the island come here for lunch. The place is really little more than a boardwalk terrace built on top of the sand a few feet from the beach. Its overhead awnings and blackboard menu encourage an attire of bathing suits, or less. Typical meals, often preceded by a frothy piña colada, might include chilled lobster, grilled chicken or fish, a selection of wine or beer, and a choice of homemade tortes and cakes. The establishment is a busy focal point of beach life.

LE PATIO, Village St-Jean. Tel. 27-61-39.
Cuisine: ITALIAN/FRENCH. **Reservations:** Required.
$ Prices: Appetizers 45F–85F ($8.65–$16.35); main courses 80F–280F ($15.40–$53.85). MC, V.
Open: Lunch Thurs–Tues noon–2:30pm; dinner Thurs–Tues 7–10:30pm. **Closed:** June–July.

Ⓢ Le Patio, 1 mile from the airport in the direction of St-Jean, enjoys a deserved reputation for offering some of the best food values on the island. A northern Italian cuisine, along with pizza and some French dishes, are featured at this restaurant, which enjoys a beautiful view. Fifteen different pastas are featured, including one made with lobster, crabmeat, and shrimp. You might begin with marinated roast peppers, then go on to one of the homemade pasta dishes, including a tricolor tortellini. The fish and meat courses are also excellent, including the sautéed seafood in a wine-and-cream sauce, and prime rib for two diners.

LE PELICAN, Plage de St-Jean. Tel. 27-64-64.
Cuisine: CREOLE/FRENCH. **Reservations:** Recommended, especially for dinner.
$ Prices: Appetizers 45F–90F ($8.65–$17.30); main courses 85F–280F ($16.35–$53.85). No credit cards.
Open: Lunch daily 11:30am–3:30pm; dinner daily 7–10pm. **Closed:** Sun in summer.
The ambience and cuisine differ so much here from day to night that you'd almost think you were in two different restaurants. Lunch is served outdoors in the shade of an elongated parasol, within earshot of the nearby surf. While sipping French wine in the Antillean sunshine, you can enjoy fish soup, lobster bisque, and a generously portioned Créole platter laden with accras, shellfish, blood pudding, and grilled fish. Dinners are more elaborate, with lobster salad, green-pepper steak, grilled chicken with mustard, and, one of the most popular items, grilled catch of the day. The setting, 1 mile east of the airport, incorporates three high-ceilinged dining rooms with pastel colors, a view of the sea, and candlelight.

MORNE LURIN

SANTA FE BAR RESTAURANT, Lurin. Tel. 27-61-04.
Cuisine: AMERICAN. **Reservations:** Not required.
$ Prices: Appetizers $3–$4; main courses $10–$20. No credit cards.
Open: Lunch Mon–Sat noon–2:30pm; dinner Thurs–Tues 5–10pm. **Closed:** June.

If you're in the area late in the day, head up to the Santa Fe Bar Restaurant, high up beyond Sapore di Mare, 1 mile east of Gustavia. Here you'll get the best American-style hamburgers on the island, juicy ones at that. You can take in the view for free. Most checks are under $12 unless you have a lot to drink.

COLOMBIER

FRANÇOIS PLANTATION RESTAURANT, Colombier. Tel. 27-78-82.
Cuisine: FRENCH. **Reservations:** Required.
$ Prices: Appetizers 50F–60F ($9.60–$11.55); main courses 70F–200F ($13.45–$38.45). AE, MC, V.
Open: Dinner only, daily 6:30–10pm. **Closed:** Sun in Apr; Sept–Oct.

Françoise and François Beret take justifiable pride in their traditional cuisine. Their dining room, part of the old plantation that stood here 2 miles northwest of Gustavia, is attractively decorated and inviting. The wine, the service, and the quality of ingredients used in the dishes presented are top-notch. The chef might tempt you with a traditional fish soup or one of the salads, and typical dishes might be escalope of wild salmon with a watercress-and-cream sauce, Oriental-style duck breast, or a baked combination of fish flavored with fresh coriander.

ANSE DU GRAND CUL-DE-SAC

BARTOLOMEO, in the Hôtel Guanahani, Anse du Grand Cul-de-Sac. Tel. 27-66-60.
Cuisine: FRENCH/SEAFOOD. **Reservations:** Recommended, especially for non-hotel guests.
$ Prices: Appetizers 65F–135F ($12.50–$25.95); main courses 145F–250F ($27.90–$48.10). AE, DC, MC, V.
Open: Lunch daily noon–5pm; dinner daily 7:30–9:30pm. **Closed:** Sept–Oct.

This is the deluxe dining choice for one of the most exclusive and expensive hotels on the island. The menu selection changes frequently, but always includes a variety of gastronomic specialty dishes, interestingly spiced, sauced, and served. The restaurant, which is a blend of casual and elegant taste in both ambience and cuisine, also offers an outside terrace for drinks and dinner. There is also nightly piano entertainment.

GRANDE SALINE

LE TAMARIN, Plage de Saline. Tel. 27-72-12.
Cuisine: FRENCH/CREOLE. **Reservations:** Required.
$ Prices: Appetizers $9–$15; main courses $18–$25. MC, V.
Open: Lunch daily 12:30–3pm; dinner daily 7–9pm. **Closed:** May–Nov.

The favored place in the sun is Le Tamarin, which picks up the beach traffic—many in stunningly revealing bikinis—from the nearby Plage de Saline. It's isolated amid rocky hills and forests east of Gustavia, in a low-slung cottage whose eaves are lined with gingerbread. Inside, you'll see Haitian paintings, exotic hardwoods, and wicker armchairs. If you have to wait, you can order an apéritif in one of the lazy hammocks stretched under a tamarind tree (hence the name of the restaurant). Fresh fish is invariably featured, but meat dishes and poultry also are cooked well. Service can be hectic, but if you're in a rush you shouldn't be here. It's for a lazy afternoon on the beach or a relaxed dinner under the stars.

GRAND CUL-DE-SAC

CLUB LAFAYETTE, Grand Cul-de-Sac. Tel. 27-62-51.
 Cuisine: FRENCH/CREOLE. **Reservations:** Recommended.
$ Prices: Appetizers $10–$15; main courses $25–$50. AE, MC, V.
 Open: Lunch daily noon–4pm; dinner daily 7–10pm. **Closed:** May–Nov.
Lunching here, at a cove on the eastern end of the island, east of Marigot, is like taking a meal at your own private beach club. After a dip in the ocean or pool, you can order a *planteur* in the shade of a sea grape, and later proceed to lunch itself: a roquefort-and-walnut salad, charcoaled langouste, grilled fresh fish, and breast of duck. In other words, this is no hamburger fast-food beach joint. Afterward, have a refreshing citrus-flavored sherbet. For dinner, you might begin with a warm goat-cheese salad, then follow with fish filet in a sorrel sauce.

LE TOQUE LYONNAISE, in El Sereno Beach Hotel. Tel. 27-64-80.
 Cuisine: FRENCH. **Reservations:** Recommended.
$ Prices: Appetizers 55F–140F ($10.60–$26.90); main courses 135F–175F ($25.95–$33.65); fixed-price meals 240F ($46.15) and 340F ($65.40). AE, DC, MC, V.
 Open: Dinner only, daily 7–10pm. **Closed:** June–Oct.
Four miles east of Gustavia, one of the premier restaurants on the island fronts a swimming pool and is partially open to the sky. Most guests come here for the *menu lyonnais*, reflecting the culinary background of Christine and Marc Llepez, the owners. They invite chefs from Lyon, the gastronomic capital of France, to visit St. Barts. Specialties are likely to include salade lyonnaise, lobster ravioli, herb-flavored lamb, or magret of duckling with ginger. But all that depends on the whim of the current chef, André Chenu. The wine list is among the finest on the island. The restaurant is open to sea breezes and contained in an angular modern pavilion decorated in a tropical style with lattices.

RESTAURANT FLAMBOYANT, Grand Cul-de-Sac. Tel. 27-75-65.
 Cuisine: FRENCH/CREOLE. **Reservations:** Required.
$ Prices: Fixed-price dinner 180F ($34.60). AE, MC, V.
 Open: Dinner only, Tues–Sun 7–9:30pm. **Closed:** Sept.
On the western edge of the island, directly east of Marigot, lies what many residents consider the best restaurant on St. Barts. It's on the veranda level of the isolated island home of Albert Balayn, a chef who studied cuisine in France before returning to his native island. The preferred seating is on a panoramic terrace, where the hillside location contributes to a view over fields, forest, and sea. You might begin with eggplant pâté or a stuffed christophine, then follow with small lobster casserole or breast of duck in a cider sauce. Dessert might include a homemade chocolate mousse or coconut flan. The wine list is also interesting.

VITET

HOTELLERIE DES 3 FORCES, Vitet. Tel. 27-61-25.
 Cuisine: FRENCH/CREOLE/VEGETARIAN. **Reservations:** Required.
$ Prices: Appetizers 40F–110F ($7.70–$21.15); main courses 45F–270F ($8.65–$51.90). AE, MC, V.
 Open: Lunch daily noon–3pm; dinner daily 7–9:45pm. **Closed:** Aug 15–Sept 7.
This place 2 miles east of the airport has a resident astrologer, a French provincial decor, well-scrubbed surfaces, and food with a genuine allure. The food is well prepared and beautifully served, and for dessert you get an astrological forecast thrown in. The heart and soul of the place is Hubert de la Motte, who arrived from Brittany with his wife and sister to create a hotel (see "Where to Stay," above) where happiness, good food, comfort, and conversation could be a way of life. Even if you don't stay here, you might want to drive out for a meal, enjoying it on a sun-washed, scrub-covered landscape. Evening meals are more formal and might include fish pâté, beef shish kebab with curry sauce, grilled fresh lobster, veal kidneys flambé with cognac, a cassolette of snails, and such succulent desserts as crêpes

Suzette flambé. "Each dish takes time," in the words of the owner, because it's prepared fresh. Count on a leisurely meal.

PUBLIC

MAYA'S, Public. Tel. 27-73-61.
    Cuisine: CREOLE. **Reservations:** Required.
$ **Prices:** Appetizers 35F–50F ($6.75–$9.60); main courses 135F–175F ($25.95–$33.65). AE, MC, V.
    Open: Dinner only, Mon–Sat 6–11pm. **Closed:** June–Oct.
This is the kind of place you might find in Martinique—because its French-Créole chef, Maya Veuzelin-Gurley, is from that island. You might begin with the salad of tomatoes, arugula, and endive, then follow with grilled fish in sauce chien (hot) or a grilled filet of beef. She also prepares what she calls "sailor's chicken" with soya sauce and coconut milk. For dessert, the coconut tart is a taste treat. Maya's is directly west of Gustavia.

SPORTS & RECREATION

BEACHES There are 14 gleaming-white sand beaches on St. Barts. Few are ever crowded, even in winter, and all are public and free. Nudism is prohibited, but topless is quite common. The most famous beach is **St-Jean,** which is actually two beaches divided by the Eden Rock promontory. It offers water sports, beach restaurants such as Chez Francine, and a few hotels, as well as some shady areas. **Flamands,** to the west, is a very wide beach with a few small hotels and some areas shaded by lantana palms. For beaches with hotels, restaurants, and water sports, **Grand Cul-de-Sac,** on the northeast shore, fits the bill. This is a narrow beach protected by a reef.

    Gouvenor, a beach on the south, can be reached by driving through Gustavia and up to Lurin. Turn at the Santa Fe Restaurant (see "Where to Dine," above) and head down a narrow road. The beach is gorgeous, but wear lots of sunscreen as there is no shade there. **Saline,** to the east of Gouvenor, is reached by driving up the road from the commercial center in St-Jean; a short walk over the sand dune and you're there. Like Gouvenor, Saline offers some waves, but again there is no shade. **Lorient,** on the north shore, is quiet and calm, with shady areas. **Marigot,** also on the north shore, is narrow but offers good swimming and snorkeling. **Colombier** is a beach difficult to get to but well worth the effort. It can only be reached by boat or by taking a rugged goat path from Petite Anse past Flamands, a 30-minute walk. Shade and snorkeling are found there, and you can pack a lunch and spend the day.

FISHING People who like fishing are fond of the waters around St. Barts. From March through July they catch dolphin (the fish, not the mammal); in September, wahoo. Atlantic bonito, barracuda, and marlin also turn up with frequency. **Marine Service,** quai du Yacht-Club (tel. 27-70-34), rents the *Merry Fisher,* which was created for big-game fishing, for 2,500F ($480.75) for the boat. The rate is for 4 hours, with captain and first mate.

TENNIS It's mainly for hotel guests. There's a court at the **St. Barths Beach Hotel,** Grand Cul-de-Sac (tel. 27-60-70).

    One of the best courts is at the **Hôtel Manapany** (tel. 27-66-55) (see "Where to Stay," above). Use of the court is free to residents both day and night. Nonresidents pay 100F ($19.25) per hour during daylight, 150F ($28.85) for nighttime illumination.

    It's also possible to play on the courts of the **Hôtel Guanahani,** at Grand Cul-de-Sac (tel. 27-66-60) (see "Where to Stay," above).

WATERSKIING Waterskiing is authorized from 9am to 1pm and again from 4:40pm to sundown. Because of the shape of the coastline, skiers must remain 80 yards from shore on the windward side of the island and 110 yards off on the leeward side.

WATER SPORTS **Marine Service,** quai du Yacht Club (tel. 27-70-34), is the most complete water-sports facility on the island. It operates from a one-story building set directly on the water at the edge of a marina, on the opposite side of the harbor from the more congested part of Gustavia. The outfit offers a series of dives from Gustavia harbor. Their program includes exploration for beginners (first dive) as well as for certified divers, night dives, and PADI certification. One dive costs 250F ($48.10). Of interest to the general tourist, they offer a series of sailing and snorkeling trips. One of the most popular outings is a sunset cruise daily from 5 to 6:30pm, costing 230F ($44.25) with an open bar. One of the most interesting half-day trips goes to Colombier Beach or Fourchue Island, the best for snorkeling. Trips are daily from 9:30am to 1pm and 1:30 to 5pm.

Ile Fourchue (Forked Island) is a popular rendezvous point for boats. Named for its configuration, with rocky peaks separated by valleys, Ile Fourchue is horseshoe-shaped, with a protected anchorage. Its only permanent residents are goats, but a few ruins bear witness to the fact that it was once the home of a Breton who lived a Robinson Crusoe–style life here for many years. Another attraction is Colombier Beach (see "Beaches," above). A full day's excursion to both Ile Fourchue and Colombian costs 450F ($86.55) per person, with a lunch included. A half-day excursion to Colombier costs 270F ($51.90) per person, including a French picnic. Each cruise features an open bar.

WINDSURFING   Windsurfing is one of the most popular sports practiced on St. Barts. Try **St. Barth Wind School,** at the Tom Beach Hotel on Pelican Beach near Chez Francine (tel. 27-71-22). It's open daily from 9am to 5pm. Windsurfing generally costs $15 to $18 per hour. Professional instructors are on hand.

SAVVY SHOPPING

You don't pay any duty on St. Barts—everything is out-of-bond—so it's a good place to buy liquor and French perfumes, which are among the lowest priced in the West Indies. Perfume, for example, is cheaper on St. Barts than it is in France itself. Champagne is cheaper than in Epernay, France. St. Barts is the only completely free-trading port in the world, with the exception of French St. Martin and Dutch St. Maarten. Only trouble is, selections are limited. However, you'll find good buys in sportswear, crystal, porcelain, watches, and other luxuries.

If you're in the market for some island crafts, try to find those convertible-brim, fine straw hats St. Bartians like to wear. *Vogue* once featured this high-crown headwear in its fashion pages. They also have some interesting block-printed resort clothes in cotton.

Shopping hours are usually Monday through Friday from 8:30am to noon and from 2 to 5pm, and on Saturday from 8:30am to noon.

THE ATELIER, Colombier. Tel. 27-61-72.
Two miles north of Gustavia is Jean-Yves Froment's shop and studio, recently completely redecorated and reorganized. Visitors can watch the hand-dyed and block-printed decorations and tropical fashion prints being made.

LA CAVE DU PORT FRANC, rue Jeanne-d'Arc. Tel. 27-65-27.
For wine devotees, there are two good choices, including La Cave in Marigot (tel. 27-63-21), and the more centrally located one above. Both carry fine French vintages, which are stored in temperature-controlled "cellars." The branch at rue Jeanne-d'Arc, lying at Le Brigatin on Gustavia's harbor, also carries a collection of contemporary paintings and antique objets d'art.

LA FONDA HERMES, rue de la République, Gustavia. Tel. 27-66-15.
This is the only outlet in the Caribbean of the famous Parisian haberdasher. It stands across the street from the port. Be warned, you'll pay dearly for some French allure.

GUCCI, bd. du Front-de-Mer, Gustavia. Tel. 27-69-46.
Gucci has dignified St. Barts with its presence, carrying the standard array of chic and expensive merchandise. Here you can get the real item, not the imitation from Asia.

LITTLE SWITZERLAND, rue de la France, Gustavia. Tel. 27-64-66.
Behind glass cases is an array of untaxed crystal, jewelry, and luxurious frill merchandise.

LOULOU'S MARINE, rue de la République, Gustavia. Tel. 27-62-74.
Some of its merchandise could come from any general store in France and some of it is so specialized that only a yacht owner could appreciate it. This is possibly the most gregarious rendezvous point in town, and amid pulleys, coils of rope, and folded sailcloth, you'll find clothing, luggage, shirts, shoes, and beachwear.

SAMSON & CO., Nya Gatan, Gustavia. Tel. 27-60-46.
Samson & Co. stocks art from the Philippines and Bali and sells batiks and hand-painted clothing for both men and women.

THE SHELL SHOP, rue du Général-de-Gaulle, Gustavia. Tel. 27-87-55.
This small shop offers shell and coral jewelry in original designs unique to St. Barts and the Caribbean. Shells and coral from all over the world, local handcrafts and block printing, free paperbacks, and U.S. sports information are available here.

SMOKE AND BOOZE, rue du Général-de-Gaulle, Gustavia. Tel. 27-60-24.
This is the place to go for wine, liquor, liqueurs, and tobacco, as well as for toys and souvenirs. They'll package your beverage purchases for you to take home.

EVENING ENTERTAINMENT

Most guests consider a French Créole dinner under the open stars near the sea (or with a view of the twinkling stars) enough of a nocturnal adventure. After that, there isn't a lot of excitement.

In Gustavia, the most popular gathering place is **Le Select,** rue de la France (tel. 27-86-87), apparently named after its more famous granddaddy in the Montparnasse section of Paris. It's utterly simple, and a game of dominoes might be under way as you walk in. In the open-air café garden, near the port, tables are placed outside on the gravel. The outdoor grill promises a "cheeseburger in Paradise." You never know who might show up here, perhaps Mick Jagger, perhaps Jimmy Buffett. Beer begins at 12F ($2.30), and the place is open Monday through Saturday from 10am to 11pm. The locals like it a lot, and outsiders are welcomed but not necessarily embraced until they get to know you a bit. If you want to spread a rumor and have it travel fast across the island, start it here.

Also in Gustavia, overlooking the harbor, is the **Hôtel Hibiscus,** rue Thiers (tel. 27-64-62), popular with yachting people who like to visit for drinks.

The island's leading disco is **Autour du Rocher,** Lorient (tel. 27-60-73), which is reached by an almost-impossible road up a steep hill. It often presents live acts; otherwise, disco music is played. On some nights the crowd tends to be French fashionable. Hours are 10pm to 4am daily, with drinks costing $5 to $7. Admission is $10. Closed: Oct.

CHAPTER 12

THE BRITISH WINDWARDS

These windward islands lie in the direct path of the trade winds, which swoop down from the northeast. British affiliated (now independent), they are Gallic in manner, West Indian in outlook.

French habits can be traced back to early Gallic invaders, as the islands changed hands many times before coming into Britain's orbit. On such islands as St. Lucia, and especially Dominica, you'll hear a Créole patois. English, however, is also spoken.

The British Windwards are made up of four main islands—St. Lucia, St. Vincent, Grenada, and Dominica—along with a scattering of isles or spits of land known as the Grenadines. Truly far-out islands, the Grenadines are a chain stretching from St. Vincent to Grenada. Some people group Barbados and Trinidad and Tobago in the British Windwards, but I have preferred to treat these independent island nations separately in the following chapters.

Topped by mountains and bursting with greenery, the British Windwards in this chapter are still far enough off the mainline tourist circuit to make a visit to them something of an adventure. At some of the more remote oases, you'll have the sand crabs, iguanas, and sea birds to enjoy all by yourself.

For the most part, the islands are small and volcanic in origin. Most of the inhabitants live on their crops. There's little or no industry, and tourism is not overly developed, especially in Dominica.

1. DOMINICA

It has been called "the most original island in the Caribbean." Covered by a dense tropical rain forest that blankets its mountain slopes, including cloud-wreathed Morne Diablotin at 4,775 feet, it has vegetation unique in the West Indies. Untamed, unspoiled Dominica (pronounced Dom-in-*ee*-ka, and not to be confused with the Spanish-speaking Dominican Republic) is known for its clear rivers and waterfalls, its hot springs and boiling lakes. According to myth, it has 365 "rivers," one for each day of the year. This is the most rugged of Caribbean islands.

Largest of the British Windwards, Dominica (or Sunday Island) was sighted by Columbus in November 1493. For centuries British and French troops fought each other for its domination, and Britain eventually paid $65,000 to France to get the French off the island. In 1805 Britain assumed control, yet it still had to deal with Carib uprisings, including a native war that broke out as late as 1930.

On March 1, 1967, Dominica got a new constitution and was declared a state in

WHAT'S SPECIAL ABOUT THE BRITISH WINDWARDS

Beaches

- ☐ Pigeon Island, St. Lucia, a white sandy beach with picnic facilities.
- ☐ Vigie Beach, St. Lucia, one of the island's most frequented.
- ☐ Anse Chastanet, St. Lucia, called the beach connoisseur's delight, with white sands against lushly overgrown foothills.
- ☐ St. Vincent beaches, ranging from the white sands of Villa Beach to the black sands of Buccament Bay or Questelle's Bay, all west-coast sites.
- ☐ Grande Anse, 3 miles of sugar-white sands on Grenada, the finest beach in the British Windwards.

Great Towns/Villages

- ☐ St. George's, capital of Grenada, considered the picture-postcard port of the British Windwards.

Ace Attractions

- ☐ Carib Indian Reservation, a 3,700-acre plot of land in Dominica, last stronghold of the Carib peoples.
- ☐ Cabrits National Park, on the northwest coast of Dominica, with mountain scenery, tropical forests, swampland, volcanic sand beaches, coral reefs, and 18th-century fort ruins.
- ☐ The Pitons, a pair of volcanic cones formed of lava and rock on St. Lucia, rising to 2,460 and 2,619 feet.
- ☐ Annandale Falls, a tropical wonderland on Grenada that's often compared to Tahiti, with a 50-foot-high waterfall.

---

association with Britain. On November 3, 1978, it became independent and today is a republic and a member of the Commonwealth of Nations (formerly the British Commonwealth). It is governed by a president as head of state and a prime minister who is head of government.

Dominica, with a population of some 80,000, lies in the eastern Caribbean, between Guadeloupe to the north and Martinique to the south. English is the official language, but a French patois is widely spoken. The Caribs, the indigenous people of the Caribbean, live as a community on the northeast of the island. The art and craft of traditional basketry is still practiced and is unique to today's Carib community.

The mountainous island is 29 miles long and 15 miles wide, with a total land area of 290 square miles, many of which have never been seen by explorers other than, presumably, the Caribs.

Most Dominicans earn their living from agriculture. The government is making a strong bid for tourism—but not with the drawing card of white sandy beaches, which the island does not have. Rather, Dominica is known for its river swimming and natural attractions. Hiking and mountain climbing are also popular, as the flora on the island is extremely rich—and often rare.

Because of the pristine coral reefs, dramatic dropoffs, and shipwrecks found in the crystal-clear waters with visibility of 100 feet plus, scuba diving is becoming increasingly popular, particularly off the west coast, site of Dominica's two dive operations.

Rainfall varies from 50 inches along the dry west coast to as much as 350 inches in the tropical rain forests of the mountainous interior, where downpours are not uncommon.

Clothing is casual, including light summer wear for most of the year. However, take along walking shoes for those trips into the mountains and a sweater for cooler evenings. Bikinis and swimwear should not be worn in the streets of the capital city, Roseau, or in the villages.

National Day celebrations on November 3 commemorate Columbus's discovery in

1493 and independence in 1978. Cultural celebrations of Dominica's traditional dance, music, song, and story telling begin in mid-October and continue to Community Day, November 4.

To sum up, come to Dominica for the beauties of nature more than *la dolce vita*.

PORTRAIT OF A GREAT LADY One of Dominica's most valuable assets is its very human and intelligent prime minister, Miss **Eugenia Charles.** Born of a prominent Dominican family, and educated in Canada and Britain, she has been in office since 1980 and is her country's most influential spokesperson. Firmly allied with the U.S., she's credited almost single-handedly with focusing world resolve on the U.S. military action that prevented Grenada from being taken over by Cuba in 1985. Once a week she returns to her private offices, where you are likely to see as many as 50 people, each with a cause to plead before the island's social and political grande dame.

As for tourism, Miss Charles foresees that because of the frequent rainfall over Dominica, the island will never have the kind of "fun in the sun" holidays that other neighboring islands have fostered. Rather, she envisions the development of a series of spas in the jungle-covered interior, amid the mineral and hot springs.

Her birthday, May 15, is somewhat of a national event, at least observed by her political allies. Gracious, hard-driving, and relentlessly realistic, she is indeed the most memorable democratic leader of the entire Caribbean.

ORIENTATION

GETTING THERE There are two airports on Dominica, neither of which is large enough to handle a jetliner; therefore, there are no direct flights from North America. The **Melville Hall Airport** is on the northeastern coast of the island, almost diagonally across the island from the capital, Roseau, on the southwestern coast. Should you land at Melville Hall, there is a 1½-hour taxi ride into Roseau, a tour across the island through the forest and coastal villages. The fare from Melville Hall to Roseau is $14 per person, and drivers have the right to gather up at least three passengers in their cabs. By private taxi the cost could be $50.

The newer **Canefield Airport** is about a 5-minute taxi ride to the north of Roseau. The 2,000-foot airstrip accommodates smaller planes than those that can land at Melville Hall. From here, the typical taxi fare into town is $6.

For many North Americans, the easiest way to reach Dominica is to take a flight to Antigua (see "Getting There" in Section 1 of Chapter 8). From there, you can take one of the six or seven daily **LIAT** (tel. 809/462-0700) flights to Dominica. Another possibility, would be to fly via St. Maarten. From there, LIAT offers three daily flights on to Dominica, usually with several intermediary stops.

It is also possible to fly to Guadeloupe (see "Getting There" in Section 2 of Chapter 11). Once on Guadeloupe, you can make a connection to Dominica on **Air Guadeloupe** (tel. 809/448-2181) or LIAT to Dominica. **Air Martinique** (tel. 809/448-2181) and LIAT also fly in from Fort-de-France. Many experienced Dominica visitors flying in from neighboring islands ultimately resort to chartering a small plane from such organizations as **Mustique Airlines** (tel. 809/458-4621) or **Air Anguilla** (tel. 809/497-2643), either of which would arrange a special expedition to Dominica from anywhere in the central or southern Caribbean.

GETTING AROUND The capital of Dominica is **Roseau,** and many of the places to stay are found there or very close by.

By Minibus The public transportation system consists of private minibus service between Roseau and the rest of Dominica. These minibuses are filled mainly with schoolchildren, workers, and country people who need to come into the city. Taxis may be a more reliable means of transport for visitors, but there are hotels at which buses call during the course of the day. A typical minibus fare from Rouseau to Portsmouth is EC$6 ($2.20).

By Taxi At either the Melville Hall or Canefield airport, you can rent a taxi, and

DOMINICA & ST. LUCIA

5 mi
0
8 km

N

ST. LUCIA

Atlantic Ocean

Grande Anse Bay

Anse Lavouette

St. Lucia Channel

Pigeon Island

Reduit Beach

Gros Islet

Grande Anse Bay

La Sorcière

Petit Piton

Dennery

Micoud

Savannes Bay

Maria Islands

Cape Moule à Chique

Hewanorra Airport

Vieux Fort

Labourie Bay

Choc Bay

Vigie Beach

Vigie Airport

Grande Cul de Sac Bay

La Toc

Castries

Fort Charlotte

Cul de Sac River

Roseau River

Anse-La-Raye

Marigot Bay

Canaries

Anse Chastenet

Anse Chastenet Beach

Soufrière

Soufrière Bay

Petit Piton

Gros Piton

Choiseul

Caribbean Sea

DOMINICA

Atlantic Ocean

Capucin Point

Carib Point

Guadeloupe Channel

Anse Noire

Woodford Hill

Marigot

Pagua Bay

Melville Hall Airport

Calibishie

Portsmouth

Morne Aux Diables

Douglas Bay

Prince Rupert Bay

Salybia

Carib Indian Reservation

Saint Sauveur

Rosalie

Morne Jaune

La Plaine

Bout Sable

Morne Fraser

Morne Trois Pitons

Emerald Pool

Boiling Lake

Trafalgar

Morne Watt

Grand Bay

Central Forest Reserve

Morne Diablotin

Colihaut

Salisbury

Mero

St. Joseph

Rodney's Rock

Mahaut

Canefield Airport

Reigate

Goodwill

Roseau

Castle Comfort

Pointe Michel

Soufrière

Berekua

Scott's Head

Martinique Channel

Caribbean Sea

Airport

DOMINICA

ACCOMMODATIONS:
Anchorage Hotel **4**
Castaways Beach Hotel **5**
Evergreen Hotel **2**
Fort Young Hotel **1**
Papillote Wilderness Retreat **6**
Reigate Hall Hotel **3**

ATTRACTIONS:
Cabrits National Park **7**
Carib Indian Reservation **1**
Emerald Pool Trail **8**
Morne Trois Pitons National Park **2**
Portsmouth **6**
Sulphur Springs **4**
Trafalgar Falls **3**

ST. LUCIA

ACCOMMODATIONS:
Anse Chastenet **1**
Club Med **7**
Club St. Lucia **8**
Couples **9**
Cunard Hotel, La Toc **2**
Green Parrot Hotel **11**
Halcyon Beach Club **3**
The Islander **12**
Le Sport **10**
The Moorings Marigot Bay Resort **4**
The St. Lucian Hotel **5**
Windjammer Landing Villa Beach Resort **6**

ATTRACTIONS:
Diamond Mineral Baths **4**
Gros Piton **3**
Marigot Bay **3**
Morne Fortune **1**
Moule-à-Chique **8**
Petit Piton **5**
Soufrière **6**
Pigeon Island National Park **2**

prices are regulated by the government (see "Getting There," above). If you want to see the island by taxi, rates are about $15 per car for each hour of touring, and as many as four passengers can go along at the same time.

By Rental Car   If you rent a car, a fee of EC$20 ($7.40) is charged to obtain a driver's license, which is available at the airports. There are 310 miles of newly paved roads, and only in a few areas is a four-wheel-drive necessary. *Driving is on the left.*

Among the major car-rental firms of North America, only Budget Rent-a-Car is represented on Dominica. The island contains a handful of small, usually family-owned car-rental companies, the condition and price of whose vehicles vary widely. Their ranks include **Valley Rent-a-Car,** Goodwill Road in Roseau (tel. 809/448-3233), **Wide Range,** 81 Bath Road, Roseau (tel. 809/448-2198), and **S.T.L. Rent-a-Car,** Goodwill Road, Roseau (tel. 809/448-2340).

Rates average about $40 a day, and from $200 to $250 a week. Drivers must be between 25 and 65 years of age. If you don't use a credit card, a substantial cash deposit is required for rentals at any of them.

Most U.S.-based renters, however, opt to reserve their car in advance from the local representative of **Budget Rent-a-Car,** whose headquarters are near the airport's major airport on the Main Highway, Canefield (tel. 809/449-2080). (For reservations and information before you leave North America, call toll free 800/527-0700.) Cars should be reserved 14 days before the anticipated pickup on the island. The establishment's least expensive car rents for $186 per week, with unlimited mileage, plus 5% tax. A car with automatic transmission and air conditioning rents for $252 per week. A collision-damage waiver (CDW) costs $8 a day, yet even if you buy it, you'll still be liable for up to the first $450 of damage to your car.

By Sightseeing Tour   **Dominica Tours,** in the Anchorage Hotel, Castle Comfort (tel. 809/448-2638), offers some of the best tours on the island, including hiking, birdwatching, and photo safaris. The most popular tour is to the Carib Reservation and to Emerald Pool, a grotto in the heart of the rain forest. A 2-hour tour to the Sulphur Springs and a visit to the Botanical Gardens is also offered. I also recommend a combined tour of Trafalgar Triple Waterfalls, Sulphur Springs (via the Morne and Botanical Gardens), and Freshwater Lake, including a picnic lunch and rum punch. Tour prices range from $20 to $50, the latter for the more extensive tour taking in the rain forest and the Carib Reservation.

FAST FACTS DOMINICA

Area Code   To call Dominica from the U.S., dial area code 809 and then the seven-digit local number. For information on calling Dominica from other islands in the same area code and on dialing local numbers when on the island, see "Telecommunications," below.

Banking Hours   Banks are open Monday through Thursday from 8am to 1pm and on Friday from 8am to 1pm and 3 to 5pm.

Currency   Dominica uses the **Eastern Caribbean dollar (EC$),** worth about 37¢ in U.S. currency. *Note:* Prices in this section are given in U.S. dollars unless otherwise indicated.

Customs   Dominica is lenient, allowing you personal and household effects, plus 200 cigarettes, 50 cigars, and 40 ounces of liquor or wine per person.

Documents   To enter, U.S. and Canadian citizens must have proof of citizenship, such as a passport, or a voter registration card or a birth certificate along with photo ID. In addition, an ongoing or return ticket must be shown.

Drugstores   Try **Jolly's Pharmacy,** 33 King George Street, Roseau (tel. 8-3388).

Electricity   The electricity is 220 to 240 volts AC, 50 cycles, so both adapters and transformers are necessary for U.S.-made appliances. It's advisable to take a flashlight with you to Dominica, in case of power outages.

Emergencies Call the police, report a fire, or summon an ambulance by dialing **999.**

Holidays These include January 1 (New Year's Day), Carnival (mid-February), Good Friday, Easter Monday, May 1 (May Day), (Whit Monday), August Monday (first Monday in August), November 4 (Independence Celebrations), November 5 (Community Service Day), December 25 (Christmas), and December 26 (Boxing Day).

Hospitals The island hospital is **Princess Margaret Hospital,** Federation Drive, Goodwill (tel. 8-2231).

Information The **Dominica Tourist Information Office** is in the Old Market Plaza, Roseau, with administrative offices at the National Development Corporation offices, Valley Road (tel. 809/448-2186); it's open Monday through Friday from 8am to 4pm and on Saturday from 9am to 1pm. Also, **information bureaus** are at Melville Hall Airport (tel. 5-7051) and Canefield Airport (tel. 9-1242). Before you go, contact the **Caribbean Tourism Association,** 20 East 46th Street, New York, NY 10017 (tel. 212/682-0435).

Language English is the official language. Locals often speak a Créole-French patois.

Safety Although crime is rare here, it would be wise to safeguard your valuables. Never leave them unattended on the beach or left alone in a locked car.

Taxes A 5% government room tax is added to every hotel accommodation bill, plus a 10% tax on alcoholic drinks and food items. Anyone who remains in Dominica for more than 24 hours must pay a $6 departure tax.

Telecommunications Dominica maintains phone, telegraph, teletype, Telex, and telefax connections with the rest of the world. International direct dialing (IDD) is available, as well as U.S. direct service through AT&T. To call Dominica from within the Caribbean's 809 area code, dial the seven-digit local number—the first two digits are 44, followed by five digits. To call a local number while you're on the island, dial only the last five digits (omit the area code and 44).

Time Dominica is on Atlantic standard time, 1 hour ahead of eastern standard time in the U.S. Dominica does not observe daylight saving time, so when the U.S. changes to daylight time, clocks in Dominica and the U.S. East Coast tell the same time.

Tips and Service Most hotels and restaurants add a 10% service charge to all bills. Where this charge has not been included, tipping is up to you.

Water The water is drinkable from the taps and in the high mountain country. Pollution is hardly a problem here.

Weather Daytime temperatures average between 70° and 85° Fahrenheit. Nights are much cooler, especially in the mountains. The rainy season is June to October, when there can be warnings of hurricane activity.

WHERE TO STAY

Air conditioning may be found in some hotels, but most establishments on Dominica are simple. The cost of living here is low, so tariffs throughout the island entice the bargain seeker. However, don't forget that the government imposes a 5% tax on hotel rooms, beverages, and food, which will probably be added to your hotel bill. Ask about this when you make your reservation to save yourself a surprise at the end of your visit.

IN ROSEAU & CASTLE COMFORT

ANCHORAGE HOTEL, P.O. Box 34, Castle Comfort, Dominica, W.I. Tel. 809/448-2638. Fax 809/448-5680. 32 rms. A/C TV TEL

$ Rates: $60–$75 single, $80–$100 double. MAP $30 per person extra. Children under 12 granted reductions of 50%. American breakfast $10 extra. AE, DC, MC, V. **Parking:** Free.

Terraced, so that its true appeal is only visible once you're inside, the Anchorage is at Castle Comfort, half a mile south of Roseau. It's a peaceful holiday hideaway. Carl and Janice Armour provide rooms with two double beds and a shower or bath, plus a balcony overlooking a pool. In spite of its location on shore, there is little or no beach available, so guests spend their days around the plant-ringed rectangular pool. However, the hotel does have its own jetty and a pebble beach for saltwater bathing, plus a squash court.

The hotel's French and Caribbean cuisine is the best on the island. The food is simple but good, with an emphasis on fresh fish and vegetables. A fixed-price lunch or dinner starts at $15. Nonresidents aren't allowed to use the swimming pool, but they can drop in for meals. A West Indian band plays music twice a week for dancing. On Tuesday night there is a buffet accompanied by piano music. Laundry, room service, and baby-sitting are provided.

EVERGREEN HOTEL, P.O. Box 309, Castle Comfort, Dominica, W.I. Tel. 809/448-3288. Fax 809/448-6800. 9 rms. A/C TV TEL

$ Rates (including MAP): $80 single; $100 double. AE, MC, V. **Parking:** Free.

Built in 1986, this pleasant family-run hotel looks a bit like a Swiss chalet from the outside. A few of the rooms have access to wraparound tile-floored verandas; all have stone accents and private baths. It sits amid a cluster of other hotels about half a mile south of Roseau, between the Anchorage and Sisserou hotels. A stony beach is visible a few steps beyond the garden. Inside and out, the airy, spacious, comfortably modern place is trimmed with the richly textured local gommier wood. Mena Winston, the Dominican-born owner, assists in the preparation of each of the well-flavored meals. Laundry service and scuba diving can be arranged.

FORT YOUNG HOTEL, Victoria St. (P.O. Box 519), Roseau, Dominica, W.I. Tel. 809/448-5000. Fax 809/448-5006. 30 rms, 3 suites. A/C TV TEL

Transportation: Taxi (a 15-minute ride from Canefield Airport).

$ Rates: $75–$85 single; $95–$105 double; from $125 suite. Continental breakfast $6 extra. AE, MC, V. **Parking:** Free.

This hotel, which opened in 1988, grew from the ruins of the 1770 Fort Young. Attracting both commercial travelers and tourists, it offers comfortable bedrooms with ceiling fans and balconies. The most desirable units open onto the sea. The modern hotel's core is embraced by the crescent-shaped sweep of the historic walls of the old fort. There is an outdoor pool plus a hotel restaurant featuring an international menu. Tours of the area can be arranged. Laundry and room service are offered.

REIGATE HALL HOTEL, Mountain Rd. (P.O. Box 200), Reigate, Dominica, W.I. Tel. 809/448-4031. Fax 809/448-4034. 6 rms, 2 suites. A/C TEL

$ Rates: $60 single; $80 double; from $150 suite for two. Continental breakfast $5.55 extra. AE, MC, V. **Parking:** Free.

On a steep hillside about a mile from Roseau, 3 miles south of Canefield Airport, this hotel was originally built in the 18th century as a plantation house. Some parts of the original structure are left, but the hotel has been substantially altered. The hotel has a comfortably airy design of hardwood floors and exposed stone. The guest rooms curve around the sides of a rectangular swimming pool; each has a private bath. The hotel has a sauna, an outdoor tennis court, a gym, and a good restaurant (see "Where to Dine," below). Laundry, baby-sitting, and room service are provided.

ALONG THE BEACHFRONT

CASTAWAYS BEACH HOTEL, P.O. Box 5, Mero, Dominica, W.I. Tel. 809/449-6244. Fax 809/449-6246. 27 rms. A/C

$ Rates: Winter, $96 single; $120 double. Summer, $72 single; $96 double. MAP $25 per person extra. AE, MC, V. **Parking:** Free.

The island's first major resort along the coast north of Roseau lies some 13 miles north of the capital, 8 miles north of Canefield Airport on the west coast. Nestled between the tropical forest and a mile-long black sand beach and ringed on the inland side with huge tamarind trees, the hotel has rooms shaded by tall coconut palms. Each accommodation has a private bath or shower and is spacious, well ventilated, and filled with simple contemporary furniture. Some of the rooms are air-conditioned; others are cooled by ceiling fans.

The hotel dining room serves some of the best food I've found on Dominica (see "Where to Dine," below). On the beach is an open-air bar built in a fashion similar to the *chikees* of the Seminole people in the Florida Everglades, thatched with palmetto fronds. Water sports can be arranged through the reception desk, as can guided excursions to the island's principal sights.

IN THE RAIN FOREST

PAPILLOTE WILDERNESS RETREAT, Macaque, Trafalgar Falls Rd. (P.O. Box 67), Roseau, Dominica, W.I. Tel. 809/448-2287. Fax 809/448-2285. 7 rms, 3 suites.

$ Rates: $45–$50 single; $50–$60 double; from $65 suite. Continental breakfast $5 extra. AE, MC, V. **Parking:** Free. **Closed:** Sept–Oct.

This hotel and restaurant is run by the Jean-Baptistes: Cuthbert handles the restaurant, and his wife, Anne Grey, is a marine scientist. Their place, 4 miles east of Roseau, stands right in the middle of Papillote Forest, at the foothills of Morne Macaque. In this remote setting they have created a unique rain-forest resort that is somewhat primitive; you can lead an Adam and Eve life here, surrounded by exotic fruits, flowers, and herb gardens. Each room or suite has a private bath. Laundry and room service are available.

Don't expect constantly sunny weather, since this part of the jungle is known for its downpours. Their effect, however, keeps the orchids, begonias, and brilliantly colored bromeliads lush. The 12 acres of sloping and forested land are pierced with a labyrinth of stone walls and trails, beside which flows a network of freshwater streams, a few of which come from hot mineral springs. Natural hot mineral baths are available, and you'll be directed to a secluded waterfall where you can swim in the river. The Jean-Baptistes also run a boutique in which they sell Dominican products, including appliquéed quilts made by local artisans. Even if you don't stay here, it's an experience to dine on the thatch-roofed terrace (see "Where to Dine," below).

WHERE TO DINE

The local delicacy is the fine flesh of the *crapaud* (a frog), called "mountain chicken." Freshwater crayfish is another specialty, as is *tee-tee-ree*, fried cakes made from tiny fish. Stuffed crab back is usually a delight. The backs of red and black land crabs are stuffed with delicate crabmeat and Créole seasonings. The fresh fruit juices of the island are divine nectar, and no true Dominican spends the day without at least one rum punch.

EXPENSIVE

ORCHARD RESTAURANT, 31 King George V St. Tel. 8-3051.
Cuisine: CREOLE. **Reservations:** Required.
$ Prices: Appetizers EC$3–EC$4 ($1.10–$1.50); main courses EC$20–EC$45 ($7.40–$16.65). AE, MC, V.
Open: Lunch Mon–Sat 11:30am–4pm; dinner Mon–Fri 7–9pm.

Late in 1986 this restaurant opened in its new home—a clean, wood-lined oasis of calm on a busy street in the capital, a 10-minute drive south of Canefield Airport. There's a bar, as well as a large dining room and a lattice-covered courtyard to one side for outdoor dining. You can order take-out food here, but most clients come for the bar and the sit-down meals. Full meals include mountain chicken, callaloo soup with crabmeat, fish court bouillon, coconut shrimp, black pudding, blood sausage, goat water, several pumpkin dishes, and breadfruit puffs. Friday night features barbecued meat dishes.

REIGATE HALL RESTAURANT, in the Reigate Hall Hotel, Mountain Rd. Tel. 8-4031.
   Cuisine: AMERICAN/CREOLE. **Reservations:** Recommended, especially if you're not a hotel guest.
$ Prices: Appetizers EC$10–EC$12 ($3.70–$4.45); main courses EC$45–EC$65 ($16.65–$24.05). AE, MC, V.
   Open: Lunch daily 1–3pm; dinner daily 7–10pm.

Reigate Hall lies only a mile east of the center of Roseau, but it seems so much longer because of the tortuous road leading up to it. On the second story of this previously recommended hotel (see "Where to Stay," above), the restaurant is an intimately lit enclave of polished tropical hardwoods and exposed stone. A masonry spillway splashing water onto the paddles of a water wheel adds an old-fashioned accent. Menu items are derived from both French and Créole recipes and might include fish soup, beef curry, coq au vin, prawns in garlic sauce, seafood au gratin, and mountain chicken in a champagne sauce.

LA ROBE CREOLE, 3 Victoria St. Tel. 8-2896.
   Cuisine: CREOLE/SEAFOOD. **Reservations:** Required.
$ Prices: Appetizers EC$10–EC$12 ($3.70–$4.45); main courses EC$15–EC$55 ($5.55–$20.35). MC, V.
   Open: Mon–Sat 10am–9:30pm.

Considered the most important independent restaurant in the capital, La Robe Créole sits in a low-slung colonial house, beside a sunny plaza on a slope above the sea, behind a facade draped with flowering vines. The staff, dressed in madras Créole costumes, serves food in a long and narrow dining room capped with heavy beams and filled with relics from the 19th century. You can enjoy pumpkin-pimiento soup, callaloo with cream of coconut soup, crab back, pizzas, mountain chicken in beer batter, and shrimp in coconut with garlic sauce. For dessert, try banana or coconut cake or ice cream.

A section of the restaurant, **The Mouse Hole** (tel. 8-2896) is a good place for food on the run. You can take out freshly made sandwiches and salads, and light meals start at $6. They make good Trinidad-inspired rôtis here—wheat pancakes wrapping beef, chicken, or vegetables. In Dominica, these rôtis are often flavored with curry.

MODERATE

CASTAWAYS BEACH HOTEL, Mero. Tel. 9-6244.
   Cuisine: CREOLE. **Reservations:** Not required.
$ Prices: Appetizers $2.50–$3; main courses $8–$12. AE, MC, V.
   Open: Lunch daily noon–2pm; dinner daily 7–9pm.

If you're touring north along the coast, consider stopping in for a meal at the Castaways, 13 miles north of Roseau. In this resort setting, managing director Linda Harris welcomes nonguests to her hotel dining room with its waterfront setting. Guests dress in casual resortwear, dine informally, and enjoy the hospitality of the staff. Here you get the cuisine for which Dominica is known, including the crapaud or mountain chicken. They have a delicacy most often compared to quail. You can also get lambi (conch), as well as island crab mixed with a savory Créole stuffing. All dishes are garnished with the fruits and vegetables of Dominica's rich soil, such as passionfruit. Before dining, try a rum punch in the lounge or beach bar.

PAPILLOTE WILDERNESS RETREAT, Trafalgar Falls Rd. Tel. 8-2287.
   Cuisine: CREOLE/CARIBBEAN. **Reservations:** Recommended.
$ Prices: Appetizers EC$10–EC$12 ($3.70–$4.45); main courses EC$17–EC$50 ($6.30–$18.50). AE, MC, V.
   Open: Mon–Sat 10am–4pm. **Closed:** Sept–Oct.

Previously recommended for its lodgings (see "Where to Stay," above), this is also one of the most alluringly located restaurants in Dominica. Even if you're not staying here, take a taxi here for lunch; it's only 4 miles east of Roseau. Amid nature trails rife with exotic flowers, century-old trees, and filtered sunlight, you dine on a masonry terrace a few steps from a sociable bar topped with a slab of samaan wood. The array of healthful food includes flying fish, river shrimp, mountain chicken, dolphin, kingfish, dasheen puffs, breadfruit puffs, and a tempting array of tropical salads. Don't forget to bring sturdy walking shoes and a bathing suit. Near the dining terrace, Cuthbert built a Jacuzzi-size basin, which is constantly filled with the mineral-rich waters of a hot spring.

INEXPENSIVE

GUIYAVE, 15 Cork St. Tel. 8-2930.

Cuisine: CREOLE. **Reservations:** Not required.

$ Prices: Appetizers EC$1.75–EC$9 (65¢–$3.35); main courses EC$24–EC$50 ($8.90–$18.50). AE, MC, V.

Open: Mon–Fri 8am–5pm, Sat 8am–2pm.

This airy restaurant occupies the second floor of a wood-frame West Indian house near the private office of the prime minister. Rows of tables almost completely fill the narrow balcony overlooking the street outside. You can enjoy a drink at the stand-up bar on the second floor. The establishment is open only for breakfast and lunch. Specialties include different preparations of conch and rabbit, octopus and lobster, spareribs, chicken, crab backs, and mountain chicken. On Saturday they prepare rôtis and "goat water." The place is known for its juices, including refreshing tropical glasses of soursop, tamarind, sorrel, cherry, and strawberry. One part of the establishment is a pâtisserie specializing in French pasteries.

WORLD OF FOOD RESTAURANT AND BAR, in Vena's Hotel, 48 Cork St. Tel. 8-3286.

Cuisine: CREOLE. **Reservations:** Not required.

$ Prices: Appetizers EC$3.50–EC$4 ($1.30–$1.50); main courses EC$8.50–EC$35 ($3.15–$12.95). No credit cards.

Open: Lunch daily noon–3pm; dinner daily 6–10:30pm.

In the 1930s the garden containing this restaurant belonged to a well-known novelist, Jean Rhys. Today it's the patio for one of the most charming Créole restaurants in Roseau. Some say that its owner, Vena McDougal, is the best Créole cook in town. You can have a drink at the stone-walled building at the far end of the garden if you want, but many guests select one of the tables in the shadow of a large mango tree. Specialties include steamed fish or fish steak, curried goat, chicken-filled rôti, black pudding, mountain chicken, breadfruit puffs, callaloo-and-watercress soup, crab backs, conch, and tee-tee-ree (fried fish cakes). She's said to make the best rum punches on the island as well. The restaurant is attached to Vena's Hotel (really a guesthouse). If you want to reach the restaurant without passing through Vena's, its entrance is on Field's Lane.

WHAT TO SEE & DO

Those making day trips to Dominica from other islands will want to see the ✪ **Carib Indian Reservation,** in the northeast. In 1903 Britain got the Caribs to agree to accept boundaries on 3,700 acres of land set aside for them. Hence, this is the last remaining domain of this once-hostile tribe who gave their name to the archipelago—Caribbean.

Their look is Mongolian, and they are no longer "pure-blooded," as they have married outside of their tribe. Today they survive by fishing, growing food, and weaving baskets and vertivert grass mats, which they sell to the outside world. They still make dugout canoes too.

It's like going back in time when you explore ✪ **Morne Trois Pitons**

National Park, a primordial rain forest, "me Tarzan, you Jane" country. Mists rise gently over lush, dark-green growth, drifting up to blue-green peaks that have earned for Dominica the title of "Switzerland of the Caribbean." Framed by banks of giant ferns, rivers rush and tumble. Trees sprout orchids, and everything seems blanketed with some type of parasitic growth. Green sunlight filters down through timeless trees, and the roar of a waterfall creates a blue mist.

One of the best starting points for a visit to the park is the village of Laudat, 7 miles from Roseau. *Note:* Exploring this green heart of Dominica is for serious botanists and only the most skilled hikers, who should never penetrate unmarked trails without a very experienced guide.

Deep in the park is the **Emerald Pool Trail,** a half-mile nature trail that forms a circuit loop on a footpath passing through the forest to a pool with a beautiful waterfall. Downpours are frequent in the rain forest, and at high elevations cold winds blow. It lies 3½ miles northeast of Pont Casse.

Five miles up from the **Roseau River Valley,** in the south-central sector of Dominica, **Trafalgar Falls** can be reached after you drive through the village of Trafalgar. There, however, you have to approach by foot, as the slopes are too steep for vehicles. After a 20-minute walk, you arrive at the base, where a trio of falls converge into a rock-strewn pool. Boulders sprout vegetation and tree ferns encircle the flowing water. On the way there you pass growths of ginger plants or vanilla orchids.

The **Sulphur Springs** are evidence of the island's volcanic past. Jeeps or Land Rovers get quite near. Not only Sulphur Springs but also the Boiling Lake are bubbling evidence of underground volcanic activity, north and east of Roseau. This seemingly bubbling pool of gray mud sometimes belches smelly sulfurous fumes—the odor is like a rotten egg. Only the very fit should attempt to go to Boiling Lake. Some Dominicans fear that volcanic activity will erupt again. Freshwater Lake lies at the foot of Mount Macaque.

On the northwestern coast, **Portsmouth** is Dominica's second-largest settlement. Once there, you can row up the Indian River in native canoes, visit the ruins of old Fort Shirley in Cabrits National Park, and bathe at Sandy Beach on Douglas Bay and Prince Rupert Bay.

Cabrits National Park, on the northwestern coast of Dominica, 2 miles south of Douglas Bay (tel. 8-2401, ext. 417), is a 1,313-acre protected site containing mountain scenery, tropical forests, swampland, volcanic sand beaches, coral reefs, and the ruins of a fortified 18th-century garrison of British, then French construction. The Cabrits Park's land area is a spectacular promontory formed by twin peaks of extinct volcanoes, overlooking fine beaches, with Douglas Bay on one side and Prince Rupert Bay across the headland. Part of Douglas Bay forms the marine section of the park. Fort Shirley, the large garrison last used as a military post in 1854, is being wrested from encroaching vegetation. A small museum highlights the natural and historic aspects of the park. The name Cabrits comes from the Spanish-Portuguese-French word for goat, because of the animals left there by early sailors to provide fresh meat on future visits.

SPORTS & RECREATION

BEACHES As for beaches, some are in the northwest of the island around Portsmouth, the second town. There are also secluded beaches in the northeast, along with spectacular coastal scenery. But all of these are hard to reach, and you might settle instead for a freshwater swimming pool or river swimming.

The finest beach, lying on the northwestern coast, is **Picard.** It stretches for about 2 miles, a strip of grayish sand with palm trees in the background. The previously recommended Castaways Hotel opens onto this beach. Snorkelers like it a lot, and windsurfing is another sport practiced here. The finest swimming, however, is said to be along the banks of the **Layou River.**

HIKING Serious hikers find Dominica a major challenge. Guides should be used for all unmarked trails. You can arrange for a guide by going to the office of the **Dominica National Park** in the Botanical Gardens in Roseau (tel. 8-2732) or the Dominica Tourist Board.

SCUBA DIVING You can discover diving on the island with **Dive Dominica Ltd.,** in the Castle Comfort Diving Lodge, P.O. Box 63, Castle Comfort, Dominica, W.I. (tel. 809/448-2188, or toll free 800/544-7631). Open-water certification (NAUI) instruction is given. A 33-foot custom dive boat, *Danny-Too*, gets you to the dive sites in comfort. There are 10 rooms available at the diving lodge, where a 7-night dive package costs $750.

SAVVY SHOPPING

Store hours are usually 8am to 4pm Monday through Friday and 8am to 1pm on Saturday. In Roseau, the **Old Market Plaza,** of historical significance as a former slave-trading market and more recently the Friday- and Saturday-morning vegetable market, now houses three craft shops, each specializing in coconut, straw, and Carib craft products.

Tropicrafts Island Mats, at Queen Mary Street and Turkey Lane (tel. 8-2747), offers the well-known grass rugs handmade and woven in several intricate patterns at Tropicrafts' factory. They also have for sale handmade bags, shopping bags, and placemats, all appliquéed by hand. The handmade dolls are popular with doll collectors. The Dominican vertivert-grass mats are known throughout the world.

Some island residents claim that the entire straw-weaving industry on Dominica was established by Iris Joseph, the dignified owner of **Caribana Handicrafts,** 31 Cork Street (tel. 809/448-2761). You'll be able to see a few of the products being crafted at wooden tables. Near the front, stacks of baskets in all sizes and shapes are stocked. Mrs. Joseph is usually pleased to explain the dying processes that turn the straw into one of three different earth-related tones. When straw is buried in the earth, it turns black; when it's soaked in saffron, it turns yellow; and when it's boiled with the bark of a tang tree, it turns purple. A selection of other goods, including Bello Hot Pepper (said to be the finest by island connoisseurs), is available.

EVENING ENTERTAINMENT

It's not very sophisticated, but there is some. A couple of the major hotels, such as **Castaways** (tel. 9-6244) and **Reigate Hall** (tel. 8-4031), have entertainment on weekends, usually a combo or "jing ping" (traditional local music).

The **Anchorage Hotel** at Castle Comfort (tel. 9-2638) also has live entertainment and a good buffet at least 1 night a week. Call for details.

The **Warehouse,** Checkhall Estate, Roseau (tel. 9-1303), a 5-minute drive from Roseau, is owned and operated by Rosie Royer and Cleve Royer who have taken a 200-year-old stone building, once used to store molasses and rum, and turned it into a disco. Every Saturday night records are played from 9pm to 2am. Entrance is EC$10 ($3.70). Drinks begin at EC$4 ($1.50).

2. ST. LUCIA

Second largest of the Windward Islands, St. Lucia (pronounced "*Loo*-sha") is a checkerboard of green-mantled mountains, gentle valleys, wide beaches, banana plantations, a bubbling volcano, giant tree ferns, wild orchids, and fishing villages. There's a hint of the South Pacific about it, and a mixed French and British heritage.

The actual discovery of this mountainous island is shrouded in conjecture. Some maintain that Columbus landed on December 13, 1502. However, records reveal that the explorer was far from St. Lucia on that date. It is often conceded that Spanish seamen discovered the island in some unknown year.

St. Lucia lies some 20 miles from Martinique. An English party from St. Kitts settled here in 1605, but the island was to change hands a total of 14 times as the French and English fought intermittently for its control for more than a century. Slaughter parties led by cannibalistic Caribs deterred permanent settlements for years.

The island was a British colony from 1803 to 1967, when it became an associated state within the British Commonwealth. St. Lucia arrived at its full sovereignty on February 22, 1979.

A mountainous island of some 240 square miles, St. Lucia has about 120,000 inhabitants. The capital, **Castries,** is built on the southern shore of a large, almost landlocked harbor surrounded by hills. The approach to the airport is almost a path between hills, and it's very impressive.

The capital was named after an 18th-century French secretary of state to the foreign colonies, Marshal de Castries. Fires have swept over the town many times, destroying its wooden buildings. The last catastrophe occurred in 1948. As a result, don't expect too many vintage structures.

ORIENTATION

GETTING THERE   Airline routings from many North American cities will require at least a touchdown in one or another Caribbean island before continuing on to St. Lucia.

Airlines   Both **American Airlines** and **American Eagle** (tel. toll free 800/ 433-7300) service St. Lucia's two widely separated airports (see below) with one daily nonstop flight to each airport from its hub in San Juan, Puerto Rico.

BWIA (tel. toll free 800/327-7401) has service to St. Lucia twice a week from Miami. Airplanes touch down in Antigua and St. Kitts before continuing on to St. Lucia. From New York, BWIA offers flights four times a week to St. Lucia, always with touchdowns in Antigua en route.

Air Canada (tel. toll free 800/776-3000) has two flights that depart each week from Toronto. Flights usually touch down in Barbados before continuing to St. Lucia. On the flight back to Canada, flights touch down in Antigua instead.

Finally, if you're already on the islands and plan to visit St. Lucia, **LIAT** (tel. 809/462-0701) has small planes flying into Vigie Airport from such international hubs as Antigua and Barbados. Be warned that LIAT flights tend to island-hop through many different islands en route to St. Lucia, although some readers consider this part of the adventure.

British Airways (tel. toll free 800/247-9297) offers two flights a week to St. Lucia from London's Gatwick airport. Each makes a brief touchdown in Antigua before continuing on to St. Lucia.

Airports   The island maintains two separate airports whose different locations cause endless confusion to most newcomers. Most international long-distance flights land at **Hewanorra International Airport** in the south, 45 miles from Castries. If you fly in here and you're booked into a hotel in the north, you'll have to spend up to about an hour and a half going along the potholed East Coast Highway. The average taxi ride costs $55. Once this airport was known as "Beane Field," when Roosevelt and Churchill agreed to construct a big air base here during the depths of World War II.

However, flights from other parts of the Caribbean usually land at the somewhat antiquated **Vigie Field** in the island's northeast, whose location just outside of Castries is much more convenient to the capital and most of the island's hotels.

GETTING AROUND   By Local Bus   Minibuses (with names like "Lucian Love") and jitneys connect Castries with such main towns as Soufrière and Vieux Fort. They are generally overcrowded and often filled with produce on the way to market. However, since taxis are expensive, it might be a reliable means of transport.

At least it's cheap. Buses for Cap Estate, the St. Lucian northern part of the island, leave from Jeremy Street in Castries, near the market. Buses going to Vieux Fort and Soufrière leave from Bridge Street in front of the department store.

By Taxi Taxis are ubiquitous on the island, and most drivers are eager to please. The drivers have to be quite experienced to cope with the narrow, hilly, switchback roads outside the capital. Special programs have trained them to serve as guides. Their cars are unmetered, but tariffs for all standard trips are fixed by the government.

Make sure you determine if the driver is quoting a rate in U.S. dollars or the EC$. One of the most popular runs—from Vigie Airport to Cunard La Toc—goes for $12.

By Rental Car First, *remember to drive on the left,* and try to avoid some of the island's more obvious potholes. You'll need a St. Lucia driver's license, which can easily be purchased at either airport when you arrive, or at the car-rental kiosks when you pick up your car. Present a valid driver's license from home to the counter attendant or government official and pay a fee of $12.

Currently, among the large U.S.-based car-rental franchises, only **Avis** (tel. 809/452-4554, or toll free 800/331-2112) is represented, maintaining no fewer than eight locations, many in the larger hotels. If arrangements are made, Avis will deliver a car to the airport in anticipation of your arrival, or directly to your hotel. The company's least expensive car rents for $270 per week, with unlimited mileage. A collision-damage waiver is available for around $11 per day. Check last-minute tariffs and ask about any promotions or discounts.

By Sightseeing Tour Most hotel front desks will make arrangements for tours that take in all the major sights of St. Lucia. For example, **St. Lucia Representative Services,** Brazil Street in Castries (tel. 809/452-3762), offers many island tours, such as a shopping tour on Monday, Wednesday, and Friday at $15, a full Round the Island Tour Monday through Friday at $45 (with lunch and drinks included), and a Rain Forest Walk at $36 on Monday and Wednesday. You can also take full-day boat trips along the west coast to the volcano for $60 per person. Tours to neighboring islands can also be arranged. Tours operate only if enough passengers are booked to satisfy minimum requirements. The company has representatives making stops at most of the major hotels.

By Boat Boat tours can usually be arranged at your hotel's activity desk or through **St. Lucia Representative Services** (see above). One of the most popular tours, costing $65 per person, is aboard the brig *Unicorn,* which takes you on a day's sail to Soufrière and the Pitons. The *Unicorn* starred as the slave ship in the TV series "Roots," among other movie roles. Built in 1948, it's a 140-foot vessel with 16 square-rigged sails, and can carry a crew of 13. You sail southward from Coal Pot, near Castries, at 9am, and head for Soufrière's Sulphur Springs. On the return voyage you're served a lunch aboard. Later, you swim at Anse Cochon and sail into Marigot Bay. You're back at dock at 4pm, where coaches await to return you to your hotel. To make reservations, call 809/452-6811.

FAST FACTS ST. LUCIA

Area Code To call St. Lucia from the U.S., dial area code 809, then the seven-digit number. For information on how to make calls once on the island, and other telecommunications, see "Telephone," below.

Banking Hours Banks are open Monday through Thursday from 8am to 1pm and on Friday from 8am to noon and 3 to 5pm.

Currency The official monetary unit is the **Eastern Caribbean dollar (EC$).** It's about 37¢ in U.S. currency. *Note:* Most of the prices quoted in this section will be in American dollars, as they are accepted by nearly all hotels, restaurants, and shops.

Customs At either airport, Customs may be a hassle if there is the slightest suspicion, regardless of how ill-founded, that you are bringing illegal drugs into St. Lucia.

Documents   U.S. and Canadian citizens need proof of citizenship, such as a passport, voter registration card, or birth certificate, plus an ongoing or return ticket. Voter cards and birth certificates also require photo ID.

Drugstore   The best is **William Pharmacy,** Williams Building, Bridge Street, Castries (tel. 2-2797).

Electricity   Bring an adapter and transformer, as St. Lucia runs on 220 to 230 volts AC, 50 cycles.

Emergency   Call the police at 999.

Hospitals   There are 24-hour emergency rooms at **St. Jude's Hospital,** Vieux Fort (tel. 4-6041), and **Victoria Hospital,** Hospital Road, Castries (tel. 2-2421).

Information   The **tourist information bureau** is on Jeremy Street, next to Customs Castries. The **St. Lucia Tourist Board** is at Point Seraphine, Castries (tel. 809/452-5968); in the United States, the office is at 820 Second Avenue, New York, NY 10017 (tel. 212/867-2950).

Language   With its mixed French and British heritage, St. Lucia has interesting speech patterns. Although English is the official tongue, St. Lucians probably don't speak it as you do. Islanders also speak a French-Créole patois, similar to that heard on Martinique.

Post Office   The General Post Office is on Bridge Street in Castries. It's open Monday through Friday from 8:30am to 4pm.

Safety   St. Lucia has its share of crime like everyplace else these days. Use common sense and protect yourself and our valuables. If you've got it, don't flaunt it! Don't pick up hitchhikers if you're driving around the island. Of course, the use of narcotic drugs is illegal, and possession or sale of such could lead to stiff fines or jail.

Service   Most hotels add a 10% service charge, and restaurants do likewise.

Taxes   The government imposes an 8% occupancy tax on hotel-room rentals. If you're flying on to one of the islands in the Caribbean Commonwealth (English-speaking islands), you must pay a departure tax of $8 (only $4 if you're flying to another Caribbean destination).

Telephone   When you're on the island, you need dial only the last five digits of the number (not the area code or "45" that precedes them). Cables may be handed in at hotel desks or at the offices of Cable & Wireless in the George Gordon Buildings on Bridge Street in Castries (tel. 2-3301).

Time   St. Lucia is on Atlantic standard time, placing it 1 hour ahead of New York or Miami. However, when the U.S. is on daylight saving time St. Lucia matches the clocks of the U.S. East Coast.

Weather   This little island, lying in the path of the trade winds, has year-round temperatures of 70° to 90° Fahrenheit.

WHERE TO STAY

Most of the lead hotels on this island are in the same price range—you have to seek out the bargains (begin at the end of this section). Once you reach your hotel, chances are you'll feel pretty isolated, but that's what many guests want. Many St. Lucian hostelries have kitchenettes where you can prepare simple meals. Prices are quoted in U.S. dollars. Don't forget the 8% hotel tax.

EXPENSIVE
Hotels & Resorts

ANSE CHASTANET, Anse Chastanet Beach (P.O. Box 7000, Soufrière),

St. Lucia, W.I. Tel. 809/454-7000, or toll free 800/223-1108. Fax 809/454-7700. 44 rms, 4 suites.

$ Rates: Winter (including MAP), $180–$290 single; $260–$400 double; $680 suite. Summer (MAP $40 per person extra), $85–$150 single; $120–$240 double; $400 suite. AE, DC, MC, V. **Parking:** Free.

My favorite retreat on the island, and one of the few places that truly merits the cliché "tropical paradise," is not only St. Lucia's premier dive resort but also an exceptional Caribbean inn, combining warm service, excellent food, a beach location, and first-class facilities. It lies 18 miles north of Hewanorra International Airport (a 50-minute taxi ride), 2 miles north of Soufrière on a forested hill, a 103-step climb above palm-fringed Anse Chastanet Beach. You're surrounded by coffee trees, mangoes, papayas, banana plants, breadfruit, grapefruit, coconut palms, flamboyants, and hibiscus. The core of the house is a main building decorated in a typical island style, with a relaxing bar and dining room.

Guests can stay on the beach in spacious accommodations styled like West Indian plantation villas, with four rooms each, two up and two down. Other units, constructed like octagonal gazebos, cooled by ceiling fans, have views of the Pitons, St. Lucia's famous twin peaks. Each accommodation is large and comfortably appointed with locally made furniture crafted from island woods. Some of the rooms have Jacuzzis.

Dining/Entertainment: You can dine or drink on a wind-cooled terrace built like a tree house over the tropical landscape. The Créole, continental, and American cuisine is exceptional, and lobster is freshly caught in the bay.

Services: Laundry, baby-sitting; transfers from the airport available with advance notification.

Facilities: Scuba diving facilities, waterskiing, sailboat rentals.

CUNARD HOTEL LA TOC, P.O. Box 399, St. Lucia, W.I. Tel. 809/452-1012. Fax 809/452-1012. 100 rms, 54 suites. A/C TV TEL

$ Rates: Winter, $210–$245 single; $230–$275 double; from $375 suite. Summer, $120–$175 single or double; from $230 suite. MAP $44 per person extra. AE, MC, V. **Parking:** Free.

Some 2½ miles south of Castries, this hotel bills itself as tropical, tranquil, and luxurious, and here's one place that delivers what it promises. The site, about a 10-minute drive from the capital on half a mile of curved beach, is on 110 secluded acres on the western side of the island. Each of the handsomely furnished rooms includes a private bath, plus balconies or patios offering views of the ocean or the exotic gardens.

Suites are like little dollhouses in pastel colors. *Town and Country* called this "one of the 10 most luxurious villa complexes in the Caribbean." Set apart, each of the villas is nestled against the mountainside facing the sea. They are connected by frequent shuttle service to the main building.

Dining/Entertainment: Dining is at the Terrace Restaurant, the casual entertainment center; at Les Pitons Restaurant, which has some of the best food on the island; or at the Quarterdeck, which has classic grills and operates only in the winter season. There is live entertainment nightly, plus two floor shows a week.

Services: 24-hour room service, laundry, massage, baby-sitting.

Facilities: Two swimming pools, one so big it has its own palm-studded island; manicured nine-hole golf course with a resident pro; three Hartru tennis courts (lit for night games) and two hard-surface tennis courts with a resident tennis pro; free Sunfish sailing, windsurfing, snorkeling, and waterskiing; private 120-foot brig, the *Unicorn,* that sails twice weekly; fitness center, beauty salon, souvenir shop, boutique, and drugstore; fishing for dorado (dolphin), swordfish, cavalle, or barracuda can be arranged.

HALCYON BEACH CLUB, P.O. Box 388, Choc Bay, St. Lucia, W.I. Tel. 809/452-5331, or toll free 800/223-9815. Fax 809/452-5434. 180 rms. A/C TEL

$ Rates: Winter, $142–$172 single; $165–$195 double. Summer, $95–$118 single; $118–$148 double. American breakfast $14 extra. AE, MC, V. **Parking:** Free.

A 4-mile drive north of Castries will take you to what's almost the classic concept of a modern Caribbean hotel today. It offers the perfect vacation for the entire family. Set in landscaped tropical gardens, the hotel contains well-furnished rooms with ocean, beach, or garden views.

Dining/Entertainment: You have a choice of two restaurants. The Wharf Chanticleer is built sea style over the ocean for cool evening enjoyment. The evening menu is filled with an international cuisine, including Danish and French specialties. A barbecue, piano bar, and disco with the latest sound equipment extends on a platform out into the sea, creating a kind of artificial island.

Services: 24-hour room service, laundry, baby-sitting.

Facilities: Two swimming pools, tennis courts (two lit at night, with a charge for their use), waterskiing, windsurfing, Sunfish sailing, snorkeling, volleyball, shuffleboard, indoor games, children's playground.

MOORINGS MARIGOT BAY RESORT, Marigot Bay (P.O. Box 101, Castries), St. Lucia, W.I. Tel. 809/452-4357, or toll free 800/535-7289 in Florida. Fax 809/453-4353. 32 cottages, 13 rooms.

$ Rates: Winter, $155 double or one-bedroom cottage. Summer, $90 double or one-bedroom cottage. MAP $40 per person extra. AE, MC, V. **Parking:** Free.

This resort is actually a complex of inns, cottages, restaurants, bars, boutiques, and yachting berths about a 45-minute drive south of Castries along the west coast. Much favored by the yachting set, the lagoon setting was described by author James Michener as "the most beautiful bay in the Caribbean." On a low-lying spit of the palm-dotted island, the complex, part of which is reached only by ferry service, is the most idyllic spot on St. Lucia.

The resort rents double rooms and a cluster of colonial-style cottages called Marigot Hillside Villas, and they are spread along a hillside. Some are privately owned while others are controlled by the hotel. Yachting types often stay at the Marigot Inn, which is decorated in the West Indian style; the comfortable and attractive double rooms open onto verandas, from which the occupants can look out at their yachts. There's also Hurricane Hole, a cottage hotel on the southeastern shore, which offers the only swimming pool in the complex.

Dining/Entertainment: You have a choice of two restaurants (see "Where to Dine," below).

Services: Laundry, baby-sitting.

Facilities: Swimming pool, PADI-approved scuba center, base for the Moorings Yacht Charter fleet.

ST. LUCIAN HOTEL, P.O. Box 512, Reduit Beach, St. Lucia, W.I. Tel. 809/452-8351. Fax 809/452-8331. 222 rms. A/C TV TEL

$ Rates: Winter, $135–$155 single; $135–$175 double. Summer, $65 single; $85 double. MAP $40 per person extra. AE, DC, MC, V. **Parking:** Free.

Some 6½ miles north of Castries, the St. Lucian not only has one of the best programs of water sports on the island but it also opens onto the most spectacular beachfront, Reduit Beach. One of the largest hotels on St. Lucia, it has well-landscaped grounds, with swaying palms, latticed breezeways, and flowering shrubs. Bedrooms are attractively furnished with a number of amenities, including queen-size beds and private baths. Some guests find the activities and food here so rich and varied that they never leave the grounds, although I recommend that you do.

Dining/Entertainment: Dining facilities here are among the finest north of Castries. Many clients book in on the MAP and take their meals in the Hummingbird Restaurant. However, if you wish to partake of an à la carte selection from both Caribbean and international food, you can head for the Flamingo. You'll also find yourself on the doorstep of some of the finest independent restaurants on the island, including Capone's. The St. Lucian has the best disco on the island, plus entertainment almost nightly, including floor shows, limbo dancing, fire-eaters, and a steel band.

Services: Room service, laundry, baby-sitting.

Facilities: Beach; water sports, including scuba diving and windsurfing (free to guests, but nonresidents can also participate; see "Sports and Recreation," below).

WINDJAMMER LANDING VILLA BEACH RESORT, Labrelotte Bay (P.O. Box 1504, Castries), St. Lucia, W.I. Tel. 809/452-1311, or toll free 800/346-5358. Fax 809/452-9454. 114 villas. A/C MINIBAR TV TEL

$ Rates: Winter, $260 one-bedroom villa for one or two; $330 two-bedroom villa for one or two, $400 for three or four; $500 three-bedroom villa for five or six. Summer, $180 one-bedroom villa for one or two; $230 two-bedroom villa for one or two, $280 for three or four; $375 three-bedroom villa for five or six. MAP $47 per person extra. AE, DC, MC, V. **Parking:** Free.

About a 15-minute drive from the capital, north of Reduit Beach, the Windjammer has completed the first phase of its development. The resort was designed with a vaguely Moorish motif heavily influenced by Caribbean themes; pastel colors of pinks, blues, and greens predominate. It is composed of a cluster of white villas climbing a forested hillside above a desirable beach. This is an all-suite or all-villa resort (the larger villas have private plunge pools). The good-size interiors offer separate living and dining rooms, fully equipped kitchens, ceiling fans, cassette players, clocks, and VCRs upon request. All bedrooms adjoin private baths and open onto sun terraces.

Dining/Entertainment: A housekeeper/cook arrives daily.

Facilities: Water sports, horseback riding, greens fees, and tennis included in rates; largest freshwater pool on island, with built-in waterfalls; guests are taken out on the 44-foot cabin cruiser *Columbus*.

All-Inclusive Resorts

CLUB MED, Savannes Bay, St. Lucia, W.I. Tel. 809/454-6547, or toll free 800/CLUB-MED. Fax 809/454-6017. 512 rms. A/C

$ Rates (including all meals and use of all facilities): Winter, $1,380 per person per week double. Summer, $750 per person per week double. Single surcharge 30%. Children under 5 stay free in parents' room in certain seasons (usually spring and fall). AE, MC, V. **Parking:** Free.

Club Med is a resort set on a 95-acre property. The carefree life-style holds forth on the southernmost tip of St. Lucia, opening onto Savannes Bay, just 5 minutes from the international airport. Completely refurbished, the club offers beachside living in four-story buildings in a coconut grove. Each room contains a private shower. This Club Med caters to children and has separate children's facilities.

Dining/Entertainment: In the heart of the complex is an open-air bar and a dance and theater area. Meals are served in the second-floor dining room with a panoramic view, and guests enjoy unlimited wine at lunch and dinner.

Services: Laundry, baby-sitting.

Facilities: Freshwater swimming pool; 8 tennis courts, volleyball, archery, soccer, basketball, calisthenics, softball; Sailing Center with two large sailboats that take about two dozen sailors on full-day or overnight sailing trips; well-equipped Workout Center; facilities (some of which cost extra) for horseback riding, windsurfing, and scuba diving; separate facilities for children.

CLUB ST. LUCIA, Smugglers Village, St. Lucia, W.I. Tel. 809/452-0551, or toll free 800/777-1250. Fax 809/452-0281. 228 rms, 16 suites. A/C

$ Rates (including all meals, drinks, and use of all facilities): Winter, $190 single; $260 double; from $320 suite. Summer, $170 single; $230 double; from $300 suite. AE, DC, MC, V. **Parking:** Free.

The most economical all-inclusive resort on the island sits in Cap Estate, an area near Le Sport, 8 miles north of Vigie Airport at the northern tip of the island. It opens onto a curved bay where smugglers of yore used to bring in brandies, cognacs, and cigars from Martinique. The club's core is a wooden building with decks from which you can look down on a free-form pool. Bungalow accommodations are scattered over landscaped grounds and feature one king-size or two twin beds, air conditioning or ceiling fans, and private baths, as well as patios or terraces.

Dining/Entertainment: The emphasis is on sports and entertainment and the inclusive package the resort puts together is an impressive one, offering all meals during your stay, even snacks, along with unlimited beer, wine, and mixed drinks both day and night. Other activities include everything from free movies to nightly entertainment.

Services: Laundry, baby-sitting, shuttle bus to Rodney Bay and Reduit Beach.

Facilities: Day or night tennis, unlimited water sports (waterskiing, Sunfish sailing, windsurfing, snorkeling, and pedal boats), unlimited golf greens fees, horseback riding at nearby stables, children's Mini Club with a playground and a supervised activities program.

COUPLES, P.O. Box 190, Malabar Beach, St. Lucia, W.I. Tel. 809/452-4211. Fax 809/452-7419. 100 rms, 3 suites. A/C TEL

$ Rates (including all meals, drinks, airport transfers, and use of all facilities): Winter, $2,295–$2,685 per week per couple; from $2,950 per week per couple in a suite. Summer, $2,185–$2,585 per week per couple; from $2,850 per week per couple in a suite. AE, DC, MC, V. **Parking:** Free.

Couples is an unusual hotel, where all meals, drinks, cigarettes, entertainment, and most incidental expenses are included in the initial price. There are several price categories, depending on the season and the accommodation; top prices are charged for oceanfront luxury suites for two. The resort lies north of Vigie Airport, near Castries. The center of the complex is under a gridwork of peaked roofs floored with tasteful terra-cotta tiles. Set on the edge of a beach bordered by palm trees, the hotel has a sprawling garden centered around a 150-year-old samaan tree. No children are allowed, and only couples (male-female) are accepted.

Dining/Entertainment: The bar opens early and closes late. Most of the lunches are buffet style, and there's even a cold-cuts buffet offered every evening after the end of the dinner hour. Evening action is fun, including a weekly toga party.

Services: A member of the staff will meet your plane at the airport with a chest of cold beer and rum punches when you arrive; laundry.

Facilities: Freshwater outdoor swimming pool, fitness center, sauna, scuba-diving facilities, waterskiing, tennis courts.

LE SPORT, P.O. Box 437, Caibule Bay, St. Lucia, W.I. Tel. 809/452-8551, or toll free 800/544-2883. Fax 809/452-0368. 102 rms, 2 suites. A/C TEL

$ Rates (including all meals, drinks, use of all facilities, and airport transfers): Winter, $260–$325 single; $220–$285 per person double; from $405 per person suite. Summer, $225–$245 single; $205–$255 per person double; $310–$380 per person suite. AE, DC, MC, V. **Parking:** Free.

Using as its logo Michelangelo's *David* and Botticelli's *Birth of Venus* (or as they call it, *Venus on the Half-Shell*), Le Sport "cares for your body." An all-inclusive resort, Le Sport is a citadel of first-class living and pampering, on a 1,500-acre beachfront estate at the northernmost tip of the island. You're an 8-mile run from Castries, and guests seem to prefer this isolation. The hotel's director is Craig Barnard, who has proved such a success with his Couples.

The resort makes a promise faithfully kept: Everything "you do, see, enjoy, drink, eat, and feel" is included in the price. That means not only accommodation, three meals a day, all refreshments, and bar drinks, but also use of all sports equipment, facilities, and instruction.

The bedrooms, all overlooking the sea and each with private bath containing a shower and hairdryer, fall into three categories: garden-view, ocean-view, and oceanfront.

Dining/Entertainment: Breakfast and lunch are buffet style. Dinner offers a choice of a lighter fixed-price menu or an à la carte menu. Meals are served in an open-air restaurant overlooking the Caribbean. The food is *cuisine légère*, modeled after the cookery pioneered by the famous French chef Michel Guérard, in his Basque retreat. The point is not to make cuisine and dieting contradictory; however, the chef also prepares "sin dishes." Live entertainment is provided, and a piano bar is popular until late at night.

Services: Room service (for breakfast), transfers to and from the airport, laundry, baby-sitting.

Facilities: Full program of daily scuba diving, windsurfing, waterskiing, snorkeling, sailing, pool swimming, use of a floodlit tennis court, fencing, archery, and riding; emphasis on European body tonics based on Thalassotherapy, involving the healthful pampering of seawater massage, thermal jet baths, toning, physical culture, and beauty treatments for both sexes.

MODERATE

GREEN PARROT HOTEL, Red Tape Lane, Morne Fortune (Good Luck Hill), St. Lucia, W.I. Tel. 809/452-3167. Fax 809/453-2272. 48 rms, 2 apartments. A/C TV TEL

$ Rates: Winter, $90 single; $110 double; from $120 apartment. Summer, $68 single; $80 double; from $120 apartment. MAP $40 per person extra. AE, MC, V. **Parking:** Free.

Connected to the Green Parrot restaurant (see "Where to Dine," below), this series of balconied accommodations winds up the side of one of the steepest slopes in Castries. Flanking both sides of the pathways are masses of flowering shrubs and vines. Near the top of the complex is a terraced swimming pool, where guests lounge in chairs with views of the harbor far below. A courtesy bus makes runs to the beach Sunday through Friday. A sunken bar is set into the floor of the Pool Room restaurant, where no one minds if patrons show up in their bathing suits. The accommodations include two apartments with kitchens.

THE ISLANDER, Rodney Bay (P.O. Box 907, Castries), St. Lucia, W.I. Tel. 809/452-8757. Fax 809/452-0958. 56 rms, 4 apartments. A/C TV TEL

$ Rates: Winter, $110 single; $120 double; $130 apartment for two. Summer, $75 single; $80 double; $90 apartment for two. Children under 12 stay free in parents' room. AE, DC, MC, V. **Parking:** Free.

North of Castries and near Pat's Pub, the St. Lucian Hotel, and Reduit Beach, this well-recommended hotel has an entrance whose walls are festooned with hanging flowers. A brightly painted fishing boat serves as a buffet table near the pool, and there's a spacious covered bar area perfect for socializing with the owner, Greg Glace. Twenty of the accommodations are self-contained, with kitchenettes and private baths or showers, while the rest have private showers and small bars with minirefrigerators. Overlooking a grassy courtyard sheltered with vines and flowers, all rooms also have radios. A network of walkways leads to a convivial restaurant. Guests walk a few hundred feet to the beach and to shop in nearby markets if their lodgings are equipped for cooking.

WHERE TO DINE

Try to break free of your resort hotel and dine in one of St. Lucia's little character-loaded restaurants. The local food is excellent and reflects the years of French, British, and Carib occupation. St. Lucia's marketplace offers the ingredients for local dishes, including callaloo soup (fresh greens, dumplings, and salted beef), Pouile Dudon (sweet, zesty chicken dish), and roasted breadfruit cooked on open hot coals. A "coal pot," made of heavy clay is especially suitable for barbecue dishes and is typical of West Indian cooking. Pumpkin soup, local flying fish, lobster, and tablette—a coconut sugar candy that resembles white coral—round out the menu choices.

IN CASTRIES

GREEN PARROT, Red Tape Lane, Morne Fortune. Tel. 2-3399.

Cuisine: AMERICAN/CARIBBEAN. **Reservations:** Recommended.
$ Prices: Appetizers EC$20–EC$60 ($7.40–$22.20); main courses EC$80–EC$100 ($29.60–$37). AE, MC, V.
Open: Lunch daily noon–3pm; dinner daily 7pm–midnight.

About a mile and a half east of the center, the Green Parrot overlooks Castries Harbour. It will take about 12 minutes to walk from downtown, and the effort will be worth it, as this is an elegant choice for dining. It's the home of its chef, Harry, who got his long years of training in prestigious restaurants and hotels in London, including Claridges. Guests take their time and make an evening of it. Many enjoy a before-dinner drink in the Victorian-style salon, where they can order the house special, the Grass Parrot (made from coconut cream, crème de menthe, bananas, white rum, and sugar).

The price of a meal in the English-style dining room includes entertainment: Harry is not only a cook, but also an entertainer of some note. Shows are Wednesday and Saturday, beginning at around 10:30pm, and feature limbo dancers and fire-eaters, followed by music for dancing. Another special night is Monday, Ladies' Night: A woman who wears a flower in her hair, when accompanied by a man in a coat and tie, receives a free dinner. Everybody can listen to the music of the Shac-Shac band.

All this may sound gimmicky, but the food doesn't suffer because of all the activity. There's an emphasis on St. Lucian specialties, using home-grown produce when it's available. Try the christophine au gratin (a Caribbean squash with cheese) or the Créole soup made with callaloo and pumpkin. There are also five kinds of curry with chutney, as well as a selection of omelets and sandwiches at lunchtime. Some of the American guests enjoy the daily specials. Steak Pussy Galore is a specialty.

JIMMIE'S, Vigie Cove Marina. Tel. 2-5142.

Cuisine: CREOLE. **Reservations:** Not accepted.
$ Prices: Appetizers $2–$5; main courses $13–$25. AE, MC, V.
Open: Mon–Sat 11am–11pm, Sun 6–11pm. **Closed:** Mid-July to Aug.

Near Vigie Airport, with a view of Castries Harbour and the Morne, Jimmie's is known for its fish menu and tasty Créole cookery prepared with fresh ingredients daily. Jimmie is a native St. Lucian, and after training in England, he returned to his homeland to open this spot popular with visitors and locals alike. Its bar is considered a prime rendezvous point. Guests like the open-air terrace dining and dishes that taste just like "mama made," provided your mother came from the islands and learned secret Créole spices. Try the conch, octopus, or red snapper in Créole sauce.

RAIN, Columbus Sq. Tel. 2-3022.

Cuisine: AMERICAN/CREOLE. **Reservations:** Required.
$ Prices: Appetizers $3–$8; main courses $12–$18; banquet $30. AE, MC, V.
Open: Mon–Sat 11:30am–10pm. **Closed:** Hols.

Rain has a touch of nostalgia: It's named for that old Somerset Maugham story made into a film featuring Joan Crawford. Behind its palm-green and white facade and under its tin roof is the inspired creation of Al Haman, a former advertising man. "Under one roof" in the center of Castries he installed a bar, restaurant, and boutique, the latter selling tropical clothing. A popular rendezvous point, Rain keeps to the Maugham decor of ceiling fans, louvered doors, peacock chairs, and oil lamps. If you're dining, head for the second-floor balcony—a gingerbread-frilled upper gallery—where you can enjoy a view over the town square and its famous spreading samaan tree.

A nightly feature is "the Champagne Banquet of 1885," a re-creation of the seven-course, four-wine dinner served on Columbus Square the year Rain's landmark house was built. Good cooks turn out a repertoire of other home-cooking in the evening that includes not only Stateside dishes, but also such West Indian specialties as dolphin St-Jacques, pepperpot, stuffed crab, beef curries, and shrimp Créole. The salads are crisp and fresh with tangy dressing. The homemade ice creams are mouth-watering, especially soursop, which is featured in season. Among the drinks, I recommend such rum refreshers as Sadie's Sin and the Reverend's Downfall! If you don't dine on the candlelit upper floor, you might prefer a nook in the garden courtyard, where an array of pizzas, burgers, and local foods are available in casually informal surroundings at bargain prices.

SAN ANTOINE, Morne Fortune. Tel. 2-4660.

Cuisine: CONTINENTAL/WEST INDIAN. **Reservations:** Recommended.
$ Prices: Appetizers $3–$12; main courses $15–$32. AE, MC, V.
Open: Lunch Mon–Fri 11:45am–2:15pm; dinner Mon–Sat 6:15–9:30pm.

What many consider the finest restaurant in St. Lucia is operated by Michael and Alison Richings in a historical setting. Constructed in the 19th century as a great house, it lies up the Morne and offers superb vistas over the capital and the water. Some time in the 1920s it was turned into the first hotel on St. Lucia by Aubrey Davidson-Houston, the British portrait painter whose subjects have included W. Somerset Maugham. However, in 1970 it was destroyed by fire. When it was restored in 1984, whatever could be retained, including the original stonework, was given a new lease on life, cleaned, and repaired.

You might begin with a fritto misto or ceviche, perhaps a seafood bisque, then follow with fettuccine carbonara, fish Créole, or lobster thermidor.

IN RODNEY BAY

Across the street from Capone's is **Sweet Dreams** (tel. 2-0688), which is called "the ultimate sweet shop." For dessert lovers, there's no finer establishment on the island. For example, it offers 25 flavors of Italian ice cream and tropical fruit sorbets, including passionfruit. Frozen yogurt is also a feature, and you can get cookies and doughnuts as well. Cones cost $1 and up. Hours are 10am to midnight Tuesday through Sunday.

CAPONE'S, Rodney Bay. Tel. 2-0284.

Cuisine: ITALIAN. **Reservations:** Required.
$ Prices: Appetizers EC$7–EC$35 ($2.60–$12.95); main courses EC$30–EC$85 ($11.10–$31.45). AE, MC, V.
Open: Tues–Sun 11:30am–10:30pm. **Closed:** July.
In vivid pink and green, Capone's could have been inspired by the old Billy Wilder film *Some Like It Hot*, starring Marilyn Monroe. Actually, this is an art deco rendition of a speakeasy along Miami Beach in the 1930s. North of Reduit Beach, near the lagoon and the St. Lucian Hotel, it's brightly lit at night. Al Haman created this place as well as the equally successful Rain (see above).

At the entrance is a self-service pizza parlor that also serves burgers and well-stuffed pita-bread sandwiches. However, I recommend that you go into the back for a really superb Italian meal, beginning with a drink, perhaps "Prohibition Punch" or a "St. Valentine's Day Massacre," served by "gangster" barmen. A player piano enlivens the atmosphere as you peruse the menu. You might begin with a pasta (the lasagne is always a favorite, especially when accompanied by a "Little Caesar" salad). For your main course, try flame-grilled chicken breast with Dijon mustard (that is, with ham and cream cheese), fresh local charcoal-grilled fish, or some of the best steaks on the island. Finish off with an Italian espresso.

CHARTHOUSE, Rodney Bay. Tel. 2-8115.

Cuisine: AMERICAN/CREOLE. **Reservations:** Required.
$ Prices: Appetizers $3–$6; main courses $11–$30. AE, MC, V.
Open: Dinner only, Mon–Sat 6–10:30pm. **Closed:** Sept.
North of Reduit Beach, in a large grangelike building with a skylit ceiling and mahogany bar, the Charthouse is built several feet above the bobbing yachts of Rodney Bay, without walls, to allow an optimum view of the water. Its exterior is crafted from weathered planking into a series of soft angles whose corners are masked with masses of hanging plants. Nautical charts of the region adorn the walls. The

menu might include callaloo soup, St. Lucian crab backs, hickory-smoked baby back spareribs, shrimp Créole, local lobster (in season), a choice of local fish, and well-prepared steaks.

THE LIME, Rodney Bay. Tel. 2-0761.
   Cuisine: AMERICAN/CREOLE. **Reservations:** Not required.
   $ Prices: Appetizers EC$5–EC$12 ($1.85–$4.45); main courses EC$20–EC$60 ($7.40–$22.20). AE, DC, MC, V.
   Open: Lunch Wed–Mon 11am–2pm; dinner Wed–Mon 6:30–11pm. **Closed:** Mid-June to July 7.

⑤ The Lime stands north of Reduit Beach in an area opposite the St. Lucian Hotel that is becoming known as restaurant row. Some of these places are rather expensive, but the Lime continues to keep its prices low, its food good and plentiful, and its service and welcome among the finest on the island, all of which attract both locals and visitors. West Indian in feeling, the Lime has an open-air setting. In honor of its namesake, the restaurant features a lime special as a drink. Specialties are stuffed crab backs and fish steak Créole, and they also serve shrimp, steaks, lamb and pork chops, and rôti. The steaks are done over a charcoal grill.

MORTAR & PESTLE, in the Harmony Apartel complex, Rodney Bay Lagoon. Tel. 2-8756.
   Cuisine: CARIBBEAN/INTERNATIONAL. **Reservations:** Recommended, especially for dinner.
   $ Prices: Appetizers EC$10–EC$15 ($3.70–$5.55); main courses EC$40–EC$85 ($14.80–$31.45). AE, MC, V.
   Open: Dinner only, daily 7–10pm.

North of Reduit Beach, Mortar & Pestle mixes Caribbean cuisine with a fine view of the marina. The menu features more than 30 à la carte specialties, such as baked Antigua clams, Guyana casareep pepperpot, frogs' legs Dominica, lobster Créole Guadeloupe, and lambi (conch) St. Lucia. The specialty of the house is red snapper Martinique, filets of red snapper sautéed in garlic butter with onions and mushrooms, simmered in a white wine–cream sauce. It's served with breadfruit balls and christophine au gratin. If you're not in the mood for "haute cuisine des Caraïbes," they also have a European, a Chinese, and an Indian menu. A good selection of wines from Germany, France, Portugal, and California is offered.

IN GROS ISLET

BANANA SPLIT, Gros Islet. Tel. 2-8125.
   Cuisine: CREOLE. **Reservations:** Recommended.
   $ Prices: Appetizers EC$5–EC$10 ($1.85–$3.70); main courses EC$35–EC$60 ($12.95–$22.20). No credit cards.
   Open: Lunch Mon–Sat 11am–2pm; dinner Mon–Sat 7:30–11pm.

⑤ Between Castries and Cap Estate is a huge barnlike wooden building with its sides open to a view of the sea. One diner suggested that it's "not unlike an American Legion hall set up for a Sunday chicken dinner." Dining at a simply set, long wooden table, you might begin with one of the soups made with local ingredients, such as lobster, pumpkin, or callaloo. Or perhaps you'd prefer a crab-back appetizer, followed by chicken Créole. Lobster also appears as a main dish, either boiled and served with lime butter or curried or offered thermidor style. For dessert, you can order the namesake banana split. On Friday, there are jump-on and reggae shows, when a band arrives.

AT MARIGOT BAY

DOLITTLE'S, in the Moorings Marigot Bay Resort, Marigot Bay. Tel. 3-4230.
   Cuisine: CREOLE/INTERNATIONAL. **Reservations:** Recommended for non-residents. **Directions:** Take one of the resort's frequent ferryboats across Marigot Bay.

$ Prices: Appetizers EC$10.50–EC$35 ($3.90–$12.95); main courses EC$9–EC$100 ($3.35–$37). AE, MC, V.

Open: Lunch daily noon–2pm; dinner daily 7–10:30pm.

Named after the big-budget movie that was filmed in the nearby bay, this is the less formal of the two restaurants in one of St. Lucia's more unusual resorts. Many of this establishment's clients arrive in T-shirts and bathing suits. In the evening, the bar serves up an array of frothy and pastel-colored drinks. The decor is appropriately breezy, as you dine on an open-sided veranda with a view of the bay. Lobster is an enduring specialty, although also desirable are a seafood version of callaloo soup, and a selection of hamburgers, sandwiches, and salads. The catch of the day, perhaps dolphin, will be grilled and served with flavored rice.

THE RUSTY ANCHOR, in the Moorings Marigot Bay Resort, Marigot Bay. Tel. 3-4230.

Cuisine: INTERNATIONAL. **Reservations:** Recommended for nonresidents.

Directions: Take one of the resort's frequent ferryboats that shuttle across Marigot Bay.

$ Prices: Appetizers EC$14–EC$26 ($5.20–$9.60); main courses EC$40–EC$115 ($14.80–$42.55). AE, MC, V.

Open: Dinner only, daily 7pm–midnight.

This is the more formal of the two restaurants in the previously recommended resort. Cozy, candlelit, and nautical, it attracts many of the owners of the private yachts in the nearby bay. The congenial bar does a brisk business before dinner, when the Love Bird (orange liqueur, cream, Cheery Heering, a local brand of rum, and mashed papaya) is especially popular. Specialties include an array of soups such as conch chowder or callaloo studded with seafood, pastas, vegetarian dishes, an enduring favorite of grilled rack of lamb (prepared only for a minimum of two diners), grilled fish with herbed butter and garlic, several different preparations of lobster, and a Créole version of baked Cornish hen. Ceiling fans spin languidly as you dine.

IN SOUFRIÈRE

THE HUMMINGBIRD, Anse Chastanet Rd. Tel. 4-7232.

Cuisine: CREOLE. **Reservations:** Required.

$ Prices: Appetizers EC$6–EC$22 ($2.20–$8.15); main courses EC$35–EC$75 ($12.95–$27.75). MC, V.

Open: Lunch daily noon–3pm; dinner daily 7:30–10pm.

At the southern tip of the island, this place was named for the tiny, darting birds that fly around it and its adjoining boutique, which sells fine-art batiks. An outdoor pool is free for use by those who drop into the restaurant for a meal or just a drink. Patrons have included Mick Jagger and the late Christina Onassis. A few larger-than-life wooden statues of mermaids support the thatch roof in back, and near the entrance is a rock garden with a wood carving made from the stump of a poinciana tree. The wide-ranging menu features many tempting drinks (for example, a Hummingbird Hangover, made of sambuca, golden rum, orange juice, and bitters) as well as English, Indian, or West Indian dishes including seafood crêpes, ceviche (raw marinated fish), beef Stroganoff, steak Diane, and chateaubriand.

THE STILL, Soufrière. Tel. 4-7224.

Cuisine: CREOLE. **Reservations:** Required for dinner.

$ Prices: Appetizers EC$7.50–EC$25 ($2.80–$9.25); main courses EC$18–EC$75 ($6.65–$27.75). AE, MC, V.

Open: Lunch daily 10am–3pm; dinner by reservation only.

S The first thing you'll see as you drive up the hill from the harbor at the southern tip of St. Lucia is a very old rum distillery set on a platform of thick timbers. The front garden blossoms with avocado and breadfruit trees, and a mahogany forest is a few steps away. The bar near the front veranda is furnished with glossy tables cut from cross sections of tropical tree trunks. A more formal and spacious dining room is nearby. A three-course lunch begins at EC$25 ($9.25) and might include chicken, pepperpot, curried lamb, or fish. A buffet, when offered, goes for EC$45 ($16.65) in the evening.

WHAT TO SEE & DO

Lovely little towns, beautiful beaches and bays, mineral baths, banana plantations—even a volcano is here to visit.

CASTRIES The capital city has grown up around its harbor, which occupies the crater of an extinct volcano. Charter captains and the yachting set drift in here, and large cruise-ship wharfs welcome vessels from around the world. Because of those devastating fires mentioned earlier, the town today has a look of newness, with glass-and-concrete (or steel) buildings replacing the French colonial or Victorian look typical of many West Indian capitals.

The **Saturday-morning market** in the old tin-roofed building on Jeremy Street in Castries is my favorite "people-watching" site on the island. The country women dress up in their traditional garb of cotton headdress; the number of knotted points on top reveals their marital status (ask one of the locals to explain it to you). The luscious fresh fruits and vegetables of St. Lucia are sold as weather-beaten men sit close by playing *warrie*, which is a fast game played with pebbles on a carved board. You can also pick up such St. Lucia handcrafts as baskets and unglazed pottery.

Government House is a charming late Victorian building. A Roman Catholic **cathedral** stands on Columbus Square, which has a few restored buildings.

Beyond Government House lies **Morne Fortune,** which means "Hill of Good Luck." No one had much luck here, certainly not the battling French and British fighting for Fort Charlotte. The barracks and guard rooms changed nationalities many times. You can visit the 18th-century barracks complete with a military cemetery, a small museum, the Old Powder Magazine, and the "Four Apostles Battery" (the apostles being a quartet of grim muzzle-loading cannons). The view of the harbor of Castries is spectacular. You can see north to Pigeon Island or south to the Pitons. To reach Morne Fortune, head east on Bridge Street.

PIGEON ISLAND NATIONAL PARK St. Lucia's first national park, Pigeon Island is connected to the mainland by a causeway. On the west coast, pirate Jamb-de-bois (Wooden Leg) used it as a hideout for his men and himself, as did Admiral Rodney's fleet much later when it set out to defeat De Grasse at the Battle of the Saints. Historical ruins and remnants of the Arawaks can still be seen. The island gained its name through the red neck pigeon, or ramier, which once made this its island home. The island is ideal for a picnic, and it also has some private beaches suitable for swimming. The park is open daily from 9am to 5pm, with an entrance fee of EC$3 ($1.15). Package tours are available from the **St. Lucia National Trust** (tel. 2-5005).

MARIGOT BAY ✪ Movie crews, such as those for Rex Harrison's *Dr. Doolittle* and Sophia Loren's *Fire Power,* like to use this bay, one of the most beautiful in the Caribbean, for background shots. Lying 8 miles south of Castries, it's narrow yet navigable by yachts of any size. Here Admiral Rodney camouflaged his ships with palm leaves while lying in wait for French frigates. The shore, lined with palm trees, remains relatively unspoiled, but some building sites have been sold. Again, it's a delightful spot for a picnic if you didn't take your food basket to Pigeon Island.

SOUFRIERE This little fishing port, St. Lucia's second-largest settlement, is dominated by two pointed hills called ✪ **Petit Piton** and **Gros Piton.** These two hills, "The Pitons," have become the very symbol of St. Lucia. They are two volcanic cones rising to 2,460 and 2,619 feet. Formed of lava and rock, and once actively volcanic, they are now clothed in green vegetation. Their rise sheer from the sea makes them a spectacular landmark visible for miles around. Waves crash around their bases.

Near Soufrière lies the famous "drive-in" volcano. Called ✪ **Mount Soufrière,** it's a rocky lunar landscape of bubbling mud and craters seething with fuming sulfur. You literally drive your car into an old (millions of years) crater and walk between the sulfur springs and pools of hissing steam. A local guide is usually waiting beside them, shrouded with sulfurous fumes that are said to have medicinal properties. For a small fee, he'll point out the blackened waters, among the few of their kind in the Caribbean.

Nearby are the ✪ **Diamond Mineral Baths,** surrounded by a tropical arboretum. Constructed on orders of Louis XVI in 1784, whose doctors told him that these waters were similar in mineral content to the waters at Aix-les-Bains, they were intended for recuperative effects for French soldiers fighting in the West Indies. Later destroyed, they were rebuilt after World War II. They have an average temperature of 106°F and lie near one of the geological attractions of the island, a waterfall that changes colors (from yellow to black to green to gray) several times a day. For EC$5 ($1.85), you can bathe and benefit from the recuperative effects yourself.

From Soufrière in the southwest, the road winds toward Fond St. Jacques where you'll have a good view of mountains and villages as you cut through St. Lucia's **Moule-à-Chique** tropical rain forest. You'll also see the Barre de l'Isle divide.

MOULE-A-CHIQUE   At the southern tip of the island, Moule-à-Chique is where the Caribbean Sea merges with the Atlantic. Here the town of Vieux Fort can be seen, as can the neighboring island of St. Vincent, 26 miles away.

BANANA PLANTATIONS   Bananas are the island's leading export. As you're being hauled around the island by taxi drivers, ask them to take you to one of these huge plantations which allow visitors to come on the grounds. I suggest a sightseeing look at one of the trio of big ones—the Cul-de-Sac, just north of Marigot Bay; La Caya, in Dennery on the east coast; and the Roseau Estate, south of Marigot Bay.

SPORTS & RECREATION

BEACHES   Since most of the island hotels are built right on the beach, you won't have far to go for swimming. All beaches are open to the public, even those along hotel properties. However, if you use any of the hotel's beach equipment, you must pay for it, of course. I prefer the beaches along the western coast, because a rough surf on the windward side makes swimming there at least potentially dangerous.

Leading beaches include **Pigeon Island,** off the northern shore, with white sand and picnic facilities. **Vigie Beach,** north of Castries Harbour, is one of the most popular on St. Lucia. It has fine sands, often a light beige in color. But for a novelty, you might try the black volcanic sand at Soufrière. The beach there is called **La Toc.**

Just north of Soufrière is that beach connoisseur's delight, the white sands of **Anse Chastanet,** set at the foothills of lush, green mountains. While here, you might want to patronize the facilities of the previously recommended Anse Chastanet Hotel. The also-recommended St. Lucian Hotel opens onto **Reduit Beach** with its fine brown sands, between Choc Bay and Pigeon Point. Water sports are available here at a hotel kiosk (see "Water Sports," below).

DEEP-SEA FISHING   The waters around St. Lucia are known for their gamefish, including blue marlin, sailfish, mako sharks, and barracuda, with tuna and kingfish among the edible catches. Most hotels can make arrangements for you to go on a fishing expedition.

GOLF   St. Lucia has two nine-hole golf courses. One is at the **Cap Estate Golf Club,** at the northern end of the island (tel. 2-8523). Greens fees are $14 per day and there are no caddies. Hours are 7:45am to sunset daily.

You can also play at the **Cunard Hotel La Toc** (tel. 2-3081), which has a resident pro. Greens fees are EC$25 ($9.25), but guests of the hotel play free. The course is open from 8am to 4pm daily.

HORSEBACK RIDING   You can hire a horse at **Cas-En-Bas and Cap Estate Stables** (to make arrangements, call René Trim at 2-8273). The cost is $25 per 1½ hours. Ask about a picnic trip to the Atlantic, with a barbecue lunch and drink included for $45. Departures are on horseback at 10am. Nonriders can be included; they are transported to the site in a van and pay half price.

SCUBA DIVING   In Soufrière, **Scuba St. Lucia,** in the Anse Chastanet Hotel (tel. 4-7355), established in 1981, offers one of the world's top dive locations. At the southern end of Anse Chastanet's quarter-mile-long, soft, secluded beach, it offers great diving and comprehensive facilities for divers of all levels. Some of the most spectacular coral reefs of St. Lucia—many only 10 to 20 feet below the surface of the water—lie a short distance from the beach and provide shelter for many denizens and a backdrop for schools of reef fish.

Many professional PADI instructors offer dive programs two or three times a day. Photographic equipment is available for rent (film can be processed on the premises), and instruction is offered in picture taking, the price depending on the time and equipment involved. Experienced divers can rent the equipment they need on a per-item basis. The packages include tanks, backpacks, and weightbelts. Through participation in the establishment's "specialty" courses, divers can obtain PADI certification. A 2- to 3-hour introductory lesson, including a short theory session, equipment familiarization, development of skills in shallow water, and a tour of the reef, with all equipment included, costs $55.

TENNIS   Most of the big hotels have their own courts. If yours doesn't, ask at the front desk for the nearest one. Some of the courts on St. Lucia are lit for night games.

WATER SPORTS   The best all-around center is **St. Lucian Watersports,** at the St. Lucian Hotel, Reduit Beach (tel. 2-8351), which offers an array of activities, including parasailing, waterskiing, snorkeling, and windsurfing, as well as Sunfish sailing. Here you can rent a Sunfish or a windsurfing board for $10 per hour. Snorkeling equipment costs $4 per hour, and parasailing goes for $25 for a 15-minute ride.

SAVVY SHOPPING

Stores are generally open Monday through Friday from 8am to 4pm and on Saturday from 8am to noon—but watch those early closings at some shops on Wednesday. Most of the shopping is in Castries, where the principal streets are William Peter Boulevard and Bridge Street. Many stores will sell you goods at duty-free prices (providing you don't take the merchandise with you but have it delivered to the airport). There are some good buys—not remarkable—in bone china, jewelry, perfume, watches, liquor, and crystal. Souvenir items include bags and mats, local pottery, and straw hats, again nothing remarkable.

Built with an eye to the cruise-ship passenger, **Pointe Seraphine** has the best all-around collection of shops on the island, together with offices for car rentals, organized taxi service (for sightseeing), a Bureau-de-Change, a Philatelic Bureau, Information Centre, and international telephones. Cruise ships berth right at the shopping center. Under red roofs in a Spanish-style setting, the complex requires the presentation of a cruise pass or an airline ticket to the shopkeeper when purchasing goods. Visitors can take away their purchases, except liquor and tobacco which will be delivered to the airport. In season the center is open Monday through Friday from 8am to 5pm and on Saturday from 8am to 2pm; off-season, Monday through Friday from 9am to 4pm and on Saturday from 9am to 2pm. It is also open when cruise ships are in port.

Among the shops represented, **Windjammer Trading Company** (tel. 2-1041) has casual clothing for the whole family. Items using cotton and natural fabrics were designed and manufactured on St. Lucia. **Images** (tel. 2-6883) offers a wide selection of perfumes, including such brand names as Estée Lauder, Oscar de la Renta, and Yves St. Laurent. A good shop for luxury goods is **J. Q. Charles** (tel. 2-2721), with its offering of fine china, crystal, glassware, jewelry, perfumes, liquor, and local arts and crafts.

BAGSHAWS, La Toc. Tel. 2-2139.

Just outside Castries is a shop offering the wares of the leading hand-print silk-screeners—in fact, they have become a legend in the Caribbean. An American, the late Sydney Bagshaw, founded the operation in the mid-1960s. His daughter-in-law, Alice Bagshaw, oversees production today. The family has devoted considerable skills to turning out a line of fabric that is as colorful as the Caribbean. The birds (look for the St. Lucia parrot), butterflies, and flowers of St. Lucia are incorporated into their designs. Linen placemats, men's shirts, women's skirts, wall hangings, and children's clothing are good buys. Each creation is an original Bagshaw design. Bagshaw's doesn't offer a mail-order service; its stock is available only on the island. Open: Mon–Fri 8:30am–4pm, Sat 8:30am–noon.

CARIBELLE BATIK, Howelton House, Old Victoria Rd., The Morne. Tel. 2-3785.

In this workshop just 5 minutes' drive from Castries, you can watch St. Lucian artists at work creating intricate patterns and colors for the ancient art of making batik. At the workshop you can purchase batik in cotton and silk, some made up in casual and beach clothing, plus wall hangings and other gift items reflecting the Caribbean. Drinks and snacks are served in the Dyehouse Bar and Terrace in the renovated Victorian-era building.

EUDOVIC ART STUDIO, Goodlands, Morne Fortune. Tel. 2-2747.

Vincent Joseph Eudovic is a master artist and wood carver whose sculptures have been exhibited in the O.A.S. headquarters in Washington, D.C., and have gained an increasing island fame. He usually carves his imaginative free-form sculptures from local tree roots, such as cobary, mahogany, and red cedar, and follows the natural pattern, sanding the grain until it's of almost satin smoothness. Some of his carvings are from lourier cannea trees, which have disappeared from the island, although their roots often remain in a well-preserved state. Native to St. Lucia, he teaches pupils the art of wood carving. In the main studio, much of the work of his pupils is on display. However, ask to be taken to his private studio, where you'll see the remarkable work of this extraordinary artist. Open: Mon–Fri 7:30am–4:30pm, Sat 8am–3pm.

NOAH'S ARKADE, Jeremy St. Tel. 2-2523.

Many of the Caribbean handcrafts and gifts here are routine tourist items, yet you'll often find something interesting if you browse around. They sell local straw placemats and rugs, wall hangings, sandals, maracas, steel drums, shell necklaces, and warri boards. Branches are found at Hewanorra International Airport and Pointe Seraphine Duty Free Shop.

RAIN BOUTIQUE, Columbus Sq. Tel. 2-3022.

In the corner of this virtual landmark restaurant (see "Where to Dine," above), a fashionable and petite boutique promises that you can "sip and sup while you shop." Rain has the reputation of having the most comprehensive collection of international clothing on the island. Chicly styled cotton clothing is offered. Even Sophia Loren bought some of her clothes here, and O. J. Simpson dropped in for some resortwear.

WEST INDIAN SEA ISLAND COTTON SHOP, Bridge St. Tel. 2-3674.

The staff here designs and creates original batik artwork entirely by hand. Wall hangings and clothing are among their merchandise, which is exclusively available in the West Indies. They also stock a full range of Kokonuts designer T-shirts; Sunny Caribbee herbs, spices, and perfume products; hand-painted jewelry; and St. Lucia souvenirs.

Y. DE LIMA'S, William Peter Blvd. Tel. 2-2898.

Here you'll find a good range of jewelry in gold and silver, as well as an array of Swiss watches, cameras, and binoculars. The store also sells perfume, souvenirs, and various gift items. It stands opposite the Bank of Nova Scotia.

EVENING ENTERTAINMENT

There isn't much except the entertainment offered by hotels. In the winter months, at least one hotel offers a steel band or calypso music every night of the week. Otherwise, check to see what's happening at **Rain** (tel. 2-3022), **Capone's** (tel. 2-0284), and **The Green Parrot** (tel. 2-3167)—see "Where to Dine," above.

Splash, in the St. Lucian Hotel, Reduit Beach (tel. 2-8351), is the best disco on the island, with a large dance floor in a roomy, air-conditioned area. The club plays an assortment of music from local reggae and calypso to American and European disco. There is a cover charge of EC$15 ($5.55) per person, and you must be 18 or over to enter. Hotel guests are admitted free. Splash is open Tuesday through Saturday from 9pm until all the patrons depart. The disco has a nightly happy hour from midnight to 1am.

3. ST. VINCENT

An emerald island 18 miles long and 11 miles wide, St. Vincent was charted by Columbus in 1498 on his third voyage. If the explorer had gone on a field expedition, he would have discovered an island of extraordinary natural beauty—assuming he hadn't been devoured by the cannibalistic Caribs.

Amazing for such a small area, St. Vincent has fertile valleys, rich forests, lush jungles, rugged peaks, waterfalls, foam-whitened beaches, outstanding coral reefs (with what experts say is some of the world's clearest water), a volcano nestled in the sky and usually capped by its own private cloud, and 4,000 feet up, Crater Lake.

The tenacious Caribs held out longer on St. Vincent against the tide of European colonization than they did almost anywhere else. However, in a 1763 treaty the British won the right to possess the island. In 1779 French troops invaded, but at the Treaty of Versailles in 1783 they gave it back to His Majesty's colonists.

A few years later Captain Bligh set off on the *Bounty* from England for Tahiti. There he loaded his vessel with breadfruit seedlings. Faced with mutiny, and after great difficulties (described in many historical novels), the captain in 1793 reached St. Vincent with his seedlings. The breadfruit trees took fantastically to St. Vincentian soil and earned for the island the title of "the Tahiti of the Caribbean."

In 1795, during the French Revolution, St. Vincent suffered yet another invasion. French revolutionaries, allied with the Caribs, burned British plantations and made a fierce war, only to be defeated by British forces the following year. The British decided St. Vincent was too small for both planters and natives. The Caribs were rounded up and shipped off to British Honduras (now called Belize) in Central America, where their descendants live to this day.

The island remained under "Rule Britannia" from that day until 1979, when, with the Grenadines, it achieved independent statehood within the Commonwealth. The governor-general is appointed by the Crown on the advice of the prime minister. Parliament consists of a House of Assembly elected every 5 years. The state of St. Vincent and the Grenadines has a population of about 113,000, mainly of African, East Indian, Carib, and European (especially Portuguese) descent. Much of its interior is inhabited and cultivated with coconut and banana groves. Arrowroot, often used as a thickening in baby foods, grows in abundance.

One of the major Windward Islands, St. Vincent is only now awakening to tourism, which hasn't yet reached massive dimensions. Sailors and the yachting set have long known of St. Vincent and its satellite bays and beaches in the Grenadines. Unspoiled by the worst fallout that mass tourism sometimes brings, the people actually treat visitors like people: Met with courtesy, they respond with courtesy. British customs predominate, along with traces of Gallic cultural influences, but all with a distinct West Indian flair.

ORIENTATION

GETTING THERE In the eastern Caribbean, St. Vincent—the "gateway to the Grenadines" (see Section 4)—lies 100 miles west of Barbados, where most visitors from North America fly first, and then make connections that will take them on to St. Vincent's **E. T. Joshua Airport** and the Grenadines. For transportation from North America to Barbados, see the "Getting There" section of the next chapter.

From Barbados, you can connect with one of five daily **LIAT** (tel. 809/458-4841) flights to St. Vincent. The flight from Barbados takes just 45 minutes. LIAT also flies in from Trinidad, St. Lucia, and Grenada.

Air Martinique (tel. 51-08-09 in Martinique) runs service between Martinique, St. Lucia, St. Vincent, and Union Island.

Increasing numbers of visitors to St. Vincent prefer the dependable service of one of the best-managed charter airlines in the Caribbean, **Mustique Airways.** For reservations, contact Mustique Airways/Grenadine Travel Company, P.O. Box 1232, St. Vincent, W.I. (tel. 809/458-4380), or their representative at the Mustique Airport (tel. 809/458-4621). The airline makes frequent runs from St. Vincent to the major airports of the Grenadines. With advance warning, Mustique Airways will arrange a specially chartered (and reasonably priced) transport for you and your party to and from many of the surrounding islands (including Grenada, Aruba, St. Lucia, Antigua, Barbados, Trinidad, and any other within the southern Caribbean). The price of these chartered flights is less than you might expect, and often matches the fares on conventional Caribbean airlines.

Currently, Mustique Airways is substituting its airplanes for many of the regularly scheduled flights of LIAT, which preferred to expend its energies elsewhere. The situation, however, is subject to change. Currently the airline owns seven small aircraft, none of which carries more than nine passengers.

GETTING AROUND   By Bus   Flamboyantly painted "al fresco" buses travel the principal arteries of St. Vincent, linking the major towns and villages. The price is really low, depending on where you're going, and the experience will connect you with the people of the island. The central departure point is the bus terminal at the New Kingstown Fish Market. Fares range from EC$1 to EC$6 (37¢ to $2.20).

By Taxi   The government sets the rates for fares, but taxis are unmetered; the wise passenger will always ask the fare and agree on the charge before getting in. Figure on spending about EC$15 ($5.55) to go from the St. Vincent E. T. Joshua Airport to your hotel, maybe more. You should tip about 12% of the fare.

If you don't want to drive yourself, you can also hire taxis to take you to the island's major attractions. Most drivers seem to be well-informed guides (it won't take you long to learn everything you need to know about St. Vincent). You'll spend EC$50 ($18.50) per hour for a car holding two to four passengers.

By Rental Car   Driving on St. Vincent is a bit of an adventure because of the narrow, twisting roads and the *drive-on-the-left requirement*. To drive like a Vincentian, you'll soon learn to sound your horn a lot as you make the sharp curves and turns. If you present your valid U.S. or Canadian driver's license at the police department on Bay Street in Kingstown, and pay an EC$20 ($7.40) fee, you'll obtain a temporary permit to drive.

Among the many leasing agents, **Avis Rent-a-Car** (tel. toll free 800/331-2112), the local branch of the U.S.-based giant, is probably the most reliable. For information and to request that an Avis car be delivered to your hotel from their headquarters at the Blue Lagoon, near Kingstown, call 809/456-9334. Avis charges $249 per week, with unlimited mileage, for their cheapest car. Drivers must be 21. A collision-damage waiver goes for $6 a day, but even if you buy it, you'll still be liable for up to $450 of damage.

FAST FACTS   ST. VINCENT

Area Code   St. Vincent can be dialed directly from the U.S. by using the Caribbean area code, 809, and the seven-digit number. For information on dialing once on the island, see "Telephone," below.

Banking Hours Banks are open Monday through Thursday from 8am to noon and on Friday from 8am to noon and 3 to 5pm (always check, as each bank may vary these hours slightly).

Currency The official currency of St. Vincent is the **Eastern Caribbean dollar (EC$),** worth about 37¢ in U.S. money. *Note:* Most of the quotations in this chapter appear in U.S. dollars unless marked EC$. Most restaurants, shops, and hotels will accept payment in U.S. dollars or traveler's checks.

Documents Canadian or U.S. citizens should have proof of identity and a return or ongoing ticket. Passports, voter registration cards, or birth certificates will do.

Drugstore Try **Deane's Pharmacy,** Middle Street, Kingstown (tel. 7-1522).

Electricity Electricity is 220 volts AC, 50 cycles, so you'll need an adapter and a transformer. Some hotels have voltage transformers, but it's best to bring your own.

Holidays These include January 1 (New Year's Day), January 22 (St. Vincent and Grenadines Day), Good Friday, Easter Monday, May 6 (Labour Day), Whit Monday, July 1 (Caricom Day), July 2 (Carnival Tuesday), August Monday (dates vary), October 27 (Independence Day), December 25 (Christmas Day), and December 26 (Boxing Day).

Information The local **Tourist Board** is on Egmont Street (P.O. Box 834), Kingstown, St. Vincent, W.I. (tel. 809/457-1502). Inquiries in the U.S. can be made to the **St. Vincent and Grenadines Tourist Office,** 801 Second Avenue, 21st Floor, New York, NY 10017 (tel. 212/687-4981, or toll free 800/729-1726).

Language English is the official language.

Medical Care There are two hospitals on St. Vincent, **Kingstown General Hospital,** Kingstown (tel. 6-1185), and **Medical Associates Clinic,** Kingstown (tel. 7-2598).

Post Office The General Post Office on Halifax Street in Kingstown is open Monday through Friday from 8:30am to 3pm and on Saturday from 8:30 to 11:30am. There are sub-post offices in 49 districts throughout the state, and these include offices on the Grenadine islands of Bequia, Mustique, Canouan, Mayreau, and Union Island.

Safety St. Vincent and its neighboring islands of the Grenadines are still considered safe islands to visit. Of course, in Kingstown, the capital of St. Vincent, you might be offered marijuana for sale on the streets, but chances are you'll encounter little serious crime. However, take the usual precautions and never leave valuables unguarded.

Taxes and Service The government imposes an airport departure tax of EC$15 ($5.55) per person. A 5% government occupancy tax is charged for all hotel accommodations. In addition, most hotels and restaurants add a 10% to 15% service charge.

Telephone Once on the island, you need dial only the last five digits of the number (not the area code or the "45"). The same is true for the Grenadines.

Time Both St. Vincent and the Grenadines operate on Atlantic standard time: When it's 6am in St. Vincent, it's 5am in Miami. During daylight saving time in the U.S., St. Vincent keeps the same time as the U.S. East Coast.

Weather The climate of St. Vincent is pleasantly cooled by the trade winds all year. The tropical temperature is in the 78° to 82° Fahrenheit range. The rainy season is May to November.

WHERE TO STAY

Don't expect massive high-rise resorts here, as everything is kept small. The places are comfortable, not fancy, and you usually get a lot of personal attention from the staff.

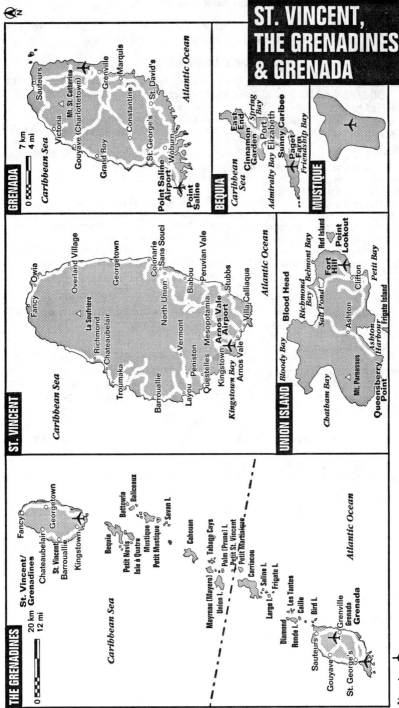

Reminder: Most hotels and restaurants add a 5% government tax and a 10% to 15% service charge to your bill; ask about this when you register.

VERY EXPENSIVE

YOUNG ISLAND, P.O. Box 211, Young Island, St. Vincent, W.I. Tel. 809/458-4826. Fax 809/457-4567. 29 cottages.
$ Rates (including MAP): Winter, $410–$550 double. Summer, $240–$380 double. Special package rates available. AE, MC, V. **Parking:** Free.

This 25-acre resort, which might have attracted Gauguin, was supposed to be where a Carib tribal chieftain kept his harem. A paradise island promising barefoot happiness, it lies just 200 yards off the south shore of St. Vincent, to which it is linked by a ferry from the pier right on Villa Beach, a 5-minute ride. Villas are set in a tropical garden, and the beach is of brilliant white sand. Hammocks are hung under thatched roofs.

You're housed in Tahitian cottages—all doubles—with a bamboo decor and outdoor showers. Floors are of seashells and terrazzo, covered with rush rugs. Ask about package rates, under the categories of "young lovers" and "lucky lovers"; these are exceptional bargain deals offered during off-season periods.

Dining/Entertainment: The food is well prepared, with an emphasis on lots of fresh fish and lobster and plenty of island-grown vegetables. Dining is by candlelight and dress is informal. Sometimes a steel band plays for dancing after dinner, and you're serenaded by strolling singers. On some nights the hotel transports guests over to the rock on its other island, Fort Duvemette, for a cocktail party. There, hors d'oeuvres are cooked over charcoal pits, and a local band plays under torchlight. Island specials are served at the Coconut Bar, a thatched bohio on stilts that actually serves many of its drinks in fresh coconuts.

Services: Room service (for breakfast), baby-sitting.

Facilities: Swimming pool (modeled on a tropical lagoon and set into landscaped grounds) and a saltwater lagoonlike pool (at the far end of the beach, where you can hear parrots and macaws chattering), a tennis court (lit for night games), Carib canoes and Sailfish; all water sports (such as scuba diving and waterskiing) available.

EXPENSIVE

GRAND VIEW BEACH HOTEL, P.O. Box 173, Villa Point, St. Vincent, W.I. Tel. 809/458-4811, or toll free 800/223-6510. Fax 809/457-4174. 20 rms, 2 honeymoon suites. MINIBAR TV TEL
$ Rates: Winter, $150 single; $210 double; from $260 suite. Summer, $95 single; $120 double; from $150 suite. MAP $30 per person extra. AE, DC, MC, V. **Parking:** Free.

Owner-manager F. A. (Tony) Sardine named this place well: The "grand view" promised is of islets, bays, yachts, Young Island, headlands, lagoons, and sailing craft. Villa Point lies just 5 minutes from the airport and 10 minutes from Kingstown. On well-manicured grounds, this resort is set on 8 acres of gardens. The converted plantation house is a large, white, two-story mansion. Rooms contain private baths, and 12 are air-conditioned. Everything is well maintained.

Dining/Entertainment: Meals are based on fresh fish and island-grown produce whenever possible. A wide variety of health food and drink is also available.

Services: Room service, laundry, baby-sitting.

Facilities: Swimming pool, tennis and squash courts, fitness club with a range of exercise options and sauna and massage.

VILLA LODGE HOTEL, P.O. Box 1191, Indian Bay Beach, St. Vincent, W.I. Tel. 809/458-4641. Fax 809/457-4468. 10 rms. A/C TV TEL
$ Rates: Winter, $95 single; $105 double. Summer, $68 single; $76 double. Continental breakfast $4 extra. AE, MC, V. **Parking:** Free.

Set at the side of a residential hillside a few minutes south of the center of Kingstown and of Arnos Vale Airport, this is a favorite of visiting businesspeople from the other islands. Because of its access to the beach and its well-mannered staff, it should be better known. Originally built as a private home, it still evokes in residents the feeling of being lodged in a well-proportioned, conservatively modern villa. It's ringed with plants growing in the gardens. Each of the air-conditioned rooms has a ceiling fan, a private bathroom, and a comfortable collection of simple furniture.

Dining/Entertainment: There's a wood-sheathed bar on the second floor, and a street-level dining room where good food is served, usually from a fixed-price menu.

Services: Room service, laundry, baby-sitting.

Facilities: Swimming pool.

BUDGET

COBBLESTONE INN, P.O. Box 867, Kingstown, St. Vincent, W.I. Tel. 809/456-1937. 21 rms (all with bath). A/C TEL **Transportation:** Taxi (a 10-minute ride south of the airport).

$ Rates (including breakfast): EC$105 ($38.85) single; EC$140 ($51.80) double. AE, MC, V. **Parking:** Free.

Originally built as a warehouse for sugar and arrowroot in 1814, the core of this historic hotel is made of stone and brick. Today it's one of the most famous hotels of St. Vincent, known for its labyrinth of passages, arches, and upper hallways. To reach the high-ceilinged reception area, you pass from the waterfront through a stone tunnel into a chiseled courtyard. At the top of a massive sloping stone staircase you are shown to one of the simple old-fashioned bedrooms. Each unit has a private bath and walls covered with wide planks. Some contain TV, and some have windows opening over the rooftops of town. Meals are served on a third-floor eagle's eyrie high above the hotel's central courtyard. Rows of windows and thick mahogany tables in its adjacent bar create one of the most unusual hideaways in town. The hotel is convenient for town; however, you'll have to drive about 3 miles to the nearest beach.

COCONUT BEACH INN, P.O. Box 355, Indian Bay, St. Vincent, W.I. Tel. 809/458-4231. Fax 809/457-2432. 9 rms (all with bath).

$ Rates (including continental breakfast): Winter, $65 single; $75 double. Summer, $55 single; $65 double. AE, MC, V. **Parking:** Free.

This owner-occupied inn, restaurant, and bar lies 5 minutes (2 miles) south of the airport and a 5-minute drive from Kingstown. Its seaside setting makes it a choice for swimming and sunbathing. Island tours, such as sailing the Grenadines, can be arranged, as can diving, snorkeling, mountain climbing, and deep-sea fishing. Each unit is furnished in a straightforward modern style. A beach bar at water's edge serves tropical drinks, and an open-air restaurant opens onto a view of Indian Bay and features West Indian and Vincentian cooking prepared from local foods. Try the locally caught fish, stuffed breadfruit, callaloo-and-pumpkin soup, as well as mango- and coconut-cream pies.

CSY HOTEL & MARINA, P.O. Box 133, Blue Lagoon, St. Vincent, W.I. Tel. 809/458-4308. Fax 809/457-4716. 19 rms (all with bath). TEL

$ Rates: Winter, $85–$95 single or double. Summer, $75–$85 single or double. Breakfast $4.50 extra. MC, V. **Parking:** Free.

A two-story grouping of rambling modern buildings crafted from local wood and stone, this hotel 4 miles from the airport on the main island road features land and sea packages; 3 nights on land and 4 days sailing the Grenadines costs $2,545 for two people, $3,290 for four people, year round. There's a pleasantly breezy bar with open walls and lots of exposed planking. As you relax, you'll overlook a moored armada of boats tied up at a nearby marina. A two-tiered swimming pool, terraced into a nearby hillside, offers two lagoon-shaped places to swim. Snorkeling, windsurfing, and daily departures on sailboats to Mustique and Bequia can be arranged through the hotel. Each of the high-ceilinged accommodations has a balcony or patio, as well as a private bath; nine are air-conditioned. Room service, laundry, and baby-sitting are provided.

HERON HOTEL, P.O. Box 226, Kingstown, St. Vincent, W.I. Tel. 809/

457-1631. 12 rms (all with bath), 1 suite. A/C TEL **Transportation:** Taxi (a 10-minute ride north of the airport).

$ Rates (including continental breakfast): EC$100 ($37) single; EC$140 ($51.80) double; from EC$150 ($55.50) suite. V. **Parking:** Free.

One of those enduring favorites with people who like a guesthouse with a lot of West Indian flavor sits in a bustling location in town. It's in a wood-frame warehouse that a century ago used to store vast quantities of copra (dried coconut) before it was shipped to Europe. Today its well-ventilated, big-windowed premises is a hotel that's more like a guesthouse. You can always read quietly in an elegantly sparse living room. American and Créole meals are served beneath the soaring ceiling of a room whose view encompasses a private courtyard encircled by some of the simple but comfortable accommodations. Each of these contains a private bathroom and simple pinewood furniture. Room 15 is particularly spacious. Room service is available from 7am to 7pm.

WHERE TO DINE

Most guests eat at their hotels on the Modified American Plan (half board). Unlike the situation on many Caribbean islands, many Vincentian hostelries serve an authentic West Indian cuisine. There are also a few independent eateries as well, but not many.

BASIL'S BAR & RESTAURANT, Bay St., Kingstown. Tel. 7-2713.

Cuisine: SEAFOOD/INTERNATIONAL. **Reservations:** Recommended.

$ Prices: Appetizers $5–$8; main courses $12–$30; lunch buffet from $12; Fri-night seafood buffet $22 plus service. AE, MC, V.

Open: Lunch Mon–Sat noon–2pm; dinner Mon–Sat 7–9:30pm, Sun 5pm "until very late."

This brick-lined enclave is a newer and less famous annex of the legendary Basil's Beach Bar in Mustique. It lies in the early 19th-century walls of an old sugar warehouse, on the waterfront in Kingstown beneath the previously recommended Cobblestone Inn. The air-conditioned interior is accented with exposed stone and brick, soaring arches, and a rambling mahogany bar, which remains open throughout the day. The bill of fare could include lobster salad, shrimp in garlic butter, sandwiches, hamburgers, and barbecued chicken. Dinners feature grilled lobster, escargots, shrimp cocktail, grilled red snapper, and grilled filet mignon.

BOUNTY, Back St., Kingstown. Tel. 6-1776.

Cuisine: AMERICAN/CREOLE. **Reservations:** Not required.

$ Prices: Appetizers EC$3.75–EC$12 ($1.40–$4.45); main courses EC$44–EC$60 ($16.30–$22.20). No credit cards.

Open: Mon–Fri 8:30am–5pm, Sat 8:30am–1:30pm.

Opposite Barclay's Bank in the center of Kingstown, you'll find Bounty behind a green-and-white facade. The color scheme is repeated inside, with a raftered ceiling and large deli-style display case. Local people who work in the shops nearby come in for a typical British breakfast, costing $3.50 and up. Later the place jumps with business at lunch, when hamburgers and snack food are the most frequently ordered items. Everything is pleasantly casual.

FRENCH RESTAURANT, Villa Beach. Tel. 8-4972.

Cuisine: FRENCH. **Reservations:** Required a day or two in advance in season.

$ Prices: Appetizers EC$16–EC$30 ($5.90–$11.10); main courses EC$40–EC$75 ($14.80–$27.75). AE, MC, V.

Open: Lunch daily noon–2pm; dinner daily 7–9:30pm. **Closed:** Sept.

In a clapboard house 2 miles from the airport, near the pier where the ferry from Young Island docks, this is one of the most consistently good restaurants on the island. It offers a long, semishadowed bar which you pass on your way to the rear veranda. There, overlooking the moored yachts off the coast of Young Island, you can enjoy well-seasoned, Gallic-inspired food. Surrounded with vine-laced lattices, you may order grilled Cornish game hen, curried conch, seafood cassoulet, fish and shrimp kebab, and stuffed crab back, followed by homemade ice cream or chocolate mousse. This is the only restaurant on St. Vincent that offers fresh lobsters from the pool. Lunch is simpler, with quiche Lorraine, omelets, tunafish salads, and cheesecake.

JULIETTE'S, Middle St., Kingstown. Tel. 7-1645.
   Cuisine: AMERICAN/CREOLE. **Reservations:** Not required.
$ Prices: Main courses EC$12–EC$14 ($4.45–$5.20). No credit cards.
   Open: Breakfast Mon–Fri 8–10:30am; lunch Mon–Fri 10:30am–2pm (restaurant open until 4pm).
In the center of town, the alleyway that stretches from Middle Street to this restaurant is so narrow you might miss it. It will lead to a concealed courtyard and a flight of exterior steps, which climb to a second-floor dining room. It's a clean, respectable West Indian restaurant where only platters of main dishes—no appetizers—are served in place of more traditional three-course meals. The restaurant closes promptly at 4:30pm, after a busy day of feeding the office workers of Kingstown. Island specialties include curried mutton, an array of fish, stewed chicken, and stewed beef. Many of the platters are garnished with fried plantain and rice.

WHAT TO SEE & DO

Special events include the week-long **Carnival** in early July, one of the largest in the eastern Caribbean, with steel-band and calypso competitions, along with the crowning of the king and queen of the carnival.

KINGSTOWN   Lushly tropical and solidly British, the capital isn't as architecturally fascinating as St. George's in Grenada. Some English-style houses do exist, many of them looking as if they belonged in Penzance, Cornwall, instead of the West Indies. However, you can still meet old-time beachcombers if you stroll on Upper Bay Street. White-haired and bearded, they can be seen loading their boats with produce grown on the mountain, before heading to some secluded beach in the Grenadines. This is a chief port and gateway to the Grenadines, and you can also view the small boats, dinghies, and yachts that have dropped anchor here. The place is a magnet for charter sailors.
   At the top of a winding road on the north side of Kingstown, **Fort Charlotte** (tel. 6-1830) was built on Johnson Point, enclosing one side of the bay. Constructed about the time of the American Revolution, it was named after Queen Charlotte, the German consort of George III. The ruins aren't much to inspect; the reason to come here is the view. The fort sits atop a steep promontory some 640 feet above the sea. From its citadel, you'll have a commanding sweep of the leeward shores to the north, Kingstown to the south, and the Grenadines beyond. A trio of cannons used to fight off French troops are still in place. You'll see a series of oil murals depicting the history of black Caribs. Admission is free, and hours are 6am to 6pm daily.
   The second major sight is the ✪ **Botanic Gardens,** on the north side of Kingstown about a mile from the center. Founded in 1765 by Gov. George Melville, they are the oldest botanic gardens in the West Indies. In this Windward Eden, you'll see 20 acres of such tropical exotics as teak, almond, cinnamon, nutmeg, cannonball, and mahogany; some of the trees are more than two centuries old. One of the breadfruit trees was reputedly among those original seedlings brought to this island by Captain Bligh in 1793. There is also a large *Spachea perforata* (the Soufrière tree), a species believed to be unique to St. Vincent and not found in the wild since 1812. The gardens are open daily from 6am to 6pm. No admission is charged.
   The **Archeological Museum,** in the Botanic Gardens, houses a good collection of stone tools and other artifacts in both stone and pottery. In front of it are shrubs that might have been found in the compound of an early Carib home.
   In the heart of town, you might pay a visit to **St. Mary's Catholic Church,** on

Grenville Street, with its curious melange of architecture. Fancifully flawed, it was built in 1935 by a Belgian monk, Dom Carlos Verbeke. He incorporated Romanesque arches, Gothic spires, and almost Moorish embellishments. The result—a maze of balconies, turrets, battlements, and courtyards—creates a bizarre effect.

St. George's Cathedral has some beautiful stained-glass windows: The three on the east are by Kempe and the large one on the south is of Munich glass. The nave and lower part of the tower date from 1820, and the galleried interior is of late Georgian architecture.

THE LEEWARD HIGHWAY ✪ The leeward or west side of the island has the most dramatic scenery. North from Kingstown, you rise into lofty terrain before descending to the water again. There are views in all directions. On your right you'll pass the Aqueduct Golf Course before reaching Layou. If you want to play golf, check its status, as it often opens and closes. Here you can see the massive **Carib Rock,** with a human face carving dating back to A.D. 600. This is considered one of the finest petroglyphs in the Caribbean.

Continuing north you reach **Barrouallie,** where there is another Carib stone altar. Even if you're not into fishing, you might want to spend some time in this whaling village, where some still occasionally set out in brightly painted boats armed with harpoons, Moby-Dick style, to seek the elusive whale. However, "Save the Whale" devotees need not harpoon their way here in anger. Barrouallie may be one of the last few outposts in the world where such whale-hunting is carried on, but Vincentians point out that it doesn't endanger an already endangered species since so few are caught each year. If one is caught, it's an occasion for festivities and a lot of blubber.

The leeward highway continues to **Chateaubelair,** the end of the line. There you can swim at the attractive **Richmond Beach** before heading back to Kingstown. In the distance, the volcano, La Soufrière, looms menacingly in the mountains.

The adventurous set out from here to see the **Falls of Baleine,** 7½ miles north of Richmond Beach on the northern tip of the island, accessible only by boat. Coming from a stream in the volcanic hills, Baleine is a freshwater fall. If you're interested in making the trip, check with the tourist office in Kingstown about a tour there.

THE WINDWARD HIGHWAY This road runs along the eastern Atlantic coast from Kingstown. Waves pound the surf, and all along the rocky shores are splendid seascapes. If you want to go swimming along this often-dangerous coast, stick to the sandy spots, as they offer safer shores. Along this road you'll pass coconut and banana plantations and fields of arrowroot.

North of Georgetown lies the **Rabacca Dry River,** which was the flow of lava from the volcano at its eruption at the beginning of the 20th century. The journey from Kingstown to here is only 24 miles, but it will seem like much longer. For those who want to go the final 11 miles along a rugged road to **Fancy,** the northern tip of the island, a Land Rover, Jeep, or Moke will be needed.

LA SOUFRIERE ✪ A safari to St. Vincent's hot volcano is possible. As you travel the island, you can't miss its cloud-capped splendor. On some occasions this volcano has captured the attention of the world. The most recent eruption was in 1979, when the volcano threw ashes and spit lava and hot mud, covering the vegetation that grew on its slopes and sending thousands of Vincentians fleeing its fury. Without warning, belched-out rock and black curling smoke filled the blue Caribbean sky. Jets of steam spouted 20,000 feet into the air. About 17,000 people were evacuated from a 10-mile ring around the volcano.

Fortunately, the eruption was in the sparsely settled northern part of the island. The volcano lies away from most of the tourism and commercial centers of St. Vincent, and even if it should erupt again, volcanologists do not consider it a danger to visitors lodged at beachside hotels along the leeward coast. The last major eruption of the volcano occurred in 1902, when 2,000 people were killed. Until its 1979 eruption the volcano had been quiet since 1972. The activity that year produced a 324-foot-long island of lava rock jutting up from the water of Crater Lake.

Even if you're an experienced hiker, don't attempt to explore this volcano without an experienced local guide. Also, wear suitable hiking clothes and be sure that you're in the best of health before making such an arduous journey.

A guide will direct you in your car through a rich countryside of coconut and banana trees, coming to a clearing at the foot of the mountain. After you get there, you go on foot through a rain forest, following the trail that will eventually lead to the crater rim of La Soufrière. Allow at least 3 hours, unless you're an Olympic athlete.

At the rim of the crater you'll be rewarded with one of the most panoramic views in the Caribbean. That is, if the wind doesn't blow too hard and make you topple over into the crater itself! Extreme caution is emphasized. Inside, you can see the steam rising from the crater.

The trail back down is much easier, I assure you.

MARRIQUA VALLEY   Sometimes known as the Mesopotamia Valley, this area is considered one of the lushest cultivated valleys in the eastern Caribbean. Surrounded by mountain ridges, the drive takes you through a landscape planted with nutmeg, cocoa, coconut, breadfruit, and bananas. The road begins at Vigie Highway, to the east of the E. T. Joshua Airport runway. At Montréal you'll come upon natural mineral springs. Only rugged vehicles should make this trip.

Around Kingstown, you can also enjoy the **Queen's Drive,** a scenic loop into the high hills to the east of the capital. From there, the view is magnificent over Kingstown and its yacht-clogged harbor to the Grenadines in the distance.

SPORTS & RECREATION

BEACHES   All beaches on St. Vincent are public, and many of the best ones border hotel properties, which you can patronize for drinks or luncheons. Most of the resorts are in the south, where the beaches have white or golden-yellow sand. However, many of the beaches in the north have sands that look like lava ash in color. The safest swimming is on the leeward beaches; the windward beaches can be dangerous.

Some of the best beaches are the white sands of **Villa Beach** or the black sands of **Buccament Bay** or **Questelle's Bay,** all west-coast sites.

FISHING   It's best to go to a local fisherman for advice if you're interested in this sport, which your hotel will usually arrange for you. The government of St. Vincent doesn't require visitors to take out a license. If you arrange things in time, it's sometimes possible to accompany the fishermen on one of their trips, perhaps 4 or 5 miles from shore. A modest fee should suffice. The fishing fleet leaves from the leeward coast at Barrouallie. They've been known to return to shore with everything from a 6-inch redfish to a 20-foot pilot whale.

SAILING & YACHTING   St. Vincent and the Grenadines are one of the great sailing centers of the West Indies. Here you can obtain yachts that are fully provisioned if you want to go bareboating, or if you're a well-heeled novice, you can hire a captain and a crew.

For boat rentals, contact **CSY Yacht Club** (tel. 8-4308) in the Blue Lagoon area of St. Vincent.

SNORKELING & SCUBA DIVING   The best area for snorkeling and scuba diving is the Villa/Young Island section on the southern end of the island.

Villa at Young Island, P.O. Box 639, St. Vincent, W.I. (tel. 809/458-4228), is owned and operated by Earl and Susan Halbich, and is located directly across from Young Island. They offer full diving service. You can rent equipment here and go on guided reef trips in the warm, fantastically clear waters. The shop also offers night dives as well as beginner and advanced diving instruction, windsurfing, waterskiing, and yacht charters. The complete resort-diving course costs $55 per person. If you're an experienced diver and want to go out on dive trips, rental of the boat, tank, kit, and weights cost about $40 per person. A minimum of two divers is required.

Dive St. Vincent, on the Young Island Dock (tel. 7-4714), has two dive boats and a capacity of 16 divers per trip. They specialize in dive tours and complete instruction from a staff of two certified instructors and three additionally trained dive guides. A one-tank dive costs $45 and a two-tank dive goes for $80, both including all equipment. Dive St. Vincent also offers water tours, such as one to Bequia and another to the Falls of Baleine, a popular trip.

TENNIS Short-term visitors to St. Vincent can play at the **Kingstown Tennis Club,** on Murray Road (tel. 6-1288). Guests are charged $6 per court per hour. You're asked to provide your own tennis balls and racquets and make arrangements through the chief steward in advance. Short-term visitors are allowed to play daily from 8:30am to noon.

Young Island and the **Grand View Beach Hotel** (see "Where to Stay," above) also have tennis courts.

SAVVY SHOPPING

You don't come to St. Vincent to shop, but once here, you might pick up some items in the Sea Island cotton fabrics and clothing that are specialties here. In addition, Vincentian artisans make pottery, jewelry, and baskets that have souvenir value at least. Most shops are open Monday through Friday from 8am to 4pm. Stores generally close from noon to 1pm for lunch. Saturday hours are 8am to noon.

Since Kingstown consists of about 12 small blocks, you can walk and browse and see about everything in a morning's shopping jaunt. Try to be in town for the colorful, noisy **Friday-morning market.** You might not purchase anything, but you'll surely enjoy the riot of color.

NOAH'S ARKADE, Bay St., Kingston. Tel. 7-1513.

Noah's sells handcrafts from the West Indies, including wood carvings, and offers locally made clothing. Noah's has shops at the Frangipani Hotel, Bequia, St. Vincent, and the Grenadines.

ST. VINCENT HANDICRAFT CENTRE, up the road from the wharf in Kingston. Tel. 7-2516.

Here you'll see a large display of the handcrafts of the island. On the site of an old cotton gin, this shop offers you a chance to see craftspeople at work, perhaps on macramé or metalwork jewelry.

ST. VINCENT PHILATELIC SERVICES LTD., Lower Bay St., Kingston. Tel. 7-1911.

This is the largest operating bureau in the Caribbean, and its issues are highly acclaimed around the world by stamp collectors. Stamp enthusiasts can visit or order by mail.

STECHERS JEWELLERY LTD., Lot 19, Lane Bay St., Kingstown. Tel. 7-1142.

Stechers offers a good selection of quality watches, china, porcelain, and jewelry. Waterford crystal is also sold. The entrance is through the courtyard of the Cobblestone Inn.

Y. DE LIMA LTD., Bay and Egmont Sts., Kingston. Tel. 7-1681.

The familiar Y. de Lima Ltd. is well stocked with cameras, stereo equipment, clocks, binoculars, and jewelry. Paragon bone china is also sold, along with a selection of gift items.

EVENING ENTERTAINMENT

The focus is mainly on the hotels, and activities are likely to include nighttime barbecues and dancing to steel bands. In season, at least one hotel seems to have something planned every night during the week. Inquire locally.

BASILS TOO, next to the Young Island landing pier. Tel. 8-4205.
The best-known spot for entertainment is still Basils Too, which "jumps up" with action, usually on Friday and Saturday nights. Guests from all the hotels come here to enjoy the music and sing-alongs. Drinks begin at $2.50. Open: Daily 9am–11pm.

THE ATTIC, Kentucky Building, at Melville and Grenville Sts., Kingstown. Tel. 7-2558.
The Attic features jazz and easy-listening music. Music is live only on Friday and Saturday; Tuesday through Thursday it's recorded. A beer costs EC$5 ($1.85). Open: Mon–Sat 8pm "until."
Admission: EC$10–EC$15 ($3.70–$5.55).

4. THE GRENADINES

South of St. Vincent, which administers them, this small chain of islands extends for more than 40 miles and offers the finest yachting area in the eastern Caribbean. The islands are strung like a necklace of precious stones, and have such wonderful names as Bequia, Mustique, Canouan, and Petit St. Vincent. We'll explore Union and Palm islands and Mayreau as well.

A few of the islands have accommodations, which we'll visit, but many are so small and so completely undeveloped and unspoiled that they attract only beachcombers and stray boaters.

Populated by the descendants of African slaves, the Grenadines collectively add up to a land mass of 30 square miles. No one has been able to ascertain why the chain of islands is called the Grenadines, but at least two main reasons are given. It was the custom of the Spaniards to name newly discovered lands after cities, towns, or villages back home, so it may well be that when they discovered Grenada (and named it after the city in southern Spain), they also found the little islands nearby, calling them Grenadines, as the plural diminutive of Granada (that is, "the little Grenadas").

It is also reported that the early roving French called the islands Grenadilles or Grenadines mainly because the islands had an abundance of wild passionfruit. The passionfruit flower is known to the French as *grenadine*.

These bits of land, often dots on nautical charts, may lack natural resources, yet they're blessed with white sandy beaches, coral reefs, and their own kind of sleepy beauty. If you don't spend the night in the Grenadines, you should at least go over for the day to visit one of them and enjoy a picnic lunch (which your hotel will pack for you) on one of the long stretches of beach.

GETTING THERE By Plane Three of the Grenadines—Mustique, Union Island, and Canouan—have small airports, the landing spots for flights on **Air Martinique** (tel. 51-08-09 in Martinique) and the well-recommended **Mustique Airways** (tel. 809/458-4621). At press time, Air Mustique anticipated landing rights (perhaps during the life of this edition) in Bequia as well. See "Getting There" in Section 3 on St. Vincent (above) and in the individual islands (below).

By Boat The ideal way to go, of course, is to rent your own yacht, as many wealthy visitors do. But a far less expensive method of transport is to go on a mail, cargo, or passenger boat as the locals do—but you'll need time and patience. However, boats do run on schedules, and generally are punctual. The **government mail boat,** M.V. *Snapper,* leaves St. Vincent on Monday and Thursday at 9:30am, stops at Bequia, Canouan, and Mayreau, and arrives at Union Island at about 3:30pm. On Tuesday and Friday, the boat leaves Union Island at about 6:30am, stops at Mayreau and Canouan, reaches Bequia at about 11am, and makes port at St. Vincent at noon. One-way fares from St. Vincent are: to Bequia, EC$10 ($3.70) Monday through Saturday and EC$12 ($4.45) on Sunday; to Canouan, EC$13 ($4.80); to Mayreau, EC$15 ($5.55); and to Union Island, EC$20 ($7.40).

You can also reach Bequia on the *Admiral I* and *II;* service on these vessels is

Monday through Saturday only. The most interesting way to go to Bequia is on a three-masted islander schooner, the *Friendship Rose*. For information on these sea trips, inquire at the **Tourist Board,** Egmont Street, in Kingstown (tel. 7-1502).

BEQUIA

Only 7 square miles of land, Bequia (pronounced *"Beck*-wee") is the largest of St. Vincent's Grenadines. It's the northernmost island in the Grenadines, offering quiet lagoons, reefs, and long stretches of nearly deserted beaches. Descended from seafarers and other early adventurers, its population of some 6,000 Bequians will probably give you a friendly greeting if you pass them along the road. Of the inhabitants, 10% are of Scottish ancestry, who live mostly in the Mount Pleasant region. A feeling of relaxation and informality prevails in Bequia.

The island lies 9 miles south of St. Vincent. There is no airport, but you can travel here by boat (see "Getting There," above).

GETTING AROUND **Rental cars,** owned by local people, are available at the port, and you can hire a **taxi** at the dock to take you around or to your hotel if you're spending the night. Taxis are reasonably priced, but an even better bet are the so-called **dollar cabs,** which take you anywhere on the island for a small fee. They don't seem to have a regular schedule—you just flag one down. Before going to your hotel, drop in at the circular **Tourist Information Centre** (you'll see it right on the beach). There you can ask for a driver who is familiar with the attractions of the island (all of them are). You should negotiate the fare in advance.

WHERE TO STAY

FRIENDSHIP BAY HOTEL, Friendship Cove (P.O. Box 9), Bequia, The Grenadines, St. Vincent, W.I. Tel. 809/458-3222. Fax 809/458-3840. 27 rms.

$ Rates (including continental breakfast): Winter, $65–$115 single; $95–$160 double. Summer, $55–$75 single; $70–$125 double. AE, MC, V. **Parking:** Free. **Closed:** Sept–Oct 15.

In this beachfront resort, the well-decorated rooms offer private verandas and lie nestled in 12 acres of tropical gardens. The entire resort complex stands on a sloping hillside above a crescent of one of the best beaches on the island, at Friendship Cove. Guests have a view of the sea and neighboring islands. Brightly colored curtains, bedspreads, handmade wall hangings, and grass rugs decorate the rooms, which are cooled by the trade winds. The owners have added a beach bar with swinging chairs in Caribbean style, and they offer Saturday-night barbecues on the beach, with music provided by a band. The food is good too, with many island specialties on the menu. You can enjoy water sports and tennis here, or take boat excursions.

JULIE'S AND ISOLA'S GUEST HOUSE, Port Elizabeth, Bequia, The Grenadines, St. Vincent, W.I. Tel. 809/458-3304. Fax 809/458-3812. 20 rms.

$ Rates (including MAP): EC$75 ($27.75) single; EC$119 ($44.05) double. No credit cards. **Parking:** Free.

These are twin establishments owned by two of the most kindhearted hoteliers on the island. Julie and Isola McIntosh are almost always on the premises, preparing meals or building extensions onto their family hotels. Julie, a mason, laid many of the bricks for both hotels, which lie across the street from one another about a block from the water in the center of Port Elizabeth. Isola's Guest House is the more modern; Julie's is slightly older. The place always seems to be full, because it is the rock-bottom cheapest place to stay on the island. Rooms tend to be hot, small, and noisy at times, but it's an enduring favorite, nonetheless. All rooms have baths or showers.

Good West Indian food is served in the dining room, which is a bougainvillea-covered veranda. The bill of fare is likely to include pumpkin fritters, very fresh fish, and curried dishes.

THE OLD FORT, Mount Pleasant, Bequia, The Grenadines, St. Vincent, W.I. Tel. 809/458-3440. Fax 809/458-3824. 7 apartments. **Transportation:** Taxi (a 10-minute ride from the port).

$ Rates: Winter, $60 single; $90 double. Summer, $50 single; $70 double. American breakfast $10 extra. MC, V. **Closed:** Aug and part of Sept.

A special hideaway has been created from the ruins of a French-built plantation house, whose location commands views of the waterways between Bequia and its neighbors. The historical records of the fort date from 1756 (it may be older), and its 3-foot-thick walls are made from cobblestones mortared together. This hotel and restaurant has only a few accommodations, each with private bath. In the reconstruction, the owner matched the original style by using the old stones with exposed ceiling beams and rafters. Spacious apartments in the towers give guests a medieval impression. There are shady garden terraces and sun decks.

The dining room is open to nonresidents in the evening, when a six-course dinner costs $30, plus 15% service. The cuisine is Mediterranean-Créole, with fresh seafood along with a house specialty, barbecued barracuda, served nightly at 7:30pm.

PLANTATION HOUSE, Admiralty Bay (P.O. Box 16), Bequia, The Grenadines, St. Vincent, W.I. Tel. 809/458-3425. Fax 809/458-3612. 25 units. MINIBAR

$ Rates (including MAP): Winter, $210–$240 single; $295–$325 double. Summer, $115–$135 single; $160–$170 double. AE, MC, V. **Parking:** Free.

Completely renovated in 1989, the Plantation House lies on Admiralty Bay, just a 5-minute walk to the center of town along the beach. An informal hotel, it has what is known as "new Caribbean style." Accommodations consist of 17 West Indian "superior" cottages painted in pink and blue, each with its own private porch, plus three luxury beachfront units with fans, and five deluxe rooms with air conditioning in the main house. Facilities include a dining room, a bar, a beach-bar grill, and a kidney-shaped beachside pool, all set in 10 acres of tropical gardens. The excellent cuisine is continental, and barbecues, tennis, and scuba diving are offered.

SPRING ON BEQUIA, Spring Bay, Bequia, The Grenadines, St. Vincent, W.I. Tel. 809/458-3414. 10 rms. **Transportation:** Taxi (a 1-mile ride from Port Elizabeth).

$ Rates: Dec 15–Mar, $105–$155 single; $130–$175 double. Nov to mid-Dec and Apr–June 15, $75–$120 single; $90–$130 double. MAP $35 per person extra. AE, MC, V. **Parking:** Free. **Closed:** June 16–Oct.

In the late 1960s the avant-garde design of this hotel won an award from the American Institute of Architects. Fashioned from beautifully textured honey-colored stone, it combines design elements from both Japan and Scandinavia; however, its flattened hip roof was inspired by the old plantation houses of Martinique. Constructed on the 18th-century foundations of a West Indian homestead, it sits in the middle of 28 acres of hillside orchards, producing oranges, grapefruit, bananas, breadfruit, plums, and mangoes. Because of the almost-constant blossoming of one crop or another, you get the feeling of springtime (hence the name of the establishment). Candy Leslie, the Minnesota-born owner, will welcome you. From the main building's stone bar and open-air dining room, you might hear the bellowing of a herd of cows. On the premises is a swimming pool and a tennis court. Each of the units is ringed with stone and contains Japanese-style screens to filter the sun. Access to the sandy beach is through a coconut grove.

For reservations, write or call Spring on Bequia, P.O. Box 19251, Minneapolis, MN 55419 (tel. 612/823-1202), or call Scott Calder International (tel. toll free 800/223-5581).

WHERE TO DINE

The food is good and healthful here—lobster, chicken, and steaks from such fish as dolphin, kingfish, and grouper, plus tropical fruits, fried plaintain, and coconut and guava puddings made fresh daily. Even the beach bars are kept spotless.

FRANGIPANI, in the Hotel Frangipani, Port Elizabeth. Tel. 8-3255.

Cuisine: CARIBBEAN. **Reservations:** Required for dinner. **Transportation:** Dollar cab to the harbor.

$ **Prices:** Appetizers EC$5–EC$15 ($1.85–$5.55); main courses EC$20–EC$60 ($7.40–$22.20); fixed-price meals EC$36–EC$60 ($13.30–$22.20); Thurs barbecue EC$60 ($22.20). MC, V.

Open: Lunch daily 10am–5:30pm; dinner daily 7:30–9pm. **Closed:** Sept to mid-Oct.

This waterside dining room is one of the best restaurants on the island. The yachting crowd often comes ashore to dine here. With the exception of the juicy steaks imported for barbecues, only local food is used in the succulent specialties. Lunches, served throughout the day, include sandwiches, salads, and seafood platters. Dinner specialties include conch chowder, baked chicken with rice-and-coconut stuffing, lobster, and an array of fresh fish. A fixed-price menu is available, or you can order à la carte. A Thursday-night barbecue with live entertainment is an island event.

FRIENDSHIP BAY RESORT, Port Elizabeth. Tel. 8-3222.

Cuisine: CONTINENTAL. **Reservations:** Required for dinner.

$ **Prices:** Appetizers $4–$5.50; main courses $7.50–$20. AE, MC, V.

Open: Lunch daily noon–3pm; dinner daily 7:30–9pm. **Closed:** Sept–Oct 15.

You'll find this dining room in the welcoming precincts of this previously recommended hotel. Guests eat in a candlelit room high above a sweeping expanse of seafront on a hillside rich with the scent of frangipani and hibiscus. Lunch is served at the beach bar, but dinner is more elaborate. It might include grilled lobster in season, curried beef, grilled or broiled fish (served Créole style with a spicy sauce), shrimp curry, and charcoal-grilled steak flambé. An island highlight is the Saturday-night jump-up and barbecue.

WHALEBONER INN, Admiralty Bay, Port Elizabeth. Tel. 8-3233.

Cuisine: CARIBBEAN/SEAFOOD. **Reservations:** Required for dinner.

$ **Prices:** Appetizers EC$5–EC$7 ($1.85–$2.60); main courses EC$44–EC$78 ($16.30–$28.85). AE, MC, V.

Open: Daily 8am–9pm.

An enduring favorite, the Whaleboner is still going strong in its new location next to the Hotel Frangipani, directly south of Port Elizabeth. Inside, the bar is carved from the jawbone of a giant whale, and the bar stools are made from the vertebrae. Dinner is served only from 6:30 to 9pm, although the bar often stays open later, depending on the crowd. The owners offer the best pizza on the island, along with a selection of fish and chips or well-made sandwiches for lunch. At night you may want one of the wholesome dinners prepared by a West Indian cook, including a choice of lobster, fish, chicken, or steak. Favored by the yachting set, the restaurant has full bar service. The Whaleboner Boutique adjoins the restaurant and offers a variety of holiday items made from batik and silk-screen-print Sea Island cotton, souvenirs, model whaling boats, and T-shirts.

WHAT TO SEE & DO

The main harbor village, **Port Elizabeth,** is known for its safe anchorage, Admiralty Bay. The bay was a haven in the 17th century for the British, French, and Spanish navies, as well as for pirates. Descendants of Captain Kydd (a.k.a. Kidd) still live on the island. Today the yachting set "from anywhere" puts in here, often bringing a kind of excitement to the locals.

If you want to see boats, just walk along the beach. There, craftspeople can be seen constructing vessels by hand, a method they learned from their ancestors.

Whalers sometimes still set out from here in wooden boats with hand harpoons, just as they do from a port village on St. Vincent.

Frankly, after you leave Port Elizabeth there aren't many sights, and you'll probably have your driver, booked for the day, drop you off for a long, leisurely lunch and some time on a beach. However, you'll pass a fort with a harbor view, and drive on to Industry Estates, which has a Beach House restaurant serving a fair lunch. At **Paget Farm,** you can wander into an old whaling village, and maybe inspect a few jawbones left over from the catches of yesterday.

At Moonhole, there's a vacation and retirement community built into the cliffs, really free-form sculpture. These are private homes, of course, and you're not to enter without permission. For a final look at Bequia, head up an 800-foot hill that the local people call **"The Mountain."** From that perch, you'll have a 360° view of St. Vincent and the Grenadines to the south.

SPORTS & RECREATION

Dive Bequia, P.O. Box 16, Bequia, W.I. (tel. 809/458-3504), specializes in diving and snorkeling. Scuba dives cost $50 for one, $90 for two in the same day, and $420 for a 10-dive package. Introductory lessons cost $25 each per person. A six-dive open-water certification course is $420. A snorkeling trip is $15 per person. Prices include all the necessary equipment.

SHOPPING

This is not a particularly good reason to come to Bequia, but there is some.

THE CRAB HOLE, next door to the Plantation House. Tel. 8-3290.
At shops scattered along the water you can buy hand-screened cotton made by Bequians. The best of these is the Crab Hole, where they invite guests to visit their silk-screen factory in back. Later you can make purchases at their shop in front.

NOAH'S ARKADE, in the Frangipani Hotel, Port Elizabeth. Tel. 8-3424.
Island entrepreneur Lavinia Gunn sells Vincentian and Bequian batiks, scarves, hats, T-shirts, dresses, and a scattering of pottery. There are also dolls, placemats, baskets, and homemade jellies concocted from grapefruit, mango, and guava, plus West Indian cookbooks and books on tropical flowers and reef fish. This place stands a few steps from the terrace bar of the Frangipani Hotel.

SARGEANT'S MODEL BOATSHOP BEQUIA, Port Elizabeth. Tel. 8-3344.
Anyone on the island can show you the way to the workshops of Sargeant's Model Boatshop Bequia. Sought out by yacht owners looking for a scale-model reproduction of their favorite vessel, Lawson Sargeant is the self-taught wood carver who established this business. Models are carved from a soft local wood called gumwood, then painted in brilliant colors of red, green, gray, or blue, whatever your fancy dictates. When a scale model of the royal family's yacht, *Britannia,* was commissioned in 1985, it required 5 weeks of work, meticulous blueprints, and cost $10,000. You can pick up a model of a Bequia whaling boat for much less. The Sargeant family usually keeps 100 model boats in many shapes and sizes in inventory.

MUSTIQUE

This island of luxury villas, which someone once called "Georgian West Indian," 15 miles south of St. Vincent, is so remote and small it almost deserves to be unknown, and it would be if it weren't for Princess Margaret, who has a cottage here.

The island is privately owned by a consortium of businesspeople. When word of Princess Margaret's retreat splashed on front pages in London, it was owned by beer baron Colin Tennant, a millionaire Scottish nobleman, now Lord Glen Conner. An eccentric dandy, he was often photographed in silk scarfs and Panama hats. On the trail of Margaret and her cousin, the Earl of Lichfield, came a host of celebrities, including Truman Capote, Paul Newman, Mick Jagger, Raquel Welch, Richard Avedon, and Prince Andrew in his bachelor days.

The island is only 3 miles long and 1 mile wide, and it has only one major hotel (see below). After settling in, you'll find many good white sandy beaches against a backdrop of luxuriant foliage. My favorite is Macaroni Beach, where the water is turquoise.

On the northern reef of Mustique you'll find the wreck of the French liner *Antilles,* which went aground on the Pillories in 1971. Today its massive hulk, now gutted, can be seen cracked and rusting a few yards offshore, an eerie sight.

If you wish to tour the small island, you can rent a Mini-Moke to see some of the most elegant homes in the Caribbean. You can even rent Les Jolies Eaux (Pretty Waters)—that is, if you can afford it. This is the Caribbean home of Princess Margaret. A five-bedroom/five-bath house, it has a large swimming pool, naturally. Accommodating 10 well-heeled guests, it's available only when HRH is not in residence. If you rent it, the princess will require references.

GETTING THERE The best way to go to Mustique is by air charter on **Mustique Airways,** which maintains two daily commuter flights between St. Vincent and Mustique. Flights depart St. Vincent daily at 7:30am and 4:30pm, and land on Mustique about 10 minutes later. Flights then head immediately back to St. Vincent. Chartered planes arrive on Mustique on the small airstrip in the middle of the bird sanctuary. The airport closes at dusk, because there are no landing lights. Once there, you'll find no taxis. But chances are, someone at Cotton House will already have seen you land.

WHERE TO STAY

THE COTTON HOUSE, Mustique, The Grenadines, St. Vincent, W.I. Tel. 809/456-4777, or toll free 800/223-1108. Fax 809/456-4777. 21 rms, 3 suites. MINIBAR TEL

$ Rates (including all meals): Winter, $375–$450 single; $475–$550 double; from $630 suite. Summer, $160–$225 single; $260–$325 double; from $350 suite. AE, MC, V. **Parking:** Free.

⭐ This exclusive hotel, once operated as a private club, is now as casually elegant as is its clientele. The 18th-century main house is built of coral and stone and was painstakingly restored, rebuilt, and redecorated by Oliver Messel, uncle by marriage to Princess Margaret. The design of the hotel is characterized by arched louvered doors and cedar shutters. The antique loggia sets the style—everything from Lady Bateman's steamer trunks to a scallop-shell fountain on a quartz base. Guests sit here and enjoy their sundowners, perhaps after a game on the tennis court, a swim in the pool surrounded by Messel's "Roman ruins," and a buffet lunch at poolside. Some of the establishment's rooms were also designed by Messel. Units are in two fully restored Georgian houses, a trio of cottages, a newer block of eight rooms, and a three-room beach house, all of which open onto windswept balconies or patios.

Dining/Entertainment: The hotel enjoys an outstanding reputation for its West Indian/continental food and service. Nonresidents are welcome to dine here, but they must make a reservation. The hotel also has three bars.

Services: Room service, laundry, baby-sitting.

Facilities: Two tennis courts, deep-sea fishing, sailboats.

FIREFLY, Mustique, The Grenadines, St. Vincent, W.I. Tel. 809/458-4621. Fax 809/456-4565. 4 rms. TEL

$ Rates (including continental breakfast): Winter, $75 single; $95 double. Summer, $65 single; $75 double. AE, MC, V. **Parking:** Free.

$ Firefly attracts those who aren't necessarily rich and famous but would still like to enjoy the beauty of Mustique. Ms. Billie Mitchell rents several rooms, each with bath and balcony, overlooking Britannia Bay from its perch high on a hill.

Some units are air-conditioned. It's a homelike, British sort of place, a hospitable guesthouse with an informal air. It was designed by a Swedish architect, with high vaulted ceilings crafted from local hardwoods and roughly textured walls of local stone. It has the feel of a small-scale castle.

WHERE TO DINE

BASIL'S BEACH BAR, 13 Britannia Bay. Tel. 8-4621.
 Cuisine: SEAFOOD. **Reservations:** Not required.
 $ Prices: Appetizers EC$25–EC$40 ($9.25–$14.80); main courses EC$50–EC$85 ($18.50–$31.45). AE, MC, V.
 Open: Lunch daily 11am–3pm; dinner daily 7:30–10:30pm (bar daily 8am "until very late").

Nobody ever goes to this island of indigenous farmers and fisherfolk without spending a night drinking at Basil's, a "South Seas island"–type establishment more authentic than any reproduction in an old Dorothy Lamour flick. It's the gathering place for yachting people, as well as owners of those luxurious villas. The bar, but mainly its owner, has received a lot of newspaper publicity. Its greeter, Basil S. Charles, is a 6-foot, 4-inch heavily muscled charmer whom *Esquire* magazine called "the island's most famous product after its sandy beaches."

Some people come here to drink and watch a beautiful view, but Basil's is also, by reputation, one of the finest seafood restaurants in the Caribbean. Both lunch and dinner are served daily at this establishment built on piers above the sea. You can dine under the open-air sun screens or with the sun blazing down on you. Expect to spend $40 and up for a meal here, and a good one at that. On Wednesday night you can "jump-up" at a barbecue, and on Friday night there's limbo dancing, fire-eating, and folk dancing. There is also a boutique on the premises.

CANOUAN

In the shape of a half circle, Canouan is surrounded by coral reefs and blue lagoons. The island is only 3½ miles by 1½ miles in size, and is visited mainly by those who want to enjoy its splendid long beaches. Canouan has a population of fewer than 1,000 people, many of whom fish for a living.

The governing island, St. Vincent, lies 14 miles to the north and Grenada 20 miles to the south. Canouan rises from its sandy beaches to the 800-foot-high peak of Mount Royal in the north. There you'll find unspoiled forests of white cedar.

GETTING THERE You can reach Canouan by first taking one of two daily flights on **Air Martinique** (tel. 809/456-4711).

You can also reach Canouan from St. Vincent by boat (see "Getting There," in the introduction to the Grenadines).

WHERE TO STAY & DINE

CANOUAN BEACH HOTEL, P.O. Box 530, Canouan, The Grenadines, St. Vincent, W.I. Tel. 809/458-8888. 43 rms. A/C MINIBAR **Transportation:** Taxi (a 5-minute ride from the airport).
 $ Rates (including all meals, drinks, and use of all facilities): Winter, $2,085–$2,453 per week single; $2,821 per week double. Summer, $927–$1,090 per week single; $1,854–$2,508 per week double. AE, MC, V. **Parking:** Free.

By far the best place to stay on Canouan, this hotel opened in 1984 and offers attractive accommodations on its 7 acres of beachfront. The location is about an eighth of a mile from the island's airport on a periwinkle-studded peninsula jutting out between the Atlantic and the Caribbean. Each of the stone accommodations has sliding glass doors, private bath, and comfortable furnishings. The resort's social center lies beneath the sun screen of a mahogany-trussed parapet whose sides are open to a water view. A pair of lush but uninhabited islands lie offshore. Snorkeling, windsurfing, small sailboats, and a catamaran are available without charge to guests. All water sports, buffet lunches, barbecue suppers, and drinks are included. Guests are booked in here for 1 week.

UNION ISLAND

Midway between Grenada and St. Vincent, Union Island is the southernmost of the Grenadines. It's known for its dramatic 900-foot peak, Mount Parnassus, which is seen by yachting people from miles away. If you're cruising in the area, Union is the port of entry for St. Vincent. Yachters are required to check with Customs upon entry.

Perhaps you'll sail into Union on a night when the locals are having a "big drum" dance—costumed islanders dance and chant to the beat of drums made of goatskin.

GETTING THERE The island is reached either by chartered or scheduled aircraft, by cargo boat, by private yacht, or by mail boat (see "Getting There" in Section 3 on St. Vincent and at the beginning of this section).

WHERE TO STAY & DINE

ANCHORAGE YACHT CLUB, Clifton, Union Island, The Grenadines, St. Vincent, W.I. Tel. 809/458-8221. Fax 809/458-8365. 15 rms. A/C TEL
$ Rates: Winter, $100–$220 single or double. Summer, $80–$180 single or double. AE, MC, V. **Parking:** Free.

The leading hotel on the island occupies a prominent position a few steps from the bumpy landing strip near a cluster of boutiques and shops. It combines a threefold function as a hotel, a restaurant and bar, and a marine-service facility. Each of the bedrooms is set between a pair of airy verandas and has white tile floors, modern furniture, and a private bath. The most expensive units are the bungalows down along the beach.

The yachting club meets in the wood-and-stone bar. There you can order lunches for $12 and dinners for $28 and up. The bill of fare is likely to include fish soup, a wide array of fresh fish, and Créole versions of lamb, pork, and beef. Try the mango daiquiri. The bar is open all day and into the night, but meals are served daily: breakfast from 7:30am to noon, lunch from noon to 2:30pm, and dinner from 7:30 to 10:30pm.

PALM ISLAND

Is this island a resort or is the resort the island? Casual elegance and privacy prevail on these 100 acres in the southern Grenadines. Surrounded by five white sand beaches, the island is sometimes called "Prune," so one can easily understand the more appealing name change. A little islet in the sun, it offers complete peace and quiet with plenty of sea, sand, sun, and sailing.

GETTING THERE To get to Palm Island, you must first fly to Union Island (see "Getting There" in Section 3 on St. Vincent for details). From Union Island, a hotel launch will take you to Palm Island.

WHERE TO STAY & DINE

PALM ISLAND BEACH CLUB, Palm Island, The Grenadines, St. Vincent, W.I. Tel. 809/458-4804. Fax 809/458-8804. 24 rms. MINIBAR
$ Rates (including all meals, afternoon tea, use of snorkeling gear, and airport transfers): Winter, $200 single; $295–$320 double. Summer, $135 single; $210 double. AE, MC, V.

The club is the fulfillment of a long-cherished wish held by John and Mary Caldwell to establish a hotel on an idyllic and isolated island. John is nicknamed "Coconut Johnny," because of his reforestation hobby of planting palms. At Prune Island, he planted hundreds upon hundreds of trees until its name was changed to Palm Island. An adventurer, this Texan once set out to sail by himself across the Pacific, coming to rest off the coast of Fiji. He made it to Australia, where he constructed his own ketch,

Outward Bound, loaded his family aboard, and took off again. Eventually he made it to the Grenadines, where he operated a charter business. His exploits, including getting embroiled in a hurricane, were documented in the autobiographical book *Desperate Voyage,* an account of his 106-day, 8,500-mile journey at sea.

Just right for the Grenadine frame of mind, he eventually built this cottage colony with enough room for 50 guests spaced under palms on the white sandy beach. Accommodations are in the Beach Club duplex cabañas or in one of the villas, which are equipped for housekeeping, and are built of stone and wood, with louvered walls as well as sliding glass doors that open onto terraces. The furniture was built by the Caldwells. All rooms are superior, with ceiling fans, window screens, rattan furniture, beach lounges, private showers, refrigerators, and outdoor walled patios on the oceanfront. Rates include afternoon tea served on the patio, a welcome drink, the manager's weekly punch party, airport transfers, tennis, and snorkel gear.

Dining is in a "South Seas island"–style pavilion where the food is good and plentiful. The nautically oriented guests like to have tall drinks at the circular beach bar.

The Caldwells still maintain a small charter fleet of yachts for day sails, with one of their amiable West Indian crewmembers aboard to assist. These natives are experts on local history, customs, and tall tales.

PETIT ST. VINCENT

A private island 4 miles from Union in the southern Grenadines, this speck of land is rimmed with white sandy beaches. On 113 acres, it's an out-of-this-world corner of the Caribbean that's only for self-sufficient types, who want to be away from just about everything.

GETTING THERE The easiest way to get to Petit St. Vincent is to fly to Union Island via St. Vincent (see "Getting There" in Section 3 on St. Vincent for details). Make arrangements with the hotel to have its "PVS boat" pick you up on Union Island.

WHERE TO STAY & DINE

PETIT ST. VINCENT RESORT, Petit St. Vincent, The Grenadines, St. Vincent, W.I. Tel. 809/458-8801, or toll free 800/654-9326. Fax 809/458-8428. 22 cottages. MINIBAR

$ Rates (including all meals): Winter, $500 single; $650 double. Summer, $425 single; $545 double. No credit cards. **Closed:** Sept–Oct.

In this offbeat island oasis there exists the Petit St. Vincent Resort, which has a kind of nautical chic. It was conceived by Haze Richardson, who had to do everything from planting trees to laying cables. The property was once owned by the archbishop of Trinidad. Open to the trade winds, this self-contained cottage colony was designed by a Swedish architect, Arne Hasselquist, who used purpleheart wood and the local stone, called blue bitch (yes, that's right), for the walls. This is the only place to stay on the island, and if you don't like it and want to check out, you'd better have a yacht waiting; but chances are, you'll be pleased.

The cottages are built on a hillside or set close to the beach, in a 113-acre setting. Units open onto big outdoor patios, all with views. Each is cooled by trade winds. Wicker and rattan along with khuskhus rugs set the Caribbean tone of the place. When you need something, write out your request, place it in a slot in a bamboo flagpole, and run up the yellow flag. One of the waiters will arrive on a motorized cart to collect your order.

To make reservations, contact Petit St. Vincent, P.O. Box 12506, Cincinnati, OH 45212 (tel. 513/242-1333, or toll free 800/654-9326).

MAYREAU

A tiny cay, 1½ square miles of land in the Grenadines, Mayreau is a privately owned island shared by a hotel and a little hilltop village of about 170 inhabitants. It's on the route of the mail boat that plies the seas to and from St. Vincent, visiting also Canouan and Union Island.

WHERE TO STAY & DINE

SALTWHISTLE BAY CLUB, Mayreau, The Grenadines, St. Vincent, W.I.
Tel. toll free 800/263-2780 in the U.S.; in Canada, call 416/430-8830 collect. Fax 613/384-6300. 5 double bungalows. **Transportation:** Private hotel launch.
$ Rates (including MAP): Winter, $280 single; $420 double. Summer, $180 single; from $270 double. No credit cards.

This is a last frontier for people seeking a tropical island paradise. A Canadian-German couple, Tom and Undine Potter, who for several years operated a beachside restaurant here catering to yachting visitors, have expanded their operation into a hotel complex. Units were built by local craftspeople, using local stone, floor tiles, and such tropical woods as purpleheart and greenheart. All units contain a private bath and are cooled by ceiling fans. Slightly less formal, and less expensive than the Petit St. Vincent Resort on Petit St. Vincent (see above), to which it is frequently compared, the place is appropriate for escapists unwilling to spend stratospheric sums for their seclusion.

The dining room at the hotel is made up of circular stone booths topped by thatch canopies, and you can enjoy seafood fresh from the waters around Mayreau—lobster, curried conch, and grouper. Guests can get acquainted at the bar. By day you can go snorkeling, fishing, windsurfing, cruising on a yacht, or just lolling in one of the hammocks strung among the trees in the 16-acre tropical garden, perhaps taking a swim along the expanse of white sand beaches which curve along both the leeward and windward sides of the island. One of the enjoyable excursions arranged by the Potters is a "Robinson Crusoe" picnic on a little uninhabited island nearby. Scuba divers will be glad to know that there's a shipwreck to explore, a 1912 gunboat lying in 40 feet of water a few hundred feet offshore.

5. GRENADA

The "Spice Island," Grenada is an independent three-island nation which includes Carriacou, the largest of the Grenadines, and Petit Martinique. The air in Grenada is full of the fragrance of spice and exotic fruits; the island has more spices per square mile than any other place in the world—cloves, cinnamon, mace, cocoa, tonka beans, ginger, and a third of the world's supply of nutmeg. "Drop a few seeds anywhere," the locals will tell you, "and you have an instant garden." The central area is like a jungle of palms, oleander, bougainvillea, purple and red hibiscus, crimson anthurium, bananas, breadfruit, birdsong, ferns, and palms.

Southernmost island of the Windward Antilles, Grenada (pronounced "Gre-*nay*-dah") lies 60 miles southwest of St. Vincent and about 90 miles north of Trinidad. An oval island, it's 21 miles long and about 12 miles wide and is volcanic in origin.

Like most of the Caribbean islands, it was sighted by Columbus, who sailed by it in 1498. Whether or not he landed is the subject of conjecture. Grenada was inhabited by the cannibalistic Carib peoples. The first Europeans who visited Grenada were probably London seafaring merchants.

The French in 1650 were the first to establish relations with the Caribs, buying their favors for two bottles of brandy and some baubles. But those peaceful relations didn't last too long, because the natives tired of their trinkets. The conflict ended in 1651 at **Le Morne de Sauteur (Leapers' Hill),** as the last band of Caribs tossed their women and children into the sea, and then, in a suicide leap, plunged to their own deaths rather than submit to European domination.

After the inevitable British-French disputes and bloody wars for domination, Grenada settled down under British rule in 1783. In 1967 it became an associated state within the Commonwealth. Before it achieved independence in early 1974, political squabbles virtually shut down the island.

Grenada was dominated by a volatile leader, Eric Gairy, who had been considered a practitioner of black magic and a UFO believer, performing voodoolike rituals to keep himself in power. On three separate occasions he proposed before a stunned United Nations that it undertake a study of UFOs. For 12 years he oppressively ruled the island until he was overthrown in the spring of 1979. The revolution cost only three lives, and boatloads of tourists, including a Soviet cruise ship, hardly noticed that they were in the middle of a revolution.

The man who ousted Gairy was Maurice Bishop, along with his radical New Jewel Movement. Bishop launched what is still a controversial 4½-year "revolution," cementing ties with the then Soviet Union and Cuba. Dramatically, in 1983 Bishop was placed under house arrest. Later he was executed along with several key supporters. An even more radical Marxist-Leninist faction took over the government and installed a revolutionary military control.

President Reagan, however, looked upon these new leaders as "thugs." In October of that year, the U.S.—backed by some other Caribbean countries—launched a successful invasion of Grenada, routing the military council and rounding up Cubans building the controversial Point Saline Airport.

Beefed up by financial aid from the U.S., Grenada has revived a sagging tourist industry. Grenada is a safe destination, and American tourists are genuinely welcomed here.

Carnival time in Grenada is in August and lasts several days, with colorful parades, music, dancing—what have you. The festivities begin on a Friday, continuing practically nonstop to Tuesday. Steel bands and calypso groups perform at Queen's Park. Jouvert, one of the highlights of the festival, begins at 5am on Monday with a parade of Djab Djab/Djab Molassi, devil-costumed figures daubed with a black substance. (Be warned: Don't wear your good clothes to attend this event—you may get sticky from close body contact.) The carnival finale, a gigantic "jump-up," ends with a parade of bands from Tanteen through the Carenage into town.

Grenada has a **People to People** program that allows you to meet the doctor, the waiter, or the spice-basket maker. This free program matches visitors to the island with Grenadians who share similar interests. For information, contact Grenada Tours and Travel, P.O. Box 46, St. George's, Grenada, W.I. (tel. 809/440-3316).

ORIENTATION

GETTING THERE   The **Point Saline International Airport**—financed in part by Cuba (and finished by the United States)—opened with much fanfare in October 1984, on the anniversary of the U.S. rescue mission of the island. At the southwestern toe of Grenada, the airport not only makes it possible for jumbo jets to land, but it also makes most of the major hotels accessible in only 5 to 15 minutes by taxi.

In 1990 **American Airlines** (tel. toll free 800/433-7300) became the first U.S.-based carrier to fly to Grenada with regularly scheduled flights. Service is via American's hub in San Juan. Using a Boeing 727-200 aircraft, which accommodates 150 passengers, the daily flight departs San Juan at 1:25pm and arrives in Grenada at 3:01pm. The daily return flight departs Grenada around 4:09pm and arrives in San Juan at 5:40pm.

BWIA (tel. toll free 800/327-7401) flies in daily from New York and Miami, with convenient connections from Toronto. Both BWIA and **LIAT** (tel. 809/422-6232) connect in Barbados with several different international airlines, including British Airways, Air Canda, American Airlines, and Air France. LIAT also offers a regularly scheduled service to Carriacou, the neighbor island of Grenada.

In addition, **British Airways** (tel. toll free 800/247-9297) flies to Grenada every Saturday from London's Gatwick airport, making a single stop in Barbados en route.

GETTING AROUND   By Bus   There are two types of buses. The most colorful and traditional ones are painted in red, blue, gold, or whatever, and are just as crazy as their names (one, for example, is called "Oo-la-la"). On plank seats, you're bounced until you're squealing just as much as the live pig with which you're likely to be sharing the ride. Most of these buses depart from Market Square in St. George's.

Minibuses have been introduced as well, and will take you on most short rides. They're not as colorful but are more comfortable.

By Taxi   You'll have to establish the price of a taxi before getting in. Most arriving visitors take a cab at the Point Saline Airport to one of the hotels near St. George's, at a cost of about $15.

You can also use most taxi drivers as a guide for a day's sightseeing, and the cost can be divided among three or four passengers. If so, count on paying about $35 to $50 per day. Again, this figure is to be negotiated.

By Rental Car   First, you must remember to *drive on the left*. A U.S. or Canadian driver's license is valid in Grenada; however, you must obtain a local permit, costing EC$60 ($22.20), before getting onto the roads. These permits can be obtained either from the car-rental companies or from the traffic department on the Carenage in St. George's.

A word of warning about local drivers: There's such a thing as a Grenadian driving machismo where the drivers take blind corners with abandon. An extraordinary number of accidents are reported in the lively local paper. Gird yourself with nerves of steel, don't drink and drive, and be extra alert for children and roadside pedestrians while driving at night.

Among the major U.S.-based car rental firms, **Budget** (tel. toll free 800/527-0700) and **Avis** (tel. toll free 800/331-2112) are represented on Grenada. Rates at Budget are usually lower. The lowest rates at Budget are awarded to anyone reserving a car at least 14 days in advance. Drivers are required to be between 23 and 70 years old, and to present a valid credit card and driver's license when picking up their car. Budget's cheapest car costs $216 per week, plus 5% tax. Avis charges $278 per week, plus 5% tax, for its cheapest car, which has air conditioning (the cheapest air-conditioned car at Budget rents for $300 a week). Both companies charge $6 a day for an optional collision-damage waiver, although both companies bill drivers for up to the first $300 in damage. (Payment with certain types of credit cards might make purchase of one of these waivers unnecessary; check with the issuer of your credit card before your trip.) Drivers at Avis need to be at least 25 years old, with no maximum age limit imposed.

It's always better (and usually cheaper) to reserve your car before leaving home, but for information once you reach Grenada, contact Avis at 3936 and Budget at 2778.

By Local Air Services   Many visitors like to fly over to Grenada's satellite island, Carriacou, for the day. **LIAT** (tel. 809/440-2796) makes the short takeoff and landing (STOL) flight in about 20 minutes. There are about three flights a day.

FAST FACTS: GRENADA

Area Code   To call Grenada from the U.S., dial area code 809, then a three-digit city code, and then a four-digit number. For information about telecommunications once you're on the island, see "Telecommunications," below.

Banks   In St. George's, the capital, you'll find **Barclays,** at Church Street and Halifax Street (tel. 3232); **Scotiabank,** Halifax Street (tel. 3274); and the **National Commercial Bank (NCB),** at the corner of Halifax Street and Hillsborough Street (tel. 3566).

Currency   The official currency is the **Eastern Caribbean dollar (EC$),** worth about 37¢. Always determine which dollars—EC or U.S.—you're talking about when someone on Grenada quotes you a price.

Documents   Proof of citizenship is needed to enter the country. A passport is preferred, but a birth certificate or voter registration card is accepted for American, British, and Canadian citizens, providing they also have photo ID.

Electricity   Not always reliable, electricity is supplied on the island by Grenada Electricity Services. It's 220/240 volts AC, 50 cycles, so transformers and adapters will be needed for U.S.-made appliances.

Embassies & High Commissions   Grenada, unlike many of its neighbors, has a **U.S. Embassy** at Point Salines, St. George's (tel. 1731). It also has a **British High Commission** on Church Street, St. George's (tel. 3536).

Emergencies   Dial 911 to summon the police, report a fire, or call an ambulance.

Holidays   Grenada celebrates the usual holidays, and has a Thanksgiving Day on October 25.

Information   Go to the **Grenada Tourist Department,** the Carenage in St. George's (tel. 809/440-2279), open daily from 8am to 4pm. Maps, guides, and general information are available. In the U.S., the **Grenada Tourist Office** is at 820 Second Avenue, Suite 900D, New York, NY 10017 (tel. 212/687-9554, or toll free 800/927-9554).

Language   English is commonly spoken on this island of 90,000 people because of the long years of British influence. However, now and then you'll hear people speaking in a French-African patois handed down from long ago.

Medical Care   There is a general hospital, **St. George's Hospital** (tel. 2051), with an X-ray department and operating theater. Private doctors and nurses are available on call.

Newspapers and Magazines   The *Grenadian Voice* is published weekly. You'll also find *Time* and *Newsweek*.

Pharmacies   Try **Gittens Pharmacy,** Halifax Street, St. George's (tel. 2165).

Post Office   The General Post Office in St. George's is open Monday through Thursday from 8am to 4pm, with a lunch break from 11:45am to 1pm. On Friday hours are 8am to 5pm. It's closed on Saturday and Sunday.

Radio   Radio Grenada, owned and operated by the government, broadcasts the news, and a lot of American pop and disco music.

Safety   Although crime is rare here, it would be wise to safeguard your valuables. Never leave them unprotected on the beach.

Service   A 10% service charge is added to most restaurant and hotel bills.

Taxes   A 10% VAT (value-added tax) is imposed on food and beverages, and there's an 8% room tax. Upon leaving Grenada, you must fill out an immigration card and pay a departure tax of EC$25 ($9.25).

Telecommunications   International telephone service is available 24 hours a day from pay phones. Public telegraph, Telex, and fax services are also provided from the Carenage offices of Grenada Telecommunications Ltd. (Grentel) in St. George's (tel. 809/440-1000 for all Grentel offices), open Monday through Friday from 7am to 7pm, on Saturday from 7am to 1pm, and on Sunday and holidays from 10am to noon. To call another number on Grenada, dial only the last four digits (not the area code or city code).

Weather   Grenada has two distinct seasons, dry and rainy. The dry season is from January through May; the rest of the year is the rainy season, although the rainfall doesn't last long. The average temperature is 80° Fahrenheit. Because of constant trade winds, there is little humidity.

WHERE TO STAY

Many of Grenada's hostelries evoke the Mediterranean more than the Caribbean in their architecture. The Ramada Renaissance Hotel is the biggest place at which you can overnight, and nearly everything else is tiny.

Don't forget that your hotel or inn will probably add a service charge to your bill. Ask in advance about this, plus the government tax on food and beverage tabs.

VERY EXPENSIVE

CALABASH, L'Anse aux Epines (P.O. Box 282, St. George's), Grenada, W.I. Tel. 809/444-4334. Fax 809/444-4804. 28 rms. A/C TEL
$ **Rates:** Winter (including MAP), $250–$450 single; $280–$450 double. Summer (including breakfast), $125–$230 single; $140–$230 double. AE, MC, V. **Parking:** Free.

Built in the early 1960s, the Calabash is today the best-established resort, and perhaps the most venerated hotel, on Grenada. Five miles south of St. George's and only minutes from the Point Saline International Airport, it occupies a landscaped 8-acre beach plot along an isolated section of Prickly Bay (L'Anse aux Epines). Many of the shrubs on the grounds, tiny when they were planted, make some of the stone outbuildings look diminutive. Foremost among the plants are the scores of beautiful calabashes (gourds) for which the resort was named. The social center of the place is a low-slung, rambling building whose walls are chiseled from blocks of dark-gray stone. Eight of the hotel units have private swimming pools and entrances nearly concealed by the thunbergia (trailing orchid) vines. Six units have their own whirlpools.

Dining/Entertainment: The hotel's restaurant serves a West Indian and continental menu. Entertainment, ranging from piano music to steel bands, is provided 4 or 5 nights a week.

Services: Room service, laundry, baby-sitting.

Facilities: One tennis court, outdoor swimming pool, sailboat rentals.

SECRET HARBOUR, Mount Hartman Bay, L'Anse aux Epines (P.O. Box 11, St. George's), Grenada, W.I. Tel. 809/444-4548. Fax 809/444-4819. 20 suites. A/C MINIBAR TV TEL
$ **Rates:** Winter, $215 single; $250 double. Summer, $125 single or double. Continental breakfast $10 extra. AE, MC, V.

Seen from the water of Mount Hartman Bay, Secret Harbour reminds one of a Mediterranean complex on Spain's Costa del Sol—a tasteful one, that is, with white stucco arches, red-tile roofs, and wrought-iron light fixtures. From all over Grenada, including some island plantation homes, antiques were purchased, restored, and installed here. The bathrooms are also luxurious, with sunken tubs lined with Italian tiles and lighting from unglazed medallion windows. Each of the suites has a dressing room, living area, and patio overlooking the water. Steps lead down to the beach.

Secret Harbour is a favorite of the yachting set. While many guests stay at the hotel, others stay on yachts anchored off the property. Owned by the Moorings, an international hotel and yacht-charter company based in Clearwater, Florida, Secret Harbour is located about 7 minutes from Point Saline Airport and 15 minutes from St. George's.

Services: Room service, laundry.

Facilities: Marina; wide range of water-sports, sailing, and boating programs, including bareboat charters and "Learn to Cruise" lessons. Tennis court, swimming pool, beach.

SPICE ISLAND INN, Grand Anse (P.O. Box 6, St. George's), Grenada, W.I. Tel. 809/444-4258. Fax 809/444-4807. 56 suites. A/C MINIBAR TEL
$ **Rates** (including MAP): Winter, $270–$400 single; $320–$420 double. Summer, $200–$260 single; $235–$295 double. AE, MC, V. **Parking:** Free.

On an estate overlooking the Caribbean, this inn is built along 1,200 feet of Grand Anse beach, directly north of the airport. The main house, reserved for dining and dancing, has a tropical aura and lots of nice touches, showing that taste and concern went into the design of the place. Most units are beach suites, plus there are 10 pool suites, all pleasantly contemporary, stretched along the white sands.

About 17 units are set back a bit and have their own private plunge pools, surrounded by high walls where guests can skinny-dip. Furnishings in the rooms are not elaborate, with outdoor pieces such as wicker chairs.

Dining/Entertainment: The waiter will arrive with your breakfast (a just-plucked red hibiscus resting on the tray), and you'll enjoy it on a shaded patio, your very own. The place is known for its Sunday buffet, and the cooks not only prepare an international cuisine but also deftly turn out good Grenadian food, including soursop ice cream (nutmeg is also a specialty), breadfruit vichyssoise, green-turtle soup, and Caribbean lobster. Sometimes a combo plays for dancing.

Services: Room service (for breakfast).

Facilities: Beach, swimming pools.

EXPENSIVE

RAMADA RENAISSANCE HOTEL, P.O. Box 441, Grand Anse Beach, Grenada, W.I. Tel. 809/444-4371, or toll free 800/228-9898. Fax 809/444-4800. 184 rms, 2 suites. A/C TV TEL

$ Rates: Winter, $158–$183 single or double. Summer, $100–$125 single or double. Year round, from $300 suite. MAP $43 per person extra. AE, DC, MC, V. **Parking:** Free.

Renovated in 1986, the Ramada reopened as the most glamorous, tastefully executed, and stylish hotel on the island, 3 miles north of the airport. It stands on a desirable stretch of beachfront, behind a cedar-shingled facade whose design might have been inspired by an 18th-century plantation house. Any comparison with another century, however, ends when visitors see the interior. Guests register beneath an octagonal roof of the entrance hall, then are ushered between a pair of manicured formal gardens to their rooms. Each of these is furnished with a formal blend of English reproduction pieces, carpeting, tile bath, and radio/alarm. Each has a balcony or veranda, some of which open onto sun-flooded views of the beach.

Dining/Entertainment: The hotel has two stylish restaurants, plus a bar featuring live entertainment.

Services: Room service, laundry, baby-sitting.

Facilities: Beach, swimming pool; water-sports kiosk for the rental of sailboats, windsurfers, and snorkeling equipment.

TWELVE DEGREES NORTH, L'Anse aux Epines (P.O. Box 241, St. George's), Grenada, W.I. Tel. 809/444-4580. Fax 809/444-4580. 8 apartments.

$ Rates: Winter, $150 one-bedroom apartment for two; from $240 two-bedroom apartment for four. Summer, $115 one-bedroom apartment for two; $185 two-bedroom apartment for four. Extra person $60. Children under 12 not accepted. No credit cards. **Parking:** Free.

On a very private beach, this complex is operated by Joseph Gaylord, a former commercial real-estate broker from New York, who greets visitors with a wide smile and an outstretched hand in front of a large flame tree on his front lawn. He owns this cluster of spotlessly clean efficiency apartments, 3 miles east of the airport at Point Saline.

Many of the staff members have been with Mr. Gaylord since he opened the place many years ago. They'll cook breakfast, prepare lunch (perhaps pumpkin soup and flying fish), do the cleaning and laundry, go food shopping, and fix regional specialties for dinner (which you heat up for yourself later). A grass-roofed beach bar faces the water. Each unit (two with two bedrooms and six with one bedroom) comes with an individual uniformed housekeeper/cook, who arrives at 8 o'clock each morning to perform the thousand small kindnesses that make Twelve Degrees North a favorite lair for returning guests from America and Europe. Each unit is equipped with an efficiency kitchen with a 12-cubic-foot refrigerator. The large beds can be separated or pushed together. The owner prefers to rent by the week, because, as he says, "a few days aren't enough to get to know Grenada."

Facilities: Beach, tennis court, two Sunfish, two sailing dinghies—all free.

MODERATE

BLUE HORIZONS COTTAGE HOTEL, P.O. Box 41, Grand Anse, Grenada, W.I. Tel. 809/444-4316. Fax 809/444-2815. 32 suites, 4 studios. A/C TV TEL
$ Rates: Winter, $105–$135 single; $120–$145 double. Summer, $85–$100 single; $90–$105 double. Continental breakfast $10 extra. AE, DC, MC, V. **Parking:** Free.

S Co-owners Royston and Arnold Hopkin purchased this place from a bankrupt estate. Sons of the famous Grenadian hotelkeepers Audrey and Curtis Hopkin (now retired), they transformed the neglected property into one of the finest on the island, with an occupancy rate second only to that of Spice Island. The units are spread throughout a flowering garden of 6¼ acres. Rates depend on the category of the cottage: standard, superior, or deluxe. Each bungalow has an efficiency kitchen and comfortable solid mahogany furniture. Children are welcome, and they can watch the 21 varieties of native birds said to inhabit the grounds.

Guests who prefer to cook in their rooms can buy supplies from a Food Fair at Grand Anse, a 10-minute walk away. Most important, Grand Anse Beach is only 5 minutes away by foot. On the grounds is one of the best restaurants on the island, La Belle Créole (see "Where to Dine," below). Lunch is served around a pool bar. Laundry, baby-sitting, and room service are provided.

COYABA BEACH RESORT, Grand Anse Beach (P.O. Box 336, St. George's), Grenada, W.I. Tel. 809/444-4129. Fax 809/444-4808. 40 rms. A/C TV TEL
$ Rates: Winter, $115 single; $165 double. Summer, $75 single; $95 double. Continental breakfast $6 extra. AE, DC, MC, V. **Parking:** Free.
On a 2½-acre site on Grand Anse beach, this resort is 6 miles from St. George's and 3 miles north of Point Saline International Airport. The hotel, opened in 1987, has views of the town and of St. George's harbor. All units have double beds, plus verandas and patios, spacious baths, and hairdryers. Laundry service is available, as are room service and baby-sitting. The hotel has an open-air restaurant serving local and international cuisine with drinks offered at the main or pool bar. Activities include tennis on a Laykold court, volleyball, and water sports offered by the H.M.C. Diving Centre on the premises.

HORSE SHOE BEACH HOTEL, L'Anse aux Epines (P.O. Box 174, St. George's), Grenada, W.I. Tel. 809/444-4244, or 718/226-8600 in New York City. Fax 809/726-6354. 12 rms, 6 suites. A/C TEL
$ Rates: Winter, $110–$115 single; $110–$125 double; from $135 suite. Summer, $70–$85 single; $85–$95 double; from $125 suite. MAP $32 per person extra. AE, DC, MC, V. **Parking:** Free.

★ This small Mediterranean-style hotel with vintage charm is set on a hilltop on the south coast of the island 3 miles east of the airport. Constructed on a small promontory, the complex captures the sea breezes at night, and you'll hear the rustling sound of wind blowing through the acres of tropical gardens. The **S** doorway to the Spanish stucco building is almost hidden by the foliage. The Grenadian-Iberian dining room and red-tile lounge has cozy nooks and original oil paintings. The dining room frames views of the beach and swimming pool, as well as of the gardens. Guests are so well coddled here that they keep returning to the appealing rooms furnished with antiques from old island-family houses.

A dozen accommodations are in six terra-cotta-roofed cottages. Each shares a kitchenette with its neighbor, and each has a canopied four-poster bed and a private terrace. In the main building are six suites, more modern in concept and slightly larger than the outlying cottages. The beach, where the hotel has scuba-diving facilities, requires a stroll down a carefully landscaped hillside.

BUDGET

LA SAGESSE NATURE CENTER, P.O. Box 44, St. David's, Grenada, W.I. Tel. 809/444-6458. Fax 809/444-4847. 3 apartments. MINIBAR TV TEL

$ Rates: Winter, $60 single; $70 double. Summer, $50 single; $60 double. Continental breakfast $3.70 extra. AE, MC, V. **Parking:** Free.

On a sandy, tree-lined beach 10 miles from Point Saline Airport, La Sagesse consists of a seaside guesthouse, restaurant, bar, and art and pottery gallery, with water sports and satellite TV. Nearby are trails for hiking and exploring the area, a haven for wading and shore birds, hummingbirds, hawks, and ducks. Rivers, mangroves, and a salt pond sanctuary enhance the natural beauty of the place. The original great house of what was once La Sagesse plantation contains three apartments, each with a fully equipped kitchen. The restaurant/bar specializes in lobster, fresh fish, and salads.

WHERE TO DINE

You may eat in most of the restaurants of the hotels previously described, but you should call first to make a reservation, as food supplies are often limited if the chef doesn't expect you. I've found hotel food better in Grenada than in the other British Windward Islands. Many of the chefs are European or European trained, and local cooks are also on hand to prepare Grenadian specialties, such as conch (called lambi here), lobster, callaloo soup (with greens and crab), conch-and-onion pie, and soursop or avocado ice cream.

Some 22 kinds of fish, including fresh tuna, dolphin, and barracuda, are caught off the island's shores. Most are good for eating. Naturally, the spices of the island, such as nutmeg, are used plentifully. The meals are often served family style in an open-air setting with a view of the sea.

EXPENSIVE

LA BELLE CREOLE, at Blue Horizons, Grand Anse Beach. Tel. 4316.
   Cuisine: CREOLE/SEAFOOD. **Reservations:** Required.
$ Prices: Appetizers EC$8–EC$15 ($2.95–$5.55); main courses EC$45–EC$60 ($16.65–$22.20); five-course dinner EC$80 ($29.60). AE, DC, MC, V.
   Open: Lunch daily 12:30–2pm; dinner daily 7–9pm.

One of the best restaurants in Grenada, a 5-minute walk from Grand Anse Beach, is run by Arnold and Royston Hopkin, sons of "Mama" Audrey Hopkin, long considered the best cook on the island if you're seeking West Indian specialties. Archways frame views of the mountains and the beach. The walls and ceilings are covered with a type of island reed called roseau (which, strangely enough, must be cut only during a certain phase of the moon to provide a durable, long-lasting building surface; if cut at any other time of the month, the covering, experience has taught, disintegrates into a powder within 6 months).

Lunch, which can be taken poolside, features soup and chicken, fish, or lobster salad. Dinner features a fixed-price menu, with a variety of choices from continental recipes with West Indian substitutions for ingredients not available on the island. A typical dinner might begin with dolphin (fish) mousse with callaloo, then conch chowder, followed by a main course such as Créole veal roll stuffed with ham, chicken livers, onions, and seasonings, baked in a wine sauce, and served with local vegetables such as a dasheen soufflé and christophines, along with candied plaintain. The meal might end with a "mango delight." Guests can also order à la carte.

SPICE ISLAND INN, Grand Anse Beach. Tel. 4258.
   Cuisine: CREOLE/SEAFOOD. **Reservations:** Required.
$ Prices: Appetizers EC$15–EC$30 ($5.55–$11.10); main courses EC$20–EC$50 ($7.40–$18.50); fixed-price dinner $35 U.S.; Fri barbecue or Sat seafood dinner $35 U.S. AE, MC, V.
   Open: Breakfast daily 7:30–10:30am; lunch daily 12:30–2:30pm; dinner daily 7:30–10pm.

A favorite way to enjoy a meal in Grenada is on an uncrowded beachfront in the full outdoors, with only a parapet over your head to protect you from sudden tropical showers. The parapet here, built of imported pine and cedar, looks like a Le Corbusier rooftop. At this inn, located directly north of the airport, the view is of one of the best beaches in the Caribbean, miles of white sand sprouting an occasional grove of sea grape or almond trees. You can eat lunch in a swimsuit. Dinner menus change frequently, and can be cooked to your specifications. Local seafood is featured on the constantly changing menu. On Friday it's barbecue night, and on Saturday it's seafood night.

MODERATE

BIRD'S NEST, Grand Anse. Tel. 4264.

Cuisine: CHINESE/CREOLE. **Reservations:** Recommended.

$ Prices: Appetizers EC$9.50–EC$12 ($3.50–$4.45); main courses EC$6–EC$60 ($2.20–$22.20). AE, MC, V.

Open: Mon–Sat 10:30am–11pm, Sun 6–11pm.

For change-of-pace dining, I suggest the Bird's Nest, in its own building with three palm trees at the entrance, opposite the Ramada Renaissance 3 miles north of the airport. This family business offers typical Chinese food, mainly Cantonese, along with Créole dishes. The most expensive main courses, of course, are those with a lobster base. You'll see the familiar shrimp eggrolls along with eight different chow meins. Sweet-and-sour fish is a favorite, and daily specials are posted. A take-out service is available.

COCONUT'S BEACH RESTAURANT, Grand Anse Beach. Tel. 4644.

Cuisine: FRENCH/CREOLE. **Reservations:** Recommended.

$ Prices: Appetizers EC$15–EC$20 ($5.55–$7.40); main courses EC$40–EC$55 ($14.80–$20.35). AE, MC, V.

Open: Lunch daily 10am–3pm; dinner daily 7–10pm; snacks daily 10am–10pm.

Closed: Mon in low season; May.

At the bottom of a bumpy, sloping road, Coconut's is actually more accessible by water than by land; many of the guests come from yachts moored offshore. The restaurant occupies a ramshackle house with clapboard siding and a green roof set directly on the beach about half a mile north of St. George's. In the dining room you can watch the chefs at work in the exposed kitchen. Meals might include Tahitian-style fish, the catch of the day with a variety of sauces, curried conch with bananas, several barbecue dishes, T-bone steak, grilled lobster, pizzas, lobster gratin, and fisherman's platter.

DELICIOUS LANDING, The Carenage, St. George's.

Cuisine: CREOLE/SEAFOOD. **Reservations:** Not required.

$ Prices: Appetizers EC$15–EC$20 ($5.55–$7.40); main courses EC$40–EC$55 ($14.80–$20.35). No credit cards.

Open: Lunch daily 10:30am–2pm; dinner daily 6:30–11:30pm; snacks daily 9:30am–midnight.

A popular restaurant at the entrance to the harbor, Delicious Landing is built on piers. Guests sit at tables supported by a mesh of beams, under a parapet of palm fronds. The setting is jauntily rickety and loaded with West Indian style. Some regular visitors argue that it offers one of the best views of whatever boat has just wandered into the harbor. The establishment is known for its soups, made with such ingredients as callaloo, pumpkin, conch, and pigeon peas. You can select from the seafood salads and dinners made of ocean denizens that are probably only hours away from the fishing vessel. The restaurant is known for its conch steaks, cinnamon-fried chicken, sirloin sukiyaki, and fish pando simmered in local herbs and spices. One of the side dishes is a cheese-laden vegetable specialty called Grumby. A favorite drink is a cinnamon daiquiri.

MORNE FENDUE, St. Patrick's. Tel. 9330.

Cuisine: CREOLE. **Reservations:** Required.

$ Prices: Fixed-price lunch EC$40 ($14.80).

Open: Lunch only, Mon–Sat 11:30am–3pm.

As you're touring north from the beach at Grand Anse and the capital at St. George's, one place is memorable. It's Betty Mascoll's Morne Fendue, 25 miles north of St. George's. This 1912 plantation house, constructed the year she was born, is her ancestral home. It was built of carefully chiseled river rocks held together with a mixture of lime and molasses, as was the custom in that day. Mrs. Mascoll and her loyal staff, two of whom have been with her for many, many years, always need time to prepare for the arrival of guests, so it's imperative to call ahead. Lunch is likely to include yam and sweet-potato casserole, curried pork with lots of hot spices, and a hotpot of pork and oxtail. Because this is very much a private home, tipping should be performed with the greatest tact. Nonetheless, the hard-working cook and maid seem genuinely appreciative of a gratuity. Mrs. Mascoll is known for introducing her house guests to her friends and neighbors on the long verandas beneath the hanging vines of her house.

THE NUTMEG, The Carenage, St. George's. Tel. 2539.
Cuisine: SEAFOOD. **Reservations:** Not required.
$ Prices: Appetizers EC$10–EC$15 ($3.70–$5.55); main courses EC$20–EC$45 ($7.40–$16.65). AE, MC, V.
Open: Mon–Sat 8am–11:30pm.

Right on the harbor, the Nutmeg is over the Sea Change Shop where you can pick up paperbacks and souvenirs. It's another rendezvous point for the yachting set and a favorite with just about everybody, both expatriates living on the island and visitors. It is suitable for a snack or a full-fledged dinner, and its drinks are very good. Try one of the Grenadian rum punches made with Angostura bitters, grated nutmeg, rum, lime juice, and syrup. An informal atmosphere prevails, as you're served your filet of fish with potato croquettes and string beans. There's always fresh fish, and usually callaloo soup, maybe lobster too. Lambi (that ubiquitous conch) is also done very well here. Lobster thermidor is the most expensive food item on the menu. There's a small wine list with some California, German, and Italian selections, and you can drop in for just a glass of beer to enjoy the sea view. Sometimes, however, you'll be asked to share a table.

THE RED CRAB, L'Anse aux Epines. Tel. 4424.
Cuisine: SEAFOOD. **Reservations:** Required in winter. **Transportation:** Taxi (a 5-minute ride from the Grand Anse Beach resorts).
$ Prices: Appetizers EC$10–EC$25 ($3.70–$9.25); main courses EC$25–EC$75 ($9.25–$27.75). AE, MC, V.
Open: Lunch Mon–Sat 11am–2pm; dinner Mon–Sat 6–10:30pm. **Closed:** Aug 15–Sept 15.

The Red Crab, popular with many Americans, is a favorite Grenadian luncheon spot, set out under the trees; however, I always like to come here in the evening. It's like an English pub in the mock-Tudor style. Before taking your order, one of the waiters will bring you a draft beer, and you can settle back to enjoy the classic fish and chips. The chef also does some of the best stuffed crab backs on the island, as well as savory seafood chowder, fried shrimp, and callaloo soup. Dessert may be blueberry pie à la mode.

RUDOLF'S, The Carenage, St. George's. Tel. 2241.
Cuisine: INTERNATIONAL. **Reservations:** Not required.
$ Prices: Appetizers EC$10–EC$14 ($3.70–$5.20); main courses EC$18–EC$45 ($6.65–$16.65). No credit cards.
Open: Daily 10am–midnight.

This long-established restaurant overlooks a deep, U-shaped inner harbor lined with commercial establishments in St. George's. Some people claim that this is the best place for dining on the entire island. On the north corner of the Carenage, it's also a good spot for drinks in the late afternoon if you want to join the yachting machismo set. If you stick around for dinner, you'll find that the food is well prepared, with more choices offered than in most places at Grenada. The menu includes about 13 different steak dishes, and if you're dining lighter, you're faced with a selection of some eight different omelets. Soups are both hot and cold, ranging from French onion to gazpacho. Try the lobster, fish, or conch. Specials are posted daily.

BUDGET

MAMMA'S, Lagoon Rd., St. George's. Tel. 1459.
   Cuisine: CREOLE. **Reservations:** Required a day in advance.
$ **Prices:** Fixed-price meals EC$45 ($16.65). No credit cards.
   Open: Dinner only, daily 8pm–midnight.

Mamma's lies on the road leading to Grenada Yacht Services. Every trip to the Caribbean should include a visit to an establishment like this. Serving copious meals, this Mamma became particularly famous during the U.S. intervention in Grenada, as U.S. servicepeople adopted her as their own island mama. Mamma (alias Insley Wardally) is now deceased, but her daughter, Cleo, carries on.

Meals, I was told, come in two sizes: "the usual" and "the special." (But I was later told that "the usual" and "the special" were the same.) Either way, meals include such dishes as callaloo soup with coconut cream, shredded cold crab with lime juice, freshwater crayfish, fried conch, and a casserole of cooked bananas, yams, and dasheen, along with ripe baked plantain, and tortillas made of curry and yellow chickpeas, followed by sugar-apple ice cream. The specialty drink of the house is rum punch, the ingredients of which are a secret. Dinner here must be reserved a day in advance so you'll be sure of having a choice of 26 to 30 different foods from Grenada.

PORTOFINO, The Carenage, St. George's. Tel. 3986.
   Cuisine: ITALIAN. **Reservations:** Recommended.
$ **Prices:** Appetizers EC$12–EC$15 ($4.45–$5.55); main courses EC$20–EC$52 ($7.40–$19.25). AE.
   Open: Mon–Fri 11am–11pm, Sat–Sun 6–10pm.

In the geographical center of town next door to the Ministry of Tourism, in a pleasant restaurant on the second floor of a waterfront building, this place offers a beautiful view of the inner harbor. The menu lists 10 varieties of pizza, costing EC$15 ($5.55) and up. Other offerings include eight types of spaghetti, different kinds of pasta, eggplant parmigiana, veal milanese, and lobster. There is also full take-out service.

WHAT TO SEE & DO
ST. GEORGE'S

The capital city of Grenada, St. George's is one of the most attractive ports in the West Indies. Its landlocked inner harbor is actually the deep crater of a long-dead volcano, or so one is told.

In the town you'll see some of the most charming Georgian colonial buildings to be found in the Caribbean, still standing in spite of a devastating hurricane in 1955. The streets are mostly steep and narrow, which enhances the attractiveness of the ballast bricks, wrought-iron balconies, and red tiles of the sloping roofs. Many of the pastel warehouses date back to the 18th century. Frangipani and flamboyant trees add to the palette of color.

The port, which some have compared to Portofino, Italy, is flanked by old forts and bold headlands. Among the town's attractions is an 18th-century, pink, Anglican **church,** on Church Street, and a **Market Square** where colorfully attired farm women offer even more colorful produce for sale.

   Fort George, on Church Street, built by the French, stands at the entrance to the bay, with subterranean passageways and old guardrooms and cells.

Everyone strolls along the waterfront of **The Carenage** or relaxes on its Pedestrian Plaza, with seats and hanging planters providing shade from the sun.

On this side of town, the **Grenada National Museum,** at the corner of Young Street and Monckton Street, is set in the foundations of an old French army barrack and prison built in 1704. Small but interesting, it houses finds from archeological digs, including the petroglyphs, native fauna, the first telegraph installed on the island, a rum still, and memorabilia depicting Grenada's history. The most comprehensive exhibit traces the native culture of Grenada. One of the exhibits shows two bathtubs—the wooden barrel used by the fort's prisoners and the carved marble tub used by Joséphine Bonaparte during her adolescence on Martinique. The museum is open Monday through Friday from 9am to 4pm. Admission is $1 for adults, 50¢ for children.

The Outer Harbour is also called the **Esplanade.** It's connected to the Carenage by the Sendall Tunnel, which is cut through the promontory known as St. George's Point, dividing the two bodies of water.

You can take a drive up to Richmond Hill where **Fort Frederick** stands. The French built this fort in 1779, but before they could finish it, British troops moved in; the English completed the structure in 1783. From its battlements you'll have a superb view of the harbor and of the yacht marina.

An afternoon tour of St. George's and its environs should take you into the mountains northeast of the capital. About a 15-minute drive takes you to ✪ **Annandale Falls,** a tropical wonderland, where a cascade about 50 feet high falls into a basin. The overall beauty is almost Tahitian, and you can have a picnic surrounded by liana vines, elephant ears, and other tropical flora and spices. The **Annandale Falls Centre** (tel. 2452) houses gift items, handcrafts, and samples of the indigenous spices of Grenada. Nearby, an improved trail leads to the falls where you can enjoy a refreshing swim. Swimmers can use the changing cubicles at the falls free. The center is open Monday through Friday from 8am to 4pm. Brochures on herbs and spices are available to guests upon arrival at the center.

In the center of the island, reached along the major interior road between Grenville and St. George's, is ✪ **Grand Etang National Park,** encompassing the island's spectacular rain forest, which has been made more accessible by hiking trails. Beginning at the park's forest center, the Morne LeBaye Trail affords a short hike along which you can see to the 2,309-foot Mount Sinai and the east coast. Down the Grand Etang Road trails lead to the 2,373-foot summit of Mount Qua Qua and the Ridge and Lake Circle Trail, taking hikers on a 30-minute trek along **Grand Etang Lake,** the crater of an extinct volcano lying in the midst of a forest preserve and bird sanctuary. Covering 13 acres, the water is a cobalt blue. All three trails offer the opportunity to see a wide variety of Grenada's flora and fauna. Guides for the park trails are available, but they must be arranged for in advance. The park's **Nature Centre** on the shores of Grand Etang Lake is open daily from 8am to 4pm, featuring a video show about the park. Phone 7425 for more information or to arrange for guided trail walks.

AROUND THE ISLAND

The next day you can head north out of St. George's along the western coast, taking in beaches, spice plantations, and the fishing villages that are so typical of Grenada.

You pass through **Gouyave,** a spice town, the center of the nutmeg and mace industry. Both spices are produces from a single fruit. Before reaching the village you can stop at the Dougaldston Estate where you'll witness the processing of nutmeg and mace.

At the **Grenada Cooperative Nutmeg Association,** near the entrance to Gouyave, huge quantities of the spice are aged, graded, and processed. Most of the work is done within the ochre walls of the factory, which sport such slogans as "Bring God's peace inside and leave the Devil's noise outside." Workers sit on stools in the natural light from the open windows of the aging factory and laboriously sort the raw nutmeg and its by-product, mace, into different baskets for grinding, peeling, and aging. It's open Monday through Friday from 9am to 4pm.

Proceeding along the coast, you reach **Sauteurs,** at the northern tip of Grenada. This is the third-largest town on the island. It was from this great cliff that the Caribs leaped to their deaths instead of facing enslavement by the French.

To the east of Sauteurs is the palm-lined **Levera Beach,** an idyll of sand where the Atlantic meets the Caribbean. This is a great spot for a picnic lunch, but swimming can sometimes be dangerous. On the distant horizon you'll see some of the Grenadines.

Heading down the east coast of Grenada, you reach **Grenville,** the island's second city. If possible, pass through here on a Sunday morning when you'll enjoy the hubbub of the native fruit-and-vegetable market. There is also a fish market along the waterfront. A nutmeg factory here welcomes visitors.

From Grenville, you can cut inland into the heart of Grenada. Here you're in a world of luxuriant foliage, passing along nutmeg, banana, and cocoa plantations up to Grand Etang, previously mentioned. You will then begin your descent from the mountains. Along the way you'll pass hanging carpets of mountain ferns. Going through the tiny hamlets of Snug Corner and Beaulieu, you eventually come back to the capital.

On yet another day, you can drive south from St. George's to the beaches and resorts spread along the already much-mentioned **Grand Anse,** which many people consider one of the most beautiful beaches in the West Indies. Water-taxis can also take you from the Carenage in St. George's to Grand Anse.

Point Saline, where the airport is now located, is at the southwestern tip of the island, where a lighthouse stood for 56 years. However, a sculpture of the lighthouse has been constructed on the grounds just outside the airport terminal building. A panoramic view ranging from the northwest side of Grenada to the green hills in the east to the undulating plains in the south can be seen from a nearby hill.

Along the way you'll pass through the village of **Woburn,** which was featured in the film *Island in the Sun,* and go through the sugar belt of **Woodlands,** with its tiny sugarcane factory.

SPORTS & RECREATION

BEACHES   One of the best beaches in the Caribbean is   ✪ **Grand Anse,** 3 miles of sugar-white sands extending into deep waters far offshore. Most of Grenada's best hotels are within walking distance of Grand Anse. You can also take off and discover dozens more beaches on your own, as they are all public.

BOAT EXCURSIONS   The *Rhum Runner* (tel. 2198), a metal-hulled catamaran with a parapet, moored at St. George's harbor, takes passengers on water tours for reef viewing, harbor trips, cocktail cruises, barbecue evenings, cruises up Grenada's coast, and all-you-can-drink punch cruises. Live, electronic, or steel-band music is offered. The cost is $20 per person.

Charters can be arranged by getting in touch with **Grenada Yacht Services,** Lagoon Road, St. George's (tel. 2508), a full-service yacht marina.

DEEP-SEA FISHING   Fisherfolk come here from November to March in pursuit of both blue and white marlin, yellowfin tuna, wahoo, sailfish, and other catches. Most of the bigger hotels have a sports desk which will arrange fishing trips for you. The **Annual Game Fishing Tournament,** held in January, attracts a number of regional and international participants.

GOLF   At the **Grenada Golf Course and Country Club,** Woodlands (tel. 4128), you'll find a nine-hole course, with greens fees of $8 for nine holes. The course is open Monday through Saturday from 8am to sunset and on Sunday from 8am to noon. From the course you'll have a view of both the Caribbean Sea and the Atlantic.

SCUBA DIVING & SNORKELING   Along with many other water sports, Grenada offers the diver an underwater world, rich in submarine gardens, exotic fish, and coral formations, sometimes with underwater visibility stretching to 120 feet. Off the coast is the wreck of the ocean liner *Bianca C,* which is nearly 600 feet long. Novice divers might want to stick to the west coast of Grenada, while more experienced divers might search out the sights along the rougher Atlantic side. *Warning:* Divers should know that Grenada doesn't have a decompression chamber for the relief of the bends. Should this happen to you, it would require an excruciatingly painful air trip to Trinidad.

Dive Grenada, in the Ramada Renaissance Hotel, Grand Anse Beach (tel. 4371, ext. 638), is directly on the beach. Considered the premier dive outfit on the island, it offers single dives for $37 or night dives for $40. A two-tank dive costs $60, and PADI instructors will offer an open-water certification program for $375 per person.

In addition, Dive Grenada is also the best center for water sports, offering snorkeling trips for $16 (1½ to 2 hours) or windsurfing with board rentals for $7 per half hour. Sunfish rentals cost $10 per half hour, and parasailing is $25 per run; waterskiing is $15 per run. Even deep-sea fishing arrangements can be made.

If you'd rather strike out on your own, take a drive to Woburn and negotiate with a fisherman for a ride to **Glovers Island,** an old whaling station, and snorkel away.

TENNIS   Tennis, like cricket and football, is a popular everyday sport in Grenada. Guests at the Secret Harbour, Ramada, Calabash Hotel, Coyaba Beach Resort, and Twelve Degrees North can avail themselves of those well-kept courts.

SAVVY SHOPPING

Everybody who visits Grenada comes home with a basket of spices, better than any you're likely to find in your local supermarket. These hand-woven panniers of palm leaf or straw are full of items grown on the island, including the inevitable nutmeg, as well as mace, cloves, cinnamon, bay leaf, vanilla, and ginger. The local stores also sell a lot of luxury-item imports, mainly from England, at prices that are almost (not quite) duty free.

Store hours, in general, are 8 to 11:45am and 1 to 3:45pm Monday through Saturday.

GIFT REMEMBERED, Cross St., St. George's. Tel. 2482.

In the center of town a block from the water, Gift Remembered sells handcrafts, straw articles, jewelry, stamps, film, postcards, books, and magazines.

HUGGINS, Grand Etang Rd. Tel. 2031.

Huggins deals in diamonds, precious stones, and gold and silver jewelry, plus china and crystal that includes such world-renowned names as Wedgwood, Aynsley, Blue Delft, Royal Doulton, Royal Brierley, Coalport, and Waterford. They also have such goods as designer sunglasses, scarves, and accessories.

IMAGINE, Grand Anse Shopping Centre. Tel. 4028.

Imagine offers an excellent line of Caribbean handcrafts in natural materials, including dolls, ceramics, straw items, clothing, and a good gift selection.

SPICE ISLAND PERFUMES LTD., The Carenage. Tel. 2006.

One of the most interesting shops in St. George's is this small store and workshop. It produces and sells perfumes, potpourri, and teas made from the locally grown flowers and spices. If you desire, they'll spray you with a number of desired scents, including island flower, spice, frangipani, jasmine, patchouli, and wild orchid. It's also the exclusive distributor in Grenada for Caribelle Batik items and Kokonuts T-shirts. The shop stands near the harbor entrance, close to the Tourist Board, post office, and public library. Open: Mon–Fri 8:30am–4:30pm, Sat 9am–noon.

TIKAL, Young St., St. George's. Tel. 2310.

This early 18th-century brick building is off the Carenage, next to the museum. You'll find a potpourri of tastefully chosen handcrafts from around the world as well as the finest crafts made in Grenada, including batiks, ceramics, wood carvings, paintings, straw work, and clothing.

YELLOW POUI ART GALLERY, Cross St., St. George's. Tel. 3001.

A 2-minute walk from Market Square, this is the most interesting shop for souvenirs and artistic items. Here you can see oil paintings and watercolors, sculpture, prints, rare antique maps, engravings, and woodcuts, with prices beginning at $10 and going up. There is also a comprehensive display of newly acquired works from

Grenada, the Caribbean area, and other sources, shown in three rooms. Open: Mon–Fri 8:30am–4pm, Sat 9am–noon.

EVENING ENTERTAINMENT

Regular evening entertainment is provided by the resort hotels and includes steel bands, calypso, reggae, folk dancing, and limbo, even crab racing. Ask at your hotel desk to find out what's happening at the time of your visit.

For those seeking culture, the 200-seat **Marryshow Folk Theatre,** Tyrell Street near Bain Alley, St. George's (tel. 2451), offers performances of Grenadian, American, and European folk music, drama, and West Indian interpretative folk dance. This is a project of the University of the West Indies School of Continuing Studies. Check with the Marryshow Theatre or the tourist office to see what's on. Tickets cost EC$15 to EC$20 ($5.55 to $7.40).

Jazz night is every Wednesday from 9pm to 1am at a small Grenadian-run inn, the **Village Hotel,** Montoo Road, St. George's (tel. 4097). It's about a block behind the Food Fair Supermarket, adjacent to the Grand Anse Beach. Call to make sure a program will be featured. Entrance is free.

The island's most popular disco is **Fantazia 2001,** in the Gem Apartments on Morne Rouge Beach (tel. 1189), which is open on Sunday, Wednesday, Friday, and Saturday from 9pm "until." Cover charges range from EC$10 to EC$20 ($3.70 to $7.40). Drinks begin at EC$8 ($2.95).

AN EXCURSION TO CARRIACOU

Largest of the Grenadines, Carriacou, "land of many reefs," is populated by about 8,000 inhabitants, mainly of African descent, who are scattered over its 13 square miles of mountains, plains, and white sand beaches. There's also a Scottish colony, and you'll see such names as MacFarland. In the hamlet of Windward, on the east coast, villagers of mixed Scottish and African descent carry on the tradition of building wooden schooners. Large skeletons of boats in various stages of readiness line the beach where workers labor with the most rudimentary of tools, building the West Indian trade schooner fleet. If you stop for a visit, a master boatbuilder will let you climb the ladder and peer inside the shell, and will explain which wood came from which island, and why the boat was designed in its particular way. Much of the population, according to reputation, is involved in smuggling. Otherwise, they are sailors, fisherfolk, shipwrights, and farmers.

GETTING THERE   Visitors arrive on the twice-weekly **produce and mail boats** from Grenada; the trip takes 5 hours (see "Getting There" in Section 4). Boat service other than this is provided by the *Alexia II* and *Adelaide B,* which leave Grenada on Wednesday and Saturday at 10am and arrive on Carriacou at 2pm. The Carriacou-Grenada voyage leaves at 10am on Monday and Thursday and reaches Grenada at 2pm. There is also the M.V. *Edna David,* which leaves Grenada on Sunday at 7am and arrives on Carriacou at 11am; it departs the island at 5pm and returns to Grenada at 7pm.

A far faster method of transport is on a nine-seat **plane,** which takes just 25 minutes from the Point Saline International Airport on Grenada to Carriacou's Lauriston Airport. For information on air service between Carriacou and Grenada, see "Local Air Services" in the "Getting Around" section on Grenada, above.

WHERE TO STAY & DINE

CARIBBEE INN AT PROSPECT, Prospect Cariacou, Grenada, W.I. Tel. 809/443-7380. Fax 809/443-7999. 8 rms, 2 suites.
$ Rates: Winter, $100 single or double; $130 suite. Summer, $90 single or double; $100 suite. MAP $32 per person extra. AE. **Parking:** Free.
Set in the rolling hills at the northern edge of the island, this inn stands on its own secluded cove with a view of a scattering of offshore islands. On the premises are a small library, a mini-menagerie of two donkeys and a handful of flying parrots, a

terrace bar, and a carefully cultivated garden. Each accommodation contains a private bathroom and a cooling system dominated by trade winds. The hotel's restaurant serves a combination of French and Créole cuisine (also to nonresidents who phone ahead) every evening at a single sitting, around 7pm, for a fixed price of around EC$75 ($27.75). Hiking, snorkeling, and boating are among the several popular daytime activities.

CASSADA BAY RESORT, Carriacou, Grenada, W.I. Tel. 809/443-7494. Fax 809/443-7672. 12 cabins. **Transportation:** Taxi (a 5-minute ride from the airport).

$ Rates: Winter, $65 single; $80 double. Summer, $55 single; $75 double. Continental breakfast EC$8–EC$20 ($2.95–$7.40). AE, MC, V. **Parking:** Free.
The Cassada Bay opened in 1988 on a site offering stunning views. Its accommodations of rough-cut timber, in 12 cabins of two units, have pine furniture, bedrooms, living rooms, baths, and verandas, plus maid service. The dining room serves traditional West Indian cuisine, and the resort has a bar. Water sports are available, with free ferry service to nearby islands for snorkeling, sunbathing, and exploring.

SILVER BEACH RESORT, Beauséjour Bay, Carriacou, Grenada, W.I. Tel. 809/443-7337, 212/545-8469 in New York City, or toll free 800/223-9815. Fax 809/443-7165. 10 rms, 6 cottages. **Transportation:** Taxi (a 5-minute ride north of the airport.

$ Rates: Winter, $80–$90 single or double; from $95 cottage. Summer, $65–$75 single or double; from $80 cottage. Continental breakfast $5. AE, MC, V. **Parking:** Free.
This small hotel is about a 5-minute walk north of Hillsborough on a mile-long white sand beach. Accommodations include spacious cottages, with bedrooms, living rooms, private baths, fully equipped kitchenettes, and patios; there are also bedrooms, each with a sea view from its own patio. The charges include gas, electricity, linen, cutlery, and crockery. The bar and dining pavilion is found between the cottages and the beach. At dinner you can sample some good Carriacouan dishes prepared by local cooks, including lobster, conch, and fresh fish. Locally grown vegetables and fruits are served. Fishing, snorkeling, scuba diving, windsurfing, and boating to nearby islands can be arranged, including trips to World's End Reef in the Tobago Cays. Tennis is also available.

WHAT TO SEE & DO

The best time to visit Carriacou is in August in time for its **regatta,** which was begun by J. Linton Rigg in 1965 with the work boats and schooners, for which the Grenadines are famous. Now work boats, three-masted schooners, and miniature "sailboats" propelled by hand join the festivities. Banana boats docking at the pier are filled with people rather than bananas, and sailors from Bequia and Union Island camp on tiny Jack-a-Dan and Sandy Isle, only 20 minutes away by outboard motor from Hillsborough. The people of the Grenadines try their luck at the greased pole, foot races, and of course the sailing races. Music fills the air day and night, and impromptu parties are held. At the 3-day celebration, Big Drum dancers perform in the Market Square.

The **Big Drum dance** is part of the heritage of Carriacou brought from Africa and nurtured here more purely than perhaps on any other Caribbean island. The "Go Tambo," or Big Drum, is an integral part of such traditional events as stone feasts (marking the setting of a tombstone) and the accompanying rites. The feast, called saraca, and setting of the tombstone may be as long as 20 years after a death. Another event involving the Big Drum and saracas is the *maroon.* This can involve a dream interpretation, but it seems actually to be just a regular festivity, held in various places during the dry season, with dancing and feasting. Boat launching may also be accompanied by the Big Drum and the saraca and usually draws crowds of participants.

The **Carriacou Parang Festival** is usually held on the weekend closest to

December 25. The festival serves to maintain the indigenous culture of the people of Carriacou. Bands are formed out of guitar, cuatro, bass drum, and violin. No electronics are needed.

Hillsborough is the chief port and administrative center, handling the commerce of the little island, which is based mainly on growing limes and cotton. The capital bustles on Monday when the produce arrives, then settles down again until "mail day" on Saturday. The capital is nestled in a mile-long crescent of white sand.

The **Carriacou Museum** has a carefully selected display of Amerindian artifacts, European china and glass shards, and exhibits of African culture. In two small rooms it preserves Carriacou's history, which parallels that of its neighbor island, Grenada.

Also in Carriacou is the **Sea Life Centre,** created by the North American Environmental Research Products organization and designed to educate both the islanders and visitors about sea life, especially the lambi (conch) and turtle. It features native paintings of fishermen at work, drawings of the life cycles of the sea's inhabitants, and microscopes and incubators set up for visitors to view the baby lambi and turtles that the center breeds.

PETIT MARTINIQUE

The only inhabited one of Carriacou's offshore islands, and also the largest, is 486-acre Petit (pronounced "pitty") Martinique, with a population of about 600. The chief occupation is listed as building and sailing fishing boats, but it's also infamous as the center of the smuggling trade among the islands. Cigarettes and liquor from St. Barts' and St. Maarten's duty-free ports are popular smuggled goods.

BARBADOS

In the 19th century Barbados became famous as "the sanatorium of the West Indies," attracting mainly British guests suffering from "the vapors" who came here for the perfect climate and the relaxed, unhurried life.

In 1751 Maj. George Washington visited Barbados with his half-brother Maj. Lawrence Washington, who had developed tuberculosis. Regrettably, the future American president contracted smallpox here, which left him marked for life. Barbados is said to have been the only place outside what is now the United States that George Washington ever visited.

The smallpox danger long gone, Barbados still remains salubrious to the spirit, with its mixture of coral and lush vegetation, along with seemingly endless miles of pink and white sandy beaches. The most easterly of the long chain of Caribbean islands, it still retains its old-world charm, an imprint of grace and courtesy left over from 300 years of British tradition.

Barbados is renowned for its hospitable people and for having the oldest parliament in the western hemisphere, with a British heritage unbroken since the first landing by Englishmen in 1625 until its independence in 1966. The 350th anniversary of the Barbados parliament was celebrated in 1989. Barbados is an independent sovereign state within the Commonwealth of Nations, of which Queen Elizabeth II is the symbolic head. And Barbados is one Caribbean island that was not explored by Columbus.

In a way, Barbados is like an England in the tropics, with its bandbox cottages with neat little gardens, its centuries-old parish churches, and a scenic, hilly district in the northeast known as "the Scotland District," where a mist rises in the morning. Narrow roads ramble through the green sugarcane fields trimmed in hedgerows. Sugar is king, and rum is queen.

The first known inhabitants of Barbados were the Arawaks, who came over from South America. But they were gone by the time of the first British expedition in 1625. Two years later Capt. John Powell returned to colonize the island with 80 settlers who arrived at Jamestown (later renamed Holetown).

A thriving colony of Europeans and African slaves turned Barbados into a prosperous land, based on trading in tobacco and cotton and, by 1640, sugarcane. More and more slaves were imported to work these sugar plantations.

Many English families settled here in the 18th and 19th centuries, in spite of the usual plagues (like yellow fever) and the intermittent wars. Because of the early importation of so many slaves, Barbados is the most densely populated per square mile of the West Indian islands, numbering some 258,000 people.

Once Barbados was the most heavily defended fortress island in the Caribbean, as 26 forts ran along its 21 miles of sheltered coast. Perhaps for that reason, the island was never invaded. Slavery was abolished in 1834, and independence within the Commonwealth was obtained in 1966.

WHAT'S SPECIAL ABOUT BARBADOS

Beaches
- ☐ The white sandy beaches, among the most beautiful in the Caribbean (all open to the public), start in the north at Heywoods—about a mile of sand—and stretch almost unbroken to Brighton Beach, a local favorite in the south.
- ☐ Needham's Point, with a lighthouse, the best of the heavily built-up south-coast beaches.

Great Towns/Villages
- ☐ Bridgetown, the island capital, with colonial buildings, modern offices, and a statue of Horatio, Lord Nelson.
- ☐ Holetown, a small old St. James coast village that's the site of the first settlement—the *Olive Blossom* landed here on May 14, 1625, and claimed the island in the name of King James of England.

Ace Attractions
- ☐ The Gold Coast, a nickname for the gilded shoreline of St. Peter and St. James, site of the posh hotels and homes of the wintering wealthy.

- ☐ Harrison's Cave, magnificent caverns graced with underground pools, waterfalls, and streams, and an array of crystal chambers.
- ☐ Barbados Wildlife Reserve, home of the rare green monkey, believed to have been imported from West Africa 300 years ago, plus deer, exotic birdlife, and tortoises.

Parks and Gardens
- ☐ Farley Hill, a national park, rich with exotic planting, dedicated by Queen Elizabeth II.
- ☐ Andromeda Tropical Gardens, visited for its terraces of lush tropical plants gathered from all over the world.

Ancient Monuments
- ☐ St. Nicholas Abbey, near Cherry Tree Hill, the oldest guesthouse on Barbados (circa 1650), noted for its Jacobean architecture and antiques.

A coral island, Barbados is flat compared to the wild, volcanic terrain of the Antilles. It is 21 miles long and 14 miles wide. Barbados lies 200 miles from Trinidad. Most of its hotels are on the western side, a sandy shoreline. The eastern side, fronting the Atlantic, is a breezy coastline with white-capped rollers. Experienced surfers like it, but it's not safe for amateur swimmers.

It's a land of hills and dales, limousines (carrying such residents as Claudette Colbert) and donkey carts. You won't find mountains, though; the highest point is Mount Hillaby, at 1,115 feet.

ORIENTATION

GETTING THERE More than 20 daily flights arrive on Barbados from all over the world. Grantley Adams International Airport is on Highway 7, on the southern tip of the island at Long Bay, between Oistins and The Crane (a village). From North America, the four major gateways to Barbados are New York, Miami, Toronto, and San Juan. Flying time to Barbados from New York is 4½ hours, from Miami it's 3½ hours, from Toronto it's 5 hours, and from San Juan 1½ hours.

American Airlines (tel. toll free 800/433-7300) has dozens of connections that pass through San Juan, Puerto Rico. From Puerto Rico, two daily nonstop flights depart for Barbados, at 1:27pm and 9:30pm. On the return trip, clients can usually speed through Customs clearance in San Juan, rather than in their home cities, which usually saves time and inconvenience.

Residents of New York and Miami can opt for nonstop flights offered daily from both of those cities by **BWIA** (tel. toll free 800/327-7401), the national airline of Trinidad and Tobago. BWIA also offers many different flights from Barbados into Trinidad, its country of origin.

Air Canada (tel. toll free 800/422-6232) has flights to Barbados that depart from Toronto between one and four times a week, depending on the season. Some of these are nonstop, although several require a connection in Antigua.

Barbados is a major hub of the Caribbean-based airline known as **LIAT (Leeward Islands Air Transport)** (tel. 809/436-6224 for reservations, or 809/428-0986 at the Barbados airport), which provides service from Barbados to a handful of neighboring islands, including St. Vincent and the Grenadines.

British Airways (tel. toll free 800/247-9297) offers nonstop service to Barbados from both London's major airports (Heathrow and Gatwick). Two of the airline's flights from London are on the world-famous supersonic Concorde, which makes a 50-minute stop in Lisbon, Portugal, before continuing on at more than twice the speed of sound into Barbados.

GETTING AROUND   By Bus   Unlike most of the British Windwards, Barbados has a reliable bus system fanning out from Bridgetown to almost every part of the island. On most major routes there are buses running every 15 minutes or so. Bus fares are $1.50 BDS (75¢) wherever you go. Exact change is required.

The nationally owned **buses** of Barbados are blue with yellow stripes. They are not numbered, but their destinations are marked on the front. Departures are from Bridgetown, leaving from Fairchild Street for the south and east; from Lower Green and the Princess Alice Highway for the north going along the west coast. Call 436-6820 for bus schedules and information.

Privately operated **minibuses** run shorter distances and travel more frequently. They are bright yellow, with their destinations displayed on the bottom left corner of the windshield. Minibuses in Bridgetown are boarded at River Road, Temple Yard, and Probyn Street. They, too, cost $1.50 BDS (75¢).

By Taxi   Typical of this part of the world, taxis aren't metered, but their rates are fixed by the government. Taxis on the island are identified by the letter Z on the license plates. One to five passengers can be transported at the same time, and can share the fare. Overcharging is infrequent; most drivers have a reputation for courtesy and honesty. Taxis are plentiful, and drivers will produce a list of standard rates.

From Grantley Adams International Airport, it costs about $25 to be driven by taxi to most hotels along the west coast, and about $15 to be taken to a south-coast destination.

For 24-hour taxi service, call **A A Taxi Service,** Broad Street, Bridgetown (tel. 426-3212).

By Rental Car   If you don't mind *driving on the left,* you may find a rental car ideal for a Bajan holiday. A temporary permit is needed if you don't have an International Driver's License. The rental agencies listed below will all issue you a visitor's permit or you can go to the police desk upon your arrival at the airport. You're charged a registration fee of $10 BDS ($5), and you must have your own license. The speed limit is 20 miles per hour inside city limits, 30 m.p.h. elsewhere on the island.

None of the major U.S.-based car-rental companies maintain affiliates in Barbados, but a host of well-managed local companies work hard to fill the need of the island's car-renting public. Except in the peak of the midwinter season, cars are usually readily available without a prior reservation. Consequently, most visitors wait until their arrival before making arrangements for a rental car.

Because of the complicated navigation of Bajan roads, most renters pay for a taxi

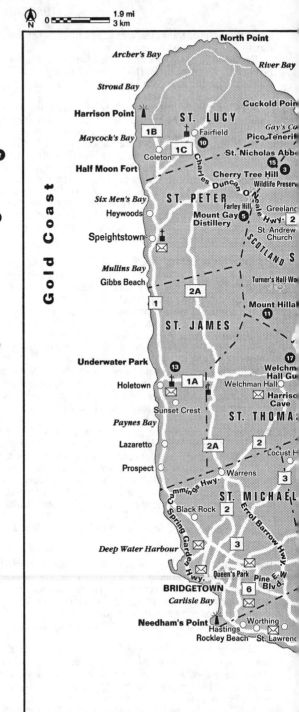

BARBADOS

Morgan Lewis Beach

Green Pond

Morgan Lewis
Sugar Windmill
Long Pond

Atlantic Ocean

⊠ Barclay's Park

ANDREW
Chalky Mount Potteries

Chalky Mount ②

DISTRICT

Tower Forest

Tent Bay ①

East Coast Road

Bathsheba

Andromeda Gardens

ST. JOSEPH

Martin's Bay

3A

Hackleton's Cliff

✝ ⑭ **Congor Rocks**

3

⊠ Blackmans

Consett Bay

ST. JOHN

④

3B

🐚 **Culpepper Island**

🔦 **Ragged Point
Lighthouse**

Gun Hill Signal Station

Three Houses

Kitridge Point

T. GEORGE

Bushy Park

Sandford

Bottom Bay

4

4B

ST. PHILIP

5

⑫

⊠ ⑯

Marchfield   Long Bay

5

Beachy Head

Crane Beach

7

CHRIST CHURCH

6

Tom Adams Hwy.

✈ ⊠

Maxwell

✝ 7

Grantley Adams Int'l Airport

⊠

Oistin

Long Bay

🔦

South Point

Lighthouse 🔦

Airport ✈

Church ✝

Post Office ⊠

from the airport to their hotel and then call for the delivery of a rental car. This is especially advisable because of the delay that is sometimes experienced waiting for a rental car to become available upon your arrival at the Barbados airport.

The island's most frequently recommended car-rental firm is **National Car Rental,** Bush Hall, Main Road, St. Michael (tel. 426-0603), which offers a wide selection of Mokes and well-maintained cars. Located near the island's national stadium (the only one on the island), it lies 3 miles northeast of Bridgetown. Maintaining an all-Japanese fleet, they charge $100 BDS to $130 BDS ($50 to $65) per day for everything from open-sided fun cars to more luxurious cars with automatic transmission and air conditioning. No taxes apply to car rentals in Barbados. Extra insurance coverage, however, is recommended, at a cost of $10 BDS ($5) per day, which reduces the responsibility of any renter to only $250 BDS ($125) in the event of an accident. Cars will be delivered to any location on the island upon request, and the driver who delivers it will carry the necessary forms for the issuance of the Bajan driver's license. This company is not affiliated in any way with the car-rental giant with the same name operating in the U.S.

Other frequently recommended companies operating on Barbados, which charge approximately the same prices and offer approximately the same services, include **Direct Rentals, Inc.** (tel. 428-3133), **Corbin's Garage** (tel. 427-9531), and **Drive-a-Matic, Inc.** (tel. 422-5017). One company which seems convenient to hotels on the remote southeastern end of Barbados is **Stout's Car Rentals,** Kirtons, St. Philip (tel. 435-4456). Set closer to the airport than any of its competitors, it can theoretically deliver a car to the airport within 10 minutes of any telephone call placed after a visitor's arrival. As at most of its colleagues, Stout's rents from an all-Japanese inventory, and also offers a handful of Portuguese-manufactured Mini-Mokes.

By Scooter or Bicycle The best place in Barbados for the rental of small machines to move you around is **Fun Seekers, Inc., Motorscooter and Bicycle Rental,** Rockley Main Road, Christchurch (tel. 435-8206). Located on the coastal road about 2 miles southeast of Bridgetown, it rents Honda motorscooters and big-wheeled, single-speed bicycles, and offers detailed maps and recommended scenic itineraries free. A deposit of $100 or $50 U.S. is required for rentals of scooters and bicycles, respectively. Two-seater motorcycles rent for $58 BDS ($29) per day, one-seaters are $32 BDS ($16) per day, and bicycles go for $19 BDS ($9.50) per day. Discounts are offered for 7-day rentals. Rental of a motorscooter requires the presentation of a valid driver's license issued from your state or country of residence, and the issuance (by Funseeker's) of a Barbadian driver's license, priced at $10 BDS ($5). In addition to bike and scooter rentals, the company also arranges day cruises on a pair of well-maintained boats.

By Sightseeing Tour Nearly all Bajan taxi drivers are familiar with the entire island, and usually like to show it off to visitors. If you can afford it, touring by taxi is far more relaxing than—and preferable to—taking one of the standardized bus tours. A 6-hour tour of the island costs about $80 to $90 U.S. for a party of up to four people.

One company which offers an unusual alternative to the usual taxi tour of the island is **Fun Seeker's, Inc.,** Rockley Main Road, Christchurch (tel. 435-8206). Mentioned earlier for their motorscooter and bike rentals, and also for their half-day and evening cruises, they offer a comprehensive land and sea tour called "The Best of Both." Their minivans collect participants at most of the island's hotels, then carry a maximum of 14 guests on a 6-hour experience which combines a 2½-hour island tour, with lunch at one of Bridgetown's most charming restaurants. This is followed with a 2½-hour cruise (with drinks and snorkeling gear provided) on a classically elegant 44-foot CSY yacht named *Limbo Lady.* The all-inclusive price for this sea-and-land tour is $100 BDS ($50). Patrick Gonsalves (a former resident of Florida) is the skipper, who usually ensures the easy transmission of both island information and a good time.

BARBADOS

American Express   The island's American Express affiliate is **Barbados International Travel Services, Inc.,** Horizon House, McGregor Street (P.O. Box 605C), Bridgetown, Barbados, W.I. (tel. 809/431-2423), located in the heart of Bridgetown.

Area Code   To phone Barbados from mainland North America, dial area code 809 and the seven-digit local number.

Bookstores   The island's best bookstore is **Cloister Bookstore Ltd.,** Hincks Street (tel. 426-2662). It carries a full line of travel, history, textbook, and resources on island lore. Its major competitor is **A. S. Bryden & Sons Ltd.** (better known simply as Bryden's), Victoria Street at Bolton Lane (tel. 431-2600).

Business Hours   Most **banks** in Barbados are open Monday through Thursday from 9am to 3pm and on Friday from 9am to 1pm and 3 to 5pm. **Stores** are open Monday through Friday from 8am to 4pm and on Saturday from 8am to noon. Most **government offices** are open Monday through Friday from 8:30am to 4:30pm.

Consulate   You can contact the following: the **U.S. Consulate,** first floor, Trident House, Bridgetown (tel. 436-4950); the **Canadian High Commission,** Bishop Court, Hill Pine Road (tel. 429-3550); and the **British High Commission,** Lower Collymore Rock, St. Michael (tel. 436-6694).

Currency   The **Barbados dollar (BDS)** is the official currency, available in $100, $20, $10, and $5 notes, as well as $1, 25¢, and 10¢ silver coins, plus 5¢ and 1¢ copper coins. The Bajan dollar is worth 50¢ in U.S. currency. *Note:* Unless otherwise specified, currency quotations in this chapter are in U.S. dollars. Most stores take traveler's checks or U.S. dollars. However, it's best to convert your money at banks and pay in Bajan dollars.

Dentist   Because of the density of its population, Barbados might have more dentists than any other Caribbean island. One who is particularly well recommended is **Dr. Derek Golding,** who, with two other colleagues, maintains one of the busiest practices in Barbados. Located at the Beckwith Shopping Mall in Bridgetown (tel. 426-3001), he accepts most of the emergency dental problems from the many cruise ships that dock in the waters off Barbados. This practice will accept any emergency and often remains open late for last-minute problems. All members of this dental team received their training in the U.S., Britain, Canada, or New Zealand.

Doctor   Take your pick—there are dozens on Barbados. Your hotel might have a list of doctors on call, although some of the best recommended are **Dr. J. D. Gibling** (tel. 432-1772), and **Dr. Adrian Lorde** or his colleague Dr. Ahmed Mohamad (tel. 424-8236), any of whom will pay house calls to patients unable or unwilling to leave their hotel rooms.

Documents   A U.S. citizen coming directly from America to Barbados for a period not exceeding 3 months must have proof of identity and national status, such as an original birth certificate, citizenship papers, a driver's license with photograph, university or school ID card with photograph, job ID with photograph, or senior-citizen card with photograph. For longer than 3 months, a passport is required. An ongoing or return ticket is also necessary.

Electricity   The electricity is 110 volts AC, 50 cycles, so at most establishments recommended you can use your U.S.-made appliances.

Emergencies   In an emergency, call **119.** Other important numbers include the **police** at 112, the **fire** department at 113, and an **ambulance** at 61113.

Holidays   Public holidays are January 1, January 21, Good Friday, Easter Monday, May 1 (May Day), Whit Monday (7 weeks after Easter), Kadooment Day (first Monday in August), United Nations Day (first Monday in October), Independence Day (November 30), Christmas Day (December 25), and Boxing Day (December 26).

Hospitals   A 600-bed facility, the **Queen Elizabeth Hospital** (tel. 436-

6450), is in Bridgetown. There are several private clinics as well, one of the most expensive and best recommended of which is the **Bayview Hospital**, St. Paul's Avenue, Bayville, St. Michael (tel. 436-5446).

Information The **Barbados Board of Tourism** is on Harbour Road (P.O. Box 242), Bridgetown, Barbados, W.I. (tel. 809/427-2623), which you can call or write for information. In the United States, you can obtain information before you go at the following offices: 800 Second Ave., New York, NY 10017 (tel. 212/986-6516), or 3440 Wilshire Blvd., Suite 1215, Los Angeles, CA 90010 (tel. 213/380-2198); the toll-free number is 800/221-9831. In Canada, offices are at Suite 1508, Box 11, 20 Queen St., Toronto, ON M5H 3R3 (tel. 416/979-2137), or 615 Dorchester Blvd. W., Suite 960, Montréal, PQ H3B 1P5 (tel. 514/861-0085).

Language The Barbadians, or Bajans, as they're called, speak English, but with their own island lilt.

Mail Most hotel desks can attend to your mailing. Otherwise, the Main Post Office is at Cheapside, St. Michael's (tel. 436-4800), on the outskirts of Bridgetown.

Safety The people of Barbados seem to know that much of the island's livelihood depends on the goodwill of its tourists (the mainstay of its economy), so crimes against visitors are rare. However, purse-snatching and pickpocketing have been reported in the capital of Bridgetown, so take precautions. You might be annoyed by the unwanted attention you get from various hawkers and peddlers on the beach. A firm and resounding "No!" should get rid of them. In any case, safeguard your possessions and never leave them unguarded on the beach.

Taxes and Service When you leave, you'll have to pay a $25 BDS ($12.50) departure tax. When you go to pay your hotel bill, you'll find you've been charged a 5% government sales tax. And while I'm on the subject, most hotels and restaurants add at least a 10% service charge to your bill.

Telecommunications You should have no trouble with telecommunications out of Barbados. Telegrams may be sent at your hotel front desk or at the Barbados External Telecommunications Ltd. office, The Wharf, Bridgetown, which is open Monday through Friday from 8am to 5pm and on Saturday from 8am to 1pm. International telephone, fax, Telex, and data-access services are also available.

Water Barbados has a pure water supply. It's pumped from underground sources in the coral rock, which covers six-sevenths of the island, and it's safe to drink.

Weather Daytime temperatures are in the 75° to 85° Fahrenheit range throughout the year.

1. WHERE TO STAY

Per square inch, Barbados has the best hotels in the West Indies. Many are small and personally run, with a quiet, restrained dignity. Most of my recommendations are sited on St. James Beach, the fashionable sector. However, you'll have to head south from Bridgetown to such places as Hastings and Worthing for the best bargains, often in self-contained efficiencies or studio apartments where you can do your own cooking.

Here's the bad news: Because of Barbados's long and continuing popularity, nowadays with back-to-back charter groups, these hotels often are extremely expensive in high season. Many hotels will also insist that you take two meals at their establishments if you're there in the winter.

However, Barbados has some very good bargains, and I've surveyed the best of these as well.

Prices cited in this section, unless otherwise indicated, are in U.S. dollars.

ON THE WEST COAST

VERY EXPENSIVE

COBBLERS COVE HOTEL, Road View, St. Peter, Barbados, W.I. Tel. 809/422-2291. Fax 809/422-1460. 39 suites. A/C MINIBAR TEL

$ **Rates** (including MAP): Winter, $530–$660 double; $1,200 Camelot Suite for two. Summer, $260–$310 double; $540 Camelot suite for two. AE, MC, V. **Closed:** Late Aug to late Sept. **Parking:** Free.

Considered one of the small, exclusive hotels of Barbados, Cobblers Cove grew out of a beachfront mansion built like a fort—with crenellations in a mock-medieval style. The home, now a Relais & Châteaux, was erected over the site of a former British fort which used to protect vessels going into the harbor at nearby Speightstown, a 10-minute walk away. Today, after an exhaustive overhaul, the hotel is a favorite honeymoon retreat offering first-class suites in a phalanx of 10 Iberian-style villas placed throughout the gardens.

Overlooking a white sand beach, each unit has a spacious living room, private balcony or patio, and a kitchenette. One of the most exclusive accommodations you can rent in all of Barbados is the Camelot Suite on the rooftop of the original mansion. It's beautifully decorated and offers panoramic views of both the beach and the garden. Meals can be delivered to your suite, reheated in the kitchenette, and consumed in privacy. The resort contains many acres of well-developed tropical gardens and lawns, including coconut palms and flowering shrubbery.

Dining/Entertainment: The open-air, shingle-roofed dining room overlooks the sea. Nearby is the resort's social center, its bar.

Services: Laundry, baby-sitting, arrangements for island tours.

Facilities: Tennis court, swimming pool, water sports (including waterskiing, Sunfish sailing, snorkeling, glass-bottomed-boat rides, and windsurfing).

COLONY CLUB, Porters, St. James Beach (P.O. Box 429, Bridge-town), Barbados, W.I. Tel. 809/422-2335. Fax 809/422-1726. 76 rms. A/C TEL

$ **Rates** (including MAP): Winter, $250–$335 single; $290–$425 double. Summer, $140–$180 single; $180–$235 double. Service and taxes extra. AE, DC, MC, V. **Parking:** Free.

Originally established by an English expatriate in the 1950s, and today a charter member of a British-owned hotel chain based in Barbados, this establishment is considered one of the well-respected and discreetly elegant hotels of the island's western coast. Set behind an impressive entrance lined with Australian pines, it's defined more as a "residential club" than a traditional hotel. It occupies an enviable site a mile north of Holetown beside one of the island's best-known beaches. An elegant feeling still prevails, even though the Colony has grown from a small "English country house party"–type establishment to a complex of carefully maintained rooms that look out over shaded verandas and handsomely landscaped grounds. About a third of the establishment's rooms lie beside the sea; the others are scattered throughout the gardens. All units have private patios. Accommodations are clustered in two- and three-story Mediterranean-style bungalows with red-tile roofs. Sliding glass doors open onto sun terraces.

Dining/Entertainment: Both continental and West Indian specialties are served on a covered terrace. The club's barbecues are well known here, and deservedly so. Entertainment, such as calypso, limbo, and dancing to a combo, is provided several nights a week. At least one of the establishment's two bars remains open throughout most of the day until late at night.

Services: Room service (7:30am–9:30pm), laundry, baby-sitting, arrangements for outings and excursions.

Facilities: Freshwater swimming pool, sailboat (Sunfish and catamaran) rentals, waterskiing, snorkeling, access to nearby tennis courts.

THE
CARIBBEAN
ISLANDS

BARBADOS

Atlantis Hotel **27**
Bagshot House Hotel **23**
Barbados Hilton
    International **16**
Casuarina Beach Club **24**
Cobbler's Cove Hotel **2**
Coconut Creek Club **10**
Colony Club **3**
Coral Reef Club **8** **6**
Cunard Paradise Village **15**
Divi Southwinds **20**
Fairholme **25**
Glitter Bay **4**
Grand Barbados Beach
    Resort **17**
Heywoods **1**
Kingsley Club **28**
Marriott's Sam
    Lord's Castle **26**
Ocean View **18**
Royal Pavillion **5**
Sandpiper Inn **9**
Sandy Lane **11**
Sandy Beach **21**
Settler's Beach **7**
Southern Palms **22**
Tamarind Cove **14**
Traveller's Palm **13**
Treasure Beach **12**
Woodville Beach
    Apartments **19**

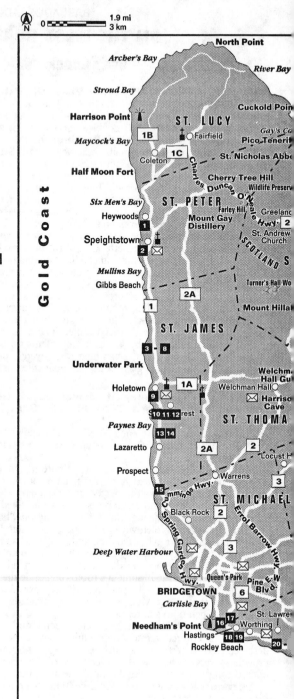

Gold Coast

North Point

Archer's Bay

River Bay

Stroud Bay

Cuckold Poin

Harrison Point

ST. LUCY

Gay's Co

1B   Fairfield   Pico Teneri

Maycock's Bay

1C   St. Nicholas Abbe

Coleton

Half Moon Fort

Cherry Tree Hill
                        Wildlife Preserv

Six Men's Bay   ST. PETER   Farley Hill   Greenlan

Heywoods   Mount Gay   Hwy. **2**
                            Distillery
1   St. Andrew
                                         Church
Speightstown

2 ✉

Mullins Bay

Gibbs Beach

2A

Turner's Hall Wo

1

Mount Hilla

ST. JAMES

3 - **8**

Underwater Park   Welchm
                                         Hall Gu
Holetown   **1A**   Welchman Hall
       9 ✉   ✉ Harriso
       10 **11** **12** rest   Cave

                            ST. THOMA

Paynes Bay
       13 **14**

Lazaretto   **2A**   **2**

Prospect   Locust H
          Warrens
15   **3**
     Cummins Hwy.
                    ST. MICHAEL
     Black Rock **2**

Deep Water Harbour   **3**

                    ✉
        ✉ Queen's Park   Pine E-W
                                    Blvd.
BRIDGETOWN   **6**
    Carlisle Bay

Needham's Point **16** **17**   St. Lawre
    Hastings   Worthing
              18 **19**
    Rockley Beach   **20**

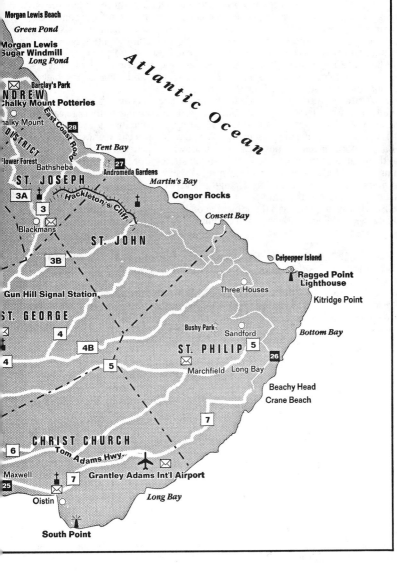

Morgan Lewis Beach

Green Pond

Morgan Lewis
Sugar Windmill

Long Pond

Barclay's Park

NDREW

Chalky Mount Potteries

alky Mount

DISTRICT

East Coast Road

28

Tent Bay

Flower Forest

Bathsheba

Andromeda Gardens

27

ST. JOSEPH

Martin's Bay

3A

Hackleton's Cliff

Congor Rocks

3

Consett Bay

Blackmans

ST. JOHN

Culpepper Island

3B

Ragged Point
Lighthouse

Gun Hill Signal Station

Three Houses

Kitridge Point

ST. GEORGE

Bushy Park

Sandford

Bottom Bay

4

4B

ST. PHILIP

5

4

5

Marchfield

Long Bay

26

Beachy Head

Crane Beach

7

CHRIST CHURCH

Tom Adams Hwy.

6

Maxwell

7

Grantley Adams Int'l Airport

25

Oistin

Long Bay

South Point

Atlantic Ocean

Lighthouse

Airport

Church

Post Office

GLITTER BAY, Porters, St. James, Barbados, W.I. Tel. 809/422-5555, or toll free 800/283-8666 in the U.S. Fax 809/422-3940. 83 suites. A/C MINIBAR TEL

$ Rates: Winter, $345–$365 double; $445–$525 suite for two; from $790 two-bedroom suites for four. Summer, $150–$215 single; $165–$300 double; $355–$515 two-bedroom suite for four. MAP $60 per person extra. Tax and service extra. AE, DC, MC, V. **Parking:** Free.

★ This carefully maintained resort has discreet charm and Mediterranean allure. Built in 1981 by a small Barbados-based hotel chain (the Pemberton Group), it lies on a 10-acre plot of manicured lowlands near a sandy beachfront a mile north of Holetown. Units are in a white mini-village of Iberian inspiration, whose patios, thick beams, and red terra-cotta tiles surround a garden whose centerpiece is a swimming pool, an artificial waterfall, and a simulated lagoon. Often the accommodations are privately owned by absentee investors, many of them British, who use them during annual holidays in Barbados; otherwise, they're available to renters. Most units contain unusual artworks, built-in furniture, louvered doors, and spacious outdoor patios or balconies ringed with shrubbery. The larger units contain small kitchenettes. All rooms are doubles, rented as singles in summer only, and some of the biggest accommodations are suitable for four or whose up to five people.

Dining/Entertainment: The establishment's social center is the Piperade Restaurant, beneath a terra-cotta roof amid a garden. Offering both classical and modern cuisine, along with West Indian specialties, it contains its own bar. On Monday a gala Bajan buffet is presented, and Friday is barbecue night. The Sunset Beach Bar is a popular rendezvous spot for a sundowner. Sheltered by shrubbery and tropical trees, guests can dance under the stars on an outdoor patio, and enjoy local entertainment, such as a steel band or calypso.

Services: Concierge (who can arrange island tours, car rentals, and almost anything else), laundry, baby-sitting.

Facilities: Two tennis courts (lit at night); complimentary water sports, including waterskiing, windsurfing, snorkeling, and catamaran sailing; golf and horseback riding can be arranged.

ROYAL PAVILLION, Porters, St. James, Barbados, W.I. Tel. 809/422-4444, or toll free 800/283-8666. Fax 809/422-3940. 75 suites, 3 suite-villas. A/C MINIBAR TEL

$ Rates: Winter, $345–$485 double; $790–$865 villa for four. Summer, $225–$290 double; $355–$515 villa for four. MAP $60 per person extra. Tax and service extra. No children under 12 in winter. AE, DC, MC, V. **Parking:** Free.

★ A spectacular place to stay, this Pemberton hotel a mile north of Holetown is next door to Glitter Bay, part of the same chain, and whose gardens it shares. The lush resort was built on the site of the former Miramar Hotel, whose walls were either completely demolished or radically redesigned in 1987 into a new pink-walled format with lily ponds and splashing fountains. British grace and Bajan hospitality blend happily in this aristocratic property, which became one of the finest resorts in Barbados the moment it opened. The architects created a California-hacienda style for their 75 waterfront junior suites and a villa consisting of three suites in 8 acres of beautifully landscaped gardens. TV is available in any room upon request. Guests staying here can visit the drinking, dining, and sports facilities at Glitter Bay (and vice versa).

Dining/Entertainment: There are two oceanfront restaurants. Tabora's serves breakfast and lunch. The more formal Palm Terrace, set below the seaside columns of an open-air loggia, is open only for dinner. Both restaurants offer an à la carte menu of Caribbean and international fare. The chef specializes in flambé dishes, and on Wednesday night in winter, an international buffet is presented.

Services: Concierge (who can arrange island tours, car rentals, and practically anything else), laundry, baby-sitting.

Facilities: Freshwater swimming pool, two tennis courts (complimentary for guests day and night), water-sports program (including complimentary snorkeling, waterskiing, sailing, and windsurfing), duty-free shops in the courtyard (including Cartier, Yves St. Laurent, and Ferrari), beauty shop and hairdresser.

SANDY LANE, St. James, Barbados, W.I. Tel. 809/432-1311, or toll free 800/225-5843 in the U.S. or Canada. Fax 809/432-2954. 97 rms, 24 suites. A/C MINIBAR TEL

$ Rates (including MAP): Winter, $600–$850 double; from $900 suite. Summer, $300–$800 double; from $490 suite. AE, DC, MC, V. **Parking:** Free.

Originally established in 1961, on the 380-acre site of a bankrupt sugar plantation less than a mile south of Holetown, this hotel once attracted many of the grandest names in Britain. In 1991, after a period of much-publicized decline, the hotel received a multi-million-dollar infusion of cash from the Forte chain, its present owners. Today the place represents luxury on an impressive and carefully orchestrated scale, with beautiful suites and rooms (all doubles), a private beach, and one of the most prestigious golf courses in Barbados. The swimming pool is surrounded by Italianate gardens, Roman fountains, and colonnaded verandas; the overall effect is one of Neo-Palladian grandeur. The buildings are made of cut coral, with shingle roofs, baronial arches, high ceilings, and a porte-cochère—in all, estatelike with tall gates, a driveway, and ornamental steps. All rooms and suites have refrigerators.

Dining/Entertainment: You can order a cool salad at the pool at lunch, and later enjoy a continental-inspired candlelight dinner. Buffet tables are frequent, as is regular native entertainment, such as calypso. You can also dine on Italian cuisine in the Seashell Restaurant, dress formally in black tie twice a week at the Sandy Bay Restaurant (the resort's culinary showcase), or munch on club sandwiches and hamburgers at either the Oasis Beach Bar or an informal bar/snack bar beside the golf course. Scattered in various corners of the place, you'll find five different bars. Live entertainment (usually from a dance band) is presented nightly, and a Bajan floorshow and cabaret is presented once a week.

Services: 24-hour room service, laundry and dry cleaning, concierge.

Facilities: 18-hole golf course, swimming pool, five all-weather tennis courts (two lit for night play), water sports (including scuba diving, windsurfing, sailboat rentals, and snorkeling), rentable bicycles.

SETTLERS BEACH, St. James, Barbados, W.I. Tel. 809/422-3052, or toll free 800/223-1108. Fax 809/223-1108. 22 villas. A/C TEL

$ Rates: Winter, $502 double; $552 triple; $602 quad. Summer, $452 double; $502 triple; $577 quad. Taxes and service extra. MAP $50 extra per adult, $25 extra per child under 12. AE, MC, V. **Parking:** Free. **Closed:** Sept.

This seaside collection of simple but comfortable villas is located on 4 acres of beachfront property 8 miles from Bridgetown, north of Holetown. Each apartment is self-contained, with two bedrooms, two bathrooms, a spacious tile-floored lounge and dining room, and a fully equipped kitchen. The apartments are decorated in sunny colors.

Dining/Entertainment: The square-roofed restaurant has won awards and is considered one of the finer ones on the island. A bar lies nearby.

Services: 24-hour room service, laundry, baby-sitting.

Facilities: Swimming pool, two tennis courts, sandy beach.

EXPENSIVE

CORAL REEF CLUB, St. James Beach, Barbados, W.I. Tel. 809/422-2372, or toll free 800/223-1108. Fax 809/422-1776. 4 rms, 75 luxury cottages. A/C TEL

$ Rates (including MAP): Winter, $230–$300 single; $360–$575 double. Summer, $133–$168 single; $233–$323 double. Taxes and service extra. AE, MC, V. **Parking:** Free.

The innkeepers of this Relais & Châteaux set standards that are hard for their competitors to attain, as this is one of the best and most respected establishments on the island. Set on elegantly landscaped and flat land beside the sea about a 5-minute drive north of Holetown, it devotes most of its efforts to maintaining a collection of veranda-fronted private cottages which surround a main building and clubhouse. This contains the reception area, a reading room, a dining area and bar, and a quartet of deluxe bedrooms on the second floor, which are the lowest prices quoted above. The cottages are scattered about a dozen handsomely landscaped acres, fronting a long strip of white sandy beach, ideal for swimming. Cottages open onto private patios, and some of the rooms have separate dressing rooms. Only a handful of the units contain private kitchens. The clientele is dignified but informal.

Dining/Entertainment: You can enjoy lunch in an open-air area. Dining and wining in the evening is in an attractive room overlooking the ocean. A first-class continental chef is in the kitchen. There's a weekly folklore show and barbecue every Thursday, and a Bajan buffet on Sunday evening, featuring a "Steamship Round of Beef," along with whole baked fish and lots of local entertainment.

Services: 24-hour room service, laundry, massage, a helpful reception staff.

Facilities: Freshwater swimming pool, tennis court, water sports (including windsurfing, snorkeling, scuba diving, and use of a minifleet of small sailboats).

SANDPIPER INN, Holetown, St. James, Barbados, W.I. Tel. 809/422-2251, or toll free 800/223-1108. Fax 809/223-1108. 24 rms, 22 suites. A/C MINIBAR TEL

$ Rates (including MAP): Winter, $320 single; $370 double; from $470 suite. Summer, $305 single; $340 double; from $440 suite. Taxes and service extra. AE, MC, V. **Parking:** Free.

The Sandpiper has more of a South Seas look than most of the hotels of Barbados. Affiliated with the also-recommended Coral Reef, it's a self-contained, intimate resort on the waterside, with a refreshing lack of pretense. The resort maintains a Bajan flavor and stands in a small grove of coconut palms and flowering trees right on the beach a 3-minute walk north of Holetown. This cluster of rustic-chic units surrounds the swimming pool, and some have a fine sea view. The rooms open onto little terraces that stretch along the second story, where you can order drinks or have breakfast.

Dining/Entertainment: Dining is under a wooden ceiling, and the cuisine is both continental and West Indian. Sometimes big buffets are spread out, with white-capped chefs in attendance. There are two bars, one of which sits a few paces from the surf.

Services: Room service (7am–9:30pm), laundry, baby-sitting.

Facilities: Swimming pool, two tennis courts.

TAMARIND COVE, Paynes Bay, St. James Beach (P.O. Box 429, Bridgetown), Barbados, W.I. Tel. 809/432-1332. Fax 809/422-1726. 67 rms, 50 suites. A/C TEL

$ Rates (including MAP): Winter, $240–$300 single; $280–$340 double; from $310 suites. Summer, $145–$180 single; $185–$220 double; from $210 suites. Taxes and service extra. AE, DC, MC, V. **Parking:** Free.

Tamarind Cove was originally established in 1969, when the daughter (Janet Kidd) of British newspaper magnate Lord Beaverbrook established a small and glamorous hotel on her own land to accommodate her friends who flew in for the polo matches on her world-class polo grounds. Shortly after its construction, it was acquired by a small but respectable British-based hotel chain (St. James Beach Properties, Ltd.) which soon transformed it into the flagship of their chain. In 1990, an $8 million restoration enlarged and expanded it into one of the most noteworthy hotels on Barbados.

Designed in an Iberian style, with pale-pink walls and red terra-cotta roofs, it occupies a desirable site beside St. James Beach 1½ miles south of Holetown. Its name derives from the presence near one of its restaurants of the largest tamarind tree in Barbados, a specimen which is considered something of a botanical marvel in its own right, and the subject of a local legend which claims that a pirate's treasure is buried beneath its tangled roots. The stylish and comfortable accommodations are in a series of hacienda-style buildings interspersed with vegetation. Each unit has a patio or balcony overlooking the gardens or ocean.

Dining/Entertainment: In addition to an informal beachfront eatery, Tamarind contains two elegant restaurants, the more memorable of which is Neptune's, which specializes in sophisticated preparations of seafood. The Flamingo is the main restaurant. A handful of bars are scattered throughout the property, and there's some kind of musical entertainment every night.

Services: Room service, baby-sitting, laundry, massage, concierge staff.

Facilities: Immediately adjacent white-sand beach, three freshwater swimming pools, complimentary water sports (including waterskiing, windsurfing, catamaran sailing, and snorkeling; golf, tennis, horseback riding, and polo available nearby.

TREASURE BEACH, St. James, Barbados, W.I. Tel. 809/432-1346. Fax 809/432-1094. 27 suites. A/C TEL

$ Rates (including breakfast): Winter, $275–$385 one-bedroom suite for one or two; $700 two-bedroom penthouse suite. Summer, $135–$210 one-bedroom suite for one or two; $350 two-bedroom penthouse suite. Service and taxes extra. Dinner supplement $43 in winter, $35 in summer. AE, DC, MC, V. **Parking:** Free.

Set on about an acre of sandy beachfront land, in a mini-village of two-story buildings arranged into a horseshoe pattern around a swimming pool and garden, Treasure Beach has one of the most loyal clienteles of any hotel on the island. It's small but choice, known for its well-prepared food and the comfort and style of its amenities. The atmosphere is both intimate and relaxed, with personalized service a mark of the well-trained staff. The hotel is set in tropical gardens in St. James in the glitter "hotel belt" of Barbados, about half a mile south of Holetown. The accommodations are beautifully furnished in a tropical motif and open onto private balconies or patios. Each contains a small kitchen for in-house preparations of meals or snacks. The clientele is about evenly divided between North American and British clients. Children under 12 are accepted only upon "special request."

Dining/Entertainment: Even if you aren't staying here, try to sample some of the culinary specialties at the Treasure Beach Restaurant, including freshly caught seafood and island favorites from the Bajan culinary repertoire. The Monday-night buffet is an island event; you choose from an array of succulent dishes, such as roast prime rib and baked whole fish, along with delectable desserts. Lunch is served daily from noon to 2pm and dinner is from 7 to 9:30pm. The bar is open to the gardens, and it is here that you can order tropical fruit drinks or whatever. The evening entertainment offered by the hotel is discreet and low-key.

Services: Room service (7:30am–9:30pm), valet and laundry service, safety-deposit boxes, concierge available to arrange for car rentals and island tours.

Facilities: Rental of sailboats, access to nearby golf and tennis courts.

MODERATE

COCONUT CREEK CLUB, Derricks, St. James, Barbados, W.I. Tel. 809/432-0803. Fax 809/422-1762. 53 rms. A/C TEL

$ Rates (including MAP): Winter, $220–$270 single; $260–$310 double. Summer, $135–$185 single; $175–$225 double. Service and taxes extra. AE, DC, MC, V. **Parking:** Free.

Small, intimate, and discreetly famous as a retreat for publicity-shy European celebrities, this is an elegantly informal and landscaped retreat on the West Coast, about a mile south of Holetown. Its developers re-created a 3-acre corner of English allure here—it resembles an exclusive country retreat in Devon, England. About half the accommodations lie atop a low bluff overlooking what might be the two most secluded beaches on the island's west coast. (Because of the configuration of the nearby coastline, access to these beaches is possible only by boat, from a handful of nearby privately owned villas, and from the gardens of the hotel.) Many of the bedrooms are built on the low cliff edge overlooking the ocean, while others open onto the pool or the flat, tropical garden. Each bedroom has a veranda or balcony where breakfast can be served.

Dining/Entertainment: The owners have created an outpost of Britannic nostalgia in the establishment's only restaurant, Cricketers, whose paneling and allure were modeled after an upscale English pub. Bajan buffets and barbecues are served on the restaurant's vine-covered open pergola, overlooking the gardens and the sea. (The inn's food has been praised by *Gourmet* magazine.) There's dancing to West Indian calypso and steel bands almost every night. Clients on the MAP are encouraged to dine at the restaurants connected to this chain's two other properties, the Tamarind Cove Hotel and the Colony Club, for no additional charge.

Services: Room service (7:30am–10pm), baby-sitting, arrangements for island tours and rental cars.

Facilities: Freshwater swimming pool, complimentary water sports (including waterskiing, windsurfing, snorkeling, and Hobie Cat sailing); scuba diving can be arranged for an extra charge; tennis available nearby.

CUNARD PARADISE VILLAGE & BEACH CLUB, Black Rock, St. Michael, Barbados, W.I. Tel. 809/424-0888, or toll free 800/222-1939. 168 rms, 4 suites. A/C TV TEL

$ Rates: Winter, $170–$230 single; $190–$250 double; suites from $310 suite. Summer, $100–$150 single; $120–$170 double; from $220 suite. Taxes and service extra. MAP $45 per person extra. AE, DC, MC, V. **Parking:** Free.

Operated by Cunard, this establishment sits 2½ miles north of Bridgetown on 13 landscaped acres of sloping hillside which rambles downhill to a point near a white sandy beach. An additional 13 acres of untamed forest belonging to the hotel await future development. The establishment's clubhouse and reception area, set near the top of the hill beside the entrance, is composed of lattices and chiseled stone in a sun-flooded position overlooking the sea. Accommodations are scattered among lattice-covered units rising amid tropical gardens and forests. Each has a modern design of big windows, comfortable furniture, and colonial-style accessories. The resort is known for the accessibility of its sports and its close communication with Cunard's Caribbean cruisers, which sometimes deposit groups of passengers seeking temporary respite from ocean-going itineraries.

Dining/Entertainment: The resort contains three different restaurants, the most formal of which is a candlelit and flower-bedecked indoor/outdoor dining room known as the Pavilion. At least two different bars provide thirst-quenchers beside the pool. There's live music nightly, and dancing, even in the rain, in a gazebo area.

Services: Room service, concierge, laundry, baby-sitting, massage.

Facilities: Two swimming pools, five tennis courts (four lit for night play; tennis lessons can be arranged from a resident tennis pro); horseback riding and golf can be arranged nearby.

HEYWOODS, Speightstown, St. Peter, Barbados, W.I. Tel. 809/422-4900, or toll free 800/822-4200. Fax 809/422-0617. 288 rms, 23 suites. A/C TEL

$ Rates: Winter, $170–$190 single or double; from $350 suite. Summer, $90–$110 single or double; from $350 suite. Children under 12 stay free in parents' room. Continental breakfast $8 extra. Tax and service extra. AE, DC, MC, V. **Parking:** Free.

A government-built collection of accommodations set amid spacious and tropically landscaped gardens, Heywoods stands on 30 acres of prime beachfront property along Highway 2A, 15 miles north of Bridgetown, and is managed by Wyndham Hotels and Resorts, an independent Texas-based company. The accommodations are clustered in seven architecturally different units that contribute to a complete self-contained ambience in the complex. One hundred units have minibars.

Dining/Entertainment: There are four restaurants, including Captains Table (an international menu), Carolines Restaurant (theme buffets), Beach Market (a coffee shop), and El Comedor (an Italian menu).

Services: Room service (7:30am–10pm), laundry, baby-sitting, craft shops, boutiques.

Facilities: Five floodlit tennis courts, nine-hole executive par-3 golf course, two air-conditioned glass-backed squash courts.

TRAVELLER'S PALM, 265 Palm Ave., Sunset Crest, St. James, Barbados, W.I. Tel. 809/432-7722. 16 apartments. A/C MINIBAR

$ Rates: Winter, $65 apartment for up to four. Summer, $40 apartment for up to four. Service and tax extra. No breakfast served. AE, MC, V. **Parking:** Free.

Designed for those who want to be independent, this is a choice collection of well-furnished apartments with fully equipped kitchens, a 5-minute drive south of Holetown. Apartments also have a spacious living- and dining-room area, as well as a patio where you can have breakfast or a candlelit dinner you've prepared yourself. The apartments are filled with bright colors and handcrafted furniture, and they open onto a well-kept lawn with a swimming pool. Serviced by maids, the apartments contain one bedroom, but are able to sleep four people. A handful of beaches lie within a 5-minute walk. Hamburgers and cheese toasties are served from a snack bar beside the establishment's pool.

SOUTH OF BRIDGETOWN

BARBADOS HILTON, Needham's Point (P.O. Box 510), St. Michael, Barbados, W.I. Tel. 809/426-0200, or toll free 800/445-8667. Fax 809/436-8946. 183 rms, 2 suites. A/C MINIBAR TV TEL

$ Rates: Winter, $189–$242 single; $281–$264 double; from $264 suite. Summer, $125–$155 single; $137–$170 double; from $266 suite. Breakfast $12 extra. Service and tax extra. AE, DC, MC, V. **Parking:** Free.

On more than 14 acres of landscaped gardens, this is a self-contained resort, although it lies on the heavily populated southern edge of Bridgetown. Built in 1966, and overhauled and redecorated several times since then, it occupies the rugged peninsula where in the 18th century the English navy built Fort Charles, today little more than a crumbling ruin. The Hilton's architecture incorporates bleached coral interspersed with jutting balconies and wide expanses of glass. The bedrooms are arranged around a central courtyard filled with tropical gardens, and vines cascade from the skylit roof. Each of the comfortable units has a balcony with a view of Carlisle Bay on the north side or the Atlantic on the south. Several kinds of water sports are offered on the nearby beach, whose outermost edge is protected from storm damage by a massive breakwater of giant rocks.

Dining/Entertainment: The Verandah restaurant, whose backdrop is a row of diminutive clapboard Bajan houses, serves island and international specialties to the accompaniment of live music. The hotel has a gaming room with slot machines and both a beachfront daytime bar and snack restaurant (the Gazebo) and a nighttime bar (the Flambeau).

Services: 24-hour room service, concierge, laundry, masseur.

Facilities: Four tennis courts (lit at night), in-house sauna and health club, access to horseback riding and golf.

GRAND BARBADOS BEACH RESORT, Aquatic Gap, Bay St. (P.O. Box 639), Bridgetown, St. Michael's, Barbados, W.I. Tel. 809/426-0890, or toll free 800/227-5475. Fax 809/436-9823. 128 rms, 5 suites. A/C MINIBAR TV TEL

$ Rates: Winter, $200–$235 single; $220–$260 double; from $450 suite. Summer, $120–$160 single; $130–$175 double; from $225 suite. Taxes and service extra. MAP $45 per person extra. AE, DC, MC, V. **Parking:** Free.

This stylish and imaginative hotel, about a mile southeast of Bridgetown, is an airy and well-designed resort that incorporates space and light into a radical overhaul of an older property, originally built in 1969. In 1986 a Trinidad-based insurance company spent several million dollars to renovate the 4-acre property, adding a cosmopolitan kind of zest. Today the bedrooms all have balconies, in-room movies, hairdryers, and safes. The higher priced units are on the two Aquatic Club executive floors, the top stories of the hotel, where the rooms come with such extra amenities as complimentary cocktails, continental breakfast, and pastries with coffee in the executive lounge at night.

Dining/Entertainment: Perhaps its most unusual feature is the massive pier jutting out into the sea, at the end of which is a seafood restaurant, the Schooner, known for its buffets. Two other restaurants provide a range of menus, including the Golden Shell, the elegant and relatively formal dining room, and a coffee shop, the Boardwalk Café on the pier, where nightly entertainment is provided. There is also the Coral Garden cocktail lounge.

Services: Room service (7:30am–10pm), laundry, concierge (to arrange car rentals and island tours).

Facilities: Shops, massage room, exercise room, sauna, Jacuzzi, 35-foot trimaran for oceangoing lunches and sunset cruises, complete facilities for disabled guests, complimentary water sports (including waterskiing and snorkeling); golf and tennis nearby.

ON THE SOUTH COAST
MODERATE

DIVI SOUTHWINDS BEACH RESORT, St. Lawrence Gap, Christ Church, Barbados, W.I. Tel. 809/428-7181, or toll free 800/367-3484. Fax 809/428-4674. 33 rms, 127 suites. A/C TV TEL

$ Rates: Winter, $200–$245 studio apartment or one-bedroom suite for one or two; $355 two-bedroom suite for two. Summer, $150–$180 studio or one-bedroom suite for one or two; $210 two-bedroom suite for two. Service and taxes extra. MAP $36 per person extra. AE, DC, MC, V. **Parking:** Free.

Midway between Bridgetown and the hamlet of Oistins, this resort was created when two distinctly different resorts (an older unit on the beachfront and a newer one built a short walk inland near a pair of swimming pools) were combined into a single coherent whole. Scattered over sandy flatlands of about 20 acres, the resorts were built in 1975 and 1986, respectively. Each enjoys a loyal clientele. The showplace of the present resort are the newer (inland) buildings consisting of one- and two-bedroom suites with full kitchens ideal for families. This section looks like a tastefully interconnected series of town houses, with spacious wooden balconies and views of a large L-shaped swimming pool. From these buildings, visitors need only cross through two groves of palm trees and a narrow lane to reach the beach. The older, more modest (but fully renovated) units lie directly on the beachfront, ringed with palm trees, near an oval-shaped swimming pool of their own.

Dining/Entertainment: The Aquarius Restaurant, which rises above the largest of the resort's swimming pools, is the resort's main dining and drinking emporium. A satellite snack bar/drink bar lies beside the beach, near the older units.

Services: Room service, laundry.

Facilities: Three swimming pools (one a wading pool reserved for children), sailboat rentals, snorkeling equipment.

SANDY BEACH HOTEL, Worthing, Christ Church, Barbados, W.I. Tel. 809/435-8000. Fax 809/435-8000. 89 suites. A/C TV TEL

$ Rates: Winter, $185–$225 one-bedroom suite for one or two; $270–$320 two-bedroom suite for one or two (additional person in any unit $30 extra). Summer, $99–$125 one-bedroom suite for one or two; $135–$170 two-bedroom suite for one or two (additional person in any unit $25 extra). Service and taxes extra. MAP $35 per person extra. AE, DC, MC, V. **Parking:** Free.

Originally established in 1980 on 2 acres of beachfront land 4 miles southeast of Bridgetown, this Bajan-owned hotel rises around its architectural centerpiece, a soaring conical cedar-sheathed structure known locally as a *palapa*. Suitable for families with children, the resort contains only one- and two-bedroom suites, plus 16 honeymoon suites with queen-size beds and completely private patios. All the tastefully decorated and spacious accommodations have fully equipped kitchenettes and private balconies or patios, and all the furniture at this informal place is locally made. Facilities for the disabled are provided in four of the ground-floor suites.

Dining/Entertainment: Ron's Green House Restaurant, which specializes in seafood and steaks, is under the previously mentioned palapa and opens onto a view of the beach and swimming pool. Every Tuesday the resort sponsors a rum-punch party, a Trinidad-style steel band, and a Bajan buffet. Then, outsiders are welcome. Caribbean specialties, such as flying fish, cou-cou, curries, plantains, and pepperpot, are served under the stars. Another restaurant, the Ocean Terrace, is a casual, open-air facility overlooking the beach and serves lighter, less expensive meals.

Services: Room service (7:30am–9pm), laundry, dry cleaning, concierge to arrange island tours.

Facilities: Swimming pool for adults, children's play area with its own wading pool; water sports, which cost extra, include 3-hour snorkeling trips, windsurfing, paddleboats, Sailfish, scuba lessons, and use of air mattresses, snorkels, fins, and masks.

SOUTHERN PALMS, St. Lawrence, Barbados, W.I. Tel. 809/428-7171.

Fax 809/428-1175. 73 rms, 20 suites. A/C MINIBAR TEL

$ Rates: Winter, $185–$235 single; $195–$245 double; from $310 suite. Summer, $100–$115 single; $110–$125 double; from $165 suite. Taxes and service extra. MAP $40 per person extra. AE, DC, MC, V. **Parking:** Free.

A seafront club with a distinct personality, Southern Palms lies on the Pink Beach of Barbados, midway between the airport and Bridgetown. The core of the resort is a mid-20th-century pink-and-white manor house built in the Dutch style, with a garden-level colonnade of arches. Spread along the sands are multiarched two- and three-story buildings. Italian fountains and statues add to the Mediterranean feeling. In its more modern block, an eclectic mixture of rooms includes some with kitchenettes, some facing the ocean, others opening onto the garden, and some with penthouse luxury. Each contains a radio, and suites have small kitchenettes. A cluster of straw-roofed buildings, which contain the drinking and dining facilities, links the accommodations together.

Dining/Entertainment: The Khus-Khus Bar and Restaurant serves both a West Indian and a continental cuisine. A local orchestra often entertains by providing merengue and steel-band music.

Services: Room service, laundry, tour desk.

Facilities: Terrace for sunning, two beachside freshwater swimming pools, sailboat rentals; snorkeling and scuba diving available.

INEXPENSIVE

BAGSHOT HOUSE HOTEL, St. Lawrence, Christ Church, Barbados, W.I. Tel. 809/435-6956. 30 rms. TEL

$ Rates (including MAP): Winter, $95 single; $133 double. Summer, $87 single; $122 double. Taxes and service extra. No credit cards. **Parking:** Free.

Custom built in 1956 as a small, family-managed hotel, the Bagshot House has flowering vines tumbling over the railing of the balconies and an old-fashioned and unhurried kind of charm. It lies within a 15-minute drive southeast of Bridgetown. In front of the inn, the beach stretches out before you. Some of the well-kept, simply furnished units have views of the water, and only two units are air-conditioned. For an extra charge, a TV can be placed in your room. A front sunbathing deck (which doubles as a kind of living room for the resort) is perched right at the edge of a lagoon; there is also a deckside lounge decorated with paintings by local artists.

CASUARINA BEACH CLUB, St. Lawrence Gap, Christ Church, Barbados, W.I. Tel. 809/428-3600. Fax 809/428-1970. 108 rms, 22 suites. A/C TEL

$ Rates: Winter, $140 single or double; $170 one-bedroom suite for one or two; $280 two-bedroom suite for four. Summer, $75 single or double; $100 one-bedroom suite for one or two; $150 two-bedroom suite for four. Service and taxes extra. MAP $32 per person extra. AE, DC, MC, V. **Parking:** Free.

You'll approach this resort, located midway between Bridgetown and Oistins, through a forest of palm trees swaying above a well-maintained lawn. Originally established in 1981, with substantial additions and improvements completed in 1991, the resort is pleasant, family run, and unpretentious. Designed with red-tile roofs and white walls, the main building has a series of arched windows leading onto verandas, although to get to your accommodation you pass through the outlying reception building and beside the pair of swimming pools. These are separated from the wide sandy beach by a lawn area dotted with casuarina and bougainvillea. On the premises is an octagonal roofed open-air bar and restaurant, two floodlit tennis courts, a gift shop, a tiny store for the purchase of foodstuffs, and a fitness room. The front desk can arrange most seaside activities through outside agencies. Each of the accommodations has a ceiling fan and wicker furniture, and each of the suites contains a kitchenette for the preparation of snacks and meals.

OCEAN VIEW, Hastings, Barbados, W.I. Tel. 809/427-7821. Fax 809/427-7826. 26 rms, 4 suites. TEL
$ Rates: Winter, $85–$105 single; $110–$135 double; $195 suite. Summer, $60–$75 single; $75–$90 double; $155 suite. MAP $40 per person extra. Tax and service extra. AE, MC, V. **Parking:** Free.

An old-timer that seems just as good as ever, this is the oldest hotel in Barbados, founded in 1901. Built between the busy road and the beach, 4 miles southeast of Bridgetown, the pink-and-white Ocean View has some of the graciousness of a colonial English house, including an open staircase with an old balustrade and a seaside porch that's good for lounging. Every bedroom is different—some large, some small and cozy—and an attractive use has been made of island antiques. Most rooms have air conditioning, and all have ceiling fans.

This vintage hostelry also serves good food. You can dine at a table overlooking the sea, helping yourself at the well-known Sunday planters' buffet lunch in winter. As in the olden days, they serve a big spread of Bajan specialties. Ernest Hemingway used to attend these lunches, and according to local legend he especially enjoyed the callaloo soup, the flying fish, and the pepperpot.

WOODVILLE BEACH APARTMENTS, Hastings, Christ Church, Barbados, W.I. Tel. 809/435-6694. Fax 809/435-9211. 28 apartments. TEL
$ Rates: Winter $70 studio apartment for one or two; $95 one-bedroom apartment for one or two; $125 two-bedroom apartment for four. Summer, $43–$56 studio apartment for one or two; $60 one-bedroom apartment for one or two; $85 two-bedroom apartment for four. Taxes and service extra. No breakfast served. No credit cards. **Parking:** Free.

These apartments represent one of the best bargains in Barbados and are ideal for families on a budget holiday. Set directly on a rocky shoreline 2½ miles southeast of Bridgetown, in the heart of the village of Hastings, on slightly less than an acre of land, this is a U-shaped apartment complex built around a pool terrace overlooking the sea. Functional and minimalist in decor, it is nevertheless clean and comfortable. The tiny kitchenettes in each accommodation are fully equipped, and a variety of rental units are offered. All have balconies or decks, and about 13 of the units contain air conditioning. There are supermarkets, stores, and banks within easy walking distance. Although a handful of athletic guests attempt to swim off the nearby rocks, most opt for a 5-minute walk to the white sands of nearby Rockley (Accra) Beach. The first of this complex's apartments was built in 1967, and many improvements and additions have been made since.

BUDGET

FAIRHOLME, Maxwell, Christ Church, Barbados, W.I. Tel. 809/428-9425. 11 rms (all with bath), 20 studio apartments. A/C
$ Rates: Winter, $25 single; $30 double; $55 studio apartment. Summer, $20 single; $25 double; $50 studio apartment. Service and taxes extra. Breakfast $5 extra. No credit cards. **Parking:** Free.

Fairholme is a converted plantation house whose sleeping quarters have been enlarged during the past 20 years with a handful of interconnected annexes. The main house and its original gardens are just off a major road 6 miles southeast of Bridgetown, a 5-minute walk to the beach and across from its neighbor hotel, the Sherringham Beach, which has a waterfront café and bar that Fairholme guests are allowed to use. The older part has 11 double rooms, each of which has a living-room area and a patio overlooking an orchard and swimming pool. Beside the pool is a lawn for sunbathing and a bar for island beverages. More recently added are 20 Spanish-style studio apartments, all with balcony or patio, built within the walls of the old plantation, with high cathedral ceilings, dark beams, and traditional furnishings. The restaurant has a reputation for home-cooking—wholesome, nothing fancy, but the ingredients are fresh. On the premises are the remnants of a very old wall, part of the ruined foundation of the original plantation complex. A note about this establishment's air conditioning: At the reception desk you buy a brass token for $3 that you insert into your air conditioner for around 8 hours of cooling-off time.

ON THE EAST COAST

EXPENSIVE

MARRIOTT'S SAM LORD'S CASTLE, Long Bay, St. Philip, Barbados, W.I. Tel. 809/423-7350, or toll free 800/228-9290. Fax 809/423-5918. 240 rms, 16 suites. A/C MINIBAR TEL

$ Rates: Winter, $195–$220 single or double; from $450 suite. Summer, $105–$130 single or double; from $250 suite. Tax and service extra. MAP $45 per person extra. AE, DC, MC, V. **Parking:** Free.

Today this resort is a smoothly operated compound maintained by the Marriott chain, but its architecturally acclaimed centerpiece was originally built in 1820 by one of Barbados's most notorious scoundrels. According to legend, Samuel Hall Lord (the "Regency Rascal") built the estate with money acquired by luring ships to their wreck on the jagged but hard-to-detect rocks of Cobbler's Reef. This he accomplished by placing lanterns along the trees of the island's relentlessly windy east coast in patterns which imitated the lights of safe harbors in other parts of the maritime world. As the ships were bashed into pieces on the rocks, Lord and his cohorts would loot them and then sell their cargoes at high (and tax-free) profits. Occasionally, sailors who survived the wrecks joined Lord's forces to loot other ships.

The Great House, near the easternmost end of the island, about 14 miles from Bridgetown, a 15-minute drive northeast of the airport, was built in the pirate's more mellow "golden years," and craftspeople were imported from England to reproduce sections of the queen's castle at Windsor. The decor includes the dubiously acquired but nonetheless beautiful art of Reynolds, Raeburn, and Chippendale.

Amid 72 landscaped acres, the estate has a wide, lengthy private sandy beach edged by tall coconut trees. Accommodations are comfortable and stylish, in a series of modern wings which ramble throughout the surrounding gardens.

Dining/Entertainment: The Sea Grill is open for breakfast, lunch, and dinner. Breakfast and dinner are also served in the Wanderer Restaurant, and you can order a hamburger at Sam's Place, right on the beach. There are many bars as well. A fiesta night in the hotel's Bajan Village is offered once a week, as is a shipwreck barbecue and beach party with a steel-drum band, a limbo show, and fire-eaters on South Beach.

Services: Beauty/barber shop, laundry, baby-sitting, concierge to arrange island tours and whatever.

Facilities: Three swimming pools, games room, exercise room, shuffleboard, table tennis, library; golf, sailing, horseback riding, snorkeling, waterskiing, fishing, luncheon and nighttime cruises, and other activities can be arranged.

INEXPENSIVE

KINGSLEY CLUB, Cattlewash-on-Sea, near Bathsheba, St. Joseph Barbados, W.I. Tel. 809/433-9422. Fax 809/433-9226. 7 rms. **Directions:** Take Hwy. 3 north of Bathsheba.

$ Rates (including breakfast): Winter, $84 single; $92 double. Summer, $72 single; $77 double. Tax and service extra. AE, MC, V. **Parking:** Free.

This establishment is a hidden-away little West Indian inn far removed from the bustle of the tourist-ridden west coast. In the foothills of Bathsheba, opening onto the often-turbulent Atlantic, Kingsley Club lies on the northeast coast. A historical inn with many associations, it offers simply furnished but clean and comfortable bedrooms. At night, you can sit back and enjoy a rum punch made from an old planter's recipe. The club enjoys a reputation for good cooking, and its Bajan food will be recommended later for those traveling to the east coast just for the day. Cattlewash Beach is one of the longest, widest, and, as the hotel brochure points out, "least crowded in Barbados." But please note: Swimming here can be extremely dangerous.

BUDGET

ATLANTIS HOTEL, Tent Bay, Bathsheba, St. Joseph, Barbados, W.I. Tel. 809/433-9445. 16 rms (all with bath).

$ Rates (including all meals): Winter, $40 single; $65 double. Summer, $30 single; $60 double. Service and taxes extra. AE. **Parking:** Free.

A tattered but respectable hostelry, the Atlantis Hotel is housed in a green-roofed villa built by a wealthy planter in 1882. Set directly on the seacoast, a short drive southeast of the island's "Scotland district," 13 miles northeast of Bridgetown, the hotel has simple bedrooms—very simple, with almost none of the electronic amenities you might have expected; five rooms contain balconies. The rates make the Atlantis one of the best bargains along the Atlantic coast of Barbados, but be warned: This place, even though it's one of the most famous and nostalgia-imbued hotels on the island, is not for everyone. The ocean at your doorstep can be turbulent—even experienced swimmers have nearly drowned here. Nevertheless, the place has its devotees and staying here might offer the opportunity for an unpretentious and offbeat adventure. Aside from inexpensive accommodations, this is the most popular luncheon spot on the east side of the island (see "Where to Dine," below).

2. WHERE TO DINE

The famous flying fish jumps up on every menu, and when prepared right, it's a delicacy—moist and succulent, nutlike in flavor, approaching the subtlety of brook trout. Bajans boil it, steam it, bake it, stew it, fry it, stuff it, or whatever.

Try also the sea urchin, or *oursin,* which you may have already sampled in Martinique and Guadeloupe. Bajans often call these urchins "sea eggs." Crab-in-the-back is another specialty, as is langouste, the Barbadian lobster. Dolphin and salt fish cakes are other popular items on the menu. Yams, sweet potatoes, and eddoes are typical vegetables. And Barbadian fruits are luscious, including papaya, passionfruit, and mangoes.

If you hear that any hotel or restaurant is having a *cohobblopot* (or more commonly, a Bajan buffet), call for a reservation. This is a Barbadian term that means to "cook up," and it inevitably will produce an array of local dishes.

Bajan dishes are a blend of cookery styles—the British, and most definitely the East Indian and African—that have been adapted to include the local meats, fruits, and vegetables. The secret of the flavorful dishes is in the "seasoning up," which is said to have changed very little since the 16th century.

At Christmas, roast ham or turkey is served with *jug-jug,* a rich casserole of Scottish derivation that includes salt beef, ground corn flour, green pigeon peas, and spices. *Cou-cou,* a side dish made from okra and cornmeal, accompanies fish, especially the "flying fish" of Barbados.

If possible, escape the dining requirements of your hotel and sample the island's varied cuisine, which is interesting but not spicy exotic.

ON THE WEST COAST

EXPENSIVE

BAGATELLE RESTAURANT, Hwy. 2A, St. Thomas Parish. Tel. 421-6767.

Cuisine: FRENCH/CARIBBEAN. **Reservations:** Recommended. **Directions:** Cut inland near Paynes Bay north of Bridgetown, 3 miles from both Sunset Crest and Sandy Lane Hotel.

$ Prices: Fixed-price dinner $105 BDS ($52.50). AE, MC, V.

Open: Nov–Apr, dinner only, daily 7–9:30pm. May–Oct, dinner only, Mon–Sat 7–9:30pm.

This restaurant is housed in one of the most historic and impressive buildings on the island. Set a 15-minute drive north of Bridgetown, and originally built in 1645 as the residence of the island's first governor (Lord Willoughby), it lies on 5 acres of forest whose trees are uplit with some of the best lighting in the Caribbean. The sylvan retreat lies in the cool uplands, just south of the island's center, and retains the allure of its original buildings. Walls of chiseled coral are at least 3 feet thick.

The Bagatelle is one of the island's finest and most elegant choices for dining on a French cuisine with a Caribbean flavor. Candles and lanterns illuminate the old archways and the ancient trees. Service is among the best I found on Barbados. Try smoked flying fish pâté, callaloo soup, or a fish chowder made from combinations of flying fish, eddoes, and shrimp. For a main course, you might enjoy superbly cooked crisp roast duck with a Bigarade sauce, or an unusual local version of beef Wellington. A catch of the day can be baked, grilled, or barbecued. Desserts include such concoctions as Key lime pie. The owners are British-born Richard and Val Richings.

LA CAGE AUX FOLLES, Summerland Great House, Prospect, St. James. Tel. 424-2424.

Cuisine: ASIAN/INTERNATIONAL. **Reservations:** Recommended, especially in winter.

$ Prices: Appetizers $22–$25 BDS ($11–$12.50); main courses $48–$72 BDS ($24–$36). AE, MC, V.

Open: Dinner only, Wed–Mon 7–10:30pm. **Closed:** June.

This restaurant is the newest statement of a pair of entrepreneurs who have established several other restaurants in both London and Barbados since their careers began in the early 1970s. Located between Batts Rock and Tamarind Cove in an old-fashioned island house, the decor is evocative of an old-fashioned plantation house, with tall ceilings, crystal chandeliers, and an old-fashioned balcony for sundowners. The most impressive room (reserved for groups and wedding receptions) centers around a reflecting pool and is lined with Bajan antiques or antique reproductions.

Try the sesame prawn pâté, sweet-and-sour shrimp, or Créole fish soup. Other courses include crispy aromatic duck and a dish inspired by the cuisine of India: tiki makhani, a creamy-and-spicy chicken cooked slowly in a tandoori and served with stir-fried vegetables. Perhaps for dessert, profiteroles with chocolate sauce and an old-fashioned English syllabub are the best choices.

CARAMBOLA, Derricks, St. James. Tel. 432-0832.

Cuisine: FRENCH/CARIBBEAN. **Reservations:** Recommended.

$ Prices: Appetizers $18–$22 BDS ($9–$11); main courses $38–$49 BDS ($19–$45). AE, MC, V.

Open: Dinner only, Mon–Sat 6:30–9:30pm.

Built beside the road that parallels the island's western coastline, a mile south of Holetown, atop the upper edge of a 20-foot seaside cliff, Carambola offers one of the most spectacular terraces for dining in the Caribbean. In the shadow of a much-enlarged Bajan house that was originally built during the 1950s as a private home, the restaurant quickly moved to the forefront of island dining experiences. The

THE
CARIBBEAN
ISLANDS

BARBADOS □

Bagatelle Restaurant ◆7
Barbados Pizza House ◆4
Barbecue Barn ◆11
Brown Sugar ◆12
Carambola ◆5
Chateau Creole ◆2
Da Luciano ◆11
David's Place ◆11
Enid's ◆9
Fathoms, The ◆6
Flamboyant ◆10
Hotel Atlantis ◆13
Ile de France ◆10
Kingsley Club ◆14
Koko's ◆8
La Maison ◆6
La Cage aux Folles ◆8
Legend Restaurant ◆1
Luigi's ◆12
Neptune's ◆6
Palm Terrace ◆3
Pisces ◆12
Reid's ◆6
Shakey's Restaurant ◆10
Ship Inn, The ◆12
Sugar Reef ◆11
T.G.I. Boomers ◆12
Virginian Restaurant ◆10
Witch Dotor ◆12

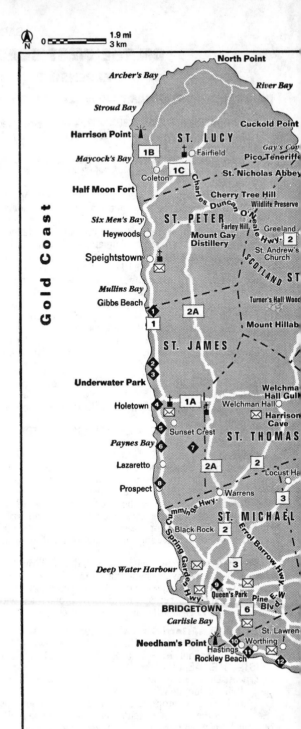

Morgan Lewis Beach

Green Pond

Morgan Lewis
Sugar Windmill
Long Pond

Atlantic Ocean

Barclay's Park

ANDREW

Chalky Mount Potteries

Chalky Mount

DISTRICT

Lower Forest

Bathsheba

Tent Bay

Andromeda Gardens

ST. JOSEPH

3A

3

Blackmans

3B

ST. JOHN

Martin's Bay

Congor Rocks

Consett Bay

Culpepper Island

Ragged Point
Lighthouse

Kitridge Point

Gun Hill Signal Station

ST. GEORGE

4

4B

5

Three Houses

Bushy Park

Sandford

5

Bottom Bay

ST. PHILIP

Marchfield Long Bay

Beachy Head

Crane Beach

7

CHRIST CHURCH

Tom Adams Hwy.

6

Maxwell

7

Grantley Adams Int'l Airport

Oistin

Long Bay

South Point

Lighthouse

Airport

Church

Post Office

cuisine is creative, with modern French-inspired touches. Owner Robin Walcott prepares jumbo shrimp served on a creamy coulis of sweet peppers, a salad of local lobster with a mango-and-basil vinaigrette, filet of kingfish cooked on a bed of onions and herbs and covered with a tomato butter sauce, and poached breast of chicken with a light sauce of its own thyme-scented juices, served on a confit of garlic. Dessert might be a passionfruit mousse on a biscuit base with its own coulis.

LA MAISON, Holetown, St. James. Tel. 432-1156.
  Cuisine: FRENCH/CARIBBEAN. **Reservations:** Recommended.
  $ Prices: Appetizers $5–$15 BDS ($2.50–$7.50) at lunch, $8–$24 BDS ($4–$12) at dinner; main courses $20–$45 BDS ($10–$22.50) at lunch, $38–$68 BDS ($19–$34) at dinner. MC, V.
  Open: Lunch Mon–Sat noon–2pm; dinner Mon–Sat 6:30–10pm.

Located on the beach north of Bridgetown near Paynes Bay, a 3-minute walk south of Holetown, this sophisticated restaurant was established in 1990 in a coral-sided building that was built in the 1970s as a copy of an older Barbadian home constructed long ago for members of the Cunard family. Open on two sides to the sea and to a flowering courtyard (whose centerpiece is a mermaid-capped fountain), the restaurant derives most of its decor from the exposed coral of its walls and the glow of its intricate ceiling, crafted solely of a Guyanan hardwood called greenheart. The French-born chef prepares a parcel of fresh scallops and mushrooms enveloped in filo pastry, a cannelloni of lobster and crabmeat, a terrine of smoked salmon, sautéed lobster studded with chanterelles, jumbo shrimp in a saffron sauce, a magret of duckling with a Bajan guava sauce, and an array of fresh seafood prepared according to the catch and the inspiration of the day. Dessert might be homemade passionfruit ice cream covered with a fresh island cherry sauce.

NEPTUNE'S, in the Tamarind Cove Beach Resort, Paynes Bay, St. James Beach. Tel. 432-1332.
  Cuisine: SEAFOOD. **Reservations:** Recommended.
  $ Prices: Appetizers $12–$20 BDS ($6–$10); main courses $40–$80 BDS ($20–$40). AE, DC, MC, V.
  Open: Daily 7–9:30pm.

By anyone's standards, this is the most avant-garde and most desirable seafood restaurant in Barbados. Located 1½ miles south of Holetown, within the pink hacienda-inspired walls of one of the island's most respected resorts, it abandons completely the "ocean breezes blowing through the hibiscus blossoms" mode that permeates most of the island's other restaurants. Instead, you'll find a stylish octagonal room sheathed in *faux* malachite, whose emerald-green tones reflect the colors of a illuminated aquarium in the room's center. Service is impeccable.

Your meal might include a sashimi of Caribbean fish, a terrine of seafood with a pimento sauce, tagliatelle of seafood, a succulent version of Bajan fish gumbo, deviled lobster, several different preparations of shrimp, and a delectable array of blackened snapper, dorado, or kingfish permeated with Cajun spices. Dessert might be a flavorful combination of honey/rum sauce, fresh pineapple, and freshly concocted ice cream.

Many visitors opt for a before-dinner drink in a coral-sided bar adjacent to the restaurant, where a polite staff serves lethal rum sours.

THE PALM TERRACE, in the Royal Pavilion Hotel, Porters, St. James, Tel. 422-4444.
  Cuisine: CARIBBEAN/INTERNATIONAL. **Reservations:** Required.
  $ Prices: Appetizers $8–$19; main courses $19–$32.50. AE, DC, MC, V.
  Open: Dinner only, daily 7:30–9:30pm.

North of Bridgetown between Sunset Crest and Gibbs Beach, in an elegant setting on a pink marble terrace evocative of the Mediterranean, this dramatic restaurant opens onto the oceanfront. In a previously recommended luxurious hotel, the Palm Terrace has a French chef who oversees a highly trained Bajan staff. Together they turn out some of the more delectable cuisine offered at any west-coast hotel. To the sounds of piano music, with the trade winds sweeping in, you can begin with hot Caribbean fish chowder, a glazed soufflé on a cream-and-cheese sauce, or duck rillettes. Main dishes might include magret of duck with green peppercorns, roast rack of lamb with fresh basil, or sea scallops with cucumbers. The poached local lobster is served with a light tarragon glaze. An international crowd frequents this restaurant.

REID'S, Derricks, St. James. Tel. 432-7623.
   Cuisine: INTERNATIONAL. **Reservations:** Recommended, especially on weekends.
$ Prices: Appetizers $8–$20 BDS ($4–$10); main courses $32–$70 BDS ($16–$35). AE, MC, V.
   Open: Dinner only, Tues–Sun 7–10pm (last order).
On the west coast, a mile south of Holetown, Reid's is in a low-slung building that was originally built early in the 19th century as the headquarters of a modest sugar plantation. Reid's one room is a breeze-filled extension of the original structure, built under a raftered ceiling which juts out toward a sloping English garden with two fountains and a rockery. Full meals might include escargots au gratin, marinated in white wine, garlic butter, and parsley; seafood crêpes with a savory cream sauce; veal St. James (veal sautéed with Pommery mustard, scallions, mushrooms, cream, and brandy); kingfish meunière; and a local version of a Sicilian cassatta made with layers of strawberries, chocolate, and vanilla ice cream, filled with cherries and walnuts and soaked in Cointreau. The British and Americanized Bajan couple who welcome you to their restaurant are Keith and Hazel Albecker.

MODERATE

THE FATHOMS, Paynes Bay, St. James. Tel. 432-2568.
   Cuisine: INTERNATIONAL. **Reservations:** Recommended for dinner.
$ Prices: Appetizers $10–$12 BDS ($5–$6); main courses $16–$20 BDS ($8–$10) at lunch, $28–$55 BDS ($14–$27.50) at dinner. AE, MC, V.
   Open: Lunch daily 11am–3pm; dinner daily 6:30–10pm (last order).
   ✪ Housed in a red-roofed stucco house close to the surf of the island's western coastline, a 10-minute drive south of Holetown near one of the island's fish markets, this pleasant restaurant serves meals on an outdoor terrace shaded by a mahogany tree and in an interior decorated with exposed accents of terra-cotta, wood, and decorative pottery.
   The lunchtime menu of sandwiches, salads, and platters of fish gives way at night to more sophisticated international specialties, such as roasted red snapper in a parsley, lemon, and thyme-flavored crust served with sorrel sauce; barbecued jumbo shrimp marinated in beer and herbs; several different versions of Bajan flying fish; and an unusual version of lightly fried filet of barracuda with a mustard-and-dill sauce.

KOKO'S, Prospect, St. James. Tel. 424-4557.
   Cuisine: BAJAN. **Reservations:** Recommended.
$ Prices: Appetizers $11–$13 BDS ($5.50–$6.50); main courses $25–$42 BDS ($12.50–$21). AE, DC, MC, V.
   Open: Dinner only, daily 6:30–9:30pm (last seating).
Koko's is an award-winning restaurant known for its excellent Caribbean cookery, a kind of Bajan *cuisine moderne.* The location alone is appealing: It's in a charming once-private house, built on coral blocks on a terrace overlooking the sea north of Bridgetown between Batts Rock and Tamarind Cove. You might begin with one of the homemade local soups, perhaps cohobblopot, made with "roots of the Caribbean," or stir-fried squid with lime-and-mayonnaise sauce as an appetizer. Shrimp and crab fritters are served with a fiery dip. Main dishes include the chef's catch of the day as well as island rabbit, west-coast style, served with a tamarind-and-ginger sauce. Each dessert is homemade and luscious.

LEGEND RESTAURANT, Mullins Bay, St. Peter. Tel. 422-0631.
   Cuisine: CARIBBEAN. **Reservations:** Recommended.
$ Prices: Appetizers $7–$12 BDS ($3.50–$6); main courses $25–$55 BDS ($12.50–$27.50). AE, MC, V.

Open: Dinner only, daily 6–10:30pm.

Designed as the centerpiece of a 12-unit condominium complex on the northwestern side of the island, about a 15-minute drive south of Speightstown, this restaurant occupies a plantation great house originally built in 1806 of coral limestone blocks by British sugar barons known as the Edmonds family. Separated from the sea by a road and a pleasant garden, the restaurant offers dining amid a maze of arches composed of chiseled blocks of coral. Selections from one of the most imaginative menus on the island include fluffy jumbo shrimp dipped in a coconut beer batter sauce and served with a tamarind tiger sauce; chicken and banana wraparound, with spicy peanut-and-coconut sauce; zaboca salad (slices of avocado with pickled green bananas splashed with herb-flavored vinaigrette); warm peanut soup studded with curried shrimp; a galaxy of jumbo curried shrimp, served on a ribbon of grilled plantain and accompanied with a jewel center of mango chutney; or lemon fettuccine on a ruby-colored pool of lobster-cream sauce surrounded by a variety of grilled fish.

RESTAURANT CHATEAU CREOLE, Porters, St. James. Tel. 422-4116.
  Cuisine: BAJAN/CREOLE. **Reservations:** Recommended.
$ Prices: Appetizers $8–$15 BDS ($4–$7.50); main courses $28–$55 BDS ($14–$27.50). AE, MC, V.
  Open: Dinner only, Mon–Sat 6:30–9:30pm (last seating).

Originally built around 1975, this stucco-and-tile house is set 2 miles north of Holetown in a tropical garden dotted with classical urns and a trio of gazebos. After passing under an arbor, you'll be invited to order a drink, served on one of the flowered banquettes that fill various parts of the house. Meals are taken on the rear terrace, al fresco style, by candlelight. Menu specialties include Créole dishes such as crab diablo and crabmeat au gratin. You might like Créole red-bean soup, a succulent version of fish chowder, "drunken chicken" (marinated and then flamed in rum), baked whitefish stuffed with crabmeat and herbs, or chicken with fresh mangoes and ginger. The establishment makes its own ice cream with local fruits.

SOUTH OF BRIDGETOWN

BROWN SUGAR, Aquatic Gap, St. Michael. Tel. 426-7684.
  Cuisine: BAJAN. **Reservations:** Recommended.
$ Prices: Appetizers $6–$9 BDS ($3–$4.50); main courses $22–$58 BDS ($11–$29) at dinner; fixed-price buffet lunch $25 BDS ($12.50). AE, DC, MC, V.
  Open: Lunch Mon–Fri 11:30am–2:30pm; dinner daily 6–9:45pm (last order).

Hidden behind lush foliage, Brown Sugar is a beautiful al fresco restaurant in an old-fashioned clapboard island house south of Bridgetown. The ceiling is latticed, with slow-turning fans, and there's an open veranda for dining by candlelight in a setting of hanging plants. The chefs prepare some of the tastiest Bajan specialties on the island. For an appetizer, try solomon gundy, a spicy-hot Jamaica favorite—it's a pâté of smoked herring, allspice, wine vinegar, onion, chives, and hot bonnie peppers, served with Jamaican water crackers. Among the soups, I suggest hot gungo-pea soup (pigeon peas cooked in chicken broth and zested with fresh coconut milk, herbs, and a touch of white wine). Of the main dishes, Créole orange chicken is popular, or perhaps you'd like stuffed crab backs. A selection of locally grown fresh vegetables is also offered. For dessert, I recommend the walnut-rum pie with rum sauce. The restaurant is known for its superb lunches, which are served buffet style to the businesspeople of the surrounding district. Dinners are romantic and leisurely.

ON THE SOUTH COAST

MODERATE

DA LUCIANO, "Staten," Hastings Hwy. 7, Christ Church. Tel. 427-5518.
  Cuisine: ITALIAN. **Reservations:** Recommended.

$ Prices: Appetizers $11–$13 BDS ($5.50–$6.50); main courses $25–$42 BDS ($12.50–$21). MC, V.
Open: Dinner only, daily 6:30–10:30pm.

Some of the finest Italian cuisine in the southern Caribbean is served in this Barbados National Trust–designated building of architectural interest, south of Bridgetown near Rockley Beach. The restaurant has gained popularity with its good service, quality ingredients, and care in preparation. I recommend cozze alla marinara (mussels in their shells sautéed in butter and parsley, with white wine and a lot of garlic). Try also the filetto battuto alla Luciano (flattened filet of beef flambéed in brandy, sautéed in butter, and served with mustard, fresh cream, and mushrooms). The pièce de résistance is the quaglia nel nido alla wolfe (charcoal-broiled filet of beef topped with croûtons of garlic bread, roast quail, and natural juice). For dessert, order fresh strawberries (in season) and finish with an espresso.

DAVID'S PLACE, St. Lawrence Main Rd., Christ Church. Tel. 435-6550.
   Cuisine: BAJAN. **Reservations:** Recommended.
$ Prices: Appetizers $7–$12 BDS ($3.50–$6); main courses $26–$50 BDS ($13–$25). AE, MC, V.
   Open: Dinner only, Tues–Sun 6–10pm (last order). **Closed:** Sept.

Owner-operator David Trotman promises that in his restaurant you'll sample "Barbadian dining at its best," and he delivers on that promise. The establishment is south of Bridgetown between Rockley Beach and Worthing, in an old-fashioned Bajan house with strongly contrasting tones of black and white both inside and outside. Tables are positioned so that diners get a view of the Caribbean. You might begin with a hot-and-creamy pumpkin soup, then follow with a Bajan pepperpot or such freshly caught fish of the day as dolphin, kingfish, or red snapper. The chef might even prepare "Baxters Road chicken" marinated in lime, salt, and herbs, then fried the way they do it on the famous nightlife street of Barbados. Desserts include coconut-cream pie.

ILE DE FRANCE, in the Windsor Arms Hotel, Hastings, Christ Church. Tel. 435-6869.
   Cuisine: CLASSIC FRENCH. **Reservations:** Recommended.
$ Prices: Appetizers $7–$35 BDS ($3.50–$17.50); main courses $30–$65 BDS ($15–$32.50). AE, MC, V.
   Open: Dinner only, Tues–Sun 6:30–9:30pm (last order).

A 12-minute drive southeast of the center of Bridgetown, this restaurant presents the finest and most authentic French cuisine in Barbados—by anyone's standards. Place yourself in the capable hands of Michel and Martine Gramaglia, two French-born *expatriés* who handle their kitchen and dining room etiquette with an enviable savoir-faire. Meals are served on a candlelit outdoor terrace overlooking a manicured garden, beside one of the oldest and most venerable hotels on the island. Ingredients are either flown in from France (or Martinique) or obtained fresh on Barbados. Specialties might include escargots de Bourgogne, a flavorful version of soupe de poissons avec langoustines (also known as *une petite soupière de la mer*), a marinade aux trois poissons whose exact composition depends on the catch of the day, imported foie gras of goose or duckling, and a dish for which the establishment is deservedly becoming famous, a tresse d'agneau (rack of lamb enveloped in a herb-laden croûte accompanied with its own juices). The atmosphere is charming and traditional.

LUIGI'S RESTAURANT, Dover Woods, St. Lawrence Gap. Tel. 428-9218.
   Cuisine: ITALIAN. **Reservations:** Recommended.
$ Prices: Appetizers $6–$14 BDS ($3–$7); main courses $27–$60 BDS ($13.50–$30). MC, V.
   Open: Dinner only, daily 6–9:45pm (last order). **Closed:** Tues in summer.

Located 4 miles south of Bridgetown between Rockley Beach and Worthing, along Highway 7, this open-air Italian trattoria with a Caribbean flavor since 1963 has operated in a green-and-white building that was originally built as a private house. Hundreds of empty chianti bottles are clustered from the rafters, so when a breeze blows, they tinkle gently against one another like wind chimes. The dining areas include a shrub-lined veranda and several inside rooms. Meals are prepared to order and so may require as much as a 30-minute wait. Specialties include seafood casserole, crab au gratin casserole, creamy seafood lasagne, and scampi broiled in garlic butter.

PISCES, St. Lawrence Gap, Christ Church. Tel. 435-6564.

Cuisine: BAJAN. **Reservations:** Recommended. **Directions:** From Bridgetown, take Hwy. 7 south for about 4 miles, then turn right toward St. Lawrence Gap at the signpost.

$ Prices: Appetizers $8–$12 ($4–$6); main courses $26–$58 BDS ($13–$29). AE, DC, MC, V.

Open: Dinner only, daily 6–9:30pm (last order).

Pisces offers al fresco dining at water's edge. A beautiful restaurant with a tropical decor, it serves primarily a Caribbean seafood menu. Some of the featured and most popular dishes are snapper Caribe, broiled fresh lobster, and a Pisces platter, which combines three kinds of fish (red snapper, Bajan flying fish, and grilled kingfish) with butterfly prawns on a single platter.

RESTAURANT FLAMBOYANT, Hastings Main Rd., Christ Church. Tel. 427-5588.

Cuisine: BAJAN/INTERNATIONAL. **Reservations:** Recommended.

$ Prices: Appetizers $7–$14 BDS ($3.50–$7); main courses $22–$48 BDS ($11–$24). AE, DC, MC, V.

Open: Dinner only, daily 6–11pm.

S This restaurant, 2 miles southeast of Bridgetown, lies within what used to be a private home, but many of the interior walls have been removed to allow ample space for dining. Owner Brian Cheeseman directs a kitchen where, because everything is prepared to order, the food may take a while to be served. Menu items include pumpkin-and-potato soup, a seafood crêpe Flamboyant, wienerschnitzel, a half chicken stuffed Bajan style, shrimp in dill sauce, and apple pie à la mode.

WITCH DOCTOR, St. Lawrence Gap, Christ Church. Tel. 435-6581.

Cuisine: BAJAN/AFRICAN. **Reservations:** Recommended.

$ Prices: Appetizers $3–$12 BDS ($1.50–$6); main courses $19–$56 BDS ($9.50–$28). MC, V.

Open: Dinner only, daily 6:30–9:30pm.

The Witch Doctor hides behind a screen of thick foliage in the heart of the southern coast. The decor, in honor of its name, features African and island wood carvings of witch doctors. The place purveys a fascinating African and Bajan cuisine with some unusual concoctions that are tasty and well prepared, a big change from a lot of the bland hotel fare. For an appetizer, try the split-pea and pumpkin soup. You'll also be offered ceviche (cold, soused in lime). Chef's specialties include various flambé dishes, shrimp Créole, flying fish, and chicken piri-piri (inspired by Mozambique).

INEXPENSIVE

SHIP INN, St. Lawrence Gap, Christ Church. Tel. 435-6961.

Cuisine: ENGLISH PUB/BAJAN. **Reservations:** Recommended for the Carvery, not needed for the pub.

$ Prices: Pub, appetizers $5–$6 BDS ($2.50–$3); main courses $12–$25 BDS ($6–$12.50). All-you-can-eat carvery, $20 BDS ($10) at lunch, $63 BDS ($31.50) at dinner. No credit cards.

Open: Lunch Sun–Fri noon–3pm; dinner daily 6–10:30pm (last order).

S South of Bridgetown between Rockley Beach and Worthing, the Ship Inn is a traditional English-style pub that contains an attractively rustic decor with dark ceiling beams, ships' engravings, and other nautical memorabilia displayed under the muted lighting of ships' lanterns. As an alternative, patrons may wish to drink and enjoy a tropical atmosphere in a garden bar. Many guests come for darts and to meet friends, and certainly to listen to the live music presented nightly by some of the island's top bands. The Ship Inn serves substantial bar food, such as homemade steak-and-kidney pie, shepherd's pie, and chicken, shrimp, and fish dishes. For more formal dining, visit the Captain's Carvery, where you can have your fill of succulent cuts from prime roasts on a nighttime buffet table, and an array of traditional Bajan food (filets of flying fish). You can drink in the pub until 2am daily. The establishment stocks beers from Jamaica, Trinidad, and Europe.

SUGAR REEF RESTAURANT AND BAR, Rockley Beach, Christ Church. Tel. 435-8074.
   Cuisine: BAJAN/INTERNATIONAL. **Reservations:** Not required.
$ **Prices:** Soups and salads $5–$10 BDS ($2.50–$5); main courses $10–$18 BDS ($5–$9). AE, MC, V.
   Open: Lunch Mon–Sat 11am–3pm, Sun 11am–4pm; dinner Mon–Sat 6–10pm.
A cliché of Caribbean charm, this open-air pavilion with a palm frond roof offers dining with a view of the sea at one of the most popular beaches along the south coast, frequented by both visitors and Bajans. It's south of Bridgetown between Hastings and Worthing. The cook specializes in kebabs, such as chicken and beef, but also lobster, these succulent tidbits flavored with herbs and served on a skewer. You can also order a freshly made soup of the day, such as pumpkin, and an assortment of salads. Other main dishes include Bajan fish cakes on a skewer and reef fish pie made with the catch of the day. For dessert, order either the fruit pie or the hot-fudge cake, both served with ice cream.

T.G.I. BOOMERS, St. Lawrence Gap, Christ Church. Tel. 428-8439.
   Cuisine: INTERNATIONAL. **Reservations:** Not required.
$ **Prices:** Appetizers $8–$10 BDS ($4–$5); main courses $19–$34 BDS ($9.50–$17); full American breakfast $7 BDS ($3.50). AE, MC, V.
   Open: Sun–Fri 8am–9:45pm (last food order), Sat 5:30–9:45pm (last food order). (Bar, Sun–Fri 8am–midnight, Sat 5:30pm–midnight.)
⑤ Four miles south of Bridgetown between Rockley Beach and Worthing along Highway 7, T.G.I. Boomers offers some of the best bargain meals on the island. An American/Bajan operation, it has an active bar and a row of tables where food is served, usually along with frothy pastel-colored drinks. The cook prepares a special catch of the day, and the fish is served with soup or salad, rice or baked potato, and a vegetable. You can always count on seafood, steaks, and hamburgers. For breakfast, you might want two eggs with bacon, toast, and coffee. For lunch, try a daily Bajan special or a jumbo sandwich. Be sure to try one of the 16-ounce daiquiris, which come in six flavors and cost $7 BDS ($3.50) each.

VIRGINIAN RESTAURANT, in the Seaview Hotel, Hastings Main Rd., Christ Church. Tel. 427-7963.
   Cuisine: BAJAN/INTERNATIONAL. **Reservations:** Recommended.
$ **Prices:** Appetizers $3–$14 BDS ($1.50–$7); main courses $28–$55 BDS ($14–$27.50). DC, MC, V.
   Open: Dinner only, daily 6–11pm.
The Virginian Restaurant is known for its good home-cookery served in a restored 18th-century manor house on the south coast, in the garrison area next to the Hastings police station, 2 miles south of Bridgetown. Guests climb a flight of exterior stone steps to reach the high-ceilinged dining room. Meals might include shrimp Suzannah, stuffed flying fish, and U.S. steaks. You might begin with Bajan ceviche.

ON THE EAST COAST

ATLANTIS HOTEL, Bathsheba, St. Joseph. Tel. 433-9445.
   Cuisine: BAJAN. **Reservations:** Required for the Sun buffet, recommended at all other times.
$ **Prices:** Two-course fixed-price lunch or dinner $29 BDS ($14.50); Sun buffet $34 BDS ($17). MC, V.
   Open: Lunch daily 1–3pm; dinner daily at 7pm (and don't be late).

Considered useful for an insight into the old-fashioned Barbados of several years ago, the slightly run-down Atlantis Hotel is often filled with both Bajans and visitors. It's located between Cattlewash-on-Sea and Tent Bay on the east coast (Atlantic Ocean). In the sunny, breeze-filled interior, with a sweeping view of the turbulent ocean, Enid I. Maxwell has been welcoming visitors from all over the world ever since she opened the place in 1945. Her copious buffets are considered one of the best food values on the island. From loaded tables, you can sample such Bajan foods as pumpkin fritters, peas and rice, macaroni and cheese, chow mein, souse, and/or a Bajan pepperpot. No one ever leaves here hungry.

KINGSLEY CLUB, Cattlewash-on-Sea, near Bathsheba, St. Joseph. Tel. 433-9422.
   Cuisine: BAJAN. **Reservations:** Required for dinner, recommended for lunch.
$ **Prices:** Appetizers $6 BDS ($3) at lunch; main courses $34 BDS ($17) at lunch; fixed-price four-course dinner $70 BDS ($35). AE, MC, V.
   Open: Lunch daily noon–3pm; dinner daily 6:30–7:30pm (last order).
A historic inn recommended previously for its rooms, the Kingsley Club also serves some of the best Bajan food on the island in a turn-of-the-century house cooled by Atlantic breezes. You're invited to "come tuck in" and enjoy your fill of split-pea-and-pumpkin soup, dolphin meunière, or planters fried chicken, followed by one of their homemade desserts, perhaps coconut pie. The inn lies amid the rolling hills of the northeastern coast of Barbados in an area called the Scotland district, a quarter mile northeast of Bathsheba, about 15 miles from Bridgetown.

3. WHAT TO SEE & DO

Barbados is worth exploring, either in your own car or with a taxidriver guide. Unlike so many islands of the Caribbean, the roads are fair and quite passable, and usually they're well marked with crossroad signs. If you get lost, the people in the countryside are generally helpful and speak English.

A DRIVING TOUR OF THE ISLAND

BRIDGETOWN   Often hot and traffic clogged, the capital, Bridgetown, merits no more than a morning's shopping jaunt. An architectural hodgepodge, it was founded by 64 settlers sent out by the Earl of Carlisle in 1628.

Begin your tour at the **Careenage,** from the French word meaning to turn vessels over on their side for cleaning. This was a haven for the clipper ship, and even though today it doesn't have its yesteryear color, it's still worth exploring.

At **Trafalgar Square** the long tradition of British colonization is perhaps immortalized. The monument here, honoring Lord Nelson, was executed by Sir Richard Westmacott and erected in 1813. The **Public Buildings** on the square are of the great, gray Victorian Gothic variety that you might expect to find in South Kensington, London. The east wing contains the meeting halls of the Senate and the House of Assembly, with some stained-glass windows representing the sovereigns of England from James I to Queen Victoria. Look for the Great Protector himself, Oliver Cromwell.

Behind the Financial Building, **St. Michael's Cathedral,** south of Trafalgar Square, is the symbol of the Church of England transplanted. This Anglican church was built in 1655, but was completely destroyed in a 1780 hurricane. Reconstructed in 1789, it was also damaged by a hurricane in 1831, but was not completely demolished as before. George Washington is said to have worshipped here on his Barbados visit.

For years, guides pointed out a house on Upper Bay Street where Washington allegedly slept during his only visit outside the United States. Beginning in 1910, the building was called "The Washington House," although historians seriously doubted the claim. Now, after a careful investigation, the house where Washington slept has

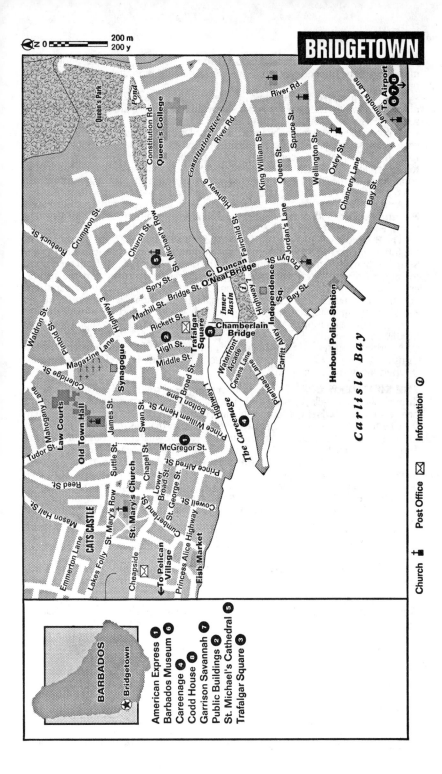

been identified by historians as the **Codd House** in Bush Hill, which lies about half a mile south of the Upper Bay Street location. The building is privately owned and is not open to the public.

The **Bridgetown Synagogue,** Synagogue Lane (tel. 432-0840), is one of the oldest in the western hemisphere and is surrounded by a burial ground of early Jewish settlers. The present building dates from 1833. It was constructed on the site of an even older synagogue, erected by Jews from Brazil in 1654. Sometime in the early 20th century the synagogue was deconsecrated, and the structure has since served various roles. In 1983 the government of Barbados seized the deteriorating building, intending to raze it and build a courthouse on the site. An outcry went up from the small Jewish community on the island; money was raised for its restoration, and the building was saved and is now part of the National Trust of Barbados and a synagogue once again.

At this point, you can hail a taxi if you don't have a car and visit **Garrison Savannah,** just south of the capital. Cricket matches and other games are played in this open-air space of some 50 acres. Horse races are often held here.

The **Barbados Museum,** the Garrison, St. Michael (tel. 427-0201), is housed in the former military prison at the impressive St. Ann's Garrison. In the exhibition "In Search of Bim," extensive collections show the island's development from prehistoric to modern times. "Born of the Sea" gives fascinating glimpses into the natural environment. There are also fine collections of West Indian maps, decorative arts, and fine arts. The museum sells a variety of quality publications, reproductions (maps, cards, prints), and handcrafts. Its Courtyard Café is a good place for a snack or light lunch. The museum is open Monday through Saturday from 10am to 6pm. It charges $4 BDS ($2) for adults, $1 BDS (50¢) for children.

Nearby, the russet-red **St. Ann's Fort,** on the fringe of the Savannah, garrisoned British soldiers in 1694. The fort wasn't completed until 1703. The Clock House survived the hurricane of 1831.

THE SOUTHERN COAST   After Bridgetown, head south on Highway 7, passing through the middle-class resorts of Hastings, Rockley, Worthing, and St. Lawrence before arriving at **Oistin,** a former shipping port that today is a fishing village. Here the Charter of Barbados was signed at the Mermaid in 1652, as the island surrendered to Commonwealth forces. The inn, incidentally, was owned by a cousin of the John Turner who built the House of the Seven Gables in Salem, Massachusetts.

From here you can head on to **Sam Lord's Castle** (see "Where to Stay," above). Although this is a hotel, it's also one of the major sightseeing attractions of Barbados. If you're not a guest, you'll have to pay $5 BDS ($2.50) to be admitted to the grounds. Built by slaves in 1820 and furnished with elegant Regency pieces, the house is like a Georgian plantation mansion. Take note of the ornate ceilings, said to be the finest example of stucco work in the western hemisphere. At the entrance to the hotel are shops selling handcrafts and souvenirs.

In the neighboring section, you can visit **Ragged Point Lighthouse,** built in 1885 on a rugged cliff. Since then the beacon has gone out as a warning to ships approaching the dangerous reef, called "The Cobblers." The view from here is spectacular.

THE EAST COAST   Continuing north along the jagged Atlantic coast, you reach **Codrington College,** which opened in 1745. A cabbage-palm-lined avenue leads to old coral block buildings, and on the grounds you can enjoy a picnic lunch. Today the gray stone buildings are a training school for men and women from the entire Caribbean to enter the ordained ministry of the Anglican church. The college is under the auspices of the Diocese of the West Indies.

Before getting back on the coast road, ask in the neighborhood for directions to **St. John's Church,** perched on the edge of a cliff opening on the east coast some 825 feet above sea level. The church dates from 1836 and in its graveyard rests a descendant of Emperor Constantine the Great, whose family was driven from the throne in Constantinople (Istanbul) by the Turks. Ferdinando Paleologus, the royal relative, died in Barbados in 1678.

While in the area, you can go to **Villa Nova** (tel. 433-1524), built in 1834, a fine sugar plantation great house, furnished with period antiques in Barbadian mahogany and set in 6½ acres of landscaped gardens and gullies. It's open Monday through Friday from 9am to 4pm, with an admission of $6 BDS ($3). To reach the place, take Highway 3B toward St. John's Church, but turn left by the fire station at Four Cross Roads, toward Mount Tabor Church. Go less than a mile before turning left again. Almost immediately turn right, and up the hill you'll see the entrance.

Before the day is over, if you move fast enough you can also visit **Andromeda Tropical Gardens,** Bathsheba, St. Joseph (tel. 433-9261). On a cliff overlooking Bathsheba on the rugged east coast, limestone boulders make for a natural 8-acre rock-garden setting, where thousands of orchids are in bloom every day of the year along with hundreds of hibiscus and heliconia. Other plants are more seasonal, including the lipstick tree, candlestick tree, mammee apple, and many more. Many varieties of ferns, bromeliads, and other species that are house plants in temperate climates grow here in splendid profusion. A section is a palm garden, with more than 100 species. A simple guide helps visitors to identify many of the plants. The garden was started in 1954 by the late Mrs. Iris Bannochie, on land that had belonged to her family for more than 200 years. On the grounds you'll occasionally see frogs, herons, guppies, and sometimes a mongoose or a monkey. With an admission of $8 BDS ($4), the gardens are open all day every day.

In the same area, **Hackleton's Cliff** also rises to a height of 1,000 feet, giving you another view of the rugged Atlantic coast. The attraction and the view were described in the book *Cradle of the Deep* by Sir Frederick Treves.

Eventually you reach **Bathsheba,** the leading town along the east coast, where ocean rollers break, forming cascades of white foam. The same Sir Frederick compared this place to a "Cornwall in miniature." Today the old fishing village is a favorite resort among Bajans. For the best dining choice in the area, I recommend the Atlantis Hotel (see "Where to Stay" and "Where to Dine," above).

The trail north from Bathsheba takes in the **East Coast Road,** which runs for many miles with views of the Atlantic. Chalky Mount rises from the beach to 500 feet, forming a trio of peaks, and a little to the south, Barclays Park is a 15-acre natural wonder presented as a gift to the country by the banking people. There's a snack bar and picnic place here.

Stopping on the western side of Chalky Mount, you can visit Chalky Mount School, and go out to see the **Potteries,** where potters turn out different products, some based on designs centuries old.

The view from the top of **Cherry Tree Hill,** on Highway 1, is the finest in Barbados. You can look right down the eastern shore past Bathsheba to the lighthouse at Ragged Point, already described. The place is about 850 feet above sea level, and from its precincts you'll see out over the "Scotland district." The cherry trees from which the hill got its name no longer stand there, having given way to mahogany.

NORTHERN BARBADOS Many visitors explore ✪ **Farley Hill National Park,** in northern St. Peter Parish. It was used in the filming of the motion picture *Island in the Sun,* with Harry Belafonte. This movie is now largely forgotten by the world, but it still holds a lot of memories for those Barbadians familiar with it. The park, which was opened by Queen Elizabeth in 1966, is open daily from 7am to 6pm. You pay a vehicular entrance fee of $5 BDS ($2.50). After disembarking in the parking area, you can walk around the grounds and enjoy the tropical flowers and lush vegetation.

The **Barbados Wildlife Reserve** (tel. 422-8826), a project operated by the Barbados Primate Research Center, Farley Hill, St. Peter, is in a mahogany forest across the road from Farley Hill National Park. From 10am to 5pm daily, for an admission charge of $10 BDS ($5) for adults (half price for children), you stroll through what is primarily a monkey sanctuary. Aside from the uncaged monkeys, you can see wild hares, deer, tortoises, otters, caymans, wallabies, and a variety of tropical birds.

I also suggest a visit to ✪ **St. Nicholas Abbey,** which stands near Cherry Tree Hill (tel. 422-8725), the Jacobean plantation great house and sugarcane fields that have been around since about 1650. It was never an abbey—an ambitious owner in about 1820 simply christened it as such. More than 200 acres are still cultivated each year. In the parish of St. Peter, the structure—at least the ground floor—is open to the public Monday through Friday from 10am to 3:30pm, with an admission of $5 BDS ($2.50) per person. The house is believed to be one of three Jacobean houses in the western hemisphere, and it's characterized by curved gables. Lt.-Col. Stephen Cave, the owner, is descended from the family who purchased the sugar plantation and great house in 1810. A movie made in 1934 with scenes of Barbados is shown at 11:30am and 2:30pm daily. Light refreshments are offered for sale.

THE WEST COAST   From Farley Hill you can head due west to **Speightstown,** which was founded around 1635 and for a time was a whaling port. The "second city" of Barbados, the town has some colonial buildings constructed after the devastating hurricane of 1831. The parish church, rebuilt in a half-Grecian style after the hurricane, is one of the places of interest. Its chancel rail is of carved mahogany.

South from Speightstown is what is known as the **Platinum Coast,** the protected western shoreline which opens onto the gentler Caribbean. Along the shoreline of the parishes of St. James and St. Peter are found the island's plushest hotels (see "Where to Stay," above).

Holetown is the center of the coast; it takes its name from the town of Hole on the Thames River. Here the first English settlers landed in the winter of 1627. An obelisk marks the spot where the *Olive Blossom* landed the first Europeans. The monument, for some reason, lists the date erroneously as 1605.

Nearby **St. James Church** is Anglican, rebuilt in 1872 on the site of the early settlers' church of 1660. In the southern porch is an old bell, bearing the inscription "God Bless King William, 1696."

INLAND   Take Highway 2 from Bridgetown and follow it to **Welchman Hall Gully** (tel. 438-6671), in St. Thomas, a lush tropical garden owned by the Barbados National Trust. You'll see some specimens of plants that were here when the English settlers landed in 1627. Many of the plants are labeled—clove, nutmeg, tree fern, and cocoa among others—and occasionally you'll spot a wild monkey. You'll also see a ravine and limestone stalactites and stalagmites, as well as breadfruit trees that are claimed to be descended from the seedlings brought ashore by Captain Bligh of the *Bounty.* Admission is $6 BDS ($3). It's open daily from 9am to 5pm.

Also at Welchman Hall in the parish of St. Thomas,   ✪ **Harrison's Cave** is the No. 1 tourist attraction of Barbados, and visitors have the chance to view this beautiful, natural, underground world from aboard an electric tram and trailer. Before the tour, a video show of the cave is shown in the presentation hall. During the tour, visitors see bubbling streams, tumbling cascades, and deep pools, which are subtly lit, while all around stalactites hang overhead like icicles. Stalagmites rise from the floor. Visitors may disembark and get a closer look at this natural phenomenon at the Rotunda Room and the Cascade Pool. Tours are conducted daily from 9am to 4pm (closed Good Friday, Easter Sunday, and Christmas Day). You should reserve by calling 438-6641. Admission is $15 BDS ($7.50) for adults and $5 BDS ($2.50) for children.

Flower Forest of Barbados, St. Joseph (tel. 433-8152), at Richmond Plantation (an old sugar plantation), stands 850 feet above sea level near the western edge of the "Scotland district," a mile from Harrison's Cave. Set in one of the most scenic parts of Barbados, it's more than just a botanical garden; it's where people and nature came together to create something beautiful. After viewing the grounds, visitors can purchase handcrafts at Best of Barbados. Hours are 9am to 5pm daily, and admission is $10 BDS ($5) for adults and $5 BDS ($2.50) for children.

HISTORICAL SIGHTS

MORGAN LEWIS SUGAR WINDMILL AND MUSEUM, St. Andrew. Tel. 426-2421.
This is typical of the wind-driven mills that crushed the juice from the sugarcane in

the 17th to the 19th century, producing sugar that made Barbados Britain's most valuable possession in the Americas. It was from the Barbados sugarcane that rum was first produced. The mill is on the northeastern coast of the island.

Admission: $4 BDS ($2) adults, $2 BDS ($1) children under 14.

Open: Mon–Sat 9am–5pm. **Directions:** Follow Hwy. 1 past Farley Hill National Park to Hwy. 2.

SUNBURY PLANTATION HOUSE, 6 Cross Roads, St. Philip. Tel. 423-6270.

On Highway 5, this is a 300-year-old lived-in historic home with a unique private collection of horse-drawn carriages, many original prints, antique furniture, and a tropical courtyard restaurant and bar. While there, you might like to inquire about the possibility of dining on the original 250-year-old Sunbury table with candelabra. Coffee and liqueurs are served later in the drawing room. Dinners are served at 8pm on Tuesday and Thursday, and reservations are essential.

Admission: $8 BDS ($4) adults, $1 BDS (50¢) children.

Open: Daily 10am–4:30pm.

GUN HILL SIGNAL STATION, Hwy. 4. Tel. 429-1358.

One of two such stations owned and operated by the Barbados National Trust, the Gun Hill Signal Station is strategically placed on the highland of St. George and commands a magnificent view from the east to the west. Built in 1818, it was the finest of a chain of signal stations and was also used as an outpost for the British army stationed here at the time.

Admission: $5 BDS ($2.50) adults, $2.50 BDS ($1.25) children under 14.

Open: Mon–Fri 9am–5pm. **Directions:** Take Hwy. 3 from Bridgetown and then go inland from Hwy. 4 toward St. George Church.

SUBMERGED SIGHTSEEING

You no longer have to be an experienced diver to see what lives 150 feet below the surface of the sea around Barbados. Now all visitors can view the wonders that lie beneath the sea aboard *Atlantis II,* a submarine for sightseeing. The air-conditioned submersible seats 28 passengers, and, with two crew members, makes 12 dives daily from 9am to 8pm. Passengers are transported from the Careenage in downtown Bridgetown aboard the *Yukon II,* a 48-foot boat, to the submarine site, about a mile from the west coast of Barbados. The ride offers a view of the west coast of the island.

The submarine has 16 2-foot-wide viewing ports, 8 on either side of the vessel, plus a 52-inch port at the front. Besides the rainbow of colors, tropical fish, and plants, you'll see a shipwreck that lies upright and intact below the surface. The total time of the trip is about 2 hours, and it costs $139 BDS ($69.50); children 4 to 12 are charged half fare. For reservations, contact **Atlantis Submarines (Barbados) Inc.,** Horizon House, McGregor Street, Bridgetown (tel. 809/436-8929).

RUM TOURS

A luncheon tour, **"Where the Rum Comes From,"** with guided visits to the home of Cockspur, makers of Barbadian rum for two centuries, is offered every Wednesday from noon to 2:15pm. The trip includes a trek through the famous rum-makers' distilleries and a buffet luncheon under a copse of coconut palms. Steel-band entertainment, free rum drinks (each featuring Cockspur's rum cocktails), and free bus transportation from your hotel and back are included. The cost is $55 BDS ($27.50) per person. For reservations, phone 435-6900.

WALKING TOURS

The **Barbados National Trust** offers Sunday-morning hikes throughout the year. The program, which gives participants an opportunity to learn about the natural beauty of Barbados, are co-sponsored by the Duke of Edinburgh's Award Scheme and the Barbados Heart Foundation and attract more than 300 participants weekly.

Led by young Barbadians and members of the National Trust, the hikes cover a different area of the island each week. Tour escorts also give brief educational talks on various aspects of the hikes, such as geography, history, geology, and agriculture. The hikes, free and open to participants of all ages, are divided into three categories: fast, for those who wish to hike for the exercise; medium, for those wishing exercise but at a slower pace than the fast walk; and slow, or fondly known as the "stop and stare" hike, for those wishing to walk at a leisurely pace.

All the hikes leave promptly at 6am and begin and end in the same place, where parking is available. Each hike is about 5 miles long and takes about 3 hours to complete. Visitors needing transportation should contact the Barbados National Trust (tel. 426-2421). The staff there will tell you where to meet for the hike.

4. SPORTS & RECREATION

The principal activities are swimming and sunning, which are far preferable on the western coast in the clear, buoyant waters, though you may also want to visit the surf-pounded Atlantic waters in the east, which are better for viewing than swimming.

BEACHES Barbadians will tell you that their island has a beach for every day of the year. If you're only visiting for a short time, however, you'll probably be happy with the ones that are easy to find. They're all open to the public, even those in front of the big resort hotels and private homes, and the government requires that there be access to all beaches, via roads along the property line or through the hotel entrance. The beaches on the west, the so-called **Platinum Coast,** are the most popular. These include Paradise Beach, Paynes Bay and Sandy Lane Bay, Treasure Beach, Gibbs Bay, Heywoods Beach, Rockley, and Bentson Beach. To reach the ones on the east, drive through the cane fields to **North Point, Cove Bay,** or **Archer's Bay,** or head down to the beautiful but more perilous one at **Bathsheba.** I could go on and on, but perhaps you'll try them all and then find your own.

BOAT TRIPS Largest of the coastal cruising vessels, the *Bajan Queen* is modeled after a Mississippi riverboat and is the only cruise ship offering table seating and dining on local fare produced fresh from the on-board galley. There is also cover available from too much sun or rain. Day cruises include two anchor stops for swimming, with snorkeling equipment provided, a buffet luncheon, water sports, open bar, and dancing to calypso music and international records. The *Bajan Queen* becomes a showboat by night, with local bands providing all kinds of music for dancing under the stars. You are treated to a dinner of roast chicken, barbecued steak, and seasoned flying fish with a help-yourself buffet of fresh side dishes and salads. Cruises are usually sold out, so you should book early to avoid disappointment. Each cruise costs $51.50 and includes transportation to and from your hotel. For reservations, contact Bajan Queen Ltd., Dunford House, Fontabelle, St. Michael (tel. 436-2149).

Another popular cruise is aboard the *Jolly Roger,* a full-size replica of a fighting ship. You can enjoy drinks from an open bar, a full steak barbecue lunch, and nonstop music for dancing on the spacious sun deck. Later the boat stops at a sheltered cove where passengers can put on their bathing suits and go for a swim. Lunch cruises are Monday through Saturday from 10am to 2pm. At night, passengers cruise and dance to the sounds of top local singing groups (in season only). Night cruises are on Thursday and Saturday from 6 to 10pm; the cost is $52, day or night (children under 12 pay half price). For information, telephone 436-6424, or visit the berth at Bridgetown Harbour.

Funseekers, Inc., Rockley Main Road, Christ Church (tel. 435-8206), is best known for its motorscooter and bicycle rentals, but this company also maintains a 44-foot CSY yacht named the *Limbo Lady,* which is the pride and joy of its Bajan-born owner, Patrick Gonsalves. Both sunset cruises and lunchtime cruises are offered and include a full roster of drinks (covered in the price), and a friendly dialogue from the skipper. Snorkeling gear is provided free as well. Lunch cruises last 4½ hours and cost $100 BDS ($50) per person; sunset cruises extend for 3 hours and cost $80 BDS ($40) per person. The organization's minivan will pick up participants at their hotels if reservations are made.

CRICKET   First made popular in 1870, this is the national pastime in Barbados—many Bajans simply live for cricket. Matches can last from a day for one inning to 5 days for two innings. The late Sir Frank Worrell became the first nonpolitical national hero after he scored 3,860 runs in 51 tests at an average of 49.48 runs; he died in 1967 of leukemia. If you'd like to see a local match, watch for announcements in the newspapers or ask at the Tourist Board.

DEEP-SEA FISHING   The fishing is first-rate in the waters around Barbados, where fishers pursue dolphin, marlin, wahoo, barracuda, and sailfish, to name only the most popular catches. There's also an occasional cobia.
   The **Dive Shop,** Pebbles Beach, Aquatic Gap, Bay Street, St. Michael (tel. 426-9947), can arrange half-day charters for one to six people (all equipment and drinks included), costing $250 per boat. Under the same arrangement, the whole-day jaunt goes for $500.

GOLF   The island's best-maintained and most prestigious links are the 18-hole championship golf course of the **Sandy Lane Hotel,** St. James (tel. 432-1311), on the west coast. Nonresidents of the hotel pay $40 for 18 holes in summer, $75 in winter. The caddy fee for 18 holes is $20.
   More crowded, but less expensive, are the fairlanes at **Heywoods,** St. Peter (tel. 422-4900). There, a publicly funded 9-hole par-3 executive golf course is open to anyone on the island. Greens fees are $16 for either 9 or 18 holes (no one will object if you opt to circumnavigate the course twice). You can rent clubs and a pull cart for $10 extra.
   A 9-hole executive course is at the **Buckley Resort Hotel,** Golf Club Road, Worthing, Christ Church (tel. 435-7880). Greens fees are $18 for the 9 holes.

HORSEBACK RIDING   A different view of Barbados is offered by the **Caribbean International Riding Centre,** c/o the Roachford family, Auburn, St. Joseph's (tel. 433-1453). Maintained by Swedish-born Elizabeth Roachford and her four daughters, it boards nearly 40 horses. Mrs. Roachford or one of her daughters (each of whom was trained in the standards of the Swedish equestrian traditions) offer a variety of trail rides for horse enthusiasts of any level of experience. Their shortest ride provides a 75-minute escorted trek through tropical forests, followed by relaxation over a cool drink in the clubroom. The price, which includes transportation to and from your hotel and a complimentary drink, is $55 BDS ($27.50). A more comprehensive 2- or 3-hour trail ride along the sublimely beautiful Atlantic coast is offered for $100 BDS ($55). Longest of all is a 4-hour equestrian tour of the historic Villa Nova Plantation, which includes a tour of the famous great house and the countryside around it, and lunch, all at a cost of $175 BDS ($87.50). Advance reservations are strongly advised.

SNORKELING & SCUBA DIVING   The clear waters off Barbados have a visibility of more than 100 feet most of the year. More than 50 varieties of fish are found on the shallow inside reefs. On night dives, sleeping fish, night anemones, lobsters, moray eels, and octopuses can be seen. On a mile-long coral reef 2 minutes by boat from **Sandy Beach,** sea fans, corals, gorgonias, and reef fish are plentiful. *J.R.,* a dredge barge sunk as an artificial reef in 1983, is popular with beginners for its coral, fish life, and 20-foot depth. The *Berwyn,* a coral-encrusted tugboat that sank in Carlisle Bay in 1916, attracts photographers because of its variety of reef fish, shallow depth, good light, and visibility.
   The **Asta Reef,** with a drop of 80 feet, has coral, sea fans, and reef fish in abundance. It's the site of a Barbados wreck sunk in 1986 as an artificial reef. **Dottins,** the most beautiful reef on the west coast, stretches 5 miles from Holetown

to Bridgetown and has numerous dive sites at an average depth of 40 feet and dropoffs of 100 feet. The S.S. *Stavronika*, a Greek freighter, is a popular dive site for advanced divers. Crippled by fire in 1976, the 360-foot freighter was sunk a quarter mile off the west coast to become an artificial reef in **Folkstone Underwater Park.** The mast is at 40 feet, the deck at 80 feet, and the keel at 140 feet. It's encrusted with coral.

The **Dive Shop,** Pebbles Beach, Aquatic Gap, Bay Street, St. Michael (tel. 426-9947), offers some of the best scuba diving in Barbados (costing about $40 per one-tank dive). Every day, two dive trips go out to the nearby reefs and wrecks. In addition, snorkeling trips and equipment rentals are possible. A 1-hour trip to a shipwreck, with equipment, goes for $8. Visitors with reasonable swimming skills who have never dived before can sign up for a resort course. Priced at $60, it includes pool-training safety instructions and a one-tank open-water dive. NAUI-certified, the establishment is open daily from 9am to 5pm.

TENNIS Most major hotels have their own tennis courts, some of which are lit for night games. Generally, if you're not a guest the hotels charge $12 BDS to $16 BDS ($6 to $8) per hour of court time.

At **Rockley Resort,** Christ Church (tel. 427-5890), courts are open from 8am to 10pm. At **Heywoods,** St. Peter (tel. 422-1581), the courts are in use daily from 7am to 11pm; day play is complimentary to guests, while there is an $8-per-hour charge for night games. You can play at the **Sunset Crest Club,** St. James (tel. 432-1309), from 8am to 11pm.

WINDSURFING Experts say that the windsurfing off **Bentson Beach** is as good as any this side of Hawaii. Judging from the crowds who flock here, it's probably true.

An establishment set up especially to handle the demand is the **Barbados Windsurfing Club,** at the Silver Sands Hotel, Christ Church (tel. 428-6001). It rents boards and gives lessons to learners. Club Mistral, a company run by Mistral A.G. of Germany, manufacturer of the finest windsurfing boards in the world, provides the rental fleet for the Barbados facility. This fleet consists of up to 100 boards, all current models with a selection of 200 sails.

5. SAVVY SHOPPING

Barbados merchants can sometimes treat you to duty-free merchandise at prices 20% to 40% lower than in the United States and Canada. Duty-free shops have two prices listed on items of merchandise, the local retail price and the local retail price less the government-imposed tax.

Some of the best duty-free buys include cameras (such as Leica, Rolex, and Fiji), watches (names like Omega, Piaget, Seiko), beautiful crystal (such as Waterford and Lalique), gold (especially jewelry), bone china (such names as Wedgwood and Royal Doulton), cosmetics and perfumes, and liquor (including Barbados rum and liqueurs), along with tobacco products and cashmere sweaters, tweeds, and sportswear from Britain.

If you purchase items made on the island of Barbados, you don't have to pay duty if you're a U.S. citizen.

The outstanding item in Barbados handcrafts is black-coral jewelry. Clay pottery is another Bajan craft, and in "What to See & Do," above, I recommend a visit to Chalky Mount and the Potteries, where this special craft originated. In the shops you'll also find a selection of locally made vases, pots, pottery mugs, glazed plates, and ornaments.

From local grasses and dried flowers, beautiful wall hangings are made, and the island craftspeople also turn out straw mats, baskets, and bags with raffia embroidery. Still in its infant stage, leatherwork is also found now in Barbados, particularly handbags, belts, and sandals.

Shopping hours, in general, are 8am to 4pm Monday through Friday and 8am to noon on Saturday.

BATIK CARIBE, Nicholas House, Broad St., Bridgetown. Tel. 436-9148.
Here you'll find original hand-dyed batik on quality 100% cotton and silk. Beautiful wall hangings are sold as well as a range of hand-hemmed scarves, beach and casual wear, and small gift items. Additional sales outlets are conveniently located, such as the Hilton Arcade and the Handicraft Shop at Marriott's Sam Lord's Castle. Visit their studio at Colleton Estate in St. John (tel. 433-1599) to see artisans working at this ancient craft.

BEST OF BARBADOS, in the Southern Palms Hotel, St. Lawrence Gap. Tel. 428-7171.
Part of an islandwide chain of seven stores, Best of Barbados sells only products designed and/or made on Barbados. It was established in 1975 by an English-born painter, Jill Walker, whose prints are bestsellers, and her husband, Jimmy. They sell articles celebrating aspects of island life, including coasters, mats, and trays with scenes of local life, T-shirts, pottery, dolls and games, and cookbooks, among other items. This tasteful shop is in a pink-and-white building around the corner from the entrance to Southern Palms.

CARIBBEAN CREATIONS, Bridge House, Careenage, Bridgetown. Tel. 431-0573.
Caribbean Creations has a fine selection of Caribbean items, including baskets, mahogany wood carvings, mats, bags, and other local souvenirs. It stands opposite Independence Arch.

CAVE SHEPHERD, Broad St., Bridgetown. Tel. 431-2121.
The best place to shop for duty-free merchandise on Barbados is Cave Shepherd, which has branches at Sunset Crest in Holetown, Speightstown, Heywoods Resort, Hastings, Grantley Adams Airport, and the Bridgetown Harbour. Cave Shepherd is the largest department store on Barbados and one of the most modern in the Caribbean. It was established in 1906, when the Cave family were the sole owners, but after a disastrous fire in 1969 it was rebuilt with the financial assistance of more than 2,000 Barbadians and went public. The store offers perfumes, cosmetics from the world's leading houses, fine full lead crystal and English bone china, sweaters, cameras, gold and silver jewelry, swimwear, leather goods, and batik, handcrafts, and souvenirs. More than 70 brands of liqueurs are sold as well as other spirits. After you finish shopping, relax on the top floor in the cool comfort of the Ideal Restaurant.

COTTON DAYS, Bridge House Complex. Tel. 431-0414.
Boutiques abound in Barbados, but Cotton Days is one of the best. It's run by Carol Cadogan, who designs tropical wear and is known for her one-of-a-kind items. For inspiration, she turns to the flora and fauna of the island and the world under the sea. She also sells the accessories to go with her apparel. *Vogue* and *Glamour* have praised her collection.

DA COSTA'S COLONNADE SHOPPE, Sunset Crest, St. James. Tel. 431-0029.
Here you'll find an excellent selection of fine china, such as Aynsley and Belleek giftware, Waterford crystal, Lladro and Florence figurines, and other items, all at duty-free prices. French fragrances and locally made handcrafts are also sold. The shop at Da Costas' Mall, Broad Street (tel. 429-4843), offers Royal Doulton, Wedgwood, and Aynsley fine china, plus articles from the other sources listed above.

HARRISON'S, 1 Broad St., Bridgetown. Tel. 431-5500.
In addition to this main shop, Harrison's has eight branch stores, all selling a wide variety of duty-free merchandise, including china, crystal, jewelry, leather goods, sweaters, and perfumes, all at fair prices. They've been in business since the 19th century.

MALL 34, Broad St. Tel. 429-9235.

Bridgetown's most modern shopping complex offers duty-free shopping in air-conditioned comfort. You can find watches, clocks, china, jewelry, crystal, linens, sweaters, and liquor, together with souvenir items and tropical fashions. A restaurant is on the top floor of the building, and shoppers can stop for a cool drink and a snack at the little café downstairs.

PELICAN VILLAGE, Princess Alice Hwy., Bridgetown. Tel. 426-1966.

While in Bridgetown, go down to the Pelican Village on Princess Alice Highway leading down to the city's Deep Water Harbour. A collection of island-made crafts and souvenirs is sold here in a tiny colony of thatch-roofed shops, and you can wander from one to the other. Sometimes you can see craftspeople at work. Some of the shops to be found here are gimmicky and repetitive, although interesting items can be found.

QUEEN'S PARK GALLERY, Queen's Park House, Bridgetown. Tel. 427-2345.

The visual arts are flowering in Barbados, as many painters, potters, and sculptors work in a wide variety of styles and media. This gallery is operated by the National Cultural Foundation and is open to the public daily. Call the above telephone number for the times of exhibitions and further information.

SEA NYMPH DRESS SHOPPE, in the Skyway Shopping Plaza, Hastings, South Coast. Tel. 429-4242.

This shop specializes in swimwear, hostess gowns, blouses, shorts, slacks, and dresses made to order.

WALKERS WORLD, St. Lawrence Gap. Tel. 431-0013.

This shop rightly claims that it sells "beautiful things from around the world." Close to the Southern Palms, it also offers many locally made items for sale, plus the famous Jill Walker prints.

6. EVENING ENTERTAINMENT

Most of the big resort hotels feature entertainment nightly, often dancing to steel bands and occasional Bajan floor shows. Sometimes beach barbecues are staged.

For the most authentic Bajan evening possible, head for **Baxters Road** in Bridgetown, a street that reaches its peak of liveliness on Friday and Saturday after 11pm. In fact, if you stick around until dawn, the joints are still jumping. The street is safer than it looks, because Bajans come here to have fun, not to make trouble. Entertainment tends to be spontaneous. Some old-time visitors have compared Baxters Road to the backstreets of New Orleans in the 1930s. If you fall in love with the place, you can "caf crawl" up and down the street, where nearly every bar is run by a Bajan mama. All prices are about the same, but each place has its own atmosphere.

The most popular "caf" on Baxters Road is **Enid's** (she has a phone, "but it doesn't work"), a little ramshackle establishment where Bajans come to devour Enid's fried chicken at 3 in the morning. Her place is open daily from 8:30pm to 8:30am, when the last satisfied customer departs into the blazing morning sun and Enid heads home to get some sleep before the new night begins. You can also stop in for a Banks beer.

PLANTATION RESTAURANT AND GARDEN THEATRE, Main Rd. (Hwy. 7), St. Lawrence. Tel. 428-5048.

This is the island's most visible showcase for evening dinner theater and Caribbean cabaret. Dinner and a show are presented every Monday, Wednesday, Friday, and Saturday. Dinner is served at 6:30pm, and one of two different shows (either *Barbados by Night* or the *Plantation Tropical Spectacular II*) is presented at 8 or 8:15pm, depending on the night of the week. Both involve plenty of exotic costumes, and lots of reggae, calypso, limbo, and Caribbean exoticism. Reservations in advance are recommended.

Admission (including unlimited drinks): Dinner and show, $42; show only, $17.50.

1627 AND ALL THAT SORT OF THING, at the Barbados Museum, St. Michael's Parish. Tel. 435-6900 or 427-0349 for reservations.

Nothing else on Barbados so effectively combines music with entertainment and dining, and on Thursday and Sunday evenings this is probably the most interesting place on the island. The format combines, in this order, a cocktail hour, a theatrical presentation (presented in two different segments as a kind of historical celebration of the Bajan experience) and an all-you-can-eat buffet. The museum that contains all this (and whose exhibits you're invited to inspect) was originally built as a British military garrison and lies close to the island's largest horseracing track, the Garrison Savannah. The price includes minivan transportation to and from the museum to your hotel. This is one of the best after-dark bargains in town, and you'll learn a lot as well as have fun. Shows are presented every Thursday and Sunday. Cocktail hour and museum inspections begin at 6pm, the first segment of the show begins at 7:30pm, the buffet is served at 8:30pm, and, as you eat, the final segment of the theater is shown between 9 and 9:45pm. Buses depart from the museum to deposit visitors back at their hotels at 10pm. Advance reservations are necessary.

Admission (including tax): $85 BDS ($42.50).

HARBOUR LIGHTS, Marine Villa, Bay St., St. Michael. Tel. 436-7225.

In theory, at least, the heart and soul of this club is a dignified seafront villa, originally built directly above the beachfront about a century ago. In reality, however, the party and its participants sprawl over the land that surrounds it, dancing and reveling to the sounds of the live bands or recorded music which fills the nighttime air. Dancing might break out anywhere, especially on the patio whose sightlines overlook the surf. No one under 18, and no one wearing shorts, is admitted. Grilled meats and hamburgers, priced at around $5 BDS ($2.50) each, are available from a barbecue pit/kiosk on the premises. The location is beside the seacoast about a mile southeast of Bridgetown. Live music can be heard Friday through Monday. Open: Daily 9:30pm–4:30am.

Admission: $10–$20 BDS ($5–$10), depending on the performers.

BEACH CLUB, Sunset Crest, St. James. Tel. 432-1309.

The Beach Club is a bar and restaurant that serves as a social focal point for Sunset Crest, with many island residents happily hobnobbing with their friends and colleagues. Happy hour at the Beach Bar is from 6 to 7pm nightly, when drinks are half price. Fish fries, barbecues, or buffets are offered from 7 to 9pm daily, costing $10 BDS to $35 BDS ($5 to $17.50). There's some kind of live entertainment every night, which might include live bands, amateur talent shows, films of Barbados, and local folk chorales. Saturday night is show night, when the entertainment is bigger and more theatrical than usual. Open: Daily 8am–3pm and 8–11pm.

Admission: Sat $5 BDS ($2.50) for nondiners; diners, and everyone Sun–Fri, free.

WATERFRONT CAFE, Cavan's Lane, The Careenage, Bridgetown. Tel. 427-0093.

By anyone's estimate, this is the busiest, most interesting, and most animated nighttime watering hole in Bridgetown. In a turn-of-the-century warehouse originally built to store bananas and freeze fish, it welcomes both diners and drinkers to its reverberating walls for Créole food, beer, and pastel-colored drinks. Live music (reggae, ragtime, rock and roll, or jazz) is presented Wednesday through Saturday from 8:30pm till closing. Hamburgers cost $14 BDS ($7), full Créole meals average $45 BDS ($22.50), and rum punch goes for $6 BDS ($3). Careenage Coffee, laced with various after-dinner potions, is an enduring favorite. Open: Daily 10am–midnight or 1am, depending on the crowd.

Admission: Free.

PIER 29, Cavan's Lane, The Careenage, Bridgetown. Tel. 429-6160.

The two-story premises here were originally built around 1900 as the first free-standing steel structure ever erected on Barbados. Devoted to the presentation of live bands and up-to-date recorded music, the establishment has a decor of dark carpeting and dozens of mirrors painted with replicas of things you might find near an underwater coral reef. There are also three bars whose different noise levels encourage either quiet dialogue or raucous shouting, depending on their proximity to the music. Open only 4 nights a week, Pier 29 draws a busy crowd which appreciates the chance to mingle. Beer costs $3 BDS ($1.50) per bottle. Open: Tues and Thurs–Sat 9:30pm–4am.

Admission: $5–$15 BDS ($2.50–$7.50), depending on entertainment.

COACH HOUSE, Paynes Bay, St. James. Tel. 432-1163.

The Coach House, named after a pair of antique coaches which stand opposite, is an ocher-colored house said to be 200 years old. The atmosphere is a Bajan version of an English pub. Businesspeople and habitués of the nearby beaches come here for the buffet lunches, offered Sunday through Friday from noon to 3pm, when Bajan food is served. The price is $20 BDS ($10) for an all-you-can-eat lunchtime assortment that includes local vegetables and salads prepared fresh daily. If you visit from 6 to 11pm, you can order bar meals, including flying fish and chips, with prices from $9 BDS ($4.50) and up. There's also a more formal evening dining room where meals, served from 6 to 11pm daily, begin at $45 BDS ($22.50) and include homemade soups and pâtés, shrimp Créole, local fish, steak, and chicken dishes. The pub is on the main Bridgetown Holetown road, just south of Sandy Lane, about 6 miles north of Bridgetown. Live music, featuring everything from steel bands to country and calypso, and an attentive crowd assemble together here Tuesday through Saturday from 9pm till closing. Open: Daily noon–2am.

Admission (including coupons worth $6 BDS/$3 U.S. of drinks at the bar): Tues–Sat $8 BDS ($4).

CLUB MILIKI, in the Heywood Hotel and Resort, St. Peter. Tel. 422-4900.

Club Miliki, which translates as "welcome" in West African dialect, plays recorded disco music by Bajan and international bands. The club is in one of the many buildings (just follow the trail markers) at the government's Heywoods Resort previously recommended (see "Where to Stay," above). All ages of clients come to drink and dance the night away. Beer costs $5 BDS ($2.50). Open: Wed–Sat 9pm–3am.

Admission: $10 BDS ($5).

PEPPERPOT, St. Lawrence Main Rd. Tel. 428-5678.

The Pepperpot is owned by international singing star Eddy Grant, who built this place on the site of the old Caribbean Pepperpot, which was for years the leading nightspot of Barbados. It features top live bands performing nightly within the precincts of this two-story open-air nightclub. Parking is available, and a taxi rank is nearby if you don't have a car. Drinks begin at $4 BDS ($2). Open: Daily 9pm–3:30am.

Admission: $10 BDS ($5).

FLAMBEAU BAR, in the Barbados Hilton, on Needham's Point, St. Michael. Tel. 426-0200.

The Flambeau Bar, an indoor-outdoor bar set in lush gardens by the sea, has a happy hour with free appetizers every evening between 5:30 and 6:30pm. Live music is presented on most nights, produced either by small groups or solo entertainers; otherwise, a disc jockey plays the latest hits. Open: Daily 5pm–1am.

Admission: Free.

CHAPTER 14

TRINIDAD & TOBAGO

- **FAST FACTS: TRINIDAD & TOBAGO**
- **WHAT'S SPECIAL ABOUT TRINIDAD & TOBAGO**
- **1. TRINIDAD**
- **2. TOBAGO**

Charted by Columbus on his third voyage in 1498, Trinidad has been peopled by immigrants from almost every corner of the world—Africa, the Middle East, Europe, India, China, and the Americas. It is against such a background that the island has become the fascinating mixture of cultures, races, and creeds that it is today.

Trinidad, which is about the size of Delaware, and its neighbor island, tiny Tobago, 20 miles to the northeast, together form a nation popularly known as "T&T." The islands of the new country are the southernmost outposts of the West Indies. Trinidad lies only 7 miles from the Paria Peninsula in Venezuela, to which in prehistoric times it was once connected.

The Spanish settled the island, which the Native Americans had called Iere, or "land of the hummingbird." The Spaniards made their first permanent settlement in 1592 and held onto it longer than they did any of their other real estate in the Caribbean. The English captured Trinidad in 1797, and it remained British until the two-island nation declared its independence in 1962. The Republic of Trinidad and Tobago is a parliamentary democracy, with a president and a prime minister.

FAST FACTS TRINIDAD & TOBAGO

Area Code To call Trinidad or Tobago from the U.S., dial area code 809 and then the local number. For information on making local calls on the islands, see "Telecommunications," below.

Banking Hours Banks stay open Monday through Thursday from 9am to 2pm and on Friday from 9am to noon and 3 to 5pm.

Currency The **Trinidad and Tobago dollar (TT)** is pegged to the U.S. dollar at an exchange rate of $1 U.S. to $4.25 TT ($1 TT is 23¢). Ask what currency is being referred to when rates are quoted to you. I've used a combination of both in this chapter, depending on the establishment. U.S. and Canadian dollars are accepted in exchange for payment, particularly in Port-of-Spain. However, you'll do better by converting your Canadian or U.S. dollars into local currency. *Note:* Unless otherwise specified, dollar quotations appearing in this chapter are in U.S. currency.

Customs Readers have reported long delays in clearing Customs on Trinidad. Personal effects are duty free, and visitors may bring in 200 cigarettes or 50 cigars plus 1 quart of "spirits."

Documents Visitors arriving in Trinidad and Tobago should have an ongoing or return ticket from their point of embarkation. You'll be asked to fill out an

WHAT'S SPECIAL ABOUT TRINIDAD & TOBAGO

Beaches

- ☐ Maracas Beach, the most splendid on Trinidad, enclosed by mountains with white sands, swaying coconut palms, and crystal-clear water.
- ☐ Pigeon Point, on the northwest coast of Tobago, the island's best-known bathing area, with a long coral-sand beach and thatched shelters.
- ☐ Man-O-War Bay, Tobago, one of the finest natural harbors in the Caribbean, with a long white sandy beach.
- ☐ Back Bay, one of Tobago's best white sandy beaches, a Robinson Crusoe fantasy—but watch those dangerous undercurrents.

Great Towns/Villages

- ☐ Port-of-Spain, capital of the nation known as T&T, home of the famous Trinidad Carnival and the most polyglot population in the West Indies.
- ☐ Scarborough, main port and villagelike capital of Tobago, "the land of the hummingbird."

Ace Attractions

- ☐ Caroni Bird Sanctuary, a 40-square-mile sanctuary in Trinidad that's the nesting ground of the scarlet ibis, the national bird of Trinidad and Tobago.
- ☐ Pitch Lake, in the geographic heart of Trinidad, one of the wonders of the world, an asphalt lake discovered, according to legend, by Sir Walter Raleigh.

- ☐ The Saddle, a humped pass on a ridge dividing Trinidad's Maraval Valley and the Santa Cruz Valley, where you'll see a panoramic sweep of the island's luxuriant vegetation.

Parks and Gardens

- ☐ Royal Botanical Gardens, covering 70 acres of Port-of-Spain's Savannah, filled with exotic tropical trees and plants, including the "raw beef tree" (if you cut it, it bleeds).
- ☐ Buccoo Reef, Tobago's sea gardens of coral sheltering hundreds of tropical fish, the natural aquarium of the island.

Historic Monuments

- ☐ Fort King George, towering 430 feet above Scarborough, built by the English in 1779, a citadel that the French and English contested for years.

Special Events

- ☐ The Carnival of Trinidad, called "the greatest show on earth," the Caribbean's most spectacular and dazzling celebration on the Monday and Tuesday preceding Ash Wednesday.

---

immigration card upon your arrival, and the carbon copy of this should be saved, as it must be returned to immigration officials when you depart. Citizens of the U.S. and Canada do not need passports to enter Trinidad and Tobago for stays of up to 2 months. However, they should have a birth certificate and a valid identification with photo ID.

Electricity The electricity is 110 or 220 volts AC, 60 cycles, but ask when making your hotel reservations so you'll know if you'll need transformers and/or adapters.

Embassies and High Commissions In Port-of-Spain on Trinidad, the **U.S. Embassy** is at 19 Queen's Park West (tel. 809/622-6371); the **Canadian High Commission** is at 72 South Quay (tel. 809/623-7254); the **British High Commission** is at Furness House, 90 Independence Square (tel. 809/625-2861); and the **New Zealand High Commission** is at 223 Western Main Road, St. James (tel. 809/622-7020).

TRINIDAD & TOBAGO

TOBAGO

N

Caribbean Sea

ST. GILES IS.
Charlotteville **9** Goat Is.
Bloody Bay
Parlatuvier
Castara **8** Speyside
LITTLE TOBAGO
Moriah Roxborough
Culloden Bay
Plymouth **7** Pembroke
Black Rock Mason Hall
Buccoo Reef **2 4**
3 SCARBOROUGH
Canaan **1** **Atlantic Ocean**
5 **6**

TRINIDAD

Caribbean Sea

Grand Rivière Galera Point
San Souci
Matelot Redhead
Blanchisseuse

5 9
Maraval **3 7** San Juan
Four Roads Tunapuna Tacarigua Matura Bay
St. Pierre **2 4 6** Arima
CHACACHACARE ISLANDS St. Joseph **9** Matura
PORT-OF-SPAIN **8** Arouca
Caroni Guanapo Guaico Sangre Grande
1 2 5 1 Chaguanas
3 4 6 7
Waterloo Upper Manzanilla

Gulf of Paria

Claxton Bay Cocos Bay
Point-à-Pitre Princess Pierreville
San Fernando Town Rio Claro
Pitch Lake La Brea Mayaro Bay
Debe Ortoire River
Preau Guayaguayure
Point Fortin Basseterre Galeota Point
Penal
Buenos Aires Moruga Moruga River
Fullarton San Francique
Icacos Point

Airport ✈

ACCOMMODATIONS:

Trinidad:
Asa Wright Nature Centre Lodge **9**
Chaconia Inn **3**
Holiday Inn **1**
Kapok Hotel and Restaurant **5**
Monique's Guest House **7**
Normandie, Hotel **4**
Pax Guest House **8**
Trinidad Hilton **2**
Valley Vue Hotel **6**
Zolina **9**
Tobago:
Blue Waters Inn **8**
Della Mira Guest House **6**

Grafton Beach Resort **1**
Kariwak Village **3**
Man-O-War Bay Cottages **9**
Richmond Great House **7**
Sandy Point Beach Club **5**
Turtle Beach **4**

DINING:
Café Savanna **3**
La Boucan **1**
La Fantasie **2**
Rafters **4**
Restaurant Singho **7**
Roof Garden Restaurant **5**
Solimar **3**
Tiki Village **3**
Veni Mange **6**

Emergency Call the **police** at 999. To report a **fire** or summon an **ambulance,** dial 990.

Holidays These include January 1 (New Year's Day), Good Friday, Easter Monday, June 7 (Whit Monday), June 18 (Corpus Christi), June 19 (Labour Day), August 1 (Emancipation Day), August 31 (Independence Day), September 24 (Republic Day), December 25 (Christmas Day), and December 26 (Boxing Day).

Information Before you go, write or call the **Trinidad & Tobago Tourism Development Authority,** 25 West 43rd Street, Suite 1508, New York, NY 10036 (tel. 212/719-0540). Locally, contact the board at 134–138 Frederick Street, Port-of-Spain (tel. 623-1932).

Language English is the official language, although you'll hear it spoken with many different accents, including cultured British. Hindi, Chinese, French, and Spanish are also spoken.

Safety As a general rule, Tobago is safer than its larger neighbor, Trinidad. Crime does exist, but it's not of raging dimensions. If you can, avoid the downtown streets of Port-of-Spain at night, especially those around Independence Square where muggings have been reported. It would also be wise to safeguard your valuables and never leave them unattended at the beach or even in a locked car.

Taxes and Service The big hotels and restaurants add at least a 10% to 15% service charge to your final tab; if not, you should tip 12% to 15%. In addition, the government imposes a 15% Value-Added Tax on room rates. It also imposes a departure tax of $50 TT ($11.75) on every passenger more than 5 years old.

Telecommunications On the islands, you don't need to dial the 809 area code, just the seven-digit number. Cables may be handed in at a hotel desk.

Time Trinidad and Tobago time is the same as the U.S. East Coast. In summer the islands go to daylight saving time.

Weather Trinidad has a tropical climate all year, with constant trade winds maintaining mean temperatures of 84° Fahrenheit during the day, 74° at night, with a range of 70° to 90°. The rainy season runs from May to November, but it shouldn't deter a visit at that time; the rain usually lasts no more than 2 hours before the sun comes out again. However, carry along plenty of insect repellent for visits during those times.

1. TRINIDAD

Trinidad is completely different from the other islands of the Caribbean, and that forms part of its charm and appeal. Visitors in increasing numbers are drawn to this island of many rhythms, where the swinging sounds of calypso, limbo, and steel-drum bands all began.

The people are part of the attraction on this island, the most cosmopolitan in the Caribbean. Its polyglot population includes Syrians, Chinese, Americans, Europeans, East Indians, Parsees, Madrasis, Venezuelans, and the last of the original Amerindians, the early settlers of the island. You'll also find Hindustanis, Javanese, Lebanese, African descendants, and Créole mixtures. The main religions are Christianity, Hinduism, and Islam. In all there are about 1.2 million inhabitants, whose language is English, although you may hear speech in a strange argot, Trinibagianese.

Port-of-Spain, in the northwestern corner of the island, is the capital, with the largest concentration of the population, about 120,000. With the opening of its $2-million cruise-ship complex in Port-of-Spain, Trinidad now has become a major port of call for Caribbean cruise lines. Many craft shops operate in the complex.

One of the most industrialized nations in the Caribbean, and the third-largest exporter of oil in the western hemisphere, Trinidad, measuring 50 by 38 miles, is also blessed with the huge 114-acre Pitch Lake from which comes most of the world's asphalt. Further, it's also the home of Angostura Bitters, the recipe for which is a guarded secret.

ORIENTATION

GETTING THERE From North America, Trinidad is one of the most distant islands in the Caribbean. Because of the legendary hostility of Trinidadian Customs, it's preferable to arrive during the day (presumably when your stamina might be at its peak) if you can schedule it.

Trinidad is the transfer point for many passengers heading on to the beaches of Tobago. For information about getting to Tobago, refer to Section 2 of this chapter.

The **American Airlines** (tel. toll free 800/433-7300) hub in San Juan receives hundreds of incoming flights every day from throughout North America, and then American offers a daily nonstop flight from San Juan to Port-of-Spain.

From New York, **BWIA** (tel. toll free 800/327-7401), the national carrier of Trinidad and Tobago, offers either two or three daily flights into Port-of-Spain, depending on the season. Only a handful of these are nonstops; many require a touchdown in Barbados before continuing without a change of aircraft on to Trinidad, the airline's home base. The others stop at either two or three other islands along the way.

From Miami, BWIA offers three daily flights to Port-of-Spain, the most convenient of which stops only once (in Aruba) before continuing on to a 7:45pm arrival in Trinidad. Earlier flights on BWIA tend to island-hop to as many as three other islands, which might include (depending on the schedule) Antigua, St. Lucia, Barbados, or Grenada.

Air Canada (tel. toll free 800/776-3000) makes two weekly nonstop flights from Toronto to Port-of-Spain.

If you're interested in including South America on your itinerary, you can go on a routing that **United Airlines** (tel. toll free 800/862-8621) acquired from the recently deceased Pan Am. United's routes to Trinidad begin in New York and go through Caracas, Venezuela. During the lifetime of this edition, a similar route originating in Miami might also reach Trinidad via Caracas. A stopover in Caracas does not add greatly to the price of your ticket, and gives an opportunity to explore one of South America's most interesting cities. Be warned, however, that if you opt for this routing, your arrival in Port-of-Spain will occur after midnight, and will probably require iron-clad hotel reservations.

ALM Airlines (tel. toll free 800/327-7230), the national airline of Curaçao, offers either direct or nonstop flights to Trinidad twice a week from its home base.

GETTING AROUND   By Bus All the cities of Trinidad are linked by regular bus service from Port-of-Spain. Fares are low: from 50¢ (for runs within the capital). However, buses are likely to be very overcrowded. Always try to avoid them at rush hours.

By Taxi There are lots of taxis in Trinidad, and they're identified by their license plates, beginning with the letter H. There are also "pirate taxis" as well—private cars that cruise around and pick up passengers like a regular taxi. Maxi Taxis or vans can also be hailed on the street. A taxi ride from Piarco Airport into Port-of-Spain generally costs about $16.

Most drivers also serve as guides. Their rates, however, are based on route distances, so get an overall quotation and agree on the actual fare before setting off. All fares are subject to 50% increases after midnight.

By Rental Car There are some 4,500 miles of good roads, but whereas touring outside Port-of-Spain goes quickly, the fierce traffic jams of the capital are legendary. And although your rental car will probably have a right-hand-mounted steering wheel, *you'll be required to drive on the left.* You'll also need a good map.

The major U.S.-based car-rental firms currently have no franchises on the island. If you want to rent a car, you have to make arrangements with a local firm (go over the terms and insurance agreements carefully). Count on spending about $50 per day or more, with unlimited mileage included. In theory you should have an international driver's license, but a valid U.S. or Canadian license will do for stays of up to 2 months.

One of the island's leading local car-rental firms is **Bacchus Taxi & Car Rental Service,** 37 Tragarete Road, Port-of-Spain (tel. 622-5588). With unlimited mileage, plus all insurance included, a functional but peppy Nissan, Sunny, or Charmant rents for $160 TT ($37.65) per day.

To avoid the anxiety of driving, you can rent taxis and local drivers for your sightseeing jaunts. Although it costs more, it alleviates the hassles of badly marked (or unmarked roads) and contact with the sometimes bizarre local driving patterns; if a rented taxi and driver is too expensive, you can take an organized tour. Night driving is especially hazardous.

By Organized Tour Sightseeing tours are offered by **The Travel Center,** Uptown Mall, Edward Street, Port-of-Spain (tel. 623-5101). The tours are made in late-model sedans, with a trained driver-guide. Prices are quoted on a seat-in-car basis. Private arrangements will cost more.

A city tour, lasting 2 hours, will take you past the main points of interest of Port-of-Spain: Whitehall, the President's House, Queen's Park Savannah, the Botanical Gardens, the National Museum and Art Gallery, the Emperor Valley Zoo, cathedrals, a mosque, temples, and through the commercial and residential centers, then to Lady Young Look-out for a view of the city. This trip leaves daily at 10am.

You'll see tropical splendor at its best on a Port-of-Spain/Maracas Bay/Saddle Road jaunt leaving at 1pm daily, lasting 3½ hours. The tour begins with a drive around Port-of-Spain, passing the main points of interest listed above and then going on through the beautiful mountain scenery over the "Saddle" of the northern range to Maracas Bay, a popular beach. You return via Saddle Road, Santa Cruz Valley, the village of San Juan, and the Lady Young Road for the view of Port-of-Spain.

An Island Circle Tour is a 7-hour journey that includes lunch and a welcome drink. Leaving at 9am daily, your car goes south along the west coast with a view of the Gulf of Paria, across the central plains, through Pointe-à-Pierre and San Fernando, and on eastward into rolling country overlooking sugarcane fields. Then you go down into the coconut plantations along the 14-mile-long Mayaro Beach for a swim and lunch before returning along Manzanilla Beach and back to the city.

An especially interesting trip is to Caroni Swamp and Bird Sanctuary, a 4-hour trek by car and boat into the sanctuary where you'll see rich Trinidad bird life.

ESSENTIALS For your medical needs, there is the **Oxford Pharmacy,** at the corner of Charlotte Street and Oxford Street in Port-of-Spain (tel. 627-4657). The **Port-of-Spain General Hospital** is on Charlotte Street (tel. 623-2951). The main **post office** is on Wrightson Road, Port-of-Spain, and is open Monday through Friday from 7am to 5pm. You can send a cable at the offices of **Textel,** 1 Edward Street, Port-of-Spain.

CARNIVAL & CALYPSO ✪ Called "the world's most colorful festival," the Carnival of Trinidad is a spectacle of dazzling costumes and gaiety. Hundreds of bands of masqueraders parade through the cities on the Monday and Tuesday preceding Ash Wednesday, bringing traffic to a standstill. The island seems to explode with music, fun, and dancing. It has been called a 48-hour orgy!

Hotel accommodations are booked months in advance, and most inns raise their prices at the time.

Some of the carnival costumes cost hundreds of dollars. For example, "bands" might depict the birds of Trinidad, such as the scarlet ibis and the keskidee; or a bevy of women might come out in the streets dressed as cats. Costumes are also satirical and comical.

The top calypsonian is proclaimed king. On one occasion, the King of Carnival appeared dressed as a "Devil Ray" with a gigantic "delta wing," his eyes glinting behind a black mask, his body bound in black leather studded with silver.

Trinidad, of course, is the land of calypso, which grew out of the folksong of the Afro-West Indian. The lyrics command the greatest attention, as they are rich in satire and innuendo. The calypsonian is considered a poet-musician, and lyrics have often been considered libelous and obscene, as capable of toppling politicians from office today as they have in the past. In banter and bravado, the calypsonian reveals and gives voice to the sufferings, hopes, and aspirations of his people. At carnival time the artist sings his compositions to spectators in places called by the traditional name of "tents." There are five or six shows a night at the calypso tents around town, from 8pm to midnight. Tickets for these are sold in the afternoon at most record shops.

Carnival parties, or fêtes, with three or four orchestras at each one, are public and are advertised in the newspapers. Tickets for these events, which go on for several weeks before Carnival ends on Shrove Tuesday, cost $50 TT to $60 TT ($11.75 to $14.10). For a really wild time, attend a party on Sunday night before Carnival Monday. To reserve tickets, contact the **National Carnival Committee,** 92 Frederick Street, Port-of-Spain, Trinidad (tel. 809/623-7510).

You can attend rehearsals of steel bands at their headquarters, called panyards, beginning about 7pm. Preliminary band competitions are held at the grandstand of the Queen's Park Savannah in Port-of-Spain and at Skinners Park in San Fernando, beginning some 3 weeks before carnival.

WHERE TO STAY

The number of hotels is limited, and don't expect your Port-of-Spain room to open directly on a white sandy beach—the nearest beach is a long, costly taxi ride away. Don't forget that 15% tax and 10% service charge will be added to your hotel and restaurant bills.

VERY EXPENSIVE

TRINIDAD HILTON, Lady Young Rd. (P.O. Box 442), Port-of-Spain, Trinidad, W.I. Tel. 809/624-3211, or toll free 800/445-8667. Fax 809/624-3211. 388 rms, 24 suites. A/C TV TEL

$ Rates: $120–$160 single; $137–$175 double; from $380 suites. Breakfast from $9 extra. AE, DC, MC, V. **Parking:** Free.

By anyone's standards, this is the most dramatic and architecturally sophisticated hotel on Trinidad. Because of its position on some of the steepest terrain in Port-of-Spain, the building's lobby lies on its uppermost floor, and the rooms are staggered in rocky but verdant terraces that sweep down the hillside. Its location just above Queen's Park Savannah provides most of its rooms with a view of the sea and mountains.

The hotel offers a wide range of accommodations, from standard rooms through rooms with minibars; the more expensive rooms, on the Plaza Level, have upgraded services and amenities and complimentary continental breakfast. Regardless of their comfort levels, all units have balconies and a comfortably neutral international decor. One of the benefits of a stay here is that some of the most sought-after musical entertainment on Trinidad appears as a standard part of the hotel's many offerings. And for the business traveler, the Hilton is the best choice of the island.

Dining/Entertainment: The main dining room, La Boucan (see "Where to Dine," below), contains museum-quality murals by one of the island's best-known artists (Geoffrey Holder). Less formal are the Pool Terrace and the Gazebo, both of which serve Caribbean and international food and colorful drinks in sun-flooded settings. Live music is played every evening in the Aviary Bar until 2am. The hotel always books plenty of activities, with pool barbecues featuring roast suckling pig, weekly fiestas, sometimes extraordinarily talented steel-band concerts, and limbo contests.

Services: Room service (6am–11:30pm daily), concierge, baby-sitting, massage, travel agency, car-rental kiosk.

Facilities: Swimming pool with a refreshment bar (the Gazebo), two all-weather tennis courts (lit at night), two-story arcade with handcraft shops, business center (with 24-hour Telex, fax, and cable facilities; worldwide courier service for documents; and secretarial and translation services).

EXPENSIVE

HOLIDAY INN, Wrightson Rd. at London Rd. (P.O. Box 1017), Port-of-Spain, Trinidad, W.I. Tel. 809/625-3361, or toll free 800/465-4329. Fax 809/625-4166. 230 rms, 5 suites. A/C TV TEL

$ Rates: $95 single; $105 double; $168 suite. Breakfast from $9 extra. AE, DC, MC, V. **Parking:** Free.

Originally built during the 1960s in an internationally modern style, and proud of its role as the second-largest hotel (after the Hilton) on Trinidad, the Holiday Inn contains all the amenities a businessperson might appreciate, as well as a handful of resort-inspired "trimmings." It lies on the northern perimeter of the city's commercial zone, a 5-minute walk from the center. Most of the hotel bedrooms have a freshness to them, with private balconies, two double beds, and radios. You forget, at least for a while, the raging traffic of the city that surrounds you.

Dining/Entertainment: The hotel is topped by La Ronde, its revolving 14th-floor restaurant, where diners have a view of the coastline of Venezuela, 9 miles across the sea. A West Indian and international menu is featured.

Facilities: Swimming pool with thatched poolside bar.

MODERATE

CHACONIA INN, 106 Saddle Rd. (P.O. Box 3340), Maraval, Trinidad, W.I. Tel. 809/628-8603. Fax 809/628-3214. 27 rms, 4 apartments. A/C TV TEL

$ Rates: $65–$75 single; $75–$85 double or twin; $120–$140 two-bedroom apartment. MAP $30 per person extra. Higher rates during Carnival. AE, DC, MC, V.

Named for the country's scarlet national flower, the Chaconia is a miniature self-contained resort 3 miles north of Port-of-Spain in the cool mountain residential valley of Maraval. Its buildings are simple, and its furnishings are in a contemporary motel idiom. Ken E. Duval, the managing director, runs one of Trinidad's finest small hotels, and does so with some flair. You'll be housed in one of three different types of accommodations, including two-bedroom apartments, superior rooms, and standard rooms. All are equipped with private baths and radios, and the superior rooms and apartments also have kitchenette facilities. In addition to the dining room/lounge, there is a Roof Garden Restaurant where an international cuisine is served.

HOTEL NORMANDIE, 10 Nook Ave., St. Ann's (P.O. Box 851), Port-of-Spain, Trinidad, W.I. Tel. 809/624-1181. Fax 809/624-1181, ext. 2315. 52 rms. A/C TV TEL

$ Rates: $60–$80 single; $70–$90 double. Continental breakfast from $6. AE, DC, MC, V. **Parking:** Free.

Originally built in the 1920s, this was already a well-established hotel when its owners drastically modernized it in 1986. It rises around a banyan- and banana-filled courtyard that surrounds a cool swimming pool accented with a jet of water. Inside, each room has a balcony or patio, and the beds in some rooms are set onto minilofts arranged in a small-scale but serviceable duplex format.

Calm and cosmopolitan, the hotel sits 3½ miles northwest of the city center, next to one of the best art galleries on Trinidad, a skylight-covered shopping center, an attractive restaurant (La Fantasie), the botanical gardens of Port-of-Spain, and the official residence of the president of Trinidad and Tobago.

KAPOK HOTEL AND RESTAURANT, 16-18 Cotton Hill, St. Clair, Trinidad, W.I. Tel. 809/622-6441. Fax 809/622-9677. 65 rms, 6 suites. A/C TV TEL

$ Rates: $65 single; $75 double; from $135 suites. Rates higher during Carnival. Continental breakfast from $3.50 extra. AE, DC, MC, V. **Parking:** Free.

The Kapok is a modern nine-floor hotel located in the pleasant residential suburb of St. Clair, a minute's drive from the city's biggest park, the Savannah. From its lounge, you have a panoramic view not only of the Savannah, but also of the Gulf of Paria. Guests who prefer small to medium-sized hotels feel at home here, and appreciate the slick neatness, the comfortably appointed bedrooms, and the rooftop restaurant serving Chinese and Polynesian food. On the ground floor of the hotel is the Café Savanna, one of the better-known restaurants of Trinidad. In the back is a small pool with a sunning area. The well-furnished, spacious rooms have private baths and are decorated with wicker furniture.

VALLEY VUE HOTEL, Ariapita Rd., St. Ann's, Trinidad, W.I. Tel. 809/624-0940. Fax 809/627-8046. 48 rms, 20 suites. A/C MINIBAR TV TEL

$ Rates: $70–$90 single; $80–$100 double; from $120 suite. Breakfast from $8 extra. AE, DC, MC, V. **Parking:** Free.

Originally built in 1986, this modern hotel about 5 miles northwest of the center of Port-of-Spain maintains a vaguely English kind of decor, lots of wicker furniture, and occasional use of marble in its floors and walls. Each of the pleasant bedrooms contains two telephones, a balcony, and comfortably unpretentious furniture. On the premises is an oval swimming pool with a "swim-through" bar and a water slide, two squash courts, a beauty parlor, gift shop, and an airy restaurant called the Prima Vera.

INEXPENSIVE

ASA WRIGHT NATURE CENTRE AND LODGE, Spring Hill Estate, Arima, Trinidad, W.I. Tel. 809/667-4655, or toll free 800/426-7781. Fax 914/273-6370 (in New York state). 22 rms (all with bath). A/C

$ Rates (including all meals, afternoon tea, and a welcoming rum punch): Winter, $124 single; $91 per person double. Summer, $97.50 single; $71 per person double. No credit cards. **Parking:** Free.

There really isn't anything else like it in the Caribbean. Known to birdwatchers throughout the world, this center sits on 196 acres of protected land at an elevation of 1,800 feet in the rain-forested northern mountain range of Trinidad, 10 miles north of Arima, beside Blanchisseuse Road. Hummingbirds, toucans, bellbirds, manakins, several varieties of tanagers, and the rare oilbird are all on the property. It's not uncommon for a guest who has not previously visited the South American tropics to record 30 "lifebirds" before breakfast, and this without leaving the veranda of the main house. Accommodations are available in the lodge's self-contained rooms, in guest bedrooms in the Edwardian main house, or in one of the cottages built on elevated ground above the main house.

Guided tours (priced at about $12 per half-day outing) are available on the nature center's grounds, which contain several well-maintained trails. The center also offers guided bird tours to a variety of different wildlife habitats.

For more information or to make reservations, call the above toll-free number or write Caligo Ventures, 156 Bedford Rd., Armonk, NY 10504.

MONIQUE'S GUEST HOUSE, 114 Saddle Rd., Maraval, Trinidad, W.I. Tel. 809/628-3334. 11 rms (all with bath). A/C TEL

$ Rates: From $40 single or double; from $45 triple. Continental breakfast $3 extra. MC, V. **Parking:** Free.

A rebuilt bungalow in the lush Maraval Valley, Monique's is about 8 minutes (3 miles) north of downtown Port-of-Spain. Mike and Monica Charbonne have an informal and comfortable home where they offer spacious rooms. Most units are furnished with two double beds, and one room is specifically designed for the aged or disabled. There's a TV room and a beautiful lawn where fellow guests can gather to exchange travel tips. Arrangements can be made for guests to go to a nearby swimming pool.

PAX GUEST HOUSE, Tunapuna, Trinidad, W.I. Tel. 809/662-4084. 14 rms (none with bath).

$ Rates (including all meals): From $60 per person. No credit cards. **Parking:** Free.

This well-run guesthouse occupies a substantial building nestled on the ledge of a hill halfway between the airport and Port-of-Spain. It's really like a spiritual retreat, and was once used as such for Catholic Dutch fathers. Capping the hillside are a church, monastery, and school, although the guesthouse is nonsectarian. The neat, clean, uncluttered rooms have twin beds and cold water. Guests use the corridor baths, which have hot water.

The food is above average, with an emphasis on local specialties. The dining room is spacious with two walls of windows providing a view of the valley, and meals are served family style. There's also a wide front veranda from which you can look out onto vistas of hibiscus, bougainvillea, and poinsettia. Bus transport is possible, but of course it's better to have your own car. Birdwatchers can discover up to 65 different species of birds around the grounds of the hotel on their first day.

ZOLLNA HOUSE, 12 Ramlogan Development, La Seiva, Maraval, Trinidad, W.I. Tel. 809/628-3731. Fax 809/627-0856. 7 rms (2 with bath).

$ Rates (including continental breakfast): $30 single without bath, $35 single with bath; $50 double without bath, $55 double with bath. No credit cards. **Parking:** Free.

On a hillside in the Maraval Valley with a view of Port-of-Spain and the Gulf of Paria, Zollna House is 2 miles from the capital and a quarter of a mile off Saddle Road. The two-story building has comfortably furnished bedrooms, two large porches, two indoor lounges, a beverage bar and games room, and dining areas on two floors, as well as a patio/barbecue set-up outdoors. The garden is lush with flowering shrubs and fruit trees, home to a variety of birds. The house, white with black trim, is almost obscured by trees, but you can find it by going along Saddle Road, turning into La Seiva Road, and going uphill for about a quarter of a mile.

WHERE TO DINE

The food on Trinidad is as varied and cosmopolitan as the islanders themselves. Although this was a British colony for years, the cookery of Olde England never made much impression on Trinidadians. Red-hot curries remind one of the island's strong East Indian influence, and some Chinese dishes are about as good here as any you'll find in Hong Kong. Créole and Spanish fare, as well as French, are also to be enjoyed.

A typical savory offering is a rôti, a king-size crêpe, highly spiced and rolled around a filling of chicken, shellfish, or meat. Of course, you may prefer to skip such local delicacies as opossum stew and fried armadillo. Naturally, your fresh rum punch will have a dash of Angostura Bitters.

EXPENSIVE

LA BOUCAN, in the Trinidad Hilton, Lady Young Rd. Tel. 624-3211.
   Cuisine: INTERNATIONAL. **Reservations:** Required.

$ Prices: Appetizers $15–$45 TT ($3.55–$10.60); main courses $44–$110 TT ($10.35–$25.90); lunch buffet $55 TT ($12.95); dinner buffet $80 TT ($18.85). AE, DC, MC, V.

   Open: Lunch Mon–Sat noon–2:30pm; dinner Mon–Sat 7–11:30pm.

Considered the finest restaurant in Trinidad, with some of the most sumptuous buffets, this establishment satisfies the eye as well as the palate. Against one of its longest walls stretches a graceful, museum-quality mural by Geoffrey Holder, one of the most famous artists of the Caribbean. (Born in Trinidad, although living in New York most of his life, he painted this mural to honor the social gatherings that used to take place in Port-of-Spain's central park, the Savannah. Today, it's considered one of the island's most famous works of art.)

Typical dishes include smoked breast of duckling with seasonal fruits, thinly sliced filet of shark (smoked on the premises over coals of guava wood), stuffed crab back, and a house specialty known as Crusoe's Treasure Chest (butter-fried tenderloins stuffed with chunks of Tobago lobster served with a tomato concasse). Also popular are the trio of fresh fish which appears every day on the menu, and which can be poached, pan-fried, or grilled any way you want them; and an array of succulently smoked pork, beef, duck, and lamb dishes. Desserts are sumptuous. As you dine, live music from a lacquered piano (and on weekends from a dance band) provides entertainment.

LA FANTASIE, 10 Nook Ave., St. Ann's Village. Tel. 624-1181.
   Cuisine: FRENCH/CREOLE. **Reservations:** Not required.
$ Prices: Appetizers $12–$15 TT ($2.85–$3.55); main courses $45–$120 TT ($10.60–$28.25). AE, DC, MC, V.
   Open: Lunch daily noon–2pm; dinner daily 7–10pm.
Off Queen's Park Savannah, and named after the 18th-century plantation that once stood here, La Fantasie is loaded with style and features a tempting modern Créole cuisine. The changing menu might include filet mignon with a tamarind-flavored sauce, locally caught Trinidadian salmon in a wine-based sauce with sultana raisins and bananas, and shrimp with Créole sauce in a pastry shell flavored with cheese. "Fish walk up the hill" is grilled fish with chopped herbs. Meals might follow with a Trinidadian fruitcake with a rum-flavored custard.

MODERATE

CAFE SAVANNA, in the Kapok Hotel, 16–18 Cotton Hill, St. Clair. Tel. 622-6441.
   Cuisine: CARIBBEAN. **Reservations:** Recommended.
$ Prices: Appetizers $15–$20 TT ($3.55–$4.70); main courses $50–$80 TT ($11.75–$18.85). AE, DC, MC, V.
   Open: Mon–Fri 11:45am–10pm, Sat 6:45–10:30pm.
On the ground floor of a previously recommended hotel, a minute's drive from the Savannah, Café Savanna serves an excellent Caribbean cuisine that is known throughout the island. The specialties change seasonally, but sizzling steaks are always available, and lobster is often available. The warmly accented haven of the dining room is embellished with slabs of opaque glass. Also in the same hotel is the popular Tiki Village Restaurant, which serves Chinese and Polynesian food (see below).

RAFTERS, 6A Warner St., Newtown. Tel. 628-9258.
   Cuisine: SEAFOOD. **Reservations:** Not required. A short walk off the Savannah.
$ Prices: Appetizers $10–$20 TT ($2.35–$4.70); main courses $25–$95 TT ($5.90–$22.35); seafood buffet from $75 TT ($17.65). AE, DC, MC, V.
   Open: Lunch Mon–Fri 11:30am–3pm; dinner Mon–Sat 6:30–11pm (seafood buffet Wed and Fri–Sat 7:30–10pm).
⑤ Rafters is housed in a century-old grocery shop in the central business district of a suburb of Port-of-Spain. Three nights a week there's a special seafood buffet, and you can also order from an à la carte menu devoted mainly to local seafood items. In the lounge, a snack-and-sandwich menu is offered daily, attracting clients of all ages and occupations. Busy crowds congregate on Friday and Saturday nights to listen to the sounds of the DJ or live local bands. Entrance is free except during live performances when a $10-TT ($2.30) cover charge is levied.

ROOF GARDEN RESTAURANT, in the Chaconia Inn, 106 Saddle Rd., Maraval. Tel. 628-8603.
   Cuisine: INTERNATIONAL. **Reservations:** Required.
$ Prices: Appetizers $12–$22 TT ($2.85–$5.20); main courses $45–$75 TT ($10.60–$17.65). AE, DC, MC, V.

Open: Lunch daily 11am–2pm; dinner daily 7–11pm.

Located 3 miles north of Port-of-Spain, the Chaconia serves some of the best hotel food on Trinidad. Ken E. Duval, the managing director, has a good wine list and lots of continental specialties as well as Trinidadian dishes. The staff is helpful and the service good. The dining room/lounge is open daily and meals are à la carte. There is a large selection of appetizers, steaks, seafood, poultry, salads, sandwiches, and desserts. The restaurant serves a barbecue dinner on Friday and Saturday from 7 to 11pm, charging $45 TT ($10.60) and up.

SOLIMAR, 6 Nook Ave., St. Ann. Tel. 624-1459.

Cuisine: INTERNATIONAL. **Reservations:** Recommended.

$ **Prices:** Appetizers $9–$26 TT ($2.10–$6.10); main courses $24–$71 TT ($5.65–$16.70). V.

Open: Dinner only, Mon–Sat 6:30–10:30pm. **Closed:** 6 weeks in midsummer (dates vary).

By some estimates, this restaurant offers the most creative cuisine and most original format in Trinidad and Tobago. Established by an English-born chef (Joe Brown) who worked for many years in the kitchens of Hilton hotels around the world, it occupies a garden-style building whose open walls are cooled by ceiling fans. As you dine, you'll hear the sound of an artificial waterfall which cascades into a series of fish ponds. The restaurant is opposite the Hotel Normandie, 3½ miles northwest of the city center.

The menu, which changes every month, presents local ingredients inspired by the cuisines of the world. They might include a Singapore-derived specialty of beef serondeng (cooked with tamarind, cilantro, and coconut), an English-inspired combination of grilled breast of chicken and jumbo shrimp dressed with a lobster sauce, and a dish from Puerto Rico composed of medallions of pork in a honey-mustard sauce.

TIKI VILLAGE, in the Kapok Hotel, 16-18 Cotton Hill, St. Clair. Tel. 622-6441.

Cuisine: POLYNESIAN/CHINESE. **Reservations:** Recommended, especially for dinner.

$ **Prices:** Appetizers $7–$15 TT ($1.65–$3.55) at lunch, $7–$20 TT ($1.65–$4.70) at dinner; main courses $45–$55 TT ($10.60–$12.95) at lunch, $45–$70 TT ($10.60–$16.45) at dinner; portions of dim sum $8 TT ($1.90) each; lunch buffet $34.50–$43.50 TT ($8.10–$10.25). AE, DC, MC, V.

Open: Lunch daily 11:30am–7pm; dinner daily at 7:30 and 9pm.

Tiki Village, named after and inspired by a South Seas theme, perches on the top floor of a previously recommended hotel and has a panoramic view of the nearby Queen's Park Savannah. Decorated in a medley of sunset colors, the restaurant prides itself on an assortment of hors d'oeuvres (which arrives flaming at your table) known as a Polynesian delight. The eggroll is among the best I've ever ordered in the West Indies. Among the main courses, I'd recommend the Hawaiian luau fish—a whole fish coated with water-chestnut flour and fried crisply before it's engulfed in a sweet-and-pungent sauce. Chicken provincial is boneless cubes sautéed in a black-bean sauce. Desserts include a Polynesian cheesecake, followed by Chinese tea. Especially charming is the assortment of dim sum (delicately fashioned Chinese versions of ravioli) which appear on the lunchtime menu only on Saturday and Sunday.

INEXPENSIVE

RESTAURANT SINGHO, Long Circular Mall, Port-of-Spain. Tel. 628-2077.

Cuisine: CHINESE. **Reservations:** Not required.

$ **Prices:** Appetizers $3–$18 TT (70¢–$4.25); main courses $12–$50 TT ($2.85–$11.75). AE, MC, V.

Open: Daily 11am–11pm.

Lined with planks of cedar, this restaurant contains an almost mystically illuminated bar and aquarium. The restaurant is on the second floor of one of the capital's largest shopping malls, midway between the commercial center of Port-of-Spain and the Queen's Park Savannah. A la carte dishes include shrimp with oyster sauce, shark-fin soup, stewed or curried beef, almond pork, and spareribs with black-bean sauce. A large percentage of this establishment's business derives from its take-away service, which is one of the best-known in town.

VENI MANGE, 13 Lucknow St. Tel. 622-7533.
   Cuisine: CREOLE. **Reservations:** Recommended for groups of six or more.
$ **Prices:** Appetizers $1–$3; main courses $5–$9. AE, MC, V.
   Open: Mon–Thurs 11:30am–2:30pm, Fri 11:30am–9pm.

Built in the 1950s of ocher stucco, Veni Mangé (which translates from the Créole argot as "come and eat") lies on a tranquil residential street right off Western Main Road, 3 miles west of the city center, on the opposite edge of the Savannah from the Hilton hotel. If you can find this tiny home, you'll get a fine welcome from Allyson Hennessy and her sister, Rosemary Hezekiah. (Allyson spends her mornings hosting a daily television talk show which is broadcast throughout Trinidad.) Best described as a new generation of Créole women, both Allyson and Rosemary (whose parents were English/Venezuelan and Afro-Caribbean/Chinese) entertain with their humor and charm.

Start with the bartender's special, a coral-colored fruit punch, which is a rich, luscious mixture of the golden papaya and a banana whose skin is allowed to turn black so that its taste is most flavorsome. On some days they do an authentic callaloo soup, which, according to Trinidadian legend, can make a man propose marriage. Save room for one of the main courses, such as curried crab or West Indian hotpot (a variety of meat cooked Créole style), perhaps a vegetable lentil loaf. The helpings are large, and if you still have room, order their pineapple upside-down cake, unless you prefer a homemade version of soursop ice cream or a coconut mousse.

Because of local zoning laws, only lunch is served, though on Friday the place stays open until 9pm as a bar and rendezvous point.

WHAT TO SEE & DO
PORT-OF-SPAIN

One of the busiest harbors in the Caribbean, Trinidad's capital, Port-of-Spain, can be explored on foot. Most tours begin at ✪ **Queen's Park Savannah,** on the northern edge of the city. Called "The Savannah," it consists of 199 acres, complete with a race course, cricket fields, and vendors hawking coconut water. What is now the park was once a sugar plantation until it was swept by a fire in 1808 that destroyed hundreds of homes.

Among the Savannah's outstanding buildings is the pink-and-blue **Queen's Royal College,** containing a clock tower with Westminster chimes. Today a school for boys, it stands on Maraval Road at the corner of St. Clair Avenue. On the same road, the family home of the Roodal clan is affectionately called **"the gingerbread house"** by Trinidadians. It was built in the baroque style of the French Second Empire.

In contrast, the family residence of the Strollmeyers was built in 1905 and is a copy of a German Rhenish castle. Nearby stands **Whitehall,** which was once a private mansion but today has been turned into the office of the prime minister of Trinidad and Tobago. In the Moorish style, it was erected in 1905 and served as the U.S. Army headquarters in World War II. These houses, including Hayes Court, the residence of the Anglican bishop of Trinidad, and others form what is known as **"the magnificent seven"** big mansions standing in a row.

On the south side of the Memorial Park, a short distance from the Savannah and within walking distance of the major hotels, stands the **National Museum and Art Gallery,** 117 Frederick Street (tel. 623-7116), open Tuesday through Sunday from 10am to 6pm. The museum contains a representative exhibition of Trinidad artists, including an entire gallery devoted to Michel Jean Cazabon (1813–88), permanent collections of historical artifacts giving a general overview of the island's history and culture, Amerindian archeology, British historical documents, and a small natural-history exhibition including geology, corals, and insect collections.

At the southern end of Frederick Street, the main artery of Port-of-Spain's shopping district, stands **Woodford Square.** The gaudy **Red House,** a large Neo-Renaissance building built in 1906, is the seat of the government of Trinidad and Tobago. Nearby stands **Holy Trinity Cathedral,** whose Gothic look may remind you of the churches of England. Inside, look for the marble monument to Sir Ralph Woodford made by the sculptor of Chantry.

Another of the town's important landmarks is **Independence Square,** dating from Spanish days. Now mainly a parking lot, it stretches across the southern part of the capital from the **Cathedral of the Immaculate Conception** to Wrightson Road. The Roman Catholic church was built in 1815 in the Neo-Gothic style and consecrated in 1832.

The cathedral has an outlet that leads to the **Central Market,** on Beetham Highway on the outskirts of Port-of-Spain. Here you can see all the spices and fruits for which Trinidad is known. It's one of the island's most colorful sights, made all the more so by the wide diversity of people who sell their wares here.

At the north of the Savannah, the **Royal Botanical Gardens** cover 70 acres. Once part of a sugar plantation, the park is filled with flowering plants, shrubs, and rare and beautiful trees, including an orchid house. Seek out also the raw beef tree—an incision made in its bark is said to resemble rare, bleeding roast beef. Licensed guides will take you through and explain the luxuriant foliage to you. In the garden is the **President's House,** official residence of the president of Trinidad and Tobago. Victorian in style, it was built in 1875. Part of the gardens is the **Emperor Valley Zoo,** Royal Botanical Gardens (tel. 622-3530), in St. Clair, which shows a good selection of the fauna of Trinidad as well as some of the usual exotic animals from around the world. The star attractions are a family of mandrills, a reptile house, and open bird parks. You can take shady jungle walks through tropical vegetation. Adults pay $3 TT (70¢); children 3 to 12, $1.50 TT (35¢). Hours are 9:30am to 5:30pm daily.

AROUND THE ISLAND

For one of the most popular attractions in the area, the **Asa Wright Nature Centre,** see "Where to Stay," above.

On a peak 1,100 feet above Port-of-Spain, **Fort George** was built by Gov. Sir Thomas Hislop in 1804 as a signal station in the days of the sailing ships. Once it could be reached only by hikers, but today it's accessible by an asphalt road. From its citadel you can see the mountains of Venezuela. The drive is only 10 miles, but to play it safe, allow about 2 hours for the excursion.

At sundown, clouds of scarlet ibis, the national bird of Trinidad and Tobago, fly in from their feeding grounds to roost at the ✪ **Caroni Bird Sanctuary.** The 40-square-mile sanctuary couldn't be more idyllic, with blue, mauve, and white lilies, oysters growing on mangrove roots, and caimans resting on mudbanks. The sanctuary lies about a half-hour drive (7 miles) south of Port-of-Spain.

The sanctuary is a big mangrove swamp interlaced with waterways. Visitors are taken on a launch through these swamps to see the birds (bring along some insect repellent). Most visitors leave their hotels at 3pm for a 4pm departure. There are also departures at 4am for early, early risers. Count on spending about $20 for the tour, which includes a pickup at your hotel. A reliable boat operator is **Winston Nanan's Bird Sanctuary Tours,** Bamboo Grove Sett, no. 1 Butler Highway (tel. 645-1305). The sanctuary is open all year, but its innermost core can be visited only from August to April.

The ✪ **Pitch Lake** lies in the geographical center of Trinidad with the village of Le Brea on its north shore. To reach Pitch Lake from Port-of-Spain, take the Solomon Hocoy Highway. It's about a 2-hour drive, depending on traffic (which can be heavy around Port-of-Spain). Once you get to Le Brea, you'll find some bars and restaurants.

One of the wonders of the world, its surface like elephant skin, the lake is 300 feet deep at its center. It's possible to walk on its rough hide, but I don't recommend that you proceed far. Legend has it that the lake devoured a tribe of Chayma Amerindians, punishing them for eating hummingbirds in which the souls of their ancestors reposed. The bitumen mined here has been used for paving highways throughout the world. This lake was formed millions of years ago, and it is believed that at one time it was a huge mud volcano into which muddy asphaltic oil seeped. Churned up and down by underground gases, the oil and mud eventually formed asphalt. According to legend, Sir Walter Raleigh discovered the lake in 1595 and used the asphalt to caulk his ships. Some say that no matter how much is dug out the lake is fully replenished in a day, but actually the level of the lake drops at the rate of about 6 inches a year. A tour of 120 miles around the lake lasts 5 hours.

The ☼ **Saddle** is a humped pass on a ridge dividing the Maraval Valley and the Santa Cruz Valley. Along this circular run you'll see the luxuriant growth of the island, as reflected by grapefruit, papaya, cassava, and cocoa. Leaving Port-of-Spain by Saddle Road, going past the Trinidad Country Club, you pass through Maraval Village with its St. Andrew's Golf Course. The road rises to cross the ridge at the spot from which the Saddle gets its name. After going over the hump, you descend through Santa Cruz Valley, rich with giant bamboo, into San Juan and back to the capital along Eastern Main Road or via Beetham Highway. You'll see splendid views in every direction. This tour takes about 2 hours and covers 18 miles.

Nearly all cruise-ship passengers are hauled along Trinidad's "Skyline Highway," the **North Coast Road.** Starting at the Saddle, it wends for 7 miles across the Northern Range, and down to Maracas Bay. At one point, 100 feet above the Caribbean, you'll see on a clear day as far away as Venezuela in the west or Tobago in the east, a sweep of some 100 miles.

Most visitors take this route to ☼ **Maracas Beach,** one of the most splendid in Trinidad. Enclosed by mountains, it has the cliché charm of a Caribbean fantasy—white sands, swaying coconut palms, and crystal-clear water.

SPORTS & RECREATION

For golf and tennis holidays, you should read some of the previous chapters.

BEACHES Trinidad isn't thought of as beach country, yet, surprisingly, it has more beach frontage than any other island in the West Indies. The only problem is that most of its beaches are undeveloped and found in distant, remote places, far removed from Port-of-Spain. The closest of the better beaches, **Maracas** (see the North Coast Road, in the previous section), is a full 18 miles from Port-of-Spain. (For lovely, inviting, and more accessible beaches, see Section 2 on Tobago, immediately following.)

GOLF The oldest golf club on the island, **Moka** (tel. 629-2314) is in Maraval, about 2 miles from Port-of-Spain. This 18-hole course has a clubhouse that offers every facility to all visitors, and the course has been internationally acclaimed since it was the setting for the 1976 Hoerman Cup Golf Tournament.

TENNIS The **Trinidad Hilton,** Lady Young Road (tel. 624-3111), has the best courts. On the grounds of the Prince's Building, there are **public courts** in Port-of-Spain (ask at your hotel for directions to these).

SAVVY SHOPPING

One of the large bazaars of the Caribbean, Port-of-Spain has luxury items from all over the globe, including Irish linens, English china, Scandinavian crystal, French perfumes, Swiss watches, and Japanese cameras. More interesting than these usual items are the Asian bazaars where you can pick up items in brass. Reflecting the island's culture are calypso shirts (or dresses), sisal goods, woodwork, cascadura bracelets, silver jewelry in local motifs, and saris. For souvenir items, visitors often like to bring back figurines of limbo dancers, carnival masqueraders, or calypso singers.

Most stores are open Monday through Friday from 8am to 4pm (some shops remain open until 5pm). Liquor and food stores close at noon on Thursday, and nearly all shops, except liquor and food, close at noon on Saturday.

ART CREATORS AND SUPPLIERS, Apt. 402, Aldegonda Park, 7 St. Ann's Rd., St. Ann's. Tel. 624-4369.

⭐ It's in a relatively banal apartment complex, but the paintings sold inside are among the finest in the Caribbean. Clara Rosa De Lima, the creative force behind the gallery, is a recognized authority on Trinidadian art. The works sold here, however, are fairly priced examples of the very best of Trinidad. Among the artistic giants represented are the Holder brothers, both Geoffrey and Boscoe, along with Robert Mackie and Noel Vaucrosson. Ms. De Lima is usually candid about the relative merits of artists she represents, and maintains dialogues with a handful of artists in Brazil and Guyana as well. Open: Mon–Fri 10am–1pm and 4–7pm, Sat 10am–noon.

GALLERY 1-2-3-4, St. Ann's Village. Tel. 625-5502.

Probably more iconoclastic and less conservative than any other gallery on the island, this art center displays its paintings in a space of minimalist walls and careful lighting. The gallery opened in 1985, and since then has attracted the attention of the art world because of its sophisticated selection of Caribbean artists. Open: Mon–Fri 10am–6pm, Sat 10am–5pm.

ST. ANN'S VILLAGE, The Marketplace, 10 Nook Ave., St. Ann's. Tel. 624-1181.

One of the most fashionable shopping complexes in Trinidad contains some 20 boutiques that represent some of the best jewelers, designers, and art dealers on Trinidad. These shops come and go, so I won't recommend any one specifically—it's more a place for window-shopping and browsing at leisure. The complex forms an interconnected bridge among three previously recommended establishments, the Hotel Normandie, the Restaurant Fantasie, and a top-notch art emporium, Gallery 1-2-3-4.

STECHER'S, 27 Frederick St. Tel. 623-5912.

For those luxury items I mentioned above, pay a call at Stecher's, which sells crystal; watches; jewelry; perfumes; Georg Jensen silver; handbags; Royal Copenhagen, Wedgwood, and Royal Doulton china; and other in-bond items which can be delivered to Piarco International Airport upon your departure. If you don't want to go downtown, you'll be glad there's a branch at the Hilton. Among the other famous names represented here are Patek-Phillippe, Piaget, Girard Perregaux, Royal Crown Derby, Bing & Grondahl, Belleek, Rosenthal, Lalique, Baccarat, and Swarovski. If you miss both shops, you can always pay a last-minute call at their tax-free airport branch, where they sell perfume, Cartier lighters, pens, leather goods, Hummel figurines, Swarovski crystal, local ceramics, cigarettes, and cigars. There's also a branch shop at the Cruise Ship Complex at the Port-of-Spain docks.

TRINIDAD AND TOBAGO BLIND WELFARE ASSOCIATION, Henry St. Tel. 624-3356.

You'll find everything from furniture to shopping baskets with rattan peel, rattan core, and sea grass. If you make a purchase here, you'll also be helping a sightless worker who is trying to help himself or herself.

Y. DE LIMA, 23A Frederick St. Tel. 623-1364.

This is another good store for duty-free cameras, watches, and local jewelry. Its third-floor workroom will make whatever you want in goldwork. You may emerge with everything from steel-drum earrings to a hibiscus-blossom brooch.

EVENING ENTERTAINMENT

SPARROW'S HIDEAWAY, Diego Martin, in Petit Valley.

Unfortunately, some of the best calypso is not in the capital, but at places such as this. Go only on a Saturday night. It's a 9-mile taxi ride from the center of Port-of-Spain, but I recently asked three taxi drivers what it would cost to take me there and each one came up with a different figure, so I don't know what the going rate will be at the time of your visit. Of course, all collectors of calypso records know that "The Sparrow" is one of Trinidad's most famous singers. He is in fact known as the "calypso king of the world." If you're devoted enough to go, don't expect to see any fellow tourists—it's strictly a local crowd. Ask at your hotel reception desk for directions on how to get there.

Admission: $45 TT ($10.60).

CALYPSO LOUNGE, in the Holiday Inn, Wrightson Rd., Port-of-Spain. Tel. 625-3361.

If you like your calypso in tamer surroundings than the famous but potentially dangerous Independence Square, try this lounge. A local band plays for dancing and some of the best calypsonians are brought in to entertain guests, especially in the winter months. Local bands play on Friday and Saturday. Open: 8pm–1am.

Admission: Fri–Sat $3.

CHACONIA INN, 106 Saddle Rd., Maraval. Tel. 628-8603.

This place becomes a "hot spot" on Friday and Saturday night when a Trinidadian band is brought in from 11pm to 1am. Drinks begin at $13 TT ($3.05).

Admission: Sat $10TT ($2.35), Sun–Fri free.

TRINIDAD HILTON, Lady Young Rd. Tel. 624-3211.

The Hilton stages a *Carnival Potpourri* show, which happens every Monday night, with a folkloric performance beginning at 7:30pm and continuing live till 9pm. It features lots of live music from calypso and steel bands after that. It is probably the most spectacular in Trinidad.

Admission: (including a buffet dinner with grills): $99 TT ($23.30).

MASCAMP PUB, French St. at Ariapata Ave. Tel. 627-8449.

This is the only venue in Trinidad where calypso music from the island's greatest bands is presented continually throughout the year. (Many similar establishments offer the art form only during Carnival.) Set on the western outskirts of Port-of-Spain, it promotes a "rootsy," sometimes raucous, and generally high-energy format that is recommended only to adventurous readers who happen to love live musical performances with an ethnic slant. Styled like a large American bar with an open stage against one wall, it charges between $2 and $5 (U.S.) for one of the array of drinks.

Although simple lunches are served here every weekday from noon to around 3pm, for a cost of around $7 (U.S.), the establishment is far more recommendable (and exciting) as a nightspot. Live music begins every night at 9pm and continues till as late as 4am, but calypso and its modern variations are the almost exclusive format every Wednesday, Friday, and Saturday.

Admission: $2–$5.

2. TOBAGO

Unlike bustling Trinidad, Tobago is sleepy, and Trinidadians come there, especially on weekends, to enjoy its wide sandy beaches. The legendary home of Robinson Crusoe, Tobago is only 27 miles long and 7½ miles wide. The people are hospitable, and their villages are so tiny they seem to blend with the landscape.

Fish-shaped Tobago was probably sighted by Columbus in 1498 when he charted Trinidad, but the island was so tiny he paid no attention to it in his log. For the next 100 years it lay almost unexplored. In 1628 when Charles I of England gave it to one of his nobles, the Earl of Pembroke, the maritime countries of Europe suddenly showed a belated interest. From then on, Tobago was fought over no fewer than 31 times by the Spanish, French, Dutch, and English, as well as marauding pirates and privateers.

After 1803 the island settled down to enjoy a sugar monopoly unbroken for decades. Great houses were built, and in London it used to be said of a wealthy man that he was "as rich as a Tobago planter." The island's economy collapsed in 1884 and Tobago entered an acute depression. The ruling monopoly, Gillespie Brothers, declared itself bankrupt and went out of business. The British government made Tobago a ward of Trinidad in 1889, and sugar was never revived.

Tobago, "the land of the hummingbird," lies 20 miles northeast of Trinidad, from which it is reached by frequent flights. It has long been known as a honeymooner's paradise. The physical beauty of Tobago is stunning, with its forests of breadfruit, mango, cocoa, and citrus, through which a chartreuse-colored iguana will suddenly dart.

The island's villagelike capital is **Scarborough,** which is also the main port. Most of the shops are clustered in streets around the market. From Scarborough one can either go cross-country toward Plymouth or head toward the southwestern part of Tobago.

ORIENTATION

GETTING THERE   By Plane   In most cases, you'll have to get to Trinidad first (see Section 1, above). Some carriers, however, such as **BWIA** (tel. toll free 800/327-7401), the national airline of Trinidad and Tobago, offer flights several days a week from both Miami and New York which continue on to Tobago after a stop on Trinidad; the availability of these flights varies with the season and the day of the week. BWIA also links the two islands with about 14 shuttle flights a day. (Since Tobago is a favorite of vacationing Trinidadians, these flights are almost always crowded and, on weekends, sometimes impossibly overbooked.) The first flight for Tobago leaves Trinidad at 6:15am and the last flight back to Trinidad departs Tobago at 8:30pm. Although the company's schedules list the flight time at 30 minutes, you're airborne for only 12 minutes. On certain BWIA flights to Trinidad, the side trip to Tobago can be included for no extra charge (ask a travel agent before flying to Trinidad how this works).

LIAT (tel. 809/462-0701) has a single daily flight from Trinidad to Tobago. From St. Vincent and many of its neighboring islands, as well as from islands which require inconvenient and expensive transfers through other hubs, many passengers opt for a specifically chartered aircraft from such operators as **Mustique Airways** (tel. 809/458-4621).

Tobago's small airport lies at Crown Point, near the island's southwestern tip.

By Boat   It's also possible to travel between Trinidad and Tobago by a boat run by the **Port Authority.** Call either the office in Port-of-Spain (tel. 626-4906) or in Scarborough on Tobago (tel. 639-2181) for departure times and more details. Ferries leave at least twice a day (trip time is 6 hours). The round-trip fare is $50 TT ($11.75).

GETTING AROUND   By Bus   The modern and very inexpensive public buses travel from one end of the island to the other several times a day. Of course, expect an unscheduled stop at any passenger's doorstep, and never, never, be in a hurry.

By Taxi   From the airport to your hotel, take an unmetered taxi, which will cost $6 to $20, depending on the location of your hotel. You can also arrange (or have your hotel do it for you) a sightseeing tour by taxi. Rates must be negotiated on an individual basis.

By Rental Car   Contact **Tobago Travel,** Milford Road, Store Bay (tel. 809/639-8778), where the average cost of a vehicle begins at $50 per day, with unlimited mileage. An international driver's license or your valid license from home entitles you to drive on the roads of Tobago. Don't forget that *you must drive on the left.*

By Motor Scooter   If you prefer to get around by motor scooter, call **Jan Ramsay** (tel. 639-8445). He offers Honda vehicles for about $25 per day.

ESSENTIALS   Nearly all passengers arrive from Trinidad, where they have already cleared Customs. The **Tobago Tourist Bureau,** Scarborough Mall, Scarborough (tel. 809/639-2125), provides general information about the island. There's a **pharmacy** in Ross Drugs in Scarborough (tel. 639-2658). The **Tobago County Hospital** is on Fort Street, Scarborough (tel. 639-2551).

WHERE TO STAY

The hotels of Tobago attract those who seek hideaways instead of action at high-rise resorts. Because of the shortage of restaurants on the island, it's best to take the MAP (breakfast and dinner) plan when reserving a room. Don't forget to ask if the 15% VAT on hotel rates and a service charge is included in the prices given when you make your reservations.

EXPENSIVE

GRAFTON BEACH RESORT, Black Rock, Tobago, W.I. Tel. 809/639-0191. Fax 809/639-0030. 113 rms, 2 suites. A/C MINIBAR TV TEL
$ Rates: Winter, $215–$240 single or double; from $600 suite. Summer, $155–$215 single or double; from $550 suite. AE, DC, MC, V. **Parking:** Free.

One of the newest resorts on the island, this luxurious complex of stone-and-stucco buildings lies on 5 acres 4 miles south of Scarborough, between a low-rising hill and the pale-dotted stretch of a white sand beach, 4 miles from the airport, on Grafton Road. Each accommodation contains a sliding glass door opening onto a balcony, a ceiling fan, and a mini-refrigerator.

Dining/Entertainment: The resort's swimming pool, traversed by an ornamental bridge, is ringed with café/restaurant tables, and there are several different bars (including a swim-up bar). Both a regional and international cuisine are served. Limbo dancing and calypso are featured at various times.

Services: 18-hour room service, laundry, baby-sitting, massages.
Facilities: Two squash courts, gym, dive shop, outdoor swimming pool, access to a nearby golf course.

MOUNT IRVINE BAY HOTEL, Mount Irvine (P.O. Box 222, Scarborough), Tobago, W.I. Tel. 809/639-8871, or toll free 800/44-UTELL. Fax 809/639-8800. 99 rms, 6 suites. A/C TV TEL
$ Rates: Winter, $185–$350 single; $195–$350 double; from $720 suites. Summer, $120–$270 single; $140–$270 double; from $510 suite. MAP $40 per person extra. Up to two children under 12 stay free in parents' room. AE, DC, MC, V. **Parking:** Free.

Originally established in 1972 on the grounds of an 18th-century sugar plantation, Tobago's most expensive resort occupies 16 acres of a recreational complex which totals more than 150 acres, about a 5-mile drive northwest of the airport. Most of this acreage is devoted to the Mount Irvine Golf Course, one of the finest in the Caribbean. The remainder is filled with sprawling lawns and tropical gardens, in the center of which rise the ruins of a stone sugar mill and a luxurious L-shaped swimming pool. The grounds slope down to a lovely beach. Most accommodations are in a two-story hacienda-inspired wing of guest rooms, each of which opens toward a view of green lawns and flowering shrubbery. The remainder of the accommodations are small cottages covered with beliconia. Each cottage has two rooms (rented separately) with a private bath and patio and a view of the fairways or the water.

Dining/Entertainment: The most impressive place to dine is the Sugar Mill Restaurant, built around the circular core of a 200-year-old stone mill, under a shingled, raftered conical roof. The cuisine is of an acceptable international standard. The hotel also offers dining at Le Beau Rivage at the golf course and at Jacaranda, featuring an international cuisine. You can order drinks in the Cocrico Lounge, named after the tropical bird of Tobago. There's dancing almost every evening on the Sugar

Mill Patio. Calypso singers are brought in, barbecues are held, and limbo dancers and occasional shows entertain you, particularly in season.

Services: Room service (7am–10pm), baby-sitting, laundry, massage.

Facilities: Tennis courts, swimming pool with swim-up bar; boat rentals, windsurfers, and snorkeling equipment available at the beach; guests become temporary members of the golf club (see "Sports & Recreation," below) and receive discounts off regular greens fees.

MODERATE

BLUE WATERS INN, Batteaux Bay, Speyside, Tobago, W.I. Tel. 809/660-4341, or toll free 800/888-3483. Fax 809/660-5195. 29 rms, 1 suite.

$ Rates: Winter, $81 single; $90 double; from $150 suite. Summer, $55 single; $64 double; from $110 suite. Continental breakfast $7 extra. AE, DC, MC, V. **Parking:** Free.

Attracting nature lovers, this property on the northeastern coast of Tobago extends into acres of tropical rain forests with myriad exotic birds, butterflies, and other wildlife. Managed by the MacLean family, the inn is about 24 miles from the airport and 20 miles from Scarborough. It's a drive of an hour and 15 minutes along narrow, winding country roads. This is a very informal place, so leave your fancy resortwear at home.

All rooms have a private shower, but only two are air-conditioned. Meals are served in their casual restaurant, and there's also a bar dispensing tropical libations. Fishing, tennis, shuffleboard, and scuba and skin diving can be arranged, as well as boat trips to Little Tobago.

KARIWAK VILLAGE, Store Bay (P.O. Box 27, Scarborough), Tobago, W.I. Tel. 809/639-8545. Fax 809/639-8441. 18 rms. A/C TEL

$ Rates: Winter, $90 single or double. Summer, $60 single or double. Breakfast $9 extra. AE, DC, MC, V. **Parking:** Free.

A self-contained cluster of cottages evoking the South Pacific, this complex is about a 6-minute walk from the beach on the island's western shoreline, a 2-minute drive from the airport. During its construction in 1982, the builders made much use of Tobago's palm fronds, raw teak, coral stone, and bamboo.

Live entertainment is provided in season on weekends. The food served in the main restaurant is among the best on the island, and you may want to come here for a meal even if you aren't staying here. A fixed-price meal, either à la carte or in the form of one of the weekend buffets, ranges from $17 to $19 per person. The establishment's name is an orthographical combination of the two native tribes that originally inhabited Tobago, the Caribs and the Arawaks.

RICHMOND GREAT HOUSE, Belle Garden, Tobago, W.I. Tel. 809/660-4467. 3 rms, 3 suites.

$ Rates (including continental breakfast): $65 single; $75 double; from $90 suite. No credit cards. **Parking:** Free.

Ⓢ One of the most charming accommodations on the island is an 18th-century great house set on a 1,500-acre cocoa-and coconut-growing estate. Near Richmond Beach, it's owned by Dr. Hollis R. Lynch, who is a professor of African history at Columbia. As befits his profession, he has decorated the mansion with African art along with a collection of island antiques. Guests are free to explore the garden and grounds and later to enjoy the pool and the barbecue. On the premises are two 19th-century tombs containing the remains of the original English founders of the plantation. All accommodations contain a private bathroom, each with an individualized decor. The hotel lies on the southern (windward) coast of Tobago, and the airport is within a 45-minute drive.

TURTLE BEACH, Courland Bay (P.O. Box 201, Scarborough), Tobago, W.I. Tel. 809/639-2851. Fax 809/639-1495. 125 rms. A/C TEL

$ Rates: Winter, $110–$130 single; $110–$150 double. Summer, $45 single; $65 double. MAP $40 per person extra. AE, MC, V. **Parking:** Free.

S Standing directly on a mile of sandy beach on Courland Bay, Turtle Beach sits on the leeward shore in the midst of a 600-acre coconut plantation. It's 8 miles from the airport and 5 miles from Scarborough. The entrance loggia is a long covered terrace where you can enjoy the relaxed, casual life-style of the hotel while seated on sofas and in armchairs with a tall fruit-and-rum drink. Lunches are served around the garden pool or at the beach. Three times a week calypso music can be heard in the evening; perhaps a steel band will be brought in. If you don't want the beach, you can swim in a freshwater pool. Fishing can be arranged, as can snorkeling at Buccoo Reef. A water-sports shop is on the hotel premises.

Accommodations lie in an interconnected series of white two-story bungalows, between beds of hibiscus and oleander. All rooms are oceanfront and have private bathrooms with both tub and shower, a patio or balcony, and smartly tailored furnishings. Rooms on the second floor have sloped open-beamed ceilings, with white walls and shuttered doors that can be pushed back to enlarge the living areas.

INEXPENSIVE

DELLA MIRA GUEST HOUSE, Windward Rd., Scarborough, Tobago, W.I. Tel. 809/639-2531. 14 rms.

$ Rates: $25–$35 single; $32–$45 double. Continental breakfast $3 extra. AE, MC, V. **Parking:** Free.

The warm hospitality of Neville Miranda and his wife, Angela, is extended in this simple West Indian guesthouse about a 10-minute walk east of the town center. The modest and intimate inn has an open living-room area with provincial furnishings. In an adjoining dining room Angela serves authentic island dishes. Tobagoans are fond of coming here, as it has a real atmosphere which most of the other hotels lack. It's on a cool, airy site overlooking the sea, about half a mile from stores and churches and some 50 yards from the beach. You can also swim in a pool set in the lawn of the garden, around which a terrace has been built for sunning. The bedrooms overlook the garden and the pool, but some cheaper units look out onto the hills. The bedrooms have a basic simplicity, nothing fancy, yet everything is clean and comfortable. All the rooms come with private bath, and about half of them are air-conditioned as well. On the premises is a somewhat sleepy nightclub, La Tropicale, plus a beauty salon. Mrs. Miranda, incidentally, is a licensed barber.

MAN-O-WAR BAY COTTAGES, Charlotteville Estate, Charlotteville, Tobago, W.I. Tel. 809/660-4327. Fax 809/660-4328. 6 cottages. **Transportation:** Charlotteville bus.

$ Rates: $55–$65 one-bedroom cottage for two; $130 large four-bedroom bungalow (big enough to sleep 10). For $5 a maid will prepare a meal or clean your cottage. No credit cards. **Parking:** Free.

If you're seeking a Caribbean hideaway—that is, a cluster of beach cottages—then the Man-o-War might be for you. The cottages are a part of Charlotteville Estate, a 1,000-acre cocoa plantation. The entire estate is open to visitors, who may wander through at will. Pat and Charles Turpin rent several cottages on a sandy beach. Each unit is complete with a kitchen, a spacious living and dining room, a private bath, and a porch opening onto the sea.

Near the colony is a coral reef that's an ideal ground for snorkelers. The couple will also arrange a boat rental if you want to explore Lovers' Beach. Birdwatchers often book these cottages, and scuba diving and guided nature tours are available. The Man-o-War Cottages are 36 miles from the bustle of the airport. The ride follows a bumpy coastal road offering views over the sea and passing through many small villages en route.

SANDY POINT BEACH CLUB, Crown Point, Tobago, W.I. Tel. 809/639-8533. Fax 809/639-8495. 20 suites, 22 studios. A/C TV TEL

$ Rates: $60–$70 single or double. Third person $10; child under 12 sharing an accommodation with two other people $5. MC, V. **Parking:** Free.

This miniature vacation village somewhat resembles a Riviera condominium. All but six of the units (those at poolside) contain a kitchenette. It's just a 3-minute run from the airport, but its shoreside position on the island's southwestern coast makes it seem remote. The little village of peaked and gabled roofs is landscaped all the way down to the sandy beach, where there's a rustic Steak Hut, which serves meals throughout the day and evening. The units are fully equipped, and each opens onto a patio, toward the sea, or onto a covered loggia. The studios contain living and dining areas with pine trestle tables, plus satellite color TV. In some of the apartments is a rustic open stairway leading to a loft room with bunk beds, although there's a twin-bedded room on the lower level as well. On the premises are two different swimming pools.

WHERE TO DINE

LE BEAU RIVAGE, in the Mount Irvine Bay Hotel, Tobago Golf Course, Buccoo Bay. Tel. 639-8871.
   Cuisine: FRENCH/CARIBBEAN. **Reservations:** Required.
$ **Prices:** Appetizers $4.50–$8.50; main courses $22.25–$28.25. AE, DC, MC, V.
   Open: Dinner only, Wed–Sun 7–9:30pm.

Run by the previously recommended hotel, this restaurant is in a clubhouse built in 1968 which until recently served as the headquarters of the golf course that surrounds it on every side. From its windows you'll have a sweeping view of one of Tobago's most historic inlets, Mount Irvine Bay. Menu choices include sophisticated combinations of local ingredients with continental inspirations of cuisine moderne, such as grilled Caribbean lobster, grilled filet of red snapper in a tomato purée, chicken Cordon Bleu (stuffed with ham and cheese and wrapped in bacon), and roast duckling stuffed with tropical fruits. Dessert might include a fresh mango flan floating on a coulis of tropical fruits. The restaurant is a 5-minute drive northwest of the airport.

THE BLUE CRAB, Robinson St., Scarborough. Tel. 639-2737.
   Cuisine: CARIBBEAN/INTERNATIONAL. **Reservations:** Recommended for lunch, required for dinner.
$ **Prices:** Appetizers $15–$20 TT ($3.55–$4.70); main courses $30–$125 TT ($7.05–$29.40). AE, MC, V.
   Open: Lunch daily 11am–3pm; dinner Wed and Fri night by reservation only.

One of my favorite restaurants in the capital, adjacent to the town's only Methodist church, this family-run establishment occupies an Edwardian-era house with an oversize veranda. This is the domain of the Sardinha family, who returned to their native country after a sojourn in New York. Keeping their establishment together with "spit and love" after setting it up in 1984, they learned to make the most of local ingredients and regional spices. Dinners might not always be available; when they are served, the menu will be dictated by whatever is available that day in the marketplace. Menu items include fresh conch, stuffed crab backs, shrimp, an array of Créole meat dishes grilled over coconut husks, flying fish in a mild curry-flavored batter, shrimp with garlic butter or cream, and a vegetable-laced rice dish of the day. Lobster is, of course, the most expensive item you could order.

KISKADEE RESTAURANT, in the Turtle Beach Hotel, Courland Bay. Tel. 639-2851.
   Cuisine: CREOLE/CARIBBEAN. **Reservations:** Recommended for those not staying in the hotel.
$ **Prices:** Appetizers $3–$6; main courses $9–$15. AE, DC, MC, V.
   Open: Lunch daily 1–2:30pm; dinner daily 7–9:30pm.

Five miles from Scarborough and informally casual, its tables sit on an outdoor veranda whose edges overlook a tropical garden and the sea. On certain nights, limbo dancers and Tobagoan musicians provide live entertainment. Cuisine minceur is available as a low-calorie alternative to the other specialties. These include lobster thermidor, breast of chicken with paprika sauce, fish filet in cider, pan-fried kingfish, callaloo, and stuffed Plymouth crab back.

OLD DONKEY CART HOUSE, Bacolet St., Scarborough. Tel. 639-3551.

Cuisine: INTERNATIONAL. **Reservations:** Recommended.

$ **Prices:** Appetizers $24–$48 TT ($5.65–$11.30); main courses $45–$115 TT ($10.60–$27.05). AE, MC, V.

Open: Lunch Thurs–Tues noon–3pm; dinner Thurs–Tues 6:30pm–midnight.

An unusual and noteworthy restaurant occupies a green-and-white Edwardian house about half a mile south of Scarborough. Its entrepreneurial owner, Gloria Jones Schoen, used to work as a fashion model in Germany. "Born, bred, and dragged up" in Tobago, she is today the island's leading authority on German wines, which she buys directly from well-established German vineyards and sells in her restaurant. Meals might include stuffed crab back, homemade pasta, shrimp-and-crabmeat cocktail, beef Stroganoff, omelets, and a succulent collection of shrimp, crabmeat, and fresh fish. When Ms. Schoen established her business in 1978, "sheep and goats scampered through the living room." Today you can dine behind a screen of bamboo and palmetto in the front garden or head for one of the plank-topped tables inside.

THE STEAK HUT, in the Sandy Point Beach Club, Crown Point. Tel. 639-8533.

Cuisine: STEAK. **Reservations:** Recommended.

$ **Prices:** Appetizers $3; main courses $13–$18. MC, V.

Open: Breakfast daily 7:30–10am; lunch daily noon–3pm; dinner daily 7–9pm.

On the island's southwestern side, the Steak Hut serves the best meat on the island, specializing in U.S. sirloin, T-bone, porterhouse, and tenderloin. The location, near the beach and swimming pool of this previously recommended hotel, is ideal, especially in the evening. The seafront restaurant also features local fish steaks from shark, flying fish, grouper, dolphin, barracuda, and kingfish. A steel band plays most Friday nights.

SUGAR MILL RESTAURANT, in the Mount Irvine Bay Hotel, Buccoo Bay. Tel. 639-8871.

Cuisine: INTERNATIONAL. **Reservations:** Required for those not staying at the hotel.

$ **Prices:** Appetizers $4.50–$8.50; main courses $8.25–$25.75. AE, DC, MC, V.

Open: Lunch noon–2:30pm; dinner daily 7–10pm.

About a 5-mile drive northwest of the island's airport, this restaurant has at its core a 200-year-old sugar mill whose walls were fashioned from chiseled blocks of coral. Out of it radiate the spidery arms of a beamed ceiling, the shingles of which protect the dozens of tables from the direct sunlight. Open-air, breezy, casually elegant, and permeated with the scent from nearby jasmine, this is probably the best restaurant on Tobago.

Lunch includes everything from salads and sandwiches to lamb chops provençal or sirloin steak. Dinner might include lobster bisque, a carbonade of beef, shrimp Newburg with rice pilaf, suprême of chicken garnished with tropical fruit, lobster sautéed in ginger, and filet of dolphin. Meals are usually accompanied by live music and entertainment, at least in season.

WHAT TO SEE & DO

In Tobago's capital, **Scarborough,** you can visit the local market Monday through Saturday morning and listen to the sounds of a Créole patois.

The town need claim your attention only briefly before you climb up the hill to **Fort King George,** about 430 feet above the town. Built by the English in 1779, it was later captured by the French. After that it jockeyed back and forth among various conquerors until nature decided to end it all in 1847, blowing off the roofs of its buildings. The cannons still mounted had a 3-mile range, and one is believed to have come from one of the ships of Sir Francis Drake (you can still see a replica of the *Tudor Rose*). One building used to house a powder magazine, and you can see the ruins of a military hospital. Artifacts are displayed in a gallery on the grounds.

From Scarborough you can drive northwest to **Plymouth,** Tobago's other town. In the graveyard of the little church is a tombstone dating from 1783 with a mysterious inscription: "She was a mother without knowing it, and a wife, without letting her husband know it, except by her kind indulgences to him."

Perched on a point at Plymouth is **Fort James,** which dates from 1768 when it was built by the British as a barracks. Now it's mainly in ruins.

From Speyside you can make arrangements with some local fisherman to go to **Little Tobago,** a 450-acre offshore island where a bird sanctuary attracts ornithologists. Threatened with extinction in New Guinea, many birds, perhaps 50 species in all, were brought over to this little island in the early part of this century.

Off Pigeon Point lies **Buccoo Reef** (see "Sports and Recreation," below) where sea gardens of coral and hundreds of fish can be seen in waist-deep water. This is the natural aquarium of Tobago. Nearly all the major hotels arrange boat trips to these acres of submarine gardens, which offer the best scuba diving and snorkeling. Even nonswimmers can wade knee-deep in the waters. Remember to protect your head and body from the tropical heat and to guard your feet against the sharp coral.

After about half an hour at the reef, passengers reboard their boats and go over to **Nylon Pool,** with its crystal-clear waters. There in this white sand bottom, about a mile offshore, you can enjoy water only 3 to 4 feet deep. After a swim, you'll be returned to Buccoo Village jetty in time for a goat and crab race.

At the **Museum of Tobago History,** on the grounds of the Mount Irvine Bay Hotel (tel. 639-8871), you'll find artifacts, implements, and pottery of the Caribs and Arawaks who used to inhabit Tobago. Tobago's archeological and historic past comes alive. The museum is open on Tuesday and Thursday from 5:30 to 8:30pm and on Sunday from 4:30 to 7:30pm. Admission is $5 TT ($1.20) for adults, 50¢ TT (10¢) for children.

SPORTS & RECREATION

BEACHES If beach-fringed Tobago wasn't in fact the alleged location of Daniel Defoe's immortal story, the visitors who enjoy its superb beaches hardly seem to care. On Tobago sands you can still feel like Robinson Crusoe in a solitary cove, at least for most of the week before the Trinidadians fly over to sample the sands on a Saturday.

A good beach, **Back Bay,** is within an 8-minute walk of the Mount Irvine Bay Hotel. Along the way you'll pass a coconut plantation and an old cannon emplacement. Sometimes there can be dangerous currents here, but you can always enjoy exploring Rocky Point with its brilliantly colored parrot fish.

Try also **Man-O-War Bay,** one of the finest natural harbors in the West Indies, at the opposite end of the island. Once there, you'll come to a long sandy beach, and you can also enjoy a picnic at a government-run rest house.

The finest for last, **Pigeon Point,** on the island's northwestern coast, is the best-known bathing area with a long coral beach. Thatched shelters provide havens for changing into bathing attire, as well as tables and benches for picnics.

BOATING The **Turtle Beach Hotel,** Courland Bay (tel. 639-2851), rents Aqua-finn sailboats and is a registered Mistral Sailing Centre.

FIELD TRIPS More than 10 different field trips offer closeup views of Tobago's exotic and often-rare tropical birds, as well as a range of other island wildlife and lush tropical flora. Naturalists of the Trinidad-Tobago area guide these excursions. The trips lead you to forest trails, coconut plantations, along rivers, and past waterfalls. Each trip lasts about 2 to 3 hours so you can take at least two per day if you like. One excursion goes to two nearby islands. The price per trip is $20 per person. For details, contact **Pat Turpin,** Man-O-War Bay Cottages, Charlottesville (tel. 660-4327).

GOLF Tobago is the proud possessor of an 18-hole, 6,800-yard golf course at Mount Irvine. Called the **Tobago Golf Club** (tel. 639-8871), it covers 150 breeze-swept acres and was featured in the "Wonderful World of Golf" TV series. The course—and even beginners agree—is considered "friendly" to golfers. As a guest of the Mount Irvine Bay Hotel you are granted temporary membership and use of the clubhouse and facilities. Resident hotel guests are entitled to discounts. All serious golfers should stay at the Mount Irvine. Nonresidents pay $35 for 18 holes.

TENNIS The **Turtle Beach Hotel** (tel. 639-2851) has courts. The best courts, however, are at the **Mount Irvine Bay Hotel** (tel. 639-8871), where two good courts are available free to guests.

WATER SPORTS Unspoiled reefs off Tobago teem with a great variety of marine life. Divers can swim through rocky canyons 60 to 130 feet deep, and underwater photographers can shoot pictures they won't find anywhere else. Snorkeling over the celebrated Buccoo Reef is one of the specialties of Tobago. Hotels arrange for their guests to visit this underwater wonderland. (See "What to See and Do," above.)

The **Turtle Beach Hotel,** Courland Bay (tel. 639-2851), is the best equipped for water sports. Sailing, windsurfing, and waterskiing are offered at reasonable rates.

Dive Tobago Ltd., Pigeon Point (tel. 639-2150), is the oldest and most established dive operation on Tobago, operated by James Young. It caters to the beginner as well as to the experienced diver. A basic resort course, taking half a day and ending in a 30-foot dive, costs $55. Young is a certified PADI diver.

Tobago Dive Experience, Grafton Beach Resort, Black Rock (tel. 639-0191), offers scuba dives, snorkeling, and boat trips. All dives are guided, with a boat following. Exciting drift dives are available for experienced divers. Manta rays are frequently seen 5 minutes from the shore, and there is rich marine life with zonal compaction.

SAVVY SHOPPING

Scarborough's stores have a limited range of merchandise, more to tempt the browser than the serious shopper.

COTTON HOUSE FASHION STUDIO, Old Windward Rd., Bacolet. Tel. 639-2727.

This is one of the island's best choices for "hands-on" appreciation of the fine art of batik. (Batik is an Indonesian tradition where melted wax, brushed onto fabric, resists the impregnation of dyes into selected parts of the cloth, thereby creating unusual colors and designs.) It contains one of the largest collections of batik clothing (for men and women) and wall hangings in Tobago, many suitable for resortwear. Dying techniques are demonstrated to clients, who can try their skills at the art form if they wish.

STECHER'S, Main St. Tel. 639-2377.

Stecher's has a more famous and better branch in Trinidad. However, this store stocks a limited range of merchandise, including crystal, pipes from Scotland, Seiko watches, and gold jewelry.

Y. DE LIMA, Burnett St. Tel. 639-2464.

With a small outlet in Scarborough (and a much bigger supply on Trinidad), this has a small range of merchandise, including jewelry and cameras. It's not duty free, however.

EVENING ENTERTAINMENT

Hotels with nightlife include the **Mount Irvine Bay Hotel** (tel. 639-8871) and the **Turtle Beach Hotel** (tel. 639-2851), both previously recommended. The Turtle Beach has a popular barbecue on Saturday night from 8 to 9:30pm, with poolside dancing to a steel band, continuing until late.

CHAPTER 15

THE DUTCH LEEWARDS

As Dutch as a wooden shoe, the so-called ABC group of islands—Aruba, Bonaire, and Curaçao—lie just off the northern coast of Venezuela. The islands cover only 363 square miles, with a widely diversified population of some 225,000 people, many of whom speak Papiamento, a patois language, although Dutch is the official tongue.

Duty-free shopping and gambling are promoted by the governments on all three islands. Curaçao has the most Dutch atmosphere, with a number of 18th-century buildings. Curaçao, along with Aruba, also has the most developed tourist centers, while Bonaire attracts the most dedicated scuba divers.

Someone once said that there are more flamingos than people on Bonaire. Aruba has the best beaches and the most hotel accommodations.

The canny Dutch emerged from the European power struggle in the West Indies with these tiny specks of land, arid and for all appearances inconsequential. But they proceeded to turn these ugly-duckling properties into some of the most valuable real estate in the Caribbean. These spotless islands still retain old-world charm and are clean and thriving.

On January 1, 1986, Aruba became a separate entity within the Kingdom of the Netherlands under a political arrangement called Status Aparte. Before that date, it was a member of the Netherlands Antilles, consisting of six Dutch Caribbean islands. With Aruba's new status, the Kingdom of the Netherlands has three separate components: the Netherlands, the Netherlands Antilles, and Aruba. The government of the Netherlands is responsible for the defense and foreign affairs of the kingdom, but other government tasks are carried out by each island country for itself.

In addition to Bonaire and Curaçao, the Netherlands Antilles encompasses Saba, St. Eustatius (Statia), and St. Maarten, already discussed in Chapter 9, "The Dutch Windwards in the Leewards."

1. ARUBA

Forget lush vegetation on Aruba—that's impossible with only 17 inches of rainfall annually. Aruba is dry and sunny year round, with clean, exhilarating air like a desert. However, trade winds keep the island from becoming uncomfortably hot. At least you can be sure of the sun every day of your vacation in Aruba.

Cactus fences surround pastel-washed houses, divi-divi trees with their wind-blown look stud the barren countryside, free-form boulders are scattered about, and on occasion you'll come across an abandoned gold mine.

WHAT'S SPECIAL ABOUT THE DUTCH LEEWARDS

Beaches

- ☐ Aruba's Palm Beach, the nerve center of Aruban tourism with the best swimming and water sports on the island, called "one of the ten best beaches in the world" by the *Miami Herald.*

- ☐ Aruba's Eagle Beach, among the last undiscovered stretches on the south coast, a once nearly deserted isle that's fast gaining in popularity.

- ☐ Manchebo Beach, Aruba, a wide stretch of white powder where women often go topless.

- ☐ The beaches of Bonaire, some of the finest white sandy beaches in the West Indies, including Playa Funchi, Boca Cai, and the "clothes-optional" Sorobon.

- ☐ Curaçao's Blauwbaai (Blue Bay), the largest and most spectacular on the island, a private beach with lots of white sandy stretches and changing facilities.

Great Towns/Villages

- ☐ Willemstad, capital of Curaçao, a favorite Caribbean cruise stop known for its gabled houses and Dutch-influenced designs.

- ☐ Oranjestad, capital of Aruba, a charming Dutch capital attracting more shoppers than sightseers, where fishing boats and schooners from Venezuela fill the harbor.

Ace Attractions

- ☐ Atlantis Submarines, Aruba, an underwater ride offering one of the Caribbean's best opportunities for nondivers to witness the underwater life of a coral reef.

- ☐ Scuba diving at Bonaire, one of the richest reef communities in the West Indies, with plunging walls that descend to a sand bottom at 130 or so feet.

Parks and Gardens

- ☐ Cunucu, which in Aruban Papiamento means "the countryside," land of the strangely shaped divi-divi tree, with its trade-wind-blown coiffure in a dramatic desert setting.

- ☐ Bonaire Marine Park, incorporating the entire coastline of the island, where all marine life is completely protected, including many species of fish and various coral formations.

- ☐ Washington/Slagbaai National Park, occupying 15,000 acres of Bonaire's northwesternmost territory and conserving the island's fauna, flora, and landscape.

- ☐ Curaçao Underwater Park, where scuba divers and snorkelers enjoy spectacular scenery in waters with visibility often exceeding 100 feet.

Historic Monuments

- ☐ Fort Nassau, northeast of Willemstad, Curaçao, completed in 1797, built high on a hill overlooking a dramatic harbor panorama.

Aruba stands outside the hurricane path. Its coastline on the leeward side is smooth and serene, with sandy beaches; but on the eastern coast, the windward side, the look is rugged and wild, typical of the windswept Atlantic.

First inhabited by the Arawak peoples, Aruba was sighted by Spaniards in 1494. It was claimed for Spain in 1499 by Alonso de Ojeda, although Madrid never considered Aruba of any value. Near the culmination of the 80-year war between Spain and Holland, the Dutch took over in 1636. Pieter Stuyvesant was named governor of Aruba, a post he held for 4 years before going on to Nieuw Amsterdam (later known as New York). The English were in control between 1805 and 1816 during the Napoleonic Wars. When the English departed, the Dutch returned.

Gold was discovered in 1824 and was mined up until 1924 when the yield became so meager that it ceased to be profitable. However, every now and then someone uncovers a big nugget and the excitement is generated all over again.

Aruba's rather bleak economic outlook changed in 1929 when Lago Oil and Transport Company, a subsidiary of Standard Oil of New Jersey, built a large refinery at the southeastern tip of the island. Aruba became one of the most prosperous islands in the West Indies; however, the refinery shut down in 1985, causing widespread unemployment.

In the 1970s Aruba entered the Caribbean resort sweepstakes when visitors discovered that it has one of the finest beaches in the West Indies stretching along its western coast. In addition to the sands, casinos in high-rise hotels draw the crowds today, as tourism has become Aruba's major industry

Many visitors come to the island for the annual pre-Lenten **Carnaval,** a month-long festival with something going on day and night. With music, dancing, parades, costumes, and "jump-ups," Carnaval is the highlight of Aruba's winter season.

ORIENTATION

GETTING THERE   On **American Airlines** (tel. toll free 800/433-7300), Aruba-bound passengers can catch a daily nonstop 4½-hour flight departing New York's JFK Airport at 10:30am. The nonstop return flight leaves Aruba at 5:15pm. From American's hub in San Juan, Puerto Rico, two daily nonstop flights depart every day for Aruba.

American's lowest fare is included as part of a "land package," whereby prearranged and prepaid accommodations at selected hotels (recommended in this guide) are booked at the same time as the airfare through American's tour department. Contact an American Airlines phone reservations clerk or a travel agent for details.

For clients who prefer to make their own hotel arrangements, American offers its least expensive tickets to those who can reserve at least 14 days in advance. Weekday travel—that is, between noon Monday and noon Thursday—is usually cheaper than travel in any direction on a Friday, Saturday, or Sunday.

From Miami, direct and sometimes nonstop service is provided by both **BWIA** (tel. toll free 800/327-7230) and **ALM** (tel. toll free 800/327-7230) as well as the Venezuela-based **VIASA** airlines (tel. toll free 800/327-5454). VIASA also offers nonstop service twice a week from Houston's Intercontinental Airport.

Tiny **Air Aruba** (tel. toll free 800/88-ARUBA), the island's national airline, offers six or seven nonstop flights to and from Miami every week, depending on the season. It also offers four to six daily round-trip flights between Aruba and Curaçao, depending on the season, each leg of which takes about 20 minutes. Air Aruba also has links to Bonaire, and connections to St. Maarten, Santo Domingo, and the South American cities of Caracas, Venezuela, and São Paulo, Brazil. European visitors usually fly to Aruba on **KLM** (tel. toll free 800/777-5553) from Amsterdam, or on Air Aruba, which flies once a week to Aruba from both Cologne and Amsterdam.

Canadian visitors can fly from Toronto via Miami on one of four daily nonstop flights on **Air Canada** (tel. toll free 800/272-1031), eventually connecting with ALM's daily flights to Aruba. Passengers in Montréal can fly to Miami on Air Canada or **Delta** (tel. toll free 800/221-1212) before connecting with the ALM flights to Aruba. Passengers from other parts of Canada and much of the Northeast usually fly to New York, where they interconnect with the daily American flight to Aruba mentioned above.

GETTING AROUND   By Bus   Aruba has a decent bus service, and the fare is 90¢. Your hotel reception desk will know the approximate times the buses pass by where you're staying. There is regular service daily from 7:40am to 6:05pm.

THE DUTCH LEEWARDS

0 ____ 6.25 mi
  ____ 10 km

CARIBBEAN ISLANDS

Dutch Leeward Islands

Caribbean Sea

BONAIRE

Spelonk
Lagoen
Boca Cai
Sorobori
Willemstoren
Nikiboko
Noord
Salinja
Antriol
Lac
Bay
Solar
Salt
Works
Pekelmeer
Kralendijk
Klein Bonaire
Punt Vierkant
Pink Beach
Boca Onima Caves
Rincon
Playa Grandi
Playa Chiquito
Bronswinkel
Mt. Brandaris
Washington
National Park
*Gotó
Meer*
Playa Funchi
Boca Slagbaai

Caribbean Sea

CURAÇAO

Noordpunt
Westpunt
Knip Bay
Westpunt
Boca Tabla
Christoffel Park
Christoffel Park
St. Christoffelberg
Soto
Barber
*Boca St.
Marie*
St. Michiel
St. Willibrordus
San Juan Bay
Boca Hato
Dr. Albert Plesman Airport
Julianadorp
Ronde Klip
Emmastad
Santa Catarina
Santa Rosa
St. Joris Bay
Montagne
*Spaanse
Water*
Duivelsklip
Curaçao Underwater Park Oostpunt
Willemstad
Schottegatt

Caribbean Sea

ARUBA

California
Lighthouse
Malmok
Palm Beach
Alta Vista Chapel
Oranjestad
Paardenbaai
*Spanish
Lagoon*
Boca Mahos
Ayó
Santa Cruz
Boca Prins
The Haystack
Indian Cave
Hubiba Cave
Boca Grandi
Savaneta
Sint Nicolaas (San Nicolas)
Rodgers Beach
Baby Beach

Airport ✈

① Aruba
② Bonaire
③ Curaçao

By Taxi In Aruba, the taxis are unmetered but rates are fixed, so tell the driver your destination and ask the fare before getting in. A ride from the airport to most of the hotels, including those at Palm Beach, costs about $12 per car, and a maximum of four passengers are allowed to take the journey. Some of the local people don't tip, although it's good to give something extra, especially if the driver has helped you with luggage.

By Rental Car Unlike most Caribbean islands, Aruba makes it easy to rent a car and explore independently. The roads connecting the major tourist attractions are excellent, and a valid U.S. or Canadian driver's license is accepted by each of the major car-rental companies. Most of the big hotels have desks that will rent cars to you. Always ask them a day in advance and you'll stand a better chance of getting the car you specify.

Three major U.S. car-rental companies maintain offices on Aruba, and a quick comparison of prices before you leave the U.S. will reveal current price differences. Many of the companies have both airport branches and kiosks at the major hotels. No taxes are imposed on car rentals on Aruba, but insurance can be tricky. Even with the purchase of a collision-damage waiver (at $8 to $10 per day), a driver is still responsible for between $300 and $500 worth of damage. (Avis doesn't even offer this waiver, so in the event of an accident—unless you have private insurance—you'll be liable for up to the full value of damage to your car.)

Budget Rent-a-Car (tel. toll free 800/472-3325) consistently offers the lowest rates. A Toyota Corolla, with manual transmission and no air conditioning, rents for $162 per week in high season, with unlimited mileage. All the rentals at **Hertz** (tel. toll free 800/654-3131) and most of the rentals from **Avis** (tel. toll free 800/331-2112) have automatic transmission and air conditioning, which raises the price. The lowest rate from Hertz is $253; from Avis, $235 per week. Budget requires that drivers on Aruba be between 25 and 60; Avis and Hertz will rent only to qualified drivers older than 23 and 21, respectively. For rental information once you reach Aruba, call Budget at 25423, Avis at 25496, and Hertz at 480-0364.

By Motorcycle & Bicycle Hondas can be rented from **Donazine Cycle Car Rental,** Soledad 3, Tanki Leendert, in the Noord District, north of Oranjestad (tel. 22633), for $35 per day, plus $5 daily insurance. Mopeds and scooters start at $22 per day at **Georges Scooter Rental,** L. G. Smith Boulevard 136, Oranjestad (tel. 25975).

By Sightseeing Tour You'll find **taxis** with English-speaking drivers available as guides. Most of them seem well informed about their island and are eager to share it with you. A 1-hour tour (and you don't need much more than that) is offered at $30 per hour for a maximum of four passengers.

De Palm Tours, L. G. Smith Boulevard 142, Oranjestad (tel. 24400), has desks at all the major hotels. Their latest attraction is De Palm Island, a complete entertainment facility built on a private island just 5 minutes by ferry from Aruba. Their tours include a wide range of activities, featuring snorkeling, beach barbecues, and folklore shows. Their office is open Monday through Friday from 8:30am to noon and 1:30 to 4pm, and on Saturday and Sunday from 8:30am to noon. The cost of their organized jaunts ranges upward from $15, depending on what activity you select.

FAST FACTS: ARUBA

Area Code Aruba is *not* part of the Caribbean 809 area-code system. See "Telecommunications," below, for complete information on making calls to and on this island.

Banking Hours Banks are open Monday through Friday from 8am to noon and 1:30 to 3:45pm.

Currency   The currency is the **Aruba florin (AFl)**, which is divided into 100 cents. Silver coins are in denominations of 5, 10, 25, and 50 cents and 1 and 2½ florins. The 50-cent piece, the square "yotin," is probably Aruba's best-known coin. The current exchange rate is 1.77 AFl to $1 U.S. (1 AFl is worth about 56¢). U.S. dollars are accepted throughout the island. *Note:* Unless otherwise stated, prices quoted in this chapter are in U.S. dollars.

Documents   To enter Aruba, U.S. and Canadian citizens may submit a valid passport or a birth certificate (or for U.S. citizens only, a voter registration card with a photo ID).

Electricity   The electricity is 110 volts AC, 60 cycles, the same as in the U.S.

Emergencies   For the **police**, dial 100. For a **medical emergency**, dial 24300. For the **fire** department, call 115.

Holidays   Aruba celebrates January 1 (New Year's Day), Carnival Monday, Good Friday, Easter Monday, March 18 (National Anthem and Flag Day), April 30 (Queen's Birthday), May 1 (Labor Day), Ascension Day, and December 25–26 (Christmas Day and second Christmas Day).

Information   Go to the **Aruba Tourism Authority**, L. G. Smith Boulevard 172 (tel. 23777), a two-story building opposite the Tamarijn Beach Hotel. Before you go, contact the Aruba Tourism Authority, 521 Fifth Avenue, 12th Floor, New York, NY 10175 (tel. 212/246-3030, or toll free 800/TO-ARUBA outside New York State).

Language   The official language is Dutch, but nearly everybody speaks English. The language of the street is often Papiamento. Spanish is also widely spoken.

Medical Care   To receive medical care, go to the **Horacio Oduber Hospital** (tel. 24300, also the number to call in case of a medical emergency). It's a modern building near Eagle Beach, with excellent medical facilities. Hotels also have medical doctors on call, and there are good dental facilities as well (appointments can be made through your hotel).

Safety   Aruba is one of the Caribbean's safer destinations, in spite of its numerous hotels and gambling casinos. Of course, pickpockets and purse-snatchers are around, but in no great numbers. However, it would be wise to guard your valuables. Never leave them unattended on the beach or even in a locked car.

Taxes and Service   The government of Aruba imposes a 5% room tax, as well as a $10 airport departure tax. At your hotel, you will have an 11% to 15% service charge added to charges for room, food, and beverages. Otherwise, tipping is up to you.

Telecommunications   Telegrams and Telexes can be sent from the Government Telegraph and Radio Office, at the Post Office Building in Oranjestad, or via your hotel. There is also an I.T.T. office at Boecoetiweg 33 (tel. 21458). Local and international telephone calls can be made at the Government Long Distance Telephone Office, also in the Post Office Building, or through hotel operators.

Aruba is *not* a part of the 809 area code that applies to most of the Caribbean. To call Aruba from the U.S., if your long-distance telephone company is equipped to handle international direct dialing, dial 011 (the international access code), then 297 (the country code for Aruba), and then 8 (the area code) and the five-digit local number. If you cannot direct-dial internationally, dial 0 ("zero," for the operator) and tell the operator you wish to make an international call; once you are transferred to the international operator, state the 297 country code, the 8 area code, and then the local number, and the operator will dial the call for you.

Once on Aruba, to call another number on the island only the five-digit local number is necessary. *Note:* In this chapter only the area code and local number are given.

Time   Aruba is on Atlantic standard time year round, so most of the year Aruba is 1 hour ahead of eastern standard time (when it's 10am in Aruba, it's 9am in New York). When daylight saving time is in effect in the U.S., clocks in New York and Aruba show the same time.

Water   The water, which comes from the world's second-largest desalination plant, is pure.

Weather   Dry and sunny, Aruba has a median temperature of 83° Fahrenheit (as mentioned, the trade winds make it more bearable).

WHERE TO STAY

Most of Aruba's hotels are of the resort variety, bustling and self-contained. There's a tremendous dearth of family or budget hotels. Guesthouses are few and tend to be booked up early in winter by faithful returning visitors. In season, it's imperative to make reservations well in advance; don't ever arrive expecting to find a room on the spot—you must have an address to give Immigration when you arrive in Aruba. Don't forget to ask if the 5% room tax and any service charge are included in the rates quoted when you make your reservation.

HOTELS
Very Expensive

AMERICAN ARUBA BEACH RESORT & CASINO, Palm Beach (P.O. Box 218), Aruba. Tel. 8/24500, 212/661-4540 in New York, or toll free 800/223-1588. 419 rms, 9 suites. A/C MINIBAR TV TEL

$ Rates: Winter, $245–$295 single or double; from $425 suite. Summer, $150–$160 single or double; from $300 suite. Continental breakfast $10 extra. AE, DC, MC, V. **Parking:** Free.

A 20-minute (6-mile) taxi ride northwest of the airport, this high-rise resort underwent a $25-million renovation and expansion in 1990. Its twin eight-story towers contain king-size and double-bedded rooms and suites, all with ocean views from balconies, refrigerators, and hairdryers.

Dining/Entertainment: Tradewinds offers lunch and dinner off the grill, and you can order breakfast or partake of a lavish buffet breakfast at the Veranda; light lunch and dinner are also available. The Jardin Bresilien, a tropical café open from 6pm to 2am, is a drink-and-ice-cream emporium, serving such delights as a raspberry daiquiri, Kahlúa banana coladas, and a "Shark Bite." Las Palmas nightclub offers a full dinner menu with a show. The hotel also has a casino.

Services: Room service, laundry, massages.

Facilities: Swimming pool with built-in current, spas, waterfalls, and swim-up bar; four tennis courts; health club; sauna.

DIVI DIVI BEACH HOTEL, Lloyd G. Smith Blvd. 93, Oranjestad, Aruba. Tel. 8/233300, or toll free 800/367-DIVI. Fax 8/34002. 204 rms, 3 suites. A/C MINIBAR TV TEL

$ Rates: Winter, $225–$305 single or double; from $235 suite. Summer, $110–$140 single or double; from $160 suite. Continental breakfast $8 extra. AE, DC, MC, V. **Parking:** Free.

Near the largest beach on the island, north of Oranjestad and 6 miles northwest of the airport, the casual, comfortable Divi Divi is one of the island's friendliest oases. A rambling, low-rise structure, it has Iberian architectural accents, offering some rooms in the bungalow style, others in two- or three-story buildings or lanais. Each unit has a private bath with tub and shower and a private terrace or balcony.

Dining/Entertainment: Meals are served on the casual Pelican Terrace or in the Red Parrot dining room. Sunday brunch is a popular occasion. All year, dancing and entertainment are offered nightly. The Alhambra Casino stands across the road from the Divi Divi.

Services: Room service for breakfast), laundry, baby-sitting.

Facilities: Two freshwater swimming pools, three Jacuzzis, tennis court.

DIVI TAMARIJN BEACH RESORT, Lloyd G. Smith Blvd. 64, Palm Beach,

Aruba. Tel. 8/24150, or toll free 800/367-DIVI. Fax 8/32300. 236 rms. A/C TV TEL

$ **Rates:** Winter, $216 single or double. Summer, $178 single or double. Continental breakfast $10 extra. AE, DC, MC, V. **Parking:** Free.

The center of a trio of hostelries owned and well managed by the Divi Hotel chain, this resort 6 miles northwest of the airport enjoys one of the longest beachfronts in Aruba. Built in a Dutch style of two-story units, it resembles a collection of connected waterfront town houses. The narrow strip of sandy turf between the accommodations and the beach is planted with copses of almonds, palms, and sea grapes. Each of the sunny rooms contains a private bathroom, radio, and big glass doors that slide open to accept the breezes from the beach.

Dining/Entertainment: At one end of the long and narrow property, the open-air Bunker Bar is perched, as its name suggests, on stilts above a lopsided fortification remaining intact from World War II. On the premises are several drinking spots and a pair of tropical restaurants, the Palm Court and the Red Parrot.

Services: Laundry, baby-sitting, electric carts transport visitors to the Alhambra Casino and the Divi Divi Beach Hotel where admission to the casino and use of the facilities is free.

Facilities: Swimming pool, hard-surface tennis courts (lit at night), water sports (including scuba diving and waterskiing).

GOLDEN TULIP ARUBA CARIBBEAN RESORT & CASINO, Lloyd G. Smith Blvd. 81, Palm Beach, Aruba. Tel. 8/33555, or toll free 800/333-1212. Fax 8/23260. 378 rms, 23 suites. A/C MINIBAR TV TEL

$ **Rates:** Winter (including breakfast and dinner), $215–$280 single or double; from $335 suite for two. Summer, $115–$145 single or double; from $190 suite for two (continental breakfast $10 extra). AE, DC, MC, V. **Parking:** Free.

Its original core was the first hotel on Aruba when it was patronized by the likes of Elizabeth Taylor and the queen of the Netherlands. The hotel reopened after renovations in 1986. Today the Golden Tulip, 6 miles northwest of the airport, qualifies as one of the finer hotels on the island. The main building's curved driveway is centered around a splashing fountain, huge weathered rocks, and a cluster of cactus. The lobby incorporates tones of blue and sea green into many different themes, ranging from traditional to beach-resort modern. Don't overlook the massive mural crafted from Delft tiles, depicting the world's first salute to the American flag, in 1776.

Accommodations are scattered among three buildings in a garden, a few steps from one of the best beaches on the island. Each unit has a private terrace or veranda and a stylishly contemporary decor of semitropical motifs.

Dining/Entertainment: There's a casino, plus four attractive restaurants, the Café Barbizon, the Gazebo, the Rib Room, and the French Room. Guests end the night at the Fandango Night Club.

Services: 24-hour room service, laundry, massages, baby-sitting.

Facilities: Swimming pool, four tennis courts, health club, shopping arcade, scuba-diving facilities.

HYATT REGENCY ARUBA, Palm Beach, Aruba. Tel. 8/31234, or toll free 800/233-1234. Fax 8/35478. 340 rms, 20 suites. A/C MINIBAR TV TEL

$ **Rates:** Winter, $260–$420 single or double; from $800 suite. Summer, $165–$275 single or double; from $400 suite. Breakfast $3.50–$11.50 extra. AE, DC, MC, V. **Parking:** Free.

A 12-acre resort, the Hyatt lies about 2 miles from Oranjestad and some 4 miles northwest of the airport. The $52-million deluxe hotel and casino has a nine-story tower flanked by two guest-room wings, built in a traditional Caribbean style. The rooms are luxurious in appointment, with many amenities. Original art, much of it commissioned from local artists, graces the walls. Furniture in the guest rooms and public areas are of bleached ash, wicker and rattan, many with leather trim. Guests in the hotel's 29 Regency Club rooms, located on the ninth floor, receive the special features of a private concierge, upgraded linens and room amenities, and a lounge where daily complimentary continental breakfast and evening cocktails and hors d'oeuvres are served.

Dining/Entertainment: Situated throughout the property are four restaurants and lounges, including the indoor/outdoor Ruinas Del Mar restaurant, with decor reminiscent of Aruba's gold mining past. Fashioned out of native island stone, it's dramatically positioned on the edge of the lagoon and offers scenic ocean views; the cuisine is Mediterranean. Palms is the hotel's beachfront restaurant, presenting an open-air Caribbean-style seafood grill for more casual dining. The Balashi Bar, accented by a swim-up bar, is conveniently located for guests lounging either poolside or on the beach. Al Fresco, an outdoor lounge of the main lobby, overlooks the courtyard, pool area, and beach.

Services: 24-hour room service, laundry, massages, baby-sitting.

Facilities: A $2.5-million multilevel pool complex and lagoon (with waterfalls, tropical gardens, and slides), health and fitness facilities (including exercise room, saunas, massage, steam rooms, outdoor whirlpool, and sun-aerobics deck), two tennis courts (lit at night); scuba diving can be arranged.

Expensive

ARUBA CONCORDE HOTEL & CASINO, Lloyd G. Smith Blvd. 77, Palm Beach, Aruba. Tel. 8/24466, or toll free 800/327-4150. Fax 8/33403. 490 rms, 90 suites. A/C MINIBAR TV TEL

$ **Rates:** Winter, $145–$210 single or double; from $255 suite. Summer, $100–$120 single or double; from $180 suite Continental breakfast $7 extra. AE, MC, V. **Parking:** Free.

One of the biggest hotels along the Palm Beach strip, 10 miles northwest of the airport, is this 18-story high-rise, with one of the largest casinos on the island—it's the quintessential Las Vegas–style hotel. The rooms offer ocean views, private balconies, closed-circuit color TV with movies shown until 3am, radio with private-channel music, and a vaguely continental decor. The designer was lavish in the use of vivid island colors, and the result is delightful and pretty.

Dining/Entertainment: A wide-ranging choice of dining options awaits guests, many of whom book in here on package tours. Restaurants include the refined Italian cuisine of Adriana and the elegant continental cuisine of La Serre. Later you can view the feather-bedecked dancers at Club Arubesque.

Services: 24-hour room service, laundry, baby-sitting.

Facilities: Olympic-size swimming pool, crowded beach, professional tennis courts (lit at night).

ARUBA PALM BEACH RESORT AND CASINO, Lloyd G. Smith Blvd. 79, Palm Beach, Aruba. Tel. 8/23900, 305/427-5488 in Florida, or toll free 800/345-2782. Fax 8/21941. 200 rms, 4 suites. A/C MINIBAR TV TEL

$ **Rates:** Winter, $160–$175 single or double; from $325 suite. Summer, $90–$115 single or double; from $240 suite. MAP $36 per person extra. AE, MC, V. **Parking:** Free.

A seashell-pink high-rise resort with Moorish-style arches, the Aruba Palm Beach rises over a choice location, on the beach 6 miles north of the airport. At this sleek, stylish resort, you're given vacation living with all the trimmings amid a profusion of palms. The rooms and cabañas were all massively overhauled in 1988. Every unit has quality and character, plus all the modern amenities, including private bath.

Dining/Entertainment: You can enjoy the 24-hour Las Vegas–style Palm Casino, nightly entertainment in the Players Club lounge, fine dining in the elegant Palm Garden café, or cozy outdoor dining in the nautical Seawatch Restaurant, featuring U.S. beef and seafood. Light fare is available at the Fantail Restaurant and High Tide Bar, or the poolside On the Rocks Bar & Grill.

Services: Room service, laundry, baby-sitting.

Facilities: Olympic-size freshwater swimming pool, children's pool, tennis; excursions, scuba diving, and windsurfing available; the Dutch Arcade, which houses a shopping center.

HOLIDAY INN ARUBA BEACH RESORT, Palm Beach, Aruba. Tel. 8/ 23600, or toll free 800/465-4329. Fax 8/25165. 602 rms, 20 suites. A/C MINIBAR TV TEL

$ Rates: Winter, $163–$250 single or double; from $313 suite. Summer, $120–$170 single or double; from $270 suite. Continental breakfast from $5.50 extra. AE, DC, MC, V. **Parking:** Free.

The Holiday Inn, a 15-minute taxi ride northwest of the airport, is the most action-packed hostelry along the sands of Palm Beach. Private balconies frame vistas of white sands, and each bedroom comes with a TV offering in-house video movies and a private tiled bath. Each unit, built to Holiday Inn traditional standards, is well furnished, with wall-to-wall carpeting, two double beds, and large closets.

Dining/Entertainment: Musicians serenade you as you dine in Le Salon, with its French cuisine, its Sunday buffet brunch, and many other specialties. The Chinese restaurant, the Empress of China, features a Cantonese menu. La Scala offers an à la carte Italian menu. In addition, the hotel has the Grand Holiday Casino.

Services: Room service, laundry, massage, baby-sitting.

Facilities: Olympic-size freshwater swimming pool with a sun terrace, health spa (with aerobics, sauna, and massage), six tennis courts including one international court (lit at night).

MILL CONDOMINIUM RESORT, Lloyd G. Smith Blvd. 330 (P.O. Box 1012), Palm Beach, Aruba. Tel. 8/37700. Fax 8/37271. 60 rms, 40 suites. A/C TV TEL

$ Rates: Winter, $185 single or double; from $310 suite. Summer, $120 single or double; from $210 suite. Continental breakfast from $3.50 extra. AE, DC, MC, V. **Parking:** Free.

Next to the old Dutch windmill that is a national landmark, a 15-minute taxi ride northwest of the airport, the Mill opened in 1990, offering beautifully furnished rooms in a U-shaped configuration around a swimming pool. The two-level complex features superior accommodations (facing botanical gardens and a bird sanctuary), and deluxe accommodations, opening onto gardens and a swimming pool. Each apartment-style unit is fully equipped. A junior suite is one room with kitchenette, full bath, king-size bed, sitting area, and patio; a studio has one room and full kitchen, dining area, bath, queen-size convertible bed, and sitting area; and a royal den is one room with a king-size bed, full bath, marble Jacuzzi, and patio.

Dining/Entertainment: Hotel amenities include breakfast and luncheon facilities around the pool.

Facilities: Swimming pool, tennis and racquetball courts, health center, coin-operated laundry facilities.

SONESTA HOTEL BEACH CLUB & CASINO, Lloyd G. Smith Blvd. 82, Oranjestad, Aruba. Tel. 8/36000, or toll free 800/SONESTA. Fax 8/34389. 275 rms, 25 suites. A/C MINIBAR TV TEL

$ Rates: Winter, $180–$220 single or double; from $280 suite. Summer, $100–$155 single or double; from $220 suite. Continental breakfast $6.50 extra. AE, DC, MC, V. **Parking:** Free.

Launched in 1991, the Sonesta stands in Oranjestad overlooking the harbor, about 10 minutes from the airport. The five-story atrium hotel offers well-furnished guest rooms and suites.

Dining/Entertainment: The hotel has a brasserie specializing in grilled food; see "Facilities," below, for information on the Sea Breeze Restaurant. The 10,000-square-foot Crystal Casino at Seaport Village features a salon with baccarat, high-stakes blackjack, and a roulette table, along with slot machines.

Services: 24-hour room service, laundry, baby-sitting.

Facilities: A special feature of the property is its own private beach club, including a 40-acre island with two beaches and an extensive array of water sports, as well as a lagoon, whirlpools, and a beach bar. Hotel boats pick up guests at a canal cut through the lobby and take them to the private island. Here, the Sea Breeze Restaurant specializes in light fare, with weekly theme nights and live entertainment daily. Two tennis courts are available within walking distance of the hotel; there are also swimming pools and a complete fitness center.

A GUESTHOUSE

Many travelers prefer to visit Aruba on a much simpler basis than what we've been considering. There are some apartments and a handful of guesthouses overlooking the sea or within walking distance of a beach. Others are on a bus route, and still others require a car. My personal favorite follows.

THE EDGE'S, Lloyd G. Smith Blvd. 458, Malmok-by-the-Sea, Aruba. Tel. 8/21072. Fax 8/31870. 11 rms, 1 suite. A/C

$ Rates (including continental breakfast): Winter, $128–$150 single or double; from $185 suite. Summer, $100–$125 single or double; from $150 suite. AE, MC, V. **Parking:** Free.

Favored by windsurfers, this is a guesthouse complex 50 yards from the beach. Only a short bus ride from Oranjestad, it's a 15-minute taxi ride east of the airport and less than a mile from the Holiday Inn Hotel and Casino going toward the lighthouse. A carpeted patio with chaise longues separates two rows of motel-style units, and each apartment has a private entrance and patio with furniture for outdoor dining. These are really efficiency units with kitchenette, refrigerator, dishes, toaster, coffee pot, and all utensils for cooking. All apartments have large tiled baths, and each unit has at least two beds and is pleasantly furnished and clean. There are two deluxe units and a luxury suite with king-size beds, sitting rooms, full kitchens, and private patios with a view of the ocean. To the right of the entrance gate, you can watch sunsets from a whirlpool spa at no charge.

TIME-SHARE PROPERTIES

Time-sharing has become a major vacation investment in Aruba. Even if you're not interested for yourself, you may want to consider renting a unit as a one-time vacationer.

ARUBA BEACH CLUB/CASA DEL MAR, Druif Beach (P.O. Box 368, Oranjestad), Aruba. Tel. 8/27000. Fax 8/26557. 280 units. A/C TV TEL

$ Rates: Winter, $170–$250 Aruba Beach Club single or double; $225–$330 Casa del Mar double. Summer, $84–$140 Aruba Beach Club single or double; $126–$200 Casa del Mar double. Continental breakfast from $7 extra. AE, DC, MC, V. **Parking:** Free.

Two properties built at different times, 4 miles north of the airport, are now connected by a common wing and a shared reception desk. The older and more staid of the properties, the Aruba Beach Club, embraces a rear courtyard, an expanse of seafront, and its own swimming pool. Dating from the late 1970s, each of its pleasant units contains a kitchenette, cable color TV, and a decor of tropical furniture.

The newer time-share section, the Casa del Mar contains tasteful, well-decorated apartments, with Jacuzzi tubs, well-equipped kitchens, verandas or patios, and sunny views of the sea. Casa del Mar wraps itself around its own stretch of beachfront and a private courtyard fringed with palms and thatch-covered cabañas. In its center, a swimming pool, shaped like a pair of connected octagons, provides an alternative to the beach.

Across from the Alhambra Casino, both resorts are encircled by urn-shaped balustrades. The establishments share the same tennis courts, bars, and an appealingly rustic restaurant.

PLAYA LINDA BEACH RESORT, Lloyd G. Smith Blvd. 87 (P.O. Box 235, Oranjestad), Palm Beach, Aruba. Tel. 8/31000. Fax 8/25210. 194 rms. A/C TV TEL

$ Rates: Winter, $200–$600 double. Summer, $110–$300 double. AE, DC, MC, V. **Parking:** Free.

Designed in a ziggurat shape of receding balconies, the terra-cotta and cream complex sits amid tropical foliage and native Aruban flora on a desirable stretch of white sandy beachfront 6 miles northwest of the airport. The units offer kitchens and private verandas. Amenities and facilities at Playa Linda include a large free-form swimming pool, outdoor whirlpool baths, tennis courts, and a shopping arcade featuring a beauty parlor, perfumery, and souvenir and gift shop. The Linda Vista Restaurant serves international food. Laundry and baby-sitting are available.

WHERE TO DINE

A few of Aruba's restaurants serve *rijstaffel,* the "Asian smörgåsbord," or *nasi goreng,* a "mini-rijstaffel." In addition, many Chinese restaurants operate in Oranjestad. More and more Aruban specialties are beginning to appear on menus. French cuisine is the second major choice of most chefs. Sometimes, at least on off-season package deals, visitors on the MAP (breakfast and dinner) are allowed to dine around on an exchange plan with the other hotels.

IN ORANJESTAD

CHEZ MATHILDE, Havenstraat 23. Tel. 34968.
 Cuisine: FRENCH. **Reservations:** Required.
 $ Prices: Appetizers $4–$14; main courses $17–$38. AE, DC, MC, V.
 Open: Dinner only, daily 6–11pm.

The *restaurant français* of Oranjestad is expensive, but most satisfied customers agree that it's worth the price, especially those diners who order the chef's bouillabaisse, made with more than a dozen different sea creatures. Not only do you get distinguished food and service, including a haute-cuisine classic French repertoire, but you can enjoy your repast in an elegant setting. The structure housing the restaurant, near the Sonesta Hotel Beach Club, a 5-minute drive north from the airport, was built in the 1800s, and it has been preserved more or less as it was originally. The intimate dining rooms contain beautifully set tables and a restrained but romantic decor. Enjoy an apéritif while you peruse the comparatively large wine list. Live piano music enhances the total experience.

FRENCH STEAK HOUSE, in the Manchebo-Bucuti Beach Hotel, Lloyd G. Smith Blvd. 5. Tel. 23444.
 Cuisine: CONTINENTAL. **Reservations:** Required.
 $ Prices: Appetizers $1.25–$8; main courses $5.25–$18.40. AE, DC, MC, V.
 Open: Dinner only, Wed–Mon 6–11pm.

The atmosphere is gracious and the food is good in this beachside bistro west of Oranjestad. Guests from the other hotels often come here for romantic candlelit dining, and no one need worry about putting on a jacket or tie. The chef's specialties are ordered à la carte and might include red snapper provençal or the classic veal Stroganoff flamed with vodka and madeira. You can also help yourself at a New York–style salad bar. Of course beef is featured, like chateaubriand or pepper steak for two people.

ALONG THE BEACHFRONT

Expensive

PAPIAMENTO, Washington 61. Tel. 24544.
 Cuisine: CONTINENTAL. **Reservations:** Recommended, especially on week-ends.

$ Prices: Appetizers $2.75–$10; main courses $16–$30. AE, DC, MC, V.
Open: Dinner only, daily 6–11pm.

One of the most desirable independent restaurants in Aruba lies at the north end of Palm Beach. Transformed into a stylish and intimate hideaway, it boasts a changing exhibition of contemporary paintings (each of which is for sale), and such old-world touches as massive brass chandeliers. A distinguishing culinary feature is the way fresh meat or seafood is served raw on sizzling marble slabs so that your dinner is cooked in front of you the way you like it. Chicken or fish is cooked in an Aruba-made clay pot, which is then broken open at your table. Meals might include fresh lobster, chicken breast, lamb chops, or mixed seafood cooked directly on the stone, or rack of lamb for two.

THE RED PARROT, in the Divi Divi Beach Resort, Lloyd G. Smith Blvd. 93. Tel. 23300.
Cuisine: SEAFOOD/INTERNATIONAL. **Reservations:** Recommended.
$ Prices: Appetizers $3–$9; main courses $16–$30. AE, DC, MC, V.
Open: Dinner only, daily 6–10pm.

You'll dine in a tropical atmosphere in the Red Parrot, one of Aruba's top hotel restaurants, and the view is through arched windows framed with draperies and plants opening onto the sea 6 miles northwest of the airport. Unusual appetizers include lobster-and-prawns romance, lightly coated in oyster sauce and seasoned vegetables. Main-dish specialties are West Indian scampi, baked jumbo shrimp stuffed with spiced scallops, as well as a local favorite, grouper caines sauté (filet of grouper with a sumptuous lobster sauce and tender chunks of fresh lobster). The chef also prepares good international specialties daily. You choose your dessert from either the trolley or the fancy dessert menu.

On Tuesday night a buffet of local dishes is presented, everything enlivened by the Divi Divi steel band, complete with a parade of award-winning carnival costumes and an island-wear fashion show.

RISTORANTE VALENTINO, Caribbean Palm Village, Noord 43. Tel. 64777.
Cuisine: ITALIAN. **Reservations:** Recommended.
$ Prices: Appetizers $6–$8.50; main courses $13–$35. AE, MC, DC, V.
Open: Dinner only, Mon–Sat 6–11pm.

Conveniently located a 3-minute drive north of Oranjestad, a 10-minute walk from the beach and some of the largest casino-related hotels in Aruba, this pastel-colored enclave is a stylish holdout of authentic Italian cuisine. The Italian chef specializes in seafood, preparing succulent versions of linguine del pescatore, richly garnished with shrimp, mussels, and lobster; seafood crêpes; and gamberoni zi Teresa (shrimp sautéed in tomatoes and fresh garlic). All pastas are made in-house and are impeccably fresh. Elegant attire is appreciated.

Moderate

BALI FLOATING RESTAURANT, off Lloyd G. Smith Blvd. Tel. 20680.
Cuisine: CHINESE/INDONESIAN. **Reservations:** Required.
$ Prices: Appetizers $3–$5; main courses $8–$35. AE, MC, V.
Open: Lunch daily noon–2:30pm; dinner daily 6–11pm.

Housed in an Asian houseboat decorated with bamboo and Indonesian art, the Bali Floating Restaurant is moored in Oranjestad's harbor. Diners are treated to the popular Indonesian rijstaffel (rice table), a complete meal of rice surrounded by 21 different dishes, served at your table in individual portions. The rijstaffel is not spicy, but the sambal (hot, hot) is served on the side for the more adventurous to try. A mini-version is served for lunch, as well as sandwiches and snacks. The rijstaffel may be ordered per person, but try to go with a group if possible, since it's a fun meal that everyone will enjoy. The menu also offers a fine selection of tenderloin steaks and fresh local fish dishes.

BUCCANEER, Gasparito 11C. Tel. 26172.

Cuisine: SEAFOOD. **Reservations:** Not required.
$ Prices: Appetizers $2–$5.50; main courses $11–$22. AE, DC, MC, V.
Open: Dinner only, Mon–Sat 6–10:30pm.

The atmosphere here evokes (or means to) a ship's cabin, complete with saltwater aquarium. Near many of the major hotels, the restaurant is about 2 miles from Palm Beach; taxis are always waiting outside. For an opener, the pirate's hotpot is a seaworthy choice (a native fish soup that somehow manages to taste different every night). Among the "fruits of the sea," the lobster thermidor is everybody's favorite. I always ask the waiter for the catch of the day, which the kitchen will prepare with a Créole sauce. Meats are frozen of course, but well prepared, including tournedos in a number of ways. Every main dish is served with the vegetable of the day, along with a stuffed potato and salad on the side. Coup Melba or homemade cheesecake is favored to finish off your meal, and the service is excellent.

CATTLE BARON, Lloyd G. Smith Blvd. 228. Tel. 22977.
Cuisine: STEAKS/SEAFOOD. **Reservations:** Recommended.
$ Prices: Appetizers $3–$6.50; main courses $11–$18. AE, MC, V.
Open: Dinner only, daily 6–10:30pm.

The Cattle Baron's location a 15-minute drive northwest of Oranjestad, amid a dry and dusty landscape beside the highway, seems appropriate to its western theme. Surrounded by ruffled gingham curtains, roughly textured planking, and wagon-wheel chandeliers, diners enjoy generous portions of aged U.S.-bred beef, as well as a scattering of seafood. Served by waiters whose costumes enhance the cattle baron theme, the specialties include Dutch steak, porterhouse steak, prime rib, barbecued ribs, and pepper steak. The seafood features red snapper San Francisco style (with crabmeat, mushrooms, and bordelaise sauce), broiled lobster, shrimp bisque, fish Oriental, and snapper arubiano (with Créole sauce, fried plantain, and funchi).

LA DOLCE VITA, Caya G. F. Betico Croes 164. Tel. 25675.
Cuisine: ITALIAN. **Reservations:** Recommended, especially in high season.
$ Prices: Appetizers $3–$6; main courses $9.95–$22. AE, MC, V.
Open: Dinner only, daily 6–11pm. **Closed:** Either June or Sept.

Once it was a private home, but since 1980 La Dolce Vita, on the main shopping street, has been the most acclaimed Italian restaurant in Aruba. It wasn't long before it was discovered by the food and wine critics of such prestigious Stateside magazines as *Gourmet.* If you like pasta with salmon and cream (which became the rage in Italy in the 1980s), you'll find it served here. You might begin with a sampling of their antipasti, including fine Italian salami and cheese, along with artichokes and marinated squid. They also do a savory, perfectly flavored "kettle" of fruits de mer. Naturally you get some good veal, along with such familiar Italian standby dishes as baked clams and linguine. Finish with an espresso or perhaps some Italian ice cream.

HEIDELBERG, Lloyd G. Smith Blvd. 136. Tel. 26888.
Cuisine: GERMAN. **Reservations:** Required.
$ Prices: Appetizers $4–$5.50; main courses $12–$28.50. AE, MC, V.
Open: Dinner only, Thurs–Tues 6–11pm. **Closed:** Sept.

About the last place you'd expect to find a restaurant with a name like Heidelberg is the desertlike island of Aruba, but here it is, a 5-minute drive west of Oranjestad. Established in 1982, it became popular immediately. Arubans even come here to celebrate Christmas by ordering a fat, juicy Christmas goose. You get traditional German fare, including wienerschnitzel, goulash and noodles, herring "hausfrau" style, sauerbraten, and a specialty of Berlin, eisbein (pork knuckle). For dessert, select something from the trolley; most diners, however, go for the strudel. Count on a big, hearty, and altogether satisfying meal.

OLD CUNUCU HOUSE, Palm Beach 150. Tel. 31666.
Cuisine: ARUBAN. **Reservations:** Recommended.
$ Prices: Appetizers $3–$9; main courses $11.95–$25. AE, DC, MC, V.

Open: Dinner only, daily 6–10pm.

Housed in a 75-year-old *cunucu* (countryside) house on a small estate, this restaurant lies in a residential neighborhood (however, it's only a 10- to 15-minute walk from the Palm Beach resorts). Restored to its original style, the restaurant maintains a warm, traditional feeling. It focuses on local recipes including fish soup, fried squid, coconut fried shrimp, and broiled swordfish. Several dishes are served with funchi (cornmeal) and pan bati (a local pancake).

DE OLDE MOLEN (The Mill Restaurant), Palm Beach, Lloyd G. Smith Blvd. 130. Tel. 22060.
Cuisine: INTERNATIONAL. **Reservations:** Not required.
$ Prices: Appetizers $4–$6; main courses $14–$26. AE, DC, MC, V.
Open: Dinner only, Mon–Sat 6–11pm.

This landmark structure is just across the street from the Concorde Hotel and within walking distance of a number of other Palm Beach hotels. The windmill in which the restaurant is housed was built in 1804 in Friesland, but it was torn down and shipped to Aruba where it was reconstructed piece by piece. Since 1960 it has been a tourist-focused destination for dinner. An international and regional cuisine is served, including thick Dutch split-pea soup, pepper steak for two people, veal Cordon Bleu, shrimp provençal, and if available, red snapper arubiano (with a Créole sauce). Many diners finish their meal with an Irish coffee.

Budget

MI CUSHINA, Cura Cabai. Tel. 48335.
Cuisine: ARUBAN. **Reservations:** Recommended.
$ Prices: Appetizers $3–$6; main courses $10–$20. AE, DC, MC, V.
Open: Lunch Fri–Wed noon–2pm; dinner Fri–Wed 6–10pm. **Closed:** Sept.

On the main road about a mile before San Nicolas, Mi Cushina serves up fried fish with funchi (cornmeal), stewed lamb with pan bati (a local pancake), and other tasty dishes. A selection of international food is also served. The decor includes a ceiling made of coffee bags, light fixtures on old wagon wheels, and family photographs, along with tools and utensils used in the past. There is a display of musical instruments used by Arubans long ago.

AROUND THE ISLAND

BRISAS DEL MAR, Savaneta 222A. Tel. 47718.
Cuisine: SEAFOOD. **Reservations:** Required.
$ Prices: Appetizers $2–$4; main courses $9–$20. AE, MC, V.
Open: Lunch Tues–Sun noon–2:30pm; dinner daily 6:30–9:30pm.

A 15-minute drive east of Oranjestad, near the police station, Brisas del Mar is like a place you might encounter in some outpost in Australia. Here in very simple surroundings, right at water's edge, Lucia Rasmijn opened this little hut with an air-conditioned bar in front of which the locals gather to drink the day away. The place is often jammed on weekends with many of the same local people, who come here to drink and dance. On Friday, Saturday, and Sunday the place offers entertainment, with home-grown talent playing everything from the guitar to the harp. In back the tables are open to the sea breezes, and nearby you can see the catch of the day, perhaps wahoo, being sliced up and sold to local buyers.

CHARLIE'S BAR AND RESTAURANT, B. v/d Veen Zeppenveldstraat 56, Mainstreet, San Nicolás. Tel. 45086.
Cuisine: AMERICAN/ARUBAN. **Reservations:** Not required. A 25-minute drive east of Oranjestad.
$ Prices: Appetizers $6.50–$10; main courses $10–$16. No credit cards.
Open: Mon–Sat noon–10pm (bar, daily noon–10pm).

Charlie's qualifies through its decor and history as the most interesting reason to visit San Nicolás; it's the most overly decorated bar in the West Indies, sporting an array of memorabilia and local souvenirs. Where roustabouts and roughnecks once brawled, you'll find tables filled with contented tourists admiring thousands of pennants, banners, and trophies dangling from the high ceiling. Two-fisted drinks are still served, but the menu has improved since the good old days when San Nicolas was one of the toughest towns in the Caribbean. You can now enjoy freshly made soup, grilled scampi, Créole-style squid, and churrasco. Sirloin steak and red snapper are usually featured.

NUEVA MARINA PIRATA, Spanish Lagoon. Tel. 27372.
   Cuisine: SEAFOOD/ARUBAN. **Reservations:** Required.
$ Prices: Appetizers $3–$10; main courses $10–$40. AE, MC, V.
   Open: Dinner only, Wed–Mon 6–11pm.
Considered by some the most authentic seafood restaurant in Aruba, this is the place to go if you want to escape hotel dining rooms. In a breezy al fresco setting on the water, with a palm-frond roof overhead, you can order a before-dinner drink at a bar constructed from rum kegs. The daily catch is delivered directly to the restaurant's pier every afternoon so you might find red snapper or octopus in a Créole sauce on the menu. Head east from Oranjestad along Lloyd G. Smith Boulevard.

WHAT TO SEE & DO

The capital of Aruba, **Oranjestad** attracts shoppers rather than sightseers. The bustling city has a very Caribbean flavor, and it's part Spanish, part Dutch in architecture. Cutting in from the airport, the main thoroughfare, Lloyd G. Smith Boulevard, goes along the waterfront and on to Palm Beach. But most visitors cross it heading for Caya G. F. Betico Croes, where they find the best free-port shopping.

After a shopping trip, you might return to the harbor where fishing boats and schooners, many from Venezuela, are moored. Nearly all newcomers to Aruba like to take a picture of the **Schooner Harbor.** Not only does it have colorful boats docked along the quay, but boatpeople display their wares in open stalls. The local patois predominates. A little farther along, at the fish market, fresh fish is sold directly from the boats. Also on the seaside of Oranjestad, **Wilhelmina Park** was named after Queen Wilhelmina of the Netherlands. A tropical garden has been planted along the water, and there's a sculpture of the Queen Mother.

Aside from shopping, the major attraction of Aruba is **Eagle Beach and Palm Beach,** considered among the finest in the Caribbean. Most of Aruba's hotels are stretched Las Vegas–strip style along these pure-white sand stretches on the leeward coast.

MUSEUMS

I know you didn't come to Aruba to look at museums, but just in case. . . .

MUSEO ARUBANO, just off Lloyd G. Smith Blvd. behind the government buildings. Tel. 26099.
In the restored Fort Zoutman, the Museo Arubano (also called the King Willem III Tower and Fort Zoutman Museum) contains material on the culture and history of Aruba, with artifacts dating from the earliest times of the island through colonial days and up to the present. The 18th-century fort, the oldest building on Aruba, has at its entrance the King Willem III Tower, which served as a lighthouse for almost 100 years.
   Admission: 1 AF1 (45¢).
   Open: Mon–Fri 9am–4pm, Sat 9am–noon.

ARCHEOLOGICAL MUSEUM, Zoutmanstraat 1. Tel. 28979.

Diagonally across the street from the Sonesta Hotel, the Archeological Museum contains on its first floor pre-Columbian artifacts found at numerous places on the island. You'll see agricultural and home equipment dating back 1,000 years, and even skeletons of people who were buried in big earthenware urns. In addition, there's a collection of skeletons and tools dating back 2,000 years.

Admission: Free.

Open: Daily 8am–noon and 1:30–4:30pm.

NUMISMATIC MUSEUM, in the Ministry of Culture Building, Irausquin Plein 2A. Tel. 28831.

In front of the post office and near St. Francis Roman Catholic Church, you can see an outstanding collection of coins and paper currency housed in the Numismatic Museum. Opened in 1981, the house and private collection of J. M. Odor contain more than 30,000 pieces from more than 400 countries.

Admission: Free (but donations are appreciated).

Open: Mon–Fri 7:30am–noon and 1–4:30pm.

DE MAN HOME, Morgenster 18. Tel. 24246 for an appointment.

A privately owned shell collection of the Adrian de Man family can be seen here, 1½ miles from Oranjestad on the road to Santa Cruz. The permanent collection, which includes a rare murex, is in a room at the rear of the de Mans' home. Shells from all over the world make up the display. The collection was started in 1951 and was acquired by beachcombing, snorkeling, and diving by the whole family. They also swapped, traded, and exchanged shells from all over the world to form the collection. Very few shells were ever purchased. Once you make an appointment, the owner requests that you be punctual.

Admission: Free.

Open: Mon–Sat by appointment only.

AN UNDERWATER JOURNEY

One of the island's most diverting pastimes involves an underwater journey on one of the world's few passenger submarines, operated by ✪ **Atlantis Submarines,** Seaport Village Marina (opposite the Sonesta Hotel), Oranjestad (tel. 36090). An underwater ride offers one of the Caribbean's best opportunities for nondivers to witness firsthand the underwater life of a coral reef, with fewer obstacles and dangers than posed by a scuba expedition. Carrying 46 passengers to a depth of up to 150 feet, the submarine organizes departures from the Oranjestad harborfront every hour on the hour, Sunday through Friday from 10am to 3pm (there are no departures on Saturday). Each tour includes a 25-minute transit by catamaran to Barcadera Reef, 2 miles southeast of Aruba, a site chosen for the huge variety of its underwater flora and fauna. At the reef, participants transfer to the submarine for a 1-hour underwater lecture and tour.

Allow 2 hours for the complete experience. The cost is $68 for adults and $34 for children 4 to 12 (no children under 4 are admitted). Advance reservations are essential, either through the concierge of one of the island's hotels, or via the telephone number listed above. In either event, a staff member will ask for a credit-card number (and give you a confirmation number) to hold the booking for you.

OUT IN THE COUNTRY

If you can lift yourselves from the sands for one afternoon, you might like to drive into the **cunucu,** which in Papiamento means "the countryside." Here Arubans live in very modest but colorful pastel-washed houses decorated with tropical plants, which require expensive desalinated water to grow. Of course, all visitors venturing into the center of Aruba want to see the strangely shaped divi-divi tree with its trade-wind-blown coiffure.

Rocks stud Aruba, and the most impressive ones are those found at **Ayo** and **Casibari,** northeast of Hooiberg. These stacks of diorite boulders are the size of buildings. The rocks, weighing several thousand tons, are a puzzle to geologists. On the rocks at Ayo are ancient Amerindian drawings. At Casibari, you can climb the boulder-strewn terrain to the top for a panoramic view of the island or wander around lower down looking at rocks nature has carved into seats and likenesses of prehistoric birds and animals. Casibari is open daily from 9am to 5pm. No admission is charged. There is a lodge at Casibari where you can buy souvenirs, snacks, soft drinks, and beer.

Guides can also point out drawings on the walls and ceiling of the **Caves of Canashito,** south of Hooiberg. While there, you may get to see the giant green parakeets.

Hooiberg is affectionately known as "The Haystack." It's Aruba's most outstanding landmark, and anybody with the stamina can take the steps all the way to the top of this 541-foot-high hill. One Aruban jogs up there every morning. From its precincts in the center of the island you can see Venezuela on a clear day.

On the jagged, windswept northern coast, the **Natural Bridge** has been carved out of the coral rock by the relentless surf. In a little café overlooking the coast you can order snacks. There you'll also find a souvenir shop with a large selection of trinkets, T-shirts, and wall hangings, all for reasonable prices.

You turn inland for the short trip to **Pirate's Castle** at Bushiribana, which stands on a cliff on the island's windward coast. This is actually a deserted gold mill from the island's now-defunct industry. Another gold mill is in the old ghost town on the west coast, Balashi.

You can continue to the village of Noord, known for its **St. Anne's Church,** with a hand-carved, 17th-century Dutch altar.

EAST TO SAN NICOLAS

Driving along the highway more or less paralleling the south coast of Aruba toward the island's southernmost section, you may want to stop at the **Spaans Lagoen (Spanish Lagoon),** where legend says pirates used to hide out as they waited to plunder rich cargo ships in the Caribbean. Today this is an ideal place for snorkeling, and you can picnic at tables under the mangrove trees.

On to the east, you'll pass an area called **Savaneta,** where some of the most ancient traces of human habitation have been unearthed. You'll see along here the first oil tanks marking the position of the Lago Oil & Transport Company Ltd., the Exxon subsidiary around which the town of San Nicolás developed, although it had been an industrial center since the days of phosphate mining in the late 19th century. A "company town" until the refinery was closed in 1985, San Nicolás, 12 miles from Oranjestad, is called the Aruba Sunrise Side, and tourism has become its main economic factor. The town has a blend of cultures—customs, style, languages, color, and tastes. In the area are caves with Arawak artwork on the walls and a modern innovation, a PGA-approved golf course with sand "greens" and cactus traps.

Boca Grandi, on the windward side of the island, is a favorite windsurfing location; or if you prefer quieter waters, you'll find them at **Baby Beach** and **Rodgers Beach,** on Aruba's lee side. Overlooking the latter two beaches is **Seroe Colorado (Colorado Point),** from which it's possible to see the coastline of Venezuela as well as the pounding surf on the windward side. You can climb down the cliffs, and perhaps spot an iguana here and there; protected by law, the once-endangered saurians now proliferate in peace.

Other sights in the San Nicolás area are the **Guadarikiri Cave** and **Fontein Cave,** where you can see the wall drawings, plus the **Huliba** and **Tunnel of Love** caves, with guides and refreshment stands. Guadarikiri Cave is a haven for wild parrots.

SPORTS & RECREATION

BEACHES The western and southern shore, called the **Turquoise Coast,** attracts sun seekers to Aruba. **Palm Beach** and **Eagle Beach** (the latter closer to Oranjestad) are the best beaches. No hotel along the strip owns the beaches, all of which are open to the public (if you use any of the hotel's facilities, however, you'll be charged, of course). You can also spread your towel on **Manchebo Beach** or **Druif**

Bay Beach—in fact, anywhere along 7 miles of uninterrupted sugar-white sands. In total contrast to the leeward side, the north or windward shore is rugged and wild.

CRUISES   Visitors interested in combining a pleasant boat ride with a few hours of snorkeling should contact **De Palm Tours,** which has offices in seven of the island's hotels and its main office at Lloyd G. Smith Boulevard 142, in Oranjestad (tel. 24400). For $35 per person they'll take you on a "fun cruise" aboard a catamaran. After a windswept sail of 1½ hours, passengers stop for 3 hours at their private De Palm island for snorkeling. Lunch and an open bar are included in the price. The tour, if participation warrants it, departs daily at 10am and returns at 4pm.

DEEP-SEA FISHING   In the deep waters off the coast of Aruba you can test your skill and wits against the big ones—wahoo, marlin, tuna, bonito, and sailfish. **De Palm Tours,** Lloyd G. Smith Boulevard 142 in Oranjestad (tel. 24400), takes out a maximum of six people (four of whom can fish at the same time) on one of its four boats, which range in length from 29 to 38 feet. Half-day tours, with all equipment included, begin at $200 for two people, at $220 for four, and at $240 for six. The prices are doubled for full-day trips. Boats leave from the docks beside the Bali Floating Restaurant in Oranjestad. De Palm maintains seven branches, most of which are in Aruba's major hotels.

GOLF   Visitors can play at the **Aruba Golf Club,** Golfweg 82 (tel. 42006), in San Nicolás at the eastern end of the island. This is a 9-hole course with 25 sand traps and 10 greens played from different tees to facilitate an 18-hole play. Greens fees are $10 for 18 holes and $7.50 for 9. The course is open daily from 7:30am to dusk and features a pro shop, bar, air-conditioned restaurant, and changing rooms with showers.

SCUBA DIVING, SNORKELING & OTHER WATER SPORTS   You can snorkel in rather shallow waters, and scuba divers find stunning marine life with endless varieties of coral as well as tropical fish in infinite hues; at some points visibility is up to 90 feet. The goal of most divers is the German freighter *Antilia,* which was scuttled in the early years of World War II off the northwestern tip of Aruba, not too far from Palm Beach.

   Red Sails Sports, Lloyd G. Smith Boulevard 83 (tel. 31603), is the best water-sports center on the island. The center has an extensive variety of activities, including sailing, windsurfing, waterskiing, and scuba diving. Scuba diving can be experienced in 1 day with Red Sail dive packages, including shipwreck dives as well as exploration of marine reefs. Guests are first given a poolside resort course where Red Sail's certified instructors teach procedures that ensure safety during dives. For those who wish to become certified, full PADI certification can be achieved in as little as 4 days. Photography equipment is available for rental.

   Divi Winds Center, Lloyd G. Smith Boulevard 41 (tel. 23300, ext. 623), near the Divi Tamarind Beach Hotel, is the windsurfing headquarters of the island. Equipment is made by Fanatic, Inc., and is rented for $20 per hour or $38 per half day. Because of the nature of Aruba's strong winds, everyone is required to take a "Learn to Windsurf" course, which is included free in the rental. The resort is on the quiet (Caribbean) side of the island, and doesn't face the fierce Atlantic waves. Catamaran rides, with an experienced skipper, can be arranged, and snorkeling gear can be rented.

TENNIS   Most of the island's beachfront hotels have tennis courts, often swept by trade winds, and some have top pros on hand to give instruction. Many of the courts can also be lit for night games (I don't advise playing in Aruba's noonday sun), usually with a $2 surcharge. Some hotels restrict their courts to use by guests.

SAVVY SHOPPING

Aruba manages to compress six continents into the half-mile-long Caya G. F. Betico Croes, in what is called the **Mainstreet Shopping Center,** in Oranjestad. Not technically a free port, the duty is so low (3.3%) that articles are attractively priced—and Aruba has no sales tax. You'll find the usual array of Swiss watches; German and Japanese cameras; jewelry; liquor; English bone china and porcelain; Dutch, Swedish, and Danish silver and pewter; French perfume; British woolens; Indonesian specialties; and Madeira embroidery. Delft blue pottery is an especially good buy. Some good buys include Holland cheese (Edam and Gouda), as well as Holland chocolate and English cigarettes in the airport departure area.

Philatelists interested in the wealth of colorful and artistic stamps issued in honor of the changed government status of Aruba can purchase a complete assortment, as well as other special issues, at the post office in Oranjestad.

Store Hours   In general, shops are open Monday through Saturday from 8am to noon and 2 to 6pm. Many stores are also closed on Tuesday afternoon and some seem to keep irregular hours off-season, especially in the fall and spring.

SHOPPING CENTERS

ALHAMBRA SHOPPING BAZAAR, adjacent to the Alhambra Casino, Lloyd G. Smith Blvd. Tel. 35000.

This is a blend of international shops, outdoor marketplaces, and cafés and restaurants. Merchandise ranges from fine jewelry, chocolates, and perfume to imported craft items, leather goods, clothing, and lingerie. Like the casino, the shopping bazaar is open daily from early afternoon until the early-morning hours.

SEAPORT VILLAGE, Lloyd G. Smith Blvd.

Comprising Seaport Village Mall, the Crystal Casino, and the Sonesta Hotel, this complex is landmarked by the Crystal tower and located across from the harbor at the "entrance" of the center of downtown, only 5 miles from the cruise terminal. Here are more than 85 stores, boutiques, and eateries, carrying a wide selection of merchandise to meet everyone's taste and budget—fashions, gifts, souvenirs, sporting goods, liquors, and fragrances. Top brands are featured, such as Gucci, Escada, Ralph Lauren Polo, Givenchy, Paloma Picasso, Lancôme, Baccarat, Lalique, Fendi, Movado, Valentino, Christofle, and many others known internationally. Most shops are open Monday through Saturday from 9am to 6pm.

One of the shops, the **Boulevard Book & Drugstore** (tel. 27358) has a complete range of goods from the latest paperback books to cosmetics, candies, gifts, toys, better-quality T-shirts and sweatshirts, sportswear, and souvenirs. You can also get stamps, roadmaps, current magazines, and newspapers.

SPECIALTY SHOPS

ARTISTIC BOUTIQUE, Caya G. F. Betico Croes 25. Tel. 23142.

The Artistic Boutique stocks fine linens, hand-embroidered madeiras, organdies, and Irish linen articles, such as napkins, placemats, and guest towels. You may be able to find just what you want in the $2 corner. Crystal figurines, Asian antiques, handmade rugs, paintings, jade and ivory artworks, silks, gold and silver jewelry, handcrafted articles of the islands, and Oriental rugs are among the treasures offered.

ARUBA TRADING COMPANY, Caya G. F. Betico Croes 14. Tel. 22600.

Next door to the New Amsterdam Store (see below), the Aruba Trading Company offers a complete range of attractive tourist items: perfumes, cosmetics, souvenirs, and gift items of porcelain, Delft, Hummel, and crystal ware, liquor, and cigarettes (the latter purchases can be delivered to your plane).

DIVI DIVI HOTEL GIFTSHOP AND MINIMARKET, in the Divi Divi Beach Hotel, Lloyd G. Smith Blvd. 93. Tel. 23300.

The boutique here is fully stocked like the Tamarijn shops, previewed below.

GANDELMAN JEWELERS, Mainstreet 5A. Tel. 32121.

Gandelman offers an extensive collection of fine gold jewelry and famous-name timepieces at duty-free prices. They also have stores in the Alhambra Shopping Bazaar, Americana Hotel, Airport Departure Hall, and Hyatt Regency Hotel.

LITTLE SWITZERLAND JEWELERS, Caya G. F. Betico Croes 47. Tel. 21192.

Famous for its duty-free 14- and 18-karat gold jewelry and watches, Little Switzerland also carries a big variety of famous-name Swiss watches. There are branches at most of the large hotels in Aruba.

NEW AMSTERDAM STORE, Caya G. F. Betico Croes 50. Tel. 21152.

Aruba's leading department store is best for linens, with its selection of napkins, placemats, and embroidered tablecloths with sources that range all the way from China. It has an extensive line of other merchandise as well, from Delft blue pottery to beachwear and boutique items, along with assorted gift items, porcelain figures by Lladró, watches, French and Italian women's wear, and leather bags and shoes.

PENHA, Caya G. F. Betico Croes 11–13. Tel. 24161.

Penha offers top-quality gifts, clothing, and perfumes. For example, they are exclusive purveyors here of Giorgio, and they also have Estée Lauder, Lancôme, and Clinique cosmetics. Men's clothing includes that of such designers as Pierre Cardin, Papillon, Lanvin, and Givenchy, and women can choose garments from Dior, Liz Claiborne, and Castoni. If you're shopping on a smaller scale, you'll find T-shirts and souvenirs here. Penha also has boutiques at the Tamarijn, Divi Divi, Holiday Inn, and Americana hotels.

TAMARIJN HOTEL GIFTSHOP AND MINIMARKET, in the Tamarijn Beach Hotel, Lloyd G. Smith Blvd. 64. Tel. 24150.

Tamarijn offers a complete selection of gifts, souvenirs, and drugstore items, plus a full range of delicatessen offerings, liquor, and wines.

EVENING ENTERTAINMENT
THE CLUB & BAR SCENE

Nongamblers or those who grow tired of the slots and tables can patronize a hotel's cocktail lounges and supper clubs. You don't have to be a guest of the hotel to visit to see the shows, but you should make a reservation. Tables at the big shows, especially in season, are likely to be booked early in the day. Usually you can go to one of the major hotel supper clubs and only order drinks. Expect to pay $4 and up for most libations.

ALADDIN THEATER, in the Alhambra, Lloyd G. Smith Blvd. 83. Tel. 35000.

Away from the gaming tables, cabaret shows are presented Monday through Saturday at 9 and 11pm at the Aladdin Theater. The stars and format change regularly. No reservations are accepted, although tickets can be purchased in advance. Seating is on a first-come, first-served basis.

The Alhambra has 28 shops including boutiques selling perfume, souvenirs, T-shirts, swimwear, Delft blue figurines, European high fashions, jewelry, leather goods, and local and South American crafts. There are also eating places, such as a New York–style deli; Munchies, for pizza, tacos, and snacks; Roseland, with a buffet dinner nightly from 6 to 10pm costing $12 for all you can eat; and Lui's Place, for tropical frozen cocktails.

Admission (including two drinks): Aladdin Theater, $20.

CASINOS

The casinos of the big hotels along Palm Beach are the liveliest nighttime destinations, and they stay open as long as business demands, often into the wee hours. In plush gaming parlors, guests try their luck at roulette, craps, blackjack, and of course the one-armed bandits. The **Americana Aruba Beach Resort** (tel. 24500) opens daily at 1pm for slots, at 3pm for blackjack and roulette, and at 9pm for all games. Early birds go to the **Aruba Concorde** (tel. 24466) at 10am for slots, 1pm for games. The **Holiday Inn Aruba Beach Resort** (tel. 23600) wins the prize for all-around action. Its casino doors are open 22 hours a day, closing only for 2 hours to clean. The **Aruba Palm Beach** (tel. 23900) opens its gambling tables from 9pm on. The **Golden Tulip Aruba Caribbean** (tel. 33555) has one of the newest casinos on the island. Newer still is the grand Crystal Casino at the **Sonesta Hotel Beach Club** (tel. 24622). Both of these open at 9pm every night. So does the casino at the **Hyatt Regency Aruba Resort & Casino** (tel. 31234).

The busiest casino on Aruba is the **Alhambra,** Lloyd G. Smith Boulevard 63 (tel. 35000). More than just a casino, it offers a collection of restaurants and boutiques, along with an inner courtyard designed like an 18th-century Dutch village. From the outside the complex looks Moorish, with serpentine mahogany columns and repeating arches rising to a pinnacle defined by a duet of sea-green domes; the desert setting of Aruba seems appropriate. A strapping "Moor" greets you at the door and shakes your hand to wish you luck. The casino and its satellites are open daily from 10am till very late at night. Dress is informal.

2. BONAIRE

Unlike some islands, Bonaire isn't just surrounded by coral reefs—it *is* the reef! And its shores are thick with rainbow-hued fish. Only 5 miles wide and 24 miles long, Bonaire is poised in the Caribbean, close to the coast of South America known for many generations as the Spanish Main. It's just 50 miles north of Venezuela. The island, whose name in Amerindian means "low country," attracts those seeking that out-of-the-way spot, that uncrowded shore.

Part of the Netherlands Antilles (an autonomous part of the Netherlands), Bonaire has a population of about 10,000. Its capital is **Kralendijk**. It is most often reached from its neighbor island of Curaçao, 30 miles to the west. Like Curaçao, it's desertlike, with a dry and brilliant atmosphere. Often it's visited by "day trippers," who rush through here in pursuit of the shy, elusive flamingo.

Boomerang-shaped Bonaire comprises about 112 square miles, making it the second largest of the ABC Dutch-affiliated grouping. Its northern sector is hilly, tapering up to Mount Brandaris, all of 788 feet. However, the southern half, flat as a flapjack, is given over to bays, reefs, beaches, and a salt lake that attracts the flamingos.

The island has powdery white beaches and turquoise waters, where underwater photographers find a visibility of 100 feet or more. Unspoiled Bonaire is one of the world's best scuba and snorkeling grounds, a beachcomber's retreat, and a birdwatcher's heaven, with 135 different species—not only the graceful flamingo, but also the big-billed pelican, as well as bright-green parrots, snipes, terns, parakeets, herons, hummingbirds, and others. Bring a pair of binoculars.

Bonaireans zealously want to protect their environment. Even though they eagerly seek tourism, they aren't interested in creating "another Aruba" with its high-rise hotel blocks. Spearfishing isn't allowed in their waters, nor is the taking or destruction of any coral or other living animal from the sea.

The big annual event is the **October Sailing Regatta,** a 5-day festival of racing sponsored by the local tourist bureau. Now an international affair, the event attracts sailors and spectators from around the world, as a flotilla of sailboats and yachts anchor in Kralendijk Bay. If you're planning to visit during regatta days, make sure you have an iron-clad hotel reservation.

ORIENTATION

HISTORY The island was sighted in 1499 by a party of explorers commanded by Amerigo Vespucci, who lent his name to the New World. Amerigo found some native tribes living on the island in Stone Age conditions. After Spanish domination, Bonaire witnessed the arrival of the Dutch in 1634, perhaps seeking to protect Curaçao's flanks, an island they already occupied. Bonaire was assigned the duty of supplying livestock, corn, and salt.

Once the British occupied the island, and eventually leased it to a New York merchant for $2,400 annually, including the services of 300 "salt-mine" slaves.

The Dutch came back in 1816 and up plantations to grow dyewood, cochenille, and aloes. At the abolition of slavery in 1863, the economy collapsed and Bonaire settled into a long, dreary depression. Relief came in the form of what was known as the "money-order economy" era, when Bonaireans migrated to Curaçao and Aruba to work in the oil industry. Automation of that industry in the 1950s caused the loss of many jobs, and Bonaireans returned to their native island. Fortunately, instead of being plunged permanently back into depression, Bonaire was discovered, along with other Caribbean islands, by international tourism, and the economy began to look up. The first hotel opened in 1951. The long-dormant salt-harvesting industry, taking full advantage of the abundant Bonaire sunshine, was reactivated and has become one of the most successful salt-mining industries in the world.

GETTING THERE   The only nonstop flights to Bonaire from North America are offered on **ALM** (tel. toll free 800/327-7230). These fly only twice a week (on Saturday and Sunday) from Atlanta and three times a week from Miami. **Air Aruba** (tel. toll free 800/88-ARUBA) touches down in Bonaire once a week as part of its Friday-morning nonstop flight from Newark, New Jersey, to Aruba. (After landing in Aruba, the aircraft continues on to Bonaire.)

When making your plans to visit Bonaire, you'll have more flexibility if you remember that connections among the ABC Islands are offered many times a day on ALM. (The airline offers eight flights a day to Bonaire from both Aruba and Curaçao.) You can get to Aruba on **American Airlines** (tel. toll free 800/433-7300) through its hubs in New York and San Juan, Puerto Rico, and then transfer to a prearranged flight to Bonaire. American will set this up for you, as well as reduced fares on hotels, if you book them simultaneously with your air passage.

GETTING AROUND   Even though the island is flat, renting Mopeds or motor scooters is not always a good idea. Roads are often unpaved, pitted, and peppered with rocks. Touring through Washington National Park, for example, is best done by van, Jeep, or automobile.

By Taxi   Taxis are unmetered, but the government has established rates. All licensed taxicabs carry a license plate with the letters TX. Each driver should have a list of prices to be produced upon request. As many as four passengers can go along for the ride unless they have too much luggage. As examples of what rates to expect, a trip from the airport to your hotel should cost about $9. From 8pm to midnight fares are increased by 25%, and from 11pm to 6am they go up by 50%.

By Rental Car   I recommend **Budget/Boncar,** with offices in Kralendijk (tel. 8300, ext. 225) and at the airport (tel. 8315). This firm rents vehicles starting at $26 per day with unlimited mileage. Your valid U.S. or Canadian driver's license is acceptable for driving in Bonaire. Driving in Bonaire is *on the right.*

By Sightseeing Tour   **Bonaire Sightseeing Tours** (tel. 8300, ext. 225) transports you on tours of the island, both north and south, taking in the flamingos, slave huts, conch shells, Goto Lake, the Amerindian inscriptions, and other sights. Each of these tours lasts 2 hours and costs $12 per person. You can take a half-day City and Country Tour, lasting 3 hours and costing $17 per person, allowing you to see the entire northern section and the southern part as far as the slave huts. A special 4-hour tour of Washington-Slagbaai National Park can be booked at a cost of $25 per person for a minimum of four. An all-day tour of the national park goes for $45 per person.

Most taxi drivers are informed about the sights of Bonaire and will take you on a tour. You must negotiate the price according to how long a trip you want and what you want to see.

FAST FACTS   BONAIRE

Area Code Bonaire is *not* part of the Caribbean 809 area code. See "Telecommunications," below, for complete information on making calls to and on this island.

Banking Hours Banks are usually open Monday through Friday from 8:30am to noon and 2 to 4pm.

Currency Like the other islands of the Netherlands Antilles (Curaçao, St. Maarten, St. Eustatius, and Saba), Bonaire's coin of the realm is the **Netherlands Antillean florin (NAf)**, sometimes called a guilder, equal to 56¢ in U.S. currency. However, U.S. dollars are also accepted.

Customs There are no Customs requirements for Bonaire.

Documents To enter Bonaire, all a U.S. or Canadian citizen needs is proof of citizenship and a return or continuing ticket.

Electricity The electrical current on Bonaire is slightly different from that used in North America (127 volts, 56 cycles, as opposed to U.S. and Canadian voltages of 110 volts, 60 cycles). It's completely suitable for any simple North American appliance, including a hairdryer, a small TV, or a contact lens sterilizer, with no need for an electric transformer or adapter. Be warned, however, that electrical current used to feed or recharge finely calibrated diving equipment should be stabilized with a specially engineered electrical stabilizer. Every dive operation on the island has one of these as part of its standard equipment for visiting divers to use.

Information For tourist information on Bonaire, go to the Bonaire Government **Tourist Bureau,** Kaya Libertad Simon Bolivar 12, Kralendijk (tel. 7/8322), open Monday through Friday from 7:30am to noon and 1:30 to 5:30pm. Before you go, contact the Bonaire Government Tourist Office, 201½ East 29th Street, New York, NY 10016 (tel. 212/779-0242, or toll free 800/U-BONAIR).

Language English is widely spoken, but you'll hear Dutch, Spanish, and Papiamento.

Medical Care The **St. Francis Hospital** is in Kralendijk (tel. 8900). A plane on standby at the airport takes seriously ill patients to Curaçao for treatment.

Police Call 8000.

Safety "Safe, safe Bonaire" might be the island's motto in this crime-infested world. But remember, any place that attracts tourists also attracts people who prey on them. Safeguard your valuables.

Taxes and Service The government requires a $2.80 daily room tax on all hotel rooms. Most hotels and guesthouses add a 10% service charge in lieu of tipping. Restaurants generally add a service charge of 15% to the bill. Upon leaving Bonaire, you'll be charged an airport departure tax of $10, so don't spend every penny. There is also an inter-island departure tax of $2.75.

Telecommunications Service for telephone, Telex, telegraph, radio, and TV is available in English. Bonaire is *not* a part of the 809 area code that applies to most of the Caribbean. To call Bonaire from the U.S., if your long-distance telephone company is equipped to handle international direct dialing, dial 011 (the international access code), then 599 (the country code for Bonaire), and then 7 (the area code) and the four-digit local number. If you cannot direct-dial internationally, dial 0 ("zero," for the operator) and tell the operator you wish to make an international call; once you are transferred to the international operator, state the 599 country code, the 7 area code, and then the local number, and the operator will dial the call for you.

Once on Bonaire, to call another number on the island only the four-digit local number is necessary. *Note:* In this chapter only the area code and local number are given.

Time Bonaire is on Atlantic standard time year round, 1 hour ahead of eastern standard time (when it's noon in Bonaire, it's 11am in Miami). When daylight saving time is in effect in the U.S., clocks in Miami and Bonaire show the same time.

Water   Drinking water is pure and safe. It comes from distilled seawater.

Weather   Bonaire is known for its climate, with temperatures hovering at 82° Fahrenheit. The water temperature averages 80°. It's warmest in August and September, coolest in January and February. The average rainfall is 22 inches, and December through March are the rainiest months.

WHERE TO STAY

Hotels, all facing the sea, are low-key, hassle-free, and personally run operations where everybody gets to know everybody else rather fast.

A Reminder: Taxes and service charges are seldom included in the prices you are quoted, so ask about them when making your reservations.

VERY EXPENSIVE

HARBOUR VILLAGE BEACH RESORT, Kaya Gobernador Deprot, Playa Lechi, Bonaire, N.A. Tel. 7/7500, or toll free 800/424-0004. Fax 7/7507. 72 rms, 8 villas. A/C TV TEL

$ Rates: Winter, $205–$265 single or double; from $365 suite. Summer, $135–$175 single or double; from $275 suite. Dive packages available. Continental breakfast $8 extra. AE, DC, MC, V. **Parking:** Free.

Opened in 1990, 4 miles north of the airport, Harbour Village offers deluxe rooms lying on a peninsula overlooking its own private beach and marina. Designed in a villagelike setting of low-rise buildings are first-class hotel accommodations, and in addition, guests can select ocean- or harbor-view villas, complete with patios or balconies overlooking the Caribbean. Rooms have hairdryers, cable movies, and well-equipped private baths.

Dining/Entertainment: Kasa Coral Gourmet Dining Terrace offers breakfast and dinner, featuring an international menu and live music. La Balandra Bar & Grill offers lunch, happy-hour, and after-dinner drinks. Lunch service also is available poolside, on the beach, or in rooms, terraces, or patios.

Services: Room service, laundry and dry cleaning, wake-up service, pickup at the airport (10 minutes from the resort).

Facilities: Swimming pool, scuba-diving shop with state-of-the-art diving and underwater photographic equipment, tennis courts, waterskiing.

EXPENSIVE

CAPTAIN DON'S HABITAT, Kaya Gouverneur Debrotweg 103, Bonaire, N.A. Tel. 7/8290; for all reservations and business arrangements, contact Captain Don's Habitat, 1080 Port Blvd., Suite 100, Miami, FL 33132 (tel. toll free 800/327-6709; fax 305/371-2337). 41 rms, 31 suites. A/C

$ Rates (including 4 nights/5 days, breakfast, airport transfers, tax, service, two boat dives daily, plus unlimited surf dives, and use of all equipment): Winter, $619 single; $300 per person double; from $421 per person suite. Summer, $434 single; $284 per person double; from $319 per person suite. AE, DC, MC, V. **Parking:** Free.

Built on a coral bluff overlooking the sea about 5 minutes north of Kralendijk, this is a unique diving, snorkeling, and nature-oriented resort, with an air of congenial informality and a philosophy and life-style for those whose souls belong to the sea. The infrastructure and staff are devoted to the many different possibilities for diving off the coast of Bonaire. Habitat and its accompanying dive shop are the creation of Capt. Don Stewart, Caribbean pioneer and "caretaker of the reefs," a former

Californian who sailed his schooner from San Francisco through the Panama Canal, arriving on a reef in Bonaire in 1962—he has been here ever since. Called the "godfather of diving" on the island, Captain Don was instrumental in the formation of the Bonaire Marine Park, whereby the entire island became a protected reef.

More than 90% of the clients coming here opt for one of the packages which incorporate a variable number of dives with accommodations in settings ranging from standard double rooms to oceanfront villas. The most popular arrangement is the 4-night/5-day package (rates are listed above).

Dining/Entertainment: This resort has an oceanfront restaurant and two seaside bars.

Services: Laundry, baby-sitting.

Facilities: Boutique, ocean-bordering pool, complete diving program.

SAND DOLLAR BEACH CLUB, Kaya Grandi, Bonaire, N.A. Tel. 7/8738, or toll free 800/345-0805. Fax 7/8760. 85 units. A/C TV

$ Rates: Mid-Dec to mid-Apr, $145 studio for two; $175 one-bedroom unit for two; $225 two-bedroom unit for four. Summer, $125 studio; $155 one-bedroom unit for two; $185 two-bedroom unit for four. Continental breakfast $6 extra. AE, MC, V. **Parking:** Free.

On the beachfront, just 1½ miles north of Kralendijk and 3 miles north of the airport, the Sand Dollar offers studio apartments and one-, two-, and three-bedroom units with all the style, comfort, and convenience of a full-service hotel. All accommodations are equipped with electric ranges, ovens, dishwashers, refrigerators, custom cabinets, and modern furnishings, with decks or balconies facing the ocean. For more information on the property, contact Travel Barn, 52 Georgetown Road, Bordentown, NJ 08505 (tel. 609/298-3844).

Dining/Entertainment: The complex has a restaurant and bar.

Facilities: Shopping center, tennis courts, freshwater swimming pool with bar and cabaña, Sand Dollar Dive and Photo (see "Sports and Recreation," below).

MODERATE

DIVI FLAMINGO BEACH RESORT & CASINO, J. A. Abraham Blvd., Bonaire, N.A. Tel. 7/8285, 305/633-1621 in Florida, or toll free 800/367-3484. Fax 7/8238. 105 rms, 40 studios. A/C

$ Rates: Winter, $125–$195 single or double (prices about 10% higher between Christmas and New Year's); from $195 studio. Apr to mid-Dec, $80–$115 single or double; from $125 studio. Continental breakfast $8 extra. AE, MC, V. **Parking:** Free.

North of Kralendijk, this complete beachfront resort, with its water-sports facilities and stylish bedrooms, was once a neglected, gone-to-seed hotel with a cluster of flimsy wooden bungalows that had been used as an internment camp for German prisoners in World War II. With foresight and taste, the owners turned it into a top-notch resort, offering individual cottages and modern seafront rooms with private balconies resting on piers above the surf, so you can stand out and watch rainbow-hued tropical fish in the water below.

The resort's original rooms were supplemented in 1986 with the addition of stylish time-sharing units, forming Club Flamingo. Each of the units is rentable by the day or week. Accommodations in both sections are spacious and sunny, with air conditioning, ceiling fans, private bathrooms, and a selection of Mexican accessories. The newer units are clustered into a green-and-white Neo-Victorian pavilion facing its own curving swimming pool. Each contains a handsome kitchenette with carved cupboards and cabinets of pickled hardwoods. Both sections benefit from the attentions of a pair of social hostesses and the proximity of a good dive operation and a beautiful beach. A pair of restaurants, the Chibi-Chibi and the Calabase Terrace, provide satisfying meals.

SUNSET BEACH HOTEL, Playa Leche (P.O. Box 333), Bonaire, N.A. Tel. 7/8448, or toll free 800/330-3322. Fax 7/8593. 106 rms, 4 suites. A/C TV

$ Rates: Winter, $100–$130 single or double; from $160 suite. Summer, $65–$85 single or double; from $125 suite. Continental breakfast $7.50 extra. AE, MC, V. **Parking:** Free.

This was formerly the Bonaire Beach Hotel before its present affiliation with the Golden Tulip chain. Set on its own beach, Playa Leche (Milk Beach), it occupies 12 acres of land half a mile north of Kralendijk and 3 miles north of the airport. From its headquarters in a low-slung, plant-filled central building, long, covered walkways lead across a sandy terrain through gardens to the comfortable accommodations in motellike annexes scattered around a freshwater pool; each unit has a small refrigerator. The hotel has good diving facilities, windsurfing equipment, two tennis courts (lit at night), a miniature golf course, and a beach bar and restaurant. Laundry, baby-sitting, and room service are available.

INEXPENSIVE

CARIB INN, J. A. Abraham Blvd. (P.O. Box 68), Kralendijk, Bonaire, N.A. Tel. 7/8819. Fax 7/5295. 6 rms, 3 suites. A/C TV
$ Rates: Winter, $59–$89 single or double; from $99 suite. Summer, $49–$69 single or double; from $89 suite. AE, MC, V. **Parking:** Free.

Set directly on the water, this hotel was established by American Bruce Bowker and is occupied by dedicated scuba divers. About half the units ring an oval swimming pool; others are in separate cottages on the beach, facing the hotel's dock. Each room has simple tropical furniture and few frills; seven units come with kitchens and all have refrigerators. Breakfast isn't served.

WHERE TO DINE

Bonaire's food is generally acceptable. Nearly everything has to be imported, of course. Your best bet is fresh-caught fish and an occasional *rijstaffel*, the traditional Indonesian rice table, or try the local dishes. Popular foods are conch cutlet or stew, pickled conch, red snapper, tuna, wahoo, dolphin, fungi (a thick cornmeal pudding), rice, beans, sate (marinated meat with curried mayonnaise), goat stew, and Dutch cheeses.

EXPENSIVE

THE BEEFEATER, Kaya Grandi 22, Kralendijk. Tel. 8081.
Cuisine: CONTINENTAL. **Reservations:** Required in season.
$ Prices: Appetizers $4.85–$10.30; main courses $13–$26. AE, DC, MC, V.
Open: Dinner only, Mon–Sat 6–11pm. **Closed:** Sept.

Outside the hotels, I prefer the Beefeater, one of the island's oldest restaurants, in the heart of the capital near the Divi Flamingo. An Englishman, Richard Dove, a former inspector for the Michelin guides, created this handsome restaurant in an old town house, decorating it with prints and pictures. An apéritif is served in an intimate bar, and in the dining room you'll enjoy excellent personal service in a dignified, somewhat elegant atmosphere. Steaks and seafood are the main feature. The chef prepares an excellent steak au poivre. Before your main course, try his pâté, crêpe, or conch.

BISTRO DES AMIS, Kaya L. D. Gerharts 1, Kralendijk. Tel. 8003.
Cuisine: AMERICAN/CARIBBEAN. **Reservations:** Required.
$ Prices: Appetizers $5–$10; main courses $17–$32. AE, MC, V.
Open: Dinner only, Mon–Sat 6:30–11pm.

In the heart of town near the Divi Flamingo, this intimate air-conditioned bistro offers such daily changing specials as the best onion soup on the island, escargots served piping hot in garlic butter, mousse of smoked eel, pepper steak in cream-cognac sauce, and scallops swimming in a velvety cream sauce. The wine selection is limited, but among the best on the island. There's also a large bar if you'd like to drop in for a drink, and there's often dancing so you can make a night of it.

CHIBI-CHIBI, in the Flamingo Beach Resort & Casino, J. A. Abraham Blvd. Tel. 8285.
　Cuisine: CONTINENTAL. **Reservations:** Recommended.
$ Prices: Appetizers $3.50–$5.75; main courses $14–$20. AE, DC, MC, V.
　Open: Dinner only, daily 6–10pm.
On the sea on the periphery of Kralendijk, this place is named after the yellow-breasted tropical birds that can be observed from your dining table. An imposing two-tier edifice of exposed planking and wooden balustrades, the restaurant is perched over a coral-encrusted sea bottom, and you can see schools of multicolored fish in the illuminated waters. The chef prepares a continental menu, which also includes Antillean onion soup, seafood crêpe, fettuccine Flamingo, keshi yena (Edam cheese stuffed with meat and then baked), and of course, some of the freshest fish on the island.

DEN LAMAN RESTAURANT, Gouverneur Debrotweg 77. Tel. 8955.
　Cuisine: SEAFOOD. **Reservations:** Not required.
$ Prices: Appetizers $3–$8; main courses $11–$29.95. AE, MC, V.
　Open: Dinner only, Wed–Mon 6–11pm. **Closed:** Sept.
Located between the Sunset Beach Hotel and the Sand Dollar Beach Club, Den Laman serves some of the best seafood on Bonaire. An excellent beginning is the fish soup, the chef's special. The fresh fish of the day depends on what was caught, of course. Perhaps you'll order conch Flamingo, a local favorite, or lobster from the tank. When it's featured, I always go for the red snapper Créole. It's easy to spend $35 here, but it's also possible to dine for less.

RAFFLES' SEASIDE RESTAURANT, Caye Helmund 5. Tel. 8617.
　Cuisine: CARIBBEAN/CONTINENTAL. **Reservations:** Recommended.
$ Prices: Appetizers $3.50–$6.50; main courses $14–$22. AE, MC, V.
　Open: Dinner only, Tues–Sun 6:30pm–midnight.
★　Named after Sir Thomas Raffles, founder of Singapore, this sea-bordering restaurant near the Divi Flamingo is one of the island's oldest houses. Intimate tables, soft jazz music, and candlelight create a romantic ambience in the main air-conditioned restaurant, although you can dine less formally outside on the terrace overlooking the harbor. Astrid and Peter Lensvelt, the Dutch-born owners, offer seafood soup made with seven different kinds of fish, and also fish pâté. The locally born chef is known for his sweet-and-sour shrimp. The menu always features the catch of the day as well as steak dishes. Another specialty, called the Royal Platter, combines prime beef with seafood. The desserts are succulent, and include a white-and dark-chocolate mousse, several different kinds of fresh-fruit sorbets, and a mango parfait.

MODERATE

CHINA GARDEN, Kaya Grandi 47. Tel. 8480.
　Cuisine: ASIAN. **Reservations:** Recommended.
$ Prices: Appetizers $2–$10; main courses $3–$22. AE, MC, V.
　Open: Lunch Wed–Mon 11:30am–2pm; dinner Wed–Mon 4–10pm.
⑤　Good-tasting Eastern dishes, with some Indonesian specialties, are served to West Indians and visitors in this restored Bonairean mansion between the Divi Flamingo and Sunset Beach hotels. Portions are enormous, and prices are low considering what you get. The chefs from Hong Kong also cook Chinese, American, and local dishes, including a variety of curries ranging from beef to lobster. Seafood dishes, prepared in a variety of styles, including lobster in black-bean sauce, are also served. Special culinary features include a Java rijstaffel and the nasi goreng special. The place is air-conditioned and seats 60 guests.

GREEN PARROT RESTAURANT, in the Sand Dollar Beach Club, Kaya Grandi. Tel. 5454.
　Cuisine: CONTINENTAL. **Reservations:** Recommended.
$ Prices: Appetizers $3–$6; main courses $5–$20. AE, MC, V.

Open: Lunch daily 11:30am–3pm; dinner daily 3:30–10pm.
Set on a breeze-filled pier, this place is part of the complex of this previously recommended resort, a 15-minute drive from airport. It serves informal food, including burgers, pasta, sandwiches, and seafood dishes. You can gaze at the waves, enjoy a tropical fruit drink, and watch the sunset. On Saturday night there's a barbecue buffet with entertainment. Try the filet mignon or the barbecued chicken wings.

ZEEZICHT, Kaya Corsow. Tel. 8434.
   Cuisine: INTERNATIONAL. **Reservations:** Not required.
$ Prices: Appetizers $3–$4; main courses $6–$24. AE, MC, V.
   Open: Daily 9am–11pm.

This is the best place in the capital to go for a sundowner. You join the old salts or the people who live on boats to watch the sun go down, and you try to see the "green flash" that Hemingway wrote about. Pronounced "*Zay*-zict" and meaning "sea view," this place has long been popular for its excellent local cookery. A two-story operation, the restaurant offers a small rijstaffel as well as fresh fish from the nearby fish market. Lobster à la Zeezicht is occasionally offered, and there's always the Zeezicht steak.

WHAT TO SEE & DO

KRALENDIJK   The capital, Kralendijk, means "coral dike" and is pronounced "*Kroll*-en-dike" although most denizens refer to it as Playa, Spanish for "beach." A dollhouse town of some 2,500 residents, it's small, neat, pretty, and Dutch-clean, and its stucco buildings are painted pink and orange, with an occasional lime green. The capital's jetty is lined with island sloops and fishing boats.

Kralendijk nestles in a bay on the west coast, opposite **Klein Bonaire,** or Little Bonaire, an uninhabited, low-lying islet a 10-minute boat ride from the capital.

The main street of town leads along the beachfront on the harbor. A Protestant church was built in 1834, and St. Bernard's Roman Catholic Church has some stained-glass windows.

At **Fort Oranje** you'll see a lone cannon dating from the days of Napoleon. If possible, try to get up early to see the **Fish Market** on the waterfront, where you'll see a variety of strange and brilliantly colored fish.

Around town you'll probably see the official tourist guide and welcoming committee of one, Richard Faneyte.

BONAIRE MARINE PARK   ✪ To maintain the coral-reef ecosystem off Bonaire and to ensure returns from scuba diving, snorkeling, fishing, and other recreational activities, the Bonaire Marine Park was created, with the help of the International Union for Conservation of Nature and Natural Resources and of the World Wildlife Fund. The park incorporates the entire coastline of Bonaire and neighboring Klein Bonaire, defined as the "seabottom and the overlying waters from the high-water tidemark down to 200 feet." All park activities are controlled by island government legislation and a marine-environment management program. The park is policed, and services and facilities provided for visitors include a Visitor Information Center at the Karpata Ecological Center, park brochures, lectures, slide presentations, films, and permanent dive-site moorings.

Visitors are asked to respect the marine environment and to refrain from activities that may damage it, such as sitting or walking on the coral. All marine life is completely protected. This means no fishing or collecting of fish, shells, or corals—dead or alive. Spearfishing is forbidden. Anchoring is not permitted—all craft must use permanent moorings, except for emergency stops; boats shorter than 12 feet may use a stone anchor. Most recreational activity in the marine park takes place on the island's leeward side and among the reefs surrounding small, uninhabited Klein Bonaire.

The reefs are home to various coral formations that grow at different depths, ranging from the knobby brain coral at 3 feet to staghorn and elkhorn up to about 10 feet deeper, and gorgonians, giant brain, and others all the way to 40 to 83 feet. Many species of fish inhabit the reefs, and the deep reef slope is home to a range of sponges, groupers, and moray eels.

THE TOUR NORTH   The road north is one of the most beautiful stretches in the Antilles, with turquoise waters on your left, coral cliffs on your right. You can stop at several points along this road where you'll find paved paths for strolling or bicycling.

After leaving Kralendijk, and passing the Sunset Beach Hotel and the desalination plant, you'll come to **Radio Nederland Wereld Omroep (Dutch World Radio).** It's a 13-tower, 300,000-watter. Opposite the transmitting station is a lovers' promenade, built by nature and an ideal spot for a picnic.

Continuing, you'll pass the storage tanks of the Bonaire Petroleum Corporation, the road heading to **Goto Meer,** the island's loveliest inland sector, with a saltwater lake. Several flamingos prefer this spot to the salt flats in the south.

Down the hill the road leads to a section called **"Dos Pos"** or two wells, which has palm trees and vegetation in contrast to the rest of the island, where only the drought-resistant kibraacha and divi-divi trees, tilted before the constant wind, can grow, along with forests of cacti.

Bonaire's oldest village is **Rincón.** Slaves who used to work in the salt flats in the south once lived here. There are a couple of bars, including the Amstel and the Tropicana, and the Rincón Ice Cream Parlour makes homemade ice cream in a variety of interesting flavors. Above the bright roofs of the village is the crest of a hill called Para Mira or "stop and look."

A side path outside Rincón takes you to some Arawak inscriptions supposedly 500 years old. The petroglyph designs are in pink-red dye. At nearby **Boca Onima,** you'll find grotesque grottoes of coral.

Before going back to the capital, you might take a short bypass to **Seroe Largu,** which has a good view of Kralendijk and the sea. Lovers frequent the spot at night.

WASHINGTON/SLAGBAAI NATIONAL PARK   ✪ Washington/Slagbaai National Park is concerned with the conservation of the island's fauna, flora, and landscape, and is a changing vista highlighted by desertlike terrain, secluded beaches, caverns, and a bird sanctuary. Occupying 15,000 acres of Bonaire's northwesternmost territory, the park was once plantation land, producing divi-divi, aloe, charcoal, and goats. It was purchased by the Netherlands Antilles government, and since 1967 part of the land, formerly the Washington plantation, has been a wildlife sanctuary. The southern part of the park, the Slagbaai plantation, was added in 1978.

The park can be seen in a few hours, although it takes days to appreciate it fully. Touring the park is easy, with two routes: a 15-mile "short" route, marked by green arrows, and a 22-mile "long" route, marked by yellow arrows. The roads are well marked and safe, but somewhat rugged, although they are gradually being improved. Tickets cost $2 per person and can be purchased at the gate.

Whichever route you take, there are a few important stops you should make. Just past the gate is **Salina Mathijs,** a salt flat that's home to flamingos during the rainy season. Beyond the salt flat on the road to the right is **Boca Chikitu,** a white sand beach and bay. A few miles up the beach lies **Boca Cocolishi,** a two-part black sand beach. Its deep, rough seaward side is separated from the calm, shallow basin by a ridge of coralline algae. Hermit crabs walk the beach and shallow water.

The main road leads to **Boca Bartol,** a bay full of living and dead elkhorn coral, seafans, and reef fish. A popular watering hole good for birdwatching is **Poosdi Mangel. Wajaca** is a remote reef where many sea creatures live, including turtles, octopuses, and trigger-fish. Immediately inland towers 788-foot **Mount Brandaris,** Bonaire's highest peak, at whose foot is **Bronswinkel Well,** a watering spot for pigeons and parakeets. Some 130 species of birds live in the park, many with such exotic names as banana quilt and black-faced grassquit. Bonaire has few mammals, but you'll see goats and donkeys, perhaps even a wild bull.

HEADING SOUTH   Leaving the capital again, you pass the **Trans World Radio antennas,** towering 500 feet in the air, transmitting with 810,000 watts. This is one of the hemisphere's most powerful medium-wave radio stations, the loudest voice in Christendom and the most powerful nongovernmental broadcast station in the world. It sends out interdenominational Gospel messages and hymns in 20 languages to places as far away as Eastern Europe and the Middle East.

Later, you come on the ✪ **salt flats** where the brilliantly colored pink flamingos live. Bonaire shelters the largest accessible nesting and breeding grounds in the world. The flamingos build high mud mounds to hold their eggs. The birds are best viewed in spring when they're usually nesting and tending their young.

The salt flats were once worked by slaves, and the government has rebuilt some primitive stone huts, bare shelters little more than waist high. The slaves slept in these huts, and returned to their homes in Rincón in the north on weekends. The centuries-old salt pans have been reactivated by the International Salt Company. Near the salt pans you'll see some 30-foot obelisks in white, blue, and orange built in 1838 to help mariners locate their proper anchorages.

Farther down the coast is the island's oldest lighthouse, **Willemstoren,** built in 1837. Still farther along, **Sorobon Beach** and **Boca Cai** come into view. They're at landlocked Lac Bay, which is ideal for swimming and snorkeling. Conch shells are stacked up on the beach. The water here is so vivid and clear you can see coral 65 to 120 feet down in the reef-protected waters.

SPORTS & RECREATION

The true beauty on Bonaire is under the sea, where visibility is 100 feet 365 days of the year, and the water temperatures range from 78° to 82° Fahrenheit. Many dive sites can be reached directly from the beach, and sailing is another pastime. Birdwatching is among the best in the Caribbean, and for beachcombers there are acres and acres of driftwood, found along the shore from the salt flats to Lac.

BEACHES   Bonaire has some of the whitest sand beaches in the West Indies. The major hotels have beaches, but you may want to wander down to the southeast coast for a swim at the "clothes optional" **Sorobon** or **Boca Cai** on Lac Bay. In the north, you may want to swim at **Playa Funchi,** on the coastline of the Washington/Slagbaai National Park.

BOATING   Every visitor to Bonaire wants to take a trip to uninhabited Klein Bonaire. The **Flamingo Beach Hotel** and **Sunset Beach Hotel** offer trips daily. You'll be left in the morning for a day of snorkeling, beachcombing, and picnicking, then picked up later that afternoon. Other hotels will also arrange a trip to the islet for you, perhaps including a barbecue.

Several resorts offer sailing cruises. The **Sand Dollar Beach Club** (tel. 5252) has day trips aboard its *Samur,* taking visitors to Klein Bonaire beach from 10am to 4pm for a day of swimming and snorkeling. With sandwiches and soft drinks included, the cost is $35 per person. A sunset cruise with rum punch leaves daily between 5 and 7pm, costing $25 per person.

The **Sunset Beach Hotel** also offers a sunset cruise, requiring a minimum of 10 guests. It departs from the hotel every evening at 5pm and returns an hour later. You ride on a vessel that resembles a pontoon-supported floating barge. There's a cash bar, but snacks are free. The price is $8 per person, and it's best to reserve a seat 24 hours in advance.

Most of the major hotels, including the Sunset Beach Hotel, rent Sunfish or windsurfers for $12 per hour.

FISHING   The island's offshore fishing grounds offer some of the best fishing in the Caribbean. A good day's catch might include mackerel, tuna, and wahoo, among the many species out there.

Your best bet is Chris Morkos, **Piscatur Fishing Supplies,** Playa Pabao 69 (tel. 8774). A native Bonairean, he has been fishing almost since he was born. A maximum of five people are taken out on a 30-foot boat with a guide and captain, at a cost of

$275 for a half day or $425 for a whole day, including all tackle and bait. Reef fishing is another popular sport, in boats averaging 15 feet. A maximum of two people can go out for a half day at $120 or a whole day at $200. For the same price, a maximum of four people can fish for bonefish and tarpon on the island's large salt flats.

SCUBA DIVING ✪ One of the richest reef communities in the entire West Indies, Bonaire has plunging walls that descend to a sand bottom at 130 or so feet, abounding with hard corals, numerous seawhips, black-coral trees, basket sponges, gorgonia, and swarms of rainbow-hued tropical fish. Most of the diving is done on the leeward side where the ocean is lake flat. There are more than 40 dive sites on sharply sloping reefs.

The waters off the coast of Bonaire received an additional attraction in 1984. A rust-bottomed general cargo ship, 80 feet long, was confiscated by the police along with its contraband cargo, about 25,000 pounds of marijuana. Known as the *Hilma Hooker* (familiarly dubbed "The Hooker" by everyone on the island), it sank unclaimed (obviously) and without fanfare one calm day in 90 feet of water. Lying just off the southern shore near the capital, its wreck is now a popular dive site.

Bonaire has a unique program for divers in that the major hotels offer personalized, closeup encounters with the island's fish and other marine life under the expertise of Bonaire's dive guides.

Dive I and **Dive II,** at opposite ends of the beachfront of the Divi Flamingo Beach Resort & Casino, J. A. Abraham Boulevard (tel. 8285), north of Kralendijk, are among the island's most complete scuba facilities. Both operate out of well-stocked beachfront buildings, rent diving equipment, charge the same prices, and offer the same type of expeditions.

Captain Don's Habitat Dive Shop, Kaya Gouverneur Debrotweg 103 (tel. 8290), is a PADI five-star training facility. The open-air, full-service dive shop includes a classroom, photo/video lab, camera-rental facility, equipment repair, and compressor rooms grouped around spacious seafront patios. Habitat's slogan is "Diving Freedom," and divers can take their tanks and dive anywhere any time of day or night, most often along "The Pike," a half mile of protected reef right in front of the property. The highly qualified staff is there to assist and advise but not to police or dictate dive plans. Diving packages include boat dives, unlimited offshore diving (24 hours a day), unlimited air, tanks, backpack, weights, and belt. Some dive packages also include accommodations and meals (see "Where to Stay," above).

The **Bonaire Scuba Center,** in the Black Durgon Inn, Playa Lechi (tel. 8978). Some of the island's best diving is available from the doorstep of this seven-room inn. A living reef just 50 feet from shore quickly drops to 150 feet. Snorkeling is also possible from the property. The center caters to both novice and advanced divers, and offers both resort courses and certification courses.

Sand Dollar Dive and Photo, at the Sand Dollar Beach Club, Kaya Grandi (tel. 8738), offers dive packages, PADI and NAUI instruction, equipment rental and repairs, and boat, land, and deep-dive trips. The photo shop offers underwater photo and video shoots, PADI specialty courses, E-6 processing, print developing, equipment rental and repair, and a weekly slide and video presentation.

SNORKELING Snorkeling equipment can be rented at such previously recommended establishments as **Harbour Village Beach Resort,** the **Carib Inn,** or at any of the scuba centers (see below), including **Sand Dollar Dive and Photo, Dive Bonaire,** or **Habitat Dive Center.**

TENNIS The **Sunset Beach Hotel** (tel. 8448) has two good tennis courts, which are illuminated for night play and covered with artificial grass. Use of the courts is free to guests of the hotel, but nonresidents pay $6 per half hour of play. A tennis instructor is available, and racquets and balls can be borrowed without charge.

In addition, there are two courts at the **Sand Dollar Beach Club** and **Divi Flamingo Beach Resort** (see "Where to Stay," above); all the courts are lit for night play.

SAVVY SHOPPING

Kralendijk features an assortment of goods, including gemstone jewelry, wood, leather, sterling, ceramics, liquors, and tobacco at 25% to 50% less than in the U.S. and Canada. Prices are often quoted in U.S. dollars, and major credit cards and traveler's checks are usually accepted. Most shops are open Monday through Saturday from 8am to noon and 2 to 6pm; they might open for a few hours on Sunday if a cruise ship is in port. Walk along Kaya Grandi in Kralendijk to sample the merchandise.

FUNDASHON ARTE INDUSTRIA BONAIRIANO, J. A. Abraham Blvd. Tel. 4363.

The foundation sells handcrafts, including wood carvings, goatskin leather articles, and coral jewelry. All items are locally made. It's on the way to the airport, next to the post office.

KI BO KE PAKUS ["What Do You Want"], in the Divi Flamingo Beach Resort & Casino, J. A. Abraham Blvd. Tel. 8239.

This place has some of the most imaginative merchandise on the island—Bonaire T-shirts, handbags, dashikis, locally made jewelry, batiks from Indonesia, and Delft blue items.

LITTMAN JEWELERS, Kaya Grandi 35. Tel. 8160.

Steve and Esther Littman have restored this old house to its original state. They sell Rolex and Tag-Heuer dive watches, plus fine Orbit timepieces. The shop also carries Daum French crystal and Lladró Spanish porcelain. Next door, the Littmans have a shop called **Littman's Gifts,** selling T-shirts from standard to hand-painted, plus Dutch cheeses, chocolates, fine wines, imported crackers, and other food items.

THINGS BONAIRE, Kaya Grande 38C. Tel. 8423.

Things Bonaire has an additional branch at the Sunset Beach Hotel (tel. 8190). All shops carry many gift items, including Delft pewter, black coral jewelry, sunglasses, postcards, and locally made shell and driftwood items. They also carry men's and women's swimsuits, shorts, T-shirts, beach towels, guayaberas, caps, hats, and visors. Things Bonaire is also the exclusive outlet for "Amazon Lily's" men's and women's wear, jewelry, and souvenirs from Bali.

EVENING ENTERTAINMENT

Underwater **slide shows** provide entertainment for both divers and nondivers in the evening. The best shows are at **Captain Don's Habitat** (tel. 8290) (see "Sports and Recreation," above). Check when you get to Bonaire about the time of these presentations.

DIVI FLAMINGO BEACH RESORT & CASINO, J. A. Abraham Blvd. Tel. 7/8285.

A casino opened here in 1984 in a former residence adjoining the property. Promoted as "The World's First Barefoot Casino," it offers blackjack, roulette, poker, wheel of fortune, video games, and slot machines. Gambling on the island is regulated by the government. Open: Mon–Sat 8pm–4am.

E WOWO, Kaya Grandi 38, at the corner of Kaya L. D. Gerharts. Tel. 8998.

Outside the hotels, check out the dance floor at "E Wowo" ("The Eye" in Papiamento), which lies right in the heart of town. Distinguished by two flashing op art eyes, the club occupies the second floor of one of the island's oldest Dutch colonial buildings. The club caters to members, but if you ask at your hotel desk you'll usually be granted an admission pass. Open: Wed–Sun 9pm until the early hours.
Admission: $3.

PIRATE HOUSE, Kaya Corsow. Tel. 8434.

Upstairs over the Zeezicht Bar and Restaurant (see "Where to Dine," above), Pirate

House is operated by the same manager, Maddy Visser. You can eat and dance to disco music from 7 to 11pm and occasionally see a show. Drinks begin at $3.

KAREL'S, on the Waterfront. Tel. 8434.

Almost Tahitian in its high-ceilinged, open-walled design, this popular bar is perched above the sea on stilts. You can sit at the long rectangular bar with many of the island's dive and boating professionals or select a table near the balustrades overlooking the illuminated surf. Drinks begin at $3 each. Open: Tues–Sun 5pm–2am.

3. CURAÇAO

Just 35 miles north of the coast of Venezuela, Curaçao, the "C" of the Dutch ABC islands of the Caribbean, is the most populous in the Netherlands Antilles. It attracts visitors because of its people, who extend a big welcome, as well as its almost duty-free shopping, lively casinos, water sports, and international cuisine. Fleets of ocean-going tankers head out from its harbor to bring refined oil to all parts of the world.

Now a peaceful, self-governing part of the Netherlands, Curaçao was discovered not by Columbus, but by one of his lieutenants, Alonso de Ojeda, as well as Amerigo Vespucci, in 1499. The Spaniards exterminated all but 75 members of a branch of the peaceful Arawaks. However, they in turn were ousted by the Dutch in 1634, who also had to fight off French and English invasions.

The Dutch made the island a tropical Holland in miniature. Pieter Stuyvesant, stomping on his pegleg, ruled Curaçao in 1644. The island was turned into a Dutch Gibraltar, bristling with forts. Thick ramparts guarded the harbor's narrow entrance; the hilltop forts (many now converted into restaurants) protected the coastal approaches.

In this century, it remained sleepy until 1915 when the Royal Dutch/Shell Company built one of the world's largest oil refineries to process crude from Venezuela. Workers from some 50 countries poured onto the island, turning Curaçao into a polyglot, cosmopolitan community.

The largest of the Netherlands Antilles, Curaçao is 37 miles long and 7 miles across at its widest point. Because of all that early Dutch building, Curaçao is the most important island architecturally in the entire West Indies, with more European flavor than anywhere else in the Caribbean. After leaving the capital, **Willemstad,** you plunge into a strange, desertlike countryside that may remind you of the American Southwest. The landscape is an amalgam of browns and russets, studded with three-pronged cactus, spiny-leafed aloes, and the divi-divi trees, with their coiffures bent by centuries of trade winds. Classic Dutch-style windmills are in and around Willemstad and in some parts of the countryside. These standard farm models pump water from wells to irrigate vegetation.

Curaçao, together with Bonaire, St. Maarten, St. Eustatius, and Saba, is in the Kingdom of the Netherlands as part of the Netherlands Antilles. Curaçao has its own governmental authority, relying on the Netherlands only for defense and foreign affairs, and a population of 171,000 representing more than 50 nationalities.

ORIENTATION

GETTING THERE The air routes to Curaçao's international airport, **Aeropuerto Internashonal Hato,** Plaza Margareth Abraham (tel. 82288), are strongly linked to those leading to and from Aruba, since several airlines combine flights from North America to both destinations.

American Airlines (tel. toll free 800/433-7300) has three daily nonstop flights to Aruba from either New York or San Juan, Puerto Rico, and then passengers transfer to one of the many shuttle flights that depart dozens of times every day to

Curaçao. An American sales representative can also sell discounted hotel packages to clients who book their airfare and overnight accommodations simultaneously.

Another popular choice is **ALM** (tel. toll free 800/327-7230), Curaçao's national carrier, which was established in 1934 as the Caribbean representative of KLM Royal Dutch Airlines. It flies every day from Miami nonstop to Aruba, and then after a brief delay it continues on to Curaçao. From Atlanta, ALM flies into Curaçao twice a week, stopping first in Aruba before continuing onward to Curaçao. For connections to the other ABC islands, ALM would be a fine choice because of its eight daily flights from Curaçao to Bonaire, and its seven daily connections between Curaçao and Aruba.

GETTING AROUND   By Bus   Some of the hotels operate a free bus shuttle that will take you from the suburbs to the shopping district of Willemstad. A fleet of DAF yellow buses operates from Wilhelmina Plein, near the shopping center, to most parts of Curaçao for an average fare of 40¢. Some limousines function as "C" buses. When you see one listing the destination you're heading for, you can hail it at any of the designated bus stops.

By Taxi   Since taxis don't have meters, ask your driver to quote you the rate before getting in. Drivers are supposed to carry an official tariff sheet, which they'll produce upon request. Charges go up by 25% after 11pm. Generally there is no need to tip, unless a driver helped you with your luggage. The charge from the airport to Willemstad is about $11, and the cost can be split among four passengers. If a piece of luggage is so big that the trunk lid won't close, you'll be assessed a surcharge of $1.

In town, the best place to get a taxi is on the Otrabanda side of the floating bridge. To summon a cab, call 290747.

By Rental Car   Since all points of tourist interest are easily accessible by paved roads, you may want to rent a car. U.S. and Canadian citizens can use their own licenses, if valid, and traffic moves on the right. International road signs are observed.

Several car-rental companies are represented on Curaçao, but **Budget Rent-a-Car** (tel. toll free 800/527-0700), the largest, offers one of the most reasonably priced high-season car-rental arrangements. A car without air conditioning is rented for an unlimited-mileage rate of $193 per week; this rate requires a 14-day advance booking and a minimum rental of 6 days. Visitors who prefer a car with air conditioning and automatic transmission can reserve one for a weekly rate of $217, which is what an equivalent car at Avis costs. (Similar cars at Hertz, however, are more expensive.) Purchase of a collision-damage waiver (between $10 and $11 per day) reduces a renter's liability in case of an accident to between $100 and $300 worth of damages.

Currently, **Hertz** (tel. toll free 800/654-3001) and **Avis** (tel. toll free 800/331-2112) usually charge higher prices. There, the least expensive vehicles, with manual transmissions and no air conditioning, cost $223 and $234 per week, respectively, with unlimited mileage. With automatic transmission and air conditioning, the least expensive cars cost $300 to $324 per week. At Hertz, renters must be 25 years old; at Budget, 23; and at Avis, only 21.

At least 2 weeks before your departure, you should phone all three companies for a comparison of the latest prices and promotional offerings.

By Sightseeing Tour   A tour by **taxi** costs about $15 per hour, and up to four passengers can go on the jaunt.

Taber Tours, Dokweg (tel. 376637), offers several tours, both day and night, to points of interest in and around Curaçao. The tour through Willemstad, to the Curaçao Liqueur distillery, through the residential area and the Bloempot shopping center, and to the Curaçao Museum (admission fee included in the tour price) costs $10 per person for adults, $5 for children under 12.

FAST

CURAÇAO

Area Code   Curaçao is *not* part of the Caribbean 809 area code. See

"Telecommunications," below, for complete information on making calls to and on this island.

Banks Banking hours are Monday through Friday from 8:30am to noon and 1:30 to 4:30pm. The only exceptions are the Banco Popular and the Bank of America, which remain open during the lunch hour, doing business Monday through Friday from 9am to 3pm.

Consulate The **U.S. Consulate** is at J. B. Gorsiraweg 1 (tel. 613066).

Currency While Canadian and U.S. dollars are accepted for purchases on the island, the official currency is the **Netherlands Antillean florin (NAf)**, also called a guilder, which is divided into 100 NA (Netherlands Antillean) cents. The exchange rate is $1 U.S. to 1.77 NAf (or 56¢ U.S. equals 1 NAf). Shops, hotels, and restaurants usually accept most major U.S. and Canadian credit cards.

Documents To enter Curaçao, U.S. or Canadian citizens need proof of citizenship such as a birth certificate or a passport, along with a return or continuing airline ticket out of the country.

Electricity The electricity is 110–130 volts AC, 50 cycles, the same as in North America, although many hotels will have transformers if your appliances happen to be European.

Holidays Curaçao celebrates New Year's Day, Chinese New Year (in January), Carnival (the weekend preceding Lent), Carnival Monday, Harvest Festival (in March), Good Friday, Easter, Easter Monday, April 30 (Queen Juliana's Birthday), May 1 (Labor Day), Ascension Day, July 2 (Curaçao Flag Day), St. Nicholas' Day (in December), Christmas Day, and December 26 (Boxing Day).

Information For tourist information in Curaçao, go to the **Curaçao Tourist Board,** Pietermaai (tel. 610000). In the United States, contact the Curaçao Tourist Board, 400 Madison Avenue, Suite 311, New York, NY 10017 (tel. 212/751-8266, or toll free 800/332-8266).

Language Dutch, Spanish, and English are spoken on Curaçao, along with Papiamento, a language that combines the three major tongues with Amerindian and African dialects.

Medical Care Medical facilities are well equipped, and the 820-bed **St. Elisabeth Hospital,** Breedestraat 193 (tel. 624900), near Otrabanda in Willemstad, is considered one of the most up-to-date facilities in the Caribbean.

Police The police emergency number is 44444.

Post Office The post office is on Waaigat in Willemstad (tel. 61125).

Safety While Curaçao is not plagued with crime, it would be wise to safeguard your valuables.

Taxes and Service Curaçao levies a room tax of 5% on accommodations, and most hotels add 12% for room service. There is a departure tax of 18 NAf ($10) for international flights, but only 10 NAf ($5.60) for flights to other islands in the Netherlands Antilles.

Telecommunications For cable service, call All America Cables (tel. 611433) or Landsradio (tel. 613500).

Curaçao is *not* part of the 809 area code that applies to most of the Caribbean. To call Curaçao from the U.S., if your long-distance telephone company is equipped to handle international direct dialing, dial 011 (the international access code), then 599 (the country code for Curaçao), and then 9 (the area code) and the local number (the number of digits in the local number varies). If you cannot direct-dial internationally, dial 0 ("zero," for the operator) and tell the operator you wish to make an international call; once you are transferred to the international operator, state the 599 country code, the 9 area code, and then the local number, and the operator will dial the call for you.

Once on Curaçao, to call another number on the island only the local number is necessary; to make calls to an off-island destination, dial 021 and then the area code and number. *Note:* In this chapter only the area code and local number are given.

Time Curaçao is on Atlantic standard time, 1 hour ahead of eastern standard time and the same as eastern daylight saving time.

Water The water comes from a modern desalination plant and is safe to drink.

Weather   Curaçao has an average temperature of 81° Fahrenheit. Trade winds keep the island fairly cool, and it is flat and arid, with an average rainfall of only 22 inches per year—hardly your idea of a lush, palm-studded tropical island.

WHERE TO STAY

Your hotel will be in Willemstad or in one of the suburbs, which lie only 10 to 15 minutes from the shopping center. The bigger hotels often have free shuttle buses running into town, and most of them have their own beaches and pools.

Remember that Curaçao is a bustling commercial center, and the downtown hotels often fill up fast with business travelers and visitors from neighboring countries on a shopping holiday. Therefore, reservations are always important.

When making reservations, ask if the room tax and service charge are included in the price you're quoted.

EXPENSIVE

CURAÇAO CARIBBEAN HOTEL & CASINO, Piscadera Bay (P.O. Box 2133, Willemstad), Curaçao, N.A. Tel. 9/625000. Fax 9/625846. 196 rms, 15 suites. A/C TV TEL
$ Rates: Winter, $150–$180 single; $160–$190 double; from $250 suite. Summer, $110–$120 single; $120–$130 double; from $190 suite. MAP $40 per person extra. AE, DC, MC, V. **Parking:** Free.

This distinguished, "honeycomb-on-stilts" high-rise resort on the outskirts of Willemstad has a free bus service to take you shopping in town. It's a self-contained complex, with a charming little beach and cove set among rocky bluffs. The structure is a block of rooms encased in a concrete facade. Glass-enclosed elevators clinging to the exterior walls of the hotel offer a panoramic view as you're whisked to your room. The refurbished, spacious bedrooms have immaculate baths with big towels, traditional furnishings, and breeze-cooled private balconies; there's an ice machine on each floor.

Dining/Entertainment: Most impressive to me is the wide, open lower lounge area, giving everyone a trade-wind-swept view of Piscadera Bay. Furnished in wicker, the Pisca Terrace bar and restaurant opens onto an eight-pointed-star–shaped pool and the ruins of a fort two centuries old. You can enjoy a buffet breakfast on this terrace. Mexican nights are popular, as are Antillean nights with folklore shows. Of course, the casino is a major attraction.

Services: Room service, laundry, baby-sitting, free bus service to town.

Facilities: A dive shop offering the best water-sports program on the island, including skin diving, sailing, deep-sea fishing, and sea Jeeps; two Grasstex tennis courts (lit at night); well-stocked shopping complex.

MODERATE

AVILA BEACH HOTEL, Penstraat 130-134 (P.O. Box 791), Willemstad, Curaçao, N.A. Tel. 9/614377. Fax 9/611493. 90 rms, 2 suites. A/C TV TEL
$ Rates: Winter, $80–$150 single; $90–$160 double; from $200 suite. Summer, $73–$120 single; $81–$130 double; from $180 suite. Breakfast buffet $8 extra. AE, DC, MC, V. **Parking:** Free.

This beautifully restored 200-year-old mansion stands on the shore road leading east out of the city from the shopping center and next to the Octagon Museum. It's the only beachfront hotel in Willemstad proper, set on its own small but lovely private beach. The mansion was built by the English governor of Curaçao during the British occupation of the island during the Napoleonic Wars. Subsequent governors, including Dutch ones, have used the place as a retreat.

The mansion was converted into a hotel in 1949; the Dutch architecture and colonial style were preserved on the exterior, while the interior of the mansion was totally rebuilt with a spacious lobby, conference room, offices, and a deluxe 45-room modern bedroom wing opening toward the sea, named La Belle Alliance. The guest rooms are all furnished with Scandinavian modern pieces; some have minibars. In all, it's a comfortable, family-style hotel.

An open-air restaurant, Belle Terrace, offers split-level dining and a bar area overlooking the beach (see "Where to Dine," below), and the Avila Café serves breakfast, lunch, light meals, and drinks until 7pm. A private hotel shuttle bus takes guests to town.

HOLIDAY BEACH HOTEL & CASINO, Pater Euwensweg 31 (P.O. Box 2178), Willemstad, Curaçao, N.A. Tel. 9/625400. Fax 9/624397. 200 rms. A/C TV TEL

$ Rates: Winter, $125–$140 single; $140–$155 double. Summer, $80–$85 single; $90–$95 double. Buffet breakfast $9 extra. AE, DC, MC, V. **Parking:** Free.

Along a sandy beach dotted with palm trees, the Holiday Beach Hotel sits near a grassy peninsula jutting out to sea about a mile from the capital and boasts all the facilities of a resort hotel. The main part of the complex houses the Casino Royale, the largest casino on the island, and the premises contains a handful of tennis courts. Local entertainment is offered in the hotel's nightclub. After dinner, you can enjoy a drink in the Cocolishi Lounge, perhaps before heading to the roulette tables.

The sleeping quarters are in two four-story wings, centering around a U-shaped garden with a large freshwater swimming pool. The modern bedrooms are well furnished, with two double beds in each unit, opening onto private balconies overlooking the water. Wall-to-wall carpeting and big tiled baths are just part of the comforts. Laundry, baby-sitting, and room service are available.

LIONS DIVE HOTEL & MARINA, De Ruyterkade 53, Willemstad, Curaçao, N.A. Tel. 9/611644, 212/545-8469 in New York, or toll free 800/451-9376. Fax 9/618200. 72 rms. A/C TV TEL

$ Rates (including American breakfast): Winter, $95 single; $110 double. Summer, $85 single; $92 double. AE, DC, MC, V. **Parking:** Free.

On the island's largest white sandy beach, a 30-minute taxi ride southeast of the airport, is a complete dive resort with programs supervised by the Underwater Curaçao staff. Each of its comfortable accommodations has a sea view as well as private bath, a balcony or terrace, and two queen-size beds. Other facilities include a freshwater pool and three restaurants specializing Italian and American cuisine plus seafood. Introductory dives and resort and certification courses are offered, and on the premises is a fully equipped rental dive shop. Two boat dives are conducted daily. Waterskiing, windsurfing, and sailing can also be arranged. Massage facilities are available, as are laundry and baby-sitting services.

LAS PALMAS HOTEL AND VACATION VILLAGE, Piscadera Bay (P.O. Box 2179, Willemstad), Curaçao, N.A. Tel. 9/625200. Fax 9/625962. 98 rms, 94 two-bedroom casitas. A/C TV TEL

$ Rates: Winter, $115–$145 single or double; $165 casita for two or three; $185 casita for four to six. Summer, $78–$88 single or double; $115 casita for two; $125 casita for three; $135 casita for four to six. MAP $28 per person extra. AE, DC, MC, V. **Parking:** Free.

Across from the Curaçao Caribbean is an ideal choice for those who seek a more moderately priced resort. The atmosphere here is casual and convivial. The location is only 2 miles from Willemstad, a 20-minute taxi ride south of the airport, on a breezy hillside a few hundred yards from its own little beach with water sports. The cacti that used to stud the hillside have now given way to a botanical garden. Accommodations are in a three-story main building or in one of the little casitas with Samoan-style roofs sprinkled through the hillside gardens. The main building has public rooms off the garden-style entry lounge. At its core is a courtyard, with a lily pond, bamboo, and flowering vines, where you can start your day with breakfast, and later enjoy drinks and entertainment.

Rooms in the main building have contemporary styling with bold colors, and each has a private bath and air conditioning. The casitas, furnished in rustic style, can accommodate four people and possibly six (although that would be crowded). Each has two well-furnished bedrooms, a living room, a kitchenette, and a porch where you can set up breakfast you prepared yourself after shopping at the minimarket on the grounds. Sporting facilities include two swimming pools—one Olympic size for adults, plus a tiny wading pool for children—and a tennis court lit for night games. Laundry, room service, and baby-sitting are available.

PRINCESS BEACH RESORT & CASINO, Dr. Martin Luther King Blvd., Willemstad, Curaçao, N.A. Tel. 9/614944. 202 rms. A/C MINIBAR TV TEL

$ Rates: Winter, $125–$210 single; $140–$225 double. Summer, $80–$140 single; $95–$155 double. MAP $35 per person extra. AE, DC, MC, V. **Parking:** Free.

A modern, low-rise condominium-style beachfront resort lies in front of the Curaçao Underwater Park and close to the Seaquarium (just a complimentary shuttle ride away from Willemstad). The hotel has the only half-kilometer-long beach on the island. It's a haven for water-sports enthusiasts, with docking facilities for deep-sea fishing and a windsurfing center. Other sports-related facilities include a tennis court, a freshwater pool with a swim-up bar, and in the vicinity, a nine-hole golf course. Many of the refurbished bedrooms look out over the beach, and all have private baths, hairdryers, and either balconies or patios shielded by tropical plants. A casino and nightly entertainment are an added feature. The hotel offers laundry, dry cleaning, and baby-sitting.

VAN DER VALK PLAZA HOTEL, Plaza Pier (P.O. Box 229), Willemstad, Curaçao, N.A. Tel. 9/612500. Fax 9/618347. 254 rms, 9 suites. A/C TV TEL

$ Rates (including continental breakfast): $105–$150 single or double; from $120 suite. MAP $30 per person extra. AE, MC, V. **Parking:** Free.

Standing guard over the Punda side of St. Anna Bay, the Van der Valk Plaza is nestled in the ramparts of an 18th-century waterside fort on the eastern tip of the entrance to the harbor, a 20-minute drive south of the airport. In fact it's one of the harbor's two "lighthouses." (The hotel has to carry marine collision insurance, the only hostelry in the Caribbean with that distinction.) The original part of the hotel followed the style of the arcaded fort. However, now there is a tower of rooms stacked 15 stories high. Each of the bedrooms—your own crow's nest—is comfortably furnished with private bath. The pool, with a bar and suntanning area, is placed inches away from the parapet of the fort. In the hotel's Waterfront Grill you can order American and continental dishes. The hotel offers laundry, baby-sitting, and room service.

INEXPENSIVE

CORAL CLIFF RESORT AND BEACH CLUB, Santa Marta Bay (P.O. Box 3782, Willemstad), Curaçao, N.A. Tel. 9/641610. Fax 9/641781. 35 units. A/C TV TEL

$ Rates: Winter, $65 single; $75 double; from $95 triple. Summer, $50 single; $60 double; $70 triple. Continental breakfast $3.75 to $6.50 extra. AE, MC, V. **Parking:** Free.

On the western part of the island is a group of bungalows with red roofs, surrounded by 18 acres of cliffs, mountains, and bays. Each of these apartments at the edge of the sea has a kitchenette. Dining is in the Santa Marta Terrace Restaurant, an open-air social center, and you can relax at the Beach Bar or toast the sunset at the Cliffhanger Bar. The resort has 600 feet of private beach, an all-weather tennis court, and a number of water sports. A free shuttle bus makes regularly scheduled trips daily to Willemstad. Scuba diving and waterskiing can be arranged, and laundry and baby-sitting are available.

HOTEL HOLLAND, F. D. Rooseveltweg 524, Curaçao, N.A. Tel. 9/ 688044. Fax 9/688114. 30 rms. A/C TV TEL
$ Rates: $55 single; $65 double; from $100 suite. Continental breakfast $6 extra. AE, DC, MC, V. **Parking:** Free.

S A 5-minute drive from the airport, the Hotel Holland contains the Flying Dutchman Bar which is a popular gathering place, plus a small casino which opened in 1991. For a few brief minutes of every day, you can see airplanes landing from your perch at the edge of the poolside terrace, where well-prepared meals are served during good weather. This property is the domain of ex-navy frogman Hans Vrolijk and his wife, Henne. Hans still retains his interest in scuba and arranges dive packages for his guests. He also directs the service at his Dutch-style restaurant, 'T Kokkeltje (see "Where to Dine," below). The comfortably furnished accommodations have baths, TVs and VCRs, refrigerators, and balconies. Laundry, baby-sitting, and room service are available.

WHERE TO DINE

The basic cuisine is Dutch, but there are many specialty items, particularly Latin American and Indonesian. The cuisine strikes many visitors as heavy for the tropics, so you may want to have a light lunch and order the more filling concoctions, such as *rijstaffel,* in the evening. You'll want to finish your meals with Curaçao, the blue-tinged orange-based liqueur that made the island famous.

Erwtensoep, the well-known Dutch pea soup, is a popular dish, as is *keshi yena,* Edam cheese stuffed with meat, then baked. *Funchi,* a Caribbean tortilla, accompanies many local dishes. *Sopito,* fish soup often made with coconut water, is an especially good local dish, and conch is featured in curries and many other dishes.

EXPENSIVE

BELLE TERRACE, in the Avila Beach Hotel, Penstraat 130-134. Tel. 614377.
Cuisine: CARIBBEAN/CONTINENTAL. **Reservations:** Required. **Directions:** See below.
$ Prices: Appetizers $5.50–$11; main courses $15.75–$21.65. AE, DC, MC, V.
Open: Dinner only, daily 7–10:30pm.

You'll find this open-air restaurant in a 200-year-old mansion on the beachfront of Willemstad. In a relaxed and informal atmosphere, it offers split-level dining. The Schooner Bar, where you can enjoy a rum punch, is shaped like a weather-beaten ship's prow looking out to sea, with a thatch roof projecting from its mast. The restaurant, sheltered by an arbor of flamboyant branches, features Scandinavian, continental, and local cuisine with such special dishes as pickled herring, barracuda, and a Danish lunch platter. Local dishes such as sopito and keshi yena are on the menu. On Saturday night the chef has a beef-tenderloin barbecue and a help-yourself salad bar. Fish is always fresh at Belle Terrace, and the chef prepares the catch of the day to perfection: grilled, poached, meunière, or amandine. Desserts include Danish pastry and cakes, as well as a cocoa sherbet served in a coconut shell.

From the airport, follow the signs to "Punda." Turn left after the second traffic light in town. Stay on the right side of that road (Plaza Smeets) and go straight ahead. If you keep to the right side of the road you'll enter Penstraat, where you will find Avila Beach Hotel on the right-hand side.

BISTRO LE CLOCHARD, on the Otrabanda side of the pontoon bridge. Tel. 625666.
Cuisine: FRENCH/SWISS. **Reservations:** Required.
$ Prices: Appetizers $5–$12; main courses $15–$30. AE, DC, MC, V.
Open: Lunch Mon–Fri noon–2pm; dinner Mon–Sat 6:30–11pm; Harborside terrace, dinner only, Mon–Sat 6–11pm.

⭐ Bistro le Clochard has been snugly fitted into the northwestern corner of the grim ramparts of Fort Rif at the gateway to the harbor. Its entrance is marked with a canopy, which leads to a series of rooms, each built under the 19th-century vaulting of the old Dutch fort. Only one table has a view of the water, since the only window is the rectangular opening that was formerly used to receive munitions from the adjacent stone quay. More panoramic is the establishment's outdoor terrace (the Harborside Terrace), built directly at the edge of the water, which receives additional guests for a view over the harbor and the sparkling lights of the nearby town.

Dishes change weekly, but a frequent specialty is "The Stone," consisting of seasoned meat or seafood grilled directly at your table on skewers atop an oven-heated stone, and there will also be a few dishes from the Alps, such as raclettes and fondues.

DE TAVEERNE, Landhuis Groot Develaar, Silena. Tel. 370669.
   Cuisine: FRENCH/SEAFOOD. **Reservations:** Required.
$ **Prices:** Appetizers $5.50–$12; main courses $16–$32. AE, DC, MC, V.
   Open: Lunch Mon–Sat noon–2pm; dinner Mon–Sat 7–11pm.

⭐ A red-brick octagonal cupola rises over the roof of this country manor house in a residential neighborhood, inland on the east side of Santa Anna Bay. Inside, where the cows used to be sheltered, the owner has created a tavern atmosphere with an antique decor, including furnishings from Curaçao's old homes. The charming restaurant, bar, and wine cellar are enhanced by burnished copper, white stucco walls, dark woods, and terra-cotta tiles. Specialties change frequently, but perhaps you'll start with smoked Dutch eel, lobster soup, or snails bourguignon. Other recommendable dishes include shrimp thermidor, sole meunière, and a chateaubriand Stroganoff for two diners.

RIJSTAFFEL RESTAURANT INDONESIA AND HOLLAND CLUB BAR,
   Mercuriusstraat 13, Cerrito. Tel. 612606.
   Cuisine: INDONESIAN. **Reservations:** Recommended.
$ **Prices:** Appetizers $3.50–$6.50; main courses $15–$22. AE, DC, MC, V.
   Open: Lunch Mon–Sat noon–2pm; dinner daily 6–9:30pm.
This is the best place on the island to sample the Indonesian rijstaffel, the traditional rice table with all the zesty side dishes. You must ask a taxi to take you to this villa in the suburbs near Salinja, near the Princess Beach Hotel, southeast of Willemstad. You're allowed to season your plate with peppers rated hot, very hot, and palate-melting. At lunchtime the selection of dishes is more modest, but for dinner, Javanese cooks prepare the specialty of the house, a rijstaffel consisting of 16, 20, or 25 dishes. Warming trays are placed on your table and the service is buffet style. It's best to go to with a party so that all of you can share in the fun and feast. The Holland Club bar is only for diners at the restaurant.

MODERATE

LA BISTROELLE, Astroidenweg/Schottagatweg, in the Promenade
   Shopping Center. Tel. 370408.
   Cuisine: CONTINENTAL. **Reservations:** Recommended.
$ **Prices:** Appetizers $3.50–$6; main courses $14–$25. AE, DC, MC, V.
   Open: Lunch Mon–Sat noon–2pm; dinner daily 7–11pm.
In Zeelandia, a residential area east of the harbor, a short drive from the center of Willemstad, this elegant, family-run restaurant offers an international cuisine and a good selection of wines, all served in a cozy, atmospheric place. The decor is one of stucco, brick accents, darkened beams, rustic chandeliers, and high-backed chairs, like a French country inn. The cuisine is largely French, beginning with such selections as snails in herb-garlic butter and rich fish or steaming French onion soup. Some of the chef's specialties include octopus in a vinaigrette sauce, sole Picasso, lobster thermidor, and chicken saltimbocca. For dessert, you might prefer the crêpes Suzette flavored with Curaçao, for two people.

FORT NASSAU, near Point Juliana. Tel. 613450.

Cuisine: CREOLE/SEAFOOD. **Reservations:** Recommended.
$ Prices: Appetizers $3.90–$7.85; main courses $14.50–$25.20. AE, DC, MC, V.
Open: Lunch Mon–Fri noon–3pm; dinner daily 7–10pm.

This restored restaurant and bar is built on a hilltop overlooking Willemstad in the ruins of a formidably buttressed fort dating from 1792, and it has retained an 18th-century decor. From its Battery Terrace a 360° panorama unfolds of the sea, the harbor, and Willemstad, just a 5-minute drive away. You'll even have a faraway view of the island's vast oil refinery. A signal tower on the cliff sends out beacons to approaching ships. Before dining, you can enjoy an apéritif in a fashionably decorated bar where many come just to have a drink and watch the sunset. On cruise-ship days, the place overflows.

Specialties include twice-cured "Thai Salmon" with lotus-root chips, bean thread, and ginger-lime vinaigrette; bamboo-steamed Curaçao lobster with wild oyster mushrooms, bellpeppers, ginger, lemongrass, and black-currant tea leaves; Amstel marinated sirloin with fried yucca chips and roasted chestnut butter; smoked sweet-and-sour pork tenderloin with tamarind sauce and sweet-potato chips; and stir-fried Surinam peanut-spiced chicken and shrimp with wild mushrooms, snow peas, and a cilantro-peanut sauce. A limited selection of international desserts, such as coffee mousse, tops a most recommendable repast. You can dress casually and enjoy your meal in air-conditioned comfort.

There's a cozy disco called Infinity in the lower depths, open on Friday and Saturday from 9pm to 2am. It has an intimate atmosphere, a waterfall wall, and good music.

FORT WAAKZAAMHEID BISTRO, Seru di Domi, Otrabanda. Tel. 623633.

Cuisine: CREOLE/AMERICAN. **Reservations:** Not required.
$ Prices: Appetizers $3–$6; main courses $10–$20. AE, MC, V.
Open: Dinner only, Wed–Mon 6–11pm (bar open until 1am, later on weekends).

Captain Bligh, of *Bounty* fame, captured this old fort in 1804 and laid siege to Willemstad for almost a month. A stone-and-hardwood tavern and restaurant have been installed in the fort, which opens onto a view of the Otrabanda and the harbor entrance. The atmosphere is that of a country tavern. Start with the fish soup and follow with curried veal, wienerschnitzel, or garlic shrimp. Lobster is the most expensive item on the menu, or you may settle instead for Curaçao snapper. Each day a fresh fried fish is offered, with a salad.

RODEO RANCH SALOON & STEAKHOUSE, at the Curaçao Seaquarium, in Bapor Kibra. Tel. 615757.

Cuisine: STEAK/AMERICAN. **Reservations:** Not required.
$ Prices: Appetizers $2.80–$5.25; main courses $14–$28. AE, MC, V.
Open: Lunch daily noon–2pm; dinner daily 5:30–11pm (bar open till "whenever?").

East of Willemstad, the Rodeo Ranch is a lot of fun. Stanley Gibbs and his Netherlands-born wife, Kathe, have created a touch of the Old West with a replica of a covered wagon set over the entrance, and an interior decor of rough-sawn planking, dark woods, and antique wagon wheels. A "sheriff" (usually Stanley) greets visitors at the door in an outfit that includes a 10-gallon hat and a silver star. You'll be presented with a cowhide-covered menu by a cowgirl/waitress. To the sounds of country-western music, you'll enjoy the specialties of soup from the kettle, a chuckwagon choice of potato specials, steak, roast prime rib, and seafood. All steaks are U.S. prime beef, and you can make as many visits as you want to the soup-and-salad bar. You don't have to dress up, and you'll enjoy your meal in air-conditioned comfort. Hot snacks are served at the happy hour from 5 to 7pm.

WINE CELLAR, Ooststraat/Concordiastraat. Tel. 612178.

Cuisine: INTERNATIONAL. **Reservations:** Required.
$ Prices: Appetizers $5–$28; main courses $11–$28. AE, MC, V.
Open: Lunch Tues–Fri noon–2pm; dinner Tues–Sun 6pm until "whenever."

Opposite the cathedral in the center of town is the domain of Ivo Cornelisse, who has one of the most extensive wine cartes on the island. You are welcomed to air-conditioned comfort in a Victorian dining room, where the food isn't ignored either. The kitchen has good meat dishes, well prepared, and a limited selection of seafood, including fresh red snapper and lobster. Lobster is the most expensive main dish; caviar, the most expensive appetizer.

INEXPENSIVE

GOLDEN STAR, Socratesstraat 2. Tel. 54795.

Cuisine: CREOLE. **Reservations:** Not required.
$ Prices: Appetizers $2.80–$5.60; main courses $8.30–$25.20. AE, DC, MC, V.
Open: Daily 11am–1am.

The best place to go on the island for "criollo" or local food is inland from the coast road leading southeast from St. Anna Bay, at the corner of Dr. Hugenholtzweg and Dr. Maalweg, southeast of Willemstad. Evoking a roadside diner, the air-conditioned restaurant is very simple, but it has a large menu of very tasty Antillean dishes, such as carco stoba (conch stew), bestia chiki (goat-meat stew), bakijauw (salted cod), and concombor stoba (stewed meat and marble-size spiny cucumbers). Other specialties include criollo shrimp (kiwa) and sopi carni. Everything is served with a side order of funchi, the cornmeal staple. The place has a large local following with an occasional tourist dropping in.

PISCES SEAFOOD, Caracasbaaiweg 476. Tel. 672181.

Cuisine: CREOLE/SEAFOOD. **Reservations:** Recommended.
$ Prices: Appetizers $2.80–$4.50; main courses $12.20–$18. AE, DC, MC, V.
Open: Daily noon–midnight. **Closed:** Last 2 weeks in Aug.

This West Indian restaurant may be difficult to find, as it's on a flat industrial coastline near a marina and an oil refinery, about 20 minutes from the capital. There has been a restaurant here since the 1930s, when sailors and workers from the oil refinery came for home-cooked meals. Today the simple frame building offers seating near the rough-hewn bar or in a breeze-swept inner room. Pisces serves combinations of seafood that depend on the catch of the day. Main courses, served with rice, vegetables, and plantains, might include sopi, "seacat" (squid), mula (similar to kingfish), shark meat, red snapper, or any of these served, if you wish, in copious quantities for two or more people in the Pisces platter. Shrimp and conch are each prepared three different ways: with garlic, with curry, or Créole style.

PLAYA FORTI, Westpunt. Tel. 640273.

Cuisine: CREOLE. **Reservations:** Not required.
$ Prices: Appetizers $3–$4.50; main courses $4–$14. AE, MC, V.
Open: Tues–Sat 10am–6pm.

A good address to know if you're touring the island, Playa Forti is built on the foundation of a fortress dating from Bonaparte's day; it's near North Point, the extreme northwestern end of Curaçao. Not only do you get good local food here, but you also get one of the most spectacular sea views on the island. If you're touring, drop in for drinks in the afternoon. The waters of Westpunt are perfect for snorkeling and scuba diving if you want to bring your own equipment.

International dishes are presented, but it would be wiser to order some of the Antillean specialties, such as cabrito, a succulent goat stew which tastes a bit like veal. Try also keshi yena, a tasty mixture of beef and chicken that has been pickled and cooked with tomatoes and onions, then wrapped in Edam cheese. Ayaca is a combination of chicken and beef, with olives, raisins, nuts, and spices wrapped in a soft corndough tortilla (it's packed and cooked in banana leaves). Sopidi plata, the fish soup, makes a zesty opening. Or try the fried red snapper Curaçao style—fried a golden brown, then covered in a sauce of tomatoes, onions, and green peppers. It's served with fried plantains and funchi, the local cornmeal preparation.

'T KOKKELTJE, in the Hotel Holland, F. D. Rooseveltweg 524. Tel. 688014.

Cuisine: DUTCH. **Reservations:** Not required.
$ Prices: Appetizers $3–$5; main courses $10–$25. AE, DC, MC, V.
Open: Daily 7am–10:30pm.

You'll find this warmly decorated hideaway on the scrub-bordered road leading to the airport, a few minutes away from the landing strips. If you want to follow your drinks with dinner, full meals (which stress a Dutch and Antillean cuisine) include fresh fish in season, Dutch-style steak, fresh herring, Caribbean-style chicken, and split-pea soup. All dishes are accompanied by fresh vegetables and Dutch-style potatoes. Patrons enjoy their meals around the pool outside or in a paneled and intimately lit room near the bar.

WHAT TO SEE & DO

Most cruise-ship passengers see only Willemstad—or, more accurately, the shops—but you may want to get out into the *cunucu*, or countryside, and explore the towering cacti and rolling hills topped by *landhuizen* (plantation houses) built more than three centuries ago.

WILLEMSTAD ✪ In Willemstad the Dutch found a vast natural harbor, a perfect hideaway along the Spanish Main. Not only is Willemstad the capital of Curaçao, it's also the seat of government for the Netherlands Antilles.

The city grew up on both sides of the canal. Today it's divided into the **Punda** and the **Otrabanda,** the latter literally meaning "the other side." Both sections are connected by the **Queen Emma Pontoon Bridge,** a pedestrian walkway. Powered by a diesel engine, it swings open many times every day to let ships from all over the globe pass in and out of the harbor.

The view from the bridge is of the old **gabled houses** in harmonized pastel shades such as deep earth-toned golds, mustards, and greens. The bright pastel colors, according to legend, are a holdover from the time when one of the island's early governors is said to have had eye trouble and flat white gave him headaches.

The colonial-style architecture, reflecting the Dutch influence, gives the town a "storybook" look. The houses, built three or four stories high, are crowned by "step" gables and roofed with orange Spanish tiles. Hemmed in by the sea, a tiny canal, and an inlet, the streets are narrow, and they're crosshatched by still narrower alleyways. Except for the pastel colors, Willemstad may remind you of old Amsterdam. It has one of the most intriguing townscapes in the Caribbean.

A **statue of Pedro Luis Brion** dominates the square known as Brionplein right at the Otrabanda end of the pontoon bridge. Born in Curaçao in 1782, he became the island's favorite son and best-known war hero. Under Simón Bolívar, he was an admiral of the fleet and fought for the independence of Venezuela and Colombia.

In addition to the pontoon bridge, the **Queen Juliana Bridge** opened to vehicular traffic in 1973. Spanning the harbor, it rises 195 feet, which makes it the highest bridge in the Caribbean and one of the tallest in the world.

The Waterfront originally guarded the mouth of the canal on the eastern or Punda side, but now it has been incorporated into the Van der Valk Plaza Hotel. The task of standing guard has been taken over by **Fort Amsterdam,** site of the Governor's Palace and the 1769 Dutch Reformed church. The church still has a British cannonball embedded in it. The arches leading to the fort were tunneled under the official residence of the governor.

A corner of the fort stands at the intersection of Breedestraat and Handelskade, the starting point for a plunge into the island's major shopping district.

A few minutes' walk from the pontoon bridge, at the north end of Handelskade, is the **Floating Market,** where scores of schooners tie up alongside the canal, a few yards from the main shopping section. Docked boats arrive from Venezuela and Colombia, as well as other West Indian islands, to sell tropical fruits and vegetables, a little bit of everything in fact. The modern market under its vast concrete cap has not replaced this unique shopping expedition, which is fun to watch.

Between the I. H. (Sha) Capriles Kade and Fort Amsterdam, at the corner of

Columbusstraat and Kerkstraat, stands the **Mikve Israel–Emanuel Synagogue,** one of the oldest synagogue buildings in the western hemisphere. Consecrated on the eve of Passover in 1732, it antedates the first U.S. synagogue (in Newport, Rhode Island) by 31 years and houses the oldest Jewish congregation in the New World, dating from 1651. A fine example of Dutch colonial architecture, covering about a square block in the heart of Willemstad, it was built in a Spanish-style walled courtyard, with four large portals. Sand covers the sanctuary floor following a Portuguese Sephardic custom, representing the desert where Israelites camped when the Jews passed from slavery to freedom. The *theba* (pulpit) is in the center, and the congregation surrounds it. Highlight of the east wall is the Holy Ark, rising 17 feet, and a raised banca, canopied in mahogany, is on the north wall.

João d'Illan led the first Jewish settlers (13 families) to the island in 1651, almost half a century after their expulsion from Portugal by the Inquisition. The settlers came via Amsterdam to Curaçao. The first Jew to arrive in Curaçao (although he stayed less than a year) was Samuel Coheno, an interpreter for the Dutch naval commander, Johan van Walbeck, who conquered Curaçao from the Spaniards in 1634.

The synagogue has services every Friday at 6:30pm and Saturday at 10am, as well as similar holiday service times. Visitors are welcome to all services, with appropriate dress required.

Adjacent to the synagogue courtyard is the **Jewish Cultural Historical Museum,** Kuiperstraat 26–28, housed in two buildings dating back to 1728. They were originally the rabbi's residence and the bathhouse. The 2½-centuries-old mikvah, or bath for religious purification purposes, was in constant use until around 1850 when this practice was discontinued and the buildings sold. They have been reacquired through the Foundation for the Preservation of Historic Monuments and turned into the present museum. On display are a great many ritual, ceremonial, and cultural objects, many of which are still in use by the congregation for holidays and life-cycle events.

The synagogue and museum are open to visitors Monday through Friday from 9 to 11:45am and 2:30 to 5pm; if there's a cruise ship in port, also on Sunday from 9am to noon. There is a $2 entrance fee to the museum. The gift shop is in the synagogue office (tel. 611633).

WEST OF WILLEMSTAD   The **Curaçao Museum,** Van Leeuwenhoekstraat (tel. 623777), can be walked to from the Queen Emma Pontoon Bridge. It was built in 1853 by the Royal Dutch Army Corps of Engineers as a military quarantine hospital for yellow fever victims and was carefully restored in 1946–48 as a fine example of 19th-century Dutch architecture. Furnished with paintings, objets d'art, and antique furniture made in the 19th century by local cabinetmakers, it re-creates the atmosphere of an era gone by. A novelty is the polka-dot kitchen. The museum contains a large collection from the Caiquetio tribes, the early inhabitants described by Amerigo Vespucci as giants 7 feet tall. There's a modest Children's Museum of Science in the basement, with hands-on exhibits. In the gardens are specimens of the island's trees and plants. There is also a reconstruction of a traditional music pavilion in the garden where Curaçao musicians give regular performances. It's open Tuesday through Saturday from 9am to noon and 2 to 5pm, and on Sunday from 10am to 4pm. Admission is 3 NAf ($1.70) for adults, 1.50 NAf (85¢) for children under 14.

The **Curaçao Seaquarium,** off Martin Luther King Boulevard at a site called Bapor Kibra (tel. 616666), has more than 400 species of fish, crabs, anemones, and other invertebrates, sponges, and coral displayed and growing in a natural environment. A rustic boardwalk connects the low-lying hexagonal buildings comprising the Seaquarium complex, which sits on a point off which the *Oranje Nassau* broke up on the rocks and sank in 1906 (the name of the site, Bapor Kibra, means "sunken ship"). Located a few minutes' walk along the rocky coast from the Princess Beach Hotel, the Seaquarium is open daily from 9am to 10pm. Admission to the Seaquarium is $6 for adults, $3 for children under 15 years of age.

The **Curaçao Underwater Park,** established in 1983 with the financial aid of the World Wildlife Fund, stretches from the Princess Beach Hotel to the east point of

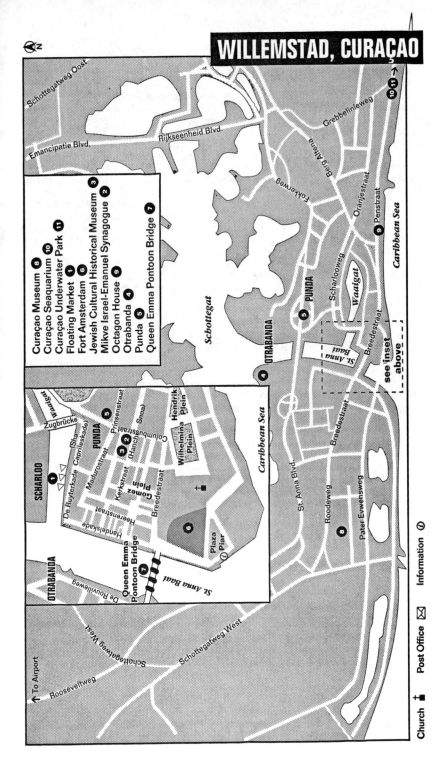

WILLEMSTAD, CURAÇAO

Curaçao Museum ⑧
Curaçao Seaquarium ⑩
Curaçao Underwater Park ⑪
Floating Market ①
Fort Amsterdam ⑥
Jewish Cultural Historical Museum ③
Mikve Israel-Emanuel Synagogue ②
Octagon House ⑨
Otrabanda ④
Punda ⑤
Queen Emma Pontoon Bridge ⑦

Church ✝   Post Office ⊠   Information ⓘ

the island, a strip of about 12½ miles of untouched coral reefs. For information on snorkeling, scuba diving, and trips in a glass-bottom boat to view the park, see "Sports and Recreation," below.

Traveling northwest along the road, you reach the tip of the island. On the road to Westpunt, the **Landhuis Jan Kock,** built in 1650, is probably the oldest building on the island. The owner once stood on its adobe porch to watch slaves gather salt from huge flat fields flooded with sea water left to evaporate in the sun. The house, said to be haunted, was restored as a museum by the late Dr. Jan Diemont in 1960. Inside are many pieces from the 18th and early 19th centuries, including a hurdy-gurdy from this century. Daily tours are 9 to 10am. Reserve in advance by phoning 648087.

Also en route to Westpunt, you'll come across a seaside cavern known as **Boca Tabla,** one of many such grottoes on this rugged, uninhabited northwest coast.

In the Westpunt area, a 45-minute ride from Punda in Willemstad, **Playa Forti** is a stark region characterized by soaring hills and towering cacti, along with 200-year-old Dutch land houses, the former mansions that housed the slaveowner plantation heads. For a dining suggestion, see my recommendation of the Playa Forti Restaurant in "Where to Dine," above.

Out toward the western tip of Curaçao, a high wire fence surrounds the entrance to the 4,500-acre ✪ **Christoffel National Park,** Savonet (tel. 640363), about a 45-minute drive from the capital. A macadam road gives way to dirt, surrounded on all sides by abundant cactus and bromeliads. In the higher regions you can spot rare orchids. Rising from flat, arid countryside, 1,230-foot-high St. Christoffelberg is the highest point in the Dutch Leewards. Donkeys, wild goats, iguanas, the Curaçao deer, and many species of birds thrive in this preserve, and there are some Arawak paintings on a coral cliff near the two caves. A folk legend surrounds Piedra di Monton, a rockheap accumulated by African slaves who worked on the former plantations. According to the legend passed down through the generations, any worker would be able to climb to the top of the rockpile, jump off, and fly back home across the Atlantic. If, however, the slave had at any time in his life tasted a grain of salt, the magic would not work and he would crash to his death below. The park has 20 miles of one-way traillike roads, with lots of flora and fauna along the way. The shortest trail is about 5 miles long, and because of the rough terrain, takes about 40 minutes to drive through. Various walking trails are available also. One of them will take you to the top of St. Christoffelberg in about 1½ hours. (Come early in the morning when it isn't so hot.) The park is open Monday through Saturday from 8am to 5pm; on Sunday it opens as early as 6am, closing at 3pm. Admission is 3.50 NAf ($1.95) for adults, half price for children. The park also has a museum with varying exhibitions year round set in an old storehouse left over from plantation days. Guided tours are available by calling 640363.

NORTH & EAST OF WILLEMSTAD   Just northeast of the capital, **Fort Nassau** was completed in 1797 and christened by the Dutch as Fort Republic. Built high on a hill overlooking the harbor entrance to the south and St. Anna Bay to the north, it was fortified as a second line of defense in case Waterfort gave way. When the British invaded in 1807, they renamed it Fort George in honor of their own king. Later, when the Dutch regained control, they renamed it Orange Nassau in honor of the Dutch royal family. Today diners have replaced soldiers (see "Where to Dine," above).

Along the coast to the southeast of the town, the oddly shaped **Octagon House** on Penstraat (tel. 623777) was where the liberator, Simón Bolívar, used to visit his two sisters during the wars for Venezuelan independence. Now a museum, it has been restored and furnished with antiques. It also contains some of the liberator's memorabilia. The house is open Monday through Saturday from 8am to noon and 2 to 6pm; admission is free.

From the house you can head north, going along the eastern side of the water, to the intersection of Rijkseenheid Boulevard and Fokkerweg. There you'll see the **Autonomy Monument,** a vibrant 20th-century sculpture representing the Dutch islands.

In the area, the **Amstel Brewery** (tel. 612944) allows visitors to tour its plant where Curaçao beer is brewed from desalinated seawater. Tours are given only on Tuesday from 10am to noon.

In addition, the **Curaçao Liqueur Distillery,** in the Salina area (tel. 623526), offers free tours and tastes at Chobolobo, the 17th-century landhuis where the famous liqueur is made. The cordial, named after the region where it originated, is a distillate of dried peel of a particular strain of orange found only on Curaçao. Several herbs are added to give it an aromatic bouquet. It's made by a secret formula handed down through generations. One of the rewards of a visit here is a free snifter of the liqueur at the culmination of the guided tours, offered Monday through Friday from 8am to noon and 1 to 5pm.

On Schottegatweg West, northwest of Willemstad, past the oil refineries, lies the **Beth Haim Cemetery,** the oldest Caucasian burial site still in use in the western hemisphere. Meaning "House of Life," the cemetery was consecrated before 1659. On about 3 acres are some 2,500 graves. The carving on some of the 17th- and 18th-century tombstones is exceptional.

Landhuis Brievengat, Brievengat (tel. 78344), gives visitors a chance to visit a Dutch version of an 18th-century West Indian plantation house. This stately building, in a scrub-dotted landscape on the eastern side of the island, contains a few antiques, high ceilings, and a frontal gallery facing two entrance towers, said to have been used to imprison slaves and even for romantic trysts. The plantation was originally used for the cultivation of aloe and cattle, but an 1877 hurricane caused the plantation to cease operation. The building was pulled down, but around 1925 the remains of the structure were donated to the Society for the Preservation of Monuments, which rebuilt and restored it. It's open daily from 9:30am to 12:30pm and 3 to 6pm; admission is $1.

SPORTS & RECREATION

BEACHES   Its beaches are not as good as Aruba's 7-mile strip of sand, but Curaçao does have some 38 of them, ranging from hotel sands to secluded coves. About 30 minutes from town, in the Willibrordus area on the west side of Curaçao, **Daaibooi** is a good beach. It's free, but there are no changing facilities. A good private beach on the eastern side of the island is **Santa Barbara Beach,** on land owned by a mining company between the open sea and the island's primary water-sports and recreational area known as Spanish Water. On the same land are Table Mountain, a remarkable landmark, and an old phosphate mine. The natural beach has pure-white sand and calm water. A buoy line protects swimmers from boats. Rest rooms, changing rooms, a snack bar, and a terrace are among the amenities. You can rent water bicycles and small motorboats. The beach, open daily from 8am to 6pm, has access to the Curaçao Underwater Park.

Blauwbaai (Blue Bay) is the largest and most frequented beach on Curaçao, with enough white sand for everybody. Along with showers and changing facilities, there are plenty of shady places to retreat from the noonday sun. Since this is a private beach, its owners charge 25¢ to enter. To reach it, follow the road that goes past the Holiday Beach Hotel, heading in the direction of Julianadorp. Follow the sign that tells you to bear left for Blauwbaai and the fishing village of San Michiel.

Other beaches include: **Westpunt,** known for the gigantic cliffs that frame it and the Sunday divers who jump from the cliffs into the ocean below. The public beach is located on the northwestern tip of the island. **Knip Bay,** just south of Westpunt, is a beach at the foot of beautiful turquoise waters. On weekends, live music and dancing make the beach a lively place. Changing facilities and refreshments are available. **Playa Abao,** with crystal turquoise water, is a beach at the northern tip of the island.

A Word of Caution to Swimmers: The sea water remains an almost-constant 76° Fahrenheit year round, with good underwater visibility, but beware of stepping on spines of the sea urchins that sometimes abound in these waters. To give temporary first aid for an embedded urchin's spine, try the local remedies of vinegar or lime juice, or as the natives advise, a burning match if you are tough. While the urchin spines are not fatal, they can cause several days of real discomfort.

BOATING TOURS **Taber Tours,** Dokweg (tel. 376637), offers a handful of seagoing tours, such as a snorkel/barbecue trip to Port Marie, which includes round-trip transportation to excellent reef sites, use of snorkeling equipment, and a barbecue for a cost of $45 per person.

A less ambitious tour involves a sunset cruise with wine, cheese, and French bread served on board, and a 2-hour sailing trip at dusk, for a cost of $30 per adult and $20 for children under 12.

Travelers looking for an easy way to see Curaçao should book a trip on the **Insulinde,** Hoogstraat 32 (tel. 626084). This 120-foot traditionally rigged sail logger is available for day trips, sunset sails, and for charter, with special weekend programs available to the islands of Klein Curaçao or Bonaire. The full-day sailing excursion takes passengers on a trip along the shoreline of Willemstad where you have a water view of the town and its old fortresses, then moves on to a secluded beach for sun, swimming, and snorkeling, followed by a luncheon barbecue on the porch of a house overlooking the ocean. The return sail ends at 5pm. The price for the full-day trip, including round-trip transportation from the beachfront hotels of Willemstad, is $37.50 per person. Sunset sails, which include wine and snacks, are $28.50 per person. Call for additional information on chartering the ship or reservations for one of the day sails.

GOLF The **Curaçao Golf and Squash Club,** Wilhelminalaan, in Emmastad (tel. 373590), is open to the general public by arrangement only—telephone the day before you wish to play. Greens fees are $15. The 10-hole course is open Monday to Friday from 8am to noon and 1 to 8pm, and on Saturday and Sunday from 8am to 8pm.

TENNIS There are tennis courts at the Curaçao Caribbean, Golden Tulip Las Palmas, Princess Beach, and Holiday Beach hotels. Las Palmas's court is open 24 hours a day.

WATER SPORTS Most hotels offer their own programs of water sports. However, if your hotel isn't equipped, I suggest that you head for one of the most complete water-sports facilities in Curaçao, **Seascape Dive and Watersports,** at the Curaçao Caribbean Hotel (tel. 625000, ext. 6056). Specializing in snorkeling and scuba-diving trips to reefs and underwater wrecks, it operates from a hexagonal kiosk set on stilts above the water, just offshore from the hotel's beach.

Open from 8am to 5pm daily, the company offers snorkeling excursions for $15 per person, glass-bottom-boat rides for $8, pedalboats for $10 per hour, waterskiing for $40 per half hour, and windsurfing at $20 per 1½ hours. A Sunfish rents for $20, and an introductory scuba lesson, conducted by a competent diver, goes for $40. Packages of four dives cost $110. Bottom fishing, with all equipment included, aboard a 22-foot Aquasport, is $100 for a half day, $180 for a full day.

One trip enthusiastically endorsed by some readers departs from the hotel at 7am (when participation warrants). The destination is Little Curaçao, midway between Curaçao and Bonaire. Clothes are optional once you get to the sugar-white sands of the island. Fishing, snorkeling, and the acquisition of an "overall tan" are highlights. The price is $40 per person, and the excursion lasts all day. Another possibility is a boat ride to one of Curaçao's more isolated beaches, Santa Barbara Beach. A full day's outing is $30 per person.

They can also arrange deep-sea fishing for $300 for a half-day tour carrying a maximum of six people, $500 for a full day. Drinks and equipment are included, but you'll have to get your hotel to pack your lunch.

Underwater Curaçao, in Bapor Kibra (tel. 618131), has a complete underwater-sports program. A fully stocked modern dive shop has retail and rental equipment. Peter Hughes designed the state-of-the-art dive boats used by the trained staff for instruction and scuba diving. Individual dives and dive packages are offered, costing $30 per dive for experienced divers. An introductory dive for novices is priced at $45, and a snorkel trip costs only $20, including equipment.

Scuba divers and snorkelers can expect spectacular scenery in waters with visibility often exceeding 100 feet at the **Curaçao Underwater Park,** off the Princess Beach Hotel. There are steep walls, two shallow wrecks, gardens of soft corals, and more than 30 species of hard corals. Although access from shore is possible at Jan Thiel Bay and Santa Barbara Beach, most people visit the park by boat. For easy and safe mooring, the park has 16 mooring buoys, placed at the best dive and snorkel sites. A snorkel trail with underwater interpretive markers is laid out just east of the Princess Beach Hotel and is accessible from shore. Spearfishing, anchoring in the coral, and taking anything from the reefs except photographs are strictly prohibited.

SAVVY SHOPPING

Curaçao is a shopper's paradise. Some 200 shops line the major shopping malls of such wooden-shoe-named streets as Heerenstraat and Breedestraat. Right in the heart of Willemstad, the Punda shopping area is a five-block district. Most stores are open Monday through Saturday from 8am to noon and 2 to 6pm (some from 8am to 6pm). When cruise ships are in port, stores are also open for a few hours on Sunday and holidays. To avoid the cruise-ship crowds, do your shopping in the morning.

Look for good buys in French perfumes, Dutch Delft blue souvenirs, finely woven Italian silks, Japanese and German cameras, jewelry, silver, Swiss watches, linens, leather goods, liquor, and island-made rum and liqueurs, especially Curaçao.

Incidentally, Curaçao is not technically a free port, but its prices are low because of its low import duty.

BERT KNUBBEN BLACK CORAL, in the Princess Beach Hotel, Dr. Martin Luther King Blvd. Tel. 614944, ext. 5048.

Bert Knubben is a name synonymous with craftsmanship and quality. Although collection of black coral has been made illegal by the Curaçao government, an exception was made for Bert, a diver who has been harvesting corals from the sea and fashioning them into fine jewelry and objets d'art for more than 30 years. The jewelry is finished with 14-karat gold.

BOOLCHAND'S, Heerenstraat 4B, Punda. Tel. 616233.

In business since 1930, Boolchand's features Seiko and Citizen watches and a complete line of cameras, photo, audio and video equipment. A branch store, La Fortunata, has clothing for men, women, and children.

GANDELMAN JEWELERS, Breedestraat 35. Tel. 611854.

This store has a large selection of fine jewelry set with diamonds, rubies, emeralds, and other stones. You'll also find timepieces by Piaget, Ebel, Corum, Concord, Baume & Mercier, Movado, Gucci, Fendi, Seiko, and Swatch. Gandelman Jewelers has five other shops in the Dutch Leewards.

LITTLE SWITZERLAND, Breedestraat 44, Punda. Tel. 612111.

Little Switzerland is known as the premier watch retailer in the Caribbean. It's the exclusive agent for many famous brands, including Bertolucci, Eterna, Kreiger, Rado, Rolex, Sector, Swiss Army, Tiffany, Zodiac and the famous Little Switzerland line of high-fashion watches. You will also find such names as Baume & Mercier, Cartier, Omega, Raymond Weil, and Tag-Heuer. The store carries only Swiss-made watches.

It offers an extensive selection of 14- and 18-karat gold, colored stone and diamond jewelry from Europe and Asia, as well as a beautiful collection of its own "private label" Little Switzerland jewelry.

Little Switzerland has the finest names in china and crystal including Aynsley, Atlantic, Baccarat, Caithness, Daum, Herend, Lalique, Marcolin, Rosenthal, Royal Albert, Royal Crown Derby, Royal Doulton, Villeroy & Boch, Waterford, and Wedgwood; figurines are from David Winter, Goebel-Hummel, Lladró, and Swarovski.

OBRA DI MAN, Bargestraat 57. Tel. 612413.

Filled with authentic local handcraft items, including printed T-shirts, handmade dolls, hand-screened fabrics, carved driftwood, and filigree jewelry, Obra di Man also has some merchandise from the Netherlands.

PALAIS HINDI, Heerenstraat 17. Tel. 616897.

To satisfy your audio and video needs, Palais Hindi sells a wide range of video and cassette recorders. They also stock a lot of photographic equipment, along with cameras and watches.

PENHA & SONS, Heerenstraat 1. Tel. 612266.

Penha & Sons occupies the oldest building in town, built in 1708. Established in 1865, it's the distributor of such names as Chanel, Jean Patou, Yves Saint Laurent, and other perfumes, and cosmetics of Lancôme, Clinique, Clarins, and Estée Lauder, among others. The collection of merchandise at this prestigious store is quite varied—Hummel figurines and Delft blue souvenirs. Don't miss their men's and ladies' boutiques, where they feature travel and sportswear. The firm has 16 other stores in the Caribbean.

SPRITZER & FUHRMANN, Gomezplein. Tel. 612600.

I always head first to the legendary Spritzer & Fuhrmann. Dating from 1927, this is the leading jeweler of the Netherlands Antilles; the name stands for great values, service, and integrity, whether you buy a $50,000 diamond ring or a $50 gold chain. The finest Swiss watches are found here. The store also carries porcelain, chinaware, and crystal.

THE YELLOW HOUSE (La Casa Amarilla), Breedestraat. Tel. 613222.

Housed in a yellow-and-white 19th-century building, and operating since 1887, this place sells an intriguing collection of perfume from all over the world, and is the exclusive distributor of such names as Christian Dior, Guerlain, and Van Cleef & Arpels.

EVENING ENTERTAINMENT

Most of the action spins around the four **casinos** at the Curaçao Caribbean, the Holiday Beach, the Princess Beach, and the Las Palmas, all hotels previously recommended. These hotel gaming houses usually start their action at 2pm, and some of them remain open until 4am. The Princess Beach serves complimentary drinks.

CLUB FACADE, Lindbergweg 8. Tel. 9/614640.

In the Salinja district, this is one of the most popular discos on the island. Spread over several different levels of a modern building, it has a huge bar and three dance floors, and is sometimes filled with balloons. Beer begins at $2, and there is live music on Wednesday, Thursday, Friday, and Sunday. Open: Wed–Mon.

Admission (including first drink): $8.25 men, $5.75 women.

THE PUB, Salinja. Tel. 9/612190.

About a mile outside town, not far from the Seaquarium, this is one of the most crowded and convivial watering holes in Curaçao and is popular with both locals and visitors. The place is dark, mysterious, and filled with shadows, music, and bodies. A beer costs $2. Open: Daily 7pm–4am.

Admission: 10 NAf ($5.70).

INDEX

GENERAL INFORMATION

DESTINATIONS

KEY TO ABBREVIATIONS: A = All-inclusive Resorts; B = Budget; B&B = Bed & Breakfast; C =
Condos & Villas; CG = Campground; E = Expensive; Gh = Guest House; Hs = Hostel; I = Inexpensive; M
= Moderate; VE = Very Expensive; * = An Author's Favorite; $ = Super Value Choice.

Now Save Money On All Your Travels by Joining
FROMMER'S ™ TRAVEL BOOK CLUB
The World's Best Travel Guides at Membership Prices

FROMMER'S TRAVEL BOOK CLUB is your ticket to successful travel! Open up a world of travel information and simplify your travel planning when you join ranks with thousands of value-conscious travelers who are members of the FROMMER'S TRAVEL BOOK CLUB. Join today and you'll be entitled to all the privileges that come from belonging to the club that offers you travel guides for less to more than 100 destinations worldwide. Annual membership is only $25 (U.S.) $35 (Canada and all foreign).

The Advantages of Membership

1. Your choice of three free FROMMER'S TRAVEL GUIDES (you can pick two from our FROMMER'S COUNTRY and REGIONAL GUIDES and one from our FROMMER'S CITY GUIDES).
2. Your own subscription to **TRIPS AND TRAVEL** quarterly newsletter.
3. You're entitled to a **30% discount** on your order of any additional books offered by FROMMER'S TRAVEL BOOK CLUB.
4. You're offered (at a small additional fee) our **Domestic Trip Routing Kits.**

Our quarterly newsletter **TRIPS AND TRAVEL** offers practical information on the best buys in travel, the "hottest" vacation spots, the latest travel trends, world class events and much, much more.

Our **Domestic Trip Routing Kits** are available for any North American destination. We'll send you a detailed map highlighting the best route to take to your destination—you can request direct or scenic routes.

Here's all you have to do to join:

Send in your membership fee of $25 ($35 Canada and foreign) with your name and address on the form below along with your selections as part of your membership package to **FROMMER'S TRAVEL BOOK CLUB, P.O. Box 473, Mt. Morris, IL 61054-0473**. Remember to select 2 FROMMER'S COUNTRY and REGIONAL GUIDES and 1 FROMMER'S CITY GUIDE on the pages following.

If you would like to order additional books, please select the books you would like and send a check for the total amount (please add sales tax in the states noted below), plus $2 per book for shipping and handling ($3 per book for all foreign orders) to:

FROMMER'S TRAVEL BOOK CLUB
P.O. Box 473
Mt. Morris, IL 61054-0473
1-815-734-1104

[ ] **YES**. I want to take advantage of this opportunity to join FROM-MER'S TRAVEL BOOK CLUB.

[ ] **My check is enclosed**. Dollar amount enclosed_____*

Name_____

Address_____

City_____ State_____ Zip_____

To ensure that all orders are processed efficiently, please apply sales tax in the following areas: CA, CT, FL, IL, NJ, NY, TN, WA and CAN.

*With membership, shipping and handling will be paid by FROMMER'S TRAVEL BOOK CLUB for the three free books you select as part of your membership. Please add $2 per book for shipping and handling for any additional books purchased ($3 per book for all foreign orders).

Allow 4-6 weeks for delivery. Prices of books, membership fee, and publication dates are subject to change without notice.

FROMMER GUIDES

	Retail Price	Code		Retail Price	Code
Alaska 1990–91	$14.95	C001	Jamaica/Barbados		
Arizona 1993–94	$18.00	C101	1993–94	$15.00	C105
Australia 1992–93	$18.00	C002	Japan 1992–93	$19.00	C020
Austria/Hungary 1991–			Morocco 1992–93	$18.00	C021
92	$14.95	C003	Napal 1992–93	$18.00	C038
Belgium/Holland/			New England 1992	$17.00	C023
Luxembourg 1993–94	$18.00	C106	New Mexico 1991–92	$13.95	C024
Bermuda/Bahamas			New York State 1992–93	$19.00	C025
1992–93	$17.00	C005	Northwest 1991–92	$16.95	C026
Brazil 1991–92	$14.95	C006	Portugal 1992–93	$16.00	C027
California 1992	$18.00	C007	Puerto Rico 1993–94	$15.00	C103
Canada 1992–93	$18.00	C009	Puerto Vallarta/		
Caribbean 1993	$18.00	C102	Manzanillo/		
The Carolinas/Georgia			Guadalajara 1992–93	$14.00	C028
1992–93	$17.00	C034	Scandinavia 1991–92	$18.95	C029
Colorado 1993–94	$16.00	C100	Scotland 1992–93	$16.00	C040
Cruises 1993–94	$19.00	C107	Skiing Europe 1989–90	$14.95	C030
DE/MD/PA & NJ Shore			South Pacific 1992–93	$20.00	C031
1992–93	$19.00	C012	Switzerland/Liechten-		
Egypt 1990–91	$14.95	C013	stein 1992–93	$19.00	C032
England 1993	$18.00	C109	Thailand 1992–93	$20.00	C033
Florida 1993	$18.00	C104	USA 1991–92	$16.95	C035
France 1992–93	$20.00	C017	Virgin Islands 1992–93	$13.00	C036
Germany 1993	$19.00	C108	Virginia 1992–93	$14.00	C037
Italy 1992	$19.00	C019	Yucatán 1992–93	$18.00	C110

FROMMER $-A-DAY GUIDES

Australia on $45 a Day			Israel on $45 a Day		
1993–94	$18.00	D102	1993–94	$18.00	D101
Costa Rica/Guatemala/			Mexico on $50 a Day		
Belize on $35 a Day			1993	$19.00	D105
1991–92	$15.95	D004	New York on $70 a Day		
Eastern Europe on $25			1992–93	$16.00	D016
a Day 1991–92	$16.95	D005	New Zealand on $45 a		
England on $60 a Day			Day 1993–94	$18.00	D103
1993	$18.00	D107	Scotland/Wales on $50 a		
Europe on $45 a Day			Day 1992–93	$18.00	D019
1993	$19.00	D106	South America on $40 a		
Greece on $45 a Day			Day 1991–92	$15.95	D020
1993–94	$19.00	D100	Spain on $50 a Day		
Hawaii on $75 a Day			1991–92	$15.95	D021
1993	$19.00	D104	Turkey on $40 a Day		
India on $40 a Day			1992	$22.00	D023
1992–93	$20.00	D010	Washington, D.C. on		
Ireland on $40 a Day			$40 a Day 1992	$17.00	D024
1992–93	$17.00	D011			

FROMMER CITY $-A-DAY GUIDES

	Retail Price	Code		Retail Price	Code
Berlin on $40 a Day 1992–93	$12.00	D002	Madrid on $50 a Day 1992–93	$13.00	D014
Copenhagen on $50 a Day 1992–93	$12.00	D003	Paris on $45 a Day 1992–93	$12.00	D018
London on $45 a Day 1992–93	$12.00	D013	Stockholm on $50 a Day 1992–93	$13.00	D022

FROMMER TOURING GUIDES

Amsterdam	$10.95	T001	New York	$10.95	T008
Australia	$10.95	T002	Paris	$ 8.95	T009
Barcelona	$14.00	T015	Rome	$10.95	T010
Brazil	$10.95	T003	Scotland	$ 9.95	T011
Egypt	$ 8.95	T004	Sicily	$14.95	T017
Florence	$ 8.95	T005	Thailand	$12.95	T012
Hong Kong/Singapore/ Macau	$10.95	T006	Tokyo	$15.00	T016
			Turkey	$10.95	T013
Kenya	$13.95	T018	Venice	$ 8.95	T014
London	$12.95	T007			

FROMMER'S FAMILY GUIDES

California with Kids	$16.95	F001	San Francisco with Kids	$17.00	F004
Los Angeles with Kids	$17.00	F002	Washington, D.C. with Kids	$17.00	F005
New York City with Kids	$18.00	F003			

FROMMER CITY GUIDES

Amsterdam/Holland 1991–92	$ 8.95	S001	Miami 1991–92	$ 8.95	S021
Athens 1991–92	$ 8.95	S002	Minneapolis/St. Paul 1991–92	$ 8.95	S022
Atlanta 1991–92	$ 8.95	S003	Montréal/Québec City 1991–92	$ 8.95	S023
Atlantic City/Cape May 1991–92	$ 8.95	S004	New Orleans 1993–94	$13.00	S103
Bangkok 1992–93	$13.00	S005	New York 1992	$12.00	S025
Barcelona/Majorca/ Minorca/Ibiza 1992	$12.00	S006	Orlando 1993	$13.00	S101
Belgium 1989–90	$ 5.95	S007	Paris 1993–94	$13.00	S109
Berlin 1991–92	$10.00	S008	Philadelphia 1991–92	$ 8.95	S028
Boston 1991–92	$ 8.95	S009	Rio 1991–92	$ 8.95	S029
Cancún/Cozumel/ Yucatán 1991–92	$ 8.95	S010	Rome 1991–92	$ 8.95	S030
			Salt Lake City 1991–92	$ 8.95	S031
Chicago 1991–92	$ 9.95	S011	San Diego 1993–94	$13.00	S107
Denver/Boulder/ Colorado Springs 1990–91	$ 7.95	S012	San Francisco 1993	$13.00	S104
			Santa Fe/Taos/ Albuquerque 1993–94	$13.00	S108
Dublin/Ireland 1991–92	$ 8.95	S013	Seattle/Portland 1992–93	$12.00	S035
Hawaii 1992	$12.00	S014	St. Louis/Kansas City 1991–92	$ 9.95	S036
Hong Kong 1992–93	$12.00	S015	Sydney 1991–92	$ 8.95	S037
Honolulu/Oahu 1993	$13.00	S106	Tampa/St. Petersburg 1993–94	$13.00	S105
Las Vegas 1991–92	$ 8.95	S016			
Lisbon/Madrid/Costa del Sol 1991–92	$ 8.95	S017	Tokyo 1992–93	$13.00	S039
London 1993	$13.00	S100	Toronto 1991–92	$ 8.95	S040
Los Angeles 1991–92	$ 8.95	S019	Vancouver/Victoria 1990–91	$ 7.95	S041
Mexico City/Acapulco 1991–92	$ 8.95	S020	Washington, D.C. 1993	$13.00	S102

Other Titles Available at Membership Prices—
SPECIAL EDITIONS

Bed & Breakfast North America	$14.95	P002	Marilyn Wood's Wonderful Weekends (within 250-mile radius of New York City)	$11.95	P017
Caribbean Hideaways	$16.00	P005			
Honeymoon Destinations	$14.95	P006	New World of Travel 1991 by Arthur Frommer	$16.95	P018
			Where to Stay USA	$13.95	P015

GAULT MILLAU'S "BEST OF" GUIDES

Chicago	$15.95	G002	New England	$15.95	G010
Florida	$17.00	G003	New Orleans	$16.95	G011
France	$16.95	G004	New York	$16.95	G012
Germany	$18.00	G018	Paris	$16.95	G013
Hawaii	$16.95	G006	San Francisco	$16.95	G014
Hong Kong	$16.95	G007	Thailand	$17.95	G019
London	$16.95	G009	Toronto	$17.00	G020
Los Angeles	$16.95	G005	Washington, D.C.	$16.95	G017

THE REAL GUIDES

Amsterdam	$13.00	R100	Morocco	$14.00	R111
Barcelona	$13.00	R101	Nepal	$14.00	R018
Berlin	$11.95	R002	New York	$13.00	R019
Brazil	$13.95	R003	Able to Travel (avail April '93)	$20.00	R112
California & the West Coast	$17.00	R102	Paris	$13.00	R020
Canada	$15.00	R103	Peru	$12.95	R021
Czechoslovakia	$14.00	R104	Poland	$13.95	R022
Egypt	$19.00	R105	Portugal	$15.00	R023
Florida	$14.00	R006	Prague	$15.00	R113
France	$18.00	R106	San Francisco & the Bay Area	$11.95	R024
Germany	$18.00	R107	Scandinavia	$14.95	R025
Greece	$18.00	R108	Spain	$16.00	R026
Guatemala/Belize	$14.00	R109	Thailand	$17.00	R114
Holland/Belgium/ Luxembourg	$16.00	R031	Tunisia	$17.00	R115
Hong Kong/Macau	$11.95	R011	Turkey	$13.95	R116
Hungary	$12.95	R012	U.S.A.	$18.00	R117
Ireland	$17.00	R110	Venice	$11.95	R028
Italy	$13.95	R014	Women Travel	$12.95	R029
Kenya	$12.95	R015	Yugoslavia	$12.95	R030
Mexico	$11.95	R016			